PENGUIN SHAKESPEARE LIBRARY

GENERAL EDITOR: T. J. B. SPENCER

A SHAKESPEARE COMPANION

F. E. Halliday, a Yorkshireman, was educated at Giggleswick School and King's College, Cambridge. He taught for many years at Cheltenham College, where he was head of the English department. Soon after the war he moved to St Ives in Cornwall to devote his time to writing. He is married and has one son and four grandchildren. He has published, among other things, *Five Arts* (an essay in aesthetics), *The Legend of the Rood*, *A History of Cornwall*, *Richard Carew of Antony*, *Indifferent Honest* (autobiography), *Meditation at Bolerium* (poems), *A Cultural History of England*. However, he is best known for his books on Shakespeare. These include *Shakespeare and His Critics*, *The Poetry of Shakespeare's Plays*, *The Cult of Shakespeare*, and *The Life of Shakespeare*. He has lectured on Shakespeare at Stratford, Ontario, and in the universities of Portugal and Spain.

F. E. HALLIDAY

A SHAKESPEARE COMPANION

PENGUIN BOOKS
BALTIMORE · MARYLAND

Penguin Books Ltd, Harmondsworth, Middlesex, England
Penguin Books Inc., 7110 Ambassador Road, Baltimore, Maryland 21207, U.S.A.
Penguin Books Australia Ltd, Ringwood, Victoria, Australia

—

First published (as *A Shakespeare Companion 1550-1950*) by Duckworth 1952
This revised edition published in Penguin Books 1964
Reissued in Penguin Shakespeare Library 1969

—

—

Made and printed in Great Britain
by Hazell Watson & Viney Ltd
Aylesbury, Bucks
Set in Monotype Bembo

TO THE MEMORY OF

E. A. BELL

AND

A. M. McINTOSH

Contents

Preface

'THIS book is more than a handbook to Shakespeare; it is a handbook not only to Shakespeare's life and works, to his friends and acquaintances, to his poems and plays and their characters, but also to the Elizabethan-Jacobean theatre, the other dramatists who wrote for it, their most important plays and the companies that performed them, and to the history up to the present day of Shakespeare's work both on the stage and in the study, to his printers and publishers, players and producers, editors and adapters, scholars and critics. There must be many readers of Shakespeare to whom, for example, Nathan Field, *Pandosto*, Worcester's Company, "Copy", *The Gull's Hornbook*, William Jaggard, Maddermarket Theatre, Nahum Tate, Leslie Hotson, Lewis Theobald, the Blackfriars Theatres, A. W. Pollard, the Master of the Revels, Assembled Texts, Cinthio, New Place, F. J. Furnivall, "Plots", William Poel, the Folger Shakespeare Library, John Norden, Kenilworth, Gervinus, Jig, Leonard Digges, the Chandos Portrait, and Queen Margaret of the Histories, are little more than names, and would welcome a single volume in which these and similar names and subjects could be investigated.

'Briefly, it is an attempt to cover all aspects of Shakespeare, and the people who have been most intimately associated with his works, in whatever capacity, in the course of more than three and a half centuries. Though I should be the last to maintain that such knowledge is essential for the appreciation of Shakespeare's works, it quite clearly adds to the understanding of them, and is in itself a fascinating extension of the subject.

'The book is neither a glossary nor a concordance, nor does it make any claim to be complete; indeed, such a book never could be complete. There is, for example, no attempt to catalogue all the editions of Shakespeare any more than all the translations, nor to recite the names of all those who have ever written about Shakespeare or acted in his plays. The list of characters in the plays is almost complete, but I have not thought it necessary to include every servant and every "gentleman" who serves to swell a scene. When the part played by a main character is sufficiently indicated in the synopsis of the play, the notice may be shorter than that of a minor character who is not mentioned in the general summary. I have included these, as I know from experience how useful it is to have an outline of the part played by a character, and it is both interesting and instructive to follow the fortunes of a character through a sequence of the

Histories in which he may appear under various names: Prince John of Lancaster, for example.

'Inevitably the mesh becomes finer and the selective process more rigorous as the present day is approached, and I have limited the names of living people, particularly of actors, to those who, it may generally be conceded, have done most to advance the understanding of Shakespeare. Many others are mentioned incidentally, or will be found in the Bibliography. Within the very wide limits imposed, I think the book will be found fairly complete, and to contain as much information as will be required by a more than average reader. But there must, in a work of this scale, be some wrong emphasis and many oversights and errors, and these must be charged entirely to my own ignorance and incompetence, though not, I think, to indolence.'

So I wrote thirteen years ago in the Preface to the first edition. There has, I think, been no deterioration in knowledge, competence and industry since then, but much has happened in the field of Shakespeare studies (the work of the new school of bibliographers, for example) and the book has been thoroughly revised and brought up to date: redundant and peripheral material has been discarded, new entries have been added and others completely rewritten.

Again to quote my original Preface: 'I began it (in 1948) mainly for my own satisfaction . . . as a means to an end, a necessary preliminary to a fuller understanding of Shakespeare.' At least its revision, a graver labour than I anticipated, has served as a refresher course, and I can only hope that the book in its new form will help others to a fuller understanding, perhaps even to a fuller appreciation of 'what, after all, matters most about Shakespeare, his poetry'.

F.E.H.

St Ives, Cornwall
1964

List of Abbreviations

BAL	British Academy Lecture
ES	*The Elizabethan Stage*, E. K. Chambers
F. Ff.	Folio, Folios
Lib.	*The Library*
NQ	*Notes and Queries*
NSS	New Shakspere Society
PBA	*Proceedings of the British Academy*
PBSA	*Proceedings of the Bibliographical Society of America*
Q. Qq.	Quarto, Quartos
RES	*Review of English Studies*
s.d.	stage direction
SJ	*Shakespeare-Jahrbuch*
SQ	*Shakespeare Quarterly*
SR	Stationers' Register
SS	*Shakespeare Survey*
TLS	*Times Literary Supplement*

A

Aaron. In *Titus Andronicus* (q.v.), a Moor, and the lover of Queen Tamora. He is ultimately responsible for the murder of Bassianus, the execution of Quintus and Martius Andronicus, and the mutilation of Titus and Lavinia. (See PEACHAM.)

Abbott, Edwin Abbott (1838–1926), grammarian, became Headmaster of the City of London School in 1865. In 1869 he published his valuable *Shakespearian Grammar*, the object of which was 'to furnish students of Shakespeare and Bacon with a short, systematic account of some points of difference between Elizabethan syntax and our own. The *words* of these authors present but little difficulty. . . . But the *differences of idiom* are more perplexing.' (See NEW SHAKSPERE SOCIETY.)

Abergavenny, Lord. In *Henry VIII*, he is arrested at the same time as his father-in-law, Buckingham, and sent to the Tower (I, i). (George Neville, 3rd Baron (d. 1535), married Mary Stafford, daughter of the 3rd Duke of Buckingham.)

Abhorson. In *Measure for Measure*, an executioner. He disapproves of Pompey the bawd as an apprentice who 'will discredit our mystery', but with him prepares to execute Barnardine (IV, ii and iii).

Abraham. In *Romeo and Juliet*, a servant of Montague (I, i).

Abridgement of Plays. Some of the plays appear to have been printed from a deliberately abridged text. For example, Q1 *Othello* omits about 100 lines found in F1, though conversely it may be argued that these lines are really interpolations. The Folio version of *2 Henry IV* contains several passages, totalling 168 lines, which appear to have been deliberately cut in the version from which Q (1600) was printed. Q2 (1604) *Hamlet* is 200 lines longer than F, though 85 lines in F are missing from Q2. It is probable that *Macbeth*, for which there is only the F text, has been severely shortened. Various reasons have been suggested for abridgement: for Court performances, for provincial performances, and for winter performance in a public theatre when there was little more than two hours' daylight between two o'clock, when playing began, and sunset. After the Restoration, plays were often abbreviated to make room for music and spectacle (cf. *The Fairy Queen*), and it is possible that this process had begun in James I's reign. (See CUTS.)

Abuses of Players, An Acte to Restraine. 27 May 1606.

> For the preventing and avoyding of the greate Abuse of the Holy Name of God in Stageplayes, Interludes, Maygames, Shewes, and such like; Be it enacted.... That if at any tyme or tymes, after the end of this present Session of Parliament, any person or persons doe or shall in any Stage play, Interlude, Shewe, Maygame, or Pageant jestingly or prophanely speake or use the holy Name of God or of Christ Jesus, or of the Holy Ghoste or of the Trinitie, which are not to be spoken but with feare and reverence, shall forfeite for everie such Offence by hym or them committed Tenne Pounds.

It should be noted that the offence is to *speak* the oath, not to write or print it. The reprints of Qq earlier than 1606 are unexpurgated, yet many of the oaths – and some mere imprecations and asseverations – have been suppressed or replaced by euphemisms in F. For example, Mistress Page's 'what the dickens' for the Q 'what the devil' is the first employment of the term. The two parts of *Henry IV* have been most severely censored, but the purge was far from systematic and thorough. Presumably the oaths had been deleted or altered in the prompt copies from which the text of much of F was set up, and the printer selected the most legible version. (See HERBERT, HENRY; CENSORSHIP OF PLAYS.)

Academic Drama. Classical or neo-classical plays, for the most part in Latin but sometimes in English, written and performed by university men. The first record of a performance of a classical play in England is of 'a goodly commedy of Plautus' at Greenwich Palace in 1519. Elizabeth's only visit to Cambridge was in 1564 when performances were given in King's College chapel of the *Aulularia* of Plautus, of *Ezechias*, an English comedy by Nicholas Udall, and of *Dido*, a Latin tragedy by Edward Halliwell. In 1566 she heard in the hall of Christ Church, Oxford, a Latin comedy, a Latin tragedy, and an English tragedy, *Palamon and Arcite*, all written by Christ Church men, the last by Richard Edwardes, Master of the Children of the Chapel. Again, in 1592, at Christ Church she attended two performances, one of a Latin comedy by William Gager, ranked by Meres with Edwardes as one 'of the best for comedy amongst us'. Both universities were invited to produce plays at Court that Christmas – in English; but English was insufficiently academic, at least for Cambridge, and neither university attended. James I was present at productions, assisted by Inigo Jones, of three Latin plays at Christ Church in 1605, and ten years later in the hall of Trinity, Cambridge, saw four plays, one of which, George Ruggles's *Ignoramus*, pleased him so much that two months later he went to a second performance. *Ignoramus* is 'Latine, and part English', satirizing, as did *3 Parnassus*, the Cambridge recorder, Francis Brackyn, 'which so nettled the lawyers, that they are almost out of all patience'.

Achilles. In *Troilus and Cressida*, a Grecian commander. He orders his myrmidons to murder the unarmed Hector (v, viii).

Act and Scene Division. Division of a play into five acts is a classical convention derived from Seneca. Scenic division is structural, a new scene naturally beginning after the stage has been left empty. Extant theatrical manuscripts show that after 1600 plays were usually divided into acts, and scenes were often marked.

There are no divisions in any of the Shakespearean Quartos, save a few indications in the 'bad' Q1 of *Romeo and Juliet*, *Pericles* and *Othello*. In F1, however, most of the plays are divided, and some of them into scenes. All begin with the heading *Actus Primus, Scena Prima*, except the sequence of *Love's Labour's Lost*, *A Midsummer Night's Dream* and *The Merchant of Venice*, which have only *Actus Primus;* for the rest they fall into four groups. (The plays are printed opposite in the order of F1.)

Jonson adopted the neo-classical convention of beginning a new scene with a change in the main characters on the stage, and as he published the first Folio of his 'Works' in 1616 it must have served as a model for the editors of the Shakespeare Folio. Their division is inconsistent, but this is probably due to the different kinds of 'copy'. We should expect division into acts by 1623, and generally division into scenes when a prompt-book was the basis of the text, though less often when set up from non-theatrical copy such as foul papers or a Quarto. The first four plays in F and *The Winter's Tale* may be from transcripts by Crane, who combined the natural and neo-classical methods of scene division, and indicated the beginning of a scene by massed entry of characters. We do not know whether Shakespeare worked in terms of acts or not; Baldwin thinks that he did, Wilson that he did not.

In his octavo edition of 1709, Rowe completed the division into acts and scenes. Pope (1725), on the French model, made scenes coincide with the entry and exit of a main character. (See ASSEMBLED TEXTS; APPENDIX I.)

Acting. In the last few years scholars have for the first time attempted to discover the Elizabethan style of acting.

The actor, it should be remembered, would be seen in daylight, on an apron stage almost devoid of scenery – in the round like a sculpture on a pedestal – and would as often as not speak verse. The evidence suggests that they adopted a rhetorical and formalized, and not a realistic style, suiting the word to conventional action, though in the private theatres the method would have to be modified. (See PLAYERS.)

'Shakespeare created a new art of acting,' wrote Granville-Barker. 'He did this incidentally, but of necessity,' for the actor had now to do more than declaim verse, he had to interpret, to realize character. (See B. L. Joseph, *Elizabethan Acting*, 1951.)

Actor-Lists. See DRAMATIS PERSONAE; CASTS.

Actors. In the Middle Ages, in addition to the guildsmen who performed the Mystery plays, there were wandering troupes of professional entertainers: clowns, acrobats and jugglers, some of the more reputable of whom were retained by the nobility as interlude players (q.v.). Henry VII maintained a company of four, raised to eight by Henry VIII and Elizabeth; the Earls of Essex had a company as early as 1468. Though these companies were attached to some great house, they continued to travel, and performed in the halls of other houses, monasteries and towns. At the same time the new secular drama of the Renaissance, classical and neo-classical plays, came to be acted at schools, the universities, and Inns of Court, but these esoteric amateurs did not cater for the growing public demand, and it was only natural that there should be a big increase of professional actors, many of whom were attracted to London by the powerful and centralized Tudor government. From the beginning of Elizabeth's reign there are plenty of records of Court performances, both by the Children of the Chapel and of Paul's, and by companies of adult actors who made their temporary, and sometimes, perhaps, almost permanent, headquarters at the City inns. Clearly this growing body of professional players could not exist on provincial, private, and Court

Acts and Scenes	*Acts and Scenes Imperfectly*	*Acts Only*	*Undivided*
*†Tempest[1] †Two Gentlemen Merry Wives *†Measure for M.[2] A.Y.L.I. Twelfth Night †Winter's Tale	Taming of Shrew	C. of Errors Much Ado L. L. Lost M. N. Dream M. of Venice All's Well	
King John Richard II 1 Henry IV †2 Henry IV Richard III Henry VIII	1 Henry VI	Henry V	2 Henry VI 3 Henry VI
Macbeth Lear †Othello Cymbeline	Hamlet	Coriolanus Titus And. J. Caesar	Tr. & Cress. Rom. & Juliet †Timon Ant. & Cleo.

* Location of Scene given: (1) 'An uninhabited island'; (2) 'The scene Vienna'.
† 'Names of the Actors' given at the end.

performances; they had to perform in the crowded capital, if possible in the most crowded part, within the City walls. The City Corporation, however, looked askance at their performances, to which the citizens flocked, as likely to cause disturbances and spread plague. The Queen and Privy Council agreed with them on these points, but they did not agree with the Puritans within and behind the Corporation, who wished to prohibit plays on religious and moral grounds. The Queen and Court were humanists, and, then, they wanted to be amused.

The main steps whereby the actors were incorporated within the ordered Tudor society and secured the privilege of playing in London, at least outside the walls, may be summarized as follows. (It must be remembered that until 1576 there were no regular theatres, only inns, most of them within the walls, converted into playhouses.)

1559: By a Proclamation the Queen forbade all plays that treated of matters of religion or politics. No play might be publicly or privately performed in any town without the licence of the Mayor or other chief officers. The Mayor and Corporation of London, therefore, as well as others, were confirmed in their traditional privilege of controlling entertainments, and it was to this right that they were continually to appeal against encroachments by the Queen and her Council with their centralizing policy.

1572: An Act, part of the Tudor Poor Law, classed as rogues and vagabonds

> all Fencers Bearewardes Comon Players in Enterludes & Minstrels, not belonging to any Baron of this Realme or towardes any other honorable Personage of greater Degree ... whiche ... shall wander abroade and have not Lycense of two Justices of the Peace at the leaste, wherof one to be of the Quorum.

As all companies had to travel for part of the year, this meant that reputable players had to find a patron among the nobility, though in fact most of them had already done so, and the effect of the Act was to strengthen the position of the genuine player and his company.

1574: A proposal by the Lord Chamberlain that 'one Holmes' should have 'the appointment of places for playes and enterludes within this citie' was rejected by the Lord Mayor, mainly on the grounds that it would be 'a precident farre extending to the hart of our liberties'.

1574: A royal patent overruled the City Corporation by authorizing Leicester's Men to perform plays allowed by the Master of the Revels 'as well within oure Citie of London and liberties of the same' as elsewhere, save in the time of common prayer and of plague in London.

1574: The City acquiesced, but not without protest and a code of regulations. The preamble to their Act of Common Council summarizes their case against plays:

> Whearas hearetofore sondrye greate disorders and inconvenyences have benne found to ensewe to this Cittie by the inordynate hauntyinge of greate multitudes of people, speciallye youthe, to playes, enterludes, and shewes, namelye occasyon of ffrayes and quarrelles, eavell practizes of incontinencye in great Innes, havinge chambers and secrete places adioyninge to their open stagies and gallyries, inveglynge and alleurynge of maides, speciallye orphanes and good Cityzens Children vnder Age, to previe and vnmete Contractes, the publishinge of vnchaste vncomelye and vnshamefaste speeches and doynges, withdrawinge of the Queenes Maiesties Subiectes from dyvyne service on Sonndaies and hollydayes, at which Tymes suche playes weare Cheflye vsed, vnthriftye waste of the moneye of the poore and fond persons, sondrye robberies by pyckinge and Cuttinge of purses, vtteringe of popular busye and sedycious matters, and manie other Corruptions of youthe and other enormyties, besydes that allso soundrye slaughters and mayheminges of the Quenes Subiectes have happened by ruines of Skaffoldes, fframes, and Stagies, and by engynes, weapons, and powder used in plaies; And whear in tyme of goddes visitacion by the plaigue suche assemblies of the people in thronge and presse have benne verye daungerous for spreadinge of Infection....

However, plays would be tolerated, provided that:

1. They should contain no 'wourdes, examples, or doynges of anie vnchastitie, sedicion, nor suche lyke vnfytt and vncomelye matter'; penalty, 14 days' imprisonment and a fine of £5.
2. They should be 'firste pervsed and Allowed' by the 'Lorde Maior and Courte of Aldermen'.
3. They were shown only by 'suche persons and in suche places' as were 'permitted and allowed by the lord maior and Aldermen'.
4. Licensees gave surety to the Chamberlain of London for the preservation of order.
5. There were no performances during times disallowed by the City authorities, as during plague, or divine service on Sundays and holidays; penalty, £5.
6. Every licensee pay 'to the vse of the poor in hospitalles of the Cyttie or of the poore of the Cyttie visited with syknes, by the dyscretion of the said lorde maiour and Aldermen'.

These regulations were not unreasonable, though no doubt irksome, and it is significant that the new theatres were built in the liberties, just outside the City jurisdiction, the Theatre and Curtain in 1576, and a house at Newington Butts before 1580. This infuriated the City Corporation, who now had to try to persuade the unpuritanical Middlesex and Surrey magistrates to enforce a similar code. Nor did the regulations of 1574 satisfy the extreme Puritans, who goaded the Corporation to renew the attack.

1580: The Lord Mayor's appeal to the Middlesex magistrates led to the indictment of John Brayne and James Burbage for unlawful assembly at the Theatre, causing a breach of the peace. After further disorder at the Theatre, the Lord Mayor appealed to the Lord Chancellor 'that the said playes and toumbelers be wholy stayed and forbidden as vngodlye and perilous, as well at those places nere our liberties as within the iurisdiction of this Cittie'.

1581: As in 1574 a royal patent overruled the City by giving Edmund Tilney, Master of the Revels, authority 'in all places within this our Realme of England' over 'all suche showes, plaies, plaiers and play-makers, together with their playing places, to order and reforme, auctorise and put downe, as shalbe thought meete or vnmeete vnto himselfe'.

1582: Having failed to secure the closing of the theatres, the Corporation tried to prevent the citizens attending them: the City guilds were to warn all their freemen 'that if they or anie of them do at annye time hereafter suffer any of ther sarvants, apprentices, journemen, or children, to repare or goe to annye playes, peices, or enterludes, either within the cittie or suburbs thereof, or to annye place witheout the same' they would be punished. This proving impossible of enforcement, they followed it up later in the year by an order that 'all such Enterludes in publique places, and the resort to the same shall wholy be prohibited as ungodly', and resolved to ask the Council that 'lyke prohibition be in places neere unto the Cittie'. The City inn-theatres, therefore, were closed.

1583: The formation of the Queen's company, under the patronage of Elizabeth herself, may have been a reply to the City attack; the Corporation had to assign them two 'playing places', 'at the sygnes of the Bull in Bushoppesgate streete, and the sygne of the Bell in Gratioustreete and nowheare els within this Cyttye'.

1584: After disorders at the Theatre and Curtain, the Corporation persuaded the Council to agree to their suppression. There was, therefore, no theatre open either in the liberties or in the City. In November the Queen's Men petitioned the Council to write 'favorable letters' to the Middlesex justices and the Lord Mayor, asking them to reopen the liberty theatres and City inns so that they could practise for the winter season at Court.

The Corporation replied to the Council's request, restating their case against players who 'shold by their profession be rogues', but granting a limited toleration.

1. The Regulations of 1574 should be revived.
2. That they play not openly till the whole death in London haue ben by xx daies under 50 a weke.

3. That no playes be on the sabbat.
4. That no playeing be on holydaies but after euening prayer.
5. That no playeing be in the dark.
6. That the Quenes players only be tolerated.

The City had failed to suppress playing, and the position was much the same as in 1574. As the Corporation had told the Council 'that the last yere [1583] when such toleration was of the Quenes players only, all the places of playeing were filled with men calling themselues the Quenes players', it may be assumed that once again the theatres were filled with 'Queen's Men', and that the attempt to limit players to one company had little effect.

1589: The conflict was renewed at the time of the Martin Marprelate controversy (q.v.), but checked in 1593–4 when the theatres were closed for most of the time on account of the plague.

1596: In August, Lord Cobham, no great friend of the players, became Lord Chamberlain, and the City succeeded in ejecting the players from the inns within their jurisdiction. (See RAWLIDGE.)

1597: The Corporation then tried to persuade the Council to order the closing of the theatres 'abowt the Citie', and after the production of the seditious *Isle of Dogs* at the Swan on 28 July, they did close them for a time, and even ordered them to be 'plucked down'; though, as so often happened, nothing came of this ferocious order.

1598: The 2nd Lord Hunsdon was now Lord Chamberlain, and the Council took a firm line. The Act of 1572 was modified, and magistrates were no longer authorized to license 'wandering abroad', so that all reputable players had to be in the service of at least a Baron. Then, an order to the magistrates of Middlesex and Surrey to enforce a limitation of the London companies to two, the Admiral's and Chamberlain's, makes it clear that the Council had assumed direct control of the London theatres and companies. Provided, therefore, the players behaved themselves, they could now feel secure in the support of the Privy Council. The City had failed to gain control of the theatres outside the walls.

1600: An Order of the Privy Council confirmed the monopoly of the Chamberlain's and Admiral's Men, playing at their own new houses of the Globe and the Fortune, with the restrictions that there should be no playing on Sunday, in Lent, in time of plague, in any 'common inn', or on more than two days a week. But other companies were soon playing in London, Worcester's were officially admitted in 1602, the other theatres continued in use, new ones were built, and plays were acted every weekday.

1603: After the accession of James I the status of the privileged companies was still further raised and secured, for the King took the Chamberlain's Men into his service as the King's Men, while Worcester's became the Queen's, and the Admiral's Prince Henry's. As Leicester's had been in 1574, so they were licensed by royal patent and authorized to play 'as well in and about our Cittye of London in such vsuall howses as themselues shall provide, as also within anye Townehalles, Mootehalles, Guildhalles, Schoolehowses or other convenient places within the lybertye and freedome of any other Cittye, vniversity, Towne, or Boroughe whatsoever within our Realmes and Domynions'. Two other companies were attached to members of the royal family: the Duke of York's (Prince Charles's) received its patent in 1610, the Lady Elizabeth's in 1611. The chief members of these five companies, of whom the King's and Prince Henry's (the Palsgrave's) were by far the most important, were no longer subject to mayors and magistrates, and at one remove from rogues and vagabonds, but privileged members of the royal household, Grooms of the Chamber, and regular performers at Court in the winter.

Travelling companies, licensed by noblemen, still performed in the provinces, and the London companies also travelled; indeed, they had to in plague years. This system of regulation remained comparatively stable until 1642, when the theatres were closed, and finally 1648, when Parliament decreed that 'all stage-players, and players of interludes, and common players, are hereby declared to be, and are, and shall be taken to be, rogues, ... whether they be wanderers or no, and notwithstanding any licence whatsoever from the King or any person or persons to that purpose'.

By 1598, therefore, when the Privy Council took over the control of dramatic entertainment in London, the relation of the actor to the government was defined; provided that he had a licence, observed – more or less – the laws forbidding playing on Sundays and in Lent, and avoided plays that were too obscene and at all seditious, he was officially recognized as a valuable member of society and free to play where he chose. But he had a number of other relationships besides that to the government: he must be a member of some nobleman's household, wear his badge and livery, and carry his warrant. The relations between patron and actor varied, no doubt, according to the patron's influence and his interest in the drama, and the protection of a powerful patron, such as the Lord Chamberlain, was a great asset. Queen Elizabeth's Men had a great advantage for nearly a decade and after 1603 so had the companies licensed by the King.

Some actors, notably Robert Browne and John Green, preferred leading a company, composed for the most part of failures, on foreign tours, particularly of Germany, where the multitudinous petty courts welcomed English players, who were highly esteemed. But it must have been a rough life: adventurous, but not remunerative.

The London player with his fine clothes and maybe affected airs was an easy mark for the satirist, though he might well have possessed nothing more substantial than his appearance of prosperity; perhaps he was in debt to Henslowe, and even the finery might have been borrowed surreptitiously from the company's wardrobe. The fortunate few, however, really were prosperous: Alleyn and Richard Burbage – though they were theatre owners as well as actors – and Shakespeare, and many of his fellows of the privileged King's Men. Such success roused the envy and indignation of impecunious playwrights like Robert Greene against 'those Puppets that spake from our mouths, those Anticks garnisht in our colours', 'upstart Crows' and 'painted monsters', and of the anonymous author of *Parnassus* (q.v.).

And there were always the Puritan pamphleteers, such men as Stephen Gosson, John Field and Phillip Stubbes, to attack the 'masking players', 'painted sepulchres' and 'doble dealing ambodexters', and to prod the City Corporation to persecute these men who 'shold by their profession be rogues'. (See ACTORS' COMPANIES; PAY OF ACTORS; M. C. Bradbrook, *The Rise of the Common Player*, 1962.)

Actors' Companies. The actor was of necessity a member of a company under the patronage of some nobleman or member of the royal family. The company was an association of actors who invested their money in a common stock of properties, costumes – often very valuable (velvet cost £1 a yard) – and plays which they bought outright from the dramatist for £6 or £7. They shared in the receipts and expenses according to the amount of their share capital, which might be more than one share, or only a fraction of one. Compare *Hamlet*:

HAMLET: Would not this, sir, and a forest of feathers ... get me a fellowship in a cry of players, sir?
HORATIO: Half a share.
HAMLET: A whole one, I.

Such members, 'full adventurers', were called 'sharers', of whom usually there would be about ten, and the total value of the stock, assuming their all having one share, might be about £700 of Elizabethan money, or some £20,000 of ours. One of these sharers, like John Heminge for the Chamberlain's, would act as business manager. The sharers employed 'hired' actors for about 6s. a week, and the boys who played the women's parts were apprenticed to the sharers, who received from the company a few shillings a week for their services. There would also be the 'book-keeper' or prompter, the tireman who looked after the properties and wardrobe, the stage-keeper who swept up the litter, musicians and 'gatherers'.

There were two main forms of organization: the one followed by companies who rented a theatre from a capitalist owner, such as Henslowe of the Rose and Langley of the Swan, the other by those who owned their own theatres, such as the Chamberlain's-King's at the Globe and Blackfriars, and Worcester's-Queen's at the Red Bull. James Burbage was 'the first builder of playhouses in London', and in return for the use of his Theatre the sharers paid him as rent the receipts from the entrance to the galleries, though this later became half these receipts. The sharers took the other half of these gallery profits, and also all those arising from entrance to the 'yard' where the groundlings stood, out of which they had to pay the hired actors, boys, musicians, lighting and other expenses. This was the method of other capitalist theatre owners, such as Henslowe and Langley. Henslowe took half the gallery money as rent, himself appointing the gatherers, kept the theatre in repair and paid the licence for its use to the Master of the Revels, the sharers being responsible for the rest of the expenses. In practice, Henslowe became the company's banker, advancing them money jointly for the purchase of plays and costumes, as well as individually; among others to Ben Jonson. It was, in fact, his policy to keep 'these fellows' in his debt, for otherwise he 'would have noe rule with them', and he could always reimburse himself by taking the half of the gallery due to the sharers. Sometimes the sharers, as well as the hired men, bound themselves to Henslowe instead of to their fellows, like Robert Dawes of the Lady Elizabeth's who, in 1614, contracted with Henslowe for three years, and agreed to pay fines: if late for rehearsal 12d.; for a performance 3s.; for missing a rehearsal altogether 2s., a play 20s.; and for drunkenness when due to perform 10s. And Henslowe sometimes bound dramatists, Henry Chettle for example, to write for nobody but 'my company'.

On the other hand, the Chamberlain's-King's Men formed a free association. When the Burbage brothers, Cuthbert and Richard, built the Globe in 1599, they kept one-half of the shares for themselves and divided the other half among five members of the company, one of whom was Shakespeare. There were originally, therefore, seven theatre owners, or 'housekeepers' as they were called. Cuthbert was not an actor, but the others as sharers were entitled to their proportion of the profits from the yard and half the gallery; as housekeepers they were entitled to the other half of the gallery, out of which they paid for the repairs and the ground-rent of £14 10s. The same system was adopted at the Blackfriars in 1608, and sometime after 1600, when the Admiral's moved to the Fortune, Alleyn made a similar arrangement. It is significant that the three great stable companies, the Chamberlain's, Admiral's, and Worcester's, all had ultimately this free form of association, whereas the companies that came under Henslowe and Langley had much more chequered and ephemeral careers. Indeed, in 1615 the Lady Elizabeth's Men accused Henslowe of having 'broken and dissmembered' five companies in three years. On the other hand, the alienation of shares in the houses of the Globe and Blackfriars led to a dispute in 1635. (See SHARERS' PAPERS.)

The history of the actors' companies may fairly easily be summarized, though the detail, particularly for 1592–4, is complex and obscure. It must also be remembered that the personnel of a company was by no means static: that not only did individual actors like the 'chameleon' Duttons frequently change their allegiance, but sometimes many, or even all, of the members of a company were temporarily or permanently absorbed by another. (For more detailed accounts see the various companies.)

1558–74: Though the Queen had her eight Court interlude players, they were allowed literally to die off, and she relied for her entertainment mainly on the Children of Paul's under Sebastian Westcott, their master from 1557 to about 1582, and on the Children of the Chapel. Of the adult companies Leicester's was the most prominent.

1574: Elizabeth herself granted Leicester's, who had recently appeared five times at Court, licence to play anywhere 'thoroughte oure Realme of England', an act that inaugurated the period of ascendancy of the adult companies until they were again challenged by the Children at the end of the century. Until 1583 Leicester's remained the most important company.

1576: James Burbage built the Theatre, and in that or the next year the Curtain was built in the same northern liberty of Holywell, where they offered better accommodation than the improvized inn-theatres of the City. (1576–84: the first Blackfriars theatre.)

1583–92: In 1583 Elizabeth selected twelve of the best men from the other companies and made them her servants, the Queen's Men. Not only had they a royal licence to play, but they also had in Tarlton the most popular comedian of the age, and the abstraction of the best men from the other companies – three came from Leicester's – was a crippling blow to them. For the next seven or eight years, the period of the University Wits and an immense advance in the drama, the Queen's Men had it all their own way, though they lost Tarlton, who died in 1588.

1590–92: Strange's Men, and the Admiral's with Alleyn became serious rivals of the Queen's.

January 1593–Spring 1594: Plague and a period of confusion. The theatres were closed for most of this time, and all the companies had to travel; Pembroke's were unable to pay their way and had to pawn their stock, the Queen's never returned to London but became a provincial company, and Alleyn of the Admiral's led a troupe of Strange's Men through the provinces.

1594: The Strange-Admiral combination broke up in June when the theatres reopened; Strange's found a new patron in the Lord Chamberlain and were joined by Shakespeare and Richard Burbage; Alleyn reorganized the Admiral's. Henceforth these two companies were much the most important.

1597: A Privy Council order limited the London companies to the Chamberlain's and Admiral's, though the order was not strictly enforced, and in 1602 the Council officially admitted Worcester's, and assigned to them the Boar's Head as a house, the Chamberlain's having been established at their own Globe since 1599, the Admiral's at Alleyn's Fortune since 1600.

1600–8: There was a revival of interest in the Boys' companies playing at Blackfriars, leading to the 'War of the Theatres', or *Poetomachia* (q.v.). It was most acute about the turn of the century, when it is referred to in *Hamlet*, but by 1608, when the King's Men took over the Blackfriars theatre, the competition was practically at an end.

1603: The three official London companies, the Lord Chamberlain's, the Admiral's and Worcester's, were taken into the royal service as the King's, Prince Henry's and Queen's respectively.

1610–15: The Duke of York's and the Lady Elizabeth's received royal patents, but from an amalgamation under Henslowe with the Queen's Revels the Duke of York's (now Prince Charles's) alone emerged, so that when Shakespeare died there were four London companies: the King's at the Globe and Blackfriars; the Palsgrave's (the former Admiral's and Prince Henry's) at the Fortune; the Queen's at the Red Bull; and Prince Charles's at the Hope, and much the most successful of these was Shakespeare's company, the King's. (See under the various companies; CHILDREN'S COMPANIES; THEATRES.)

Actresses. Before the Restoration (1660), women's parts were acted by boys, though there are a few references to women on the stage in Shakespeare's time. Thomas Coryate in his *Crudities* (1611) writes: 'I saw women acte in Venice, a thing that I never saw before, though I have heard that it hathe beene sometimes used in London.' But if the Epilogue to Middleton's and Dekker's *The Roaring Girl, Or Moll Cut-Purse*, performed at the Fortune (*c.* 1610):

> The Roring Girle her selfe some few dayes hence,
> Shall on this Stage give larger recompence,

really refers to the forthcoming appearance of Moll herself on the stage (Moll, or Mary Frith, was a real person), it could scarcely be as an actress. Apart from these possible exceptions, the first appearance of a professional actress on the London stage seems to have been that of Margaret Hughes as Desdemona in 1660. On 18 February 1662 Pepys recorded: 'I went to the Opera, and saw "The Law against Lovers", a good play and well performed, especially the little girl's, whom I never saw act before, dancing and singing; and were it not for her, the losse of Roxalana [Elizabeth Davenport] would spoil the house.' Even after 1660, however, boys sometimes took women's parts. (See BOY ACTORS; APPRENTICES; KYNASTON.)

Adam. In *As You Like It*, the faithful old servant who follows Orlando into exile. According to William Oldys (*c.* 1750), 'One of Shakespeare's younger brothers, who lived to a good old age,' told some actors that a long time ago he had seen 'his brother Will ... act a part in one of his own comedies, wherein being to personate a decrepit old man, he wore a long beard, and appeared so weak and drooping and unable to walk, that he was forced to be supported and carried by another person to a table, at which he was seated among some company, who were eating, and one of them sung a song.' This, for what it is worth, must refer to Adam. (He is the Adam Spencer (the steward) of Lodge's *Rosalynde*.)

Adams, John Cranford (b. 1903). American scholar; President of Hofstra College since 1944; senior research fellow at the Folger Shakespeare Library; author of *The Globe Playhouse*, etc. Plays at the Hofstra College Shakespeare Festival are performed in his replica of the Globe.

Adams, Joseph Quincy (1881–1946). American scholar; Professor in English at Cornell University, 1919–31; Director of the Folger Shakespeare Library, 1931–46. Editor of the *New Variorum* Shakespeare. Author of *Shakespearean Playhouses*, *A Life of William Shakespeare*, etc.

Adaptation of Plays. In its more moderate form, the opinion that Shakespeare adapted other men's plays is confined to his early work, particularly the first part of *Henry VI* and *Titus Andronicus*, but some extend adaptation to the plays of the middle period, to *Henry V* and *Julius Caesar*. (See AUTHENTICITY OF PLAYS.)

After the Restoration many of Shakespeare's plays were adapted: trimmed and tidied, and furnished with all manner of music, dance, and spectacle. D'Avenant adapted *Measure for Measure* (1662), *Macbeth* (1663), *Tempest* (1667); Lacy, *Taming of the Shrew* (1663); Duffet, *Tempest* (1675); Ravenscroft, *Titus Andronicus* (1678); Shadwell, *Timon* (1678); Dryden, *Troilus and Cressida* (1679); Otway, *Romeo and Juliet* (1679); Tate, *Richard II* (1680), *Lear* (1681), *Coriolanus* (1682); Crowne, *Henry VI* (1681); D'Urfey, *Cymbeline* (1682); Gildon, *Measure for Measure* (1699); Colley Cibber, *Richard III* (1700); Granville, *Merchant of Venice* (1701); Dennis, *Merry Wives* (1702). Betterton, to his credit, played often in the original versions, and in the 18th century Garrick claimed to have returned to the original texts, yet he fiddled with *The Taming of the Shrew*, *The Winter's Tale*, *A Midsummer Night's Dream*, even with *Hamlet*, which so far had survived, and he gave *Romeo and Juliet* a happy ending. It remained for the 19th century gradually to restore the original Shakespeare, and for the 20th century producer to revert to adaptation; e.g. *A Midsummer Night's Dream*: 1933, Reinhardt's open-air production; 1939, *Swingin' the Dream* in New York, with Louis Armstrong as Bottom; 1959, a 'Texan Version'; 1959, Peter Hall's Stratford production. (See the Stage History of each play, and Hazelton Spencer, *Shakespeare Improved*, 1927.)

Addenbrooke, John. On 17 December 1608 the Stratford Court of Record issued a precept, signed by Thomas Greene, to arrest 'Johannem Addenbrooke generosum ... ad respondendum Willielmo Shackspeare generoso, de placito debiti'. Again, on 15 March 1609, it issued a similar precept to produce Addenbrooke

> ad satisfaciendum Willielmo Shackspere generoso, tam de sex libris debiti quas predictus Willielmus in eadem curia versus eum recuperavit quam de viginti et quatuor solidis qui ei adiudicati fuerunt pro dampnis et custagiis suis quos sustinuit occacione detencionis debiti predicti.

But Addenbrooke had moved outside the jurisdiction of the Court: 'Infranominatus Johannes non est inventus infra libertatem hujus burgi', and Shakespeare had to proceed against his surety, Thomas Horneby, for the recovery of his £6, and 24s. damages and costs. Nothing more is known of Addenbrooke.

Addison, Joseph (1672–1719). There are a number of passages of Shakespearean criticism in the *Spectator*. Though an Augustan, Addison could appreciate Shakespeare's 'Fairy way of Writing', and though he subscribed to the classical conception of Shakespeare as a wild, irregular genius, yet, 'Our Criticks do not seem sensible that there is more Beauty in the Works of a great Genius who is ignorant of the Rules of Art, than in those of a little Genius who knows and observes them'. (*Spectator*, 592.)

Adlington, William. Translator of the *Metamorphose*, or *Golden Ass*, from the Latin of Lucius Apuleius, to whom Shakespeare may be indebted for Bottom's transformation. Little is known of Adlington; the dedication of his book to the Earl of Sussex was 'From University College in Oxford, the xviii of September 1566'. It was reprinted in 1571, 1582 and 1596. Adlington worked from a French version of Apuleius, and his fine prose must have made an impression on Shakespeare.

Admiral's Men. After the Chamberlain's, the most important of all the players' companies, and thanks to the *Diary* of Philip Henslowe the one about which we know most. Until 1603 their patron was Charles Howard, 1st Earl of Nottingham (1536–1624), the son of William, 1st Baron Howard of Effingham, whom he succeeded as 2nd Baron in 1573. In 1585 he became Lord High Admiral, and commanded the fleet that destroyed the Armada in 1588. After the Cadiz raid of 1596, the command of which he shared with Essex, he was created Earl of Nottingham. In 1618 he resigned the office of Lord High Admiral, and in 1624 he died. He was one of the most attractive characters of the time, his actions being beyond reproach. The company of players, generally known as the Admiral's, was successively Lord Howard's, Lord Admiral's (1585), Earl of Nottingham's (1596), Prince Henry's (1603), Elector Palatine's (Palsgrave's) (1612).

There are records of a company of Lord Howard's Men both in the provinces and at Court in 1576–9. They are next heard of as the Admiral's in 1585, when it is possible that Edward Alleyn and others left Worcester's to join them. The years 1583–94 were difficult for a new company: first there was the competition of the Queen's Men, and then the plague years of 1593–4, events which broke many of the companies. The Admiral's survived, however, though they had to join forces with Strange's, possibly as early as 1590 (see OTTEWELL), and in the plague years of 1593–4 Alleyn led the combined companies on a prolonged provincial tour, though according to the Privy Council licence of 6 May 1593, all the chief players except Alleyn himself were Strange's:

> Edward Allen, servaunt to the right honorable the Lord Highe Admiral, William Kemp, Thomas Pope, John Heminges, Augustine Phillipes, and Georg Brian, being al one companie, servauntes to our verie good Lord the Lord Strainge.

In October 1592, Alleyn married Henslowe's step-daughter, Joan Woodward, and began the lucrative partnership that lasted until Henslowe's death in 1616. When, therefore, the theatres reopened, Henslowe recorded, 'begininge the 14 of Maye 1594, by my lord Admeralls men; *The Jewe of Malta, The Rangers comodey, Cutlacke.*' For ten days in June they played for Henslowe at Newington Butts with the Chamberlain's, then apparently the companies reorganized, Shakespeare, Richard Burbage and Kempe among others joining the Chamberlain's, and the two companies went triumphantly their own ways, becoming great rivals and much the most important of the London companies.

But their organization was very different: while the Chamberlain's were self-governing, after 1599 owning their own theatre, and performing the plays of one of their own actors, Shakespeare, the Admiral's paid rent to their landlord, Henslowe, who in time became virtually their employer and banker, to whom many of them were chronically in debt. As rent, Henslowe normally received half the money paid for admission to the galleries, the other half and the profits arising from entrance to the yard being divided among the actor-sharers, who had to buy their costumes, pay the hired actors, the dramatists who supplied them with plays, and so on. In practice, Henslowe came to advance money for these purposes, often buying plays himself, binding dramatists to write for the Admiral's alone, and recouping himself from the half share of the galleries that nominally went to the actor-sharers. In a normal year they would play at the Rose every weekday from about October to the beginning of Lent, with two or three Court performances at Christmas; playing was forbidden during Lent, but this rule was by no means always kept; then from Easter to midsummer at the Rose, after which they might go on a provincial tour for about three months. According to Chambers's analysis, in the three years 1594–7 they gave 728 London performances and produced 55 new plays, in addition to older plays, in particular those of Marlowe, which always remained popular. During these years their principal actors were: Edward Alleyn, John Singer, Richard Jones, Thomas Towne, Martin Slater, Edward Juby, Thomas Downton and James Donstone.

In 1597 Jones and Downton joined Pembroke's at Francis Langley's Swan theatre, but after the disastrous episode of their production of *The Isle of Dogs*, which led to the closing of all the theatres from the end of July to October, they returned, bringing with them three of Pembroke's Men: Robert Shaw, Gabriel Spencer and William Bird (or Borne), whom Henslowe bound fast to the Admiral's. Humphrey and Anthony Jeffes joined the company in the same year, and in March 1598 Thomas Heywood the dramatist 'came and hiered hime seallfe with me [Henslowe] as a covenante searvante for ij yeares'. But, though strengthened by the addition of Pembroke's men, particularly Shaw, they were sadly weakened by the loss of Alleyn, who retired from acting until 1600, when he returned at the Queen's request. On the other hand, the Admiral's and the Chamberlain's were given the monopoly of London playing by the Privy Council. In 1598 they also lost Gabriel Spencer, who was 'slayen in Hogesden fylldes by the handes of Bengemen Jonson bricklayer'. Their main playwrights at this time were Drayton, Hathway, Munday, Wilson,

Dekker, Chettle, Chapman, Heywood: the first four, for example, collaborating in *Sir John Oldcastle*, the first part of which was later attributed to Shakespeare and included in the Third Folio.

In 1600 Alleyn resumed playing, and shortly afterwards the Admiral's moved to the Fortune theatre, which he had built on the north side of the river, a venture in which Henslowe joined him in 1601. In 1602 Jones and Shaw left the company, and in 1603 Elizabeth died, and the Admiral's, or more strictly the Earl of Nottingham's Men, became the servants of James I's son, Prince Henry. Like the King's and Queen's Men, the sharers in the Prince's received 4½ yards of red cloth for James's coronation procession, their names being given as, 'Edward Allen, William Bird, Thomas Towne, Thomas Dowton, Samuell Rowley, Edward Jubie, Humfry Jeffes, Charles Massey, and Anthony Jeffes'. In the royal patent of 1606 the roll is the same except for Alleyn, who must have retired about 1605, though he still drew rent for the Fortune from the Prince's.

With the accession of James, the number of Court performances increased greatly. From 1594 to 1603 the Chamberlain's had given 32 Court performances as against the Admiral's 20, 5 by other adult companies, and 7 by the Boys'. The figures for 1603–16 are: 177, 47, 57, 18. In November 1612 Prince Henry died, and the company came under the patronage of James's son-in-law, the Elector Palatine, the players named in the patent of 1613 being: 'Thomas Downton, William Bird, Edward Juby, Samuell Rowle, Charles Massey, Humfrey Jeffs, Frank Grace, William Cartwright, Edward Colbrand, William Parr, William Stratford, Richard Gunnell, John Shank, and Richard Price'. Downton was the one survivor of the original company of 1594. Henslowe, whose detailed *Diary* ended in 1603, died in 1616, but Alleyn survived at his Dulwich manor another ten years.

It is possible that as early as 1608 Alleyn sold part of his interest in the Fortune to the company. Ten years later they rented the theatre from him for £200 and two rundlets of wine annually. In 1621 it was burned down, and rebuilt by Alleyn, who again leased shares to the company.

Adrian. In *The Tempest*, 'A Lord', ingenuous and pedantic, shipwrecked with Alonso.

Adriana. In *The Comedy of Errors* (q.v.), the wife of Antipholus of Ephesus. (Unnamed in the *Menaechmi* of Plautus.)

Aegeon. In *The Comedy of Errors*, a merchant of Syracuse, husband of Aemilia, and father of the Antipholus twins. (Called Moschus in the *Menaechmi.*)

Aemilia. In *The Comedy of Errors*, the wife of Aegeon and mother of the Antipholus twins, after the imagined loss of whom she becomes an Abbess at Ephesus. She protects the bewildered Antipholus of Syracuse, who takes refuge with her when he is thought to be mad. (There is no such character in the *Menaechmi.*)

Aemilius. In *Titus Andronicus*, 'a noble Roman'; he first acknowledges Lucius as Emperor (v, iii).

Aeneas. A Trojan commander in *Troilus and Cressida.* He breaks the news to Troilus that he 'must give up to Diomedes' hand The Lady Cressida' (iv, ii).

Agamemnon. In *Troilus and Cressida*, the Grecian commander-in-chief, brother of Menelaus, and King of Mycenae. Though he appears often, he affects the action but little.

Agas, Ralph (*c.* 1540–1621), surveyor, was born in Suffolk. He is best known for his maps of Oxford (1578), Cambridge (1592), and London. Of the last, two copies remain, six feet long and printed from wooden blocks made sometime between 1569 and 1590. As they were not printed until 1633, they are unreliable guides to the shapes and positions of the Elizabethan theatres.

Agrippa. In *Antony and Cleopatra*, a friend of Octavius, whose sister, Octavia, he suggests that Antony should marry (II, ii). (M. Vipsanius Agrippa (63–12 B.C.) commanded the fleet at Actium for Octavius, and later married his daughter.)

Aguecheek, Sir Andrew. In *Twelfth Night*, a foolish knight, a suitor of Olivia, gulled by Sir Toby and beaten by Sebastian.

Ajax. In *Troilus and Cressida*, one of the Grecian commanders. Alexander's description of him in I, ii is thought by some to refer to Ben Jonson, and to be Shakespeare's *purge* referred to in *3 Parnassus* in return for Jonson's *pill* in *The Poetaster*. (See POETOMACHIA.)

Alabaster, William. See ROXANA.

Alarbus. In *Titus Andronicus*, the eldest son of Tamora. He is sacrificed by the sons of Titus (I, i).

Albany, Duke of. In *King Lear*, the husband of Goneril, whose unfilial actions he comes to detest. Though his sympathies are with Lear, he has to repel the French forces brought to his aid by Cordelia. After Lear's death he becomes King of Britain.

'Alchemist, The.' Perhaps the best of Ben Jonson's plays, registered in October 1610, and published in 1612. In the Folio, 1616, is the note:

> This Comœdie was first acted, in the yeere 1610. By the Kings Maiesties Seruants. The principall Comœdians were, Ric. Burbadge, Ioh. Hemings, Ioh. Lowin, Will. Ostler, Hen. Condel, Ioh. Vnderwood, Alex. Cooke, Nic. Tooley, Rob. Armin, Will. Eglestone. With the allowance of the Master of the Revells.

Alcibiades. In *Timon of Athens*, 'an Athenian Captaine' (F). He asks the Senate to pardon a friend, is refused, answers angrily, and is banished. The misanthropic Timon gives him gold to support his attack on Athens, which he takes and avenges himself on his and Timon's ungrateful enemies. (Alcibiades lived *c.* 450–404 B.C.)

Aldridge, Ira Frederick (*c.* 1805–67), negro actor, 'the African Roscius' was born in Senegambia, went to New York, and then to Glasgow to train for missionary work, but turned actor and played Othello and Aaron with great success in the provinces and on the Continent, where he died.

Alençon, Duke of. In *1 Henry VI*, a supporter of the Dauphin, and an admirer of Joan of Arc's prowess. He talks of the English much as do the French lords in *Henry V*:

> They want their porridge and their fat
> bull-beeves ...
> Lean raw-boned rascals! who would e'er
> suppose
> They had such courage and audacity?

(John, 2nd Duke of Alençon (d. 1476), was the son of the 1st Duke, mentioned in *Henry V* as fighting with Henry, and killed at Agincourt.)

Alexander. In *Troilus and Cressida*, a servant of Cressida to whom in I, ii he describes Ajax (q.v.).

Alexander, Peter. Regius Professor of English Language and Literature at Glasgow University since 1935. In his *Shakespeare's Henry VI and Richard III* (1929), he showed that *1 Contention* and *True Tragedy* are 'bad' Quartos (q.v.). Author of *Shakespeare's Life and Art*, *Hamlet: Father and Son*, etc.

Alexandrines. Lines of six iambic feet, instead of the five iambics of regular blank verse. They are, like the short lines, substitutions of feet, and so on, an irregularity that becomes more frequent in the later plays. According to Fleay, *A*

Midsummer Night's Dream has none, and *Othello* the most with seventy-three, from which the following examples are taken:

For nought but provender, and when he's old cashier'd (I, i, 48).

That can thy light relume. When I have pluck'd the rose (V, ii, 13).

Alexas. In *Antony and Cleopatra*, an attendant on Cleopatra. His treachery to Antony and death are related by Enobarbus (IV, vi).

Alice. In *Henry V*, a lady attending on Princess Katharine of France, to whom she gives an English lesson (III, iv). This is one of the scenes 'discarded' by Hanmer as 'a wretched piece of ribaldry'. (In F 'an old Gentlewoman'. J. Q. Adams suggests that Shakespeare may have got his French from Mary Mountjoy (q.v.).)

Aliena. The name assumed by Celia in *As You Like It*, and by Alinda in Lodge's *Rosalynde*.

Allde, Edward (*c.* 1583–1624). A printer, like his father, John, of the Long Shop in the Poultry. He had two presses, but his work was poor. Edward printed,

1600, possibly Q1 *A Midsummer Night's Dream*, for T. Fisher.

1611, Q3 *Titus Andronicus*, for E. White.

1611, Q2 *The Phoenix and Turtle*, for M. Lownes.

He may have printed the second half of Q1 *Romeo and Juliet*.

Allen, Giles. Ground landlord of James Burbage's Theatre (q.v.).

Alleyn, Edward (1566–1626). Actor and founder of Dulwich College, was born in London, his father being an innholder and porter to the Queen. According to Fuller, he was 'bred a stage player', and certainly in 1583 he was a member of a provincial company of the Earl of Worcester. Soon afterwards he joined the Admiral's, of which company his brother John was a member. In 1592 he married Joan Woodward, stepdaughter of Philip Henslowe, with whom he formed a partnership that lasted until Henslowe's death in 1616. From 1590 to 1594 there seems to have been an amalgamation of Strange's and the Admiral's under the leadership of Alleyn, and when, owing to the plague in 1593, this joint company was forced to travel, a special licence was issued by the Privy Council to 'Edward Allen, servaunt to the right honorable the Lord Highe Admiral, William Kemp, Thomas Pope, John Heminges, Augustine Phillipes and Georg Brian, being al one companie, servauntes to our verie good the Lord the Lord Strainge'. Presumably these were the more important actor-sharers, and presumably there were four or five hired men, of whom Shakespeare may have been one.

That Alleyn's acting was already remarkable is clear from Nashe's *Pierce Penilesse* of 1592, in which he says: 'Not Roscius nor Aesope, those admyred tragedians that haue liued euer since before Christ was borne, could euer performe more in action than famous Ned Allen.' From 1594 to 1597 he was with the Admiral's at Henslowe's Rose, then 'leafte playnge' for a time, but in 1600 was at the Fortune. which he and Henslowe built. In 1603 the Admiral's became Prince Henry's Men, and their leader Alleyn, as Genius of the City, delivered an Address to James I, with, according to Dekker, 'excellent action and a well-tun'de, audible voyce'.

Alleyn was now a wealthy man; since 1594 he had had a financial interest in the Beargarden (later the Hope), he was part owner of the Fortune, he had leasehold investments in London and Sussex, and in 1604 he and Henslowe succeeded in buying jointly the office of Master of the Game of Paris Garden. In 1604, therefore, he retired and the next year bought the manor of Dulwich, though it was not till 1614 that he consolidated the estate at a total cost of nearly £10,000. In 1613 he moved from Southwark to Dulwich, where he began the building of the College which was opened in 1617. His father-in-law, Henslowe, died in 1616, and his wife Joan in 1623, but in the same year he married Constance, the daughter of John Donne, the poet and Dean of St Paul's. He died 25 December 1626.

We know that Alleyn played Tamburlaine, Faustus and Barabas in Marlowe's plays, and there are numerous references to his genius besides those of Nashe and Dekker, notably by Weever, Johnson, Fuller and Heywood. Dover Wilson and G. B. Harrison think Shakespeare was satirizing the acting of Alleyn in Hamlet's advice to the players. (See APOLOGY FOR ACTORS; SS, 7.)

Alleyn, John (*c.* 1556–96). Elder brother of Edward Alleyn. An actor, with the provincial company of Lord Sheffield in 1580, with the Admiral's 1589–91.

'All for Love, or The World Well Lost.' Dryden's version of the Antony and Cleopatra story, produced at Drury Lane in 1678. The action is simpler than Shakespeare's; the attempt of Dolabella, Ventidius and Octavia to detach Antony from Cleopatra. They fail because Antony begins to suspect Dolabella's motives. In his Preface Dryden wrote:

> In my style I have professed to imitate the divine Shakespeare; which that I might perform more freely, I have dis-incumbered myself from rhyme. ... I hope I need not to explain myself, that I have not copied my author servilely: words and phrases must of necessity receive a change in succeeding ages: but 'tis almost a miracle that much of his language remains so pure; and that he who began dramatic poetry amongst us, untaught by any, and, as Ben Jonson tells us, without learning, should by the force of his own genius perform so much, that in a manner he has left no praise for any who come after him. ... Yet I hope I may affirm, and without vanity, that by imitating him, I have excell'd myself throughout the play.

'All is True.' The name given to *Henry VIII* – presumably because of the triple insistence of the Prologue on the truth of the events – by Sir Henry Wotton in a letter describing the burning of the Globe on 29 June 1613:

> Now, to let matters of state sleep, I will entertain you at the present with what has happened this week at the Bank's side. The King's players had a new play, called *All is True*, representing some principal pieces of the reign of Henry VIII, which was set forth with many extraordinary circumstances of pomp and majesty, even to the matting of the stage....

Alliteration. The repetition of the same letter either at the beginning or in the body of closely related words. The device is more obvious in Shakespeare's early work, when he favoured the alliterative use of the consonants *p, b, v, f*, as in *Love's Labour's Lost*:

> Good Lord Boyet, my beauty, though but mean,
> Needs not the painted flourish of your praise:
> Beauty is bought by judgment of the eye,
> Not utter'd by base sale of chapmen's tongues.

Even in this play Shakespeare parodies alliteration when Holofernes 'something affects the letter':

> The playful princess pierced and prick'd a pretty pleasing pricket ...

and of course it is parodied again in *A Midsummer Night's Dream*:

> Whereat, with blade, with bloody blameful blade,
> He bravely broach'd his boiling bloody breast.

The later poetry is remarkable less for the bravery of its consonants than for the richness of its vowel music:

> Where souls do couch on flowers, we'll hand in hand,
> And with our sprightly port make the ghosts gaze:
> Dido and her Æneas shall want troops,
> And all the haunt be ours.

Allot, Robert. Bookseller, in business 1625–35. He was one of the syndicate that published F2 in 1632. He died in 1635. (See BLOUNT.)

'ALL'S WELL THAT ENDS WELL.'

WRITTEN: 1602–3. A very difficult play to date, as there is more than one style. At about the time of the writing of *Hamlet* Shakespeare seems to have revised a play written some five or six years before (perhaps the *Love's Labour's Won* mentioned by Meres). He may have given it a further revision after his retirement to Stratford, for parts (e.g. I ii) are written in his latest manner. (See 'JACK DRUM'S ENTERTAINMENT'.)

PERFORMED: First recorded performance at Goodman's Fields, 1741.

REGISTERED: 1623, 8 November. One of the sixteen plays registered by Blount and Jaggard before publishing F1.

PUBLISHED: 1623, F1. 'All's Well, that Ends Well.' The twelfth play in the Comedy section: pp. 230–54. *Actus primus. Scaena prima*, and Acts II to V marked. Not a very good text; some indications of cutting. Set up from foul papers.

SOURCE: Boccaccio: the *Decameron*; the tale of *Giglietta di Nerbona*, translated by William Painter in his *Palace of Pleasure*, 1566.

STAGE HISTORY: 1741, Goodman's Fields.

1742, Drury Lane: Peg Woffington as Helena.

1794, Drury Lane: J. P. Kemble as Bertram; Dora Jordan as Helena.

1811, Covent Garden: Charles Kemble as Bertram.

1832, Covent Garden: an operatic version.

1852, Sadler's Wells: Samuel Phelps as Parolles.

1927, Birmingham Repertory Theatre: modern dress.

1953, Stratford (Ontario) Festival.

Helena, daughter of a famous physician who has recently died, is taken into the household of the kindly dowager Countess of Rossillion, who is overjoyed when she discovers that she is in love with her son Bertram, a haughty young man. Unaware of Helena's love, Bertram goes to the French court as the king's ward; Helena follows him, cures the king of a serious disease with a remedy of her father's, and as a reward asks him to give her Bertram as her husband. At the king's command Bertram unwillingly marries her, but at once sets off for the wars as a volunteer in the Florentine army, sending a message to Helena: 'When thou canst get this ring upon my finger, which never shall come off, and show me a child begotten of thy body hat I am father to, then call me husband.' In Florence Helena discovers that he is attempting to seduce her hostess's daughter Diana, persuades her to let her take her place in bed at night, is got with child by Bertram, and secures his ring in exchange for one given her by the king. She is, therefore, able to claim Bertram as her husband and, after some complications, all is well.

The sub-plot of the cowardly braggart Parolles is but loosely attached, though his dramatic function is to corrupt Bertram, as Falstaff corrupts Prince Hal, and so make the hero's faults more readily pardonable.

For Coleridge, Helena was Shakespeare's 'loveliest character', and of the Countess Bernard Shaw wrote: 'The most beautiful old woman's part ever written.'

Allusions. Topical allusions are useful as evidence of the date of a play's composition. For example, Gloucester's reference in *King Lear* to 'these late eclipses in the sun and moon' is almost certainly to the eclipses of October and September 1605; if so, and assuming the play to be a homogeneous composition, it must have been written after that date. Topical allusions, however, are much rarer in Shakespeare than in most of his contemporaries, as none of his plays deals with a contemporary theme, and there are no other references as definite as that to Essex's Irish expedition in *Henry V*, which dates the play between March and September 1599.

Alonso. In *The Tempest*, the King of Naples, who helped Antonio to eject Prospero from Milan, in return for the Dukedom's becoming subject to Naples (q.v.). On his return from Tunis after marrying his daughter to the King, he is shipwrecked on Prospero's magic island, made to repent, and willingly agrees to the marriage of his son Ferdinand to Prospero's daughter, Miranda.

'Amends for Ladies.' A comedy by Nathan Field, a sharer in the King's *c.* 1615–19. The play was written *c.* 1611, and published 1618:

Amends for Ladies. A Comedie. As it was acted at the Blacke-Fryers, both by the

Princes Seruants, and the Lady Elizabeths. By Nat Field.

The Blackfriars theatre was Porter's Hall (1615–17). There is a reference to *1 Henry IV*, and to Falstaff by his original name of Oldcastle:

The Play where the fat Knight, hight Old-
Castle,
Did tell you truly what his honour was?

America. See UNITED STATES.

Amiens. In *As You Like It*, a lord attending the banished Duke. He sings 'Under the greenwood tree', and 'Blow, blow, thou winter wind'. (See ARNE.)

Amner, Richard (1736–1803). Born at Hinckley, Leicestershire. He became a Presbyterian minister, from 1764 to 1777 being in charge of a chapel at Hampstead, where George Steevens was living. They quarrelled, and when Steevens published his 1793 edition of *Shakespeare* he attributed to Amner and another clergyman, John Collins, a number of obscene interpretations of the text.

Amyot, Jacques (1513–93). French writer and translator of Plutarch. His origin was poor, but he went to Paris University, and became professor of Greek and Latin at Bourges, tutor to the sons of Henry II, and finally Bishop of Auxerre. His fine French version of Plutarch's *Lives, Vies des hommes illustres* (1559–65), was translated into English by Sir Thomas North (1579). North's *Plutarch* was Shakespeare's source for his Roman plays.

Anachronisms. Errors in chronology, whereby the historical sequence of events is confused and things put out of place. Generally speaking, the artists of the Renaissance, whether painters or poets, paid little attention to historical accuracy, and Shakespeare was no exception. Thus clocks strike in Rome and Cleopatra plays billiards. In Troy, ancient Athens, and Rome they wear hats and gloves; Caesar wears a doublet, Chiron carries a rapier, and Gloucester in pre-Christian Britain needs spectacles. Froth lives in Vienna, Sir Toby Belch in Illyria, Dogberry in Messina, and Bottom in Athens. In the mid 19th century realist producers tried, with disastrous results, to resolve these apparent discords. Thus, in 1856 Charles Kean complained of *The Winter's Tale*: 'chronological contradictions abound, inasmuch as reference is made to the Delphic Oracle, Christian burial, an Emperor of Russia, and an Italian painter of the sixteenth century.' His remedy was drastic: the period became that when Syracuse was 'at the summit of her political prosperity'; Bohemia became Bithynia, the costume that of Asia Minor, and the sheep-shearing scene a Dionysiac Festival.

Anapaest. A trisyllabic foot consisting of two unstressed and one stressed syllable (⏑ ⏑ –). According to Saintsbury, 'perhaps the chief enlivening and inspiriting force in English poetry'. It is used by Shakespeare with progressive frequency to vary the regular iambics of blank verse; e.g.:

There they hoist us
To cry | tŏ thĕ sēa | that roared to us; to
sigh
Tŏ thĕ wīnds | ...

'Anatomy of Abuses, The: *Contayning a Discoverie, or briefe Summarie of such Notable Vices and Imperfections, as now raigne in many Christian Countreyes of the Worlde: but (especiallie) in a verie famous Ilande called Ailgna.*' By Phillip Stubbes, 1583. One of the most violent of the Puritan attacks on the stage, the book is a dialogue between Spudeus and Philoponus, and is a general denunciation of the abuses of the age. 'Ailgna' is England (Anglia). It was answered by Nashe in his *Anatomie of Absurditie*. The following extracts indicate the nature of Stubbes's attack on the stage:

I would not haue thee so to take mee, as though my speaches tended to the ouerthrowe and vtter disliking of all kynd of exercyses in generall: that is nothing my simple meaning. But the particulare Abuses which are crept into euery one of these seuerall exercyses is the only thing which I think worthie of reprobation.... But being vsed (as now commonly they be) to the prophanation of the Lord his sabaoth, to the alluring and inuegling of the People from the blessed word of God preached, to Theaters and vnclean assemblies, to ydlenes, vnthriftynes, whordome, wantonnes, drunkennes, and what not; and which is more, when they are vsed to this end, to maintaine a great sort of ydle Persons, doing nothing but playing and loytring, hauing their liuings of the sweat of other Mens browes, much like vnto dronets deuouring the sweet honie of the poore labouring bees, than are they exercyses (at no hand) sufferable....

All Stage-playes, Enterluds, and Commedies are either of diuyne or prophane matter: If they be of diuine matter, then are they most intollerable, or rather Sacrilegious. ... Vpon the other side, if their playes be of prophane matters, then tend they to the dishonor of God, and norishing of vice, both which are damnable. So that whither they be the one or the other, they are quite contrarie to the Word of grace, and sucked out of the Deuills teates to nourish vs in ydolatrie, hethenrie and sinne....

But if there were no euill in them saue this, namely, that the arguments of tragedies is anger, wrath, immunitie, crueltie, iniurie, incest, murther, & such like, the Persons, or Actors are Goddes, Goddesses, Furies, Fyends, Hagges, Kings, Queenes, or Potentates. Of Commedies the matter and ground is loue, bawdrie, cosenage, flattery, whordome, adulterie; the Persons, or agents, whores, queanes, bawdes, scullions, knaues, Curtezans, lecherous old men, amorous yong men, with such like of infinit varietie. If, I say, there were nothing els but this, it were sufficient to withdraw a good christian from the vsing of them; For so often as they goe to those howses where Players frequent, thei go to *Venus* pallace, & sathans synagogue, to worship deuils, & betray Christ Iesus....

Away therfore with this so infamous an art! for goe they neuer so braue, yet are they counted and taken but for beggars. And is it not true? liue they not vpon begging of euery one that comes? Are they not taken by the lawes of the Realm for roagues and vacaboundes? I speak of such as trauaile the Cuntries with playes and enterludes, making an occupation of it, and ought so to be punished, if they had their deserts.

Anderson, Mary (1859–1940). American actress, born at Sacramento, California. Her first appearance on the stage was in 1875 at Louisville, Kentucky, as Juliet. Between 1883 and 1889 she played often in London, and took the part of Rosalind at the opening of the Memorial Theatre at Stratford. Her chief Shakespearean roles were Rosalind, Juliet, and Perdita, which last part she contrived to double with that of Hermione. She retired from the stage in 1889, married Antonio de Navarro, and settled at Broadway at the foot of the Cotswolds.

Andrewes, Robert (d. 1616). The scrivener who prepared the conveyance and mortgage of the Blackfriars Gatehouse for Shakespeare in March 1613. His shop was near St Paul's, and his clerk was 'Henry Lawrence, servant to the same scr'.

Andromache. In *Troilus and Cressida*, the wife of Hector. In v, iii she tries to prevent his going to fight the Greeks.

Andronicus, Marcus. In *Timon of Athens*, brother of Timon and tribune of the people. He discovers the ravished and mutilated Lavinia (II, v), and helps Titus to avenge his wrongs.

Andronicus, Titus. A victorious Roman general, and the chief character in *Titus Andronicus* (q.v.).

Angelo. 1. In *The Comedy of Errors*, a goldsmith who makes a chain for Antipholus of Ephesus, but in mistake gives it to his twin brother and then demands payment from the former.

2. In *Measure for Measure* (q.v.) 'the Deputie' (F). (He is the Promos of Whetstone's *Promos and Cassandra*, and the Juriste of Cinthio's *novella*.)

Angus. In *Macbeth*, a Scottish nobleman who supports Malcolm against Macbeth.

Anne. In *Richard III* she curses Richard who, however, woos and marries her

(I, ii). She is crowned (IV, i), but dies mysteriously, and her ghost appears to Richard before Bosworth. (Anne Neville (1456–85) was the daughter of Warwick the Kingmaker. She was betrothed to Edward, Prince of Wales, killed, possibly by Richard, at Tewkesbury.)

Anne Hathaway's Cottage. See HEWLAND.

Anne of Denmark (1574–1619). Wife of James I of England and daughter of King Frederick II of Denmark. She was married to James by proxy in 1589 when he was King of Scotland only; Prince Henry was born in 1594, Elizabeth (of Bohemia) in 1596, and the future Charles I in 1600. She was crowned with James in London in July 1604 after his accession to the English throne. Anne had been brought up a Lutheran, but her Catholic sympathies caused some scandal both in Scotland and England. However, she was more interested in pleasure than in religion: in the 6,000 dresses of Elizabeth which she inherited, in her jewellery, and, above all, in the masque. At her father's Court she would have seen Shakespeare's future fellows, Will Kempe, Thomas Pope and George Bryan, and other English players in 1586; and Laurence Fletcher and 'Inglis Comedians' were at the Scottish Court from 1594 onwards. In England the pleasure-loving Queen gave herself up to the delights of the masque, a spectacular and excessively expensive form of entertainment, in which she herself used to take part. The first Queen's Masque was given at Winchester in 1603, the plague year, next at Hampton Court, and after that at Whitehall, where in 1607 a stone hall was built as a worthy setting for them. Inigo Jones supplied the scenery and mechanical devices for Ben Jonson's *Masque of Blackness* of 1604, one of a series culminating in the celebrations of the Lady Elizabeth's marriage to the Elector Palatine in the winter of 1612–13. *The Masque of the Twelve Goddesses* is said to have cost £2,000–£3,000, and Anne, as Pallas, wore jewellery worth £100,000. Nor did the Queen forget the common players; Court performances were far more frequent than in Elizabeth's time, and she attended a public theatre at least once; she was patroness of the Queen's Revels, and in 1603 took Worcester's Men into her service as the Queen's Servants.

Antenor. In *Troilus and Cressida*, a Trojan commander described by Pandarus as 'one o' the soundest judgements in Troy' (I, ii). He is captured by the Greeks and exchanged for Cressida.

Antigonus. In *The Winter's Tale*, a Sicilian lord and husband of Paulina. Leontes sends him to expose the 'female bastard' Perdita in some desert place. He leaves her on the shore of the deserts of Bohemia, where a bear eats him (III, iii).

Antiochus. In *Pericles*, the King of Antioch. Pericles discovers his incestuous relations with his daughter. Antiochus pursues him with poison, but is shrivelled up by a fire from heaven (II, iv).

Antipholus. In *The Comedy of Errors* (q.v.), the name of the twin sons of Aegeon. (In the *Menaechmi* of Plautus, Antipholus of Syracuse is Menaechmus Sosicles; Antipholus of Ephesus is Menaechmus Surreptus.)

Antonio. 1. In *The Two Gentlemen of Verona*, the father of Proteus, whom he sends 'to the emperor's court' (I, iii).

2. The merchant in *The Merchant of Venice* (q.v.).

3. In *Much Ado*, the brother of Leonato, and Hero's uncle. He tries to comfort Leonato, bids him 'Make those that do offend you suffer too', and himself challenges the 'fashion-monging boy' Claudio. The repentant Claudio promises to marry Antonio's 'daughter'.

4. In *Twelfth Night*, a sea-captain and friend of Sebastian, to whom he lends his purse, demanding it later of Viola when he is arrested by Orsino's officers for

fighting in her defence, mistaking her for Sebastian.

5. In *The Tempest*, Prospero's brother, the usurping Duke of Milan, shipwrecked on Prospero's island, where he is compelled to restore the dukedom.

Antonius, Marcus (*c.* 83–30 B.C.). In *Julius Caesar*, one of the triumvirs after the death of Caesar and the flight of his murderers. He and Octavius defeat Brutus and Cassius at the battle of Philippi. He is the hero of *Antony and Cleopatra* (q.v.).

'ANTONY AND CLEOPATRA.'

WRITTEN: 1606–7. (See DEVIL'S CHARTER.)

PERFORMED: No record of a 17th-century production. (See SS, 6.)

REGISTERED: 1608. '20 Maij. Edward Blount. Entered for his copie under thandes of Sir George Buck knight and Master Warden Seton. A booke called The booke of Pericles prynce of Tyre, vjd. Edward Blount. Entred also for his copie by the like Aucthoritie. A booke called Anthony and Cleopatra, vjd.'

1623, 8 November. One of the sixteen plays registered by Blount and Jaggard before publishing F1.

PUBLISHED: 1623, F1. 'The Tragedie of Anthonie, and Cleopatra.' The eleventh play in the Tragedy section: pp. 340–68. *Actus Primus. Scaena Prima* marked. A fair text. Set up from Shakespeare's manuscript.

SOURCE: North's translation of Plutarch's *Life of Antonius*.

STAGE HISTORY: At the Restoration the play passed to Killigrew's King's Company, but it does not seem to have been performed. Dryden's version of the story, *All for Love* (1678), held the stage to the exclusion of Shakespeare's for about a hundred years.

1759, Drury Lane: Garrick as Antony in the original play.

1813, J. P. Kemble produced a mixture of Shakespeare and Dryden, enlivened by a battle of Actium, and solemnized with an epicedium or funeral dirge.

1833, Shakespeare and Dryden with Macready as Antony.

1849, Phelps returned to the original Shakespeare text.

1906, His Majesty's: Tree's production.

1922, Old Vic: Robert Atkins's 'non-stop' production.

1953, Stratford: Michael Redgrave, Peggy Ashcroft.

Antony, ensnared by the beauty of Cleopatra, lingers in Egypt until recalled to Rome by the threat of civil wars and the death of his wife Fulvia. There a quarrel with Octavius Caesar is patched by Antony's marrying his sister Octavia, and the triumvirs make peace with Pompey. Caesar, however, attacks and defeats Pompey, gets rid of Lepidus, and 'speaks scantly' of Antony, who returns to Cleopatra and makes ready for war. At the battle of Actium, Antony's fleet is defeated owing to the flight of the Egyptian squadron, and Caesar closes in on Alexandria where Antony is finally defeated. Deserted by his friend Enobarbus, and hearing a false report of Cleopatra's death, he stabs himself, is carried to Cleopatra, and dies in her arms. To avoid being led in triumph by Caesar, Cleopatra kills herself with the bite of an asp.

Apemantus. In *Timon of Athens*, a churlish philosopher who warns Timon of the falseness of his friends. Finally Timon, 'sick of this false world', becomes even more misanthropic than Apemantus, and stones him away from his cave (IV, iii).

Apocrypha. The Shakespearean Apocrypha consists of the plays attributed to Shakespeare, but not included in the Canon of the First Folio. They may be divided into four groups:

1. The seven plays added to the second issue of F3, 1664:

> Unto this impression is added seven Playes, never before Printed in Folio, viz. Pericles, Prince of Tyre. The London Prodigall. The History of Thomas Ld. Cromwell. Sir John Oldcastle, Lord Cobham. The Puritan Widow. A Yorkshire Tragedy. The Tragedy of Locrine.

These had all been printed as Quartos and attributed either to W. S. or openly to Shakespeare; but *Pericles* is the only one that can seriously be considered as being, at least in part, by Shakespeare.

2. *The Two Noble Kinsmen*. Registered 1634 as being 'by John ffletcher and William Shakespeare'.

Cardenio. A lost play, acted at Court in 1613, and registered 1653 as being by 'Mr. Fletcher & Shakespeare'.

3. *Sir Thomas More*, *Edward III*. There is no external evidence, but on the basis of internal evidence some passages have been ascribed to Shakespeare.

4. Other plays ascribed to Shakespeare, either by the publishers or by booksellers, but certainly spurious: *The Troublesome Reign of King John*, *The Birth of Merlin*, *Arden of Feversham*, *Faire Em*, *The Merry Devil of Edmonton*, *Mucedorus*, etc. The last three plays were bound together in Charles II's library and labelled 'Shakespeare Vol 1'. (See B. Maxwell, *Studies in the Shakespeare Apocrypha*, 1956.)

'Apollonius of Tyre.' See Gower.

'Apology for Actors.' *Containing three briefe Treatises. 1. Their Antiquity. 2. Their ancient Dignity. 3. The True Use of their Quality.*

Thomas Heywood's reasoned and moderate reply to the Puritan attacks on the stage, published in 1612 but probably written a few years earlier. It is important for its reference to contemporary theatrical affairs.

A description is only a shadow, received by the eare, but not perceived by the eye; so lively portraiture is meerely a forme seene by the eye, but can neither shew action, passion, motion, or any other gesture to moove the spirits of the beholder to admiration: but to see a souldier shap'd like a souldier, walke, speake, act like a souldier: to see a Hector all besmered in blood, trampling upon the bulkes of kinges; a Troilus returning from the field.... To turne to our domesticke hystories: what English blood, seeing the person of any bold Englishman presented, and doth not hugge his fame, and hunnye at his valor, pursuing him in his enterprise with his best wishes, and as beeing wrapt in contemplation, offers to him in his hart all prosperous performance, as if the personator were the man personated?... So of Henry the Fift.

To see your youths attired in the habit of women, who knowes not what their intents be? who cannot distinguish them by their names, assuredly knowing they are but to represent such a lady, at such a tyme appoynted? Do not the Universities ... admit the like in their colledges? ... In the time of my residence at Cambridge, I have seen tragedyes, comedyes, historyes, pastorals, and shewes, publickly acted, in which the graduates of good place and reputation have been specially parted.

The King of Denmarke ... entertained into his service a company of English comedians, commended unto him by the honourable the Earle of Leicester: the Duke of Brunswicke and the Landgrave of Hessen retaine in their courts certaine of ours of the same quality.... And amongst us one of our best English Chroniclers records, that when Edward the Fourth would shew himselfe in publicke state to the view of the people, hee repaired to his palace at S. Johnes, where he accustomed to see the citty actors: and since then that house, by the prince's free gift, hath belonged to the Office of the Revels, where our court playes have beene in late daies yearely rehersed, perfected, and corrected before they come to the publike view of the prince and the nobility....

Here I must needs remember Tarleton, in his time gratious with the queene, his soveraigne, and in the people's generall applause, whom succeeded Wil Kemp, as wel in the favour of her majesty, as in the opinion and good thoughts of the generall audience. Gabriel, Singer, Pope, Phillips, Sly, all the right I can do them is but this, that, though they be dead, their deserts yet live in the remembrance of many. Among so many dead, let me not forget one yet alive, in this time the most worthy, famous Maister Edward Allen....

I also could wish, that such as are condemned for their licentiousnesse, might by a generall consent bee quite excluded our society; for, as we are men that stand in the broad eye of the world, so should our manners, gestures, and behaviours, savour of such government and modesty, to deserve the good thoughts and reports of all men, and to abide the sharpest censures even of those that are the greatest opposites to the quality. Many amongst us I know to be of substance, of government, of sober lives, and temperate carriages, house-keepers, and contributory to all duties enjoyned them, equally with them that are rank't with the most bountifull; and if amongst so many of sort, there be any few degenerate from the rest in that good demeanor which is both requisite and expected at their hands, let me entreat you not to censure hardly of all for the misdeeds of some.

In his *Epistle* to the printer Heywood protests against Jaggard's incorporation of his two 'Loue Epistles' in the 1612 reprint of *The Passionate Pilgrim*, and adds, 'The Author [Shakespeare?] I know much offended with M. *Jaggard* that (altogether vnknowne to him) presumed to make so bold with his name'.

'Apolonius and Silla.' See Rich, Barnabe.

Apprentices. A somewhat misleading term when applied to actors, for the Statute of Apprentices, 1563, excluded those in the households of the nobility and gentry, and therefore actors. It seems that a boy might be apprenticed, though apprenticeship was not a necessary qualification, for two or three years to an actor-sharer, who maintained him and taught him the art of acting. Apparently a trained boy could be sold, for Henslowe bought his 'boye Jeames Brystow of William Agusten player the 18 Desember 1594 for viij^{li}', and then hired him to the Admiral's for 3s. a week. James Sands was apprentice to Augustine Phillips when he made his will in 1605, and Samuel Gilburne his 'late apprentice'. When John Shank of the King's Men answered the petitioners of 1635 he pleaded that he had

> still of his own purse supplyed the company for the service of his Majesty with boyes as Thomas Pollard, John Thompson deceased (for whome hee payed 40^{li}) your suppliant haveing payd his part of 200^{li} for other boyes since his comming to the company, John Honiman, Thomas Holcome and diuerse others, and at this time maintaines three more for the sayd service.

Apron Stage. The part of the stage that projects into the pit or 'yard'; 'to the middle of the yarde' in the Fortune, the apron stage of which was 27½ ft deep and 43 ft wide. (See Stage.)

Apuleius, Lucius (fl. 2nd century A.D.). Platonic philosopher, and author of the *Metamorphose*, or *Golden Ass*, was born in Numidia, and educated at Carthage and Athens. The adventures of Don Quixote and of Gil Blas owe something to *The Golden Ass*, and possibly Shakespeare remembered Adlington's English version when Bottom was translated, and when Cornelius in *Cymbeline* substituted a sleeping-draught for the Queen's poison. (See Adlington.)

Arber, Edward (1836–1912). An Admiralty clerk 1854–78, Professor of English at Birmingham 1881–94, and then Emeritus Professor in London and Fellow of King's College. He is important as the editor of numerous old books, tracts, and documents. The thirty volumes of his *English Reprints* (1868–80) include Gosson's *School of Abuse* and Tottel's *Miscellany*. Between 1875 and 1894 he edited the invaluable *Transcript of the Registers of the Stationers' Company*, 1553–1640.

Archer, William (1856–1924). Dramatic critic, born at Perth and educated at Edinburgh University. He is best known, perhaps, as the editor and translator of Ibsen's plays. He wrote 'What We Know of the Elizabethan Stage' in *The Quarterly Review*, 1908. In *The Old Drama and the New* (1923) he shows little sympathy for any of the Elizabethans except Shakespeare.

Archidamus. In *The Winter's Tale*, a Lord of Bohemia who opens the play and then disappears into obscurity.

Arcite. In *The Two Noble Kinsmen* (q.v.), the cousin of Palamon.

Arden Family. According to the Grant of Arms of 1596, Shakespeare's father, John, 'maryed the daughter & one of the heyres of Robert Arden of Wilmcoote ['Wellingcote' in the draft of 1599] in the saide Counte ['Warwike'] esquire'. The Ardens of Wilmcote, a village three miles north-west of Stratford, were a minor branch of the Ardens of Park

Hall, between Birmingham and Coleshill, one of whom was sheriff of Warwickshire in 1438, another in 1575, and another had been sheriff in the reign of Edward the Confessor. They are one of the three families who can prove a male line of descent from Saxon times.

THOMAS ARDEN of Wilmcote and his son Robert in 1501 bought an estate in Snitterfield, a village three miles north of Stratford. Thomas died *c.* 1547.

ROBERT ARDEN inherited his father's property, and in 1547 had two holdings at Snitterfield, on one of which Richard Shakespeare, the poet's grandfather, was a tenant. By his first wife, whose name is unknown, Robert had eight daughters, six of whom were married, Joan to Edmund Lambert, and Mary to John Shakespeare (see p. 542). Robert was married a second time, to Agnes, the widow of John Hill, but there were no more children. When he died in 1556 he owned a farmhouse and land at Wilmcote, and two farmhouses and about 100 acres at Snitterfield. To Mary he left £6 13s. 4d. and his chief property at Wilmcote, Asbies (q.v.), consisting of about sixty acres of land. It seems probable that he had already settled other Wilmcote property upon her, and she also had a share in the reversion of the Snitterfield estate. The Arden house at Wilmcote was bought by the Birthplace Trustees in 1930.

MARY ARDEN was the youngest of Robert's eight daughters. About 1557 she married John Shakespeare, who had recently moved from Snitterfield to Stratford. Their first child, a daughter, Joan, was born in 1558, and it must be assumed that she died in infancy, though there is no record of her death. Their next child, Margaret, was born in December 1562, but only lived five months. Then in April 1564 their third child and first son, William, was born. There were three other sons, Gilbert, Richard and Edmund, and two more daughters, Joan and Anne. Little more is known of Mary; when her husband was in difficulties in 1579–80 he sold her reversion in Snitterfield for £4, let Asbies on a lease of twenty-one years for a nominal rent and, apparently, an advance of money, and mortgaged her other Wilmcote property to Edmund Lambert, the husband of her sister Joan, for £40. John and his son William later tried to recover this property, but failed. Mary died in 1608, and was buried in Stratford churchyard 9 September: 'Mayry Shaxspere, wydowe'.

'Arden of Feversham.'

The Lamentable and True Tragedie of M. Arden of Feuersham in Kent. Who was most wickedlye murdered, by the meanes of his disloyall and wanton wyfe, who for the love she bare to one Mosbie, hyred two desperat ruffins Blackwill and Shakbag, to kill him. Wherin is shewed the great mallice and discimulation of a wicked woman, the vnsatiable desire of filthie lust and the shameful end of all murderers.

The play was published in 1592, and reprinted in 1599 and 1633. It was first assigned to Shakespeare in the edition of 1770 by the printer Edward Jacob, who lived at Faversham. The play has some merit, and Swinburne accepted it as Shakespeare's, but most critics reject it, Fleay and others suggesting Kyd as the author.

'Arden' Shakespeare. Published 1899–1924 in 37 vols. under the general editorship of W. J. Craig and R. H. Case. Revision was begun in 1951 (*The New Arden*) with Una Ellis-Fermor as general editor, succeeded on her death in 1958 by Dr H. F. Brooks and Professor Harold Jenkins.

Ariel. In *The Tempest*, an airy spirit confined by the witch Sycorax into a cloven pine until freed by Prospero to do his spiriting. At the end of the play Prospero releases him 'to the elements'. Ariel sings the songs 'Come unto these yellow sands', 'Full fathom five', and 'Where the bee sucks'.

'Ariodante and Genevra.' See ARIOSTO; MERCHANT TAYLORS' SCHOOL.

Ariosto, Ludovico (1474–1533). Italian poet, born at Reggio in Lombardy. His *Orlando Furioso*, an epic on the subject of Roland and Angelica, daughter of the King of Cathay, was translated by Sir John Harington in 1591, and the story of Ariodante and Genevra in Canto V may have suggested the deception of Claudio by Margaret's impersonation of Hero in *Much Ado*. The sub-plot of Bianca and her lovers in *The Taming of the Shrew* is probably derived from Ariosto's comedy *I Suppositi*, englished by George Gascoigne as the *Supposes*, performed at Gray's Inn 1566, and published 1573.

Aristotle (384–322 B.C.), the Greek philosopher, was born at Stagira, whence comes his name of 'the Stagirite'. His *Poetics* is a fragmentary discourse 'of Poetry in itself and of its various kinds', but it treats most fully of Tragedy. It is important to remember that his conclusions were necessarily based on Greek tragedy alone, the only model he had, and there is no reason to doubt that, as Dryden said, 'if he had seen ours he might have changed his mind'.

He argued moderately that a Tragedy should represent one action only, and that the time for the sequence of events should be such as would 'admit of a change from bad fortune to good, or from good fortune to bad'. Of the so-called Unity of Place he says nothing.

The *Poetics* was unknown in Europe during the Dark and Middle Ages, but was rediscovered *c.* 1500 and reduced to a rigid set of rules by 16th-century Italian scholars. Thus Castelvetro wrote in 1570:

> But it is evident that, in tragedy and comedy, the plot contains one action only, or two that by their interdependence can be considered one ... not because the fable itself is unsuited to contain more actions than one, but because the space of time, of twelve hours at most, in which the action is represented, and the strait limits of the place in which it is represented likewise, do not permit a multitude of actions.

These are the Three Unities – of Action, Time and Place – of Neo-Classicism (q.v.). (See SIDNEY.)

Armado, Don Adriano de. In *Love's Labour's Lost*, a fantastical Spaniard and the rival of Costard for the love of Jaquenetta. In the interlude of *The Nine Worthies* he presents Hector. (See MONARCHO; PHILIP II OF SPAIN.)

Armin, Robert (d. 1615). One of the 'Principall Actors' in Shakespeare's plays (see p. 90). He seems to have been a goldsmith's apprentice, and a pupil of Richard Tarlton, the principal comedian of the Queen's Men. He was one of Lord Chandos's Men, but probably joined the Chamberlain's in 1599 to replace Kempe. His fooling was more subtle than Kempe's, and Shakespeare probably wrote the parts of Touchstone, Feste, and the Fool in *Lear* for him. In his *Phantasma, the Italian Tailor and his Boy* (1609) Armin refers to 'his constableship' and to having been 'writ down an ass in his time', which presumably means that he played Dogberry in *Much Ado*. He is mentioned in the lists of the King's Men in 1603, 1604, 1610. Armin was also an author; in addition to *Phantasma* he wrote *Quips upon Questions*, *A Nest of Ninnies*, and a play, *The Two Maids of Moreclacke*. He was buried 30 November 1615.

Arms, Grant of. At about the time that he was bailiff of Stratford in 1568–9 John Shakespeare had approached the College of Heralds for a grant of arms, but had got no further than a suggested 'patierne' if a grant were made. In 1596, probably at the instance of the poet, he applied again, and the grant was made on the grounds that John's 'great grandfather' had performed 'faithefull & approved service to H7 ... & rewarded with Landes and Tenements ... in ... Warwikeshere', while John himself had 'maryed the daughter & one of the heyrs of Robert Arden of Wellingcote'. The coat is described (in 1599) as:

> In a field of Gould vppon a Bend Sables A Speare of the first the poynt vpward hedded Argent, and for his creast or cognizance A Falcon, with the wynges displayed, standing on a wrethe of his coullers Supporting a Speare Armed hedded or & steeled sylvor fixed vppon a helmet with mantelles & tasselles.

In 1599 John applied again for the right to impale the arms of Arden, but it seems improbable that the grant was made, for the privilege was not exercised by him or any of his descendants. In 1602 there was some criticism of the grant, to which Garter and Clarenceux Kings-of Arms replied that 'the man was A magestrat in Stratford vpon Avon. A Iustice of peace he maryed A daughter and heyre of Ardern, and was of good substance and habilité.'

It is possible that Jonson jests at the motto 'Non Sans Droict', which, however, the Shakespeares never used, in *Every Man out of His Humour* (1600), when Sogliardo, a 'clown', is chaffed about his newly-bought coat-of-arms, 'a Bores head Proper', and it is suggested that an appropriate motto would be 'Not Without Mustard'. (See G. R. French, *Shakspeareana Genealogica*; C. W. Scott-Giles, *Shakespeare's Heraldry*, 1950; DETHICK.)

Arne, Thomas Augustine (1710–78). English composer, born in London and educated at Eton. In 1733 he produced his opera *Rosamund*, in which his sister, Susannah Cibber (q.v.), played the heroine's part. This was followed by the burlesque *Opera of Operas*, based on Fielding's *Tragedy of Tragedies*, and the *Masque of Alfred*, which contains his 'Rule, Britannia!' In 1740 he wrote the music for the songs in the Drury Lane production of *As You Like It*: 'Under the greenwood tree', and 'Blow, blow, thou winter wind'. He also composed settings for 'Where the bee sucks', and 'When daisies pied', and the music for Garrick's *Ode* for the Shakespeare jubilee at Stratford in 1769.

Arnold, Matthew (1822–88). Author of the famous sonnet on Shakespeare:

> Others abide our question. Thou art free.
> We ask and ask: Thou smilest and art still,
> Out-topping knowledge ...

It is worth noting that Arnold thought of Shakespeare as one 'self-schooled'.

Arragon, Prince of. In *The Merchant of Venice*, one of the suitors of Portia. He chooses the silver casket and finds 'the portrait of a blinking idiot' (II, ix).

Artemidorus of Cnidos. In *Julius Caesar*, a teacher of rhetoric. He tries to save Caesar by writing him a note warning him of the conspiracy, but Caesar refuses to read it (II, iii; III, i).

Arthur. In *King John* (q.v.). Arthur (1187–1203) was the posthumous son of Geoffrey Plantagenet, fourth son of Henry II and Constance of Brittany. As Geoffrey was John's elder brother, Arthur should have been King, and many in the French dominions acknowledged him, but in England the Great Council chose John. (See HUBERT.)

Arviragus. In *Cymbeline*, younger son of Cymbeline, and brother of Imogen. He and his brother Guiderius are brought up by Belarius, a banished lord who assumes the name of Morgan, in the belief that they are his sons Cadwal and Polydore. Arviragus discovers Imogen apparently dead, and he and Guiderius 'say their song' over her body, 'Fear no more the heat o' the sun'. They help to repel the Roman invasion, and are restored to their father.

Asbies. In his will, dated 24 November 1556, Robert Arden wrote: 'I give and bequethe to my youngste dowghter Marye all my lande in Willmecote, cawlide Asbyes.' It was probably in the following year that Mary married John

Shakespeare, who, when he was in financial difficulties in 1579–80, sold or alienated his wife's property. It used to be assumed that the Wilmcote estate mortgaged to Edmund Lambert in November 1578 for £40, to be repaid at Michaelmas 1580, referred to Asbies. This mortgaged estate consisted of a house, fifty acres of arable, and six acres of meadow and pasture. But there is no mention of a house in Robert's will, and just before the completion of the mortgage John and Mary Shakespeare leased to Thomas Webbe land at Wilmcote consisting of seventy acres of arable and sixteen acres of meadow and pasture, with no mention of a house. It may be that the two properties are the same, but the considerably bigger acreage of the leased estate without a house, and the lack of mention of a house attached to Robert Arden's 'lande cawlide Asbyes', suggest that the leased estate of eighty-six acres was Asbies. If so, the mortgaged property may have been a settlement, possibly a marriage settlement on Mary in anticipation of her marriage with John Shakespeare. There is no trace of a house called Asbies, though John Jordan in the late 18th century identified it with a house, with land attached, bought by George Gibbes and Adam Palmer in 1562. In 1575 there was a partition, Gibbes taking as part of his share 'the small messuage and all houses and buildings, with their appurtenances, which he then dwelt in and occupied', Palmer, as part of his, 'one parcel of meadow and lees called the Meadow-Piece, adjoining to the close of John Shakesperes of the west side'.

Ashbourne (Kingston) Portrait. Inscribed 'Ætatis suæ. 47 A° 1611'. According to Spielmann, it is 'an acceptable likeness of Shakespeare'; but as nothing is known of its history before its possession by the Rev. C. U. Kingston in 1847, it cannot be accepted as an authentic portrait of the poet. It is a pleasant three-quarter-length painting.

Ashcroft, Peggy (b. 1907), first appeared at the Birmingham Rep. in 1926. In 1930 she played Desdemona to Paul Robeson's Othello, and since then has had many seasons at Stratford and the Old Vic, where she has played Cleopatra, Imogen, Rosalind, Beatrice, Viola, etc. Created D.B.E. 1956.

Ashley (or Astley), Sir John (d. 1641). One of the gentlemen of the privy-chamber and Master of the Revels. In 1612 he obtained a reversionary grant of the Mastership, succeeding to the office 29 March 1622, when Sir George Buck was mad, but on 20 July 1623 he appointed Henry Herbert as his deputy in return for £150 a year. The Office Book of Henry Herbert begins with a few records of Ashley; for example, an account of 'Revels and Playes performed and acted at Christmas in the court at Whitehall, 1622. ... At Candlemas *Malvolio* was acted at court by the kings servants'.

Aspley, William. Bookseller. His shops were the Tiger's Head, and the Parrot in St Paul's Churchyard. He became a freeman of the Stationers' Company in 1598, and Master in 1640, in which year he died.

> 23 Augusti [1600] Andrew Wyse William Aspley. Entred for their copies....Two Bookes, the one called Muche a Doo about nothinge. Thother the second parte of the history of Kinge Henry the iiijth with the humours of Sir John Falstaff; Wrytten by master Shakespere. xij^{d}.

Both these Quartos were printed in 1600 by Simmes for Wise and Aspley. In 1609 some of the copies of Thorpe's edition of the *Sonnets* were 'to be solde by William Aspley'. He was a member of the syndicates that published F1 in 1623, and F2 in 1632.

Assembled Texts. The theory that copy for the printers of F1 was assembled for some of the plays from the 'parts' transcribed for the actors. If there were no Quarto of a play, or no 'good'

Quarto, and the 'book' had been lost – perhaps in the Globe fire of 1613 – the text would have to be reconstructed somehow, and the only way might be to put together the actors' parts with the aid of the 'plot', the prompter's abstract of the play. The theory was first suggested by Malone, and has recently been supported by Dover Wilson and others – though not generally accepted – to account for certain peculiarities in the Folio texts of some of the plays, particularly of *The Two Gentlemen of Verona* and *The Merry Wives of Windsor*. Stage directions are very few, and all the characters in a scene are named at the beginning in the order of their appearance, later entrances and most exits being generally unmarked: a characteristic that we should expect if a plot were used, for the prompter had to mark quite clearly at the beginning of a scene what characters were due to appear. McKerrow and Greg, however, suggest that this arrangement was based on the neo-classical method, adopted by Jonson and others, of beginning a new scene with every fresh group of characters, whose names are given at the head. There are other minor arguments in favour of 'assembly', and other plays suggested as having assembled texts: *As You Like It*, *Measure for Measure*, *Comedy of Errors*, *Merchant of Venice*, *Winter's Tale*. (See CRANE; ACT AND SCENE DIVISION.)

Aston Cantlow. A village about two miles north-west of Wilmcote, which lies within its parish. Presumably John Shakespeare married Mary Arden in the parish church of Aston Cantlow, but the church registers begin after 1557.

'AS YOU LIKE IT.'

WRITTEN: 1599–1600.

PERFORMED: ? 1603, 2 December, at Wilton (q.v.).

REGISTERED: 1600. '4 Augusti. As you like y^t, a booke to be staid.' (Possibly an attempt by the Chamberlain's Men to prevent piratical publication.)

1623, 8 November. One of the sixteen plays registered by Blount and Jaggard before publishing F1.

PUBLISHED: 1623, F1, 'As you Like it'. The tenth play in the Comedy section: pp. 185–207. Acts and scenes marked. A fairly good text. Wilson finds evidence of an assembled text, and of the revision of an earlier version of 1593. Set up from prompt-book or a transcript of it.

SOURCE: Thomas Lodge: *Rosalynde, or Euphues golden legacie* (1590). Lodge's source was the pseudo-Chaucerian *Tale of Gamelyn*, which, though not printed until 1721, existed in manuscripts to which Shakespeare may have referred. Shakespeare alters the beginning of Lodge's story, and adds new characters, notably Jaques and Touchstone.

STAGE HISTORY: 1669, Granted by royal warrant to the King's company.

1723, Drury Lane: Charles Johnson's adaptation, *Love in a Forest*, with Colley Cibber as Jaques.

1740, Drury Lane: Shakespeare's text with Arne's settings of the songs; Quin as Jaques, Macklin as Touchstone, Mrs Pritchard as Rosalind and Mrs Clive as Celia.

After this the play was often revived, Jaques being played by J. P. Kemble, Macready, Charles Kean, Phelps, and other leading actors; Rosalind by Peg Woffington, Dora Jordan, Mrs Siddons and many others.

The unique copy of Thomas Morley's *First Booke of Ayres* (1600) containing his setting of 'It was a lover and his lass' is in the Folger Shakespeare Library.

Oldys and Capell record the tradition that Shakespeare acted the part of Adam.

The satirical Jaques has been thought by some to be Shakespeare's 'purge' for Jonson's 'pill' in *The Poetaster*. (See PARNASSUS.)

Frederick, father of Celia, has usurped the dominions of the rightful Duke, father of Rosalind, who is living with his followers, including the melancholy Jaques, in the Forest of Arden. Orlando sees Rosalind and falls in love with her, but when he hears that his elder brother Oliver plans to kill him he flies with the old family servant, Adam, to the forest. Duke Frederick banishes Rosalind, who has been living at Court as a companion for Celia, but both girls disguise themselves, Rosalind as a boy, and with the court fool Touchstone also seek refuge in Arden. There Orlando meets Rosalind, who persuades him to pretend that she really is Rosalind, and to make love to her. Eventually she discloses her identity, is restored to her father, and marries Orlando. At the same time Celia is paired off with a repentant Oliver, Touchstone with Audrey and Silvius with Phebe. Duke Frederick repents, restores the dukedom to Rosalind's father, and is followed by Jaques, who finds much matter in 'these convertites'.

Adam Spencer is common both to the *Tale of Gamelyn* and Lodge's *Rosalynde*; in the latter Orlando is called Rosader, Oliver being Saladyne.

Atkins, Robert (b. 1886). Actor and producer, joined the Old Vic Company in 1915 and after war service directed plays at the Old Vic, 1920–25. He took his own Shakespeare Company to Egypt 1927–8, and was Director of the Shakespeare Memorial Theatre 1944–5. Since the last war he has produced Shakespeare in the Open Air Theatre, Regent's Park.

Atkinson, William. One of the witnesses of Shakespeare's purchase and mortgage of the Blackfriars Gatehouse in 1613. He lived in St Mary Aldermanbury, the parish of John Heminge, one of Shakespeare's trustees in the transaction, and as Clerk of the Brewers' Company he would know the other trustees, John Jackson and William Johnson of the Mermaid.

'Attempt to Ascertain the Order in which the Plays of Shakespeare were Written.' This very important essay by Edmond Malone was first published in 1778 in Steevens's second edition of Shakespeare's Plays, revised in 1790, and in its final form in the Third Variorum of 1821. It is the first serious attempt to establish the chronology, and Malone bases his conclusions not only on recently discovered contemporary records – the Stationers' Registers, the Henslowe Papers, Herbert's Office Book and so on – and contemporary plays and pamphlets such as *Parnassus*, Greene's *Groatsworth of Wit* and the invaluable *Palladis Tamia* of Meres, but also on elementary verse tests that laid the foundation of Furnivall's elaborate 19th-century structure. The following extracts are from the version of 1790. Malone begins with a summary of the achievements of the scholars of the second half of the 18th century:

An ardent desire to understand and explain his [Shakespeare's] works is, to the honour of the present age, so much increased within the last forty years, that more has been done towards their elucidation, during that period, than in a century before. All the ancient copies of his plays, hitherto discovered, have been collated with the most scrupulous accuracy. The meanest books have been carefully examined, only because they were of the age in which he lived, and might happily throw a light on some forgotten custom, or obsolete phraseology: and, this object being still kept in view, the toil of wading through *all such reading as was never read* has been cheerfully endured, because no labour was thought too great, that might enable us to add one new laurel to the father of our drama. Almost every circumstance that tradition or history has preserved relative to him or his works, has been investigated, and laid before the publick....

However, after the most diligent inquiries, very few particulars have been recovered, respecting his private life or literary history; and while it has been the endeavour of all his editors and commentators to illustrate his obscurities, and to regulate and correct his text, no attempt has been made to trace the progress and order of his plays....

The materials for ascertaining the order in which his plays were written, are indeed so few, that, it is to be feared, nothing very decisive can be produced on the subject.... Little then remains, but to collect into one view, from the several dramas, and from the ancient tracts in which they are mentioned, or alluded to, all the circumstances that can throw any light on this new and curious inquiry. From these circumstances, and from the entries in the books of the Stationers' Company, extracted and published by Mr Steevens (to whom every admirer of Shakespeare has the highest obligations) it is probable that our author's plays were written nearly in the following succession....

Of the twenty-one plays which were not printed in our author's lifetime, the *majority* were, I believe, late compositions. (This supposition is strongly confirmed by Meres's list of our author's plays, in 1598.)...

The following is the order in which I

suppose the plays of Shakespeare to have been written:

1	First Part of King Henry VI	1589
2	Second Part of King Henry VI	1591
3	Third Part of King Henry VI	1591
4	A Midsummer Night's Dream	1592
5	Comedy of Errors	1593
6	Taming of the Shrew	1594
7	Love's Labour's Lost	1594
8	Two Gentlemen of Verona	1595
9	Romeo and Juliet	1595
10	Hamlet	1596
11	King John	1596
12	King Richard II	1597
13	King Richard III	1597
14	First Part of King Henry IV	1597
15	Second Part of King Henry IV	1598
16	The Merchant of Venice	1598
17	All's Well that Ends Well	1598
18	King Henry V	1599
19	Much Ado about Nothing	1600
20	As You Like It	1600
21	Merry Wives of Windsor	1601
22	King Henry VIII	1601
23	Troilus and Cressida	1602
24	Measure for Measure	1603
25	The Winter's Tale	1604
26	King Lear	1605
27	Cymbeline	1605
28	Macbeth	1606
29	Julius Caesar	1607
30	Antony and Cleopatra	1608
31	Timon of Athens	1609
32	Coriolanus	1610
33	Othello	1611
34	The Tempest	1612
35	Twelfth Night	1614

Malone then treats each play in detail, adducing the evidence that leads him to ascribe its date. In a significant note to *Love's Labour's Lost* he writes:

As this circumstance [frequent rhymes] is more than once mentioned ... it may not be improper to add a few words on the subject of our author's metre. A mixture of rhymes with blank verse, in the same play, and sometimes in the same scene, is found in almost all his pieces, and is not peculiar to Shakespeare.... It is not, therefore, merely the use of rhymes, mingled with blank verse, but their *frequency*, that is here urged, as a circumstance which seems to characterize and distinguish our poet's earliest performances. In the whole number of pieces which were written antecedent to the year 1600, and which, for the sake of perspicuity, have been called his *early compositions*, more rhyming couplets are found, than in all the plays composed subsequently to that year, which have been named his *late productions*. Whether in process of time Shakespeare grew weary of the bondage of rhyme, or whether he became convinced of its impropriety in a dramatick dialogue, his neglect of rhyming (for he never wholly disused it) seems to have been *gradual*. As, therefore, most of his early productions are characterized by the multitude of similar terminations which they exhibit, whenever of two early pieces it is doubtful which preceded the other, I am disposed to believe (other proofs being wanting) that play in which the greater number of rhymes is found, to have been first composed.

Of *The Comedy of Errors* he observes:

The doggerel measure, which, if I recollect right, is employed in none of our author's plays except *The Comedy of Errors*, *The Taming of the Shrew*, and *Love's Labour's Lost*, also adds support to the dates assigned to these plays.... He was imperceptibly infected with the prevailing mode in these his early compositions; but soon learned to 'deviate boldly from the common track,' left by preceding writers.

And of *The Winter's Tale*, a play that gave him some difficulty and which he first placed in 1594, he writes:

The metre of *The Winter's Tale* appears to me less easy and flowing than many other of our poet's dramas; and the phraseology throughout to be more involved and parenthetical than any other of his plays. In this harshness of diction and involution of sentences it strongly resembles *Troilus and Cressida*, and *King Henry the Eighth*, which I suppose to have been written not long before.

(See also MALONE; CHRONOLOGY; VERSE-TESTS; NEW SHAKSPERE SOCIETY.)

Aubrey, John (1626-97). English antiquary, was born at Easton Pierse, near Malmesbury. He was educated at Malmesbury Grammar School, where he met Thomas Hobbes, whose *Life* he wrote, and at Trinity, Oxford. His father died in 1652, leaving him large estates which, through his love of good living, passion for gossip, and legacy of law-suits, he lost one by one until he was reduced to living with friends. In 1667 he met Anthony à Wood, for whom he agreed to gather material for his *Athenae Oxonienses*. Aubrey was unmethodical and tactless, his notes on the first Earl of Clarendon leading to Wood's expulsion from Oxford in 1693, an event that probably accounts for his sour estimate of Aubrey's character:

> He was a shiftless person, roving and magotie-headed, and sometimes little better than crased. And being exceedingly credulous, would stuff his many letters sent to A. W. with follies and misinformations, which sometimes would guide him into the paths of Errour.

Aubrey obtained some of the material for his famous *Brief Life* of Shakespeare from William Beeston, an actor who died in 1682, the son of Christopher Beeston, a fellow of Shakespeare in the Chamberlain's Company:

> Mr William Shakespear was borne at Stratford vpon Avon, in the County of Warwick; his father was a Butcher, & I have been told heretofore by some of the neighbours, that when he was a boy he exercised his father's Trade, but when he kill'd a Calfe, he would doe it in a *high style*, & make a Speech.... This Wm. being inclined naturally to Poetry and acting, came to London I guesse about 18, and was an Actor at one of the Playhouses and did act exceedingly well: now B. Johnson was never a good Actor, but an excellent Instructor. He began early to make essayes at Dramatique Poetry, which at that time was very lowe; and his Playes tooke well: He was a handsome well shap't man: very good company, and of a very readie and pleasant smooth Witt. The Humour of ... the Constable in a Midsomersnight's Dreame, he happened to take at Grendon in Bucks which is the roade from London to Stratford, and there was living that Constable about 1642 when I first came to Oxon. ... Ben Johnson and he did gather Humours of men dayly where ever they came. One time as he was at the Tavern at Stratford super Avon, one Combes an old rich Usurer was to be buryed, he makes there this extemporary Epitaph:
>
> Ten in the Hundred the Devill allowes
> But *Combes* will have twelve, he sweares & vowes:
> If any one askes who lies in this Tombe:
> Hoh! quoth the Devill, 'Tis my John o' Combe.
>
> He was wont to goe to his native Country once a yeare. I thinke I have been told that he left 2 or 300^{li} per annum there and thereabout: to a sister. I have heard S^{r} Wm. Davenant and Mr Thomas Shadwell ... say, that he had a most prodigious Witt, and did admire his naturall parts beyond all other Dramaticall writers. He was wont to say, That he never blotted out a line in his life: sayd Ben: Johnson, I wish he had blotted out a thousand. His Comœdies will remaine witt, as long as the English tongue is understood; for that he handles mores hominum.... Though as Ben: Johnson sayes of him, that he had but little Latine and lesse Greek, He understood Latine pretty well: for he had been in his younger yeares a Schoolmaster in the Countrey.

In another note, Aubrey adds: 'the more to be admired [because] he was not a company keeper, lived in Shoreditch, wouldnt be debauched, & if invited to writ; he was in paine.' (See D'AVENANT; SAVAGE.)

Audience. It used to be thought that the Elizabethan audience was an ignorant and ill-smelling assembly, capable of nothing but bawdiness, inexplicable dumb-shows and noise. Ill-smelling they may have been, but in those days when few could read, and talk took the place of books, the ear must have been delicately trained and quick to appreciate fine language. No doubt some of the gallants who sat on the stage and smoked, and some of the ladies in the galleries, came to be seen rather than to listen, but recent research discovers an audience made up for the most part of eager and attentive listeners, generous with their applause, though equally ready to hiss and mew their disapproval. (See A. Harbage, *Shakespeare's Audience*.) Malone, drawing his material from Heywood, Jonson, Beaumont, and Fletcher, describes an audience before the beginning of a play, for as there were no reserved seats they came early:

> While some part of the audience entertained themselves with reading, or playing

at cards, others were employed in less refined occupations; in drinking ale, or smoking tobacco: with these and nuts and apples they were furnished by male attendants, of whose clamour a satirical writer of the time of James I loudly complains ('To be made adder-deaf with pippin-cry': *Notes from Black-fryers*, 1617). In 1633, when Prynne published his *Histrio-mastix*, women smoked tobacco in the playhouses as well as men.

(See also 'GULL'S HORNBOOK'.)

The audience at a private theatre like the Blackfriars – which Anne of Denmark attended at least once – where the prices were higher, must have been more fastidious, but were perhaps no more appreciative. Here is the description by Orazio Busino of a visit to a London theatre in 1617, possibly the Blackfriars, or Cockpit:

> They took me ... to one of the numerous theatres here in London where plays are recited and we saw a tragedy performed there, which moved me little, especially as I cannot understand a single word of English, though one may derive some little amusement from gazing on the sumptuous dresses of the actors and observing their gestures, and the various interludes of instrumental music, dancing, singing and the like. The best treat was to see and stare at so much nobility in such excellent array that they seemed so many princes, listening as silently and soberly as possible.

Audrey. In *As You Like It*, a country wench whom Touchstone discovers in the Forest of Arden and eventually marries.

Aufidius, Tullus. In *Coriolanus*, General of the Volscians and the opponent of Coriolanus. When Coriolanus is banished from Rome he seeks alliance with Aufidius, who murders him when he fails in his resolve to attack Rome.

Aumerle, Duke of. In *Richard II*. (See YORK, 2ND DUKE OF.)

Auriol Miniature. Has no history before it was claimed as a portrait of Shakespeare in 1826. It was subsequently acquired by the collector Charles Auriol, and is now in America. It is the portrait of a fashionably dressed man 'Aet 33', with beady eyes and a hooked nose.

Austria. In 1948 the Österreichische Shakespeare-Gesellschaft was founded with Raoul Aslan, acting manager of the Vienna Burgtheater, as president, and having the same aims as the Deutsche Shakespeare-Gesellschaft. Post-war interest in Shakespeare was further quickened by the scholarship and enthusiasm of Richard Flatter, whose translations have largely superseded the classical Schlegel-Tieck version. The plays, particularly the comedies, are regularly performed both in Vienna and the provinces.

Austria, Archduke of. In *King John*, confused by the author of Shakespeare's source-play, *The Troublesome Reign*, and by Shakespeare himself with the Vicomte de Limoges. Austria supports Arthur and France against John, and is mocked by the Bastard Falconbridge, who kills him in battle. (Leopold V, Duke of Austria, captured and imprisoned Richard I, who was killed at the siege of the castle of the Vicomte de Limoges.)

Authenticity of Shakespeare's Plays. This is not the frivolous question of whether Shakespeare really was the author of the plays attributed to him, but of how much 'alien matter' there is in the Shakespearean canon of the First Folio.

The evidence in favour of Shakespeare's being the author of all, or of all but an inconsiderable amount of, the thirty-six plays of the First Folio may be summarized as follows:

1. (*a*) The Title-page of F1: 'Mr. William Shakespeares Comedies, Histories, & Tragedies. Published according to the True Originall Copies.'

(*b*) The Preface of the editors, Heminge and Condell, *To the great Variety of Readers*, in which they claim so to have published the plays 'as where (before) you were abus'd with diuerse stolne, and surreptitious copies, maimed, and deformed by the frauds and stealthes of iniurious impostors, that expos'd them: euen those, are now offer'd to your view cur'd, and perfect of their limbes: and all the rest, absolute in their numbers, as he conceiued them'. They seem to distinguish between the deformed 'bad' Quartos and 'all the rest', but all are now perfect, as Shakespeare wrote them. They also claim to have worked from, or at least to have referred to some of, Shakespeare's original manuscripts, for, they say, 'wee haue scarce receiued from him a blot in his papers'.

If any two men knew what Shakespeare wrote they were Heminge and Condell, his fellows as Chamberlain's and King's Men for twenty years, and friends to whom he left legacies.

2. The Stationers' Register: Three plays were entered as being by Shakespeare before publication as Quartos. Sixteen of the eighteen plays not published as Quartos were entered as Shakespeare's by Blount and Jaggard before the publication of the Folio in 1623.

3. Title-pages: Of the eighteen plays published as Quartos, fifteen have Shakespeare's name on the title-page either of the first or later editions.

4. *Palladis Tamia*, 1598: Meres names twelve plays – perhaps thirteen, for he does not specify both parts of *Henry IV* – as being Shakespeare's. (By '*Loue labours wonne*', he may mean *All's Well*.)

5. The Revels Accounts of 1604–5 mention three plays as being by 'Shaxberd'.

6. Other contemporary references in which Shakespeare is mentioned as the author of a particular play.

A table will make this clearer:

	S.R.	Q	*Meres*	*Other References*
2 Henry VI		Q3.1619		
3 Henry VI		Q3.1619		
1 Henry VI	1623			
Richard III		Q2.1598	M	*Parnassus*, 1601
T. Andronicus			M	
C. of Errors	1623		M	Revels Account, 1604–5
Two G. of Ver.	1623		M	
L. L. Lost		Q1.1598	M	
R. and Juliet			M	Weever, 1599
Richard II		Q2.1598	M	Weever, 1599
T. of Shrew				
M. N. Dream		Q.1600	M	
King John			M	
M. of Venice		Q1.1600	M	Revels Account, 1604–5
1 Henry IV		Q2.1599	M	
2 Henry IV	1600	Q. 1600	M?	
Merry Wives		Q1.1602		
Henry V				
Much Ado	1600	Q. 1600		
As Y. L. It	1623			
Twelfth Night	1623			
J. Caesar	1623			Jonson, *c.* 1630
Hamlet		Q1.1603		Harvey, 1601
T. & Cressida		Q. 1609		
All's Well	1623		M?	
M. for Measure	1623			Revels Account, 1604–5
Othello		Q1.1622		
Timon	1623			
King Lear	1607	Q1.1608		
Macbeth	1623			
A. & Cleopatra	1623			
Coriolanus	1623			
Cymbeline	1623			
Winter's Tale	1623			Jonson, 1619
Tempest	1623			
Henry VIII	1623			

On the other hand:

1. Seventeenth-century editors were not as accurate as they are today.

2. Title-pages are not conclusive evidence. Of the seven additional plays in F3, 1664, three had been published as being written by W. S. and four by Shakespeare. *The Troublesome Reign* was attributed to W. Sh. in 1611, and to W. Shakespeare in 1622.

3. Inclusion in F1 is not an absolute guarantee of authenticity. *Henry VIII* is almost certainly largely Fletcher's. (Nor is exclusion from F1 necessarily a sign of spuriousness: *Pericles* is for the most part Shakespeare's.)

The evidence against Shakespeare's authorship of any of the plays, or of part of a play, is:

EXTERNAL: Edward Ravenscroft, in the *Address* to his adaptation of *Titus Andronicus* (1687), wrote: 'I have been told by some anciently conversant with the Stage, that it was not Originally his, but brought by a private Author to be Acted, and he only gave some Master-touches to one or two of the Principal Parts or Characters.' This is the only piece of external evidence – such as it is – against Shakespeare's authorship of any of the plays.

INTERNAL: In the 18th century Theobald and Warburton questioned, on stylistic grounds, the authenticity of the three parts of *Henry VI*, and Coleridge found *1 Henry VI*, the opening at least, un-Shakespearean. In 1850 James Spedding asked *Who wrote Henry VIII?* and most scholars agree today that much of it is by Fletcher.

If, therefore, *Titus Andronicus* and *Henry VI* at one end are adaptations by Shakespeare of other men's work, and *Henry VIII* at the other end is collaboration, can we be sure that the plays in between are entirely Shakespeare's? Most competent judges will agree that the Hecate speeches in *Macbeth* are not Shakespeare's work. But once disintegration of the canon begins, where is it to end? What of *The Taming of the Shrew*, *All's Well* and *Timon of Athens*? What of *Henry V*, *Julius Caesar* and *Hamlet*?

Disintegration is pursued in two ways; one method is mainly subjective: by the ear 'to assign alien matter to alien hands'; if a passage is reminiscent of the style of Greene, or Marlowe, or Chapman, then it is, or may be, assigned to him. J. M. Robertson was the leader of this school. The other method is objective and bibliographical: the detection of alien matter from peculiarities and inconsistencies in the original texts, by stage-directions, spelling, punctuation, and so on.

There are four ways in which alien matter may have come to be in the plays:

1. Adaptation by Shakespeare of work by his predecessors. Though possible – for adaptation was a common Elizabethan practice – there is no clear proof of this; and certainly he did not make a practice of it. The source plays that we possess, *The Taming of A Shrew*, *The Troublesome Reign of John*, *The Famous Victories of Henry V*, and *King Leir*, are sources only. Shakespeare did not adapt them; he abstracted what he wanted, altered and added to the plot and characters, and completely rewrote them.

2. Adaptation by Shakespeare of work by his contemporaries. The same arguments apply. It seems improbable that Shakespeare made a practice of adapting Chapman as Robertson suggests, though he may have begun his career as a 'dresser' of other men's plays, e.g. *1 Henry VI*.

3. Collaboration. This was a common practice, and almost certainly Shakespeare collaborated with Fletcher towards the end of his career in *The Two Noble Kinsmen* and *Henry VIII*. There is, however, no external evidence that Shakespeare collaborated with anybody else.

4. Other men's adaptation of Shakespeare's work. There is no evidence of wholesale adaptation, but it is clear that certain speeches, scenes and episodes, such as the Hecate speeches, are interpolations. And no doubt many actors' gags have crept into the text.

Finally, though this does not affect authenticity, Shakespeare may have revised his own work – probably he revised *All's Well* – though it seems unlikely that he would make a practice of this when he was for ever advancing the frontiers of his art. A creative genius is more interested in what is to be achieved than in what has been achieved.

We are all disintegrators up to a point: that there is alien matter in some of the plays of the canon few will deny, but that whole plays are substantially the work of other men is another matter.

Autolycus. In *The Winter's Tale*, 'a Rogue': a pedlar and pick-pocket of Bohemia. He is made to change clothes with Florizel to help the prince's escape to Sicilia, and then abuses his finery in extorting money from the shepherd and his son. He sings the songs 'When daffodils begin to peer' and 'Lawn as white as driven snow'.

Auvergne, Countess of. In *Henry VI* (1, iii) she tries, but fails, to trap the English commander, Talbot, in her castle.

Ayrer, Jakob (d. 1605). German dramatist who became imperial notary at Nuremberg, where he died. His dramatic works were published in 1618 as *Opus Theatricum*. He was much influenced by the English drama through the visits of English 'comedians' like Kempe, Pope and Bryan in 1586–7, and Robert Browne from 1590 onwards, to the German Courts and towns where they were so well received. From their repertoire Ayrer borrowed the Elizabethan clown and many melodramatic devices. Shakespeare and Ayrer seem to have used the same source, Bandello, for *Much Ado* and *Die Schöne Phänicia* (*c.* 1595). The plot of Ayrer's *Die Schöne Sidea* is similar to that of *The Tempest*, and as Ayrer died in 1605, it has been suggested that Shakespeare was indebted to him. As in *Much Ado*, however, a common source, though unknown, seems more probable.

Ayscough, Samuel (1745–1804). 'The Prince of Indexers', obtained a post in the British Museum, where he became assistant librarian, catalogued an immense number of books and documents, and in 1790 published the first *Index* or Concordance of the Works of Shakespeare.

B

Back-cloths were certainly used in the Restoration theatre, and though the evidence for their use in Shakespeare's time is slender, they would be an obvious and simple device hung on the tiring-house wall. The Admiral's had a 'clothe of the Sone and Mone' (though this was probably for the 'heavens') and a 'sittie of Rome'. (See CURTAINS.)

Bacon, Mathias. Son of Thomas Bacon of Norfolk and his wife Anne (Blackwell). In 1590 Mathias inherited the Blackfriars Gatehouse from his mother, selling it in 1604 for £100 to Henry Walker, from whom Shakespeare bought it in March 1613 for £140. In April 1615 Shakespeare and others issued a friendly Bill of Complaint against Mathias so that he might have the sanction of the Court of Chancery to surrender the title-deeds of the Lodging of the Prior of Blackfriars, of which estate Shakespeare's Gatehouse formed a part.

Bacon, Francis, 1st Baron Verulam and Viscount St Albans (1561–1626). Son of Sir Nicholas Bacon, he was born in London and educated at Trinity College, Cambridge. In 1584 he entered Parliament, in 1606 married Alice Barnham, becoming successively Solicitor-General 1607, Attorney-General 1613, Lord Keeper 1617, Lord Chancellor 1618. In 1621 he was found guilty of taking bribes in his official capacity, fined and condemned to prison. Both fine and imprisonment, however, were modified, and he devoted the rest of his life to literature and philosophy. His chief works are: in English: *Essays* 1597–1625, *The Advancement of Learning* 1605, *History of Henry VII* 1622, *New Atlantis* 1627; in Latin: *Novum Organum* 1620, *De Augmentis Scientiarum* 1623.

In July 1600 Bacon wrote to Essex who, by his influence, had helped him in his career: 'I love few persons better than yourself, both for gratitude's sake and for your own virtues', but warned him of the danger of his course, and after the Rebellion of February 1601 he was instrumental in securing Essex's conviction. In his *Declaration of the Practises and Treasons . . . by Robert late Earle of Essex* Bacon refers to the extraordinary production of Shakespeare's *Richard II*, with the deposition scene, by the Chamberlain's Men at the Globe on the day before the rising:

> The afternoon before the rebellion, Merricke, with a great company of others, that afterwards were all in the action, had procured to be played before them, the play of deposing King Richard the second. Neither was it casual, but a play bespoken by Merrick. And not so only, but when it was told him by one of the players, that the play was old, and they should have loss in playing it, because few would come to it: there was forty shillings extraordinary given to play it, and so thereupon played it was. So earnest he was to satisfy his eyes with the sight of that tragedy which he thought soon after his lord should bring from the stage to the state, but that God turned it upon their own heads.

Baconian Heresy. In the middle of the 19th century Shakespeare was still thought of as 'self-schooled' (Arnold), 'the Stratford Peasant' (Carlyle), and in his *Life of Shakespeare* Halliwell-Phillipps concluded that when Shakespeare left Stratford he must have been 'all but destitute of polished accomplishments'. At the same time, the critics, from Swinburne to Masson, were exhausting the superlatives of the language; Shakespeare was capable of all things: 'Thought, History, Exposition, Philosophy, all within the round of the poet. It is as if into a mind poetical in form there had been poured all the matter which existed in the mind of his contemporary Bacon.' How could the Stratford Peasant be reconciled with this Prince of Poets and Philosophers? This was a question asked by a thoughtful American consul, Joseph C. Hart, in his *Romance of Yachting* (1848), and answered in 1857 by his compatriot, Delia Bacon. The principal author was undoubtedly her namesake, Francis Bacon. Mr W. H. Smith of London came to the same conclusion, as did Mrs Henry Pott, who edited Bacon's *Promus of Formularies and Elegancies*, demonstrating the parallelism of expression in Bacon's commonplace book and the works of 'Shakespeare'. When pressed, however, this phraseology was found to be common to all the Elizabethan and Jacobean writers, and it became necessary to assume that Bacon had also written most of the Elizabethan drama, Burton's *Anatomy of Melancholy* and Florio's translation of Montaigne's *Essays*. Meanwhile the Americans were not idle: the two volumes of Nathaniel Holmes's *Authorship of the Plays attributed to Shakespeare* reached its fourth edition in 1886, and was quickly followed by another two volumes from the pen of Ignatius Donnelly, ex-Senator of Minnesota: *The Great Cryptogram: Francis Bacon's Cypher in the so-called Shakespeare Plays*. It was sensational; Shakespeare was revealed as a profligate son of a poor peasant, 'born in a hole'. No wonder a Baconian Society was founded in London in 1886 with its magazine *Baconiana*, and that Chicago followed in 1892 with a quarterly periodical of the same name.

The cryptographic approach was further explored by Mrs E. W. Gallup, who unintentionally revealed that Bacon must have made use of Pope's translation of Homer, and by Sir Edwin Durning-Lawrence, who discovered the all-revealing word in *Love's Labour's Lost*. This is 'honorifacabilitudinitatibus', the 27 letters of which form the anagram, 'Hi ludi F Baconis nati tuiti orbi': 'These plays, F. Bacon's offspring, are preserved for the world.' But the whole of the page on which the word occurs in the Folio is cryptographic, and the revelations are really very remarkable, that of Bacon's intention to disclose his identity in 1910, the very year of Sir Edwin's discovery, being almost incidental.

Up till this time the Baconians had had it all their own way: Shakespeare, the illiterate Stratford actor, could not have written the plays, and Bacon could. But in the 20th century the continent of Europe joined the attack, only to split the anti-Stratfordian ranks, however: Germany and Belgium discovered *der wahre Shakespeare* in Roger Manners, 5th Earl of Rutland, France in William Stanley, 6th Earl of Derby, and Mr Looney produced another nobleman in Edward de Vere, 17th Earl of Oxford. America has recently added another candidate – Marlowe.

The Baconians still base their crazy structures on the scholarship of a century ago, but it will be a pity when their magazines fail to publish their entertaining fantasies. (See W. and E. Friedman, *The Shakespearean Ciphers Examined*; F. E. Halliday, *The Cult of Shakespeare*; H. N. Gibson, *The Shakespeare Claimants*.)

'Bad' Quartos. When the 18th-century editors began the study of the Quarto texts they assumed that the reference of Heminge and Condell in their Preface to the Folio, 'to diuerse stolne, and surreptitious copies, maimed, and deformed by frauds and stealthes of iniurious impostors' applied to *all* the Quartos, though Malone recognized the superiority of many of the Quarto texts. But in his *Shakespeare's Folios and Quartos* (1909) A. W. Pollard showed that Heminge and Condell distinguish between some ('diverse copies') and 'all the rest', and to the former he gave the name 'bad' Quartos, not because they were badly printed, but because the text is out of all measure corrupt. These Quartos were Q1 *Romeo and Juliet*, *Henry V*, *The Merry Wives*, and Q1 *Hamlet* (discovered only in 1823). When compared with the good texts of a corrected Q or with F, they are found to have gaps in the sense, changes in the word order, synonyms, and paraphrases of speeches; some scenes have lines taken from another part of the play, and even from another play, not necessarily Shakespeare's; verse is often unmetrical and printed as prose, prose as verse.

At first it was thought that these texts were put together from shorthand notes taken in the theatre, but Greg (*Two Elizabethan Stage Abridgments*, 1923) and R. C. Rhodes (*Shakespeare's First Folio*, 1923) noted that some of the smaller parts were less corrupt than the others, and argued that the plays were reconstructed from memory by one or more actors who had played minor parts in a London production, and tried to reproduce the play for a provincial performance. This theory is generally accepted.

To the four 'bad' Quartos noted by Pollard, Peter Alexander (*Shakespeare's Henry VI and Richard III*, 1929) has been able to add *The First Part of the Contention* (1594), and *The True Tragedy* (1595), previously thought to be source-plays, but now recognized as pirated versions of *2, 3 Henry VI* as printed in F. His thesis that *A Shrew* is not a source of *The Shrew* but a 'bad' Quarto of it has not been generally accepted. (See REPORTED TEXTS; PIRACY OF PLAYS.)

Badges. Actors, as members of their patron's household, wore his livery (q.v.) and badge. In 1588 a Norwich cobbler was imprisoned for 'lewd words uttered against the ragged staff' of Leicester's Men, and the mock company of players in *Histrio-mastix* assume the badge of their patron, Sir Oliver Owlet, an owl in an ivy-bush.

Bagehot, Walter (1826–77), born in Somerset, educated at London University, and called to the Bar. In 1860 he became editor of *The Economist*. In his essay on *Shakespeare – The Man* (1853) he reconstructs Shakespeare's character, emphasizing his love and knowledge of the country, sympathy with the common people, disbelief in the middle classes, and his power of delineating women.

Bagley, Edward. 'Citizen and pewterer of London', and a cousin of Shakespeare's granddaughter Elizabeth, Lady Bernard (d. 1670), either through the Shakespeares or the Halls, or possibly the Ardens. He probably bought the Blackfriars Gatehouse *c.* 1647, and was the sole executor and residuary legatee of Lady Bernard's will, by which he acquired the Old Stratford estate and New Place, which he sold to Sir Edward Walker in 1675. (See WILL OF SHAKESPEARE.)

Bagot, Sir William (d. *c.* 1400). In *Richard II*, one of the 'creatures to King Richard'. He, Bushy, and Green were, according to Bolingbroke, 'the caterpillars of the commonwealth', the last two of whom he captured and executed; Bagot was imprisoned and informed against Aumerle (IV, i).

Baker, Daniel. Nephew and one of the correspondents of Richard Quiney, and the brother-in-law of Abraham Sturley. He came from Henley-in-Arden, and like Quiney and Sturley was a member of the Stratford Corporation.

Baker, George Pierce (1866–1935). American educationalist; Professor of English at Harvard University 1905–24, and in his '47 Workshop' trained his students in the drama, on the theory of which he lectured. In 1925 he became director of the Yale Department of Drama. His *Development of Shakespeare as a Dramatist* (1907) was a pioneering study of the plays as written by a successful actor-dramatist. He also wrote *Dramatic Technique* (1910). (See J. B. MATTHEWS.)

Baldwin, Thomas Whitfield (b. 1890). American scholar. Professor of English at New York University. His *Organization and Personnel of the Shakespearian Company* (1927) is important. In *William Shakespeare's Five-Act Structure* (1947) he maintains that Shakespeare was influenced by classical dramatic construction and wrote his plays in five acts. (See LOVE'S LABOUR'S WON.)

Bales, Peter (1547–*c.* 1610). English calligraphist, and one of the first experimenters in shorthand writing since Roman times, was born in London. Of his micrography Evelyn wrote: 'Famous Peter Bales, who, in the year 1575, wrote the Lord's Prayer, the Creed, Decalogue, with two short prayers in Latin, his own name, motto, day of the month, year of the Lord, and reign of the Queen ... all of it written within the circle of a single penny ... so accurately wrought as to be very plainly legible'. In 1590 he was headmaster of a school in London, and in that year published *The Writing Schoolemaster*, one part of which contained *The Arte of Brachygraphie*; but the art seems still too clumsy and undeveloped to have been applied to reporting the texts of plays in the theatre. (See REPORTED TEXTS.)

Balthasar. 1. In *The Comedy of Errors*, a merchant. He persuades Antipholus of Ephesus not to use violence when his wife locks him out of his own house.

2. In *The Merchant of Venice*, a servant to Portia. He speaks one line, when Portia sends him with a letter to her cousin, Doctor Bellario of Padua. (Portia adopts the name when she disguises herself.)

3. In *Much Ado*, servant to Don Pedro. He sings the song, 'Sigh no more, ladies'. The part was played by Jack Wilson, for instead of the Q 'Enter ... Musicke', F reads 'Enter ... Iacke Wilson'. (See WILSON, JOHN.) Presumably he sang also, 'Pardon, Goddess of the night' in V, iii.

4. In *Romeo and Juliet*, servant to Romeo. He brings the news to Romeo, banished in Mantua, of Juliet's supposed death, and accompanies him to the Capulets' monument, outside which he hides, meets Friar Lawrence, and is captured by the Watch.

Bandello, Matteo (*c.* 1480–1562). Italian novelist, was born at Castelnuovo near Tortona. After the battle of Pavia he fled to France, where Francis I made him

Bishop of Agen. He wrote a number of *novelle*, prose romances similar to those of Boccaccio's *Decameron*, which were translated into French by Belleforest (1565), from whose version they were freely translated into English by Sir Geoffrey Fenton (1567). William Paynter included a number of these in his anthology of romances, *The Palace of Pleasure* (1565–7). Shakespeare was indebted to Bandello, though probably indirectly, for:

Romeo and Juliet: Arthur Brooke's poem *Romeus and Juliet* (1562) is a version of Belleforest's and Boaistuau's adaptation of Bandello's II, 9.

Much Ado: The Hero story is number 22 of Bandello's *Novelle*, a French version of which is in Belleforest's *Histoires Tragiques*.

Twelfth Night: Barnabe Rich's *Apolonius and Silla* in his *Farewell to Militarie Profession* (1581) is approximately the Viola-Orsino story as told by Bandello II, 36.

Rape of Lucrece: Bandello's *novella* is one of the possible sources.

Bankside. A district of Southwark, extending for roughly half a mile to the west of London Bridge, on the south bank of the Thames, and backed in Shakespeare's day by an area of swamp, open drains, and scattered houses. Along the river front from west to east there was, according to Stowe (1598), 'a continuall building of tenements': the bear garden, the stews, the Clink prison, Winchester House, and the church of St Mary Overie. About this area ran primitive roads: on the west Love Lane, on the east Deadman Place, and connecting them, about two hundred yards from the river, Maid Lane. By the river to the west was the Liberty of Paris Garden with its landing-steps, where the old amphitheatres for bear and bull baiting once stood. Adjoining this Liberty on the east was the Liberty of the Clink, within which Shakespeare was living apparently in 1596–9, and perhaps longer. Henslowe and his son-in-law Alleyn also lived in the Bankside district. The Bankside theatres, running from west to east, were the Swan *c.* 1594, the Hope 1614, the Rose *c.* 1587 and the Globe 1599. (See *Bankside: Survey of London Series*, 1950.)

Banquo. In *Macbeth*, a Scottish nobleman and general who, with Macbeth, defeats the rebel Macdonwald and his Norwegian allies. Because the Witches prophesy that Banquo shall be the ancestor of Scottish kings, Macbeth has him murdered, but his son Fleance escapes. Macbeth's betrayal of his horror when he sees Banquo's ghost first arouses the suspicions of the thanes. (An unhistorical character.)

Baptista Minola. In *The Taming of the Shrew*, a rich gentleman of Padua and the father of Katharina the shrew, and of the gentle Bianca. The plot depends on his resolve not to bestow his youngest daughter before he has a husband for the elder. (Called Alfonso in *A Shrew*.)

Bardolfe, George. One of the 'nyne persons' who in 1592 were reported for not 'comminge monethlie to the Church' at Stratford, two others being Shakespeare's father John, and William Fluellen.

Bardolph. In *1* and *2 Henry IV*, a follower of Falstaff. 'His face is all bubukles, and whelks, and knobs, and flames of fire.' In *The Merry Wives* Falstaff finds him 'a life that he has desired', that of a tapster at the Garter Inn. In *Henry V* he is hanged for looting churches in the French wars, or as Pistol has it, his 'vital thread is cut with edge of penny cord and vile reproach'. (See HARVEY.)

Bardolph, Lord. In *2 Henry IV*, one of the Northumberland faction. He brings the Earl false news of Hotspur's victory at Shrewsbury. In Q he is called Sir John Umfrevile, a correction that is not fully carried out in F (cf. I, i, 34). He advises the rebel Archbishop and Hastings to be cautious, and, with Northumberland, apparently deserts their cause, but news of their defeat is brought in IV, iv. (Thomas Bardolph, 5th Baron (1368–1408), was killed at Bramham Moor.)

Barker, John. See TITHES.

Barksted, William. Minor poet, dramatist, and 'one of the servants of his Maiesties Revels'. At the end of his poem, *Myrrha, the Mother of Adonis; or Lustes Prodegies* (1607), he compares unfavourably the merit of his Muse with that of Shakespeare, both of whom sang the Adonis theme:

His Song was worthie merrit (*Shakspeare* hee)
sung the faire blossome, thou the withered tree
Laurell is due to him, his art and wit
hath purchast it, *Cypres* thy brow will fit.

Barnard. See BERNARD.

Barnardine. In *Measure for Measure*, 'a dissolute prisoner ... a Bohemian born. ... A man that apprehends death no more dreadfully but as a drunken sleep.' The Duke orders the Provost to have Barnardine executed instead of Claudio, but Barnardine refuses to die: 'I will not consent to die this day, that's certain. ... Not a word: if you have anything to say to me, come to my ward.' Eventually he is pardoned.

Barnes, Barnabe (*c.* 1569–1609). English poet, 'Petrarch's scholar'; son of the Bishop of Durham, was educated at Brasenose, Oxford. He wrote *Parthenophil and Parthenophe, Sonnettes, Madrigals, Elegies and Odes* (1593), and *A Divine Centurie of Spirituall Sonnetts* (1595). There are critics who assign some of Shakespeare's Sonnets to Barnes, and Sir Sidney Lee found in him the 'rival poet' referred to by Shakespeare: 'All the conditions of the problem are satisfied by the rival's identification with the young poet and scholar Barnabe Barnes, a poetic panegyrist of Southampton and a prolific sonnetteer, who was deemed by contemporary critics certain to prove a great poet.' (See DEVIL'S CHARTER.)

Barnes, Joshua (1654–1712), Professor of Greek at Cambridge University. Malone (*Var*, II, 143) writes that in a MS. *History of the Stage*, *c.* 1730, full of forgeries and falsehoods, and probably by William Chetwood, is a story of how Barnes (*c.* 1690) gave an old woman of Stratford a new gown for two stanzas of a ballad on Sir Thomas Lucy (q.v.) that she was singing:

Sir Thomas was too covetous,
To covet so much deer,
When horns enough upon his head
Most plainly did appear.

Had not his worship one deer left?
What then? He had a wife
Took pains enough to find him horns
Should last him during life.

Barnfield, Richard (1574–1627). English poet, born at Norbury, Staffordshire, and educated at Brasenose, Oxford. In 1594, when he was only twenty, he published *The Affectionate Shepherd*, 'the complaint of Daphnis for the love of Ganymede', a poem in the manner of Shakespeare's *Venus and Adonis*. Next year he followed this with *Cynthia*, a panegyric on the Queen in Spenserean stanzas, and *Certain Sonnets*, a sequence of twenty, resembling those of Shakespeare. His third volume was *The Encomium of Lady Pecunia*, which included *Poems of Divers Humours*, one of which, 'A Remembrance of some English Poets', contains the first tribute in verse to Shakespeare (this was 1598, the year of Meres's *Palladis Tamia*):

And *Shakespeare* thou, whose hony-flowing Vaine,
(Pleasing the World) thy Praises doth obtaine.
Whose *Venus*, and whose *Lucrece* (sweete, and chaste)
Thy Name in fames immortall Booke haue plac't.
Liue euer you, at least in Fame liue euer:
Well may the Bodye dye, but Fame dies neuer.

In the next year *The Passionate Pilgrim*, 'by W. Shakespeare', was published. Of the twenty-one poems only five are certainly by Shakespeare, and two are certainly by Barnfield, numbers 8 and 21,

'If music and sweet poetry agree', and 'As it fell upon a day', probably also 18, 'My flocks feed not', and possibly others. Barnfield published no more poetry, retiring to his estate of Dorlestone in Staffordshire, where he died in 1627. Apart from the great merit of some of his poetry, Barnfield is interesting as one of the first admirers and imitators of Shakespeare.

Barrett, Lawrence (1838–91). American actor with Irish parents. He played many Shakespearean parts: Richard III, Shylock, Lear, Hamlet, Cassius to Booth's Brutus, and Othello to his Iago. From 1867 to 1870 he was joint-manager with John M'Cullough of the California Theatre, San Francisco. He acted in London a number of times in the eighties.

Barry, Ann (1734–1801). English actress; the second wife of Spranger Barry, was born in Bath. Her first husband was an actor called Dancer, but the first record of her appearance is with Barry at his Crow Street Theatre, Dublin, where in 1758 she played Cordelia to his Lear. As Desdemona she was said to rival Mrs Siddons. After Barry's death she married a third time, went on acting until 1798, and in 1801 was buried in Westminster Abbey.

Barry, Spranger (1719–77). Actor, born in Dublin. He first appeared in London at Drury Lane in 1746 as Othello, his greatest part. In 1749 he played Mahomet to Garrick's Demetrius in Johnson's *Irene*, and aroused Garrick's jealousy by his success as Macbeth, Hamlet, and Romeo. His going to the rival house of Covent Garden in 1750 led to the 'Romeo and Juliet War', simultaneous productions with Garrick at Drury Lane and Barry at Covent Garden. In 1758 he built and began the management of the Crow Street Theatre, Dublin, but when he married Mrs Dancer he returned to the stage at Drury Lane under Garrick. In 1774 he and his wife moved to Covent Garden, where he died in 1777.

'Bartholomew Fair.' 'A Comedie, Acted in the Yeare, 1614. By the Lady Elizabeths Seruants ... By ... Beniamin Iohnson.' First printed in the unsatisfactory F2 of Jonson's *Workes*. The satire is directed largely against the Puritans in the person of Zeal-of-the-Land Busy, 'a Banbury man' (i.e. a Puritan) who is eventually put in the stocks. Apart from its merit as a play, it is important because of its references to the theatre, to actors, and to Shakespeare.

THE THEATRE: In the *Induction* a Scrivener makes pretended 'Articles of Agreement ... between the spectators or hearers, at the Hope on the Bankside ... and the author ... the one and thirtieth day of October 1614'. (The play was given at Court the next day, 1 November.) 'And though the Fair be not kept in the same region that some here, perhaps, would have it: yet think, that therein the author hath observed a special decorum, the place being as dirty as Smithfield, and as stinking every whit.' (The Hope was the rebuilt Beargarden.)

ACTORS: In the *Induction* the Stage-keeper says, 'I am an ass! I! and yet I kept the stage in master Tarleton's time, I thank my stars. Ho! an that man had lived to have played in Bartholomew Fair, you should have seen him have come in, and have been cozen'd in the cloth-quarter, so finely.'

v, iii Which is your Burbage now?
What mean you by that, sir?
Your best actor, your Field?...
And here is young Leander, is as proper an actor of his inches, and shakes his head like an hostler ...
One Taylor, would go near to beat all this company, with a hand bound behind him.

(Tarlton, Queen's 1583–8; Richard Burbage, Chamberlain's-King's 1594–1619; Nathan Field, Jonson's favourite, Lady Elizabeth's 1613–15, King's 1615–*c.* 1619; William Ostler, King's *c.* 1610–14; Joseph Taylor, Lady Elizabeth's 1611–14, Duke of York's 1614–19, King's 1619–42.)

SHAKESPEARE: From the *Induction*: 'He that will swear, *Jeronimo*, or *Andronicus*, are the best plays yet, shall pass unexcepted at here, as a man whose judgment shews it is constant, and hath stood still these five and twenty or thirty years....

'If there be never a servant-monster in the

fair, who can help it, he says, nor a nest of antiques? he is loth to make nature afraid in his plays, like those that beget tales, tempests, and such like drolleries, to mix his head with other men's heels.' (A reference to *The Winter's Tale*, and *The Tempest*.)

IV, ii Well, my word is out of the Arcadia, then; *Argalus*.
And mine out of the Play, *Palemon*.

(Probably a reference to Shakespeare's and Fletcher's *Two Noble Kinsmen*, which must have been written about this time.)

Bartlett, John (1820–1905). American publisher, born in Plymouth, Mass. In 1855 he published his *Familiar Quotations*, and in 1894 his massive *New and Complete Concordance or Verbal Index to Words, Phrases and Passages in the Dramatic Works of Shakespeare; with a Supplementary Concordance to the Poems*.

Barton-on-the-Heath. A village on the border of Warwickshire, about fifteen miles south of Stratford and four miles east of Moreton in Marsh. Here lived Shakespeare's aunt and uncle, Joan and Edmund Lambert, and their son John. Christopher Sly in *The Taming of the Shrew* came from there, 'Old Sly's son of Burton-heath'.

Bassanio. In *The Merchant of Venice*, a friend of the merchant Antonio, from whom he borrows money to go to Belmont and woo Portia. He chooses the leaden casket and so wins her.

Basse, William. 'William Basse, according to Wood, "was of Moreton, near Thame in Oxfordshire, and was sometime a retainer to the Lord Wenman of Thame Park". There are some verses by him in Annalia Dubrensia, 1636; and ... there is a poem by Dr Bathurst "to Mr William Basse, upon the *intended* publication of his Poems, Jan. 13, 1651. ... In a collection of manuscript poems ... these [the following] verses are entitled "Basse his Elegie one poett Shakespeare, who died in April 1616". The MS. appears to have been written soon after the year 1621. In the edition of our author's poems in 1640, they are subscribed with the initials W. B. only. They were erroneously attributed to Donne ... in 1633' (Malone). There are many versions of this elegy, to which Jonson alludes in his poem in F1:

Renowned Spenser, lie a thought more nigh
To learned Chaucer; and rare Beaumont lie
A little nearer Spenser, to make room
For Shakespeare, in your three-fold, four-fold tomb.
To lodge all four in one bed make a shift
Until doomsday; for hardly will a fift
Betwixt this day and that by fate be slain,
For whom your curtains may be drawn again.
But if precedency in death doth bar
A fourth place in your sacred sepulchre,
Under this carved marble of thine own,
Sleep, rare tragedian, Shakespeare, sleep alone.
Thy unmolested peace, unshared cave,
Possess as lord, not tenant, of thy grave;
That unto us and others it may be
Honour hereafter to be laid by thee.

Basset. In *1 Henry VI*, of the Red-rose, or Lancaster faction. He quarrels with Vernon, who wears the white rose of York. (Either Robert or Philip Basset, both of whom fought at Agincourt.)

Bassianus. In *Titus Andronicus*, brother of the Emperor Saturninus. He marries Lavinia, but is murdered by Tamora's sons, Demetrius and Chiron (II, iii).

Bastard of Orleans. See ORLEANS.

Bates. In *Henry V*, an English soldier who, though he wishes the King were at Agincourt alone, is determined 'to fight lustily for him'. He implores his friend Williams and the disguised King to stop quarrelling (IV, i).

Bathurst, Charles. His *Remarks on the differences of Shakespeare's versification in different periods of his life* (1857) is one of the early essays to determine by metrical tests the order in which Shakespeare wrote his plays.

Bawd. In *Pericles*, the wife of the Pandar, the brothel-keeper of Mytilene. Boult brings in Marina (IV, ii), and the Bawd tells him to 'crack the glass of her virginity' (IV, vi).

Baylis, Lilian Mary (1874–1937), was born in London and trained as a violinist. In 1890 her family moved to S. Africa, but in 1898 she returned to England to help her aunt, Emma Cons, in the management of the Royal Victoria Hall, the Old Vic (q.v.). She developed the musical activities of the hall, particularly after the death in 1912 of Miss Cons, who had been interested mainly in welfare work, renamed it 'The People's Opera House', and made it not only the home of opera and ballet, but also of Shakespeare, where people could see for a modest sum all his plays performed by leading actors under the direction of leading producers. She herself took no part in the production of the plays, confining herself to encouragement and management, and when the Sadler's Wells theatre was acquired in 1931 as a similar people's theatre for north London, she helped in its management as well. (See S. and R. Thorndike, *Lilian Baylis*, 1938.)

Baynes, Thomas Spencer (1823–87). English man of letters. In 1864 he was appointed Professor of Logic and English Literature at St Andrews University, and in 1873 editor of the *Encyclopaedia Britannica*, to the 9th edition of which he contributed an article on Shakespeare which, with other essays, was republished in 1894 as *Shakespeare Studies*.

Beargarden. Bear baiting and bull baiting were favourite sports of the 16th and 17th centuries. The office of 'Maister, Guyder and Ruler of all our Beres and Apes' appears to have been created by Richard III. In 1573 Elizabeth appointed Ralph Bowes 'Cheif Master Overseer and Ruler of all and singular our game pastymes and sportes, that is to saie of all and everie our beares bulles and mastyve dogges'. This was a lucrative monopoly, for 'the Master of her Majesty's Game at Paris Garden' received £5 whenever the Queen was a spectator, in addition to the profits made out of public baiting and the granting of licences. Henslowe and Alleyn paid Bowes's successor £40 a year for licence to bait, and in 1604 succeeded in buying for £450 the Mastership which they held jointly until Henslowe's death in 1616, after which Alleyn continued as sole Master. One of their bills, or posters, gives a good idea of the 'sport':

> Tomorrowe beinge Thursdaie shalbe seen at the Beargardin on the banckside a greate mach plaid by the gamstirs of Essex who hath chalenged all comers what soeuer to plaie v dogges at the single beare for v pounds and also to wearie a bull dead at the stake and for your better content shall haue plasant sport with the horse and ape and whipping of the blind beare.

The whipping of the blind bear, Harry Hunks, 'till the blood ran down his old shoulders' was a humorous interlude, as was also the baiting by dogs of a horse with an ape tied to its back. Thursdays were reserved for public baiting, in 1591 the Privy Council prohibiting plays at the theatres on that day, an order that was by no means strictly kept. (See ES, IV, 307.)

The site of the Beargarden is not very clear. Contemporary writers refer to it as Paris Garden, the Liberty at the extreme west of the Bankside: thus Stowe in 1583, 'The Beare-garden, commonly called the Paris Garden'. But the maps (e.g. Norden's *Speculum Britanniae*, 1593, and *Civitas Londini* 1600) show the Beare howse or Bearegarden farther to the east, in the Liberty of the Clink, and just to the north-west of the 'play howse', i.e. the Rose. Probably an early 16th-century bear garden in Paris Garden continued to be known by that name even when moved farther east into the Clink.

On Sunday, 13 January 1583, eight people were killed when the scaffolds round about the Bear Garden collapsed, an accident attributed by the Puritans to the wrath of God. However, it was in use again after a few months. In 1613 it was pulled down by Henslowe and Meade and newly built as the Hope Theatre on the model of the Swan, but with a movable stage so that it should be 'fitt & convenient in all thinges, bothe for players to playe in, and for the game of Beares and Bulls to be bayted in the same'. It was ready by 31 October 1614, on which day the Lady Elizabeth's performed Jonson's *Bartholomew Fair* there. Baiting was prohibited by Parliament at the beginning of the Civil War, but restored with the Stuarts, and the Hope seems to have been used for baiting as late as 1682. On 14 August 1666, Pepys records, 'After dinner, with my wife and Mercer to the Beare Garden; where I have not been, I think, of many years, and saw some good sport of the bull's tossing the dogs – one into the very boxes. But it is a very rude and nasty pleasure.' (See also BULL-BAITING; HOWES.)

Beatrice. In *Much Ado*, niece of Antonio and cousin of Hero; Benedick's 'dear lady Disdain', who is tricked into confessing her love for him. 'There was a star danced, and under that was I born', she says of herself. (See CASTIGLIONE.)

Beaufort, Henry, In *1 Henry VI*, great-uncle of the King, Bishop of Winchester and Cardinal. He quarrels with the Protector Gloucester, who accuses him of having murdered Henry V (I, iii). He crowns Henry VI in Paris (IV, i), and in V, i appears as a Cardinal.

In *2 Henry VI* he is partly instrumental in securing the disgrace of the Duchess of Gloucester, Gloucester's arrest on a false charge of treason, and his murder. The short scene of his death, III, iii, is perhaps the finest in the play. (Henry Beaufort (d. 1447) was the son of John of Gaunt by his third wife, Katharine Swynford, and therefore step-brother of Henry IV; created Bishop of Winchester and Chancellor by Henry V; Cardinal 1426.)

Beaufort, Thomas, first appears in *Henry V* as Duke of Exeter (q.v.). In *1 Henry VI* he plays the part of peacemaker, but foresees the outbreak of the Wars of the Roses 'so plain, that Exeter doth wish His days may finish ere that hapless time.' (Thomas Beaufort, Earl of Dorset (d. 1426), was the younger brother of the Cardinal. He was not created Duke of Exeter until 1416, after the death of Henry V.)

Beaufort, John. In *1 Henry VI*, Earl, afterwards Duke, of Somerset. Though he tries to keep the peace between Gloucester and the Bishop of Winchester, he quarrels with the Duke of York throughout the play, plucking a red rose in the Temple Garden scene (II, iv). (John Beaufort (1404–44) was a nephew of the Cardinal and of Thomas Beaufort, and grandfather of Henry VII. He was created 1st Duke of Somerset in 1443. Shakespeare sometimes confuses him with his brother Edmund, 2nd Duke.)

Beaufort, Edmund. In *2 Henry VI*, he continues the feud of his brother John against the Duke of York. In I, iii he is made Regent of France, but in III, i has to report that all is lost. York demands his removal, and his finding him at liberty precipitates the Wars of the Roses (V, i). He is killed by York at St Albans (V, ii). (Edmund Beaufort, 2nd Duke of Somerset (1404–55), was the younger brother of the 1st Duke.)

Beaufort, Edmund. In *3 Henry VI*, he joins Warwick when Edward IV marries Lady Grey, and sends Henry Richmond to Brittany for safety (IV, vi). He is captured at Tewkesbury and executed (V, v). (Edmund Beaufort, 4th Duke of Somerset (*c.* 1438–71), was the younger son of the 2nd Duke, succeeding to the title after Edward IV's execution of his brother in 1464. Richmond, later Henry VII, was the son of his cousin Margaret Beaufort.)

Beaumont, Francis (1584–1616). English poet and dramatist, was born at

Grace Dieu in Leicestershire, the third and youngest son of Sir Francis Beaumont, Justice of Common Pleas. In 1597 he entered Broadgates Hall, later Pembroke College, Oxford, and in 1600 was entered a member of the Inner Temple. In London he became friendly with Ben Jonson, *c.* 1606 wrote *The Woman Hater* for the Children of Paul's, and the next year his *Knight of the Burning Pestle* was produced. His collaboration with John Fletcher began about 1608 and lasted until Beaumont's marriage with Ursula Isley, an heiress, in 1613. According to Aubrey, Beaumont and Fletcher 'lived together on the Banke Side, not far from the Playhouse, both batchelors; lay together; had one wench in the house between them, which they did so admire; the same cloathes and cloake, &c., between them'. Beaumont died in March 1616 when he was only 32, and was buried in Westminster Abbey.

It is difficult to assign definitely to Beaumont alone any plays other than *The Woman Hater* and *The Knight of the Burning Pestle*, for the thirty-four plays of F1 (1647) and the fifty-two of F2 (1679) were all published as being by Beaumont and Fletcher. The plays in which Beaumont certainly collaborated with Fletcher are, *Philaster*, *A Maid's Tragedy*, *A King and No King*, *Four Plays in One*, *Cupid's Revenge*, *The Coxcomb*, *The Scornful Lady*. After his marriage Beaumont appears to have stopped writing plays, and Fletcher turned to other collaborators, one of whom was Shakespeare. In a persuasive paper (SS, I) G. E. Bentley suggests that in 1608 the King's Men enlisted the support of Beaumont and Fletcher in their new enterprise of the Blackfriars private theatre with its more exclusive audience, because of their social standing, and because they had had experience of writing for private theatres. Certainly their plays of the next few years were all written for the King's, and of the fifty-two plays of F2, forty-five belonged to them. Probably, too, as Bentley says, Shakespeare's tragi-comedies, which have something in common with those of Beaumont and Fletcher, were written for the Blackfriars rather than for the Globe.

In a poem (*c.* 1615) addressed to Ben Jonson, 'FB', almost certainly Francis Beaumont, wrote:

heere I would let slippe
(If I had any in mee) schollershippe,
And from all Learninge keepe these lines as cleere
as Shakespeare's best are, which our heires shall heare
Preachers apte to their auditors to showe
how farr sometimes a mortall man may goe
by the dimme light of Nature ...

Bedford, Duke of. See LANCASTER, PRINCE JOHN OF.

Beeching, Henry Charles (1859–1919). English divine and man of letters. He edited a number of 16th- and 17th-century poets, in 1904 publishing *The Sonnets of Shakespeare* with a valuable introduction and critical notes, and in 1916 contributing to *A Book of Homage to Shakespeare*. In 1911 he was appointed Dean of Norwich.

Beeston, Christopher. Actor. He appears in the actor list of the Chamberlain's Men as one of the 'principall Comœdians' when they played *Every Man in His Humour* in 1598, but is not in the Folio list, and probably, therefore, was not a sharer. Like Kempe, he joined Worcester's (Queen Anne's) in 1602, but Augustine Phillips of the Chamberlain's-King's in his will of 1605 left him 30s. as his 'servant'. He became the owner of the Cockpit (Phoenix, q.v.) theatre, where he was joined by Queen Anne's (1617), Prince Charles's (1619), Lady Elizabeth's (1622), Queen Henrietta's (1625–37), and 'the King's and Queen's young company' ('Beeston's Boys') (1637).

Beeston, William (d. 1682). Actor, and son of Christopher Beeston. It was from William that Aubrey gathered some of his information about Shakespeare: that

Shakespeare 'understood Latine pretty well: for he had been in his younger yeares a Schoolmaster in the Countrey'. And apparently, 'the more to be admired q he was not a company keeper lived in Shoreditch, wouldnt be debauched, & if invited to writ; he was in paine'. (See AUBREY.)

Belarius. In *Cymbeline*, a banished lord who, under the assumed name of Morgan, brings up in the wilds of Wales the two sons of Cymbeline as his own. He somewhat clumsily explains his role at the end of III, iii:

O Cymbeline! heaven and my conscience knows
Thou didst unjustly banish me: whereon
At three and two years old, I stole these babes;...
Myself, Belarius, that am Morgan call'd,
They take for natural father.

He helps to repel the Roman invasion, and restores the boys to Cymbeline, who says, 'Thou art my brother; so we'll hold thee ever.'

Belch, Sir Toby. In *Twelfth Night*, a drunken uncle of Olivia in whose house he is staying. He plucks the gull Sir Andrew, helps to set the device against Malvolio, and marries Maria in recompense for her writing the letter.

Belgium. The Belgian National Theatre has one French theatre (in Brussels) and three Flemish, the most important of which is the Royal Netherlands Theatre in Antwerp. Shakespeare was first performed there in 1876, and between 1884 and 1950 there were 63 productions, 17 of *The Merchant of Venice*, much the most popular play. The standard translation is that of L. J. Burgersdyk. (See SS, 5.)

'Believe As You List.' A play by Massinger, important as an example of an author's revision of his work after disallowance by the Master of the Revels. Herbert refused to allow it on political grounds in January 1631, but after revision passed it for the King's in May. The play is in manuscript in Massinger's hand (though not his original draft), in the revision the action being shifted from dangerous Portugal to innocuous Syria. The manuscript was used as a prompt-copy; there are additions by the book-keeper indicating properties and, more important, the fact that there were 'long' intervals after Acts I and III. (See KNIGHT, EDWARD; Greg, *Dramatic Documents*.)

Bell Inn. One of the City inns used by the players as a theatre. In November 1583 the City Corporation licensed the newly formed Queen's Men to play 'at the sygnes of the Bull in Bushoppesgate streete, and the sygne of the Bell in Gratioustreete and nowheare els within this Cyttye'. Tarlton, who was with the Queen's from 1583 to his death in 1588, with his fellows, played 'at the Bel by ... the Crosse-keyes in Gracious [Gracechurch] streete'. After the prohibition of playing within the City in 1596 'the Playhouses in Gracious street ... were put down'. (See RAWLIDGE.)

Bel Savage Inn. One of the City inns used by the players as a theatre. It was in Ludgate Hill. In 1575 George Gascoigne wrote contemptuously of 'Bellsavage fayre'. Tarlton played there in 1588, presumably with the Queen's, for in that year 'a sorrowfull newe sonnette' was published, 'intituled Tarltons Recantacion uppon this theame gyven him by a gentleman at the Belsavage without Ludgate (nowe or els never) beinge the laste theame he songe'. *Faustus* was one of the Admiral's plays, and Prynne's reference in *Histrio-mastix* (1633) would seem to be to a performance by that company: 'The visible apparition of the Devill on the stage at the Belsavage Play-house, in Queen Elizabeth's dayes ... while they were there prophanely playing the History of Faustus ... there being some distracted with that feareful sight.' According to Richard Rawlidge (q.v.), a playhouse 'on Ludgate Hill' was 'put down' sometime before 1628. The site is now occupied by the publishing house of Cassell, whose device is 'une belle sauvage', though the derivation is doubtful.

Belleforest, François de (1530–83). A favourite of Margaret of Navarre, he aspired to poetry, but had to content himself with prose, most of it compilation, translation and imitation. His *Histoires Tragiques Extraites des Œuvres Italiennes de Bandello* were collected and published in 7 volumes in 1580. Shakespeare may have been indebted to Belleforest's French version for part of the plots of some or all of the following: *The Rape of Lucrece*, *Romeo and Juliet*, *Much Ado*, *Twelfth Night*, *Hamlet*. The first four are translations from Bandello's *Novelle*, but there were English versions of all these stories, and these were generally Shakespeare's main source.

Bellenden (or Ballantyne), John. Sixteenth-century Scottish poet, and translator of Hector Boece's Latin history of Scotland. His translation was probably used by Holinshed for the Scottish part of his *Chronicles*, which in turn was Shakespeare's source for *Macbeth*.

Belott-Mountjoy Suit. In London on 11 May 1612, Shakespeare made his deposition in the Belott-Mountjoy lawsuit. Stephen Belott had been the apprentice of the tire-maker, or manufacturer of women's headdresses, Christopher Mountjoy, a Huguenot who lived at the corner of Silver and Monkwell streets in Cripplegate ward. In 1604 he married his master's daughter Mary, and in 1612 brought a suit accusing Mountjoy of failing to provide his daughter with a promised dowry of £60 and a further £200 in his will. Joan Johnson, a maidservant of Mountjoy, deposed that Shakespeare, at Mountjoy's request, had helped to persuade Belott to marry Mary:

> And as she remembereth the defendant did send and perswade one Mr Shakespeare that lay in the house to perswade the plaintiff to the same marriadge.

Another deponent, Daniell Nicholas, confirmed this and added that Belott asked him to go to Shakespeare

> to vnderstande the truthe howe muche and what the defendant did promise to bestowe on his daughter in marriadge with him the plaintiff, who did soe. And asking Shakespeare thereof, he answered that he promissed yf the plaintiff would marrye with Marye his the defendantes onlye daughter, he the defendant would by his promise as he remembered geue the plaintiff with her in marriadge about the some of ffyftye poundes in money and certayne household stuffe.

Shakespeare testified to Belott's good character, admitted his part in the persuasion, but could not remember the vital evidence of what Mountjoy had promised to settle on Mary:

> William Shakespeare of Stratford vpon Aven in the Countye of Warwicke gentleman of the age of xlviij yeres or thereaboutes ... deposethe ... To the first interrogatory this deponent sayethe he knowethe the partyes plaintiff and deffendant and hathe knowne them bothe as he now remembrethe for the space of tenne yeres or thereaboutes....
>
> To the third interrogatory this deponent sayethe ... that the said deffendantes wyeffe did sollicitt and entreat this deponent to move and perswade the said complainant to effect the said marriadge, and accordingly this deponent did moue and perswade the complainant thervnto ...
>
> To the ffourth interrogatory this deponent sayth that the defendant promissed to geue the said complainant a porcion in marriadge with Marye his daughter, but what certayne porcion he rememberethe not, nor when to be payed, nor knoweth that the defendant promissed the plaintiff two hundered poundes with his daughter Marye at the tyme of his decease.... And more he cannot depose.... Willm Shaksp.

As Shakespeare's evidence was so unsatisfactory, the case was referred to the overseers of the Huguenot church in London, who awarded Belott twenty nobles.

From all this it appears that Shakespeare had lodged with Mountjoy sometime between 1602 and 1604, and that in May 1612 he was living in Stratford. There seems no good reason why he should have remembered the details of an arrangement made some eight years before; or it may be that he did not wish to be involved in the affairs of the Mountjoy family, who were described 'tous 2 pere & gendre desbauchéz'; or again it is possible that his memory was beginning to fail him. (See WALLACE.)

Benedick. In *Much Ado*, a young lord of Padua. He considers himself a confirmed bachelor, but when he overhears that Beatrice loves him he changes his mind, 'brushes his hat o' mornings', and declares his love for her. She tests it by ordering him to 'kill Claudio', his friend, who has slandered her cousin Hero. (See CASTIGLIONE.)

'Benedicte and Betteris.' The title given to a Court performance of *Much Ado* in the Chamber Account 1612–13.

Benfield, Robert. One of the twenty-six 'Principall Actors' in Shakespeare's plays (see p. 90). He was probably with the Lady Elizabeth's in 1613, and may have joined the King's in 1614 to replace Ostler who died in December, and whose part of Antonio in *The Duchess of Malfi* he played. He is in the 1619 patent of the King's Men, and Sir Henry Herbert notes in his *Office Book*:

> Received of Mr Benfielde, in the name of the kings company, for a gratuity for ther liberty gaind unto them of playinge, upon the cessation of the plague, this 10 of June, 1631, £3 10. 0. This was taken upon Pericles at the Globe.

Benfield was one of the three King's Men who petitioned the Lord Chamberlain in 1635 for the right to acquire shares in the houses of the Globe and Blackfriars (see SHARERS' PAPERS). He signed the *Players' Dedication* to the 4th Earl of Pembroke (q.v.) of the Beaumont and Fletcher Folio published by the King's Men in 1647 after the closing of the theatres.

Benson, Francis Robert (1858–1939). English actor and theatre manager, was born at Tunbridge Wells, and educated at Winchester and New College, Oxford, where he produced the *Agamemnon* and gained a running blue. His first appearance as a professional actor was as Paris in *Romeo and Juliet*, at the Lyceum under Irving in 1882. In the following year he formed his famous touring company, in which his wife acted with him. He did invaluable work in popularizing Shakespeare and rescuing the plays from the tyranny of spectacle, acting as many of the plays with as little scenery and as few cuts as possible. In 1900 at the Lyceum he gave the complete *Hamlet*, and in 1906 at Stratford, where he had assumed the managership of the Festival in 1888, his company played the whole of the Histories. 'We were the first', he wrote, 'to achieve the notable feat of playing the whole list of Shakespeare's plays.' He was knighted in 1916, during the war, when he worked in a canteen managed by Lady Benson.

Benson, John (d. 1667). A London bookseller who specialized in the publication of ballads and broadsides. He published the 1640 edition of Shakespeare's *Poems* (q.v.).

Bentley, Gerald Eades (b. 1901). American scholar, and Professor of English Literature at Princeton University since 1945. Author of *Shakespeare and Jonson*, and of *The Jacobean and Caroline Stage* (2 vols. 1941), etc.

Benvolio. In *Romeo and Juliet*, nephew of Montague, friend of Romeo and Mercutio, and the innocent cause of the tragedy. His fight with Tybalt leads to the Prince's decree that street brawls shall be capital offences, and his persuading Romeo to go to Capulet's dance leads to Romeo's falling in love with Juliet. After Mercutio's death he does not appear again.

Berkeley, Earl. Minor character in *Richard II*. He speaks only eight lines – to Bolingbroke, who insults him (II, iii).

Berlioz, Hector (1803–69), French composer, inspired by the Shakespearean actress Henrietta Smithson, who became his first wife, wrote an overture to *King Lear*, and the dramatic symphony *Roméo et Juliette.*

Bernard (or Barnard), Elizabeth. Shakespeare's granddaughter. (See HALL.)

Bernard (or Barnard), John. Second husband of Shakespeare's granddaughter, Elizabeth Hall, whom he married at Billesley, a village four miles west of Stratford, 5 June 1649. He was a widower, owned the manor of Abington, near Northampton, and was knighted by Charles II in 1661. He and his wife lived at New Place for a time after their marriage, but in 1653 moved to Abington. 'The house, which is situated very near the church, still remains, but in a modernised state. ... No tradition respecting the family has been preserved.' Elizabeth died there in 1670, and John in 1674. 'His remains, with probably those of Lady Bernard, have long since disappeared, for beneath his memorial slab is now a vault belonging to another family. Administration of his effects was granted to his son-in-law, Henry Gilbert of Locko, co. Derby.' (Halliwell-Phillipps, 1886.)

Bernardo. In *Hamlet*, an officer. He and Marcellus have twice seen the ghost of Hamlet's father before they persuade Horatio to visit their watch. The three of them report what they have seen to 'young Hamlet', but Bernardo is not on the battlements when Hamlet meets the Ghost, nor is he heard of again.

Berners, Lord (1469–1533). John Bourchier, 2nd Baron, helped to secure the position of Henry VII on the throne, was created Lord Chancellor by Henry VIII in 1516, and finished his days as Deputy of Calais. His translation of the *Cronycles* of Sir John Froissart (q.v.), in which he apologizes for being only a 'lerner of the language of Frensshe', was published in 2 vols. (1523–5). His translation of the French romance *Huon de Bordeaux* (q.v.) as *The Boke of Duke Huon of Burdeux* was printed by Wynkyn de Worde (*c.* 1534).

Bernhardt, Sarah (1834–1923). French actress. One of her first successes was as Cordelia in a French translation of *King Lear.* In 1899 she played the part of the prince in Dumas's version of *Hamlet*, a 'preposterous undertaking' enjoyed by Max Beerbohm.

Berowne (or Biron). In *Love's Labour's Lost*, one of the three lords attending the King of Navarre. They take an oath to study and avoid the sight of women for three years. However, the King falls in love with the Princess of France, Berowne with Rosaline, one of her ladies, and the other two with her other ladies. They discover that each is forsworn, but Berowne defends their conduct in a great speech in IV, iii. (Armand and Charles de Gontaut, Ducs de Biron, supported Henry of Navarre in his fight for the French throne, 1589–93. See CHAPMAN.)

Bertram. In *All's Well*, son of the Countess of Rossillion. The King of France forces him to marry Helena, who loves him; he deserts her, but is recovered by a trick.

'Bestrafte Brudermord, Der.' The full title of the play is: *Tragoedia Der bestrafte Brudermord oder: Prinz Hamlet aus Dännemark.* It was printed in 1781 from a MS, now lost, dated 1710. It appears to be a corrupt version of the *Hamlet* play that was part of the repertory performed by the English actor John Green and his touring company at Dresden in 1626. It has resemblances to the 'bad' Q1, for example Polonius is called Corambus, and it has characteristics peculiar to itself. On the other hand, in many places it resembles the good texts of Q2 and F. On the whole it seems probable that it is a memorial reconstruction of Shakespeare's play with recollections of Q1 and the *Ur-Hamlet.*

Betterton, Thomas (*c.* 1635–1710). English actor and dramatist, son of a cook to Charles I, was born in London. His first appearance on the stage was at the Cockpit in 1660. The next year he joined D'Avenant's company at Lincoln's Inn Fields, from 1671 assisted in the management of the Dorset Garden Theatre, and in 1695 opened the new playhouse in Lincoln's Inn Fields. In 1662 he married Mary Saunderson, the first actress to play a number of Shakespeare's heroines. In a profligate age, a favourite of Charles II and of the Court, Betterton was remarkable for his simplicity, integrity, and devotion to his art, in particular to Shakespeare. According to Rowe (1709), 'his veneration for the memory of Shakespeare ... engaged him to make a journey into Warwickshire, on purpose to gather up what remains he could of a name for which he had so great a value'. Downes, the prompter, tells us in his *Roscius Anglicanus*, 1708, that Betterton derived his acting of Hamlet and of Falstaff from D'Avenant, who had the one from Taylor and the other from Lowin, who in turn, as King's Men, were instructed by Shakespeare. Pepys testifies to Betterton's greatness as an actor: 'Saw "Hamlet", done with scenes very well, but above all, Betterton did the Prince's part beyond imagination' (24 August 1661); 'Saw "Hamlet" ... and mightily pleased with it, but, above all, with Betterton, the best part, I believe, that ever man acted' (30 August 1668). (See FAIRY QUEEN.)

Bevis. See GEORGE BEVIS.

Bianca. 1. In *The Taming of the Shrew* (q.v.), daughter of Baptista (called Philema in *A Shrew*).

2. In *Othello*, the mistress of Cassio. Desdemona drops the handkerchief given to her by Othello; it is found by Emilia, whose husband Iago leaves it in Cassio's lodging. Cassio gives it to Bianca, asking her to take the work out, and Othello sees her return it to him. Iago also contrives to make Othello think that when Cassio is jesting about Bianca he is talking of Desdemona.

Bible. The only mention of the Bible by name is made by Dr Caius in *The Merry Wives* (II, iii): 'He has pray his Pible well', though there are three mentions of Holy Writ, and one of God's Book. *Numbers* is the only book of the Bible mentioned, and that is in a transcript from Holinshed in *Henry V*. Nor are Shakespeare's allusions to biblical characters and stories particularly numerous, though, as they are drawn from all parts of the Old and New Testaments, they suggest a wide knowledge. But Shakespeare's *language* was much influenced by the Bible, by its phraseology, rhythms and homely imagery. Until the Authorised Version of 1611, he would rely on the Genevan version of 1560 and the Bishops' revision of 1568. (See Richmond Noble, *Shakespeare's Biblical Knowledge*, 1935.)

Bibliographical Criticism. A field of Shakespearean research opened up at the beginning of this century by A. W. Pollard, with whom were associated W. W. Greg and R. B. McKerrow. It involves the study of Elizabethan book production, type, printers' and publishers' devices, water-marks, and so on; of MS. plays, their handwriting, prompters' additions, and their relation to printed copies, etc. The London Bibliographical Society was founded in 1892, with its journal *The Library* and Pollard as Honorary Secretary. (See TEXTUAL CRITICISM.)

Bidford. A village on the Avon some eight miles west of Stratford, and the site of one of the many apocryphal stories about Shakespeare. It occurs in the *British Magazine*, June 1762. The author is anonymous.

> On the road thither, at a place called Bidford, he shewed me in the hedge, a crab-tree, called Shakespear's canopy, because under it our poet slept one night; for he, as well as Ben Johnson, loved a glass for the pleasure of

society; and he, having heard much of the men of that village as deep drinkers and merry fellows, one day went over to Bidford, to take a cup with them. He enquired of a shepherd for the Bidford drinkers; who replied they were absent; but the Bidford sippers were at home; and, I suppose, continued the sheepkeeper, they will be sufficient for you: and so, indeed, they were. He was forced to take up his lodging under that tree for some hours.

'Shakespeare's Crab' is still marked on the Ordnance map.

Bigot, Robert, Earl of Norfolk. He plays a minor part in *King John* as a representative of the nobles who join the Dauphin on the discovery of Arthur's death, but later return to their allegiance. (Roger, not Robert, Bigot, 2nd Earl, died 1220.)

'Bills'. The earliest extant play-bills are those of the late 17th century, but they are mentioned as early as 1564, and there is a Jacobean bill for the Bear Garden (q.v.). Players set up their bills on posts (cf. our modern 'poster'), and sometimes distributed handbills advertising their plays. (See NORTHBROOKE.)

Biography. Thomas Heywood's projected *Lives of all the Poets* came to nothing, and it is almost as unfortunate that Dugdale, Wood and Walton made no attempt to write a life of Shakespeare. However, in the second half of the 17th century some biographical matter was recorded by Fuller, Aubrey and R. Davies.

At the beginning of the 18th century came the first attempt at a formal *Life*, written by N. Rowe, who got some of his information from Betterton. At the end of the century Malone incorporated a mass of new material collected from Stratford, Dulwich, and London in his *Life*, which almost fills Vol. II of the Third Variorum.

The most important biographies of the 19th century were J. O. Halliwell-Phillipps's *Outlines of the Life of Shakespeare*, 1881, and Sidney Lee's *Life of William Shakespeare*, 1898, the standard work until superseded by J. Q. Adams's *Life of William Shakespeare*, 1923, and E. K. Chambers's *William Shakespeare*, 1930.

Some important biographical discoveries have been made in the 20th century, notably by C. W. Wallace, C. C. Stopes, and Leslie Hotson. (See Bibliography, p. 547; SS, 3, *Studies in the Life and Environment of Shakespeare since 1900*, by C. J. Sisson.)

Biondello. One of the servants of Lucentio in *The Taming of the Shrew*. He has to pretend that his master is the other servant, Tranio, with whom Lucentio, to gain Bianca, changes places. (Called Catapie in *A Shrew*.)

Birmingham Repertory Theatre. Financed and directed by Barry Jackson (q.v.), it opened on 5 February 1913 with a production of *Twelfth Night*. All Shakespeare's plays have been produced there, the most celebrated and influential being those in modern dress, particularly the *Hamlet* of 1925. In 1935 Sir Barry transferred the theatre to a Board of Trustees, though he remained as Director. In 1945 Peter Brook (aged 20) produced *King John* with Paul Scofield (aged 23) as the Bastard, and both went to Stratford with Jackson, who became Director of the Memorial Theatre in 1946. There Brook produced *Love's Labour's Lost* with Scofield as Don Armado.

Birmingham Shakespeare Memorial Library, was founded, largely through the efforts of George Dawson, on 23 April 1864, the tercentenary of Shakespeare's birth, and opened four years later when it had 1,200 volumes. There were 7,000 by 1879, when it was destroyed by fire. By 1884 the loss had been made good, and there are now 35,000 books and pamphlets in 65 languages. There is a copy of each of the four Folios and 70 Quarto editions published before 1709. The Library is particularly rich in 18th-century editions, in illustrations to Shakespeare, play-bills, newspaper cuttings and photographs of modern productions of the plays.

'Birth of Merlin.' A play assigned partly to Shakespeare by the publisher Kirkman, in his play-list of 1661. It can scarcely be Shakespeare's, but may well be by Rowley:

> Q. 'The Birth of Merlin: Or, the Childe hath found his Father. As it hath been several times Acted with great Applause. Written by William Shakespear, and William Rowley. Tho. Johnson for Francis Kirkman and Henry Marsh. 1662.'

Birthplace. The property in Henley Street, Stratford, known as the Birthplace of Shakespeare, consists of two adjoining houses, the western and the eastern. Tradition assigns the western half as the house where Shakespeare was born, but there is no other evidence that Shakespeare was born there, or indeed in either of the houses. The facts are as follows:

1552. John Shakespeare was fined for making a 'sterquinarium' or dunghill 'in vico vocato Hendley Strete', where presumably he was living either as tenant or owner of a house.

1556. He bought a house in Greenhill Street, and the eastern one of the two in Henley Street, the 'Woolshop', where he may already have been living as tenant.

1564. William Shakespeare was born, but we do not know whether his father had yet acquired the western, or was living in the eastern half.

1575. He bought two more houses, sites unknown, but probably the Birthplace.

1597. He was living in the western house in Henley Street when he sold a strip of land to his neighbour, George Badger.

1601. William Shakespeare inherited the property on the death of his father.

1603? The eastern half let as an inn known as the Maidenhead.

1616. Shakespeare left the property to his elder daughter Susanna, from whom it passed to her daughter Elizabeth, who on her death in 1670 left it to her cousin, Thomas Hart. Shakespeare's sister, Joan Hart, was living in the western half in 1616, and the Harts occupied it until 1806.

1769. For the Garrick Jubilee at Stratford a 'birthroom' was assigned and an engraving of the Birthplace was published in the *Gentleman's Magazine*. After this the house became a place of pilgrimage.

1806. The Harts sold the property, in a decayed condition, to Thomas Court for £210, the western half becoming a butcher's shop.

1846. The property was put up for auction on the death of Court's widow, who had respectfully invited 'the nobility and gentry ... to gratify their own laudable curiosity and honour her by inspecting the house in which the immortal Poet of Nature was born'.

1847. The property was bought for £3,000 by the Birthplace Committees of Stratford and London, in the hope that the government would take it over.

1857. The property was restored and contiguous buildings demolished.

1891. An Act incorporated The Trustees and Guardians of Shakespeare's Birthplace, and vested in them the Birthplace as well as the New Place estate, which had been acquired by public subscription in 1862. In 1892 they bought Anne Hathaway's Cottage, in 1930 Mary Arden's House at Wilmcote, and Hall's Croft in 1949. (See SS, 1.)

Bishop, Henry Rowley (1786–1855). English musician, knighted 1842. He composed music for many of Frederick Reynolds's adaptations of Shakespeare's comedies, so popular in the early 19th century. He also wrote 'Home, sweet home'.

Bishop, Sir William (1626–1700). Lived in Bridgetown on the southern outskirts of Stratford, and was responsible for the story told by John Roberts in 1729 that two large chests full of Shakespeare's loose papers and manuscripts

> in the hands of an ignorant baker of Warwick (who married one of the descendants from Shakespear) were carelessly scattered and thrown about, as garret lumber and litter, to the particular knowledge of the late Sir William Bishop, till they were all consumed in the general fire and destruction of the town [i.e. Warwick in 1694].

And William Oldys wrote, *c.* 1750:

> Old Mr Bowman the player reported from Sir William Bishop, that some part of Sir John Falstaff's character was drawn from a townsman of Stratford, who either faithlessly broke a contract, or spitefully refused to part with some land for a valuable consideration, adjoining to Shakespeare's, in or near that town.

Blackfriars Gatehouse. A house bought by Shakespeare from Henry Walker, 'Minstrell of London', for £140 on 10 March 1613. It was part of the estate of the old Lodging of the Prior of Blackfriars, a big house that was occupied towards the end of the 16th century by the Earl of Northumberland, while the gatehouse descended to Mathias Bacon, who sold it in 1604 to Henry Walker for £100. It was close to the Blackfriars Theatre, and is described in the conveyance as 'abutting vpon a streete leading down to Pudle wharffe on the east part, right against the Kinges Maiesties Wardrobe; part of which said Tenement is erected over a great gate leading to a capitall Mesuage. ... And also all that plott of ground on the west side ...' The witnesses were Will. Atkinson, Ed. Overy, Robert Andrews and Henry Lawrence. The next day Shakespeare mortgaged the house to Walker for £60, apparently as security against the payment of the balance of the purchase money. He signed both conveyance and mortgage, associating with himself three trustees, William Johnson, John Jackson and John Heminge, the effect of which, whether deliberately or not, was to deprive his wife or her legal dower of a life interest in the property. Shortly afterwards Shakespeare leased the house to John Robinson (q.v.). It was completely destroyed in the Great Fire of 1666. (See FETHERSTON.)

Blackfriars Theatre. The Dominican priory, built in 1275, was surrounded by walls enclosing an area of some five acres which, until 1608, formed a liberty within the City, lying roughly between Ludgate Hill and the river, with the long western wall flanking the east bank of the Fleet ditch. The priory was suppressed in 1538 and the estate split up into a number of holdings, one of which was given to the Master of the Revels, Sir Thomas Cawarden, and passed on his death in 1559 to Sir William More, who held it until he died in 1601. This holding consisted mainly of the two-storied buildings running from north to south on the western side of the cloisters.

In 1576 More leased half of the upper frater, which had been partitioned, forming a room some 140 by 25 feet, to Richard Farrant, Master of the Children of the Chapel, for the public performance of their plays before production at Court. Farrant died in 1580, but the enterprise was carried on by William Hunnis and then by Henry Evans, the Children of the Chapel and of Paul's performing Lyly's plays there. In 1584 More recovered the buildings and brought to an end the first Blackfriars Theatre.

The second Blackfriars Theatre was adapted from the buildings bought from More for £600 by James Burbage in 1596. These seem to have been all the rooms that had once been the upper frater, and some rooms beneath them. Exactly how these were converted is uncertain, but according to C. W. Wallace there was a hall 66 by 46 feet, with a stage at one end, galleries, and seats. James Burbage died in 1597 and left the property to his son Richard, who in 1600 leased it to Henry Evans and Nathaniel Giles for performances by the Children of the Chapel (q.v.), the serious competitors for a time of the adult companies. In 1608, however, Evans surrendered the lease, and Richard Burbage formed a company of owners, or 'housekeepers', consisting of himself, his brother Cuthbert, the four King's Men, Shakespeare, Heminge, Condell, and Sly, and Thomas Evans, presumably a relation of Henry. In 1608 or 1609 the King's Men took possession of their new private theatre, which was to become more important than the Globe, and lead to a modification of their style of acting and of the type of play performed – Beaumont's and Fletcher's plays, and Shakespeare's romances date from this time. The theatre was demolished in 1655. (See SHARERS' PAPERS.)

Blanch (d. 1254). In *King John*, daughter of Alphonso, King of Castile, and niece of King John. Her marriage to the Dauphin leads to a temporary alliance between John and the French, soon broken by the papal legate, Pandulph, who excommunicates John. The distracted Blanch follows the Dauphin, 'There where my fortune lives, there my life dies'.

Blank Verse. Unrhymed verse, a term usually confined to verse with five iambic feet in a line (⏑ – | ⏑ – | ⏑ – | ⏑ – | ⏑ –), a measure introduced into England by the Earl of Surrey in the first half of the 16th century. It was applied to the drama by Sackville and Norton in *Gorboduc*, *c.* 1560, and further developed by the University Wits, notably by Marlowe, in the eighties. Early blank verse is very regular, and therefore monotonous: the lines are end-stopped, a pause after the second foot, and there is little substitution of other feet for the basic iamb. Briefly, the progress of Shakespeare's verse is from regularity to variety: by enjambement, or running one line into the next, by varying the position of the pause and length of the line, by substituting other feet for the iamb, by the use of the redundant syllable, or feminine ending, and by varying the weight of the stressed syllables, notably at the end of the line. By imposing, in fact, a secondary rhetorical rhythm on the primary one of the metre. The following examples will illustrate this progress:

Love's Labour's Lost, 1594 (IV, iii)

From women's eyes this doctrine I derive:
They sparkle still the right Promethean fire;
They are the books, the arts, the academes,
That show, contain, and nourish all the world:
Else none at all in aught proves excellent.

2 Henry IV, 1598 (II, iii)

For those that could speak low and tardily
Would turn their own perfection to abuse
To seem like him: so that in speech, in gait,
In diet, in affections of delight,
In military rules, humours of blood,
He was the mark and glass, copy and book,
That fashioned others.

Antony and Cleopatra, 1607 (V, ii)

For his bounty,
There was no winter in't; an autumn 'twas
That grew the more by reaping: his delights
Were dolphin-like; they show'd his back above
The element they liv'd in; in his livery
Walk'd crowns and crownets; realms and islands were
As plates dropp'd from his pocket.

The Tempest, 1611 (II, i)

She that is queen of Tunis; she that dwells
Ten leagues beyond man's life; she that from Naples
Can have no note, unless the sun were post,–
The man i' the moon's too slow, – till new-born chins
Be rough and razorable; she that from whom
We all were sea-swallowed, though some cast again,
And by that destiny, to perform an act
Whereof what's past is prologue; what to come,
Is yours and my discharge.

(See VERSE PARAGRAPH: VERSE-TESTS; RHYME.)

Blount, Edward (1564–1632). Bookseller; he became a freeman of the Stationers' Company in 1588. In 1601 he published *Love's Martyr*, the volume containing *The Phoenix and Turtle*, assigned to Shakespeare. In 1608 he registered *Antony and Cleopatra* and *Pericles*, but did not publish. In 1623 he and Isaac Jaggard entered sixteen of the eighteen plays that had not been published as Quartos, and in the same year he was one of the syndicate at whose charges F1 was printed. In 1630 he transferred his rights in the sixteen plays to Robert Allot, one of the publishers of F2. Blount also published Florio's translation of Montaigne, Marlowe's *Hero and Leander*, and Lyly's *Sixe Court Comedies*. He also did some translation from Italian and Spanish. In 1622 he published Leonard Digges's translation, *Gerardo, the Unfortunate Spaniard*, and no doubt obtained the verses of Digges (q.v.) and 'I.M.' (James Mabbe) for the Folio.

Blunt (Blount), Sir Walter. In *1 Henry IV*, a faithful supporter of the King, between whom and Hotspur he is anxious to make peace. He acts as mediator before the Battle of Shrewsbury, in which he is killed by Douglas, who mistakes him for the King. (He was an executor and legatee of John of Gaunt's will; killed 1403.)

SIR JOHN. In *2 Henry IV*, he is given charge of the rebel Colevile (IV, iii). (The son of Sir Walter, he died 1418.)

SIR JAMES. In *Richard III*, he supports Richmond (V, iii). (Great-grandson of Sir Walter.)

Boaistuau, Pierre (d. 1566). French translator, associated with Belleforest in his anthology of *Histoires Tragiques*. Boaistuau's version of Bandello's *novella* of Romeo and Juliet was published in 1559, and is the source of Arthur Brooke's poem, from which Shakespeare took the story.

Boar's Head Theatre. The name of the Eastcheap tavern is not mentioned by Shakespeare in *Henry IV*, though it is implied in the text ('Doth the old boar feed in the old frank? ... At the old place, my lord, in Eastcheap'. *1 Henry IV*, II, ii, 159). There was a Boar's Head tavern in Eastcheap, but it seems unlikely that it became the Boar's Head theatre, as playhouses within the City were suppressed in 1596. Queen Anne's Men were licensed *c.* 1604 to play at 'the Curtayne, and the Bores head, within our County of Middlesex', i.e. outside the City and the liberties. This was the Boar's Head inn, east of Aldgate, in the yard of which plays had been performed since at least 1557.

Boas, Frederick S. (1862–1957), Shakespeare scholar, Professor of English at Queen's College, Belfast, 1901–5; editor of *The Year's Work in English Studies*; author of *Shakspere and his Predecessors*, etc.

Boccaccio, Giovanni (1313–75). Italian poet and novelist, the illegitimate son of a Florentine merchant, was born probably at Certaldo. In 1341 he met Maria d'Aquino, natural daughter of King Robert of Naples, with whom he fell in love and immortalized as Fiammetta. After 1350 he spent much of his time between Florence and Certaldo, where he died in 1375, the news of the death of his dearest friend, Petrarch, in 1374, being said to have hastened his end. Boccaccio is best known as the author of the *Decameron*, a hundred tales supposed to have been told by seven young ladies and three young men who withdrew from Florence into the country during the plague of 1348. His *Teseide*, an epic poem on the subject of Palamon and Arcite, was the source of Chaucer's *Knight's Tale*. Shakespeare was indebted to Boccaccio, though indirectly through English versions, for the following:

Merchant of Venice: the casket theme (*Decameron* X, 1).

All's Well: the story of *Giglietta di Nerbona* (III, 9).

Cymbeline: the wager theme, from the story of *Bernabo of Genoa* (II, 9).

Troilus and Cressida: *Filostrato*, a narrative poem, and the source of Chaucer's *Troilus and Criseyde*.

Two Noble Kinsmen: *Teseide*, the source used by Chaucer, from whom Shakespeare and Fletcher took the story.

Bodenstedt, Friedrich von (1819–92), German author, became a schoolmaster at Tiflis, and professor at Munich. He was a student of Elizabethan literature, in 1862 published a translation of Shakespeare's *Sonnets*, and with F. Freiligath and Paul Heyse a complete translation of the plays (1867–71). (See DEUTSCHE SHAKESPEARE-GESELLSCHAFT.)

Bodleian Library, Oxford, was founded by Sir Thomas Bodley and opened in 1602. As Bodley's views were puritanical, most of the early books were theological, and it was not until 1821, when it acquired the cream of Edmond Malone's collection, that the Bodleian became a great Shakespeare library. There are two First Folios, copies of the other three, and 43 Quartos published before 1623. It is particularly rich in early editions of the poems, and of the five Bodleian editions of *Venus and Adonis* three, including the first, are unique. The most important manuscripts are Aubrey's *Life* and Forman's *Bocke of Plaies*.

Bodmer Library, the property of Martin Bodmer, was rehoused in 1951 at Cologny, near Geneva. It is the finest private Shakespeare collection in the world, with copies of the four Folios, 32 Quartos, all different editions, six being the first and *Troilus and Cressida* uncut.

Boece (or Boyce), Hector (*c.* 1465–1536). Scottish historian, born at Dundee, becoming a professor at Paris University. His *Scotorum Historiae*, a Latin history of Scotland (1527), was translated by John Bellenden (1536), and probably used by Holinshed for the Scottish part of his *Chronicles*, from which Shakespeare took the story of *Macbeth*.

Bolingbroke. In *2 Henry VI*, 'a conjuror' who pretends to call up a prophetic spirit for the benefit of the Duchess of Gloucester who aspires to the throne (I, iv). They are discovered, Bolingbroke and his accomplices being condemned to be 'strangled on the gallows'.

Bolingbroke, Henry (1367–1413). In *Richard II* (q.v.) the cousin of Richard, whom he deposes to make himself Henry IV. (See also *1, 2 Henry IV*.) (The son of John of Gaunt, Duke of Lancaster, he took the name Bolingbroke from his father's castle in Lincolnshire. As Earl of Derby he married Mary de Bohun, daughter of the Earl of Hereford, and was himself created Duke of Hereford in 1397. He succeeded to the Lancaster estates, seized by Richard, on the death of his father in 1399, in which year he returned from exile and deposed Richard. Pronounce *Bullingbrook*.)

Bolton, Edmund (*c.* 1575–*c.* 1633), historian and poet, was educated at Trinity Hall, Cambridge, entered the Inner Temple, and secured the patronage of Buckingham and James I. He wrote *Hypercritica*, *c.* 1616, a critical account of contemporary authors, in the draft MS. of which, though not in its final form, occurs the passage:

> The bookes also out of which wee gather the most warrantable English are not many to my Remembrance, of which in regard they require a particuler and curious tract, I forbeare to speake at this present. But among the cheife, or rather the cheife are in my opinion these ... Shakespere, Mr Francis Beamont and innumerable other writers for the stage and presse tenderly to be vsed in this Argument.

Bona. In *3 Henry VI*, she has agreed, at Warwick's suggestion, to marry Edward IV, when news comes that he has already married Lady Grey. The insulted Bona then urges Louis to support Margaret, wife of the deposed Henry VI, in her struggle against Edward, an alliance joined by Warwick (III, iii). (Princess Bona, or Bonne (d. 1485), was the daughter of the Duke of Savoy. Her eldest sister was the Queen of Louis XI of France.)

'Bonduca.' A tragedy by Beaumont and Fletcher, performed about 1613 by the King's Men. 'The Principal Actors were Richard Burbage, Henry Condel, William Eglestone, Nich. Toolie, William Ostler, John Lowin, John Underwood, Richard Robinson' (F2, 1679). There is a MS. copy of the play, *c.* 1630, a careful transcript by the book-keeper Edward Knight, who added the informative note: 'The booke where by it was first Acted from [i.e. prompt-book] is lost: and this hath beene transcrib'd from the fowle papers of the Authors wch were founde.'

Bonian, Richard. Bookseller, 1607–11. In January 1609 he and Henry Walley entered for their copy of *Troilus and Cressida*, and published it the same year with a remarkable Preface to a second issue. (See TROILUS AND CRESSIDA.)

'Book'. The 'book' of the play is a technical term, and is to be distinguished from the printed book. When a company bought a play it would have to be revised for stage performance. This was, apparently, one of the duties of the book-keeper, presumably at the direction of the leading members of the company. Modifications would have to be made according to the resources of the company: cuts made in the text, either merely to shorten the play or to purge dangerous political or religious matter, and even minor characters and over-elaborate episodes might have to go. Then the stage directions, particularly the entries of characters, would have to be checked, properties noted, and any ambiguities made clear. Finally the acting version would have to be submitted to the Master of the Revels for his endorsement as the 'allowed book' of the play. This revised stage version might be the author's original MS. with additions in the margin, or it might be a transcript, in which event it might be used as the prompt-copy. There is no surviving example of an original draft being used as a prompt-book.

Book-keeper, or book-holder, was the prompter. It is not clear where he stood during a performance, though *Cynthia's Revels* (*Induction*) seems to indicate the tiring-house. *Bartholomew Fair* begins with a scene between the book-holder and the stage-keeper. He was responsible for preparing the acting-copy of the play, or 'book' as it was called, and submitting it to the Master of the Revels for his 'allowance'. That he also prepared the actors' 'parts' – long scrolls each containing the part and cues of an actor – is clear from a curt note of 1633 to Knight (q.v.), book-keeper of the King's Men, from Sir Henry Herbert, Master, when he returned the book of Beaumont's and Fletcher's *Tamer Tamed*: 'In many things you have saved mee labour; yet wher your judgment or penn fayld you, I have made boulde to use mine. Purge ther parts, as I have the booke.' (See KNIGHT, EDWARD; GASCOIGNE, WILLIAM.)

Booth, Barton (1681–1733). English actor, was befriended by Betterton with whom he acted. After 1708 he was at Drury Lane, and succeeded Betterton as the great tragic actor of the age, playing many of the main parts in Shakespeare's plays, notably Lear, Brutus and Hotspur. He was buried in Westminster Abbey. (See VICTOR.)

Booth, Edwin (1833–93). American actor, and son of the actor Junius Brutus Booth. He established his reputation in the fifties, and in 1862 became manager of the Winter Garden theatre, New York, where he produced a number of Shakespeare's plays. In 1865 his brother, John Wilkes Booth, shot President Lincoln. A few years later Edwin built Booth's Theatre in New York and there gave a series of Shakespearean productions in their original versions. He played most of the main Shakespearean parts, his finest performance being Hamlet. He visited London three times. In 1874 he lost his fortune, and turned his house into an actors' club, where he died.

Booth, Junius Brutus (1796–1852). Actor, was born in London, and after his first appearance at Covent Garden in 1815 became a rival of Kean. He played many of Shakespeare's heroes, notably Richard III and Hamlet, and popularized the plays in America, where he settled in 1821. He was the father of three actor sons, Junius Brutus, Edwin and John Wilkes, the assassinator of President Lincoln.

Borachio. In *Much Ado*, one of the followers of Don John, to whom he suggests the plot whereby he makes love to Margaret so that Claudio mistakes her for Hero. After the deception he is arrested by the Watch, cross-examined by Dogberry, and confesses.

Boswell, James (1778–1822), third son of James Boswell, Johnson's biographer. He was educated at Brasenose, Oxford, and after his father's death in 1795 helped his friend, Edmond Malone, in the preparation of the later editions of *The Life of Johnson*. When Malone died in 1812 he was engaged on a new edition of Shakespeare, which was brought out by Boswell in 1821. This is the Third Variorum, or 'Boswell's Malone' (21 vols.), one of the most important of all editions of Shakespeare. To it Boswell prefaced an *Advertisement*, and a *Memoir* of Malone, 'one whom I loved and honoured from my infancy – mine own and my father's friend'.

Bottom, Nick. In *A Midsummer Night's Dream*, a weaver of Athens. He plays the part of Pyramus in the 'tedious brief scene' of *Pyramus and Thisbe*, but at rehearsal Puck gives him an ass's head, and the spell-bound Titania, Queen of the fairies, falls in love with him.

Boult. In *Pericles*, servant of the pander and bawd who keep the brothel at Mitylene. There Boult brings Marina, but eventually she bribes him to find her a place 'amongst honest women' as a needlewoman (IV, ii, v).

Bourbon, Duke of. In *Henry V*, at Agincourt, where he is captured, he urges attacking the English, whom he calls 'bastard Normans' (III, v; IV, v). (John, Duke of Bourbon, was the uncle of Charles VI, and died in England in 1433.)

Bourchier, Cardinal. In *Richard III*, he weakly agrees to the Duke of York's and the Queen-Mother's being brought out of sanctuary, by force if necessary (III, i). (Thomas Bourchier, or Bouchier (*c.* 1404–86), was created Archbishop of Canterbury 1454, and Cardinal 1473. He crowned Edward IV, Richard III, and Henry VII.)

Bowdler, Thomas (1754–1825), was born near Bath, studied medicine at Edinburgh, and eventually settled in South Wales, where he died. He was an active philanthropist, and the friend of Elizabeth Montagu, to whom he dedicated his *Family Shakespeare*, first published in 1818. The text is that of Steevens, but purged of all profanity, indecency, and 'whatever is unfit to be read aloud by a gentleman to a company of ladies'. The plays that most taxed his ingenuity were *Measure for Measure*, *Henry IV* and *Othello*. He followed this success with a 'bowdlerized' edition of Gibbon's *Decline and Fall*, published posthumously in 1826.

Bowers, Fredson Thayer (b. 1905). Bibliographer, since 1949 Professor of English at the University of Virginia. Author of *On Editing Shakespeare and Other Elizabethan Dramatists*, *Textual and Literary Criticism*, etc. Editor of *The Dramatic Works of Thomas Dekker*.

Bowman, John. 'An actor more than half an age on the London theatres' from whom William Oldys (1696–1761) professed to gather information about Shakespeare. Bowman was 'unwilling to allow that his associate and contemporary Betterton had ever undertaken' a journey to Stratford as Rowe claimed. Presumably Oldys wished to belittle Rowe's source of information and to advance his own. (See also BISHOP, SIR WILLIAM.)

Boy Actors. Actresses, with a very few possible exceptions, did not appear on the public stage before 1660, and women's parts were taken by boys with unbroken voices (cf. *Hamlet*: 'Pray God, your voice, like a piece of uncurrent gold, be not cracked within the ring'), though characters like Mistress Quickly might be played by men. Boys appear to have been apprenticed, probably for two or three years, to an actor-sharer; for example, in 1605 James Sands was apprentice to Augustine Phillips, and Samuel Gilburne was his late apprentice. The two or three boy actors in an adult company should be distinguished from those in companies composed entirely of boys, who had to act men's parts as well as women's. This is well illustrated by Ben Jonson's *Epitaph on Solomon Pavy*, 'a Child of Queen Elizabeth's Chapel', who played the parts of old men:

> Years he number'd scarce thirteen
>   When fates turn'd cruel,
> Yet three fill'd zodiacs had he been
>   The stage's jewel;
> And did act, what now we moan,
>   Old men so duly,
> As sooth, the Parcae thought him one,
>   He play'd so truly.

Underwood, Field, and Ostler of the King's Men all started as Children of the Chapel under Evans at the Blackfriars theatre. Even after the Restoration women did not at once entirely displace boys. (See APPRENTICES; ACTRESSES; CHILDREN'S COMPANIES; KYNASTON.)

Boyet. In *Love's Labour's Lost*, a lord attending on the Princess of France. He talks greasily, and does little but run errands, though he discovered to the ladies that the Muscovite masquers are the King and his companions.

Brabantio. In *Othello*, a Venetian senator. When Othello secretly marries his daughter Desdemona, Brabantio charges him before the Senate with stealing her 'by spells and medicines', and his parting words are ominous (I, iii):

> Look to her, Moor, if thou hast eyes to see:
> She has deceived her father, and may thee.

He does not appear after Act I, but we are told (V, ii) that Desdemona's 'match was mortal to him'.

Bracciano. Orsini, Duke of Bracciano, the ancient Roman family, was in London during the winter of 1600–1. If Shakespeare took his name for that of Orsino in *Twelfth Night* the play was probably not written before this date. Orsini is the boy Giovanni, son of Brachiano, in Webster's *White Devil*. (See Hotson, *The First Night of 'Twelfth Night'*.)

Bracegirdle, Anne (*c.* 1670–1748). English actress who appeared often with Betterton, playing Desdemona to his Othello, and a number of Shakespearean parts, though often in 'improved' versions: Juliet, Portia, Ophelia, Cordelia and Isabella. She retired in 1707 when eclipsed by Mrs Oldfield, though she returned for Betterton's benefit in 1709. She was very beautiful, and the friend, mistress, or wife of Congreve, to the success of whose comedies she largely contributed.

Brackets. In extant manuscript plays they are used mainly to mark parentheses. They are so used in the printed texts of Shakespeare's plays, but also as commas. Normally F follows the Quartos in the printing of brackets, but tends to increase their number, compositor B being particularly fond of them: e.g. in the 21 pages that he set of *Richard III* there are 66, only 10 of them taken from Qq. *The*

Winter's Tale is remarkable for the number of its brackets; cf.:

Leo. You haue mistooke (my Lady)
Polixenes for *Leontes*: O thou Thing,
(Which Ile not call a Creature of thy place,
Least Barbarisme (making me the precedent)
Should a like Language vie to all degrees,
And mannerly distinguishment leaue out,
Betwixt the Prince and Beggar:) I haue said
Shee's an Adultresse, I haue said with whom:

This was probably set (by A) from a transcript by Crane, who was also fond of brackets.

According to Wilson (*Tempest*, lvii), 'Brackets affect intonation rather than speed. Often they denote the drop in the voice which a parenthesis demands; but there are many beautiful instances which mark a much more significant change of tone; a hushed whisper, a touch of anxiety, a note of tenderness, surprise or awe.' (See PUNCTUATION.)

Bradley, Andrew Cecil (1851–1935). English critic, and younger brother of F. H. Bradley, the philosopher, was Professor of Poetry at Oxford 1901–6, publishing his *Oxford Lectures on Poetry* in 1909. He is, perhaps, best known for his *Shakespearean Tragedy* (1904), a brilliant analysis of *Hamlet*, *Othello*, *Lear*, and *Macbeth*, but criticized today for its treatment of the characters as though they were real, and not merely *dramatis personae* in 17th-century plays. (See MACKENZIE.)

Bradock, Richard. Printer from 1581 to 1615. He printed:

Midsummer Night's Dream. Q1. 1600, for Fisher (or the printer might have been Allde).

A Yorkshire Tragedy. Q1. 1608, for Pavier.

Venus and Adonis. O4. 1599, O5. 1602? for Leake.

Brakenbury, Sir Robert. As lieutenant of the Tower in *Richard III* he surrenders the sleeping Clarence to the two murderers on the warrant of Richard (I, iv). Presumably he also surrenders the young Princes to Tyrrel on a similar warrant (IV, iii). (He was killed at Bosworth, 1485.)

Brandes, Georg (1842–1927). Danish critic, born in Copenhagen. By 1870, after the publication of his *Aesthetic Studies*, *The French Aesthetics*, and *Criticisms and Portraits* he had established himself as the foremost critic of northern Europe. In 1877 he went to Berlin, but returned to Copenhagen in 1883 owing to his advanced political views. In 1896 he published his massive and original *William Shakespeare*, which has done much to popularize Shakespeare on the Continent.

Brandon. In *Henry VIII*. (See SUFFOLK, DUKE OF.)

Brayne, John (d. 1586). A London grocer whose sister Ellen married James Burbage. In 1567 he had an interest in the theatre at the Red Lion Inn, Stepney. Nine years later he financed the building of the Theatre on the land leased to Burbage, an arrangement that led to disputes and even to blows. After Brayne's death Burbage brought an action against his widow, who retorted with a counter-action, and when she died in 1593 the suit was inherited by Brayne's friend, Robert Miles, of the George Inn, Whitechapel. (See THEATRE.)

Brend, Nicholas, of West Molesey, was the owner of the land on which was built the Globe theatre (q.v.). His son was Sir Matthew Brend. (See HOWES.)

Bretchgirdle, John (d. 1565), a staunch Protestant, was vicar of Stratford when John Shakespeare was one of the Chamberlains, 1561–5. Presumably he christened John's son, William, on 26 April 1564. He took his B.A. at Oxford in 1545 and went to Stratford from Witton,

Northwich. He was buried in Stratford parish church on 21 June 1565, and left an estate of £23 2s. 8d., half of it in books.

Bright, Timothy (1550–1615), one of the pioneers of modern shorthand. He was a doctor of medicine who entered the Church, being rewarded with a Yorkshire living by Queen Elizabeth, to whom he dedicated his *Characterie. An Arte of Shorte, Swifte and Secrete Writing by Character* (1588). The method involved memorizing 537 signs. (See REPORTED TEXTS.) *Hamlet* owes something to Bright's *Treatise of Melancholie*, 1586. (See Wilson, *What Happens in Hamlet*, and G. Keynes, *Dr Timothie Bright.*)

British Empire Shakespeare Society, founded in 1901 by Miss Moritt 'to promote greater familiarity with Shakespeare's Works among all classes throughout the British Empire. It is the rule of the Society to organize Dramatic Readings and Acted Scenes from Shakespeare's plays as often as possible, and lectures on his life and works.'

British Museum Library. When opened in 1759 it had virtually no early editions of Shakespeare. The foundation of its collection was Garrick's 1779 bequest of old English plays, containing 37 Quartos. The acquisition of George III's library in 1823 added 23 more. In 1858 the Museum bought 18 books from Halliwell-Phillipps, including one of the two known copies of *Hamlet*, 1603, the 'bad' Q1. There are now five copies of the First Folio, and copies of the other three. Among the manuscripts are five of the seven known 'plots' of plays, John Manningham's *Diary*, Shakespeare's mortgage of the Blackfriars Gatehouse and *The Booke of Sir Thomas Moore.*

Britten, Benjamin (b. 1913). Composer; founded the Aldeburgh Festival of Music in 1948; his opera, *A Midsummer Night's Dream*, was produced by John Gielgud in 1961.

Broadcasting. The first complete sound production of a Shakespeare play by the B.B.C. was *Twelfth Night*, broadcast in the National Programme 28 May 1923. The first television production was *Julius Caesar*, in modern dress, on 24 July 1938. A few of the plays have not yet been broadcast, either on sound or television, but in 1960 a sequence of all the English Histories, except *King John* and *Henry VIII*, was produced on television as *An Age of Kings: Richard II, 1, 2 Henry IV, Henry V, 1, 2, 3, Henry VI, Richard III.* (For U.S.A., see SQ, XII, 3, *Shakespeare on Television.*)

Brooke (or Broke), Arthur (d. 1563). English poet, and author of *The Tragicall Historye of Romeus and Juliet* (1562), a version of the Bandello story taken from the French translation of Boaistuau and Belleforest in their *Histoires Tragiques.* As Brooke adds incidents incorporated by Shakespeare, it seems certain that his poem was the main source of *Romeo and Juliet.* For example, compare with the end of I, v, Juliet's asking the Nurse the names of the masquers, mentioning Romeo last:

What twayne are those quoth she that
  prease unto the doore,
Whos pages in theyr hand doe beare two
  toorches light before?
And then as eche of them had of his household name,
So she him namde. Yet once agayne the
  yong and wyly dame:
And tell me who is he with vysor in his
  hand,
That yender doth in masking weede besyde
  the window stand.

And with the imagery of Romeo's last speech compare:

God graunt, no dangers rock, ylurking in
  the dark
Before thou win the happy port, wracke
  thy sea-beaten barke.

But Brooke's verse rarely rises to the plane of poetry. He was drowned in 1563 on an expedition to assist the Huguenots.

Brooke, C. F. Tucker (1883–1946). American scholar; Professor of English at Yale University in 1920; author of *The Tudor Drama* (1911), *Shakespeare of Stratford* (1926), *Shakespeare's Sonnets* (1936); editor of *The Shakespeare Apocrypha* (1908), *Shakespeare's Plutarch* (1909), *The Yale Shakespeare* (with W. L. Cross) (1917–27).

Brown, John. An importunate creditor of John Shakespeare who, in 1585–6, in the Stratford Court of Record pressed for settlement of his debt, and obtained a writ of distraint, but 'Johannes Shackspere nihil habet unde distringi potest', a legal formula that is not to be taken too literally.

Browne, Robert. Player, was with Alleyn in Worcester's company in 1583. In 1590 he was at Leyden, and in 1592 began his foreign tours when he obtained a passport for himself, John Bradstreet, Thomas Sackville, and Richard Jones. He and his company toured Germany (q.v.) with a repertory of English plays in 1592–3, *c.* 1594–9, 1601–7, 1618–20.

Brutus, Decius. In *Julius Caesar*, one of the conspirators. He brings Caesar to the Capitol by interpreting the ominous dreams of Calpurnia as 'a vision fair and fortunate' (II, ii). He does not appear after the assassination. (Shakespeare follows North and Amyot in calling him Decius. He was really Decimus Junius Brutus (*c.* 84–43 B.C.), named by Caesar as one of his heirs. He was captured and put to death by Antony.)

Brutus, Junius. In *Coriolanus*, he and Sicinius are tribunes of the people, whom they incense against Coriolanus and succeed in getting him banished on a charge of affecting tyrannical power. When Coriolanus returns with the Volscians to attack Rome, the tribunes deny their responsibility and implore Menenius to try to stop his advance. (He and Sicinius were the leaders of the plebeians in their secession to the Mons Sacer in 464 B.C.)

Brutus, Marcus Junius. The real hero of *Julius Caesar* (q.v.). He joins the conspiracy against Caesar, not out of envy, but 'in a general honest thought, and common good to all'. (He was born *c.* 85 B.C. On the outbreak of civil war in 49 he joined Pompey against Caesar, who pardoned him after Pharsalia and made him Governor of Cisalpine Gaul. His wife was Portia, Cato's daughter. He killed himself after his defeat at Philippi in 42 B.C.)

Bryan, George. One of the twenty-six 'Principall Actors' in Shakespeare's plays (see p. 90). He was one of the English actors who visited the Courts of Denmark and Saxony in 1586–7; he played in Tarlton's *Seven Deadly Sins*, *c.* 1591, possibly with Strange's, with whom he travelled in the plague year 1593, and it seems reasonable to suppose that he was with that company when it was reorganized under the patronage of the Lord Chamberlain in 1594. He was certainly a Chamberlain's man in 1596 when, with Heminge, he was joint-payee for a Court performance. He occurs in none of the actor-lists, so perhaps by the time of the earliest one, 1598, he had retired, for in 1603, and again in 1611–13, he is mentioned as an ordinary Groom of the Chamber with household duties.

Buck, Sir George. Master of the Revels, 1610–22. He was knighted in 1603 when James I appointed him Deputy-Master with a reversion to the office which had been held by his uncle, Edmund Tilney, since 1579. When Tilney died in 1610, Buck succeeded him and remained Master until 1622, when John Chamberlain wrote, 'Old George Buck, master of the revels, has gone mad.' He was succeeded by Sir John Ashley, who sold the office to Sir Henry Herbert for £150 in 1623, the year in which Buck died.

'Buckingham.' A play acted by Sussex's. (See RICHARD III.)

Buckingham, George Villiers, Duke of (1592–1628). 'On Teusday [29 July

1628], his Grace [Buckingham] was present at ye acting of K. Hen. 8 at ye Globe, a play bespoken of purpose by himself; whereat he stayed till ye Duke of Buckingham was beheaded, & then departed. Some say, he would rather have seen ye fall of Cardinall Woolsey, who was a more lively type of himself, having governed this kingdom 18 yeares, as he hath done 14.' (Letter of Robert Gell.) A month later Buckingham was assassinated by John Felton.

Buckingham, John Sheffield, Duke of (1648–1721). 'At the conclusion of the advertisement prefixed to Lintot's edition of Shakespeare's poems [*c.* 1709], it is said, "That most learned prince and great patron of learning, King James the First, was pleased with his own hand to write an amicable letter to Mr. Shakespeare; which letter, though now lost, remained long in the hands of Sir William D'Avenant, as a credible person now living can testify". Mr. Oldys, in a MS note to his copy of Fuller's *Worthies*, observes, that "the story came from the duke of Buckingham, who had it from Sir William D'Avenant".' (Steevens's *Shakespeare*, ed. 1778, p. 205.)

Buckingham, Humphrey Stafford, 1st Duke of (1402–60). In *2 Henry VI*, the chief agent in uncovering the practices of the Duchess of Gloucester, and one of those who bring about the disgrace of the Duke of Gloucester. He persuades the followers of Cade to disperse on a false promise of pardon, and in the Wars of the Roses supports the King against York. His death is reported in the first scene of *3 Henry VI*, though as a matter of history he was killed at Northampton in 1460, and not at St Albans in 1455.

Buckingham, Henry Stafford, 2nd Duke of (1454–83). In *Richard III*, grandson of the 1st Duke, the professed friend of Edward IV, his widow, and children, but really the supporter of Gloucester, at first secretly and then openly. They arrest, and have executed, Rivers, Grey and Hastings, and Buckingham secures the succession of Gloucester as Richard III. When he hesitates over the murder of the Princes, Richard throws him over, and after an attempt to join Richmond he is captured and executed. His Ghost appears to Richard the night before Bosworth Field.

Buckingham, Edward Stafford, 3rd Duke of (1478–1521). In *Henry VIII*, son of the Buckingham executed by Richard III, and father-in-law of Lord Abergavenny, he is the enemy of Wolsey, whom he accuses of being 'corrupt and treasonous'. Wolsey secures his arrest; he is accused by his own surveyor of threatening to murder Henry, and is found guilty and carried to execution. His last speech in II, i was almost certainly written by Fletcher.

Budbrooke. A village eight miles northeast of Stratford and one mile west of Warwick. The following entries occur in the church Register:

> 1573. Nov. 14. Antony Shaxspere Jonne Whetrefe were maried.
>
> 1575. Mar. 24. Henri Shackespere the sonne of Shackespere and Jone his wif [was christened].

This Anthony may be the Anthony mentioned as his brother by John Shakespeare of Clifford Chambers in his will (1610). An Anthony of Hampton, probably the same, occurs in the Stratford Register.

Hampton Corley is a hamlet of Budbrooke, where, according to a subsidy Roll, one Richard Shakyspere lived in 1524–5. It is possible that this is the poet's grandfather, who first appears at Snitterfield in 1528–9. A Nicolas Shakespeare was living at Budbrooke in 1640–1.

Bull Inn. One of the City inns converted into a theatre, as Richard Flecknoe records in his *Short Discourse of the English Stage*, 1664:

> They acted nothing here but plays of the holy Scripture, or Saints' Lives; and that

without any certain Theatres or set Companies, till, about the beginning of Queen Elizabeth's Reign, they began here first to assemble intoCompanies, and set up Theatres, first in the City (as in the Inn-yards of the Cross-Keyes, and Bull in Grace and Bishops-Gate Street at this day is to be seen) ...

The Bull stood on the west side of Bishopsgate Street, just within the walls. It is mentioned by John Florio in his English-Italian phrase-book, *First Fruites*, 1578:

Where shall we goe?
To a playe at the Bull, or els to some other place ....
I beleeue there is much knauerie vsed at those Comedies: what thinke you?
So beleeue I also.

In 1583 the City Corporation licensed the newly formed Queen's Company to perform 'at the sygnes of the Bull in Bushoppesgate streete, and the sygne of the Bell in Gratioustreete and nowheare els within this Cyttye'; and at the Bull they played *The Famous Victories of Henry V*.

Bull-baiting. A 'bolrynge' is marked in Southwark High Street in a map of 1542, and in those of Höfnagel (1554–72) and Agas (1569–90) there is a 'bolle bayting' ring on the Bankside close to the site of the later Hope theatre. The baiting is described in 1584 by Lupold von Wedel:

There is a round building three stories high, in which are kept about a hundred large English dogs, with separate wooden kennels for each of them. These dogs were made to fight singly with three bears, the second bear being larger than the first and the third larger than the second. After this a horse was brought in and chased by the dogs, and at last a bull, who defended himself bravely ...

And in 1592, by J. Rathgeb, the secretary of Frederick, Duke of Württemberg (Mömpelgart), who witnessed the sport:

His Highness was shown in London the English dogs, of which there were about 120, all kept in the same enclosure, but each in a separate kennel. In order to gratify his Highness, and at his desire, two bears and a bull were baited; at such times you can perceive the breed and mettle of the dogs, for although they receive serious injuries from the bears, are caught by the horns of the bull, and tossed into the air so as frequently to fall down again upon the horns, they do not give in, so that one is obliged to pull them back by their tails, and force open their jaws. Four dogs at once were set on the bull; they, however, could not gain any advantage over him, for he so artfully contrived to ward off their attacks that they could not well get at him; on the contrary, the bull served them very scurvily by striking and butting at them.

(See also BEARGARDEN.)

Bullcalf. In *2 Henry IV*, one of the 'half a dozen sufficient men' provided by Shallow for the King's service. He protests that he is a sick man, having 'a whoreson cold, sir, a cough', but Falstaff presses him. He escapes by bribing Bardolph with 'four Harry ten shillings' (III, ii).

Bullen, Anne. In *Henry VIII*. The King first meets her at a masque at Cardinal Wolsey's (the scene in which the Globe caught fire in 1613), after which she is created Marchioness of Pembroke. Wolsey's latter to the Pope attempting to thwart Henry's marriage with Anne is intercepted, and is the immediate cause of his downfall. Anne is sympathetically treated, but as she was in fact executed for adultery, she is kept in the background, and attention concentrated on the birth of Elizabeth. She is not heard after II, iv and is not seen after IV, i, even at the christening of her daughter. (Anne (*c.* 1507–36) was the daughter of Sir Thomas Bullen.)

Burbage (or Burbadge), James (*c.* 1530–97). 'By occupacion a joyner and reaping but a small lyving by the same, gave it over and became a commen player in playes', as one of Leicester's Men. He married Ellen, sister of John Brayne, who supplied the capital for the building of the Theatre on ground rented by Burbage, and in 1596 he bought for £600 part of the Blackfriars priory which he converted into a private theatre. He was the father of Cuthbert and Richard, the former of whom stated in 1635, 'The father of vs Cutbert and Richard Burbage was the first builder of Playhowses, and was him selfe in his younger yeeres a Player.' He is said to have been 'a stubborne fellow', and not over-scrupulous. He certainly quarrelled, and even fought, with Brayne.

Burbage, Cuthbert (*c.* 1566–1636). The elder son of James Burbage, was not an actor, but a theatre manager, having an interest in the Theatre, Globe, and Blackfriars, about which he gave invaluable information in his Answer to the Petition of 1635 (see SHARERS' PAPERS). He married Elizabeth Cox and had two sons and a daughter. He was friendly with a number of the King's Men, being mentioned in the wills of Sly, Cowley, and Tooley.

Burbage, Richard (*c.* 1568–1619). The younger son of James Burbage, and one of the twenty-six 'Principall Actors' in Shakespeare's plays (see p. 90). He disputes with Alleyn the claim to have been the greatest actor of the age; as Alleyn played the heroes of Marlowe's plays, so Burbage played those of Shakespeare's. According to an elegy on Burbage,

No more young Hamlett, ould Heironymoe,
Kind Leer, the greued Moore, and more beside,
That liued in him, haue now for ever dy'de.

The first mention of Richard is in 1590 when he supported his father in resisting a Chancery Order granting half the profits of the Theatre to the widow of John Brayne. John Alleyn, like his brother Edward, an Admiral's man, describes the scene: how he

found the foresaid Ry. Burbage the yongest sone of the said James Burbage there, wt a broome staff in his hand, of whom when this deponente asked what sturre was there, he answered in laughing phrase how they came for a moytie. But quod he (holding vppe the said broomes staff) I haue, I think, deliuered him a moytie with this & sent them packing.

He may have been playing with the Admiral's at his father's Theatre at the time, and about the same date he took parts in *The Dead Man's Fortune* and *The Seven Deadly Sins*. He may have gone on tour with the Admiral-Strange combination under Alleyn in the plague year of 1593, but certainly was a member of Strange's as reorganized under the Lord Chamberlain's patronage in 1594, when he and Kempe and Shakespeare were payees for a Court performance. John Manningham (q.v.) relates a story about Burbage and Shakespeare, and that they remained friends to the last is made clear by the will in which Shakespeare left his 'ffellowe' Burbage 26s. 8d. to buy a ring. Burbage was also a painter, and he and Shakespeare combined in 1613 to make an 'impresa' for the Earl of Rutland, for which each received 44s. in gold. (See CHANDOS PORTRAIT.)

Richard and Cuthbert held jointly half the housekeepers' interest in the Globe, and probably owned jointly the freehold of the Blackfriars. Both were married and lived as neighbours in Halliwell Street, Shoreditch. Richard had at least eight children, one of whom, William, was alive at the time of the Petition of 1635, as was his widow Winifred who had married Richard Robinson of the King's Men. The shortest and most pregnant of the many epitaphs on Burbage is 'Exit Burbage'. (See CORBET.)

Burby, Cuthbert (d. 1607). Bookseller from 1592 to 1607, sometimes confused with Cuthbert Burbage, was the son of a Bedfordshire farmer. In 1599 he published the 'newly corrected and augmented' Q2 of *Romeo and Juliet* after Danter's 'bad' Q1 of 1597; and as his Q1 (1598) of *Love's Labour's Lost* also claims to be 'newly corrected and augmented' it seems probable that this too replaced a 'bad' Q, now lost. Burby registered neither of these plays, but transferred them to Ling in 1607.

Burdett-Coutts Portrait. A good painting, supposed to represent Shakespeare at the age of 37, but with no history to support its claim. The Baroness Burdett-Coutts (1814–1906) owned also the 'Felton', the 'Lumley', and the 'Bath' or 'Archer' portraits, and one of the finest copies of the First Folio (the Sheldon) now in the Folger Library.

Burgundy, Duke of, Philip the Good (1396–1467). In *Henry V*, he brings together Henry of England and Charles VI of France, and arranges the Treaty of Troyes and Henry's marriage with Katharine. He appears only in this last scene, in which he makes his great plea for peace and for 'this best garden of the world, Our fertile France', followed by a less elevated conversation with Henry.

In *1 Henry VI*, he is at first the ally of the English, the Duke of Bedford having married his sister. He refers to Joan of Arc as a trull, vile fiend, and shameless courtezan, but Joan, in a speech resembling that of Burgundy's own in *Henry V*, appeals to him to bring peace to 'fertile France', and he forsakes the English alliance (III, iii).

Burgundy, Duke of. In *King Lear*, one of the 'great rivals' in Cordelia's love; ut when Lear disinherits Cordelia andb offers her to Burgundy, dowered only with his curse, he knows no answer, excuses himself, and disappears from the play.

Burnaby, William (b. *c.* 1675), often wrongly called Charles, was of Merton, Oxford, and the Middle Temple. He wrote four comedies, one of them, *Love Betray'd*, or *the Agreeable Disappointment*, being a disagreeable version of *Twelfth Night*, performed at Lincoln's Inn Fields in 1703.

Burt, Nicholas. Caroline actor; one of the 'Old Actors' of Killigrew's Company. Pepys saw him play Othello at the Cockpit on 11 October 1660. He also took the part of the Prince in an early Restoration revival of *1 Henry IV*.

Busby, John. Bookseller. In 1600 he and Millington published the 'bad' Q1 of *Henry V*, which had been registered 4 August as 'to be staied', presumably by some agent of the Chamberlain's Men in an attempt to stay a threatened piratical publication (see JAMES ROBERTS). In 1602 Busby entered for his copy of *The Merry Wives*, but transferred it on the same day to Arthur Johnson, who brought out in the same year the 'bad' Q1. In 1607 Busby and Butter registered *King Lear*, though the title-page of the very poor Q1 of 1608 reads, 'Printed for Nathaniel Butter', only. Busby's record is not a good one. He is last heard of in 1619.

Bushy. In *Richard II*, one of the 'creatures to King Richard'. He, Bagot, and Green are 'the caterpillars of the commonwealth' according to Bolingbroke, who captures Bushy and Green at Berkeley Castle and has them executed (III, i). (Sir John Bushy (d. 1399) was Speaker of the House of Commons in 1394.)

Butter, Nathaniel. Bookseller. In 1607 Butter and Busby registered *King Lear*, a poor Q1 of which was 'Printed for Nathaniel Butter' in 1608. William Jaggard reprinted this in 1619 'for Nathaniel Butter' with the false date 1608. In 1605 Butter published *The London Prodigal*, 'by William Shakespeare', without registration, and in the same year pirated Heywood's *If You Know not Me, You Know Nobody*, which the author claimed was reproduced by stenography. (See PIDE BULL EDITION.)

Butts, Doctor. In *Henry VIII*, Physician to the King. In a curious little scene (V, ii) Butts discovers Cranmer ignominiously kept waiting outside the Council

Chamber by order of Bishop Gardiner. He tells the King who, 'at a window above', sees Cranmer without being seen. (Sir William Butts (d. 1545) was the favourite physician of Henry VIII. His portrait was painted by Holbein.)

Byrd, William (1543–1623). English musician and composer. He was 'bred up to music under Thomas Tallis', became organist of Lincoln Cathedral, and in 1569 joined Tallis as organist of the Chapel Royal. He composed for strings, for the virginals, was one of the founders of the English madrigal, and wrote both church and secular choral music. It is possible that some of his *Sonets and Songs of Sadnes and Pietie* were composed for the plays given by the Children of the Chapel.

C

Cade, Jack (d. 1450). In *2 Henry VI*, the rebel leader. Seduced by York, he claims to be John Mortimer and marches with his mob on London, plundering and killing. In Southwark, Buckingham and Clifford persuade his followers to desert him; Cade escapes, but is killed by Alexander Iden in his garden. (He was probably an Irishman, living in Kent, who married a lady of good position.)

Cadwal. In *Cymbeline*. (See ARVIRAGUS.)

Caesar, Julius (100–44 B.C.). Caesar is dictator of the Roman world, in command of a victorious army. A conspiracy is formed against him by those who, like Brutus, really fear, and those who, like Cassius, pretend to fear a tyranny. In fact Caesar refuses the crown when Antony offers it to him, but the conspirators murder him in the Senate-house. Not Caesar, portrayed as a weak man, but Brutus, is the hero of *Julius Caesar*, though after his death Caesar is Brutus's real adversary.

Caesar, Octavius (63 B.C.–A.D. 14). In *Julius Caesar*, he becomes one of the triumvirs after the murder of his great-uncle, and with Antony defeats Brutus and Cassius at Philippi. In *Antony and Cleopatra* he gets rid of the other triumvirs: first Lepidus, and then Antony, who had married his sister Octavia, and then deserted her for Cleopatra. He defeats Antony at Actium, invades Egypt, and though he fails to capture Antony and Cleopatra, who kill themselves (30 B.C.), he is left sole master of the Empire. (Caius Octavius was the son of J. Caesar's niece, and became first Emperor of Rome (Augustus) in 27 B.C.)

Caesura. In English prosody, the principal pause in a line of verse. Shakespeare's variation of pause and caesura is one of the great qualities of his later verse. Compare lines from *The Two Gentlemen of Verona* with others from *Cymbeline*:

O hateful hands, | to tear such loving words!
Injurious wasps, | to feed on such sweet honey,
And kill the bees that yield it, with your stings.

He hath a kind of honour sets him off
More than a mortal seeming. | Be not angry,
Most mighty princess, | that I have adventur'd
To try your taking of a false report.

Caius, Doctor. In *The Merry Wives of Windsor*, a French physician in love with Anne Page whose mother supports his suit. He challenges Sir Hugh Evans who, he discovers, is furthering Slender's advances to Anne. The Host appoints them contrary places, and they unite against him, cozening him of three horses. Mistress Page arranges that Caius shall lead away and marry Anne while they are baiting Falstaff at night, but thanks to the plot of Fenton and the Host, he finds that he has 'married un paysan, by gar, a boy'. (See BIBLE.)

Caius Lucius. In *Cymbeline*, general of the Roman army invading Britain. He discovers Imogen, disguised as a boy, and takes her into his service. The Romans are defeated by the Britons, Caius and Imogen captured and brought before Cymbeline, who recognizes his daughter and releases Caius.

Caius Marcius. See CORIOLANUS.

'Caius Marius.' Thomas Otway's adaptation (1679–80) of *Romeo and Juliet*. The scene is ancient Rome, the feud that between patricians and plebeians, the lovers Young Marius and Lavinia. Lavinia wakes before Marius dies, a feature that was preserved until the 19th century.

Calchas. In *Troilus and Cressida*, a Trojan priest who 'incurr'd a traitor's name' by abandoning Troy and joining the Greeks, whom he asks, in return for his services, to exchange the Trojan prisoner Antenor for his daughter Cressida, who is still in Troy (III, iii). When she comes, Calchas makes no objection to Diomedes's seduction of her (V, ii). (See SAINTE-MAURE.)

Caliban. In *The Tempest*, a savage and deformed slave 'not honour'd with a human shape', the litter of the witch Sycorax. Prospero finds him on the island, teaches him language, and makes him his servant. With the shipwrecked Stephano and Trinculo he plans to murder Prospero, but the plot is defeated and Caliban learns wisdom and seeks for grace.

Calpurnia. In *Julius Caesar*, the fourth, last, and childless wife of Caesar. Frightened by her dreams and the portents of the night, she persuades Caesar not to go to the Capitol, but Decius makes him change his mind (II, ii).

Cambridge, Richard Earl of (*c.* 1374–1415). In *Henry V*, with Scroop and Grey he plans to murder Henry at Southampton as he sets out on his French campaign. But 'The King hath note of all that they intend', exposes them, and orders their execution (II, ii). (He was the 2nd son of the 1st Duke of York (in *Richard II*), and brother of the York in *Henry V* (Aumerle in *Richard II*). He married Anne Mortimer, whose brother Edmund he wished to place on the throne. His son is the York of *Henry VI*, and his grandsons Edward IV and Richard III.)

'Cambridge' Shakespeare. The most important of the 19th-century editions of Shakespeare, prepared with the help of Capell's bequest of books to Trinity College, Cambridge. The 1st ed. (9 vols., 1863–6) was edited by W. G. Clark and W. A. Wright (vol. 1 by Clark and J. Glover); 2nd ed. 1867; 3rd ed. revised by Wright 1891–3. For long the standard text, though the notes include many inferior readings from previous editions, which might have been discarded. (See GLOBE SHAKESPEARE; NEW CAMBRIDGE SHAKESPEARE.)

Cambridge University. Though the universities did not directly play a large part in the development of the popular Elizabethan drama, they produced the men who, in London, were responsible for its startling advance in the eighties of the 16th century. Of the group of dramatists called by the actors 'The University Wits', Marlowe, Greene and Nashe were Cambridge men, and Lyly after being at Oxford studied at Cambridge. The university drama was largely 'academic': classical Latin plays, or neoclassical plays, either in Latin or English, written and performed by university men, such as those witnessed by Elizabeth and James I, or Alabaster's *Roxana*, *c.* 1592. The three parts of *Parnassus*, however, were more popular and topical Christmas entertainments in English (*c.* 1600), containing references to Shakespeare and his company, and probably inspired by a visit of the Chamberlain's Men to Cambridge. Q1 *Hamlet* (1603) states that the play had been acted 'in the two Universities of Cambridge and Oxford'. (See ACADEMIC DRAMA; VOLPONE.)

In 1779 Capell gave his Shakespeare collection to Trinity College. This included copies of the four Folios and 55 Quartos. (See SS, 5.)

Camden, William (1551–1623). English antiquary and historian, was educated at Christ's Hospital, St Paul's, Magdalen, and Christ Church, Oxford, in 1593 becoming Headmaster of Westminster. He published the first edition of his *Britannia* in 1586, the sixth and final edition in 1607, and in 1615 the first part of his *Annales*, a history in Latin of Elizabeth's reign, the second part being published posthumously in 1625. The *Britannia*, also written in Latin, was translated by Philemon Holland in 1610. It is a description of England, Scotland, and Ireland, full of archaeological and historical information from which Camden in 1605 published selections as *Remaines of a greater Worke concerning Britaine*. He founded a Chair of History at Oxford, and the Camden Society for historical research was founded in 1838. In the *Remaines* Shakespeare might have read the story of King Lear, and the fable of the belly and the members recited by Menenius in *Coriolanus*, as well as a reference to his name (Camden was made Clarenceux King-of-Arms in 1597), names being derived 'from that which they commonly carried, as ... Shakespeare, Shotbolt, Wagstaffe', and an appreciation of his work:

> If I would come to our time, what a world could I present to you out of Sir Philipp Sidney, Ed. Spencer, Samuel Daniel, Hugh Holland, Ben: Johnson, Th. Campion, Mich. Drayton, George Chapman, Iohn Marston, William Shakespeare, & other most pregnant wits of these our times, whom succeeding ages may iustly admire.

(See also CAREW.)

Camillo. In *The Winter's Tale*, a Lord of Sicilia. Leontes makes him promise to poison Polixenes whom he suspects of being the lover of his wife, Hermione; Camillo tells Polixenes and they sail secretly for Bohemia. Sixteen years later Polixenes with the help of Camillo discovers that his son Florizel is in love with a shepherd's daughter, Perdita, and orders him to renounce her, but Camillo helps the lovers to escape to Sicilia. (Called Franion in Greene's *Pandosto*.)

Campbell, Lily Bess (b. 1883). American scholar, Professor of English in the University of California in 1922. Author of *Scenes and Machines on the English Stage during the Renaissance* (1923). In her *Shakespeare's 'Histories', Mirrors of Elizabethan Policy* (1947) she maintains that the *Histories* reflect current politics, that, for example, King John's attitude towards Arthur reflects that of Elizabeth towards Mary Queen of Scots.

Campbell, Oscar James (b. 1879). American scholar, Professor of English at Columbia University in 1936. Author of *Shakespeare's Satire*, etc.

Campeius, Cardinal (1472–1539). In *Henry VIII*, the legate who, with Wolsey, is commissioned by the Pope to consider the divorce of Katharine of Aragon. He speaks smoothly, but does little, as Henry perceives: 'These cardinals trifle with me: I abhor This dilatory sloth and tricks of Rome' (II, iv). (He was Bishop of Salisbury 1524–34.)

Canada. After the last war the Canadian theatre was in a poor way, but in 1949 the semi-professional Earle Grey Shakespeare Company was formed, and inaugurated an annual Shakespeare Festival in the grounds of Trinity College, Toronto. This ran for ten years. Meanwhile, in 1953 the first Shakespeare Festival was celebrated at Stratford, Ontario, under the direction of Tyrone Guthrie. There were two plays: *Richard III* with Alec Guinness, and *All's Well*, the audience sitting round the stage in a temporary canvas-covered auditorium. In 1956 it was decided to build a permanent theatre, and with the help of the

Canada Council the Festival has become a successful and established institution. The first Seminar on Shakespeare, sponsored by the universities of Canada, was held at Stratford in 1960. (See *Stratford Papers on Shakespeare*, ed. B. W. Jackson, Toronto; SS, 8.)

Cancel. The name given to a leaf inserted in a book to replace the original one. In Shakespeare's day a serious mistake discovered while printing was in progress might be corrected in this way. There is a famous example in the *Troilus and Cressida* Quarto (1609), the title-page of the first issue being cut out and two new leaves inserted, the first with a new and unsigned title-page, the other with an epistle to the reader.

Canidius. In *Antony and Cleopatra*, lieutenant-general to Antony. At Actium he advises Antony to fight by land instead of by sea, and after his defeat renders his legions and his horse to Caesar.

Canon, The Shakespearean. The thirty-six plays of the First Folio, 1623, which, on the whole, are generally accepted as being Shakespeare's work. (See AUTHENTICITY.)

'Canons of Criticism.' See EDWARDS.

Canterbury, Archbishop of. In *Henry V*, he prepares the audience for the regenerated Henry. Then, in order to avoid the threatened confiscation of Church property, he cynically urges Henry to assert his title to the French crown, promising that the Church will help to finance a campaign. His disingenuous speech 'proving' Henry the rightful King of France is transcribed almost verbatim from Holinshed, and is perhaps the most tedious in Shakespeare (I, ii). (Henry Chicheley (*c.* 1362–1443) was created Archbishop in 1414. He founded All Souls', Oxford.)

Capell, Edward (1713–81), the seventh editor of Shakespeare, and the first of the great scholars, was born at Troston Hall in Suffolk. In 1737 he became deputy-inspector of plays, and in 1745 groom of the privy chamber. He died in the Temple in 1781, leaving his priceless collection of Shakespeare Quartos to Trinity College, Cambridge, where they proved invaluable to the editors of the *Cambridge Shakespeare* of 1863–6. (See SS, 5.) The fastidious Capell was horrified by the reckless emendations of Rowe, and so astonished by Hanmer's edition of 1744 that he resolved to attempt to save Shakespeare's text from further ruin. He describes his method:

> Hereupon he [Capell] possess'd himself of the other modern editions, the folio's, and as many quarto's as could presently be procur'd; and, within a few years after, fortune and industry help'd him to all the rest, six only excepted; adding to them withal twelve more, which the compilers of former tables had no knowledge of. Thus furnish'd, he fell immediately to collation, – which is the first step in works of this nature; and, without it nothing is done to purpose, – first of moderns with moderns, then of moderns with ancients, and afterwards of ancients with others more ancient.... He had not proceeded far in his collation, before he saw cause to come to this resolution; – to stick invariably to the old editions (that is, the best of them), which hold now the place of manuscripts.

Twenty-four years later, during which period he is said to have transcribed Shakespeare's works ten times, his edition in ten volumes was published (1768). It forms a landmark in Shakespearean scholarship, for he was the first editor thoroughly to study and minutely to collate the Quartos; he went to contemporary sources, made use of the Stationers' Register, and of Meres's *Palladis Tamia*, and he investigated the 'Origin of Shakespeare's Fables'. He concludes his Introduction with an apology for the lack of an adequate Life of Shakespeare,

> especially, with the addition of one proper and even necessary episode – a brief history of our drama, from its origin down to the poet's death: even the stage he appear'd upon, its form, dressings, actors should be

enquir'd into, as every one of those circumstances had some considerable effect upon what he compos'd for it: The subject is certainly a good one, and will fall (we hope) ere it be long into the hands of some good writer.

It very soon fell into the capable hands of Malone.

Capell published his commentary on nine of the plays in 1774, but his complete work, the fruit of thirty years of unremitting toil, *Notes and Various Readings* and *The School of Shakespeare*, was delayed until 1779 and completed in 1783, two years after his death, and ten years after Steevens's first edition of the Plays, a fact that has tended to obscure Capell's originality and importance. Then again, his prose is such a formless succession of relative clauses stumbling over prepositions that Johnson dismissed him in one sentence in the *Life*, 'If the man would have come to me, I would have endeavoured to endow his purpose with words, for as it is, he doth gabble monstrously'. (See PBA, XLVI, 1962.)

Caphis. In *Timon*, one of 'Seuerall Seruants to Vsurers' (F). He is sent by his master, a Senator, to ask Timon for the settlement of a debt, which Timon finds he is unable to repay (II, i and ii).

Capital Letters. In the manuscript 'copy' for the printer verse lines probably began with minuscules (see SPELLING); these were capitalized by the compositor (Q1 *M. of Venice* is exceptional in having many lines beginning with lower case letters), and some words, mainly nouns, were printed with capitals, perhaps as written by Shakespeare. The Folio is much more lavish in its use of capital letters. (See PUNCTUATION.)

Wilson thinks that Shakespeare used capital letters to indicate emphasis (*Tempest*, lix):

> Shakespeare generally conveyed emphasis by the use of the pause. Sometimes, however, he indicated the emphatic word by beginning it with a capital letter. The Folio teems with emphasis-capitals, which ... in bulk ... are non-Shakespearian. Yet here and there we can catch a Shakespearian emphasis even in the Folio, while in the Quartos, where they are far less frequent, the dramatist's hand is more often in evidence.

'Captain, The.' A comedy by Fletcher, possibly with the collaboration of Beaumont, performed by the King's Men at Court, 1612–13. According to F2 of Beaumont's and Fletcher's *Works* (1679), 'The principal actors were, Richard Burbage, Henry Condel, William Ostler, Alexander Cooke'. These would be actors in the original performance, some time after 1609, when Ostler joined the company, and before the Court performance.

Capucius. In *Henry VIII*, ambassador from the Emperor Charles V. He brings kind messages to the dying Katharine from Henry, to whom she asks him to deliver a letter commending her daughter and her servants (IV, ii).

Capulet. In *Romeo and Juliet*, the head of the family opposed to the Montagues. Ignorant of Juliet's secret marriage to the Montague, Romeo, he insists on her marrying Paris, an action that precipitates the tragedy.

Capulet, Lady. In *Romeo and Juliet*, she supports her husband in the proposed marriage of Juliet to Paris. She is one of the four mothers of heroines in Shakespeare's plays: the others, Mistress Page, Hermione, and Thaisa. (See INNOGEN.)

'Cardenio.' On 20 May 1613, Heminge was payee for Court performances of 'sixe severall playes ... One other Cardenno'; and two months later he received the customary £6 13s. 4d. for the performance at Greenwich by the King's Men of 'a playe before the Duke of Savoyes Embassadour on the viij^th^ daye of June, 1613, called Cardenna'.

1653. Humphrey Moseley, a stationer and collector of play-manuscripts, registered 'The History of Cardennio, by Mr. Fletcher & Shakespeare'.

1727. *Double Falsehood, or the Distressed Lovers* was produced at Drury Lane, and in 1728 published with the title-page:

> Double Falsehood; Or, The Distrest Lovers. A Play. As it is Acted at the Theatre-Royal in Drury-Lane. Written originally by W. Shakespeare; and now Revised and Adapted to the Stage By Mr. Theobald, the Author of Shakespeare Restor'd.

The play is based on the story of Cardenio and Lucinda in Don Quixote, Thomas Shelton's translation of which had appeared in 1612, and was probably the source of the original *Cardenno* or *Cardenna*. In his preface to *Double Falsehood*, Theobald wrote:

> One of the Manuscript Copies, which I have, is of above Sixty Years Standing, in the handwriting of Mr. *Downes*, the famous Old Prompter; and, as I am credibly inform'd, was early in the possession of the celebrated Mr. *Betterton*, and by him design'd to have been usher'd into the World.... There is a Tradition .... that it was given by our Author, as a Present of Value, to a Natural Daughter of his, for whose Sake he wrote it, in the Time of his Retirement from the Stage. Two other Copies I have ..., which may not, perhaps, be quite so old as the Former; but One of them is much more perfect, and has fewer Flaws and Interruptions in the Sense.... Others, again to depreciate the Affair, as they thought, have been pleased to urge, that tho' the Play may have some resemblances to *Shakespeare*, yet the *Colouring*, *Diction*, and *Characters* come nearer to the Style and Manner of *Fletcher*. This, I think, is far from deserving any Answer.

There is nothing Shakespearean about Theobald's 'revised and adapted' version. The manuscripts that he claimed to possess have never been found, nor did he in his edition of Shakespeare (1733), although he ascribed the original play to Shakespeare alone, make any attempt to publish it. On the other hand, a play on the same subject was twice acted by Shakespeare's company in 1612–13; it is unlikely that Theobald knew of this record in the Chamber Accounts; and at about this date Fletcher was almost certainly collaborating with Shakespeare in *Henry VIII* and *The Two Noble Kinsmen.*

Cardinal. See BEAUFORT; BOURCHIER; CAMPEIUS; PANDULPH; WOLSEY.

Carew, Richard (1555–1620), English poet and antiquary, was born in Cornwall, of which he wrote a *Survey* (1602). He was a friend of William Camden (q.v.), to whom in 1605 he wrote *An Epistle concerning the Excellencie of the English Tongue*, which was added to the second (1614) edition of Camden's *Remaines*. It is significant that Carew thinks of Shakespeare and Marlowe as writers of poems and not as dramatists:

> Add hereunto, that whatsoever grace any other language carrieth in verse or prose, in tropes or metaphors ... they may all be lively and exactly represented in ours:... Will you read Virgil? take the Earl of Surrey, Catullus? Shakespheare and Marlowes fragment. Ovid? Daniell, ... will you have all in all for prose and verse? take the miracle of our age, Sir Philip Sidney.

Carey, Elizabeth. Daughter of Sir George Carey, 2nd Lord Hunsdon in 1596, Lord Chamberlain 1597, and patron of Shakespeare's company. In 1595 there were preliminaries of a betrothal between Elizabeth Carey and William Herbert (later Earl of Pembroke), then aged 15: a slender piece of evidence in favour of the Mr W. H. of the *Sonnets* being William Herbert. In 1596, however, Elizabeth married Lord Berkeley, in celebration of which event Shakespeare may have written *A Midsummer Night's Dream.*

Carleton, Dudley (1573–1632), diplomatist, was educated at Westminster and Christ Church, Oxford. In 1603 he was elected to the first Parliament of James I, and knighted in 1610 when he succeeded Sir Henry Wotton as ambassador at Venice, after which he was from 1616 to 1621 ambassador at The Hague. In 1626 he was created Lord Carleton of Imbercourt, and in 1628 Viscount Dorchester. After this he became chief Secretary of State to Charles I. Carleton was one of the ablest diplomatists of his age, and a brilliant and voluminous writer of letters and despatches, some of which were published in T. Birch's *Court and Times of James I and Charles I* (1848). His letters contain a number of important references to the theatre of his time. (See CHAMBERLAIN, JOHN; LOVE'S LABOUR'S LOST.)

Carlisle, Bishop of. In *Richard II*, a loyal supporter of Richard. He puts heart into the King when he lands in Wales after his disastrous Irish expedition, and is with him when he surrenders to Bolingbroke at Flint Castle. When in IV, i Bolingbroke says that he will 'ascend the regal throne' Carlisle protests, and is arrested for capital treason. He becomes involved in the abortive plot against Bolingbroke, but is pardoned. (Thomas Merke (d. 1409), Bp of Carlisle 1397.)

Carlyle, Thomas (1795–1881). Carlyle gave a course of lectures *On Heroes, Hero-worship, and the Heroic in History*, in the third of which, on *The Hero as Poet*, delivered in May 1840, he said:

> That Shakspeare is the chief of all Poets hitherto; the greatest intellect who, in our recorded world, has left record of himself in the way of Literature ...
>
> Alas, Shakspeare had to write for the Globe Playhouse: his great soul had to crush itself, as it could, into that and no other mould....
>
> Which Englishman we ever made, in this land of ours, which million of Englishmen, would we not give up rather than the Stratford Peasant? ... For our honour among foreign nations, as an ornament to our English Household, what item is there that we would not surrender rather than him? Consider now, if they asked us, Will you give up your Indian Empire or your Shakspeare? ... Indian Empire will go, at any rate, some day; but this Shakspeare does not go, he lasts forever with us; we cannot give up our Shakspeare!

Cartwright, William. An actor in a King's Revels company of 1629–37, who, during the Civil War, became a bookseller and collector of play manuscripts, one of which, *Thomas of Woodstock* or *1 Richard II* (*c.* 1592), may have served as a source for the earlier part of Shakespeare's *Richard II*. On 2 November 1667 Pepys saw a performance of *1 Henry IV*, and 'was pleased in nothing more than in Cartwright's speaking of Falstaffe's speech about "What is Honour?"'

Casca. In *Julius Caesar*, one of the conspirators against Caesar. 'A blunt fellow', but 'quick mettle ... in execution Of any bold or noble enterprise.' He gives a humorous description of Caesar's rejection of 'one of these coronets', is persuaded by Cassius to join the faction, is the first to stab Caesar, and then disappears from the play. (P. Servilius Casca, tribune, fought at Philippi and died soon afterwards.)

'Cases'. In typography, the compositor's trays for holding the type. The lower case contains the small letters; above it is the upper case with the capitals. Each case is divided into compartments for the different letters. (See PRINTING.)

Cassandra. In *Troilus and Cressida*, a prophetess and daughter of King Priam of Troy. She foretells the destruction of Troy (II, ii) and the death of her brother Hector (V, iii).

Cassio. In *Othello* (q.v.), 'an Honourable Lieutenant' (F).

Cassius. In *Julius Caesar* (q.v.). C. Cassius Longinus supported Pompey against Caesar in the Civil War, but surrendered to him after Pharsalia (48 B.C.), was pardoned, made Praetor in 44, and promised the province of Syria. After the murder of Caesar he went to

Syria, which he plundered, before joining Brutus at Sardis.

Castiglione, Baldassare (1478–1529). Italian writer and diplomatist. His most famous book *Il Cortegiano* (*The Courtier*), was published in 1528 and translated into English by Thomas Hoby in 1561. It is written in the form of a discussion on the qualities that go to make the ideal gentleman, one of them being a proficiency in music. The verbal duels of Benedick and Beatrice may owe something to those of two of the disputants, Gaspare Pallavicino and Emilia Pia.

Casts. There are eight actor-sharers (excluding Fletcher) named in the Patent of 1603 for the King's Men, twelve in that of 1619, the increase taking place in 1603–4. A company of ten or twelve with their boys and hired men would be ample for the performance of most plays, though *Henry VIII* would require much doubling and a number of 'supers'. The book-keeper sometimes noted in his prompt-copy the names of actors against their parts, though generally minor ones, and more completely in the 'plots', and from other sources we know that certain actors played certain parts: that Burbage, for example, played Hamlet, Lear, Othello and Richard III, that Alleyn played Faustus, Tamburlaine, Barabas and Orlando in Greene's *Orlando Furioso*, and that Armin played Dogberry. But the only complete cast for the King's Men is that for a revival of *The Duchess of Malfi* (q.v) about 1621, in which were seven sharers, Lowin, Taylor, Robinson, Benfield, Rice, Underwood and Tooley, the last two doubling their parts, three boys, Pollard, Sharpe and Thompson, and one hired man, Pallant, though it is possible that he also was a boy. (See DRAMATIS PERSONAE.)

Castle, William, was parish-clerk and sexton at Stratford in 1693 when 'Mr Dowdall' (q.v.) wrote his letter to 'Mr Southwell' describing his visit to Stratford. 'The clarke that shew'd me this Church is aboue 80 y^{rs} old', he wrote. There was a William Castle christened at Stratford 17 July 1614, and another 10 August 1628.

Catchword. The word printed below, and to the right of the last line of a page, which is also the first word of the next page. As the pages of plays were generally unnumbered, catchwords formed a guide to pagination. The pages of the Folio are numbered, though sometimes wrongly, but it is printed with catchwords. For example, the bottom right-hand column of the first page, *The Tempest*, reads as follows:

Scena Secunda.
Enter Prospero and Miranda.
Mira. If by your Art (my deerest father) you haue
Put the wild waters in this Rore; alay them:
The skye it seemes would powre down stinking pitch,
But that the Sea, mounting to th' welkins cheeke,
Dashes the fire out. Oh! I haue suffered
With those that I saw suffer: A braue vessell

A (Who

Page 2 begins:

(Who had no doubt some noble creature in her)

The letter A at the foot of page 1 is the 'signature' indicating the number of the sheet.

Catesby, Sir William (d. 1485). In *Richard III*, a follower of Richard and Buckingham, who send him to sound Lord Hastings, 'How he doth stand affected to our purpose', but, as Catesby predicted, Hastings is loyal (III, i and ii). He takes part in the humbug of III, vii, where the Mayor and Citizens are persuaded of Richard's holy zeal, and remains faithful to Richard to the end, his last words being at Bosworth: 'Withdraw, my lord; I'll help you to a horse.' (Richard III made him Chancellor of the Exchequer for life.)

'Catharine and Petruchio.' Garrick's three-act version of *The Taming of the Shrew*, which held the stage for more than a hundred years, was produced at Drury Lane in 1754. The action is concentrated on the main theme, the Induction being omitted, and the sub-plot modified on the lines of *A Shrew*.

'Catiline.' 'Catiline his Conspiracy. A Tragœdie. Acted in the yeere 1611. By the Kings Maiesties Seruants. The Author B.I. ... The principall Tragœdians were, Ric. Burbadge, Ioh. Hemings, Alex. Cooke, Hen. Condel, Ioh. Lowin, Ioh. Underwood, Wil. Ostler, Nic. Tooley, Ric. Robinson, Wil. Eglestone.' (From F1 of Ben Jonson's *Works*, 1616.)

Cato, Young. In *Julius Caesar*, the son of Marcus Cato, and friend of Brutus and Cassius. He appears only at Philippi, where he is killed.

Caxton, William (*c.* 1422–91). Printer and translator, was born in Kent, but lived for thirty years in Bruges, where he began his translation of the French romance of Troy in 1469. This translation, The *Recuyell of the Historyes of Troye*, was the first book he printed, in 1475: 'this said book . . . is not wreton with penne and ynke as other bokes ben, . . . for all the bookes of this storye . . . thus enpryntid as ye here see were begonne in oon day, and also fynysshid in oon day'. Shakespeare used Caxton's *Recuyell* for the Grecian camp-scenes in *Troilus and Cressida.*

Cecil, Robert (1563–1612). The only surviving son of William Cecil, Lord Burghley, by his second marriage. He was Secretary of State to Elizabeth, and mainly responsible for the peaceful accession of James I, who created him Lord Cecil of Essendine (1603), Viscount Cranborne (20 August 1604), and Earl of Salisbury (4 May 1605). In 1608 he assumed complete control of public affairs. Cecil was physically small, weak, and ill-formed, and therefore an easy target for malicious criticism; for example, a remark of October 1596, which seems to be directed against him, as 'St Gobbo', with 'bumbasted legs', is presumably a reference to the decrepit Old Gobbo of *The Merchant of Venice*. It is just possible that there is something of Lord Burghley in Polonius, and of Robert Cecil in Laertes and Reynaldo. There are two references to Cecil's probably seeing Shakespeare's plays: in December 1595 Sir Edward Hoby (q.v.) invited him to supper and 'K. Richard', and in January 1605 there seems to have been a performance of *Love's Labour's Lost* at his house. It was Cecil's intervention in 1601 that saved Shakespeare's patron, Southampton, who had been sentenced to death for his part in the Essex rebellion.

Cecil, William (1520–98). Principal minister to Queen Elizabeth, he was created Lord Burghley in 1571.

Celia. In *As You Like It* (q.v.). (The Alinda of Lodge's *Rosalynde.*)

Censorship of Plays. Licence to *print* should be distinguished from licence to *perform* plays. (See LICENSING OF PLAYS.) In 1559 Elizabeth ordered mayors of towns and justices of the peace in the counties to examine 'al maner Interludes' before they were played, and to 'permyt none to be played wherein either matters of religion or of the gouernance of the estate of the common weale shalbe handled'. But the Mayor and Corporation of London, partly for hygienic, but mainly for puritanical reasons, abused their rights and tried to suppress plays altogether, not only in the City, but also in the liberties and suburbs over which they had no jurisdiction. The result was that in December 1581 Elizabeth authorized Edmund Tilney, Master of the Revels, 'to order and reforme, auctorise and put downe as shalbe thought meete or vnmeete vnto himselfe' all plays whatsoever 'in all places within this our Realme of England.' Henceforth plays had to be submitted for the allowance and endorsement of the Master, who automatically became responsible for seeing that the provisions of the Act of 1606 *To Restraine Abuses of Players* (see ABUSES OF PLAYERS) were observed. The Master, as censor and licenser for performance of plays, was concerned mainly with the suppression of profanity and of any criticism of the established political and religious order. The Office Book of Henry Herbert (q.v.) reveals a Master at work as censor. Shakespeare seems to have had little trouble with his plays, for they contain little satire and few topical allusions, while his political philosophy agreed well enough with that of Elizabeth, James I and Cecil. But the deposition scene in *Richard II* was not printed until Q4, 1608; Oldcastle's name had to be changed to Falstaff, and the Brook of the reported Q of *The Merry Wives* becomes the less appropriate Broome of F, and therefore presumably of the 'allowed book' on which the text would be based. In the Folio many of the oaths have been altered or deleted, but as the Act of 1606 applied only to the spoken and not to the written word, the censorship is by no means logical or complete. An expurgated F text is, therefore, evidence of a stage revival of the play before 1623. (See Greg, *First Folio*.)

'Centurie of Prayse.' An anthology of 17th-century allusions to Shakespeare, compiled by C. M. Ingleby (q.v.), and published for the New Shakspere Society in 1875 as *Shakespeare's Centurie of Prayse; being Materials for a History of Opinion on Shakespeare and his Works, 1591–1693*. It was revised and enlarged by L. T. Smith (1879), F. J. Furnivall (1886), by J. Munro in 1909 as *The Shakespeare Allusion Book, 1591–1700*, and re-edited by Sir Edmund Chambers in 1932.

Ceres. In *The Tempest*, one of the spirits called up by Prospero to celebrate the betrothal of Ferdinand and Miranda (IV, i). Iris summons Ceres to meet Juno, and the two goddesses sing their blessings, probably addressed to the Elector Palatine and Princess Elizabeth at the Court performance before their marriage in February 1613.

Cerimon. In *Pericles*, a lord of Ephesus, to whose house the apparently dead body of the sea-buried Thaisa is brought, where he restores her with blest infusions, warmth, and music (III, ii). He recommends her to the temple of Diana at Ephesus, where she takes a vestal livery. In the recognition scene Cerimon plays something like the part of Paulina in *The Winter's Tale*.

Cervantes Saavedra, Miguel de (1547–1616), Spanish novelist and dramatist. At the Battle of Lepanto he lost the use of his left hand, and then in 1575 was captured by pirates and spent five years as a slave in Algiers. The first part of *Don Quixote* was published in 1605 and translated into English by Thomas Shelton (1612). From it probably came the plot of the lost play *Cardenio*, attributed to Shakespeare and Fletcher. Fletcher made liberal use of Cervantes's stories for the plots of his plays.

Cesario. The name adopted by Viola in *Twelfth Night*. The heroine of C. Gonzaga's *Gl'Inganni* calls herself Cesare.

Chalmers, Alexander (1759–1834). Scottish journalist and editor. In 1797 he published a *Glossary to Shakspeare*, and in 1810 an edition of Steevens's *Shakespeare*.

Chalmers, George (1742–1825). Scottish antiquarian and writer. His most important work is his *Caledonia*, an unfinished history of Scotland from the 1st to the 13th century. In 1797 he published his *Apology for the Believers in the Shakespeare-Papers*. These *Papers* were the forgeries of William Henry Ireland (q.v.), which were exhibited in 1795 by his father, Samuel, at his house in Norfolk Street, and Chalmers was one of those who were convinced that they were genuine. In 1796 Ireland confessed his forgery, and Chalmers then wrote his *Apology*, and in 1799 *A Supplemental Apology*, in which he sought to prove that the *Papers*, though admittedly forgeries, might nevertheless have been genuine. He incurred the hostility of Malone and Steevens who had pronounced them spurious, but his perverse essays contain valuable work on Shakespeare's punctuation and the history of the stage. See also his *Further Historical Account of the English Stage* in the Variorum editions.

Chamber Accounts. Under Henry VII and Henry VIII the importance of the Treasurer of the Chamber was considerably increased by the deliberate policy of making him, an officer of the royal household and not of the state, instead of the Chancellor of the Exchequer, responsible for a number of accounts, many of which could scarcely be called personal. In the first year of her reign Elizabeth reorganized her household, placing her personal expenditure in the hands of a Keeper of the Privy Purse, and a number of less personal accounts in those of the Treasurer of the Chamber. These included payment of the Keepers of Paris Garden, Rat and Mole Takers, and Musicians and Players, the last of whom were to be paid on warrant from the Privy Council. Two officers of the Exchequer called Auditors of the Prests were appointed, and to these the Treasurer sent an account in duplicate, the 'Original Account', made out by the Revels Office. If passed, one was signed and returned to him, the other kept by the auditors, who made a summary, the 'Declared Account', and sent a duplicate to the Pipe Office for record. The Declared Accounts for the office of the Treasurer of the Chamber are very full, though, unfortunately, the names of the plays performed are generally omitted; thus the Declared Account for 1594 (according to the Old Style the year began on 25 March) states:

> To Willm Kempe Willm Shakespeare & Richarde Burbage seruantes to the Lord Chambleyne vpon the councelles warr^{t} dated at Whitehall xv^{to} Marti 1594 for twoe seuerall comedies or Enterludes shewed by them before her Matie in xrmas tyme laste paste viz^{d} vpon St Stephens daye & Innocentes daye xiij^{l} vj^{d} viij^{s} and by waye of her ma^{tes} Rewarde vj^{l} xiij^{s} iiij^{d}.

The Treasurers of the Chamber in Shakespeare's time were: 1570–95 Sir Thomas Heneage, 1595–6 William Killigrew, 1596–1617 Sir John Stanhope (cr. Lord Stanhope in 1605). (See REVELS ACCOUNTS.)

Chamberlain. In *1 Henry IV* the chamberlain of the inn at Rochester tells Gadshill when the guests are to set out, and is promised a share of the booty (II, i).

Chamberlain, John (1553–1627), was born in London and educated at Trinity, Cambridge. He was delicate and led a quiet life as scholar and entertaining letter-writer, 'the Horace Walpole of his day', one of his correspondents being Dudley Carleton (q.v.), whom he accompanied on his Venetian embassy in 1610–11. *Letters written by John Chamberlain during the Reign of Queen Elizabeth* were published for the Camden Society in 1861, and some are included in *Court and Times of James I.* Chamberlain described the burning of the Globe (29 June 1613) in a letter to Sir Ralph Winwood:

> The burning of the Globe, or play-house, on the Bankside, on St. Peter's day, cannot escape you; which fell out by a peal of chambers (that I know not upon what occasion were to be used in the play), the tamplin or stopple of one of them lighting in the thatch that covered the house, burn'd it down to the ground in less than two hours, with a dwelling-house adjoining, and it was a great marvaile and fair grace of God, that the people had so little harm, having but two narrow doors to get out.

(See GOWRIE.)

Chamberlain, Lord. See LORD CHAMBERLAIN.

Chamberlain's-King's Men. Their patrons were:

1. Henry Carey, cr. 1st Lord Hunsdon 1559; Lord Chamberlain 1585; d. 22 July 1596. (See HUNSDON.)

2. George Carey, succeeded as 2nd Lord Hunsdon 1596; Lord Chamberlain 17 March 1597; d. 9 September 1603.

3. James I succeeded Elizabeth 24 March 1603. The Chamberlain's became the King's Servants by patent dated 19 May 1603.

1564–7; 1581–3. Records exist of provincial companies of Lord Hunsdon, and one Court performance in December 1582.

1585. Hunsdon became Lord Chamberlain, and this company is traceable to 1590, with one Court performance jointly with the Admiral's, January 1586.

1594. As Ferdinando Stanley, 5th Earl of Derby, died 15 April 1594, at about the same time as the theatres reopened after the plague, Strange's-Derby's (q.v.) sought and found a new patron in Lord Chamberlain Hunsdon, and another Chamberlain's company was formed. After acting with the Admiral's for ten days in June at Henslowe's Newington Butts theatre the companies appear to have separated, the Admiral's under Alleyn going to his father-in-law Henslowe's theatre, the Rose, the Chamberlain's to the Theatre of James Burbage, who had been with Hunsdon's in 1584, and whose son Richard was now with the Chamberlain's. In the winter they played at the Cross Keys Inn, for in October Hunsdon wrote to the Lord Mayor for his permission. The first official record of the company occurs in the Chamber Account for 15 March 1595, when Kempe, Shakespeare, and R. Burbage were payees for two performances at Greenwich Palace on 26–27 December 1594.

Kempe, Pope, Heminge, Phillips, Bryan, and Cowley were with Strange's-Derby's in 1593, and these six were probably original sharers in the company reorganized as the Chamberlain's in 1594, when they were joined by Shakespeare and Burbage. There seem to have been eight sharers until 1603, when Lawrence Fletcher, who came from Scotland with James I, joined them, though not as an active member. In 1604 their number was increased to twelve, and so remained until 1619, one more being added before 1625.

The following abstract, based on Chambers, who sometimes differs from Baldwin, may be helpful in tracing the personnel of the company, though some of the entries are conjectural. The first column shows the original eight sharers, the others those who replaced members who retired or died, giving the dates of their becoming sharers (not always the same as the dates of joining; Lowin, for example, was a hired man in 1603), and the companies from which they came. At the bottom of column two are the four actors who raised the number of sharers from eight to twelve.

Shakespeare ?	Field (1616) *Elizabeth's*	Rice (1620) *Elizabeth's*	
Burbage *Admiral's?*	Taylor (1619) *Prince Charles's*		
Heminge	(*d.* 1630)		
Phillips	Gilburne (1605) *boy with King's*	Gough (1611) *boy or hireling with King's*	
Kempe	Armin (1599) *Chandos's?*	Shank (1615) *Palsgrave's*	
Pope	Condell (*c.* 1600) *hireling with Ch'lain's*		
Bryan	Sly (*c.* 1598) *hireling with Ch'lain's*	Ostler (1608) *Revels*	Benfield (1614) *Elizabeth's*

Cowley	Robinson (1619)	
	boy with King's	
	[Fletcher (1603)	Underwood (1608)
	from Scotland]	*Revels*
	Lowin (1604)	
	Worcester's	
	Crosse (1604?)	Tooley (1605)
	?	*boy or hireling with King's*
	Cooke (1604)	Ecclestone (1614)
	boy or hireling with King's?	

These, with the exception of Fletcher, are the twenty-six 'Principall Actors' in Shakespeare's plays, as given in the list in the Folio. In the following table their names are given as in F. It is constructed mainly from the actor-lists given in the First Folio of Ben Jonson, 1616, and the Second Folio of Beaumont and Fletcher, 1679, and shows who were the principal actors in these plays performed by the company. The last four names do not occur in the Folio list. (See the various plays, in particular THE DUCHESS OF MALFI.)

a 1598 *Every Man in His Humour.*
b 1599 *Every Man out of His Humour.*
c 1603 Royal patent, licensing the King's Men.
d 1603 *Sejanus.*
e 1604 Account of the Master of the Great Wardrobe.
f 1605 Will of Augustine Phillips, showing his legacies. Gilburne was his 'late apprentice', Sands his apprentice and Beeston his 'servant'. The rest were his 'fellows'. (Gough was left a legacy by Pope in 1603.)
g 1605 *Volpone.*
h 1610 *The Alchemist.*
i 1611 *Catiline.*
j *c.* 1612 *The Captain.*
k *c.* 1613 *Bonduca.*
l *c.* 1613 *Valentinian.*
m *c.* 1614 *The Duchess of Malfi.*
n 1619 March. Royal Patent.
o 1619 May. Lord Chamberlain's warrant for liveries.
p 1621 Lord Chamberlain's warrant for liveries.
q *c.* 1621 *The Duchess of Malfi.*
G 1599 Original housekeeper of the Globe.
B 1608 " " " Blackfriars theatre.

The dates are those (sometimes approximate) of an actor's joining the company, either as a hired man or sharer, and his death or retirement.

The first list of the Chamberlain's Men is in the cast of *Every Man in His Humour* of 1598, in which seven of the original sharers appear, though we have notice of Heminge and Bryan in 1596, and of Pope in 1597 as payees for the company. It was on 28 December 1594, the night after their two Court performances, that 'a Company of base and common Fellows', presumably Shakespeare and his crew, performed *The Comedy of Errors* at Gray's Inn.

1596 (22 July). The 1st Lord Hunsdon died, but they secured the patronage of his son, the 2nd Lord Hunsdon, being known as Hunsdon's Men until he became Lord Chamberlain on 17 March 1597 (cf. Q1, *Romeo and Juliet*, 1957, 'As it hath been often plaid publiquely, by the right Honourable the L. of Hunsdon his Seruants'). In 1596 the City Corporation managed permanently to prevent the

CHAMBERLAIN'S–KING'S MEN

William Shakespeare	a cdef	G B	1594–d. 1616
Richard Burbadge	abcdefghijklmn	G B	1594–d. 1619
John Hemmings	abcdefghi nop	G B	1594–d. 1630
Augustine Phillips	abcde	G	1594–d. 1605
William Kempt	a	G	1594– 1599
Thomas Poope	ab	G	1594–*c.* 1600
George Bryan			1594–*c.* 1600
Henry Condell	abcdefghijklmnop	B	1594–d. 1627
William Slye	abcdefg	B	1594–d. 1608
Richard Cowly	c ef		1594–d. 1619
John Lowine	d ghi kl nopq		1603–d. 1669?
Samuel Crosse			1604–d. 1605?
Alexander Cooke	d fghij		1603–d. 1614
Samuel Gilburne	f		1605– ?
Robert Armin	c ef h		1599–d. 1615
William Ostler	hijklm		1608–d. 1614
Nathan Field	no		1616–d. 1620
John Vnderwood	hi kl nopq		1608–d. 1624
Nicholas Tooley	hi k nopq		1605–d. 1623
William Ecclestone	hi k nop		1610–d. 1625?
Joseph Taylor	opq		1619–d. 1652
Robert Benfield	nopq		1614–d. 1650?
Robert Goughe	nop		1603–d. 1624
Richard Robinson	i k nopq		1611–d. 1648
Iohn Shancke	nop		1615–d. 1636
Iohn Rice	pq		1620–*c.* 1626
Christopher Beeston	a		
John Duke	a		
Lawrence Fletcher	c ef		
James Sands	f		

players performing in the City inns, such as the Cross Keys, and the Chamberlain's probably went to the Swan, and in 1597 to the Curtain where they remained until they had built their own Globe in 1599.

1597. The Privy Council limited the London Companies to two, the Chamberlain's and the Admiral's. They had to travel in the autumn owing to the prohibition of plays from July to October, but gave four performances at Court that winter. Altogether, between their formation in 1594 and Elizabeth's death in March 1603, they gave thirty-two Court performances. Their greatest rivals, the Admiral's, gave twenty.

1598. The first list of the Chamberlain's Men is that of the cast of Jonson's *Every Man in His Humour*, produced in September 1598. 'The principall Comœdians were, Will. Shakespeare, Aug. Philips, Hen. Condel, Will. Slye, Will. Kempe, Ric. Burbadge, Ioh. Hemings, Tho. Pope, Chr. Beeston, Ioh. Duke.' It was also in September of this year that Francis Meres's *Palladis Tamia* was entered in the Stationers' Register and published shortly afterwards. From this we learn that Shakespeare had already written, and presumably the Chamberlain's had performed 'his *Gentlemen of Verona*, his *Errors*, his *Loue labors lost*, his *Loue labours wonne*, his *Midsummers night dreame*, & his *Merchant of Venice*; his *Richard the 2*, *Richard the 3*, *Henry the 4*, *King Iohn*, *Titus Andronicus* and his *Romeo and Iuliet*'. Meres does not mention the three parts of *Henry VI*, or specify both parts of *Henry IV*.

1599 (February). The lease for the site of the Globe, owned by the Burbages, was signed: half the shares were kept by Cuthbert and Richard Burbage, the other half assigned equally to Shakespeare, Phillips, Pope, Heminge and Kempe. Kempe, however, soon left the company, being replaced as comedian by Robert Armin, and assigned his share to the other four. The new theatre was probably open in the autumn, for it may have been at the Globe that Thomas Platter saw a play of *Julius Caesar* on 21 September. Again it was at the Globe in 1599, 'this fair-fitted [filled?] Globe', as Jonson calls it in the play, that *Every Man out of His Humour* was produced, the 'principall Comœdians' being Burbage, Heminge, Phillips, Condell, Sly and Pope.

1601 (7 February). The Chamberlain's were persuaded by the offer of 'xl*s*. more than their ordynary' to perform 'the play of the deposyng and kyllyng of Kyng Rychard the second'. The promoters of the performance were Essex's supporters who wished to show a precedent for the rising that took place next day. It failed, and Augustine Phillips had to answer for the production, but no proceedings were taken against the company.

1603 (24 March). Elizabeth died, and Hunsdon was relieved of his office of Lord Chamberlain, but by letters patent of 19 May 1603, the Chamberlain's Men were taken into the service of James I as the King's Servants and Grooms of the Chamber:

> Knowe yee that Wee ... doe licence and aucthorize theise our Servauntes Lawrence Fletcher, William Shakespeare, Richard Burbage, Augustyne Phillippes, Iohn Heninges, Henrie Condell, William Sly, Robert Armyn, Richard Cowly, and the rest of their Assosiates freely to vse and exercise the Arte and faculty of playinge ... when the infection of the plague shall decrease, as well within theire nowe vsual howse called the Globe within our County of Surrey, as alsoe within anie towne halls or Moute halls or other conveniente places within the liberties and freedome of anie other Cittie, vniversitie, towne, or Boroughe whatsoever within our said Realmes and domynions.

Fletcher was not an active member of the company, but is mentioned as a King's Man because he had led a company of players at James's Scottish Court. Pope is not mentioned, and he died in the winter. 1603 was a plague year, and it was probably then that they visited Oxford and Cambridge, as recorded on the title-page of Q1 *Hamlet*. The last mention of Shakespeare as an actor is in the cast of *Sejanus*:

> This Tragœdie was first acted, in the yeere 1603. By the Kings Maiesties Seruants. The principall Tragœdians were, Ric. Burbadge, Aug. Philips, Will. Sly, Ioh. Lowin, Will. Shake-Speare, Ioh. Hemings, Hen. Condel, Alex. Cooke.

Lowin, from Worcester's, and Cooke are new men.

Between December 1603 and February 1604 they performed eight plays at Court, more than twice as many as the average during Elizabeth's reign, yet the fewest in James's reign up to 1616. Altogether from 1603 to 1616 they performed 175 times at Court, an average of twelve performances a year.

1604 (15 March). James supplied the nine members of his company, mentioned in the Licence of 1603, each with 4½ yards of red cloth for his coronation procession. Shakespeare heads the list. Between November 1604 and February 1605 they performed eleven times at Court: two of the plays were Jonson's, seven were Shakespeare's: *Othello*, *The Merry Wives*, *Measure for Measure*, *The Comedy of Errors*, *Henry V*, *Love's Labour's Lost*, and *The Merchant of Venice* (twice). The company was increased to twelve. (See SOMERSET HOUSE; GOWRIE.)

1605. Augustine Phillips died in May, leaving legacies to his fellows Shakespeare, Condell, Fletcher, Armin, Cowley, Cooke, Tooley, Heminge, Burbage, Sly, and his apprentice James Sand, his late apprentice Samuel Gilburne, and £5 to 'the hyred men of the company which I am of'.

1606 (July). Three performances were given at Court in honour of the King of Denmark, followed by a provincial tour in the autumn, and nine Court plays in the winter, including *King Lear*: 'yt was played before the Kinges maiestie at Whitehall vppon Sainct Stephens night at Christmas ... by his maiesties servantes.'

1608. A plague year, and the theatres were closed July-December, the King's Men going on tour. In August, shares in the Blackfriars theatre, owned by the Burbages, were distributed among seven housekeepers: Cuthbert Burbage and Thomas Evans, and five of the King's Men, Richard Burbage, Shakespeare, Heminge, Condell and Sly, but as Sly died a few days later his share was divided among the other six. Despite the plague they performed twelve Court plays at Christmas.

1609. A plague year during which the company travelled. The Blackfriars theatre was probably ready as their winter quarters. They gave thirteen plays at Court.

1610. In April they played *Othello* at the Globe, *Sejanus*, too, was produced this year, the cast according to Jonson being, Burbage, Lowin, Condell, Cooke, Armin, Heminge, Ostler, Underwood, Tooley, Ecclestone. Ostler and Underwood came from the Queen's Revels, but Ecclestone's origin is unknown. They gave fifteen Court plays in the winter.

1611. In April and May, Simon Forman saw productions of *Macbeth*, *Cymbeline* and *The Winter's Tale* at the Globe. The cast of Jonson's *Catiline* was the same as that for *Sejanus*, except that Richard Robinson took Armin's place. Between October 1611 and April 1612 they performed twenty-two plays at Court, including *The Tempest* and *The Winter's Tale*. Significantly one of the plays was *A King and No King* by Beaumont and Fletcher, who were beginning to fill the gap created by Shakespeare's retirement to Stratford.

1612. In the winter occurred the Court festivities in honour of the marriage of James's daughter Elizabeth to the Elector Palatine, the King's Men contributing twenty plays. Of Shakespeare's there were seven: *Much Ado* (twice), *Tempest*, *The Winter's Tale*, *1* and *2 Henry IV*, *Othello* and *Julius Caesar*; Jonson had one, and Beaumont and Fletcher four. There was also *Cardenno*, the lost play, supposedly by Shakespeare and Fletcher, a performance that was repeated in June 1613 'before the Duke of Savoyes Embassadour'.

1613 (29 June). The Globe was 'casually burnt downe and consumed with fier', but 'the next spring it was new builded in far fairer manner than before'.

1614. Cooke and Ostler died and were replaced by Ecclestone and possibly Benfield as sharers.

1616 (23 April). Shakespeare died. He appears to have stopped acting soon after 1603, and about 1610 had retired to New Place in Stratford.

1619 (27 March). The King's Men received a new patent in which the names are R. Burbage, Heminge, Condell, Lowin, Underwood, Tooley, Ecclestone, Gough, Robinson and the new men Nathan Field, Robert Benfield and John Shank. But Burbage died 13 March, before the patent was issued, and Joseph Taylor from the Duke of York's (Prince Charles's) Men took his place. According to John Downes (1708) it was Taylor and Lowin who handed down the tradition of Shakespeare's company by way of D'Avenant to the Restoration stage, Taylor having played Hamlet, Lowin Henry VIII.

1623. Heminge and Condell published the First Folio of Shakespeare's plays 'to keepe the memory of so worthy a Friend, & Fellow aliue, as was our Shakespeare', dedicating it to the brothers the Earls of Pembroke and of Montgomery. Condell died in 1627 and Heminge in 1630, the last of the original company.

1642. The theatres were closed from the beginning of the Civil War to the Restoration in 1660, and the history of the King's Men comes to an end. But some of them sought to emulate Heminge and Condell, and in 1647 published the First Folio of those plays of Beaumont and Fletcher that had not been printed as Quartos. Their dedication of the volume to the 4th Earl of Pembroke, the younger of the two brothers to whom the Shakespeare Folio had been dedicated, then Earl of Montgomery, is not without pathos:

But directed by the example of some, who once steered in our quality, and so fortunately aspired to choose your Honour, joined with your (now glorified) brother, patrons to the flowing compositions of the then expired sweet swan of Avon Shakespeare; and since, more particularly bound to your Lordship's most constant and diffusive goodness, from which we did for many calm years derive a subsistence to ourselves, and protection to the scene (now withered, and condemn'd, as we fear, to a long winter and sterility) we have presumed to offer to yourself, what before was never printed of these authors ...

John Lowin,	Joseph Taylor,
Richard Robinson,	Robert Benfield,
Eylærd Swanston,	Thomas Pollard,
Hugh Clearke,	William Allen,
Stephen Hammerton,	Theophilus Byrd.

Chambers, Edmund Kerchever (1866–1954). Shakespeare scholar, was educated at Marlborough and Corpus Christi, Oxford, an official in the Education Department 1892–1926, and knighted 1925. He is the author of the standard works on Shakespeare and the stage: *The Mediaeval Stage*, 2 vols. 1913; *The Elizabethan Stage*, 4 vols. 1923; *William Shakespeare*, 2 vols. 1930.

Chambers, Raymond Wilson (1874–1942), scholar, was educated at University College, London, where he became Professor of English in 1922. He was associated with A. W. Pollard in *Shakespeare's Hand in Sir Thomas More*. (See BIBLIOGRAPHY.)

'Chances, The.' A play by John Fletcher, based on a novel by Cervantes, and in the mid 17th century one of the many plays advertised by booksellers as being by Shakespeare.

Chandos Portrait. So called because it belonged to the Duke of Buckingham and Chandos; at the sale of his belongings in 1847 it was bought by Lord Ellesmere and presented to the National Portrait Gallery. Tradition has it that this so-called portrait of Shakespeare was painted by Richard Burbage, who gave it to Joseph Taylor, who bequeathed it to Sir W. D'Avenant. Yet Taylor joined the King's Men after Burbage's death, indeed he replaced him, and he died intestate. It is not generally accepted as being a genuine portrait, partly because the facial dimensions are quite unlike those of the Stratford bust and Folio engraving. (See KNELLER; THIRD VARIORUM.)

Chapel Lane Cottage. On 28 September 1602 Shakespeare acquired from Walter Getley the copyhold of a cottage and garden with a frontage of forty feet in Chapel Lane, 'alias Dead Lane'. It lay within the Manor of Rowington, a Survey of which states that in October 1604 'William Shakespere lykewise holdeth there one cottage and one garden, by estimation a quarter of one acre, and payeth rent yeerlye ij^{s}, vj^{d}.' As it stood opposite the garden of New Place it may be that Shakespeare bought it for his gardener. In his will he provided for the surrender by Judith of her interest in this 'parcel of the mannour of Rowington' to her sister Susanna Hall, in consideration of a legacy of £50. It remained with the Halls until at least 1633, was rebuilt in brick and tile about 1690, and in the early 18th century was in the hands of the Cloptons. (See GETLEY, ROWINGTON.)

Chapel Royal. Not a building, but part of the establishment of the royal household, consisting of clergy, musicians, Gentlemen of the Chapel, and choirboys, or Children of the Chapel (q.v.). Representatives travelled about the country listening to the cathedral choirs and pressing the best boys for service in the Chapel Royal. Members of the Chapel accompanied the progress of the sovereign, and they were with Henry VIII at the Field of the Cloth of Gold in 1520. The Chapel Royal has been very important in the development of English music and drama. (See CHILDREN OF THE CHAPEL.)

Chapman, George (*c.* 1560–1634). Chapman was born near Hitchin, and, according to Anthony Wood, about 1574 went to the university, 'but whether first to this of Oxon. or that of Cambridge, is to me unknown'. In 1594 he published his philosophical poem *The Shadow of Night*, to which there are possible allusions in *Love's Labour's Lost* (IV, iii), and he is often identified with the poet, 'the proud full sail' of whose great verse Shakespeare refers to in the *Sonnets*. His first extant play, *The Blind Beggar of Alexandria*, was produced by the Admiral's in 1596, and during the next three years he supplied Henslowe with a number of plays for 'his' company, and was mentioned by Meres in 1598 as one of the best both for tragedy and comedy. From 1600 to 1608 he wrote mainly for the Children playing at Blackfriars, though *Bussy D'Ambois* was 'presented at Pauls', and it was for an uncomplimentary reference to the Scots in one of these plays, *Eastward Ho!*, that he and one of his collaborators, Jonson, were imprisoned in 1605. He also got into trouble by offending French susceptibilities in his *Charles, Duke of Byron*, 1608. Soon after this he turned to his translation of Homer, finding a patron first in Prince Henry, then in Robert Carr, Earl of Somerset. He was buried in 1634 at St Giles in the Fields, where Inigo Jones erected a monument to his memory.

The stylistic disintegrators find much of Chapman in Shakespeare, J. M. Robertson attributing to him the greater part of *All's Well*, *Measure for Measure*, *Troilus and Cressida*, and passages in many other plays. Chapman's laurel is withered, and he is remembered mainly as the inspirer of Keats's sonnet on Homer. He was not a great dramatist, but he was a considerable poet. 'Of all the English play-writers', Lamb wrote, 'Chapman perhaps approaches nearest to Shakespeare in the descriptive and didactic. Dramatic imitation was not his talent. ... He would have made a great epic poet ... I have often thought that the vulgar misconception of Shakespeare, as of a wild irregular genius "in whom great faults are compensated by great beauties", would be really true, applied to Chapman.' (See Jean Jacquot, *George Chapman*, 1951.)

Character. The aspect of Shakespeare's genius on which critics, after the time of Jonson and Milton, for the most part concentrated. At the risk of being too trim and Procrustean, it may be said that the most successful characters of the first period, that of verse, are those of low life, who speak prose. The poetry of this period is more decorative than functional, more lyrical than dramatic. In the second period Shakespeare applied prose to his main characters, to Benedick and Beatrice, Falstaff and Prince Henry, and by this discipline learned to write functional, dramatic verse. In the tragedies verse again predominates over prose, but it is poetry, almost every word of which is creative of character, the poetry *is* the character: Hamlet, Othello, Macbeth, Lear, Antony, Cleopatra. In the final period the poetry is again more lyrical, and from it spring the almost tragic heroines, Marina, Imogen, Perdita and finally Miranda.

Charlecote. A village on the Avon, four miles east of Stratford. The manor of Charlecote had been held by the Lucy family since the 12th century. The house was rebuilt for Sir Thomas Lucy (q.v.) *c.* 1558, and there Elizabeth visited him on her progresses of 1566 and 1572. Richard Davies, *c.* 1700, noted that Shakespeare stole 'venison & Rabbits from Sr Lucy'; Rowe, in 1709, that he stole deer from 'a Park that belong'd to Sir *Thomas Lucy* of *Cherlecot*'. He does not say that Charlecote was the scene of the episode, though no doubt that is what he meant. Strictly speaking, Lucy did not possess a park, 'an enclosure stocked with beasts of the chase', but a warren for keeping 'beasts and fowls of warren' such as hares and partridges, though roe-deer came to be included as beasts of warren. (See FULBROOK; A. Fairfax-Lucy, *Charlecote and the Lucys*, 1958.)

Charles I (1600–49). The second son of James I and Anne of Denmark. In 1605 he was created Duke of York, and after him in 1608 was named a company of players that included the dramatist William Rowley, and Joseph Taylor, who joined the King's in 1619 on the death of Burbage. When Charles's elder brother, Henry, died in 1612 he became heir-apparent and his company was known as Prince Charles's Men. He saw the performance of *Benedicte and Betteris* given at Court by the King's Men in 1612, and more than twenty years later wrote this alternative title to *Much Ado* in his copy of the Second Folio.

Charles II (1630–85). The second son of Charles I and Henrietta Maria. At the Restoration in 1660 he reopened the theatres, introduced the French fashion of actresses on the public stage, and granted patents to two companies, the King's under his own patronage to Killigrew, the Duke of York's under that of his brother to D'Avenant, dividing between them the exclusive right to produce, 'reform' and 'make fit' most of Shakespeare's plays. Copies of three spurious plays, *The Merry Devil of Edmonton*, *Mucedorus* and *Fair Em*, were bound and labelled 'Shakespeare Vol. I' in Charles's library.

Charles. In *As You Like It*, the Duke Frederick's wrestler who is thrown by Orlando in I, ii.

Charles VI. In *Henry V*, the King of France. He makes the Treaty of Troyes (v, ii) with Henry V, whereby Henry is to marry his daughter Katharine and to succeed him as King of France. (Charles VI (1368–1422) suffered from insanity, as did his grandson Henry VI of England. He died a few weeks before Henry V, and was succeeded by his son Charles VII, wrongly called the Dauphin in *1 Henry VI*.)

Charles (1403–61). In *1 Henry VI*, the Dauphin and son of Charles VI, after 1422 King Charles VII of France. He falls in love with Joan of Arc, and frankly attributes to her the French successes. After her capture he submits to being merely viceroy of his dominions, subject to Henry VI (v, v).

Charlton, Henry Buckley (1890–1961). Professor of English at Manchester University; author of *Shakespearian Tragedy*, etc.

Charmian. In *Antony and Cleopatra*, one of the attendants of Cleopatra. The soothsayer tells her in I, ii that she shall outlive the lady whom she serves, to which Charmian replies, 'O, excellent, I love long life better than figs.' She outlives Cleopatra by a few minutes, dying like her from the bite of an asp that leaves its trail of slime on the fig-leaves.

Chateaubriand, François René, Vicomte de (1768–1848). One of the first French Romantic writers; his *Génie du Christianisme* is a revolt against the classicism that belittled Shakespeare, to whom he turned as a source of the Romantic beauty that he preached.

Chatillon. In *King John*, a French ambassador. He opens the play by threatening John with war in the name of Philip of France, if he does not renounce the throne in favour of Arthur. In II, i he brings the news to Philip at Angiers that John has already begun the invasion of France.

Chaucer, Geoffrey (1340?–1400). Shakespeare did not borrow from Chaucer as much, perhaps, as might be expected, but he was indebted to him for the following:

The Legend of Good Women: one possible source of *The Rape of Lucrece*.

The Knight's Tale: supplied the material for the Theseus theme in *A Midsummer Night's Dream*, and is certainly the source of *The Two Noble Kinsmen*.

Troilus and Criseyde: the main source of the Troy scenes in *Troilus and Cressida*.

Chester, Robert (*c.* 1566–1640), probably the son of Edward Chester of Roysdon. He was the author of *Love's Martyr* (1601), the volume that contains *The Phoenix and Turtle* (q.v.).

Chettle, Henry (*c.* 1560–*c.* 1607). Printer, and for a time a partner of John Danter. By 1598, however, he had turned dramatist, for Meres mentions him as one of the best for comedy, and during the next five years he wrote, or collaborated in, forty-eight plays for the Admiral's under Henslowe, to whom he was chronically in debt. His only extant printed play is *The Tragedy of Hoffman.* He is best known for his *Kind-Harts Dreame. Conteining fiue Apparitions with their Inuectiues against abuses raigning,* 1592. In this pamphlet Chettle apologizes for the part he played in editing Greene's *Groatsworth of Wit,* with its attack on Shakespeare:

> I am as sory as if the originall fault had beene my fault, because my selfe haue seene his [Shakespeare's] demeanor no lesse ciuill than he exelent in the qualitie he professes: Besides, diuers of worship haue reported, his vprightnes of dealing, which argues his honesty, and his facetious grace in writting, that aprooues his Art.

Chettle's hand has been identified as one of those in the manuscript of *Sir Thomas More.*

Chetwind, Philip. The publisher of the Third Folio 1664, to the second impression of which he added *Pericles* and six spurious plays. He married the widow of Robert Allot, one of the publishers of F2, and so secured the copyright of Shakespeare's plays.

Chetwood, William Rufus (d. 1766). Bookseller, dramatist, and prompter at Drury Lane and in Ireland. His *General History of the Stage,* 1749, states for the first time in print that 'Sir William Davenant was by many suppos'd the natural Son of Shakespear.' He is one of the earliest Shakespearean forgers, publishing in his *British Theatre,* 1750, a list of Quartos, many of them fictitious.

Child, Harold Hannyngton (1869–1945), novelist, dramatic critic, and authority on the history of the drama. He contributed to the *New Cambridge Shakespeare* (Stage Histories), *A Companion to Shakespeare Studies,* etc.

Children's Companies. Until 1576 there was no permanent theatre, and until the decade of the University Wits (*c.* 1583–93) the plays performed by the adult companies were on the whole rough-and-tumble affairs, or simply 'feates of activitie'. It is, therefore, easy to understand why Elizabeth and the Court preferred the more cultured performances given by the schoolboys of Westminster and Eton, and those of the choristers of Paul's, the Chapel Royal, and Windsor, trained by scholars and accomplished musicians. Between 1558 and 1576 boys gave forty-six Court performances to the adults' thirty-two. After the building of James Burbage's Theatre in 1576, adult companies, particularly Leicester's, came more into favour, though in the same year Farrant replied for the Children by renting the (first) Blackfriars theatre for public performances by the Chapel Children. After Farrant's death the venture was continued until 1584 by Hunnis, who was joined by the Paul's Children with Lyly's plays. From 1584 to 1600 there was no public competition from the boys, and their position at Court was shaken first by the Queen's Men, and then after 1590 by the Admiral's with Marlowe's plays, and by the Strange-Chamberlain company with Shakespeare's. From 1600–8 came another period of competition from the boys. Under Edward Peers the Paul's Children performed both 'at Powles' and at Court plays by Chapman, Marston and others, but more serious was the competition from the second Blackfriars theatre rented by Nathaniel Giles and Henry Evans, where the Chapel Children performed Jonson's plays. This came to an end in 1608 when the King's Men moved into the Blackfriars theatre, the Chapel children had to find new quarters, and the Paul's boys were bought off.

Children of the Chapel (The Queen's Revels). 'The Chapel' was established in the 12th century as part of the royal household, the personnel having grown by 1603 to consist of a Dean, Sub-dean, thirty-two Gentlemen (priests and laymen), including the Master of the Children, and twelve children. They accompanied the Court in its progresses. In the early 16th century plays were given by the Gentlemen, but William Cornish, Master of the Children 1509–23, formed the boys into a dramatic company who performed Court interludes.

Richard Edwardes was Master 1561–6; at Christmas 1564 the boys played one of his tragedies, probably *Damon and Pythias*, at Court, and at Candlemas 1565 and 1566 they performed at Lincoln's Inn. Under Edwardes's successor William Hunnis (1566–97) and his deputy Richard Farrant (1576–80), who was also Master of the Windsor Children, the boys played fairly regularly at Court until 1584. In 1576, the year of the building of the first public theatre, Farrant began a venture of the greatest significance. He rented rooms in the Blackfriars priory, and there the boys gave public performances, an experiment that was continued after his death by Hunnis, who however transferred his interest to Henry Evans, a scrivener, in 1583, but in the following year Sir William More, the landlord, recovered his buildings, and the first Blackfriars theatre came to an end. Apparently in 1583–4 the Chapel boys acted with those of Paul's and the Earl of Oxford's, two of their plays being Lyly's *Campaspe* and *Sapho and Phao*. Though in 1584 the boys ceased acting at Court and at Blackfriars, they gave some performances in the provinces.

From 1597 to 1634 Nathaniel Giles was Master, and he, in partnership with Henry Evans, in 1600 leased from Richard Burbage the Blackfriars buildings which had been converted into a theatre by James Burbage in 1596. There the boys acted, and again at Court, for the first time since 1584, the Queen's Men, and then the Chamberlain's and Admiral's, having in the meantime been the favoured companies. Again they became serious rivals of the adult players, thanks largely to the support of Ben Jonson. In 1601 they produced his *Poetaster* ridiculing Marston and Dekker, who replied in *Satiromastix*, Shakespeare referring to the squabble in *Hamlet* (1601):

> There is, sir, an eyrie of children, little eyases, that cry out on the top of question and are most tyranically clapped for 't: these are now the fashion, and so berattle the common stages – so they call them – that many wearing rapiers are afraid of goose-quills, and dare scarce come thither.

'Nat. Field, Ioh. Underwood, and Wil. Ostler', all future King's Men and 'fellows' of Shakespeare, were in the cast of *The Poetaster*.

In this year Giles was accused of making secular profit at Blackfriars out of his more spiritual office at the Chapel with its authorization to 'take as manye well singinge children as he shall thinke mete'. Apparently, like Falstaff, he had 'misused the queen's press damnably', and carried off boys 'noe way able or fitt for singing ... to exercyse the base trade of mercynary enterlude player', nor were they 'by anie the sayd confederates endeavoured to be taught to singe'. Giles abandoned the Blackfriars business, and Evans went abroad, but returned in 1603 and with Edward Kirkham secured a royal licence 'to provide keepe and bring uppe a convenient nomber of Children, and them to practize and exercise in the quality of playinge by the name of Children of the Revells to the Queene within the Blackfryers in our Cytie of London'. The Children of the Chapel, therefore, were now known as The Children of the Queen's Revels, but after a number of unfortunate episodes, including the production of *Eastward Ho!* in 1605, they lost the favour of the Court and the royal title, becoming merely The

Children of the Revels, and in 1606 The Children of the Blackfriars, the severance between the Chapel and Blackfriars becoming complete according to the commission given to Giles:

> Wee doe straightlie charge and commaunde that none of the saide Choristers or Children of the Chappell so to be taken by force of this commission shalbe vsed or imployed as Comedians or Stage players, or to exercise or acte any Stage plays Interludes Comedies or tragedies, for that it is not fitt or decent that such as shoulde singe the praises of God Allmightie shoulde be trayned vpp or imployed in suche lascivious and prophane exercises.

When the King's Men took over the Blackfriars theatre in 1608 the boys had to find new quarters and, under Robert Keysar, moved to Whitefriars to the west of the City walls, being known as the Children of Whitefriars until 1610 when they were restored to royal favour under Philip Rosseter, and became again The Children of the Queen's Revels. Nat Field was in their production of Jonson's *Epicoene* (1609), and shortly afterwards they acted both at Court and Whitefriars Field's own play, *A Woman is a Weathercock*. About 1616 Field joined the King's Men, and soon the career of this company of the Queen's Revels came to an end, though a new one was formed by Rosseter in 1617.

Children of the King's Revels. A short-lived company, playing at Whitefriars, was formed *c.* 1606 by a syndicate, of which Michael Drayton was a member. It is just possible that the children were those of Paul's, who appear to have ceased playing at this time. The King's Revels began at an unfortunate time of plague and inhibition, and in 1609 perished in litigation among members of the syndicate. A second but provincial company was formed in 1615.

Children of Paul's. The grammar school attached to St Paul's Cathedral was founded in the 12th century, and at the same time a cathedral choir school was established with its headquarters at St Gregory's church to the south-west of the cathedral. These two foundations are distinct, though the boys of the choir school appear to have gone to the grammar school for their more academic education. It is the boys of the choir school who are known as the Children of Paul's. Sebastian Wescott was Master *c.* 1557–82, and under him the boys acted plays, probably in St Gregory's, but also at Court, where they performed twenty-seven times during his mastership, far more than any other company. In 1583–4 the boys acted at the Blackfriars theatre with the Chapel Children, and under the Mastership of Thomas Giles (1584–*c.* 1599) they performed a number of Lyly's plays at Court, where they appeared nine times 1587–90, but in 1590 were suppressed, possibly because Lyly used them, though with the government's encouragement, against the Marprelate tracts. When Edward Peers became Master *c.* 1599 another period of performances began both 'at Powles' and at Court, the boys acting plays by Marston, Chapman, Middleton, Dekker and Webster (see POETOMACHIA), but their last appearance at Court was in 1606, and the Paul's Boys appear to have ceased playing, their potential competition being bought off by the King's Men and the Queen's Revels syndicate in 1608.

Children of Windsor. There was an old ecclesiastical college at Windsor, consisting of a dean, a number of clergy, and about ten children under a Master. From 1564 to his death in 1580 Richard Farrant was Master, and between 1567 and 1575 the Children gave ten Court performances of plays. From 1576 the Children of Windsor and the Chapel appear to have combined for Court performances under Farrant who, in the same year, rented the rooms in Blackfriars priory (the 'first' Blackfriars theatre), where the Children performed their plays in public. From 1595 to 1634 Nathaniel Giles was Master of the

Children of Windsor, and after 1597 of the Chapel as well, but after Farrant's death there are no records of performances of plays by the Windsor Children.

China. Although it is only fifty years since the Western drama was introduced, Shakespeare is becoming comparatively popular. To reach a largely uneducated audience, however, translation has to be a simple prose paraphrase, and performances are further limited by the old Chinese etiquette: for example, a man may not touch the hand of a woman.

Chiron. In *Titus Andronicus*, the youngest son of Tamora. He and his brother Demetrius ravish and then mutilate Titus's daughter Lavinia; they also secure the deaths of two of Titus's sons by making them appear guilty of their own murder of Bassianus, the Emperor's brother. Titus cuts their throats, and bakes them in a pie which their mother eats.

Chorus. In *Henry V* Shakespeare prefaces each act with a Chorus. He apologizes for the deficiencies of the stage, but appeals to the audience to use their imaginations, and in magnificent narrative verse unifies the action, 'turning the accomplishment of many years Into an hour-glass'. Gower acts as Chorus to the five acts of *Pericles*. There is a Chorus to the first two acts of *Romeo and Juliet*, Rumour acts as Prologue to *2 Henry IV*, and there is a Prologue to *Henry VIII*. In *The Winter's Tale*, Time, as chorus, bridges the gap of sixteen years between Acts III and IV.

Chronology of the Plays. Malone was the first scholar scientifically to attempt to date the plays, his conclusions appearing as *An Attempt to Ascertain the Order in which the Plays of Shakespeare were Written* (q.v.) in 1778, revised in 1790, and in its final form in the Third Variorum of 1821. Malone used elementary verse-tests, as well as other evidence, internal and external. In 1833 came William Spalding's *Letter ... on the characteristics of Shakespeare's style*, in 1850 James Spedding's *Who wrote Henry VIII?*, and in 1857 Charles Bathurst's *Remarks on ... Shakespeare's versification*. In 1850 the German scholar Gervinus published his *Shakespeare*, with the results of his researches into chronology, and in England F. J. Furnivall (*Leopold Shakspere*, 1877) and the New Shakspere Society worked along similar lines, for, said Furnivall, 'Shakspere *must* be studied chronologically, and as a whole.' Others who made a special study of chronology are F. G. Fleay and C. M. Ingleby, and in Germany W. König, H. Conrad and G. Sarrazin.

These were all engaged in the quantitative method of verse-tests: the percentage of rhyme, of feminine endings, and so on, by which to establish a date within limits generally fixed by other evidence. Evidence that a play was written before a certain date may be furnished by entry in the Stationers' Register, by the title-page of Q, by record of performance, or by contemporary mention, particularly by Meres, who named twelve plays in 1598. Negative evidence that a play was written after 1598 is lack of mention by Meres; positive evidence that it was later than a certain date may be supplied by topical allusions, of which, however, there are tantalizingly few in Shakespeare. Thus *Troilus and Cressida* is not mentioned by Meres and was registered on 7 February 1603, and was probably written, therefore, between the end of 1598 and the end of 1602. On stylistic grounds it is placed immediately after *Hamlet*, probably in 1602, though in its first form it may be as early as 1598. (See VERSE-TESTS.)

Some scholars now question the generally accepted chronology, particularly Dover Wilson, editor of the New Cambridge Shakespeare, with his concept of constant revision of plays. T. W. Baldwin in his *William Shakspere's Five-Act Structure* (1947) supports the hypothesis of revision, and places the first version of

Love's Labour's Lost as early as 1588, followed by that of *All's Well* (in which he finds Meres's '*Love's Labour's Won*'), *The Comedy of Errors, The Two Gentlemen of Verona, Romeo and Juliet*. Hotson, too, pushes some of the plays further back; *1, 2 Henry IV* and *Merry Wives* to 1596–spring 1597, *Troilus* (which he claims as '*Love's Labour's Won*') to 1598 and the *Sonnets* (q.v.), or some of them, to 1588–9.

In the table below, the plays are divided into five main periods: early; lyrical; histories and comedies; tragedies; romances. Though they must have been written in something like this order, dates of most of them can only be approximate. (See SS, 3.)

1589–90	1 Henry VI
1590–1	2 Henry VI
	3 Henry VI
1592–3	Richard III
	Titus Andronicus
1593–4	Comedy of Errors
	Taming of the Shrew
1594–5	Two Gentlemen of Verona
	Love's Labour's Lost
1595–6	Romeo and Juliet
	Richard II
	Midsummer Night's Dream
1596–7	King John
	Merchant of Venice
1597–8	1 Henry IV
	2 Henry IV
1598–9	Much Ado
	Henry V
	Merry Wives
1599–	Julius Caesar
1600	As You Like It
	Twelfth Night
1600–1	Hamlet
1601–2	Troilus and Cressida
1602–3	All's Well
	Othello
1603–4	Measure for Measure
1604–5	Timon
1605–6	Lear
	Macbeth
1606–7	Antony and Cleopatra
1607–8	Coriolanus
1608–9	Pericles
1609–10	Cymbeline
1610–11	Winter's Tale
1611–12	Tempest
1612–13	Henry VIII
1613–14	Two Noble Kinsmen

Cibber, Colley (1671–1757), son of the sculptor Caius Gabriel Cibber, was born in London and educated at Grantham. In 1690 he joined Betterton at Drury Lane, married in 1693, and produced his first play, *Love's Last Shift*, in 1696. He was successful as actor, joint-manager of Drury Lane, and as dramatist, and was created Poet Laureate in 1730. In 1740 he published his *Apology for the Life of Colley Cibber, Comedian*, containing a valuable *View of the Stage during his Own Time*. He offended Pope, who in revenge substituted him for Theobald as the hero of the *Dunciad*. Cibber played a number of Shakespearean parts, including Wolsey, Jaques, and Iago, though generally in the 'improvised' versions of the period. He himself adapted *Richard III* (1700), in the version that held the stage until 1821, with its famous 'Off with his head. So much for Buckingham.' His last appearance as an actor was as Pandulph in his own *Papal Tyranny in the Reign of King John*, a production inspired by the threatened Jacobite rebellion of '45.

Cibber, Theophilus (1703-58), son of Colley Cibber, and like him an actor and dramatist. He produced a version of *Henry VI, Parts 2 and 3*, in 1723, and of *Romeo and Juliet* in 1744, and contrived to work into a production of *Henry VIII* the spectacle of the Champion in Westminster Hall, which was so successful that it was incorporated in other plays. The nature of his acting may be gauged from his having played Parolles and Pistol, the last his most successful part. In 1753 was published *The Lives of the Poets* ... 'By Mr Cibber'. Johnson said the book was written mainly by his amanuensis, Robert Shiels, and that the publisher had paid Theophilus for the use of his surname, which would be taken for that of his father Colley. In his *Life of Shakespeare* Cibber (or Shiels) adds only one incident unrecorded by Rowe, the story, derived in a wonderful sequence from D'Avenant, of how Shakespeare began his theatrical career by holding horses' heads at the playhouse door, and hiring boys, who came to be known as 'Shakespear's boys', to help him.

Cibber, Susannah Maria (1714–66). The sister of Dr Arne who, in 1734, married Theophilus Cibber, though she lived with him but a short time. She had a beautiful voice and began her stage career in opera, but later joined Garrick, playing Constance, her best part, to his King John in a rival production to Colley Cibber's version in 1745, and among other parts, Ophelia to his Hamlet, and Perdita to his Leontes.

Cicero, M. Tullius. In *Julius Caesar*, a Roman senator. Brutus speaks of his ferret and fiery eyes, says that 'he will never follow any thing that other men begin', and overrules the other conspirators who wish to approach him. (In his Philippic orations he attacked Antony, who had him murdered, 43 B.C.)

Cimber. See METELLUS.

Cinema. The earliest films were, of course, silent, and most of them made in U.S.A., though a film (*c.* 1899) of Sarah Bernhardt as Hamlet in the duel scene is still extant, and the first film of a play is apparently Tree's *King John* (*c.* 1899), now lost. The first talkie seems to have been the Pickford-Fairbanks *Taming of the Shrew* in 1929. Only half of the plays have been filmed, and the earliest and most notable versions are given below.

As You Like It: U.S.A. 1908. G.B. 1936, with Elisabeth Bergner and L. Olivier.

Cymbeline: U.S.A. 1913.

Hamlet: France 1910. Denmark 1911, filmed at Kronberg Castle. G.B. 1913, with Forbes Robertson. G.B. 1948, L. Olivier.

Henry V: G.B. 1944, L. Olivier.

Henry VIII: G.B. 1911, Tree's production at His Majesty's.

King Lear: U.S.A. 1909. 906 ft!

Julius Caesar: U.S.A. 1908. Italy 1909; 1914 with cast of 20,000. U.S.A. 1952, with J. Gielgud.

Measure for Measure: *c.* 1908 (Lubin).

Merchant of Venice: U.S.A. 1912. France 1913. France-Italy 1952.

Macbeth: G.B. 1902 (?), an early attempt at a super-film with Arthur Bourchier and Violet Vanbrugh. U.S.A. 1908. Italy 1909. France 1910. Germany 1913. U.S.A. 1915, production D. W. Griffith with Beerbohm Tree. U.S.A. 1948, Orson Welles. Japan 1956.

Merry Wives: U.S.A. 1910. France 1911. Germany 1950, based on Otto Nicolai's opera.

Midsummer Night's Dream: U.S.A. 1909; 1935 directed by Reinhardt. Czechoslovakia 1958, puppet film.

Othello: Italy 1914. Germany 1922, with Emil Jannings. G.B. 1946. Morocco 1950, Orson Welles. U.S.S.R. 1955.

Richard III: U.S.A. 1908, 1913. G.B. 1911; 1955, L. Olivier, J. Gielgud.

Romeo and Juliet: U.S.A. 1908. G.B. 1912, Godfrey Tearle, Mary Malone. France 1913. U.S.A. 1936, Leslie Howard, Norma Shearer. G.B.-Italy 1954, directed by Renato Castallani.

Taming of the Shrew: U.S.A. 1908, directed by D. W. Griffith. G.B. 1911. France 1911. U.S.A. 1929, Mary Pickford, Douglas Fairbanks, Snr.

Tempest: U.S.A. 1911. France 1912.

Twelfth Night: U.S.A. 1910. U.S.S.R. 1955.

Winter's Tale: U.S.A. 1910.

(See SQ, III, 'The Shakespeare Film as Record'; IV, VI, VII, 'Shakespeare through the Camera's Eye'.)

Cinna, Helvius. In *Julius Caesar*, the poet, a friend of Catullus, mistaken for Cinna the conspirator, and murdered by the frenzied mob.

Cinna, L. Cornelius. In *Julius Caesar*, one of the conspirators. His part is to place anonymous 'instigations' where Brutus shall find them (I, iii; II, i). He does not appear after the assassination.

Cinthio (1504–73). Giovanni Battista Giraldi, surnamed Cinthio, was scholar, poet and novelist. He was born and educated at Ferrara, where he became a professor, and then Professor of Rhetoric at Pavia. He wrote nine tragedies and an epic, *Ercole*, but is best known for his *Hecatommithi* (1565), a sequence of prose romances in the manner of Boccaccio and Bandello. From the *Hecatommithi* (iii, 7) Shakespeare took the plot of *Othello*, modifying it, and supplying the characters with names. He was indirectly indebted to Cinthio for the plot of *Measure for Measure*, which he found in George Whetstone's *Promos and Cassandra* (q.v.), 1578, a dramatic version of Cinthio's *novella* viii 5.

Cittern. A simple form of lute with only four strings and a flat back like a guitar. It was very popular in Shakespeare's day, and barbers kept them in their shops for the use of waiting customers. Cf. Jonson, *Epicoene*: 'That cursed barber! I have married his cittern!'

City Authorities. For an account of the attempt of the Lord Mayor and Corporation to suppress theatres in London, and their defeat by the Privy Council, see ACTORS.

'Civitas Londini.' A view of London 'performed', i.e. drawn, by John Norden 'from the Pitch of the Hill towards Dulwich College' in 1600. His map of 1593 shows only the Beargarden and the Rose; an inset map in the *View* adds the Swan, built *c.* 1595, and the Globe, built 1599. All four buildings are shown as cylindrical, the Globe being on the south side of Maid Lane and just to the east of the Rose, misnamed 'The Stare'. (See SS, 1.)

Clarence, George Duke of. In *3 Henry VI*, he is created Duke of Clarence by his brother Edward IV after the Yorkist victory at Towton (II, vi), but with Warwick deserts him when he marries Lady Grey. Before Barnet he deserts Warwick and rejoins Edward (v, i).

In *Richard III*, Edward IV imprisons him and orders his death. Richard intercepts his reprieve and he is murdered (I, iv). (Clarence (1449–78) was a younger brother of Edward IV, and elder brother of Richard III. He married a daughter of Warwick the Kingmaker.)

Clarence, Thomas Duke of. In *2 Henry IV*, the second son of the King, who appeals to him to guide Prince Henry when he becomes King (IV, iv).

In *Henry V* (v, ii, 84) he is addressed by Henry. (Clarence (1388–1421) was killed at Beaugé.)

Clark, William George (1821–78), was born at Darlington and educated at Sedbergh, Shrewsbury, and Trinity, Cambridge, of which college he became a fellow. He was a fine classical scholar, in 1857 being appointed Public Orator. He is best known as one of the three editors of the *Cambridge Shakespeare*, 1863–6, the other two being John Glover and W. Aldis Wright. He left money to Trinity for the foundation of an annual lectureship in English literature, the Clark Lectures.

Clarke, Charles Cowden (1787–1877). The friend and encourager of Keats, and acquaintance of Shelley, Coleridge, Lamb and other writers of the period. In 1828 he married Mary Novello (1809–98), and so began their enthusiastic partnership in the study of Shakespeare. In 1863 Clarke published some of his lectures as *Shakespeare's Characters, chiefly those subordinate*; in 1868 came their joint edition of Shakespeare, and in 1879 their *Shakespeare Key, unlocking the Treasures of his Style*. Mary's famous *Complete Concordance* was published in 1845, and in 1850–2 the three volumes of her *Girlhood of Shakespeare's Heroines*.

Claudio. 1. In *Much Ado* (q.v.), a young lord of Florence. (He is called Timbreo di Cardona in Bandello's *novella*.)

2. In *Measure for Measure* (q.v.), the brother of Isabella. (In Cinthio's *novella* the corresponding character, Vico, really is executed.)

Claudius. 1. In *Hamlet*, the uncle of Hamlet, and King of Denmark. (His name is mentioned only in s.d. I, ii, '*Enter Claudius King of Denmarke ...*' He is called Fengo in the *Historiae Danicae* of Saxo Grammaticus.)

2. In *Julius Caesar*, a servant of Brutus, who slept in his tent the night before Philippi.

Clayton, John. In 1600 a William Shakespeare recovered a debt of £7, outstanding since 1592, from one John Clayton of Willington, Bedfordshire. As a William Shakespeare of Bedfordshire has been discovered it is reasonable to assume that it was he and not the poet who brought the action.

Clemen, Wolfgang (b. 1909), German Shakespeare scholar, Professor at the University of Munich, visiting Professor at Columbia University, N.Y., Director of the Shakespeare-Gesellschaft, author of *The Development of Shakespeare's Imagery* (1951, translation of revised edition of *Shakespeares Bilder*, 1936), *English Tragedy before Shakespeare*, 1961, and *A Commentary on Shakespeare's Richard III* (English translation, 1968).

Cleomenes. In *The Winter's Tale*, a lord of Sicilia. Leontes sends him and Dion 'To sacred Delphos, to Apollo's temple' to ask the oracle the truth about Hermione. They return with the answer that she is chaste.

Cleon. In *Pericles* (q.v.), husband of Dionyza, and governor of Tarsus.

'Cleopatra.' A play by Samuel Daniel, published in 1594, and again 'newly altered' in 1607. Some maintain that the 1607 version shows the influence of Shakespeare's *Antony and Cleopatra*, thus suggesting that the latter play was written at least a year before its registration in May 1608. Others argue that a re-reading of Plutarch would account for Daniel's alterations. (See SS, 6.)

Cleopatra. The heroine of *Antony and Cleopatra* (q.v.). She was born 68 B.C., and on the death of her father in 51 succeeded to the throne of Egypt jointly with her younger brother Ptolemy. In 49 she was deposed by her guardians, but restored by Julius Caesar, whose mistress she became, and bore him a son, Caesarion. After Caesar's murder she supported the Triumvirate, met Antony in 41, and became his mistress. After their defeat at Actium in 31 she negotiated with Octavius and promised to get rid of Antony, but when she realized that she was to be carried captive to Rome she killed herself (30 B.C.).

Clifford, Lord. In *2 Henry VI*, a supporter of the King. In IV, viii, he and Buckingham persuade the mob to desert Cade. In V, i, he takes the King's part at the beginning of the Wars of the Roses, but is killed by York at St Albans (V, ii). (Thomas Clifford (1414–55), 12th Baron.)

Clifford, Lord. He appears in *2 Henry VI* as Young Clifford, and sees his father killed at St Albans, from which battle he escapes. In *3 Henry VI* he follows Queen Margaret, who continues the war against York, stabs York's son Rutland at Wakefield, and the captured York himself after the battle. He is killed at Towton (II, vi). (John Clifford (d. 1461), the son of Thomas.)

Clifford Chambers. A village two miles south of Stratford. The lady who was the *Idea* of Michael Drayton's *Sonnets* married Sir Henry Rainsford, who lived at Clifford Chambers. As Drayton used to stay there, there may be some truth in the note of John Ward, vicar of Stratford 1662–81, that 'Shakespeare, Drayton, and Ben Jonson, had a merry meeting, and it seems drank too hard, for Shakespeare died of a fever there contracted'. There were Shakespeares living on the Rainsford manor: in 1560 John Shaxspere married Julian

Hobbins, who died in 1608, John dying in 1610. (See SNITTERFIELD.)

Clink. The prison and liberty on the Bankside (q.v.).

Clitus. In *Julius Caesar*, a servant of Brutus, who, after the defeat at Philippi, refuses Brutus's request to kill him. He runs away at the approach of Octavius and Antony.

Clive, Catherine [Kitty] (1711–85). Comic actress, mainly at Drury Lane, which she joined under Colley Cibber in 1728. Her surname was Raftor until she married George Clive, a relation of Clive of India. She played Portia to Macklin's Shylock in the first play produced by Garrick as manager of Drury Lane (1747), and Catherine in his *Catherine and Petruchio*; some of her other Shakespearean parts were Celia, Olivia, and Ophelia. She retired in 1769, and on her death Horace Walpole wrote,

> The comic muse with her retired,
> And shed a tear when she expired.

'Mrs Clive', said Johnson, 'in the sprightliness of humour, I have never seen equalled.'

Clopton. A hamlet two miles north of Stratford, owned by the Clopton family. Sir Hugh Clopton, who was Lord Mayor of London in 1491, rebuilt the bridge over the Avon and the Guild Chapel. Before he died in 1496 he built New Place (q.v.). The park of Clopton House was leased to Shakespeare's friend, John Combe. Thomas Russell tried to buy the house and estate from William and Anne Clopton, but the agreement fell through, and the house passed to Lord Carew and his wife Joyce Clopton, sister of Anne. At Michaelmas 1605 it was rented by Ambrose Rookwood and used as a base for Gunpowder Plot.

Cloten. In *Cymbeline*, the son of King Cymbeline's Queen by a former husband. He loves his step-sister Imogen, to whom he makes insulting remarks about her banished husband Posthumus. Imogen tells him that she loves the meanest garment of Posthumus better than him. When Cloten hears that she has gone to Milford Haven to meet her husband, he puts on the clothes of Posthumus and plans to 'kill him, and in her eyes', then ravish her. However, he is killed by Guiderius. Imogen finds his headless body, and thinking it is Posthumus is prostrated with grief.

Clown. The word is probably connected with 'clod', a stupid, rustic fellow. The Elizabethans appear to have used 'clown' and 'fool' indiscriminately: thus Dekker in *The Gull's Hornbook* (1609), 'Tarlton, Kemp, nor Singer, nor all the litter of fools that now come drawling behind them, never played the clowns more naturally than the arrantest sot of you all shall.' And Hamlet: 'Let those that play your clowns speak no more than is set down for them ... that's villanous, and shows a most pitiful ambition in the fool that uses it.'

The Clown is a stock character in Shakespeare's plays, from Launce in *The Two Gentlemen of Verona* to Stephano in *The Tempest*, commonest of course in the Comedies: the Dromios, Grumio, Costard, the Gobbos, Bottom, Dogberry, and the delightful shepherd's son in *The Winter's Tale*; rarer in the Histories, though no doubt Mistress Quickly was played by a 'clown'; and there are few Tragedies without a clown, from the poor shadowy creature in *Titus Andronicus* to the gravediggers in *Hamlet*, the porter in *Macbeth*, and the clown who brings the asps to Cleopatra. But the broad comedy of most of these parts should be distinguished from that of the much more subtle and intellectual comedy of the professional 'fools' (apparently descended from the Vice of medieval drama), Touchstone and Feste, with their music, and the tragic jesting of Lear's Fool, parts probably played by Armin, much less of a clown than Tarlton and Kempe. The chief comedians of

Shakespeare's company appear to have been Kempe, Pope, Armin, Cowley, Robinson and Shank.

In 1694 Charles Gildon wrote,

> I'm assured from very good hands, that the person that acted Iago was in much esteem for a comedian, which made Shakespear put several words, and expressions into his part (perhaps not so agreeable to his character) to make the audience laugh, who had not yet learnt to be serious a whole play.

Shakespeare had written (*Hamlet* III, ii):

> And let those that play your clowns speak no more than is set down for them: for there be of them that will themselves laugh, to set on some quantity of barren spectators to laugh too, though in the mean time some necessary question of the play be then to be considered.

In *Shakespeare's Motley* Hotson shows that the fool's motley was a long coat woven of different coloured threads; though portraits of Henry VIII's jester, Tom Skelton, depict him in a long checked coat. (See SS, 13; Douce, *Illustrations of Shakespeare*, p. 496.)

Cobham, William Brooke, 7th Lord. Lord Chamberlain after the death of Henry Carey, 1st Lord Hunsdon, from 8 August 1596 to his own death on 5 March 1597, when George Carey, 2nd Lord Hunsdon succeeded him. The seven months of Cobham's office are important, for he can have made little attempt to defend the players from the attacks of the City authorities, who then carried their first objective of banishing 'all players from playing within the City', while the inhabitants of Blackfriars successfully petitioned the Privy Council to disallow the opening of James Burbage's new private theatre. It was probably he or his son who secured the alteration of his ancestor's name, Sir John Oldcastle, to Falstaff, and in *The Merry Wives*, of Ford's assumed name of Brooke to the less appropriate Broome, and perhaps the exclusion of Falstaff from *Henry V*. His son, Henry Brooke, 8th Lord, was an enemy of Essex, who ridiculed him in a note to Cecil in February 1598, the first Falstaffian allusion:

> I pray you commend me allso to Alex. Ratcliff and tell him for newes his sister is maryed to S^r^ Jo. Falstaff.

This was a jest, as Margaret Ratcliffe did not marry Cobham. A similar jest was made in July 1599 when the Countess of Southampton wrote to her husband, Shakespeare's patron, then with Essex on the Irish campaign, describing the birth of an illegitimate son to Cobham:

> Al the nues I can send you that I thinke wil make you mery is that I reade in a letter from London that Sir John Falstaf is by his Mrs Dame Pintpot made father of a goodly milers thum, a boye thats all heade and veri litel body, but this is a secrit.

In 1603 Cobham was arrested for his part in the Raleigh conspiracy, and died in prison in 1618. (See Hotson, *Shakespeare's Sonnets Dated.*)

Cobweb. In *A Midsummer Night's Dream*, one of the fairy attendants of Titania. Bottom promises to make use of him if he cuts his finger.

Cockpit Theatre. In 1616 the roofed Cockpit in Drury Lane was converted into a private theatre, officially called the Phoenix. It was owned by Christopher Beeston, a Chamberlain's man *c.* 1600, but from 1602 to 1619 with Worcester's-Queen Anne's, which company made the Cockpit their headquarters 1617–19, after which it was occupied by Prince Charles's. It was badly damaged by apprentices in a riot on Shrove Tuesday 1617. In their address *To the great Variety of Readers* in F1, Heminge and Condell wrote in 1623, 'And though you be a Magistrate of wit, and sit on the stage at *Black-Friers* or the *Cock-pit*, to arraigne Playes dailie, know, these Playes haue had their triall alreadie.' The first Shakespearean play to be produced when the theatres were reopened in 1660 was *Pericles* at the Cockpit.

Cockpit-at-Court. There was a Cockpit at Whitehall Palace, which was sometimes used as a theatre when the audience was not too big. At Worcester College, Oxford, is a plan and elevation by Inigo Jones for the new Cockpit-at-Court, *c.* 1632: a rectangular building in the Palladian style, with a stage 35 ft wide and 16 ft deep. In 1639 Court performances of *Henry IV*, *Julius Caesar* and *The Merry Wives* were given 'at the Cocpit'.

Cokain, Sir Aston (1608–84). In his *Small Poems of Divers Sorts* (1658) occur verses addressed 'To Mr. Clement Fisher of Wincott':

Shakspeare your *Wincot*-Ale hath much renowned
That fox'd a Beggar so (by chance was found
Sleeping) that there needed not many a word
To make him to believe he was a Lord:
But you affirm (and in it seem most eager)
'Twill make a Lord as drunk as any Beggar.
Bid *Norton* brew such Ale as *Shakspeare* fancies
Did put *Kit Sly* into such Lordly trances:
And let us meet there (for a fit of Gladness)
And drink our selves merry in sober sadness.

Cokain seems to identify the Wincot of Marian Hacket, the fat ale-wife of *The Taming of the Shrew*, with the Wilnecote of north Warwickshire, near which he and Clement Fisher lived. It was almost certainly the tiny Wincot four miles south of Stratford in the parish of Quinton, for on 21 November 1591 'Sara Hacket, the daughter of Robert Hacket' was baptized in Quinton church. (See WILMCOTE.)

Coleridge, Samuel Taylor (1772–1834). His Shakespearean criticism is of the first importance, even though much of it is scrappy and desultory, and some of it downright *un*critical in its adulation. He led the new Romantic school of poets and critics (though, in Germany, A. W. Schlegel disputed the precedence with him) against the classical concept of Shakespeare as 'a wild irregular genius, in whom great faults are compensated by great beauties' and showed that 'the judgment of Shakspeare is commensurate with his genius ... that the true ground of the mistake lies in the confounding mechanical regularity with organic form'; that Shakespeare's form is not mechanically impressed from without, but like natural forms is organic, shaping itself as it develops from within. And he was the first critic to proclaim and demonstrate that Shakespeare was not only a great dramatist, a creator of character, but also a great poet, for the eighteenth century appears to have been almost deaf to the poetry. It is by means of these two new conceptions of Shakespeare, as a great artist and a great poet, that Coleridge communicates to the reader 'those thrills of wonder and exaltation which he has felt in contact with Shakespeare's imaginative work'. The *Biographia Literaria* was published in 1817, *Notes and Lectures upon Shakspeare* posthumously in 1849, but some of the notes were compiled and some of the lectures delivered as early as 1802. (See WORDSWORTH; *Coleridge's Writings on Shakespeare*, ed. T. Hawkes, 1959.)

Collaboration. This was a common practice among Elizabethan dramatists. Sackville and Norton wrote *Gorboduc*, the University Wits sometimes worked together, and for a period of five or six years there was the famous partnership of Beaumont and Fletcher. Of the 130 odd plays that Henslowe notes as bought for the Admiral's and Worcester's between 1597 and 1604 more than half were collaborations, sometimes by as many as five dramatists. Thus:

March 1598. *Earl Goodwin and his three Sons*, by Drayton, Chettle, Dekker, and Wilson.

November 1602. *Lady Jane*, by Chettle, Dekker, Heywood, Smith, and Webster.

October 1599. 'Received by me Thomas

Downton of Philip Henslowe, to pay Mr Monday, Mr Drayton, Mr Wilson, and Hathway, for *The first part of the Lyfe of Sir Jhon Ouldcastell*, and in earnest of the *Second Pte.* for the use of the company, ten pound.' (This play was reprinted by Jaggard in 1619 as 'Written by William Shakespeare'.)

Jonson boasted that he wrote *Volpone* 'in five weeks without a co-adjutor', but in *Sejanus* 'a second Pen had good share', though he re-wrote this himself before publication.

Collaboration was practised, no doubt, because of the big demand for plays, most of which had a very short life, and the collaboration of experienced playwrights, a division of labour applied to literature, would immensely quicken production. They did not write together scene by scene, but after drafting the action one man would contribute the main plot, another the sub-plot, one the tragedy, another the comedy; or one might begin the main themes leaving their development to another, as appears to have been the method of Shakespeare and Fletcher in *Henry VIII*. The only external evidence of collaboration by Shakespeare, however, is at the end of his career, when apparently he worked with Fletcher in *The Two Noble Kinsmen* and the lost *Cardenio*. Internal evidence points to collaboration in *Henry VIII*, and he may have written a scene for *Sir Thomas More*. As Shakespeare wrote entirely for one company and had therefore a steady market, as he was not in need of ready money as so many of his contemporaries were, and as he was a great artist who must have taken a pride in his own work, it is a reasonable assumption that the amount or collaboration in his plays is very limited. (See K. Muir, *Shakespeare as Collaborator*, 1960.)

Collier, John Payne (1789–1883). A journalist working for the *Morning Chronicle* and *The Times*, he was called to the Bar in 1829. His *History of Dramatic Poetry and Annals of the Stage* (1831) led to his appointment as librarian to the Duke of Devonshire, and between 1835 and 1850 he published a number of books on Shakespeare: *New Facts*, *New Particulars* and *Further Particulars*, as well as *Memoirs of Edward Alleyn*, and *Of the Principal Actors in the Plays of Shakespeare*, etc. With Halliwell-Phillipps and others he founded the Shakespeare Society in 1840. In 1852 he announced that a copy of the Second Folio that he had brought for 30s., inscribed 'Tho Perkins his Booke', contained annotations in a 17th-century hand, and these he published as *Notes and Emendations to the Text of Shakespeare's Plays*. Their authenticity was questioned by S. W. Singer in *The Text of Shakespeare Vindicated* (1853), by A. E. Brae in *Literary Cookery* (1855), and in 1859 they were shown by N. E. Hamilton of the British Museum to be forgeries. Not only this, but many passages in his other works have been proved to be fabrications; for example, a petition from the Chamberlain's Men to the Privy Council in reply to that of the inhabitants of Blackfriars who protested against the proposed opening of Burbage's theatre in 1596; a list showing Shakespeare as living in Southwark in 1609; a ballad on the apprentices' riot at the Cockpit in March 1617, and another called *The Inchanted Isle*, suggesting a source for *The Tempest*. He has even been charged by Tannenbaum of forging all the accounts, which include the famous Jacobean Revels Accounts, discovered by Cunningham in 1842, but of this he was almost certainly innocent. It is, however, an example of the doubt and confusion caused by his fabrications. Collier did much valuable work, but on balance he has scarcely made the solution of Shakespearean problems any easier. (See INGLEBY; his *Shakspere Controversy*, 1861, gives the best account of Collier's forgeries.)

Collins, Francis (d. 1617). The solicitor who drew up Shakespeare's will, of which he was one of the overseers and witnesses. He was also a legatee: 'to ffrauncis Collins of the Borough of Warr in the countie of Warr gent thirteene poundes Sixe Shillinges & Eight pence', though this would include his fee. When the will was first drafted in January 1616, Collins was living in Warwick, but moved to Stratford when he was appointed Steward to the Corporation on 8 April, shortly before Shakespeare's death. He himself died the next year.

Collins, John (1741–97), Shakespeare scholar, was born in Cornwall, and became vicar of Ledbury. He defended Capell against Steevens, and on Capell's death in 1781 published his *Notes and Various Readings to Shakespeare* (2 vols.) and *The School of Shakespeare*. Steevens replied by fathering on Collins indecent notes in his 1793 edition of Shakespeare. (See AMNER.)

Collins, John Churton (1848–1908). English critic, was born at Bourton, Glos., and educated at King Edward's, Birmingham, and Balliol, Oxford, in 1904 being appointed Professor of English Literature at Birmingham University. He wrote *Studies in Shakespeare*, *Essays in Poetry and Criticism*, etc. In his essay, *The Porson of Shakespearean Critics*, he vindicated the reputation of the neglected Theobald as a textual critic.

Colman, George (the Elder) (1732–94). Was born in Florence and educated at Westminster and Christ Church, Oxford. He became friendly with Garrick, in 1761 produced his first successful play, *The Jealous Wife*, and in 1768 was elected to the Literary Club. From 1767 to 1774 he was acting manager of Covent Garden, where he produced a number of Shakespearean adaptations, though in *Lear* he returned in part to the original Shakespeare in place of the spurious Tate. In 1777 he bought the Haymarket theatre from Foote, but on the failure of his health in 1789 resigned the management to his son George (the Younger). He wrote about thirty plays, and produced an edition of Beaumont and Fletcher in 1778.

Colonne, Guido delle. Thirteenth-century Sicilian writer who translated Benoît de Saint-Maure's poem, the *Roman de Troie*, into the Latin prose of *Historia destructionis Trojae* (1270–87). Boccaccio used both these for his *Filostrato*, and Chaucer all three for his *Troilus and Criseyde*, which in its turn was Shakespeare's main source for his *Troilus and Cressida*.

Colophon. 'Finishing-stroke'. The final paragraph of a manuscript or early printed book, giving the information which later came to be supplied on the title-page: the author, scribe or printer, date, and place of production. After 1520 with the development of the title-page the colophon, if retained, was reduced to the name of the printer. Colophons are uncommon in plays.

Colvill, Sir John. In *2 Henry IV*, 'a famous rebel', yet he yields to Falstaff without a blow when they meet in Gaultree Forest. Lancaster sends him 'to York, to present execution'. (IV, iii.)

Combe. A family who were neighbours of Shakespeare at Stratford, and with various members of which he had relations, both friendly and business. They came originally from Astley in Worcestershire, acquired the Manor of Crowle, five miles east of Worcester, and became connected with Stratford through the marriage of John Combe i (d. 1550) to Katherine, widow of Adrian Quiney i of Stratford. (See p. 543.)

WILLIAM i (1551–1610) was the second son of John i 'of Stratford on Avon Esq.' and Katherine Quiney. Of the Middle Temple, he practised in London as a lawyer, was M.P. for Warwick, where he lived, in 1592, for the county in 1597, and High Sheriff in 1608. He was twice married, but had no children, It was from this William and his nephew John iii that Shakespeare bought his Welcombe estate in 1602.

JOHN iii (d. 1614) was the third son of William's elder brother, John ii of

Crowle. He was associated with his uncle William i in the sale of the estate to Shakespeare in 1602, and in his will, dated January 1613, he left 'to Mr William Shackspere five pounds'. He died without children, and was buried in the chancel of Stratford church. In 1619 Richard Brathwaite, in his *Remains after Death*, recorded:

An Epitaph vpon one Iohn Combe of Stratford vpon Auen, a notable Vsurer, fastened vpon a Tombe that he had caused to be built in his life time.

Ten in the hundred must lie in his graue,
But a hundred to ten whether God will him haue?
Who then must be interr'd in this Tombe?
Oh (quoth the Diuell) my *John a Combe*.

In September 1634 one Lieutenant Hammond visited Stratford to make his *Short Survey of 26 Counties*, and saw,

A neat Monument of that famous English Poet, Mr William Shakespeere; who was borne heere. And one of an old Gentleman a Batchelor, Mr Coombe, vpon whose name, the sayd Poet, did merrily fann vp some witty, and facetious verses, which time would nott giue vs leaue to sacke vp.

Then,

In 1673 I Robert Dobyns being at Stratford upon Avon & visiting the church there transcribed these two Epitaphs, the first is on William Shakespeare's monument....
the other is upon ye monument of a noted usurer.

Tenn in the hundred here lyeth engraved
A hundred to tenn his soule is now saved
If anny one aske who lyeth in this Tombe
Oh ho quoth the Divell tis my John a Combe.

Since my being at Stratford the heires of Mr Combe have caused these verses to be razed, so yt now they are not legible.

The epitaph is a variation on an old theme, and there is nothing original about it. Brathwaite says it was 'fastened upon a tomb', Dobyns that it was 'upon the monument' from which it had to be 'razed'. Their versions by no means tally. Hammond was the first to ascribe the verses to Shakespeare.

THOMAS i (d. 1609). The second son of John ii of Crowle, and brother of John iii. He bought the sub-lease of part of a parcel of tithes, the other part of which Shakespeare bought in 1605. According to his will of December 1608 he lived at College House in Stratford. On the death of his elder brother Edward in 1597 he had acquired Crowle and the manor of Ryen Clifford near Stratford, and these he left to his elder son, William ii. In 1740 Francis Peck, a Leicestershire clergyman, wrote in his *New Memoirs of Milton*:

Every body knows *Shakespeare's* epitaph for *John a Combe*. And I am told he afterwards wrote another for *Tom a Combe*, alias *Thin-Beard*, brother of the said *John*; & that it was never yet printed. It is as follows.

Thin in *beard*, and thick in purse;
Never man beloved worse:
He went to th' grave with many a curse:
The Devil & He had both one nurse.

This is very sour.

WILLIAM ii (1586–1667), elder son of Thomas i, entered the Middle Temple in 1602, lived at College House, and was High Sheriff in 1616. In 1611 Shakespeare complained that he was not paying his share of the mean rent for the tithes which he held, so endangering his own holding. He was one of the promoters of the Welcombe enclosure (q.v.) in 1614.

THOMAS ii (1589–1657), younger son of Thomas i, entered the Middle Temple in 1608. In his will Shakespeare left 'to mr Thomas Combe my Sword'. At the beginning of the Civil War both he and his brother William were living at Old Stratford. His sister Mary married Edward Lane. (See C. Whitfield, *The Kinship of Thomas Combe II*, 1961.)

Comedies. There are fourteen plays in the comedy section, which is printed first in the Folio. The two parts of *Henry IV* are printed with the Histories, and *Cymbeline*, the last play in the volume, with the Tragedies, where it is called 'The Tragedie of Cymbeline'. *Pericles* was added to F3 in 1664. The Comedies fall into four groups of varying styles and moods, the third one containing the more enigmatic plays, the fourth the romances (the figures in brackets represent the order of printing in the Folio):

1. 1593–7	The Comedy of Errors (5)
	The Taming of the Shrew (11)
	Two Gentlemen of Verona (2)
	Love's Labour's Lost (7)
	A Midsummer Night's Dream (8)
	The Merchant of Venice (9)
2. 1598–1600	Much Ado about Nothing (6)
	The Merry Wives of Windsor (3)
	As You Like It (10)
	Twelfth Night (13)
3. 1602–4	All's Well that Ends Well (12)
	Measure for Measure (4)
4. 1608–11	(Pericles)
	(Cymbeline)
	The Winter's Tale (14)
	The Tempest (1)

(See SS, 8, in which the Comedies are the central theme.)

'COMEDY OF ERRORS.'

WRITTEN: 1593–4. Mentioned by Meres, 1598.

PERFORMED: 1594, 28 December, at Gray's Inn. 1604, at Court: 'By his Maiesties plaiers. On Inosents night. The plaie of Errors. Shaxberd'. (REVELS ACCOUNT.)

REGISTERED: 1623, 8 November. One of the sixteen plays registered by Blount and Jaggard before publishing F1.

PUBLISHED: 1623, F1. 'The Comedie of Errors.' The fifth play in the Comedy section: pp. 85–100. Acts marked. A fair text. The shortest of Shakespeare's plays; according to Wilson an abridgement, and an 'assembled' text; for Greg, from foul papers.

SOURCES: Plautus: the *Menaechmi* (q.v.), for the confusion of twins. The play was translated by William Warner, registered June 1594, and published 1595. As it was dedicated to Lord Hunsdon, patron of the Chamberlain's, Shakespeare may have seen the manuscript.

Plautus: the *Amphitruo*, for the double master-servant theme, and the husband locked out of his own house. There is no known translation that Shakespeare might have used.

Gower: *Confessio Amantis*, for the Aegeon-Aemilia theme, from the story of *Apollonius of Tyre*. (Compare Pericles-Thaisa in *Pericle of Tyre*.)

STAGE HISTORY: 1594, 28 December. 'And after such Sports, a Comedy of Errors (like to *Plautus* his *Menechmus*) was played by the Players.' (GESTA GRAYORUM, q.v.)

1734, Covent Garden: An adaptation called *See if You Like It*.

1741, Drury Lane: A version with Macklin as Dromio of Syracuse.

1790–1850: Various versions produced at Covent Garden.

1855, Sadler's Wells: Phelps returned to Shakespeare's text.

1938, Stratford: Komisarjevsky's production.

Aegeon, a Syracusan merchant, and his wife Aemilia are shipwrecked with their twin baby sons, both called Antipholus, and twin slaves called Dromio. Aegeon, one son, and one slave get back to Syracuse, the other three reach Ephesus, though Aemilia is separated, and thinking she has lost all her family enters a convent of which she becomes abbess.

When eighteen, Antipholus of Syracuse goes with his Dromio in search of his brother; Aegeon has no news, and spends five years looking for him. All arrive at Ephesus on the same day, but as Syracuse and Ephesus are at enmity Aegeon is condemned to death unless he can pay a ransom of a thousand marks by the evening.

Antipholus of Ephesus is married to Adriana, who mistakes A. of S. for her husband, whom she locks out. The two Dromios are also confused. Both Antipholuses are so bewildered that they are in danger of being confined as lunatics; A. of E. appeals to the Duke as he accompanies Aegeon to his execution, and the Abbess intercedes for A. of S. who has taken refuge with her, and the recognition scene follows.

Comicall Gallent, The: or The Amours of Sir John Falstaffe.' A vulgar perversion of *The Merry Wives of Windsor* by John Dennis, produced unsuccessfully at Drury Lane in 1702. In his *Epistle* Dennis records the tradition that Shakespeare wrote his play at Elizabeth's command, 'and she was so eager to see it Acted, that she commanded it to be finished in fourteen days; and was ... very well pleased at the Representation'.

Cominius. In *Coriolanus*, Consul and commander-in-chief of the Roman army against the Volscians. He tells the people how Coriolanus in the campaign 'lurch'd all swords of the garland', and tries to reverse their decision to banish him. When Coriolanus joins the Volscians he pleads with him in vain to halt his projected attack on Rome.

Commedia dell'Arte, or *commedia all'improvviso*, was the popular Italian drama of the 16th and 17th centuries, in which the dialogue was improvised, and the players were stock characters such as the two *zanni* or rascally servants, Harlequin and Brighella, Pulcinello (Punch) the egoist, the pedantic Dottore, the avaricious and cheated Pantalone, and the cowardly braggart the Capitano. How far the *commedia dell'arte* influenced Elizabethan actors and dramatists is still uncertain. Travelling companies of Italian actors were in England in the 16th century, particularly between 1570 and 1580, and many of the characters of Shakespeare's early comedies may easily be identified with those of the *commedia dell'arte*: for example, Holofernes (the Dottore) and many of the others in the sub-plot of *Love's Labour's Lost*, and Parolles, and even Falstaff, may be the Capitano. As regards improvisation, Falstaff asks, 'Shall we have a play *extempore*?'; on the other hand, Valentine in Jonson's *The Case is Altered* (1597) says that English plays are 'all premeditated things'. (See K. M. Lea, *Italian Popular Comedy*, 1934; V. Capocci, *Shakespeare e la commedia dell'arte*, 1950.)

Compositors. The latest phase in textual criticism is the intensive study of the peculiarities of individual Elizabethan-Jacobean compositors. In 1920 (TLS, 3 June) T. Satchell distinguished by their spelling two compositors, A and B, in the setting of *Macbeth*. In his *Printing of the First Folio* (1932) E. E. Willoughby assigned parts of other plays to these two men, *Richard II*, *Julius Caesar*, *Hamlet*, *Tempest*, for example, and concluded that 'there was another pair of compositors at work'. Alice Walker (*Textual Problems*, 1953) demonstrated the greater accuracy of A, and Charlton Hinman (*The Prentice Hand*, 1957) showed that Compositor E, an apprentice incapable of dealing with manuscript copy, set *Titus* and *Romeo* (from Quartos) and certain pages of *Troilus*, *Hamlet*, *Lear* and *Othello*. 'It is already apparent', wrote Greg (*Shakespeare First Folio*, 1955), 'that a study of the habits of compositors will in the future not only influence editorial procedure but may even affect basic assumptions respecting the nature of the text.'

Of the Comedies, Histories, Tragedies in the Folio, the five compositors set approximately the following number of pages:

	C	H	T	Total
A	74	80	40	194
B	143	89	213	445
C	79	22	19	120
D	35½	—	—	35½
E	—	—	71½	71½

E was probably John Leason, bound apprentice 4 November 1622. One of the other four may have been John Shakespeare, son of a Warwickshire butcher, apprenticed to Jaggard in 1610, and took up his freedom in May 1617. (See Hinman, *Printing . . . of the First Folio*, 1963.)

Conceit. An elaborate and often far-fetched comparison, a figure frequently employed by Shakespeare in his early work. Thus Arthur in *King John*:

The iron of itself, though heat red-hot
Approaching near these eyes, would drink my tears
And quench his fiery indignation
Even in the matter of mine innocence;
Nay, after that, consume away in rust,
But for containing fire to harm mine eye.

Concordances, etc. Some of the most important are:

(1768 See R. Warner.)
1790 S. Ayscough, *Index*.
1822 Robert Nares, *Glossary*.

1845 Mrs Cowden Clarke, *Complete Concordance to ... the Dramatic Works*
1859 J. O. Halliwell and T. Wright. (A revision of Nare's *Glossary*.)
1864 A. Dyce, *Glossary*.
1872 Mrs H. H. Furness. *A Concordance to the Poems of Shakespeare*.
1874 A. Schmidt, *Shakespeare Lexicon*.
1895 J. Bartlett, *New and Complete Concordance* (to Plays and Poems).
1911 C. T. Onions, *Shakespeare Glossary*.

Condell, Henry (d. 1627). One of the twenty-six 'Principall Actors' in Shakespeare's plays (see p. 90). He appears in all the actor and official lists up to 1623, with the exception of that of the revival of *The Duchess of Malfi*, *c.* 1621, when his part of the Cardinal was taken by Robinson. The first mention of him is in 1598 in *Every Man in His Humour*, but from his position in the Folio list, 8th, it seems probable that he joined the Chamberlain's at the same time as Shakespeare in 1594, though not then as a sharer. He married in 1599, and had nine children, living first in Almondbury and then in Fulham. Augustine Phillips left him and Shakespeare each 'a thirty shillings peece in gould' (1605), and Shakespeare left Condell 26s. 8d. to buy a ring. In 1623 he and Heminge prepared the First Folio 'to keepe the memory of so worthy a Friend, & Fellow aliue, as was our Shakespeare'. He was one of the original housekeepers of the Blackfriars theatre (1608), and by 1612 had acquired shares in the Globe, which he left to his widow. He was buried in St Mary Almondbury 29 December 1627. (See SALISBURY, SIR HENRY.)

Conrade. In *Much Ado*, one of the followers of Don John, whom he promises to help in the deception of Claudio, though his fellow Borachio is the main agent. Conrade was not present at the deception itself, for it is while Borachio is telling him of it that they are arrested by the Watch. After calling Dogberry an ass, he does not speak.

Constable of France. 'Charles Delabreth'. In *Henry V* he tells the French King of Henry's new reputation, yet urges attacking the English as they retreat. He is confident of victory before Agincourt, jesting and boasting with the Dauphin and the other lords, but is killed in the battle.

Constance. In *King John*, mother of Arthur, whose claim to the English throne on behalf of her son is supported by France and Austria. Their temporary defection drives her almost distracted, and she goes mad indeed when John defeats her allies and captures Arthur. In IV, ii a messenger tells John that 'the Lady Constance in a frenzy died'. (She was the daughter of the Duke of Brittany, and married twice after the death of her first husband, Geoffrey Plantagenet, Arthur's father. She died in 1201.)

'Contention Between ... Lancaster and York.' See 2, 3 HENRY VI.

Continuous Copy. The theory that a dramatist's original manuscript, after being licensed, became the promptbook; was annotated by the bookkeeper; over a number of years was cut, expanded, revised and rewritten; and sometimes sent as copy to the printer. The theory was developed by Dover Wilson, though he has modified his views. It is improbable that an author's foul papers were used as the promptbook, such altered copy would be too confused for a printer, and though there is evidence that Shakespeare sometimes revised his work (e.g. *All's Well*) it is unlikely that he rewrote much during his active career.

Cooke, Alexander. One of the 'Principall Actors' in Shakespeare's plays (see p. 91). Apparently he was first apprenticed to Heminge. He is not in the King's Men patent of May 1603, nor in the Account of the Master of the Wardrobe of March 1604. Yet in the winter of 1603 he was a 'principall Tragœdian' in *Sejanus*, and in May 1605 is mentioned by Phillips in his will as 'my fellowe'. Presumably, therefore, he became a sharer in 1604, when the number of Grooms was increased from nine to twelve, after having served as a hired man. He occurs regularly in the actor lists until 1612–13. He was married, and had four children, for whom he appointed 'my master Hemings' and Condell trustees in his will made shortly before his death in February 1614.

Cooke, George Frederick (1756–1811). Actor, was born in London, and made his name in the part of Othello in Dublin. After 1800 he played many of Shakespeare's leading parts in London, Falstaff, Henry VIII, Shylock, Richard III, Jaques, becoming a rival of Kemble, whom, with Mrs Siddons, he joined at Covent Garden. Towards the end of his career he spoiled his acting by his intemperance. He died in New York.

Cope, Sir Walter (d. 1614), politician and antiquary, was knighted in 1603 and became Chamberlain of the Exchequer. At Kensington he built Cope Castle, later renamed Holland House. In the winter of 1604 he wrote to Robert Cecil, Viscount Cranborne,

> I have sent and bene all thys morning huntyng for players Juglers & Such kinde of Creaturs, but fynde them harde to finde, wherfore Leavinge notes for them to seeke me, Burbage ys come, & Sayes ther ys no new playe that the quene hath not seene, but they have Revyved an olde one, Cawled *Loves Labore lost*, which for wytt & mirthe he sayes will please her excedingly. And thys ys apointed to be playd to Morowe night at my Lord of Sowthamptons, unless yow send a wrytt to Remove the Corpus Cum Causa to your howse in Strande. Burbage ys my messenger Ready attendyng your pleasure.

From a letter of Dudley Carleton to John Chamberlain it is clear that the performance was given, either at Southampton's or Cranborne's, in the second week of January 1605.

Copy is the manuscript or printed text from which a compositor sets the type. The copy from which the good Quartos could have been printed was: either *foul papers* or their transcript by the author or another; or *prompt-book* or its transcript. (*Richard III* is exceptional.) For the Folio the good Quartos were also available. Thus, Q *Love's Labour's Lost* was printed from foul papers, and F from Q. Often, however, copy was more complex: many F texts being set from Quartos collated with the prompt-book, so that Q and F texts sometimes vary widely.

Copy probably used for Quartos and Folio is tabulated in Appendix I, though it must be emphasized that, in the words of Greg, 'all are conjectural'. The following is a summary. For the 14 good Quartos the main copy was probably:

10 – Shakespeare's foul papers
3 – transcript of foul papers
1 – a good memorial reconstruction

For the 36 plays of the Folio:

14 – the good Quartos
8 – foul papers
4 – Shakespeare's transcript of foul papers
3 – Crane's transcript of foul papers
7 – prompt-book or its transcript

It will be seen that all but one of the 14 good Quartos were printed from Shakespeare's original scripts, his foul papers, or a transcript of them. For the Folio the 14 good Quartos were used; 15 plays were set from foul papers or a transcript of them, and the remaining 7 from the prompt-book or its transcript.

Characteristic of foul papers used as copy are: confusions and duplications in the printed text; inconsistent designation of characters and substitution of an actor's name: indefinite and explanatory stage-directions. Characteristic of prompt-book copy: preliminary warnings for actors and properties to be ready; an actor's name duplicating that of a character. (See TEXTUAL CRITICISM; TRANSCRIPTS; ASSEMBLED TEXTS; PARALLEL TEXTS; Greg, *First Folio*; Alice Walker, *Textual Problems*.)

Copyright. Until the Act of 1709 there was no copyright in the modern meaning of the word: an author's rights in his own work. In Shakespeare's time copyright was concerned not with authors but stationers (printers, publishers, booksellers) who had the right to print, or have printed for them, any work in their possession, provided they had ecclesiastical or other official licence. (Cf. George Wither's *Schollers Purgatory*, 1624: 'If he get any written Coppy into his powre, likely to be vendible, whether the Author be willing or no, he will publish it.') This right was conferred by the Stationers' Company (q.v.). (See DERELICT PLAYS; Greg, *First Folio*, Chap. 2.)

Corbet, Richard (1582–1635). A friend of Ben Jonson and of other dramatists, he became Bishop of Oxford in 1628, being translated to Norwich in 1632. He wrote a number of poems, in one of which, *Iter Boreale*, he describes a visit to the scene of the battle at Bosworth:

Mine Host was full of Ale and History ...
Besides what of his knowledge he can say,
He had authentic notice from the Play ...
For when he would have said, King Richard died,
And call'd, a horse, a horse; he *Burbage* cried.

Cordelia. In *King Lear* (q.v.), the youngest daughter of Lear.

Corin. In *As You Like It*, an old shepherd. (Coridon in Lodge's *Rosalynde*.)

'CORIOLANUS.'

WRITTEN: 1607–8.

PERFORMED: No record of an early performance.

REGISTERED: 1623, 8 November. One of the sixteen plays registered by Blount and Jaggard before publishing F1.

PUBLISHED: 1623, F1. 'The Tragedy of Coriolanus.' The second play in the Tragedy section (including the inserted *Troilus and Cressida*); pp. 1–30. Acts marked, and 1, i. A faulty text, with many mislineations. Set up from foul papers.

SOURCES: North's translation of Plutarch's *Life of Coriolanus*. Camden: *Remaines* (1605) gives a more detailed version of the fable of the belly and the members than Plutarch or Livy.

STAGE HISTORY: 1682, Drury Lane: *Coriolanus, The Ingratitude of a Commonwealth*. A grisly political adaptation by Nahum Tate.

1719, Drury Lane: *The Invader of his Country, or the Fatal Resentment*. John Dennis's adaptation, driven off the stage after three performances.

1754, Drury Lane: Garrick produced Shakespeare's text with Mrs Pritchard as Volumnia.

In return for his exploits at the siege and capture of the Volscian town of Corioli, Caius Marcius, a Roman general, is rewarded with the surname Coriolanus and offered the consulship. But his arrogance and contempt for the common people, encouraged by the jealous tribunes, so infuriate the masses that he is banished. In revenge he joins his former opponent Aufidius, and leads the Volscian army against Rome. His old friends, Cominius and Menenius, vainly plead with him to spare the city, but eventually he succumbs to the entreaties of his mother, Volumnia, who, with his wife Virgilia, and son, comes to his tent. Coriolanus returns with spoils and an advantageous peace to Corioli where, however, he is murdered by conspirators under Aufidius, who is jealous of his success and popularity.

Cornelius. 1. In *Hamlet*, a courtier who, with Voltimand, is sent by Claudius to the King of Norway in a successful attempt to stop the threatened invasion of Fortinbras.

2. A doctor in *Cymbeline*. The Queen asks him for poison, but he rightly suspects her motives, and gives her a drug that makes a 'show of death' only. It is this that Imogen takes when she feels ill.

Cornet. In Shakespeare's day, a leather-covered wooden instrument with finger-holes, blown like a horn or trumpet. It was softer in tone than the trumpet, which it may have replaced in the private theatres.

Cornwall, Duke of. In *King Lear*, the husband of Regan. He puts Kent, Lear's messenger, in the stocks, and orders Gloucester to shut the doors on the distracted King out in the storm. When Gloucester helps Lear, Cornwall puts out his eyes, but is killed by one of the servants. (In *King Leir* he is Gonorill's husband.)

Coryat, Thomas (*c.* 1577–1617). Traveller, wit, member of the Mermaid Tavern circle, and author of *Coryats Crudities*, in which he tells how in Venice he 'saw women act, a thing I never saw before ... and they performed it with as good a grace ... as ever I saw any masculine actor'. (See ACTRESSES; JACKSON, JOHN.)

Costard. In *Love's Labour's Lost*, a clown, and rival of Don Armado for the love of Jaquenetta. He acts as messenger, confusing letters from Berowne to Rosaline, and Armado to Jaquenetta. In the interlude of The Nine Worthies he plays 'Pompion the Great'.

Costume. The finery of the Elizabethan actors 'sooping it in their glaring satten sutes' was one of the main targets of contemporary satire and abuse, and that they wore 'sumptuous dresses' on the stage we know from the letter of Orazio Busino written in 1617 (see AUDIENCE), while the players in Greene's *Groatsworth of Wit* (1592) tell Roberto that his 'very share in playing apparel will not be sold for two hundred pounds', though this is doubtless an exaggeration. We have the drawing by Henry Peacham of a production of *Titus Andronicus* in 1595, and from this, Henslowe's inventories of apparel, other contemporary references, and 18th-century prints of actors, Allardyce Nicoll (*The Development of the Theatre*) comes to the conclusion that, while most of the actors wore Elizabethan costume, there were special costumes for (i) Roman and Grecian characters, (ii) certain abnormal characters such as deities, ghosts, and even Falstaff, and (iii) Eastern characters. Thus the first entries under 'The Enventary of the Clownes Sewtes and Hermetes Sewtes, with dievers other sewtes' in Henslowe's 'Booke of the Inventory of the goods of my Lord Admeralles men, tacken the 10 of Marche in the yeare 1598' illustrate these three classes:

> *Item*, j senetores gowne, j hoode, and 5 senetores capes.
> *Item*, j sewtte for Nepton; Fierdrackes sewtes for Dobe.
> *Item*, iiij genesareyes [janizaries] gownes, and iiij torchberers sewtes.

Such costumes were conventional rather than historically correct: thus a breastplate and a plumed helmet represented a Roman, while baggy trousers and a scimitar suggested an Oriental (see the figures on the left of the Peacham drawing). These conventional costumes were retained by the 18th-century stage. (See PLANCHÉ; PLATTER; M. C. Linthicum, *Costume in the Drama of Shakespeare*, 1936.)

Cotes, Thomas. The printer of the Second Folio, 1632, for Robert Allot and William Aspley, and of John Benson's edition of Shakespeare's *Poems*, 1640. Thomas and his brother Richard took over the Jaggard business on Isaac Jaggard's death in 1627, used their devices, and were partners until Thomas's death in 1641.

Cotgrave, Randle (d. 1634), lexicographer, was from Cheshire, educated at St John's, Cambridge, and became secretary to Lord Burghley. His French-English Dictionary (1611), like the Italian one of Florio, is valuable for its explanation of 17th-century words, and, therefore, for the editing of Shakespeare's plays. (See LIGHTING.)

Cotton, William. Bookseller, 1602–9, at the Long Shop, Ludgate. Apprenticed to William Leake in 1594, he became a freeman of the Stationers' Company in 1602, in which year he registered *Thomas Lord Cromwell*, though Q1, 1602, was published by William Jones.

Court, Alexander. In *Henry V*, one of the soldiers to whom the King talks on the night before Agincourt (IV, i).

Court, Thomas. See BIRTHPLACE.

Court Performances. The period of the Court Revels was normally from All Saints (1 November) to the beginning of Lent, but the plays were most concentrated during the twelve days of Christmas; excluding Christmas Day itself, there were nearly always plays on the feasts of St Stephen, St John, and the Innocents (26-7-8 December), on New Year's Day, and on Twelfth Night (6 January). Then would come a play at Candlemas (2 February) and a few more before the beginning of Lent. There were far more Court performances under James I and Anne of Denmark than under Elizabeth, the Revels sometimes extending until after Easter. Between 1594 and 1603 Shakespeare's company, much the most popular, gave 32 Court performances; from 1603 to 1616 they gave 177.

The plays were given in the great Hall of one of the palaces: Whitehall, Greenwich, Hampton Court, Richmond or Windsor, though at Whitehall they might be held in the Banqueting House, the Great Chamber or even the Cockpit-at-Court. The Master of the Revels was responsible for the scenery (though not for the erection of the stage itself or the seating of the spectators), for the costume, and the selection of the plays, normally from those acted in the public theatres where the players 'practised' for their Court performances. There was, therefore, no cleavage between the courtly and popular play, but a healthy partnership between the two. Most of our information comes from the Accounts of the Revels Office, and from those of the Treasurer of the Chamber who was responsible for paying the expenses incurred by the Master of the Revels. The fee for a Court performance had been fixed by Henry VIII at 10 marks (£6 13s. 4d.), but by 1575 this had come to be £10, the extra £3 6s. 8d. being 'by way of special reward' if the sovereign were present.

Court plays in the 16th century seem to have been staged with curtains and multiple setting, that is, with a number of 'houses' constructed of lath and painted canvas to represent different localities. This is quite clear in Lyly's *Campaspe* (1584), a Court play by the Blackfriars Children, with its simultaneous staging of a palace, a shop and Diogenes' tub. *The Comedy of Errors*, performed at Gray's Inn, could easily be staged in this way. Apparently Court plays were sometimes staged in the middle of the Hall, 'in the round'. Thus, when *Gorboduc* was presented at Whitehall in 1561, the hall was 'to be furnished with skaffolds to sit upon ... on each side', and for the Revels of 1601, the Office of Works was responsible for 'framing and setting up a broade stage in the middle of the haule'. In the 17th century, with the influence of Inigo Jones and the masque, productions became more elaborate and spectacular. (See STAGING; RARE TRIUMPHS OF LOVE AND FORTUNE; Hotson, *The First Night of 'Twelfth Night'*.)

Covell, William (d. 1614), was educated at Christ's, Cambridge, a Fellow of Queen's, sub-dean of Lincoln, and Fellow of King James's College at Chelsea. One of the first printed mentions of Shakespeare's name occurs in a side-note in *Polimanteia*, a tract printed at Cambridge in 1595, purporting to distinguish between true and false astrology. In *The Centurie of Prayse* it was attributed to William Clarke, but now to William Covell, as there is a copy with his name, instead of W. C., to the Epistle. The note reads, 'All praiseworthy. Lucrecia Sweet Shakspeare. Eloquent Gaveston. Wanton Adonis. Watsons heyre.'

Covent Garden Theatre. The site is the old 'convent garden' of the Abbey of Westminster, laid out in the first half of the 17th century by Inigo Jones as a square with a piazza on two sides. By the middle of the century it was becoming a market for vegetables, fruit, and flowers. The first Covent Garden theatre was opened by John Rich, its first manager, in 1732. The Licensing Act of 1737 confined the 'legitimate drama' to Covent Garden, Drury Lane, and the Haymarket until 1843. The first theatre was burned down in September 1808, and its successor in 1856. The present theatre was designed by E. M. Barry and opened in 1858. John Philip Kemble became manager of the first theatre in 1803 and was nearly ruined by the fire of 1808. Macready was manager 1837–9.

Cowley, Richard. One of the twenty-six 'Principall Actors' in Shakespeare's plays (see p. 91). He played in Tarlton's *Seven Deadly Sins*, *c.* 1590, and though not mentioned in the licence to travel of the Strange-Admiral combination of 1593, Alleyn refers to him in a letter to his wife on 1 August: 'I reseved your letter att Bristo by Richard Couley'. He may have joined the Chamberlain's, as a sharer, on their formation in 1594, but does not appear in any of their actor-lists, his first mention being as payee with Heminge for Court performances in the winter of 1600–1. He was a sharer in 1603, but appears never to have been a housekeeper. Malone says he 'appears to have been an actor of a low class, having performed the part of Verges in *Much Ado About Nothing*'. This we know from the speech-prefix that has crept into the text in II, ii. Kempe played Dogberry. Phillips left Cowley a legacy in 1605. He married, had four children, and died in 1619.

Craig, Gordon (1872–1968), son of Ellen Terry, was educated at Bradfield College and Heidelberg. He became an actor, producer, scenic and costume designer, and in Florence, where he went to live, studied and wrote on the relation between the English and Continental theatres. Like William Poel in England, and Adolphe Appia and Georg Fuchs abroad, he returned to simplified settings for Shakespeare, on a stage that approximated to the Elizabethan. Granville-Barker put many of Craig's ideas into practice in England, and his has been one of the greatest influences on modern stage design. Created C.H. 1956.

Craig, Hardin (1875–1968). American scholar, Professor of English in the University of Missouri. Author of *The Enchanted Glass: the Elizabethan Mind in Literature*, *An Interpretation of Shakespeare*, etc. His approach was historical: 'We must make ourselves at home in the Renaissance.'

Craik, George Lillie (1798–1866). Born at Kennoway, Fifeshire, but went to London in 1824 and devoted himself to literature, becoming Professor of History and English Literature at Queen's College, Belfast, in 1849. He was an original member of the Council of the Shakespeare Society founded by J. P. Collier in 1840, and in 1856 published *The English of Shakespeare*, one of the early studies of Shakespeare's versification.

Crane, Ralph. A professional scribe who was sometimes employed as copyist by the King's Men after Shakespeare's death. His work was identified by F. P. Wilson (*Lib.* Sept. 1926, VII). He transcribed Middleton's *Game at Chess*, in which the names of all the characters appearing in a scene are massed in the opening stage-direction. Certain plays of Shakespeare, notably *Two Gentlemen* and *Merry Wives*, have similar massed entries, and it seems probable that Crane transcribed the first four plays and *The Winter's Tale* for the Folio. (See ASSEMBLED TEXTS.)

Cranmer, Thomas (1489–1556). In *Henry VIII*, to Wolsey 'a heretic', to Norfolk 'a worthy fellow'. He secures the King's divorce from Katharine, is made Archbishop of Canterbury and crowns Anne. When charged with heresy by Gardiner and other members of the Council, the king intervenes and makes Gardiner embrace him and asks him to be godfather to Elizabeth.

Creede, Thomas. Printer, one of the best of his time, at the Catherine Wheel in Thames Street, 1593–1600, and at the Eagle and Child in the Old Exchange, 1600–17. In 1616 Bernard Alsop became his partner and took over Creede's business on his retirement or death in 1617. Creede printed:

2 Henry VI, Q1, 1594 (a 'bad' Quarto).
Richard III, Qq 2, 3, 4, 5, 1598, 1602–5–12.
Romeo and Juliet, Q2, 1599 (the 'good' Quarto).
Henry V, Qq 1, 2, 1600–2 ('bad' Quartos).
Merry Wives, Q1, 1602 (a 'bad' Quarto).

In 1594 Creede entered in the Stationers' Register '*The lamentable Tragedie of Locrine*', which he published in 1595 as 'Newly ... corrected, By W.S.' In 1605 he printed for Nathaniel Butter, without registration, '*The London Prodigall* ... By William Shakespeare.'

Creizenach, Wilhelm (1851–1919). German critic and historian of the theatre; Professor at Cracow. His work includes *Schauspiele der englischen Komödianten*, and *Geschichte des neueren Dramas*, the fourth volume of which is translated as *The English Drama in the Age of Shakespeare*. He traces the relationship between the English and European drama, finding, for example, a possible model for the English theatre in the mid-16th-century theatres of Ghent and Antwerp.

Cressida. In *Troilus and Cressida* (q.v.) daughter of Calchas.

Criticism. Criticism of Shakespeare by his contemporaries, such as it is, is generally brief and either affected or conventional, of the 'honey-tongued', 'honey-flowing', 'mellifluous' variety. Ben Jonson's elegy in the Folio is a noble tribute, though a few years earlier he had told Drummond that 'Shaksperr wanted Arte'. The first considered criticism of Shakespeare is that of Dryden, himself a dramatist, and though he was generous in his praise of 'the divine Shakespeare', he too found that he wanted art, that 'the fury of his fancy often transported him beyond the bounds of judgment'.

Dryden died in 1700, but the burden of 18th-century criticism is much the same. It was the age of Shakespearean editors and textual critics, from Rowe to Malone, and Pope and Johnson both produced editions of his plays with important critical Prefaces in which the triumphs of imagination are judicially balanced against the failures of judgement. But as Dryden had defended Shakespeare against the pedantic neo-classicism of Rymer, so did Johnson defend him against the arid excesses of Voltaire and the French school, for whom Shakespeare was little more than a 'bouffon'.

It was Coleridge who, at the beginning of the 19th century, exploded this conception of Shakespeare as 'a wild irregular genius', by showing that his judgement was equal to his genius, and that his 'irregularity' was *organic* form, not a mechanical impression from without. And with Coleridge and the Romantic critics, Hazlitt and Lamb, came for the first time an appreciation of Shakespeare's divinest gift, his poetry. In Germany, Lessing, Goethe and Schlegel, in Russia Pushkin, and in France Hugo, rejected 17th- and 18th-century French models and turned for inspiration to Shakespeare.

Later 19th-century critics, seizing on Coleridge's thesis that Shakespeare's irregularity was only another aspect of his genius, began to lose themselves in superlatives and 'O altitudo', and became either exclamatory like Swinburne, or sentimental and domestic like Dowden. What Croce calls 'objectivistic' criticism became fashionable, 'detaching the characters from the creative centre of the play and transferring them into a pretended objective field, as though they were made of flesh and blood'. The finest example of this school is A. C. Bradley's *Shakespearean Tragedy*, 1904.

The 20th century has changed all this. In 1906 appeared Lytton Strachey's essay on *Shakespeare's Final Period*, upsetting Furnivall's and Dowden's cosy conception of Shakespeare's serenity and bliss 'by his quiet Avon's side'. In 1907 came the *Shakespeare* of Sir Walter Raleigh, who turned from the excesses of the exclamatory school to the 'cool and manly utterances of Dryden, Johnson and Pope'; and in the same year the American E. E. Stoll published *The Ghosts*. Stoll, whose best-known work is *Art and Artifice in Shakespeare* (1933), was the leader of a new 'realist' school of criticism, whose aim was the reverse of 19th-century 'objectivism': that is, to place Shakespeare and his characters in their real environment, on the Elizabethan stage, an aim stimulated by the discovery of De Witt's sketch of the Swan theatre. Levin Schücking pursued a similar 'realist' line in his *Character Problems in Shakespeare's Plays* (1922). As a producer, Granville-Barker was necessarily concerned with placing Shakespeare's characters in their real environment, but in his *Prefaces to Shakespeare* the theatrical approach was an approach only, a means to an end, the end being the revelation and interpretation of Shakespeare's plays.

The original realist, or theatrical, school of criticism inevitably developed into a broader historical school. In *Shakespeare's Problem Comedies* (1931) W. W. Lawrence analysed the medieval elements surviving in these plays, and in 1936 another American, Hardin Craig, published his *Enchanted Glass: the Elizabethan Mind in Literature*. Here was the fully developed historical approach that sought to relate Shakespeare to his age as a whole, instead of merely to his theatre; 'We must make ourselves at home in the Renaissance' if we are to understand him. This was followed in 1942 by Theodore Spencer's *Shakespeare and the Nature of Man* and in 1943 by E. M. W. Tillyard's *Elizabethan World Picture*, illustrating the belief in a divine natural order.

Meanwhile there had been a revolt against the realist school, which seemed to be the negation of Jonson's claim that Shakespeare was 'not of an age, but for all time'. In 1930 Lascelles Abercrombie had made his 'Plea for the Liberty of Interpreting', and in the same year Wilson Knight put it into practice in his *Wheel of Fire*. His interpretation is in terms of symbolism instead of character, a Shakespeare play being a development of a central idea to which everything else is immediately related. Similarly, for L. C. Knights in his satirical essay directed against Bradley, *How Many Children had Lady Macbeth?* (1933), 'the only profitable approach to Shakespeare is a consideration of his plays as dramatic poems, of his use of language to obtain a total emotional response'. The poetry, or rather the imagery, is the important thing, and in *Shakespeare's Imagery* (1935) Caroline Spurgeon reduced its study to a science, while Wolfgang Clemen in *Shakespeares Bilder* (1936) traced the dramatic function of the imagery and its relation to character.

This close analysis of the plays and search for a pattern was largely inspired by the work of T. S. Eliot, and had much in common with the new Cambridge school of criticism led by I. A. Richards and F. R. Leavis, the arch-anti-Bradleyite. The 'interpreters' also received support from Italy and France, from N. Orsini in *La Critica Shakespeariana* (1946) who protested against a Shakespeare who is merely a product of his age and not of his own genius, and from Henri Fluchère, whose *Shakespeare* (1948) is an admirable introduction to modern criticism.

Yet there were still those who supported Bradley: Dover Wilson, T. M. Parrott, John Palmer and George Gordon, for example, and H. B. Charlton attacked the citadel of Cambridge itself when in 1946 he delivered the Clark Lectures with the provocative title of *Shakespearian Tragedy*, insisting on the importance of characterization in the plays. And the realist, historical school was still vocal, Lily B. Campbell tracing a political instead of an aesthetic pattern in *Shakespeare's 'Histories': Mirrors of Elizabethan Policy* (1947).

The psychology of Freud and Jung is a new weapon in the hands of those who support the classical approach by way of character, and as early as 1910 Ernest Jones had analysed Hamlet and found him suffering from an Oedipus complex. S. L. Bethell applied psychology to the audience in *Shakespeare and the Popular Dramatic Tradition* (1944), to which T. S. Eliot wrote an illuminating preface, showing that poetry reveals, beneath the vacillating superficial character, the indomitable unconscious will. J. I. M. Stewart developed this theme in his *Character and Motive in Shakespeare* (1949), a book that attempted to reconcile Bradleyism with the school of Knight.

The gap has narrowed a little. As early as 1946 Knights confessed that his initial ridicule of Bradley sprang from 'the exhilaration of attacking what was still the orthodox academic view of Shakespeare', and in 1955 admitted that the meaning of a play does not reside 'exclusively or even predominantly in the imagery'. Yet characters are 'persons' and apparently little more than symbols. For Leavis in 1952 Bradley was 'still a very potent and mischievous influence'; in *Shakespeare: The Last Phase* (1954) D. A. Traversi found a symbolic unity in the romances; in *The Sovereign Flower* (1958) Wilson Knight reproclaimed his original manifesto of thirty years before, with its emphasis on symbolism, and in *Some Shakespearean Themes* (1959) Knights subordinates 'character' and 'plot' to the poetry, its imagery and symbols.

There have been protests; thus Stewart in 1949: 'The New Bowdlers ... who would give us not merely *Hamlet* without the Prince but the Complete Works without their *dramatis personae*', and ten years later D. J. Enright: 'the effort to remove the barriers which imagery-hunting, excessively ingenious "ambiguity" studies and the taste for abstract "symbolism" have in their turn set up between the author and his audience. Perhaps a more overt concern with character and realistic motivation – but chastened by the work of the great critics of the past forty years – will be part of the means to this.'

The result of this conflict between the old and the new criticism has been a lack of coherence, a fragmentation, and an extravagant liberty of interpreting, an attempt to find whatever the critic wishes to find in the plays of Shakespeare. Much of this analysis has been very valuable, but the time has come for the synthesis to which Una Ellis-Fermor looked forward in 1950. There must be a compromise, for the conflict is an unreal one; character and poetry are equally important, for they are the same thing: the poetry is the characters, the characters are the poetry – the words in which they talk themselves alive. Perhaps the great work of synthesis and reconciliation will appear, appropriately, in 1964. (See F. E. Halliday, *Shakespeare and his Critics*, revised edition 1958; SS, 4.)

Croce, Benedetto (1866–1952). Italian philosopher and literary critic. His criticism of Shakespeare in *Ariosto, Shakespeare and Corneille* is an analysis of his poetical personality, of the character and development of his art, and a protest against the irrelevance of the biographical, objectivistic, exclamatory and realistic schools of Shakespearean criticism. (*Shakespeare* was published separately in 1943 with an introduction by N. Orsini.)

Cromwell, Thomas. In *Henry VIII*, a servant of Wolsey. He appears in the long III, ii, and serves as audience for Wolsey's farewell to all his greatness. As secretary to the Council he defends Cranmer against Gardiner's vicious attack. (Lord Cromwell 1536, Earl of Essex 1539, executed for high treason 1540. (See THOMAS LORD CROMWELL.)

Cross Keys Inn. One of the City inns used by the players before the erection of the permanent theatres in the suburbs after 1576, and for the next twenty years mainly as winter quarters, until the 'putting down' of playhouses within the City in 1596. Yet James Burbage, who had built the Theatre in 1576, was arrested for a debt of £5 in the summer of 1579 'as he came down Gracious [Gracechurch] Street towards the Cross Keys there to a play'. Not only plays were to be seen there, for Tarlton, who died in 1588, saw Banks's performing horse at 'the Crosse-Keyes in Gracious streete'. In November 1589 Edward Tilney, Master of the Revels, ordered 'the staie of all playes within the Cittie' because he 'did vtterly dislike the same'. The Lord Mayor told the Admiral's and Strange's Men 'to forbere playinge', yet Strange's 'in a very Contemptuous manner ... went to the Crosse keys and played that afternoon'. Strange's, recently reorganized as the Chamberlain's, were using the Cross Keys as their winter quarters in 1594, for on 8 October Lord Chamberlain Hunsdon wrote to the Lord Mayor,

> Where my now company of players have been accustomed ... to play this winter time within the City at the Cross Keys in Gracious Street. These are to require and pray your Lo .... to permit and suffer them so to do; the which I pray you rather to do for that they have undertaken to me that, where heretofore they began not their plays till towards four o'clock, they will now begin at two, and have done between four and five, and will not use any drums or trumpets at all for the calling of people together, and shall be contributories to the poor of the parish where they play according to their habilities.

They could have had only one more winter season at the Inn.

Crosse, Samuel. One of the twenty-six 'Principall Actors' in Shakespeare's plays (see p. 91), yet this is the only reference to him. He was not one of the nine sharers and Grooms of the Chamber in the patent for the King's Men of May 1603, but in the summer of 1604 the number of Grooms was increased to twelve, and it may have been then that Lowin, Crosse and Cooke became sharers, their names occurring together in that order in the Folio list. Crosse probably died before May 1605 and was succeeded by Tooley, who was a 'fellow' in Phillips's will of that date.

Crown Tavern. See D'AVENANT.

Crowne, John (*c.* 1640–1703). A writer of heroic tragedies and political comedies, whose patrons were Rochester and Charles II. His best play is *Sir Courtly Nice*. After the Popish Plot he combined the last two acts of *2 Henry VI* with *3 Henry VI* in an adaptation directed against the Whigs, called *The Misery of Civil War*, and followed this with another political adaptation of the first three acts of *Part 2*. The plays were produced at Dorset Garden in 1680 and 1681.

Cumberland, Richard (1732–1811). Educated at Westminster, and Trinity, Cambridge, he held a number of minor political posts and wrote numerous plays, for the most part sentimental comedies, of which the best are *The Brothers* and *The West-Indian*. He is satirized by Sheridan in *The Critic* as Sir Fretful Plagiary. In 1771 his adaptation of *Timon of Athens* was produced at Drury Lane.

Cunningham, Peter (1816–69). Fourth of the five sons of Allan Cunningham, the Scottish poet. The youngest, Francis, was the editor of Marlowe, Massinger and Jonson. Peter wrote *The Life of Drummond of Hawthornden* and a *Handbook of London*. He was treasurer of the London and Stratford Committees that bought the 'Birthplace' in 1847. In 1842 he published for the Shakespeare Society *Extracts from the Accounts of the Revels at Court*, including the highly informative Original Accounts for 1604–5 and 1611–12, the only extant ones for the Jacobean period. Shortly before his death he stated that he had found them, separate from the Elizabethan Accounts, 'under the vaults of Somerset House', but when they came into the hands of the British Museum their authenticity was questioned. However, as there is evidence that Malone, who died in 1812, knew of the 1604–5 Accounts, or a similar record, it seems certain that they are genuine. (See MUSGRAVE.)

Curan. In *King Lear*, a shadowy character who appears only in II, i (unless he is also the 'Gentleman' of III, i), when he tells Edmund that Cornwall and Regan are coming to Gloucester's castle, and of rumours of wars between Cornwall and Albany.

Curio. In *Twelfth Night*, a gentleman attending on the Duke. He speaks only four times, and is of no importance in the action.

Curle, Edward. A barrister of the Middle Temple. He seems to have told the story recorded by John Manningham (q.v.) in his *Diary*, 13 March 1602, of Shakespeare, Burbage, and the 'citizen'. Manningham's writing of his informant's name is indistinct and has been variously interpreted, but Curle was his authority for other entries.

Curtain Theatre. It stood just north of Bishopsgate and to the south of the Theatre, in Shoreditch. In his description of the liberty of Holywell, Stow records in his *Survey* of 1598, 'and near thereunto are builded two public houses for the acting and show of Comedies, Tragedies, and Histories, for recreation. Whereof the one is called the Courtein, the other the Theatre: both standing on the Southwest side towards the field.' It is shown in the recently discovered 'View of the Cittye of London from the North' as a three-storey circular building with a hut over the tiring-house. (See Hotson, *Shakespeare's Wooden O*.) The name was derived from a piece of land called Curtain Close, on which a number of houses were built in Elizabeth's reign. The Curtain theatre is first mentioned in 1577 by John Northbrooke in his *Treatise wherein ... plays ... are reproved*, as one of 'those places also, which are made up and builded for such plays and enterludes, as the Theatre and Curtain is'. As the first playhouse was James Burbage's Theatre built in 1576, the Curtain must have followed soon afterwards. Presumably it was built by Henry Laneman, who rented property on Curtain Close in 1581, and in 1585 made a seven-year agreement with Burbage to pool the profits of the two theatres, the Curtain becoming an 'easer' to the Theatre. Little is known about which companies used the Curtain, but it is almost certain that the Chamberlain's were there from the re-opening of the theatres in the autumn of 1597 after the inhibition of the summer, until their occupation of the Globe two years later (see SCOURGE OF VILLANIE). In 1603 it became the home of the Worcester's-Queen's Men (see SHIRLEY, ANTHONY), though by 1609 they had moved permanently to the Red Bull. It is last mentioned in 1627. (See PLATTER.)

Curtains. There are no curtains in the De Witt drawing of the Swan theatre, though there are hangings at the back of the *Roxana*, *Messalina*, and *Witt* stages. These appear to be the curtains through which the players entered from the *skene* or tiring-house, which, according to Florio, was 'trimmed with hangings' (see PROSCENIUM). The orthodox view is that there were curtains in front of an inner and upper stage in the tiring-house wall, though there is no real evidence for these subsidiary stages. The 'canvas' and 'painted cloths' supplied by the Revels Office for Court performances were to cover the 'houses', and Hotson argues that the curtains in the public theatres were hangings that were drawn about similar erections on the apron stage.

For his Jacobean masques Inigo Jones employed a proscenium arch with a perspectively-painted front curtain that was lowered (not raised) like the Roman *auleum*, but there was no front curtain at the Globe and the other public theatres. The front curtain of the Restoration theatre rose at the beginning and fell at the end of a play, there being no attempt to hide the shifting of scenery, and it was not until the middle of the 19th century, with the disappearance of the fore-stage, that the uses of a front curtain were fully exploited. (See TRAVERSE; BACK-CLOTHS; HEAVENS.)

Curtis. In *The Taming of the Shrew*, a servant in Petruchio's country house. He appears only in IV, i, where he prepares for the arrival of Petruchio and Katharine, announced by Grumio. (See GREVILLE.)

Cushman, Charlotte (1816–76). An American actress who began her career as an operatic singer. Her first Shakespearean part, and perhaps her best, was Lady Macbeth, which she played in New Orleans. After that she accompanied Macready on an American tour and made her name as a great tragic actress. In 1845 she played Romeo at the Haymarket to her sister Susan's Juliet. She also played Wolsey in *Henry VIII*, and one of her best parts was Queen Katharine in the same play.

Cuts. In the Stationers' Address in the First Folio of Beaumont's and Fletcher's *Works* (1647) Humphrey Moseley wrote,

> One thing I must answer before it be objected; 'tis this: When these Comedies and Tragedies were presented on the stage, the actors omitted some scenes and passages (with the Authors' consent) as occasion led them; and when private friends desired a copy, they then (and justly too) transcribed what they acted.

Presumably the same thing happened to Shakespeare's plays: *Macbeth*, for example, of which there is no Quarto text, may be an abridged acting version. (See ABRIDGEMENT; DELETION.)

'CYMBELINE.'

WRITTEN: 1609–10. See PHILASTER.

PERFORMED: 1611. Simon Forman saw a performance, probably at the Globe in April, but at any rate before his death on 12 September.

1634. 'On Wensday night the first of January, Cymbeline was acted at Court by the Kings players. Well likte by the kinge.' (*Office Book*.)

REGISTERED: 1623, 8 November. One of the sixteen plays registered by Blount and Jaggard before publishing F1.

PUBLISHED: 1623, F1. 'The Tragedie of Cymbeline.' The last play in the Tragedy section, and therefore the last play in the Folio: pp. 369–99 (the last page is wrongly numbered 993). Acts and scenes marked. A fair text. Set up from prompt-book (or transcript of foul papers).

SOURCES: The wager theme: from Boccaccio's *Decameron* (the story of *Bernabo of Genoa*).

The Belarius theme: possibly from *The Rare Triumphs of Love and Fortune*, an anonymous play performed before Elizabeth in 1589. The historical parts: from Holinshed's *Chronicles*. There are resemblances to Beaumont's and Fletcher's *Philaster*, but it is impossible to say whether *Cymbeline* or *Philaster* came first.

STAGE HISTORY: 1682. *The Injured Princess, or The Fatal Wager*. A tidy version by Thomas D'Urfey spiced with attempted rape, and Cloten's blinding of Pisanio, at Drury Lane.

1761. Garrick returned largely to Shakespeare's text. Posthumus being one of his best parts.

1923. Barry Jackson's production in modern dress.

1937. Produced with a new Act V by Bernard Shaw.

Imogen, daughter of Cymbeline, King of Britain, has secretly married Posthumus. This is revealed to Cymbeline by his second wife, who wishes her son, Cloten, to marry Imogen, and Posthumus is banished. In Rome, Posthumus makes a wager with Iachimo that Imogen is incorruptible, but Iachimo comes to Britain, by a trick gains access to Imogen's bedroom while she is asleep, and obtains evidence which convinces Posthumus of her unchastity. He therefore writes to Imogen, telling her to meet him at Milford Haven, at the same time ordering his servant Pisanio to kill her on the way. Pisanio, however, persuades her to disguise herself as a man, and to join Lucius, the Roman general, who is invading Britain.

Imogen meets Belarius, a banished lord,

and her two brothers, the sons of Cymbeline, whom Belarius stole as babes, and has brought up in his mountain cave. Cloten, in pursuit of Imogen, is killed by them. Imogen, feeling ill, takes a drug which gives her the appearance of death, and she is left beside the headless body of Cloten whom she mistakes for Posthumus. She joins Lucius, but in the ensuing battle the Romans are defeated, largely owing to the courageous action of Belarius, the sons of Cymbeline, and Posthumus who has returned. All are brought before Cymbeline, and the recognition scene follows.

D

Daborne, Robert (d. 1628). Dramatist, and one of the syndicate who reorganized the Queen's Revels Children at Whitefriars in January 1610. The Revels joined the Lady Elizabeth's in 1613 under the management of Henslowe, and Daborne is interesting mainly as illustrating the relations between Henslowe and the dramatists in his pay. About 1615 he wrote to 'Mr. Hinchlowe' from his bed, praying him 'in my extremity forsake me not', and Henslowe noted, 'Lent Mr. Daborne upon this note, in earnest of a play called *The Bellman of London*, xxs.' *A Christian Turned Turk* and *The Poor Man's Comfort* are Daborne's, but many plays were written for Henslowe in collaboration with other dramatists, with Field, Fletcher, Massinger and Tourneur. He died, presumably in prosperity, as Dean of Lismore.

Dactyl. A trisyllabic foot, in English prosody a stressed syllable followed by two slacks (– ⏑ ⏑). Like all irregularities in Shakespeare's verse, the substitution of dactyls for iambs, though never frequent, becomes commoner in the later plays. (See TROCHEE.)

Daly, Augustin (1838–99). The American theatre manager and dramatist who in 1879, opened Daly's theatre in New York, and in 1893 Daly's Theatre in London. With Ada Rehan and Fanny Davenport in his company he produced most of Shakespeare's comedies, generally in rearranged and abbreviated versions, to make room for his sumptuous elaborations.

Dance, James (1722–74), son of the architect, George Dance. He assumed the name of Love, and became an actor, his best part being Falstaff. He wrote an heroic poem on *Cricket*, and an adaptation of *Timon of Athens* (1768), based partly on Shadwell's version, producing it at his theatre in Richmond, where it was well received.

Dances. It was customary to finish the performance of a play with a dance, and sometimes this is indicated in the text, as in *A Midsummer Night's Dream* and *Much Ado*. Thomas Platter of Basle describes a visit in September 1599 to a playhouse, probably the Globe, where he saw a performance of the 'Tragedy vom ersten Keyser Julio Cæsare', possibly Shakespeare's *Julius Caesar*: 'at the end, as is their custom, they danced, two in men's and two in women's clothes, wonderfully well together'. A month later he saw another play, probably at the Curtain, and again 'at the end they performed both English and Irish dances'. This concluding dance was a jig, in *Much Ado* performed to the music of the simple pipe, and perhaps tabor. With Tarlton and Kempe the jig became a comic ballad, danced and sung to a popular tune, so that 'whores, bedles, bawdes, and sergeants filthily chaunt Kemps Jigge'.

It may be that in the 17th century the adult companies followed the Children of Paul's and the Chapel in giving musical interludes, and sometimes dances *between* the acts. Certainly dances were frequently introduced into the plays themselves, as in *The Winter's Tale* and *The Tempest*. The music for these dances would be in the form either of the stately pavan or of the sprightly galliard, as would normally be any instrumental music that was required. (See PLATTER.)

Daniel, Samuel (*c.* 1563–1619). Was born near Taunton, the son of a music master, and educated at Magdalen Hall, Oxford. He became tutor to William Herbert, the Countess of Pembroke's son, at Wilton House, and in 1592 published his sonnet sequence to *Delia*, a lady who lived by the Avon, and *The Complaint of Rosamond*, written in rhyme-royal, as was Shakespeare's *Lover's Complaint*, and *Lucrece*. In 1594 came his academic tragedy of *Cleopatra*, and in the following year the epic *History of the Civil Wars*. He is said to have become poet laureate after Spenser's death in 1599, at about which time he became tutor to Anne Clifford, daughter of the Earl of Cumberland. By a patent of 1604 he was appointed licenser of the plays of the Queen's Revels, for whom he wrote *Philotas*, a play that caused him some trouble owing to its supposed sympathy for Essex. However, it did not prevent his becoming Groom, and then Gentleman Extraordinary of Queen Anne's Privy Chamber. He wrote two pastoral tragi-comedies, and two masques, one being the famous *Vision of the Twelve Goddesses*. Towards the end of his life he lived 'retiredly to enjoy the company of the Muses', and Shakespeare is said to have been one of the few admitted to his house in Old Street.

It is probable that Daniel's *Delia* and *Rosamond* influenced Shakespeare, as did his *Civil Wars* (registered Oct. 1594) *Richard II*, v, iv, but it seems equally probable that Shakespeare's *Antony and Cleopatra* led to Daniel's revising his *Cleopatra* (q.v.). The poets are mentioned together in *2 Parnassus* (*c.* 1599):

Guillio. Antonio's Cleopatra a black browed milkmaid, Helen a dowdy.

Ingenioso. (Mark, Romeo and Juliet! O monstrous theft! I think he will run through a whole book of Samuel Daniel's!)

If 'Mr W. H.' is William Herbert, it is possible that Daniel is the rival poet in Shakespeare's *Sonnets*.

Danter, John. Was active as a printer of poor quality and dubious reputation from 1589, when he was in partnership with Chettle, to his death in 1598–9. His business seems to have been carried on by Simon Stafford who was admitted a Freeman of the Stationers' Company in May 1599, and in the same year employed the device used by Danter for Q1, *Romeo and Juliet*: Opportunity standing on a floating wheel. Danter appears as a character in the Cambridge play, *3 Parnassus* (*c.* 1601). He printed:

Titus Andronicus. Q1, 1594. This he registered, and it was to be sold by White and Millington.

Romeo and Juliet. Q1, 1597. The first part of the 'bad' Quarto, which he printed without registration, and without his address on the title-page. His press was seized while printing. (See ALLDE.)

Dardanius. In *Julius Caesar*, a servant of Brutus. After his defeat at Philippi, Brutus asks Dardanius to kill him, but he refuses and runs away at the approach of Octavius and Antony, v, v.

'Dark Lady.' See SONNETS.

Dauphin. (Pronounce 'dolphin' or 'dawfin'.) See CHARLES; LOUIS.

D'Avenant, Sir William (1606–68). Son of John D'Avenant, a vintner of Oxford, of which city he became Mayor in 1621, the year before his death at 'my house, the taverne'. This house was the Crown Tavern, now 3 Cornmarket Street, where D'Avenant's 'Painted Chamber' was uncovered in 1927. It may have been here that William, the fourth and youngest child, was born in 1606. He went to the grammar school of All Saints, and to Lincoln College, thence passing into the service of the Duchess of Richmond, and then into that of Fulke Greville, Lord Brooke. He produced his first tragedy, *Albovine*, in 1629, following it with *The Cruel Brother* and *The Just Italian*, and then in collaboration with Inigo Jones produced three masques. On Jonson's death in 1637 he was made Poet Laureate. A staunch Royalist in the

Civil War, he was knighted by Charles I in 1643 after the siege of Gloucester, but was captured and imprisoned 1650–2, during which time he composed his epic, *Gondibert*. He is said to have been released at the instance of Milton, a service that he was able to repay when Milton was in danger at the Restoration. Although plays were forbidden, he obtained permission to perform 'operas' at a makeshift theatre 'at the back part of *Rutland-House*' where, in 1656, he produced his *Siege of Rhodes*, 'Made a Representation by the Art of Prospective in Scenes. And the Story sung in *Recitative* Musick'. This is the first English opera, but in addition, the elaborate scenery and theatrical machines were something new, as was the appearance on the stage of an actress, Mrs Coleman. At the Restoration D'Avenant organized one of the two authorized companies of players, the Duke of York's, joined by Betterton in 1661, and opened a theatre in Lincoln's Inn Fields. There he produced a number of Shakespeare's plays, the monopoly of the most popular of which he was granted, mostly in 'improved' versions, the most famous – or notorious – being that of *The Tempest*, polished by him and Dryden. He was buried in Poet's Corner, Westminster Abbey.

D'Avenant is said to have been the godson of Shakespeare, but tradition, first recorded in Aubrey's manuscript, *c.* 1680, makes him Shakespeare's illegitimate son:

> Sr William Davenant Knight Poet Laureate was borne in — street in the City of Oxford, at the Crowne Taverne. His father was John Davenant a Vintner there, a very grave and discreet Citizen: his mother was a very beautifull woman, & of a very good witt and of conversation extremely agreable ... Mr William Shakespeare was wont to goe into Warwickshire once a yeare, and did commonly in his journey lye at this house in Oxon: where he was exceedingly respected. I have heard parson Robert D [William's elder brother] say that Mr Wm. Shakespeare here gave him a hundred kisses. Now Sr. W^m^ would sometimes when he was pleasant over a glasse of wine with his most intimate friends, e.g. Sam: Butler (author of Hudibras) &c. say, that it seemed to him that he writt with the very spirit that Shakespeare, and was seemed contentended enough to be thought his Son: he would tell them the story as above, in which way his mother had a very light report, whereby she was called a whore.

It was not until 1749, however, that the story was printed, by W. R. Chetwood: 'Sir William Davenant was by many suppos'd the natural Son of Shakespear.' It is only fair to the memory of John's wife, Jane, to add that she was elsewhere described as 'a vertuous wife'. (See WILLOBIE.)

D'Avenant is said to have preserved and transmitted a number of Shakespearean theatrical traditions; for example, Downes wrote that Shakespeare instructed Taylor in the playing of Hamlet, that D'Avenant saw Taylor, and passed on his knowledge to Betterton. And he had the part of Henry VIII from 'Old Mr Lowen'. D'Avenant was said to have 'an amicable letter' written to Shakespeare by James I 'with his own hand'. (See DUKE'S COMPANY.)

D'Avenant Bust. See ROUBILIAC.

Davenport, Edward Loomis (1816–77). American actor of Shakespearean parts. He first appeared with Junius Brutus Booth, and played also with Macready in London. His daughter Fanny (1850–98) played in Shakespearean comedy with Daly's company.

Davenport, James, was from 1787 to 1841 vicar of Stratford, and on behalf of Malone 'most obligingly made every inquiry in that town and the neighbourhood' that might throw any light on the life of Shakespeare. Davenport's information about the mulberry-tree, cut down by the Rev. Francis Gastrell in 1758, appeared in Malone's edition of Shakespeare, 1790.

> The Rev. Mr Davenport informs me, that Mr Hugh Taylor, (the father of his clerk),

who is now eighty-five years old, ... and an alderman of Warwick, where he at present resides, says, he lived when a boy at the next house to New-Place; that his family had inhabited the house for almost three hundred years; ... that this tree (of the fruit of which he had often eaten in his younger days, some of its branches hanging over his father's garden), was planted by Shakspeare; and that till this was planted, there was no mulberry tree in that neighbourhood. Mr Taylor adds, that he was frequently, when a boy, at New-Place, and that this tradition was preserved in the Clopton family, as well as in his own.

Davenport, Robert (*c.* 1590–1640). Dramatist. His extant plays are *King John and Matilda* (published 1655), and two comedies, *The City Nightcap* (licensed 1624), and *A New Trick to Cheat the Devil* (published 1639). In 1624 'The Historye of Henry the First, written by Damport' was licensed for the King's Men, but when Humphrey Moseley in 1653 registered 'Cardennio, by Mr Fletcher, & Shakespeare', he added, 'Henry y[e] first, & Hen: y[e] 2[d]. by Shakespeare, & Dauenport'. And John Warburton, the antiquary (1682–1759), in a list of his lost manuscript plays records, 'Henry y[e] 1st. by Will. Shakespear & Rob. Davenport'. All but three of his valuable collection were 'unluckily burned or put under pye bottoms' by his servant Betsy Baker.

Davies, John (*c.* 1565–1618). Poet and writing-master of Hereford. His *Microcosmos* (1603) and *Civil Wars of Death and Fortune* (1605) contain complimentary references to players in general, and to W. S. and R. B., presumably Shakespeare and Richard Burbage, in particular. His *Scourge of Folly* is important for its references to contemporary dramatists, for example, it helps to date Beaumont's and Fletcher's *Philaster*. Epigram 159 is addressed 'To our English Terence, Mr. Will. Shake-speare':

Some say (good *Will*) which I, in sport, do sing,
Had'st thou not plaid some Kingly parts in sport,
Thou hadst bin a companion for a *King*;
And, beene a King among the meaner sort.
Some others raile; but, raile as they thinke fit,
Thou hast no rayling, but, a raigning Wit:
And honesty *thou sow'st, which they do reape;*
So, to increase their Stocke *which they do keepe.*

(See EDWARD I.)

Davies, Richard (d. 1708). An Oxford man, probably of Queen's College. He became curate of Sandford-on-Thames, and in 1695 rector of the Cotswold village of Sapperton, near Cirencester. In 1703 he was appointed Archdeacon of Coventry, but was buried at Sapperton in 1708. When William Fulman, vicar of Maisey Hampton, Gloucestershire, died in 1688, his papers came into the hands of Davies. (After Davies's death his executor gave them to Fulman's old College, Corpus Christi.) Among these papers were some notes on Shakespeare, to which Davies added the first account of the deer-stealing, and the only reference to Shakespeare's religion. (Davies's additions are printed in italics.)

William Shakespeare was born at Stratford upon Avon in Warwickshire about 1563–4.
much given to all unluckinesse in stealing venison & Rabbits particularly from S[r] Lucy who had him oft whipt & sometimes Imprisoned & at last made him fly his Native Country to his great Advancem[t], but His reveng was so great that he is his Justice Clodplate and calls him a great man & y[t] in allusion to his name bore three lowses rampant for his Arms.
From an Actor of Playes, he became a Composer

Ætat. 53.

He dyed Apr. 23, 1616, probably at Stratford, for there he is buryed, and hath a Monument on *w[c] He lay[s] a Heavy curse vpon any one who shal remoove his bones He dyed a papist.* (See RELIGION OF SHAKESPEARE.)

Davy. In *2 Henry IV*, Justice Shallow's factotum, who appears to look after his legal, farming, and household business. Davy makes an ingenious defence (v, i) of William Visor of Woncot against Clement Perkes o' the hill, both places near Dursley (q.v.) on the Cotswold escarpment.

Day, John (*c.* 1574– *c.* 1640). Dramatist, born in Norfolk, and educated at Ely and Caius College, Cambridge, from which he was sent down. He was one of the team of impecunious playwrights who wrote for Henslowe and the Admiral's 1599–1603, producing some fifteen plays in collaboration with Haughton, Chettle, Dekker and Hathway. Six of his own plays are extant, one of which, the satirical *Isle of Gulls*, led to the disgrace of the Revels Children who performed it, and to the imprisonment of some of those concerned (1606). His best-known work is the delightful half play, half masque, *The Parliament of Bees*. He killed Henry Porter, apparently in self-defence, in June 1599.

'Dead Man's Fortune.' A 'plot', or prompter's abstract of a play, probably once in the Alleyn collection of papers at Dulwich. It does not give the complete cast, but four actors are mentioned in addition to the 'tyre-man' (wardrobe-man): Burbage, Darlowe, Robert Lee (Queen's 1604–19), and 'b. Samme' (possibly the boy Samuel Rowley). The play must have belonged either to the Admiral's or Strange's, and was probably acted about 1590. (See Greg, *Dramatic Documents*.)

Decius Brutus. In *Julius Caesar*. See BRUTUS, DECIUS.

'Declaration of Popish Impostures.' See HARSNETT.

Declared Accounts. See CHAMBER ACCOUNTS.

Dedications. The only works that Shakespeare himself published and saw through the press were the two early poems, and both of these have elaborate dedications. The plays were not written for publication, and in any event were sold to his company whose property they became.

Venus and Adonis (1593) and *The Rape of Lucrece* (1594) were both dedicated by William Shakespeare to Henry Wriothesley, Earl of Southampton, and Baron of Titchfield.

The Sonnets (1609) were dedicated by their publisher, Thomas Thorpe, to 'Mr W. H.'.

The Folio (1623) was dedicated by its editors, Heminge and Condell, to the brothers, the Earls of Pembroke and Montgomery.

Deer Stealing. See CHARLECOTE; DAVIES, RICHARD; LUCY, SIR THOMAS; SHALLOW.

Deiphobus. In *Troilus and Cressida*, one of the sons of Priam, and brother of Troilus. He speaks only half a line: at the beginning of IV, i.

Dekker, Thomas (*c.* 1572–*c.* 1632). Of Dekker's early life practically nothing is known, though he seems to have been a Londoner, and the first reference to him is, ominously enough, in Henslowe's *Diary* at the beginning of 1598. A month later Henslowe 'lent unto the company, to discharge Mr. Dicker owt of the cownter in the powltrey, the some of fortie shillinges'. Dekker seems always to have been in financial difficulties, and it is improbable that his years of hack-writing for Henslowe, from 1598, and perhaps earlier, to 1602, were very lucrative. During this time he wrote nine or ten plays and had a hand in some thirty more, as well as in five plays for Worcester's in the second half of 1602. His *Satiromastix*, registered in November 1601, was, however, for the Chamberlain's and Paul's Children. It is his reply to *The Poetaster*, in which Jonson ridicules Dekker as Demetrius, 'a dresser of plays about the town'. Dekker good-naturedly gives as much as he takes (See POETOMACHIA). Soon after this he took to pamphleteering; first came *The Wonderful Year 1603*, a description of the plague in London, followed by *The Seven Deadly Sins of London*, *News from*

Hell and the dramatically important *Gull's Hornbook* (q.v.) of 1609. Perhaps pamphleteering was no more profitable than playwriting, or perhaps Dekker was incorrigibly prodigal, for in 1613 he was imprisoned for debt in the King's Bench, where he remained for six years. In later life he collaborated with Massinger and Ford. His best-known plays are, perhaps, *The Shoemaker's Holiday* (1599), *Old Fortunatus* (1599) and the masterpiece, *The Honest Whore* (1604), though Middleton had a hand in this. He is one of the most attractive of Shakespeare's contemporaries; he 'had poetry enough for anything', and a kindliness and charm, even in his satire, which is a pleasant contrast to the arrogance of Jonson (who told Drummond 'That Sharpham, Day, Dicker, were all rogues') and the bitterness of Marston. His industry, capacity, and reputation as a dresser of plays have led the disintegrators to find traces of his dressing in some of Shakespeare's: in *Henry V* and *Julius Caesar*, for example. (*The Dramatic Works of Thomas Dekker*, ed. F. Bowers.)

Deletion. In the extant play manuscripts that once belonged to a company of actors, passages that were to be cut are either crossed out or, more commonly, marked with a vertical line or bracket in the left margin. The second method, even if it were generally recognized as an arbitrary sign in printing, must often have been missed by the compositor, and the passage included. A manuscript used as printer's copy, therefore, with a revised and rewritten passage, might be printed with two versions of the same speech. A famous example is in Berowne's great speech in IV, iii of *Love's Labour's Lost*.

Delius, Nikolaus (1813–88). German Shakespeare scholar, Professor at Bonn University. Between 1854 and 1861 he published his valuable edition of Shakespeare, the text of which was used by Furnivall for the *Leopold Shakespeare*. Delius was a pioneer in the study of the Elizabethan stage, and wrote *Über das englische Theaterwesen zu Shaksperes Zeit* (1853), and in 1878 and 1888 published the two volumes of his *Abhandlungen zu Shakspere*. He also published a *Shakspere-Lexicon* in 1852.

Deloney, Thomas (*c.* 1550–1600). Silk-weaver, ballad-writer, and pamphleteer. He wrote three broadsides on the Spanish Armada, and prose narratives celebrating various crafts, *The Gentle Craft* containing the story of Simon Eyre, the shoemaker's apprentice who became Lord Mayor, adapted by Dekker in *The Shoemaker's Holiday*. The twelfth poem, 'Crabbed age and youth', in *The Passionate Pilgrim* (1599), attributed to Shakespeare, occurs in Deloney's poetical miscellany *Garland of Goodwill*. This was published in 1631, though there may have been earlier editions. There are four additional and inferior stanzas.

Demetrius. 1. In *Titus Andronicus*, the brother of Chiron (q.v.).

2. In *A Midsummer Night's Dream*, an Athenian whose love of Hermia is changed by fairy magic into love of Helena.

3. In *Antony and Cleopatra*, a friend of Antony. He appears only in the first scene.

Denmark. Frederick II (1559–88) of Denmark was the father of Christian IV (1588–1648) and of Anne, wife of James I. After the accession of James to the English throne in 1603 the Danish influence at Court was strong, and Shakespeare had to modify his references to Denmark in *Hamlet*: for example, to the deep drinking, and his comparison of Denmark to a prison. But Anne had married James in 1589 when he was King of Scotland, and Danish relations went back earlier than 1603. Frederick II 'entertained into his service a company of English comedians, commended unto him by the honourable the Earl of Leicester.' There were English 'instrumentister' at the Danish Court in 1580, and again in 1586 George Bryan and Thomas Pope, later of the Chamberlain's, were there with three other English players.

In 1606 Christian IV paid a visit to James, and the Chamber Accounts record, for performances at Greenwich and Hampton Court in July and August, payment to 'John Hemynges, one of his Maiesties players . . . for three playes before his Maiestie and the kinge of Denmarke.' That there was some truth in Hamlet's gibe about deep drinking in Denmark is made clear by Sir John Harington's (q.v.) comment and description of the masque of *Solomon and the Queen of Sheba* presented before James and Christian in July:

> I think the Dane hath strangely wrought on our good English nobles; for those whom I could never get to taste good liquor now follow the fashion and wallow in beastly delights. The ladies abandon their sobriety and are seen to roll about in intoxication ...

Danish interest in Shakespeare began in the second half of the 18th century, when some of his plays were translated, though the first performance – of *Hamlet* – was in 1813. The principal translations are those of Edward Lembcke, 1873, and of Valdemar Österberg, published 1888–1945. The publication of Georg Brandes's *William Shakespeare* in 1895 did much to popularize Shakespeare, as did the *History of Theatrical Art* (1897–1907) by Karl Mantzius who, as manager of the Royal Theatre, Copenhagen, produced and acted in the plays, a work continued in the twenties and thirties by Johannes Poulsen. The open-air performances of *Hamlet* at the Castle of Kronborg, Elsinore, began in 1916; in 1937 it was given by the Old Vic company with Laurence Olivier and Vivien Leigh, in 1939 by John Gielgud and Fay Compton, in 1949 by the State Theatre of Virginia with Robert Breen, in 1950 by the Old Vic. (See A. Henriques, *Shakespeare and Denmark*, 1900–49, in SS, 3.)

Dennis. He plays a tiny part in *As You Like It* as servant of Oliver (I, i).

Dennis, John (1657–1734), dramatist and critic, was born in London and educated at Harrow, and Caius and Trinity Hall, Cambridge. His poems and plays are worthless; his *Comical Gallant* (q.v.), 1702, is a vulgar perversion of *The Merry Wives*, and his adaptation of *Coriolanus*, as *The Invader of his Country*, was driven from the Drury Lane stage after three performances in 1719. Many of his plays were violently anti-French, for example, the successful *Liberty Asserted* (1704), and in 1713, such was his vanity, he asked the Duke of Marlborough to add a special clause to the Treaty of Utrecht as a protection from French reprisals. His criticism is better, but his *Essay on the Genius of Shakespeare* (1712) is almost as pedantic and insensible as anything in Rymer. He quarrelled with Addison, and with Pope who pilloried him as Appius in *An Essay on Criticism*, and as one of the 'monkey-mimics' in *The Dunciad*. He died in poverty. (See GILDON.)

Denny, Sir Antony (1501–49). He appears once in *Henry VIII* (V, i), where he brings Cranmer to see the King.

De Quincey, Thomas (1785–1859). His criticism is desultory, like all his work, and one feels that he was more interested in what he was writing than in what he was writing about, more interested in himself than his subject. But his essay *On the Knocking at the Gate in Macbeth* (1823) is one of the most penetrating critical footnotes in our literature.

Derby, Earls of. Henry Stanley became 4th Earl of Derby on the death of his father in 1572. He was Lord Lieutenant of Lancashire, and one of the commissioners who tried Mary, Queen of Scots. An illegitimate daughter, Ursula, married Sir John Salisbury, to whom Robert Chester dedicated *Love's Martyr*

(1601), the volume in which Shakespeare's *Phoenix and Turtle* was published.

His eldest son was Ferdinando Stanley, Lord Strange (the courtesy title of the eldest sons of the Earls of Derby), who became 5th Earl on his father's death on 25 September 1593 (the plague year). He was born about 1559, was a writer of verse, and it was he who, as Lord Strange, became patron of the company that bore his name. This patronage may be glanced at by Spenser in *Colin Clout's Come Home Again* (1595), where he laments the recent death of Derby as Amyntas,

Amyntas, flower of shepherds' pride forlorn:
He whilst he lived was the noblest swain,
That ever piped in an oaten quill:
Both did he other, which could pipe, maintain,
And eke could pipe himself with passing skill.

And it is possible that Aetion in the next line is Shakespeare, whose *Venus and Adonis* and *Lucrece* had already made a name for him:

And there, though last not least, is Ætion;
A gentler shepherd may nowhere be found:
Whose Muse, full of high thoughts' invention,
Doth like himself heroically sound.

Shakespeare's name certainly sounds heroically, and the mention of Derby may have suggested to Spenser Derby's Men and the early Histories of Shakespeare.

Strange's Men were Derby's only for seven months, for he died 16 April 1594. He was succeeded by his brother, William Stanley, the patron of a provincial company of players. In January 1595 he married Elizabeth Vere, and died in 1642.

Derby's (Strange's) Men. Henry Stanley had a company of players traceable in the provinces as Strange's Men in the sixties, and as Derby's in the seventies, after his succession to the Earldom in 1572.

In the eighties appears another Strange's company, presumably under the patronage of Ferdinando, Lord Strange. They performed at Court during the Revels of 1580, 81, 83, 85, 86, their leader and payee being John Symons, 'the Tumbler'. They were, in fact, a troupe of acrobats, performing 'sundry feates of Tumbling and Activitie'. In 1588 there seems to have been some sort of reorganization; Symons joined the Queen's, perhaps taking some of Strange's tumblers with him, and it is possible that they were replaced by Bryan, Pope, and Kempe, who had all been in Holland, the last, and possibly the others, in the service of Leicester who died in September 1588. Perhaps they were also joined by some of Hunsdon's Men, records of whom disappear about this time. Henceforth Strange's were primarily players, though all these early companies were capable of putting on a tumbling turn.

They were in London in November 1589, for when the Lord Mayor ordered them to forbear playing they showed their contempt by at once going to the Cross Keys and giving a performance. The Court records for the following winter (1590) suggest the beginning of an affiliation with the Admiral's, for 'George Ottewell and his companye the Lorde Straunge his players' were paid for 'plays and other feats of activity' given by the Admiral's.

In 1591 the Admiral's were at the Theatre, and Strange's probably at the neighbouring Curtain, the owners of which two theatres, James Burbage and Henry Laneman, were working together. If so, it seems likely that the 'plot' of *The Dead Man's Fortune* represents a performance by the Admiral's, that of *The Second Part of the Seven Deadly Sins* by Strange's. The actors named in the former are Burbage, Darlowe, Robert Lee, and 'b. Samme'; in the latter they are Mr Brian, Mr Phillipps, Mr Pope, R. Cowley, R. Burbadge, John Duke, W. Sly, John Sincler, Ro. Pallant, J. Holland, Tho. Goodale and nine others playing minor parts or boys playing women. Richard

Burbage is in both lists, and this may mean that the two companies had already combined for public as well as Court performances. The first four actors in the cast of *The Deadly Sins* were with Strange's in 1593, and the first five were to become original members of the Chamberlain's company in 1594. In the winter of 1591 Strange's gave six Court performances.

From 19 February to 23 June 1592 Strange's played at Henslowe's Rose in a repertory of 23 plays, which included '*Harry the vj*', probably Shakespeare's *1 Henry VI*. On 23 June the Privy Council inhibited plays in London and the players were driven to make provincial tours. That winter Strange's gave three Court performances, and on 29 December began another season with Henslowe, which was cut short on 28 January 1593 by the outbreak of serious plague.

It was not until 6 May 1593 that Strange's received from the Privy Council their licence to travel:

> Whereas it was thought meet that during the time of the infection and continuance of the sickness in the city of London there should no plays or enterludes be used ... and though the bearers hereof, Edward Allen, servant to the right honorable the Lord High Admiral, William Kemp, Thomas Pope, John Heminges, Augustine Phillipes and Georg Brian, being all one company, servants to our very good Lord the Lord Strainge, are restrained their exercise of playing within the said city and liberties thereof, yet it is not thereby meant but that they shall and may ... exercise their quality of playing comedies, tragedies and such like in any other cities, towns and corporations where the infection is not, so it be not within seven miles of London or of the Court, that they may be in the better readiness hereafter for her Majesty's service ...

This list again suggests an alliance between Strange's and the Admiral's, for though all the actors mentioned, except Alleyn, are Strange's, obviously they must have worked under the capable leadership of the famous Alleyn of the Admiral's. That Richard Cowley was also with them is clear from Alleyn's correspondence with his wife, Joan Woodward, Henslowe's step-daughter. Their travels took them into Kent, along the south coast to Southampton, to Bath and Bristol, north to Shrewsbury, possibly to Chester and York, and south again by Leicester and Coventry. During this tour, on 25 September 1593, Ferdinando Stanley succeeded his father as Earl of Derby, so that Strange's became Derby's Men until the new Earl's death on 16 April 1594.

When Derby died the company were in East Anglia, in May in Hampshire, but were back in London in June, for the plague was over and the theatres reopening. There they found a new patron in the Lord Chamberlain, Henry Lord Hunsdon, and are first mentioned as the Chamberlain's by Henslowe when they played with the Admiral's from 5 to 15 June 1594, at Newington Butts. After that the two companies reorganized and went their own highly successful ways: the Admiral's under Alleyn to his father-in-law's Rose, the Chamberlain's to the Theatre of Richard Burbage's father, and for the winter season to the Cross Keys Inn in the City. The personnel of the original Chamberlain's company was probably Kempe, Pope, Heminge, Phillips, Bryan, Cowley, R. Burbage, perhaps Sly, and by the end of the year Shakespeare.

The first official notice of Shakespeare as a player occurs in the Chamber Accounts for performances at Court on 26, 27 December 1594, for which he was one of the payees on 15 March 1595: 'William Kempe William Shakespeare & Richard Burbage seruantes to the Lord Chamberleyne.' If he were with Strange's before this, as he may have been, it is odd that he should not have been mentioned in the cast of *The Deadly Sins*, in the Licence of 1593, or by Alleyn in his correspondence, for after all Strange's had acted one of his plays, and perhaps more, while Greene's oblique attack and Chettle's apology of 1592 testify to his importance. (See CHAMBERLAIN'S-KING'S MEN.)

Dercetas. In *Antony and Cleopatra*, a friend of Antony. When Antony stabs himself, Dercetas takes the sword to Caesar, to whom he offers his services (v, i).

Derelict Plays. If a book were not registered, or if a publisher died or retired without selling or otherwise transferring his copyright in a play, it became derelict, and the property of the Stationers' Company, though in practice it might be appropriated by any enterprising stationer.

Dering MS. A version made from Q5 *1 Henry IV* and Q *2 Henry IV* about 1613, probably for a Court or private performance, with alterations by Sir Edward Dering (1598–1644) of Surrenden, Kent, where it was found. It is the earliest extant manuscript of a Shakespearean play, and is now in the Folger library.

Desdemona. The heroine of *Othello*. (Disdemona in Cinthio's *novella*.)

Dethick, Sir William (1543–1612). Garter King-of-Arms who issued the Grant of Arms to John Shakespeare in 1596. Dethick and Clarenceux King-of-Arms drafted the second grant of 1599, which does not seem to have been issued, and in 1602 defended the original grant against the attack of Ralph Broke, York Herald. Dethick was unpopular with the College of Heralds, and though he was knighted in 1603 he was deprived of his office in the same year owing to his mismanagement of the investiture of the Duke of Württemberg (Mömpelgart).

Deutsche Shakespeare-Gesellschaft. The German Shakespeare Society, founded at Weimar (1865) after the tercentenary celebrations. It publishes the *Jahrbuch der Deutschen Shakespeare-Gesellschaft* (first editor Friedrich von Bodenstedt (q.v.)). In 1964 the society divided into East and West, under separate direction. The West German section has its seat at Bochum.

Device. A printer's or publisher's device is defined by McKerrow, in his *Printers' and Publishers' Devices 1485–1640*: 'any picture, design, or ornament (not being an initial letter) found on a title-page, final leaf, or in any other conspicuous place in a book, and having an obvious reference to the sign at which the printer or publisher of the book carried on business, or to the name of either of them, or including the arms or crest of either of them, is – whatever its origin – that printer's or publisher's device.'

'Devil's Charter, The.' 'A Tragedie Conteining the Life and Death of Pope Alexander the sixt. As it was plaide before the King's Maiestie, vpon Candlemasse night last: by his Maiesties Seruants', 1607, by Barnabe Barnes. The play is interesting for its detailed stage-directions; even the main characters sometimes have to bring their furniture with them: for example, Lucrezia Borgia is to carry in a chair 'which she planteth upon the Stage.' After the performance the play was corrected and augmented by the author 'for the more pleasure and profit of the Reader', and registered for publication in October. As Alexander Borgia calls the asps with which he works in poison 'Cleopatra's birds', it may be that Shakespeare's *Antony and Cleopatra* had been produced before October, and perhaps before February, 1607.

De Witt, Johannes. After a visit to London about 1596 de Witt wrote his *Observationes Londinienses*, to the manuscript of which he attached a sketch and description of the Swan Theatre (q.v.), now lost. However, his friend, Arend van Buchel, who was a fellow-student with de Witt at Leyden in 1583, made a copy which was discovered and reproduced by K. T. Gaedertz in his *Zur Kenntnis der altenglischen Bühne*, 1888.

Diana. 1. In *All's Well*, daughter of the Florentine widow with whom Helena stays. (She signs herself 'Diana Capilet' in v, v.)

2. In *Pericles*, the goddess Diana appears to Pericles in a vision, and tells him to go to the Temple of Diana at Ephesus (v, i). There he discovers his wife Thaisa who is High Priestess. (Cf. the Aegeon-Aemilia theme in *The Comedy of Errors.*)

'Diana.' See MONTEMAYOR.

Dick. In *2 Henry VI*, a butcher of Ashford and a follower of Cade. He makes shrewd and sceptical remarks when Cade recites his claims (IV, ii), yet is as eager as any for blood and destruction.

Diderot, Denis (1713–84). French philosopher, dramatist, and critic, is best known as the main founder of the Encyclopédie. He wrote sentimental comedies, *Le Neveu de Rameau*, and *La Poésie Dramatique*. He was one of the first to protest against Voltaire's generally accepted view of Shakespeare as a 'barbarian'.

Digges, Leonard (1588–1635). Younger son of Thomas Digges (1545–95), the astronomer and mathematician, and of Anne St Leger who in 1603 married, as her second husband, Thomas Russell, Shakespeare's friend. Leonard went to University College, Oxford, where he met James Mabbe (q.v.), and became 'a great master of the English language, a perfect understander of the French and Spanish, a good poet, and no mean orator'. His translation of *Gerardo, the Unfortunate Spaniard* was published in 1622 by Edward Blount, who was then busy with the publication of Shakespeare's Folio. Digges must have known Shakespeare through his stepfather, and he wrote one of the commendatory poems in the Folio, beginning:

Shake-speare, at length thy pious fellowes giue
The world thy Workes: thy Workes, by which, out-liue
Thy Tombe, thy name must: when that stone is rent,
And Time dissolues thy *Stratford* Moniment,
Here we aliue shall view thee still....

The longer poem, printed in Benson's 1640 edition of Shakespeare's *Poems*, five years after Digges's death, may have been written at the same time. It contains the well-known lines describing the popularity of Shakespeare's plays:

when let but *Falstaffe* come,
Hall, *Poines*, the rest you scarce shall have a roome
All is so pester'd: let but *Beatrice*
And *Benedicke* be seene, loe in a trice
The Cockpit Galleries, Boxes, all are full
To heare *Maluoglio* that crosse garter'd Gull.

Digges's elder brother was Sir Dudley Digges, member of the council for the Virginia Company. In 1610 he visited his stepfather, Russell, at Alderminster, where Shakespeare may have heard the story that inspired *The Tempest*.

Diomedes. 1. In *Troilus and Cressida* (q.v.), one of the Grecian commanders, outspoken and cynical.

2. In *Antony and Cleopatra*, a servant of Cleopatra, who sends Mardian to tell Antony that she is dead, then 'fearing how it might work', sends Diomedes, too late however, to proclaim the truth. He takes the dying Antony to Cleopatra's monument (IV, xiv and xv).

Dion. In *The Winter's Tale*, a lord of Sicilia. (See CLEOMENES.)

Dionyza. In *Pericles* (q.v.), wife of Cleon, Governor of Tarsus.

Disintegrators. There are two main groups of disintegrators. First, those who like Fleay and Robertson, following stylistic clues, find much alien matter in the Shakespearean canon, either because a passage is inferior, or resembles the work of another dramatist, or is in some other way 'abnormal'. Then there are those who, following mainly bibliographical clues, find that Shakespeare's plays are rarely homogeneous: that most of them have been more or less drastically revised, though generally by Shakespeare himself. Briefly, and in the geological metaphor they themselves assume, the one school finds outcrops of other men's work, the other finds successive strata of Shakespeare's own work. (See AUTHENTICITY OF PLAYS.)

Dobyns, Robert. See COMBE, JOHN.

Doctor. In *Macbeth*, an English doctor tells Malcolm the King is coming to cure the sick with his touch (IV, 3). In V, i a Scottish doctor witnesses Lady Macbeth's sleep-walking. (See CORNELIUS; FORMAN.)

'Doctor Faustus.' Written by Marlowe 1588–9; a stock play of the Admiral's in which Alleyn played Faustus. A corrupt version was published in 1604. In November 1602 Henslowe paid Bird and Rowley £4 for their additions, which are probably the comic scenes in the longer version of 1616. The play is an interesting example of the 'dressing' of old plays. (See DEKKER.)

Dodsley, Robert (1703–64). His first published work was *Servitude; a Poem*, written while he was a footman. After the production of his farce, *The Toyshop*, at Covent Garden in 1735, he set up as a bookseller at 'Tully's Head' in Pall Mall. He published work by Pope, Johnson, Young, Akenside, Goldsmith, Gray (the *Elegy*), and with Burke founded *The Annual Register* in 1758. He is best known for his *Select Collection of Old Plays* (12 vols. 1744), the first of its kind, and invaluable for the 18th-century editors and critics of Shakespeare. Lamb found it useful when compiling his *Specimens of English Dramatic Poets* (1808).

Dogberry. In *Much Ado*, a constable. According to Aubrey, Shakespeare 'happened to take' the 'humour' of Dogberry 'at Grendon in Bucks which is the road from London to Stratford'. The part was played by Kempe, and then by Armin. Dogberry sets the Watch that captures Borachio and Conrade, examines them, and is called an ass for his pains.

Doggerel. Verses of four to seven lame and irregular feet. It was a measure much used in the plays of the middle 16th century, for example, in *Ralph Roister Doister* and *Gammer Gurton's Needle*. Shakespeare experiments with it in his early plays, but it is very rare after 1595–6. The Dromio twins in *The Comedy of Errors* often speak in doggerel:

Say what you will, sir, but I know what I know;
That you beat me at the mart, I have your hand to show:
If the skin were parchment, and the blows you gave were ink,
Your own handwriting would tell you what I think.

Dogget, Thomas (d. 1721). English comic actor for whom Congreve wrote the part of Ben in his *Love for Love*, the play with which Betterton opened the Lincoln's Inn Fields theatre in 1695. In 1715, to celebrate the accession of the Hanoverians, Dogget founded the annual race for 'Dogget's Coat and Badge'. He played Shylock in George Granville's *Jew of Venice*, 1701, a feeble adaptation, but the part of Shylock is scarcely altered. Of this production Rowe remarked in the Preface to his edition of Shakespeare (1709), 'Tho' we have seen that Play Receiv'd and Acted as a Comedy, and the Part of the *Jew* perform'd by an Excellent Comedian, yet I cannot but think it was design'd Tragically by the Author.'

Dolabella. In *Antony and Cleopatra*, a friend of Caesar. Caesar sends him to bid Antony yield, but Antony is dead, and he tells Cleopatra that Caesar intends leading her in triumph, that she has only three days in which to make use of his information. When he returns to prepare her for Caesar's arrival, he finds her dead (v, i and ii).

Doll Tearsheet. In *2 Henry IV*, a harlot. She goes to supper with Falstaff and Mistress Quickly at the Boar's Head Tavern, where they are discovered by Prince Henry and Poins (II, iv). In v, iv she is dragged off to prison, for 'there hath been a man or two lately killed about her'. Doll does not appear in *Henry V*, but Pistol, having married Mistress Quickly, tells Nym to console himself by 'espousing' 'the lazar kite of Cressid's kind, Doll Tearsheet she by name.' In v, i, Pistol hears that his 'Doll is dead i' the spital', which seems to be an error for Nell Quickly, though Wilson argues that 'Doll' is correct as Shakespeare originally wrote the speech for Falstaff, for whom Pistol had to be substituted in some of the episodes.

Donalbain. In *Macbeth*, the younger son of Duncan. After the murder of their father, Malcolm decides to go to England, Donalbain to Ireland. This (II, iii) is the only scene in which Donalbain speaks, and the last in which he appears.

Donne, John (1572–1631), poet and divine, was the son of a wealthy merchant. His mother, Elizabeth Heywood, was the daughter of John Heywood, the interlude writer, and of a niece of Sir Thomas More. In 1621 Donne was appointed Dean of St Paul's. He was a friend of Ben Jonson, who told Drummond that he esteemed 'John Done the first poet in the world in some things', yet 'for not keeping of accent, deserved hanging', and 'for not being understood, would perish'. Edward Alleyn, after the death in June 1623 of his first wife, Henslowe's step-daughter, married Donne's daughter, Constance, in the following December. At the wedding dinner was 'Mr. Wilson, the singer', probably the Jack Wilson who played Balthazar in *Much Ado*, and sang 'Sigh no more, ladies'.

Dorcas. In *The Winter's Tale*, a shepherdess, in love with the 'Clown'. In the sheep-shearing scene (IV, iv) she is one of the dancers, and with Autolycus and Mopsa sings her part in 'Get you hence, for I must go'.

Doricles. The name assumed by Prince Florizel in *The Winter's Tale*.

Dorrell, Hadrian. The Oxford friend of Henry Willobie (q.v.) and editor of *Willobie his Avisa*. In a preface written at Oxford, and dated '1 Oct', Dorrell says that the author, Willobie, has gone abroad, that he found the poem in his friend's study, debates the question whether it is all 'a poetical fiction', concludes that at least the name 'Avisa' is feigned, though one 'A.D.' is her equal in virtue. In a second edition, probably of 1599, he decides that not only her name, but Avisa herself is fictitious. He says nothing, however, about Willobie's 'familiar friend W.S. . . . the old player'.

Dorset, Thomas Sackville, 1st Earl of (1536–1608). Statesman and poet. He became successively, Baron Buckhurst, Chancellor of Oxford University, Lord Treasurer, and in 1604 Earl of Dorset. He contributed the *Induction*, and *The Complaint of Buckingham* to the second edition of *A Mirror for Magistrates*, 1563, and with Thomas Norton was the author of the first real English tragedy, *Gorboduc*, *c.* 1560. He built Knole House, about which W. H. Ireland, in his *Confessions* (1805) relates a dubious story:

> It has been stated in the public prints, and I conjecture with truth, that two letters from the pen of Shakespeare were discovered some time since at Knole in Kent, among the papers of the Dorset family, written by our bard to the then lord-chamberlain [treasurer] upon mere official business relative to theatrical matters.

Malone's attempt to find the papers was unsuccessful.

Dorset, Marquis of. In *Richard III*, eldest son of Elizabeth Woodville, afterwards Queen of Edward IV, by her first husband Sir John Grey. After Richard's execution of his brother Lord Grey, and his uncle Rivers, Dorset joins Richmond in Britanny (IV, i and ii), but is not present at Bosworth. (Thomas Grey (d. 1501) created M. of Dorset 1475.)

Dorset Garden Theatre. Opened 9 November 1671 and used by the Duke of York's company until they went to the new Lincoln's Inn Fields theatre in 1695. The Duke's theatre in Dorset Garden was the most ornate of the Restoration theatres, with a music-room above the proscenium arch, and proscenium doors leading on to the apron stage. It appears to have been abandoned because of its poor acoustics.

Double Endings. See FEMININE ENDINGS.

'Double Falsehood.' See CARDENIO.

Doubling of Parts. The actor-list sometimes printed with a play is usually a plain recital of the names of the 'principal comedians' or 'principal tragedians' without mention of the parts they played, and for Shakespeare's plays, save the composite one in the Folio, there are no actor-lists at all. It is, therefore, difficult to say to what extent doubling was practised. Obviously minor parts must have been doubled, and the bigger the number of characters, and the smaller the number of players – as on a provincial tour – the more doubling (and the more cutting) there would have to be. On the other hand, the stage-keeper, tireman and gatherers might be called on for small parts. The actor-list for the revival of *The Duchess of Malfi* (q.v.) by the King's Men *c.* 1620 gives the parts as well as the actors, and there Underwood doubled the not inconsiderable role of Delio with that of one of the madmen; Tooley also played two parts, and the boy Pallant played Cariola, the Doctor and a court officer.

Douce, Francis (1757–1834), English antiquary, became keeper of manuscripts in the British Museum, and in 1807 published *Illustrations of Shakespeare and Ancient Manners*, the two volumes of which, though containing some trivial and erroneous matter, explained many obscure references in Shakespeare. (See HUNTER.)

Douglas, Archibald 4th Earl of (d. 1424). In *1 Henry IV*, after being defeated by Hotspur at Holmedon he joins his rebellion, and is one of those who keep faith with him at Shrewsbury. In the battle he kills Blunt, almost kills the King, but is captured in the rebel rout. Prince Henry delivers him 'ransomless and free'.

Dowdall, Mr. On 10 April 1693 a Mr Dowdall wrote a letter from Butler's Marston, Warwickshire, to his 'Dr. Cousin . . . Mr Southwell'. The letter, which is in the Folger Shakespeare Library, is signed 'John at Stiles', and endorsed, presumably by Southwell, 'From Mr Dowdall'. Dowdall quotes Shakespeare's epitaph accurately, and is the first to record its being 'made by himselfe', the fear of the curse, and the 'earnest desire' of his wife and daughters. He corroborates Aubrey's story that Shakespeare was a butcher's apprentice, but does not add that the butcher was his father.

The 1st Remarkable place in this County y^t I visitted was Stratford super avon, where I saw the Effigies of our English tragedian, m^r Shakspeare . . .

Neare the Wall where his monument is Erected Lyeth a plaine free stone, underneath wch his bodie is Buried with this Epitaph, made by himselfe a little before his Death.

Good friend, for Jesus sake forbeare
To digg the dust inclosed here.
Bles't be the man that spares these stones
And Curs't be he that moves my bones!

the clarke that shew'd me this Church is aboue 80 y^rs old; he says that this Shakespear was formerly in this Towne bound apprentice to a butcher; but that he Run from his master to London, and there was Rec[d] Into the playhouse as a serviture, and byt his meanes had an oppertunity to be w[t] he afterwards prov'd. he was the best of his family but the male Line is extinguished; not one for feare of the Curse aboues[d] Dare Touch his Grave Stone, tho his wife and Daughters Did Earnestly Desire to be Layd in the same Graue wth him.

Dowden, Edward (1843–1913). Irish man of letters, was born at Cork and educated at Queen's College, Cork, and at Trinity College, Dublin, where in 1867 he was elected Professor of English Literature. His first important book was *Shakspere: A Critical Study of his Mind and Art* (1875), which was a response to Furnivall's reproach when he founded the New Shakspere Society in 1873: 'It is a disgrace to England . . . that no book by an Englishman [Gervinus had written one in German] exists which deals in any worthy manner with Shakspere as a whole.' Dowden's interpretation is somewhat idealized and sentimental, but it is the first attempt in English to trace the growth of Shakespeare's 'intellect and character from youth to full maturity', that is, through the four periods established by Furnivall with the help of his verse-tests. In 1877 Dowden published his *Shakespeare Primer*, and followed this with editions of the *Sonnets* and a number of the plays.

Dowland, John (1563–1626), was for a time lutenist to Christian IV of Denmark, to whose sister Anne, wife of James I, he dedicated his *Lachrymae*. He was also lutenist to Charles I. He published three books of *Songes or Ayres of Foure Partes with Tableture for the Lute*. Cf. *Passionate Pilgrim*, 8, a sonnet by Barnfield:

> Dowland to thee is dear, whose heavenly touch
> Upon the lute doth ravish human sense.

Downes, John (*c.* 1640–*c.* 1710), was 'book-keeper and prompter' of the Duke of York's company from 1662 to 1706. With further information supplied by Charles Booth, prompter of the King's company, he was able to write his valuable, though not highly informative *Roscius Anglicanus, or, an Historical Review of the Stage* (1708), our main source of information about the Restoration theatre. The following extracts come from *Roscius Anglicanus*, though it is improbable that Shakespeare coached Taylor, who joined the King's Men three years after Shakespeare's death.

> The Tragedy of *Hamlet*; *Hamlet* being Perform'd by Mr. Betterton, Sir *William* [D'Avenant] (having seen Mr *Taylor* of the *Black-Fryars* Company Act it, who being Instructed by the Author Mr *Shaksepeur*) taught Mr *Betterton* in every Particle of it . . .
>
> King *Henry* the 8*th* . . . The part of the King was so right and justly done by Mr *Betterton*, he being instructed in it by Sir *William*, who had it from Old Mr *Lowen*, that had his Instructions from Mr *Shakespear* himself, and I dare and will aver, none can, or will come near him in this Age, in the performance of that part.

'Downfall of Robert, Earl of Huntingdon.' A play of 'Robin Hood of merrie Sherwodde' by Munday. This and its sequel, *The Death of Robert, Earl of Huntingdon*, by Munday and Chettle, were Admiral's plays performed in 1598. Shakespeare wrote *As You Like It* at about the same time, and the three plays are a good illustration of intercompany competition on similar themes. (Compare also *Henry IV* and *Sir John Oldcastle*.)

Downton, Thomas. Actor. He may have been the 'Mr Doutone' who was with the Strange's-Admiral's company during their provincial tour of 1593. In 1594 he was with the Admiral's, of which he became a prominent member.

Drake, Nathan (1766–1836), was born at York and became a doctor, practising at Hadleigh in Suffolk, where he died. He wrote a number of essays, but his most important work, published in two volumes in 1817, is *Shakespeare and his*

Times, including the Biography of the Poet, Criticisms on his Genius and Writings; a new Chronology of his Plays; a Disquisition on the Object of his Sonnets; and a History of the Manners, Customs and Amusements, Superstitions, Poetry and Elegant Literature of his Age. (See SOUTHAMPTON.)

Dramatis Personae. None of the Shakespearean Quartos has a list of Dramatis Personae. In the First Folio 'The Names of the Actors', that is, of the characters, are given after *The Tempest*, *The Two Gentlemen of Verona*, *Measure for Measure*, *The Winter's Tale*, *2 Henry IV*, *Timon of Athens* and *Othello*. In the Third Folio of 1664 a similar list was added to *Pericles*. Nicholas Rowe, in his edition of 1709, completed the lists of Dramatis Personae. F1 Ben Jonson (1616), F2 Beaumont and Fletcher (1679) have lists of the actors themselves, and Q *Duchess of Malfi* (1623) has a list of the actors with the parts they played. (See CHAMBERLAIN'S MEN; CASTS.)

Dramatists. In his *Palladis Tamia* of 1598 Francis Meres wrote:

As Plautus and Seneca are accounted the best for Comedy and Tragedy among the Latines: so Shakespeare among the English is the most excellent in both kinds for the stage ...

These are our best for Tragedie, The Lord Buckhurst, Doctor Leg of Cambridge, Doctor Edes of Oxford, Master Edward Ferris, the author of the *Mirror for Magistrates*, Marlow, Peele, Watson, Kid, Shakespeare, Drayton, Chapman, Decker, and Beniamin Iohnson ...

The best for Comedy amongst vs bee Edward, Earle of Oxforde, Doctor Gager of Oxforde, Master Rowley, once a rare scholler of learned Pembrooke Hall in Cambridge, Maister Edwardes, one of her Maiesties Chappell, eloquent and wittie Iohn Lilly, Lodge, Gascoyne, Greene, Shakespeare, Thomas Nash, Thomas Heywood, Anthony Mundye, our best plotter, Chapman, Porter, Wilson, Hathway, and Henry Chettle.

A list of the most important dramatists writing at about the same time as Shakespeare (1590–1612) is given below. The dates of many of these writers are only approximate.

Wilson, Robert	*c.* 1550–*c.* 1605
Lyly, John	*c.* 1554–1606
Peele, George	*c.* 1557–96
Lodge, Thomas	*c.* 1557–1625
Greene, Robert	1558–92
Kyd, Thomas	1558–94
Munday, Anthony	*c.* 1560–1633
Chettle, Henry	*c.* 1560–1607
Chapman, George	*c.* 1560–1634
Daniel, Samuel	*c.* 1563–1619
Drayton, Michael	1563–1631
Marlowe, Christopher	1564–93
Shakespeare, William	1564–1616
Nashe, Thomas	1567–*c.* 1601
Barnes, Barnabe	*c.* 1569–1609
Hathway, Richard	*c.* 1570–*c.* 1610
Middleton, Thomas	*c.* 1570–1627
Rowley, Samuel	*c.* 1570–*c.* 1630
Dekker, Thomas	*c.* 1572–*c.* 1632
Jonson, Benjamin	1572–1637
Heywood, Thomas	1573–1641
Day, John	*c.* 1574–*c.* 1640
Haughton, William	*c.* 1575–1605
Marston, John	*c.* 1575–1634
Tourneur, Cyril	*c.* 1575–1626
Fletcher, John	1579–1625
Daborne, Robert	*c.* 1580–1628
Rowley, William	*c.* 1580–*c.* 1635
Webster, John	*c.* 1580–*c.* 1630
Massinger, Philip	1583–1640
Beaumont, Francis	1584–1616
Ford, John	1586–*c.* 1639

For further information, see the names of the dramatists and SS, 14.

Drayton, Michael (1563–1631), was born at Hartshill in Warwickshire. In 1593 he published *Idea: The Shepherd's Garland*, and in 1594 *Idea's Mirror*, the first a collection of nine pastorals, the second a sequence of sixty-four sonnets addressed to 'Idea', the name he gave to Anne, the daughter of his patron, Sir Henry Goodere of Polesworth. Drayton's suit failed, he died a bachelor, and Anne married Sir Henry Rainsford of Clifford Chambers (q.v.), near Stratford, where Drayton used to stay. He wrote a number of historical poems, but is best known for his *Poly-Olbion* (1613–22), thirty 'Songs' each of some four hundred lines, forming a survey of England in hexameter couplets. His best work, perhaps, is in his volume of 1627, which includes *The Battle of Agincourt*, and *Nimphidia*.

For a period of about ten years Drayton was associated with the theatre. Between 1597 and 1602 he collaborated in some twenty plays for Henslowe and the Admiral's, one of them, *Sir John Oldcastle*, which he wrote with Hathway, Munday and Wilson, being printed in 1619 by Jaggard as Shakespeare's. The disintegrators find traces of Drayton's work in some of Shakespeare's plays, and there are those who favour his claim to be the rival poet of the *Sonnets*. In 1607–8 he was one of the syndicate that promoted the short-lived King's Revels company.

Drayton's connexion with Shakespeare and the Stratford district is interesting. Shakespeare's son-in-law, Dr John Hall, cured him, 'an excellent poet', of a fever by an infusion of violets. But Hall was unable to cure of a fever an even more excellent poet, for according to John Ward (*c.* 1662), 'Shakespear, Drayton, and Ben Jhonson, had a merry meeting, and itt seems drank too hard, for Shakespear died of a feavour there contracted.' Of Shakespeare, Drayton wrote (1627),

And be it said of thee,
Shakespeare, thou hadst as smooth a
Comicke vaine,
Fitting the socke, and in thy naturall
braine,
As strong conception, and as Cleere a rage,
As any one that trafiqu'd with the stage.

Drew. A family of American actors. John Drew (1827–62) was an Irish actor who settled in Philadelphia, his wife being Louise Lane Drew, an English actress. Their eldest son, John Drew, played in Shakespearean comedy with Daly's company. His sister Georgiana married Maurice Barrymore, and was the mother of Ethel, John, and Lionel, all actors.

Droeshout, Martin (1601–*c.* 1650), the engraver of Shakespeare's portrait in the First Folio, seems to have been the son of Michael Droeshout, a Flemish engraver who joined his parents and settled in London *c.* 1590. As he was only fifteen when Shakespeare died, he can scarcely have drawn the picture from life, and he was still only an inexperienced, and doubtless inexpensive, artist when he made the engraving sometime before the end of 1623. There is reason to believe that Droeshout worked from a line drawing, by some unknown artist, depicting Shakespeare as a youngish man, and himself added the unsuccessful chiaroscuro and dress. The engraving, which was on copper, exists in three states. Only a few impressions of the first, the 'proof state', were made before modification. In state two there is shading on the ruff under the ear, and in state three, the commonest, shadows are intensified, the lines are harder, the moustache and beard exaggerated, and the jaw covered with stubble. (See Hinman, *Printing . . . of the First Folio*, I, 248.) The plate was used for the later Folios. The 'Flower Portrait' (q.v.) can scarcely have been the original from which Droeshout worked, but was probably painted from the engraving.

Of Droeshout's portrait Ben Jonson wrote in the Folio:

This Figure, that thou here seest put,
It was for gentle Shakespeare cut:
Wherein the Grauer had a strife
With Nature, to out-doo the life:
O, could he but haue drawne his wit
As well in brasse, as he hath hit
His face, the Print would then surpasse
All, that was euer writ in brasse.
But, since he cannot, Reader, looke
Not on his Picture, but his Booke.

Droeshout made portrait engravings of George Villiers, John Donne, John Fox and others. (See FAITHORNE.)

'Drolls'. The name given to the adaptation of comic scenes extracted from Elizabethan and Jacobean plays when the theatres were closed 1642–60. The law against the public performance of plays was often circumvented by attaching these drolls, for example, *The Merry conceited Humours of Bottom the Weaver*, to other permissible forms of entertainment. (See KIRKMAN.)

Dromio. The name of the twin slaves attendant on the twin Antipholuses in *The Comedy of Errors*. (There is only one slave, Messenio, in the *Menaechmi* of Plautus.)

Drum. The drum was used with the trumpet in battle scenes; Stephen Gosson in his *School of Abuse* (1579) describes how the players 'come to the scaffold with drum and trumpet to proffer skirmish, and when they have sounded alarm, off go the pieces to encounter a shadow'. And again, the inhabitants of Blackfriars protested in 1596 that 'the noise of the drums and trumpets' would disturb divine service. This may have referred also to the use of drums and trumpets for summoning people to the theatre (see also CROSS KEYS INN).

In February 1600 Henslowe bought a drum and two trumpets for the Admiral's 'when to go into the country'. The small drum, or tabor, was played with one hand while the other played the pipe. Tarlton is shown playing pipe and tabor, as is the man who accompanied Kempe on his dance to Norwich.

Drummond, William (1585–1649), Scottish poet, was born at Hawthornden, near Edinburgh, and educated at Edinburgh High School and University. He spent two years in France studying civil law, but when he succeeded his father as Laird of Hawthornden in 1609 he abandoned law for literature. His first published work was an elegy on the death of Henry, Prince of Wales (1613). In 1616 came *Poems*, an account of his love for Mary Cunningham, who died on the eve of their wedding. Some of his best work occurs in the volume of 1623, *Flowers of Sion*, to which was adjoined his *Cypress Grove*, a prose meditation on death. He was a royalist and episcopalian, and in his later years wrote a number of pamphlets in support of his faith, dying soon after the execution of Charles I.

Drummond was a friend of Drayton, with whom he corresponded from 1618 till Drayton's death in 1631. In the winter of 1618 Ben Jonson paid a visit to Hawthornden. Drummond's notes of their conversations were discovered by David Laing and published for the Shakespeare Society in 1842. Jonson's censure of Drummond's verses was, 'that they were all good, especially my Epitaph of the Prince, save that they smelled too much of the Schools, and were not after the fancy of the time'. Jonson told Drummond:

> That Shaksper wanted arte ... Sheakspear, in a play, brought in a number of men saying they had suffered Shipwrack in Bohemia, wher ther is no Sea neer by some 100 Miles.
>
> His epitath, by a companion written, is
>
> Here Lyes Benjamin Johnson dead,
> And hath no more wit than [a] goose in his head;
> That as he was wont, so doth he still,
> Live by his wit, and evermore will.

That the 'companion' was Shakespeare was suggested in the notes of an anonymous writer and by Thomas Plume, both of whom about 1650 quote a similar epitaph which, they say, was written by Shakespeare.

Drury Lane Theatre. A Theatre Royal, sometimes called 'the first Drury Lane', between Bridges Street and Drury Lane, was opened in May 1663 by Killigrew and the King's company. This was destroyed by fire in January 1672, and a new Theatre Royal was built in Drury Lane by Wren and occupied by the King's company in 1674. It was here that many of Shakespeare's plays were revived in 'improved' versions: for example, Ravenscroft's *Titus Andronicus* (1678), Tate's *Richard II* (1680) and *Coriolanus* (1682), Cibber's *Richard III* (1700) and Dennis's *Comical Gallant* (1702). In 1794 the theatre was rebuilt 'upon a much larger scale than that of any other theatre in Europe', but in February 1809 it was burned to the ground, and the present theatre opened in 1812. Alterations were made in 1812 and 1821 to improve the acoustic properties. After Killigrew, managers of Drury Lane were Cibber, Rich, Garrick (1747–76), J. P. Kemble (1788–1802), Macready (1841–3). Until 1843, when the monopoly lapsed, Drury Lane was one of the 'patent' theatres.

Dryden, John (1631–1700). Poet, dramatist, and critic. His Shakespearean criticism, which is of the first importance, is to be found mainly in *An Essay of Dramatick Poesie* (1688), *Essay on the Dramatique Poetry of the Last Age* (1672) and *Preface to Troilus and Cressida* (1679). Dryden was a very great critic and generous in his judgements. For him 'the divine Shakespeare, the father of our dramatic poets ... was the man who of all modern, and perhaps ancient poets, had the largest and most comprehensive soul.' Yet, as Dryden lived in an age which he considered so much more refined, and with trim French models before him, Shakespeare had his faults, as was only to be expected of one 'untaught, unpractis'd in a barbarous Age ... the fury of his fancy often transported him beyond the bounds of judgment.' With D'Avenant he wrote an adaptation of *The Tempest* (1667), and in 1679 made an equally unfortunate adaptation of *Troilus and Cressida* (q.v.). His best play, and first in blank verse, is *All for Love* (q.v.), his version of the Antony and Cleopatra story, produced at Drury Lane in 1677–8. (See KNELLER.)

Du Bellay, Joachim (*c.* 1524–60). After Ronsard, the most important of the group of seven French poets known as the Pléiade. Du Bellay wrote their manifesto, *La Défense et Illustration de la Langue Française*, in which they asserted that French as a literary medium was the equal of Latin and Greek, which, however, should serve as models. The sonnets of du Bellay influenced the Elizabethans; Spenser translated some of them, Drayton imitated them in addressing his sonnets to Idea, and Shakespeare sometimes was indebted to them for a figure or a phrase.

'Duchess of Malfi, The.'

The Tragedy of the Dutchesse of Malfy. As it was Presented priuately, at the Black-Friers; and publiquely at the Globe, By the Kings Maiesties Seruants. The perfect and exact Coppy, with diuerse things Printed, that the length of the Play would not beare in the Presentment. Written by John Webster.... The Actors Names. Bosola, *I. Lowin*. Ferdinand, *1 R. Burbidge*, *2 J. Taylor*. Cardinall, *1 H. Cundaile*, *2 R. Robinson*. Antonio, *1 W. Ostler*, *2 R. Benfeild*. Delio, *I. Vnderwood*. Forobosco, *N. Towley*. Pescara, *I. Rice*. Silvio, *T. Pollard*. Madmen, *N. Towley*, *I. Vnderwood*, etc. Cardinals Mis, *I. Tomson*. The Doctor, Cariola, etc., *R. Pallant*. Dutchesse, *R. Sharpe*.

The actor-list attached to this first edition (1623) refers to two productions; the first, which included Burbage and Condell, was probably shortly before Ostler's death in December 1614; the revival, for which the cast is complete, was presumably between the death of Burbage in March 1619 and that of Tooley in June 1623.

Dudley, Robert. See LEICESTER, EARL OF.

Duffet, Thomas. A Restoration milliner turned playwright. In 1675 his *Mock Tempest* was produced at Drury Lane to compete with the Dryden-D'Avenant version of *The Tempest* running at Dorset Garden.

Dugdale, Sir William (1605–86), was born at Shustoke, near Coleshill, Warwickshire. In 1635 he went to London to pursue his antiquarian studies and was commissioned to make drafts of the monuments in Westminster Abbey and the principal churches of England. Until its surrender in 1646 Dugdale was with Charles I at Oxford, collecting material from the Bodleian. At the Restoration he was made Norroy King-at-Arms, and in 1677, when he was knighted, Garter King-at-Arms. His principal works are *Monasticon Anglicanum* (1655–73), *History of St Paul's Cathedral* (1658), and *Antiquities of Warwickshire* (1656). In the last of these appears an engraving of Shakespeare's monument in Stratford church, but very different from that now to be seen. This, however, is not very remarkable, as other monuments in Dugdale's book are similarly misrepresented. (See JANSSEN.)

Duke, John. Actor. In the 'plot' of the *Seven Deadly Sins* Duke is named as playing the part of 'Will foole'; this probably represents a performance by Strange's at the Curtain, *c.* 1590. It is probable that he was an original member of the Chamberlain's in 1594, but the only actor-list in which he occurs is that of *Every Man in His Humour* (1598), and as he is not mentioned in the Folio list he may never have been a sharer. From 1602 to 1609 he was with the Worcester-Queen Anne company.

'Duke Humphrey.' One of the lost plays, registered in June 1660 by Humphrey Moseley as 'by Will: Shakespeare'. John Warburton (1682–1759), in a list of his burned manuscript plays, records 'Duke Humphrey Will. Shakespear'.

Duke of York's (Prince Charles's) Men. The Duke of York was the future Charles I, the second son of James I, becoming after his brother Henry's death in November 1612, Prince of Wales. The Duke of York's company first appeared in 1608, in the provinces, but in February 1610 were at Court where for some years they played fairly regularly. In the patent of 1610 their names are given as, 'Iohn Garland, Willyam Rowley, Thomas Hobbes, Robert Dawes, Ioseph Taylor, Iohn Newton, and Gilbert Reason', authorized to play 'about our Cittye of London in such usuall howses as themselues shall provide'. Their leader was the dramatist Rowley who supplied them with plays. In 1612 they became known as Prince Charles's, then for a short time, *c.* 1614–16, they joined forces with the Lady Elizabeth's, and in 1619 when Christopher Beeston joined them they moved to his theatre, the Cockpit. In the same year Taylor left them for the King's.

Duke's Company. One of the two companies of players to whom Charles II issued patents in 1660. This company, under D'Avenant, was named after the Duke of York, the future James II, their home being first at Salisbury Court, then in 1661 when Betterton joined them, at Lincoln's Inn Fields, and in 1671 at the Dorset Garden theatre. In December 1660, Charles II granted the Duke's the exclusive right to perform, and 'reform', *The Tempest*, *Measure for Measure*, *Much Ado*, *Romeo and Juliet*, *Twelfth Night*, *Henry VIII*, *King Lear*, *Macbeth*, *Hamlet* and *Pericles*. In 1668 the list was extended to include *Timon of Athens*, *Troilus and Cressida* and *Henry VI*.

Duke 'Senior'. In *As You Like It*, Rosalind's father, who is driven into exile by his brother, Duke Frederick. (In Lodge's *Rosalynde* he is Gerismond, King of France.)

Dull, Anthony. In *Love's Labour's Lost*, a constable who arrests Costard at the suit of Armado for breaking the King's decree by 'consorting' with Jaquenetta. In v, i he promises to 'make one in a dance, or so; or I will play on the tabor to the Worthies, and let them dance the hay', but he is not mentioned after this.

Dulwich. The manor was bought by Edward Alleyn in 1605, the purchase being completed in 1614 at a cost of about £10,000. In 1613 he began the building of the College of God's Gift, or Dulwich College, which was opened in September 1619. Invaluable theatrical records were preserved at Dulwich, including Alleyn's diary (1617–22) and papers, and those of his father-in-law, Henslowe, who died in 1616. At the College are paintings of Alleyn, Richard Burbage, Nathan Field and William Sly.

Dumain. In *Love's Labour's Lost*, one of the three lords attending the King of Navarre. He falls in love with Katharine, to whom he addresses the lyric 'On a day – alack the day!', published by Jaggard in *The Passionate Pilgrim*, 1599. (See HENRI IV; MAYENNE.)

In *All's Well* the two French Lords are the brothers Dumain. They take part in the untrussing of Parolles.

Dumb-show. In some of the early Elizabethan plays the acts were preceded by dumb-shows, either summarizing or symbolizing the action, each accompanied by appropriate music. For example, in *Gorboduc* (*c.* 1560) the music for the dumb-shows is successively violins, cornets, flutes, hautboys, and, for the battle of Act v, drums and flutes. Before Act IV 'first the music of hautboys began to play, during which time there came forth from under the stage, as though out of hell, three furies ... Hereby was signified the unnatural murders to follow'. So, for the dumb-show introducing the 'most unnatural murder' of the King in the interlude in *Hamlet* 'hautboys play'. There are similar dumb-shows in Gascoigne's *Jocasta* (1566) and in *Pericles.* The dumb-show, though attached to plays on the Senecan model, is not classical in origin, and seems to have come from Renaissance Italy.

Duncan (d. 1040). In *Macbeth*, King of Scotland.

D'Urfey, Thomas (1653–1723), familiarly called Tom D'Urfey, a member of a Huguenot family of Exeter, was a dramatist and writer of songs. He was generally popular, favoured by Charles II, James II, William III and Anne, and his friends John Blow, Purcell, and Thomas Farmer helped to popularize his songs by setting them to music. These were published in six volumes in 1720 as *Wit and Mirth; or Pills to Purge Melancholy*. Twenty-nine of his plays were produced, his comedies being more successful than his tragedies. In 1682 his adaptation of *Cymbeline* as *The Injured Princess, or The Fatal Wager* was produced at Drury Lane. In this tidy version Pisanio is given a daughter and is blinded by Cloten for saving her from attempted rape. The play appears to have held the stage for some fifty years.

Dursley. An old market town at the foot of the Cotswold escarpment. There is a tradition that Shakespeare lived here for a time after leaving Stratford, and before going to London; and Aubrey says that 'he had been in his younger years a schoolmaster in the country'. In *2 Henry IV* (v, i) Davy asks Justice Shallow 'to countenance William Visor of Woncot against Clement Perkes o' the hill'. The village of Woodmancote, or Woncot as it is pronounced locally, adjoins Dursley, and both lie under Stinchcombe Hill. Arthur Vizar was buried in Dursley churchyard in 1620, and there was a family of Perkes at Stinchcombe in the 16th century. Dursley is only a dozen miles west of Sapperton, where Richard Davies lived, the man who first recorded Shakespeare's 'unluckiness in stealing venison and rabbits', and a few miles east of Berkeley Castle, which Caroline Spurgeon thought Shakespeare had in mind when he wrote *Macbeth.* Some of the scenes in *Richard II* must have taken place in the neighbourhood of Dursley.

'Dutch Courtesan.' Marston's masterpiece, written 1603–4, and published 1605, 'As it was played in the Blacke-Friars. by the Children of her Maiesties Reuels'. It contains possible references to the title of *All's Well that Ends Well*, thus giving some clue to the date of this enigmatic play.

Duthie, George Ian (1915–67). Professor of English at McGill University

1947–54, and at Aberdeen 1955–67. Author of *Elizabethan Shorthand, Shakespeare*, etc.

Dutton, John and Laurence. Actors and brothers, satirically called the 'chameleon' Duttons, from their practice of often changing companies. Between 1571 and 1591 Laurence was a member of Lane's, Clinton's, Warwick's, Oxford's and the Queen's.

Dyce, Alexander (1798–1869), was born in Edinburgh and educated at Edinburgh High School and Exeter College, Oxford. He entered the Church, settling in London in 1827. His literary work was mostly that of editor and literary historian. He edited Kempe's *Nine Day's Wonder* for the Camden Society, and *Sir Thomas More* for the Shakespeare Society, of which he was one of the founders. His *Strictures on Collier's new Edition of Shakespeare* cost him the friendship of Collier. His own edition of Shakespeare appeared in 1857, and in its revised form in 1866. His valuable *Glossary* was published in 1864.

E

'Eastward Ho!' A comedy performed and published in 1605: 'As it was played in the Black-friers. By the Children of her Maiesties Reuels. Made by Geo: Chapman. Ben Ionson, Ioh: Marston.' It is a pleasant play about idle and industrious apprentices, but because it contained uncomplimentary remarks about the Scots, Chapman was put in prison where Jonson voluntarily joined him, but Marston escaped. The Revels Children lost the Queen's patronage as a result. (See TATE.)

Ecclestone, William. One of the twenty-six 'Principall Actors' in Shakespeare's plays (see p. 91). He played for the King's in 1610–11, was with the Lady Elizabeth's 1611–13, and then rejoined the King's, presumably becoming a sharer, possibly in place of Cooke, and appearing in their lists until 1623.

Eden, Richard (*c.* 1521–76), translator, was born in Herefordshire, and educated at Queens', Cambridge. After being private secretary to Sir W. Cecil he spent the years 1562–73 mainly abroad. His translations of John Taisner's *De Natura Magnetis*, and of Ludovico Barthema's *Travels in the East in 1503* were posthumously published in 1577 as *The History of Travayle in the East and West Indies*. Shakespeare knew the book, for Setebos is given as a Patagonian god.

Edgar. In *King Lear*, the legitimate son of Gloucester. (In Sidney's *Arcadia*, the Prince of Paphlagonia has such a son, Leonatus.)

Editors of Shakespeare.

1623 First Folio, edited by John Heminge and Henry Condell.
1632 Second Folio, editors unknown.
1663 Third Folio, editors unknown. A second impression of 1664 added *Pericles* and six spurious plays.
1685 Fourth Folio, editors unknown.
1709 Nicholas Rowe, 6 vols. octavo.
1725 Alexander Pope, 6 vols. quarto.
1733 Lewis Theobald, 7 vols. octavo.
1744 Thomas Hanmer, 6 vols. quarto.
1747 William Warburton, 8 vols. octavo.
1765 Samuel Johnson, 8 vols. octavo.
1768 Edward Capell, 10 vols. octavo.
1773 George Steevens, 10 vols. octavo.
1790 Edmond Malone, 10 vols. octavo.
1803 First Variorum, 21 vols. Johnson-Steevens, edited by Isaac Reed.
1813 Second Variorum, 21 vols. A reprint of the First Variorum.
1821 Third Variorum, 21 vols. Malone, edited by James Boswell.

From the First Folio to the Third Variorum is 200 years, but the 17th-century reader had to rely on the clumsy and often inaccurate Folios, or, where they existed, on the Quartos. The Folio is the only text for those plays not printed as Quartos, and is superior to that of the plays of which only 'bad' Quartos were issued (*2* and *3 Henry VI*,

Henry V, *The Merry Wives*), but for the rest, though Heminge and Condell professed to offer the plays absolute in their numbers, as Shakespeare conceived them, the Quarto version is generally the better, as the printers of F1 normally used the latest Quarto (though generally with reference to the prompt-book or foul papers) and added to the original errors.

F2 is printed from F1, and though there are improvements in spelling, metre, and stage directions, most of the old errors are perpetuated, and new ones made. There are, however, some 600 good emendations.

F3 is printed from F2, and F4 from F3; the number of errors accumulates, and the text becomes more and more corrupt.

The first improvement of the 18th-century editors was to make Shakespeare easier to read by printing him in handier form, normally in octavo, and in six to ten volumes. From Rowe to Capell the editors were concerned mainly with textual emendation: Rowe, being the first, was able to make many, but as he worked largely from the corrupt F4 most of them were conjectural; he wrote the first Life of Shakespeare, added uniform stage directions, and completed the lists of Dramatis Personae. Pope worked from Rowe's text, collated a few Quartos, but added little of value. Theobald was the first Shakespeare scholar: he collated Quartos, made many brilliant emendations, and studied Shakespeare's sources and the chronology of the plays. Hanmer worked from Theobald's text, and from intuition. Warburton, too, used Theobald, whom he maligned, and added 'his own chimerical conceits'. Johnson based his text on Warburton's, but was too indolent either to improve the text by collation, or to make researches into Shakespeare's life and theatre. His edition is valuable because of its splendid Preface. Capell was the last of the important amenders, and the first fully to realize the importance of the Quartos, which he collected and collated for thirty years.

Capell was also the first of the great Shakespeare scholars, a student not only of the Quartos, but also of Elizabethan literature, making use of material such as Mere's *Palladis Tamia*, the Stationers' Register, Holinshed, North's *Plutarch* and the Italian novel. He began the work that was carried on by Steevens and Malone, the search for original material, and the systematic study of 'all such reading as was never read' in the hope of discovering anything that would throw light on Shakespeare and his work. Steevens, using Johnson's text, illuminated it with quotations from Shakespeare's contemporaries, and his second edition of 1778 contains a mass of new material. Malone made his momentous *Attempt to ascertain the order in which Shakespeare's plays were written*, and wrote the first account of the Elizabethan theatre, based on a knowledge of the Henslowe papers, the Revels Accounts, the Dulwich 'Plots' and other contemporary records. The three volumes of Prolegomena to the Variorum editions are the priceless legacy of the 18th century to the 19th.

The 18th century had been concerned first with Shakespeare's text, then with Shakespeare's life and times: with his theatre, but not with his poetry. Indeed, the first two Variorums do not print the *Poems*, though they are in Vol. xx of the third. The early 19th-century critics, particularly Coleridge and Hazlitt, seized on the poetry and inaugurated the era of aesthetic criticism.

In the 19th century there were scores of editions, the most important being the great *Cambridge Shakespeare* of Clark, Glover and Wright (1863) and the *New Variorum* of H. H. Furness (1871–).

Perhaps the most important of the 20th-century editions are the *Yale*, *Arden*, *New Arden* and *New Cambridge*. (For a more complete list see BIBLIOGRAPHY. See also QUARTOS; FOLIOS; VARIORUM; the various editors.)

Edmund. In *King Lear*, the illegitimate son of Gloucester. (In Sidney's *Arcadia* the Prince of Paphlagonia has a similar hard-hearted son, Plexirtus.)

Education of Shakespeare. Rowe tells us that Shakespeare was 'bred ... at a Free-School', and it seems certain that he went to Stratford Grammar School, which for the sons of burgesses was free, and provided a liberal education for boys up to the age of sixteen. The successive masters in Shakespeare's time (*c.* 1570–80) were, Walter Roche (1569–71), Fellow of Corpus, Oxford, Simon Hunt (1571–5), also of Oxford, and later a Jesuit at Douai and Rome, Thomas Jenkins (1575–9), Fellow of St John's, Oxford, and John Cottam (1579–81). In his *Essay on the Learning of Shakespeare* (1767) Richard Farmer maintained that Shakespeare knew no language except English, but as no English version then existed of some of the books that he used for his plots, it seems certain that he had some French and Italian, picked up probably in London. At school he would begin with elementary phrase books such as the *Sententiae Pueriles* of Leonhard Culmann, and with the aid of Lily's Latin Grammar go on to read Aesop's *Fables*, Caesar, Cicero, Virgil, Horace and above all Ovid; perhaps also Plautus, Terence, and Seneca, and the *Bucolica* of the popular Renaissance poet Baptista Mantuanus. Probably Shakespeare learned no Greek, but he would be well acquainted with the Bible, either in the Genevan or the Bishops' version of 1560 and 1568. (See T. W. Baldwin, *William Shakspere's Small Latin and Lesse Greek*; SS, 3; SS, 10.)

Edward, Earl of March (1442–83), afterwards Edward IV, first appears in *2 Henry VI* as the eldest son of Richard Plantagenet, Duke of York (v, i). In the opening scene of *3 Henry VI* he tells his father how he killed Buckingham at St Albans, and helps to persuade him to break his oath to King Henry. After the murder of his father at Wakefield, 'the wanton Edward' defeats the Lancastrians at Towton and becomes Edward IV (1461) and marries Lady Grey. He is captured, but escapes, and returns to win the battles of Barnet and Tewkesbury. In *Richard III* he appears only in II, i, when Richard tells him of Clarence's murder. His own death is reported in the next scene.

Edward, Prince of Wales (1453–71), only son of Henry VI, in *3 Henry VI*. When his father promises to leave the crown to York, Edward protests 'you cannot disinherit me'. When Warwick joins Margaret and the Lancastrians, Prince Edward is betrothed to his daughter, but is captured at Tewkesbury, and stabbed by Edward IV and his brothers when he addresses them as 'Lascivious Edward, and thou perjured George, And thou mis-shapen Dick'.

Edward, Prince of Wales (1470–83), the son of Edward IV, appears as a baby in the last scene of *3 Henry VI*. In *Richard III*, as the young Edward V, he and his brother York are put in the Tower where they are murdered by order of their uncle, Richard Duke of Gloucester, who seizes the crown.

'Edward I.' A historical play by Peele, written 1592–3, following up the success of Marlowe's *Edward II*. It has been suggested, on the slender evidence of a few lines in the play, that Shakespeare played Edward. Queen Elinor tells the newly crowned John Baliol to admit Edward's overlordship:

> Shake thy spears, in honour of his name,
> Under whose royalty thou wearest the
> same.

John Davies of Hereford (q.v.) in 1610 mentions Shakespeare's 'Kingly parts'.

'Edward II.' A historical play by Marlowe, written in 1592, performed by Pembroke's, published 1594, and in their play-list of 1656 attributed to Shakespeare by the booksellers Richard Rogers and William Ley. It may have influenced Shakespeare's *Richard II*.

'Edward III.' An anonymous historical play published for Cuthbert Burby in 1596 as 'The Raigne of King Edward the third: As it hath bin sundrie times plaied about the Citie of London'. There is no external evidence of Shakespeare's authorship save its ascription to Shakespeare in the play-list of Rogers and Ley (1656). Capell reprinted it in his *Prolusions* in 1760, and described it as 'thought to be writ by Shakespeare', on the grounds that he was the only man who could have written so well in 1595. Tennyson agreed with Capell, and Swinburne disagreed.

There seem to be two hands in the play, one of which may be Shakespeare's. The best writing is in Act II and IV, iv. The line 'Lilies that fester smell far worse than weeds' occurs in II, i as well as in Sonnet 94. But we cannot assign any part in the play to Shakespeare with any confidence on the basis of internal evidence only. (See SS, 6.)

'Edward IV.' A historical play, possibly by Heywood, written *c.* 1594, and published anonymously in 1600 as 'The First and Second Parts of King Edward the Fourth. Containing ... his loue to faire mistrisse Shoare. As it hath diuers times beene publikely played by the Right Honorable the Earle of Derbie his seruants'. It was ascribed to Shakespeare by Rogers and Ley in their play-list of 1656, and the anonymous author of *Pimlyco or Runne Red-Cap* (1609) couples a play of 'Shore' with *Pericles*:

Amazde I stood, to see a Crowd
Of *CiuillThroats* stretched out so lowd;
(As at a *New-play*) all the Roomes
Did swarme with *Gentiles* mix'd with
Groomes,
So that I truly thought all These
Came to see *Shore* or *Pericles*.

Edwardes, Richard (*c.* 1523–66). Musician and dramatist, was born in Somerset, and educated at Corpus, Oxford. In 1556 he became a Gentleman of the Chapel, and in 1561 Master of the Children. He entered Lincoln's Inn, and at Candlemas 1564 and 1565 produced plays there by the Children. His *Damon and Pithias* was acted at Court by the Children in 1565, and on 2 and 4 September 1566 Elizabeth saw the two parts of his *Palamon and Arcite* in the Hall of Christ Church, Oxford. The play is lost, but an analysis of the plot shows that though the source was Chaucer's *Knight's Tale*, it is improbable that Shakespeare and Fletcher used it for their *Two Noble Kinsmen*. In *Romeo and Juliet* (IV, v) Shakespeare quotes a verse from Edwardes's poem *In Commendation of Musique*, published in *The Paradise of Dainty Devises* (1575):

When griping grief the heart doth wound
And doleful dumps the mind oppress,
Then music with her silver sound
With speedy help doth lend redress.

Edwardes is thought to be the composer of the early madrigal 'In going to my naked bed'. (See INNS OF COURT.)

Edwards, Thomas (1699–1757), critic, was educated privately, entered Lincoln's Inn, but devoted himself to literature when he inherited his father's estate. In 1747 he published his *Supplement to Warburton's Edition of Shakespeare*, renamed the following year *The Canons of Criticism*. It is an able exposure of Warburton's shortcomings as an editor of Shakespeare. Johnson compared Edwards to a gad-fly: 'A fly, Sir, may sting a stately horse, and make him wince; but one is but an insect, and the other is a horse still.'

Egerton, Thomas (*c.* 1540–1617). One of the most trusted advisers of Elizabeth, by whom he was knighted and made Lord Keeper. James I created him Lord Ellesmere and Lord Chancellor in 1603, and Viscount Brackley in 1616. He did his best to bring Essex to reason, and befriended Bacon, who succeeded him as Lord Chancellor in 1618. John Donne was his secretary from 1596 to 1601. His son was created Earl of Bridgewater. The *Egerton Papers*, a collection of public and private documents, were edited by J. P. Collier for the Camden Society in 1840. (See HUNTINGTON LIBRARY.)

Egeus. In *A Midsummer Night's Dream*, the father of Hermia. He appeals to Theseus to enforce his wish that she marry Demetrius, but at the end of the play acquiesces in her marriage to Lysander.

Eglamour. In *The Two Gentlemen of Verona*, he helps Silvia to escape from Milan and the attentions of Thurio whom her father wishes her to marry. They set off together to find Valentine, but he deserts her (v, iii).

Elbow. In *Measure for Measure*, 'a simple constable' who twice arrests the bawd Pompey. He resembles Dull and Dogberry.

Eld, George. Printer, in business from about 1604 to his death of the plague in 1624, when Miles Fletcher, who had been his partner since 1617, succeeded to the business. Eld printed:

Troilus and Cressida	Q 1609
The Sonnets	Q 1609

On 6 August 1607 he registered 'the comedie of the Puritan Widowe', the Q of which he printed: 'The Puritaine Or the Widdow of Watling-streete. Acted by the Children of Paules. Written by W. S. Imprinted at London by G. Eld. 1607'. He also printed Stow's *Annales* and Camden's *Remains*.

Elector Palatine. Frederick V (1596–1632) became Elector Palatine of the Rhine on the death of his father in 1610, and on 4 November 1619 was crowned King of Bohemia by the Protestant Bohemians who refused to recognize the new Emperor Ferdinand II. On 8 November Frederick was easily defeated by the imperial army under Tilly at the White Hill, near Prague, and the 'Winter King', as he was derisively called, fled to the Netherlands. He lost his electorate and died in comparative obscurity at Mainz.

In February 1613 Frederick married Elizabeth, daughter of James I. He arrived 16 October 1612; a fortnight later, Henry, Prince of Wales, was taken ill, and died 6 November. Yet the festivities were only postponed; the betrothal took place 27 December, and on 14 February 1613, the wedding. During the winter revels the King's Men gave twenty performances, eight of which were of Shakespeare's plays: *1, 2 Henry IV*, *Julius Caesar*, *Much Ado* (twice), *Othello*, *Winter's Tale*, *Tempest*; there was also the lost *Cardenio* by Shakespeare and Fletcher. On 11 January Prince Henry's Men (formerly the Admiral's) became the servants of the Elector Palatine. On 10 April Frederick and Elizabeth left London. Among their numerous children were Sophia, who became the mother of George I of England, and Prince Rupert of the Rhine, Charles I's cavalry leader in the Civil War, who, incidentally, visited Queen Henrietta Maria in July 1643 when she was staying at New Place.

Elinor. In *King John*, the mother of John, about whose claim to the throne she has no illusions, yet she supports his 'strong possession' against Arthur. She recognizes in the bastard Falconbridge the son of her eldest son Richard I, and he becomes her devoted follower. Elinor accompanies John on his French campaign, stays in France, and in IV, ii John receives news of her death. (Elinor (*c.* 1122–1204), daughter of the Duke of Aquitaine, married Louis VII of France before marrying Henry II (1152), by whom she was the mother of Richard I, Geoffrey (father of Arthur), John, and Eleanor (mother of Blanch).)

Eliot, John (b. 1562). A Warwickshire and Oxford man, possibly a friend of Shakespeare, who certainly made use of his *Ortho-epia Gallica*, a series of lively dialogues in French and English. (See SS, 6.)

Elision. Strictly, the suppression of the final vowel of a word before the initial vowel of the next, but by extension it has come to mean the omission of any syllable in a word. Obviously the rhythm of Shakespeare's blank verse is greatly modified by elision, yet we cannot be certain exactly how Shakespeare intended his verse to be spoken; generally speaking, there is more elision in the Folio than in the Quarto text of a play. It is generally indicated by an apostrophe:

> There they hoyst vs
> To cry to th' Sea, that roard to vs; to sigh
> To th' windes ...

Sometimes, however, there is no apostrophe, as in *roard*, or *theyle* for *they will*; or sometimes the consonants are altered or reversed: *pluckt*, *stolne*. Shakespeare also gave rhythm and emphasis to his prose by means of elision:

> Why then 'tis time to doo't ... What will these hands nere be cleane? No more o' that my Lord, no more o' that ... I tell you yet againe *Banquo's* buried; he cannot come out on's graue.

Elizabeth of Bohemia (1596–1662). The eldest daughter of James I and Anne of Denmark, 'Th' eclipse and glory of her kind' of Wotton's lyric, and in her misfortunes 'The Queen of Hearts'. On 14 February 1613 she married Frederick V, Elector Palatine (q.v.), and spent five happy years in Heidelberg. For a few days in 1619 she was the crowned Queen of Bohemia, but after Frederick's defeat by the imperial army she spent the rest of her life in exile and comparative poverty. Frederick, by whom she had thirteen children, died in 1632; in 1648 she succeeded in restoring her eldest son to the Rhenish Palatinate, but like all her children he quarrelled with her, and refused to give her a home. In 1661 she came, unwanted, to England, and died in February 1662.

In the winter of 1612–13, during the time of her wedding celebrations, the King's Men gave twenty performances, eight of which were of Shakespeare's plays. One of these was *The Tempest*, and it is probable that the masque was inserted in honour of the occasion. Elizabeth had her own company of players, The Lady Elizabeth's (q.v.), licensed by a patent of March 1611, and they gave three performances during the celebrations.

Elizabeth, Queen (1533–1603), was born at Greenwich Palace, 7 September 1533, the only surviving child of Henry VIII and Anne Boleyn. She succeeded to the throne on the death of Mary on 17 November 1558. Elizabeth was a great patron of literature and the theatre, and it was in no small measure due to her that the early drama developed as healthily as it did. She inherited the Court interlude players of her father and grandfather, but these she neglected for the more cultured performances of the Children of Paul's and of her own Chapel. In 1583 she formed an adult company of her own, the Queen's Men (q.v.), which was part of her policy of supporting the professional players in their struggle against the hostile City authorities. She had already issued in 1574 a royal patent to Leicester's Men, authorizing them to play in London without further permission, and another in 1581, giving Edmund Tilney, Master of the Revels, authority over all plays 'in all places'. Elizabeth was not as lavish as James I, for whose Court between 1603 and 1616 there were 299 performances; for a similar period, 1590–1603, Elizabeth gave about 90 performances.

There are not many references to Elizabeth by Shakespeare in his works. The climax of *Henry VIII* is the birth of Elizabeth; the reference to the 'fair vestal throned by the west ... the imperial votaress' in *A Midsummer Night's Dream*, appears to be conventional flattery of the Queen; and in *Sonnet 107* he may refer to her: 'The mortal moon hath her eclipse endured.' (But see SONNETS.) Shakespeare and the Chamberlain's narrowly escaped trouble when they were bribed to produce, on the day before Essex's rebellion of February 1601, Shakespeare's *Richard II*, about the deposition of whom Elizabeth was very sensitive. However, nothing came of the affair, and that Elizabeth appreciated Shakespeare's work is suggested by Ben Jonson in his lines:

Sweet Swan of Avon! what a sight it were
To see thee in our waters yet appear,
And make those flights upon the banks of Thames,
That so did take Eliza, and our James,

and by Rowe (1709), who coherently records the 17th-century tradition:

Queen Elizabeth had several of his plays acted before her, and without doubt gave him many gracious marks of her favour: ... She was so well pleas'd with that admirable character of Falstaff, in the two Parts of *Henry the Fourth*, that she commanded him to continue it for one play more, and to show him in love. This is said to be the occasion of his writing *The Merry Wives of Windsor*.

And it would be pleasant to be able to believe the anonymous story told in the *Dramatic Table Talk* (1825), probably by Richard Ryan, though there is no record of Elizabeth's visiting a theatre:

It is well known that Queen Elizabeth was a great admirer of the immortal Shakspeare, and used frequently (as was the custom of persons of great rank in those days) to appear upon the stage before the audience, or to sit delighted behind the scenes, when the plays of our bard were performed. One evening, when Shakspeare himself was personating the part of a King, the audience knew of her Majesty being in the house. She crossed the stage when he was performing, and, on receiving the accustomed greeting from the audience, moved politely to the poet, but he did not notice it! When behind the scenes, she caught his eye, and moved again, but still he would not throw off his character, to notice her: this made her Majesty think of some means by which she might know, whether he would depart, or not, from the dignity of his character while on the stage. Accordingly, as he was about to make his exit, she stepped before him, dropped her glove, and re-crossed the stage, which Shakspeare noticing, took up, with these words, immediately after finishing his speech, and so aptly were they delivered, that they seemed to belong to it:

'And though now bent on this high embassy,
Yet *stoop* we to take up our *Cousin's* glove!'

He then walked off the stage, and presented the glove to the Queen, who was greatly pleased with his behaviour, and complimented him upon the propriety of it.

Elizabeth (1437–92). In *Richard III*, the Queen of Edward IV. She plays a passive part, her one definite action being the vain attempt to save her children by taking them into sanctuary. Her husband dies, her brother, Earl Rivers, and three of her sons, Lord Grey, Edward V, and the Duke of York are murdered by Richard. We last see the 'shallow, changing woman', in IV, iv, promising Richard to persuade her daughter to marry him. (In *3 Henry VI* she appears as Lady Grey (q.v.).)

Elizabethan English. The Elizabethan was a period of rapid change in the English language. The old process of discarding the numerous inflexions of Early English went on apace; at the same time many words were adopted from Latin and Greek to express the new ideas and discoveries of the Renaissance, and all kinds of experiments, successful and unsuccessful, were made with words. The syntax, however, remained English; constructions were more compressed than ours, and grammar was sacrificed to clarity and vigour. Some of the more important differences in grammar are:

NOUNS: Genitive singular formed by *his* instead of *'s*: 'Mars *his* sword.'

PRONOUNS: *His* or *it* for *its*:

'The action lies in *his* true nature.'
'It had *it* head bit off by *it* young.'

Confusion of nominative and accusative case in personal pronouns: 'Which of *he* or Adrian?' 'Is she as tall as *me*?' The indiscriminate use of *which* and *who*: 'The mistress *which* I serve.' 'A lion *who* glared.'

ADJECTIVES: Freely used as adverbs: 'Grow not *instant* old'; and as nouns: 'Caviare to the *general*.' Double comparative and superlative: 'A *more larger* list.' 'The *most unkindest* cut.'

VERBS: Often formed from nouns and adjectives: 'Such stuff as madmen *tongue* and *brain* not.' 'Time will *unfair* that fairly doth excel.'

3rd person singular with plural subject: 'What *cares* these roarers?'

The impersonal verb: '*It yearns* me not.'

The frequent use of the subjunctive: 'Where *be* thy brothers?'

ADVERBS: *Still* for *always*. *Merely* for *entirely*. *Presently* for *at once*.

PREPOSITIONS: We have more prepositions than the Elizabethans, so that their use is now more strictly defined; for example, *by* was used where we should say *on* or *about*: 'Fed his flocks *by* the fat plains.' 'How say you *by* the French lord?'

CONJUNCTIONS: The emphatic use of *and*, meaning *also*, *even*.

'The friends thou hast, *and* their adoption tried.'

But meaning *except*, *without*, *if not*, etc.

'God defend *but* I should still be so.'

'You salute not at the court *but* you kiss your hands.'

'Beshrew my soul *but* I do love.'

Elizabethan pronunciation was approximately half-way between that of Chaucer and today. Though the final *e* was rarely sounded (though they said *achés*, *statuá*), long vowels were broader and flatter than ours (*ō* approximating to its sound in *core*, *ā* to that in *care*), and the *i* in words ending in *-ion -ian*, *-ient*, *-ience*, was distinctly pronounced, as was normally the *-er* in words like *prayer*. The vowel sounds of many words have changed: *Rome* was practically indistinguishable from *room*, and *Thames* rhymed with *James*. The accentuation of words, particularly of Latin derivatives, sometimes differed from ours, the accent being thrown farther back: *aspéct*, *revénue*, *sepúlchre*. It is important to realize that Shakespeare anglicized foreign names: thus *dauphin* was pronounced *dáwfin* or *dolphin*; and lines like the following should be given a frank English pronunciation:

Then do I give Volquessen, Touraine, Maine,
Poictiers, and Anjou, these five provinces.

See E. A. Abbott's *Shakespearian Grammar*; H. Kökeritz, *Shakespeare's Pronunciation*; SS, 7.)

Elizabethan Stage Society. Founded by William Poel (q.v.) in 1895, with the object of producing plays under approximately Elizabethan conditions, often at Oxford, Cambridge and the Inns of Court.

Ellis-Fermor, Una (1894–1958). Professor of English, University of London, 1947. General editor of the *New Arden Shakespeare*.

Elliston, Robert William (1774–1831). Actor, born in London and educated at St Paul's, from which he ran away. He began his stage career in Bath in 1791, where he soon played leading parts in Shakespearean tragedy and comedy. In 1796 he moved to London, after 1804 playing at Drury Lane, of which he became lessee in 1819, and there presented with over elaborate stage effects, Kean and Macready. He last appeared at Drury Lane as Falstaff in 1826.

Elvetham. See HERTFORD'S MEN.

Ely, Bishop of. 1. In *Henry V* he appears in the first two scenes, first as a pretext for Canterbury's exposition to the audience, then as a cynical supporter of the war against France. (John Fordham, Bp of Ely 1388, d. 1425.)

2. In *Richard III*. See MORTON, JOHN.

Ely Palace Portrait. This so-called portrait of Shakespeare was discovered in 1845 in a broker's shop and bought by the Bishop of Ely, Thomas Turton, after whose death in 1864 it was presented by Henry Graves to the Birthplace. It is inscribed 'Æ 39 + 1603'. The moustache, beard and eyebrows are almost identical with those in the 'first state' of the Droeshout engraving, of which it *may* be the original.

Elyot, Sir Thomas (*c.* 1490–1546). Diplomatist and author, his most famous work being the *Boke named the Governour* (1531), important in the evolution of English prose. It is a treatise on education, politics and the principles that should guide the actions of those in authority. Shakespeare may have been indebted to the book for some of his history; for example, Prince Henry's striking the Chief Justice, and his estimate of Caesar's character.

Elze, Karl (1821–89). German Shakespeare scholar, was in 1875 appointed Professor of English Philology at Halle University. His contributions to the Shakespeare-Gesellschaft were collected as *Abhandlungen zu Shakespeare* and published in English as *Essays on Shakespeare* in 1874; his *Life of Shakespeare* appeared in 1876, and the three volumes of *Notes on Elizabethan Dramatists* in 1880–6.

Emendations. Dover Wilson calculates that the Folio compositor, working from Q *Love's Labour's Lost*, corrected 117 errors, retained 59, and added 137 of his own. If, therefore, a compositor, setting up his type from printed copy, made about 100 errors in a play, we may assume that in working from a manuscript he would make quite as many in setting up a first edition.

There was, therefore, plenty of scope for amending Shakespeare's text, and this was primarily the work of the early editors, particularly of Rowe (1709) and Theobald (1733). By the time Capell published his edition in 1768 most of the obvious emendations had been made, as well as many conjectural alterations. The Globe edition (1864) marked about 130 lines as incapable of emendation, but with modern bibliographical knowledge and a knowledge of the kind of hand that Shakespeare wrote, it has been possible to make many more emendations, and the new study of the peculiarities of individual Elizabethan compositors will help to produce yet more accurate texts of the plays. (See MISPRINTS; PROOF-READING.)

Emerson, Ralph Waldo (1803–82). For his appreciation of Shakespeare, see his *Representative Men: Shakespeare; or, the Poet.*

Emilia. 1. In *Othello*, wife of Iago and companion to Desdemona. She innocently helps to bring about the tragedy, by keeping the fatal handkerchief instead of returning it at once to Desdemona, and by assisting Cassio to 'some brief discourse with Desdemona alone'. (Unnamed in Cinthio's *novella*, she plays a passive part.)

2. In *The Winter's Tale*, a lady attending on Hermione. She accompanies the Queen to prison, where she tells Paulina of the birth of Perdita (II, ii).

3. Sister of Hippolyta and heroine of *The Two Noble Kinsmen* (q.v.).

Enclosure. The consolidation of holdings in the medieval open fields was a progressive and beneficial movement. But the enclosure of common and waste impoverished the country folk by the loss of valuable grazing and other rights. In addition, as Tudor and early Stuart enclosure was mostly for sheep rearing, the conversion of arable into pasture led to unemployment. 'Sheep', wrote Sir Thomas More, 'be become so great devourers and so wild, that they eat up and swallow down the very men themselves.' (See WELCOMBE ENCLOSURE.)

End-stopped Lines. Before the time of Shakespeare blank verse was generally a series of lines, each complete in itself: a main or subordinate clause of ten syllables with a grammatical pause at the end. Marlowe's 'mighty line' was the development of this single-moulded verse to its extreme limits. Shakespeare's early verse is for the most part end-stopped, as in *The Comedy of Errors* (I, i, 113–18):

At length, another ship had seized on us;
And, knowing whom it was their hap to save,
Gave healthful welcome to their shipwreck'd guests;

And would have reft the fishers of their
prey,
Had not their bark been very slow of sail;
And therefore homeward did they bend
their course.

(See RUN-ON LINES; VERSE-TESTS.)

England's Helicon. One of the best of the Elizabethan Miscellanies (1600), Numbers 17, 18, 20, and part of 21 of *The Passionate Pilgrim* (1599) were reprinted in it.

Enjambment. See RUN-ON LINES.

Enobarbus. In *Antony and Cleopatra*, the dearest friend of Antony. On their return to Rome he gives Maecenas and Agrippa the famous description of Cleopatra in her barge (II, ii). When Antony's power and judgement decline he 'seeks some way to leave him', and joins Caesar. Antony sends after him all his treasure 'with his bounty over-plus', and Enobarbus dies of a broken heart (IV, ix). (Cn. Domitius Ahenobarbus was consul in 32 B.C. and deserted Antony before Actium, shortly after which he died.)

Entrances and Exits. In the early editions of Shakespeare's plays entrances are more accurately marked than exits, presumably because the book-keeper, from whose prompt-copy the printer often worked, was responsible for getting the characters on the stage but not for getting them off. Rowe, in his edition of 1709, completed the marking of entrances and exits. (See STAGE DIRECTIONS.)

'Epicoene, Or the Silent Woman. A Comœdie. Acted in the yeere 1609. By the Children of her Maiesties Revells. The Author B[en] I[onson].' One of the 'principall Comœdians' was Nat. Field. Truewit's 'you have lurch'd your friends of the better half of the garland' in the last speech of the play, may be an echo of Cominius in *Coriolanus* (II, ii, 99), 'He lurched all swords of the garland.' If so, it gives a final date for the composition of *Coriolanus*.

Epilogue. The epilogue was generally spoken by one of the main characters of the play, for which it was an apology and an appeal for applause. After it might come a prayer for the sovereign, as in *2 Henry IV*, and then a jig. Sometimes, at least in Charles I's reign, the next play in the repertory would be announced. This is clear from the verses prefatory to the Beaumont and Fletcher Folio of 1647:

As after th' Epilogue there comes some one
To tell spectators what shall next be shown.

Towards the end of the 16th century the epilogue appears to have been preferred to the prologue: cf. *The Birth of Hercules*, *c.* 1597, 'Thepilogue is in fashion; prologues no more'. There is an epilogue to the following plays of Shakespeare: *A Midsummer Night's Dream*, *As You Like It*, *Twelfth Night*, *All's Well*, *Pericles*, *The Tempest*, *2 Henry IV*, *Henry V*, *Henry VIII*. None of the tragedies has an epilogue.

Epitaphs. See MONUMENT; DOWDALL.

Eros. In *Antony and Cleopatra*, a servant of Antony. He plays a small part, but after the defection of Enobarbus it becomes more important. When Antony is told that Cleopatra is dead, he orders Eros to kill him. He turns his back and Eros draws his sword, but kills himself.

Erpingham, Sir Thomas. In *Henry V*, an officer in the English army. He appears only in IV, i, in the early morning before Agincourt. After telling him that he is too old for such a campaign, Henry borrows his cloak. (Erpingham (1357–1428) helped Bolingbroke to the throne. At Agincourt he set the army in order of battle.)

Escalus. I. In *Romeo and Juliet*, the Prince of Verona, who threatens death to the Capulets and Montagues if ever they disturb the streets again. He banishes Romeo and tidies up the threads of the story at the end of the play. (So called in Brooke's *Romeus and Juliet*. See SCALA.)

2. In *Measure for Measure*, 'an ancient Lord' (F). In the Duke's absence he advises Angelo, publicly supporting his severity but privately disapproving; he pleads for Claudio, and dismisses Froth and Pompey with a warning. Nevertheless, he orders the disguised Duke to be sent to prison on the testimony of Lucio.

Escanes. In *Pericles*, a lord of Tyre. He appears with Helicanus in I, iii and speaks half a dozen words to him in II, iv.

Eschenburg, Johann Joachim (1743–1820), German scholar, and Professor at the Collegium Carolinum in Brunswick. His prose translation of Shakespeare (1775–82), based on that of Wieland, is the first complete German version of the plays.

Essex, Earl of. In *King John*. He appears only in I, i, where he announces the Faulconbridge brothers to John. (Geoffrey Fitz-Piers, died 1212.)

Essex, Robert Devereux, 2nd Earl of (1566–1601), succeeded to the title on the death of his father in 1576. In 1585 he accompanied his stepfather, the Earl of Leicester, on his campaign in Holland, where he distinguished himself at the battle of Zutphen. After Leicester's death in 1588 Essex succeeded him as Elizabeth's favourite. His marriage with the widow of Sir Philip Sidney in 1590 occasioned one of the many quarrels with the queen, but she forgave him, making him one of the commanders of the successful Cadiz expedition of 1596, and in 1597 creating him Earl Marshal. Relations, however, between the vain and ambitious young man and the ageing queen became very strained. Opposed to him was Cecil, who trapped him into accepting the Lord-Deputyship of Ireland with the unenviable task of putting down Tyrone's rebellion, and after some delay he made a spectacular departure from London in March 1599 with Shakespeare's patron, Southampton, as his Master of Horse. At this time Shakespeare was finishing *Henry V*, in the Chorus to the last Act of which he compares Henry's return to England with the expected return of Essex from Ireland:

> As, by a lower but loving likelihood,
> Were now the general of our gracious
>   empress,
> As in good time he may, from Ireland
>   coming,
> Bringing rebellion broached on his sword,
> How many would the peaceful city quit,
> To welcome him!

Essex, however, did not bring home rebellion broached on his sword; instead he made a disastrous truce with Tyrone, lost his nerve, and fled to England, where on 28 September he burst into the Queen's room and threw himself upon her mercy. But Elizabeth did not forgive him this time; he was a discredited and ruined man, and became thenceforth the rallying-point of other malcontents. The Council was alarmed and demanded an explanation; this forced Essex's hand, and on 8 February 1601 he led his small band of supporters, Southampton among them, into the City, hoping to raise the citizens and train-bands; but few followed him, and he was forced to surrender. Essex and Southampton were brought to trial on 19 February and both were condemned to death. Southampton, however, was spared, but Essex was executed on 25 February. There was a curious incident on the day before the rising. Essex's supporters paid Shakespeare's company, the Chamberlain's, 'xl*s*. more than their ordynary' for a performance of *Richard II*, apparently with the idea that the presentation of 'the deposyng and kyllyng of Kyng Rychard' would influence the people in their favour. Augustine Phillips (q.v.) had to explain the Chamberlain's part in the affair, but no action was taken against the company, and on 24 February, the day before Essex's execution, they played before the Queen at Whitehall. (See BACON; LAMBARDE; L. Strachey, *Elizabeth and Essex*.)

Essex's Men. Walter Devereux, 1st Earl of Essex, had a provincial company of players traceable from 1572 to his death in 1576, after which for a time it was called after his widow, 'The Countess of Essex's'. They appeared at Court in February 1578. From 1581–96 his son, Robert 2nd Earl, had a provincial company, and there is mention of another in 1601, the year of his execution.

Etkyns, Thomas. Shakespeare's uncle; a farmer of Aston Cantlow who married Mary Arden's sister, Katharine. He had a son Thomas, a yeoman, and it may have been his son, a third Thomas, and the clerk of Abraham Sturley, who died of the plague in Stratford in 1597.

Eton College. Christmas plays were given by the boys in the middle of the 16th century. 'Elderton and the Children of Eyton' received the customary £6 13s. 4d. for their only Court performance on 6 January 1573. A year later William Elderton was payee for the Children of Westminster. (See UDALL.)

Euphronius. In *Antony and Cleopatra*, an ambassador, described by Dolabella as Antony's 'schoolmaster'. After his defeat at Actium, Antony sends Euphronius to Caesar to beg that he may be allowed to live in Egypt or Athens, and that Cleopatra may remain Queen. Caesar refuses (III, xii).

Euphuism. The name given to the elaborate and highly artificial language popularized by John Lyly (q.v.). He was only about twenty-five when, in 1579, he published *Euphues, the Anatomy of Wit*, the second part, *Euphues and his England*, appearing in the following year. It is a romance, though the greater part is made up of letters and dialogues on education and love. The characteristics of the style are balance, antithesis, alliteration, allusions to classical history and mythology, and similes drawn from medieval natural history:

For although the worm entereth almost into every wood, yet he eateth not the cedar tree. Though the stone Cylindrus at every thunder clap roll from the hill, yet the pure sleek stone mounteth at the noise: though the rust fret the hardest steel, yet doth it not eat into the emerald: though Polypus change his hue, yet the salamander keepeth his colour: though Proteus transform himself into every shape, yet Pigmalion retaineth his old form ...

Euphuism left its mark on all forms of Elizabethan literature, from the prose of the pamphleteers to the poetry of the dramatists. Its influence can be seen in the early work of Shakespeare, particularly in *Love's Labour's Lost*; but Shakespeare never treated it very seriously, and parodied the style as often as he imitated it.

Evans, Edith (b. 1888), made her first stage appearance at King's Hall, Covent Garden, as Cressida with the Elizabethan Stage Society. She was the first West End artist 'to learn her job in Shakespeare' at the Old Vic, which she joined in the 1925 season, playing Portia, Beatrice, Cleopatra, etc. She returned to the Old Vic in 1932 and 1936. In 1946 she was created D.B.E. At Stratford in 1959 she played the Countess of Rossillion and Volumnia.

Evans, Henry, a London scrivener and theatre manager, associated with W. Hunnis in 1583–4 in the first Blackfriars theatre. In 1600 he became the partner of Nathaniel Giles, Master of the Children of the Chapel, and after 1602 of Edward Kirkham, in the second Blackfriars theatre, where the Children of the Chapel gave public performances. In September 1600 Richard Burbage leased the theatre to him for a rent of £40, but in May 1602, owing to some irregularities Lord Chamberlain Hunsdon ordered Evans 'to avoyd and leave the same', and he went abroad. In 1603, however, with a new King and a new Lord Chamberlain, he returned, the syndicate receiving a patent for their enterprise from James I. Evans soon sold one-sixth of the interest in the business to John Marston, who later sold it for £100 to Robert Keysar, after 1606 one of the syndicate. In August 1608 Henry Evans surrendered the lease in the Blackfriars to Burbage, who divided shares in the theatre into seven parts, one each for himself and his brother Cuthbert, one each for four of the King's Men, including Shakespeare, and the seventh for Thomas Evans, presumably the representative of Henry Evans. In 1610 Keysar brought a suit against the King's Men, claiming a share in their profits, as he maintained that when he bought his interest they had promised not to make an arrangement with Evans prejudicial to him. Burbage replied that Evans had no right to sell his interest. Kirkham, too, in 1611–12, brought a number of suits against Evans, vainly claiming damages sustained by the surrender of the lease.

Evans, Sir Hugh. In *The Merry Wives*, a Welsh parson. In the final baiting of Falstaff, Evans undertakes to teach the children, and himself delightfully leads the revels as Fairy Queen. (See CAIUS.)

'Every Man in His Humour.' The play was registered 4 August 1600, along with *As You Like It*, *Henry V* and *Much Ado*, as 'to be staied'. However, it was published in 1601. The 1616 Folio reads: 'Euery Man in his Humour. A Comœdie. Acted in the yeere 1598. By the then Lord Chamberlaine his Seruants. The Author B[en]I[onson]... The principall Comœdians were, Will. Shakespeare, Ric. Burbage, Aug. Philips, Ioh. Hemings, Hen. Condel, Tho. Pope, Will. Slye, Chr. Beeston, Will. Kempe, Ioh. Duke'. This is the first actor-list of the Chamberlain's. It has been hazarded that the Droeshout engraving of Shakespeare shows him in the part of old Knowell in this play, and Rowe credits him with having been responsible for his company's acceptance of this, Jonson's first or second play, when he was 'altogether unknown to the World'. The Prologue, first printed in the Folio, may have been written for the Court performance by the King's Men in February 1605, though probably later, as it appears to criticize Shakespeare's *Henry VI*, and his attempt in *Henry V* to give unity by means of the Chorus, and to represent Agincourt 'with four or five most vile and ragged foils'. There may also be references to the long lapses of time in *Pericles* and *The Winter's Tale*:

> To make a child, now swaddled, to proceed
> Man, and then shoot up, in one beard, and weed,
> Past threescore years: or, with three rusty swords,
> And help of some few foot-and-half-foot words,
> Fight over York, and Lancaster's long jars:
> And in the tiring-house bring wounds, to scars.
> He rather prays, you will be pleas'd to see
> One such, to-day, as other plays should be.
> Where neither Chorus wafts you ore the seas;
> Nor creaking throne comes down, the boys to please ...

'Every Man out of His Humour.' Three Quartos were published in 1600. F1, 1616, reads, 'A Comicall Satyre. Acted in the yeere 1599. By the then Lord Chamberlaine his Seruants. The Author B[en] I[onson] ... The principall Comœdians were, Ric. Burbadge, Ioh. Hemings, Aug. Philips, Hen. Condel, Wil. Sly, Tho. Pope.' The play contains a reference to Silence in *2 Henry IV*: 'No, lady, this is a kinsman to Justice Silence' (v, ii), and possibly to *Julius Caesar* ('O judgment, thou art fled to brutish beasts', III, ii) in III, i: 'reason long since is fled to animals', and again, 'Et tu, Brute' (v, iv). (See 'WISDOM OF DR DODIPOLL'.) There may also be an allusion to Shakespeare and his motto, *Non Sans Droit*, in III, i. Sogliardo describes his newly acquired coat of arms: 'On a chief argent, a boar's head proper', and Puntarvolo suggests as an appropriate motto, *Not Without Mustard*.

Exeter, Duke of. 1. In *Henry V*, Thomas Beaufort (*c.* 1375–1426), uncle of the King, urges Henry to claim the French throne, arrests Cambridge, Scroop, and Grey for high treason, acts as ambassador to France, and accompanies Henry on the Harfleur-Agincourt campaign. He describes the deaths of Suffolk and York in the battle (IV, vi). He appears in *1 Henry VI* as Thomas Beaufort (q.v.) Duke of Exeter.

2. In *3 Henry VI*. This is Henry Holland (1430–73), Duke of Exeter. He plays a small part as a supporter of Henry in the Wars of the Roses. (He was attainted by Edward IV, and died in poverty.)

Exits. See ENTRANCES AND EXITS.

Exton, Sir Piers. In *Richard II*, he overhears Henry IV wishing for the death of Richard, and murders him in Pontefract Castle, though Henry does not thank him for the deed (v, iv–vi). (Shakespeare follows Holinshed's account. Sir Nicholas Exton, Sheriff of London, probably a near relation, was a violent opponent of Richard in Parliament.)

F

Fabian. In *Twelfth Night*, one of Olivia's household. He is not one of the originators of the plot against Malvolio, but joins in the fun because the puritanical steward has brought him out of favour with Olivia about a bear-baiting.

Fabyan, Robert (d. 1513). A member of the Drapers' Company, and Sheriff of London 1493–4. In 1516 his *New Chronicles of England and of France* was published, a history that goes up to 1485. In a second edition of 1533 another hand brings the chronicle up to 1509; but that Fabyan left a manuscript of events up to 1511 seems certain from references by Stow and Hakluyt. Shakespeare probably made use of Fabyan for his history of Henry VI.

Facsimiles of Early Editions. Some of the most important are:

QUARTOS:
- Lithographic, J. O. Halliwell-Phillipps, 48 vols., 1862–76.
- Photolithographic, F. J. Furnivall, 43 vols., 1880–9.
- Collotype, the Shakespeare Association and Clarendon Press, 1939– .

FIRST FOLIO:
- Type facsimile, L. Booth, 1862–4.
- Photolithographic, H. Staunton, 1866.
- Photographic, reduced facsimile, J. O. Halliwell-Phillipps, 1876. (See SQ, 5, 395.)
- Collotype, Sidney Lee, 1902. (Oxford.)
- Photographic, selected plays, J. D. Wilson.
- Photographic, reduced facsimile, H. Kökeritz and C. T. Prouty (Yale), 1955.
- Photographic, Charlton Hinman, 1969.

THE FOUR FOLIOS:
- Photozincographic, 1904–10 (Methuen).

POEMS: Collotype, Sidney Lee, 1905.

(See F. Bowers, PBSA, xlvi.)

'Fair Em.' An anonymous play written *c.* 1590 and published without date:

> A Pleasant Comedie of Faire Em, the Millers Daughter of Manchester. With the loue of William the Conqueror. As it was sundry times publiquely acted in the Honourable Citie of London, by the right Honourable the Lord Strange his Seruants.

Fair Em was bound with *Mucedorus* and *The Merry Devil of Edmonton* in Charles II's library, and labelled 'Shakespeare, Vol. 1'. R. Simpson argues that the play is Shakespeare's reply to Robert Greene's attacks.

Fairholt, Frederick William (1814–66). Antiquary and wood engraver, was born in London and entered his father's tobacco business. His publications include an edition of Lyly's plays (1856). He illustrated Halliwell-Phillipps's folio edition of Shakespeare (1853–65), and was one of the committee for the purchase of the Birthplace in 1847. He left his collection of Shakespearean books to the Stratford library.

Fairies. Shakespeare was not the first Elizabethan dramatist to introduce fairies into his plays, though he was the first to use them on the scale of *A Midsummer*

Night's Dream. There are fairies in Lyly's delicate comedies, *Galathea*, and *Endymion*, written for the Children of the Chapel about 1588, and Robert Greene's *James IV* is 'presented by Oboram, King of Fayeries'. They were also popular ingredients in the 'entertainments' given to Elizabeth on her progresses; for example at Woodstock in 1575 'the Queen of the Fayry drawen with six children in a waggon of state' presented her with an embroidered gown; at Norwich in 1578 she was met by fairies and the Fairy Queen, and at Elvetham in 1591 there were dancing fairies and their Queen Aureola. From childhood Shakespeare must have been acquainted with the fairies of Warwickshire folk-lore, and Puck, or Robin Goodfellow, is one of these. Oberon, however, is French, in the romance of *Huon de Bordeaux*, from Berners's translation of which Shakespeare may have taken him, though he would certainly have met him in Greene's *James IV*. Titania he got from Ovid who, in his *Metamorphoses* gives the name to Circe, Diana, Latona and Pyrrha, as descendants of the Titans. In *Romeo and Juliet*, however, she is Queen Mab, a Celtic name, and Shakespeare appears to have been the first to apply it to the Fairy Queen. (See M. C. Latham, *The Elizabethan Fairies*, 1930; K. M. Briggs, *The Anatomy of Puck*, 1959.)

'Fairy Queen.' Betterton's adaptation of *A Midsummer Night's Dream*, produced at Dorset Garden theatre in 1692. It is reduced to the Fairy and Bottom story to make room for song, dance, spectacle and the music of Purcell. It is magnificent, but it is not Shakespeare. The original production surpassed all that the courtly masques had done: there was a fountain, swans that turned into fairies, peacocks with spreading tails, a monkey ballet and Chinese singers.

Faithorne, William (1626–91). Painter and engraver. As a Royalist he was driven to France during the Civil War and studied under Robert Nanteuil. About 1650 he returned to London, where he set up as printseller and engraver, executing portrait engravings, among others of Milton and Cromwell, and in 1655, of Shakespeare. It is a reversed copy of the Droeshout engraving, and was published as frontispiece to Quarles's edition of *The Rape of Lucrece*.

'False Folio'. The collected edition of ten 'Shakespearean' plays, mostly pirated or spurious, projected by W. Jaggard (q.v.) in 1619. (See Greg, *First Folio*, pp. 11–17.)

Falstaff, Sir John. The most famous comic character in English literature, not only witty in himself, but the cause that wit is in other men.

In *1 Henry IV* he is seen as the boon companion of Prince Henry; he robs the travellers at Gadshill, is himself robbed, and talks himself out of the charge of cowardice. Against the Hotspur rebellion he is given a company of foot, misuses the king's press damnably, and at Shrewsbury, after feigning death, pretends to have killed Hotspur himself.

In *2 Henry IV* he insults the Lord Chief Justice, defrauds Mistress Quickly, sups with Doll Tearsheet, captures the rebel Coleville, borrows a thousand pounds from Justice Shallow, and is finally disowned and banished by his old companion Prince Hal, now Henry V. His death is reported by Mistress Quickly in *Henry V* (II, iii): 'his heart is fracted and corroborate', comments Pistol.

In *The Merry Wives of Windsor*, according to tradition written at Elizabeth's command to show Falstaff in love, Falstaff is little more than a butt. He makes love to Mistress Page and Mistress Ford, escapes Ford's jealous search, once in a buck basket which is thrown into the Thames, another time in the disguise of the old witch of Brentford, and is cudgelled. Finally he is persuaded to dress up as Herne the Hunter and baited in Windsor Forest at night by Pistol, Mistress Quickly, Sir Hugh Evans and his fairies.

In *Henry IV* as Shakespeare originally wrote it, Falstaff was called Sir John Oldcastle, but probably in deference to the Lords Cobham, who were descendants of Oldcastle and prominent at Court, changed it to Falstaff before publication. He chose the new name for two reasons: Falstaff, like Oldcastle, was 'Sir John', and this would necessitate fewer alterations, and then Sir John Fastolfe in *1 Henry VI* had a kind of alacrity in running away. Unfortunately the real Sir John Fastolfe was no more a coward than Sir John Oldcastle, and the substitution led to new protests. (See FASTOLFE; OLDCASTLE; COBHAM; SOUTHAMPTON; FULLER; 'FAMOUS VICTORIES OF HENRY V'; MORGANN; JAMES, RICHARD.)

'Famous Victories of Henry V.' This anonymous play was registered 14 May 1594, the earliest extant edition being published in 1598 as 'The Famous Victories of Henry the fifth: Containing the Honourable Battell of Agin-court: As it was plaide by the Queenes Maiesties Players'. It may have been written by 1588, for Tarlton of the Queen's Men, who died in that year, is said to have doubled the parts of the judge and the clown at a performance 'at the Bull in Bishopsgate'. For his *Henry IV* and *Henry V* Shakespeare took from *The Famous Victories* the name of Sir John Oldcastle, Gadshill and the dissolute Prince Henry.

Fanfare. A flourish of trumpets. It was used to announce the beginning of a play (see SOUNDINGS), and in a performance the arrival of royalty; cf. *The Order of the Coronation* in *Henry VIII* (IV, i), which begins with 'a lively flourish of trumpets', and ends with 'a great flourish of trumpets'. The alarms, retreats and tuckets of battle and warlike scenes may be classed as fanfares.

Fang. In *2 Henry IV*, one of the '2 Serieants' sent to arrest Falstaff at the suit of Mistress Quickly (II, i).

Farmer, Richard (1735–97), was born at Leicester, from its grammar school going to Emmanuel, Cambridge, of which in 1775 he became Master, and in the same year Vice-Chancellor. He lived mostly in Cambridge, and enjoyed the things he loved most: old port, old clothes and old books. In 1767 appeared his short but important *Essay on the Learning of Shakespeare*. This was written as a refutation of those critics who, like Gildon, Sewell and Upton, had too vehemently asserted the learning of Shakespeare, and in it he showed that Shakespeare's Greek came from North and Chapman, not from Plutarch and Homer, his Latin from Golding, his Italian from Painter, and his Spanish from Shelton. He concludes:

> He [Shakespeare] remembered perhaps enough of his school-boy learning to put the *Hig, hag, hog* into the mouth of Sir Hugh Evans; and might pick up in the writers of the time, or the course of his conversation, a familiar phrase or two of French or Italian: but his *studies* were most demonstratively confined to *nature* and *his own language*.

Scholars do not agree with this today, but Farmer offers the sound critical suggestion, a hint that was taken by Capell, Steevens and Malone:

> In the course of this disquisition, you have often smiled at 'all such reading, as was never read;' and possibly I may have indulged it too far: but it is the reading necessary for a comment on Shakespeare. Those who apply solely to the ancients for this purpose, may with equal wisdom study the Talmud for an exposition of Tristram Shandy. Nothing but an intimate acquaintance with the writers of the time, who are frequently of no other value, can point out his allusions, and ascertain his phraseology. The reformers of his text are for ever equally positive, and equally wrong. The cant of the age, a provincial expression, an obscure proverb, an obsolete custom, a hint at a person or a fact no longer remembered, hath continually defeated the best of our *guessers*....

(See EDUCATION OF SHAKESPEARE.)

Farrant, Richard (1530?–80). About 1553 Farrant became a Gentleman of the

Chapel Royal, and in 1564 Master of the Children of Windsor, a post which, from 1576, he combined with that of Deputy Master of the Children of the Chapel. In 1567 he began a series of Court plays with the Windsor Children, then in 1576 took a lease of some rooms in the dissolved Blackfriars Priory, and converted them into the first Blackfriars theatre where the Children gave public performances of their plays. He also gave performances at Lincoln's Inn. As Master of the Children of Windsor, Farrant was organist to the Queen at St George's Chapel, Windsor. He composed some church music, the anthem, *Lord, for Thy Tender Mercies' Sake*, may be his, and some of his secular music may have been written for the Children's plays. (See INNS OF COURT.)

Fastolfe, Sir John. In *1 Henry VI*, a cowardly knight. In I, i, a messenger describes how Talbot was captured at Patay because Fastolfe 'cowardly fled, not having struck one stroke'. Again, he deserts Talbot at Rouen and saves himself by flight (III, ii). In IV, i Talbot tears the Garter from the craven's leg and the King banishes him on pain of death.

The real Sir John Fastolf (d. 1459) was a distinguished, though apparently grasping and pitiless soldier, governor of Maine and Anjou in 1423, and victor of the 'Battle of the Herrings'. He did, however, desert Talbot at Patay, though, according to an eye-witness, only when the situation was hopeless; and he was deprived of the Garter, though afterwards honourably reinstated. But his reputation as a coward and as a Lollard clung to him, and this was one reason why Shakespeare changed the original name of Oldcastle in *Henry IV* to Falstaff. Fastolf owned a Boar's Head Tavern in Southwark, and like Falstaff had been in the service of Thomas Mowbray, Duke of Norfolk. (See also JAMES, RICHARD; FULLER, THOMAS.)

Faucit, Helena Saville (1817–98). Shakespearean actress, was born in London. Her first appearance was in 1836 at Covent Garden, under Macready, whom she joined at Drury Lane in 1842, and accompanied on a Paris tour of 1844–5. She played most of Shakespeare's heroines, both in comedy and tragedy, one of her last appearances, when she was over sixty, being as Beatrice at the opening of the Memorial Theatre in 1879. In 1851 she married Sir Theodore Martin, who presented the pulpit to Stratford church in her memory. In 1885 she published her book *On Some of Shakespeare's Female Characters.*

Faulconbridge. In *King John.* Lady Faulconbridge is the mother of the Bastard Philip, and of Robert. In I, i, Philip forces her to admit that Richard I was his father. (In *The Troublesome Reign* she is Lady Margaret.)

Philip F., generally known as the Bastard. In I, i, Queen Elinor recognizes him as her grandson, and John knights him. Henceforth he serves John as faithfully as Kent serves Lear. (In *Tr. Reign* he aspires to the hand of Blanch. Historically, he may be identified with Foulke de Breante, who died in disgrace in 1228.)

Robert F., the legitimate and younger son of Lady F., maintains that Philip is illegitimate, and appeals to John to let him have his father's inheritance. This John grants (I, i).

Fechter, Charles Albert (1824–79). Actor, born of French parents. At first he worked in Paris, mainly as a sculptor, but in 1846 began a successful career as an actor. In 1860 he came to London, where his playing of Hamlet, Othello and Iago was enthusiastically received. In 1870 he went to America, where he died. He was one of the Romantic school of actors who followed naturalism in acting and verse-speaking.

Feeble, Francis. In *2 Henry IV*, one of the half-dozen sufficient men supplied by Justice Shallow, from whom Falstaff is to select four for the army. Francis Feeble is a woman's tailor who philosophically accepts his lot when chosen (III, ii).

'Felix and Philiomena.' A lost play acted at Court (Greenwich) by Queen Elizabeth's Men in January 1585: 'The history of felix & philiomena ... by her maiesties servauntes on the Sondaie next after new yeares daye' (*Revels Accounts*). This is the story of Montemayor's *Diana Enamorada* from which Shakespeare took his *Two Gentlemen of Verona*. No doubt he knew the play as well.

Felton Portrait. A head painted on a panel, with a forehead so high as to amount almost to a deformity. It takes its name from Samuel Felton, who bought it in London for £5 in 1792. On the back of the panel was inscribed 'Gul. Shakespear 1597 R.B.', which, if genuine, would suggest that Richard Burbage was the painter. Steevens, who rejected 'the canvas Chandois picture', considered that the Felton portrait, engravings of which by J. Neagle and William Holl were prefixed to the Variorum editions of 1803 and 1813 respectively, 'had the fairest chance of being a genuine likeness'. The printseller Richardson found it profitable to sell engravings of the Felton head in the Droeshout costume, which he was then able to claim as the Droeshout original.

Feminine Endings. The extra or 'redundant' unstressed syllable at the end of a line, usually that of a disyllabic or polysyllabic word, but often in Fletcher's verse, rarely, though with increasing frequency in Shakespeare's, an unstressed monosyllable. 'When Shakspere uses the extra syllable, he does it generally in moments of passion and excitement, – in questions – in quarrel – seldom in quiet dialogue or narrative, and seldom in any serious or pathetic passage' (E. A. Abbott). Fletcher, on the other hand, was very fond of the falling cadence of the feminine ending, particularly for increasing the pathos. Cf. *Henry VIII*, the dying Katharine, almost certainly a Fletcher passage:

Whom I most hated Liuing, thou hast made | mee
With thy Religious Truth, and Modestie,
(Now in his Ashes) Honor: Peace be with | him.
Patience, be neere me still, and set me low | er,
I haue not long to trouble thee. Good *Griff* | *ith*,
Cause the Musicians play me that sad note
I nam'd my Knell; whil'st I sit meditat | ing
On the Cœlestiall Harmony I go | too.

The proportion of feminine endings increases fairly regularly in Shakespeare's plays and for establishing the chronology is one of the most helpful of the verse-tests (q.v.).

Fenton. In *The Merry Wives*, a young gentleman in love with Anne Page. Her father objects to his suit because of his rank, his extravagance and riotous past, and Fenton himself admits that his wealth was the first motive of his wooing. He bribes the Host, who helps him in his scheme of running away with Anne and marrying her.

Fenton, Geoffrey (*c.* 1539–1608). Writer and diplomatist. While he was in Paris in 1567 he translated Belleforest's version of Bandello's *novelle*, published as *Certaine tragicall discourses written oute of Frenche and Latin*, a book that Shakespeare must have been well acquainted with. In 1580 he joined Edmund Spenser in Ireland, as secretary to the Lord Deputy, and made himself unpopular by reporting the activities of his fellows to Elizabeth, who knighted him in 1589. He was buried in Dublin.

Fenton, Richard (1746–1821), author, was born at St David's, Pembrokeshire, entered the Middle Temple, became a barrister and took to literature. He was, apparently, a charming and well-informed man. In 1773 he published his *Poems*, and in 1811 the anonymous *A Tour in Quest of Genealogy through* *several Parts of Wales*. In the latter he quotes passages from 'a curious journal of Shakespeare, an account of many of his plays, and memoirs of his life by himself.' He professed to have found the manuscript in the house of a Welsh gentleman who had married a Hathaway, and that it was a copy in the hand of 'Mrs. Shakespeare'. Chambers is probably right in thinking it only a *jeu d'esprit*.

Ferdinand. 1. In *The Tempest*, son of the King of Naples.

2. In *Love's Labour's Lost*, the King of Navarre. (See HENRI IV.)

Feste. In *Twelfth Night*, the lady Olivia's fool. He takes part in the jest against Malvolio who has discredited him before Olivia. Disguised as the parson Sir Topas, he baits Malvolio and pretends to believe that he really is mad. He sings the songs, *O mistress mine*; *Come away, come away, death*; *When that I was and a little tiny boy*. (See ARMIN.)

Fetherston(haugh). The Blackfriars Gate-house, bought by Shakespeare in 1613, formed part of his entailed estate, but by 1667 it was the property of Edward Bagley, who sold it in that year to Sir Heneage Fetherston. The family became Fetherstonhaugh, and it was among their papers that the vendor's copy of the original conveyance and the subsequent mortgage were found in 1796 and 1768 respectively.

Field, Nathan (1587–1620). An actor-dramatist like Shakespeare, Heywood, Rowley and Daborne. His father was the puritanical preacher John Field, who wrote *A godly exhortation* after the Paris Garden disaster of 1583. With Underwood and Ostler he was one of the Chapel Children, where he met Ben Jonson, who told Drummond that 'Nid Field was his schollar', and in *Bartholomew Fair* (1614) asks 'Which is your best actor, your Field?' Field played in Jonson's *Cynthia's Revels* 1600, *Poetaster* 1601 and *Epicoene* 1609. It was probably not until 1616 that he joined the King's, possibly to replace Shakespeare, his name being 17th in the Folio list of the 'Principall Actors' in Shakespeare's plays. As a dramatist he wrote two robust comedies, *A Woman's a Weathercock*, *c.* 1609, and *Amends for Ladies*, *c.* 1611, and with Massinger, *The Fatal Dowry*. He wrote for Henslowe when he was managing the Revels-Lady Elizabeth combine, of which Field was a member, and he may have had a hand in some of the plays of Beaumont and Fletcher. He was married and had children, but was a notoriously loose liver. (See W. Peery, *The Plays of Nathan Field*, 1950.)

Field, Richard, printer, was the son of Henry Field, a Stratford tanner with whom Shakespeare's father did business. In 1579 Richard was apprenticed to the London printer Thomas Vautrollier, on whose death in 1587 he married his widow and took over the business, one of the best in London. Field and Shakespeare probably knew one another in Stratford and renewed their acquaintance or friendship in London, for Field was responsible for Shakespeare's first published work, in April 1593 registering *Venus and Adonis*, of which he printed an admirable Quarto in the same year. The two early poems, both carefully printed by Field, are probably the only works the publication of which Shakespeare supervised. Field printed:

Venus and Adonis, Q1, 1593; Q2, 1594; O1, 1595; O2, 1596.
Rape of Lucrece, Q, 1594.
Phoenix and Turtle, Q1, 1601.

When Field died in 1624 his business passed to George Miller and Richard Badger, who took over his devices, most of which incorporated an anchor with the motto *Anchora Spei*.

Fife. A small, shrill instrument of the cross-blown flute family. It came from Switzerland in the 16th century, when it was made of wood and known as the

Swiss pipe. It was used for military music; cf. *1 Henry IV* (III, iii): *Enter the Prince marching, and Falstaffe meets him, playing on his Truncheon like a Fife.*

Fine. The conveyance, or sale, of landed property in Shakespeare's time was often conducted by means of a fine, or 'amicable composition' of a fictitious lawsuit. The seller was the defendant, who owned himself in the wrong and suggested a compromise, fine or price, in settlement of the imaginary breach of covenant. A recovery was a similar practice, a method of conveying entailed property by means of an action brought by the purchaser, alleging that the tenant-at-tail had no legal title to the land. Cf. *Hamlet* (v, i):

> This fellow might in 's time be a great buyer of land, with his statutes, his recognizances, his fines, his double vouchers, his recoveries; is this the fine of his fines, and the recovery of his recoveries, to have his fine pate full of fine dirt?

Finsbury. In Shakespeare's time, a liberty lying to the north of Moorgate and Moorfields, and to the west of the parish of Shoreditch where the Theatre and Curtain stood. It was for the most part open fields, much frequented by 'Sunday citizens'. Cf. Hotspur in *1 Henry IV* (III, i):

> And givest such sarcenet surety for thy oaths,
> As if thou never walk'st further than Finsbury.

First Folio. See FOLIOS.

'First Part of the Contention.' The title of the pirated Quarto (1594) of *2 Henry VI* (q.v.).

Fisher, Clement. In 1658 Sir Aston Cokain (q.v.) addressed verses to him on the subject of Shakespeare and 'Wincot-Ale'. Fisher was then probably living at Wilnecote in north Warwickshire as a neighbour of Cokain at Pooley Hall, Polesworth. Later he inherited his father's estate at Great Packington, Warwickshire, and became a baronet.

Fisher, Thomas, draper and bookseller, 1600–2. On 8 October 1600 he registered *A Midsummer Night's Dream*, published it the same year, and sold it 'at his shoppe, at the Signe of the White Hart, in Fleetestreete'.

Fiske, Minnie Maddern (1865–1932). American actress. When she was nine she played Arthur to John McCullough's Faulconbridge in a New York production of *King John*. Later she played a number of Shakespeare's and Ibsen's heroines. In 1901 she opened the independent Manhattan theatre in New York, in opposition to the theatrical trust.

Fitton, Mary (*c.* 1578–1647). On the assumption that Shakespeare addressed his *Sonnets* to William Herbert, later Earl of Pembroke, Thomas Tyler and Frank Harris argued that the 'dark lady' was Herbert's mistress, Mary Fitton. She was the daughter of Sir Edward Fitton of Gawsworth, Cheshire, about 1595 became one of Elizabeth's Maids of Honour, and in 1600 Herbert's mistress. She bore him a child which died soon after its birth; Herbert was sent to the Fleet prison, and Mary dismissed from Court. Apparently she went to live with her sister, Lady Newdigate, at Arbury, where two portraits show her as fair, with brown hair and grey eyes, though her monument in Gawsworth church is said to represent a dark woman.

Fitzwater, Lord (*c.* 1368–1407). In *Richard II*, a young peer who 'intends to thrive in this new world'. He seconds Bagot when he accuses Aumerle of Gloucester's murder, and challenges him and his supporter, Surrey (IV, i).

Flags. Flags were flown from the tops of the theatres as a sign that they were open for performance; cf. *A godly exhortation* (1583) of John Field, father of the actor-dramatist Nathan Field, 'Those flags of defiance against God, and trumpets that are blown to gather together such company ...' They were taken down when playing was prohibited in Lent or time of plague; cf. Middleton's *A Mad World, my Masters* (*c.* 1605), ''Tis Lent in your cheeks; the flag's down.'

Flaminius. In *Timon of Athens*, a faithful servant whom Timon sends to borrow fifty talents from Lucullus. Lucullus offers him three 'solidares' to say that he could not find him, and Flaminius flings the money at him (III, i).

Flats. As designed by Inigo Jones for his later masques, flats were side-wings within the proscenium arch, those in front two-sided and stationary, those behind one-sided and movable, sliding in grooves. Beyond the side-wings were more sliding flats, called shutters, which ran together and met in the middle of the stage. Above and behind the shutters was the painted sky-cloth. (See SERLIO.)

Flatter, Richard (1891–1960). Austrian Shakespeare scholar and translator, author of *Shakespeare's Producing Hand*, *Hamlet's Father*, etc. (See AUSTRIA.)

Flavius. 1. In *Julius Caesar*. See MARULLUS.

2. In *Timon of Athens*, the faithful steward of Timon. He tries to warn his master of his reckless generosity, but he will not hear him until it is too late. When Timon is broken, Flavius shares what wealth he has with the abandoned servants. He visits Timon in his cave, and is the 'singly honest man' whom Timon does not abuse.

Fleance. In *Macbeth*, the young son of Banquo. As the witches have prophesied that Banquo shall beget kings, Macbeth plans to murder both father and son, but Fleance escapes (II, i). (Fleance is an invention of Boece.)

Fleay, Frederick Gard (1831–1909), was educated at Trinity, Cambridge, ordained, and became a schoolmaster 1856–76. He was one of the leading members of the New Shakspere Society, and his paper *On Metrical Tests as Applied to Dramatic Poetry* was read at their opening meeting in March 1874. His tables of verse-tests for Shakespeare are valuable pioneering work, though often inaccurate. After publishing a number of books on Shakespeare, and the Elizabethan-Jacobean stage and drama (see BIBLIOGRAPHY), he turned to Egyptology and Assyriology. Fleay was the first of the 'disintegrators'.

'Fleir.' 'A Comedie called The Fleare' was registered on 13 May 1606, and published in 1607: 'The Fleire. As it hath beene often played in the Blacke-Fryers by the Children of the Reuells. Written by Edward Sharpham of the Middle Temple, Gentleman'. As Sharpham (q.v.) imitates the conversation of Lear and the disguised Kent (I, iv), it seems certain that *King Lear* was written before May 1606.

Fletcher, John (1579–1625). Was born in Sussex, son of the vicar of Rye, Richard Fletcher, who became successively Bishop of Bristol, Worcester, and London. He was the cousin of the poets Phineas and Giles (the younger) Fletcher. He may have gone to Benet College, Cambridge, but little is known of him before he appears as a dramatist for the King's Men in collaboration with Beaumont, *c.* 1608, though he may have written before this for the Queen's Revels. After Beaumont's marriage in 1613, and death in 1616, Fletcher wrote a number of plays on his own, and also in collaboration with Massinger, Rowley, and others. *The Two Noble Kinsmen* and the lost *Cardenio* were written with Shakespeare, and it seems certain that he had a large part in *Henry VIII*. It is difficult to disengage the plays written by Fletcher alone, but it is probable that the following are mainly his: *The Woman's Prize*, *The Faithful Shepherdess*, *Monsieur Thomas*, *Valentinian*, *Bonduca*, *Wit With-*

out Money. He wrote almost entirely for the King's Men, his romances and tragicomedies being eminently suitable for performance in the Blackfriars private theatre. After the Restoration his plays were more popular than Shakespeare's. (See also BEAUMONT.)

Fletcher, Lawrence. Actor. In the Licence for the King's Men of 19 May 1603, Fletcher heads the list, and Augustine Phillips left 'my Fellowe Lawrence Fletcher' a legacy of 20s. in 1605. But as he is not mentioned in any of the King's actor-lists, nor in the Folio list of the principal actors in Shakespeare's plays, it looks as though he was merely a Groom of the Chamber and not an active member of the company. When James was King of Scotland only, Fletcher had been 'comediane to his Majesty', and was, therefore, already a 'King's Man' before James's accession to the English throne in 1603, and this would account for his inclusion in the Licence. 'Lawrence Fletcher, a player, the King's servant', was buried in St Saviour's 'with an afternoon knell of the great bell', 12 September 1608.

Florence, Duke of. In *All's Well*. He appears in two short scenes only: III, i, where he says how just is his cause in the war against Siena, and in III, iii, where he appoints Bertram general of his horse.

Florio, Giovanni (*c.* 1553–1625). Born in London, the son of Italian Protestant refugees, he was educated at Magdalen, Oxford, and became a university teacher of Italian and French. In 1598 he published his Italian-English dictionary, *A World of Words*, and in 1603 his famous translation of the *Essayes on Morall, Politike, and Millitarie Discourses of Lo. Michaell de Montaigne*. He was appointed tutor to Prince Henry, reader in Italian to Queen Anne, a Groom of the Privy Chamber, and among his patrons numbered Southampton and Pembroke. He married Rosa, the sister of Samuel Daniel, and the Rosalind of Spenser's *Shepherd's Calendar*. It is probable that Shakespeare knew Florio through their common patron, Southampton, and he certainly knew his translation of Montaigne (q.v.), and, like Jonson, may have got information from him about Italy. It has been suggested that Shakespeare wrote the sonnet by 'Phæthon' prefixed to Florio's *Second Fruits* of 1591:

PHÆTHON TO HIS FRIEND FLORIO

Sweet friend, whose name agrees with thy increase,
How fit a rival art thou of the Spring!
For when each branch hath left his flourishing,
And green-locked Summer's shady pleasures cease,
She makes the Winter's storms repose in peace
And spends her franchise on each living thing:
The daisies sprout, the little birds do sing;
Herbs, gums, and plants do vaunt of their release.
So that when all our English wits lay dead
(Except the Laurel that is ever green),
Thou with thy fruits our barrenness o'erspread
And set thy flowery pleasance to be seen.
Such fruits, such flow'rets of morality,
Were ne'er before brought out of Italy.

Florizel. In *The Winter's Tale*, the son of Polixenes, and the Prince of Bohemia. (The Dorastus of Greene's *Pandosto*.)

'Florizel and Perdita.' Garrick's adaptation, mainly of the last two acts, of *The Winter's Tale*, produced at Drury Lane in 1756. Garrick played Leontes, Mrs Pritchard Hermione, and Mrs Cibber Perdita.

Flower Family. See ROYAL SHAKESPEARE THEATRE.

Flower Portrait. This was bought from a dealer about 1840 by H. C. Clements of Peckham Rye, who pasted a note on the box in which he kept it: 'The original portrait of Shakespeare, from which the now famous Droeshout engraving was taken and inserted in the first collected edition of his works ... The picture was publicly exhibited in London seventy years ago, and many thousands went to see it.' On the death of Clements in 1895 it was bought by Mrs Charles Flower and presented to the Shakespeare Museum at Stratford. It is painted on a panel made of two strips of elm, and inscribed in the upper left-hand corner 'Willm. Shakespeare, 1609'. It resembles more closely the third state of the Droeshout engraving, and is therefore suspect, for if it were 'The Droeshout Original' it should have the characteristics of the first state. Again, the inscription is in cursive script, no other example of which is known as early as 1609. It may have been painted in the first half of the 17th century – from the Droeshout print, and is possibly the earliest painted portrait of Shakespeare. (See *The Times*, 28 May 1966.)

Fluellen. In *Henry V*, a loyal and humourless Welsh officer on Henry's French campaign, well grounded in the disciplines of the pristine wars of the Romans. He quarrels with the Irish captain Macmorris, and with Pistol whom he forces to eat a leek for insulting the Welsh, while the King, by giving him the glove of Williams to wear in his cap, involves him in a quarrel with that soldier. (In September 1592 John Shakespeare, William Fluellen, George Bardell (or Bardolf), and six others were reported as Stratford recusants.)

Flute. Though the cross-blown flute was played in Tudor times – Henry VIII had seventy-eight of them – the popular instrument was the end-blown flute, or recorder. As it was made in at least four different sizes – treble, alto, tenor, bass – it was used for music in parts, whereas the cross-blown flute is purely treble.

Flute, Francis. In *A Midsummer Night's Dream*, an Athenian bellows-mender. Although he has a beard coming, he plays Thisbe to Bottom's Pyramus in the interlude.

Folger, Henry Clay (1857–1930). American collector, was born at Brooklyn, educated at Amherst College, and in 1889 began the serious collection of a Shakespeare library by buying a Fourth Folio. The wealth that he later acquired as President and Chairman of the Standard Oil Company he spent mainly on his books. He died a fortnight after the laying of the foundation-stone of the library that he planned to house them in Washington. On 23 April 1932 the building and books were presented to the American people 'for the promotion and diffusion of knowledge in regard to the history and writings of Shakespeare'. The richness of the collection in the Folger Shakespeare Library may be gauged from the fact that it contains 79 First Folios and 205 Shakespearean Quartos, in addition to thousands of rare or unique copies of books relating to all branches of Shakespearean scholarship. (See SS, 1.)

Folios. THE FIRST FOLIO of 1623 is the first collected edition of Shakespeare's plays. It was edited, or overseen, by Shakespeare's friends and fellow-actors in the Chamberlain's-King's company, John Heminge and Henry Condell. The title-page reads:

> Mr William Shakespeares Comedies, Histories, & Tragedies. Published according to the True Originall Copies. [Portrait, signed *Martin Droeshout sculpsit London*] London. Printed by Isaac Iaggard, and Ed. Blount. 1623.

And the colophon:

> Printed at the Charges of W. Jaggard, Ed. Blount, I. Smithweeke, and W. Aspley, 1623.

The preliminary matter, the order of which differs slightly in various copies, consists of (*a*) Verses *To the Reader* by Ben Jonson on the Droeshout engraving. (*b*) Title-page and Droeshout engraving. (*c*) Dedication by Heminge and Condell to the Earls of Pembroke and Montgomery. (*d*) Address *To the great Variety of Readers* by Heminge and Condell. (*e*) Verses to the memory of Shakespeare by Ben Jonson, Hugh Holland, Leonard Digges and 'I.M.'. (*f*) Head-title, and 'The Names of the Principall Actors in all these Playes'. (*g*) 'A Catalogue of the seuerall Comedies, Histories, and Tragedies contained in this Volume.'

The plays are printed in three sections: Comedies, Histories, Tragedies, totalling 908 pages of double columns enclosed within printer's rules. The price was probably £1, and about 1,000 copies were printed, of which some 200 are known, though only 14 are in perfect condition. The largest copies measure $13\frac{1}{2} \times 8\frac{1}{2}$ inches.

Of the thirty-six plays in the Folio, eighteen had already been published as Quartos, though of these four had 'bad' Quartos only (*2, 3 Henry VI*, *Henry V*, and *The Merry Wives*). The Folio, therefore, gives eighteen unpublished plays, and, according to Heminge and Condell, 'perfect' texts of the imperfect Quartos. Sixteen of the eighteen unpublished plays were registered 8 November 1623:

> Mr Blounte Isaak Jaggard. Entred for their Copie vnder the hands of Mr Doctor Worrall and Mr Cole, warden, Mr William Shakspeers Comedyes Histories, and Tragedyes soe manie of the said Copies as are not formerly entred to other men, vizt. Comedyes. The Tempest. The two gentlemen of Verona. Measure for Measure. The Comedy of Errors. As you Like It. All's well that ends well. Twelft night. The winters tale. Histories. The thirde parte of Henry the sixt. Henry the eight. Coriolanus. Timon of Athens. Julius Cæsar. Tragedies. Mackbeth. Anthonie and Cleopatra. Cymbeline.

King John and *The Taming of the Shrew* were not registered, probably because they passed as reprints of the Quartos of Shakespeare's source-plays, *The Troublesome Reign of John* and *The Taming of A Shrew*. William Jaggard, one of the publishing syndicate, and the printer of the Folio, died shortly before this registration by his son Isaac, and by Blount, who was not a printer. *Troilus and Cressida* (q.v.) was inserted at the last moment as the first play in the Tragedy section, and is not mentioned in the 'Catalogue' of plays. (See SHELDON. The copy given by W. Jaggard to his friend Augustine Vincent is in the Folger Library.) The Address of Heminge and Condell *To the great Variety of Readers*, after appealing to the public to buy the Folio, contains the very important passage (see TEXTUAL CRITICISM):

> It had bene a thing, we confesse, worthie to haue bene wished, that the Author himselfe had liu'd to haue set forth, and ouerseen his owne writings; But since it hath bin ordain'd otherwise, and he by death departed from that right, we pray you do not envie his Friends, the office of their care, and paine, to haue collected & publish'd them; and so to haue publish'd them, as where (before) you were abus'd with diuerse stolne, and surreptitious copies, maimed, and deformed by the frauds and stealthes of iniurious impostors, that expos'd them: even those, are now offer'd to your view cur'd, and perfect of their limbes; and all the rest, absolute in their numbers, as he conceiued them. Who, as he was a happie imitator of Nature, was a most gentle expresser of it. His mind and hand went together: And what he thought, he vttered with that easinesse, that wee haue scarce receiued from him a blot in his papers.

In 1619 the Jaggards (q.v.) were associated with Pavier in the abortive 'False Folio', which may have led to the King's Men's offering Jaggard material for a genuine collected edition, and preparation for the Folio began in 1620. William Jaggard was ill, and his son Isaac assumed the main responsibility, both as printer and publisher, though Blount joined him later. Smethwick and Aspley were junior partners, having rights in some of the Quartos. Heminge and Condell probably did little more than supply copy for Jaggard, and Edward Knight, the King's Men's bookkeeper, may have done the detailed editing. Printing probably began in April 1621, was interrupted in October, resumed a year later, and the Folio was on sale by the end of 1623, by which time William Jaggard was dead.

The most important studies of the Folio are: A. W. Pollard, *Shakespeare Folios and Quartos*, 1909 (the beginning of modern textual criticism). R. Crompton Rhodes, *Shakespeare's First Folio*, 1923 (often inaccurate). E. E. Willoughby, *The Printing of the First Folio of Shakespeare*, 1932 (traces the course of its printing from 1621 to 1623, and identifies compositors A and B and probably 'another pair'). Alice Walker, *Textual Problems of the First Folio*, 1953 (that many of the F plays were printed from corrected Quartos, and a study of the characteristics of compositors A and B). W. W. Greg, *The Shakespeare First Folio* ('Its bibliographical and textual history'. An invaluable survey.) C. K. Hinman, *The Printing and Proof-Reading of the First Folio*, 1963. (See COMPOSITORS; MISLINEATION; MISPRINTS; PROOF-READING.)

THE SECOND FOLIO, 1632. Isaac Jaggard died in 1627, and in 1630 Blount transferred to Robert Allot his rights in the sixteen plays registered for F1 in 1623. The Second Folio was printed by Thomas Cotes for Allot, Smethwick, Aspley, Richard Hawkins, and Richard Meighen. It is a reprint of F1 with some modernization of spelling and correction of stage-directions and proper names.

THE THIRD FOLIO, 1663. Allot's widow married Philip Chetwinde, for whom the Third Folio, a reprint of F2, with some corrections and some new errors, was printed. To a second impression of 1664 were added 'seven Playes, never before Printed in Folio, viz. Pericles, Prince of Tyre. The London Prodigall. The History of Thomas Ld. Cromwell. Sir John Oldcastle, Lord Cobham. The Puritan Widow. A Yorkshire Tragedy. The Tragedy of Locrine'. The Third Folio is relatively scarce, possibly because a number of unsold copies perished in the Fire of London in 1666.

THE FOURTH FOLIO, 1685, a yet larger and clumsier volume, was printed for H. Herringman, E. Brewster, R. Chiswell and R. Bentley. It is a reprint of F3, again with corrections and new mistakes of its own, and includes *Pericles* and the six spurious plays. The last three Folios, printed without reference to early Quartos or manuscripts, are of no authority.

Folk-music. The jig at the conclusion of a performance of a play was often danced to a traditional air, and the fragments of old songs and ballads so often introduced by Shakespeare were probably sung to these popular tunes.

Fool. 1. In *King Lear*, he is wise enough to realise the tragic blunder that Lear has made, and though he keeps reminding him of it he pitifully tries to hold the King's madness at bay with his jesting. After Cordelia's going into France he 'much pined away', and apparently dies after following Lear into the storm, his last words being, 'And I'll go to bed at noon' (III, vi). (See ARMIN.)

2. In *Timon of Athens* there is a fool, the servant of a courtesan, who exchanges ribaldries with Apemantus and the servants of Timon's creditors, in II, ii. (See CLOWN.)

Foote, Samuel (1720–77), actor and dramatist, was born at Truro in the year that John Potter built the Haymarket theatre (q.v.). His first appearance on the stage, as Othello, was a failure, but in 1747 he found fame by his genius for mimicry in the *Diversions of the Morning*. As the result of a practical joke in 1766, he was thrown from a horse and broke his leg which had to be amputated, in reparation for which the Duke of York secured him a royal patent for the Haymarket. By the Licensing Act of 1737 all theatres save Drury Lane and Covent Garden should have been closed, but 'the little theatre' in the Haymarket now became the third authorized house as the Theatre Royal. Foote's patent, however, was limited to the summer months and his own lifetime.

Footlights. In his *Pratica di fabricar Scene e Machine ne' Teatri*, 1638, Nicola Sabbatini recommended lights placed behind a parapet at the front of the stage. There are crude footlights in the illustration of Francis Kirkman's *The Wits*, 1672. (See LIGHTING.)

Forbes-Robertson, Johnston (1853–1937). Actor, was educated at Charterhouse and the Royal Academy schools, but in 1874 abandoned painting for acting, which he studied under Samuel Phelps. In 1882 he played Claudio to Irving's Benedick and Ellen Terry's Beatrice, and ten years later appeared as Buckingham in Irving's sumptuous revival of *Henry VIII*, with Irving as Wolsey and Ellen Terry as Katharine. His finest performance was as Hamlet, which play he produced, as well as *Romeo and Juliet* and *Macbeth*, after assuming the management of the Lyceum in 1895. In 1900 he married the actress Gertrude Elliott, to whose Desdemona he played Othello in 1902. He was knighted in 1913 and retired from the stage in the next year.

Ford, John (1586–*c.* 1639), one of the last of the Elizabethan-Jacobean dramatists, was born at Ilsington in Devon, and seems to have entered Exeter College, Oxford, in 1601, and the Middle Temple in 1602. Little is known of his later life, but it is assumed from the lines in the *Choice Drollery* (1656) that he left London and lived in seclusion:

Deep in a dump alone John Ford was gat,
With folded arms and melancholy hat.

His first publication was in 1606, *Fame's Memorial*, an elegy on Lord Mountjoy; his first acted play was probably *A Bad Beginning Makes a Good Ending*, performed at Court by the King's, 1612–13. He wrote some sixteen plays, alone or in collaboration with Dekker, Webster, and Rowley, his best, *'Tis Pity She's a Whore* (*c.* 1625) and *The Broken Heart* (*c.* 1629) illustrate his passion for abnormal subjects. *The Witch of Edmonton* (with Dekker and Rowley) is good domestic drama, and *Perkin Warbeck* one of the best English historical plays outside Shakespeare. There was a story, without foundation, that Ford stole *The Lover's Melancholy* from Shakespeare's papers. (See C. MACKLIN.)

Ford. In *The Merry Wives of Windsor*, Pistol tells him that Falstaff is making love to his wife, so to test her chastity he disguises himself as Master Brooke, and offers Falstaff money to woo her on his behalf. (In the Folio Ford's assumed name is changed to the less appropriate Broome, presumably because Lord Cobham, whose family name was Brooke, objected.)

Ford, Mistress. She and Mistress Page are the Merry Wives of Windsor to whom Falstaff writes identical love-letters. They teach Falstaff a lesson, and cure Ford of his jealousy.

Fordun, John of (d. *c.* 1384). The writer of the first, largely fabulous, history of Scotland, the *Scotichronicon*. This was used by Hector Boece for his *Scotorum Historiae* of 1527, the source of Holinshed's Scottish *Chronicles*.

Fore-stage. That part of the old apron-stage that remained in front of the proscenium arch, within which it was gradually squeezed until in 1837 it was entirely absorbed at the Haymarket. It is not the same thing as the proscenium (q.v.).

Forgeries. The hundred years from 1750 to 1850, when public interest in Shakespeare had been stimulated by Garrick, and scholars were eagerly searching for biographical information, naturally produced a crop of fabrications to satisfy curiosity. The most notorious forgeries are those of William Henry Ireland (1777–1835) and John Payne Collier (1798–1883). Others guilty of minor fabrications, or some of whose information is open to suspicion, are: Lewis Theobald (1688–1744), Charles Macklin (1697?–1797), W. R. Chetwood (d. 1766), George Steevens (1736–1800), John Jordan (1746–1809), Richard Fenton (1746–1821), Peter Cunningham (1816–69). For details see under the various names.

Forman, Simon (1552–1611). Physician and astrologer, was born near Wilton and educated at Magdalen, Oxford. He pursued his medical studies in Holland, practised in London, but as he held no diploma was more than once imprisoned. Eventually, however, he received a diploma from Cambridge University. He died 12 September 1611, while crossing the Thames in a boat. He may have committed suicide, as he had predicted the day of his death. Forman's manuscript *Booke of Plaies* is preserved in the Bodleian, and contains notes of his visits to three of Shakespeare's plays: 'In Mackbeth at the Glob, 1610 (1611?), the 20 of Aprill'; 'In the Winters Talle at the glob 1611 the 15 of maye'; and without date or theatre, 'Of Cimbalin king of England'. He also saw a play of Richard II at the Globe on 30 April, but not Shakespeare's. The entries are mainly summaries of the action of the plays. As a doctor he notes:

> Obserue Also howe Mackbetes quen did Rise in the night in her slepe, & walke and talked and confessed all, & the docter noted her wordes.

And he draws a moral from *The Winter's Tale:*

> Remember also the Rog that cam in all tottered like coll pixci and howe he feyned him sicke & to haue bin Robbed of all that he had and howe he cosened the por man of all his money, and after cam to the shep sher with a pedlers packe & ther cosened them Again of all their money And howe he changed apparrell with the kinge of Bomia his sonn, and then howe he turned Courtier &c. Beware of trustinge feined beggars or fawninge fellouss.

The *Booke of Plaies* has been suspected as one of Collier's forgeries, but it is generally accepted as genuine. (See RES, xxiii, 193.)

Forme. The block, or blocks, of type set for printing one side of a sheet of paper. Some early books were printed page by page, but the Shakespeare Folio was printed from two-page formes.

Forrest, Edwin (1806–1872). First of the great American actors, was born at Philadelphia. He began his stage career at the age of fourteen, and achieved fame in 1826 by his performance of Othello in New York. His finest performance appears to have been that of Lear. In England, however, he was not popular; he was jealous of Macready, and his Macbeth was hissed. His last appearance was in 1871.

Fortescue, John. When Shakespeare bought the Blackfriars Gatehouse in March 1613 the tenant was William Ireland; before him it had been 'John Fortescue gent'. He and his wife were Catholics, and in 1598 the house was searched for hidden priests. Later they went to St Omer, their daughter Elizabeth marrying Sir John Beaumont, brother of the dramatist.

Fortinbras. In *Hamlet*, nephew of old Fortinbras, King of Norway. He is secretly preparing an invasion of Denmark to recover lands lost by his father, but Claudius succeeds in preventing this, and grants him the right to march through Denmark and use his army against Poland instead. Hamlet meets Fortinbras and his army in IV, iv. Fortinbras has 'some right of memory' in Denmark, and when Hamlet has killed Claudius he gives him his 'dying voice'.

Fortune Theatre. In 1599 the Chamberlain's moved from the Curtain on the north side of the City to the new Globe on the Bankside; in the following year the Admiral's moved from the Rose near the Globe to the new Fortune about half a mile to the west of the Curtain. The Fortune was authorized by an Order of the Privy Council in June 1600, provided 'there shall bee about the Cittie two howses and no more', one for the Admiral's, another for the Chamberlain's. Neither the Rose nor the Curtain, however, was 'ruined and plucked down'. In December 1599 Edward Alleyn had acquired a lease of the site, just to the north of Cripplegate, between Golding (Golden) Lane and Whitecross Street in the liberty of Finsbury. In April 1601 Henslowe became his partner, though he was a party to the contract of January 1600 with Peter Street, who agreed to build the theatre for £440.

This contract has been preserved: the Globe was to be the model, though the Fortune was to be square, 80 ft outside and 55 ft inside; the framework was wood; there were three galleries, 12, 11, and 9 ft high, 12½ ft deep, and provided with seats; four 'gentlemens roomes' were partitioned off, and there was an unspecified number of 2d. rooms. There was 'a shadowe or cover over the Stadge', which was 43 ft broad and extended to the middle of the yard (27½ ft). The windows and lights to the 'Tyreinge howse' were glazed. Alleyn's total expenses were £240 for the lease, £520 for building and painting the theatre, £100 for a reversionary lease in 1610, £340 for the freehold, and £120 for 'other priuat buildings'. Street began work at once and finished probably in the autumn, when it was occupied by the Admiral's, who made it their permanent home, later as Prince Henry's, and then the Palsgrave's. It is illustrated in Hotson's *Shakespeare's Wooden O*. On 9 December 1621 it was destroyed by fire; in the words of John Chamberlain:

> On Sonday night here was a great fire at the Fortune in Golden-Lane, the fayrest playhouse in this towne. It was quite burnt downe in two howres & all their apparell & play-bookes lost, wherby those poore companions are quite undone.

It was rebuilt in 1623, a round building of brick costing £1,000, and dismantled in 1649. (See MAPS OF LONDON.)

Foul Case. The commonest cause of error in printing: when type has got into the wrong compartment of the compositor's case.

Foul Papers. The original manuscript of a dramatist, as opposed to a *fair* copy. Thus, in November 1613 Daborne wrote to Henslowe: 'I promysd to bring you the last scean which that you may see finished I send you the foule sheet & the fayr I was wrighting ... I will not fayle to write this fayr and perfit the book.' (See also BONDUCA.) It seems probable that a dramatist's foul sheets, or papers, were kept in the theatre after preparation of the prompt-book. Shakespeare seems rarely to have made fair copies, and many of his plays were apparently printed from his foul papers. The three pages that he added to the *Sir Thomas More* manuscript, if they really are his, are presumably foul papers. (See ORIGINAL.)

Foxe, John (1516–87), was born at Boston, Lincolnshire, and educated at Magdalen, Oxford. In 1545 he resigned his fellowship and was for a time tutor in the family of the Lucys at Charlecote, near Stratford. During Mary's reign he lived in Germany, where he finished the Latin edition of his *Book of Martyrs*, an account of the martyrs of the Christian Church, particularly of the Protestant martyrs of his own time. On his return to England he worked as translator and editor for John Day, who, in 1563, printed his *Actes and Monuments*, known as *The Book of Martyrs*. The attack on Cranmer in *Henry VIII* (v, i–iii) is taken from Foxe's account of the Marian persecutions.

France. French drama was based firmly on classical models and neo-classical precepts, severe and restrained, a drama of concentration conforming to the unities, without the exuberant variety and bewildering irrelevancies of the popular English stage. Corneille (1606–84) and Racine (1639–99) were too late to influence the English drama before the closing of the theatres in 1642, but after the Restoration the impact was felt; Shakespeare was simplified and polished till he shone again, Dryden showed what could be made out of the Antony and Cleopatra story, and Addison out of that of Cato. But England never accepted whole-heartedly the neo-classical doctrines, and Shakespeare, despite his excesses and want of taste, remained the darling of the English stage. It was different, however, in France. There Racine was the man, and Shakespeare for the critics, for Voltaire and La Harpe, and for the polite audiences of the French theatre, was little more than a barbarian, at times indeed almost a drunken barbarian: 'Il avait un génie plein de force et de fécondité, de naturel et de sublime, sans la moindre étincelle de bon goût et sans la moindre connaissance des règles.' (See, however, DIDEROT; LETOURNEUR.) After the political revolution of 1789 writers began to recognize that the age of Voltaire was over, and Mme de Staël, though not without regret, turned to Shakespeare. (See GRIMM.) But it was Victor Hugo (1802–85) who proclaimed the full Romantic faith in France and did most to popularize Shakespeare. In his *Préface de Cromwell* (1827) he pronounced him a god of the theatre who united in himself the genius of Corneille, Molière, and Beaumarchais. A Frenchman could scarcely go further than this, and Taine (1828–93), with reservations, was almost as enthusiastic. For the last hundred years there has been in France a generous admiration of Shakespeare, though it is perhaps as difficult for the Frenchman to appreciate Shakespeare as it is for the Englishman to appreciate Racine, and the contribution of French scholars has been inconsiderable in comparison with that of the Germans.

Nevertheless, in this century there has been a great advance. Emile Legouis did much to stimulate interest in Elizabethan literature, and Albert Feuillerat was an authority on the Elizabethan theatre. Among the critics should be mentioned Louis Cazamian, André Suarès, Louis Gillet, Paul Reyher, Henri Fluchère, and important biographical studies have been written by the Countess Longworth Chambrun, Léon Lemonnier, and Abel Lefranc (a Derbyite). There have been numerous translations, the most popular being the Pléiade one with a preface by Gide, who translated *Antony and Cleopatra* and *Hamlet*. Jacques Copeau has revolutionized the production of Shakespeare in France. In recent years the most interesting productions have been at summer festivals in the provinces, often staged in or against some historical building, as at Angers, Avignon, Orange, Nîmes, Arles, Carcassonne. (See DE VIGNY; BERNHARDT; J. Jacquot, *Shakespeare en France*, 1960; SS, 2; SS, 16.)

The principal French translations of Shakespeare's works are:

Letourneur, P., 20 vols., 1776–82. Revised by F. Guizot, 1821.

Michel, M. F., 3 vols., 1839.

Laroche, B., 2 vols., 1839–40; 7 vols., 1842–3.

Hugo, F. V., 18 vols., 1859–66. Revision by René Lalou in progress.

Montégut, E., 10 vols., 1867–73.

Duval, G., 8 vols., 1908–9.

Collection Aubier (bilingual) in progress.

France, King of. 1. In *All's Well*. He suspects Bertram of having murdered Helena, but at length disentangles the threads of the story. He acts as Epilogue to the play.

2. In *King Lear*. He appears only in the first scene, when he agrees to marry Cordelia though she is dowered only with her father's curse. He brings the French army to the rescue of Lear, but suddenly returns to France because of 'something he left imperfect in the state' (IV, iii).

3. In *King John*. See PHILIP II.

4. In *Henry V*. See CHARLES VI.

France, Princess of. In *Love's Labour's Lost* she and her three attendant ladies upset the tranquillity of the Court of the King of Navarre. Ostensibly she comes to settle a debt, but stays to return Navarre's love. (See HENRI IV.)

Francis. In *1 Henry IV*, a tavern drawer made sport of by Prince Henry and Poins (II, iv).

Francisca. In *Measure for Measure*, a nun of the order of St Clare who receives

Isabella when she begins her novitiate (I, iv).

Francisco. 1. In *Hamlet*, a soldier. At the opening of the play he is on guard on the battlements of the castle at Elsinore, but after being relieved by Bernardo he is not heard of again.

2. In *The Tempest*, a courtier shipwrecked with Alonso, King of Naples, whom he comforts with the thought that Ferdinand is still alive (II, i).

Frederick V. See ELECTOR PALATINE.

Frederick. In *As You Like It*, the usurping Duke, and father of Celia. (Called Torismond in Lodge's *Rosalynde*, in which he is killed.)

Freeman, Thomas (*c.* 1590–?), was a Gloucestershire man, entered Magdalen, Oxford, in 1607, and in 1614 published a collection of epigrams in two parts: *Rubbe and a Great Cast*, and *Runne and a Great Cast*. In the latter there is a sonnet 'To Master W. Shakespeare':

Shakespeare, that nimble *Mercury* thy braine,
Lulls many hundred *Argus*-eyes asleepe,
So fit, for all thou fashionest thy vaine,
At th' *horse-foote* founteine thou hast drunk full deepe,
Vertues or vices theame to thee all one is:
Who loues chaste life, there's *Lucrece* for a Teacher:
Who list read lust there's *Venus* and *Adonis*,
True modell of a most lasciuious leatcher.
Besides in plaies thy wit windes like *Meander*:
Whence needy new-composers borrow more
Then *Terence* doth from *Plautus* or *Menander*.
But to praise thee aright I want thy store:
Then let thine owne works thin owne worth upraise,
And help t' adorne thee with deserued Baies.

French, George Russell (1803–81), architect, temperance reformer, and antiquary. After tracing the descent of Nelson and the Duke of Wellington from Edward I, he turned his attention to Shakespeare and in 1869 published his valuable *Shakespeareana Genealogica*, an identification of the dramatis personae in the historical plays, notes on characters in *Macbeth* and *Hamlet*, on persons and places in Warwickshire alluded to in the plays, and on the Shakespeare and Arden families and their connexions.

Friar Francis. In *Much Ado*, he begins the marriage ceremony of Claudio and Hero, and when Claudio slanders Hero suggests the device of pretending that she has died of grief, so changing slander to remorse, and reviving Claudio's love. The scheme succeeds, and eventually Friar Francis marries not only Claudio and Hero, but Benedick and Beatrice as well.

Friar John. In *Romeo and Juliet*, a Franciscan sent by Friar Laurence to Mantua to tell Romeo to fetch the apparently dead Juliet from the Capulet tomb; but the constables think that he may be infected with the plague and prevent his going (V, ii).

Friar Laurence. In *Romeo and Juliet*, the Franciscan who secretly marries the lovers.

Friar Peter. In *Measure for Measure*, he is in the confidence of the disguised Duke of Vienna, whose schemes he helps to mature in Act V. He marries Angelo and Mariana.

Friar Thomas. In *Measure for Measure*. The Duke of Vienna persuades him to let him disguise himself as a friar of his order so that he can watch the conduct of his deputy Angelo (I, iii).

Fripp, Edgar Innes (d. 1931), was a Life-Trustee of Shakespeare's Birthplace and William Noble Research Fellow at Liverpool University in 1930. He devoted much of his life to the study of Shakespeare's Stratford, his friends, and Shakespeare himself, dying shortly before the completion of his chief work, *Shakespeare, Man and Artist* (2 vols. 1938), the standard book on Shakespeare and his native town. Fripp sees in Shakespeare a well educated man who was trained in an attorney's office, and attributes to Halliwell-Phillipps the concept of 'the Stratford Boor'.

Froissart, Jean (1338–1410). French chronicler, born in Hainaut, who wrote a splendid and picturesque account of the chivalry of western Europe in the 14th century. It is concerned mostly with the first half of the Hundred Years War. His *Chroniques* were translated by Lord Berners, 1523–5. In *Richard II* (v, v), Richard's reference to 'roan Barbary' being ridden by Bolingbroke is probably an echo of Froissart's account of the greyhound, Mathe, that deserted Richard for Bolingbroke. The author, or authors, of *Edward III* took some of their material from Froissart.

Froth. In *Measure for Measure*, 'a foolish Gentleman' of fourscore pound a year. He is arrested with Pompey the bawd, who has been swindling him, and dismissed by Escalus with a warning (II, i).

Fulbrook. A hamlet half-way between Stratford and Warwick, and some two miles north of Charlecote (q.v.). Rowe, in 1709, first suggested Charlecote as the scene of Shakespeare's deer-stealing, but there was no park there in the legal sense, only a warren. About 1790 John Jordan informed Malone that Sir Thomas Lucy 'had at the time also another park at a place called Fullbroke, two miles distant from the other; and there tradition reports it was that Shakespeare and his companions made a practise of following their favourite diversion'. The story had become more picturesque by 1828 when Sir Walter Scott entered in his Diary:

> April 8. Charlecote is in high preservation, and inhabited by Mr. Lucy, descendant of the worshipful Sir Thomas ... He told me the park from which Shakespeare stole the buck was not that which surrounds Charlecote, but belonged to a mansion at some distance, where Sir Thomas Lucy resided at the time of the trespass. The tradition went that they hid the buck in a barn, part of which was standing a few years ago, but now totally decayed. The park no longer belongs to the Lucys.

Yet Fulbrook was disparked shortly before Shakespeare's birth, bought by the Lucys a year before his death, and afterwards re-emparked. (See IRELAND, WILLIAM HENRY.)

Fuller, Thomas (1608–61), was born at the Northamptonshire village of Aldwinkle, where Dryden was born twenty-three years later, and educated at Queen's, Cambridge. His uncle, the Bishop of Salisbury, made him vicar of Broadwindsor, Dorset, in 1634. During the Civil War he served as army chaplain to the royalist Sir Ralph Hopton. He was little persecuted during the Commonwealth period, and at the Restoration became chaplain to the King, but died of typhus the following year. His great *Church History of Britain* was published in 1658, and his most famous work, the *Worthies of England*, after his death, in 1662. Fuller's fanciful prose appealed much to Lamb and Coleridge.

In his *Worthies*, the preparation of which he began while some of Shakespeare's contemporaries were still alive, Fuller protests, in the Norfolk section, against Shakespeare's misuse of the names of Oldcastle and Fastolfe:

> John Fastolfe Knight the *Stage* hath been overbold with his memory, making him a *Thrasonical Puff*, & emblem of *Mock-valour*.
>
> True it is, *Sir John Oldcastle* did first bear the brunt of the one, being made the *make-sport* in all plays for a *coward* ... Now as I am glad that *Sir John Oldcastle* is *put out*, so I am sorry that *Sir John Fastolfe* is *put in*, to relieve his memory in this base service, to be the *anvil* for every *dull wit* to strike upon. Nor is our Comedian excusable, by some alteration of his name, writing him *Sir John Falstafe* (and making him the *property* of *pleasure* for King *Henry* the fifth, to abuse), seeing the

vicinity of sounds intrench on the memory of *that worthy Knight*, and few do heed the *inconsiderable difference* in spelling of their name.

In the Warwickshire section he writes a few notes on Shakespeare himself:

William Shakespeare was born at *Stratford* on *Avon* in this County, in whom three eminent Poets may seem in some sort to be compounded. 1. *Martial* in the *Warlike* sound of his Sur-name ... 2. *Ovid*, the most *naturall* and *witty* of all Poets ... 3. *Plautus*, who was an exact Comædian, yet never any Scholar, as our *Shake-speare* (if alive) would confess himself...

He was an eminent instance of the truth of that Rule, *Poeta non fit, sed nascitur*, one is not *made*, but *born* a Poet. Indeed his Learning was very little, so that as *Cornish diamonds* are not polished by any Lapidary, but are pointed and smoothed even as they are taken out of the Earth, so *nature* it self was all the *art* which was used upon him.

Many were the *wit-combates* betwixt him and *Ben Johnson*, which two I behold like a *Spanish great Gallion* and an English *man of War*; Master *Johnson* (like the former) was built far higher in Learning; *Solid*, but *Slow* in his performances. *Shake-spear*, with the *English-man of War*, lesser in *bulk*, but lighter in *sailing*, could turn with all tides, tack about and take advantage of all winds, by the quickness of his Wit and Invention. He died *Anno Domini* 16 ..., and was buried at *Stratford* upon *Avon*, the Town of his Nativity.

Fullom, S. W. See LUDDINGTON.

Fulman, William (1632–88), was born at Penshurst, Kent, and elected a scholar of Corpus Christi, Oxford, whence he was ejected by the Parliamentary forces and became a private tutor. After the Restoration he was elected a fellow of his college and presented to the living of Maisey Hampton, near Cirencester, where he died. He was a scholar of repute, corresponded with Anthony Wood, and began the collection of biographical notices of English poets. On his death he left his papers to his friend Richard Davies, rector of Sapperton, in the Cotswolds, who made his own additions. Davies's executor gave the combined collection to Corpus Christi College. (For their notes on Shakespeare, see DAVIES, RICHARD.)

Furness, Horace Howard (1833–1912). American Shakespeare scholar, was born in Philadelphia and educated at Harvard. In 1871 he published the first volume, *Romeo and Juliet*, of his New Variorum edition of Shakespeare, a vast work with annotations, textual notes, and critical extracts from the most eminent authorities of all nations. The work was continued by his son, H. H. Furness, Jr, and on his death by the Modern Language Association of America, with J. Q. Adams as general editor. Mrs Helen Kate Furness (1837–83) compiled *A Concordance to the Poems of Shakespeare*, 1872. (See VARIORUM EDITIONS.)

Furnivall, Frederick James (1825–1910), was born at Egham, Surrey, and educated at University College, London, and Trinity Hall, Cambridge. In 1861 he succeeded Herbert Coleridge as editor of the projected Oxford English Dictionary, and in 1864 founded the Early English Text Society. He was also founder of the Chaucer, Ballad, New Shakspere, Wyclif, Shelley, and Browning Societies, honorary secretary of the Philological Society, and editor of the *Percy Ballads* and the 'Six-Text' edition of the *Canterbury Tales*.

As a Shakespeare scholar Furnivall wrote important prefaces to the English translation of Gervinus's *Commentaries*, 1875, and to his own *Leopold* edition of Shakespeare, 1876. He explained the object of his New Shakspere Society (q.v.) as the study of 'the growth, the oneness of Shakspere', and pursued this end by directing the verse-tests establishing the order of the plays and the division of Shakespeare's writing career into four periods. The result was the first book 'by an Englishman ... which deals in any worthy manner with Shakspere as a whole': Dowden's *Shakspere: his Mind and Art*, 1875. Between 1880 and 1889 Furnivall supervised the production of facsimiles of Shakespearean Quartos in forty-three volumes.

G

Gabriel. See SPENCER, GABRIEL.

Gadshill. In *1 Henry IV*, the setter of the robbery, confusingly enough, at Gadshill. He finds from the chamberlain of the Rochester inn the time of the travellers' departure, and helps Falstaff, Bardolph, and Peto to waylay and rob them. They are robbed in their turn by the disguised Prince Henry and Poins, and Gadshill encourages Falstaff in his lies when they explain their adventure in the Boar's Head tavern, though in Qq these lines are given to Ross[ill] (q.v.). After this, Gadshill disappears from the plays.

Gaedertz, Karl Theodor (1855–1912). German literary historian; Librarian at Berlin and Greifswald. It was in his *Zur Kenntnis der altenglischen Bühne* that John de Witt's famous drawing of the Swan theatre with van Buchel's copy of his observations was published in 1888.

Gag. An actor's interpolation in his part. That gagging was a common practice is clear from Hamlet's advice to the players (III, ii): 'And let those that play your clowns speak no more than is set down for them.' (See CLOWN.)

Gager, William (*c.* 1560–1621), of Christ Church, Oxford, where his academic Latin plays, *Meleager* 1582, *Rivales* and *Dido* 1583, *Ulysses Redux* and *Hippolytus* 1592, were produced. Gager championed the academic drama against the puritanical John Rainolds (q.v.) of Corpus Christi College. (See GENTILI.)

Galleries. There were normally three galleries for spectators in the public theatres. In the Fortune, starting from the bottom they were 12, 11, and 9 feet high, and 'twelve foot and a half in breadth throughout, besides a jutty forwards in the two upper stories, of ten inches'. These were ceiled with lath, lime, and hair, boarded with deal, and supplied with seats. The top gallery of the Fortune was tiled, but the Globe was thatched. Part of the galleries was partitioned to form 'private rooms' – there were four 'gentlemens roomes' at the Fortune – doubtless the sixpenny or twelvepenny rooms, where each seat cost 6d. or 12d. There were also 2d. rooms in the top gallery, and perhaps in parts of the other galleries as well. Entrance to a theatre cost 1d. which gave a spectator the right to stand and see the play, payment of another 1d. at an inner door secured a seat in a 2d. room, and of a third penny at another door a better seat with a cushion. (See PLATTER.) Prices rose in the 17th century, and were always higher in the private theatres. The middle gallery was continued behind or 'over' the stage (cf. *Every Man out of His Humour*, 1599: 'over the stage, i' the Lords room'). In de Witt's sketch of the Swan the six rooms in the gallery over the stage appear to be occupied by spectators, though the orthodox view is that this gallery was generally used as an upper stage (q.v.).

Galley. A shallow tray of wood or metal into which the compositor slips the lines of type from his composing-stick, until it is full. Today the type in a galley is not made up into pages, but in Shakespeare's time a full galley represented the printed page.

Galliard. A lively dance of Italian origin with five steps – hence its name *Cinque-pace* or *Sink-a-pace* – to six beats. In Shakespeare's time the galliard form was already being treated as pure music and combined with the pavane into a rudimentary suite.

Gallus. In *Antony and Cleopatra*, a friend of Caesar. In V, ii he is one of those who capture Cleopatra in her monument; he orders the others to 'guard her till Caesar come', and himself goes to fetch him.

'Gamelyn, Tale of.' The 14th-century pseudo-Chaucerian verse romance from which Lodge took his novel *Rosalynde*, the source of *As You Like It*. Gamelyn corresponds to Orlando, and takes to the forest with Adam the spencer, or steward. Lodge adds the Rosalind-Alinda (Celia) theme.

Ganymede. The name, 'no worse a name than Jove's own page', adopted by Rosalind in *As You Like It* when she disguises herself as a boy.

Gardiner. In *Henry VIII*, the Bishop of Winchester. He is depicted as a creature of Wolsey, raised by his hand (II, ii). In the first three scenes of Act V, derived from Foxe's *Book of Martyrs*, he is the leader of the attack on Cranmer as 'a most arch-heretic'. The King, however, makes them embrace (V, iii). (Stephen Gardiner became Bp of W. 1531, and died 1555.)

Gardiner, William (1531–97). The Surrey magistrate against whom and William Wayte (q.v.) Francis Langley, owner of the Swan theatre, craved sureties of the peace in November 1596, shortly before Wayte craved sureties against him and Shakespeare. Gardiner was J.P. 1580–97, and High Sheriff of Surrey and Sussex 1594–5. He married Frances, daughter of Robert Luce and widow of Edmund Wayte, cheated her brothers and sisters of their father's fortune, and defrauded his step-son, William Wayte. Partly on the evidence of his arms, *Gardiner impaling Luce* – a golden griffin and three white luces (pike) – Hotson in his *Shakespeare versus Shallow* concludes that Shallow in *The Merry Wives* and *2 Henry IV* is a satirical portrait of Gardiner, with whom Shakespeare had quarrelled, and not of Sir Thomas Lucy of the tradition.

Gargrave, Sir Thomas. In *1 Henry VI*, an officer in the English army besieging Orleans. With Salisbury he is killed by a shot from a cannon (I, iv).

Garnet, Henry (1555–1606), was born in London and educated at Winchester. He became a Roman Catholic, joined the Society of Jesus in Italy, and in 1587 became head of the Jesuit mission in England. He knew of the Gunpowder Plot, and after its failure concealed himself at Hindlip Hall, Worcester, but gave himself up 30 January 1606. On 28 March he was tried on a charge of high treason, and was said to have defended himself by equivocation. He was found guilty and hanged on 3 May. The Porter in *Macbeth* (II, iii) seems to refer to Garnet: 'Faith, here's an equivocator, that could swear in both the scales against either scale; who committed treason enough for God's sake, yet could not equivocate to heaven.' If so, it helps to fix the date of *Macbeth*. One of Garnet's *aliases* was Farmer, and the Porter's previous reference to 'a *farmer* that *hanged* himself' may have suggested to Shakespeare the equivocator passage.

Garnier, Robert (*c.* 1545–1600). French dramatist, was born at Ferté Bernard, Le Maine, studied law, and became a distinguished magistrate in his native province. His early tragedies are in the Senecan manner, a series of declamations, with chorus and little action. One of these, *Cornélie* (1573), was translated by Thomas Kyd in 1593, and is one of the many Elizabethan plays on the subject of Julius Caesar. Kyd also considered translating Garnier's *Porcie*, which deals with the deaths of Portia, Brutus and Cassius. In his later plays, *Bradamante* and *Les Juives*, Garnier broke away from the Senecan model. He is the greatest of the French tragic poets of the 16th century.

Garrick, David (1717–79), of French Protestant descent, was born at Hereford, though his home was at Lichfield, where he was educated. For a few months in 1736 he was a pupil of Samuel Johnson at his short-lived Academy at Edial, then in March 1737 both master and pupil set out to make their fortunes in London. Garrick's burlesque, *Lethe*, was performed at Drury Lane in 1740. In March 1741 he made his first appearance on the stage as Harlequin at Goodman's Fields, in the summer his first appearance as an actor in *Oroonoko* at Ipswich, and in October burst into fame as Richard III, again at the Goodman's Fields theatre. From 1742 to 1745 he played at Drury Lane, 1746 in Dublin, 1746–7 at Covent Garden, then in 1747, in association with Lacy, he took over Drury Lane theatre, where he remained until he sold his share for £35,000 in 1776, though he acted little after 1766. In 1749 he married the dancer Eve Maria Violetti (1724–1822). He was a member of the Literary Club, and wrote three volumes of plays and two of verse.

Garrick revolutionized the art of acting, substituting speed, variety, and naturalism for the traditional declamatory intonation of Quin and the actors of the old school. As theatre manager and producer he improved stage lighting, and employed the romantic Loutherbourg to design more realistic scenery and stage effects. He did more than all the scholars to popularize Shakespeare, producing twenty-four of the plays at Drury Lane, and himself playing seventeen Shakespearean parts. In his productions of *Coriolanus*, *The Tempest*, *Antony and Cleopatra*, *Cymbeline* and *Macbeth* he returned very nearly to the text of Shakespeare, though he could not resist writing a dying speech for Macbeth, and some of the original text he restored to *Romeo and Juliet*, *Lear*, and *Timon*. On the other hand he made a little opera, *The Fairies* (1755), of *A Midsummer Night's Dream*, and of *The Tempest* (1756), adapted *The Taming of the Shrew* as *Catharine and Petruchio* (1754), and *The Winter's Tale* as *Florizel and Perdita* (1756), and produced Benjamin Victor's adaptation of *The Two Gentlemen of Verona* (1762). Then in 1772 he produced his own version of *Hamlet*, until then one of the few plays that the improvers had left alone, omitting the grave-diggers and Ophelia's funeral to make room for his additions to his own part. Garrick thus set an example to his successors, who felt justified in treating Shakespeare as material to be cut and refashioned as they pleased. (See 3 *Variorum*, II, p. 691.)

In 1769 Garrick organized the Shakespeare Jubilee (q.v.) at Stratford. Eleven years earlier he had commissioned the statue of Shakespeare by Roubiliac, and ten years later was buried in Westminster Abbey at the foot of Scheemakers's statue of Shakespeare.

Gascoigne, George (*c.* 1530–77), son of Sir John Gascoigne of Cardington, Bedfordshire, was educated at Trinity, Cambridge, and entered Gray's Inn in 1555. He led a riotous youth, was known as 'a notorious ruffianne', married the widow Elizabeth Breton, mother of the poet Nicholas Breton, and 1572–4 served under William of Orange in the Low Countries, where he was captured by the Spaniards. In 1575 he published *The Posies of G. G.* He was a pioneer in many forms of literature; his *Notes concerning the making of verse* (1575) is one of the earliest English critical essays, *The Steele Glas* (1576) has been called the earliest regular English satire, his *Jocasta* is the second English blank verse tragedy, and his adaptation of Ariosto's *I Suppositi* is 'the earliest play in English prose'. This last was first performed in 1566, and published in 1573 with the title-page, 'Supposes: A Comedie written in the Italian tongue by Ariosto, and Englished by George Gascoyne of Grayes Inne Esquire, and there presented'. The author of the Bianca subplot in *The Taming of the Shrew*, whether Shakespeare or a collaborator, took his material either direct from Ariosto or more probably from Gascoigne's *Supposes*. (See KENILWORTH.)

Gascoigne, William. One of the 'necessary attendants' of the King's Men exempted from arrest by Sir Henry Herbert in December 1624 during the season of the Revels. The book-keeper's note on the prompt-copy of Massinger's *Believe as You List*, allowed for the

King's in 1631, makes it clear that he was a stage-hand: 'Gascoigne: & Hubert below: ready to open the Trap doore for Mr Taylor.' (See PROTECTION OF PLAYERS.)

Gastrell, Francis. '*The New Place* was sold by Henry Talbot, Esq., son-in-law and executor of Sir Hugh Clopton, in or soon after the year 1752, to the Rev. Mr Gastrell, a man of large fortune, who resided in it but a few years, in consequence of a disagreement with the inhabitants of Stratford. Every house in that town that is let or valued at more than 40s. a year, is assessed by the overseers, according to its worth and the ability of the occupier, to pay a monthly rate toward the maintenance of the poor. As Mr Gastrell resided part of the year at Lichfield, he thought he was assessed too highly; but being properly compelled by the magistrates of Stratford to pay the whole of what was levied on him, on the principle that his house was occupied by his servants in his absence, he peevishly declared, that *that* house should never be assessed again; and soon afterwards pulled it down, sold the materials, and left the town. Wishing, as it should seem, to be "damn'd to everlasting fame", he had some time before cut down Shakspeare's celebrated mulberry-tree, to save himself the trouble of showing it to those whose admiration of our great poet led them to visit the poetick ground on which it stood.' (Malone, 1 *Variorum*, I, 76.)

Gates, Sir Thomas (fl. 1596–1621), Governor of Virginia, was knighted in 1596 for his services on the Cadiz campaign, entered Gray's Inn in 1598, served in the Netherlands, and was appointed Lieutenant-General of Virginia. In May 1609 nine ships sailed for the colony, but the *Sea Venture* with Gates and Admiral Somers on board was wrecked on Bermuda, where six of the passengers died. The survivors, including William Strachey, Sylvester Jourdan and Richard Rich, reached Jamestown in May 1610 in two pinnaces made out of the wreck. In July Gates, Jourdan and Rich sailed for England with a dispatch from the Governor, Lord Delawarr, and an account of the wreck by Strachey, dated 15th July. They reached London in September; Rich's ballad, Jourdan's *Discoverie*, and the official account of the wreck were published October–November. (See TEMPEST.) Gates was Governor of Virginia 1611–14. Later, he is said to have sailed to the East Indies and died there.

Gatherers. The collectors, men and women, of the entrance money to the theatre and galleries (q.v.). Half the gallery receipts were taken as rent by the owners of the theatre, or house-keepers, who appear to have reserved the right of appointing the gatherers. The sharers paid the gatherers, who collected the money in boxes, and were sometimes known as box-holders (cf. box-office). They were not above shaking the money out of the boxes for themselves; cf. *The Actors Remonstrance*, written in 1643, after the closing of the theatres: 'they cannot now ... seem to scratch their heads where they itch not, and drop shillings and half crown-pieces in at their collars'. The gatherers sometimes acted as supers. (See 'GULL'S HORNBOOK'.)

Gebon. In the 'bad' Quarto (1600) of *Henry V*, the name given to Rambures in III, vii and IV, v by the reporter of the text. Presumably Gebon was the name of an actor in the Chamberlain's company in one of the early performances, 1599–1600. It may be a corruption of Samuel Gilburne who, in 1605, is mentioned by Augustine Phillips in his will as 'my late apprentice'. (See GIBBORNE.)

'Gelyous Comodey.' This play, marked 'ne[w]', was entered by Henslowe in his *Diary* under 5 January 1593. The performance was almost certainly at Henslowe's Rose, and probably by Strange's company. Fleay thought that it might refer to an early version of *The*

Merry Wives, of which 'The Jealous Comedy' would be a good description. Chambers suggests that it may refer to *The Comedy of Errors*.

Genest, John (1764–1839), was educated at Westminster and Trinity, Cambridge, took Orders, and retired to Bath, where he wrote his valuable and accurate *Some Account of the English Stage from the Restoration in 1660 to 1830* (10 vols. 1832), the basis of all later histories of the stage.

Gentili, Alberico (1552–1608), Italian jurist, and one of the founders of the science of international law. As a Protestant he found refuge in England, arrived in Oxford in 1580, and in 1587 was appointed Regius Professor of Civil Law. In the nineties he supported the playwright William Gager against the Puritan John Rainolds as to the propriety of plays at the university.

'Gentleman's Magazine.' A periodical founded by Edward Cave who, in its first number in 1731, described it as 'a Monthly Collection to store up, as in a Magazine, the most remarkable Pieces on the Subjects above-mentioned'. From this usage 'magazine' has come to mean a periodical pamphlet. Dr Johnson was a regular contributor 1739–44. In August 1850 it published the important article by James Spedding, 'Who wrote Henry VIII?' *The Gentleman's Magazine* lasted until 1914.

Gentlemen of the Chapel. The name given to the chaplains and clerks, the former priests and the latter laymen, on the establishment of the Chapel Royal (q.v.). After the subdean the most important of the Gentlemen was the Master of the Children. (See FARRANT; GILES, NATHANIEL.)

Geoffrey of Monmouth (*c.* 1100–54), Bishop of St Asaph. His *Historia Regum Britanniæ* claims to be an account of the British kings up to the time of King Arthur, translated from 'a very old book in the British tongue', but it appears to be based on Bede, Nennius, tradition and imagination. The book established the Arthurian legend, and popularized a number of others that were drawn on by later writers: Sackville and Norton (*Gorboduc*), Spenser (*Faerie Queene*), Drayton (*Polyolbion*), Milton (*Comus*) and Shakespeare (*King Lear* and *Cymbeline*). Shakespeare's immediate source, however, or one of his sources for these two plays, was Holinshed, who for the early part of his *Chronicles* used Geoffrey of Monmouth.

George Bevis. In *2 Henry VI*, one who with 'Iohn-Holland' throws in his lot with Jack Cade. He appears in IV, ii, but the Folio stage-direction reads simply 'Enter Beuis and Iohn Holland'. In IV, vii a stage-direction reads 'Enter George', and editors have assumed that Bevis and George are the same character, and run the two names together as George Bevis. As Holland was certainly an actor, it seems clear that Bevis too was an actor whose name has slipped into the text. He may have been a hired man with Strange's or Pembroke's.

George Inn. An inn in Whitechapel. In 1578 John Brayne, the partner of James Burbage in the Theatre venture, bought it for conversion into a theatre, but failed to obtain a licence.

George III. In 1785 Madame D'Arblay (Fanny Burney) recorded the King's private opinion of Shakespeare:

> Was there ever such stuff as great part of Shakspeare? only one must not say so! But what think you? – What? Is there not sad stuff? What? – What? I know it's not to be said! but it's true. Only it's Shakspeare, and nobody dare abuse him.

Gerald. In *The Two Noble Kinsmen*, a schoolmaster who teaches the country folk a dance which they perform before Theseus and his companions while they are resting in the forest during a hunt (III, v).

Germany. In the 16th and 17th centuries English players visited Germany where they were enthusiastically received both at the numerous courts and in the towns. Fynes Moryson describes them at Frankfort in 1592:

> Germany hath some few wandering Comedians, more deserving pity than praise, for the serious parts are dully penned, and worse acted, and the mirth they make is ridiculous ... So as I remember that when some of our cast despised stage players came out of England into Germany, and played at Frankfort in the time of the Mart, having neither a complete number of Actors, nor any good Apparel, nor any ornament of the Stage, yet the Germans, not understanding a word they said, both men and women, flocked wonderfully to see their gesture and Action rather than hear them, speaking English which they understood not, and pronouncing pieces and patches of English plays, which myself and some English men there present could not hear without great wearisomeness.

The most important of these English players were Robert Browne and Thomas Green, who were in Germany with their companies for long periods between 1590 and 1626. To begin with they spoke English, but eventually German, the language of all the plays that have been preserved, the most interesting of which is *Der Bestrafte Brudermord*, a version of *Hamlet*. German dramatists, notably Jacob Ayrer (q.v.), were influenced by these Elizabethan plays.

Until the 18th century, Germany had no great native literature; her polite society spoke French, her writers imitated French models and affected to despise the barbarous Shakespeare. But in 1767–8 Lessing in his *Hamburgische Dramaturgie* proclaimed the superiority of Shakespeare to the French dramatists. A few years later the Sturm und Drang movement swept Germany, and Shakespeare was hailed as a 'pure virgin genius, ignorant of rules and limits, a force as irresistible as those of nature'. Lessing's teaching was developed by Herder, who fired the youthful Goethe with his enthusiasm; Wieland began his prose translation of Shakespeare's plays, completed by Eschenburg (1775–83), and this was followed by the brilliant verse translation of A. W. Schlegel (1797–1801), completed by Tieck, perhaps the most significant achievement of the Romantic movement in Germany. In 1808 Schlegel delivered his *Lectures on Dramatic Art*, like Coleridge, maintaining that Shakespeare's art was equal to his genius.

In the course of the 19th century German scholars and critics were tireless in their pursuit of Shakespeare; 'through industry and love', wrote Gervinus, 'we have won the great poet for ourselves.' Gervinus published his massive *Shakespeare* in 1849–50; Ulrici had already produced his *Shakespeares dramatische Kunst* in 1839; and Delius followed with his *Abhandlungen zu Shakspere* in 1888; the German Shakespeare-Gesselschaft was founded in 1865, and began the publication of its *Jahrbuch*. At the same time Gustav Rümelin in his *Shakespeare Studies by a Realist* protested against the conventional adulation of Shakespeare and inaugurated the period of more critical criticism, of F. Kreyssig, F. Gundolf, M. J. Wolff and L. L. Schücking. Karl Simrock (1831) was the first scholar to write about Shakespeare's sources since Charlotte Lennox in 1753. In 1888 Gaedertz, by his publication of De Witt's drawing of the Swan theatre, revolutionized ideas about the Elizabethan stage and inspired scholars everywhere – Creizenach, Brodmeier, Neuendorff and Wegener in Germany – to study Shakespeare's theatre, and critics to consider Shakespeare primarily as a man of the theatre. The study of verse-tests was carried on by Hertzberg, König and Conrad, and the plays of Shakespeare were lavishly staged by Max Reinhardt and the Saxe-Meiningen players, with their insistence on the importance of the crowd, and with great simplicity by the Swiss scenic designer, Adolphe Appia (1862–1928), who used lighting to integrate the setting and the actors, and to emphasize three-dimensional form. Today the leading Shakespeare scholar is Wolfgang Clemen.

The principal German translations of Shakespeare's works are:

Wieland, C. M.	8	vols.	1762–6 (prose)
Eschenburg, J. J.	13	,,	1775–82 ,,
	22	,,	1778–83 ,,
Schlegel, A. W.	8	,,	1797–1801
Voss, J. H.	9	,,	1818–29
Benda, J. W. O.	19	,,	1825–6
Schlegel and Tieck	12	,,	1839–40
Ortlepp, E.	16	,,	1838–9
Böttger, A.	12	,,	1839
Keller, A., and Rapp, M.	37	,,	1843–7
Dingelstedt, F.	10	,,	1867
Bodenstedt, F.	9	,,	1867–71
Gundolf, F.	10	,,	1908–23
Rothe, Hans			1922–
Flatter, R. (q.v.)			

The popularity of Shakespeare in Germany today may be gauged from the fact that even in The Festival year of Schiller's bicentenary (1959) there were far more performances of Shakespeare than of Schiller. (See E. L. Stahl, *Shakespeare und das deutsche Theater*, 1947; SS, 16.)

Gertrude. In *Hamlet*, the mother of Prince Hamlet. Her marriage to Claudius largely accounts for the melancholy and cynicism of her son, who violently attacks her for her lust.

Gervinus, Georg Gottfried (1805–71), was born at Darmstadt, where he was educated, later attending the universities of Giessen and Heidelberg. In 1844 he became Professor at Heidelberg, and in 1849–50 published the four volumes of his *Shakespeare*, translated into English as *Shakespeare Commentaries* in 1863, and followed it in 1868 with his *Händel und Shakespeare*. Comparative neglect and the union of Germany by force under Prussia embittered him, and he died at Heidelberg in 1871. Gervinus, by means of verse-tests, divided the work of Shakespeare into three periods, and was the first critic to trace the development of his art, 'to deal with Shakespeare as a whole'.

'Gesta Grayorum.' The records of Gray's Inn. Masques and revels, elaborate festivities presided over by a Master of the Revels or Lord of Misrule, were an ancient custom of the Inns of Court, particularly of Gray's Inn and the Inner Temple. The *Gesta Grayorum*, printed in 1688 (ed. by W. W. Greg for Malone Society), contain a contemporary account of the Revels on 28 December 1594, when Shakespeare and his fellows played *The Comedy of Errors*. The Gray's men invited an 'ambassador' and his followers from the Inner Temple, but the festivities were so riotous that the Templarians retired. On the next day Gray's held a mock trial, and found a sorcerer guilty of the confusion.

> The next grand Night was intended to be upon *Innocents-Day* at Night.... The Ambassador came ... about Nine of the Clock at Night ... there arose such a disordered Tumult and Crowd upon the Stage, that there was no opportunity to effect that which was intended.... The Lord Ambassador and his Train thought that they were not so kindly entertained, as was before expected, and thereupon would not stay any longer at that time, but, in a sort, discontented and displeased. After their Departure the Throngs and Tumults did somewhat cease, although so much of them continued, as was able to disorder and confound any good Inventions whatsoever. In regard whereof, as also for that the Sports intended were especially for the gracing of the *Templarians*, it was thought good not to offer any thing of Account, saving Dancing and Revelling with Gentlewomen; and after such Sports, a Comedy of Errors (like to *Plautus* his *Menechmus*) was played by the Players. So that Night was begun, and continued to the end, in nothing but Confusion and Errors; whereupon, it was ever afterwards called, *The Night of Errors*.... We preferred Judgments ... against a Sorcerer or Conjuror that was supposed to be the Cause of that confused Inconvenience.... And, lastly that he had foisted a Company of base and common Fellows, to make up our Disorders with a Play of Errors and Confusions; and that Night had gained to us Discredit, and itself a Nickname of Errors.

'Gesta Romanorum.' A collection of stories in Latin, compiled *c.* 1400 either in England, France or Germany. It is not limited to 'Deeds of the Romans', there being stories of the Greeks and Middle Ages, legends of the Saints and Oriental tales, all with a moral significance. An English translation was published by Wynkyn de Worde *c.* 1510, and a revised edition by Richard Robinson in 1577. The work was very popular, and the source of many later stories; for example, it contains the moral tale of the choosing of the leaden casket, and that of Apollonius of Tyre, both of which were used by Gower in his *Confessio Amantis*, and by Shakespeare, the former in *The Merchant of Venice*, the latter in *The Comedy of Errors* and *Pericles*, though Shakespeare did not take them directly from the *Gesta Romanorum*.

Getley, Walter. The man from whom Shakespeare bought the copyhold estate of the Chapel Lane Cottage (q.v.) 28 September 1602. The Court-rolls of the Manor of Rowington record the transaction:

> Rowington . . . Ad hanc curiam venit Walterus Getley, per Thomam Tibbottes iuniorem attornatum suum unum customariorum tenencium manerii prediciti ... et sursumreddidit in manus domine manerii predicti vnum cotagium cum pertinenciis scituatum iacens ct existens in Stratford super Avon, in quodam vico ibidem vocato Walkers Streete alias Dead Lane, ad opus et vsum Willielmi Shackespere et heredum suorum imperpetuum. . . .

Ghost. In *Hamlet*. The ghost of the elder Hamlet has twice appeared to Marcellus and Bernardo before they see it a third time in the presence of the sceptical Horatio. It appears again to Hamlet, Horatio, and Marcellus. Hamlet follows, and it tells him how he was poisoned by Claudius, who had already seduced Hamlet's mother, and enjoins him to revenge his murder, but to leave his mother to the punishment of heaven. The ghost appears again in III, iv when Hamlet, having made no attempt to kill Claudius, appears to be on the point of killing his mother. According to Rowe (1708), Shakespeare himself acted the part: 'the top of his performance was the Ghost in his own *Hamlet*.' (See R. Flatter, *Hamlet's Father*, 1949.)

Ghosts. One of the elements borrowed from Seneca's tragedies by the Elizabethans, particularly for their popular revenge-tragedies, of which *Hamlet* is an example. The ghost in *Hamlet* should be compared with that of Tantalus in Seneca's *Thyestes*, and of Thyestes in his *Agamemnon*. There is a ghost, or ghosts, in *Richard III*, *Julius Caesar*, *Hamlet*, *Macbeth* and *Cymbeline*.

Gibbons, Orlando (1583–1625), born at Cambridge, where he became a choirboy at King's College. In 1604 he was appointed organist of the Chapel Royal, and in 1623 of Westminster Abbey. He died at Canterbury, whither he was sent in charge of the Chapel Royal musicians to welcome Henrietta Maria, Charles I's bride. He was one of the greatest composers of the early 17th century, writing church music, madrigals, and music for virginals and viols.

Gibborne, Thomas. Actor, and housekeeper in the Palsgrave's at the Fortune in 1624. It is just possible that he is the 'Gebon' (q.v.) whose name occurs in the Quarto of *Henry V*.

Gide, André (1869–1951). French essayist and novelist, was born in Paris and educated at the École Alsacienne and the Lycée Henri IV. He wrote the preface to the Pléiade edition of a number of Shakespeare's plays, and himself translated *Antony and Cleopatra* and *Hamlet*.

Gielgud, John (b. 1904). His first stage appearance was at the Old Vic in 1921 as the Herald in *Henry V*. In 1924 he was Romeo in Barry Jackson's production. He has played in many Old Vic seasons, was Malvolio at the reopening of Sadler's Wells in January 1931, and produced *Hamlet*, *Romeo and Juliet*, *Macbeth*, etc. At Elsinore in 1939 he played Hamlet, at Stratford Lear, Leontes, and Benedick in 1950, Prospero in 1957, etc.; in films Cassius and Clarence. Among his recordings is *The Ages of Man*, and he produced Britten's opera *A Midsummer Night's Dream* in 1961. Knighted 1953.

Gilburne, Samuel. One of the twenty-six 'Principall Actors' in Shakespeare's plays (see p. 90). The only other mention of him is in the will of Augustine Phillips (1605) who left him, 'my late apprentice', 40s. and 'my mouse coloured velvit hose and a white taffety dublet, a blacke taffety sute, my purple cloke, sword, and dagger, and my base viall'. He may be the 'Gebon' (q.v.) of the Quarto of *Henry V*, probably took Phillips's place as a sharer in the King's company, and died a few years later.

Gild of Holy Cross. A 13th-century fraternity at Stratford. In 1269 it was granted a licence to build the Gild Chapel, rebuilt by Sir Hugh Clopton in 1492. The Gild, which was governed by a Master and Aldermen, had founded the school in the 13th century, and maintained priests to sing masses for the souls of its dead brothers and sisters, whose names are recorded in its register. It was dissolved in 1547 and the Gild Chapel was granted to the Corporation when the town received its charter in 1553.

Gildon, Charles (1665–1724), the critic, was born near Shaftesbury, trained as a Roman Catholic priest, and after spending his patrimony turned hack-writer. His *Reflections on Rymer's Short View of Tragedy* contains a note on Iago (see CLOWN). In 1698 he edited *The Lives and Characters of the English Dramatick Poets. First begun by Mr. Langbain, improv'd and continued down to this Time*, to which he, or a collaborator, added a Shakespeare anecdote (see also HALES, JOHN):

> I have been told that he writ the scene of the Ghost in *Hamlet*, at his House which bordered on the Charnel-House and Church-Yard.

In 1699 appeared,

> Measure for Measure, or Beauty the best Advocate. As it is acted at the Theatre in Lincoln's Inn Fields; written originally by Mr. Shakespeare, and now very much altered: with additions of several Entertainments of Musick. By Mr. Gildon.

It is a simplified version of D'Avenant's adaptation, *The Law Against Lovers*, without Benedick and Beatrice, but with the masque of Dido and Aeneas and music by Purcell. Betterton played Angelo, and Anne Bracegirdle Isabella. In 1710 Gildon issued a volume containing Shakespeare's *Poems*; this was made to look like a seventh volume of Rowe's six-volume edition of the plays (1709), though the publisher was Curll instead of Tonson. Pope pilloried Gildon in *The Dunciad* (III, 173):

> Ah Dennis! Gildon ah! what ill-starr'd rage
> Divides a friendship long confirm'd by age?
> Blockheads with reason wicked wits abhor,
> But fool with fool is barbarous civil war ...'

Giles, Nathaniel (*c.* 1559–1634), was educated at Magdalen, Oxford, and became organist of Worcester Cathedral, in which town he was probably born. After being a Clerk in St George's Chapel, Windsor, he was in 1595 appointed Master of the Windsor Children, and two years later Master of the Children of the Chapel as well, holding both Masterships until his death in 1634. He composed mainly church music. In 1600 he was associated with Henry Evans in the second Blackfriars theatre, where the Chapel Children gave public performances, but appears to have retired from the venture after the Star Chamber complaint of 1602, when he was accused of exploiting his privilege of pressing children for service in the Chapel for his own profit.

Giles, Thomas, brother of Nathaniel, became Master of the Children of Paul's in 1584, and was authorized by the Queen to press into the service of the choir any 'apt and meet' boy in England or Wales. He produced Lyly's plays at Court 1587–90, but when Lyly used the boys, at the Government's request, to attack Marprelate, their dramatic activities were suppressed. By 1600 Giles had been succeeded by Edward Peers, and he became the musical instructor of Princes Henry and Charles.

Giovanni (Fiorentino), Ser. 14th-century Florentine notary, and author of a collection of stories called *Il Pecorone*. The tales are modelled on those of Boccaccio, and are supposed to be related by two lovers, a monk and a nun, in the parlour of the monastery of Forlì. They were written about 1378, but not published until 1558. Shakespeare used the story of Gianetto for his *Merchant of Venice*. It contains the themes of the lover's elderly friend, his winning of a wife, by a test less moral than that of the caskets, the pound of flesh, the woman disguised as a lawyer, and that of the ring. Shakespeare probably read the original Italian, as there does not appear to have been an English translation.

Giustinian, Zorzi. Venetian ambassador to England from 5 January 1606 to 23 November 1608. Sometime between these dates he saw a performance of *Pericles*, for according to evidence given at the trial in 1618 of Antonio Foscarini (Venetian ambassador 1611–15),

> All the ambassadors who have come to England have gone to the play more or less. Giustinian went with the French ambassador and his wife to a play called *Pericles*, which cost Giustinian more than 20 crowns. He also took the Secretary of Florence.

Glansdale, Sir William. In *1 Henry VI*, an officer in the English army. At the siege of Orleans, I, iv.

Glendower, Owen (*c.* 1359–1415?). In *1 Henry IV*, he defeats and captures Hotspur's brother-in-law, Mortimer, who then marries his captor's daughter. They join Hotspur's rebellion, but neither is present at Shrewsbury where Hotspur is killed. After the battle the King and Prince Henry set off to deal with Glendower and Mortimer. (Glendower was educated in England, claimed to be independent Prince of Wales, and led a national revolt 1401–15. His end is unknown.)

Globe Theatre. When the lease of the Theatre site expired, Giles Allen, owner of the land, threatened to pull it down because of 'the greate and greevous abuses that grewe by the Theater', but his move was anticipated by the Burbages, the owners of the building. In December 1598 or January 1599 they and Peter Street

> and divers other persons, to the number of twelve ... armed themselves ... and throwing downe the sayd Theater in verye outragious, violent and riotous sort ... did then alsoe in most forcible and ryotous manner take and carrye awaye from thence all the wood and timber thereof unto the Bancksyde in the parishe of St. Marye Overyes, and there erected a newe playehowse with the sayd timber and woode.

The site of the new Globe theatre has been disputed, but it now seems clear that it was just south of Maid Lane and south-east of the Rose, so becoming the most easterly of the four Bankside theatres. It was built at the charge of the Burbage brothers, probably by Peter Street, the carpenter who erected the Fortune in 1600, and seems to have been completed by the autumn, when it was occupied by the Chamberlain's. The land belonged to Nicholas Brend who, for a rent of £14 10s. granted a thirty-one year lease running from December 1598 to December 1629; it was conveyed in two halves, one half to the Burbages, Richard and Cuthbert, and the other half in five equal shares to Shakespeare, Heminge, Phillips, Pope and Kempe (see LEVESON). How the money was raised for the building is not clear. Each member of this syndicate of housekeepers was entitled to his proportion of half the gallery takings, and was liable for his proportion of the ground-rent and cost of upkeep of the theatre. (See SHARERS' PAPERS; WITTER.)

The Globe was the model for the Fortune (q.v.) built for Alleyn by Peter Street in the following year, with the one important difference that the Fortune was rectangular while the Globe was almost certainly cylindrical. Unfortunately it was thatched, which led to the fire of 29 June 1613, when it was burned to the ground during a performance of *Henry VIII*, described by Sir Henry Wootton in a letter of 2 July:

> Now, King Henry making a masque at the Cardinal Wolsey's house, and certain chambers being shot off at his entry, some of the paper, or other stuff, wherewith one of them was stopped, did light on the thatch, where being thought at first but an idle smoke, and their eyes more attentive to the show, it kindled inwardly, and ran round like a train, consuming within less than an hour the whole house to the very grounds. This was the fatal period of that virtuous fabric, wherein yet nothing did perish but wood and straw, and a few forsaken cloaks; only one man had his breeches set on fire, that would perhaps have broiled him, if he had not by the benefit of a provident wit put it out with bottle ale. (See also LORKIN; J. CHAMBERLAIN.)

It was rebuilt in the following year 'in far fairer manner than before', and open by June 1614. The Burbages would have to pay half the cost, and the other housekeepers, of whom there were then seven, the other half; the total cost appears to have been about £1,400. This time it was tiled, and, according to Holler's *Long View of London* (1647) and the original drawing (*c.* 1640) for his etching, circular. The second Globe was 'pulled downe to the ground, by Sir Matthew Brand, on Munday the 15 of April, 1644, to make tenements in the room of it'. (See HOWES; J. C. Adams, *The Globe Playhouse*; Irwin Smith, *Shakespeare's Globe Playhouse*; C. W. Hodges, *The Globe Theatre*; L. Hotson, *Shakespeare's Wooden O.*)

'Globe' Shakespeare. The one-volume edition edited by W. G. Clark and W. A. Wright in 1864. It gives the text of the *Cambridge Shakespeare* of 1863–6, and is the standard edition for line numbering.

Glossaries. See CONCORDANCES.

Gloucester, Duchess of. 1. In *Richard II*, Eleanor de Bohun (d. 1399), widow of Thomas of Woodstock, Duke of Gloucester, brother of John of Gaunt. (Gloucester had been engaged with Bolingbroke and Mowbray in a plot against King Richard. Mowbray betrayed it and murdered Gloucester at the King's command.) The Duchess appeals in vain to Gaunt to avenge her husband's murder, and then apparently retires to die of grief (I, ii).

2. In *2 Henry VI*, Eleanor Cobham (d. 1454), second wife of Humphrey, Duke of Gloucester. She wishes to be Queen, and practises sorcery against the King, is discovered (I, iv), and banished (II, iii), her accomplices being sentenced to death. As she sets out for the Isle of Man she warns Gloucester against Suffolk, York and Henry Beaufort, Bishop of Winchester.

Gloucester, Humphrey, Duke of (1391–1447), fourth son of Henry IV. He first appears in *2 Henry IV* as Prince Humphrey of Gloucester (IV, v), speaks a few lines, but plays no important part in the action. In *Henry V* as Duke of Gloucester, brother of the King, he appears in a number of scenes, and is present at Agincourt, but plays an unimportant part. In *1 Henry VI* he is the King's uncle, and Protector. The English scenes in the play are concerned largely with his quarrel with Henry Beaufort, Cardinal Bishop of Winchester. In *2 Henry VI*, when his wife is banished for sorcery, Gloucester is deprived of the Protectorship. His enemies, the Queen, Cardinal Beaufort, Suffolk, and York, secure his arrest and murder (III, i and ii).

Gloucester, Richard, Duke of (1452–85), fourth son of Richard Plantagenet, 3rd Duke of York, and the future Richard III. He first appears in *2 Henry VI*, and kills Somerset in fight at the Battle of St Albans, though as a matter of history he was only eight at the time. In *3 Henry VI* his brother Edward creates him Duke of Gloucester (II, vi), and though in his seventy-two line soliloquy he wishes Edward 'wasted, marrow, bones and all', he supports him loyally when Clarence and Warwick desert him. After the Battle of Tewkesbury he stabs the Prince of Wales and hurries to London to murder Henry VI in the Tower, so getting rid of the Lancastrians who stand in his way to the throne. In *Richard III* he gets rid of the Yorkists. Of his three elder brothers, Rutland had been killed at Wakefield, Edward IV dies, and he secures the murder of Clarence. Before murdering the two young sons of Edward IV he is proclaimed King by Buckingham, although Clarence's children are still alive. When he is defeated and killed by Richmond at Bosworth he has murdered or executed Rivers, Grey, Vaughan, Hastings, Buckingham and apparently the Lady Anne, his wife.

Gloucester, Earl of. In *King Lear*, father of Edgar and the illegitimate Edmund. (In Sidney's *Arcadia* he is the Prince of Paphlagonia.)

Gloucestershire. Shakespeare makes a number of references to Gloucestershire and the Cotswolds, particularly in his earlier plays: in *The Taming of the Shrew*, *Richard II*, *1* and *2 Henry IV*, *The Merry Wives*, and Dr Spurgeon suggests that Shakespeare had Berkeley Castle in mind when he wrote *Macbeth*. There are Shakespeares in that part of the county, and there is a tradition that Shakespeare lived at Dursley, at the foot of the Cotswolds and a few miles from Berkeley, between leaving Stratford and going to London.

Gobbo. In *The Merchant of Venice*, Launcelot Gobbo is a 'clown', the servant of Shylock. He follows the advice of the fiend against that of his conscience, and decides to leave the Jew's for Bassanio's service. He helps Lorenzo to carry off Jessica, and accompanies Bassanio to Belmont. For the rest, he acts as messenger and buffoon. His father is the sand-blind Old Gobbo who appears in II, ii with a present for Shylock. Launcelot persuades him to give it to Bassanio instead and to help him into his service. (There was a family of Gobbos at Titchfield in Hampshire, the home of Shakespeare's patron, the Earl of Southampton. See CECIL.)

Godfrey of Viterbo (*c.* 1120–*c.* 1196). A chronicler in the service of the Emperor Frederick I and of his son Henry VI. He wrote a verse history of the world beginning at the creation, in its revised form called *Pantheon*, first printed in 1559. From this Gower took the story of Apollonius of Tyre for his *Confessio Amantis*, in its turn the main source of *Pericles, Prince of Tyre*.

Goethe, Johann Wolfgang von (1749–1832). The Sturm und Drang movement may be said to have begun in Strasbourg in the winter of 1770–71, when Herder opened the young Goethe's imagination to the beauties of Shakespeare. Goethe tells how the first page of Shakespeare that he read made him a life-long admirer, and how he was overwhelmed by the colossal scale of his characters and his elemental power. Goethe's championship assured the position of Shakespeare in Germany. His Shakespearean criticism, concerned mainly with the philosophical significance of character, is scattered throughout his works, the most famous passage being in *Wilhelm Meister* (1795), where he analyses the character of Hamlet, 'a lovely, pure, noble and most moral nature'; a passage that Gervinus claimed to be 'like a key to all works of the poet'. From 1791 to 1813 Goethe was director of the Court theatre at Weimar, and though he thought Shakespeare's plays unsuitable for the stage, he produced a version of *Romeo and Juliet*.

Golding, Arthur (*c.* 1536–*c.* 1605). It is probable that he was born in London, and may have gone to Queen's, Cambridge. In 1549 he was in the service of the Protector Somerset, and later appears to have been in that of Sir William Cecil. In 1567 appeared his famous translation into English verse of Ovid's *Metamorphoses*, written in fourteeners:

The gods sat down. The aged wife, right chare and busy as
A bee, set out a table, of the which the third foot was
A little shorter than the rest. A tilesherd made it even
And took away the shoringness; and when they had it driven
To stand up level, with green mints they by and by it wiped.

Shakespeare's references to Ovid are numerous, to the story of Philemon and Baucis, for example, quoted above, and Prospero's farewell to his art owes something to Golding's version of Medea's invocation, beginning:

Ye airs and winds, ye elves of hills, ye brooks and woods alone.

Shakespeare probably made some use of Golding's translation for his *Venus and Adonis*, though he seems to have been well enough acquainted with the original Latin; certainly he took Titania direct from Ovid. Golding was a confirmed Puritan, the translator of Calvin, but he reconciled the translating of the anything but puritanical stories of Ovid by drawing a Christian moral from them.

Gollancz, Sir Israel (1864–1930), Professor of English at King's College, London. In 1903 he became secretary of the British Academy, and was knighted in 1919. He edited the *Temple Classics*, including the *Temple Shakespeare* (40 vols. 1894–6), *Ambales-Saga* (1898) and *The Book of Homage to Shakespeare* (1916). (See SHAKESPEARE ASSOCIATION.)

Goneril. In *King Lear*, the eldest daughter of Lear and wife of Albany, whom she despises. (Gonorill in *King Leir*.)

Gonzaga. The family name of the Renaissance Dukes of Mantua. Vincentio Gonzaga was Duke of Mantua 1587–1612; the name of Shakespeare's Duke of Vienna in *Measure for Measure* is Vincentio; and Hamlet describes his play as 'the image of a murder done in Vienna: Gonzago is the Duke's name'. There was also a Fernando Gonzaga, governor of the province of Milan, who in 1547 played something the same part as the Duke in *Measure for Measure*; but this story Shakespeare took from Whetstone, who had it from Cinthio.

Gonzaga, Curzio. 16th-century Italian author of *Inganni* (1592), to which John Manningham compared *Twelfth Night* when he saw it performed at the Inner Temple in February 1602.

Gonzalo. In *The Tempest*, 'an honest old Councellor'. When Antonio usurped Milan and put Prospero and Miranda to sea to drown, Gonzalo gave them 'rich garments, linens, stuffs and necessaries', and above all, books. When, therefore, he falls into Prospero's power with the others, Prospero addresses him as 'good Gonzalo, My true preserver, and a loyal sir To him thou follow'st'.

Goodale, Thomas. Actor. In 1581, as one of Lord Berkeley's company, he was imprisoned for a brawl with the Inns of Court men. He appears as 'Tho. Goodale' in the cast of *The Second Part of the Seven Deadly Sins*. In the manuscript of *Sir Thomas More* (q.v.), *c.* 1595, he was cast to play the part of a messenger; at the beginning of Addition V, 'C' inserted the stage-direction 'Mess/T Goodal'.

Goodman's Fields Theatre. The first mention of a theatre at Goodman's Fields, Leman Street, near the Tower, is in 1703. Shortly before 1730 Thomas Odell opened a second Goodman's Fields theatre in Leman Street, and appointed Henry Giffard as manager. The puritanical City authorities attacked it as obscene and seditious, and eventually Odell sold it to Giffard, who rebuilt it. It was at this theatre, unfashionable and unauthorized, that Garrick first appeared in 1741.

'Gorboduc, or Ferrex and Porrex,' is important as the first English tragedy in blank verse. It was published in September 1565:

> The Tragedie of Gorboduc. Where of three Actes were wrytten by Thomas Nortone, and the two laste by Thomas Sackuyle. Sett forthe as the same was shewed before the Quenes most excellent Maiestie, in her highnes Court of Whitehall, the xviij day of Ianuary, Anno Domini 1561. By the Gentlemen of Thynner Temple in London.

It is a wearisome affair on the strict Senecan model ('climbing to the height of Seneca his style', wrote Sidney), with a chorus, and long rhetorical and narrative speeches in stumping end-stopped lines to explain the action that takes place off-stage. A non-Senecan feature is the dumb-show before each of the five acts.

Gosson, Henry. Publisher of the first two Quartos (1609) of *Pericles.* Edward Blount had registered the play on 20 May, and there is no record of a transfer of copyright. The text is corrupt. Gosson was in business 1601–40, and specialized in popular literature.

Gosson, Stephen (1554–1624), was born at or near Canterbury, and educated at Corpus Christi, Oxford. In London he made a name for himself as playwright and poet, Meres in 1598 mentioning him as one of the 'best for pastorall', and Lodge reports that he became a player. He soon recanted, however, for in 1579 he published *The Schoole of Abuse, Containing a pleasaunt inuective against Poets, Pipers, Plaiers, Iesters and such like Caterpillers of a Commonwealth,* dedicating it, quaintly enough, to Sir Philip Sidney, only to be, according to Spenser, 'for hys labor scorned, if at leaste it be in the goodnesse of that nature to scorne'. Gosson followed this in the same year with *The Ephemerides of Phialo and a short Apologie of the Schoole of Abuse,* again dedicated to Sidney, whom it appears to have inspired to write his *Apologie for Poetrie.* Lodge replied in his *Defence of Playes* (1580), and the players by reviving Gosson's own plays, now lost, but three of which he mentions as pigs of his own sow: *Catiline's Conspiracies,* The Comedy of *Captain Mario,* and a Moral, *Praise at Parting.* In 1582 Gosson answered his opponents in his *Playes Confuted in fiue Actions, Prouing that they are not to be suffred in a Christian common weale.* Meanwhile he had taken Orders, becoming Rector of Great Wigborough, Essex, and in 1600 of St Botolph's, Bishopsgate. Gosson is outspoken: the theatres are 'a generall market of bawdrie', and the players 'vncircumcised Philistines ... daunsing Chaplines of Bacchus', yet he does not condemn indiscriminately: 'And as some of the players are far from abuse: so some of their plays are without rebuke: which are as easily remembered as quickly reckoned,' one of them being his own *Catiline's Conspiracies.*

Gottsched, Johann Christoph (1700–66). German critic of the neo-classic school, who maintained that German literature must follow French rules, and himself laid down rules for the drama. He attacked Milton and Shakespeare, but his influence speedily crumbled before the liberal criticism of the Swiss Bodmer and Breitinger, of Lessing and the German romantics.

Götz, Hermann (1840–76), German composer of the opera *Der Widerspenstigen Zähmung* (*Taming of the Shrew*).

Gough, Robert (d. 1624). One of the twenty-six 'Principall Actors' in Shakespeare's plays (see p. 90). He is probably the 'R. Go.' mentioned as playing a woman's part in the Plot of *The Seven Deadly Sins,* performed probably by Strange's *c.* 1591. He may have joined the Chamberlain's-King's as a hired man, for in 1603 Thomas Pope left him a legacy, and in 1605 he witnessed the will of Augustine Phillips, whose sister he appears to have married. Baldwin suggests that Gough became a sharer on Phillips's death, but Chambers thinks that Gilburne replaced Phillips, and that Gough succeeded Gilburne some time before 1611, for there is some chronology in the Folio list, in which Gough is four from the end. He cannot have been a very important actor, he is in none of the actor-lists, but appears in the official lists of 1619 and 1621.

Gounod, Charles François (1818–93). The French composer who achieved fame with his opera *Faust* (1859). After Goethe he turned to Shakespeare, and in April 1867 his operatic version of *Romeo and Juliet* was produced in Paris; but, as Dr Scholes remarks, 'those who love Shakespeare do not love Gounod'.

Gower, John (*c.* 1330–1408). Poet, contemporary, and friend of Chaucer, who calls him 'moral Gower', and admirer of Richard II's cousin Bolingbroke, who became Henry IV in 1399. Gower came of a good Kentish family, lived mostly in London, and went blind some years before his death. He was buried in the church of St Mary Overie's, now St Saviour's, Southwark, in a splendid tomb with a recumbent effigy, the poet's head resting on the three volumes of his most famous works, the *Speculum Meditantis*, *Vox Clamantis*, and *Confessio Amantis*. The first, called also *Mirour de l'Omme*, is a 30,000-line allegory in French; the second, a 10,000-line poem in Latin elegiacs describing the Peasants' Revolt of 1381; the third, and much the most important, is in English, a poem of some 35,000 lines written in octosyllabic couplets. Gower is himself the lover and confesses to the priest of Venus, Genius, who illustrates his precepts with a series of classical and medieval tales. Gower is absolved, but dismissed from her court by Venus, as one too old to be a lover.

Shakespeare probably took the Aegeon-Aemilia theme of *The Comedy of Errors* from Gower's version of the old romance of Apollonius of Tyre, and for *Pericles*, in which Gower himself appears as Chorus, almost certainly used the same story. Possibly, too, Shakespeare took from Gower the moral story of the caskets for his *Merchant of Venice*. (See GODFREY OF VITERBO.)

Gower. 1. In *Pericles* the poet Gower acts as Chorus, summarizing and moralizing the play, and bridging the years. He appears before each act, before V, ii, as Epilogue, and IV, iv is a scene of his own. He speaks for the most part in the octosyllabic couplet of the *Confessio Amantis*, but sometimes in decasyllabics, rhyming either in couplets or alternately. In II; III; IV, iv, his speeches are illustrated by dumb-shows.

2. In *2 Henry IV*, Gower, presumably the poet and admirer of Henry IV, appears in II, i, where he announces the approach of the King to the Lord Chief Justice.

3. In *Henry V*, a captain on the Agincourt campaign. The most modest of men himself, he has no illusions about Pistol. His main function in the play is to listen to his friend Fluellen, and to restrain his fiery temper.

Gowrie Conspiracy. According to King James this was an attempt by John Ruthven, Earl of Gowrie, and his brother Alexander, to assassinate him at Gowrie House, Perth, on 5 August 1600. The affair has never been satisfactorily cleared up, but Gowrie and his brother were killed in a struggle with James's followers. James used to observe 5 August as a day of delivery from death. Towards the end of 1604 the King's Men seem to have caused offence by the production of a play on the Gowrie affair, for on 18 December John Chamberlain wrote to Ralph Winwood:

> The Tragedy of *Gowry*, with all the Action and Actors hath been twice represented by the King's Players, with exceeding Concourse of all sorts of People. But whether the matter or manner be not well handled, or that it be thought unfit that Princes should be played on the Stage in their Life-time, I

hear that some great Councellors are much displeased with it, and so 'tis thought shall be forbidden.

However, the King's Men gave eleven Court performances that winter, seven of the plays being Shakespeare's.

Grafton, Richard (*c.* 1512–72), printer and chronicler, was born at Shrewsbury. In 1538–9, with Coverdale and Edward Whitchurch he printed a modified version of Coverdale's translation of the Bible, known as the Great Bible. In 1543 he printed his *Chronicle* of the period from the time of Edward IV, a continuation of Hardyng's *Chronicles*, and in 1548 Edward Halle's *The Union of the Two Noble and Illustre Famelies of Lancastre and Yorke*, himself adding the history of the years 1532–47. On the accession of Edward VI Grafton was appointed the Royal Printer, but on the King's death printed the proclamation of Lady Jane Grey, signing himself the Queen's Printer, for which he was imprisoned by Mary. After this he devoted himself to adapting and publishing the work of other chroniclers; for example, *An Abridgement of the Chronicle of England* (1562). Graftons's daughter Joan married the printer Richard Tottell, publisher of *Tottell's Miscellany*. Shakespeare made use of Grafton's *Chronicles* for his *Henry VI*, though Grafton follows Halle so closely that it is often impossible to say which was his source.

Grandpré. In *Henry V*, a French lord. He appears only in IV, ii, where he describes the ragged English army on the morning of Agincourt. His name is in the list of those killed in the battle (IV, viii).

Granville, George (1667–1735), was educated at Trinity, Cambridge, in 1702 returned as M.P. for Fowey, in 1710 made Secretary of War, and in 1711 Lord Lansdowne. From 1715 to 1717 he was imprisoned for Jacobite activities in Cornwall, lived in France 1722–32, devoting himself to literature, and publishing his complete works in the latter year. These have little value today, but they include an adaptation of *The Merchant of Venice* called *The Jew of Venice*, produced at Lincoln's Inn Fields in 1701 with Betterton as Bassanio and the low comedian Thomas Doggett as Shylock. The version was popular and held the stage until the Drury Lane production of the original Shakespeare with Charles Macklin as Shylock in 1741.

Granville-Barker, Harley (1877–1946), the first modern producer of Shakespeare in the commercial theatre, was born in London, educated privately, and in 1890 went to the dramatic school of the Theatre Royal, Margate; a year later he made his first appearance on the London stage. He acted in Shakespeare with Ben Greet and William Poel, and himself wrote a number of plays, his first in 1893; he produced his *Voysey Inheritance* in 1905, and *Waste*, banned by the Censor, was played privately by the Stage Society in 1907. In 1904 he had joined J. E. Vedrenne in the management of the Court theatre, where he produced plays by Ibsen, Shaw and other modern dramatists. He retired from acting in 1910. His productions at the Savoy theatre, of *The Winter's Tale* and *Twelfth Night* in 1912, and of *A Midsummer Night's Dream* in 1914, were revolutionary; with the aid of a false proscenium, proscenium doors, and built-out apron-stage without footlights, he converted the picture-frame theatre into something like the Elizabethan; then, to make time for the unabridged texts, scenery was formalized, there was only one interval, the pace of acting and speaking was quickened, and traditional 'business' cut out. After these productions he retired from the theatre, but their influence for good on later productions has been incalculable. In 1927 appeared the first of his *Prefaces to Shakespeare*, a series of original and stimulating essays on the plays, written from the point of view of a producer and playwright.

Gratiano. 1. In *The Merchant of Venice*, a friend of Antonio and Bassanio, one who 'speaks an infinite deal of nothing'. He marries Nerissa.

2. In *Othello*, brother of Brabantio, whose death he announces, and uncle of Desdemona. In v, i he comes to Cyprus in time to answer Cassio's cry for help when Roderigo attacks him, and in the next scene to answer the similar cry of Emilia. He is bewildered and ineffective.

Gray, Thomas (1716–71), was educated at Eton, and Peterhouse, Cambridge, where he became Professor of Modern History. He was buried at Stoke Poges, the village celebrated in his *Elegy in a Country Churchyard*. As in his friend Horace Walpole, the seeds of romanticism were stirring in Gray, and in an age of prose he was exceptional in drawing attention to the *poetry* of Shakespeare. Thus, he wrote to Richard West in 1742:

> In truth, Shakespeare's language is one of his principal beauties; and he has no less advantage over your Addison's and Rowe's in this, than in those other great excellencies you mention. Every word in him is a picture.

Gray's Inn. See INNS OF COURT; 'GESTA GRAYORUM'.

Green. In *Richard II*, one of the 'creatures to King Richard'. See BAGOT; BUSHY. (Sir Henry Green of Drayton, Northants, d. 1399.)

Green, John. One of the English players who toured Europe in James I's reign. He was in Germany (q.v.) with Robert Browne's company in 1608, then with his own company 1615–20, and again in 1626. In his repertory of 1626 were plays of *Romeo and Juliet*, *Julius Caesar*, *Lear König von Engelandt*, and *Hamlet einen printzen in Dennemark*.

Green, Thomas. An entry in the Stratford Parish Register states that 'Thomas Green alias Shakspere' was buried 6 March 1590. It is not clear what the *alias* means; perhaps one of the names was his mother's. He may be the Thomas of the entry in the Snitterfield Register, 10 March 1581, 'Baptizatus fuet John filius Thome Shaxper'. John Shakespeare of Clifford Chambers, who died in 1610, left a legacy to 'John Shakespeare, son to my brother Thomas Shakespeare'. Fripp suggests that he was the cousin of Thomas Greene of Warwick, father of Thomas Greene, Town Clerk of Stratford, who called Shakespeare 'cousin'.

Greene, John. The brother of Thomas Greene, Shakespeare's 'cousin'. He was of Clement's Inn, becoming solicitor to the Stratford Corporation in 1612, and deputy Town Clerk in the following year. In 1609 he married Margaret Lane, sister of John Lane, against whom Shakespeare's daughter Susanna brought an action for slander in 1613. In 1618 the trustees of Shakespeare's Blackfriars Gatehouse conveyed the property to Greene and Mathew Morrys of Stratford, in accordance with the terms of the entail. (See p. 543.)

Greene, Joseph (1712–90). In 1735 Greene was appointed Master of Stratford Grammar School, and later Rector of Welford. He supplied James West with information about Shakespeare, sending him an extract from the Stratford Register; 'In the margin of this paper Mr. Greene has written, opposite the entry relative to our poet's baptism, "*Born on the 23rd*"; but for this, as I conceive, his only authority was the inscription on Shakespeare's tomb' (Malone, *Var.*, II, 63). In 1747 Greene discovered a copy of Shakespeare's will, and sent a copy to West. He was concerned with the restoration of the Shakespeare monument (q.v.) in 1749. (See NEW PLACE; SS, 4.)

Greene, Robert (1558–92), one of the University Wits, was born at Norwich, and educated at St John's, Cambridge. In 1588 he took an Oxford degree, so becoming what he styled himself, 'Utriusque Academiæ in Artibus Magister'. It is possible to reconstruct the outlines of his life from his pamphlets, the autobiographic *Repentance of Robert Greene* (1592), his *Never Too Late* (1590), and *Groatsworth of Wit* (1592). He led a dissolute youth 'among wags as lewd as himself', travelled extensively 1578–83, married, but as his wife 'would persuade me from my wilful wickedness, after I had a child by her, I cast her off, having spent up the marriage-money which I obtained by her'. He went to London, where the sister of 'Cutting Ball', a notorious thief, became his mistress and bore him a son, Fortunatus. In London he soon made a reputation as a playwright, became the rival of Marlowe, and jealous of the players whom he attacked as covetous and insolent, 'pranct with the glory of others feathers'; and Nashe contributed a prefatory Epistle to Greene's prose romance *Menaphon* (1589), attacking the 'vainglorious Tragedians'. Greene became involved in a quarrel with Gabriel Harvey, who describes his end; after 'a surfeit of pickle herringe and Rennish wine' he fell sick and died in the squalor of a poor shoemaker's house, attended by his landlady and his mistress.

Greene's famous attack on the players in general, and on Shakespeare in particular, is in his *Greenes Groatsworth of Wit bought with a Million of Repentance*, written on his death-bed (see SS, 4):

> Yes trust them not: for there is an upstart Crow, beautified with our feathers, that with his *Tygers hart wrapt in a Players hyde*, supposes he is as well able to bombast out a blanke verse as the best of you: and beeing an absolute *Iohannes fac totum*, is in his owne conceit the onely Shake-scene in a countrey.

Greene's extant plays, written *c.* 1587–92, are: *Alphonsus*, *A Looking Glass for London and England* (with Lodge), *Friar Bacon and Friar Bungay*, *Orlando Furioso* and *James the Fourth*. In a reply to his moral tracts on 'cony-catching', one 'Cuthbert Conycatcher' wrote:

> What if I should prove you a cony-catcher, Master R.G., would it not make you blush at the matter? ... Ask the Queen's players if you sold them not Orlando Furioso for twenty nobles, and when they were in the country sold the same play to the Lord Admiral's men for as many more.

The disintegrators have found Greene's hand in much of Shakespeare's early work, in *Titus Andronicus*, *Henry VI*, *The Comedy of Errors*, *The Two Gentlemen of Verona* and traces even in *Henry V* and *All's Well*. His novel *Pandosto* is the source of *The Winter's Tale*. Greene's liveliness, humour and poetry make him one of the most attractive of the Elizabethan dramatists. (See HARVEY, GABRIEL.)

'Greene's Funeralls.' Poems by 'R. B. Gent' (possibly Richard Barnfield), published in 1594. The author seems to support Greene's attack on Shakespeare, though the sonnet may refer to Harvey's attack on Greene. (See SQ VI, 4.)

> Greene, is the pleasing Object of an eye:
> Greene, pleased the eyes of all that lookt upon him.
> Greene, is the ground of every Painter's dye:
> Greene, gave the ground, to all that wrote upon him.
> Nay more the men, that so Eclipst his fame:
> Purloined his Plumes, can they deny the same?

Greene, Thomas. The eldest son of Thomas Greene of Warwick, he entered the Middle Temple in 1595, was called to the Bar in 1602, and in the following year appointed Town Clerk of Stratford. He married Lettice, widow of one Chandler of Leicester, and lived for a time at New Place, presumably with his wife and two young children, as guests of Anne Shakespeare, for on 9 September 1609 he wrote that he perceived he 'mighte stay another yere at newe place'. He bought the other part of Shakespeare's holding of tithes, so that his position was difficult when the enclosure of 1614 was broached; he stood to gain by enclosure, but as Town Clerk he had to support the Corporation's opposition to the scheme. During the controversy he naturally had to consult Shakespeare, and more than once in his notes he calls him 'my Cosen Shakspeare', though what his relationship was is not at all clear. (See GREEN, THOMAS; and p. 543.) His lukewarmness in the matter may explain why he was replaced by Francis Collins, the solicitor who drew up Shakespeare's will on 8 April 1616, a fortnight before Shakespeare's death. He went to live in Bristol, and a year later wrote to the Stratford Corporation of the 'golden days' when he had been their Clerk: 'we cannot doubt that it was the Poet's friendship and kinship which made these days of strenuous labour "golden" and his death which turned sunshine into night.' He became a barrister in London, and died in 1640.

Greenwich Palace stood on the site of the present Greenwich Hospital. As early as 1300 it was a royal residence, but in the early 15th century became the property of Humphrey, Duke of Gloucester, who improved it and called it *Placentia* or *Pleasaunce*. On his death in 1447 it reverted to the Crown. It was enlarged by Henry VIII, who was born there, as were his daughters Mary and Elizabeth. It was demolished by Charles II, and the present buildings, designed by John Webb and Wren, erected. Court performances of plays were often given at Greenwich Palace; the first official record of Shakespeare as an actor is that of his being payee for the Chamberlain's for performances given there on 26 and 27 December 1594.

Greet, Phillip Barling Ben (1857–1936), the actor-manager who, like his contemporary William Poel, insisted that the words that Shakespeare wrote really should be heard, and by as wide an audience as possible. His first London appearance was in 1883 as Caius Lucius in *Cymbeline*, then in 1886 he began his work of popularizing Shakespeare by giving open-air performances of the plays, by touring the United Kingdom and United States with his repertory company, by joining Lilian Baylis at the Old Vic in 1914 and making that theatre into the home of Shakespeare, and after 1918 by arranging performances for London school-children. In 1929 he was knighted for his services to drama and education. (See THORNDIKE, SYBIL.)

Greg, Walter Wilson (1875–1959), bibliographer and Shakespeare scholar, was educated at Harrow and Trinity, Cambridge. He was Librarian of Trinity 1907–13, General Editor of the Malone Society 1907–39, and President of the Bibliographical Society 1930–2. He was associated with Pollard in his revolutionary work on the transmission of Shakespeare's text (see TEXTUAL CRITICISM), and has written and edited numerous indispensable books, including Henslowe's *Diary* and *Papers*, and *Dramatic Documents of the Elizabethan Playhouses*. His monumental *Shakespeare First Folio* appeared in 1955. One of the greatest of all Shakespeare scholars, he was knighted in 1950.

Gregory. In *Romeo and Juliet*, a servant of Capulet. In the first scene he and his fellow-servant Sampson begin the brawl with the Montagues, the result of which is the Prince's decree:

If ever you disturb our streets again,
Your lives shall pay the forfeit of the peace.

Gremio. In the sub-plot of *The Taming of the Shrew*, one of the suitors of Bianca. In the Folio stage-direction (I, i) he is called 'Gremio a Pantelowne', and in III, i Lucentio refers to him as 'the old pantaloon'. He employs as Bianca's tutor the disguised Lucentio, who eventually marries her. In III, ii, Gremio gives a brilliant description of the marriage of Petruchio and Katharina. (Called Cleandro in Ariosto's *I Suppositi*.)

Greville, Curtis. Actor. In the Quarto (1634) of *The Two Noble Kinsmen* the prompter's notes are printed in the stage-directions; in IV, ii, 'Curtis' was a messenger, in V, iii an attendant. He is probably the Curtis Greville who joined the Palsgrave's in 1622, and by 1626 was with the King's. Wilson thinks he is the Curtis of *The Shrew*.

Greville, Sir Edward. The Grevilles lived at Milcote Manor, two miles south-west of Stratford. In 1562 Elizabeth had granted the manor of Stratford to Ambrose Dudley, Earl of Warwick, after whose death in 1590 it was bought by Ludovic Greville, whose son Edward inherited it soon afterwards. In 1610 the manor was sold to William Whitmore and John Randoll.

Greville, Fulke (1554–1628), the poet, whose father was a cadet of the Greville's of Milcote, was born at Beauchamp Court, Warwickshire, and educated at Shrewsbury School with his friend Philip Sidney, and at Jesus College, Cambridge. He became a member of the Leicester House 'Areopagus', which included Spenser, Gabriel Harvey, Sidney, and Edward Dyer, advocates of classical metres in English verse. He was a favourite of Elizabeth, who appointed him Treasurer of the Navy, and of James I, who granted him Warwick Castle, made him Chancellor of the Exchequer in 1614, and in 1621 Baron Brooke. He was stabbed and killed by his servant Ralph Haywood, who thought he was omitted from his will. His epitaph, composed by himself, on his tomb in St Mary's, Warwick, reads: 'Folk Greville Servant to Queene Elizabeth Concellor to King James Frend to Sir Philip Sidney. Trophaeum Peccati.'

His two tragedies on the classical model, 'rigid with intellect', *Alaham* and *Mustapha*, were not intended for the stage. His most famous work is his *Life of the Renowned Sr. Philip Sidney*. In 1665 David Lloyd, in his *Statesmen and Favourites of England*, wrote of Brooke:

> One great argument for his worth, was his respect of the worth of others, desiring to be known to posterity under no other notions than of *Shakespear's* and *Ben Johnson's* Master, Chancellor *Egerton's* Patron, Bishop *Overal's* Lord, and Sir *Philip Sidney's friend.*

Though Anthony Wood discounts Lloyd's reliability, and though there is no other evidence, it is possible that Greville knew Shakespeare, and helped him at the beginning of his career. (See G. Bullough, *Poems and Dramas of Fulke Greville.*)

Grey, Lady (1437–92). In *3 Henry VI*, daughter of Richard Woodvile, Earl Rivers. She first appears in III, ii as a suppliant to Edward IV for the restoration of the estates lost by her husband, Sir Richard [John] Grey, killed at St Albans. The 'wanton Edward' falls in love with her and marries her, an action that costs him the support of Warwick, who was negotiating a marriage for him with the Lady Bona of France. In the last scene she appears as Queen with her baby son, the future Edward V. (See also ELIZABETH.)

Grey, Lord. In *Richard III*, youngest son of Elizabeth, Queen of Edward IV, by her former husband Sir John Grey. Lord Grey and the Queen's brother, Lord Rivers, are imprisoned and executed at Pomfret Castle by order of Richard (III, iii). (Really Sir Richard Grey, youngest brother of Thomas Grey, Marquis of Dorset.)

Grey, Sir Thomas (d. 1415). In *Henry V*, a knight of Northumberland, and one of the conspirators, Cambridge and Scroop being the others, bribed by the French to kill the King at Southampton as he sets out on his French campaign. But 'The king hath note of all that they intend', exposes them, and orders their execution. Grey professes joy at the discovery of his treason (II, ii).

Griffin, Bartholomew (d. 1602), poet, probably of Northamptonshire, was buried at Coventry in 1602. His sonnet sequence *Fidessa* was published in 1596. No. xi in *The Passionate Pilgrim* (q.v.), on the Venus and Adonis theme, is a version of his sonnet iii, and the otherwise unknown iv, vi, ix of *P.P.* may also be his.

Griffith. In *Henry VIII*, a Gentleman-usher of Queen Katharine. He appears only in IV, ii with the dying Queen, to whom he describes the death of Wolsey.

Grimm, Friedrich Melchior (1723–1807). French critic, son of a German pastor, was born at Ratisbon and educated at Leipzig University. He went to Paris, his friendship with Rousseau and the encyclopaedists leading to his adoption of the French language. In 1775 he was created a Baron of the Holy Roman Empire. His *Correspondance Littéraire* (1753–90) was published 1812–14. Wordsworth had been reading this when he wrote in the *Essay Supplementary to the Preface to the Lyrical Ballads* (1815):

> At this day the French Critics have abated nothing of their aversion to this darling of our Nation: 'the English, with their bouffon de Shakspeare', is as familiar an expression among them as in the time of Voltaire. Baron Grimm is the only French writer who seems to have perceived his infinite superiority to the first names of the French Theatre: an advantage which the Parisian Critic owed to his German blood and German education.

'Groatsworth of Wit.' See GREENE, ROBERT.

Grooms of the Chamber. The royal players of Elizabeth and the Stuarts were sworn in by the Lord Chamberlain as Grooms of the Chamber. Thus, Tarlton of the Queen's Men is described in 1587 as an 'ordenary grome of her majestes chamber', and after James's accession, when there was a King's, Queen's, and Prince's company, the members were sworn in as 'grooms of the chamber in ordinary without fee'. This seems to mean that, like 'ordinary' grooms, they were part of the ordinary household establishment, but like 'extraordinary' grooms, whose position was nominal, they were unpaid because normally not in attendance. In 1604, however, the King's and Queen's Men acted as grooms to the Spanish ambassador, the Constable of Castile, though in the Chamber accounts for their payment they are distinguished from the ordinary and extraordinary grooms. As grooms the royal players received 'watching' liveries in the winter, and 'summer' liveries of scarlet, renewed every two years. Shakespeare heads the list of the nine sharers in the King's company who received 4½ yards of red cloth for James's coronation procession in March 1604. Grooms ranked between Gentlemen and Yeomen of the Chamber, and formed part of the establishment of the Lord Chamberlain (q.v.). (See SOMERSET HOUSE.)

Groto, Luigi. 16th-century Italian dramatist, and author of *La Hadriana* (1578), a tragedy of Romeo and Juliet, based on the version of Luigi da Porto's *Istoria di due Nobili Amanti* (*c.* 1524). There are some details, for example Juliet's mistaking the lark for the nightingale, common to Groto and Shakespeare. William Alabaster's *Roxana* (q.v.) is a Latin version of Groto's *La Dalida* (1576).

Groundlings. At a theatre, the spectators who paid a penny to stand on the ground, probably unfloored, of the yard or pit, the open space into which the apron stage projected. There are numerous references by the dramatists to this humble part of the audience. The first is in *Hamlet* (1600):

> 'O, it offends me to the soul to hear a robustious periwig-pated fellow tear a passion to tatters, to very rags, to split the ears of the groundlings, who, for the most part, are capable of nothing but inexplicable dumb-shows and noise.' Dekker, *Gull's Hornbook* (1609): 'your *Groundling*, and *Gallery Commoner* buys his sport by the penny.'

The groundlings are sometimes jestingly referred to as 'understanders', or 'understanding men';

> Jonson, *Bartholomew Fair* (1614): 'the understanding gentlemen o' the ground here ask'd my judgment.'

Grumio. In *The Taming of the Shrew*, a servant of Petruchio. In IV, i, he gives Curtis a humorous description of the journey of Petruchio and Katharina from Padua to Petruchio's country house. (Sander in *A Shrew*. There is a Grumio in the *Mostellaria* of Plautus (q.v.).)

Guiderius. In *Cymbeline*, elder son of Cymbeline, and brother of Imogen and Arviragus (q.v.).

Guildenstern. In *Hamlet*, a university acquaintance of Hamlet. Claudius invites him and his inseparable friend Rosencrantz to the Danish Court to spy on Hamlet. When Hamlet kills Polonius, Claudius sends him to England guarded by Rosencrantz and Guildenstern bearing sealed orders for his death. Hamlet substitutes their names for his, and himself escapes. (Their names are those of well-known Danish families of Shakespeare's time, connected by marriage, and in the records of Wittenberg University.)

Guildford, Sir Henry (1489–1532). In *Henry VIII* 'young Sir Harry Guildford' welcomes the guests on behalf of Wolsey to the feast at York Place (I, iv). This is his only appearance. (He became Henry VIII's Comptroller of the Household, and *ad hoc* Master of the Revels, before the appointment of the first permanent Master, Sir Thomas Cawarden, in 1545.)

Guizot, François (1787–1874). French statesman and writer; the minister of Louis Philippe. He revised Letourneur's translation of Shakespeare, and wrote *Sur la Vie et les Œuvres de Shakespeare* (1821), and *Shakespeare et son Temps* (1852). He maintained that Shakespeare essayed all styles save simplicity.

'Gull's Hornbook.' A satire by Thomas Dekker (q.v.), published in 1609. He gives ironical advice to a Gallant as to how he 'should behave himself in a Playhouse' and other public places if he wishes to attract attention to himself by his bad manners. Chapter VI is a valuable source of information about the early Jacobean theatre:

Whether therefore the gatherers of the public or private Playhouse stand to receive the afternoon's rent, let our Gallant (having paid it) presently advance himself up to the throne of the Stage. I mean not into the Lords room (which is now but the Stages Suburbs). No, those boxes, by the iniquity of custom, conspiracy of waiting-women and Gentlemen-Ushers, that there sweat together, and the covetousness of Sharers, are contemptibly thrust into the rear, and much new Satten is there dambd by being smothered to death in darkness. But on the very Rushes where the Commedy is to dance, yea and under the state of *Cambises* himself must our feathered *Estridge*, like a piece of Ordnance be planted valiantly (because impudently) beating down the mews and hisses of the opposed rascality ...

Present not yourself on the Stage (especially at a new play) until the quaking prologue hath (by rubbing) got colour into his cheeks, and is ready to give the trumpets their Cue that he's upon point to enter: for then it is time, as though you were one of the *Properties*, or that you dropt out of the *Hangings*, to creep from behind the Arras, with your *Tripos* or three-footed stool in one hand, and a teston mounted between a forefinger and a thumb in the other.... It shall crown you with rich commendation to laugh aloud in the midst of the most serious and saddest scene of the terriblest Tragedy ...

Before the Play begins, fall to cards ... throw the cards (having first torn four or five of them) round about the Stage, just upon the third sound, as though you had lost ...

Now, sir, if the writer be a fellow that hath either epigramd you ... you shall disgrace him ... if, in the middle of his play ... you rise with a skreud and discontented face from your stool to be gone: no matter whether the Scenes be good or no, the better they are the worse do you distaste them: and being on your feet, sneak not away like a coward, but salute all your gentle acquaintance, that are spread either on the rushes, or on stools about you, and draw what troop you can from the stage after you ...

Marry if either the company, or indisposition of the weather bind you to sit it out, my counsel is then that you turn plain Ape, take up a rush and tickle the earnest ears of your fellow gallants, to make other fools fall a laughing: mew at passionate speeches, blare at merry, find fault with the music, whew at the childrens Action, whistle at the songs: and above all, curse the sharers ...

Gundolf, Friedrich (1880–1931). Professor at Heidelberg University; author of *Shakespeare, Sein Wesen und Werk*, 1928–9. His *Shakespeare und der deutsche Geist*, 1911, is an important analysis of the effect of Shakespeare on German culture. He translated the plays, 1908–23.

Gunpowder Plot. There are two possible references in Shakespeare. Gloucester's speech in *King Lear* (I, ii): 'in cities, mutinies; in countries, discord; in palaces, treason; ... machinations, hollowness, treachery and all ruinous disorders follow us disquietly to our graves.' The Porter in *Macbeth* (II, iii) seems to refer to the Jesuit Henry Garnet (q.v.), who knew of the Plot: 'an equivocator ... who committed treason enough.'

The plot would be a great shock to Shakespeare, who must have known some of the conspirators; the Catesbys, for example, held the manor of Bishopton in Stratford, and had another estate at Lapworth, ten miles north of the town. In London the conspirators frequented the Mermaid Tavern, and in Stratford Clopton House was used as a base.

Gurney, James. In *King John*, a servant of Lady Faulconbridge (I, i). (The only character that Shakespeare added to *The Troublesome Reign*.)

Guthrie, Tyrone (b. 1900), perhaps the most adventurous of English producers, associated particularly with the Old Vic (q.v.) to which he returned 1951–2. In 1953, and subsequent years, he produced the plays of the new Shakespeare Festival at Stratford, Ontario. Knighted 1961.

Gwinne, Matthew (*c.* 1558–1627). Fellow of St John's College, Oxford, and author of the Latin play *Vertumnus*, which sent James I to sleep when he saw it performed at Christ Church in August 1605. On his entry into the City, James was greeted by Gwinne's device of *Tres Sibyllae*, which may have furnished a hint for the witches in *Macbeth*.

H

Hacket. In *The Taming of the Shrew* (Ind., ii) Christopher Sly says, 'Ask Marian Hacket, the fat ale-wife of Wincot, if she know me not.' And 'the woman's maid of the [ale-]house' is Cicely Hacket. On 21 November 1591, 'Sara Hacket, the daughter of Robert Hacket', was baptized at Quinton, within the parish of which lay the Gloucestershire hamlet of Wincot (q.v.). (See COKAIN.)

Hakluyt, Richard (*c.* 1552–1616), came of a Welsh family long settled in Herefordshire, and was educated at Westminster and Christ Church, Oxford. Fascinated by maps and stories of discovery, he devoted much of his life to recording English voyages of exploration, and in 1589 published his *Principall Navigations, Voiages, and Discoveries of the English Nation*. This was revised and enlarged to three volumes 1598–1600, and some copies include Molyneux's 'new map with the augmentation of the Indies' to which Maria compares Malvolio's smiling face. William Strachey's account of the wreck on the Bermudas, which partly inspired *The Tempest*, was published in *Purchas his Pilgrimes* (1625), a continuation of Hakluyt's book by his friend Samuel Purchas (q.v.).

Hales. The brothers John and Bartholomew Hales held successively the principal manor at Snitterfield, a farm on which was occupied by Richard Shakespeare (d. 1561) and his son Henry, the poet's grandfather and uncle.

Hales, John (1584–1656). 'The ever memorable John Hales' was born at Bath and educated at Corpus Christi, Oxford. In 1605 he was elected a fellow of Merton, and in 1613 a fellow of Eton, where he lived until forced to leave during the Commonwealth. He returned to Eton and died there in poverty. The following anecdote is told by Charles Gildon (1694):

Mr. *Hales* of Eaton affirm'd that he wou'd shew all the Poets of Antiquity outdone by Shakespear, in all the Topics, and common places made use of in Poetry. The Enemies of Shakespear wou'd by no means yield him so much Excellence: so that it came to a Resolution of a trial of skill upon that Subject; the place agreed on for the Dispute was Mr. Hales's Chamber at Eaton; a great many Books were sent down by the Enemies of this Poet, and on the appointed day my Lord Falkland, Sir John Suckling, and all the Persons of Quality that had Wit and Learning, and interested themselves in the Quarrel, met there, and upon a thorough Disquisition of the point, the Judges chose by agreement out of this Learned and Ingenious Assembly, unanimously gave the Preference to Shakespear. And the Greek and Roman Poets were adjudg'd to Vail at least their Glory in that of the English Hero.

Rowe (1709) gives a slightly different version in which Ben Jonson's 'frequently reproaching him [Shakespeare] with the want of Learning, and Ignorance of the Antients' led to the challenge.

Hales, John Wesley (1836–1914). Fellow of Christ's College, Cambridge, and Professor of English Literature at King's College, London. Author of *Notes and Essays on Shakespeare* (1884) and of the Introduction to *The Age of Shakespeare* by Seccombe and Allen.

Hall, Arthur (*c.* 1540–1604), was born at Grantham and brought up as a ward of Sir William Cecil. He was M.P. for Grantham, and more than once got into trouble both inside and outside the House. In 1581 he published the first English translation of Homer, his *Ten Bookes of Homers Iliades* (I–X). It is based on the French version of Hugues Salel (1555), and written in rhyming fourteeners. Shakespeare may have used the version for his *Troilus and Cressida.*

Hall, Elizabeth (1608–70). Shakespeare's granddaughter, the daughter of Susanna Shakespeare and Dr John Hall, was christened at Stratford 21 February 1608: 'Elizabeth dawghter to John Hall gentleman.' In his will Shakespeare left her 'All my Plate (except my brod silver and gilt bole)', and, as Susanna had no more children, Elizabeth inherited New Place and all the other entailed property. On 22 April 1626 she married Thomas Nash of Stratford, who died at New Place in 1647. Two years later, on 5 June 1649, at Billesley, a village four miles from Stratford, she married the widower John Bernard. A month later her mother died. Elizabeth went to live at Abington, Northants, the home of her husband, who was knighted in 1661. She died without children, the last of Shakespeare's direct descendants, and was buried at Abington on 17 February 1670. She left the Henley Street houses to her cousins, the Harts, and the rest of Shakespeare's entailed estate was sold after her husband's death in 1674. (See MACKLIN.)

Hall, John. The Bristol limner who was commissioned in 1748 to 'repair and beautify, or have the direction of repairing and beautifying the original monument' of Shakespeare in Stratford church. Hall painted a picture of the monument as it was before he recoloured the bust.

Hall, John (1575–1635), was born at Carlton in Bedfordshire; with his elder brother, Dive, entered Queen's College, Cambridge, in 1589, took his B.A. in 1593 and M.A. in 1597, studied medicine in France, and settled in Stratford *c.* 1600. On 5 June 1607 he married Shakespeare's elder daughter Susanna in Stratford church, and appears to have lived in the Old Town near the church at Hall's Croft. In 1608 his only child, Elizabeth, was born. He and Susanna were residuary legatees and executors of the poet, after whose death they moved into New Place. He died there and was buried in the chancel of Stratford church 26 November 1635: 'Johannes Hall, medicus peritissimus'. On his gravestone was inscribed:

Heere lyeth ye Body of Iohn Hall gent: hee marr: Svsanna, ye daughter, & coheire of Will: Shakespeare, gent. Hee deceased Nover: 25. A°. 1635, aged 60.

Hallius hic situs est medica celeberrimus
arte;
Expectans regni Gaudia laeta Dei;
Dignus erat meritis, qui nestora vinceret
annis;
In terris omnes, sed rapit aequa dies.
Ne tumulo, quid desit adest fidessima
coniux,
Et vitae comitem nunc quoque mortis
habet.

Hall was a physician of some reputation; 'His advice was solicited in every direction, and he was summoned more than once to attend the Earl and Countess of Northampton at Ludlow Castle, a distance of over forty miles.' He left a medical note-book in Latin, which was translated by a Warwick surgeon, James Cooke, as *Select Observations on English Bodies* (1657). He records illnesses and cures of himself, Susanna, Elizabeth and Michael Drayton, but as the earliest dated case is 1617 there is no mention of Shakespeare, whom he must have attended before his death. He is said to have had puritanical leanings, and if so can scarcely have approved of his father-in-law's poetry and plays.

Hall, Susanna. Shakespeare's elder daughter, who married John Hall. See SHAKESPEARE, SUSANNA.

Hall, W. In the Bodleian is a copy of Ovid's *Metamorphoses*, printed at Venice by Aldus in 1502, with the note, 'This little Booke of Ovid was given to me by W. Hall who sayd it was once Will Shakespere's. T.N. 1682.' Opposite this, on the title-page, is the signature, the authenticity of which is generally rejected, 'W^{m} Sh^{r}', 'W^{m} Sh^{e}', or 'W^{m} Sh^{re}'.

Hall, William. Son of the proprietor of the White Hart Inn, Lichfield, who took his B.A. degree from Queen's, Oxford, in 1694. In that year he wrote to his friend 'Neddy' Thwaites, also of Queen's, and later Regius Professor of Greek, about a visit to Stratford, through which he must have passed on his way home:

... There is in this Church a place which they call the bone-house, a repository for all bones they dig up; which are so many that they would load a great number of waggons. The Poet being willing to preserve his bones unmoved, lays a curse upon him that moves them ... Nor has the design mist of its effect; for lest they should not only draw this curse upon themselves, but also entail it upon their posterity, they have laid him full seventeen foot deep, deep enough to secure him.

This is the first mention of the improbable tradition. The charnel-house has been destroyed.

Hall, William. The printer, identified by Sidney Lee as the 'Mr W. H.' of Shakespeare's *Sonnets*. In 1577 Hall was apprenticed to John Allde, and seven years later admitted to the freedom of the Stationers' Company. He appears to have begun printing on his own account in 1598 and retired about 1614. Lee assumes that Thorpe's dedication to Mr W. H. as 'the onlie begetter' of the *Sonnets* means 'procurer of the copy', that he was the W. H. who wrote a dedication to Robert Southwell's *Fourefold Meditation* (1606), like the *Sonnets* printed by George Eld, and that both W. H.'s were William Hall.

Halle, Edward (*c.* 1498–1547), a member of a staunchly Protestant Shropshire family, was educated at Eton and King's, read law at Gray's Inn, became a Common Serjeant and entered Parliament. His *The Union of the Two Noble and Illustre Famelies of Lancastre and Yorke* is the history of the period 1399–1532. It was written to glorify the Tudors and to show 'that as by discord greate thynges decaie and fall to ruine, so the same by concord be revived and erected'. A second issue of 1548 contained the addition of Richard Grafton (q.v.) 1532–47. Halle, rather than Holinshed, was Shakespeare's main source for his early histories, and he observed Halle's moral pattern of the discord following the overthrow of the established order being resolved by its restoration. Alan Keen thinks that the annotations in a copy of the 1550 issue of Halle's history may be Shakespeare's. (See TLS, 21 April 1950.)

Halliwell-Phillipps, James Orchard (1820–89), one of the most important 19th-century Shakespeare scholars, was born in London, the son of Thomas Halliwell, and educated privately and at Jesus, Cambridge, of which he became librarian. He was one of the founders of the first Shakespeare Society in 1840, published his *Life of Shakespeare* in 1848, a scholarly edition of Shakespeare in fifteen folio volumes (1853–61), and from 1850 onwards the Stratford archives and extant legal documents connected with Shakespeare. Much of this information was included in his *Outlines of the Life of Shakespeare* (1881), which in its seventh and final form of 1887 is the basis of all later Lives. Altogether he published more than sixty volumes. He assumed the name of Phillipps in 1872 according to the terms of the will of the antiquary Sir Thomas Phillipps, grandfather of his first wife. (See JUBILEE; HENRIETTA MARIA; FRIPP.)

Hamlet. As a Christian name Hamlet in its various forms was not uncommon in Warwickshire. Hamnet Sadler, the Stratford baker, called Hamlett in Shakespeare's will, was probably the godfather of Shakespeare's son, Hamnet. It is a derivative of the Norman Hamon. As a surname: Katherine Hamlett of Tiddington was drowned in the Avon in December 1579. The name in Shakespeare's play is, of course, of immediate Scandinavian origin. (See SAXO GRAMMATICUS.)

'HAMLET.'

WRITTEN: 1600–1.

PERFORMED: 1602, July; it had then been 'latelie Acted'.
1603, it had been acted at Cambridge and Oxford.
1607, on board Captain Keeling's East Indiaman.
1619, at Court?
1637, at Hampton Court, 24 January, 'before the kinge and Queene'.

REGISTERED: 1602. 'xxvj^{to} Julij. James Robertes. Entred for his Copie vnder the handes of master Pasfield and master Waterson warden A booke called the Revenge of Hamlett Prince Denmarke as yt was latelie Acted by the Lord Chamberlayne his servantes'.

PUBLISHED: 1603. Q1. 'The Tragicall Historie of Hamlet Prince of Denmarke. By William Shake-speare. As it hath beene diuerse times acted by his Highnesse seruants in the Cittie of London: as also in the Vniuersities of Cambridge and Oxford, and elsewhere. At London printed for N. L. and Iohn Trundell. 1603.' A 'bad' Quarto, less than half the length of Q2. Probably a memorial reconstruction of the full text, made for provincial performance by an actor who played Marcellus. (See G. I. Duthie, *The 'Bad' Quarto of Hamlet*.)

1604. Q2. 'Newly imprinted and enlarged to almost as much againe as it was, according to the true and perfect Coppie. At London, Printed by I. R. for N. L. ... 1604.' The longest version, set up from foul papers with some reference to Q1. Eighty-five lines which appear in F1 were omitted, probably in deference to Anne of Denmark, the Queen.

1611. Q3 set up from Q2; Q4 (undated) from Q3; Q5 (1637) from Q4.

1623. F1. 'The Tragedie of Hamlet, Prince of Denmarke.' The eighth play in the Tragedy section: pp. 152–6, 257–80. Acts and scenes marked as far as II, ii. A good text, probably set up from Q2 collated with prompt-book. It is 200 lines shorter than Q2, no doubt owing to cuts.

SOURCES: Belleforest's French version in his *Histories Tragiques* (1576) of the *Historia Danica* of Saxo Grammaticus (q.v.). There was an old play of *Hamlet* (the *Ur-Hamlet*), now lost, acted in 1594, which may have been written by Kyd and used by Shakespeare. (Belleforest's version was translated into English in 1608 as *The Hystorie of Hamblet*, and contains a few scraps taken from the play. See 'BESTRAFTE BRUDERMORD'.)

STAGE HISTORY: 1661. Revived by D'Avenant at Lincoln's Inn Fields, with cuts and textual alterations.

1772. At Drury Lane, Garrick produced a refined version that was never printed, omitting the grave-diggers and making his own part still larger. (See 3 *Variorum*, II, 691.)

1881. William Poel's Q1 *Hamlet*.

1900. Benson's complete text (Lyceum).

1925. Barry Jackson's modern dress.

1930. Harcourt Williams's production with John Gielgud (Old Vic).

1961. Dubrovnik Summer Festival. (See DENMARK.)

1963. National Theatre Company at the Old Vic.

Prince Hamlet is the son of Hamlet, King of Denmark, who has recently died, and of Gertrude who, soon after her husband's death, has married his brother Claudius, the new King. The ghost of Hamlet's father appears and tells his son that Claudius murdered him after seducing Gertrude, and orders him to be revenged on his uncle, though to spare his mother. Hamlet pretends to be mad, and repulses Ophelia whom he loves. He arranges a play representing the crimes of his uncle, who betrays his guilt when he sees it. Immediately after this Hamlet fails to take the opportunity of killing the defenceless King while he is praying, seems about to kill his mother, and does kill Polonius, Ophelia's father, who is spying behind the curtains. Thereupon Claudius sends Hamlet to England, and orders the English king to put him to death. Meanwhile Ophelia goes mad, and her brother Laertes returns from France to be revenged on Claudius, who, however, persuades him that Hamlet is responsible. News comes that Hamlet has returned from his English journey, and the two hatch a plot to kill him. When Hamlet arrives, he sees the funeral of Ophelia, who has drowned herself. The King then arranges a fencing match in which Laertes is to use a poisoned and unbuttoned sword. Laertes wounds Hamlet, who seizes the sword and mortally wounds Laertes, who tells him of the King's treachery. Meanwhile the Queen drinks of a poisoned cup prepared for Hamlet, and dies. Hamlet then stabs the King, and forces him to drink the poison, and after preventing his friend Horatio from drinking too, he dies. (See SS, 9, devoted mainly to *Hamlet*.)

Hammond, Lieutenant. See COMBE, JOHN.

Hampton Court. One of the five most important of Elizabeth's palaces; the others being Whitehall, Windsor, Greenwich and Richmond. Under James I the last two lost some of their importance. Both sovereigns usually spent Christmas at Whitehall, but in time of plague the Court was held farther away from London; for example, in the plague winter of 1603–4 James was at Hampton Court, where the King's Men gave seven performances between 26 December and 2 February. The palace was built by Cardinal Wolsey, who gave it to Henry VIII. It was partly rebuilt by Wren in William III's reign.

Hampton Lucy. A village, originally Bishop's Hampton, four miles east of Stratford, on the opposite side of the river to the Lucy manor of Charlecote. The parish register has the entries:

1582 June 10. [Christened.] Lettyce the Daughter of Henrye Shakespere.

1585 Oct. 16. [Christened.] Jeames the sonne of Henry Shakespere.

1589 Sept. 25. [Buried.] Jeames Shakespere of Yngon.

This may be Shakespeare's uncle, Henry, for in the year 1570 a John Shakespeare or his assigns 'held, under William Clopton ... a field of about fourteen acres, known by the name of "Ingon, alias Ington meadowe", situated at a small distance from that estate which his son afterwards purchased ... the annual rent was eight pounds ... Probably there was a good dwelling-house and orchard upon it'. (*Var.*, II, 94.) (See INGON.)

Handwriting. Shakespeare, like most of his contemporaries, wrote the angular late medieval hand, which in the 17th century was generally replaced by the round and much more beautiful and legible Italian hand of the Renaissance. The only certain examples of Shakespeare's handwriting are six signatures, that on the last sheet of the will being prefixed by the words 'by me'. From peculiarities in the formation of certain letters (*a*, *k*, *m*, *p*, *s*, *w*) it has been sought to prove that Shakespeare wrote Addition 'D' of the manuscript play of *Sir Thomas More* (q.v.). (See SIGNATURES.)

Hanmer, Sir Thomas (1677–1746), fourth editor of Shakespeare, a country gentleman, and in 1714 Speaker of the House of Commons. His sumptuous edition of Shakespeare with Gravelot's engravings after Francis Hayman's designs, published at Oxford in six quarto volumes in 1744, rose from its original price of three guineas to nine or ten by the time of its reprinting in 1770. Johnson considered that Hanmer had 'the first requisite to emendatory criticism, that intuition by which the poet's intention is immediately discovered'. Unfortunately he worked almost entirely by intuition and without consulting any edition older than that of Pope, like whom he 'threw to the bottom of the page' passages that displeased him, in particular 'that wretched piece of ribaldry in *King Henry the Fifth*, put into the mouths of the French princess and an old gentlewoman, improper enough as it all is in French, and not intelligible to an English audience'. He was also responsible for the famous emendation of 'Cassio ... A fellow almost damn'd in a fair wife' to 'damn'd in a fair phyz'. His intuition sometimes served him better than this, but as Johnson mildly remarked, 'by inserting his emendations, whether invented or borrowed, into the page, without any notice of varying copies, he has appropriated the labours of his predecessors, and made his own edition of little authority'.

Harbage, Alfred (b. 1901), American scholar, Professor of English at Harvard since 1952; authority on Shakespeare's theatre, author of *Shakespeare's Audience*, etc., and editor of the *Pelican Shakespeare*.

Harcourt. In *2 Henry IV*, he reports to the King the defeat of the Earl of Northumberland and the Lord Bardolph at the battle of Bramham Moor in Yorkshire (IV, iv).

Harington, Sir John (1561–1612), the godson of Queen Elizabeth, was educated at Eton and Christ's, Cambridge. He became a courtier, but retired to his home at Kelston, near Bath, to translate Ariosto's *Orlando Furioso*, published in 1591. In 1596 he published his Rabelaisian trilogy on *Ajax* ('a jakes'; cf. *Love's Labour's Lost*; V, ii, 'your lion, that holds his poll-axe sitting on a close-stool, will be given to Ajax'). He served with Essex in Ireland, where he was knighted on the field, but escaped being involved in the catastrophe. He was less popular at James I's Court, ironical accounts of which he, no puritan, recorded (see DENMARK), though he became a tutor of Prince Henry. Shakespeare may have referred to his translation of *Orlando Furioso* for the Claudio-Hero plot of *Much Ado*. The poem was printed by Richard Field, and is interesting as one of the two extant examples of used printer's copy; it shows the author's alteration in proof, and more important, the fact that the printer modernized some of Harington's spellings.

Harleian MSS. Robert Harley, 1st Earl of Oxford (1661–1724) and his son Edward, 2nd Earl (1689–1741), formed a magnificent collection of manuscripts and books. The former were bought for the nation in 1753 and are now in the British Museum. The library was bought by the bookseller Thomas Osborne in 1742, and described by Dr Johnson, who also wrote a preface to the *Harleian Miscellany* (1744–6), a selection from the library's rarer books and pamphlets, edited by William Oldys (q.v.).

Harris, 'Frank' [James Thomas] (1856–1931), adventurer and author, ran away from home and was Kansas cowboy and war correspondent before becoming editor of the *Evening News*, *Fortnightly Review* and *Saturday Review* (1886–98). In 1909 he published *The Man Shakespeare and His Tragic Life Story*, an imaginative interpretation in which he finds Shakespeare revealing himself in the *Sonnets*, in the characters of Berowne, Romeo, Jaques, Hamlet and so on, an embittered man, dying broken-hearted for love of the Dark Lady, whom, like Thomas Tyler, he identified with Mary

Fitton. Harris also wrote *The Women of Shakespeare*, and a play, *Shakespeare and his Love*. (See G. B. Shaw, *Dark Lady of the Sonnets*; Ivor Brown, *Shakespeare*, p. 196.)

Harris, Henry (*c.* 1630–81), sometimes confused with Joseph Harris of the King's Company, was a prominent actor with D'Avenant's Duke of York's. In 1661 he played Horatio, in 1662 Romeo, and subsequently a number of Shakespearean roles, comic and tragic. In 1671 he became joint manager of the Dorset Garden theatre with Betterton, whose equal in some parts he was reported to be, or as Pepys has it, 'a more ayery man'.

Harrison, George Bagshawe (b. 1894), educated at Brighton College and Queen's, Cambridge; Professor of English at Queen's University, Ontario, in 1943 and at the University of Michigan in 1949. He is an authority on Shakespeare's background (cf. his *Elizabethan Journals*, *Shakespeare at Work*, etc.) and editor of the *Penguin Shakespeare*, based on the Folio text.

Harrison, John. One of a family of London booksellers. In June 1594 Field transferred *Venus and Adonis* to Harrison, for whom he printed O1 1595, and O2 1596. In May 1594 Harrison registered *Lucrece*, and published Q 1594 (printed by Field), O1 1598 (by Short), O2 and O3 1600 he printed himself, O4 1607 (by Okes).

Harrison, William (1534–93), was born in London, educated at St Paul's Westminster, Cambridge and Oxford, and successively rector of Radwinter, Wimbish, and canon of Windsor. He collaborated with Holinshed in the production of *The Chronicles of England, Scotland and Ireland* (1577), Holinshed contributing the history, and Harrison the topography. His shrewd *Description of England* is an invaluable survey of Elizabethan life in its social, political and religious aspects; Furnivall included Books 2 and 3 in his *Shakspere's England*, edited for the New Shakspere Society, 1877–8.

'Harry the V.' A new play performed thirteen times by the Admiral's between 28 November 1595 and 15 July 1596. The play is lost, but it cannot be Shakespeare's, and appears to be distinct from the older Queen's *Famous Victories*.

Harsnett, Samuel (1561–1631), was born at Colchester and educated at Pembroke Hall, Cambridge, of which college he became Master, and also Vice-Chancellor of the University. In 1609 he was appointed Bishop of Chichester, and in 1629 Archbishop of York. As one of the official deputies for the censoring of books, he had licensed in 1599 John Hayward's *Life and Reign of King Henry IV*, dedicated to Essex as 'magnus et presenti iudicio et futuri temporis expectatione', a description that was brought against him at his trial. Harsnett's famous *Declaration of Egregious Popish Impostures* (1603) supplied Shakespeare with the names of the devils mentioned by Edgar in *King Lear*, IV, i.

Hart Family. WILLIAM HART (d. 1616). His marriage to Shakespeare's sister Joan is not entered in the Stratford Register, the first record of him being that of the christening of his son on 28 August 1600: 'Wilhelmus filius Wilhelmi Hart'. He is a shadowy character, all that is known being that he was a hatter; at the christening of his second son he is called 'Wilhelmus Hart Hatter', and his burial on 17 April 1616 is recorded as 'Will. Hartt, hatter'.

JOAN HART (1569–1646), William's wife, was Shakespeare's younger sister, apparently the only other member of the family who married. She was the fifth child of John Shakespeare and Mary Arden, christened 15 April 1569. In his will Shakespeare left 'my Sister Johane Harte … xx^{li} & all my wearing Apparrell … And … the house with thappurtenances in Stratford wherein she dwelleth for her naturall lief vnder the yearlie Rent of xij[d].' Joan's husband was buried just a week before her brother, and she continued to live as a widow in the western Henley Street house, the 'birthplace', until her death. 'Joan Hart, widow' was buried 4 November 1646. Joan and William Hart had four children (Shakespeare left the three surviving sons £5 each):

1. WILLIAM (1600–39), was an actor, and is mentioned in a royal warrant of 17 May 1636 as one of 'his Majesties comedians, and of the regular company of players in the Blackfryars London'. Apparently he died unmarried, but Charles Hart (q.v.) is reputed to have been his illegitimate son.

2. MARY (1603–7). Buried 17 December 1607; 'Mary dawghter to Willyam Hart'.

3. THOMAS (b. 1605, died before 1670). He married, and after his mother's death succeeded her in the Birthplace, the property of his cousin Susanna Hall, and then of her daughter Elizabeth. Thomas had two sons, Thomas (b. 1634), and George (1636–1702), to whom Elizabeth, Lady Bernard, left both the Henley Street houses on her death in 1670. George's descendants occupied the Birthplace until 1806, when the property was sold to Thomas Court.

4. MICHAEL (1608–18). Buried 1 November 1618: 'Micael filius to Jone Harte widowe'.

The sixth descendant of Joan was John Shakespeare Hart (1753–1800), who settled at Tewkesbury as a chair-maker, and was buried on the north side of the Abbey Church with the misleading inscription on his headstone: 'In Memory of John Hart, who died January 22nd, 1800, the sixth descendant from the poet Shakespeare, aged 45 years'. His son William, and grandson Thomas, were buried in the old Baptist burial-ground at Tewkesbury in 1834 and 1850 respectively. The 11th descendant of Shakespeare's sister is H. G. Shakespeare Hart (b. 1898), who has a daughter, born 1940. (See PHILLIPS, SIR RICHARD.)

Hart, Charles (d. 1683), is said to have been the illegitimate son of William Hart, son of Joan Hart, Shakespeare's sister. He was Richard Robinson's apprentice at the Blackfriars theatre, fought for the King in the Civil War, and at the Restoration joined Killigrew's company, of which he was one of the leading actors, playing Hotspur, Brutus, and Othello. He is said to have been the first lover of Nell Gwyn and to have trained her as an actress.

Harvard '47 Workshop'. See BAKER, GEORGE PIERCE.

Harvard, John (1607–38). On 8 April 1605, Robert Harvard of Southwark married Katharine, daughter of Alderman Thomas Rogers of Stratford, their son John being christened at St Mary Overy's 29 November 1607. John went to Emmanuel, Cambridge, became a Puritan minister, emigrated to America, and bequeathed £780 and some 300 books to the newly founded college at Cambridge, Massachusetts, which in 1639 was called Harvard College in his honour. (In 1611 Katharine Rogers's younger sister, Frances, married Robert Harvard's brother, William.)

Harvey. In *1 Henry IV*, apparently Shakespeare's first name for Bardolph. As he changed Oldcastle's name to Falstaff, so he seems to have changed Harvey to Bardolph, and Rossill (Russell) to Peto, no doubt owing to protests from the Harveys and Russells at Court. F retains their names in Poins's speech (I, ii): '*Falstaffe*, *Haruey*, *Rossill*, and *Gadshill*, shall robbe those men that wee haue already way-layde', but Bardolph and Peto made up the four at the robbery.

Harvey, Gabriel (*c.* 1545–1630), was born at Saffron Walden, educated at Christ's, Cambridge, and in 1570 elected a fellow of Pembroke Hall, where he formed his friendship with Edmund Spenser. Later he practised as a barrister in London, then retired to Saffron Walden, where he died. He was a fanatical supporter of the movement to apply classical rules of prosody to English verse, for which he was mocked by Thomas Nashe. He quarrelled with many of the writers of his age, notably with Robert Greene, who ill-naturedly taunted him with being the son of a ropemaker in *A Quip for an Upstart Courtier*, 1592. In his copy of Speght's edition of Chaucer, Harvey wrote, sometime between 1598, when it was published, and, possibly, 25 February 1601, when Essex was executed:

... The Earle of Essex much commendes Albions England ... The younger sort takes much delight in Shakespeares Venus, & Adonis: but his Lucrece, & his tragedie of Hamlet, Prince of Denmarke, haue it in them, to please the wiser sort. Or such poets: or better: or none.

Vilia miretur vulgus: mihi flavus Apollo
Pocula Castaliæ plena ministret aquæ:

quoth Sir Edward Dier, betwene iest, & earnest. Whose written deuises farr excell most of the sonets, and cantos in print. His Amaryllis, & Sir Walter Raleighs Cynthia, how fine & sweet inuentions? Excellent matter of emulation for Spencer, Constable, France, Watson, Daniel, Warner, Chapman, Siluester, Shakespeare, & the rest of owr florishing metricians.

Harvey, Martin (1863–1944), was born at Wyvenhoe, Essex, and educated at King's College School, London. His first stage appearance was in 1881, and in the following year he joined Irving's company, with which he stayed for fourteen years. He married the actress Helena de Silva, who played with him in many of his Shakespearean productions both in London and the provinces. He was knighted in 1921.

Harvey (or Hervey), Sir William (d. 1642). In 1598 he married the widow of the 2nd Earl of Southampton (d. 1581), mother of Shakespeare's patron Henry Wriothesley, 3rd Earl, and has been claimed as 'Mr W. H.', the 'begetter' or 'procurer' of Shakespeare's *Sonnets* for the printer Thorpe. He may be the 'W. Har' who wrote *Epicedium. A funeral Song, upon the Lady Helen Branch*, who died in April 1594, containing the first known reference to Shakespeare's *Lucrece*:

You that have writ of chaste Lucretia,
Whose death was witness of her spotless life:
Or penn'd the praise of sad Cornelia,
Whose blameless name hath made her fame
  so rife,
As noble Pompey's most renowned wife:
  Hither unto your home direct your eyes,
  Whereas, unthought on, much more
    matter lies.

Harvey first distinguished himself against the Armada, then after 1600 as a soldier in Ireland. He was knighted in 1596, created an Irish peer by James I in 1619, and Baron Harvey of Kidbrooke, Kent, in 1628.

Hastings, Lord. 1. In *2 Henry IV*, one of the rebel leaders. In I, iii he advises going on without Northumberland's help, but in IV, i he favours making terms with Prince John, who treacherously offers peace. When the rebel army has been dismissed, he is arrested and sent to execution with the Archbishop and Mowbray. (Really Sir Ralph Hastings.)

2. In *3 Henry VI*, a faithful supporter of Edward IV, whom he helps to escape after his capture by Warwick. He first appears in IV, i. In *Richard III*, although the Queen and her kindred are his enemies, he refuses to join Richard in his attempt to seize the throne. Richard, therefore, accuses him of being a traitor, the protector of the witch and strumpet Jane Shore, and orders his immediate execution (III, iv). (William, Lord Hastings (*c.* 1430–83) was made Lord Chamberlain by Edward IV.)

Hathaway Family. There is no record of the solemnization of Shakespeare's marriage, but in the Bishop of Worcester's *Register* there is the record of the granting of a special licence on 27 November 1582 for the marriage of 'Willelmum Shaxpere et Annam Whateley de Temple Grafton'. But on the next day Fulk Sandells and John Richardson of Shottery entered into a bond to exempt the bishop from all liability if there should be any irregularity in the speedy marriage of 'William Shagspere ... and Anne Hathwey of Stratford in the Dioces of Worcester maiden'. Presumably the clerk made an error in the *Register* entry and the bond is correct. And Rowe, who knew nothing of the bond, wrote in 1709: 'His Wife was the Daughter of one *Hathaway*, said to have been a substantial Yeoman in the Neighbourhood of *Stratford*.' (See TEMPLE GRAFTON.)

Hathaway was a common name in Warwickshire, common in Stratford, and even in Shottery, where Sandells and Richardson came from, there was more than one family of the name. But Anne's grandfather appears to have been John Hathaway, *alias* Gardiner, who in 1556 held land and a house called Hewland (q.v.) on the manor of Shottery. His son was probably the Richard Hathaway who married, had a large family, and was buried 7 September 1581. In his will of 1 September 1581 he mentions his wife Joan, his sons Bartholomew, Thomas, John and William, and daughters Agnes, Catherine and Margaret. Fulk Sandells was a supervisor, and John Richardson a witness. Richard's wife, Joan, died in 1599, and his eldest son Bartholomew in 1624, John Hall, Shakespeare's son-in-law, being the overseer of his will. Hewland was held by Joan Hathaway, and on her death passed to Bartholomew, who bought the freehold in 1610. Presumably Agnes Hathaway, Richard's eldest daughter, was born there, and this is the farmhouse now known as Anne Hathaway's Cottage. The names Agnes and Anne were, in popular usage, freely interchangeable in the 16th century.

Anne Hathaway, Shakespeare's wife, was born in 1555 or 1556 (she was 67 when she died on 6 August 1623), and was therefore eight years older than her husband, whom she married about the end of November 1582. Her eldest child, Susanna, was christened six months later on 26 May 1583, and the twins Hamnet and Judith on 2 February 1585. She is next mentioned in the will of Thomas Whittington of Shottery, once her father's shepherd, 25 March 1601:

> Item I geve and bequeth unto the poore people of Stratford 40s. that is in the hand of Anne Shaxspere, wyf unto Mr Wyllyam Shaxspere, and is due debt unto me, beyng payd to myne Executor by the sayd Wyllyam Shaxspere or his assigns.

Shakespeare does not mention her by name in his will: 'Item I gyve vnto my wief my second best bed with the furniture.' Anne would by law have a third share for life in her husband's estates and the right to live at New Place. 'Mrs Shakspeare' was buried 8 August 1623 in the chancel of Stratford church next to her husband (see DOWDALL). A brass plate on the gravestone bears the inscription and elegiacs, probably written by her son-in-law John Hall:

> Heere lyeth interred the body of Anne wife of William Shakespeare who departed this life the 6th day of August 1623 being of the age of 67 yeares.
>
> Vbera, tu mater, tu lac, vitamque dedisti.
> Vae mihi: pro tanto munere saxa dabo?
> Quam mallem, amoueat lapidem, bonus angelus orem
> Exeat ut, christi corpus, imago tua.
> Sed nil vota valent, venias cito Christe; resurget
> Clausa licet tumulo mater et astra petet.

Hathway, Richard. A dramatist contemporary with Shakespeare, and according to Meres in 1598 one of the 'best for comedy'. Henslowe records eighteen plays in which he collaborated for the Admiral's and Worcester's between 1598 and 1603, including *1, 2 Sir John Oldcastle*, the first part of which was attributed to Shakespeare by Jaggard in Q2, 1619.

Hautboy. The reed instrument of Shakespeare's day; the English form of the French hautbois and Italian oboe. Like the recorder, it was made in various sizes, the smaller and shriller instruments being the hautboys, sometimes called shawms or waits; the bigger variety was the gros-bois or bassoon. At Wolsey's feast in *Henry VIII* (I, iv) the stage directions begin with *Hautboys.* (See DUMB-SHOW.)

Hawkins, Richard. Bookseller; he became a freeman of the Stationers' Company in 1611, and published miscellaneous literature and plays, including *The Maid's Tragedy* (1630) and *A King and No King* (1631). He was one of the syndicate that published the second Folio of Shakespeare in 1632, and died in the following year.

Hawkins, William (1722–1801). Professor of Poetry at Oxford, author of an *Essay on Drama*, and of a version of *Cymbeline*, produced at Covent Garden with little applause in 1759.

Haymarket Theatre. 'The Little Theatre in the Hay' was built by John Potter, a carpenter, in 1720. It was taken over by Foote (q.v.) in 1747, and in 1766, in reparation for the loss of his leg, he was granted a life patent for it; it thus became the Theatre Royal. Foote was succeeded by George Colman and his son. Ira Aldridge, 'the African Roscius', played Aaron and Othello at the Haymarket at the beginning of the 19th century, and Tree began his Shakespearean productions there towards the end. The Queen's Theatre in the Haymarket was built by Vanbrugh in 1705, and became the home of opera.

Hayward, Sir John (*c.* 1560–1627), was born near Felixstowe and educated at Pembroke, Cambridge. He was knighted in 1619. In 1599 he published a prose history of *The First Part of the Life and Raigne of King Henry IV*, dedicated to Essex. This, like Shakespeare's *Richard II*, of which a special performance was given the day before Essex's rising, dealt with the deposition of Richard II, a theme abhorrent to Elizabeth, and Hayward was imprisoned. Essex's approval both of Hayward's book and Shakespeare's play was brought as evidence against him. (See HARSNETT.)

Hazlitt, William (1778–1830), was born at Maidstone, the son of a Unitarian minister who emigrated to America in 1783 but returned three years later and settled at Wem in Shropshire, where William was brought up. He met Coleridge and visited him and Wordsworth at Nether Stowey in 1799, and formed a friendship with Lamb. He abandoned his first ambition of being a portrait painter and turned to literature, publishing *The Characters of Shakespear's Plays* in 1817. The book is of the greatest importance, though the title is conventional enough; 18th-century critics had all written about the characters, but Hazlitt is carried away by the poetry, and nobody before him had written a book with such understanding and such gusto on the *poetry* of Shakespeare. Yet he did not like the Poems; *Venus and Adonis* and *Lucrece* are 'like a couple of ice-boxes', and he did not well know what to say about the *Sonnets*, for it seemed to him that 'in expressing the thoughts of others Shakespear was inspired; in expressing his own he was a mechanic'. (See also his *Lectures on the English Poets*, 1818.)

Hazlitt, William Carew (1834–1913), bibliographer, and grandson of William Hazlitt, was educated at Merchant Taylors' School and called to the bar of the Inner Temple in 1861. He edited the valuable *Shakespeare's Library* (2nd ed. 1875, 6 vols.), the most complete 'collection of the plays, romances, novels, poems, and histories employed by Shakespeare in the composition of his works'.

Hearne, Thomas (1678–1735), the antiquary and 'Wormius' of *The Dunciad*, was born in Berkshire, and educated at St Edmund Hall, Oxford. In 1699 he was appointed assistant keeper of the Bodleian, and in 1712 second keeper. He refused several posts rather than take the oath of allegiance to the Hanoverians. In his *Diary* for 1709 he relates the legend of Shakespeare's being the father of Sir William D'Avenant:

> ye said Mr Shakespear was his God-father & gave him his name. (In all probability he got him.) 'Tis further said that one day going from school a grave Doctor in Divinity met him, and ask'd him, *Child whither art thou going in such hast?* to wch the child reply'd, *O Sir my God-father is come to Town, & I am going to ask his blessing.* To wch the D^r. said, *Hold Child, you must not take the name of God in vaine.*

Heavens. The 'shadowe or cover' over the apron stage of the Elizabethan theatre; cf. Heywood's *Apology for Actors*, 'the covering of the stage, which we call the heavens'. Apparently the loft so formed was connected with the hut at the top of the tiring-house, and from the heavens 'some god appeared or spoke', and actors and properties descended. A painted cloth might be slung below the heavens; cf. the opening line of *1 Henry VI*, 'Hung be the heavens with black!' The Admiral's had a 'clothe of the Sone and Mone'.

Nicola Sabbatini describes the heavens in the Italian theatre (1638):

> When it is necessary for machines to ascend to the sky or descend thence to the stage, one must have a 'cut' heaven, both for convenience and for the delight and wonder which audiences take in it, since they cannot see how the machines which rise from the earth disappear or how they descend from the heavens to the stage.

The trap-door in the floor of the apron stage sometimes represented hell-mouth, and the space below was known as 'hell'. The heavens and hell are relics of the staging of medieval miracle plays. (See MACHINES; HOPE THEATRE.)

Hecate. The triple goddess of the moon, earth and underworld, and patroness of witches. She appears in *Macbeth*, III, v, and IV, i, where she scolds the witches for acting without her knowledge. Her sing-song speeches are out of harmony with the play and are undoubtedly interpolations, probably by Thomas Middleton, author of the songs which appear in full in his *The Witch* (q.v.).

Hector. In *Troilus and Cressida*, eldest son of Priam King of Troy, and husband of Andromache. He thinks that Helen should be returned to the Greeks, yet with his brothers Paris and Troilus resolves to keep her (II, ii). He challenges any of the Greeks to single combat, and fights inconclusively with Ajax. He is murdered by the jealous Achilles and his Myrmidons when he is caught unarmed (V, viii).

Heine, Heinrich (1797–1856), the German poet, a son of Jewish parents, was born in Düsseldorf. In 1825, he became a Christian, and in 1830 settled permanently in Paris. His *Shakespeares Mädchen und Frauen* appeared in 1839, and contains the well-known passage about *The Merchant of Venice*, beginning:

> When I saw a performance of this play at Drury Lane, a beautiful pale-faced English woman stood behind me in the box and wept profusely at the end of the fourth act, and called out repeatedly: 'The poor man is wronged.' I have never been able to forget those big dark eyes weeping for Shylock.

The one fault Heine found with Shakespeare was that he was an Englishman.

Helen. 1. In *Troilus and Cressida*, wife of the Greek Menelaus, who has been carried off to Troy by Paris. She plays a small and unimportant part in the action.

2. In *Cymbeline*, a lady attending on Imogen. She is called by name at the beginning of II, ii.

Helena. 1. In *A Midsummer Night's Dream*, she loves Demetrius, but both he and Lysander love Hermia. Then, owing to Puck's muddled magic, both fall in love with Helena. Puck makes all well, and Helena has her Demetrius, Hermia her Lysander.

2. The heroine of *All's Well*, an orphan, the daughter of a doctor; for Coleridge, Shakespeare's 'loveliest character'. (She is Giglietta di Nerbona in Boccaccio's story.)

Helenus. In *Troilus and Cressida*, one of the sons of Priam King of Troy, and a priest. In the debate as to whether to keep Helen (II, ii) he accuses Troilus of lack of reasons, to which Troilus replies: 'You are for dreams and slumbers, brother priest; You fur your gloves with reason.'

Helicanus. In *Pericles*, a lord of Tyre. Pericles leaves him to govern his dominions while he goes to Tarsus. He remains faithful even though Pericles is away so long.

Hell. See TRAP-DOORS.

Heminge, John (d. 1630). One of the twenty-six 'Principall Actors' in Shakespeare's plays (see p. 90). In 1588 'John Hemminge, gent' of St Mary Cornhill married Rebecca, widow of William Knell, by whom he had at least twelve children. In 1593 he was one of Strange's Men who toured the provinces under Alleyn, and probably in the following year joined the Chamberlain's when that company was formed. With them, after 1603 known as the King's Men, he remained, and though the last record of his acting is in *Catiline*, 1611, he appears to have been their business manager – he was the regular payee for Court performances – until his death. Malone asserts that he was the first to play the part of Falstaff, and he is described in the lines on the burning of the Globe, 1613,

Then with swolne eyes, like druncken Flemminges,
Distressed stood old stuttering Heminges.

In this year Shakespeare appointed him a trustee for his Blackfriars Gatehouse, and in his will left him 26s. 8d. to buy a ring. In 1619 Heminge is described as being of 'greate lyveinge wealth and power', and at his death seems to have held a quarter of the shares in the Globe and Blackfriars theatres, in both of which he was one of the original housekeepers.

In 1623 Heminge and Condell prepared the first collected edition of Shakespeare's plays, the First Folio, 'without ambition either of selfe-profit, or fame: onely to keepe the memory of so worthy a Friend, & Fellow aliue, as was our Shakespeare'.

Heminge had trouble with one of his daughters, Thomasine, who had married William Ostler of the King's Men. When Ostler died intestate in 1614 Heminge seized his shares in the Globe and Blackfriars, and Thomasine brought a suit in Chancery for their recovery. There was a reconciliation, but Heminge failed to keep his promise and Thomasine brought an action for £600 damages. Heminge appears to have kept the shares which passed to his son William, the playwright, who sold most of them to John Shank, an action that led to the Petition to the Lord Chamberlain in 1635. Like his friend Condell, he was buried in the church of St Mary Almondbury. (See SHARERS' PAPERS; SALISBURY, SIR HENRY.)

Henderson, John (1747–85), actor, was born in London, and made his first stage appearance at Bath in 1772, as Hamlet. Garrick, who was jealous, refused to have him at Drury Lane, but in 1777 Colman gave him the part of Shylock at the Haymarket. The performance was a great success, and the veteran Macklin, who had rescued the part from low comedy, congratulated him. After this he played for Sheridan at Drury Lane, and at Covent Garden, in a number of Shakespeare's plays, in which he excelled.

Henley Street. The Stratford thoroughfare leading to the market town of Henley-in-Arden, some ten miles to the north. (See BIRTHPLACE.)

Henri IV (1553–1610), King of Navarre and France. On the assassination of Henri III in August 1589 (see SONNETS), Henry of Navarre really became the King of France, but as he was a Protestant he had to fight for the throne against the Catholic League. In July 1593, however, he decided that 'Paris is worth a Mass', became a Catholic, and was acknowledged as King. Shakespeare punningly refers to the civil war in *The Comedy of Errors* (III, ii), which means that the play, or at least the allusion, was written before July 1593:

Ant. S. Where France?
Dro. S. In her forehead; armed and reverted,
making war against her heir.

The main theme of *Love's Labour's Lost* may have been suggested by a visit to Henry of Navarre at Nérac in 1578, of Marguerite de Valois, his estranged wife. She was accompanied by a number of ladies, there were great festivities, and there were negotiations about a dowry and the sovereignty of Aquitaine. Henry of Navarre's supporters in his war for the throne were the Ducs de Biron, de Longueville, de Mercade, and the Marquis de la Mothe. The Duc de Mayenne (Dumain) was one of his chief opponents. There was no published account of the Nérac visit when Shakespeare wrote the play.

In *The Merchant of Venice* (III, ii), Portia's,

Then music is
Even as the flourish when true subjects bow
To a new-crowned monarch,

may be an allusion to Henri IV's coronation in February 1594.

Henrietta Maria (1609–66). The daughter of Henri IV of France, she married Charles I in 1625. Her love of dramatic entertainment is illustrated by the entries in the *Office Book* of Sir Henry Herbert, Master of the Revels:

On Saturday the 17th of Novemb, being the Queens birth-day, Richarde the Thirde was acted by the K. players at St. James, wher the king and queene were present, it being the first play the queene sawe since her M^tys^. delivery of the Duke of York. 1633.

On tusday night at Saint James, the 26 of Novemb. 1633, was acted before the King and Queene, The Taminge of the Shrew. Likt.

Her visit, during the Civil War, to New Place, then occupied by Shakespeare's daughter, the widow Susanna Hall, is described by Halliwell-Phillipps (II, 108, ed. 6):

In the month of July, 1643, New Place was the temporary residence of Queen Henrietta Maria in the course of her triumphant march from Newark to Keinton. This fact, which there is no reason to dispute, rests upon a tradition told by Sir Hugh Clopton to Theobald early in the last century, and the anecdote exhibits a continuation in the family of the sincere loyalty which the favours of previous sovereigns must have riveted to the poet's own affections. According to the last-named editor, the Queen 'kept her Court for three weeks in New Place' ... She was, however, at Stratford only three days, arriving there on July 11th with upwards of two thousand foot and a thousand horse, about a hundred waggons, and a train of artillery. This was a memorable day for Stratford, for here the Queen was met by Prince Rupert at the head of another body of troops, the most stirring event of the kind the ancient town has ever witnessed. The Corporation bore at least some of the expense of entertaining Henrietta, who left Stratford on the 13th of the same month, meeting the King in the vale of Keinton, near the site of the battle of Edgehill.

From 1644 to 1660 she lived in exile in France, returned to England at the Restoration, but died near Paris.

Henry I and **Henry II.** See DAVENPORT, ROBERT.

Henry IV (1367–1413). See BOLINGBROKE.

'HENRY IV, PART I.'

WRITTEN: 1597–8. Meres mentions '*Henry the 4*' in 1598.

PERFORMED: 1600, 6 March. 'In the After Noone his [the Lord Chamberlain's] Plaiers acted, before Vereiken [the Flemish

Ambassador], Sir John Old Castell, to his great Contentment.'

1612. 'The Hotspur', at Court.

1625. 1 January. 'The First Part of Sir John Falstaff, by the kings company, Att Whitehall.'

1638. 'At the Cocpit the 29th of May .... ould Castel.'

REGISTERED: 1598, 25 February, by Andrew Wise; transferred to Mathew Law, 25 June 1603.

PUBLISHED: 1598, Q1. 'The History of Henrie the Fourth; With the battell at Shrewsburie, betweene the King and Lord Henry Percy, surnamed Henrie Hotspur of the North. With the humorous conceits of Sir Iohn Falstalffe ... Printed by P. S. for Andrew Wise.' Q1, set up from foul papers, is the authoritative text, later Qq being set up from their immediate predecessors.

1599, Q2. 'Newly corrected by W. Shakespeare.'

1604, Q3; 1608, Q4; 1613, Q5; 1622, Q6; 1632, Q7; 1639, Q8. (See DERING MS.)

1623, F1. 'The First Part of Henry the Fourth, with the Life and Death of Henry Sirnamed Hot-spvrre.' The third play in the History section; pp. 46–73. Acts and scenes marked. Set up from Q5.

SOURCES: Holinshed's *Chronicle* for the history. *The Famous Victories of Henry the Fifth*, an anonymous play, gave hints for the comic scenes. (See FALSTAFF.)

STAGE HISTORY: Heminge, Lowin, and Hart are said to have played Falstaff. The play was revived at the Restoration by the King's Company, and Pepys saw it in December 1660. Betterton produced an abbreviated version in which he played Hotspur, and later Falstaff. Garrick made little of Hotspur; Quin was the most famous 18th-century Falstaff.

Hotspur, his father Northumberland, and his uncle Worcester, join with Mortimer, Glendower, and Douglas in a rebellion. Only Worcester and Douglas, however, are at Shrewsbury with Hotspur, who is killed in the battle by the Prince of Wales. Worcester is executed and Douglas freed. The period of the action is June 1402 to July 1403. The Prince of Wales is shown as the boon companion of Falstaff, with whom he takes part in the robbery at Gadshill. In the Boar's Head Tavern they stage mock interviews between the Prince and the King; the real interview follows in III, ii; the Prince promises to reform and there is a reconciliation. Falstaff is at the battle of Shrewsbury, where he makes his famous speech on Honour, and pretends to have killed Hotspur.

'HENRY IV, PART 2.'

WRITTEN: 1597–8. '*Henry the* 4', though not necessarily Part 2, mentioned by Meres in 1598.

PERFORMED: 'Sundrie times publikely acted' before Q, 1600.

1612. *Sir John Falstaffe* and *The Hotspur* were acted at Court.

1619. '[Seco]nd part of Falstaff' at Court?

REGISTERED: 1600. 'Andrew Wyse William Aspley. Entred for their copies ... the second parte of the history of Kinge Henry the iiijth, with the humours of Sir John Falstaffe: Wrytten by master Shakespere.'

PUBLISHED: 1600, Q. 'The Second part of Henrie the fourth, continuing to his death, and coronation of Henrie the fift. With the humours of sir Iohn Falstaffe, and swaggering Pistoll. As it hath been sundrie times publikely acted by the right honourable, the Lord Chamberlaine his seruants. Written by William Shakespeare ... Printed by V. S. for Andrew Wise, and William Aspley.' In the first issue III, i was accidentally omitted. Set up from foul papers.

1623, F1. 'The Second Part of Henry the Fourth, Containing his Death: and the Coronation of King Henry the Fift.' The fourth play in the History section: pp. 74–100. 'The Actors Names' at the end. Acts and scenes marked. Contains 168 lines omitted from Q, probably censored as dealing with the deposition of Richard II, but omits forty lines of Q. Set up from Q collated with prompt-book.

SOURCES: Holinshed's *Chronicle*, and *The Famous Victories*.

STAGE HISTORY: The play was revived by Betterton *c.* 1700; *The Sequel of Henry the Fourth*, *c.* 1720, may be his version. Quin and Cooke played Falstaff; Garrick, J. P. Kemble and Macready played the King. In 1853 Phelps doubled Shallow and the King.

The action covers the years 1403–13, from Shrewsbury to the death of Henry IV, and deals with the rebellion of Archbishop Scrope, Hastings and Mowbray, who are tricked into disbanding their forces, and executed. Pistol makes his first appearance, and Falstaff has a long scene with Mistress Quickly and Doll Tearsheet. He goes recruiting in the Cotswolds, where he falls in with Justice Shallow, whom he persuades to lend him a thousand pounds on the security of the accession of his friend, the Prince of Wales; but when he goes to London, the reformed Prince, now Henry V, banishes him from his presence and sends him to prison.

Henry V. See HENRY, PRINCE OF WALES; HENRY V, the play.

'HENRY V.'

WRITTEN: 1598–9. The reference to Essex in the Prologue to Act v suggests that most of the play was written between Essex's departure for Ireland on 27 March 1599 and his return on 28 September.

PERFORMED: 'Sundry times playd' before Q1, 1600. It may have been the first play to have been performed in the newly built Globe, probably the 'wooden O' of the Prologue.

1605. 'By his Maiesties plaiers. On the 7 of January was played the play of Henry the fift,' at Court.

REGISTERED: 1600? '4 Augusti. Henry the ffift; a booke. to be staied.' This may have been an attempt by the Chamberlain's to prevent piratical publication. (See ROBERTS, JAMES.)

1600. '14 Augusti. Thomas Pavyer. Entred for his Copyes by Direction of master White warden vnder his hand wrytinge. These Copyes followinge beinge thinges formerlye printed and sett over to the sayd Thomas Pavyer. viz. ... The historye of Henry the Vth with the battell of Agencourt.'

PUBLISHED: 1600, Q1. 'The Chronicle History of Henry the fift, With his battel fought at Agin Court in France. Togither with Auntient Pistoll. As it hath bene sundry times playd by the Right honorable the Lord Chamberlaine his seruants. Printed by Thomas Creede, for Tho. Millington, and Iohn Busby. And are to be sold at his house in Carter Lane, next the Powle head. 1600.' A 'bad' Quarto; a reported version, possibly by an actor who played Gower, Exeter, or the Governor of Harfleur. The omission of Chorus, three scenes, and long passages, suggests that the report was based on a shortened version.

1602, Q2. Set up from Q1.

1619, Q3. Set up from Q1. Dated 1608. One of the ten plays published in 1619 by Jaggard, many of them with false dates.

1623, F1. 'The Life of Henry the Fift.' The fifth play in the History section: pp. 69–95 (wrongly numbered). Acts marked. A fair text. According to Wilson, set up from 'the manuscript exactly as Shakespeare handed it to his company ... in 1599.'

SOURCES: Holinshed's *Chronicle*. The wooing scene occurs in *The Famous Victories of Henry the Fifth*.

STAGE HISTORY: Wilson argues that Falstaff was in the play as originally written, but that Kempe's departure left Shakespeare without a suitable actor, so that before production he had to fill in with fresh episodes, and substituted Pistol for Falstaff in the leek-eating scene. The 'noble play of Henry the Fifth' seen by Pepys was written by Lord Orrery, 1664. Shakespeare's play was adapted by Aaron Hill in 1723. Garrick played the Chorus. 19th-century revivals, which were not many, concentrated on spectacle.

Encouraged by the Archbishop of Canterbury, Henry V sets out on his campaign to win the French crown. Before embarking he discovers the plot of Cambridge, Scrope, and Grey to assassinate him at Southampton. He takes Harfleur, marches towards Calais, but is intercepted at Agincourt by the French whom he defeats. By the Treaty of Troyes Henry marries the French King's daughter, Katharine. At the beginning of the play Falstaff's death is reported by the quondam Quickly who has married Pistol. Pistol, Bardolph and Nym go on the campaign; the last two are hanged for looting, and Pistol is beaten by Fluellen and forced to eat leeks for insulting the Welsh. King Henry involves Fluellen in another quarrel, with the English soldier Williams.

Henry VI (1421–71), hero of the three parts of *Henry VI*, was the son of Henry V and Katharine, daughter of Charles VI of France. He became King of England in 1422, was crowned at Westminster in 1426, and in Paris in 1431. He founded Eton College and King's College, Cambridge, in 1440–1, and in 1445 married Margaret of Anjou. A mild and patient man, he was neither strong enough to save the French inheritance, nor to prevent the civil Wars of the Roses. He was murdered after the battle of Tewkesbury in 1471.

'HENRY VI, PART 1.'

WRITTEN: 1589–90. Not mentioned by Meres, 1598.

PERFORMED: 1592. In his *Diary* Henslowe records a performance on 3 March of a new play, 'Harey the vj', by Strange's. This may be Shakespeare's *1 Henry VI*, also alluded to by Nashe in his *Pierce Penilesse* (q.v.), 1592, as a play about *Talbot*.

REGISTERED: 1623, 8 November. One of the sixteen plays registered by Blount and Jaggard before their publication of the Folio. It is entered as "The thirde parte of Henry ye Sixt', but the entry must refer to *1 Henry VI*.

PUBLISHED: 1623, F1. 'The first Part of Henry the Sixt.' The sixth play in the History section: pp. 96–119. Acts marked, and scenes in III and IV. From author's fair copy used as prompt-book.

SOURCES: Halle's *Union*, with Holinshed's *Chronicles* for Joan of Arc.

STAGE HISTORY: There is practically none. Benson produced all three parts at Stratford in 1906, and BBC television in 1960. Parts 1, 2 and 3 were produced at the Birmingham Repertory Theatre in 1951–2. (See SS, 6.) John Barton's adaptation of the three parts and *Richard III* was produced at Stratford by Peter Hall in 1963.

It is probable that there is more than one author in the play. The English scenes may be mostly by Shakespeare writing under the influence of Marlowe, but the majority of the French scenes appear to be the work of another and inferior hand. II, iv and IV, ii, at least, are generally ascribed to Shakespeare. It is possible that 'Harey the vj' was merely Shakespeare's source-play, revised by him as late as 1594–5.

The play begins just after the death of Henry V, and finishes with the marriage of young King Henry VI to Margaret, the daughter of the King of Naples. It deals with the attempt of the English to hold their possessions in France, with the successes of Joan of Arc, who is portrayed as a strumpet and a witch, and with the defeat and death of the English leader Talbot. The English scenes are concerned mainly with the struggle between the Protector Gloucester and Henry Beaufort, Bishop of Winchester and Cardinal. The beginning of the wars of Lancaster and York is foreshadowed by the plucking of the red and white roses in the Temple garden (II, iv).

'HENRY VI, PART 2.'

WRITTEN: 1590–1. Not mentioned by Meres, 1598.

PERFORMED: No recorded performance.

REGISTERED: 1594. 'xij° Marcij. Thomas Myllington ... the firste parte of the Contention of the twoo famous houses of York and Lancaster ...'

1602. April 19. Assigned by Millington to Thomas Pavier.

PUBLISHED: 1594, Q1. 'The First part of the Contention betwixt the two famous Houses of Yorke and Lancaster, with the death of the good Duke Humphrey: And the banishment and death of the Duke of Suffolke, and the Tragicall end of the proud Cardinall of Winchester, with the notable Rebellion of Iacke Cade: And the Duke of Yorkes first claime vnto the Crowne. London. Printed by Thomas Creed, for Thomas Millington, and are to be sold at his shop vnder Saint Peters Church in Cornwall.' A 'bad' Quarto; a reported text, perhaps by actors who had played Suffolk and Cade. (It used to be thought that this was an old play revised by Shakespeare as the *2 Henry VI* of F. See ALEXANDER, PETER.)

1600, Q2. 'Printed by Valentine Simmes for Thomas Millington.'

1619, Q3. 'The Whole Contention betweene the two Famous Houses, Lancaster and Yorke. With the Tragicall ends of the good Duke Humfrey, Richard Duke of Yorke, and King Henrie the sixt. Diuided into two Parts: And newly corrected and enlarged. Written by William Shakespeare, Gent. Printed at London for T. P.' One of the ten plays printed by William Jaggard in 1619, many of them with false dates. *The Whole Contention* is a reprint of *The First part of the Contention* with *The true Tragedie*.

1623, F1. 'The second Part of Henry the Sixt, with the death of the Good Duke Hvmfrey.' The seventh play in the History section: pp. 120–46. Unmarked save for *Actus Primus. Scœna Prima*. The authoritative text. From author's fair copy used as prompt-book.

SOURCES: Holinshed, Halle and perhaps Grafton and Stow.

STAGE HISTORY: In 1680 John Crowne ran together the last two acts of Part 2 and the whole of Part 3 in an adaptation called *The Misery of Civil War*. Theophilus Cibber produced his version in 1723. See 1 HENRY VI.

The Protector Gloucester, angry at the cession of Anjou and Maine as the price of Margaret's marriage to Henry, incurs the enmity of Margaret, Cardinal Beaufort, Suffolk, and York. They secure the banishment of the Duchess of Gloucester for practising sorcery against the King, and then arrest and murder Gloucester himself. Suffolk, the Queen's lover, is banished for the murder and killed by pirates. Act IV is given up mainly to Cade's rebellion and death. In Act V the Wars of the Roses begin: Henry, Margaret, Somerset and Clifford for Lancaster, Warwick and Salisbury in support of York and his sons. The play ends with the battle of St Albans (1455), in which Somerset and Clifford are killed.

'HENRY VI, PART 3.'

WRITTEN: 1590–1. Not mentioned by Meres, 1598 .

PERFORMED: Before September 1592 when Robert Greene (q.v.) in his *Groatsworth of Wit* parodied the line 'O tiger's heart wrapp'd in a woman's hide' (I, iv, 137). It had been 'sundrie times acted' by 1595.

REGISTERED: There is no entry before publication, but on 19 April 1602 'Thomas Pavier. Entred for his copies by assignment from Thomas Millington ... The firste and Second parte of Henry the vj[t] ij bookes xij[d]', i.e. *2, 3 Henry VI.*

PUBLISHED: 1595, Q1. 'The true Tragedie of Richard Duke of Yorke, and the death of good King Henrie the Sixt, with the whole contention betweene the two Houses Lancaster and Yorke, as it was sundrie times acted by the Right Honourable the Earle of Pembrooke his seruants. Printed at London by P. S. for Thomas Millington, and are to be sold at his shoppe vnder Saint Peters Church in Cornwal.' A 'bad' Quarto; a reported text, perhaps by actors who had played Warwick and Clifford. (It used to be thought that this was an old play revised by Shakespeare as the *3 Henry VI* of F. See TRUE TRAGEDY.)

1600, Q2. Printed by William White for Thomas Millington.

1619, Q3. 'The Whole Contention ...' Jaggard's reprint. (See 2 HENRY VI.)

1623, F1. 'The third Part of Henry the Sixt, with the death of the Duke of Yorke.' The eighth play in the History section: pp. 147–72. Unmarked save for *Actus Primus. Scœna Prima*. The authoritative text. From author's fair copy used as prompt-book.

SOURCES:
STAGE HISTORY: } See 2 HENRY VI.

After St Albans, Henry VI makes York his heir, but Margaret, supported by Young Clifford, continues the struggle on behalf of her son Edward, Prince of Wales. At Wakefield Clifford kills York's youngest son Rutland, and York himself is captured, mocked, and stabbed to death by Clifford and Margaret. (York speaks the line. referring to Margaret, 'O tiger's heart wrapp'd in a woman's hide.') York's sons, Edward (IV) and Richard (III), defeat the Lancastrians at Towton (1461), where Clifford is killed; Henry VI is captured and Edward IV crowned. When Edward marries Elizabeth Woodville, Warwick joins Margaret, releases Henry and captures Edward who, however, escapes, recaptures Henry, and defeats and kills Warwick at Barnet (1471). At Tewkesbury (1471) the Lancastrians are finally defeated, the Prince of Wales is stabbed, and Richard Duke of Gloucester rushes to the Tower to murder Henry VI.

Henry VII. See RICHMOND, HENRY TUDOR.

Henry VIII (1491–1547), the hero of *Henry VIII*, was the second son of Henry VII, whom he succeeded in 1509. The play deals with the period 1520–33, from the Field of the Cloth of Gold to the christening of Elizabeth. His first wife, Katharine of Aragon, was the widow of his elder brother, Arthur, who died in 1502.

'HENRY VIII.'

WRITTEN: 1612.

PERFORMED: 1613, 29 June, at the Globe (q.v.), when it was burned down.

1628, 29 July, at the Globe. (See BUCKINGHAM, GEORGE VILLIERS.)

REGISTERED: 1623, 8 November. One of the sixteen plays registered by Blount and Jaggard before publishing F1.

PUBLISHED: 1623, F1. 'The Famous History of the Life of King Henry the Eight.' The tenth and last of the plays in the History section; pp. 205–32. Acts and scenes marked. Elaborate stage directions. From foul papers, or a transcript, prepared for a production.

SOURCES: Holinshed's *Chronicle*; Foxe's *Book of Martyrs* for the Cranmer episode (V, i–iii), and perhaps the play by Samuel Rowley (q.v.). *When you see me, You know me, Or the famous Chronicle Historie of King Henry the eight*. (*c.* 1604.)

STAGE HISTORY: John Lowin is said by

Downes (1708) to have played the original King Henry, and to have 'had his Instructions from Mr *Shakespear* himself'. The play is half pageant, and this element has always been exploited. D'Avenant's production with Betterton as the King was seen by Pepys in January 1664, and after this it was produced with mounting expense and realism by, among others, Garrick, Charles Kean, Irving and Tree.

1949. Stratford: Tyrone Guthrie's production.

1958. Old Vic: Michael Benthall's production, with Edith Evans and John Gielgud.

Scholars are generally agreed that there are two authors in this play. As early as 1850 James Spedding asked, '*Who wrote Henry VIII?*' and, basing his opinion on a study of the verse, attributed to Shakespeare only I, i and ii; II, iii and iv; III, ii, 1–203; V, i; and the rest to Fletcher. Alexander and Wilson Knight reject the Spedding-Hickson thesis of joint authorship, but A. C. Partridge supports it in his *Problem of Henry VIII Reopened*, 1950, in which he adduces new evidence of Fletcher's hand.

Henry VIII is a sequence of themes, a series of private disasters, rather than a play. First there is the trial and execution of Buckingham on a charge of high treason raised by Wolsey. Then comes the divorce and death of Queen Katharine, and the King's marriage with Anne Bullen, in spite of Wolsey's intrigues, which bring about his disgrace and death. Cranmer is made Archbishop of Canterbury for his services, and is rescued from the malicious attacks of Gardiner by the intervention of the King. The play ends with another grand spectacle, the christening of the Princess Elizabeth.

Henry, Prince (1207–72). In *King John*, the young son of John; he appears only in the last scene. When his father dies he becomes Henry III, to whom the Bastard and the other lords swear loyalty. (He was only nine when John died in 1216.)

Henry, Prince of Wales (1387–1422). In *Henry IV*, eldest son of Bolingbroke, King Henry IV. In *Part 1* he and Poins rob Falstaff, Bardolph, Peto and Gadshill of what they have taken from the travellers; then in the Boar's Head Tavern he and Falstaff rehearse the expected interview with the King. This occurs in III, ii; Prince Henry promises to reform, and the King gives him a command in the army sent against the rebels. At Shrewsbury the Prince kills Hotspur in single combat.

In *Part 2* the Prince and Poins 'idly profane the precious time' with their practical joking, and he plays a small part until IV, v, when he comes from the tavern to see his dying father, thinks him dead, and takes away the crown. The King awakes, reproaches his son, and counsels him 'to busy giddy minds in foreign quarrels' when he is King, advice that he is not slow to take. In the last scene, as Henry V, he disowns Falstaff and banishes him from his presence. (See HENRY V, the play.)

Henry Frederick, Prince of Wales (1594–1612), eldest son of James VI of Scotland and I of England, was born in Scotland 19 February 1594. He was very popular, fond of the tilt, and when he was created Prince of Wales, 31 May–6 June 1610, there were great festivities, including a water triumph in which Richard Burbage and John Rice of the King's Men delivered speeches written by Anthony Munday. It was a sad blow when he died suddenly on 6 November 1612, in the middle of the festivities for the marriage of his sister Elizabeth to the Elector Palatine. Sometime between August 1603 and February 1604 he became the patron of the Admiral's Men (q.v.), though their patent as 'Servauntes to our dearest sonne the Prince' was not published until 30 April 1606. On the Prince's death the company came under the patronage of the Elector Palatine.

Henryson, Robert (*c.* 1430–*c.* 1506), Scottish poet and schoolmaster of Dunfermline, about whose life little is known. He was author of *The Testament of Cresseid*, a continuation of the story of Troilus and Cressida, told by 'worthy Chaucer glorious', describing the final degradation of Cressida. She becomes a common harlot of the Greek camp, and is stricken with leprosy. Shakespeare only hints at this later history in his *Troilus and Cressida*, but that he knew the poem is clear not only from this play, but from *Twelfth Night*, 'Cressida was a beggar' (III, i) and *Henry V* (II, i):

Fetch forth the lazar kite of Cressid's kind,
Doll Tearsheet she by name, and her espouse.

Henslowe, Philip (d. 1616), theatre manager, was the son of Edmund Henslowe of Lindfield, Sussex, Master of the Game in Ashdown Forest and Brill Park. Philip was employed by the bailiff of Viscount Montague, who owned property in Southwark, and by 1577 he was living on the Bankside in the Liberty of the Clink, which became his permanent home. About this time he married his master's widow, Agnes Woodward, who had a fair fortune and a daughter Joan. In the eighties he is described as a dyer, in the nineties he was a pawnbroker, and always he was a buyer of Southwark property, among which were some of the Bankside Stews. In 1592 he was appointed a Groom of the Chamber, probably Extraordinary, in 1603 Gentleman Sewer of the Chamber, and in the next year he became with Alleyn joint Master of the Game of Paris Garden, that is, of the bear-baiting in which he had been financially interested for ten years. The shrewd and ambitious man of business knew the value of respectability; he became a churchwarden of St Saviour's, Southwark, and a governor of the local grammar school. He died 6 January 1616, and his wife a year later.

Henslowe was not slow to see that there was a future in the theatre business; in 1585 he acquired the lease of a plot of land north of Maid Lane, on which in 1587 he built the first Bankside theatre, the Rose, and by 1594 he seems to have owned the theatre at Newington Butts. In 1592 his step-daughter Joan married Edward Alleyn of the Admiral's, vhen began a triumphant and a profitable partnership with the great actor; he was associated with Alleyn in the Fortune, built in 1600, and in the Hope, which was the old Bear Garden rebuilt in 1613 for plays and baiting.

Most of Henslowe's property was inherited by Alleyn, on whose death Henslowe's *Diary* and other papers passed to the library of Dulwich College, where they were forgotten and mislaid until in 1790 they were unearthed by Malone who prepared an abstract for his Variorum edition. These documents, edited by W. W. Greg (1904–8), throw a flood of light on Henslowe's relations with the theatre, on theatre management and finance, and the Elizabethan stage in general. The *Diary*, which is more of an account or memorandum book, covers the years 1592–1603, and falls into two sections. In the first Henslowe records the companies who performed at his theatre, presumably the Rose, the names of the plays, and the amount he received as housekeeper or theatre owner: one-half of the gallery takings. (It must be remembered that according to the Old Style of reckoning the year began on 25 March; thus 24 March 1591, is 1592 in our calendar.) He begins with a run by Strange's, from 19 February to 23 June 1592, some of the entries for which are as follows:

In the name of god Amen 1591 begininge the 19 of febreary my g. lord Stranges mene as ffoloweth 1591.

R. at fryer bacone, the 19 of febreary (saterday)		xvii^{s}.	iii^{d}.
mulomurco the 20 of febr.		xxix^{s}.	
orlando the 21 of febreary		xvi^{s}.	vi^{d}. . . .
Harey the vj the 3 of marche 1591 ne	iii^{li}.	xvi^{s}.	8^{d}. . . .
the seconde pte of tamber came the 28 of April 1592 ne	iii^{li}.	iiij^{s}.	

(Presumably 'ne' means 'new', but whether a first performance, or new to Henslowe's theatre, or 'newly corrected', is not clear. *Harey the vj*, if Shakespeare's

1 Henry VI, may have been about a year old in March 1592. The money represents Henslowe's receipts.)

Another season, probably with Strange's, follows from 29 December to 31 January 1593. This was the plague year, but Sussex's were with him 26 December to 6 February 1594, playing *Titus & Ondronicous* (ne), and the Queen's and Sussex's together 1–9 April; and 3–13 (or 5–15) June the Admiral's and Chamberlain's, back from their travels, played at Newington Butts. After this the Chamberlain's went their own way, leaving the Admiral's at the Rose, where Henslowe records their performances down to November 1597.

After 1597, when the Admiral's were reorganized, there is a change in the nature of Henslowe's entries. Instead of the daily list of plays and receipts, there are records of the advances he made to the company for the purchase of plays, costumes, properties, for the licensing of plays, and of advances made to the players themselves. Henslowe, in fact, became the banker of the Admiral's, both corporately and individually, after July 1598 securing his advances by taking the profits of 'the wholle gallereys'. Players and poets alike were in his hands, or clutches; as he himself wrote later: 'Should these fellowes come out of my debt I should have noe rule over them.' A few examples of his entries are given:

Lent Bengemyn Johnson, the 5 of Jeneware 1597 in redy money the some of vs.

Paid unto the Master of the Revells man for lycensyng of a boocke called the Tragedie of Agamemnon the 3 of June 1599, viis.

The 16th of October, 99. Received by me Thomas Downton of Philip Henslowe, to pay Mr. Monday, Mr. Drayton, Mr. Wilson, and Hathway, for The first part of the Lyfe of Sir Jhon Ouldcastell, and in earnest of the Second Pte, for the use of the company, ten pound.

P^{d}. unto Thomas Hewode, the 20 of september [1602] for the new *adycions* of Cutting Dick, the some of xxs.

Henslowe notes the plays and 'goodes' he bought for the company, and his inventories of their goods, 'sewtes', 'aparell ... Leaft above in the tier-house in the cheast', and properties:

Item, j rocke, j cage, j Hell mought.

Item, j tome of Guido, j tome of Dido, j bedsteade ...

Item, Cupedes bowe, and quiver; the clothe of the Sone and Mone ... *etc.*

Henslowe continued his transactions when the Admiral's moved to the Fortune, but in 1604 struck a final balance showing that 'all reconynges consernynge the company in stocke generall descarged & my sealfe descarged to them of al deates'. From 1602–4 he had a similar arrangement with Worcester's at the Rose, and 1611–15 he financed the Lady Elizabeth's, for a time amalgamated with the Queen's Revels and Prince Charles's.

In 1615 they drew up an indictment, including nine 'Articles of oppression against Mr Hinchlowe', among them being:

For lending of vj^{ll} to pay them theire wages, hee made vs enter bond to give him the profitt of a warraunt of tenn poundes due to vs att Court. Alsoe wee have paid him for plaie bookes 200^{ll} or thereaboutes and yet hee denies to give vs the Coppies of any one of them.

Also within 3 yeares hee hath broken and dissmembred five Companies.

(See Malone, *Var.*, III; Greg, *Henslowe's Diary* and *Henslowe Papers*. In their edition of the *Diary* (1961) R. A. Foakes and R. T. Rickert view Henslowe in a more favourable light than Greg.)

Hentzner, Paul, wrote an account, in Latin, of his travels in Germany, France, England and Italy, published in 1612. It was translated by R. Bentley and published by Horace Walpole in 1757. Hentzner describes the Presence Chamber at Greenwich in August 1598, and refers briefly to the London theatres and the bear-baiting in Paris Garden.

Herbert. See PEMBROKE, EARLS OF.

Herbert, Sir Henry (1595–1673), son of Richard Herbert of Montgomery Castle, and brother of the first Lord

Herbert of Cherbury, and of George Herbert the poet, and a relation of William Herbert, Earl of Pembroke and Lord Chamberlain (1615–26). Sir John Ashley became Master of the Revels (q.v.) in March 1622, but on 20 July 1623 he appointed Herbert his deputy in consideration of a payment of £150 a year. Though Herbert was strictly only deputy until Ashley's death in January 1641, when he became Master in his own right, he was knighted in August 1623 and recognized as Master, the duties of whom he rigorously fulfilled. His *Office Book* has been lost, but it was used by Malone and Chalmers, who published extracts which give invaluable information about the work of the Revels Office, the censorship and licensing of plays for performance, the plays performed, the closing of the theatres in time of plague, and the fees received by the Master. The regular salary of the office was only £10 a year, but by 1603 'fees and other perquisites' brought in another £90–£100; twenty years later, when Herbert farmed it for £150, it must have been worth much more. Not only did he receive 'benefits', but it became the custom for all places of public entertainment to pay him for permission to perform in Lent. For example:

1622. 21 Martii. For a prise at the Red-Bull, for the howse; the fencers would give nothing. 10*s*. [This was received by Ashley.]

From Mr. Gummel, [Manager of the Fortune] in the name of the dancers of the ropes for Lent, this 15 March, 1624. £1.0.0.

From Mr. Blagrave, in the name of the Cockpit company, for this Lent, this 30th March, 1624. £2.0.0.

March 20, 1626. From Mr. Hemminges, for his Lent allowance, £2.0.0.

The kinges company with a generall consent and alacritye have given mee the benefitt of too dayes in the yeare, the one in summer, thother in winter, to be taken out of the second daye of a revived playe, att my owne choyse. The housekeepers have likewyse given their shares, their dayly charge only deducted, which comes to some 2*l*. 5*s*. this 25 May 1628.

The benefitt of the winters day from the kinges company being brought mee by Blagrave, upon the play of The Moor of Venise, comes, this 22 of Nov. 1629, unto 9*l*. 16*s*. 0*d*.

Received of Mr. Benfielde, in the name of the kings company, for a gratuity for ther liberty gaind unto them of playinge, upon the cessation of the plague, this 10 of June 1631, 3*l*. 10*s*. 0*d*. ... This was taken upon Pericles at the Globe.

The following extracts are typical:

To the Duchess of Richmond, in the kings absence, was given The Winter's Tale, by the K. Company, the 18 Janu. 1623. Att Whitehall.

For the king's players. An olde playe called Winter's Tale, formerly allowed of by Sir George Bucke, and likewyse by mee on Mr. Hemmings his worde that there was nothing profane added or reformed, thogh the allowed booke was missinge; and therefore I returned it without a fee, this 19 of August, 1623.

17 July, 1626, from Mr. Hemmings for a courtesie done him about their Blackfriers hous, – 3*l*.0.0.

from Mr. Hemming, in their company's name, to forbid the playing of Shakespeare's plays, to the Red Bull Company, this 11 of April 1627, – 5*l*.0.0.

This day being the 11 of Janu. 1630. I did refuse to allow of a play of Messinger's, because itt did contain dangerous matter, as the deposing of Sebastian king of Portugal ... I had my fee notwithstandinge, which belongs to me for reading itt over, and ought to be brought always with the booke.

This morning being the 9th of January 1633, the kinge was pleasd to call mee into his withdrawinge chamber to the windowe, wher he went over all that I had croste in Davenants play-booke, and allowing of *faith* and *slight* to bee asseverations only, and no oathes, markt them to stande, and some other few things, but in the greater part allowed of my reformations. This was done upon a complaint of Mr. Endymion Porters in December. The kinge is pleased to take *faith*, *death*, *slight*, for asseverations, and no oaths, to which I doe humbly submit as my masters judgment; but under favour conceive them to be oaths, and enter them here, to declare my opinion and submission.

At the increas of the plague to 4 within the citty and 54 in all. – This day the 12 May, 1636, I received a warrant from my lord Chamberlin for the suppressing of playes and shews, and at the same time delivered my several warrants to George Wilson for the four companys of players, to be served upon them.

Herbert ends his *Office Book* with the note: 'Here ended my allowance of plaies, for the war began in August 1642.'

At the Restoration new companies were formed, and 'Sir Henry Herbert, who still retained his office of Master of the Revels, endeavoured to obtain from these companies the same emoluments which he had formerly derived from the exhibition of plays; but after a long struggle, and after having brought several actions against Sir William D'Avenant, Mr. Betterton, Mr. Mohun, and others, he was obliged to relinquish his claims, and his office ceased to be attended with either authority or profit.' (Malone, *Var.*, III, 243.) (See OFFICE BOOK; KNIGHT; KILLIGREW.)

Herbert, Sir Walter. In *Richard III*, a supporter of Henry Richmond (v, ii).

Herder, Johann Gottfried (1744–1803), born in East Prussia, became one of the most influential of German writers. Himself influenced by his reading of English ballad poetry and Shakespeare, he became the leader of the Sturm und Drang movement and of a German literature freed from French and classical models. Here he differed from Lessing, who rejected French models, but favoured a national literature based on the ancients and Shakespeare. In Strassburg in 1771 Herder met the young Goethe and fired him with his own enthusiasm for Shakespeare.

Herford, Charles Harold (1853–1931), scholar and critic, entered Trinity, Cambridge, in 1875, was Professor of English at Aberystwyth 1887–1901, and at Manchester 1901–21. He edited the *Eversley* Shakespeare (1899) and with P. Simpson, the *Works of Jonson.*

Hermia, in *A Midsummer Night's Dream,* loves Lysander, but her father Egeus insists on her marrying Demetrius. Hermia and Lysander run away to the forest where Puck muddles his magic and makes both Lysander and Demetrius fall in love with Helena. However, he undoes the spell, and Hermia has her Lysander.

Hermione. In *The Winter's Tale,* the wife of Leontes, King of Sicilia. (In Greene's *Pandosto* she is called Bellaria, and really dies.) (See RARE TRIUMPHS.)

Hero. In *Much Ado,* the daughter of Leonato. (The Fenicia of Bandello's *novella.*)

Heroes and Heroines. Shakespeare's young heroes are less heroic than his heroines, some of those in the comedies, indeed, are cads; the heroes are doubtful and inconstant, the heroines heavenly true, though sometimes perhaps over-persistent. Orsino explains the difference:

> Our fancies are more giddy and unfirm,
> More longing, wavering, sooner lost and worn,
> Than women's are.

And Proteus, king of cads, apologizes for himself and the others who were yet to come:

> O heaven, were man
> But constant, he were perfect! That one error
> Fills him with faults; makes him run through all the sins.

And the 'divine air' in *Much Ado,* of which Claudio is the hero, is not without irony:

> Sigh no more, ladies, sigh no more,
> Men were deceivers ever,
> One foot in sea and one on shore,
> To one thing constant never.

But Shakespeare rarely invented a plot, and never wrote a play of contemporary English life, and the faults of the main characters are in the main those of the originals in the romantic stories that he borrowed. He makes amends when he is free to create his own characters.

His borrowed plots partly, though not entirely, account for the curious fact that only four of his heroines have mothers: Juliet, Anne Page, Perdita and Marina, and of these the last two grow up in the belief that their mothers are dead. The mother-daughter relationship is scarcely treated by Shakespeare. When the heroine has a parent, it is generally a father, but often she is an orphan, and apparently an only child.

It is worth noting that there is no passionate love-making in Shakespeare's plays. In the comedies hero and heroine keep their distance, on guard with the rapiers of their wit; in the tragedies they are rarely seen alone; Romeo once, as he leaves Juliet; Othello once, when he murders Desdemona; Antony and Cleopatra never. This, no doubt, is Shakespeare's happy solution of the problem created by a boy's playing the heroine's part.

Heroic Couplets. Strictly, the iambic pentameter couplets of the 'heroic' poem and play of the late 17th century, but loosely applied to all five-footed iambic couplets. Though the measure was employed in poems in the 16th century: for example, Marlowe's *Hero and Leander*, it was not much used in plays, and Shakespeare's employment of it in his early 'lyrical' period was something of an innovation. The percentage of rhyming couplets to all verse lines is very high in *Love's Labour's Lost* (62), in *A Midsummer Night's Dream* it is 43, in *Richard II* 19 and in *Romeo and Juliet* 17. The proportion of feminine endings is correspondingly low in these plays; 8, 7, 11, 8 respectively. Apart from these plays and *1 Henry VI*, *The Comedy of Errors*, *Twelfth Night* and *All's Well*, the proportion of heroic to blank verse is fairly constant, averaging about 5 per cent, for Shakespeare continued to use rhyme for certain purposes, such as aphorisms and definition at the end of a scene; but with *Antony and Cleopatra* and the romances there is a rapid declension, until in the last plays the heroic couplet has disappeared. (See RHYME; VERSE-TESTS.)

Hertford's Men. Edward Seymour, son of the Protector Somerset, was born in 1539, created Earl of Hertford in 1559, married three times, and died in 1621. He had a company of players traceable in the provinces from 1582 to 1607. They would almost certainly take part in the Earl's entertainment of Elizabeth in 1591 at Elvetham, his Hampshire home. There was an artificial pond, a water pageant with sea-gods, and there were fireworks. It is possible that Shakespeare was thinking of this when he wrote in *A Midsummer Night's Dream* (II, i),

> And certain stars shot madly from their spheres,
> To hear the sea-maid's music.

Chambers suggests that Elizabeth's enjoyment of this entertainment led to the one appearance of Hertford's Men at Court a few months later, in January 1592, and that Bottom and his crew may represent the provincial players.

Hertzberg, Wilhelm A. B. (1813–79), German scholar, finally Headmaster of a school in Bremen. See his *Introduction to Cymbeline* (Schlegel-Tieck) 1871, and *Jahrbuch* 1878. (See VERSE-TESTS.)

Hewins, John. The first husband of Shakespeare's aunt, Anne Arden. They lived at Bearley. He died sometime before 1550, when she married Thomas Stringer of Stockton in Shropshire. She died sometime before October 1576.

Hewland. The original name of the Elizabethan farmhouse in Shottery, now known as Anne Hathaway's Cottage. A survey of 1556 records that John Hathaway, Anne's grandfather, was a tenant of the house and attached land in 1543, for which, with another holding, he paid a rent of 33s. 8d.:

> Johannes Hathewey tenet, per copiam curie datam xx. die Aprilis, anno regni nuper regis Henrici Octavi xxxiiij. to, unum messuagium et dimidiam virgatam terre, jacentem in Shotterey, vocatam Hewland ...

In 1590 it was held by Joan, widow of his son Richard, whose son Bartholomew bought the property from William Whitmore and John Randoll in 1610. On Bartholomew's death in 1624 it was inherited by his son John, and the house remained in the possession of the family until 1838, though the male line became extinct in 1746. It was bought by the Birthplace Trustees in 1892.

It is first mentioned as Anne Hathaway's Cottage by Samuel Ireland in his *Picturesque Views on the Warwickshire Avon* (1795), in which he published an engraving, and observed, 'it is still occupied by the descendants of her family, who are poor and numerous'. The house underwent substantial alterations, in the late 18th century being converted into two, and afterwards into three cottages.

Heyes, Thomas, publisher of *The Merchant of Venice* Quarto, 1600. The play had been registered by James Roberts 22 July 1598, though it was not to be printed 'without lycence first had' from the Lord Chamberlain. On 28 October 1600 Roberts transferred the copyright to Heyes:

> Thomas Haies. Entred for his copie under the handes of the Wardens and by Consent of master Robertes. A booke called the booke of the merchant of Venyce.

The text is a good one, and the redundancy, 'A booke called the booke', suggests that the MS submitted for registration was the 'allowed book', the acting version authorized by the Master of the Revels. When Thomas died in 1603 he left the copyright to his son Laurence, then a boy, but when it was surreptitiously printed by William Jaggard in 1619 he at once put in a claim to the Stationers' Company, who pronounced it his:

> 8° Julij 1619. Laurence Hayes. Entred for his Copies by Consent of a full Court theis two Copies following which were the Copies of Thomas Haies his fathers viz[t]. A play Called 'The Marchant of Venice ...

Laurence became a freeman of the Stationers' Company in 1614; he published another edition of *The Merchant of Venice* in 1637, in which year he probably died.

Heywood, John (1497–*c.* 1580), interlude writer, seems to have been born in London and educated at Broadgates Hall, Oxford. He was a chorister in the Chapel Royal, and in 1521 became player on the virginals to Henry VIII. He married Elizabeth Rastell, niece of Sir Thomas More, was a fervent Catholic, and a favourite of Henry VIII and Queen Mary. When Elizabeth succeeded to the throne he fled to Malines, whence he is said to have returned in 1577.

In 1538 Heywood received 40s. for 'playeng an enterlude with his children' before Princess Mary, and it is probable, though not certain, that he supplied the Children of Paul's with plays under their Master, Sebastian Westcott, much as Lyly supplied them for Westcott's successor, Thomas Giles. Heywood is important as the writer of interludes that link the religious medieval to the secular modern drama, by the substitution of real characters for the abstractions of the Moralities. His most famous interlude is *The Four P's*, the story of how a Palmer, a Pothecary, a Pardoner and a Pedlar compete as to who shall tell the biggest lie, and of how the prize is won by the Palmer, who maintains that he has never seen a woman out of patience.

Heywood, Thomas (1573–1641), dramatist and actor, was a native of Lincolnshire, and educated at Cambridge. The first record of him is in a payment of October 1596 'for Hawodes booke' for the Admiral's. It must have been to this company that he bound himself as an actor, for Henslowe records:

> Memorandum that this 25 of Marche 1598 Thomas Hawoode came and hiered hime seallfe with me as a covenante searvante for ij yeares by the receuenge of ij syngell pence acordinge to the statute of Winchester & to begine at the daye a boue written & not to playe any wher publicke a bowt London not whille these ij yeares be expired but in my howsse yf he do then he doth forfett vnto

me by the receuinge of these ij^{d}. fortie powndes.

In 1602 he was with Worcester's (Queen Anne's after 1603), with whom he stayed until the company was disbanded on the Queen's death in 1619. After this he does not appear again as an actor, though he continued to pour out plays. His *Preface to The English Traveller* (1633) is worth quoting, for the light that it throws both on him and on the contemporary drama:

This tragi-comedy (being one reserved amongst 220 in which I had either an entire hand or at the least a main finger) coming accidentally to the press, and I having intelligence therof, thought it not fit that it should pass as *filius populi*, a bastard without a father to acknowledge it: true it is that my plays are not exposed to the world in volumes, to bear the title of works (as others): one reason is, that many of them by shifting and change of companies have been negligently lost. Others of them are still retained in the hands of some actors, who think it against their peculiar profit to have them come in print, and a third that it never was any great ambition in me to be in this kind voluminously read ...

Of these 220 plays, many of them written for the Admiral's and Worcester's-Queen Anne's, about twenty remain, and the names of some dozen more; and of these only one is really remembered, *A Woman Killed with Kindness* (1603), 'the first bourgeois tragedy of our Elizabethan literature'. 'Heywood', wrote Lamb, 'is a sort of *prose* Shakespeare.' 'Tho. Heywood, Poet', was buried at St James's, Clerkenwell, 16 August 1641. (See SS, 7.)

Heywood began to write *Lives of all the Poets*, unhappily unfinished, and like most of his plays, unprinted and unknown. His important *Apology for Actors* (q.v.), however, was published in 1612, and contains his protest against the printing of two of his poems in the 1612 edition of *The Passionate Pilgrim* (q.v.). In his *Hierarchie of the Blessed Angels* (1635) there is an allusion to Shakespeare:

Our modern Poets to that pass are driven,
Those names are curtal'd which they first had given;
And, as we wisht to have their memories drown'd,
We scarcely can afford them half their sound ...
Mellifluous *Shake-speare*, whose inchanting Quill
Commanded Mirth or Passion, was but *Will*.

Hiccox, Lewis. Tenant of the land in Old Stratford, bought by Shakespeare in 1602. In 1603 Hiccox was granted a licence for an inn in Henley Street, and in the same year his wife Alice was so rough with her next-door neighbour, Mrs Robert Brookes of the Bell Inn, that she was bound over to keep the peace. The Hiccox's inn was probably that known in 1642 as the Maidenhead, the 'Woolshop' to the east of the 'Birthplace'. In 1639 'Jane Hiccox, widdowe' was living there.

Higgins, John (*c.* 1545–1602), is said to have been of Christ Church, Oxford, 'a poet, antiquary, and historian of great industry'. He is best known for his work in *The Mirrour for Magistrates*, first published 1559, to which in 1574 he added *The Firste parte*, consisting of an induction and sixteen fables in verse, *of the first unfortunate Princes of this lande*, including the story of King Lear, a version probably consulted by Shakespeare.

Hill, Aaron (1685–1750), son of George Hill of Malmesbury Abbey, was born in London and educated at Westminster School. An undistinguished author, he was satirized in *The Dunciad* to which he replied in 1730 in *The Progress of Wit*. His version of *Henry V* was produced in 1723. He was a pioneer in theatrical costume, like the Italians Antonio Conti and P. J. Martelli, suggesting historical dress for the characters, and he himself designed the costumes for one of his own plays in 1731.

Hill, Agnes, sister of Alexander Webbe, and wife of John Hill, 'a substantial farmer of Bearley', by whom she had two sons and two daughters. In his will of August 1545 he made Agnes residuary legatee and left her 'the lease of my farme in Berely duringe her lyff'. She became the second wife of Robert Arden, Shakespeare's maternal grandfather, by whom she had no children. In his will of 23 November 1556, made just before his death, he wrote:

> Allso I gyve and bequethe to Annes my wife vj. *li.* xiij. *s.* iiij. *d.* apone this condysione, that shall sofer my dowghter Ales quyetlye to ynyoye halfe my copye-houlde in Wyllmecote dwring the tyme of her wyddowe-whodde; and if she will nott soffer my dawghter Ales quyetlye to ocupye halfe with her, then I will that my wyfe shall have butt iij. *li.* vj. *s.* viij. *d.* and her gintur in Snyterfylde.

When Agnes made her will in 1579, she left most of her property to her son John Hill, including 'my second potte, my best panne', and the 'cowe with the white rump'.

Hilliard Miniature, sometimes called the Somerville miniature. In 1818 this supposed portrait of Shakespeare was in the hands of Sir James Bland Burges, who in that year sent it to James Boswell junior, editor of the *Third Variorum* edition of Shakespeare, to the second volume of which he prefixed an engraving of it by 'that excellent artist Mr Agar'. Burges wrote to Boswell:

> Mr. Somerville of Edstone, near Stratford-upon-Avon, ancestor of Somerville, author of the Chace, &c. lived in habits of intimacy with Shakespeare, particularly after his retirement from the stage, and had this portrait painted, which, as you will perceive, was richly set, and was carefully preserved by his descendants, till it came to the hands of his great grand-son, the poet, who, dying in 1742, without issue, left his estates to my grand-father, Lord Somerville, and gave this miniature to my mother.

Though the miniature is by Hilliard, and in spite of the assertion of Burges that it bears 'a general resemblance to the best busts of Shakespeare', it bears no resemblance either to the Stratford bust or to the Droeshout engraving, and is not accepted as a portrait of the poet.

Sir William Somerville (d. 1616) lived at Wooton Wawen in Warwickshire, and knew a number of the inhabitants of Stratford. His brother John married a daughter of Edward Arden of Park Hall.

Hilliard, Nicholas (*c.* 1537–1619), 'the first true English miniature painter', seems to have been the son of Richard Hilliard of Exeter, high sheriff in 1560. He became portrait painter to Elizabeth, engraved her second Great Seal in 1586, made a portrait of Mary Queen of Scots when he was eighteen, was a favourite of James I, and author of a treatise on miniature painting. Donne mentions him in his poem, *The Storme* (1597):

> And, a hand, or eye
> By *Hilliard* drawn, is worth an history,
> By a worse painter made.

Hinman, Charlton K. (b. 1911), American scholar, Professor of English at the University of Kansas, who, with the aid of a machine that he invented, has collated 50 copies of the First Folio in the Folger Shakespeare Library. He has published his revolutionary discoveries in *Cast-off Copy for the First Folio* (SQ, 1955), *The Prentice Hand ... Compositor E* (1957), *Six Variant Readings* (1961), and finally in *The Printing and Proof-Reading of the First Folio of Shakespeare*, 1963. (See MISLINEATION; MISPRINTS; PROOF-READING; COMPOSITORS.)

Hippolyta. 1. In *A Midsummer Night's Dream*, queen of the Amazons, and the betrothed of Theseus. She appears in I, i, but does not speak; in IV, i she speaks the lines beginning 'I was with Hercules and Cadmus once'; and in V, i she is a sympathetic member of the audience at Bottom's play.

2. In *The Two Noble Kinsmen* she is now the wife of Theseus, her sister Emilia being the heroine of the play. She helps to persuade Theseus to avenge

the three queens on 'cruel Creon', and to spare Palamon and Arcite. She is a spectator at the tournament which Emilia refuses to attend.

Hired Men, or hirelings, were employed and paid about 6s. a week by the actor-sharers of a company. Some were actors, others musicians, others stage-hands and perhaps gatherers; the book-keeper (prompter) and tireman (wardrobe-master) were also hired men. All, except the book-keeper, might be pressed into service to swell a scene, as in the Order of the Coronation in *Henry VIII*, or as in *Titus Andronicus*:

Sound Drums and Trumpets, and then enter two of Titus *sonnes, and then two men bearing a Coffin couered with black, then two other sonnes, then* Titus Andronicus, *and then* Tamora *the Queene of Gothes & her two sonnes* Chiron *and* Demetrius, *with* Aron *the More, and others as many as can be.*

In December 1624 Sir Henry Herbert signed a warrant of protection from arrest during the season of the Revels for twenty-one hired men 'all employed by the kings Ma[ties] servants in theire quallity of playinge as musitions, and other necessary attendants'. Of these, seven were actors, Knight was book-keeper, John Rhodes wardrobe-master, Henry Wilson and William Toyer musicians, and William Gascoigne a stage-hand. We do not know what parts the other nine played, but it looks as though Shakespeare would have been able to count on six or seven regular hired actors, and ten or twelve supers, as well as the twelve actor-sharers (nine before 1604) of the company. (See PROTECTION OF PLAYERS.)

His Majesty's Theatre, originally Her Majesty's. The theatre with which are associated the Shakespearean productions of Beerbohm Tree, who opened it 19 April 1897.

Histories. There are ten plays in the History section of the Folio, all English histories; the Roman historical plays, *Coriolanus*, *Julius Caesar*, *Antony and Cleopatra*, being printed with the Tragedies. They are arranged in historical order, and appear in the Catalogue of contents as follows (the dates prefixed are those, approximately, of their composition):

1596–7	*The Life and Death of King John.*	*Fol.* 1
1595–6	*The Life and death of Richard the second.*	23
1597–8	*The First part of King Henry the fourth.*	46
1597–8	*The Second part of K. Henry the fourth.*	74
1598–9	*The Life of King Henry the Fift.*	69
1589–90	*The First part of King Henry the Sixt.*	96
1590–1	*The Second part of King Hen. the Sixt.*	120
1590–1	*The Third part of King Henry the Sixt.*	147
1592–3	*The Life & Death of Richard the Third.*	173
1612–13	*The Life of King Henry the Eight.*	205

The history play as a genre developed out of the moral interlude by way of Bale's *King John* (*c.* 1547), in which all the characters save John are abstractions, and history is used merely as a means to a didactic end. In *The Troublesome Reign of John* (*c.* 1588) the abstractions have given way to real characters, but the didacticism is still there. Shakespeare, apparently the first to write a real history play, treats his material as a dramatist, not as a preacher or mere chronicler of events, and there is nothing comparable to this great series of Histories in any other literature.

'What can no longer be doubted, is that, whether by design or not, the history plays have a collective unity, deriving from an Elizabethan view of history and a common fund of ideas and ideals about the ordering of man's society.'

(See SS, 6, in which the Histories are the central theme.)

'Histrio-mastix.' 1. An anonymous play registered and printed in 1610 for Thomas Thorpe as 'Histrio-mastix. Or the Player whipt'. It appears to be a revision made by Marston in 1599 of a play written some ten years before. It is an attack on the insolence of the professional players (see GREENE, ROBERT), which suggests that it was written for one of the boys' companies, or it may be a University or Inn of Court play. The story is of a company of vagabonds, 'Sir Oliver Owlet's Men', and their poet Posthaste, who announce their forthcoming performances in a town-hall, but in fact play before Lord Mavortius. Their performance is a series of fragments, the first being Troilus and Cressida. As the lovers are parting, Troilus boasts of the favour Cressida has given him to wear:

Come, Cressida, my Cresset light,
Thy face doth shine both day and night;
Behold behold thy garter blue
Thy knight his valiant elbow wears,
That when he shakes his furious Speare
Thy foe in shivering fearful sort
May lay him down in death to snort.

It has been argued that this is a punning reference to Shakespeare, that he is Posthaste, and that *Troilus and Cressida* must have been written by 1599, though Posthaste is almost certainly Anthony Munday. After their performance Owlet's Men behave insolently and quarrel, and are finally pressed for the army. The play is important for the light it throws on theatrical conditions.

2. *Histrio-mastix, The Players Scourge* was a pamphlet published by William Prynne (q.v.) in 1633. It is a violent attack on plays, players, and playwrights in general:

... popular Stage-playes (the very Pompes of the Divell which we renounce in Baptisme, if we beleeve the Fathers) are sinfull, heathenish, lewde, ungodly Spectacles, and most pernicious Corruptions; condemned in all ages, as intolerable Mischiefes to Churches, to Republickes, to the manners, mindes, and soules of men. And that the Profession of Play-poets, of Stage-players; together with the penning, acting, and frequenting of Stage-playes, are unlawfull, infamous and misbeseeming Christians.

It was interpreted also as a reference to Charles I and to Henrietta Maria, who was then taking part in the rehearsal for a ballet. Prynne was imprisoned and sentenced by the Star Chamber to have both his ears cut off.

Hoby, Sir Edward (1560–1617), courtier and diplomatist, was the son of Sir Thomas Hoby, translator of the *Cortegiano* of Castiglione (q.v.). In 1592 he entertained Elizabeth at Bisham, in Berkshire, and James I visited him there several times. In 1595 he had a house in Canon Row, Westminster, and on 7 December wrote to Sir Robert Cecil inviting him, apparently, to a performance of 'K. Richard', probably Shakespeare's *Richard II*:

Sir, findinge that you wer not convenientlie to be at London to morrow night I am bold to send to knowe whether Teusdaie may be anie more in your grace to visit poore Channon rowe where as late as it shal please you a gate for your supper shal be open: & K. Richard present him selfe to your vewe.

'Hoffman.' In December 1592 Henslowe advanced Henry Chettle 5s. for his tragedy of 'Howghman' which was published anonymously in 1631 as 'The Tragedy of Hoffman or A Reuenge for a Father, As it hath bin diuers times acted with great applause, at the Phenix in Druery-lane.' In the booksellers' play-lists of the mid 17th century the play is ascribed to Shakespeare.

Holcombe, Thomas. A boy actor with the King's Men; an apprentice of John Shank.

Holinshed, Raphael (*c.* 1529–*c.* 1580), seems to have come of a Cheshire family, and may have been a Cambridge man. In London he worked as a translator for the publisher Reginald Wolfe who was preparing a history of the world. Wolfe died in 1573, and in 1577 the work appeared in a more modest form as *The Chronicles of England, Scotland, and Ireland*. It was written by a number of hands: Holinshed wrote the History of England, William Harrison the Description of England; the History of Scotland is mainly a translation of Boece's *Scotorum Historiae*; the Description of Scotland and the History of Ireland are adaptations, and the Description of Ireland was written by Richard Stanyhurst and Edward Campion. The first edition was in two volumes, and illustrated. A second and enlarged edition without illustrations, published in 1587, contained passages about Ireland offensive to Elizabeth, and a number of pages were cut out. It was from Holinshed's *Chronicles*, probably the 1587 edition, that Shakespeare took much of the history for his English historical plays, and for *Macbeth*, part of *Cymbeline*, and perhaps *King Lear*. Holinshed's style is undistinguished, and Shakespeare does not follow him as closely as he does North, whose translation of Plutarch is the source of his Roman histories. When Holinshed made his will in October 1578 he was the steward of Thomas Burdett of Bramcote, Warwickshire, who was also lord of the manor of Packwood, near Stratford. As Burdett's steward, Holinshed used to go to Packwood to preside over the manor court, so that it is just possible that Shakespeare met him before his death *c.* 1580–1. (See SHAKESPEARE, JOHN.)

Holland, Hugh (d. 1633), author of one of the commendatory poems prefixed to the Folio: the sonnet 'Upon the Lines and Life of the Famous Scenicke Poet, Master William Shakespeare':

Those hands, which you so clapt, go now, and wring
You *Britaines* brave; for done are *Shakespeares* dayes:
His dayes are done, that made the dainty Playes,
Which made the Globe of heau'n and earth to ring.
Dry'de is that veine, dry'd is the *Thespian* Spring,
Turn'd all to teares, and *Phoebus* clouds his rayes:
That corp's, that coffin now bestick those bayes,
Which crown'd him *Poet* first, then *Poets* King.
If *Tragedies* might any *Prologue* have,
All those he made, would scarse make one to this:
Where *Fame*, now that he gone is to the grave
(Deaths publique tyring-house) the *Nuncius* is.
For though his line of life went soone about,
The life yet of his lines shall never out.

Holland came from Denbigh, and was educated at Westminster School and Trinity, Cambridge, where he became a fellow. He had some reputation as a poet, publishing *Pancharis* in 1603, *A Cypres Garland* in 1625, and a number of commendatory verses.

Holland, John, actor, appears in the cast of *The Second Part of the Seven Deadly Sins*, performed probably by Strange's *c.* 1591. A prompter's note has led to his name appearing in the stage-directions and speech-prefixes of *2 Henry VI*, where in IV, ii, vii he appears as a follower of Jack Cade and a friend of George Bevis (q.v.). This probably indicates an early performance of the play by Strange's, in which company Holland was a hired man.

Holland, Philemon (1552–1637), was born at Chelmsford and educated at Trinity, Cambridge. About 1595 he became a doctor in Coventry, and in 1628 headmaster of the free school. The poverty of his last years was relieved by a small pension from the town council. He is remembered as 'the translator-general in his age', and one of his translations at least was used by Shakespeare: Pliny's *Natural History* (1601). When he wrote *Othello*, Shakespeare must have been reading or re-reading Holland's Pliny, from which he took the Anthropophagi, the Pontick sea, the Arabian tree, and other allusions. Holland also translated the *Britannia* of Camden (q.v.).

Hollar, Wenceslas (1607–77), Bohemian etcher, was born at Prague, whence his family fled to Germany at the beginning of the Thirty Years' War. In Cologne he attracted the attention of Thomas, Earl of Arundel, who in 1637 brought him to England, where he worked for publishers at ridiculously low prices. In the Civil War, like Inigo Jones and Faithorne, he was a Royalist, was captured, but escaped to Antwerp, his famous 'Long View' of London being published at Amsterdam in 1647. He returned to England in 1652, and died in poverty despite his brilliance and immense industry – he etched more than 2,700 plates. His very fine 'Long View' of London includes the Globe and the Hope, the earliest detailed representations of theatre exteriors. This is the second Globe, built in 1614, and 'pulled down to the ground' in April 1644, the year in which Hollar was captured at the defence of Basing House. He must have made the engraving from drawings made between 1637 and 1644. It is important to note that in the print the names of the Globe and the 'Beere bayting h' (the Hope) have been interchanged.

Holofernes. In *Love's Labour's Lost*, a pedantic schoolmaster, probably the stock pedant, the old Dottore, of the Italian *commedia dell'arte* (q.v.). When Don Armado, as *ad hoc* Master of the Revels, is to present the princess 'with some delightful ostentation' Holofernes at once suggests The Nine Worthies, with himself as Judas Maccabaeus. His audience prevents his speaking more than one line.

Holywell. A London liberty north of the City, in which stood James Burbage's Theatre (q.v.).

Homer. Shakespeare would have learned Latin at Stratford Grammar School, but probably no Greek. Arthur Hall's *Ten Bookes of Homers Iliades* (I–X) was published in 1581, and in 1598 came Chapman's *Seaven Bookes of the Iliades* (I, II, VII–XI) and *Achilles Shield* (XVIII). These Shakespeare must have used for his *Troilus and Cressida* (1598–1602), and perhaps he knew the complete French translation of Hugues Salel and Amadis Jamyn (1584, 1597).

Hondius, Jodocus. 17th-century Dutch engraver, and founder, *c.* 1602, of a firm of map-makers. (See MAPS OF LONDON.)

'Honest Whore, The.' Dekker's masterpiece, written in collaboration with Middleton. Part I was registered 9 November 1604, and published in the same year, as 'The Honest Whore, With The Humours of the Patient Man, and the Longing Wife. Tho: Dekker'. In the first scene occur the lines,

HIPP. Oh, you ha' killed her by your cruelty!
DUKE. Admit I had, thou kill'st her now again;
And art more savage than a barbarous Moor.

This is almost certainly an allusion to *Othello*, which must therefore have been written by the middle of 1604.

Honiman, John. A boy actor with the King's Men; an apprentice of John Shank.

Hope Theatre. Since 1594 Henslowe and Alleyn had been licensees of the Bear Garden on the Bankside, and in 1604 succeeded in acquiring the joint Mastership of the Game of Paris Garden, that is, of bear- and bull-baiting. In 1611 Alleyn sold his interest in the property for £580 to Henslowe, who thereupon took Jacob Meade into partnership. On 29 August 1613 the carpenter Gilbert Katherens contracted to pull down the Bear Garden and to build for Henslowe and Meade a theatre on or near the same site at a cost of £360:

> Gilbert Katherens ... shall ... before the last daie of November next ensuinge ... not onlie take downe or pull downe all that same place or house wherin Beares and Bulls haue been hertofore vsuallie bayted, and also one other house or staple wherin Bulls and horsses did vsuallie stande, sett, lyinge, and beinge vppon or neere the Banksyde in the saide parishe of St Saviour in Sowthworke, comonlie called or knowne by the name of the Beare garden, but shall also ... newly erect, builde, and sett vpp one other same place or Plaiehouse fitt & convenient in all thinges, bothe for players to playe in, and for the game of Beares and Bulls to be bayted in the same, and also a fitt and convenient Tyre house and a stage to be carryed and taken awaie, and to stande vppon tressels ...; And shall new builde ... the saide plaie house or game place neere or vppon the saide place, where the saide game place did heretofore stande; And to builde the same of suche large compasse, fforme, widenes, and height as the Plaie house called the Swan in the libertie of Parris garden in the saide parishe of St Saviour now is; And shall also builde two stearecasses without and adioyninge to the saide Playe house in suche convenient places, as shalbe moste fitt and convenient for the same to stand vppon, and of such largnes and height as the stearecasses of the saide playehouse called the Swan nowe are or bee; And shall also builde the Heavens all over the saide stage, to be borne or carryed without any postes or supporters to be fixed or sett vppon the saide stage, and all gutters of leade needfull for the carryage of all suche raine water as shall fall vppon the same.

The Globe was being rebuilt at the same time, and this may have had something to do with the delay in the building of the Hope, as the Bear Garden was now called, which does not appear to have been open until October 1614. On the 31st of that month Ben Jonson's *Bartholomew Fair* was produced there by the Lady Elizabeth's. Apparently the animals gave the 'plaie house or game place' something of the smell of Smithfield where the Fair was held, for Jonson calls it in the play 'as dirty as Smithfield, and as stinking every whit'. On Henslowe's death in 1616 Alleyn inherited his interest in the Hope, which he leased to Meade whom he appointed deputy Master of the Game. Bear-baiting was forbidden in 1642 and the Hope 'pulled downe to make tennements, by Thomas Walker, a peticoate maker in Cannon Streete, on Tuesday the 25 day of March 1656'. In Hollar's 'Long View' of London, the drawings for which were made between 1637 and 1644, the 'Beere bayting h' is shown as a cylindrical building to the north and slightly to the west of the Globe, the names of the two houses being interchanged.

Horatio. In *Hamlet*, the prince's quiet and stoical friend. He sees the Ghost, and is the only person to whom Hamlet confides the revelation of his father's murder. Dramatically he is invaluable as a foil, and as a confidant to whom Hamlet can unburden himself, yet he scarcely influences the course of events. It is characteristic of him that he looks after the distracted Ophelia. The dying Hamlet prevents his committing suicide as he must live to report his cause aright to the unsatisfied. (Horatio of *The Spanish Tragedy* may be a link between that play and *Hamlet*.)

Horn. Horns were employed in the Elizabethan theatre solely for hunting music. For example, in *A Midsummer Night's Dream*, IV, i, is the stage-direction, *Horns winded within. Enter Theseus* ... Then:

> A cry more tuneable
> Was never holla'd to, nor cheer'd with horn ...
> Go, bid the huntsmen wake them with their horns.
>
> *Horns and shouts within.*

Again, in the hunting scene in *The Two Noble Kinsmen* (III, v) there is the repeated stage-direction, *Wind horns.*

Hornby, Mrs. The wife of Thomas Hornby, cousin of John Shakespeare Hart, from whom he rented the Birthplace. She lived there 1793–1820, and is described in the *Sketch Book* of Washington Irving, who visited Stratford in 1815:

> It is a small and mean-looking edifice of wood and plaster.... The walls of its squalid chambers are covered with names and inscriptions in every language....
>
> The house is shown by a garrulous old lady, in a frosty red face, lighted up by a cold blue anxious eye, and garnished with artificial locks of flaxen hair, curling from under an exceedingly dirty cap. She was peculiarly assiduous in exhibiting the relics with which this, like all other celebrated shrines, abounds. There was the shattered stock of the very matchlock with which Shakespeare shot the deer, on his poaching exploits. There, too, was his tobacco-box; which proves that he was a rival smoker of Sir Walter Raleigh; the sword also with which he played Hamlet; and the identical lantern with which Friar Laurence discovered Romeo and Juliet at the tomb! There was an ample supply also of Shakespeare's mulberry-tree, which seems to have as extraordinary powers of self-multiplication as the wood of the true cross; of which there is enough extant to build a ship of the line. (See PHILLIPS, RICHARD.)

Horneby, Thomas, the Henley Street blacksmith who was surety for John Addenbrooke (q.v.), and against whom Shakespeare had to proceed in 1609 for the recovery of his debt when Addenbrooke was not to be found.

Horner. In *2 Henry VI*, an armourer accused by his apprentice Peter Thump of affirming that 'Richard Duke of York was rightful heir unto the English crown'. Gloucester orders a trial by combat in which Peter kills his drunken master, who confesses treason (II, iii). Horner begins the fight with the words, 'and therefore, Peter, have at thee with a downright blow'. The Quarto adds, 'as Bevis of Southampton fell upon Ascaprt', which Chambers suggests is a gag of the actor George Bevis (q.v.), who played the part.

Hortensio. In *The Taming of the Shrew*, he persuades his friend Petruchio to woo and marry Katharine the Shrew so that he may try to win her younger sister Bianca. (Called Polidor in *A Shrew*.)

Hortensius. In *Timon*, a servant of one of Timon's creditors (III, iv).

Host. 1. In *The Two Gentlemen of Verona*, he takes Julia to find Proteus, who also lodges at his house (IV, ii).

2. In *The Merry Wives*, the Host of the Garter fools Evans and Caius, who avenge themselves by robbing him of his horses (IV, v). He helps Fenton to gain Anne Page.

Hostess. In *The Shrew* (Ind.), she goes to fetch the thirdborough to arrest the drunken Sly. Presumably she is Marian Hacket (q.v.). (See also QUICKLY.)

Hôtel de Bourgogne. The only public theatre in Paris at the beginning of the 17th century. In 1548 a long rectangular hall was converted into a theatre by the Confrérie de la Passion, and in 1608 taken by the Comédiens du Roi with Alexandre Hardy as their chief dramatist (cf. the King's Men and Shakespeare). The method of staging was that of *décor simultané*, or multiple setting (q.v.), as is clear from the sketches of Laurent Mahelot for the production, *c.* 1630, of the *Pandoste* (the *Winter's Tale* story) of Hardy, who also describes the setting:

> Au milleu du théâtre, il faut un beau palais; à un des costez, une grande prison où l'on paroist tout entier. A l'autre costé, un temple; au dessous, une pointe de vaissaeu, une mer basse, des rozeaux et marches de degrez.

This may have been the method of staging plays at Court in Elizabeth's reign, and perhaps in the private theatres. (See HOUSES.)

Hotson, Leslie (b. 1897), Professor of English, Haverford College, Pennsylvania (1931–41) and Shakespeare scholar, was born in Canada and educated at Harvard. He specializes in literary detection, and has discovered who killed Kit

Marlowe, the lost letters of Shelley to Harriet, Shakespeare's relations with Francis Langley, Justice Gardiner, Thomas Russell, Leonard Digges and others, clues to the date of the *Sonnets*, and the first performance of *Twelfth Night*. His *Shakespeare's Wooden O* is a revolutionary reconstruction of the Elizabethan theatre.

Hotspur. In *Richard II*, with his father, Northumberland, he joins Bolingbroke (II, iii), and in v, iii first mentions his rival, Prince Henry.

In *1 Henry IV* he leads the Percy rebellion against Bolingbroke, but, deserted or betrayed by most of his allies, he is killed at Shrewsbury by Prince Henry. Henry Percy (1364–1403), called Hotspur 'for his often pricking', was the eldest son of Henry, 1st Earl of Northumberland, and nephew of the Earl of Worcester. He married Elizabeth Mortimer, daughter of the 3rd Earl of March. Though Shakespeare makes him of the same age as Prince Henry (b. 1387), he was older than Henry IV (b. 1367).

Housekeepers. The name given to the owners of a theatre. James Burbage, owner of the Theatre, received as rent from the companies of actors who played there all the money taken for entrance to the galleries. Later, the customary rent became half the gallery takings, and this is what Henslowe received at the Rose from the Admiral's until, in 1598, he began to take 'the whole gallereys' in return for the advances he had made. The Chamberlain's-King's had a different arrangement: the actors themselves or some of them, were housekeepers, the Globe and Blackfriars being run as joint stock companies, the shares in which were saleable. The original housekeepers of the Globe (1599) were Cuthbert and Richard Burbage (25 per cent each), and Shakespeare, Phillips, Pope, Heminge, and Kempe (10 per cent each); in the Blackfriars (1608) there were seven equal shares held by the Burbage brothers, Shakespeare, Heminge, Condell, Sly, and Thomas Evans. The sale and alienation of shares led to a dispute in 1635. (See SHARERS' PAPERS.) The housekeepers were responsible for the payment of ground-rent and the upkeep of the theatre.

Houses. The English name for the French *mansions* of medieval plays. Instead of changing the scene, all the different localities were placed on the stage at the same time, and called *houses* or *mansions*. In the Donaueschingen Mystery play there were twenty-two mansions, representing Hell, Heaven, the Garden of Gethsemane, the Sepulchre, the Cross, and so on. This convention of *décor simultané* or multiple setting (q.v.) was used even in Renaissance times, and from the accounts of the Revels Office appears to have been the method of staging plays at Court in Shakespeare's day. These note 'sparres to make frames for the players howses', 'canvas to cover diuers townes and howses', etc. It is probable that *The Comedy of Errors*, performed at Gray's Inn in 1594, was written to be produced in this way, as it was produced by Komisarjevsky at Stratford in 1938. All the action takes place out of doors, and the *houses*, literally houses in this case, can be represented by painted canvas stretched over frames, and grouped about the stage: the Phoenix in the centre, the Porpentine on one side, and the Priory and Centaur on the other. (See ROUNDS; HÔTEL DE BOURGOGNE.)

Howard, Charles. See ADMIRAL'S MEN.

Howard, James (*c.* 1630–*c.* 1680), son of Thomas Howard, 1st Earl of Berkshire, and brother of the better-known dramatist Sir Robert Howard. James Howard wrote two comedies, *All Mistaken* and *The English Monsieur*, the latter of which was seen by Pepys, 8 December 1666, 'a mighty pretty play, very witty and pleasant. And the women do very well; but, above all, little Nelly', that is, Nell Gwyn, who played Lady Wealthy. According to John Downes, *Romeo and Juliet* was made 'into a Tragi-comedy by Mr. James Howard, he preserving Romeo and Juliet alive; so that when the Tragedy was Reviv'd again, 'twas Play'd Alternately, Tragical one Day, and Tragicomical another; for several Days together'.

Howes, Edmund (*c.* 1580–*c.* 1640), chronicler, lived in London. After Stow's death in 1605 he brought out a fifth edition of his *Annales* in 1615 with new matter, and in 1631 the final and most valuable edition of all, 'Continued and Augmented unto 1631' and dedicated to Charles I. A manuscript continuation, written 1656–8, found in a copy of the 1631 edition, describes the destruction of the theatres:

The Globe play house on the Banks side in Southwarke, was burnt downe to the ground, in the yeare 1612. And now built vp againe in the yeare 1613, at the great charge of King Iames, and many Noble men and others. And now pulled downe to the ground, by Sir Matthew Brand, On Munday the 15 of April 1644, to make tenements in the room of it.

The Blacke Friers players playhouse in Blacke Friers, London, which had stood many yeares, was pulled downe to the ground on Munday the 6 day of August 1655, and tennements built in the rome.

The play house in Salsbury Court, in Fleetstreete, was pulled downe by a company of souldiers, set on by the sectuaries of these sad times, On Saterday the 24 day of March 1649.

The Phenix in Druery Lane, was pulled downe also this day, ... by the same souldiers.

The Fortune Playhouse betweene White Crosse streete and Golding Lane was burnd downe to the ground in the yeare 1618. And built againe with brick worke on the outside in the yeare 1622. And now pulled downe on the inside by the souldiers this 1649.

The Hope, on the Banks side in Southwarke, commonly called the Beare Garden, a Play House for Stage Playes on Mundayes, Wedensdayes, Fridayes, and Satredayes, and for the baiting of the Beares on Tuesdayes and Thursdayes, the stage being made to take vp and down when they please. It was built in the year 1610, and now pulled downe to make tennementes, by Thomas Walker, a peticoate maker in Cannon Streete, on Tuesday the 25 day of March 1656. Seuen of Mr. Godfries beares, by the command of Thomas Pride, then the Sheriefe of Surry, were then shot to death, on Saterday the 9 day of February 1655, by a company of souldiers.

In his 1615 edition, Howes mentions 'Willi. Shakespeare gentleman' as one of 'Our moderne, and present excellent Poets which worthely florish in their owne workes'.

Huband, Ralph, 'of Ippesley in the countye of Warr. Esquier', was the man from whom in 1605 Shakespeare bought a leasehold interest in a parcel of tithes. This interest had been left to Ralph by his brother Sir John Huband (d. 1583), steward to the Earls of Warwick and Leicester. Thomas Nash, grandfather of the Thomas Nash who married Shakespeare's granddaughter Elizabeth Hall, was a cousin of Sir John, for whom he was either agent or farmer of the tithes.

Hubert de Burgh. In *King John*. When John captures his nephew Arthur, he hands him over to Hubert with instructions to put him to death. Apparently, however, his written warrant is to *blind* the boy, and this he reluctantly prepares to do, but overcome by pity he cannot bring himself to do it, hides Arthur and tells John that he is *dead*. Naturally, when Arthur is found dead after his attempt to escape, Hubert is suspected by Salisbury and the other lords, from whom he is rescued by the Bastard. Peter of Pomfret is also delivered to Hubert. (The historical Hubert de Burgh (d. 1243) was a descendant of Charlemagne and 'the greatest subject in Europe', regent for Henry III, and Duke of Kent, 1226.)

Hudson, Henry Norman (1814–86), American clergyman and scholar, edited Shakespeare 1852–7. He published his *Lectures on Shakespeare* in 1848.

Hughes, Margaret (d. 1719), was probably the first professional actress to appear on the English stage. In 1660 she played Desdemona with the King's Company, but in 1676 joined the Duke's. She was the mistress of Prince Rupert, by whom she had a daughter, Ruperta.

Hughes, William. It has been suggested, not very plausibly, that the Mr W. H. of the *Sonnets* was William Hughes, a boy actor who played women's parts. The so-called 'Will sonnets' (135–6, 143) supply the 'William'. The 'Hughes' is derived from the line in Sonnet 20, 'A man in hew all *Hews* in his controwling'. There is, however, no record of a William Hughes likely to have been Shakespeare's friend.

Hugo, François Victor (1828–73), son of the poet, in 1859–66 published a prose translation of Shakespeare, which, in the superlatives of Swinburne, was 'a monument of perfect scholarship, of indefatigable devotion, and of literary genius'.

Hugo, Victor Marie (1802–85), the poet and dramatist, claimed Shakespeare as an ally in the Romantic cause. In his *Préface de Cromwell* (1827) he honoured Shakespeare on the other side idolatry as 'ce dieu du théâtre', and his *William Shakespeare* (1864) is scarcely less exclamatory or more critical. Hugo rescued Shakespeare from the 18th century conception of him as a wild irregular genius and firmly established his reputation in France, but his extravagant eulogies led to his being passively and somewhat uncritically accepted.

Hull, Thomas (1728–1808), actor and dramatist, was born in London and educated at Charterhouse. He first appeared at Covent Garden in 1759 and stayed at that theatre until his death, playing much Shakespeare, though generally secondary parts. He made adaptations of *Timon of Athens* (1786), and of *The Comedy of Errors* (1793).

Humanism. The revolt in the 15th and 16th centuries against the ecclesiastical authority of the Middle Ages; more positively, the realization of the dignity and potentialities of man, stimulated by the discovery of Greek and Roman culture. The interest in the secular drama was part of this movement of thought underlying the Renaissance, and it was the drama that was most bitterly attacked by the opponents of humanism, the Puritans. (See ACTORS.)

Hume, John. In *2 Henry VI*, a priest. He is bribed by Cardinal Beaufort and Suffolk 'to undermine the aspiring humour' of the Duchess of Gloucester to be Queen. He encourages her experiments in black magic and produces the witch Margery Jourdain and the conjurer Bolingbroke. They are discovered at their ceremonies (I, iv), and Hume is sentenced to be 'strangled on the gallows'.

Humour. The original meaning of the word was that of the Latin *humor*, 'liquid' or 'moisture' (cf. *humid*), and in this sense it is sometimes used by Shakespeare: 'the humours of the dank morning' (*Julius Caesar*, II, i). It then came to be used by the old physicians as the moisture in man's body, there being four different kinds of moisture or humour: blood, phlegm, yellow bile (choler), and black bile (melancholy). Humour then came to mean the temper of mind determined by the admixture of these humours, particularly a temper determined by the morbid excess of any one: thus too much black bile would produce a melancholy type. It is in this sense that Ben Jonson uses it in his comedies of humours, where a ruling passion is abstracted and caricatured. Jonson himself explains the word at the beginning of *Every Man out of His Humour*:

> So in every human body,
> The choler, melancholy, phlegm, and blood,
> By reason that they flow continually
> In some one part, and are not continent,

Receive the name of humours. Now thus
far
It may, by metaphor, apply itself
Unto the general disposition:
As when some one peculiar quality
Doth so possess a man, that it doth draw
All his affects, his spirits, and his powers,
In their confluctions, all to run one way,
This may be truly said to be a humour.

Such one-sided, unbalanced characters are inevitably flat and stagey creatures, admirable puppets for Jonson's brilliant satirical comedies. Shakespeare satirized them in the person of the grotesque Corporal Nym, who can scarcely speak without using the refrain 'that's the humour of it'. The 'melancholy Jaques' is perhaps his only essay in 'the humourous man'.

'Humour out of Breath,' a play by John Day, registered 12 April 1608, and published in the same year as 'Humour out of breath. A Comedie Diuers times latelie acted, By the Children of the Kings Reuells. Written by Iohn Day'. There is a character mad 'as the lord that gave all to his followers, and begged more for himself', a possible allusion to *Timon of Athens*. If it is, *Timon* must have been written before the beginning of 1608.

Hunnis, William (d. 1597), musician and poet, became a Gentleman of the Chapel, *c.* 1550, but was imprisoned for his complicity in plots against Queen Mary. On Elizabeth's accession he was freed, and in 1566 succeeded Richard Edwardes as Master of the Children of the Chapel. Under his Mastership, and that of his deputy Farrant (1576–80), the Children continued to give Court performances of plays, some of which may have been written by Hunnis himself, and in addition probably played publicly for profit in their Chapel, and certainly at the first Blackfriars Theatre (1576–84). Hunnis's extant works include *Certain Psalmes in English metre*, *A Hive full of Hunnye*, *Seven Sobbes*, and *Hunnies Recreations*. (See KENILWORTH.)

Hunsdon, Henry Carey, 1st Lord (*c.* 1524–96), son of William Carey and Mary Boleyn, sister of Anne Boleyn, and thus a first cousin of Queen Elizabeth. He was knighted in 1558, created Baron Hunsdon the next year, and in 1561 a Privy Councillor and Knight of the Garter. He became Governor of Berwick in 1568, and in 1585 Lord Chamberlain. On 16 April 1594 died Ferdinando, Earl of Derby, formerly Lord Strange, patron of the company of players known as Strange's and, for a short time, Derby's Men. Soon afterwards Hunsdon became their patron, for at the beginning of June 'my Lorde Chamberlen men' were playing for Henslowe, and on 8 October of the same year Hunsdon wrote to the Lord Mayor of London asking him to allow 'my nowe companie of Players' to continue their practice of playing at the Cross Keys Inn. It was at about this time that Shakespeare joined the Chamberlain's Men, the company with which he was to be associated for the next twenty years. Henry Lord Hunsdon died 22 July 1596, and was succeeded as second Baron by his son George Carey.

Hunsdon, George Carey, 2nd Lord (1547–1603), was Captain-General of the Isle of Wight at the time of the Armada (1588), succeeded his father as Lord Hunsdon in 1596 and, at the same time apparently, took over the patronage of his father's company of players. These were known as Hunsdon's Men from the death of Henry Lord Hunsdon on 22 July 1596 to 17 March 1597, when George Lord Hunsdon became Lord Chamberlain. He married Elizabeth, daughter of Sir John Spencer of Althorp, the patroness of her kinsman Edmund Spenser, and their daughter Elizabeth married Thomas Berkeley in 1596. He was a sick man when James I ascended the throne in March 1603, was relieved of his duties as Lord Chamberlain in April, and died 9 September 1603, four months after the King had assumed the patronage of his company of players.

Hunsdon also had a company of musicians on whom, presumably, his players would be able to draw for their performances. There are records of his entertaining in March 1600 the Flemish Ambassador, Verreyken, to a 'delicate dinner' at Hunsdon House, Blackfriars, 'and there in the After Noone his Plaiers acted, before Vereiken, Sir John Old Castell, to his great Contentment'. And on 29 December 1601, 'The Q. dined this day priuatly at my Ld Chamberlains; I [Dudley Carleton] came euen now from the Blackfriers, where I saw her at the play with all her *candidæ auditrices.*'

Hunsdon's Men. Henry Carey, 1st Lord Hunsdon, had a company of players traceable 1564–7. In 1581 the records begin of a second company, who performed at Court 27 December 1582, and, in conjunction with the Admiral's, on 6 January 1586. They are traceable in the provinces until 1590. Hunsdon had become Lord Chamberlain in July 1585, but this provincial Hunsdon's-Chamberlain's company is distinct from the famous London company formed from Strange's-Derby's in 1594. The latter was known as Hunsdon's from the death of the 1st Lord on 22 July 1596 until 17 March 1597, when the 2nd Lord Hunsdon succeeded Lord Cobham as Lord Chamberlain. This period of nine months is referred to in Q1 (1597) of *Romeo and Juliet*, the title-page of which states that 'it hath been often (with great applause) plaid publiquely, by the right Honourable the L. of Hunsdon his Seruants'.

Hunt, Simon, took his degree at Oxford in 1569, and at Michaelmas 1571 was nominated by the Earl of Warwick and licensed by Bishop Bullingham as Master of Stratford Grammar School after Roche's resignation, Adrian Quiney being bailiff and John Shakespeare his deputy. Hunt was, or became, a Catholic, left the school for Douai in the summer of 1575, went to Rome where he joined the Jesuits, succeeded Parsons as English Penitentiary in 1580, and died in 1585. If Shakespeare went to Stratford Grammar School, he would be under Hunt's influence from the age of seven to eleven.

Hunter, Joseph (1783–1861), the antiquary, was born at Sheffield, in 1809 became a Presbyterian minister at Bath, and moved to London in 1833, when appointed a sub-commissioner of the Public Records. In 1845 he published *New Illustrations of the Life, Studies, and Writings of Shakespeare. Supplementary to all the editions* (2 vols.). The first section deals with the Shakespeare and allied families (see FRENCH); the other three consist of notes on the plays in the manner of the *Illustrations* of Francis Douce (q.v.).

Huntington Library, at San Marino, California, is the creation of Henry E. Huntington, a self-made businessman who left his collection, his home and gardens to the people of California. It includes four great libraries bought *en bloc*, the Elihu D. Church, Devonshire, Halsey and Bridgewater, thus earning the name of 'a library of libraries'. It is particularly rich in books of the Renaissance, and contains copies of all first Quartos of Shakespeare's plays except *Titus Andronicus*, four First Folios, including the Bridgewater, ten Second, including the Perkins, seven Third and eight Fourth. There is also a very fine collection of Elizabethan music. (See EGERTON; COLLIER; ILLUSTRATIONS; SS, 6.)

Huntsmen appear in *The Taming of the Shrew* (Ind. i), and there is a huntsman in *3 Henry VI* (IV, v). Though not mentioned as huntsmen in the stage-directions, the 'train' of Theseus in *A Midsummer Night's Dream* (IV, i) and *The Two Noble Kinsmen* (III, v) are huntsmen, as are the Foresters in *As You Like It*.

'Huon de Bordeaux,' the 13th-century French *chanson de geste* from which, or from Greene's *James IV*, Shakespeare took the name Oberon for his King of the Fairies in *A Midsummer Night's Dream*. Huon, the hero of the romance, unwittingly kills the emperor's son and is condemned to death, but reprieved on condition that he goes to Babylon and brings back a handful of the Amir's beard, four of his back teeth, kisses his daughter three times, and kills his most famous knight. With the aid of the fairy dwarf Oberon, Huon succeeds in his mission. The romance was translated into English *c.* 1540 by Lord Berners as *Huon of Burdeuxe*. A play of '*Hewen of Burdoche*' formed part of Sussex's repertory at Henslowe's Rose, December 1593–February 1594.

Hymen, God of Marriage. In *As You Like It* he restores Rosalind to her father (v, iv). He appears, carrying a burning torch, at the beginning of *The Two Noble Kinsmen*, the action of which begins just after the marriage of Theseus and Hippolyta.

I

Iachimo. In *Cymbeline*, a Roman whom the banished Posthumus meets at the house of his friend Philario. After deceiving Posthumus he joins the army invading Britain, is captured, confesses, and is pardoned.

Iago. In *Othello*, 'a Villaine' (F). (In Cinthio's story he is 'the Ensign' who kills Disdemona with a stocking filled with sand while the Moor looks on. He dies under torture.)

Iambic Foot. A metrical unit of two syllables, the first short, the second long, or in English prosody the first unstressed, the second stressed (˘ -). It is the regular foot of blank verse (q.v.).

Iden, Alexander. In *2 Henry VI*, a Kentish gentleman into whose garden Cade escapes. Iden is reluctant to fight with a starving man, but when Cade attacks him with a sword he kills him. On discovering who he is, he takes his head to the King, who knights him (IV, x; V, i). (Iden was Sheriff of Kent at the time, 1450.)

'If You Know Not Me, You Know Nobody.' A play by Thomas Heywood, the first part of which was registered 5 July 1605, and published by Nathaniel Butter in the same year: 'If you Know not me, You Know no bodie: Or The troubles of Queene Elizabeth.' In a Prologue written later, Heywood complained

> that some by Stenography drew
> The plot: put it in print: (scarce one word trew:).

But Heywood wrote the Prologue for a revival of the play nearly thirty years later, and internal evidence suggests a reconstruction from memory rather than a shorthand report. (See REPORTED TEXTS.)

Illustrations to Shakespeare. The first is of *Titus Andronicus* (*c.* 1595), attributed to Henry Peacham (q.v.). The first book illustration is the title-page of the 1655 edition of *Lucrece*, but Shakespeare illustration really begins with Vandergucht and du Guernier in Rowe's edition of 1709. Francis Hayman's illustrations sold Hanmer's edition of 1744, and since that date there have been innumerable illustrated editions. Hayman also popularized the painting of scenes from Shakespeare, and works by Reynolds, West, Wheatley, Smirke, Peters, Fuseli and others were among the most popular at the Royal Academy after its opening in 1769, also the year of Garrick's Stratford Jubilee. Twenty years later Alderman Boydell opened his Shakespeare Gallery (q.v.). Fuseli is popular in Italy today. Cesare Lodovici's recent translation of Shakespeare is illustrated with Fuseli's plates, and Giulio Argan has written on 'Fuseli, Shakespeare's Painter'. In the Huntington Library are prints contained in the extra-illustrated book collection, notably George Steevens's *Dramatic Works of Shakespeare Revived* (1802), extended to 44 large folio volumes, and Knight's *Pictorial Edition*, extended from 8 to 100 volumes. (See W. M. Merchant, *Shakespeare and The Artist*, 1959.)

Imagery. It is a fair generalization that much of Shakespeare's early imagery, particularly in the poems, is conventional, drawn from the common stock of Elizabethan literary images, and often expressed in the leisurely form of simile and conceit; for example, in *Venus and Adonis*:

The night of sorrow now is turn'd to day:
Her two blue windows faintly she up-
heaveth,
Like the fair sun, when in his fresh array
He cheers the morn, and all the earth
relieveth:
And as the bright sun glorifies the sky,
So is her face illumined with her eye.

In the plays of the middle period the conventional and literary gives place to the original and observed image, generally in the more dramatic, because more compressed and rapid, form of metaphor:

better be with the dead,
Whom we, to gain our peace, have sent to
peace,
Than on the torture of the mind to lie
In restless ecstasy. Duncan is in his grave;
After life's fitful fever he sleeps well ...

In *Antony and Cleopatra* and the later romances, Shakespeare sometimes wonderfully combines the early lyrical imagery with the later dramatic form, as when Charmian speaks of Cleopatra dead:

Now boast thee, death, in thy possession
lies
A lass unparallel'd. Downy windows, close;
And golden Phœbus never be beheld
Of eyes again so royal.

It should be observed that a sequence of Shakespearean images is rarely a succession of flashing and isolated pictures, but a coherent pattern, as in Prospero's speech, where the dissolution of the great *globe* is related to our little life *rounded* with a sleep.

The study of Shakespeare's imagery has been stimulated by the discovery of the workings of the unconscious mind, though this psychological approach was anticipated in the 18th century by Walter Whiter, whose *Specimen of a Commentary on Shakspeare* is based on a 'new principle of criticism derived from Mr. Locke's Doctrine of the Association of Ideas' (1794). Whiter shows that certain ideas were always associated in Shakespeare's mind; for example, flatterers suggested dogs, and dogs suggested sweetmeats, as in *1 Henry IV* (I, iii) and *Antony and Cleopatra* (IV, xii):

Why, what a candy deal of courtesy
This fawning greyhound then did proffer
me!
The hearts
That spaniel'd me at heels, to whom I gave
Their wishes, do discandy, melt their sweets
On blossoming Cæsar.

The most methodical study of the subject is Caroline Spurgeon's *Shakespeare's Imagery* (1935), in which she shows that in addition to recurrent symbolic imagery common to all, or to groups of plays, certain plays, notably the tragedies, have imagery peculiar to themselves. Thus, in *Romeo and Juliet* the dominating image is light, in *Hamlet* sickness and disease. In *The Frontiers of Drama* (1945) Una Ellis-Fermor developed the work of Miss Spurgeon, who did not live to complete it, and in *Shakespeare's Imagination* (1946) E. A. Armstrong developed Whiter's theory in what he called 'image-clusters'.

Since 1930 imagery has been one of the main themes of Shakespeare criticism. This is an aspect of the revulsion from 'Bradleyism' and traditional criticism with its emphasis on character (though M. M. Morozov applies imagery to the revelation of character: for example, the artificial imagery of Laertes and natural imagery of Hamlet). The new criticism 'interprets' the plays as poems, in terms of imagery and symbolism. Thus, in *The Wheel of Fire* (1930)

Wilson Knight wrote: 'we should see each play as an expanded metaphor'; 'we should regard each play as a visionary unit, close-knit in personification, atmospheric suggestion, and direct poetic-symbolism.' Apart from Spurgeon's, perhaps the most influential books have been those of Knight and Wolfgang Clemen. Knight's interpretation verges on mysticism, but Clemen is not given to rapture. In *Shakespeares Bilder* (1936) he looks for 'a truly organic method of understanding the images, considers the plays chronologically, and traces the imagery from the merely iterative to the fully symphonic.' By its insistence on the poetry the new criticism has been salutary, but there is now a reaction against the over-insistence on imagery and symbolism. (See CRITICISM; J. L. LOWES.)

Imogen. The heroine of *Cymbeline*, and according to Swinburne, 'the woman best beloved in all the world of song and all the tide of time'. (Simon Forman calls her Innogen. See RARE TRIUMPHS.)

Impressa. See RUTLAND.

Imprint. The name of the publisher of a book, with the date and place of publication. In Shakespeare's time this was printed at the bottom of the title-page (q.v.), and generally included the name or initials of the printer and address of the publisher, or of the bookseller who was to sell it on commission. Thus, the imprint of *Shakespeare's Sonnets* reads:

At London
By *G. Eld* for *T.T.* and are
to be solde by *William Aspley*.
1609.

But there was another bookseller, and some imprints read: 'and are to be solde by Iohn Wright, dwelling at Christ Church gate. 1609'. Similarly, when there were two or more publishers there would be different imprints for each one.

Income of Shakespeare. It is impossible accurately to compare the purchasing power of money at the beginning of the 17th with that in the middle of the 20th century, but it would probably not be far wrong to say that £1 then was worth about £20 of our money. Sidney Lee estimated Shakespeare's average income before 1599 at £130, and 'at a later period of his life' at £600. This, however, appears to be a great over-estimate. Working from the figures given in the suit of 1635, Chambers calculates that if Shakespeare had been alive in the playing year May 1634–May 1635, as an actor-sharer he would have received £90, as a housekeeper in the Globe £25, and in the Blackfriars £90: a total of £205, including rewards for Court performances. There would be no profit from apprentices, as they paid no premium; the King's Men were Grooms of the Chamber, but without fee; and it is probable that after 1603 Shakespeare was a playwright-sharer rather than an actor-sharer, giving his plays to the company in lieu of his services as an actor. Moreover, this was a full playing year, no plague, and no inhibitions for other reasons, and prices had risen in the twenty-five years since Shakespeare had taken an active part in the affairs of the company. On the other hand, there were fewer housekeepers in the Globe and Blackfriars in 1610, and profits would be correspondingly greater. On the whole, it seems probable that £200 would be about the largest income Shakespeare ever received, and the average for 1600–10 would be considerably less. (See PAY OF ACTORS.)

'Inganni.' In his *Diary*, 2 February 1602, John Manningham (q.v.) of the Middle Temple wrote:

At our feast wee had a play called 'Twelue Night, or What You Will', much like the Commedy of Errores, or Menechmi in Plautus, but most like and neere to that in Italian called *Inganni*.

He probably refers to *Gl'Ingannati*, a comedy written by a member of the Sienese academy of Intronati, who produced it in 1531. The play is the source of Bandello's novel, from which Barnabe Riche took his story of Apolonius and Silla, in its turn the source of *Twelfth Night.*

Ingleby, Clement Mansfield (1823–86), Shakespeare scholar, was born in Birmingham, educated at Trinity, Cambridge, and for some years practised as a lawyer. In 1859 he abandoned law for literature, in that year exposing J. P. Collier's forgeries in *The Shakespeare Fabrications*, following it in 1861 with *A complete View of the Shakspere Controversy*. In 1875 came his *Shakespeare Hermeneutics*, and his *Centurie of Prayse*, an anthology of allusions to Shakespeare, 1591–1693. The two volumes of his *Shakespeare, The Man and the Book* appeared in 1877 and 1881. *Shakespeare's Bones* (1882) was a proposal to dig up the poet's body in order to examine his skull. He was one of the original Birthplace trustees, and a vice-president of the New Shakspere Society.

Ingon. A hamlet two miles north-east of Stratford, in the parish of Hampton Lucy. In 1570 a John Shaxpere, or his assigns, was tenant of Ingon Meadow, a 14-acre estate belonging to William Clopton. As the rent was £8, there was probably a house attached to it. The son and daughter of Henry Shakespere were christened at Hampton Lucy in 1582 and 1585, the son being buried in 1589 as 'Jeames Shakespere of Yngon'. It is possible that this John was the poet's father, and that Henry was John's brother, his assign, who occupied the Ingon farm. According to Halliwell-Phillipps,

> The Rev. S. Cooper, of Loxley, writing to Jordan in 1788, mentions a farm 'at Ingon containing now about two hundred acres of land adjoining to the old park, now deparked, from which it is said William Shakespere stole Mr Lucy's deer'.

But Charlecote is three miles east of Ingon. (See HAMPTON LUCY.)

Ingram, John Kells (1823–1907), Irish scholar, economist and poet, was educated at Trinity College, Dublin, where he became Vice-Provost. He was a member of the New Shakspere Society, and read a paper *On the Weak Endings of Shakspere* at their tenth meeting in November 1874. His table of light and weak endings (*N.S.S. Trans.*, 1874, p. 450) is generally accepted.

'Ingratitude of a Common-wealth, The.' An adaptation (1681) of *Coriolanus* by Nahum Tate (q.v.).

'Injured Princess, The.' An adaptation (1682) of *Cymbeline* by Thomas D'Urfey (q.v.).

Inner Stage. It is clear that the stage of the Elizabethan theatre had some sort of compartment that could be used as a cave (*Tempest*), tomb (*Romeo and Juliet*), or room, sometimes called the 'study' (cf. *Titus Andronicus*, v, ii: *They knocke and Titus opens his studie doore*). This may have been an alcove in the tiring-house wall, across which curtains could be drawn. But the only contemporary picture that we have of the interior of an Elizabethan theatre, de Witt's sketch of the Swan, *c.* 1596, shows no central opening. The details of this sketch cannot be trusted as a safe guide, yet it is not clear how a scene played in an alcove could have been visible to many of the spectators, unless it were very shallow and wide. Perhaps it was little more than a corridor with a door at either end, and one in the middle. G. F. Reynolds suggests that, at the Red Bull at least, the inner stage was a curtained frame that could be set up at the back of the outer stage. The frontispieces to Alabaster's *Roxana* (1632), a Cambridge play, and Richards's *Messalina* (1640), a public play, have curtains. More elaborate scenery and properties could be used on the inner than on the outer stage, as it could be set while the curtains were drawn. (See STAGE.)

Innogen. The first stage-direction in Q and F of *Much Ado* reads: *Enter Leonato Gouernour of Messina, Innogen his wife,*

Hero his daughter, and Beatrice his Neece. Again at the beginning of Act II: *Enter Leonato, his brother, his wife.* Yet Innogen does not speak, is not spoken to, and is not referred to by the other characters. This supports Wilson's argument that Shakespeare revised his play, though it may be that he simply struck out Hero's mother – she has one in the Bandello story – when he found that a sensible woman, as she would have to be, would be in the way.

Inns of Court. The hostels or colleges established in Edward I's reign, *c.* 1300, for the accommodation of law students. Sir John Fortescue, *c.* 1470, wrote that the students learned not only law and divinity, but also music and dancing, 'so that these hostels, being nurseries or seminaries of the Court, are therefore called Inns of Court'. The members of an Inn of Court are benchers, barristers and students, the benchers being senior members who manage the affairs of the society. There are four Inns of Court: Gray's Inn, Middle Temple, Inner Temple and Lincoln's Inn. The Inns, particularly the first two, were famous for their elaborate masques and revels, and it was at Gray's Inn that *The Comedy of Errors* was played by the Chamberlain's on 28 December 1594 (see 'GESTA GRAYORUM'). And John Manningham (q.v.) of the Middle Temple records a performance of *Twelfth Night* at their feast on 2 February (Candlemas) 1602. In the early 17th century the Inner Temple had a play at Candlemas or on All Saints' Day (1 November), often on both, on which they spent £5, and after 1612, £6 13s. 4d. In 1614 and 1615 the players were the King's Men. In 1565 and 1566 the Children of the Chapel under Richard Edwardes played at Lincoln's Inn, and Farrant took them in 1580. Sometimes, of course, the Inns of Court men produced their own plays.

Inn-Theatres. The first building erected as a playhouse in London was James Burbage's Theatre in 1576. Before this, plays were acted in private houses, public halls and above all at the inns, where there was lodging for the players, drink for the spectators, and the yard surrounded by galleries made an admirable auditorium. An inn would be hired for a period by a company of players, and it seems certain that some of the inn-yards were converted into something like permanent theatres. The following list gives the most important inns known to have been used as theatres, (*a*) within the City, (*b*) in the suburbs outside the City jurisdiction, and the dates of the earliest records of their being so used:

(*a*)	1557	Boar's Head, Aldgate
	1575	Bull, Bishopsgate St
	1576	Bell, Gracechurch St
	1579	Cross Keys, Gracechurch St
	1579	Bel Savage, Ludgate Hill
(*b*)	1557	Saracen's Head, Islington
	1557	Boar's Head, Whitechapel
	1567	Red Lion, Stepney

In 1574 the City Corporation issued regulations to control the performance of plays because of 'ffrayes and quarrelles, eavell practizes of incontinencye in greate Innes, havinge chambers and secrete places adioyninge to their open stagies and gallyries'. This seems to have led the shrewd James Burbage to build his Theatre in 1576 in Shoreditch, outside the City jurisdiction. Other theatres were built outside the walls, but the City inns were convenient in the winter, with its bad weather and short days, and they continued to be used; for example, the Chamberlain's were using the Cross Keys in the winter of 1594. In 1596, however, the City Corporation secured the consent of the Privy Council to the prohibition of plays within the City, and 'the Play-houses in *Gracious street*, *Bishops-gate-street*, nigh *Paules*, that on *Ludgate* hill, the *White-Friars* were put down'. (See RAWLIDGE, and under names of inns.)

Instrumental Music. The favourite Elizabethan instruments were the lute, viol, recorder and hautboy. Strings and wind instruments were rarely combined as in modern music, but played in 'consort', that is, in groups of the same family; thus a consort of viols was composed of the different-sized instruments of the viol family. *Whole consort* was when the instruments were all strings or all wind. *Broken consort* or *broken music* was that played by both strings and wind. Shakespeare's company probably had one or two musicians permanently attached – it is probable that Augustine Phillipps was musician as well as actor – and when they needed supplementing, there were musicians to be hired. After 1608, when the company took over the Blackfriars theatre, they probably kept more musicians in permanent employment; the twenty-one hired men mentioned by Herbert in 1624 were 'musitions and other necessary attendantes'. (See PROTECTION OF PLAYERS.)

Interlude Players. Critically, the term Interlude is used to designate the kind of play that, in the 15th and 16th centuries, formed the transition between the medieval Moralities and the Elizabethan drama. It was a short secular play, usually comic, and, as the name suggests, meant to be acted in the intervals of some other entertainment: for example, Thomas Medwall's *Fulgens and Lucres*, *c.* 1495, was to be played in the two intervals between three rounds of feasting in the hall of Cardinal Morton. The best-known writer of interludes was John Heywood (q.v.), and his best-known interlude *The Four P's*. More loosely the term was used, as early as the 14th century, to describe any kind of play, and by the Puritans as a term of abuse.

Many of the nobility had interlude players among their retainers: the Earl of Oxford had a troupe in 1492, but the earliest records are those of a company belonging to Henry Bourchier, Earl of Essex, in 1468. The first royal company of interlude players, or Lusores Regis, was that of Henry VII, established apparently in 1493 and consisting of four men. Henry VIII increased the number to eight, and the company used to visit the houses of the nobility, monasteries, and perform publicly in town halls. In the latter half of the century they were sadly neglected; Mary was too fanatical to be interested in plays, and Elizabeth preferred the Boys' companies. Though she kept eight interlude players on her establishment, they appear not to have performed at Court after 1559, though they can be traced in the provinces up to 1573, and the last of them died in 1580. A new company, the Queen's Men, was formed in 1583.

Interpolations. As cuts were made for the acting version of a play as written by Shakespeare, so additions were made by other hands, many of them no doubt in the ten years between Shakespeare's retirement and the printing of the Folio (1613–23). For example, the hearty octosyllabics of Hecate in *Macbeth* quite clearly are an interpolation, almost certainly by Middleton. Before she 'retires' there is music and a song, examples of another kind of interpolation that became increasingly popular in the 17th century. Again the spectacle in *Cymbeline* v, iv:

> Iupiter descends in Thunder and Lightning, sitting uppon an Eagle. hee throwes a Thunder-bolt. The Ghostes fall on their knees,

may have been interpolated to tickle the deteriorating palates of the Jacobean courtly and popular audiences. Gags are not so likely to have got into the printed text, as they would rarely be in the 'copy' from which it was set up; though apparent gags occur in the 'bad' Quartos, where we should expect to find them (see HORNER). The amount of interpolation in the Folio is not very great, but in the hundred years after the Restoration Shakespeare's plays were mercilessly cut, stuffed with interpolated spectacle and music, and otherwise adapted. Indeed, it may be said that only in the 20th century has it become customary to play the text approximately as Shakespeare wrote it, when the dreary realism of most 19th-century actor-managers gave place to a producers' competition in the distractingly fantastic.

Intervals. In the Elizabethan public theatres it seems probable that there were, sometimes at least, short intervals between the acts, though the players did not necessarily leave the stage: cf. *M.N.D.* '*They sleepe all the Act*', i.e. the lovers lie on the stage throughout the interval between acts 3 and 4. In the plot of *The Dead Man's Fortune* (see p. 376) the end of an act is marked by crosses and a marginal note for music. Intervals for music, however, were much more of a feature in the boys' private theatres (see 'MALCONTENT'), and as the practice was popular, intervals were probably extended in the Jacobean public theatres. (See MUSIC; ORGAN.)

Inverted Commas are rare in the early texts, but sometimes, in their double form, are placed at the beginning of a line to indicate an aphorism or proverbial saying.

'Iphis and Iantha.' On 29 June 1660 the bookseller Humphrey Moseley registered 'Iphis and Iantha, or a marriage without a man, a Comedy. by Will: Shakspeare'. There is no other record of the play, which certainly was not written by Shakespeare.

Iras. In *Antony and Cleopatra*, one of Cleopatra's attendants. She plays a smaller part than Charmian. In the last scene she dresses Cleopatra in her 'best attires', then when the Queen bids her farewell and kisses her, she falls and dies.

Ireland, William. Citizen and haberdasher of London to whom, on 12 December 1604, Henry Walker granted a twenty-five years' lease of the Blackfriars Gate-house at a rent of £7. He seems to have surrendered the lease when Shakespeare bought the property in March 1613. His name is preserved in Ireland Yard, the entrance to which from St Andrew's Hill was probably spanned by the Gate-house.

Ireland, William Henry (1777–1835), son of Samuel Ireland, engraver, antiquary and author. He was born in London, where he became a conveyancer's clerk. In 1794, when he was only seventeen, he accompanied his father on a visit to Stratford, where they were shown round by John Jordan (q.v.), a local poet and unreliable antiquary. In the following year Samuel published his *Picturesque Views on the Warwickshire Avon*, an account of his visit with illustrations of Anne Hathaway's Cottage, the lodge (at Fulbrook) where Shakespeare was confined when caught deer-stealing, and so on. His son was more enterprising; as a lawyer's clerk he was well acquainted with old documents and handwriting, and was able to forge leases, contracts between Shakespeare, Heminge and Condell, letters written to Southampton and Anne Hathaway (with a lock of hair), and Shakespeare's profession of faith. These, he said, came from a gentleman to whose ancestor they had been left by Shakespeare, who had rescued him from drowning. His credulous father exhibited the manuscripts at his house in 1795, and in 1796 published them as *Miscellaneous Papers and Legal Instruments under the Hand and Seal of William Shakespeare*. In the same year a Shakespearean tragedy came to light, *Vortigern and Rowena*, which was bought by Sheridan and produced at Drury Lane, where it was received with laughter. Ireland had also written a Shakespearean history, *Henry II*, but this was not produced. Many scholars, including George Chalmers, were deceived, but Malone recognized the forgery and wrote his *Inquiry into the Authenticity of Certain Miscellaneous Papers and Legal Instruments* (1796). Samuel Ireland became suspicious, and when pressed, his son confessed his fraud, and published *An Authentic Account of the Shakespearian Manuscripts* (1796), in which he showed that his father was innocent of complicity.

Samuel wrote *A Vindication of his Conduct* (1796), and died in 1800, his end probably hastened by the disgrace. Chalmers wrote *An Apology for the Believers in the Shakespeare Papers*, in which he ingeniously argued that, although the papers were forgeries, they might well have been genuine. Driven from home and his profession, Ireland turned to literature, wrote *Confessions of William Henry Ireland* (1805), and a number of unsuccessful novels, and died in poverty. (See J. Mair, *The Fourth Forger*, 1938.)

Iris. In the Masque in *The Tempest* (IV, i), the personification of the rainbow, 'the watery arch and messenger' of Juno. She summons Ceres, naiads and sunburn'd sicklemen to celebrate the betrothal of Ferdinand and Miranda.

'Iron Age, The.' A play in two parts by Thomas Heywood, written probably *c.* 1613, and published 1632, Part I as 'The Iron Age, Contayning the Rape of Hellen: The siege of Troy: The Combate betwixt Hector and Aiax: Hector and Troilus slayne by Achilles: Achilles slaine by Paris: Aiax and Vlesses contend for the Armour of Achilles: The Death of Aiax, &c.'. There are some resemblances to Shakespeare's *Troilus and Cressida*, but if *The Iron Age* is as late as 1613, Heywood borrowed from Shakespeare, not Shakespeare from Heywood, though it has been conjectured that the anonymous *Troy*, produced by the Admiral's in 1596, was an early version of *The Iron Age*.

Irving, Henry (1838–1905), the actor, whose original name was John Henry Brodribb, was born at Keinton-Mandeville in Somerset. After a short period as a clerk in London, he turned to the stage and first appeared, as 'Henry Irving', in Lytton's *Richelieu* at Sunderland in 1856. After ten years in the provinces he found engagements in London, and in 1871 began his connexion with the Lyceum, the fortunes of which he revived by his success as Mathias in *The Bells*. Irving then turned to Shakespeare, and between 1874 and 1877 his playing of Hamlet, Macbeth, Othello and Richard III established him as one of the leading actors of the day. From 1878 to 1902, when he was his own manager at the Lyceum, he produced a series of Shakespearean plays in association with Ellen Terry: *Hamlet*, *The Merchant of Venice* (1879), *Othello*, *Romeo and Juliet*, *Much Ado*, *Twelfth Night*, *Macbeth*, *Henry VIII*, *King Lear*, *Cymbeline* and *Coriolanus* (1901). He was knighted in 1895, the first actor to be so honoured, and died suddenly after performing at the Theatre Royal, Bradford, in 1905.

Irving inherited the Charles Kean tradition of spectacular production; in *Macbeth*, for example, he brought back the flying and singing witches, and *Henry VIII*, which ran for 172 performances in 1892, cost more than £30,000. His lighting and settings were said to be the finest in Europe. As an actor he was mannered and prepared to sacrifice Shakespeare's text to find time for patches of significant mime.

Irving had two sons, Henry Brodribb (1870–1919), and Laurence (1871–1914), both of them actors and authors.

Irving, Washington (1783–1859), American author, spent the years 1815–32 in England. *The Sketch Book*, published in 1820, contains an account of his visit to Stratford in 1815 (see HORNBY).

Isabel (1370–1435). In *Henry V*, Queen of Charles VI of France. She appears only in the last scene, where she gives her blessing to the proposed marriage of her daughter Katharine to Henry V.

Isabella. The heroine of *Measure for Measure*. (The Cassandra of Whetstone's *Promos and Cassandra*, and Epitia of Cinthio's *novella* and play, in all three of which she sacrifices her honour for her brother, who, however, is executed.)

'Isle of Dogs, The.' A lost play by Thomas Nashe. The Privy Council, considering that it contained 'very seditious and sclanderous matter', on 28 July 1597, after a performance, ordered the closing of all the theatres 'during this time of sommer'. The players, Pembroke's at the Swan, were 'comytted to pryson, whereof one of them was not only an actor, but a maker of parte of the said plaie'. This last was Ben Jonson, who was released from the Marshalsea with Gabriel Spencer and Robert Shaw on 3 October. Nashe escaped to Yarmouth. This is a good example of the sensitiveness of Elizabeth and the Privy Council to political criticism, and of the dangers besetting playwrights and players.

Italian Script. In Shakespeare's day most people, like Shakespeare himself, wrote an English hand, though the Italian form was just coming into popular use, and sometimes the two were mixed. In play manuscripts, the dialogue of which is generally in English script, Italian script is often used as italics in print to differentiate proper names, speech-prefixes, and stage-directions.

Italics. Both in the Quartos and Folio, italics are normally used for proper names, speech-prefixes, songs, letters and stage-directions, though occasionally the Quartos use roman type for the last. The following extract comes from the Folio version of *Hamlet*:

Enter Ophelia diſtracted

Ophe. Where is the beauteous Maieſty of Denmark.

Qu. How now *Ophelia*!

Ophe. *How ſhould I your true loue know from another one?*

By his Cockle hat and ſtaffe, and his Sandal ſhoone.

Qu. Alas ſweet Lady: what imports this Song?

Ophe. Say you? Nay pray you marke.

He is dead and gone Lady, he is dead and gone,
At his head a graſſe-greene Turfe, at his heeles a ſtone.

Enter King.

This page, 273 in the Tragedies, was set by compositor B. Compositor A had a greater liking for italics, and would probably have set *Denmark* in italics.

Italy. 'Why did the Italians of the Renaissance do nothing above the second rank in tragedy?' asks Burckhardt in his *Civilization of the Renaissance*. 'Why did Italy produce no Shakespeare?' Apart from the obvious answer that all Europe produced but one Shakespeare, partly, he replies, because the Italians of the Middle Ages smothered their religious drama in a wealth of decorative splendour which they applied to the secular drama when it appeared, stifling their plays with fantastic intermezzi, or interludes; partly because of the pedantry of the academies, which favoured the performance of classical plays, often in Latin; but chiefly because the Counter Reformation with its Inquisitors and Spanish rulers withered the best flowers of the Italian spirit. The Italians, therefore, had little to offer the Elizabethans in the way of the legitimate drama, and indeed there was a real danger that the neo-classical doctrines of their critics would wither the infant drama of England as well. The spontaneous and popular Italian drama, however, the *commedia dell'arte* (q.v.) and its stock characters, Pantalone, the Doctor, the Capitano, and so on, did influence the English comedy of manners, and even Shakespeare's romantic comedies. There were Italian actors and actresses (see NORTON) in England in the seventies of the 16th century, including Drusiano, the well-known Arlecchino of the *commedia dell'arte*. And again, Italian methods of staging influenced Inigo Jones and the 17th-century English theatre. (See SERLIO; PALLADIO.)

Though Shakespeare owed little to the Italian drama, yet he was under a great debt to the Italians, for, as Croce writes, 'it seems undeniable that the historical origin of Shakespeare is to be found in the Renaissance, which is generally admitted to have been chiefly an Italian movement. Shakespeare got from Italy, not only a great part, both of his form and of his material, but what is of greater moment, many thoughts that went to form his vision of reality. In addition to this, he obtained from Italy that literary education, to which all English writers of his time submitted.' The sonnet came from Italy, as did the classical concept of a play as an architectural whole, 'the representation of an action with a beginning, a middle, and an end'; and the works of Ariosto, Bandello, Boccaccio, Cinthio and Petrarch supplied him with an almost inexhaustible amount of romantic material. Mario Praz concludes (SS, 7) that Shakespeare knew some Italian and was acquainted with Italian literature, but only superficially, for he generally resorted to English translations. There is no evidence that he visited Italy, and he probably got his information about the country from John Florio, as did Ben Jonson.

The Italians of the 17th and 18th centuries, like the French, dominated by neo-classical rules, thought of Shakespeare as a wild, irregular genius when they thought of him at all, but for the most part they neglected him. There was an Italian blank verse translation of a French adaptation of *Hamlet* in 1774; but the Romantic movement in Europe stimulated interest, and a translation of the plays in verse was made by Michele Leoni (1819–22), and in prose by Carlo Rusconi (1831); and Verdi's operas, *Otello* and *Falstaff*, have helped to popularize Shakespeare.

In the 20th century critics and scholars have produced valuable contributions. Benedetto Croce's important *Ariosto, Shakespeare, and Corneille*, censuring the 'realists' and emphasizing Shakespeare's art, appeared in 1919, and Napoleone Orsini (*La Critica Shakespeariana*) develops similar themes. There have also been many new translations: *Shakespeare Teatro*, the complete plays edited by Mario Praz, was completed in 1948, Cesare Lodovici's translation was published, with Fuseli's illustrations, in 1960, and Eugenio Montale and Alberto Rossi have recently translated the Sonnets. Another translator is Gabriele Baldini, who in many ways has done much to popularize Shakespeare, as has John Gielgud with his recitals in various Italian towns in 1959–60. As a result of all this, Shakespeare is now frequently performed in Italy, not only on the stage – there is an annual Shakespeare Festival at Verona – but also on film, radio and television. (See FLORIO; RISTORI; SALVINI; CINEMA.)

J

'Jack Drum's Entertainment.' An anonymous play, but almost certainly by Marston, registered 8 September 1600, and published in 1601: 'Iacke Drums Entertainment: Or the Comedie of Pasquill and Katherine. As it hath bene sundry times plaide by the Children of Powles'. It is just possible that the remark about Parolles in III, vi of *All's Well*, 'if you give him not John Drum's entertainment', is an allusion to Marston's play; if so, it helps to date the elusive *All's Well*. But 'to give John Drum's entertainment' was a fairly common cant phrase for 'to give a good beating'. The play is interesting as an episode in the *Poetomachia* (q.v.), being Marston's reply to Jonson's criticism in *Every Man out of His Humour*. The cuckold, Brabant Senior, is meant to be Jonson.

Jackson, Barry Vincent (1879–1961), theatre manager and playwright, was born at Birmingham, where he founded the Birmingham Repertory Company in 1913. He was a Governor of the Old Vic and Sadler's Wells, Director of the Shakespeare Memorial Theatre 1946–8 and manager of the Malvern Summer Festivals 1929–37. Knighted 1925. (See PRODUCTION; SS, 6, 8.)

Jackson, John (1576–1625). With Heminge and William Johnson of the Mermaid Tavern, he acted as trustee when Shakespeare bought the Blackfriars Gatehouse in 1613. He was a wealthy 'gentleman of London' with shipping interests in Hull, and married Jane, the widow of the brewer Jacob James, brother of Elias James (q.v.). He was one of the Mermaid Tavern set, a patron of John Taylor the water poet, and a friend of Tom Coryat, to whose *Crudities* he contributed 'Panegyircke Verses'.

Jackson, Roger. Bookseller, 1601–25. In 1614 Harrison transferred *Lucrece* to Jackson, for whom Snodham printed O5, 1616.

Jacobean Drama. The drama of Elizabeth's reign was the reflection of an heroic age, a spontaneous growth healthily fostered by Court and people alike; though actors were by law in the service of some nobleman, they did not play for him and his friends alone, but for the whole of London, and the dramatists supplied the material for this mixed audience. There was only one company under royal patronage, the Queen's Men, established in 1583, and even they had a short life, the competition of Strange's and the Admiral's reducing them to the status of provincial players ten years later. There was a change with the accession of James I in 1603. The three leading companies, the Chamberlain's, Admiral's, and Worcester's, were all taken under royal patronage as the King's, Prince Henry's and Queen's, and to these were added in 1610–11 the Duke of York's and the Lady Elizabeth's. The actor-sharers in these companies became Grooms of the Chamber, and this, together with the great increase in the number of Court performances, led inevitably to plays being written with an eye on a courtly audience.

That this courtly audience was not what it had been in Elizabeth's day we have the testimony of Sir John Harington (q.v.) and others. The heroic age was finished. Masque and spectacle, dance and song, and a delightful titillation of trivial emotions were demanded – and after 1608 supplied, notably by Beaumont and Fletcher. This was the year in which the King's Men took over the Blackfriars, and it was for the Court and this theatre, with its more exclusive audience, that Beaumont and Fletcher supplied their romances and tragi-comedies. In the years 1603–8, Shakespeare offered *Othello*, *Timon*, *Lear*, *Macbeth*, *Antony and Cleopatra* and *Coriolanus*, but in 1608 he, too, turned to romance, but romance very different in spirit from that of Fletcher.

Though there are numerous exceptions, Shakespeare himself, and one hesitates to include Webster, it is true that the drama, at any rate after about 1608, begins to decline; for the strength, virility, vitality and health of the earlier drama, there is sometimes a softness, effeminacy, morbidity of violence or sentiment, a sickly and laboured prettiness. With Fletcher the medium itself, blank verse, declines into a sweet surfeit of feminine endings calculated to start a delicious tear.

Jaggard, William and Isaac, printers, at the sign of the Half-Eagle and Key in Barbican. The first association of W. Jaggard with Shakespeare was his publication in 1599 of an octavo edition of *The Passionate Pilgrime*. Although the volume was said to be 'by W. Shakespeare', it is doubtful whether more than five of the twenty poems are his. In 1612 Jaggard himself printed a 'newly corrected and augmented' edition, the 'augmentation' being two pieces from Heywood's *Troia Britannica* which Jaggard had printed in 1609. Heywood protested in his *Apology for Actors* (q.v.), and perhaps also Shakespeare, whom Heywood knew to be 'much offended with M. *Jaggard*', for Jaggard seems to have replaced the title-page with its ascription to Shakespeare by one without his name.

About 1605 Jaggard took over the printing business of James Roberts, and some ten years later, with his friend Thomas Pavier and his son Isaac, who had recently become his partner, he conceived the idea of publishing a collected edition of some of Shakespeare's plays. Eventually these were issued as Quartos, many of them with false imprints, but there is ample bibliographical evidence, as revealed by Pollard, Greg and W. Neidig, to show that they all came from Jaggard's press in 1619; they are all the same size and slightly taller than the normal Quarto, carry Jaggard's device, and are printed on paper with the same water-mark; *The Whole Contention* and *Pericles* even have continuous signatures. The plays and their imprints are:

The Whole Contention betweene ... Lancaster and Yorke [*2, 3 Henry VI*]. Printed at London, for T.P.

Pericles. Printed for T.P. 1619.

A Yorkshire Tragedie. Printed for T.P. 1619.

The Merry Wiues of Windsor. Printed for Arthur Johnson, 1619.

The first part of ... Sir Iohn Old-castle. London, printed for T.P. 1600.

Henry the fift. Printed for T.P. 1608.

King Lear. Printed for Nathaniel Butter 1608.

The Merchant of Venice. Printed by J. Roberts, 1600.

A Midsommer nights dreame. Printed by James Roberts, 1600.

Of these ten plays, five, those printed 'for T.P.', were Thomas Pavier's copyright, and no doubt Jaggard was ready to risk those printed by his predecessor Roberts, though Laurence Heyes at once appealed and established his claim to *The Merchant of Venice*. But *A Yorkshire Tragedy*, *Oldcastle* and perhaps the first two acts of *Pericles* were not by Shakespeare; four of the others were reprints of 'bad' Quartos, *The Whole Contention*, *The Merry Wives* and *Henry V*; and *Lear* was a poor Quarto. Probably the King's Men protested, certainly Lord Chamberlain Pembroke wrote to the Stationers' Company on 3 May 1619, ordering them to prevent the reprinting of Shakespeare's plays without the King's Men's consent. It seems probable that the plays dated '1619' had already been issued when the Jaggards heard of this, and that they altered the dates on the others so that they might be confused with copies of the earlier editions.

According to the ideas of the time there was nothing particularly dishonest about the venture, and the Jaggards were the printers of the First Folio of 1623, which was 'Printed at the Charges of W. Jaggard, Ed. Blount, I. Smithweeke, and W. Aspley'. William Jaggard, who had been ill and blind for the last ten years, died shortly before publication, and the plays that had not previously been printed as Quartos, or at least sixteen of the eighteen, were registered 8 November 1623, by 'Mr Blounte Isaak Jaggard', and their names appear on the title-page, 'Printed by Isaac Iaggard, and Ed. Blount. 1623'. Blount, however, was not a printer but a reputable publisher, and the printing was done by the Jaggards. Isaac died in 1627, and his widow transferred the Jaggard copyright of Shakespeare's plays to Thomas and Richard Cotes. (See FOLIOS; Greg, *Shakespeare First Folio*.)

'Jahrbuch der Deutschen Shakespeare-Gesellschaft.' The annual publication of the Deutsche Shakespeare-Gesellschaft (q.v.), published without a break 1865–1943, resumed 1948 (vol. 80/1). From 1964 (vol. 100), with the division of the society into East and West there have been two annual volumes, one published in Weimar, the other (West) in Heidelberg.

Jailor. In *The Two Noble Kinsmen*, the keeper of Palamon and Arcite, and the father of the girl who frees Palamon, whose executioner he is to be after his defeat in the tournament.

Jailor's Daughter. In *The Two Noble Kinsmen*, is loved by the 'Wooer', but herself loves Palamon, whom she sets free. When she thinks that her action has led to the deaths of Palamon and her father she goes mad, but is cured by the Wooer's pretending to be Palamon.

James I (1566–1625), only child of Mary Queen of Scots and her second husband, Lord Darnley, was born at Edinburgh in June 1566, and proclaimed James VI of Scotland, in July 1567. In 1589 he married Anne, daughter of

Frederick II, King of Denmark, by whom he had three children who survived infancy: Henry, Prince of Wales (1594–1612), Elizabeth, wife of the Elector Palatine (1596–1662), and Charles, the future Charles I (1600–49). He succeeded to the English throne on the death of Elizabeth in March 1603.

James seems always to have taken an interest in the drama; to celebrate his marriage with Anne of Denmark in 1589, he asked Elizabeth for the loan of 'her Majesties players for to repayer into Scotland', and in 1594 English players were at the Scottish Court, probably under Laurence Fletcher, for the baptism of Prince Henry. Fletcher's company appears to have been in the service of James shortly before he became King of England, and his name stands first in the royal patent of 1603, establishing the Chamberlain's as the King's Men, though he seems to have taken no active part in the company. The two other leading companies were taken under royal patronage, the Admiral's as Prince Henry's, and Worcester's as the Queen's, and to these were added in 1610–11 the Duke of York's and the Lady Elizabeth's. The actor-sharers in these royal companies were sworn as Grooms of the Chamber. At the laxer Court of James and Anne, plays and masques were much more numerous than at that of Elizabeth, though the Act of Abuses (1606) led to a stricter censorship of plays, to prevent the speaking of oaths on the stage.

That James had a high opinion of Shakespeare is suggested not only by the number of his plays acted at Court but also by Ben Jonson's lines:

Sweet Swan of Avon! what a sight it were
To see thee in our waters yet appear,
And make those flights upon the banks of Thames,
That so did take Eliza and our James!

No doubt he was flattered by *Macbeth*, and there was a tradition that 'King James the First, was pleas'd with his own Hand to write an amicable Letter to Mr. Shakespeare'. (See BUCKINGHAM, JOHN SHEFFIELD.)

'James IV.' A play by Robert Greene, written probably *c.* 1591, registered 14 May 1594, and published 1598: 'The Scottish Historie of Iames the fourth, slaine at Flodden. Entermixed with a pleasant Comedie, presented by Oboram, King of Fayeries: As it hath bene sundrie times publikely plaide. Written by Robert Greene, Maister of Arts.' It is interesting as an early history play 'entermixed with comedie' like *Henry IV*, and for its 'Oboram, King of Fayeries', adopted by Shakespeare in his *Midsummer Night's Dream* either from Greene's play, or from Berners's translation of *Huon de Bordeaux* (q.v.).

James, Elias (*c.* 1578–1610). In the Bodleian is a MS. of *c.* 1630–40 (*Rawlinson Poet. MS.* 160, f. 41) with an epitaph ascribed to Shakespeare:

When god was pleas'd (ye world vnwilling yet)
Elias James to nature payd his debt,
And here reposeth; as he liv'd he dyde,
The saying in him strongly verefi'de,
Such life, such death. Then, ye known truth to tell,
He liv'd a godly life, and dy'de as well.
Wm: Shakespeare.

Leslie Hotson has discovered who Elias James was (*Sh's Sonnets Dated*), and strengthened the case for Shakespeare's authorship. He was the grandson of a Dutch immigrant, and the son of Dericke James, whose brewery near Puddle Wharf he took over in 1600. He died unmarried in 1610, and left the business to his brother Jacob, who died 1613. That Shakespeare knew Elias is probable, for his brewery was near the Blackfriars theatre and the Gate-house which Shakespeare bought in 1613, one of his trustees being John Jackson (q.v.), who married Jacob James's widow shortly afterwards. (See STANLEY, SIR THOMAS.)

James, Richard (1592–1638), scholar, was born at Newport, Isle of Wight and educated at Corpus Christi, Oxford. He became librarian to Sir Robert Cotton and, after his death in 1631, to his son Sir

Thomas. Anthony Wood says that he was 'a very good Grecian, poet, an excellent critic, antiquary, divine, and admirably well skilled in the Saxon and Gothic languages'. In an *Epistle* to Sir Harry Bourchier, written *c.* 1625, referring to Occleve's *Legend and Defence of Sir John Oldcastle*, James wrote:

> A young Gentle Lady of your acquaintance, having read ye works of Shakespeare, made me this question. How Sr John Falstaffe, or Fastolf, as he is written in y Statute book of Maudlin Colledge in Oxford, where everye day that society were bound to make memorie of his soul, could be dead in ye time of Harrie ye fift and again live in ye time of Harrie ye Sixt to be banished for cowardice: Whereto I made answear that it was one of those humours and mistakes for which Plato banisht all poets out of his commonwealth. That Sr John Falstaffe was in those times a noble valiaunt souldier, as apeeres by a book in ye Heralds Office dedicated unto him by a Herald who had binne with him, if I well remember, for the space of 25 yeeres in ye French wars; that he seems also to have binne a man of learning, because, in a Library of Oxford, I find a book of dedicating Churches sent from him for a present unto Bishop Wainflete, and inscribed with his own hand. That in Shakespeares first shew of Harrie the fift, the person with which he undertook to playe a buffone was not Falstaffe, but Sir Jhon Oldcastle, and that offence beinge worthily taken by Personages descended from his title (as peradventure by many others allso whoe ought to have him in honourable memorie) the poet was putt to make an ignorant shifte of abusing Sir Jhon Falstophe, a man not inferior of Vertue, though not so famous in pietie as the other, who gave witnesse unto the truth of our reformation with a constant and resolute Martyrdom, unto which he was pursued by the Priests, Bishops, Moncks, and Friers of those days.

Jameson, Anna Brownell (1794–1860), was born in Dublin, the daughter of Denis Brownell Murphy, a miniature painter. Her marriage with Robert Jameson was unsuccessful. In 1832, she published her *Shakespeare's Heroines; Characteristics of Women*, a book that appealed to Victorian England.

Jamy, Captain. In *Henry V*, the Scots captain who, at the siege of Harfleur has a conversation with the Welshman Fluellen and the Irishman Macmorris. He does not appear in the 'bad' Quarto, 1600, possibly, though improbably, out of deference to James VI of Scotland.

Jamyn, Amadis (*c.* 1538–85), French poet, a sonneteer and the translator of Homer. Shakespeare may have made some use of his version in *Troilus and Cressida.*

Janssen, Gheerart, was the Gerard Johnson who, according to the *Diary* of Sir William Dugdale (1653), made the Shakespeare monument in Stratford church. He was the son of Gheerart Janssen, the elder, who came from Amsterdam *c.* 1567, and established himself as a stonemason on the Bankside. He died in 1611, and Gheerart the younger was one of the four sons who carried on the business. As he worked near the Globe, it is probable that he knew Shakespeare, at least by sight. Janssen also made the monument with recumbent effigy of Shakespeare's friend John Combe (d. 1614), which stands in the chancel of Stratford church; 'Shakespeare's and John Combe's monuments were made by onc Gerard Johnson,' wrote Dugdale. (See MONUMENT.)

Janssen Portrait. The first notice of this portrait of Shakespeare was in the 18th century, when it was owned by Charles Jennens; later it came into the possession of the Duke of Somerset. It is inscribed *Aet. 46. 1610*, but the *6* of *46* is not above suspicion. It is a good portrait, and may well have been painted by Cornelius Janssen, though whether it is a portrait of Shakespeare is another matter. Cornelius Janssen (1593–1664) was born in London, and became a fashionable portrait-painter, but at the beginning of the Civil War he went to Holland, where he died.

Jaquenetta. In *Love's Labour's Lost*, a country wench, for 'consorting' with whom contrary to the King's edict, Costard is imprisoned on the information of his rival Don Armado, with whom he almost comes to blows about her in v, ii.

Jaques. In *As You Like It*, a lord attending the banished Duke. He is one of the few 'humorous' characters in Shakespeare, the melancholy man; he thinks and talks but scarcely affects events, though he does insist on Touchstone's being properly married to Audrey. (There is no corresponding character in Lodge's *Rosalynde*.)

Jaques de Boys. In *As You Like It*, the second son of Sir Rowland de Boys, and elder brother of Orlando, who mentions him as 'my brother Jaques' in his first speech. He appears only at the end of the play, where F. calls him 'second brother', to announce the restoration of his lands to the banished Duke.

'Jealous Comedy.' On 5 January 1593 Henslowe notes a single performance, probably by Strange's at the Rose, of '*the gelyous comodey*', a new play about which nothing more is known. Fleay, Robertson, and Wilson think that this may be an early version of *The Merry Wives of Windsor*; Chambers suggests that it may refer to *The Comedy of Errors*.

Jeffes, Humphrey. On p. 158 of the Histories in the Folio (the beginning of Act III of *3 Henry VI* in modern editions) is the stage-direction, *Enter Sinklo and Humfrey, with Crosse-bows in their hands*. 'Humfrey' is probably Humphrey Jeffes, who in 1597, with his brother Anthony, was with Pembroke's, the company that owned *3 Henry VI* in 1595. Jeffes may have been with the Chamberlain's for a time; 1598–1616 he was with the Admiral's-Prince Henry's, and died in 1618.

Jenkins, Thomas, succeeded Simon Hunt as Master of Stratford Grammar School. He was at St John's, Oxford, of which college he became a Fellow, took his M.A. in 1570, became Master of Warwick School, and moved to Stratford in 1575. In 1579 he resigned his mastership for £6 in favour of John Cottam. Jenkins was a Welshman and may be the original of Sir Hugh Evans in *The Merry Wives*. Shakespeare was eleven–fifteen while he was Master.

'Jeronimo.' An anonymous play, what is probably a reported text of which was published by Thomas Pavier in 1605: 'The First Part of Ieronimo. With the Warres of Portugall, and the life and death of Don Andræa'. It is not to be confused with *The Spanish Tragedy*, to which Henslowe seems to refer as *Jeronymo* in a run of sixteen performances by Strange's in 1592. *1 Jeronimo* appears to have belonged to the King's and to have been pirated by the Revels Children at Blackfriars, for in the Induction to Marston's *Malcontent* (1604), originally a Blackfriars play, Condell is made to answer Sly's question of how the King's came by *The Malcontent*, 'Why not Malevole in folio with us, as Jeronimo in decimo-sexto with them? They taught us a name for our play; we call it *One for Another*'. '*Jeronimo*' was attributed to Shakespeare by the booksellers of the mid 17th century.

'Jerusalem.' A play performed by Strange's at the Rose on 22 March 1592. (See TITUS AND VESPASIAN.)

Jessica. In *The Merchant of Venice*, the daughter of Shylock. She disguises herself as a boy and runs away with Lorenzo.

'Jew, The.' A play commended by the Puritan Stephen Gosson in his *Schoole of Abuse* (1579): 'The *Jew* ... showne at the Bull ... representing the greedinesse of worldly chusers, and bloody mindes of usurers' is one of the few plays 'without rebuke'. Nothing more is known about *The Jew*, though some think that *The Merchant of Venice* may be derived from it.

'Jew of Malta.' A play by Marlowe, written *c.* 1590, registered 17 May 1594, and published in 1633: 'The Famous Tragedy of the Rich Jew of Malta. As it was played before the King and Queene, in his Majesties Theatre at White-Hall, by her Majesties Servants at the Cock-pit. Written by Christopher Marlo.' The play was a great success, and seems to have belonged to Henslowe, for it was performed by a number of companies, seventeen times by Strange's in 1592–3. There is an interesting stage-direction at the end, showing that there was a trap-door in the upper stage: 'Ferneze *cuts the cord: the floor of the gallery gives way, and* Barabas *falls into a caldron*'. Henslowe's 1598 inventory of the Admiral's properties has the entry 'j cauderm for the Jewe'. The *Merchant of Venice* was influenced by *The Jew of Malta*; for example, Jessica may have been suggested by Barabas's daughter Abigail.

'Jew of Venice.' 1. A lost play registered by Humphrey Moseley, 9 September 1653, as being by Dekker.

2. John Green's company of English actors played a *Joseph the Jew of Venice* at Dresden in 1626.

3. A popular version of *The Merchant of Venice* by George Granville (q.v.), produced and published in 1701. Shylock was played by the low comedian, Thomas Dogget, Bassanio by Betterton, and Portia by Mrs Bracegirdle.

Jig. The dance which generally followed the performance of a play at the public theatres. The jig, as popular in England and Scotland as in Ireland (cf. *Much Ado*, 'Hot and hasty, like a Scotch jig'), was originally a solo song-and-dance, but developed into a primitive comic opera with a number of characters and a series of songs, often coarse, in ballad metre and sung to popular ballad tunes. Cf. Dekker, *A Strange Horse Race* (1613): 'As I have often seen, after the finishing of some worthy Tragedy, or Catastrophe in the open Theatres, that the scene after the Epilogue hath been more black (about a nasty bawdy jigge) than the most horrid scene in the play was.' Tarlton and Kempe were famous performers of jigs. (See PLATTER; C. R. Baskerville, *The Elizabethan Jig*.)

Joan of Arc (1412–31). In *1 Henry VI*, she is introduced to the Dauphin as 'a holy maid', rejects his offer of love, raises the siege of Orleans, and persuades Burgundy to desert the English cause for the French. In v, iii she conjures up fiends and offers them her soul and body for a French victory, but is captured by the Duke of York. At her trial she disowns her father, professes to be 'issued from the progeny of Kings' and a virgin chaste and immaculate, but when sentenced to be burned, reveals that she is with child, and is carried off cursing England and the English. (See G. B. Shaw, Preface to *Saint Joan*.)

Jodelle, Étienne (1532–73), French dramatist and poet and member of the Pléiade, was one of the first to write on the Cleopatra theme, his *Cléopâtre Captive* being produced at Court in 1552. It is a lyrical play in the classical manner, indeed the beginning of French classical tragedy, with chorus and reported action. Lee finds a parallel to the hunting of the harc in *Venus and Adonis* in Jodelle's *Ode de la Chasse*, and draws attention to the similarity between Shakespeare's satirical and vituperative sonnets and those of Jodelle's sequence *Contr' Amours*:

My mistress' eyes are nothing like the sun;
Coral is far more red than her lips' red:
If snow be white, why then her breasts are dun;
If hairs be wires, black wires grow on her head.

(*Sonnet 130*)

Combien de fois mes vers ont-ils doré
Ces cheveux noirs digne d'une Meduse?
Combien de fois ce teint noir qui m'amuse,
Ay-ie de lis et roses coloré?

'John a Kent and John a Cumber.' A manuscript prompt-book signed 'Anthony Mundy', and below the signature, in a different hand, the date. This used to be read 1595 or 1596, but I. A. Shapiro has shown (SS, 8) that it is really 1590, and that the play was probably written by 1589. As it has some resemblances to *A Midsummer Night's Dream* – Turnop and his crew of rustics resemble Bottom and his cronies, and Shrimp plays a part similar to Puck – it seems clear, from this revised dating, that Shakespeare borrowed from Munday and not the other way round. (See Greg, *Dramatic Documents*.)

John, Don. The mischief-maker in *Much Ado*, bastard brother of Don Pedro, Prince of Arragon, and a man 'not of many words'. Because Claudio has all the glory of his own overthrow, he eagerly falls in with Borachio's plan 'to misuse the prince, to vex Claudio, to undo Hero, and kill Leonato'. (There is a similar character in Bandello's story: Gironda, who is in love with Fenicia (Hero).)

John, King (1167–1216). The hero of *King John* (q.v.). (The youngest son of Henry II and Elinor of Aquitaine, he seized the throne on the death of his eldest brother, Richard I, in 1199, in spite of the claims of Arthur, the young son of his elder brother Geoffrey.)

John of Gaunt, Duke of Lancaster (1340–99). In *Richard II*, his end is hastened by Richard's banishment of his son, Bolingbroke. On his death-bed he speaks the famous panegyric on England, 'This royal throne of kings, this sceptr'd isle'. Richard's confiscation of his estates leads to Bolingbroke's return, and his own downfall. (He was the fourth son of Edward III, and by his first wife, Blanche of Lancaster, the father of Bolingbroke (Henry IV), the first of the Lancastrian kings. By his third wife, Katharine Swynford, he was the ancestor of the Beaufort-Tudor line.)

Johnson, Arthur. Bookseller in London from 1602 to *c.* 1621, when he went to Dublin, where he died in 1631. He published the 'bad' Quarto of *The Merry Wives*, 1602. The play was registered 18 January 1602 by John Busby, who transferred it to Johnson on the same day. It was reprinted in 1619 by William Jaggard as 'Printed for Arthur Johnson, 1619'.

Johnson, Charles (1679–1748). Author of *The Cobler of Preston*, a satire on the 1715 Rebellion, based on the Christopher Sly episode in *The Taming of the Shrew*, and produced at Drury Lane in February 1716. Johnson's gentlemanly version of *As You Like It*, called *Love in a Forest*, was played in 1723, also at Drury Lane, with Colley Cibber as Jaques. Orlando and Charles fight a duel, Jaques marries Celia, and the Pyramus and Thisbe interlude is introduced into the last scene. Johnson was a prolific writer of plays; he was satirized by Pope, whom he offended in the Prologue to his *Sultaness* (1717).

Johnson, Gerard. See JANSSEN.

Johnson, Richard (1573–*c.* 1659), romance and ballad writer. His *Tom a Lincolne* (1607) has a poison-drug theme, similar to that in *Cymbeline*, and his *Golden Garland* (1620) contains a ballad on the Lear story and one on Titus Andronicus. This last is probably the one registered by Danter 6 February 1594 at the same time as the play, on which it is based.

Johnson, Robert (*c.* 1585–*c.* 1634), lutenist. George Carey, 2nd Lord Hunsdon, patron of Shakespeare's company, took Johnson into his musical establishment in March 1596 as a 'covenount servaunt'. From 1604 to 1633 he was one of the Musicians of the Lute to James I and Charles I, and wrote settings for the songs in *The Tempest*, 'Where the bee sucks', and 'Full fathom five', probably for the Court performance given in 1612–13 during the celebrations of the Lady Elizabeth's marriage. (See SS, 9.)

Johnson, Robert, lived in Henley Street, near the Birthplace, his house being severely damaged by the fire of September 1594. In the inventory of his goods, 5 October 1611, after his death, is the item, 'A lease of a barne that he holdeth of Mr Shaxper, xx[li]'. This is the only record of Shakespeare's Henley Street property in his lifetime, apart from the will. The barn was in the Gild Pits, and is mentioned by Lady Bernard in her will, 1670, as being occupied by Michael Johnson, Robert's son.

Johnson, Samuel (1709–84), the sixth editor of Shakespeare. His *Miscellaneous Observations on the Tragedy of Macbeth* (1745), containing proposals for a new edition of Shakespeare, 'was fortunate enough to obtain the approbation even of the supercilious Warburton himself'. Eleven years later, again in the words of Boswell, 'He issued Proposals of considerable length, in which he shewed that he perfectly well knew what a variety of research such an undertaking required; but his indolence prevented him from pursuing it with that diligence which alone can collect those scattered facts, that genius, however acute, penetrating, and luminous, cannot discover by its own force'. The result was that his edition of 1765 (twenty years after the original Proposals) was perfunctory, and based largely on Warburton. Though he recognized the authority of the First over the later Folios, and made some collation of the Quartos, he added little of value to the elucidation of the text, or to the knowledge of Shakespeare and his theatre. The edition is important, mainly because it became the basis of Steevens's scholarly work, and because of the Preface, a splendid and generous tribute from the Age of Reason. Boswell's comment is worth quoting:

> If it had no other merit but that of producing his Preface, in which the excellencies and defects of that immortal bard are displayed with a masterly hand, the nation would have had no reason to complain. A blind indiscriminate admiration of Shakespeare had exposed the British nation to the ridicule of foreigners. Johnson, by candidly admitting the faults of his poet, had the more credit in bestowing on him deserved and indisputable praise; and doubtless none of all his panegyrists have done him half so much honour. ... What he did as a commentator has no small share of merit, though his researches were not so ample, and his investigations so acute, as they might have been; which we now certainly know from the labours of other able and ingenious critics who have followed him.

Few would quarrel with this judgement today, though E. A. Poe (q.v.) did. (See KENRICK.)

Johnson, William. One of the trustees of Shakespeare when he bought the Blackfriars Gate-house in 1613, in the conveyance and mortgage of which he is called 'citizein and Vintener of London'. He was born *c.* 1575, and was apprenticed to William Williamson of the Mermaid Tavern, the management of which he took over in 1603. Shakespeare must have known Johnson well as one of the company that used to meet at the Mermaid on the first Friday of every month. It is interesting to note that Johnson was charged with serving meat instead of fish on Fridays in Lent in 1613. (See Hotson, *Shakespeare's Sonnets Dated.*)

Jones, Ernest, Freudian psycho-analyst, first applied the new science to the study of Shakespeare in his *Oedipus-Complex as an Explanation of Hamlet's Mystery* (1910). According to this theory, Claudius succeeds in doing the two things that Hamlet had unconsciously wished to do: killed his father and married his mother, yet his power to act against his hated rival is paralysed by his own sense of guilt.

Jones, Inigo (1573–1651), was born in London, the son of a Roman Catholic clothworker. His skill at drawing led to his being sent to study painting in Italy by his patron, probably William, 3rd Earl of Pembroke, but he turned to architecture, and in Venice made such a name for himself that in 1604 he was employed by Christian IV of Denmark, brother of Anne, James I's Queen. In 1605 he came to England as architect to the Queen, and later as surveyor-general of royal buildings, his best-known work in London being the Banqueting House in Whitehall and the piazza of Covent Garden. He was also designer of Court masques, often in collaboration with Ben Jonson, with whom he quarrelled and by whom he was satirized in *A Tale of a Tub*. As a royalist Jones was persecuted after the Civil War, and died in poverty.

His designs for the production of Court masques are important in the history of the theatre. He brought to bear his knowledge of the Italian stage, designed appropriate and elaborate proscenium arches behind which the scene was set and concealed by a curtain, and experimented with various methods of changing the scene. Finally he evolved that of movable flats and shutters; there are four sets for *Salmacida Spolia* (1640), with a corresponding sky-cloth for each scene. This production of masques with changes of scene inevitably led to the staging of Court plays in the same way, and must have influenced production in the private theatres, where there is evidence to show that by 1630–40 changes of scene were employed, and that the picture-frame stage was being evolved. He left interesting drawings of painted 'perspectives' in the manner of Serlio, and his plan and elevation of the Cockpit-at-Court (q.v.) is a modification of a Palladian design. His costume designs for the Court masques also had their effect on the theatres.

Jones, Robert (fl. 1590–1615). Musician, and composer of the *First Book of Songs and Airs* (1600), which contains the song 'Farewell, dear heart', sung by Sir Toby and Feste in *Twelfth Night* (II, iii). In 1615 he was one of a syndicate who obtained a patent for converting his house in Blackfriars into a theatre for the Revels Children, an enterprise that was suppressed by the City authorities. (See PORTER'S HALL.)

Jones, Thomas (*c.* 1613–1703). According to Capell (1780),

> Mr Thomas Jones, who dwelt at Tarbick [Tardebigge] a village in Worcestershire a few miles from Stratford on Avon, and dy'd in the year 1703, aged upwards of ninety, remember'd to have heard from several old people at Stratford the story of Shakespeare's robbing sir Thomas Lucy's park; and their account of it agreed with Mr Rowe's, with this addition – that the ballad written against sir Thomas by Shakespeare was stuck upon his park gate, which exasperated the knight to apply to a lawyer at Warwick to proceed against him.

Capell adds that 'Mr Jones was also the hander-down' of the story that a very old man of Stratford, 'related to Shakespeare',

> saw him once brought on the stage upon another man's back; which answer was apply'd by the hearers, to his having seen him perform in this scene the part of Adam: That he should have done so, is made not unlikely by another constant tradition, that he was no extraordinary actor, and therefore took no parts upon him but such as this: for which he might also be peculiarly fitted by an accidental lameness, which, – as he himself tells us twice in his '*Sonnets*', v. 37, and 89, – befell him in some part of life.

William Oldys, who gives versions of the same anecdotes, *c.* 1750, probably got them from the same source as Capell. (See SHAKESPEARE, GILBERT.)

Jones, William, bookseller, at the Gun near Holborn Conduit. He was apprenticed to John Judson in 1578, became a Freeman of the Stationers' Company in 1587, and died 1618. He published Q1 *Thomas Lord Cromwell*, 'by W.S.' in 1602, and in 1611 transferred it to John Browne.

Jonson, Benjamin (1572–1637), was born at Westminster after the death of his father, who was of Scottish descent. His mother married again, a master bricklayer, to whose trade Jonson was apprenticed after a successful career at Westminster School, then under William Camden. He enlisted, and served for a time in the Netherlands, but by 1597 had begun his stage career as an actor, apparently with Pembroke's. In that year Henslowe lent him £4, on 28 July, the day on which the theatres were closed because of the production of the slanderous *Isle of Dogs*, of which he was part author. He was imprisoned, but in October released from the Marshalsea with two of Pembroke's Men, Robert Shaw and Gabriel Spencer, the latter of whom he killed in a duel a year later, as a result of which he turned Catholic for twelve years. Between 1598 and 1602 Jonson wrote for Henslowe and the Admiral's, for the Chamberlain's, and for the Children of the Chapel. Shakespeare acted in *Every Man in His Humour* (1598), and is said by Rowe to have been responsible for its acceptance. The years 1600–2 were those of the *Poetomachia* (q.v.), or War of the Theatres, Jonson on the one side with his *Poetaster*, Marston and Dekker on the other with their *Satiromastix*. In 1605 he was again imprisoned for a short time for his share in *Eastward Ho!* Between 1606 and 1610 he wrote his best plays, *Volpone*, *Epicoene* and *The Alchemist*, and a number of very successful Court masques. 1616 is the central date of his career; in that year his *Works* were published in Folio, he and Drayton are said to have drunk Shakespeare into his fatal fever, and he received a royal pension of a hundred marks, so becoming the first, though unofficial, Poet Laureate. In 1619 he paid his famous visit to William Drummond at Hawthornden, and in the twenties turned again to the writing of plays, though towards the end with failing powers owing to ill-health, and in 1631 a quarrel with Inigo Jones put an end to his masques. He died in 1637, the acknowledged head of English literature, and was buried in Westminster Abbey. His wife, whom he married sometime before 1592, was a 'shrew, but honest', and bore him a number of children.

Rowe (1709) says that Shakespeare and Jonson became friends over the production of *Every Man in His Humour*; Fuller (*c.* 1650), that there were many '*wit-combates* betwixt him and *Ben Johnson*'; the anonymous author of *3 Parnassus* (*c.* 1601), that 'our fellow Shakespeare puts them all down, ay, and Ben Jonson too. O that Ben Jonson is a pestilent fellow, he brought up Horace giving the Poets a pill, but our fellow Shakespeare hath given him a purge that made him beray his credit'; Drummond (1619), that Jonson told him 'that Shaksperr wanted Arte' (see also HALES, JOHN); and John Ward (*c.* 1662), that 'Shakespear, Drayton, and Ben Jhonson, had a merry meeting, and itt seems drank too hard, for Shakespear died of a feavour there contracted'.

In his *Works* Jonson made a few references, some of them by no means certain to Shakespeare; in *Every Man out of His Humour* to *Julius Caesar*, and to Shakespeare's Grant of Arms; in *The Poetaster*, Virgil may stand for Shakespeare; in a late prologue to *Every Man in his Humour* he laughs at Shakespeare's failure to obey the unities, and in *Bartholomew Fair* at *The Winter's Tale* and *The Tempest*. His most important and considered utterance is that in his *Discoveries*, written *c.* 1630:

> I *remember*, the Players have often mentioned it as an honour to *Shakespeare*, that in his writing, (whatsoever he penn'd) he never blotted out line. My answer hath been, would he had blotted a thousand. Which they thought a malevolent speech. I had not told posterity this, but for their ignorance, who choose that circumstance to commend their friend by, wherein he most faulted. And to justify mine own candour, (for I lov'd the man, and do honour his memory (on this side idolatry) as much as any.) He was (indeed) honest, and of an open, and free nature: had an excellent *Phantsie*; brave notions, and gentle expressions: wherein he flow'd with that facility, that sometime it was necessary he should be stopp'd: *Sufflaminandus erat*; as *Augustus* said of *Haterius*. His wit was in his own power; would the rule of it had been so too. Many times he fell into those things, could not escape

laughter: As when he said in the person of *Cæsar*, one speaking to him; *Cæsar thou dost me wrong*. He replied: *Cæsar did never wrong, but with just cause* and such like: which were ridiculous. But he redeemed his vices, with his virtues. There was ever more in him to be praised, than to be pardoned.

Sometime before this Jonson had written his tribute, 'To the memory of my beloved, the author Mr William Shakespeare: and what he hath left us', published in the Folio of 1623:

To draw no envy (Shakespeare) on thy name,
 Am I thus ample to thy Book, and Fame:
While I confess they writings to be such,
 As neither Man, nor Muse, can praise too much ...
  Soul of the Age!
 The applause! delight! the wonder of our Stage!...
Triumph, my Britain, thou hast one to show,
 To whom all Scenes of Europe homage owe.
He was not of an age, but for all time!
 And all the Muses still were in their prime,
When like Apollo he came forth to warm
 Our ears, or like a Mercury to charm!

(The standard edition of Jonson is that of C. H. Herford and P. Simpson, 11 vols., 1925–52. For Jonson's conception of comedy, see his *Prologue* to *Every Man in His Humour*. See also HUMOUR.)

Jordan, Dorothea (1762–1816), actress, was born near Waterford in Ireland, her father's name being Bland. Her first appearance was at Dublin in 1777 as Phoebe in *As You Like It*. In the eighties she toured in Yorkshire as Mrs Jordan, and in 1785 was engaged at Drury Lane, where she stayed until 1809, playing mostly in comedy, her most famous Shakespearean parts being Rosalind, Viola and Imogen. From 1790 to 1811 she was the mistress of the Duke of Clarence (William IV), by whom she had ten children, ennobled as FitzClarence, the eldest as Earl of Munster. She played in Ireland's *Vortigern* (q.v.).

Jordan, John (1746–1809), was born at Tiddington near Stratford. He was a wheelwright of little formal education, but also a writer of verses, publishing *Welcombe Hills* in 1777, antiquary, and Stratford guide, in which last capacity he conducted Samuel Ireland and his son William Henry about the town and district on their visit in 1794. Many of the anecdotes in the former's *Picturesque Views* were derived from Jordan, and the latter had one of Jordan's manuscripts written about 1770, which contained among other things an elaborated version of the crab-tree story. In his *Original Collections on Shakespeare, c.* 1780, Jordan gave a somewhat conjectural account of the Shakespeare family, and mentioned John Shakespeare's 'religious Testament', the text of which is in his *Original Memoirs*, and the original of which was sent to Malone, who published it in his 1790 edition of Shakespeare. This was said to have been found by one Joseph Mosely, a bricklayer, in the Birthplace in 1757, and is a profession of the Catholic faith. Malone later rejected this 'spiritual will', not necessarily as spurious, but because he had 'documents that clearly prove it could not have been the composition of any one of our poet's family'.

Jordan also professed to have found the ballad, mentioned by Rowe, that Shakespeare was said to have written in revenge upon Sir Thomas Lucy. The first two stanzas, printed as one, had already been quoted by Oldys and Capell, but Jordan produced the entire song, which in the words of Malone (*Var.*, II, 140), 'was found in a chest of drawers, that formerly belonged to Mrs Dorothy Tyler, of Shottery, near Stratford, who died in 1778, at the age of eighty, and which I shall insert in the Appendix; being fully persuaded that one part of this ballad is just as genuine as the other; that is, that the whole is a forgery'. (See LUCY, SIR THOMAS.)

Jourdain, Margery. In *2 Henry VI*, the witch who helps to conjure up the 'spirit' for the scheming Duchess of Gloucester (I, iv). She is arrested and sentenced to be burned at Smithfield.

Jourdan, Sylvester (d. 1650), came from Lyme Regis, as did Sir George Somers, admiral of the Virginia Company, whom he accompanied on his voyage of 1609. On 28 July they were shipwrecked on the uninhabited island of Bermuda, which they claimed for the English crown. Jourdan's *A Discovery of the Barmudas, otherwise called the Ile of Divels*, a picturesque account telling of the mysterious noises that he ascribed to spirits and devils, was published in 1610, and furnished Shakespeare with material for *The Tempest*. Jourdan died in London in 1650. (See GATES.)

Joyce, James (1882–1941). In *Ulysses* (I, 188–225) there is a remarkable discussion of Shakespeare's character, and of his relations with his family as revealed in his works.

Jubilee of 1769. Halliwell-Phillipps gives a sour summary of the occasion:

> The Jubilee of 1769 was the name given to a series of entertainments at Stratford that were devised and arranged in that year by Garrick, a celebrated actor of the day, under the ostensible pretence of doing honour to Shakespeare. And the great poet was dignified in this fashion. – The opening of the celebration having been duly announced in early morn by a powder cannonade, the lady visitors were serenaded in rotation by young men attired in fancy costume, and when everybody had thus been thoroughly aroused, Garrick was presented by the Corporation with a medal and a wand, both made from relics of the famous mulberry-tree, bells and cannon loudly uniting to proclaim the acceptance of the gifts. Then there were public feasts, more serenading, an oratorio at the church, elaborate processions, a masquerade, balls, illuminations, fireworks, horse-races, and an unlimited supply of drummers. In the midst, however, of all this tomfoolery, the presiding genius of the show recited an ode in praise of the great dramatist, that achievement and some of the gaieties taking place in a large wooden theatre that had been erected for the occasion on the Bancroft.

Boswell was there, and 'almost every man of eminence in the literary world was happy to partake in this festival of genius', but not Johnson. (See SS, 9.)

Judson, Thomas, London printer, 1584–99. He printed Q1 *The Passionate Pilgrim* for W. Jaggard in 1599, in which year he was forbidden to print epigrams, satires, etc.

Julia. In *The Two Gentlemen of Verona*, the faithful lover of the unfaithful Proteus. (The Felismena of Montemayor's *Diana*.)

Juliet. 1. The heroine of *Romeo and Juliet*, and daughter of Capulet.

2. In *Measure for Measure*, Juliet is with child by Claudio, for which offence he is condemned to death. In II, iii she confesses that her sin was the heavier. In the last scene the Duke orders Claudio to marry her.

'JULIUS CAESAR.'

WRITTEN: 1599–1600. (See 'EVERY MAN OUT OF HIS HUMOUR'; WEEVER; WISDOM OF DOCTOR DODIPOLL.)

PERFORMED: 1599, 21 September. Thomas Platter (q.v.) of Basel saw a 'Tragedy vom ersten Keyser Julio Caesare' at a Bankside theatre; possibly Shakespeare's play at the Globe.

1612–13. 'Caesars Tragedye' was one of the twenty plays given by the King's during the Revels celebrating Lady Elizabeth's marriage.

1636, 31 January. 'at St James, the tragedie of Cesar.'

1638, 13 November. 'At the Cocpit – Ceaser.'

REGISTERED: 1623, 8 November. One of the sixteen plays registered by Blount and Jaggard before publishing F1.

PUBLISHED: 1623, F1. 'The Tragedie of Ivlivs Caesar.' The sixth play in the Tragedy section: pp. 109–30. Acts marked. A very good text, though possibly cut. In IV, iii Brutus's account of Portia's death may be revision, the later report by Messala the undeleted original version. The play is much attacked by the disintegrators. Set up from a transcript of the prompt-book.

SOURCE: Plutarch's *Lives* of Brutus, Caesar and Antony, translated by Sir

Thomas North (1579) from the French of Jacques Amyot (1559).

STAGE HISTORY: *Julius Caesar* was one of the three or four plays spared by 17th- and 18th-century improvers. At the Restoration it went to the King's company, who produced it in 1672 with Charles Hart as Brutus, a part played later by Betterton. It was often revived in the 18th century, though not by Garrick.

At the beginning of the year 44 B.C., Cassius forms a conspiracy against Caesar, partly because he is jealous, partly because he fears a dictatorship. Brutus, because he loves the Roman republic even better than he loves Caesar, reluctantly joins the conspirators, who murder Caesar in the Senate House. In a great speech over Caesar's body, Mark Antony so infuriates the people against the assassins that they are driven from Rome, where a triumvirate of Octavius, Antony and Lepidus is formed. Brutus and Cassius go to Asia Minor and join forces at Sardis. Brutus accuses Cassius of accepting bribes, and there is a quarrel followed by a reconciliation and the news of the death of Portia, Brutus's wife. At Philippi in Macedonia in 42 B.C. they meet the forces of Antony and Octavius, are defeated, and kill themselves.

Juno. In *The Tempest*, 'the queen o' the sky', who is one of the characters in the masque (IV, i). She and Ceres sing their blessings on the newly betrothed Ferdinand and Miranda.

K

Katharina. Heroine of *The Taming of the Shrew*. (In *A Shrew* she is Kate, eldest of Alfonso's (Baptista's) three daughters.)

Katharine. 1. In *Love's Labour's Lost*, one of the ladies attending the Princess of France. She falls in love with Dumain (q.v.), for whom she promises to wait a year. She had a sister who died for love (V, ii).

2. In *Henry V*, daughter of Charles VI of France. In III, iv her lady Alice gives her an English lesson (see HANMER), and in V, ii Henry V woos her and insists on marrying her as part of the price of peace with France. (Katharine of Valois (1401–37) was the mother of Henry VI. After the death of Henry V (1422), she married Owen Tudor; their eldest son Edmund married Margaret Beaufort, and their only child became Henry VII.)

3. In *Henry VIII*, the first Queen of Henry. She pleads for a fair trial for Buckingham, distrusts Wolsey, yet pities him in his disgrace. Soon after her divorce she dies. Katharine of Aragon (1485–1536) was the daughter of Ferdinand and Isabella of Spain. She married Henry's elder brother, Arthur, in 1501, Henry himself in 1509, and was divorced in 1533. Mary (Queen 1553–8) was her only surviving child.)

Kean, Edmund (1787–1833), son of an actress who abandoned him, he led an adventurous youth, between 1801 and 1814 acting with various companies, mainly in the provinces. In 1814 he secured an engagement at Drury Lane, then in low water, where his performance of Shylock was a triumph, and his subsequent playing of the parts of Richard III, Hamlet, Othello, Macbeth and Lear established him as the leading tragic actor of the day. His last performance was in 1833 at Covent Garden, where he collapsed while playing Othello to his son Charles's Iago, and died shortly afterwards. Kean's contemporaries, even Coleridge, bear witness to his greatness as a tragic actor; but he was the first of the stars to whom all else was subordinated, the other players, their parts, and often the play itself.

Kean, Charles John (1811–68), son of Edmund Kean, was born at Waterford, the home of his mother, Mary Chambers, whom his father had married in 1808 and who left him in 1825. Charles was educated at Eton, and made his name as an actor mainly in the provinces, though it was his Hamlet at Drury Lane in 1838 that placed him high on the list of tragic actors. In 1842 he married the actress Ellen Tree, with whom he paid his second visit to America, and in 1848, appeared in Shakespeare at the Haymarket. In 1850 he became lessee of the Princess theatre, where he produced a series of Shakespeare's plays with a sumptuous and pedantic realism that served as a model for the yet more lavish spectacles of Irving and Tree. As an example, in his production of *The Winter's Tale* in 1856, in which his wife played Hermione and Ellen Terry was Mamillius, he changed the scene from Bohemia to Bithynia, introduced a Pyrrhic dance, a Dionysiac festival, allegorical tableaux with figures taken from Flaxman, and the vegetation peculiar to Bithynia.

Keats, John (1795–1821), was much influenced by Shakespeare, and thought of him as his presiding Genius. His letters are full of Shakespearean allusions and criticism; for example, 'It struck me what quality went to form a Man of Achievement, especially in Literature, and which Shakespeare possessed so enormously – I mean *Negative Capability*, that is, when a man is capable of being in uncertainties, mysteries, doubts, without any irritable reaching after fact and reason.' His copy of the 1808 Folio reprint is in the Keats Museum. (See C. Spurgeon, *Keats's Shakespeare*.)

Keeling, Captain William (d. 1620), naval commander, was captain of the *Susanna* on the ill-fated second voyage of the East India Company (1604). In 1607 he sailed in command of the third voyage, his ship being the *Dragon*, Captain William Hawkins being in the *Hector*. It was off Sierra Leone on the outward voyage that Keeling made the September entries in his journal:

> 1607. Sept. 5. I sent the interpreter, according to his desier, abord the Hector whear he brooke fast, and after came abord mee, wher we gaue the tragedie of Hamlett.
>
> 30. Captain Hawkins dined with me, wher my companions acted Kinge Richard the Second.
>
> [1608. Mar. 31.] I envited Captain Hawkins to a ffishe dinner, and had Hamlet acted abord me: which I permitt to keepe my people from idleness and unlawful games, or sleepe.

All but the first leaf of Keeling's journal has been lost, and its authenticity has been questioned, but it is probably genuine. Keeling was appointed Captain of Cowes Castle, *c.* 1618, and died in the Isle of Wight.

Kemble, John Philip (1757–1823), second of the twelve children of the actor Roger Kemble and the actress Sarah Wood, and brother of Sarah Siddons. He started his training as a priest, but turned to the stage and first appeared at Wolverhampton in 1776. In 1783 he began his long connexion with Drury Lane by playing Hamlet, then he and his sister played together as Macbeth and Lady Macbeth, King John and Constance, Othello and Desdemona. His favourite part was that of Coriolanus in his own version of the play. From 1788 to 1802 he was manager of Drury Lane, but after a disagreement with Sheridan, the proprietor, he became manager of Covent Garden in 1803. The fire of 1808 almost ruined him, but he was saved by the generosity of the Duke of Northumberland, and retired in 1817, when Edmund Kean had become his rival.

In his acting Kemble abandoned, inevitably perhaps, owing to the great size of the new theatres, the naturalism of Garrick for the earlier formalism of Quin, but in his productions he advanced some way in the direction of realism by dressing the players in approximately historical costume and employing the romantic scenic-designer William Capon. Though he often preferred 'improved' versions of Shakespeare, such as Tate's *King Lear*, he did at least produce a large number of his plays.

Kemble, Charles (1775–1854), a younger brother of John Philip. His first stage appearance was at Sheffield as Orlando in *As You Like It*, his first London appearance at Drury Lane in 1794 as Malcolm to his brother's Macbeth. He played in numerous Shakespearean revivals, and was called by Macready 'a first-rate actor of second-rate parts', such as Laertes and Macduff. In 1806 he married the actress Marie Therèse de Camp, and in 1809 his elder daughter, Fanny, was born. He succeeded his brother as joint-proprietor of Covent Garden and there, in 1823, with the aid of the antiquary J. R. Planché, inaugurated the vogue of the antiquarian-spectacular with a remarkable production of *King John*, in which every character appeared 'in the precise Habit of the Period, the whole of the Dresses and Decorations being executed from indisputable Authorities such as Monumental Effigies, Seals, Illumined MSS. &c.'

Kemble, Frances Anne (1809–93). Fanny was the elder daughter of Charles Kemble, whose first stage appearance, as Juliet at Covent Garden, saved her father's theatre from threatened collapse. She followed up this success by playing a number of Shakespeare's heroines, notably Portia and Beatrice. In 1832 she accompanied her father to America, where she married, divorced her husband in 1847, returned to the stage, and in 1877 came back to England. She wrote a number of books, including *Notes on some of Shakespeare's Plays* (1882).

Kempe, William. One of the twenty-six 'Principall Actors' in Shakespeare's plays (see p. 90). He was in the Low Countries in 1585–6, probably with Leicester's (see SIDNEY), and in 1590 is referred to by the anonymous author (probably Nashe) of *An Almond for a Parrat* as 'that most Comicall and conceited Caualeire Monsieur du Kempe, Jestmonger and Vice-gerent generall to the Ghost of Dicke Tarlton'. In 1593 he toured the provinces with Strange's under Alleyn, and in 1594 joined the newly-formed Chamberlain's company. From Shakespeare's directions and speech-prefixes reproduced in the texts, it is clear that Kempe played Peter in *Romeo and Juliet* and Dogberry in *Much Ado*. He was one of the original shareholders in the Globe, February 1599, but soon sold his share, and it is probable that he then left the Chamberlain's and the Globe or, as he put it, 'daunst my selfe out of the world', for in the next year, between 11 February and 11 March, he danced from London to Norwich, an event that he described in his *Kemps morris to Norwiche*. It was indeed as a dancer that he excelled, and examples of the music of 'Kemps jiggs' were collected by John Dowland and are now preserved in the Cambridge University library. Kempe went to Italy and Germany, but returned to England in September 1601, when it is possible that he rejoined the Chamberlain's, for in *3 Parnassus* he is described as a fellow of Burbage and Shakespeare, and reference made to his 'dancing the morrice ouer the Alpes'. In 1602 Henslowe lent him money, and in 1602–3 he was with Worcester's. There is no further reference to him, and he was certainly dead by 1608. Kempe's comedy was broad clowning in the manner of Tarlton, and it seems certain that Shakespeare wrote the more subtle parts of the Court fools in *As You Like It*, *Twelfth Night* and *Lear* for his successor, Robert Armin.

Kenilworth. A small town, twelve miles north-east of Stratford, the castle of which was granted by Elizabeth to Robert Dudley, Earl of Leicester, in 1562. There he entertained the Queen in the summers of 1566, 1572, and 1575. 'The Princelye pleasures' of the last entertainment, 9–27 July, were very elaborate, and mainly under the direction of George Gascoigne and William Hunnis of the Chapel Royal. There, on 18 July, the young Shakespeare may have seen the principal device of *The Delivery of the Lady of the Lake*, and 'Arion on the dolphin's back', an image that crops up in *Twelfth Night* (I, ii).

Kenrick, William (*c.* 1725–79), was born near Watford. In 1765 he published his *Review of Dr Johnson's new edition of Shakespeare; in which the Ignorance, or Inattention of the Editor is exposed*, and issued proposals for a new edition of Shakespeare, which came to nothing. He delivered a course of lectures published as *Introduction to the School of Shakespeare* (1774).

Kent, Earl of. In *King Lear*. He is banished by Lear for warning him of his folly in disinheriting Cordelia, but disguises himself, and Lear takes him into his service as 'Caius'. He trips up Oswald for insulting the King, and later beats him, for which he is put in the stocks by Cornwall although he is the King's messenger. He follows Lear into the storm and manages to take him to Cordelia in the French camp at Dover. After the battle, a dying man, he comes to bid his 'king and master aye good night'. (Perillus in *King Leir* plays a similar part.)

Kesselstadt Death Mask. A cast acquired by Dr Ludwig Becker in 1849, after the sale of Count Kesselstadt's belongings among which it was reputed to be. It is a cast made from a mask, with the date A° Dm 1616, which appears to be the only reason for associating it with Shakespeare. If the Droeshout engraving be taken as approximately representing the shape of Shakespeare's head, the Kesselstadt mask, which bears no resemblance to it, can scarcely represent the same man.

Keysar, Robert. A London goldsmith who, *c.* 1606, bought for £100 from John Marston, the dramatist, a share of one-sixth in the premises, properties, and plays of the Queen's Revels Children at Blackfriars. In 1600, Henry Evans had been granted by Richard Burbage a twenty-one years' lease of the Blackfriars theatre, but in August 1608 he surrendered it. In 1610, Keysar brought a suit against the Burbages, Heminge, Condell, Evans, 'and others' (presumably the other housekeepers, including Shakespeare), for breaking an agreement that they would not come to any arrangement with Evans prejudicial to his interests, and claiming one-sixth of the subsequent profit of £1,500. The King's Men denied the profit, and maintained that the theatre was in such bad repair that they had to take it back. The result of the case is unknown. Keysar moved the Children to the Whitefriars theatre, and in 1609–10 gave five Court performances. (See KIRKHAM; WALLACE.)

Killigrew, Thomas (1612–83), dramatist, was born in London, became page to Charles I, and when the Royalist cause was lost went to France with Prince Charles who, when he became King, made him Groom of the Bedchamber. At the Restoration, he and D'Avenant received royal patents giving them the exclusive right each to form a company of players and build a theatre. Killigrew formed the King's Company (q.v.), who played first in Vere Street, and after 1663 at the new Theatre Royal in Drury Lane. Though the office of Master of the Revels had lapsed with the closing of the theatres in 1642, Sir Henry Herbert was still alive and tried to assert his old authority, but the new companies were authorized to perform without his censorship. On Herbert's death in 1673, Killigrew succeeded him as Master. His plays were published in 1664. Pepys called him 'a merry droll, but a gentleman of great esteem with the king'.

'Kind-Harts Dreame.' See CHETTLE.

'KING JOHN.'

WRITTEN: 1596–7. Mentioned by Meres, 1598. (Wilson dates it before 1590.)

PERFORMED: First recorded performance, 1737.

REGISTERED: No entry. On 8 November 1623 Blount and Isaac Jaggard entered for their copy of all Shakespeare's plays that had not previously been published as Quartos, except *King John* and *The Taming of the Shrew*, possibly because they passed as reprints of the older plays, *The Troublesome Reign* and *The Taming of A Shrew*.

PUBLISHED: 1623, F1. 'The life and death of King Iohn.' The first play in the History section: pp. 1–22. Acts and scenes marked (Act v marked iv). A good text, set up from author's fair copy used as prompt-book?

SOURCE: *The Troublesome Raigne of Iohn King of England* (q.v.), an anonymous play in two parts published in 1591. Shakespeare follows the action of the old play fairly closely, but entirely rewrites it.

STAGE HISTORY: The revival by Rich at Covent Garden in 1737 is the first recorded performance. In 1745. Colley Cibber's adaptation, *Papal Tyranny in the Reign of King John*, was inspired by the threatened '45 Rebellion, as was Garrick's rival production of the original Shakespeare at Drury Lane. The production of Charles Kemble (q.v.), in 1823, was remarkable for its attempted historical fidelity. (See PLANCHÉ.)

King John is threatened with war by King Philip of France and the Duke of Austria, who support the claim of his nephew Arthur to the English throne. John, with his mother Elinor, and Philip, bastard son of Richard I, invade France, but peace is made by the marriage of John's niece, Blanch, to the Dauphin. However, the papal legate, Cardinal Pandulph, threatens King Philip with excommunication if he makes an alliance with the arch-heretic John, and Philip deserts him. In the ensuing battle, the English are victorious, the Bastard kills Austria, and Arthur is captured and sent to England to be put to death by Hubert de Burgh. Arthur's mother, Constance, goes mad with grief and dies. Hubert cannot bring himself to injure Arthur, who, however, kills himself in trying to escape. Salisbury and many of the English nobility suspect John of Arthur's murder and join the Dauphin, who is invading England. John gives the Bastard 'the ordering of this present time', and is himself poisoned by a monk and dies at Swinstead Abbey. Meanwhile the revolted English lords, having discovered the Dauphin's treachery, return to their allegiance, and the play ends with the retreat of the French before a united England faithful to the new King, Henry III.

'KING LEAR.'

WRITTEN: 1605–6. (See FLEIR.)

PERFORMED: 1606, 26 December, 'yt was played before the Kinges maiestie at Whitehall vppon Sainct Stephens night ... by his maiesties servantes.'

REGISTERED: 1607. '26 Novembris. Nathanael Butter John Busby. Entred for their Copie under thandes of Sir George Buck knight and Thwardens A booke called. Master William Shakespeare his historye of Kinge Lear, as yt was played before the Kinges maiestie at Whitehall vppon Sainct Stephens night at Christmas Last, by his maiesties servantes playinge vsually at the Globe on the Banksyde vj^{d}.'

PUBLISHED: 1608, Q1. 'M. William Shakspeare: His True Chronicle Historie of the life and death of King Lear and his three Daughters. With the vnfortunate life of Edgar, sonne and heire to the Earle of Gloster, and his sullen and assumed humor of Tom of Bedlam: As it was played before the Kings Maiestie at Whitehall vpon S. Stephens night in Christmas Hollidayes. By his Maiesties seruants playing vsually at the Gloabe on the Bancke-side. London, Printed for Nathaniel Butter, and are to be sold at his shop in Pauls Church-yard at the signe of the Pide Bull neere St. Austins Gate. 1608.' The 'Pide Bull' edition is not a 'bad' Quarto, but there is much mislineation, little punctuation, and prose printed as verse and verse as prose. Q1 omits about 100 lines found in F1. Perhaps set up from a surreptitious transcript of foul papers, by boys who played Goneril and Regan. (Alice Walker.)

1619. Q2. One of the ten plays reprinted by Jaggard (q.v.), many of them with false dates. The imprint on this Q is merely 'Printed for Nathaniel Butter 1608.'

1623, F1. 'The Tragedie of King Lear.' The ninth play in the Tragedy section: pp. 283–309. Acts and scenes marked. F omits about 300 lines found in Q, including the whole of iv, iii, but includes the Fool's prophecy at the end of iii, ii. Set up from Q1 collated with prompt-book. It is the more authoritative Text.

1655, Q3.

SOURCES: The Lear story is told in Holinshed's *Chronicles*, Spenser's *Faerie Queene* (ii, x), *The Mirrour for Magistrates*, and the anonymous play *King Leir* (q.v.). Sidney's *Arcadia* (ii, x) gives the outline of the Gloucester story.

STAGE HISTORY: The play was produced soon after the Restoration, and again in 1675, but this was the last original version for more than 160 years. In 1681, Nahum Tate rectified 'what was wanting in the Regularity and Probability of the Tale' and gave the play a happy ending in which Lear is restored to his kingdom and Cordelia marries Edgar. This version was approved by Johnson and acted by Betterton, Garrick, J. P. Kemble and Edmund Kean. In 1838, Macready returned to Shakespeare's text.

Lear, King of Britain, intends dividing his kingdom among his three daughters, Goneril, Regan, and Cordelia, but because Cordelia is unable to make a public profession of her love for him he disinherits her and banishes Kent for protesting. The King of France marries the dowerless Cordelia, and Lear divides the kingdom between Goneril and Regan and their husbands Albany and Cornwall, though he retains the title of King. These two elder daughters refuse to have their father in their houses with his retinue of a hundred knights, and Lear, broken by their hard hearts and ingratitude, goes out into the storm where he loses his reason. There he meets the apparently mad Edgar, the son of Gloucester, who has banished him owing to the machinations of his other and illegitimate son Edmund. The disguised Kent and Gloucester assist Lear, and Gloucester is blinded by Cornwall for doing so. Edgar then guides his father towards Dover, where Cordelia has landed with French troops in aid of her father, and Kent does the same for Lear. There is a reconciliation between Lear and Cordelia, but in the battle they are defeated and captured, Cordelia being hanged by order of Edmund. Goneril poisons Regan for love of Edmund, and when he is killed in combat with his brother Edgar she stabs herself. Edgar tells how his father died when he revealed himself to him. Lear then comes in with Cordelia dead in his arms, and dies, imagining that after all she lives. Like Gloucester, his flawed heart bursts "twixt two extremes of passion, joy and grief'. Albany is left to govern the kingdom.

'King Leir.' An anonymous play registered 14 May 1594, and again 8 May 1605, and printed in 1605 as 'The True Chronicle History of King Leir, and his three daughters, Gonorill, Ragan, and Cordella. As it hath bene diuers and sundry times lately acted'. The play was produced at Henslowe's Rose on 6 and 9 April 1594, by 'the Quenes men & my lord of Susexe to geather'. The authorship has been variously attributed to Lodge, Peele, Greene and Kyd. Shakespeare certainly knew *King Leir*, the closest version to his own play, a production of which in 1605 may have inspired him to write *King Lear*. The old play, which like all other versions ends happily, does not, of course, contain the Gloucester sub-plot.

'King Stephen.' A play registered by Humphrey Moseley 29 June 1660: 'The History of King Stephen. by Will: Shakespeare'. Nothing more is known about the play.

King's Company. On 21 August 1660 Charles II made the following grant:

We ... doe hereby giue and grante vnto the said Thomas Killigrew and Sir William Dauenant full power and authority to erect two companies of players ... and to purchase, builde and erect, or hire ... two houses or theatres ... And in regard of the extraordinary licentiousness that hath been lately used in things of this nature, our pleasure is that there shall be noe more places of representations, nor companies of actors of playes ... in our citties of London and Westminster, or in the liberties of them, then the two to be now erected by vertue of this authority.

Killigrew formed his company, the King's, mainly from the older actors, but with the addition of Kynaston, and they moved from the Red Bull, where plays had been given some months before the Restoration, to the theatre converted from Gibbons's tennis-court in Vere Street. In May 1663 they occupied the newly-built Theatre Royal in Drury Lane ('the first Drury Lane'). This was burned down in 1672, but Wren built a second Drury Lane which was ready for them in March 1674. In 1682 they were joined by the other company, the Duke's. A royal warrant of January 1669 had given the King's the exclusive right to perform twenty of Shakespeare's plays, but of these, between 1660 and 1682, they produced only four: *Othello*, *1 Henry IV*, *The Merry Wives* and *Julius Caesar*. 'Such', comments Malone, 'was the lamentable taste of those times that the plays of Fletcher, Jonson and Shirley, were much oftener exhibited than those of our author.' *Othello* was produced 8 December 1660, with Margaret Hughes as Desdemona, and this is probably the first appearance of an actress on the English public stage.

King's Men. See CHAMBERLAIN'S-KING'S MEN.

King's Revels. See CHILDREN OF THE KING'S REVELS.

Kirkham, Edward, Yeoman of the Revels from 1586 to sometime after 1617, was probably the Edward Kirkham who was a member of the Chapel Children syndicate of 1601. When Henry Evans surrendered the lease of the Blackfriars theatre to Burbage in 1608, so driving the Children from their home, Kirkham brought a number of suits against Evans, and in 1612 a Chancery action against Evans, Burbage, and Heminge. In his evidence, Kirkham makes the interesting claim that the King's Men made £1,000 more by their winter performances at the closed Blackfriars than they used to make at the open Globe. The sum refers, presumably, to the gross takings, not the net profits, of the housekeepers. (See KEYSAR.)

Kirkman, Francis (b. 1632), the son of a London blacksmith, he became a bookseller and author. In 1661 he published a valuable *Catalogue* of 690 printed *English Stage Playes*, revised in 1671 to include 806. In these lists he attributed *The Birth of Merlin* to Shakespeare and Rowley, publishing it as theirs in 1662. In 1672 appeared *The Wits; or Sport upon Sport*, a collection of drolls (q.v.) performed by the comedian Robert Cox at fairs and taverns while the theatres were closed, 1642–60. One of these is *The Merry conceited Humours of Bottom the Weaver. The Wits* is important for its frontispiece illustrating a 17th-century stage during the performance of a play. (See 'ROXANA'; 'MESSALINA'.)

Kittredge, George Lyman (1860–1941), American scholar, was educated at Harvard, where he became Professor of English Literature, 1894–1936. In addition to editing Shakespeare's plays, his *Shakspere* (1916) is a valuable introduction to the historical approach.

'Knacke to Knowe a Knave.' An anonymous play with a reference to the story of Titus Andronicus and the Goths. It was performed by Strange's 10 June 1592, when Henslowe marked it as new, registered 7 January 1594, and published in 1594 as 'A most pleasant and merie new Comedie, Intituled, A Knacke to knowe a knave. Newlie set foorth, as it hath sundrie tymes bene played by Ed. Allen and his Companie. With Kemps applauded Merrimentes of the men of Goteham, in receiuing the King into Goteham'. The reference is:

As Titus was vnto the Roman Senators,
When he had made a conquest on the Goths.

This suggests a performance of *Titus Andronicus* before June 1592, for Shakespeare's play is the only known version of the story with Goths instead of Moors. (But see NQ, II, 1955.)

Kneller, Sir Godfrey (1648–1723), portrait painter, was born at Lübeck. He came to England in 1674, and after the death of Sir Peter Lely in 1680 was appointed court painter by Charles II, a position that he held until George I's reign. Kneller painted what is apparently a copy of the Chandos portrait of Shakespeare and presented it to Dryden, who acknowledged it in his *Fourteenth Epistle* (1694):

Shakspeare, thy gift, I place before my sight;
With awe, I ask his blessing ere I write;
With reverence look on this majestic face;
Proud to be less, but of his godlike race ...

Kneller's portrait is now in the Folger Library. (See WORSDALE.)

Knight, Charles (1791–1873), publisher and author, was born at Windsor.

He published in serial form a number of works for the diffusion of useful knowledge, including *The Penny Magazine* and *The Penny Cyclopædia*. In 1843 appeared his *Pictorial Shakespeare* (8 vols.), which had been issued in parts, 1838–41, and his Library Edition (12 vols.), 1842–4. Knight was one of the original members of the council of the first Shakespeare Society (1840), and a pioneer of the study of Shakespeare's dramatic development.

Knight, Edward. Anthony and Edward Knight are among the twenty-one 'musitions and other necessary attendantes' of the King's Men mentioned by Sir Henry Herbert on 27 December 1624 (see PROTECTION OF PLAYERS). Edward was their book-keeper. On 12 October 1632, Herbert received a fee from Knight for allowing Jonson's *Magnetic Lady*, and on 21 October 1633 he returned the book of Fletcher's *Woman's Prize, or, The Tamer Tamed* with his expurgations and a curt note 'to Knight, their book-keeper':

Mr Knight,
In many things you have saved mee labour; yet wher your judgment or penn fayld you, I have made boulde to use mine. Purge ther parts, as I have the booke. And I hope every hearer and player will thinke that I have done God good servise, and the quality no wronge; who hath no greater enemies than oaths, prophaness, and publique ribaldrye, wh^ch^ for the future I doe absolutely forbid to bee presented unto mee in any playbooke, as you will answer it at your perill.

(The play was acted before the King and Queen at St James's on 28 November and 'very well likt'.) This is an interesting indication that the book-keeper was responsible for the acting version of a play, and actors' 'parts'. Knight transcribed *Bonduca* and annotated *Believe as you List*. Greg suggests that he did the detailed work of editing the Shakespeare Folio. If so, he 'would be a person of hitherto unexpected importance in the history of English literature'.

Knight, George Wilson (b. 1897), Shakespeare critic and producer, was educated at Dulwich College and St Edmund Hall, Oxford. After being a schoolmaster, he was successively Professor of English at Toronto University and Leeds. He is a leader of the symbolic method of interpretative criticism, finding 'tempests and music as dominant contrasted symbolic impressions'. (See BIBLIOGRAPHY.)

'Knight of the Burning Pestle.' A comedy by Beaumont, published in 1613, but written probably in 1607 for the Queen's Revels. Jasper's lines at the beginning of Act v seem to refer to Banquo's ghost, and afford a clue to the date of *Macbeth*:

When thou art at thy table with thy friends,
Merry in heart, and fill'd with swelling wine,
I'll come in midst of all thy pride and mirth,
Invisible to all men but thyself,
And whisper such a sad tale in thine ear,
Shall make thee let the cup fall from thy hand,
And stand as mute and pale as death itself.

Knowle. A Warwickshire village, some eight miles south-east of Birmingham. A fraternity called the Guild of St Anne was formed in 1413, and shortly afterwards a college of ten chantry priests. A number of Shakespeares, men and women, were members before the dissolution (see WROXALL), and in 1612 an Elizabeth Shaksper was a copyholder on the manor. (See W. B. Bickley, *Register of the Guild at Knowle*, 1894.)

Kreyssig, Friedrich A. T. (1818–79), German critic, and Headmaster in Frankfort-on-Main. Author of the important *Vorlesungen über Shakespeare* (3 vols. 1858–60).

Kyd, Thomas (1558–94), son of Francis Kyd, a London scrivener. He was baptized in St Mary Woolnoth, Lombard Street, November 6 1558, and in 1565 entered Merchant Taylors' School. There is no indication that he went to a university, and he may have followed his father's profession before turning to literature. If so, this makes clearer the reference in Nashe's Epistle to Greene's *Menaphon* (registered 23 August 1589), which is directed, like Greene's *Groatsworth of Wit* (1592), against upstart crows, playwrights without a university education, and the following passage may be directed against Kyd in particular:

It is common practise now a dayes amongst a sort of shifting companions, that runne through euery Art and thriue by none, to leaue the trade of *Nouerint* [scrivener], whereto they were borne, and busie themselues with the indeuours of Art, that could scarcely Latinize their neck verse if they should haue neede; yet English *Seneca* read by Candlelight yeelds many good sentences, as *Blood is a begger*, and so forth; and if you intreate him faire in a frostie morning, hee will affoord you whole *Hamlets*, I should say handfuls of Tragicall speeches.

It was probably in 1588–9 that Kyd's *Spanish Tragedy* (q.v.) was first performed, one of the most popular and influential plays of the age, in which the Senecan ingredients of revenge, ghosts, chorus, and rhetoric are adapted to the Elizabethan stage. The *Hamlet* reference is to the old play of *Hamlet*, the lost *Ur-Hamlet*, and on the strength of this the authorship has been attributed to Kyd. Nashe continues:

But O grief! *Tempus edax rerum*, whats that will last alwayes? The Sea exhaled by droppes will in continuance be drie, and *Seneca*, let blood line by line and page by page, at length must needes die to our Stage; which makes his famished followers to imitate the Kidde in *Æsop*, who, enamoured with the Foxes newfangles, forsooke all hopes of life to leape into a newe occupation; and these men, renouncing all possibilities of credite or estimation, to intermeddle with Italian translations.

Certainly, the popular horrors of *The Spanish Tragedy* led to imitations, of which *Titus Andronicus* is one, and Kyd intermeddled with translations, though his *Cornelia* was from the French of Robert Garnier's academic *Cornélie*, and written probably in 1593. This was dedicated to the Countess of Sussex, and it is probable, therefore, that the nobleman who had a company of players for whom Marlowe wrote, and whose service Kyd entered, *c.* 1587, was the Earl of Sussex. In May 1593 Marlowe was arrested on charges of lewd libels and blasphemies in which Kyd was involved, papers of his, one of 'vile heretical conceits denying the divinity of Jesus Christ', being found with those of Marlowe, to whom Kyd attributed their authorship. A month later Marlowe was killed, and Kyd was released, but he was dismissed by his patron and died in poverty before the end of 1594, his parents refusing to administer his estate. Kyd's hand has been traced by the disintegrators in a number of Shakespeare's plays, particularly in the Senecan *Titus Andronicus*, and *Hamlet*.

Kynaston, Edward (*c.* 1645–1706). At the Restoration professional actresses did not at once displace boys in women's parts on the public stage. On 18 August 1660 Pepys saw Fletcher's *Loyal Subject* at the Cockpit, 'where, one Kinaston, a boy, acted the Duke's sister, but made the loveliest lady that ever I saw in my life'. Shortly after this, Killigrew took him into the newly formed King's Company, with whom Pepys saw him on 7 January 1661 in Jonson's *Silent Woman* (*Epicoene*):

Among other things here, Kinaston, the boy, had the good turn to appear in three shapes: first as a poor woman in ordinary clothes, to please Morose; then in fine clothes, as a gallant; and in them was clearly the prettiest woman in the whole house; and lastly, as a man; and then likewise did appear the handsomest man in the house.

John Downes, in his *Roscius Anglicanus* (1708), refers to this period when he,

being then very Young made a compleat Female Stage Beauty, performing his Parts so well ... being Parts greatly moving Compassion and Pity; that it hath since been Disputable among the Judicious, whether any

Woman that succeeded him so Sensibly touch'd the Audience as he.

Later, he played men's parts; for example, Antony to Charles Hart's Brutus in a revival of *Julius Caesar* in 1672. In 1695, with Betterton, he left Drury Lane for the new theatre in Lincoln's Inn Fields.

L

Lacy, John (d. 1681), was a dancing-master who, in the Civil War, secured a commission in the King's army; after the Restoration he turned actor with Killigrew's company and became Charles II's favourite comedian. He wrote four plays, one of them a coarse prose version of *The Taming of the Shrew*, called *Sauny the Scot*, in which Grumio (Sauny) becomes the chief character. Pepys saw the play 9 April 1667:

> To the King's house, and there saw 'The Tameing of a Shrew', which hath some very good pieces in it, but generally is but a mean play; and the best part, 'Sawny', done by Lacy; and hath not half its life, by reason of the words, I suppose, not being understood, at least by me.

Lady Elizabeth's Men. The Lady Elizabeth (1596–1662) was the daughter of James I, and is best known as Elizabeth of Bohemia (q.v.), who married the Elector Palatine in 1613. A company under her patronage received a patent 27 April 1611, and on 29 August signed a bond to Henslowe, among the actors being three future members of the King's Men, Joseph Taylor, William Ecclestone and John Rice. They are first heard of in the provinces, but in 1612 they performed four times at Court. In 1613 there was an alliance with the Queen's Revels, which included Nathan Field, and *c.* 1614–16 with the Duke of York's. As the company was financed by Henslowe, they probably played for a time at the Rose, but in 1614 were at his newly-built Hope, where they played *Bartholomew Fair* (q.v.). In 1615 they quarrelled with Henslowe (q.v.) and drew up the famous 'Articles of Oppression against Mr. Hinchlowe'. Henslowe died in 1616, and the Lady Elizabeth's are not heard of again in London until 1622, when they were with Christopher Beeston at his Cockpit, where they were replaced in 1625 by Queen Henrietta's Men.

'Laelia.' An academic play performed at Queen's College, Cambridge, in 1595. It is a Latin adaptation of the Sienese comedy, *Gl'Ingannati*, from the French version, *Les Abuses* (1543), of Charles Estienne. *Gl'Ingannati* is the ultimate source of the main plot in *Twelfth Night.*

Laertes. In *Hamlet* (q.v.), the son of Polonius and brother of Ophelia, whom he warns against Hamlet's overtures of love.

Lafew. In *All's Well*, an old lord who takes Helena from Rousillon to Paris, and presents her to the King. He quarrels with Parolles, and warns Bertram not to trust him, but when Parolles proves to be the inflated coward that he thought, he behaves generously to him.

Lamb, Charles (1775–1834). Lamb wrote little Shakespearean criticism, but it is all the more precious for its scarcity. In 1807 was published *Tales founded on the Plays of Shakespeare*, in which he described the tragedies and his sister Mary the comedies. In the following year came his *Specimens of English Dramatic Poets who lived about the time of Shakespeare*, a book that did much to stimulate interest in Shakespeare's contemporaries, and the notes to which show a sensitive appreciation of the Elizabethans. His essay *On the Tragedies of Shakespeare, considered with reference to their fitness for Stage Representation* first appeared in 1811, in Leigh Hunt's quarterly periodical, *The Reflector*, and in it he maintains 'that the plays of Shakespeare are less calculated for performance on a stage, than those of almost any other dramatist whatever', and that 'the Lear of Shakespeare cannot be acted', the fine abstraction of reading the plays being preferable to the distraction of a performance.

Lamb, George (1784–1834), youngest son of the 1st Viscount Melbourne, and secretary of state in Grey's Whig ministry of 1830. On 28 October 1816 his adaptation of *Timon of Athens* was produced at Drury Lane and published the same year, as 'an attempt to restore Shakespeare to the stage, with no other omissions than such as the refinement of manners has rendered necessary'.

Lambarde, William (d. 1601), the antiquary, became Keeper of the records in the Tower, and on 4 August 1601 he made a note of a conversation with the Queen:

... her Majestie fell upon the reign of King Richard II, saying, 'I am Richard II. know ye not that?'

W. L. 'Such a wicked imagination was determined and attempted by a most unkind Gent. the most adorned creature that ever your Majestie made.'

HER MAJESTIE. 'He that will forget God, will also forget his benefactors; this tragedy was played 40tie times in open streets and houses.'

This is a reference to the performances of *Richard II* which Essex at his trial was said to have frequented, being accused of aspiring to play Bolingbroke to Elizabeth's Richard.

The 1596 edition of Lambarde's *Perambulation of Kent*, first published in 1576, contains the interesting note that pilgrims to the shrine at Boxley,

no more than such as goe to Parisgardein, the Bell Sauage, or Theatre, to beholde Beare baiting, Enterludes, or Fence play, can account of any pleasant spectacle, unlesse they first pay one pennie at the gate, another at the entrie of the Scaffolde, and the thirde for a quiet standing.

In a copy of Lambarde's *Archaionomia* (1568) in the Folger Library is the signature 'W. Shakspere', which some accept as genuine.

Lambert, Edmund (d. 1587), lived at Barton-on-the-Heath (q.v.) and married Shakespeare's aunt, Joan Arden. In November 1578 Shakespeare's father, John, mortgaged a house and land at Wilmcote, the property of his wife Mary Arden, to Lambert as security for a loan of £40, which was not repaid, and on Edmund's death in April 1587 the property passed to his son John. In September 1587, according to a Bill of Complaint of 1588 in the case of *Shakespeare* v. *Lambert*, 'Johannes Shackespere et Maria vxor eius, simulcum Willielmo Shackespere filio suo' made an offer, apparently verbal, to sell the estate outright to John Lambert in consideration of a further payment of £20. Lambert, however, kept the property in spite of the attempts of the Shakespeares to recover it. This mention of the poet in the Bill of 1588 is the only record we have of him between that of the baptism of his children Hamnet and Judith on 2 February 1585, and Greene's oblique reference in his *Groatsworth of Wit* of September 1592. The fact that Shakespeare was a party to the verbal offer of September 1587 does not imply that he was in Stratford at the time.

The parish register at Barton-on-the-Heath records:

Edmund Lambarte, senior, buried 23 April, 1587.

1593. Joanna Lambarte, vidua, buried 30 November.

Lampe, John Frederick (1703–51), German musician, was born in Saxony and died in Edinburgh. He married the singer Isabella Young, the sister-in-law of Arne. Lampe was a bassoon player, and composer of songs, theatre music, and of hymn tunes for his friend Charles Wesley. In 1745, his elaborated version of Richard Leveridge's 'Comic Masque', made out of the Pyramus and Thisbe episodes in *A Midsummer Night's Dream*, was performed at Covent Garden.

Lancaster, Prince John of (1389–1435), third son of Henry IV. He first appears in *1 Henry IV* (v, i) at the Battle of Shrewsbury, after which he is congratulated by the Prince of Wales and sent to deal with the northern rebels. The leaders of these he captures in *2 Henry IV* by persuading them to dismiss their forces on his promise to redress their wrongs; he then arrests them and sends them to execution with Colevile, whom Falstaff has captured. Falstaff says of him (IV, iii), 'this same young sober-blooded boy doth not love me; nor a man cannot make him laugh'.

In 1414, Prince John was created Duke of Bedford, as which he plays a small part in *Henry V*, though he was not in fact at Agincourt. In *1 Henry VI*, as Regent of France, he takes Orleans (II, i, ii) and Rouen, where he dies and is buried (III, ii).

Landor, Walter Savage (1775–1864). There is a certain amount of Shakespearean criticism, or rather of eulogy, in the *Imaginary Conversations*: for example, '*Landor.* A rib of Shakespeare would have made a Milton: the same portion of Milton, all poets born ever since'. (Vol. II. *Southey and Landor.*) Swinburne, who belonged to the same exclamatory school, surprisingly wrote at the end of his *Study of Shakespeare* (1880):

> The time is wellnigh come now for me to consecrate in this book my good will if not good work to the threefold and thrice happy memory of the three who have written of Shakespeare as never man wrote, nor ever man may write again; to the everlasting praise and honour and glory of Charles Lamb, Samuel Taylor Coleridge, and Walter Savage Landor.

Lane, John (senior), was of Alveston Manor, at the western end of Clopton Bridge, Stratford. In 1584, he married Frances Nash, aunt of Thomas Nash, the first husband of Shakespeare's granddaughter, Elizabeth Hall. In July 1613 Elizabeth's mother, Shakespeare's daughter Susanna Hall, brought an action of slander in the Ecclesiastical Court of Worcester against his son John, aged 23, who 'about five weekes past reported that the plaintiff had the runninge of the raynes, and had bin naught with Rafe Smith at John Palmer'. Robert Whatcott, who was to be a witness of Shakespeare's will, was chief witness on behalf of Susanna, but Lane failed to appear, and her character was cleared by his excommunication. In 1619 he led an attack on the Puritan vicar, Wilson, and was presented by the Churchwardens as a drunkard. (See GREENE, JOHN.)

Lane, Richard, was John Lane senior's elder brother, and held tithes in Stratford worth £80 a year. It was probably in 1611 that he 'and William Shackspeare, and some few others' drafted a Bill of Complaint protesting that William Combe was not paying his share of the mean rent which they themselves had to pay 'for preservacion of their estates', for failure to pay gave the owner, Henry Barker, the right of reentry. He died in 1613. His son Edward married Mary, daughter of Thomas Combe. (See p. 543.)

Lane's Men. Sir Robert Lane, of Horton, Northants, had a company of players who performed twice at Court during the Revels of 1571–2, the payee being Laurence Dutton, who in the following year led the Earl of Lincoln's. Probably, owing to the Act of 1572, whereby players were to belong to a 'Baron of this Realme', Lane's Men had to exchange their knightly patron for a peer.

Laneman, Henry. See CURTAIN THEATRE.

Langbaine, Gerard (1656–92), son of the Provost of Queen's, Oxford, was educated at University College, and after a lively youth married and settled down to literature. In 1687 he published *Momus Triumphans, or the Plagiaries of the*

English Stage exposed, in which he pedantically, but valuably, catalogued the sources used by the early dramatists, including Shakespeare. In 1691 appeared *An Account of the English Dramatick Poets*, which unfortunately adds nothing to our knowledge of Shakespeare. The book was revised and brought up-to-date by Charles Gildon in 1699. William Oldys (q.v.) annotated two copies of the 1691 edition, one of which was used by Theophilus Cibber for his *Lives of the Poets* (1753).

Langley, Francis (1550–1601). A London goldsmith who, in May 1589, bought the Manor of Paris Garden from Thomas Cure for £850. On 3 November 1594 the Lord Mayor wrote to Lord Burghley, 'I vnderstand that one Francis Langley, one of the Alneagers for sealing of cloth, intendeth to erect a niew stage or Theater (as they call it) for thexercising of playes vpon the Banck side', and protesting against the proposal. However, the new theatre, the Swan (q.v.), appears to have been built by 1595–6, for in February 1597 Pembroke's Men bound themselves to Langley to play for a year at the Swan, and at that date 'the said howse was then lately afore vsed to have playes in hit'. It is probable that Pembroke's predecessors were the Chamberlain's, for in a recently discovered writ of November 1596, William Wayte (q.v.) craves sureties of the peace against William Shakspere and Francis Langley, and in 1596 the City inn-theatres were suppressed, the Admiral's were at the Rose, and of the other two theatres the Curtain was old, and the Burbages were quarrelling with the owner of the land on which their Theatre stood. In July 1597 Pembroke's played the seditious *Isle of Dogs*, the theatres were closed for the summer, and when re-opened five of Pembroke's joined the Admiral's, and Langley sued them for breach of contract. Like Henslowe, Langley was a financier; he let his theatre in return for half the gallery takings, lent apparel for which he recouped himself out of the other half 'of the gains for the several standynges in the galleries', and again like Henslowe, bound actors to play for him alone.

Lartius. See TITUS LARTIUS.

Launce. In *The Two Gentlemen of Verona*, 'a clownish seruant to Proteus', whom he accompanies to Milan. Most of his scenes are either with Speed, Valentine's 'clownish servant', or with his dog Crab, which he offers to Silvia as a present from his master instead of the 'little jewel' of a dog that Proteus had bought for her and Launce had lost.

Lavinia. The heroine of *Titus Andronicus* (q.v.), and daughter of Titus.

'Law Against Lovers, The.' D'Avenant's improved version of *Measure for Measure*, in which Beatrice and 'Benedict' strangely appear from *Much Ado*. The low comedy is cut out; Benedict is the brother of Angelo, who is only testing Isabella's virtue before declaring his lawful love; and Beatrice has a younger sister Viola, whose dancing and singing so delighted Pepys when he saw the play on 18 February 1662:

> I went to the Opera, and saw 'the Law against Lovers', a good play and well performed, especially the little girl's, whom I never saw act before, dancing and singing; and were it not for her, the losse of Roxalana [Elizabeth Davenport] would spoil the house.

Law, Matthew (d. 1629). Bookseller. On 25 June 1603 Andrew Wise, who had originally registered them, transferred the copyright in three of Shakespeare's Histories to Law:

> 25 Junij Mathew Lawe. Entred for his copies in full courte Holden this Day. These ffyve copies followinge ij^{s} vj^{d} viz. iij enterludes or playes. The ffirst is of Richard the 3. The second of Richard the 2. The Third of Henry the 4 the first parte, all kinges ... all whiche by consent of the Company are sett ouer to him from Andrew Wyse.

Law thereupon published:

1 Henry IV: Q3, 1603; Q4, 1608; Q5, 1613; Q6, 1622.
Richard III: Q4, 1605; Q5, 1612; Q6, 1622.
Richard II: Q4, 1608; Q5, 1615.

Law's shop was 'In Pauls Churchyard, at the Signe of the Foxe, neere S. Austines gate', and he was fined several times for opening it on Sundays, as well as for selling pirated editions of books.

Lawrence, Henry. See ANDREWES.

Lawrence, William Witherle (1876–1958), American scholar, Professor of English at Columbia University; author of *Shakespeare's Problem Comedies*, 1931, etc.

Leake, William. Bookseller. He began business *c.* 1586, was elected Master of the Stationers' Company in 1618, retired after his year of office, and died in 1633. In 1596 Harrison transferred *Venus and Adonis* to Leake, who published O3–O8 between 1599 and 1602.

'Lear König von Engelandt.' A tragedy played at Dresden in 1626 by John Green's touring company of actors. It may have been a version of Shakespeare's play, or of the earlier *King Leir*.

Le Beau. In *As You Like It*, an affected courtier attending Duke Frederick. In I, ii he announces the wrestling-match, and later advises Orlando to leave the palace. (In F, except in the first stage-direction, he is called Le Beu.)

Lectures on Shakespeare. The first public lectures on Shakespeare of which there is record are those of the actor Charles Macklin, who in November 1754, at his tavern, began a series of evening lectures 'upon each of Shakespear's Plays', followed by a debate. The next series appears to have been that of William Kenrick, who published them in 1774 as *Introduction to the School of Shakespeare*. The most famous are the courses by Coleridge in 1811–12 and 1818.

Lee, Robert. An actor named in the plot of *The Dead Man's Fortune*, probably an Admiral's play, *c.* 1591. In 1593 he entered into a bond to Edward Alleyn. 1604–19 he was with Queen Anne's, and in 1622 with the Revels.

Lee, Sidney (1859–1926), Shakespeare scholar, was born in London and educated at the City of London School and Balliol, Oxford. In 1883 he became assistant editor of the *Dictionary of National Biography*, and in 1891 succeeded Sir Leslie Stephen as editor. His article on Shakespeare was the basis of his *Life of William Shakespeare* (1898), for thirty years the standard work on the subject. Other publications were, *Stratford-on-Avon from the Earliest Times to the Death of Shakespeare* (1885), *Shakespeare and the Modern Stage* (1906), *Shakespeare and the Italian Renaissance* (1915). In 1902 he edited the Oxford facsimile edition of the First Folio. He was knighted in 1911, and in 1917 became President of the English Association. From 1913 to 1924 he was Professor of English in London University. Lee's scholarship is now out of date.

Lefranc, Abel (1863–1952), French scholar, and Professor of French, Collège de France, 1904–37. He maintained that William Stanley, 6th Earl of Derby, was the author of Shakespeare's works. Though his main thesis will be found generally unacceptable, there is valuable material in his *A la Découverte de Shakespeare* (1945).

Legge, Thomas (1535–1607), was educated at Corpus Christi, Cambridge, in 1573 becoming Master of Caius, and in 1593 Vice-Chancellor. According to Meres (1598), 'Doctor *Leg* hath penned two famous tragedies, ye one of *Richard the 3*, the other of *The destruction of Ierusalem*'. The second of these has been lost, but the first is preserved at Cambridge. *Richard Tertius* is an academic Latin play, and was acted at St John's in 1580. Its influence on Shakespeare's *Richard III* is doubtful.

Legh, Gerard (d. 1563), writer on heraldry. His *Accedens of Armorie* (1563) contains the story of King Lear, and his description of the arms of Alexander furnished Shakespeare with the jest of Ajax, the lion, and the close-stool in *Love's Labour's Lost*, v, ii. (See HARINGTON.) Legh followed his father's trade, becoming a member of the Drapers' Company, with whom he quarrelled, entered the Middle Temple, and died of the plague.

Legouis, Émile (1861–1937), French scholar, by his lectures at the Sorbonne did much to stimulate interest in Shakespeare and the Elizabethans. He wrote a number of critical works on English literature, including *Shakespeare* (1899), and, with L. Cazamian, the well-known *Histoire de la Littérature Anglaise* (1924).

Leicester, Robert Dudley, Earl of (1532–88), was the fifth son of the ambitious Protector Northumberland, who married another of his sons, Guildford Dudley, to Lady Jane Grey, whom on Edward VI's death in 1553 he declared Queen. With his father and brother, Robert Dudley was condemned to death by Mary, but was pardoned. Under Elizabeth he rose to high favour, and there was the possibility of his marrying her. His first wife, Amy Robsart, who stood in the way of such an ambition, died under suspicious circumstances in 1560: she was said to have broken her neck in falling down stairs. Two years later Elizabeth granted him Kenilworth Castle, in 1564 created him Earl of Leicester, and it was at Kenilworth (q.v.) that he entertained the Queen in 1566, 1572, and 1575. As Earl of Leicester, honours were showered upon him, but his marriage in 1578 to the widow of the Earl of Essex displeased Elizabeth and brought him for a time into disgrace. He was, however, restored to favour, and in 1585 given the command of the expedition to help the Dutch against Spain. He died 4 September 1588, shortly after the defeat of the Armada, during which crisis he was Lieutenant-General of the army. His sister, Mary Dudley, married Sir Henry Sidney, whose eldest son was Sir Philip Sidney, fatally wounded at Zutphen in 1586 on Leicester's campaign in the Low Countries.

Leicester's Men. There are fairly continuous records of Leicester's Men (until 1564 known as Dudley's) from 1559 onwards, mostly in the provinces, though at Court in the winters of 1560–62. In 1572, after the proclamation against unlawful retainers, Leicester's petitioned their patron 'to certifye that we are your houshold Servaunts when we shall have occasion to travayle amongst our frendes as we do usuallye once a yere, and as other noble-mens Players do'. The petition is signed by 'Iames Burbage. Iohn Perkinne. Iohn Laneham. William Iohnson. Roberte Wilson. Thomas Clarke'. In 1574 the favourite's Men received a licence from Elizabeth herself:

> We ... do licence and auctorise, oure lovinge Subiectes, Iames Burbage, Iohn Perkyn, Iohn Lanham, William Iohnson, and Roberte Wilson, seruantes to our trustie and welbeloued Cosen and Counseyllor the Earle of Leycester, to vse, exercise, and occupie the arte and facultye of playenge Commedies, Tragedies, Enterludes, stage playes, and such other like ... as well within oure Citie of London and liberties of the same, as also ... thoroughte oure Realme of England ... Prouyded that the said ... stage playes be by the master of oure Revells for the tyme beynge before sene & allowed ...

This patent is important in the history of the theatre; not only is it the first of its kind, but in allowing the company to play anywhere in England, even in the City of London, Elizabeth overrode the cherished privilege of the Corporation to regulate all public entertainments. For the next ten years they were the most important of the actors' companies, performing regularly at Court, and in 1576 they would have James Burbage's new Theatre as their headquarters. After 1583, however, their position declined, for in that year Laneham, Johnson and Wilson joined the newly formed Queen's Company, of which Tarlton, the popular jester, also became a member, and for the next decade the Queen's took the lead. In 1585 Leicester went on his expedition to Holland, and with him was 'Mr Kemp. called Don Gulihelmo', referred to by Sir Philip Sidney, Leicester's nephew, as 'my lord of Lester's jesting plaier'. Kempe, then, seems to have been one of Leicester's Men, but it is not clear whether the five English players, including George Bryan and Thomas Pope, afterwards fellows of Shakespeare, who visited the Courts of Denmark and Saxony in 1586–7, were in his service. Probably not, for Leicester's played at Court in December 1586, and were in Stratford the same year, but there is no evidence to support the popular belief that Shakespeare joined them there and went with them to London. Soon after Leicester's death on 4 September 1588 the company came to an end. Baldwin thinks they joined Strange's in a body.

Leland, John (*c.* 1506–52), the antiquary, was born in London and educated at St Paul's and Christ's, Cambridge. He became chaplain and librarian to Henry VIII, who appointed him King's Antiquary and commissioned him to search for records in the cathedrals and monasteries of England. His antiquarian tour lasted from 1534 to 1542, when he began to write a history of the antiquities and a topography of England. By 1550, however, he was insane, and died in April 1552. His manuscripts were used by the later antiquaries, Stow, Camden and Dugdale, the account of his journey being edited and published by Thomas Hearne in 1710–12 as *The Itinerary of John Leland* (9 vols.). In the *Itinerary* Leland describes New Place (q.v.) as it was *c.* 1540.

Lena, Popilius. In *Julius Caesar*, a senator whose ambiguous speech suggests that he is about to reveal the conspiracy to Caesar just before the assassination (III, i). (Really, Laenas, a family of the Popilia gens.)

Length of Performances. There were four main kinds of performance: those in the London public and private theatres, at Court, and in the provinces. In October 1594 Lord Chamberlain Hunsdon told the Lord Mayor that his new company of players at the Cross Keys, who formerly 'began not their Plaies till towardes fower a clock, they will now begin at two, & haue don betwene fower and fiue'. A playing time of two to two and a half hours, which would probably mean a text of some 2,500 lines, seems to have been common in the public theatres; cf. *Romeo and Juliet* (1595), 'the two hours' traffic of our stage', *Henry VIII* (1612), 'two short hours', *Bartholomew Fair* (1614), 'the space of two hours and a half and somewhat more'. But the full text of *Hamlet* and of *Antony and Cleopatra* could scarcely be played in under three and a half hours, and it looks as though performances varied considerably in length. It is probable that plays were cut for provincial performance owing to the reduced number of players, and plays written primarily for the private theatres were probably shorter, to make time for more elaborate production and incidental music. (See 'MALCONTENT'.)

Lennox. In *Macbeth*, a Scottish nobleman. When Macduff has discovered the murdered Duncan, Lennox accompanies Macbeth to Duncan's room and apparently approves of Macbeth's murder of the drunken grooms. After Banquo's murder and Macbeth's strange behaviour he realizes the truth (III, vi) and joins in the rebellion.

Lennox, Charlotte (1720–1804), daughter of Colonel James Ramsay, lieutenant-general of New York. In London, after her father's death, she turned unsuccessfully to the stage and more successfully to literature. In 1752 she published her novel, *A Female Quixote*, and in 1753–4 her *Shakespear Illustrated; or the Novels and Histories on which the Plays are founded*. This is important as the first published collection of the sources of more than half of Shakespeare's plays, though she maintained that Shakespeare often spoiled the original stories by elaborating them. According to Bennet Langton,

> Dr Goldsmith, upon occasion of Mrs Lennox's bringing out a play [*The Sisters*, a comedy performed one night only, at Covent Garden, in 1769], said to Dr Johnson at the Club, that a person had advised him to go and hiss it, because she had attacked Shakespeare in her book called 'Shakespear Illustrated'.

Johnson had a very high opinion of her, considering her superior to Hannah More and Fanny Burney, and writing a dedication for her *Shakespear Illustrated*, though he made little use of it in his edition of Shakespeare (1765). She died in London in 1804 'in distressed circumstances'. (See LANGBAINE.)

Lennox's Men. Ludovic Stuart (1574–1624), cousin of James I, succeeded as 2nd Duke of Lennox in 1583, and was created Earl and then Duke of Richmond in 1613 and 1623 respectively. A company of his men is traceable in the provinces 1604–8. It may have been a continuation of Queen Elizabeth's Men under a new patron, for two of its members, John Garland and Francis Henslowe, were of that company, and possibly Lennox's in turn became the Duke of York's, formed in 1608, for Garland was with them in 1610. (See RICHMOND, LUDOVICK.)

Lent. In theory, there was to be no playing in Lent; this is made clear by a Privy Council Minute of 13 March 1579, addressed to the Lord Mayor of London and the J.P.s of Middlesex, 'that there be no plaiers suffered to plaie during this tyme of Lent, until it be after the Ester weke'. In practice, the order was difficult to enforce and was often ignored. In 1592 Strange's played almost every weekday from 19 February to 23 June, though they observed Good Friday; towards the end of the century the Admiral's compromised by playing only three days a week during Lent. In 1600 the Privy Council ordered the two authorized London companies, the Chamberlain's and Admiral's, to 'refraine to play on the Sabboth daie', and to 'forbeare altogether in the time of Lent'. And on 29 March 1615 John Heminge, Richard Burbage and other leading actors of the London companies were summoned before the Privy Council for playing 'notwithstanding the commaundement of the Lord Chamberlayne signified vnto them by the Master of the Revells' during 'this prohibited time of Lent'. This explains the note of Sir Henry Herbert (q.v.), Master of the Revels, 'Received of the King's players for a *lenten dispensation*, the other companys promising to doe as muche, 44s. March 23, 1616'.

Leonardo. In *The Merchant of Venice*, a servant of Bassanio, who sends him to buy a livery for Launcelot Gobbo (II, ii).

Leonato. In *Much Ado*, Governor of Messina, and father of Hero. (Lionato de' Lionati in Bandello's story.)

Leonine. In *Pericles*, 'a murtherer, servant to Dionisia', who persuades him to kill Marina. As he is about to do so he is attacked by pirates and runs away. Nevertheless, he tells Dionyza that Marina is dead, and she poisons him.

Leontes. In *The Winter's Tale*, the King of Sicilia. (Pandosto, King of Bohemia, in Greene's *Pandosto*.)

'Leopold Shakespeare.' The one-volume edition of Shakespeare, with the text of Delius and an introduction by F. J. Furnivall on the subject of verse-tests, published in 1877. So called because dedicated to H.R.H. Prince Leopold, Duke of Albany.

Lepidus, M. Aemilius (d. 13 B.C.). In *Julius Caesar* he is a witness of Caesar's assassination, after which he joins Octavius and becomes one of the Triumvirate, 'a slight unmeritable man', according to Antony. In *Antony and Cleopatra* he tries to keep the peace between Antony and Octavius, is carried away drunk from Pompey's banquet, and in III, v, Eros reports his overthrow and imprisonment by Octavius. (Consul 46 B.C., he was confined in Circeii by Octavius after trying to seize Sicily in 36 B.C.)

Lessing, Gotthold Ephraim (1729–81), the German dramatist and critic: for Macaulay, 'beyond all dispute, the first critic in Europe', for Gervinus, 'the man who first valued Shakespeare according to his full desert'. In 1767–8 Lessing wrote a series of articles in connexion with the newly established but short-lived German National Theatre in Hamburg; these are known as the *Hamburgische Dramaturgie*, in which, by his enlightened interpretation of Aristotle's *Poetics*, he freed German dramatists from the tyranny of French classical models and urged them to study Greek tragedy and Shakespeare.

L'Estrange, Sir Nicholas (d. 1655), eldest son of Sir Hamon L'Estrange, knt, of Hunstanton, Norfolk, and brother of Sir Roger L'Estrange, became a baronet in 1629, when his father bought the title for him. His *Merry Passages and Feasts* is a manuscript collection of 600 anecdotes, 141 of the more decent of which were published by the Camden Society in *Anecdotes and Traditions* (1839). They are anonymous, but those given on the writer's authority are signed S. N. L. The authority for the following anecdote was 'Mr Dun', probably Capt Duncomb, the source of other stories:

> Shake-speare was Godfather to one of *Ben: Johnsons* children, and after the christning being in a deepe study, Johnson came to cheere him vp, and askt him why he was so Melancholy? no faith *Ben:* (sayes he) not I, but I haue beene considering a great while what should be the fittest gift for me to bestow vpon my God-child, and I haue resolu'd at last; I pry'the what, sayes he? I faith *Ben:* I'le e'en giue him a douzen good Lattin Spoones, and thou shalt translate them. [Latten: a kind of brass.]

Letourneur, Pierre (1736–88), published his twenty-volume translation of Shakespeare, 1776–82. His admiration for Shakespeare infuriated the aged Voltaire, who wrote in 1776:

> Auriez-vous lu les deux volumes de ce misérable [Letourneur] dans lesquels il veut nous faire regarder Shakespeare comme le seul modèle de la véritable tragédie? Il sacrifie tous les Français sans exception à son idole (il l'appelle le Dieu du théâtre) comme on sacrifiait autrefois les cochons à Cérès ... Avez-vous une haine assez vigoureuse contre cet impudent imbécile? ... Ce qu'il y a d'affreux, c'est que le monstre a un parti en France; et pour comble de calamité, et d'horreur, c'est moi qui autrefois parlai le premier de ce Shakespeare, c'est moi qui le premier montrai aux Français quelques perles que j'avais trouvées dans son énorme fumier.

Leveridge, Richard (*c.* 1670–1758), bass singer and composer, made a short burlesque of Italian opera out of the Pyramus and Thisbe episodes in *A Midsummer Night's Dream*. It was successfully performed at Lincoln's Inn Fields in 1716. (See LAMPE.)

Leveson, William. When the Globe theatre was built in 1599 the ground-lease was conveyed in two halves, one half to the Burbage brothers, the other half to Shakespeare, Heminge, Phillips, Pope and Kempe. To make their half into tenancies held in common, and therefore alienable property, the five players made it over to two trustees, who regranted a fifth part to each of them. These trustees were William Leveson and Thomas Savage. In 1599 Leveson was churchwarden of St Mary's, Aldermanbury, the parish of Heminge and Condell; he was a member of the Old Merchant Adventurers, and in 1607 was commissioned by the Virginia Company to raise funds for the development of the colony. He was thus connected with Sir Dudley Digges, and indirectly with Leonard Digges and Thomas Russell, Shakespeare's friends.

Ley, William. A bookseller in whose play-list of 1656 a number of plays were wrongly attributed to Shakespeare.

Liberty. A district enjoying certain privileges, and exempt from the jurisdiction of the sheriff. In Elizabeth's reign the London liberties, such as that of Blackfriars, lay outside the jurisdiction of the City Corporation, though they constantly tried to gain control. On the Bankside, the Clink, where Shakespeare lived, possibly as early as 1596, was a liberty subject to the Bishop of Winchester. By the charter of September 1608 the City gained control of most of the liberties, including Blackfriars and Whitefriars.

'Library, The.' A quarterly review of bibliography and literature: 1889–98 the magazine of the Library Association; 1899–1918 an independent publication; since 1920 amalgamated with *The Transactions of the Bibliographical Society*, though retaining its own name.

Licensing of Plays. Distinction must be made between (*a*) the licensing of all books for printing, (*b*) the licensing of plays for printing, (*c*) the licensing of plays for performance. (See CENSORSHIP.)

(*a*) By a Decree of the Star Chamber of 23 June 1586 all books had to be licensed for printing by the Archbishop of Canterbury or the Bishop of London, who in 1588 issued an official list of their deputies, mostly London clergymen. The book would then be entered by the publisher in the Register of the Stationers' Company, under the hands of the licenser and of one or both of the Wardens of the Company, when a payment of 6d. would secure its copyright. For example:

> 8 Octobris [1600]. Thomas Fyssher. Entred for his copie vnder the handes of master Rodes and the Wardens. A booke called A mydsommer nightes Dreame vj^d^.

Plays and pamphlets, however, were often printed with no other authority than that of the Wardens, a practice that was sharply checked in 1599, when the Bishops warned the Wardens 'that noe playes be printed except they be allowed by suche as haue authority'.

(*b*) At the beginning of James I's reign, *c.* 1606, the licensing of plays for printing appears to have been delegated to the Master of the Revels, who in 1607 licensed sixteen, and after this date there are no references to other licensers or correctors. For example:

> 26 Novembris [1607]. Nathanael Butter John Busby. Entred for their Copie under thandes of Sir George Buck knight and Thwardens A booke called. Master William Shakespeare his historye of Kinge Lear ... vj^d^.

In 1607 Edmund Tilney was Master of the Revels, but a sick man, and Buck was his deputy. It is probable that a play licensed for performance by the Master came to be automatically licensed for printing.

(*c*) The Master of the Revels was responsible for censoring and allowing the plays performed at Court, and gradually his authority was extended to licensing plays for performance in the public theatres. In Elizabeth's patent of 1574, Leicester's Men were authorized to perform anywhere 'prouyded that the said ... playes be by the master of our Revells ... before sene & allowed'. By a patent of 1581 Edmund Tilney, as Master, was authorized and commanded to control all plays, players, playmakers, and playing places, and to 'auctorise and put downe, as shalbe thought meete or vnmeete'. In his Diary, 1592–7, Henslowe records fees of 7s. paid to Tilney for the licensing of new plays, and by 1607 he, or his deputy, was also licensing plays for publication. The *Office Book* of Sir Henry

Herbert (q.v.) describes his lucrative work as Master from 1623 to 1642. For example:

> Received of Knight [book-keeper of the King's Men], for allowing of Ben Johnsons play called Humours Reconcil'd, or the Magnetick Lady, to bee acted, this 12th of Octob. 1632. 2*l*.0.0.

Lieutenant of the Tower. In *3 Henry VI*, when the King is rescued by Warwick, the Lieutenant (Earl of Worcester?) craves pardon for having been his keeper (IV, vi). He (or Lord Dudley) appears again in V, vi, before Gloucester murders Henry.

Lieutenant to Aufidius. In *Coriolanus*, he tells Aufidius how Coriolanus has eclipsed him by his victories (IV, vii).

Ligarius, Caius. In *Julius Caesar*, despite his illness he joins the conspiracy against Caesar, though he is not present at the assassination. (This is really Quintus Ligarius, but Plutarch calls him Caius, and Shakespeare copies the mistake.)

Light Endings. Lines ending with lightly stressed monosyllables, usually pronouns and auxiliaries, but excluding the relational conjunctions and prepositions which are known as weak endings (q.v.). They make an extreme form of run-on line; for example:

> If, or for nothing or a little, *I*
> Should say myself offended, and with you
> Chiefly i' the world; more laugh'd at, that
> I *should*
> Once name you derogately ...

Light endings form part of the verse-tests (q.v.) which help to establish the chronology of Shakespeare's plays; the more there are, the later the play. They are not very helpful, however, as they do not vary much before the writing of *Antony and Cleopatra*, when there is a leap to 71 from 5 in *Lear* and 21 in *Macbeth*, the two preceding plays. (See INGRAM.)

Lighting in Theatres. According to the author of *Historia Histrionica* (1699), probably James Wright, 'The Globe, Fortune, and Bull were large houses, and lay partly open to the weather: and there they always acted by daylight'. As plays in the public theatres began at two o'clock, there was no need of artificial light, save perhaps in mid-winter, when it seems that cressets were used; see Cotgrave's *French Dictionary* (1611): '*Falot:* a cresset light (such as they use in play-houses), made of ropes wreathed, pitched, and put into small and open cages of iron.' But in the summer of 1594 the Chamberlain's 'began not their Plaies till towardes fower a clock'. (See LENGTH OF PERFORMANCES.)

In the roofed private theatres artificial lighting was necessary, even though the plays were performed in the afternoon; 'The Blackfriars, Cockpit, and Salisbury Court were called Private Houses; and were very small to what we see now .... Here they ... acted by candlelight' (*Historia Histrionica*). Compare the stage-direction in Marston's *What You Will*, a Blackfriars play of 1601: 'They sit a good while on the stage before the candles are lighted. ... Enter Tire-man with lights.' In 1664 Richard Flecknoe complains that the English do not know 'how to place our lights, for the more advantage and illuminating of the scenes'. The frontispiece to Francis Kirkman's *The Wits* (1672) shows a scene lighted by two candelabra hung over the stage and by primitive footlights. Side-lighting was introduced in the 18th century, Garrick and Loutherbourg being pioneers, and footlights (q.v.) were the corollary of the picture-frame stage. It is only in this century that the restrictive tyranny of footlights has been abolished, first in Germany, then in England by Gordon Craig, Granville-Barker and Barry Jackson.

Court performances were given late at night, starting about ten, and were lighted as in the private theatres by candelabra and lanterns.

Lillo, George (1693–1739), dramatist, was born in London, son of a Dutch jeweller in whose business he was for some time a partner. He is best known for his moral melodrama *George Barnwell* (1731). In August 1738 his version of *Pericles*, re-named *Marina*, was produced at Covent Garden. The action is confined to the last two acts of Shakespeare's play; Philoten, daughter of Cleon and Dionyza, mentioned merely in *Pericles*, becomes a main character and instigator of the attempted murder of Marina.

Lily, William (*c.* 1468–1522), scholar, was born at Odiham, educated at Oxford, and after a pilgrimage to Jerusalem settled in London, where he is said to have been the first to teach Greek. In 1510 Dean Colet appointed him the first High Master of his new school of St Paul's. Lily's and Colet's *Latin Grammar*, appointed for use in schools, would form the basis of Shakespeare's education at Stratford Grammar School, and there are many references to it in the plays; e.g. *Titus Andronicus*, IV, ii,

O, 'tis a verse in Horace; I know it well:
I read it in the grammar long ago.

And Sir Hugh Evans's examination of William Page in *The Merry Wives*, IV, i, etc.

Lincoln, Bishop of. In *Henry VIII*, the King reminds his confessor, John Longland, Bishop of Lincoln, that he first mentioned to him his uneasy conscience caused by his marriage to Katharine, and the Bishop admits that he advised the divorce (II, iv).

Lincoln's Inn, is on the site of a house owned by Henry Lacy, Earl of Lincoln, shortly after whose death in 1310 it became an Inn of Court (q.v.). As at the other inns, it was customary to give a play during the season of the Revels, usually at Candlemas. In 1565, 1566 and 1580 the Children of the Chapel performed, and in 1570 Lord Rich's Men. On the day after the wedding of Princess Elizabeth and the Elector Palatine the 'gent. of the Myddle temple and Lincolns Inne' combined to perform a masque before the King at Whitehall (15 February 1613): 'Inuented, and fashioned, with the ground, and speciall structure of the whole worke, By our Kingdomes most Artfull and Ingenious Architect Innigo Iones. Supplied, Aplied, Digested, and Written, By Geo. Chapman.'

Lincoln's Inn Fields, just to the west of the City, were laid out by Inigo Jones *c.* 1620. After the Restoration a theatre was built there and occupied by D'Avenant's Duke's Company in June 1661. In 1671 they moved to the new Salisbury Court theatre, and in the following year, when the first Drury Lane was burned down, the King's Company moved to the Lincoln's Inn Fields theatre until Wren's new Drury Lane was ready for them in 1674. From 1695 to 1705 Betterton and other seceders from Drury Lane acted at a second theatre in Lincoln's Inn Fields. In 1714 yet another small Lincoln's Inn Fields theatre was opened and was, until superseded by Covent Garden in 1732, with Drury Lane one of the two privileged theatres in London. (See THEATRES.)

Lincoln's Men. Edward de Clinton (1512–85) succeeded as 9th Baron Clinton in 1517, was created Lord High Admiral in 1550 and 1st Earl of Lincoln in May 1572. His son, Henry de Clinton, born *c.* 1541, succeeded his father as 2nd Earl in 1585 and died in 1616. It is possible that Sir Robert Lane's Men (q.v.) secured Lincoln as their patron after the Act of 29 June 1572, which insisted that all players should be the servants of a baron or 'honorable Personage of greater Degree'. Laurence Dutton played at Court with Lane's in December 1571 and February 1572, but with Lincoln's at Christmas 1572–3. The Earl seems to have transferred his company to his son, for in 1576–7 they appear as Clinton's. From 1599 to 1609 there are records of a provincial Earl of Lincoln's company.

Ling, Nicholas, bookseller from 1580 to 1607. With John Trundell he published Q1 *Hamlet*, the 'bad' Quarto (1603). This had been registered by James Roberts, who presumably transferred his copyright to Ling, though there is no entry, for in 1604 Ling published the corrected and augmented Q2.

In 1607 Cuthbert Burby transferred to Ling his copyright in *Love's Labour's Lost* and *Romeo and Juliet*, and in the same year Ling transferred them and *Hamlet* to John Smethwick:

> 22 Januarij Master Linge Entred for his copies by direccon of A Court and with consent of Master Burby vnder his handwrytinge These iij copies. viz. Romeo and Juliet. Loues Labour Lost ...
>
> 19 Novembris. John Smythick. Entred for his copies vnder thandes of the wardens, these bookes followinge Whiche dyd belonge to Nicholas Lynge. viz.... A booke called Hamlett ... Romeo and Julett ... Loues Labour Lost ...

Ling registered nothing after 1590, but from that date was associated with Busby, Millington, Burby and Allot. He died between 1607 and 1610.

Lion. In *A Midsummer Night's Dream.* (See SNUG.)

'Li Tre Satiri.' One of the *scenari* for *commedie dell'arte* in which there are resemblances to *The Tempest*: shipwreck, an island, and a magician; the islanders take the crew for gods, and Pantalone and the *zanni* steal the Mago's book. The *scenari* must be older than the manuscript book (1622) in which they are preserved. Italian actors visited England in Shakespeare's time, and it is just possible that he saw them in one of these *commedie dell'arte* (q.v.).

Livery of Players. Players were provided by their patron with his badge (q.v.) and livery, which they normally wore, at least when they were on tour. In their letter to Leicester of 1572 his players wrote: 'not that we meane to crave any further stipend or benefite at your Lordshippes hands but our lyveries as we have had, and also your honors License to certifye that we are your houshold Servaunts.' The royal livery was red; thus at Norwich, in June 1583, Queen Elizabeth's newly-formed company wore red coats, or rather were not wearing them just before a performance when they killed a man with whom they quarrelled; and to York in September 1587 they 'cam in her Majesties lyvereys'. In 1604 each of the actor-sharers of the three royal companies, the King's, Queen's and Prince's, received 4½ yards of red cloth for his coronation livery. These were state liveries, their everyday or 'watching' liveries being of cheaper material.

Lives of Shakespeare. See BIOGRAPHY.

Livy (59 B.C.–A.D. 17). Titus Livius, the Roman historian, was born at Padua, lived the greater part of his life in Rome, and retired to Padua shortly before his death. His great work is his history of Rome, from the landing of Aeneas in Italy and the founding of the City to the death of Drusus in 9 B.C. Of the 142 books of his *Annales*, only thirty-five remain (i–x, xxi–xlv), though there are later epitomes of all but two of the others. The story of Lucrece is told by Livy (i, 56–60), as also the fable of the belly and the members (ii, 32), related by Menenius in *Coriolanus*. Shakespeare probably knew Livy's version of both stories.

Lloyd, David (1635–92). The author of *Statesmen and Favourites of England since the Reformation* (1665), in which he wrote that Fulke Greville, Lord Brooke, was '*Shakespear's* and *Ben Johnson's* Master'. Anthony Wood in his *Athenae Oxonienses* (1692) dismissed Lloyd as a 'false writer and meer scribbler'. (See GREVILLE, FULKE.)

Locality Boards. There is evidence to suggest that in the early Elizabethan plays a locality was indicated by the players' entering through a door above which was a board bearing the name of a place; thus, the stage-direction in *Sir Clyomon and Clamydes* (*c.* 1570), 'Here enter Lamphedon out of Phrygia', may mean that one door was labelled 'Phrygia' and that the actor's entrance through it indicated that the stage then represented Phrygia. Sir Philip Sidney appears to refer to some such convention in his *Defence of Poesie* (1583): 'What Child is there, that, coming to a play, and seeing *Thebes* written in great letters upon an old door, doth believe that it is Thebes?' He also refers to a similar but earlier and simpler convention where the two sides of the stage represent different localities, 'where you shall have *Asia* of the one side, and *Affrick* of the other, and so many other under-kingdoms, that the Player, when he cometh in, must ever begin with telling where he is'. It is uncertain to what extent locality boards were used in later plays for the public stage; Shakespeare, for example, often contrives to indicate scene by means of dialogue or Chorus. On the other hand, Dekker in his *Gull's Hornbook* (1609) writes, 'And first observe your doors of entrance, and your exit; not much unlike the players at the theatres ... if you prove to be a northern gentleman, I would wish you to pass through the north door ... and so, according to your countries, take note of your entrances.'

Locke, John (1632–1704), the philosopher and author of *An Essay concerning Human Understanding* (1690). It was on Locke's doctrine of the association of ideas – 'Ideas, that in themselves are not at all of kin, come to be so united in some men's minds, that it is very hard to separate them; they always *keep in company*, and the one no sooner at any time comes into the understanding, but its *associate* appears with it; and if they are more than two which are thus united, *the whole gang* always inseparable shew themselves together' – that Walter Whiter based his *Specimen of a Commentary on Shakespeare* (1794), anticipating the 20th-century study of imagery (q.v.).

Locke, Matthew (*c.* 1630–77), musician, was born at Exeter, where he became a cathedral chorister. He composed some of the music for the first English opera, D'Avenant's *Siege of Rhodes* (1656), and in 1661 was appointed Composer in Ordinary to Charles II. He wrote anthems for the Chapel Royal and a good deal of theatre music, including that for the D'Avenant-Dryden adaptation of *The Tempest* (1667), and perhaps for D'Avenant's version of *Macbeth* (1672), with its popular and spectacular flying and singing witches. But the *Macbeth* music was first attributed to Locke by Downes in 1708, and other composers, Purcell, Leveridge, Eccles and Robert Johnson, have been suggested.

'Locrine.' One of the seven plays included by Philip Chetwind in the Third Folio of Shakespeare, 1664. It was registered by Creede, 20 July 1594, and published the following year:

> The Lamentable Tragedie of Locrine, the eldest sonne of King Brutus, discoursing the warres of the Britaines, and Hunnes, with their discomfiture: The Britaines victorie with their Accidents, and the death of Albanact. No lesse pleasant than profitable. Newly set foorth, ouerseene and corrected, by W. S. London Printed by Thomas Creede.

It is fustian in the manner of Pistol, certainly not Shakespeare's work, and it is improbable that he 'oversaw and corrected' it for publication. There is a copy in which is a note, said to be in the handwriting of Sir George Buck, Master of the Revels 1610–22; the inscription is cut at the edge, but Greg emends:

> Char, Tilney wrote [e a]
> Tragedy of this mattr [w^ch^]
> hee named Estrild: [& w^ch^]
> I think is this. it was [lost?]
> by his death. & now (?) [some]
> fellow hath published [it]
> I made dūbe shewes for it.
> wch I yet have. G.B. [ ]

Charles Tilney was a cousin of Edmund Tilney, Master of the Revels, and was executed in 1586 for his part in the Babington conspiracy; *c.* 1586 would not be an impossible date for the play.

Lodge, Thomas (*c.* 1557–1625), one of the University Wits, was the son of a Lord Mayor of London, educated at Merchant Taylors' School and Trinity, Oxford, and entered Lincoln's Inn in 1578. He began his literary career with a pamphlet defending poety, music and plays against Gosson's attack in his *School of Abuse* (1579), and during the next ten years occupied himself with writing romances, poetry and plays. His tragedy, *The Wounds of Civil War*, was an Admiral's play of *c.* 1588; *A Looking Glass for London and England* was written *c.* 1590, in collaboration with Greene; his volume of poems, *Scilla's Metamorphosis*, published in 1589, probably provided Shakespeare with hints for *Venus and Adonis*, and his prose romance, *Rosalynde*: *Euphues Golden Legacy* (1590) was to be the source of *As You Like It*. *Rosalynde* was published on his return from a voyage with Captain Clarke to the Azores and Canaries, and in 1591–3 he was with Thomas Cavendish on his expedition to South America, so being absent when his friend Robert Greene died in 1592. About 1596 he turned Catholic, in 1600 took a degree in medicine at Avignon, in 1602 another at Oxford, and wrote little more of importance. His dramatic output was small, but Fleay and others profess to have found his hand in a number of plays, including Shakespeare's *1 Henry VI*, *The Taming of the Shrew*, and *King John*.

Lodovico. In *Othello*, a kinsman of Desdemona's father, Brabantio. In IV, i he gives the letter of recall to Othello and sees him strike Desdemona. He goes to the help of Cassio when attacked by Roderigo, in whose pockets he finds letters revealing the treachery of Iago, to whom he promises lingering tortures.

Lodowick, Friar. The name assumed by Duke Vincentio in *Measure for Measure*.

London. The London of Shakespeare's day, as distinct from Westminster, was essentially the City, its southern boundary the Thames, its wall running approximately as a semicircle from the Fleet Ditch on the west to the Tower on the east, and pierced by a number of gates. Two main thoroughfares among the maze of narrow lanes cut the City from west to east and north to south; from Newgate to Aldgate ran Cheapside-Cornhill-Leadenhall Street, and from Bishopsgate to London Bridge ran Bishopsgate-Gracechurch Streets. The medieval cathedral of St Paul's stood on top of the hill to the east of Ludgate. Most of the 200,000 inhabitants were crammed within the huddled and overhanging houses of the City, though to the north of the walls in the neighbourhood of Moorfields and Finsbury the suburbs were rapidly developing. To the west, and following the line of the river up to Westminster, were the great houses of the nobility and courtiers, Somerset House (q.v.), the Savoy, and the royal palace of Whitehall. The Inns of Court, too, lay just to the west of the walls. The river was spanned by only one bridge, London Bridge, carrying houses on its twenty arches, and on the south bank was the borough of Southwark with its great church of St Mary Overie's, and the Bankside with its stews, Paris Garden, bear-baiting and theatres.

The City was the home of the merchants and master craftsmen, their apprentices and journeymen, and was governed by a Lord Mayor and Corporation elected by the twelve great Livery companies, jealous of any interference with their privileges by the Privy Council and Court of Westminster, though they were themselves continually striving to extend the area of their own authority. This was confined virtually to the area within the walls, and even here there were small 'liberties', such as that of Blackfriars, which were for the most part beyond their jurisdiction, though in 1608 they gained control of a number of them, including Blackfriars and Whitefriars.

In the Middle Ages London was not,

like York, Chester, Wakefield and Coventry, a great centre for mystery cycles, but with the strong centralized Tudor dynasty the secular drama established itself firmly in the capital. The City authorities, not altogether unreasonably, opposed theatres as potential sources of fire, rioting and plague, and, more questionably, of immorality, so that the permanent theatres, as opposed to the earlier converted inns, were built beyond their jurisdiction: the Theatre, Curtain, Fortune and Red Bull to the north, the Rose, Swan, Globe, Hope and Newington Butts to the south, and Blackfriars was a liberty within the City.

Of these theatres Shakespeare at one time or other was associated with the Theatre, Curtain, Rose, Swan, Globe and Blackfriars. In 1596 he appears to have moved from St Helen's parish, Bishopsgate, to the liberty of the Clink on the Bankside, where he was certainly living in 1599. About 1603 he lodged with Christopher Mountjoy, the Huguenot tire-maker, who lived at the corner of Silver Street and Monkwell Street in Cripplegate ward. In August 1607 his nephew, Edward, the illegitimate son of his brother Edmund, was buried at St Giles's, Cripplegate, and on 31 December 1607 Edmund himself, 'a player', was buried at St Saviour's (St Mary Overie's), Southwark. In 1613 Shakespeare bought the gatehouse of the Blackfriars Priory in the south-west corner of the City. (See MAPS OF LONDON.)

'London Prodigal.' One of the seven additional plays included by Philip Chetwind in the 2nd issue of the Third Folio of Shakespeare, 1664. It was published in 1605 without registration:

The London Prodigall. As it was plaide by the Kings Maiesties seruants. By William Shakespeare. London. Printed by T.C. for Nathaniel Butter, and are to be sold neere S Austins gate, at the signe of the pyde Bull. 1605.

The author of the play is unknown; he certainly was not Shakespeare. It is a comedy of the reformation of the prodigal Matthew Flowerdale by his faithful wife.

Long Lines. Either alexandrines (q.v.) or lines of five feet with more than one redundant syllable at the end; e.g. *Cymbeline*, III, v, 21–6:

Lucius hath wrote already to the emperor
How it goes here. It fits us therefore ripely
Our chariots and our horsemen be in
  readiness:
The powers that he already hath in Gallia
Will soon be drawn to head, from whence
  he moves
His war for Britain.

There are more long lines, as there are more irregularities of every sort, in the later verse, but there is little order in the development; *Richard II* has more than *The Tempest*. Many of them must be due to the compositor. (See SQ, vi, 3, 268.)

'Long View of London.' See HOLLAR.

Longaville. In *Love's Labour's Lost*, one of the three lords attending the King of Navarre.

He falls in love with Maria, to whom he addresses the sonnet, 'Did not the heavenly rhetoric of thine eye', published by Jaggard in *The Passionate Pilgrim*, 1599. (Henri, Duc de Longueville, was a supporter of Henry of Navarre in his fight for the French crown, 1589–93.)

Lope de Vega (1562–1635), Spanish poet and founder of the modern Spanish drama. About the time that Shakespeare was writing *Romeo and Juliet*, Lope de Vega was also dramatizing the story in his *Castelvines y Monteses* (Capulets and Montagues). The apparently dead and concealed Julia speaks to her father who thinks it is her ghost and promises to forgive the husband whom she had secretly married. Roselo and Julia appear, and their marriage is ratified.

Lopez, Roderigo. A Portuguese Jew who became physician to Queen Elizabeth. He was accused of attempting to poison the Queen and Don Antonio, pretender to the throne of Portugal, and hanged on 7 June 1594. It may be that Shakespeare had Lopez in mind when he wrote the Pythagorean passage in which Gratiano alleges that Shylock's 'currish spirit Govern'd a wolf (lupus) ... hang'd for human slaughter'. (*M.V.*, IV, i.)

Lord, A. In the Induction to *The Taming of the Shrew* (q.v.). There are unnamed and dramatically unimportant Lords in *Titus Andronicus, Love's Labour's Lost, Richard II, As You Like It, All's Well, Macbeth, Cymbeline* and *The Winter's Tale*.

Lord Chamberlain. In Tudor and Stuart times the royal household was, as it still is, divided into three principal departments, each under a great officer. The Master of the Horse was concerned mainly with affairs out of doors, the Lord Steward with affairs below stairs, with food and drink, light and fuel, the Lord Chamberlain with 'all things above stairs', with the sovereign's accommodation, wardrobe, travel, reception of guests, and entertainment. The Chamber was divided into two departments: the Privy Chamber, the personnel of which, according to one account, in Elizabeth's reign consisted of The Lord Chamberlain, Vice-Chamberlain, four Knights, Knight-Marshall, eighteen Gentlemen, four Gentlemen-Ushers, Groom-Porter, fourteen Grooms, four Carvers, three Cupbearers, four Sewers, four Squires to the Body, four Yeomen-Ushers, four Pages, four Messengers, two Clerks of the Closet, and numerous Ladies and Chambermaids: then there was the Outer or Presence Chamber with Esquires of the Body, and more Gentlemen Ushers and Grooms. The actor-sharers in the companies under royal patronage, including Shakespeare, as one of the King's Men, were sworn in by the Lord Chamberlain as 'grooms of the chamber in ordinary without fee'. The Lord Chamberlain was responsible also for the Chapel, the musicians and players, and for certain 'standing offices', including that of the Revels, established by Henry VII with a Master, originally to supply entertainment at Court, but who, though he remained immediately responsible to the Lord Chamberlain, came to exercise very wide and almost independent powers of control over the theatres. The Lord Chamberlains from Elizabeth's accession to the closing of the theatres in 1642, were:

1558–72	William, 1st Lord Howard of Effingham.
1572–83	Thomas Radcliffe, 3rd Earl of Sussex.
1583–5	Charles, 2nd Lord Howard of Effingham (patron of the Admiral's).
1585–96	Henry Carey, 1st Lord Hunsdon (patron of the Chamberlain's).
1596–7	William Brooke, 7th Lord Cobham.
1597–1603	George Carey, 2nd Lord Hunsdon (patron of the Chamberlain's).
1603–14	Thomas Lord Howard of Walden; Earl of Suffolk.
1614–15	Robert Carr, Earl of Somerset.
1615–26	William Herbert, 3rd Earl of Pembroke.
1626–41	Philip Herbert, Earl of Montgomery, and 4th Earl of Pembroke.

Most of these were good friends to the players, many of them having their own companies; the First Folio of Shakespeare was dedicated by Heminge and Condell to the brothers William and Philip Herbert, and in 1619 the former warned the Stationers' Company to prevent the printing of the King's Men's plays without their consent. They defended the players against the attacks of the City authorities and Puritans, the one exception being Lord Cobham, during whose brief tenure of office the Lord Mayor and Corporation succeeded in expelling the players from the City and closing the inn-theatres.

Lord Chamberlain. In *Henry VIII*, he acts as controller at Wolsey's feast, where he presents Anne Bullen to the King, and is one of the Council before whom Cranmer is arraigned. In v, iv he is seen superintending the arrangements for the christening of Elizabeth. (The Lord Chamberlains at the time were Charles Somerset, Earl of Worcester (1509–26), and Lord Sands (1526–43).)

Lord Chamberlain's Men. See CHAMBERLAIN'S-KING'S MEN.

Lord Chancellor. In *Henry VIII*, he (Sir Thomas Wriothesley) is president of the Council before whom Cranmer is arraigned. When the King intervenes, he explains that the imprisonment of Cranmer was not malicious (v, iii). (The Lord Chancellor in IV, i was Sir Thomas Audley, who succeeded Sir Thomas More in 1532.)

Lord Chief Justice. In *2 Henry IV*, he warns Falstaff against his ill life, and orders him to make restitution to Mistress Quickly. When Henry IV dies, he fears that Henry V will avenge himself for the imprisonment he suffered at his hands as the mad-cap Prince of Wales; but the new King confirms him in his office, and orders him to enforce the banishment and imprisonment of Falstaff. (Sir William Gascoigne, *c.* 1350–1419.)

Lords' Room. The first mention is in 1592 when Henslowe paid 13s. for the repair of the ceiling of 'my Lords Roome' at the Rose, perhaps the 'box' reserved for the patron of the company then performing. In *Every Man out of His Humour* (1599) Jonson speaks of lords táking tobacco 'over the stage i' the lords roome', and this may, perhaps, be identified with the gallery above and at the back of the stage in de Witt's drawing of the Swan (*c.* 1596). Towards the end of the century it became fashionable to sit on the stage or in the lower side gallery, and the old lords' room might then be available as an upper stage (q.v.).

Lorenzo. In *The Merchant of Venice*, he elopes with Shylock's daughter Jessica, not forgetting to take some of Shylock's ducats.

Lorkin, Thomas (d. 1625), was educated at Emmanuel, Cambridge, and 1611–13 travelled with Thomas Puckering with whom he continued a correspondence. In 1623 he was secretary to the Embassy in Paris, and was drowned in the Channel *c.* 1625. In a letter to Puckering, 30 June 1613, he described the burning of the Globe:

> No longer since than yesterday, while Burbage's company were acting at the Globe the play of Henry VIII, and there shooting off certain chambers in way of triumph, the fire catched and fastened upon the thatch of the house, and there burned so furiously, as it consumed the whole house, all in less than two hours, the people having enough to do to save themselves.

Louis, The Dauphin (1187–1226). 1. In *King John*, the son of Philip II of France. (His marriage with John's niece, Blanch, in 1202 was idyllic. He succeeded as Louis VIII in 1223.)

2. In *Henry V*, son of Charles VI. He sends Henry a derisory present of tennis-balls, boasts of the easy victory France will have at Agincourt, but when defeated threatens to stab himself. (Louis (1396–1415) died soon after Agincourt, at which he was not present.)

Louis XI (1423–83). In *3 Henry VI*, the King of France. In III, iii he first promises to help Margaret against Edward IV, but then agrees to Warwick's suggestion that Edward should marry the Lady Bona (q.v.). (Louis succeeded his father, Charles VII, in 1461. He was the grandson of Charles VI and first cousin both of Henry VI and Queen Margaret.)

Loutherbourg, Philip James de (1740–1812), was born at Strassburg, the son of a Polish miniature painter. In Paris he became a highly successful painter of romantic landscapes and battle-scenes, in 1767 being elected a member of the Académie Royale. He came to England in 1771 and was employed by Garrick at Drury Lane, where he revolutionized scenic design, stage lighting, and theatrical costume. In 1781 he was elected R.A. His scenic effects were both romantic and realistic; in his famous *Eidophusikon* he represented the progress and fury of a storm, a device adopted by Edmund Kean in his production of *King Lear* in 1820.

'Love Betray'd; or, The Agreeable Disappointment.' An adaptation of *Twelfth Night* by William Burnaby (q.v.), produced at Lincoln's Inn Fields in 1703.

'Love in a Forest.' An adaptation of *As You Like It* by Charles Johnson (q.v.).

Lovel, Lord (d. *c.* 1487). In *Richard III*, the willing servant of Richard, at whose order he carries off Hastings to execution and returns with his head (III, iv and v). He is 'Lovel our dog' of the rhyme, who 'barked and bit whom Richard would'. (Sir Francis Lovel, cr. Viscount Lovel, 1483.)

Lovell, Sir Thomas (d. 1524). In *Henry VIII*, Chancellor of the Exchequer, and a courtier in the King's confidence. He appears in a number of scenes: in II, i he conducts the condemned Buckingham to the water side, and in V, i sympathizes with Gardiner's estimate of Cranmer.

'Lover's Complaint, A.' The poem was published by Thomas Thorpe without registration in the same volume as Shakespeare's *Sonnets*: 'At London By G. Eld for T.T. and are to be solde by Iohn Wright, dwelling at Christ Church gate. 1609'. (Some copies read 'and are to be solde by William Aspley'.) The head-title states simply, 'A Louers complaint. By William Shake-speare'. It was reprinted in 1640, in John Benson's edition of Shakespeare's *Poems*: 'Poems: Written by Wil. Shake-speare. Gent. Printed at London by Tho. Cotes, and are to be sold by Iohn Benson, dwelling in St Dunstans Church-yard. 1640'. There is no other external evidence for Shakespeare's authorship of *A Lover's Complaint*, which on the internal evidence has often been rejected, though there are passages that might well be his early work. There are forty-seven stanzas in rhyme-royal, the form employed by Shakespeare in *Lucrece*, and by Daniel in *The Complaint of Rosamond* (1592).

'LOVE'S LABOUR'S LOST.'

WRITTEN: 1594–5. Mentioned by Meres in *Palladis Tamia* 1598.

PERFORMED: If the title-page of Q1 is not the repetition of an earlier one, 'it was presented before her Highnes this last Christmas', i.e. 1597–8, though presumably it was acted soon after being written. Wilson suggests that the play as we have it is a revision of an early version that was acted at the Earl of Southampton's house in the plague year of 1593–4. It certainly seems to be written for a courtly rather than a popular audience.

1605. 'By his Maiesties plaiers. Betwin Newers Day and Twelfe day A play of Loues Labours Lost.' (*Revels Account.*) This is probably the performance referred to by Sir Walter Cope (q.v.) in his letter to Robert Cecil, Lord Cranborne, of 1604–5 (January 1605?), and by Dudley Carleton to John Chamberlain on 15 January: 'The last nights revels were kept at my Lord of Cranbornes, where the Q. with the D. of Holst and a great part of the Court were feasted, and the like two nights before at my Lord of Southamptons.' Apparently this was a private performance for the Queen at either Cranborne's or Southampton's house, but *after* Twelfth Night, between 8 and 15 January.

REGISTERED: No original registration.

1607. '22 Januarij. Master Linge Entred for his copies by direccon of A Court and with consent of Master Burby vnder his handwrytynge ... Loues Labour Lost.'

1607. '19 Novembris. John Smythick. Entred for his copies vnder thandes of the wardens. these bookes followinge Whiche dyd belonge to Nicholas Lynge. viz. ... Loues Labour's lost.'

PUBLISHED: 1598, Q1. 'A Pleasant Conceited Comedie Called, Loues labors lost. As it was presented before her Highnes this last Christmas. Newly corrected and augmented

By W. Shakespere. Imprinted at London by W. W. for Cutbert Burby. 1598.' Not a 'bad' Quarto, but a badly printed text. Set up from foul papers. The fact that there was no entry in the Stationers' Register before Q1 suggests that there may have been an earlier, surreptitious Quarto from which Q1 was 'newly corrected and augmented', though it is possible that Shakespeare rewrote the play for its publication in 1598. It is the first play to be published with his name.

1623, F1. 'Loues Labour's lost.' The seventh play in the Comedy section: pp. 122–44. Acts marked (V marked VI). Set up from Q1 which is therefore the authoritative text. There are many corrections, but many new errors are introduced.

1631, Q2. 'Loues Labours lost. A Wittie And Pleasant Comedie, As it was acted by his Maiesties Seruants at the Blacke-Friers and the Globe. Written by William Shakespeare. London, Printed by W.S. for Iohn Smethwicke, and are to be sold at his Shop in Saint Dunstones Churchyard vnder the Diall.'

SOURCE: The plot appears to be Shakespeare's own, though there are many topical allusions: the Ducs de Biron and de Longueville were the supporters, and the Duc de Mayenne (Dumain) the opponent of Henry of Navarre in his fight for the French crown 1589–93.

STAGE HISTORY: The next recorded performance after that of 1605 is that of 1839 at Covent Garden, with Madame Vestris as Rosaline.

The King of Navarre and three of his lords take an oath to study for three years, during which time they will avoid the sight of women. When the Princess of France arrives, however, the King falls in love with her, and his lords with her ladies: Berowne with Rosaline, Longaville with Maria, Dumain with Katharine. Each discovers that the others are secretly forsworn, but Berowne argues that they are not really perjured, for women's eyes 'are the books, the arts, the academes, That show, contain and nourish all the world'. News comes of the death of the Princess's father, and she and her ladies hastily depart, promising to marry their lovers in a year's time. As a contrast to this courtly comedy of wits is that of Don Armado and Costard, rivals for the love of Jaquenetta, and of Holofernes and Nathaniel, the four of whom present the interlude of the Nine Worthies and finish the play with the song 'When daisies pied and violets blue'.

'Love's Labour's Won.' In his *Palladis Tamia* of 1598 Francis Meres mentions six of Shakespeare's comedies and six tragedies:

> For Comedy, witnes his *Gentlemen of Verona*, his *Errors*, his *Loue labors lost*, his *Loue labours wonne*, his *Midsummers night dreame*, & his *Merchant of Venice*: for Tragedy his *Richard the 2. Richard the 3. Henry the 4. King Iohn, Titus Andronicus* and his *Romeo* and *Iuliet*.

We should expect the otherwise unknown *Love's Labour's Won* to be an alternative title for *The Taming of the Shrew*, the only other early comedy, as far as we know, that Meres fails to mention. But in 1953 a London bookseller discovered a list of the books that the stationer Christopher Hunt had in stock in August 1603, and these include '*marchant of vennis, taming of a shrew, loves labor lost, loves labor won*'. Evidently *Love's Labour's Won* is not another name for *The Taming of the Shrew*, but either a lost comedy, or more probably one that was later included in the Folio but had been published by 1603 under another title, possibly *All's Well that Ends Well.* (See T. W. Baldwin, *Shakespere's Love's Labor's Won*, 1957.)

'Love's Martyr.' The title of the volume of poems by Robert Chester, published in 1601, and containing *The Phoenix and Turtle* (q.v.), ascribed to Shakespeare.

Lowes, John Livingston (1867–1945), Professor of English at Harvard University. *The Road to Xanadu* (1927) is a remarkable and exhaustive study of Coleridge's imagery, and shows how it was derived from his reading and stored in his unconscious memory. The book has influenced the course of much recent Shakespeare criticism in the direction of the study of his imagery.

Lowin, John (1576–1669?). One of the twenty-six 'Principall Actors' in Shakespeare's plays (see p. 91). In 1602–3 he was with Worcester's at Henslowe's

Rose, but in 1603 played with Shakespeare and the King's Men in *Sejanus*, and in 1604, when the Grooms were increased from nine to twelve, probably became a sharer in the company, with whom he stayed until the closing of the theatres in 1642, living in Southwark 'near the playhouse'. When Heminge died in 1630, he bought an eighth of the shares in the Globe and Blackfriars theatres, and with Joseph Taylor became the business manager of the company. James Wright, in his *Historia Histrionica* (1699), wrote, 'Lowin used to act, with mighty applause, Falstaff; Morose; Vulpone; and Mammon in the *Alchemist*; Melancius in the *Maid's tragedy*', and John Downes added in 1708 that Shakespeare himself instructed Lowin in the part of Henry VIII. According to Wright, Lowin 'in his latter days kept an inn (the Three Pigeons) at Brentford, where he dyed very old (for he was an actor of eminent note in the reign of King James the First), and his poverty was as great as his age'. He was one of the King's Men who signed the *Players' Dedication* to the 4th Earl of Pembroke (q.v.) of the Beaumont and Fletcher Folio which they published in 1647, and with Joseph Taylor the edition of Fletcher's *The Wild Goose Chase* in 1652. A John Lowen was buried at St Paul's, Covent Garden, 16 March 1669. There is a portrait of Lowin in the Ashmolean Museum at Oxford, inscribed 'Ætat 64, 1640'.

Lownes, Humphrey, in 1602 printed for William Leake the seventh octavo edition of *Venus and Adonis*. Lownes was bookseller and printer from 1587 to his death in 1629. In 1604 he married the widow of Peter Short, and acquired his business. In 1609 he registered *Troilus and Cressida* as a Warden of the Stationers' Company, of which he was Master 1620–1 and 1624–5.

Lucan (A.D. 39–65). Marcus Annaeus Lucanus, the Roman poet, was born at Corduba (Cordova), joined Piso's conspiracy against Nero, was discovered, and committed suicide. His chief work is the unfinished *Pharsalia*, describing the struggle between Caesar and Pompey. It is possible that Shakespeare referred to the poem when writing *Julius Caesar*.

Luce. In *The Comedy of Errors*, a servant of Adriana. In III, i she refuses to admit Antipholus of Ephesus into his house, thinking he is already inside.

Lucentio. In *The Taming of the Shrew*, the son of Vincentio of Pisa, and the successful suitor of Bianca. (Aurelius in *A Shrew*.)

Lucetta. In *The Two Gentlemen of Verona*, a 'waighting-woman to Iulia' (F). She supports Proteus in his suit of Julia, brings her a letter from him, but tries to dissuade her from following him to Milan.

Lucian (*c.* A.D. 120–180), Greek satirical writer, was born at Samosata on the Euphrates. His *Timon the Misanthrope* is a witty dialogue that was one source of the anonymous manuscript comedy *Timon*, probably an academic play of 1581–90. Shakespeare may have read Lucian's *Misanthropos* in a Latin or French translation, for his *Timon of Athens* has points in common with it, and not in Plutarch, though they are in the manuscript *Timon*, which also, like Shakespeare's tragedy, has a faithful steward and mock feast, neither in Lucian nor Plutarch.

Luciana. In *The Comedy of Errors*, the sister of Adriana. She confuses Antipholus of Syracuse with his twin brother of Ephesus, Adriana's husband, and is dismayed when he makes love to her. Presumably she marries him after the resolution of the errors in the last scene.

Lucianus. In the Mouse-trap play in *Hamlet*, 'nephew to the king. ... He poisons him i' the garden for his estate'. (III, ii.)

Lucilius. 1. In *Julius Caesar*, a friend of Brutus and Cassius, he first appears in

IV, ii, when he describes to Brutus the cooling friendship of Cassius. He is captured at Philippi.

2. In *Timon of Athens*, a servant of Timon, who 'builds his fortune' so that he becomes a suitor acceptable to the father of the girl he loves. (I, i.)

Lucio. In *Measure for Measure*, a 'fantastique' (F.). He asks Isabella to intercede for Claudio, and accompanies her to Angelo. He slanders the Duke, disguised as a friar, and then maintains that the friar spoke the slander. When the Duke reveals himself he forgives Lucio, but orders him to marry the woman 'whom he begot with child'.

Lucius. 1. In *Titus Andronicus*, the eldest son of Titus. After the execution of his two brothers, the rape of his sister, and his father's mutilation, he goes to the Goths to raise a power to be revenged on the Emperor Saturninus. On his return he kills Saturninus, is hailed as Emperor, orders Tamora's body to be thrown to the beasts, and Aaron to be set breast-deep in earth and famished.

2. In *Titus Andronicus*, 'young Lucius', a boy, the son of Lucius. His 'aunt Lavinia' indicates her rape by turning to the story of Philomel in his copy of Ovid's *Metamorphoses*. He gives her ravishers, Chiron and Demetrius, a present of arrows wrapped in a threatening note from Titus.

3. In *Julius Caesar*, a boy, servant to Brutus. In II, i he admits the conspirators, and on the morning of Caesar's assassination is sent by Portia to see that all is well with Brutus. Twice he falls asleep on duty, the second time while playing and singing to Brutus just before the appearance of Caesar's ghost.

4. In *Timon of Athens*, a 'flattering lord' who makes Timon a present of 'four milk-white horses, trapp'd in silver', but refuses to lend him money when in need. In III, iv his servant, sent to recover a debt from Timon, is called by his master's name.

Lucullus. In *Timon of Athens*, a 'flattering lord' who makes Timon a present of two brace of greyhounds, but when Timon sends Flaminius to ask for a loan he tries to bribe him to say that he could not find him. He is one of those invited to Timon's mock banquet.

Lucy, Sir Thomas (1532–1600), eldest child of Sir William Lucy, knight, of Charlecote (q.v.) near Stratford. He married the heiress Joyce Acton, and inherited Sutton Park in Worcestershire, and on his father's death in 1552 succeeded to Hampton Lucy and Sherborne as well as Charlecote, which he rebuilt *c.* 1558. He was knighted in 1565, became member for Warwick in 1571, and high sheriff of the county in 1586. John Foxe, author of the *Book of Martyrs*, is said to have been tutor at Charlecote from 1545 to 1547, and to have instilled in Lucy his own Puritan principles. In 1585 he was active in promoting a bill for the better preservation of grain and game. He died at Charlecote 7 July 1600.

Richard Davies was the first to associate Shakespeare's name with Lucy's. Sometime before 1708 he made a note that Shakespeare stole venison and rabbits from Lucy, who had him whipped, imprisoned and driven from Stratford, and that in revenge Shakespeare called him Justice Clodpate who 'bore three lowses rampant for his Arms'. The Lucy arms were 'three luces hauriant argent', that is, three vertical silver pike. Davies is clearly referring to *The Merry Wives of Windsor*, in which Justice Shallow complains that Falstaff has killed his deer, and cousin Slender boasts that the Shallows 'may give the dozen white luces in their coat', and Parson Evans replies, 'The dozen white louses do become an old coat well.' Dugdale in his *Warwickshire* (1656) illustrates a Lucy coat-of-arms with the three luces in each of the four quarterings, so making a 'dozen white luces'. Hotson, however, claims William Gardiner (q.v.) as the original of Shallow.

In his *Life of Shakespeare* (1709)

Nicholas Rowe says that Shakespeare 'more than once' stole deer from 'a Park that belong'd to Sir Thomas Lucy of Cherlecot', for which he was prosecuted by Lucy, and in revenge Shakespeare made 'a Ballad upon him' which was 'so very bitter' that it redoubled the prosecution and drove him from Stratford to London. William Oldys (d. 1761) professes to give 'the first stanza of that bitter ballad' which had been written down after its repetition by 'a very aged gentleman' who lived near Stratford and died *c.* 1700:

A parliemente member, a justice of peace,
At home a poor scare-crowe, at London an asse,
If lowsie is Lucy, as some volke miscalle it,
Then Lucy is lowsie whatever befall it:
He thinks himselfe greate,
Yet an asse in his state,
We allowe by his ears but with asses to mate.
If Lucy is lowsie, as some volke miscalle it,
Sing lowsie Lucy, whatever befall it.

Edward Capell (1780) quotes the same stanza and tells much the same story; the old gentleman was Mr Thomas Jones of Tardebigge, near Stratford, who died in 1703 'upwards of ninety', and Shakespeare's ballad had been stuck upon Lucy's park gate. In 1790 John Jordan claimed to have found a 'complete copy' of the ballad 'in a chest of drawers that formerly belonged to Mrs Dorothy Tyler, of Shottery, near Stratford'. Malone (1790) quotes two verses of a different ballad overheard and transcribed, *c.* 1690, by Joshua Barnes (q.v.) on a visit to Stratford.

Lucy, Sir William. In *1 Henry VI*, he implores York and Somerset to go to the aid of Talbot, and accuses them of causing his death by their quarrels. He secures the bodies of Talbot and his son from the Dauphin (IV, iii, iv and vii). (This may be the Lucy (d. 1466) of Charlecote, an ancestor of Sir Thomas.)

Luddington. A village on the north bank of the Avon, about three miles west of Stratford. In his *History of William Shakespeare* (1862) S. W. Fullom claimed to have discovered a tradition that Shakespeare married Anne Hathaway at Luddington, the register having been burned some years before 'to boil a kettle'. Malone (*Var.*, II, 116) states that 'some persons of the name of Hathaway' were tenants of Sir John Conway of Luddington 'early in the reign of Elizabeth, though one of them is said to have had a little patrimony of his own, probably at Weston'. Weston is just across the river from Luddington, and Malone thinks that the marriage may have been celebrated there, but again the register has been lost.

Ludwig, Otto (1813–65), German dramatist and novelist whose masterpiece is the novel *Zwischen Himmel und Erde*. His plays were influenced by those of Shakespeare, his intense admiration for whom is described in his *Shakespeare Studien*, published in 1871.

Lumley Portrait of Shakespeare, so called because it is said to have been originally in the collection of John, Lord Lumley (d. 1609) of Lumley Castle, Durham, where James I stayed on his progress from Scotland. It was first openly claimed as a portrait of Shakespeare and the original of the Chandos painting, which it resembles, about 1848 by the then owner, George Rippon. It *may* be a genuine portrait of Shakespeare. (See BURDETT-COUTTS.)

Lute. The most popular musical instrument of Shakespeare's time, often mentioned in his plays and those of his contemporaries. It is pear-shaped, unbridged, with a variable number of strings plucked by the fingers. Elizabeth had a musician called 'the Lute of the Privy Chamber'; compare the scene in *Henry VIII*, where Queen Katharine says,

Take thy lute, wench: my soul grows sad with troubles;
Sing, and disperse 'em, if thou canst: leave working.

And her lady sings 'Orpheus with his lute made trees'.

Lyance. The name of a piece of land, now the Moat Farm, in Hatton, a village eight miles north of Stratford, rented by a Rowington family of Shakespeares from 1547 to 1578. It has been suggested that the place-name Lyance indicates a family of Levelaunce, or Lyvelaunce, from which is derived Shakelaunce and Shakespeare.

Lyceum Theatre, in London, was built in 1794, given a special licence for 'English Opera' in 1810, burned down, and rebuilt in 1834. From 1878 to 1899 Henry Irving was lessee and manager, and with Ellen Terry there produced his series of sumptuous Shakespearean revivals. It was at the Lyceum in 1900 that F. R. Benson and his company played the complete text of *Hamlet*.

Lychorida. In *Pericles*, Marina's nurse. In the storm (III, i) she brings the newly-born Marina to Pericles and tells him his Queen is dead. She is left in charge of Marina in the house of Cleon and Dionyza at Tarsus. Gower reports her death in the Prologue to Act IV.

Lydgate, John (*c.* 1370–*c.* 1451), the poet, was born at Lydgate, near Newmarket, possibly educated at the school attached to the monastery of Bury St Edmunds, and may have attended the Universities of Oxford, Paris, and Padua. He was ordained priest in 1397 and at about the same time met Chaucer, of whom he was a great admirer. His *Troy Book* (1412–20), taken from the Latin of Guido delle Colonne, probably supplied Shakespeare with material for his Greek scenes in *Troilus and Cressida*.

Lyly, John (*c.* 1554–1606), the oldest of the University Wits, and a little apart from the others, was the grandson of William Lily, High Master of St Paul's. He was probably born at Canterbury, went to Magdalen, Oxford, taking his M.A. in 1575 and at Cambridge in 1579. Failing to gain a fellowship, he settled in London and in 1579–80 published the two parts of his romance, *Euphues* (q.v.), the 'new English' of which established him as the most fashionable writer of the age. (See PETTIE.) Lyly then turned to the theatre and applied his prose to the writing of courtly comedies for performance by the boys' companies. In 1584 he was associated with William Hunnis and Henry Evans, possibly under the patronage of the Earl of Oxford, at the first Blackfriars theatre, and in January and March of that year his *Campaspe* and *Sapho and Phao* were played at Court by the joint Blackfriars company of the Children of the Chapel and of Paul's. The first Blackfriars theatre came to an end in 1584, but Lyly continued to write for the Paul's boys until they were suppressed in 1590. During these years he wrote *Galathea*, *Endimion*, *Midas*, *Mother Bombie* and *Love's Metamorphosis*, all performed by the Paul's boys, and most of them given at Court. *The Woman in the Moon* is his only verse play and may have been written for another company after the dissolution of the Children of Paul's. But after 1590 Lyly wrote little, and between 1589 and 1601 he was four times returned as member of parliament. He had been led to expect the reversion of the profitable office of Master of the Revels, but about 1597 this was promised to George Buck, and Lyly complained, 'thirteen yeres your highnes servant but yet nothing'. He was buried at St Bartholomew's the Less 30 November 1606. Shakespeare's early comedies, particularly *Love's Labour's Lost*, are indebted to Lyly's *Euphues* and the courtly and witty dialogue of his plays (see SS, 14) and this debt is suggested by Ben Jonson:

I should commit thee surely with thy peeres,
And tell, how farre thou didstst our Lily out-shine,
Or sporting Kid, or Marlowes mighty line.

Lymoges (pronounce Lĭm'-ō-gēs). In *King John*. Richard I was mortally wounded at the siege of the castle of the Viscount of Limoges. Shakespeare follows the author of *The Troublesome Reign* in confusing Limoges with the Archduke of Austria (q.v.) who captured and imprisoned Richard. It was Limoges, not Austria, who was killed by Faulconbridge in 1200.

Lyrical Period. Shakespeare's so-called 'lyrical period' is that of the years when he was writing *Venus and Adonis*, *Lucrece*, and the *Sonnets*, probably *c.* 1593–6, and to these years belong *Love's Labour's Lost*, *Romeo and Juliet*, *Richard II* and *A Midsummer Night's Dream*, the most lyrical of the plays. The last act of *The Merchant of Venice* seems to mark the end of this period, and after the discipline of the next period of prose, the poetry becomes the stuff of the plays and cannot be detached. The songs (q.v.) are different; though they are used dramatically, they are not part of the dialogue, and are as frequent in the late romances as in the comedies of the early and middle periods.

Lysander. In *A Midsummer Night's Dream*, in love with Hermia, with whom he runs away.

Lysimachus. In *Pericles*, the Governor of Mytilene who frequents the brothel where he finds Marina. Her virtue overcomes him with shame, and when he visits the speechless Pericles he summons her to 'win some words of him'. After the reunion of Pericles with Marina and Thaisa he announces that Lysimachus is to marry Marina at Pentapolis.

M

M., I. Author of the verses 'To the memorie of M. *W. Shake-speare*' prefixed to F1 (1623):

Wee wondred (*Shake-speare*) that thou
 went'st so soone
From the Worlds-Stage, to the Graues-
 Tyring-roome.
Wee thought thee dead, but this thy printed
 worth,
Tels thy Spectators, that thou went'st but
 forth
To enter with applause. An Actors Art,
Can dye, and liue, to acte a second part.
That's but an *Exit* of Mortalitie;
This, a Re-entrance to a Plaudite.

Lee suggests that I. M. is Jasper Mayne (1604–72), but Mayne was only nineteen when F was published. He was a Devonshire man, educated at Westminster and Christ Church, Oxford, was dispossessed of his living during the Commonwealth, but at the Restoration became chaplain to the King. He was the author of a comedy, *The City Match* (1639), a tragi-comedy, *The Amorous War*, some poems, and a translation of Lucian's *Dialogues*. I. M. is more likely to have been James Mabbe (q.v.). (See MILTON.)

M., J. See MARKHAM.

Mabbe, James (1572–1642), was educated at Magdalen, Oxford, of which college he was a fellow when Leonard Digges was an undergraduate. He is best known for his translation of Fernando de Rojas's important *Celestina, or the Tragi-Comedy of Calisto and Melibea*, and is probably the I. M. of the verses to Shakespeare in F1. (See SS, 16.)

'MACBETH.'

WRITTEN: 1605–6. Wilson suggests that it was written 1601–2, and performed in Edinburgh, whither Shakespeare had fled after the Essex rebellion. (See GARNET; KNIGHT OF THE BURNING PESTLE; SOPHONISBA.)

PERFORMED: 1611. 'In Macbeth at the Glob, ... the 20 of Aprill.' There must have been many performances before this one seen by Simon Forman (q.v.).

REGISTERED: 1623, 8 November. One of the sixteen plays registered by Blount and Jaggard before publishing F1.

PUBLISHED: 1623, F1. 'The Tragedie of Macbeth.' The seventh play in the Tragedy section: pp. 131–51. Acts and scenes marked. An unsatisfactory text. There has been cutting (according to Wilson, by Shakespeare himself) – apart from *The Comedy of Errors* and

The Tempest it is the shortest of the plays – adaptation and interpolation: the Hecate scenes are probably by Middleton, for the songs indicated in the stage-directions of III, v and IV, i, 'Come away' and 'Black spirits', occur in full in his *The Witch*. F was printed from the prompt-book, for the book-keeper's note, *Ring the Bell* (II, iii), has been printed in the text:

Malcolme, Banquo,
As from your Graues rise vp, and walke
like Sprights,
To countenance this horror. Ring the Bell.
Bell rings. Enter Lady.

SOURCE: The *Chronicles* of Holinshed, the Scottish history of which comes from the Latin *Scotorum Historiae* of Hector Boece. (See SS, 4.)

STAGE HISTORY: At the Restoration, Macbeth was 'improved' by D'Avenant: 'being drest in all its finery, as new clothes, new scenes, machines, as flyings for the witches, with all the singing and dancing in it, (the first composed by Mr. Lock, the other by Mr. Channel and Mr. Joseph Priest,) it being all excellently performed, being in the nature of an opera'. (Downes, *Roscius Anglicanus*, 1708.) Pepys thought the version 'one of the best plays for a stage, and variety of dancing and musick, that ever I saw' (19 April 1667). In 1744 Garrick returned for the most part to the original text. J. P. Kemble seems to have been the first to produce the banquet scene without the appearance of Banquo's ghost.

After defeating an army of Norwegians and Scottish rebels, Macbeth and Banquo, generals of Duncan, King of Scotland, meet three witches who hail Macbeth as Thane of Cawdor and 'king hereafter', and Banquo as begetter of kings. As they vanish, news arrives that Duncan has created Macbeth Thane of Cawdor. Macbeth describes his adventure in a letter to Lady Macbeth who, when she hears that Duncan is coming to stay in her castle, decides that he 'must be provided for'. Macbeth, prompted by the witches, the fulfilment of the first part of their prophecy, and his own ambition, is persuaded by his wife to kill the sleeping King. Duncan's sons, Malcolm and Donalbain, are suspected, as they run away, and Macbeth is crowned king. He now acts alone, and tries to frustrate the witches' promise to Banquo by plotting his murder and that of his son Fleance, but Fleance escapes. Haunted by the ghost of Banquo, and suspected by his nobles, in particular by Macduff, he seeks out the witches, who tell him to beware of Macduff, though 'none of woman born shall harm Macbeth' who 'shall never vanquish'd be until Great Birnam wood to high Dunsinane hill Shall come against him'. When he hears that Macduff has joined Malcolm in England, he orders the murder of Lady Macduff and her son, then, deserted by his friends and finally by Lady Macbeth who goes mad and kills herself, he awaits the attack of the Scottish nobles and their English allies. When the attackers cut branches from Birnam wood and under their cover advance on his castle of Dunsinane, he goes into the field where he meets Macduff, who tells him that he was not born, but untimely ripped from his mother's womb. Macduff kills Macbeth, and Malcolm is hailed as King of Scotland.

Macbeth. The historical Macbeth was ruler of Moray and Ross, becoming King of Scotland when he murdered Duncan in 1040, though his only claim to the throne was through his wife, Gruach. His reign is said to have been a prosperous one, though various attempts were made by the royal family to regain the throne. The first attempt by Malcolm, Duncan's son, and his uncle Siward, in 1054, was unsuccessful, but in 1057 they again invaded Scotland, and Macbeth was killed at Lumphanan.

Macbeth, Lady, was the daughter of Kenneth IV's eldest son. She had a son by her first husband, the Thane of Moray. Holinshed merely says that she 'was very ambitious, burning in unquenchable desire to have the name of a queen', and Shakespeare makes use of his more dramatic account of the murder of King Duff by servants suborned by Donwald's wife.

McCarthy, Lillah (1875–1960), born and educated in Cheltenham, her first husband was Harley Granville-Barker, in whose famous productions of *The Winter's Tale*, *Twelfth Night* and *A Midsummer Night's Dream*, at the Savoy theatre in 1912–14, she played Hermione, Viola and Helena.

McCullough, John Edward (1837–85), actor, was born in Ireland and went to America in 1853, first appearing on the stage in Philadelphia in 1857. With Edwin Forrest and Edwin Booth, he played both leading and secondary parts in Shakespearean tragedy.

Macduff. In *Macbeth* (q.v.), the Thane of Fife. It is he who finds the murdered Duncan, and is perhaps the first to suspect Macbeth, whose coronation and feast he refuses to attend. He goes to England and joins Malcolm, who thinks he is an agent of Macbeth until news comes of the murder of Lady Macduff and her son. He kills Macbeth in battle.

Macduff, Lady. In *Macbeth*, she and her son are murdered by order of Macbeth when he hears of Macduff's flight to England (IV, ii).

Machines. It is clear that the 'heavens' often played an important part in an Elizabethan production. By means of a trap-door in the canopy, spectacular effects could be produced; Q of *2 Contention* has the s.d. '*Three sunns appear in the air*', and the corresponding passage in *3 Henry VI* reads:

EDW. Dazzle mine eyes, or do I see three suns?
RICH. Three glorious suns, each one a perfect sun; ...
See, see! they join, embrace, and seem to kiss ...
Now are they but one lamp, one light, one sun.

In his *Apology for Actors* (1608) Dekker writes that the Romans, like the Jacobeans, had 'the covering of the stage, which we call the heavens (where upon any occasion their gods descended)', and in his *Old Fortunatus* (1599), Fortunatus puts on the Soldan's magic hat, and 'like a magician breaks he through the clouds' – presumably on a wire through the trap-door hidden by a suspended cloud. Bulky properties, particularly the throne of state, appear to have been let down from the heavens by means of cords and pulleys, as in *Dr Faustus*, where there is '*Musicke while the Throne descends*', and in June 1595 Henslowe paid carpenters £7 2s. for 'mackinge the throne in the heuenes' at the Rose. The traps in the stage were similarly used for effects, and mysterious appearances and vanishings, as when the mist rises in *Arden of Faversham* (IV, ii), or '*the Spirit riseth*' in *2 Henry VI* (I, iv), or when in *The Tempest* '*with a quaint device, the banquet vanishes*'. (See also 'JEW OF MALTA'.) For the masques Inigo Jones designed more elaborate machinery particularly for the changing of scenes, and these devices were sometimes applied to plays at Court. Compare John Pory's account of the Ben Jonson-Inigo Jones masque of *Hymenaei* (January 1606):

> But before the sacrifice could be performed, Ben Jonson turned the globe of the earth standing behind the altar, and within the concaue sate the 8 men-maskers representing the 4 humours and the fower affections which leapt forth to disturb the sacrifice to vnion; but amidst their fury Reason that sate aboue them all, crowned with burning tapers, came down and silenced them. These eight together with Reason their moderatresse mounted aboue their heades, sate somewhat like the ladies in the scallop shell the last year. Aboue the globe of erth houered a middle region of cloudes in the center wherof stood a grand consort of musicians, and vpon the cantons or hornes sate the ladies 4 at one corner, and 4 at another, who descended vpon the stage, not after the stale downright perpendicular fashion, like a bucket into a well; but came gently sloping down. (See L. B. Campbell, *Scenes and Machines on the English Stage*.)

Mackail, John William (1859–1945), educated at Edinburgh and St Andrews, became Professor of Poetry at Oxford University, 1906–11. His *Lectures on Poetry* appeared in 1911, and his *Approach to Shakespeare* in 1930.

Mackenzie, Henry (1745–1831), Scottish writer, was born and educated in Edinburgh, his first and most famous work, *The Man of Feeling*, being published anonymously in 1771. He became the editor of the short-lived weekly periodical, *The Mirror* (1779–80), in which he wrote of Hamlet:

> We see a man, who in other circumstances would have exercised all the moral and social virtues, placed in a situation in which even the amiable qualities of his mind serve but to aggravate his distress and to perplex his conduct.

According to Bradley, Mackenzie 'was, it would seem, the first of our critics to feel the "indescribable charm" of Hamlet, and to divine something of Shakespeare's intention'. To Hazelton Spencer he 'seems to have been the first of the obscurantists'.

McKerrow, Ronald Brunlees (1872–1940), bibliographer, was educated at Harrow, King's College, London, and Trinity, Cambridge. In 1912 he became joint honorary secretary, with A. W. Pollard, of the Bibliographical Society, edited their organ, the *Library*, 1934–7, and founded and edited the *Review of English Studies*, 1925–40. He worked with Pollard and Greg, and was the first to suggest (in 1931) that the copy of a play sent by the actors to a printer was generally the author's original draft. This marks an important stage in textual criticism. He devoted the last years of his life to the preparation of the *Oxford Shakespeare*, but the only volume issued before his death was *Prolegomena for the Oxford Shakespeare*, 1939, in which he explains his conception of an editor's duties. (See 'COPY'; BIBLIOGRAPHY.)

Macklin, Charles (*c.* 1697–1797), Irish actor and dramatist, played much in Shakespearean comedy. His most famous part was that of Shylock, his impersonation of whom at Drury Lane in 1741 as 'the Jew that Shakespeare drew' was very different from the traditional representations by low comedians. In 1735 he killed a fellow actor in a quarrel at Drury Lane, and in 1754 began the first recorded series of lectures on Shakespeare. He wrote two successful comedies, *Love à la Mode* (1759) and *The Man of the World* (1781). His last stage appearance was as Shylock at Covent Garden in 1789, when he forgot his part and had to retire.

'In May 1742, when Mr. Garrick, Mr. Macklin, and Mr. Delane visited Stratford, they were hospitably entertained under Shakspeare's mulberry-tree, by Sir Hugh Clopton ... who ... mentioned to Mr. Macklin ... an old tradition that she [Lady Bernard] had carried away with her from Stratford many of her grandfather's papers.' (Malone, *Var.*, II, 522, 623.) In 1748, Macklin wrote a letter to the *General Advertiser* containing 'gleanings' from 'a pamphlet written in the reign of Charles I, with the quaint title: "Old Ben's Light Heart made heavy by Young John's Melancholy Lover",' containing anecdotes about Ben Jonson, Shakespeare and John Ford's *Lover's Melancholy*. Unfortunately the pamphlet 'was lost in its passage from Ireland'. Steevens published the matter as genuine in his edition of 1778, but Malone exposed it as a fabrication in his of 1790.

McManaway, James Gilmer (b. 1901). American scholar; Acting Director of the Folger Library 1946–8; editor of *Shakespeare Quarterly* since 1950.

Macmorris. In *Henry V*, an Irish officer in King Henry's army, who has 'a few disputations' with Fluellen 'concerning the disciplines of the war' (III, ii).

Macready, William Charles (1793–1873), actor, was born in London and educated at Rugby. He made his first stage appearance in Birmingham as Romeo in 1810, and his first London appearance in 1816 at Covent Garden, of which theatre he was manager 1837–9. He was manager of Drury Lane 1841–3, retired in 1851, and died in Cheltenham. Though Macready was an actor-manager, a star, and a believer in the elaborate and spectacular production, he returned to Shakespeare's text in *Coriolanus*, *Tempest* and *King Lear*.

Madden, Dodgson Hamilton (1840–1928), Vice-Chancellor of Dublin University 1895–1919, and Attorney-General for Ireland. Among his publications are *The Diary of Master William Silence; a Study of Shakespeare and of Elizabethan Sport* (1897), and *Shakespeare and his Fellows; an attempt to decipher the Man and his Nature* (1916).

Maddermarket Theatre. A 16th-century house at Norwich, converted by Nugent Monck (q.v.) into an Elizabethan theatre, the first of its kind to be constructed since the closing of the theatres in 1642. The first performance was *As You Like It* on 23 September 1921. All the plays of Shakespeare have been acted there, as well as many of those of his contemporaries. (See SS, 12.)

Madrigal. The word is Italian (*madrigale*), and originally meant a poem almost synonymous with lyric; the madrigals of Drummond of Hawthornden, for example, are short poems of irregular structure. As a musical form it is a contrapuntal setting of a lyric for a number of unaccompanied voices, and became popular in England after the publication in 1588 of *Musica Transalpina*, a collection of Italian madrigals with English words. Thomas Morley, possibly a friend of Shakespeare, was perhaps the finest composer of English madrigals, and in his *Plaine and Easie Introduction to Practicall Music* (1597) describes how any lady or gentleman is expected to sing a part at sight.

Maecenas, C. Cilnius. In *Antony and Cleopatra*, a friend of Octavius who tries to heal the breach between him and Antony. He is present at the conference and feast with Pompey, and supports Octavius in his attack on Antony. (Maecenas (d. 8 B.C.) is famous as the patron of Virgil and Horace.)

Maid Lane, or Maiden Lane. The Southwark road, the modern Park Street, running parallel to the Bankside, and about 200 yards from the river. The Globe was built just to the south of it.

Maidenhead Inn. In the 17th century, perhaps as early as 1603, certainly by 1647, the house to the east of Shakespeare's birthplace, called by Halliwell-Phillipps the 'Woolshop', became an inn known as the Maidenhead. It was later known as the Swan and Maidenhead, and remained an inn until both houses were bought by the Birthplace Committee in 1847. The signboards that hung at the front and back from 1806 to 1847, the smaller one with the name of the proprietress, 'Elizth Court' (d. 1846), are preserved at the Birthplace.

'Maid's Tragedy, The.' A play by Beaumont and Fletcher (*c.* 1611); one of those performed by the King's Men during the Court Revels of 1612–13 preceding the marriage of the Princess Elizabeth. In 1619 it was registered and published as 'The Maides Tragedy. As it hath beene divers times Acted at the Blacke-friers by the Kings Maiesties Seruants.'

Mainwaring, Arthur, son of Sir George Mainwaring of Ightfield, Shropshire, and nephew and steward of Lord Chancellor Ellesmere, a supporter of enclosure. Mainwaring was a landowner in Welcombe, and it was he and his cousin William Replingham who in 1614 began proceedings for the enclosure of certain fields in Welcombe and Old Stratford. (See WELCOMBE ENCLOSURE.)

Malapropism. The misapplication of words; a form of verbal blunder humorously applied in literature long before Sheridan and his Mrs Malaprop. Witness Bottom: 'And there we may rehearse most obscenely and courageously.' And Dogberry: 'Is our whole dissembly appeared? ... Dost thou not suspect my place? dost thou not suspect my years?'

Malcolm. In *Macbeth*, elder son of Duncan, King of Scotland, who proclaims him Prince of Cumberland and heir to the throne. (Malcolm Canmore became King after his defeat of Macbeth in 1057, and died 1093.)

'Malcolm King of Scots.' A lost play bought from the actor-dramatist Charles Massey by the Admiral's and performed in April 1602. It is possible that it was a version of the Macbeth story earlier than Shakespeare's.

'Malcontent, The.' A tragi-comedy by John Marston, registered and published in 1604. It was originally played by the Queen's Revels Children at Blackfriars (see JERONIMO), but was soon afterwards performed by the King's at the Globe, and a second edition published: 'The Malcontent. Augmented by Marston. With the additions played by the Kings Maiesties servants' (1604). In the Induction, written by Webster, the King's Men appear in person, and Burbage explains that the additions are not really 'greatly needful; only as your salad to your great feast, to entertain a little more time, and to abridge the not-received custom of music in our theatre'. This is interesting, as it shows that plays at the private theatre of Blackfriars were shorter, with longer intervals for music, than at the Globe public theatre.

Malone, Edmond (1741–1812), was born in Dublin, educated at Trinity College, and called to the Irish bar, but after his father's death he went to London where he became a member of the 'Club', and a friend of Johnson, Reynolds and Boswell, whose *Life of Johnson* he helped to prepare. He also became friendly with George Steevens, the Shakespeare scholar, who in his second edition of Shakespeare's Plays, 1778, incorporated Malone's *Attempt to ascertain the Order in which the Plays of Shakespeare were written*. In 1780 Malone added two volumes to Steevens's edition, containing the *Poems*, the doubtful plays of the Third Folio and a *History of the Stage*. In 1790 he published his own 10-volume edition of Shakespeare, which stimulated Steevens, with whom Malone had quarrelled over matters of scholarship, to produce his 15-volume edition of 1793. In 1796 Malone denounced the Ireland MSS. as forgeries, and in 1801 Dublin University made him an LL.D. When he died in 1812 he was engaged on a new edition of Shakespeare which was brought out in 1821 by James Boswell the younger, and known as the Third Variorum (21 volumes). Capell, Steevens, and Malone were the three giants of Shakespearean scholarship in the second half of the 18th century, working along similar lines and not always in very friendly rivalry, and reading 'all such reading as was never read ... the reading necessary for a comment on Shakespeare'. Malone's contribution to Shakespearean scholarship can scarcely be overestimated. He was not so much concerned with textual emendation, though Boswell claimed that 'his text is beyond all comparison, the most faithful that had yet been produced', as with new material that would throw light on Shakespeare's work. He was tireless in his researches, and his *History of the Stage*, based on a knowledge of the Henslowe papers, the Revels Accounts, Sir Henry Herbert's Office Book and other contemporary records, is of the first importance, as is also his *Attempt to ascertain the Order*. Something of his contribution may be gauged by comparing the twenty or thirty pages of Rowe's *Life of Shakespeare*, the standard biography of the 18th century, with the 500 pages of Malone's, the basis of all later *Lives*. (See VARIORUM.)

Malone 'Scrap'. A document found among Edmond Malone's papers, giving a list of Court plays and dates of performance for 1604–5. This agrees with the Revels Account for the period, published in 1842, and considered by some scholars to be a forgery by Peter Cunningham, the finder. But if the Malone scrap is genuine, the Revels Accounts for 1604–5, and similar accounts for 1611–12 and 1638, are almost certainly genuine. (See MUSGRAVE.)

Malone Society, named after Edmond Malone, was founded by Pollard and Greg in 1906 with the primary object of reprinting Elizabethan plays in type facsimile.

Malvolio. In *Twelfth Night*, Olivia's conceited and humourless steward, an important officer in an Elizabethan household. (Sir Henry Herbert called *Twelfth Night* 'Malvolio' in his *Office Book*, 2 February 1623: 'At Candlemas Malvolio was acted at court, by the kings servants.' See also DIGGES.)

Mamillius. In *The Winter's Tale*, the young son of Leontes and Hermione. As soon as Leontes pronounces the oracle to be false, news comes that Mamillius has died 'with mere conceit and fear of the queen's speed' (III, ii). (Called Garinter in Greene's *Pandosto*.)

Manningham, John. A barrister of the Middle Temple whose *Diary* was edited for the Camden Society in 1868. On 13 March 1602 he related the only anecdote of Shakespeare that we possess by a contemporary, apparently on the authority of 'Mr Curle', also of the Middle Temple:

> Vpon a tyme when Burbidge played Rich. 3. there was a citizen greue soe farr in liking with him, that before shee went from the play shee appointed him to come that night vnto hir by the name of Ri: the 3. Shakespeare overhearing their conclusion went before, was intertained, and at his game ere Burbidge came. Then message being brought that Rich. the 3^{d} was at the dore, Shakespeare caused returne to be made that William the Conquerour was before Rich. the 3. Shakespeare's name William.

Six weeks earlier, at Candlemas (2 February), Manningham saw a production of *Twelfth Night* at the Middle Temple:

> At our feast wee had a play called 'Twelue Night, or What You Will', much like the Commedy of Errores, or Menechmi in Plautus, but most like and neere to that in Italian called *Inganni*. A good practise in it to make the Steward beleeve his Lady widdowe was in love with him, by counterfeyting a letter as from his Lady in generall termes, telling him what shee liked best in him, and prescribing his gesture in smiling, his apparaile, &c., and then when he came to practise making him beleeue they tooke him to be mad.

Mansfield, Richard (1857–1907), American actor, was born in Berlin. He played first in Gilbert and Sullivan opera, made his name in London in 1888 with Irving at the Lyceum, and in the following year produced *Richard III* at the Globe. His lavish production of *Henry V* ran for a whole season in New York.

Mantuanus, Baptista Spagnolo (1448–1516), a Carmelite friar of Mantua whose Latin *Eclogues* had a considerable influence on Elizabethan poetry, and were often used in schools. Probably Shakespeare came across them at Stratford Grammar School, for in *Love's Labour's Lost* Holofernes quotes the beginning of the first Eclogue: 'Fauste, precor gelida quando pecus omne sub umbra Ruminat, – and so forth. Ah, good old Mantuan! ... who understandeth thee not, loves thee not.' They were translated in 1567 by George Turberville.

Manuscript Plays. Many of the extant manuscript plays are academic, either in Latin or in English, but a few manuscripts of English plays for the professional companies have survived, some of which have been produced in photographic facsimile in J. S. Farmer's *Tudor Facsimile Texts*, and others in type facsimile by the Malone Society. Of these the most important is *Sir Thomas More* (q.v.), part of the alteration to which is in the hand of Shakespeare or of one whose writing was very like his. The general practice seems to have been to write on both sides of folio paper, in English script, speech prefixes and stage directions being generally in Italian script, the former in the left margin, the latter in the right or in the centre of the page. Some of these manuscripts show the censorship or allowance of the Master of the Revels, some the revision and additions for stage performance by the book-keeper. Apart from *Sir Thomas More*, some of the most important of these manuscript plays are Massinger's *Believe as You List*, Munday's *John a Kent*, and the anonymous *Second Maiden's Tragedy*, *Edmond Ironside*, *Thomas of Woodstock*, *Sir John Van Olden Barnevelt*, *The Welsh Embassador*, and *The Launching of the Mary*. Heywood's *The Captives* appears to be his foul papers, annotated by the book-keeper. There are also the three parts of the Cambridge play, *Parnassus*. The manuscripts of *Henry IV* (see DERING MS.), *The Merry Wives*, and *Twelfth Night* are later and probably transcribed from the printed text.

There are a few manuscripts carefully written for the study, and not for the theatre, by professional scribes, of whom Ralph Crane is the best known. (See PROMPT-BOOK; PARTS; PLOTS; Greg, *Dramatic Documents*.)

Maps of London. Maps of London, 1550–1650, are not accurately measured plans, but for the most part 'views', often bird's-eye views, the detail of which may be conventional and inaccurate. They are generally taken from the south side of the river, so that some or all of the Bankside theatres – Rose, Swan, Globe, and Hope (Beargarden) – are in the foreground. The most important London maps are:

HÖFNAGEL: drawn 1554–72; published 1572 at Cologne in the *Civitates Orbis Terrarum* of G. Braun and F. Hohenburg. The view shows the Bull and Bear baitings, and may be by Georg Höfnagel.

AGAS: drawn 1569–90; published 1633; reproduced in 1737 by G. Vertue, who assigned it to Ralph Agas. It is based on the Höfnagel.

NORDEN: (*a*) drawn *c.* 1590 by John Norden; engraved by Pieter van den Keere for Norden's *Speculum Britanniae* (London, 1593), it shows 'the Beare howse' and 'the play howse' (Rose) as cylindrical buildings. (*b*) Norden revised his view of London in 1600, when it was reproduced by an unknown engraver as an inset map in a panorama of London called *Civitas Londini*. Norden's inset shows all four Bankside theatres as cylindrical; the panorama itself, probably not by Norden, shows them as polygonal. Norden's maps are the first to show the theatres.

VISSCHER: a View of London engraved by J. C. Visscher *c.* 1616; unauthoritative, being based on Höfnagel and the panorama of *Civitas Londini*.

HONDIUS: drawn 1605–11, and engraved by Jodocus Hondius as an inset to the map of Britain in John Speed's *Theatre of the Empire of Great Britain* (1611). It shows only the Beargarden and Globe, the former polygonal, the latter cylindrical; the last view before their rebuilding in 1613–14.

DELARAM: an equestrian portrait of James I with a background similar to the *Hondius View*, on which it seems to be based; engraved by Francis Delaram (b. 1590) *c.* 1615–24.

RYTHER: a map of London, almost two-dimensional, attributed to Augustine Ryther *c.* 1604, but published at Amsterdam by Cornelius Danckerts, probably 1635–45.

MERIAN: engraved by Matthias Merian and published at Frankfort in J. L. Gottfried's *Neuwe Archontologia Cosmica* (1638). Unauthoritative, being based on the *Civitas Londini* panorama and Visscher.

HOLLAR: the *Long View* engraved by Wenceslas Hollar from his drawings made between 1637 and 1644, and published in 1647 at Amsterdam by Cornelius Danckerts. This shows the new Beargarden (Hope), and new Globe, both as cylindrical, though their names are interchanged. (See SS, 1.)

In 1954 (*The Times*, 26 March) Hotson published an engraving found in the library of the University of Utrecht:

'The View of the Cittye of London from the North towards the Sowth'. It was drawn *c.* 1600, and shows the Curtain and Fortune, which was then being built.

Marcellus. In *Hamlet*, an officer who persuades Horatio to visit the battlements where he and Bernardo have twice seen the ghost. They tell Hamlet of what they have seen, and Marcellus and Horatio accompany him when he speaks to it and swears them to secrecy. He does not appear after this. (The text of Q1 may have been reported by an actor who played Marcellus.)

March Music in plays was mainly that of drum and fife; cf. s.d. in *1 Henry IV* (III, iii), '*Enter the* Prince *and* Peto, *marching, and* Falstaff *meets them playing on his truncheon like a fife*'; and *Timon of Athens* (IV, iii), '*March afar off … Enter* Alcibiades, *with drum and fife, in warlike manner*'. At the end of a tragedy a dead march on the drum was often struck or sounded, as in *Hamlet*, *Timon*, and *King Lear*. In *Coriolanus* we have, 'Beat thou the drum' … *A dead march sounded.*

Marcius. In *Coriolanus*, the young son of Coriolanus who goes with Volumnia and Virgilia to beg his father to spare Rome. He speaks only two lines (V, iii).

Mardian. In *Antony and Cleopatra*, a eunuch attending Cleopatra, who sends him to tell Antony that she has killed herself (IV, xiii and xiv).

Margaret. In *Much Ado*, a gentlewoman attending Hero. She favours Borachio, who so contrives it that she leans out of Hero's window at night while he makes love to her, Claudio and the Prince thinking that she is Hero. When Borachio confesses, he assures Leonato that Margaret 'knew not what she did when she spoke to me' (V, i).

Margaret of Anjou (1430–82). In *1, 2, 3 Henry VI* and *Richard III*, the daughter of Reignier (René, Duke of Anjou), and wife of Henry VI. In *1 Henry VI* she is captured by Suffolk, who undertakes to make her Henry's queen if she will be his mistress.

In *2 Henry VI* she appears as Queen, quarrels with the Duchess of Gloucester, secures Gloucester's dismissal, persuades Suffolk to murder him, and when Suffolk is banished and killed openly shows her love for him. Before the Wars of the Roses begin, York calls her a 'blood-bespotted Neapolitan', and after the Lancastrian defeat at St Albans she and Henry flee to London.

In *3 Henry VI* Margaret continues the struggle against York when Henry makes him his heir, so disinheriting his own son. She defeats York at Wakefield, taunts him, and stabs him, but is herself defeated at Towton, goes to France for aid and is joined by Warwick. After her defeat at Tewkesbury and the murder of her husband and son, she is sent back to her father, who ransoms her.

In *Richard III* she appears as a fateful figure recalling the dreadful past, prophesying disaster, and cursing the House of York, particularly Richard, who had murdered her husband and son. (As a matter of history, Margaret did not return to England after her defeat and dismissal to France.)

Maria. 1. In *Love's Labour's Lost*, one of the ladies attending the Princess of France on her visit to Navarre. She falls in love with Longaville (q.v.).

2. In *Twelfth Night*, a gentlewoman attending on Olivia. It is she who devises the plot against Malvolio, writes the love-letter in a hand like Olivia's, leaves it where he shall find it, and when he behaves so strangely suggests to Olivia that he is mad. She also persuades Feste to imitate Sir Topas the curate and talk to Malvolio in his prison. In the last scene Fabian announces that Maria has married Sir Toby.

Mariana. 1. In *All's Well*, a Florentine, and friend of the mother of Diana, whom she warns against Bertram and Parolles (III, v).

2. In *Measure for Measure*, betrothed to Angelo, but deserted by him when her brother was drowned and her dowry lost in a shipwreck. Isabella agrees to visit Angelo at night, and the disguised Duke arranges that Mariana shall take her place, unknown to Angelo. When the Duke reveals himself, he makes Angelo marry Mariana. (There is no corresponding character in Cinthio or Whetstone.)

Marina. The heroine of *Pericles*, she is the daughter of Pericles, so called because she is born at sea. (Gower calls her Thaise in *Confessio Amantis.*)

'Marina.' An Adaptation of *Pericles* by George Lillo (q.v.).

Markham, Gervase (or Jervis) (*c.* 1568–1637), poet, was the son of Sir Robert Markham of Cotham, Notts. He was a soldier and accompanied Essex on his Irish expedition, a horse-breeder, and a voluminous author. Because his poem, *The Tragedy of Sir Richard Grenville* (1595), was dedicated, among others, to Shakespeare's patron the Earl of Southampton, Fleay suggested that Markham might be the rival poet of the *Sonnets* as does R. Gittings in *Shakespeare's Rival.* He is probably the J.M., the author of *The New Metamorphosis* (*c.* 1615), a manuscript poem containing a contemporary reference to Shakespeare:

it seems 't is true that W.S. said,
when once he heard one courting of a
 Mayde,–
Beleve not thou Mens fayned flatteryes,
Lovers will tell a bushell-full of Lyes!

Marlowe, Christopher (1564–93), one of the University Wits, was the son of a shoemaker of Canterbury, where he was born 6 February 1564, some two months before Shakespeare. In 1579 he entered King's School, Canterbury, and matriculated at Benet (Corpus Christi) College, Cambridge, in 1581, taking his B.A. in 1584 and M.A. in 1587, the year in which his first play, *Tamburlaine*, was produced. His great series of tragedies with their titanic heroes, most of them written, apparently, for Edward Alleyn, was continued in *Dr Faustus, The Jew of Malta, Edward II, The Massacre at Paris* and *Dido Queen of Carthage*, plays that were to Alleyn and the Admiral's what Shakespeare's were to Burbage and the Chamberlain's. Marlowe was one of the group of freethinkers gathered about Sir Walter Ralegh, and when in May 1593 certain 'atheistic' notes of his were found among the papers of Thomas Kyd, who had been arrested on a charge of 'lewd and mutinous libels', a warrant was issued for his arrest. But on 30 May he was stabbed and killed in a Deptford inn by his companion, Ingram Frizer, in a quarrel over the 'recnkynge'. He was buried at Deptford on 1 June. Frizer, who seems to have acted in self-defence, was pardoned.

If Shakespeare had died, as he was born, in the same year as Marlowe, there can be no doubt as to which would now be considered the greater poet and more important dramatist. Marlowe's contemporary, Drayton, wrote of his bright and fiery genius:

Marlowe, bathed in the Thespian springs,
Had in him those brave translunary things
That our first poets had: his raptures were
All air and fire, which made his verses
 clear:
For that fine madness still he did retain,
Which rightly should possess a poet's brain.

And Swinburne's panegyric is, for once, without hyperbole: 'He is the greatest discoverer, the most daring and inspired pioneer, in all our poetic literature. Before him there was neither genuine blank verse nor a genuine tragedy in our language. After his arrival the way was prepared, the paths were made straight, for Shakespeare.'

Shakespeare lived to 'outshine ... Marlowe's mighty line', but Marlowe's influence is strong in Shakespeare's early plays, so strong that some critics find Marlowe himself in parts not only of the earliest plays, *Henry VI, Richard III, Titus Andronicus* and even *The Comedy of Errors*, but also in *Richard II, Henry V* and *Julius Caesar*. Shakespeare's one clear allusion to a contemporary poet is to Marlowe, a line from whose *Hero and Leander* he quotes in *As You Like It*:

Dead shepherd, now I find thy saw of might,
Whoever loved, that loved not at first sight?

(See L. Hotson, *The Death of Christopher Marlowe*; F. P. Wilson, *Marlowe and the Early Shakespeare*; SS, 14.)

Marlowe, Julia (1865–1950), American actress, was born in England, but first appeared on the stage in New York in 1887. In 1904 she began her association with E. H. Sothern and acted with him for a number of years in a series of Shakespeare's plays, her most successful part being that of Viola.

Marprelate Controversy (1588–90). In 1586 the Star Chamber issued a decree whereby all printed matter had to be licensed by the Archbishop of Canterbury and Bishop of London, or their deputies, so checking the flow of Puritan pamphlets. In 1588 a Welsh Puritan, John Penry, set up a secret press at Molesey in Surrey, whence, in November of that year, was issued the first of the 'Martin Marprelate' tracts, *The Epistle to the Terrible Priests*. 'Martin Marprelate' was the assumed name of the author, whose attacks were directed for the most part against the bishops. The press was constantly moved and a series of pamphlets was printed:

The Epitome, from Fawsley near Northampton.

Hay any Worke for Cooper, from Coventry, March 1589. (A reply to *An Admonition* by Thomas Cooper, Bishop of Winchester.)

Theses Martinianae, by Martin Junior, *The Just Censure of Martin Junior*, by Martin Senior } from Wolston, July 1589.

More Work for Cooper, from Manchester, August 1589.

The Protestation of Martin Marprelate, from Wolston or Haseley, September 1589.

While *More Work for Cooper* was being printed the press was seized, but Penry fled to Scotland. He returned to London in 1592, was arrested in March 1593, and hanged on a charge of sedition. The author of the pamphlets is unknown; it is improbable that Penry wrote them, and the most likely candidate appears to be his associate Job Throckmorton, who was acquitted.

Apart from the literary merit of the tracts themselves, the controversy is interesting in that the bishops called to their aid the popular pamphleteers Lyly and Nashe, and apparently Munday, to reply to Martin in his own vigorous style. *Pappe with an Hatchet* (October 1589) is almost certainly Lyly's, and *An Almond for a Parrat* (1590) probably Nashe's. They also ridiculed Martin on the stage, in plays unfortunately lost, an action that probably led to the suppression of the Paul's boys.

Marshall, William (fl. 1630–50), engraver, worked entirely for booksellers, such as Humphrey Moseley. Some of his best-known portraits are those of Donne (engraved apparently from an original, perhaps by N. Hilliard) in *Poems*, 1635, of Milton in Moseley's edition of his *Poems*, 1645, and of Shakespeare in Benson's 1640 edition of the *Poems*. This last is a smaller and reversed copy of the Droeshout engraving.

Marston, John (*c.* 1575–1634), dramatist, was born at Coventry, the son of a lawyer and an Italian mother. After Brasenose, Oxford (1592–4), he entered the Middle Temple, but to his father's regret abandoned law for literature, in 1598 publishing his satires, *The Metamorphosis of Pygmalion's Image* and *The Scourge of Villainy* (q.v.), under the name of W. Kinsayder. It is probable that he is the 'Mr Maxton the new poete' to whom Henslowe paid 40s. as part payment for a play for the Admiral's in September 1599, but by 1600 Marston was writing for the Children's companies, 1600–3 for the Paul's boys, and after 1604 for the

Queen's Revels at the Blackfriars theatre, of which syndicate he became a member. In June 1608 he was 'committed to Newgate', and this seems to have ended his dramatic career. He married Mary Wilkes, daughter of one of James I's chaplains, Jonson remarking that 'Marston wrott his Father-in-lawes preachings, and his Father-in-law his Commedies'. By 1616 he held the living of Christchurch, Hampshire, which he resigned in 1631, dying in London 25 June 1634.

In 1619 Jonson told Drummond that 'he had many quarrels with Marston, beat him, and took his pistol from him, wrote his Poetaster on him; the beginning of them were, that Marston represented him in the stage, in his youth given to venerie'. This is a reference to an episode in the War of the Theatres, or Poetomachia (q.v.): to Marston's satirical representation of Jonson as Brabant senior in *Jack Drum's Entertainment*, to which Jonson replied in *The Poetaster* (1601), satirizing Marston as Crispinus. They were friends again by 1604, when Marston dedicated *The Malcontent* to Jonson, but Jonson was with some justice annoyed over the *Eastward Ho!* affair. This play was written by Chapman, Jonson and Marston, and contained uncomplimentary references to the Scots. On its performance and publication in 1605, Chapman and Jonson were imprisoned for a time, but Marston, who was mainly responsible for the offensive passages, escaped. Marston's plays are for the most part distinguished by their misanthropy, sensational incident and rhetoric. His extant plays are: *Antonio and Mellida* 1599, *Jack Drum's Entertainment* 1600, *What You Will* 1601, *The Dutch Courtesan* 1603–4, *The Malcontent* 1604, *The Fawn* c.1605, *Sophonisba* 1606, *The Insatiate Countess* c. 1608.

Martext, Sir Oliver. In *As You Like It*, the vicar who is about to marry Touchstone and Audrey in the forest when Jaques tells them to go to church 'and have a good priest' (III, iii).

Martius. In *Titus Andronicus*, one of the four sons of Titus. He and his brother Quintus fall into the pit where lies the body of Bassianus, of whose murder they are accused (II, iii), and executed.

Marullus. In *Julius Caesar*, he and his fellow-tribune, Flavius, fear the growing power of Caesar and dissuade the people from celebrating his triumph over Pompey. He appears only in the first scene; in I, ii Casca reports that 'Marullus and Flavius, for pulling scarfs off Caesar's images, are put to silence'.

Masefield, John (1878–1967), O.M., and Poet Laureate 1930. His first publication was *Salt Water Ballads* in 1902; his *William Shakespeare*, short appreciations of the poems and plays, appeared in 1911, the same year as *The Everlasting Mercy*.

Masque. The old form of the word is 'Mask' or 'Maske'; Lyly and Jonson established the French form, 'Masque', which has become customary. In the 14th century the masque became a well-defined entertainment in which friends unexpectedly visited a house and danced before the host and his company, afterwards inviting the spectators to take part. They brought musicians, wore masks and carried torches, and generally brought presents with them. In the 15th century the spectacular and mimetic elements in the masque were emphasized and elaborated, leading to a divorce between performers and spectators in these 'disguisings', as they were called. In the early 16th century the original practice of spectators joining the dance, which had survived in Italy, returned to England as something new. On Twelfth Night 1512, the young King Henry VIII

> with xi other wer disguised, after the manner of Italie, called a maske, a thyng not seen afore in Englande, thei were appareled in garmentes long and brode, wrought all with gold, with visers and cappes of gold, and after the banket doen, these maskers came in, with sixe gentlemen disguised in silke

bearyng staffe torches, and desired the ladies to daunce, some were content, and some that knew the fashion of it refused, because it was not a thyng commonly seen. And after thei daunced and commoned together, as the fashion of the maskes is, thei toke their leave and departed, and so did the Quene, and all the ladies.

For a time masques and disguisings remained distinct, but by the middle of the century the various elements were fused and the masque of Elizabeth's reign combined the original dancing and 'commoning' of performers and spectators, with the pageantry, generally allegorical, of the disguisings.

With the accession of James I there was a rapid development of the Court masque, owing mainly to Queen Anne's fondness for and participation in the Revels, and the consequent employment of poets and dramatists such as Chapman, Jonson and Beaumont, and of Inigo Jones, the brilliant architect and scenic designer. Masques became fabulously expensive forms of entertainment, and at the same time more dramatic. The Elizabethan masque was for the most part mimed, any necessary explanation being given by a presenter, interpreter, or 'truchman' as he was called; dialogue and even songs were rare. In Jonson's masques dialogue and song became important elements, and it was Jonson who added variety by means of the anti-masque, a comic or grotesque interlude analogous to the sub-plot or comic relief of the contemporary drama. Jonson describes his first 'foil, or false masque ... an anti-masque of boys' in *The Hue and Cry after Cupid* (1608),

Wherewith they fell into a subtle, capricious dance, to as odd a music, each of them bearing two torches, and nodding with their antic faces, with other variety of ridiculous gesture, which gave much occasion of mirth and delight to the spectators.

But in spite of its high literary, musical, and spectacular qualities, the masque remained only an introduction to the main business of the evening, to the revels, the dancing of galliards and corantos by masquers and spectators alike (see MASQUE OF OBERON). *Comus* (1634), therefore, lacks the essential element of a masque, and is more strictly a play. It is easy to see how the professional English opera of D'Avenant developed from the courtly and amateur masque.

Shakespeare introduces Elizabethan masques in *Love's Labour's Lost* and *Romeo and Juliet*, and the growing influence of the masque on his later plays and those of other Jacobean dramatists is clear enough. It was inevitable that *Henry VIII* should have one, the Masque of Juno is of the very stuff of *The Tempest*, but even *Timon of Athens* has a Masque of Amazons with Cupid as truchman. (See Chambers, *Elizabethan Stage, I.*)

Masque of the Inner Temple and Gray's Inn, was to have been given 16 February 1613, two days after the Princess Elizabeth's wedding, but as 'the King was so wearied and sleepy' it was put off to the 20th, when it was given in the Banqueting House, Whitehall. The second anti-masque of a 'rurall company' had a pedant, a May lord and lady, a serving-man and chambermaid, a host and hostess, a shepherd and wench, and two Bavians: a 'Hee Baboone' and a 'Shee Baboone'. As these are the characters, though with only one Bavian, in the morris-dance in *The Two Noble Kinsmen* (III, v), it seems clear that the play followed the masque, probably at no distant date.

'Masque of Oberon.' A masque devised by Ben Jonson and Inigo Jones, and given at the Banqueting House, Whitehall, 1 January 1611, in honour of Prince Henry, who played Oberon. From divers parts of a dark rock appeared a Silene and ten Satyrs leaping and making antic actions. After some dialogue the whole scene opened and discovered a glorious palace whose gates and walls were transparent. The Satyrs chattered and sang a catch which wakened two sleeping Sylvan guards, who said that the gates would not open before the second cock-crow. To pass the time, the Satyrs sang a song to the moon, and fell into an antick dance. The cock crew, and 'the whole palace opened, and the nation of Faies were discovered, some with instruments, some bearing lights, others singing; and within, afar off in perspective, the knights masquers sitting in their several sieges: at the farther end of all, Oberon in a chariot which, to a loud triumphant music, began to move forward, drawn by two white bears'. This was followed by a song, speeches by a Sylvan and Silene, a song by two Faies, and a dance by the lesser Faies. Then 'Oberon and the knights danced out the first masque-dance' followed by a song, 'after which, they danced forth their second masque-dance, and were again excited by a Song.' Then the Queen and her ladies joined in the Revels and danced 'corantos, galliards &c.' until half an hour before sunrise. After a song the masquers 'danced their last dance into the work. And with a full Song the star vanished, and the whole machine closed.'

It is possible that this masque helps to date *The Winter's Tale*; that the dance of twelve satyrs, 'one three of them ... hath danced before the king' (IV, iv) was suggested by *Oberon*. That the bear that dined on the gentleman in III, iii is one of those that drew Oberon's chariot is more doubtful.

'Massacre at Paris, The.' A play by Marlowe, written in 1593 and published without date as 'The Massacre at Paris: With the Death of the Duke of Guise. As it was plaide by the right honourable the Lord high Admirall his Seruants. Written by Christopher Marlow'. This must be 'the tragedey of the gvyes' noted by Henslowe as 'ne[w]' when played by Strange's 26 January 1593. It is odd that the Duke of Guise, just before his murder, should speak the same line as Caesar (*Julius Caesar*, II, ii), 'Yet Caesar shall go forth', and that his dying words should be, 'Thus Caesar did go forth, and thus he died'. Line 953, 'And we are graced with wreaths of victory', is the same as *3 Henry VI*, V, iii, 2, and 1376–7 are almost the same as II, i, 68–9.

Sweet Duke of Guise, our prop to lean upon,
Now thou art dead, here is no stay for us.

Sweet Duke of York, our prop to lean upon,
Now thou art gone, we have no staff, no
stay.

Massey, Charles, actor-dramatist, author of *Malcolm King of Scots*, which he sold to his company, the Admiral's, in 1602. He was with the Admiral's from 1597 until his death sometime before 1635, and in 1618 became a housekeeper in the Fortune.

Massinger, Philip (1583–1640), dramatist, was born at Salisbury and educated at St Alban Hall, Oxford, which he left without a degree in 1606. His father had been in the service of Henry Herbert, 2nd Earl of Pembroke, but there is no indication that the poet secured the patronage of William Herbert, 3rd Earl, possibly because he may have become a Roman Catholic. The 4th Earl, Philip Herbert, was his patron, however, and Massinger supported him in his opposition to Buckingham, who is satirized as Gisco in *The Bondman*. He appears to have begun his dramatic career as a collaborator; about 1613 he was writing for Henslowe, to whom he, Field, and Daborne appealed for an advance of £5 for the 'play of Mr Fletchers and ours', and he was still in Henslowe's clutches in 1615 when he and Daborne owed him £3. He was the unacknowledged collaborator with Fletcher in a number of plays after Henslowe's death in 1616, writing almost entirely for the King's Men. Massinger's democratic ideas were not popular with Charles I and his Master of the Revels, Sir Henry Herbert, the former remarking of *The King and the Subject*, 'This is too insolent, and to bee changed', the latter refusing to allow the first version of *Believe as You List* (q.v.) with its 'dangerous matter as the deposing of Sebastian, king of Portugal'.

The first of his plays to be published was *The Virgin Martyr* (1622), written with Dekker, to whom the best things in it may be due. Massinger himself thought his tragedy *The Roman Actor* 'the most perfect birth of my Minerva', but he is best remembered by his comedy *A New Way to Pay Old Debts* with its aspiring and avaricious Sir Giles Overreach. Massinger marks the beginning of the decline of the Jacobean drama; he is steady and workmanlike, but lacks the spontaneity and inspiration of his predecessors. Technically much of his verse resembles that of Shakespeare, of whom there are many echoes in his plays, and some critics credit him instead of Shakespeare with the non-Fletcher parts of *Henry VIII* and *The Two Noble Kinsmen*. His *Roman Actor* was ascribed to Shakespeare in the middle of the 17th century.

Masson, David (1822–1907), was successively Professor of English at University College, London, and at Edinburgh University (1865–95), his great work being the six volumes of *The Life of Milton* (1858–80). His *Shakespeare Personally* helped to popularize the mid-Victorian sentimental view of Furnivall and Dowden.

Master of the Revels. The Revels Office with Master, Clerk Comptroller, Clerk, Yeoman and Groom was a 'standing office' within the department of the Lord Chamberlain. The Master of the Revels first appears in Henry VII's reign as a temporary Court official, but under Henry VIII the office became permanent on the appointment of Sir Thomas Cawarden in 1545 as 'Magister Iocorum, Revelorum et Mascorum omnium et singularium nostrorum'. Cawarden died in 1559, the Masters of Shakespeare's time being:

1560–72	Sir Thomas Benger
1573–9	Thomas Blagrave (acting Master)
1579–1610	Edmund Tilney
1603–10	Sir George Buck (deputy Master)
1610–22	Sir George Buck
1622–3	Sir John Ashley
1623–73	Sir Henry Herbert

The traditional period of the Court Revels was from All Saints' Day (1 November) to the beginning of Lent, but Elizabeth's celebrations were normally concentrated within the twelve days of Christmas, with a play or masque on the festivals of St Stephen, St John, the Innocents, New Year's Day and Twelfth Night (26, 27, 28 December, 1, 6 January), and sometimes a play at Candlemas (2 February), and one or two just before Lent. Under James I the Revels normally began 1 November and occasionally lasted with intervals until Easter.

The Revels Office was originally created to arrange and organize the Court Revels, but the powers of the Master were gradually extended, partly because of the government policy of concentration, and partly because it was to the Masters' advantage. In 1574 the royal patent for Leicester's Men authorized them to play in the City of London, subject only to the allowance of the Master, and in 1581 Edmund Tilney was given power 'to order and reforme, auctorise and put downe' all plays for public performance. The Master's powers of censorship became more important after the Act to Restrain Abuses of Players (1606), and from 1607 he acted as licenser of plays for printing, as deputy to the Archbishop of Canterbury who, by the Star Chamber Decree of 1586, was responsible for the licensing of all printed matter. The office of Master became extremely lucrative; Herbert bought it from Ashley for £150 a year, but made much more than this out of it. Apart from his normal rewards for Court services – the regular salary was £10 a year – he received fees for licensing theatres, plays and provincial companies, for lenten dispensations, and in addition received numerous gratuities such as the benefit of two performances a year from the King's Men.

From the closing of the theatres to the Restoration the Office was in abeyance, and though Herbert was still Master when the theatres reopened, he had neither authority nor profit. The work of a Master of the Revels is recorded in his *Office Book*. (See HERBERT, SIR HENRY; OFFICE BOOK; REVELS OFFICE; ABUSE OF PLAYERS; CENSORSHIP; LICENSING.)

Master-Gunner of Orleans. In *1 Henry VI*, he lays his gun on a window from which the English were 'wont ... to overpeer the city'. His son fires it and kills Lord Salisbury and Sir Thomas Gargrave (I, iv).

Masuccio of Salerno (*c.* 1415–*c.* 1477), whose real name was Tomaso Guardato, was the earliest of the south Italian novelists. His important and original *Novellino*, printed at Naples in 1476, contains a hundred stories. One of these is substantially that of Romeo and Juliet, though the young wife dies of grief after the execution of her exiled husband, caught opening her tomb.

Mathews, Charles James (1803–78), actor, was born at Liverpool, son of the actor Charles Mathews, and educated at Merchant Taylors' School. In 1838 he married Madame Vestris, and in the following year they began their management of Covent Garden with *Love's Labour's Lost*, the first recorded performance since 1605, following it with *The Merry Wives of Windsor*. In 1840, with careful and elaborate designs by J. R. Planché, they produced *A Midsummer Night's Dream* which, though severely cut, was at least Shakespeare's text. Mathews played mainly in light comedy.

Matthews, James Brander (1852–1929), American scholar, playwright and critic, was educated at Columbia University, where he became Professor of English in 1892, and of Dramatic Literature in 1900. His work was similar to that of G. P. Baker at Yale; he founded the Theatre Museum at Columbia, and his *Shakespeare as a Playwright* (1913), with its insistence on Shakespeare as dramatist, is typical of the criticism of the period.

Mayenne, Charles Duc de (1554–1611), brother of the Duc de Guise, and the Catholic opponent of Henry of Navarre in his struggle for the French throne, 1589–93. He appears as Dumaine in Marlowe's *Massacre at Paris*, and as the unhistorical Dumain in *Love's Labour's Lost*.

Mayne, Jasper. See M., I.

Mayor of London. 1. In *1 Henry VI*, he stops the fighting in the City between Gloucester's and the Bishop of Winchester's men, and begs the King to intervene (I, iii; III, i). (John Coventry, Lord Mayor 1425.)

2. In *Richard III*, he supports Richard's actions and claim to the throne (III, v and vii). (Sir Edmund Shaw, Lord Mayor 1482 and brother of Dr Shaw, III, v.)

3. In *Henry VIII*, the Lord Mayor, Sir Stephen Pecocke, is present in the last scene at the christening of Elizabeth.

Mayowe, Thomas, in 1580 brought an action for the recovery of a Snitterfield estate that had been sold by his ancestor, William Mayowe, in 1440, and passed into the hands of the Arden family. He claimed that the property was entailed and could not be alienated. In 1550, Richard Shakespeare was tenant, and John and Henry Shakespeare were witnesses in the case of 1580, records of which have perished.

'MEASURE FOR MEASURE.'

WRITTEN: 1603–4. One of the 'problem' plays, about the composition and ethics of which critics are divided. (See SQ, I, 208.)

PERFORMED: 1604, 26 December. 'By his Maiesties plaiers. On St Stiuens night in the Hall A play Caled Mesur for Mesur. Shaxberd.' (*Revels Account*.)

REGISTERED: 1623, 8 November. One of the sixteen plays registered by Blount and Jaggard before publishing F1.

PUBLISHED: 1623, F1. 'Measvre, For Measure.' The fourth play in the Comedy section: pp. 61–84. Acts and scenes marked. '*The Scene Vienna*', and 'The names of all the Actors' at the end. There are few stage-directions. An unsatisfactory text, with mislineation of verse and indications of cutting. Wilson finds evidence of revision and assembly of text from 'parts'. Perhaps set up from Crane's transcript of foul papers.

SOURCES: George Whetstone's *Promos and Cassandra* (1578), a two-part play based on a story in Giraldi Cinthio's *Hecatommithi* or *Hundred Tales* (1565). (In 1582 Whetstone translated Cinthio's *novella* in his *Heptameron of Civil Discourses*, and Cinthio dramatized his own story as the tragi-comedy *Epitia*, published 1583.)

STAGE HISTORY: 1662, 18 February, D'Avenant's adaptation, *The Law Against Lovers* (q.v.) was seen by Pepys: 'a good play and well performed'.

1699. A version by Charles Gildon with a masque of Dido and Aeneas and Purcell's music produced by Betterton at Lincoln's Inn Fields.

1720. Revived by John Rich with Quin as the Duke; perhaps an approximation to Shakespeare's text.

1908. William Poel's production at Stratford.

1963, 15 June, the last play performed by the Old Vic Company.

The Duke of Vienna leaves Angelo as his Deputy to enforce strict laws against immorality while he pretends to go on a visit to Poland, but remains in Vienna disguised as a friar. Angelo condemns to death Claudio, who has seduced Juliet, but when Claudio's sister Isabella intercedes, he promises Claudio's life if she will be his mistress. Isabella refuses in spite of her brother's entreaty that she sacrifice her honour for his life. The disguised Duke persuades Isabella to pretend to agree to Angelo's suggestion that she go to his house at night, and arranges that Mariana, betrothed to Angelo but deserted by him, shall take her place. Nevertheless Angelo orders Claudio's execution, which the provost secretly refuses to obey. The Duke reveals himself, at first pretends to disbelieve the stories of Isabella and Mariana, then forces Angelo to marry Mariana, Claudio to marry Juliet, and declares his own love for Isabella. At the beginning of Act IV a boy sings to Mariana 'Take, O take those lips away'.

Meighen, Richard. One of the publishers of F2.

Melun. In *King John*, a French lord whose 'grandsire was an Englishman'. He acts as intermediary between Salisbury and the Dauphin, but when mortally wounded tells 'the revolts of England' that the Dauphin intends to kill them when they have served his purpose (V, iv).

'Menaechmi.' A comedy by Plautus in which Menaechmus of Epidamnus is discovered by his long-lost twin brother with whom he is confused. The play is the source of *The Comedy of Errors*, though Shakespeare adds the twin slaves and the story of Aegeon and Aemilia. When John Manningham saw the performance of *Twelfth Night* at the Middle Temple, 2 February 1602, he wrote that it was 'much like the Commedy of Errores, or Menechmi in Plautus'.

'Menaphon.' Robert Greene's prose romance (1589) of the love of the shepherd Menaphon for the shipwrecked Princess Sephestia. Thomas Nashe prefixed an epistle *To the Gentlemen Students of Both Universities* in which he appears to couple the *Ur-Hamlet* with the name of Kyd (q.v.).

Menas. In *Antony and Cleopatra*, a 'famous pirate' and friend of Pompey. When the triumvirs are feasting with Pompey in his ship, Menas whispers 'let me cut the cable; And, when we are put off, fall to their throats.' Pompey replies that he should have done it, 'And not have spoke on't.'

Mendelssohn, Felix (1809–47), was born at Hamburg, son of a banker. He became director of music at Düsseldorf and then of the Conservatory at Leipzig, where he died. He wrote his *Midsummer Night's Dream* music for Ludwig Tieck's Berlin production of 1827.

Menecrates. In *Antony and Cleopatra*, a pirate and friend of Pompey. He appears only in II, i.

Menelaus. In *Troilus and Cressida*, King of Sparta and husband of Helen. He is depicted as a nonentity, and though he appears in a number of scenes, he says little.

Menenius Agrippa. In *Coriolanus*, a patrician and friend of Coriolanus. He persuades the mutinous plebeians that the patricians have a most charitable care for them, supporting his argument with the fable of the belly and the members (I, i), and he does his best to make Coriolanus ask for their confirmation of his appointment as Consul without contempt. When Coriolanus marches against Rome, he appeals to him to spare the city, but in vain.

Mennis, John. Thomas Plume (q.v.) made a note *c.* 1657 that Sir John Mennis once saw Shakespeare's 'old father in his shop'. But John Shakespeare died in September 1601, and the only John Mennis of whom there is record was born 1 March 1599, later becoming Admiral Sir John Mennis. His brother, Sir Matthew Mennis, was about six years older, and might have remembered John Shakespeare.

Menteith. In *Macbeth*, a Scottish nobleman. He first appears in V, ii leading the Scottish forces to join those of Malcolm and Siward against Macbeth.

Mercade. In *Love's Labour's Lost*, at the end of the play he brings the news to the Princess of France that her father is dead.

'MERCHANT OF VENICE.'

WRITTEN: 1596–7. Mentioned by Meres in his *Palladis Tamia*, 1598.

PERFORMED: It had 'beene diuers times acted by the Lord Chamberlaine his Seruants' before Q1, 1600.

1605. 10, 12 February, at Court. 'By his Maiesties plaiers. On Shrousunday A play of the Marthant of Venis ... On Shroutusday A play Cauled the Martchant of Venis Againe Commanded By the Kings Maiestie. Shaxberd.' (*Revels Account.*)

REGISTERED: 1598. 'xxij° Julij. James Robertes. Entred for his copie vnder the handes of bothe the wardens, a booke of the Marchaunt of Venyce, or otherwise called the Jewe of Venyce, Prouided, that yt bee not prynted by the said James Robertes or anye other whatsoeuer without lycence first had from the Right honorable the lord Chamberlen vj^{d}.'

1600. '28 Octobris. Thomas Haies. Entred for his copie under the handes of the Wardens and by Consent of master Robertes. A booke called the booke of the merchant of Venyce vj^{d}.'

PUBLISHED: 1600, Q1. 'The most excellent Historie of the Merchant of Venice. With the extreame crueltie of Shylocke the Iewe towards the sayd Merchant, in cutting a iust pound of his flesh: and the obtayning of Portia by the choyse of three chests. As it hath beene diuers times acted by the Lord Chamberlaine his Seruants. Written by William Shakespeare. At London, Printed by I. R. for Thomas Heyes, and are to be sold in Paules Churchyard, at the signe of the Greene Dragon. 1600.' A good text. Wilson finds evidence of revision and of assembly from players' parts. Set up from foul papers.

1619, Q2. One of the ten plays issued by W. Jaggard, some of them with false dates. This Q is dated 1600. Set up from an annotated Q1.

(After Jaggard's piratical reprint, Laurence Heyes, on 8 July 1619, applied for and was granted confirmation of his father's copyright in the play.)

1623, F1. 'The Merchant of Venice.' The ninth play in the Comedy section: pp. 163–84. Acts only marked. Set up from Q1 with reference to prompt-book.

1637, Q3, with a list of dramatis personae.

1652, Q4.

SOURCES: The Bond theme came from *Il Pecorone* (The Simpleton), by Ser Giovanni Fiorentino, printed 1558; the Casket theme from the 66th story of Richard Robinson's version of the *Gesta Romanorum*, 1577. (See VORAGINE.) Shakespeare may have worked from an earlier play, *The Jew* (q.v.), which apparently combined the two themes. There are some parallels to Marlowe's *Jew of Malta*, both in Shylock-Barabas and Jessica-Abigail. The Jew, Roderigo Lopez, was executed in 1594 for the attempted poisoning of Elizabeth and Don Antonio of Portugal.

STAGE HISTORY: 1701. There is no recorded revival between 1605 and 1701, when George Granville's version, *The Jew of Venice*, which includes a masque, was produced and held the stage for forty years. Betterton played Bassanio, and the low comedian Dogget was Shylock. In 1741 Charles Macklin rescued Shylock from farce in the famous Drury Lane production of Shakespeare's play. (See KEAN, EDMUND; HEINE.)

Bassanio asks his friend Antonio, merchant of Venice, for a loan of three thousand ducats so that he may go to Belmont in pursuit of the heiress Portia. As Antonio's capital is in ships and merchandise, he offers them as security for a loan of ready money from Shylock the Jew, who agrees, but demands as security a pound of Antonio's flesh. The bond is signed, and Bassanio, accompanied by his fellow fortune-hunter Gratiano, goes to Belmont. There he wins Portia by passing the casket-test in which he chooses the leaden one containing her portrait. Gratiano marries Portia's gentlewoman Nerissa. Another Venetian, Lorenzo, arrives with Shylock's daughter Jessica, who has run away with him and her father's ducats.

News comes that Antonio's ventures have miscarried, that he is unable to repay the loan, and that Shylock is demanding his pound of flesh. Bassanio and Gratiano go to his aid and, unknown to them, Portia disguises herself as a lawyer and Nerissa as her clerk in defence of Antonio. Portia saves Antonio by warning Shylock that his life is forfeit if he sheds a drop of Antonio's blood, and that in any event his fortune is forfeit for practising against the life of a Venetian citizen. The presiding Duke grants Shylock his life and, at Antonio's request, half his fortune, provided that he bequeathes it to Lorenzo and becomes a Christian. The only reward that Portia and Nerissa will accept is the rings that they gave their husbands, whom they charge with infidelity when they meet again in Belmont.

Merchant Taylors' School, was founded in 1561, its first headmaster being Richard Mulcaster (1561–86). He was interested in the drama, and in 1572–3 plays were publicly performed in the Common Hall, but were stopped by an order of the Company in 1574 owing to the bad behaviour of the audience. However, Mulcaster took his plays to Court where 'Richard Mulcaster with his Scholers' appeared six times between 1573 and 1583. The last performance was 12 February 1583: 'A historie of Ariodante and Geneuora ... On Shrovetuesdaie ... by m^r Mulcasters children'. The play is lost, but was a dramatization of the story of Ariodante and Genevra in Ariosto's *Orlando Furioso*, which is a version of the Hero story in *Much Ado*.

Mercutio. In *Romeo and Juliet*, a kinsman of the Prince of Verona, and a friend of Romeo. On the way to present a masque at Capulet's house he describes dreams and dreamers in his famous Queen Mab speech (I, iv). He is mortally wounded in a quarrel with the Capulet Tybalt, when Romeo, secretly married to Juliet, tries to stop the brawl (III, i).

Meres, Francis (1565–1647), was born at Kirton in Lincolnshire, and educated at Pembroke, Cambridge, where he took his B.A. in 1587 and M.A. in 1591, two years later being incorporated M.A. at Oxford. In 1597–8 he lived in London, and in 1602 became rector and schoolmaster at Wing, Rutland. On 7 September 1598 his *Palladis Tamia: Wit's Treasury* was registered, and published shortly afterwards. The book is a collection of apothegms on philosophy and the arts, but contains the invaluable 'Comparative discourse of our English Poets with the Greeke, Latine, and Italian Poets', in which he assesses in a highly artificial manner the work of English writers from Chaucer to his own day. Of Shakespeare he writes:

> As the soule of *Euphorbus* was thought to liue in *Pythagoras*: so the sweete wittie soule of *Ouid* liues in mellifluous & hony-tongued *Shakespeare*, witnes his *Venus* and *Adonis*, his *Lucrece*, his sugred Sonnets among his priuate friends, &c.
>
> As *Plautus* and *Seneca* are accounted the best for Comedy and Tragedy among the Latines: so *Shakespeare* among the English is the most excellent in both kinds for the stage: for Comedy, witnes his *Gentlemen of Verona*, his *Errors*, his *Loue labors lost*, his *Loue labours wonne*, his *Midsummers night*

dreame, & his *Merchant of Venice*: for Tragedy his *Richard the 2. Richard the 3. Henry the 4, King Iohn, Titus Andronicus* and his *Romeo* and *Iuliet*.

As *Epius Stolo* said, that the Muses would speake with *Plautus* tongue, if they would speak Latin: so I say that the Muses would speak with *Shakespeares* fine filed phrase, if they would speake English ...

As *Pindarus, Anacreon* and *Callimachus* among the Greekes; and *Horace* and *Catullus* among the Latines are the best Lyrick Poets, so in this faculty the best among our Poets are *Spencer* (who excelleth in all kinds), *Daniel, Drayton, Shakespeare, Bretton* ...

These are our best for Tragedie, the Lorde *Buckhurst*, Doctor *Leg* of Cambridge, Doctor *Edes* of Oxforde, maister *Edward Ferris*, the Author of the *Mirrour for Magistrates, Marlow, Peele, Watson, Kid, Shakespeare, Drayton, Chapman, Decker*, and *Beniamin Johnson* ...

The best for Comedy amongst us bee, *Edward* Earle of Oxforde, Doctor *Gager* of Oxforde, Maister *Rowley* once a rare Scholler of learned Pembrooke Hall in Cambridge, Maister *Edwardes* one of her Maiesties Chappell, eloquent and wittie *John Lilly, Lodge, Gascoyne, Greene, Shakespeare, Thomas Nash, Thomas Heywood, Anthony Mundye* our best plotter, *Chapman, Porter, Wilson, Hathway*, and *Henry Chettle*.

Meres also classes Shakespeare as one of 'the most passionate among us to bewaile and bemoane the perplexities of Loue'.

It is interesting to note that a competent contemporary thought Shakespeare the best both for comedy and tragedy, but the really important thing about this catalogue is that Meres tells us that Shakespeare's *Sonnets* were in circulation among his friends in 1598, and that he had then written the six comedies and six tragedies he mentions. It is invaluable as an aid for dating the plays. The list accounts for all those which, on other evidence, we credit Shakespeare with at that date, save the three parts of *Henry VI* and *The Taming of the Shrew*. *Love's Labour's Won* (q.v.) is a puzzle. Thomas Tyrwhitt in 1766 was the first to use *Palladis Tamia*.

Merian, Matthew (1593–1650), Swiss engraver, was born at Basel, and married the daughter of a publisher and bookseller of Frankfort whose business he took over in 1625. He is best known for his engravings of towns, one of which was a view of London (1638). Wenceslas Hollar was his pupil. (See MAPS OF LONDON.)

Mermaid Tavern. This was just to the east of St Paul's Cathedral, in Bread Street, with an entrance in Friday Street. It was the meeting-place of the Friday Street Club, founded by Sir Walter Ralegh, of which Jonson, Beaumont, Fletcher, Donne and Coryate were members, and presumably Shakespeare. The best known reference to the Mermaid is in *Master Francis Beaumont's Letter to Ben Jonson*:

> What things have we seen
> Done at the *Mermaid*! heard words that have been
> So nimble, and so full of subtle flame,
> As if that every one (from whence they came)
> Had meant to put his whole wit in a jest,
> And had resolved to live a fool the rest
> Of his dull life.

The landlord was William Johnson (q.v.), Shakespeare's trustee.

'Merry Conceited Humours of Bottom the Weaver.' A droll extracted and adapted from *A Midsummer Night's Dream*, printed separately in 1661, and in Francis Kirkman's collection, *The Wits* (1672).

'Merry Devil of Edmonton.' An anonymous play registered 22 October 1607, and published in 1608 as 'The Merry Devill of Edmonton. As it hath beene sundry times Acted, by his Maiesties Seruants, at the Globe, on the bankeside'. On 9 September 1653 Humphrey Moseley, the stationer, registered 'The merry devil of Edmonton, by Wm: Shakespeare'. In their play-lists of 1656 and 1661 Edward Archer and Francis Kirkman attributed the play to Shakespeare, and Charles II had a copy bound with *Fair*

Em and *Mucedorus* in a volume called 'Shakespeare, Vol. I'.

'MERRY WIVES OF WINDSOR.'

WRITTEN: 1598–9? Not mentioned by Meres.

PERFORMED: 'Diuers times Acted' before Q1, 1602.

1604, on Sunday, 4 November at Whitehall: 'By his Maiesties plaiers. A play of the Merry wiues of winsor.' (*Revels Account.*)

1638, 'At the cocpit the 15th of November – The merry wifes of winsor.' (Hotson concludes (*Shakespeare* v. *Shallow*) that 'Lord Hunsdon's servants presented the hastily prepared *Merry Wives* before the Queen at Westminster at the Feast of the Garter on April 23, 1597'. See WINDSOR.)

REGISTERED: 1602. '18 Januarij. John Busby. Entred for his copie vnder the hand of master Seton, A booke called An excellent and pleasant conceited commedie of Sir John Faulstof and the merry wyves of Windesor vj^{d}. Arthur Johnson. Entred for his Copye by assignement from John Busbye, A booke Called an excellent and pleasant conceyted Comedie of Sir John Faulstafe and the merye wyves of Windsor. vj^{d}.'

PUBLISHED: 1602, Q1. 'A most pleasaunt and excellent conceited Comedie, of Syr Iohn Falstaffe, and the merrie Wiues of Windsor Entermixed with sundrie variable and pleasing humors, of Syr Hugh the Welch Knight, Iustice Shallow, and his wise Cousin M. Slender. With the swaggering vaine of Auncient Pistoll, and Corporall Nym. By William Shakespeare. As it hath bene diuers times Acted by the right Honorable my Lord Chamberlaines seruants. Both before her Maiestie, and elsewhere. London Printed by T. C. for Arthur Iohnson, and are to be sold at his shop in Powles Churchyard, at the signe of the Flower de Leuse and the Crowne. 1602'. A 'bad' Quarto, based on a report, possibly that of the actor who played the Host. Passages are incorporated from *1, 2 Henry IV*, and *Hamlet*.

1619. Q2. One of the ten plays printed by W. Jaggard in 1619, many of them with false dates. This Q is dated 1619. Set up from Q1.

1623, F1. 'The Merry Wiues of Windsor.' The third play in the Comedy section: pp. 39–60. Acts and scenes marked. A good text. Greg finds evidence of some revision by another hand. Wilson suggests that the original play was the *Jealous Comedy*, revised by Shakespeare, that the original amorist was not Falstaff, and that F was assembled from actors' parts. Perhaps set up from Crane's transcript of the prompt-book.

1630, Q3. Set up from F1.

SOURCES: The plot is essentially Shakespeare's. The theme of the lover hidden by the unfaithful wife is common enough in the literature of the period. (See B. RICH.) There are obvious references to the visit of the Count of Mömpelgart to England, including Windsor, in 1592, and to that of his envoy (also to Windsor) in 1595, who urged his master's claim to the Garter promised by Elizabeth. Mömpelgart was elected to the Order in 1597; in 1598 he sent an embassy to express his gratitude and in 1600 a third embassy to obtain the insignia. The investiture was eventually granted by James I in 1603 (see DETHICK). (Cf. 'Cosen *garmombles*' of IV, V, the *Garter* Inn and the Garter references in V, V.) The envoy of 1595 was also commissioned to buy horses. Shallow may be a caricature of Sir Thomas Lucy (q.v.), or, according to Hotson, of William Gardiner (q.v.).

STAGE HISTORY: 1660, 6 December. Pepys saw the King's company in their production, and again in 1661 and 1667, but it did not please him.

1702. John Dennis's perversion, *The Comical Gallant: or The Amours of Sir John Falstaffe*, failed at Drury Lane, where in 1705 Quin appeared as Falstaff in Shakespeare's play. In 1824 Frederic Reynolds made an operatic version with music by Henry Bishop. In 1851 Charles Kean returned to Shakespeare's text.

1954. Yale Shakespeare Festival, the actors coached by H. Kökeritz in 'the language of the day'.

Falstaff writes identical love-letters to Mistress Ford and Mistress Page, the wives of two substantial burgesses of Windsor who are informed of Falstaff's intentions by his dismissed followers Pistol and Nym. Ford is suspicious and tests his wife's fidelity by disguising himself as 'Master Brooke' (changed to 'Broome' in F) and paying Falstaff to woo her on his behalf. To teach Falstaff a lesson, Mistress Ford invites him to her house, and when her jealous husband arrives she and Mistress Page hide him in a basket full of dirty linen which is thrown into the Thames to be washed. At a second assignation Falstaff is disguised as the fat woman of Brentford and only escapes after being beaten as a witch.

Meanwhile Page's daughter Anne is being wooed by Slender whom Page favours, by Doctor Caius his wife's favourite, and by Fenton whom Anne loves. All three suitors are helped by Mistress Quickly, and Sir Hugh Evans's intervention on behalf of Slender almost leads to a duel between him and Caius. When Ford discovers his wife's fidelity, another assignation is arranged with Falstaff in Windsor Forest at night, and he is made a public laughing-stock. In the confusion, and helped by the Host of the Garter, Fenton runs away with Anne and marries her, while Slender and Caius are tricked into eloping with boys.

Messala. In *Julius Caesar*, a friend of Brutus and Cassius, to whom he brings the news of Cicero's and Portia's deaths (IV, iii). He is captured at Philippi, but taken into Octavius's service.

'Messalina.' A play by Nathaniel Richards, produced by the Revels company, and published as 'The Tragedy of Messalina by N. Richards. London printed for Dan: Frere. 1640'. It is important because of the small picture of a stage at the bottom of the title-page. It shows a curtained window above, painted curtains in front of the tiring-house, and an apron tapering towards the front, and protected by low rails. The Revels Company acted mainly at Salisbury Court the stage of which this may represent. (See ROXANA; KIRKMAN.)

Metellus Cimber. In *Julius Caesar*, one of the conspirators. He suggests sounding Cicero and Caius Ligarius. His suit to Caesar for the repeal of his banished brother Publius is the signal for the assassination (III, i). (Really L. Tillius Cimber.)

Metre and **Metrical -Tests.** See BLANK VERSE; VERSE-TESTS.

Michael. In *2 Henry VI*, a follower of Cade, appearing only in IV, ii.

Michael, Sir. In *1 Henry IV*, probably a clergyman. The Archbishop of York sends him with letters to the Lord Marshal and his cousin Scrope (IV, iv).

Middle Temple. One of the Inns of Court (q.v.). The hall in which the revels used to be held was built 1562–72. John Manningham (q.v.) describes the performance of *Twelfth Night* given there 2 February 1602. Hotson draws attention to the large number of men from Stratford and neighbourhood who entered the Middle Temple, including William Combe and his great-nephews William and Thomas, Fulke Greville, Henry Rainsford of Clifford Chambers and Thomas Hales of Snitterfield, and suggests that *Love's Labour's Lost* and *Troilus and Cressida* ('*Love's Labour's Won*') 'were prepared in the first instance ... for the revels of the Middle Temple'.

Middleton, Thomas (*c.* 1570–1627), dramatist. Little is known of his early life, though it is probable that he was born in London of good family, and entered Gray's Inn, either in 1593 or 1596. By 1602 he was writing for Henslowe, collaborating with Dekker in the Admiral's *The Honest Whore* (1604), and at the same time working for the Children of Paul's. When that company came to an end, *c.* 1607, he wrote plays for various companies, and pageants for the City, of which he was appointed Chronologer in 1620. Towards the end of his career he worked for Prince Charles's Men with William Rowley who had a hand in his greatest play, *The Changeling*, 1623. In 1624 he was summoned before the Privy Council for his *Game of Chess*, which delighted the public but offended the Spaniards, and he may have been imprisoned.

Middleton's earlier comedies, for example *A Chaste Maid in Cheapside* (1611), are, like Dekker's, about contemporary London life; his later comedies, such as *The Spanish Gipsy* (1623), are for the most part romantic. After *The Changeling* his best tragedy is, perhaps, *Women beware Women*. *The Witch* (q.v.), of uncertain date, was first printed from a manuscript in 1778 (see REED), and is important because it contains the full text of the songs mentioned in the stage directions of the witch scenes in *Macbeth*, where they are almost certainly interpolations. In the middle of the 17th century the booksellers attributed Middleton's *A Trick to Catch the Old One* to Shakespeare.

Mid-line Extra Syllables. A redundant syllable before a pause within a line: *Othello* I, iii, 166,

And that would woo her. Upon this hint I
spake.

They are more numerous in the later plays, and range from none in *Love's Labour's Lost* to 208 in *Othello*, but are of little value as a test for dating the plays. They are similar to feminine endings (q.v.).

Mid-line Pauses. In Shakespeare's early verse the main pause is generally at the end of a line. As his verse develops there is a fairly steady decrease in the number of end-stopped lines, and a corresponding increase in strong mid-line pauses. The earlier mid-line pause is generally after the second or third foot; later, they occur also after the first or fourth and in the middle of a foot. (See VERSE-TESTS.) The following examples come from (*a*) *3 Henry VI* (1590); (*b*) *2 Henry IV* (1598); (*c*) *Pericles* (1608); (*d*) *Winter's Tale* (1610).

(*a*) O tiger's heart wrapp'd in a woman's
hide!
How couldst thou drain the life-blood
of the child,
To bid the father wipe his eyes withal,
And yet be seen to bear a woman's
face?

(*b*) In the grey vault of heaven, and by his
light
Did all the chivalry of England move
To do brave acts. He was indeed the
glass ...

(*c*) Wilt thou spit all thyself? The seaman's
whistle
Is as a whisper in the ears of death,
Unheard. Lychorida! – Lucina, O ...

(*d*) It cannot fail but by
The violation of my faith; and then
Let nature crush the sides o' the earth
together
And mar the seeds within! Lift up thy
looks ...

Mid-line Speech-endings. It follows from what is said above about mid-line pauses, that in the early plays speeches generally finish at the end of a line, and in the later plays more often in mid-line. This is a valuable verse-test (q.v.): the percentage of mid-line speech-endings increasing steadily from about 1 in the earliest plays to 80 or 90 in the latest ones. Compare a typical short speech from *2 Henry VI* with one from *The Tempest*:

Ah, what a sign it is of evil life,
Where death's approach is seen so terrible!

I might call him
A thing divine; for nothing natural
I ever saw so noble.

(See VERSE PARAGRAPHS.)

'MIDSUMMER NIGHT'S DREAM, A.'

WRITTEN: 1595–6. Mentioned by Meres, 1598.

PERFORMED: 'Sundry times publickley acted' before Q1, 1600.

1604, at Court: 'On New yeares night we had a play of Robin goode-fellow' (q.v.). (Dudley Carleton to John Chamberlain, 15 January 1604.) (See WILLIAMS, JOHN.)

REGISTERED: 1600. '8 Octobris. Thomas Fyssher. Entred for his copie vnder the handes of master Rodes and the Wardens. A booke called A mydsommer nightes Dreame vj^{d}.'

PUBLISHED: 1600. Q1. 'A Midsommer nights dreame. As it hath beene sundry times publickely acted, by the Right honourable, the Lord Chamberlaine his seruants. Written by William Shakespeare. Imprinted at London, for Thomas Fisher, and are to be soulde at his shoppe, at the Signe of the White Hart, in Fleetstreete. 1600'. A fair text. Set up from foul papers.

1619, Q2. Dated 1600. One of the ten plays printed by Jaggard in 1619, many of them with false dates. Set up from Q1.

1623, F1. 'A Midsommer Nights Dreame.' The eighth play in the Comedy section: pp. 145–62. Acts only marked. Set up from Q2, but with a few additional stage-directions, including at the end of Act III 'They sleepe all the Act', meaning 'Interval'. (See *The Changeling*, 1623, '*In the act-time De Flores hides a naked rapier behind a door*', which must refer to the interval between Acts II and III.) Set up from Q2 with some reference to prompt-book.

SOURCES: It is probable that the play was written for a wedding entertainment, and altered for the public stage by substituting Puck's epilogue for the preceding fairy masque. The fantasy is essentially Shakespeare's, but he was probably indebted to Munday's *John a Kent*, and the following books may have furnished hints:

Theseus and Hippolyta: Plutarch's *Life of Theseus*, and Chaucer's *Knight's Tale*.

Pyramus and Thisbe, and the name 'Titania': Ovid's *Metamorphoses*.

Robin Goodfellow and the ass-head: Scot's *Discovery of Witchcraft*. (See ADLINGTON.)

Oberon: Greene's *James IV* or *Huon de Bordeaux*.

STAGE HISTORY: The droll, *The Merry Conceited Humours of Bottom the Weaver*, was acted while the theatres were closed, 1642–60.

1662, 29 September. Pepys saw the King's company's production: 'The most insipid, ridiculous play that ever I saw in my life.'

1692. *The Fairy Queen* adaptation with Purcell's music.

1755. Garrick's version, *The Fairies*, without the workmen. (See also LEVERIDGE; JOHNSON, CHARLES; LAMPE; REYNOLDS, FREDERIC; MATHEWS.)

1911. Tree's production with live rabbits.

1914. Granville-Barker's golden fairies.

1961. Benjamin Britten's opera.

To celebrate the wedding of Theseus and Hippolyta, Bottom and other Athenian workmen arrange to perform the play of Pyramus and Thisbe, and find a convenient place for their rehearsals in the wood near Athens. To the wood also come the lovers Lysander and Hermia who are running away together, followed by Demetrius who loves Hermia, and by Helena who loves Demetrius. In the wood are the fairy King and Queen, Oberon and Titania, who quarrel, and in revenge Oberon squeezes a magic juice on Titania's eyes so that she will fall in love with the first creature she sees on waking. This is Bottom, whose head has mischievously been changed to that of an ass by Oberon's servant, Puck, when he finds the workmen rehearsing.

Meanwhile, Oberon has seen the forlorn state of Helena and orders Puck to squeeze the juice on Demetrius's eyes, but by mistake Puck anoints Lysander who falls in love with Helena, as does Demetrius when Oberon anoints him. After quarrelling and confusion deliberately made worse by Puck, the lovers fall asleep, and the charm on Lysander is removed. So too are the spells on Titania and Bottom. Theseus finds the sleeping lovers, sanctions the marriage of Lysander to Hermia and of Demetrius to Helena, and the three couples celebrate their weddings together, and witness the memorable performance of Pyramus and Thisbe.

Milan, Duke of. 1. In *The Two Gentlemen of Verona*, father of Silvia. Proteus treacherously tells him that his friend Valentine is planning to elope with Silvia, and the Duke orders him to leave his Court. When Silvia follows Valentine the Duke pursues her, is captured by outlaws, but released by Valentine, to whose marriage with Silvia he now agrees.

2. See PROSPERO; ANTONIO.

Mildmay, Sir Henry (d. 1664?), of Danbury Place, Essex, was Master of the King's Jewel-house. He deserted Charles I at the beginning of the Civil War, and at the Restoration was called to account for the jewels, sentenced to transportation to Tangier, but died at Antwerp on the way. In his *Diary* for 1635, he writes, 'Maij 6: not farre from home all day att ye bla:ffryers & a play y^{is} day called ye More of Venice'.

Miller, James (1706–44), wrote his satirical comedy, *The Humours of Oxford*, while he was at Wadham. He took orders and continued to write plays, many of which were successfully performed. They are mostly adaptations from the French, *The Universal Passion*, produced at Drury Lane in 1737, being a combination of *Much Ado* with Molière's court entertainment *La Princesse D'Élide*.

Millington, Thomas. A stationer of dubious reputation who had a hand in the publication of some of Shakespeare's early plays:

1594. John Danter's Q1 *Titus Andronicus* was 'to be sold by Edward White & Thomas Millington, at the little North doore of Paules at the signe of the Gunne'.

1594. Registered and published Q1, the 'bad' Quarto, of *The First Part of the Contention (2 Henry VI)*.

1595. Published Q1, the 'bad' Quarto of *The True Tragedy (3 Henry VI)*, without registration.

1600. With John Busby published Q1, the 'bad' Quarto, of *Henry V*, in spite of the entry in the Stationers' Register, 'to be staied'.

1600. Published Q2 of *The First Part of the Contention* and Q2 of *The True Tragedy*, reprints of the 'bad' First Quartos.

1602. 19 April. Transferred to Thomas Pavier copyright in *The First Part of the Contention* and *The True Tragedy* (entered as 'The firste and Second parte of Henry the vj[t]'), and in *Titus Andronicus*. (On 14 August 1600 Pavier had acquired the copyright of *Henry V*.)

The Contention was the first book registered by Millington, his last was in 1603. He was at various times in partnership with Busby, Ling and Thomas Gosson.

Mills, John (d. 1736). An actor with Betterton at Drury Lane, playing a great number of parts, mostly tragic. On Betterton's death in 1710 he took over the part of Macbeth, but the other great Shakespearean characters went to Barton Booth and Robert Wilks.

Milton, John (1608–74). The first of Milton's poems to be published was *An Epitaph on the admirable Dramaticke Poet, W. Shakespeare*. This appeared anonymously in the prefatory matter of F2 (1632), and with the initials I. M. in John Benson's edition of Shakespeare's *Poems* (1640). In 1645 it was published in the first collected edition of *Poems of Mr John Milton* (see MOSELEY):

On Shakespear, 1630.

What needs my *Shakespear* for his honour'd
  Bones,
The labour of an age in piled Stones,
Or that his hallow'd reliques should be hid
Under a Star-ypointing *Pyramid*?
Dear son of memory, great heir of Fame,
What need'st thou such weak witnes of thy
  name?
Thou in our wonder and astonishment
Hast built thy self a live-long Monument.
For whilst to th' shame of slow-endeavouring
  art,
Thy easie numbers flow, and that each
  heart
Hath from the leaves of thy unvalu'd Book,
Those Delphick lines with deep impression
  took,
Then thou our fancy of it self bereaving,
Dost make us Marble with too much
  conceaving;
And so Sepulcher'd in such pomp dost lie,
That Kings for such a Tomb would wish to
  die.

The lines were included in F3 (1663–4) and F4 (1685). About 1633, at the beginning of his six years' stay at Horton, near Windsor, Milton wrote *L'Allegro*, with its reference to Shakespeare:

Then to the well-trod stage anon,
If Jonson's learned sock be on,
Or sweetest Shakespeare, Fancy's child,
Warble his native wood-notes wild.

Miracle Plays. Strictly, the medieval plays dealing with the lives of the saints, but the term is applied to cover Mystery plays as well, which dramatized the stories of the Bible. They were originally written in Latin and performed by priests inside the church, but by the 14th century were in English, and acted outside by gildsmen on movable stages, or 'pageants', notably on the Feast of Corpus Christi. They were arranged in cycles, a series of short plays ranging from the Creation to the Crucifixion, each of which was acted by an appropriate craft-gild: thus, the Shipwrights might perform the story of Noah and the Ark. The four great extant cycles are those of York, Wakefield (or Towneley), Chester and Coventry, but there are records of the performance of Miracle plays in nearly a hundred towns and villages between 1300 and 1600. The didactic element in the Miracle plays led to the 15th-century Moralities and the comic element had its influence on the 16th-century Interludes and secular drama, but these medieval plays were still being performed in the provinces when Shakespeare was writing his great tragedies; the last performance of the York plays was in 1579, the Chester plays lasted until 1600, and those of Beverley until 1604. (See ROUNDS.)

Miranda. The heroine of *The Tempest* (q.v.).

'Mirror for Magistrates.' A book published in 1559, consisting of nineteen 'tragedies' by William Baldwin, George Ferrers and others. The 'tragedies' are stories in verse, supposed to be told by characters from English history who describe their own downfalls after the manner of those in Lydgate's version of Boccaccio's *Falls of Princes*. Thomas Sackville's famous *Induction* (to his own contribution) and his *Complaint of Buckingham* (Richard III's supporter) appeared in the second edition of 1563. Other editions with fresh matter followed in 1574, 1587, and 1610. The *Complaint of Buckingham* probably furnished Shakespeare with hints for *Richard III*.

'Miseries of Enforced Marriage.' A play by George Wilkins, registered as 'a tragedie' and published in 1607 as 'The Miseries of Inforst Mariage. As it is now played by his Maiesties Seruants. By George Wilkins'. Like *A Yorkshire Tragedy*, published in 1608 as Shakespeare's, it deals with the story of Walter Calverley, who was executed for the murder of his children in August 1605, though this play ends happily. (See WILKINS; PERICLES.)

'Misery of Civil War.' See CROWNE.

Mislineation. The incorrect printing of verse. In the plays of Shakespeare and his contemporaries the compositor sometimes set up verse as prose, occasionally prose as verse, and when verse was printed as verse he sometimes muddled the scansion. In the 'good' Quartos and the Folio the main causes of mislineation are probably: the beginning of verse lines with minuscules in the author's manuscript; verse passages in prose scenes; confusing marginal insertions. In Shakespeare's later plays, where speeches often begin and end in mid-line, there may be mislineation in otherwise fair texts, as in the F texts of *Antony and Cleopatra* and *Coriolanus*. In the 'bad' Quartos, where the original verse is often the reporter's paraphrase, mislineation is naturally more frequent.

The Folio is in sixes: that is, 3 sheets of paper are doubled to form a quire or gathering of 6 leaves, making 12 pages. As Hinman has shown, the setting of the type was not by successive pages, but by two-page formes: thus the outer side of the first sheet makes pages 1 and 12, the inner side 2 and 11, and so on. If, therefore, page 12 was set after page 1, 11 after 2, 10 after 3, and so on, the copy had to be cast off: that is, the lines or words to be printed on each page had first to be marked in the copy. If the copy were an unannotated Q this would be easy, but if it were a manuscript with alterations it might be very difficult, and miscalculations were frequent. If too many lines or words were cast off, the compositor had to compress: print verse as prose, run one line into another, or even omit a passage. Conversely, if there were not enough lines or words he sometimes made one line of verse into two, as in *Titus*, at the foot of the second column of p. 40:

> Who markes the waxing tide,
> Grow waue by waue,

(See C. K. Hinman, 'Cast-off Copy for the First Folio', SQ, VI, 3.)

Misprints, etc. Plays formed an unimportant part of a printer's business, and as they generally belonged to an actors' company to whom the authors had sold them, it is probable that the printer himself was often the only corrector of his compositor's work. Jonson was exceptional in checking the printing of his plays; Shakespeare does not seem to have bothered, and there was very little proof-correction of the Folio. Pollard estimates that Simmes, one of the best printers, made 227 errors and 26 corrections in printing the first three Quartos of *Richard II*. In *The Folio Text of 1 Henry IV*, Alice Walker analyses the errors made by compositor A, who set 11 pages, and B who set 14½. Working from Q5 as copy, they produced the following variants:

	A	B
Literal errors	2	24
Omissions	2	30
Interpolations	6	28
Substitutions	7	23
Transpositions	1	7
	18	112

Compositor E was an apprentice, and even more given to error than B, and in his *Six Variant Readings in the First Folio* (1961) Hinman concludes: 'Whatever textual integrity the First Folio may in fact possess depends almost exclusively upon the skill and accuracy of the various compositors (there were five in all) who put the book into type; it owes almost nothing to the activities of the proof-reader who occasionally reviewed their work. The optimism of a few years ago was certainly not so well grounded as it seemed. We are a long way still from the fullest possible knowledge of what Shakespeare actually wrote!' (See PROOF-READING.)

Modern Dress Productions. Barry Jackson's *Cymbeline* in 1923, followed by *Hamlet* in 1925, were the first of a number of modern dress productions of Shakespeare. It was part of the reaction against the heavy antiquarianism of the Kean-Irving-Tree tradition. Presumably the Chamberlain's-King's Men produced *Hamlet* in modern dress. (See SS, 8, 78; COSTUME.)

Modjeska, Helena (1844–1909), was born at Cracow, and made her name as an actress in Shakespearean tragedy and comedy at Warsaw. In 1876 she went with her husband to America where, in spite of the language difficulty, she became one of the leading Shakespearean actresses. She was occasionally seen in London.

Mohun, Michael (*c.* 1625–84), played at the Cockpit before the Civil War, in which, as a Royalist, he served with distinction. At the Restoration he joined Killigrew's company and played with Charles Hart, often in secondary rôles, as Cassius and Iago, for example, to Hart's Brutus and Othello.

Molyneux, Emerie, cartographer, made a new map of the world, the 'Hydrographical Description' (1598–9), which is sometimes found in copies of the second edition of Hakluyt's *Navigations*, 1598–1600. Maria refers to it in *Twelfth Night* (II, ii) as 'the new map with the augmentation of the Indies'.

Mömpelgart, Frederick, Count of (1557–1608), became Duke of Württemberg, in 1593, the year after his visit to England. (See THE MERRY WIVES; BULL-BAITING.)

Monarcho. A half-witted Italian who frequented Elizabeth's Court in the capacity of Fool, and believed that the ships arriving in London belonged to him. In his *Chance* (1580), T. Churchyard wrote 'The Phantasticall Monarkes Epitaphe'. Boyet, in *Love's Labour's Lost* (IV, i), describes Armado as 'A phantasime, a Monarcho, and one that makes sport to the prince'. And Helena in *All's Well* (I, i) greets Parolles as 'monarch'.

Monck, Nugent (1877–1958), was born in Shropshire, but in 1909 settled at Norwich where in 1911, he founded the Norwich Players. His work was interrupted by the war, but in 1919 he reorganized his company and in 1921 opened the Maddermarket Theatre (q.v.), with an Elizabethan stage. His Shakespeare productions, simple and swift, in the tradition of William Poel, have had a great influence. He produced *Pericles* at Stratford in 1947.

Montagu, Elizabeth (1720–1800), made her Mayfair home an intellectual centre, and earned for herself the title of 'The Madame du Deffand of the English capital'. In 1769 she published her *Essay on the Writings and Genius of Shakespeare*, in which she attempted to answer the misrepresentations of Voltaire. 'There is no real criticism in it,' Johnson pronounced. Bowdler dedicated his *Family Shakespeare* to her memory.

Montague. In *Romeo and Juliet*, the father of Romeo. In the first scene he is eager to fight with his rival Capulet, but the deaths of Romeo and Juliet lead to a reconciliation, and he promises to raise a statue in pure gold to Juliet.

Montague, Lady. In *Romeo and Juliet*, the mother of Romeo, she speaks only in the first scene. In v, iii Montague announces that 'Grief of my son's exile hath stopp'd her breath'.

Montague, Marquis of (d. 1471). In *3 Henry VI*, a Yorkist, but when Edward IV marries Lady Grey, he and his brother, Warwick the Kingmaker, join the Lancastrians and are killed at Barnet (v, ii). (Sir John Neville, 3rd son of the Earl of Salisbury, cr. M. of M. 1470.)

Montaigne, Michel de (1533–92), was born near Bordeaux, where he was educated. He spent much of his youth in travel and at Court, married, and in 1571, having succeeded to his father's estates, retired to his chateau to pursue his studies and write his *Essays*, a literary form that he originated. After travels in Italy and Germany, and four years as Mayor of Bordeaux, he died at his chateau still engaged on his *Essays*. The first two books were published in 1580, a complete edition in 1595, and were first translated into English by John Florio in 1603. They reveal the author as a delightful man and a sceptical philosopher. 'Que sais-je?' he asks, and because we can be certain of so little it follows that man must be tolerant of the opinions of his fellows. Tolerance is a Shakespearean virtue, and obviously Shakespeare knew the *Essays*. Florio and he had a common patron in Southampton, and may have been friends, and Shakespeare may have read Florio's translation in manuscript before writing *Hamlet*, the scepticism of which suggests the influence of Montaigne. But that influence is most patent in *The Tempest*, where Gonzalo explains how he would colonize the island (II, i), the passage being taken from Montaigne's essay *Of the Cannibals*, describing an ideal community in America. In the British Museum is a copy of Florio's Montaigne with the signature 'Wllm Shakspere', about the authenticity of which scholars are divided; but it was there in 1780 when Capell first drew attention to Shakespeare's indebtedness to Montaigne. (See G. C. Taylor, *Shakespeare's Debt to Montaigne*.)

Montano. In *Othello*, 'Gouernour of Cyprus' (F). He is wounded by the drunken Cassio, and in the last scene disarms Othello.

Montemayor, Jorge de (*c.* 1521–61), poet and novelist, was born near Coimbra in Portugal, but spent much of his adult life in Spain and wrote in Spanish. His fame rests chiefly on a prose romance, the *Diana*, which was translated into French by Nicolas Colin (1578), and into English by Bartholomew Yonge by 1582, though not published until 1598. On a story in the second book of the *Diana* Shakespeare based his *Two Gentlemen of Verona*. Felismena (Julia) disguises herself as a boy and follows her lover Felix (Proteus), whose page she becomes and is employed by him in wooing Celia (Silvia). In the *Diana*, however, there is no character corresponding to Valentine, and therefore no *Sonnet*-like theme of the treacherous friend; Celia falls in love with the disguised Felismena and dies. The Revels Accounts for 1585 record a Court performance by the Queen's Men of *the history of felix and philiomena*, and this lost play may have been Shakespeare's immediate source.

Montgomery, Sir John. In *3 Henry VI*, he persuades Edward, Duke of York, to proclaim himself Edward IV, by offering him help as King, but not as Duke (IV, vii). (Historically, Sir Thomas Montgomery, d. 1495.)

Montgomery, Earl of. See PEMBROKE, PHILIP HERBERT, 4TH EARL OF.

Montjoy. In *Henry V*, the principal French herald, or King at Arms. Twice (III, vi; IV, iii) before Agincourt he asks Henry if he will compound for his ransom, but in IV, vii comes to acknowledge the French defeat.

Monument. The Shakespeare monument on the north chancel wall in Stratford church is made of marble inlaid with touchstone, and consists of an inscribed base supporting two Corinthian columns with black marble shafts and gilt capitals, in turn supporting a cornice and pediment, in the centre of which are Shakespeare's arms, and surmounted by a skull and flanked by figures symbolizing Labour and Rest, the one holding a spade, the other an inverted torch and skull. The base, columns and cornice enclose a round-arched niche, within which is the coloured Cotswold-stone bust of Shakespeare holding a pen and paper, his hands resting on a cushion. The inscription on the base, composed by an unknown hand, reads:

Ivdicio Pylivm, genio Socratem, arte Maronem:
Terra tegit, popvlvs maeret, Olympvs habet.
[In judgement a Nestor, in genius a Socrates, in art a Virgil:
The earth covers him, the people mourn him, Olympus has him.]

Stay, Passenger, why goest thov by so fast?
read if thov canst, whom enviovs Death hath plast
with in this monvment Shakspeare: with whome,
qvick natvre dide: whose name doth deck ys Tombe,
Far more than cost: sieh all, yt He hath writt,
Leaves living art, bvt page, to serve his witt
obiit ano doi 1616
Aetatis. 53 die 23 apr.

The monument must have been erected between 1616 and 1623, between Shakespeare's death and the publication of the Folio in which Leonard Digges refers to it in his verses. In his *Diary*, 1653, Sir William Dugdale ascribed it to Gerard Johnson, that is Gheerart Janssen (q.v.), the Southwark stone-mason and sculptor. The monument itself is good Jacobean work: the bust is less satisfactory, though it must have been approved by Shakespeare's widow (d. 1623) and by his son-in-law, John Hall, who is said to have commissioned it, and the dimensions of the skull agree with those of the Droeshout engraving. Dugdale illustrated the monument in his *Antiquities of Warwickshire* (1656), but very inaccurately, and with no feeling for proportion.

In 1749 'Mr. John Hall, Limner' was commissioned to repair the monument which was 'much impair'd and decay'd', most of the money, about £16, having been supplied by John Ward, grandfather of Mrs Siddons, whose company of players gave a benefit performance of *Othello*. Joseph Greene, headmaster of Stratford Grammar School, in a letter of September 1749, wrote:

> In repairing the whole (which was done by contribution of ye Neighbourhood early in ye current year) Care was taken, as nearly as cou'd be, not to add or to diminish what ye work consisted of, & appear'd to be when first errected: And really, except changing ye Substance of ye Architraves from white Alabaster to white Marble, nothing has been done but Supplying with ye Original Materials whatsoever was by Accident broken off; reviving the old Colouring, and renewing the Gilding that was lost.

Halliwell-Phillipps says that the right forefinger and thumb and pen were also restored, and that in 1790 the original lead pen was replaced by a quill. In 1793 Malone 'restored' the bust 'by painting it a good stone-colour'. In 1861 this was removed and the original colours, where visible, restored. The eyes are hazel, and the hair auburn.

Moorfields. 'The great fen or moor' lying just to the north of the City walls and south of Finsbury, which probably took its name from the fen. It was drained in the 16th century and laid out as public grounds in 1606. The Curtain theatre was described in 1601 as being in Moorfields.

Mopsa. In *The Winter's Tale*, a shepherdess who supplies dance and song in IV, iv. (Mopsa is the name of the Shepherd's wife in Greene's *Pandosto*.)

Morality Plays, were a development of the Miracle plays, which were dramatic versions of the Bible stories, religious rather than didactic, and having real characters: Noah and his wife, Abraham and Isaac. But Moralities were essentially didactic, with abstractions as characters: Strength and Good Deeds, Gluttony and Strife. The one was a dramatic form of the Bible lesson read in church, the other a dramatic form of the sermon. There is mention of a Morality play at York in the second half of the 14th century, but the earliest extant Morality is *The Castle of Perseverance*, *c.* 1450, and the finest and best known is the late 15th-century *Everyman*. In the first half of the 16th century the Morality influenced the development of the native secular Interlude, in the second half that of the Renaissance drama based on classical models.

Marlowe's *Faustus* is at only one remove from the morality, and in *The Fortunes of Falstaff* Dover Wilson shows how Falstaff and Prince Hal derive from the morality tradition, comparing the sub-plot of *Henry IV* to the moral interlude *Youth* (*c.* 1520), in which Riot corrupts Youth, heir to his father's estate, who eventually repents. There is an element of the morality in *Macbeth* with its 'supernatural soliciting', and Aaron, Richard III, and Iago, all self-proclaimed ebullient villians without real motive for their mischief, may be traced back to the medieval Vice. (See B. Spivack, *Shakespeare and the Allegory of Evil*; SQ, I.)

More, Sir Thomas (1478–1535), succeeded Wolsey as Lord Chancellor in 1529. In 1534 he was imprisoned for refusing to accept the Act of Supremacy which made Henry VIII supreme head of the Church in England, and next year was found guilty of high treason and beheaded. His most famous book is the Latin *Utopia* (1516), but among his English works is a *History of Richard III*, written in 1513, published in a corrupt form in Grafton's *Chronicle* (1543), and in a good text by William Rastell in 1557. Both Halle and Holinshed used More's account of Richard III, and as Shakespeare took his material from them his *Richard III* is derived, in part at least, indirectly from More. More himself is said to have got his information from Cardinal Morton, in whose household he served as a boy. (See SIMPCOX.)

Morgan, McNamara (d. 1762). Author of *The Sheep-Shearing: or, Florizel and Perdita*, 'a very compleat and entertaining farce' adapted from *The Winter's Tale*, produced in 1754 and made into an opera in 1761. Morgan was born in Dublin, where he practised as a barrister. His friend Spranger Barry produced his first play, *Philoclea*, a tragedy based on an episode in Sidney's *Arcadia*, at Covent Garden in 1754.

Morgann, Maurice (1726–1802), was Under-Secretary of State in Shelburne's ministry, 1782, and the author of several very able pamphlets on political affairs. Though he ordered all his papers to be destroyed at his death, he had published in 1777 his *Essay on the Dramatic Character of Sir John Falstaff*, in which he defends

Falstaff from the charge of cowardice, maintains that Shakespeare's characters have a 'wholeness' that distinguishes them from the creations of other writers, and inaugurates the 'objectivistic' school of criticism by lifting Falstaff out of his dramatic environment and considering him as a real person. But most remarkable, coming from the age of reason, is Morgann's discovery of the magic of Shakespeare's poetry.

Morley, Thomas (1557–1603), musician, was a pupil of William Byrd. In 1588 he was admitted Mus. Bac. at Oxford, in 1592 a Gentleman of the Chapel Royal, and in 1598 was granted a monopoly of music printing. Apparently he suffered from illness, for in his valuable *Plaine and Easie Introduction to Practicall Music* (1597), he writes that he was 'compelled to keepe at home'. He was one of the greatest of Elizabethan composers, particularly of lute songs and madrigals. Possibly he was a friend of Shakespeare, and may have composed the settings for two of his songs, though Shakespeare may have fitted his words to Morley's music. In the unique copy in the Folger Shakespeare Library of Morley's *First Booke of Ayres. Or Little Short Songs* (1600) is a setting of 'It was a lover and his lass' (*As You Like It*, v, iii); and in his *First Book of Consort Lessons* (1599) is an air, though without words, called 'O mistress mine' (*Twelfth Night*, II, iii).

Morley's Men. There are mentions of a provincial company of players in the service of Edward Parker, Lord Morley (d. 1618); in March 1583 they were 'of one companye' with Hunsdon's at Bristol, in 1591 with the Queen's at Aldeburgh, in 1593 with the Admiral's at Newcastle, and in May 1594 with Derby's (Strange's) at Southampton.

Morocco, Prince of. In *The Merchant of Venice*, one of the unsuccessful suitors of Portia, he chooses the golden casket (II, i and vii). He and Aragon were left out of the 18th-century versions of the play.

Morozov, Mikhail (1897–1952). Professor of English in Moscow University, translator and critic, did much to popularize Shakespeare in the U.S.S.R. See his *Shakespeare on the Soviet Stage*.

Morris Dance. A traditional English folk-dance, possibly evolved from the sword-dance. The name may be derived from the blackened ('Moorish') face of one of the dancers, or from the dancing interludes (*moresche*) in Italian plays. Morris-dances often formed part of the entertainments given to Elizabeth on her progresses, and appear sometimes to have been included in the Court Revels. In 1600 Will Kempe danced his famous Morris from London to Norwich, though strictly, a one-man Morris is impossible. See York's description of Cade in *2 Henry VI* (III, i):

> In Ireland have I seen this stubborn Cade
> Oppose himself against a troop of kernes,
> And fought so long, till that his thighs with darts
> Were almost like a sharp-quill'd porpentine;
> And, in the end being rescued, I have seen
> Him caper upright like a wild Morisco,
> Shaking the bloody darts as he his bells.

Mortimer, Edmund, 5th Earl of March (1391–1424). In *1 Henry VI*, he is depicted as an old man who, before he dies, tells Richard Plantagenet that he is imprisoned because he is the real King of England, and that Richard is his heir (II, v). (This is unhistorical and is a confusion with his uncle, Sir Edmund; though he had a better claim to the throne, the 5th Earl was a friend of Henry V, and died of plague in 1424.)

Mortimer, Sir Edmund (1376–1409). In *1 Henry IV*, Shakespeare confuses him with his nephew Edmund, 5th Earl of March, heir presumptive of Richard II. He is defeated and captured by the Welsh rebel Glendower, whose daughter he marries. Mortimer's sister is the wife of Hotspur, who joins the rebellion, and in III, i he, Mortimer, and Glendower anticipate victory by dividing England and Wales among themselves.

Mortimer, Lady. In *1 Henry IV*, daughter of Owen Glendower and wife of Edmund Mortimer. She appears in III, i, but can speak only Welsh.

Mortimer, Sir John and Sir Hugh. In *3 Henry VI*, illegitimate sons of Roger Mortimer, and uncles of Richard Plantagenet, Duke of York, whose claim to the throne they support (I, ii). All three were killed at Wakefield.

Morton. In *2 Henry IV*, he brings Northumberland news of the defeat and death of his son Hotspur at Shrewsbury (I, i).

Morton, John (1410–1500). In *Richard III*, the Bishop of Ely. He sends for strawberries for Richard, is arrested, escapes, and joins Richmond. (In Henry VII's reign Morton became Archbishop of Canterbury, Cardinal, and Lord Chancellor. Sir Thomas More was brought up in his household, and is said to have obtained from him material for his *History of Richard III*, an indirect source of Shakespeare's play.)

Moryson, Fynes (1566–1630), a native of Lincolnshire and fellow of Peterhouse, Cambridge. After extensive travelling he became secretary to the Lord Deputy of Ireland, in 1617 publishing his *Itinerary*, a valuable account of early 17th-century Europe.

Moseley, Humphrey (d. 1661), bookseller in St Paul's Churchyard, became a freeman of the Stationers' Company in 1627 and a Warden in 1659. He published the work of a number of 17th-century poets, including Donne and Milton (see MARSHALL), and the Beaumont and Fletcher Folio of 1647. Moseley collected old plays during the Interregnum, and appears to have claimed their acting rights at the Restoration. Many of these are lost, but he registered:

1653, 9 September. The Merry Devil of Edmonton. The History of Cardennio, by Mr. Fletcher. & Shakespeare. Henry ye first, & Hen: ye 2^d^. by Shakespeare, & Dauenport.

1660, 29 June. The History of King Stephen. Duke Humphrey, A Tragedy. Iphis & Iantha, or a marriage without a man, a Comedy. By Will: Shakespeare.

All these plays except the first, a Globe play first published anonymously in 1608, are lost. *Cardenio* (q.v.) has an interesting history.

Mosely, Joseph, a bricklayer. On 29 April 1757, while retiling Shakespeare's birthplace, in which Thomas Hart was then living, he discovered John Shakespeare's 'religious Testament', which he gave to Mr Payton of Shottery, who sent it to Malone *c.* 1789. The document was first mentioned by John Jordan (q.v.) in his *Original Collections on Shakespeare … written about the year 1780*.

Moth. 1. In *Love's Labour's Lost*, the pert page of Armado. In the interlude of The Nine Worthies he presents the infant Hercules. (Pronounce 'Mote', i.e. speck. Shakespeare probably took him from Epiton, Sir Tophas's page in Lyly's *Endimion*.)

2. In *A Midsummer Night's Dream*, one of Titania's fairies (III, i).

Mouldy, Ralph. In *2 Henry IV*, one of the Cotswold peasants pressed by Falstaff for the army. He buys his release for forty shillings (III, ii).

Moulton, Richard Green (1849–1924), educated at Christ's, Cambridge, was Professor of Literary Theory and Interpretation, University of Chicago, 1892–1919. His *Shakespeare as a Dramatic Artist: A Popular Illustration of Scientific Criticism* (1885) is a more 'realist' approach than the sentimental one of Furnivall and Dowden.

Mountjoy, Christopher. See BELOTT-MOUNTJOY SUIT, the documents relating to which were discovered by C. W. Wallace and published in 1910.

'Mouse-trap Play.' The name ironically given by Hamlet to *The Murder of Gonzago*, the play which he sets to 'catch the conscience of the king'. See also III, iv, 182–3:

Let the bloat king tempt you again to bed;
Pinch wanton on your cheek, call you his
mouse ...

Mowbray, Thomas, 1st Duke of Norfolk (*c.* 1366–1400). In *Richard II*, he denies Bolingbroke's accusation of treason and the murder of Richard's uncle Gloucester, though he admits neglect of his prisoner. Richard exiles him for life, and his death at Venice is reported in IV, i.

Mowbray, Lord (1386–1405). In *2 Henry IV*, eldest son of the 1st Duke of Norfolk, he joins the rebellion of Scrope and Hastings, with whom he is treacherously arrested by Prince John and sent to execution (IV, ii). (See NORFOLK.)

Moxon, Joseph (1627–1700), mathematician and hydrographer, who at the Restoration became also a type-founder. His *Mechanick Exercises* of 1683 contains an account of contemporary printing methods, and as these were much the same as those of a hundred years earlier, it is an invaluable description of the way in which Shakespeare's works were printed, and an aid to bibliographical criticism. (See R. B. McKerrow, *An Introduction to Bibliography*, 1927.)

'Mr W. H.' See SONNETS.

'Mucedorus.' An anonymous play published in 1598 as 'A most pleasant Comedie of Mucedorus, the Kings sonne of Valentia and Amadine the Kings daughter of Arragon, with the merie conceites of Mouse. Newly set foorth, as it hath bin sundrie times plaide in the honorable Cittie of London. Very delectable and full of mirth'. It was reprinted in 1606; the 1610 Q was 'Amplified with new additions, as it was acted before the Kings Maiestie at White-hall on Shroue-sunday night. By his Highness Seruants vsually playing at the Globe'. (Collier claimed to have found a 1609 Q with these additions.) *Mucedorus* was ascribed to Shakespeare by Edward Archer in his play-list of 1656, and it was bound with *Fair Em* and *The Merry Devil of Edmonton* as 'Shakespeare. Vol. I' in Charles II's library. Greene, Peele and Lodge have all been suggested as the original author; the author of the 1609–10 additions is also unknown, but almost certainly not Shakespeare.

'MUCH ADO ABOUT NOTHING.'

WRITTEN: 1598–9. It is not mentioned by Meres in his *Palladis Tamia*, 1598, though it has been claimed as the '*Love's Labour's Won*' that he mentions.

PERFORMED: 'Sundrie times publikely acted' before Q 1600.

1612–13. Twice performed at the Court Revels during the festivities preceding the Lady Elizabeth's marriage, and entered in the Chamber Accounts as 'Much Adoe abowte Nothinge' and 'Benedicte and Betteris'.

That it was a popular play is clear from Leonard Digges's lines in the 1640 edition of Shakespeare's *Poems*:

let but Beatrice
And Benedicke be seene, loe in a trice
The Cockpit Galleries, Boxes, all are full.

REGISTERED: 1600. '4 Augusti. The Commedie of muche A doo about nothing a booke. to be staied.' This may have been an attempt by the Chamberlain's to prevent piratical publication.

1600. '23 Augusti. Andrew Wyse William Aspley. Entred for their copies vnder the handes of the wardens Two bookes, the one called Muche a Doo about nothinge. Thother the second parte of the history of Kinge Henry the iiijth with the humours of Sir John Falstaff: Wrytten by master Shakespere. xij^{d}.' This is the first appearance of Shakespeare's name in the Stationers' Register.

PUBLISHED: 1600, Q. 'Much adoe about

Nothing. As it hath been sundrie times publikely acted by the right honourable, the Lord Chamberlaine his seruants. Written by William Shakespeare. London Printed by V.S. for Andrew Wise, and William Aspley. 1600.'

A 'good' Q, printed from foul papers. The names of the actors Kempe and Cowley appear for Dogberry and Verges in IV, ii. From various irregularities (see INNOGEN) and the early character of the verse Wilson argues that Q is Shakespeare's revision of his earlier version of the play, the Benedick-Beatrice theme being expanded and rewritten in prose, and other parts correspondingly, and often imperfectly, abridged.

1623, F1. 'Much adoe about Nothing.' The sixth play in the Comedy section: pp. 101–21. Acts marked. Set up from Q with some reference to the prompt-book, F printing 'Enter Iacke Wilson', the singer, for Q's 'Enter Musicke' in II, i.

SOURCES: The Claudio-Hero plot occurs in a *novella* by Bandello, translated by Belleforest in his *Histoires Tragiques*; in Ariosto's *Orlando Furioso*, translated by Sir John Harington, and in the *Faerie Queene*, II, iv. (See also MERCHANT TAYLORS' SCHOOL.) The Beatrice-Benedick plot is Shakespeare's own (see CASTIGLIONE), as is Dogberry-Verges. According to Aubrey (*c.* 1681), 'The Humour of the Constable in a Midsomernight's Dreame [Much Ado], he happened to take at Grendon in Bucks which is the roade from London to Stratford.' (See 'PANECIA'; C. T. Prouty, *The Sources of Much Ado*.)

STAGE HISTORY: 1662. D'Avenant's *Law Against Lovers*, in which Benedick and Beatrice are added to a version of *Measure for Measure*.

1721. *Much Ado* revived by John Rich at Lincoln's Inn Fields.

1737. James Miller's *The Universal Passion*, a combination of *Much Ado* and Molière's *La Princesse d'Élide*.

1748. Garrick's first appearance as Benedick, one of his favourite parts, which he played until 1776.

1882. Henry Irving and Ellen Terry at the Lyceum.

1903. Gordon Craig's production with Ellen Terry, his mother, as Beatrice.

Claudio, a young lord in the service of Don Pedro, falls in love with Hero, daughter of Leonato. Don John, bastard brother of Don Pedro, plans to thwart the marriage, and arranges that Claudio and Don Pedro shall see at night his follower Borachio apparently making love to Hero at her window, though the lady is really Hero's gentlewoman, Margaret, who loves Borachio. When they come to church to be married, Claudio denounces Hero as unchaste; she faints, and on the advice of Friar Francis it is given out that she is dead, in the hope that her good name will be re-established.

Meanwhile Borachio has been captured by constable Dogberry and his watch, and confesses. The repentant Claudio promises to make amends to Leonato by marrying his 'niece', who, of course, turns out to be Hero herself.

The sub-plot is that of Benedick and Beatrice, Hero's cousin, the one professing to be a confirmed bachelor, the other a confirmed spinster. Benedick is tricked into overhearing a conversation in which Don Pedro, Leonato, and Claudio say that Beatrice is dying for love of him, and in the same way Beatrice is led to believe by Hero that Benedick loves her. They declare their love for one another, and Beatrice tests Benedick by making him challenge Claudio for his slander of Hero, but as Claudio discovers his error there is no duel, and Benedick and Beatrice arrange to be married at the same time as Claudio and Hero. The play ends with news of the capture of Don John, who had run away.

Mulberry Tree. Sir Hugh Clopton lived at New Place until his death in 1751, and in 1756 the house was bought by the Rev. Francis Gastrell, who pulled it down in 1759, having in the previous year cut down the mulberry tree said to have been planted by Shakespeare, in revenge for which 'Gothic barbarity' boys broke Gastrell's windows. In 1609 a number of mulberry trees had been distributed throughout the Midlands by order of James I, who wished to encourage the silk industry, and it is possible that Shakespeare planted the one in New Place garden, but there is no written or printed mention of the tree until after its being cut down in 1758. The first notice of it seems to be in a letter of April 1788 from Malone to Davenport (q.v.), in which he says that Macklin (q.v.) told him that he and Garrick on their visit to Stratford in 1744 (1742?) sat under the tree with Sir Hugh Clopton. According to Halliwell-Phillipps, 'within a few months after its removal, tobacco-stoppers made of its wood were publicly sold as Shakespearean relics by one Moody, a toy-seller at Birmingham'.

Mulcaster, Richard (*c.* 1530–1611), was of Eton, King's, Cambridge, and Christ Church, Oxford. In 1561 he became Headmaster of Merchant Taylors' School, where Spenser was his pupil, and from which he resigned in 1586 after a quarrel with the Company, ten years later being appointed High Master of St Paul's. Mulcaster held advanced views on education; though he believed firmly in the value of classics, he maintained that all boys could not profit from a purely classical education, and advocated elementary teaching in English. His *Elementary* (1580) is partly an elementary course in English, partly a defence of English instead of Latin as a medium for the writing of serious books.

Sir James Whitelocke, who was at Merchant Taylors' from 1575 to 1588, wrote,

> I was brought up at school under Mr Mulcaster, in the famous school of the Merchantaylors in London ... Yeerly he presented sum playes to the court, in which his scholers wear only actors, and I on among them, and by that meanes taughte them good behaviour and audacitye.

(See MERCHANT TAYLORS' SCHOOL.)

Multiple Setting, or *décor simultané*, was the convention of placing on the stage at the same time all the localities in which the action of a play takes place. It originated in the medieval liturgical drama where changes of scene were out of the question; the Cross, for example, being at the altar, Heaven and the Holy Sepulchre on one side of the sanctuary, and Hell on the other. The various localities, called 'mansions' or 'houses', were indicated by some sort of framework hung with curtains; in the 12th-century French *Adam*, Paradise was on a platform hung with silk cloths and decorated with fruit and flowers.

If, as in classical and neo-classical plays, there is unity of place, there is no difficulty about change of scene; one set, conventional or realistic, will suffice. If there is more than one scene, as became the rule in the more romantic plays of the Renaissance, they can be indicated in three ways: by multiple setting, by dispensing with scenery altogether, by changing of scenes. Multiple setting with painted scenery and 'perspective' was practised in the 16th-century Italian theatre of Serlio and in the courtly theatre of 17th-century France (see HÔTEL DE BOURGOGNE). In England, painted canvas 'houses' were used in Elizabethan Court performances, and apparently at the private Blackfriars theatre, while the Children's companies were there, Lyly's plays, performed also at Court, being designed for multiple setting. In the open public theatres there are traces of multiple setting. *The Comedy of Errors*, for example, clearly lends itself to the method, though it may not have been designed for the regular theatre, for there was little scenery on the Elizabethan public stage. With Inigo Jones and the Court masque came devices for changes of scene, and this modern method of production may have begun to spread to the private and public theatres in the first half of the 17th century.

Munday, Anthony (*c.* 1560–1633), son of a London draper. He 'first was a stage player', then in 1576 was apprenticed to the printer, John Allde, whom he left in 1578 to go on a journey to Rome where he collected material for an attack on English Catholics in France and Italy. On his return he wrote a number of anti-popish tracts, one of which was *A Discoverie of Edmund Campion*, the English poet and Jesuit executed in 1581, against whom he was one of the chief witnesses. In an anonymous reply, *A True Reporte of the death of M. Campion* (1581), Munday is taunted with having been hissed off the stage when he attempted to 'play extempore', and with beginning 'againe to ruffle upon the stage', apparently as one of Oxford's Men. He probably ceased acting in 1584, when his anti-Catholic services were rewarded with the Court post of Messenger of the Chamber. His earliest extant play, *Fedele and Fortunio*, was published in 1585. Between 1594 and 1602 he was writing for Henslowe and the Admiral's, and in 1598 was noted by Meres as one of 'the best for comedy' and as 'our best plotter'. In addition to plays he wrote ballads and lyrics, translated romances, and edited the 1618 edition of Stow's *Survey of London*. From 1605, and probably before, he was much employed, like Jonson and Middleton, in writing pageants for the City and City companies. He is satirized as Posthaste in the anonymous *Histrio-mastix* (*c.* 1589).

As a dramatist, Munday is interesting rather than distinguished, most of his plays, only four of which remain, being written in collaboration for the Admiral's. *John a Kent* (q.v.) is important because it is one of the few extant manuscript plays in the hand of its author. The original copy of the manuscript *Sir Thomas More* was written by Munday, but that he was the author is uncertain. *1 Sir John Oldcastle*, for which Henslowe paid £10 to Munday, Drayton, Wilson, and Hathway in October 1599, was one of the ten plays published by William Jaggard as Shakespeare's in 1619. In 1598 Munday wrote *The Downfall of Robert Earl of Huntingdon* and, with Chettle, *The Death of Robert Earl of Huntingdon*, Admiral's plays about Sherwood Forest and Robin Hood which may have inspired Shakespeare to write *As You Like It*.

I. A. Shapiro (SS, 14) suggests that Munday may have brought back from Italy 'something like the improvisation of the *Commedia dell'Arte*', and that Meres called him 'our best plotter' because he wrote scenarios for other dramatists to amplify.

Murderers, unnamed and hired for the purpose, kill Gloucester in *2 Henry VI*, Clarence in *Richard III*, Banquo and Macduff's family in *Macbeth*. It has been suggested that the mysterious 'third murderer' in *Macbeth* (III, iii) is Macbeth himself.

Muret, Marc Antoine (1526–85), or Muretas, was born near Limoges. After lecturing in France where he was persecuted, he went to Rome, where his teaching gained him a European reputation. Among his works is a Latin tragedy of *Julius Caesar* (1553), one of the earliest Renaissance plays on the subject.

Murry, John Middleton (1889–1957), critic, educated at Christ's Hospital and Brasenose, Oxford; editor of the *Athenæum* 1919–21, of the *Adelphi* 1923–30; author of *Keats and Shakespeare* 1925, *Shakespeare* 1936. His two volumes of *Countries of the Mind*, 1922 and 1931, contain penetrating Shakespearean criticism.

Musgrave, Sir William, Commissioner for auditing the Public Accounts, 1785 to 1800. Malone applied to him for help in unearthing the Revels and Chamber Accounts, and in a letter of November 1791 (*Var.*, III, 363) Musgrave told him that a number of *Elizabethan* Accounts awaited his inspection. There is no record of Musgrave's supplying Malone with any *Jacobean* Accounts, but in December 1799 he wrote, 'I enclose a memorandum about a MS. which you have probably met with already – if not it may furnish matter for some of your illustrations of Shakespear'. This *may* refer to the Malone 'Scrap' (q.v.), an abstract of the Revels Accounts for 1604–5, the latter of which Peter Cunningham professed to have found in 1842. These have been suspected as forgeries, but if the Malone Scrap is genuine, and it may be in Musgrave's hand, the Jacobean Accounts are almost certainly genuine, and are generally accepted as such, though S. A. Tannenbaum considers both Accounts and Scrap to be forgeries by J. P. Collier.

Music. The Elizabethans excelled in vocal music, particularly in the madrigal, to be able to take a part in which was considered a necessary social accomplishment. But much secular instrumental music was written, particularly for the lute, viol, recorder and virginal. Instruments were normally combined in 'consort', that is in families of the same instrument, and not as in a modern orchestra composed of strings, woodwind, brass and percussion. Thus, a Consort of Viols was a group of players on the different-sized instruments of the viol family. When the families were mixed, as sometimes they inevitably were, it was called 'broken music' or 'broken consort'.

Like the 'Comon players in Enterludes', 'Minstrels', as they are called in the Act of 1572, were liable to be treated as 'Roges, Vacaboundes and Sturdy Beggers' unless they had some settled employment, preferably in the service of a Baron of the Realm. Elizabeth, of course, had her musicians, and many of the nobility entertained musicians in their households, as does Orsino in *Twelfth Night*. Lord Chamberlain Hunsdon had musicians who, no doubt, supplied Shakespeare's company at need, and in 1624 Herbert mentions the 'musitions' attached to the King's Men (see PROTECTION OF PLAYERS). Some of the actor-sharers were themselves musicians, possibly Shakespeare, and probably Augustine Phillips, who left his 'base viall, a citterne, a bandore and a lute' to his apprentices. Armin certainly was a singer.

Shakespeare and his contemporaries made a more or less conventional use of some instruments in their plays; thus, apart from announcing the beginning of a performance, trumpets indicated the appearance of royalty and added realism to battle scenes with their alarms and retreats, drum and pipe suggested an army on the march, and horns a hunting scene. Songs are generally introduced for more dramatic reasons, particularly in tragedies, where they emphasize abnormal states of mind, as do the mad song of Ophelia and the Willow song of Desdemona. Instrumental music may be called for at times of quiet tension, as when Lear recovers from his madness, and is often associated with magic, as in *The Tempest*. Music seems rarely to have been specially composed for a play; popular tunes were generally played, and lyrics written to fit existing airs.

The adult companies, then, could offer their audience vocal and instrumental music in their plays, but their open theatres and nut-cracking groundlings did not encourage music before the play or during the intervals. Here the boys at the Blackfriars were at an advantage; their theatre was closed, and as they were choir-boys they were able to entertain their more educated audience with incidental music as well as with music within the play. That this was so is clear from Marston's *Malcontent*, a Blackfriars play, which when acted at the Globe had to be padded to make up for the music that the King's Men were unable or unaccustomed to supply (see ORGAN). When the King's took over the Blackfriars in 1608 they seem to have continued the musical tradition, music being a common feature in their plays after this, in Shakespeare's romances and Beaumont's and Fletcher's tragi-comedies. In 1634 'the Blackfryers Musicke' was reputed to be the best theatre music in London.

That Shakespeare knew a great deal about music is certain, and it is only reasonable to suppose that he could himself play at least one instrument. Not only does he make dramatic use of vocal and instrumental music, but his plays are full of musical references and images. Wilson Knight finds music and tempests as dominant contrasted symbols throughout the plays. (See MASQUE; OPERA; SONGS; and various instruments and composers. *Also* SS, 11 and 15; E. W. Naylor, *Shakespeare and Music*; *New Oxford History of Music, IV*; J. H. Long, *Shakespeare's Use of Music.*)

Music Room. It is clear that in the Elizabethan (or Jacobean) theatre musicians occupied a curtained room somewhere above the main stage. At the Globe, according to J. C. Adams (*The Globe Theatre*), the music room was on a level with the top gallery, above the 'upper stage'. R. Hosley (SS, 13) distinguishes between 'dramatic' music performed during a play's action and the 'inter-act' music peculiar to private theatres until about 1604. Public theatres, therefore, 'did not develop music-rooms before that date', dramatic music being performed either on-stage or 'within'. After 1604 the 'upper stage' was used primarily as a music room.

This is the orthodox view – that the music room was in the tiring-house wall above the stage, though there is no contemporary illustration showing musicians in a gallery. Hotson's solution (*Shakespeare's Wooden O*) is that the music room was the upper part of the 'house' of Heaven, to the right of spectators sitting in the lords' room. (See ROUNDS.)

In the illustrations of the production of *The Empress of Morocco* at Dorset Garden theatre in 1673 the music room is above the proscenium arch. It was only towards the end of the 17th century, when the apron was retreating, that the musicians took up their position in front of the stage. (See ORCHESTRA.)

Mustard-seed. In *A Midsummer Night's Dream*, one of Titania's fairies.

Mutes. Shakespeare sometimes refers to characters who do not appear in the play: for example, to Petruchio's 'cousin Ferdinand' in *The Taming of the Shrew* (IV, i) and, more important, to the 'brave son' of Antonio, usurping Duke of Milan, who was wrecked with the others in *The Tempest* (I, ii). Sometimes characters mentioned in stage-directions never speak and are never referred to by the others, the most famous example being 'Innogen' (q.v.), wife of Leonato in *Much Ado*. Such apparent discrepancies may, as Wilson argues, be evidence of revision.

Mutius. In *Titus Andronicus*, youngest son of Titus. When Bassianus carries off his sister Lavinia, he attempts to stop the interference of his father, who stabs him (I, i).

N

Naples. In *The Tempest*, Alonso (q.v.) is King of Naples, and Ferdinand is his son. There was an historical Alonso, King of Naples, who was succeeded by his son Ferdinand in 1495.

Nares, Robert (1753–1829), philologist, was educated at Westminster School and Christ Church, Oxford, ordained, became Keeper of Manuscripts at the British Museum, and died as Rector of Allhallows, London Wall. He published his principal work in 1822, *A Glossary; or, Collection of Words, Phrases, Names, and Allusions to Customs, Proverbs, etc. ... in the Works of English Authors, particularly Shakespeare and his Contemporaries.* It was edited 'with considerable additions' in 1859, by J. O. Halliwell [-Phillipps] and Thomas Wright, who describe the book as 'quite indispensable to the reader of the literature of the Elizabethan period'.

Nash, Anthony (d. 1622), eldest son of Thomas Nash of Old Stratford, who was buried at Aylesbury in 1587. Anthony, described as of Welcombe and Old Stratford, married Mary Baugh, of Twyning, near Tewkesbury, their eldest son being Thomas, future husband of Shakespeare's granddaughter Elizabeth. His sister, Frances, married John Lane (see p. 543). He farmed Shakespeare's tithes and witnessed his agreement with Replingham safeguarding him against loss by enclosure in 1614. In his will Shakespeare left him and his brother John (d. 1623) 26s. 8d. 'A peece to buy them Ringes.' He and John witnessed his purchase of land from the Combes in 1602. (See OLD STRATFORD.)

Nash, Thomas (1593–1647), eldest son of Anthony Nash, was christened at Stratford parish church 20 June 1593: 'Thomas filius Anthonij Nash generosi'. In 1616 he entered Lincoln's Inn, and in 1622 was executor under the will of his father, who left him two houses and a piece of land. On 22 April 1626 he married Shakespeare's granddaughter, Elizabeth Hall, daughter of Dr John Hall and Susanna Shakespeare. In a nuncupative will made a few hours before his death on 25 November 1635, Hall left Nash his 'study of books', which must have included some of Shakespeare's, as the Halls were his residuary legatees. Nash was a Royalist, and in September 1642 is noted as much the largest of the Stratford contributors to the King's cause: 'Thomas Nashe esqr. in plate or money paid in at Warr: 100 *li*'. A month before this he had made his will, in which he left his wife the house next to New Place in Chapel Street, still known as Nash's House. At that date it was occupied by a tenant, Joan Norman. Perhaps Nash lived there until Hall's death in 1635, and then moved into his mother-in-law's house next door, where he died 4 April 1647. He was buried in the chancel of Stratford church, with the inscription on his gravestone: 'Here resteth the body of Thomas Nashe, esquier; he mar. Elizabeth, the daug. of John Hall, gentleman; he dyed Aprill 4, anno 1647, aged 53'. There were no children, and two years later his widow married John Bernard.

Nashe, Thomas (1567–*c.* 1601), pamphleteer and dramatist, was of a Herefordshire family, though born at Lowestoft. From 1582 to 1589 he was at St John's, Cambridge, where he must have met Robert Greene, who published his *Menaphon* in 1589. To this Nashe wrote a preface addressed to 'The Gentlemen Students of Both Universities' in which he attacked the players as parasites, and Kyd as an upstart outside the charmed circle of the University Wits to which he himself belonged, much as Greene was to attack the players and Shakespeare in 1592. His ready pen, which wrote 'as fast as his hand could trot', was employed by Archbishop Whitgift against 'Martin Marprelate', though which pamphlets are his it is difficult to say; *An Almond for a Parrat* (1590) is probably his. He also became involved in a quarrel with Richard and Gabriel Harvey, largely over Greene, who died in 1592 and whom he passionately defended. His *Have With You to Saffron Walden* (1596) is the best known of this war of pamphlets which was suppressed by Whitgift in 1599.

If, as is probable, Nashe is the 'young Juvenal, the byting Satyrist' of Greene's *Groatsworth of Wit*, he had collaborated with Greene in a comedy before 1592, and in 1594 *Dido Queen of Carthage* was published as the work of 'Christopher Marlowe and Thomas Nash. Gent'. His only extant and unaided play is *Summer's Last Will and Testament*, a masque-like comedy written in the plague year of 1592. *Pierce Penilesse* (q.v.) appeared in this year, by which time he had changed his attitude towards players whom he here defends, as well as poetry and plays. It contains the famous reference to 'brave Talbot' in *1 Henry VI*. *The Unfortunate Traveller, or the Life of Jack Wilton* (1594) is important in the history of the novel as the first English picaresque romance, written with the convincing realism of Defoe, with whom he has affinities. In 1597 came the performance of his 'seditious and sclanderous' *Isle of Dogs* (q.v.), which led to the closing of the theatres and his flight to Yarmouth. He was dead in 1601, when an elegy on him appeared in Fitzgeffrey's *Affaniæ*. (*Works of Thomas Nashe*, ed. R. B. McKerrow.)

Nathaniel. 1. In *Love's Labour's Lost* Sir Nathaniel is a curate and a crony of Holofernes. In the interlude of the Nine Worthies he presents Alexander, but breaks down and is defended by Costard as 'a foolish mild man; an honest man, look you, and soon dashed. He is a marvellous good neighbour, faith, and a very good bowler: but, for Alisander, – alas, you see how 't is, – a little o'er-parted' (v, ii).

2. In *The Taming of the Shrew* one of Petruchio's servants is called Nathaniel (IV, i).

National Theatre. Established in 1962 with Laurence Olivier as Director. Until the theatre is built (on the South Bank), the National Theatre Company will perform at the Old Vic (q.v.), where their first production was *Hamlet*, 22 October 1963.

Navarre. French Navarre in the Pyrenees survived as a small independent kingdom until incorporated in France by Henry of Navarre. It is the scene of *Love's Labour's Lost*. (See HENRI IV.)

'NE.' See HENSLOWE; TITUS AND VESPASIAN.

Neilson, Adelaide (1846–80), actress, whose real name was Elizabeth Ann Brown, was born at Leeds. She appeared at Margate in 1865, and after that soon made a name for herself as a Shakespearean actress, mostly in comedy, though she played Juliet. She was a great success in America, which she first visited in 1872.

Neilson, Julia (1868–1957), actress, made her first stage appearance in 1888. She married Fred Terry, brother of Ellen Terry, and with him went into management in 1900. She played mostly in comedy, her most famous Shakespearean part being Rosalind.

Neo-classicism. The new classicism of the Renaissance, but a term often applied to the uncompromising classicism of the extremists among the Renaissance scholars and artists and those of the 17th and 18th centuries. The art of Greece and Rome was held to be the only model, and from it laws were deduced which the artist disobeyed at his peril. In the drama this meant following Aristotle (q.v.), whose *Poetics* was made into a rigid code demanding the unities of time, place and action; all must be probable, reasonable and restrained. The neo-classicism of Italy passed into France and England, but in England it was never very rigorously imposed; fanatics like Gabriel Harvey and Thomas Rymer were exceptional, and Shakespeare and the Elizabethans broke all the rules. For the French, Shakespeare was a barbarian; for 18th-century England he was an irregular genius, whose excesses were more than balanced by his virtues. Pope admirably states the neo-classic creed in his *Essay on Criticism*:

Those RULES of old discovered, not devis'd,
Are Nature still, but Nature methodiz'd;
Nature, like liberty, is but restrain'd
By the same laws which first herself ordained ...
Learn hence for ancient rules a just esteem;
To copy nature is to copy them.

Nerissa. In *The Merchant of Venice*, Portia's gentlewoman who marries Gratiano.

Nestor. In *Troilus and Cressida*, the old King of Pylos and one of the Grecian commanders. He is present in a number of scenes, but plays only a small part in the action. He supports the advice of Ulysses and tries to rouse Achilles by making him jealous of Ajax.

Netherlands. When Shakespeare was a boy a stream of Protestant refugees from the Spanish Netherlands was pouring into England, bringing with them their art, craftsmanship and skill. The visual arts were much influenced by these Flemish immigrants: the Antwerp Bourse was the model for Sir Thomas Gresham's Royal Exchange; Hans Eworth, John de Critz and Marcus Gheeraerts were among the chief painters of the period, and the mason Gheerart Janssen was father of the younger

Gheerart who was to make the Shakespeare monument in Stratford church.

Interest in Shakespeare grew in the Netherlands during the last war, and his plays are frequently performed, though in new translations, many by Bert Voeten, rather than in the standard 19th-century version of Burgersdijk. The Elizabethan Exhibition at the Hague in 1958 was a further stimulus.

'New Cambridge' Shakespeare. An edition based on Pollard's 'new scientific method – critical Shakespearian bibliography'. The first play, *The Tempest*, was published in 1921. Quiller-Couch and Dover Wilson were the original editors, but after the former's death Wilson acted for the most part alone. (See Q's General Introduction and Wilson's Textual Introduction in *The Tempest*; RECORDINGS.)

New Place. The Stratford house, second largest in the town, which Shakespeare bought for £60 from William Underhill 4 May 1597:

> Inter Willielmum Shakespeare querentem et Willielmun Underhill generosum deforciantem, de vno mesuagio duobus horreis et duobus gardinis cum pertinenciis in Stratford super Avon ... Et pro hac recognicione ... fine et concordia idem Willielmus Shakespeare dedit predicto Willielmo Underhill sexaginta libras sterlingorum.

William Underhill was poisoned by his son Fulke, and Shakespeare had to complete the transfer with the younger brother Hercules, who succeeded to the estate in 1602. Here Shakespeare is described as *generosus*, or gentleman, and the house as having not only two barns and two gardens, but two orchards (*duobus pomariis*) as well.

New Place was built *c.* 1490 by Sir Hugh Clopton, at the corner of Chapel Street and Chapel Lane, opposite the Guild Chapel which he rebuilt for the town. About 1540, Leland visited Stratford and wrote:

> there is a right goodly chappell, in a fayre street towardes the south end of the towne, dedicated to the Trinitye; this chappell was newly re-edified by one Hugh Clopton, major of London; this Hugh Clopton builded also by the north syde of this chappell a praty house of bricke and tymbre, wherin he lived in his latter dayes and dyed.

(According to Halliwell-Phillipps, it had a frontage of 60 ft and a depth of 70 ft.) In 1543 William Clopton let the house to Dr Thomas Bentley, Physician to Henry VIII, on whose death in 1549 it is described as being 'in great ruyne and decay and unrepayred'. In 1563 it was bought by William Bott, who sold it in 1567 to William Underhill for £40, when it was described as one messuage and one garden. The house may have been occupied by Shakespeare's wife and daughters in 1597 (Hamnet had died a few months earlier), and in the following year the Stratford Corporation 'pd to mr Shaxspere for on lod of ston x^{d}', possibly stone left over from repairs to the house. In 1737 George Vertue made a sketch of the original New Place, possibly from a description by Shakespeare Hart, who was then 'about 70'. (SS, 5.) Shakespeare himself did not live there permanently until his retirement, *c.* 1610, and in 1609 his 'cousin' Thomas Greene, the Town Clerk, was lodging there, presumably with the Shakespeares.

Shakespeare left New Place to his daughter Susanna Hall, by whom it was occupied, and by her daughter Elizabeth and her first husband, Thomas Nash, and for a time by her second husband, John Bernard. In 1643 Queen Henrietta Maria stayed there two nights. After the death of the Bernards and extinction of Shakespeare's descendants, it was sold to Sir Edward Walker, whose daughter married Sir John Clopton (d. 1719), and the house returned to the family that built it. Sir John rebuilt it with a modified ground-plan, and left it to his son Sir Hugh, after whose death it was bought by the Rev. Francis Gastrell. After cutting down the mulberry-tree in the garden, Gastrell demolished the house in 1759. The site was bought by public subscription in 1862, and is now the property of the Birthplace trustees.

Richard Grimmitt, a Stratford shoemaker born in 1683, described the original house to Joseph Greene, appointed Master of Stratford Grammar School in 1735:

> This Rich[d] the younger, Said He in his youth had been a playfellow with Edw[d] Clopton Sen[r] eldest son of S[r] John Clopton Kn[t]. & had been often with him in y[e] Great House near y[e] chapel in Stratford, call'd New-place: that to y[e] best of his remembrance there was a brick Wall next y[e] Street, with a kind of porch at that end of it near y[e] chapel; when they cross'd a small kind of Green Court before they enter'd y[e] House which was bearing to y[e] left, & fronted with brick, with plain windows, consisting of common panes of Glass set in lead, as at this time.

Malone (1790) reproduces a supposed illustration of the original New Place, Halliwell-Phillipps the 18th-century one. A theatre was built on the site in 1827; this was a failure, and it was converted into a ballroom in 1842. The theatre was revived in 1869 but demolished in 1872, and the present gardens laid out. Nash's house, next door, is a museum.

New Shakspere Society. Founded by F. J. Furnivall in 1873, twenty years after the collapse of the original Shakespeare Society. He explained the purpose of the Society (*Transactions*, 1874, p. vi):

> The purpose of our Society is, by a very close study of the metrical and phraseological peculiarities of Shakspere, to get his plays as nearly as possible into the order in which he wrote them; to check that order by the higher tests of imaginative power, knowledge of life, self-restraint in expression, weight of thought, depth of purpose; and then to use that revised order for the purpose of studying the progress and meaning of Shakspere's mind, the passage of it from the fun and word-play, the lightness, the passion, of the Comedies of Youth, through the patriotism (still with comedy of more meaning) of the Histories of Middle Age, to the great Tragedies dealing with the deepest questions of man in Later Life; and then at last to the poet's peaceful and quiet home-life again in Stratford, where he ends with his Prospero and Miranda, his Leontes finding again his wife and daughter in Hermione and Perdita; in whom we may fancy that the Stratford both of his early and late days lives again, and that the daughters he saw there, the sweet English maidens, the pleasant country scenes around him, past as it were again into his plays.

At the opening meeting at University College on 13 March 1874, Dr E. A. Abbott read a paper by F. G. Fleay 'On Metrical Tests as applied to Dramatic Poetry: Part 1, Shakspere'. But verse-tests were only a means to the revelation of Shakespeare 'as a whole', and to the 'higher aesthetic criticism', and the *Transactions*, 1874–92, are by no means confined to this scientific and mechanical criticism. A number of valuable reprints were edited for the Society: e.g. Arthur Brooke's *Romeus and Iuliet*, and Painter's *Rhomeo and Iulietta* (ed. by P. A. Daniel, 1875); *The Two Noble Kinsmen*, 1876 (see SPALDING. See also CENTURIE OF PRAYSE). The Society came to an end in 1894. (See ABBOTT; DOWDEN; FLEAY; SIMPSON, RICHARD.)

New York Shakespeare Society. The Shakespeare Society of New York was incorporated 20 April 1885, 'to promote the knowledge and study of the works of Wm. Shakespeare, and the Shakespearean and Elizabethan Drama'. It issued thirteen publications 1885–1903.

Newcastle, Margaret Cavendish, Duchess of (*c.* 1625–73), daughter of Sir Thomas Lucas of St John's, Colchester. In 1645 she met in Paris the Duke of Newcastle (1592–1676), who had deserted the Royalist cause after Marston Moor, and became his second wife. She published a number of books, including a *Life* of her husband, and in 1664 her *Sociable Letters*, one of which (CXXIII) contains a remarkable defence of Shakespeare:

> ... so Well he hath Express'd in his Playes all Sorts of Persons, as one would think he had been Transformed into every one of those

Persons he hath Described ... And in his Tragick Vein, he Presents Passions so Naturally, and Misfortunes so Probably, as he Peirces the Souls of his Readers with such a true Sense and Feeling thereof, that it Forces Tears through their Eyes ... Indeed *Shakespear* had a Clear Judgment, a Quick Wit, a Spreading Fancy, a Subtil Observation, a Deep Apprehension, and a most Eloquent Elocution; truly, he was a Natural Orator, as well as a Natural Poet.

The Duchess of Newcastle was one of Lamb's favourite authors, though for Horace Walpole she was little more than a pedantic scribbler.

Shortly before the Restoration, the Duke wrote to Prince Charles (II) advising him about 'Devertisementes for your Matie People', and recites an interesting but slightly muddled account of the theatres before they were closed in 1642, confusing the Globe with the Phoenix (Cockpit), though he is the only chronicler to mention the Boar's Head:

Firste for London Paris Garden will holde good for the meaner People.
Then for severall Playe Houses as there weare att leaste In my Time, –
Black-Friers, the Cock-Pitt, Salsburye Courte, the Fortune, & the Redd Bull, – Ther weare the Boyes thatt played at Black-Friers, & Paules, and then the Kinges Players played att the Globe – which is nowe calde the Phenix – Some Played, att the Bores heade, & att the Curtin In the feildes & some att the Hope whiche Is the Beare Garden, and some at White Friers, – Butt five or Sixe Playe Houses Is enough for all sortes off Peoples divertion & pleasure In thatt kinde.

Charles II licensed only two companies, the King's and the Duke's, and in his *Historia Histrionica* (1699) James Wright (q.v.) gives a reason:

Lovewit. Which I much admire at. That the Town, much less than at present, could then ['Before the Wars'] maintain Five Companies; and yet now Two can hardly subsist.

Truman. Do not wonder, but consider! That though the Town was then, perhaps, not much more than half so populous as now; yet then the prices were small (there being no scenes [i.e. scenery]), and better order kept among the company that came: which made very good people think a play an innocent diversion for an idle hour or two; the plays being then, for the most part, more instructive and moral.

Newington Butts Theatre. A theatre, about which little is known, in the Surrey village of Newington, where the archery butts were, about a mile to the south-west of London Bridge. The first mention of plays at Newington is in a Privy Council letter of 13 May 1580, ordering the Surrey Justices to prohibit playing because of infection: 'Neverthe-les certen players do playe sunderie daies every weeke at Newington Buttes.' A similar letter of 11 May 1586 tells the Lord Mayor that 'their Lordships have taken the like order for the prohibiting of the use of playes at the theater and th' other places about Newington out of his charge'. It was probably in the summer of 1592 that the Privy Council withdrew an order restraining 'the Lorde Straunge his servauntes from playinge at the Rose on the banckside, and enjoyning them to plaie three daies at Newington Butts'. Apparently the theatre was Henslowe's by 1594, for when the theatres were reopened in that year after the plague of 1593, Henslowe records performances by the Admiral's and Chamberlain's from 5 to 15 June: 'In the name of god Amen begininge at Newington my Lord Admeralle men & my Lorde Chamberlen men As ffolowethe 1594.' Among the play-houses mentioned by Howes in the 5th edition of Stow's *Annales* (1631) is 'one in former times at *Newington* Buts'.

Nichols, John (1745–1826), was born at Islington and apprenticed to the printer William Bowyer, to whose business he succeeded, and his *Anecdotes* of whom were expanded into the important *Literary Anecdotes of the 18th Century*, and *Illustrations of the Literary History of the 18th Century*. The 3 vols. of his valuable *Progresses and Public Processions of Queen Elizabeth* were published 1788–1807, and the 4 vols. of *The Progresses, Processions,* *and Magnificent Festivities of King James the First* in 1828. From 1788 until his death he edited the *Gentleman's Magazine*.

Nicoll, Allardyce (b. 1894), educated at Stirling High School and Glasgow University. Professor of English and founder and Director of the Shakespeare Institute (q.v.) 1951–61. Editor of *Shakespeare Survey* (1948–65), and author of numerous books on the history of the theatre. (See Bibliography.)

Nicoll, Basil. A scrivener, and one of the executors of Thomas Pope (d. 1604), a housekeeper of the Globe. Pope left part of his share in the theatre to Thomas Bromley, for whom, apparently, Nicoll acted as trustee, for when in 1615 Ostler's widow (Heminge's daughter) brought an action for the recovery of her husband's shares, Nicoll is named with Shakespeare, Heminge and the other housekeepers.

Nine Worthies. In *Love's Labour's Lost*, the 'delightful ostentation' presented before the King of Navarre and his guests by Costard (Pompey), Sir Nathaniel (Alexander), Holofernes (Judas Maccabaeus), Moth (Hercules) and Armado (Hector).

'Nobleman, The.' A lost tragi-comedy by Cyril Tourneur, registered 15 February 1612. It was acted at Court by the King's Men 23 February 1612 and was one of the twenty plays – eight of which were Shakespeare's – given by the King's during the 1612–13 Revels preceding the marriage of the Lady Elizabeth.

Nokes, James (d. 1692), the comic actor nicknamed 'Nurse Nokes' from his taking the part of the Nurse in Otway's version of *Romeo and Juliet, The History and Fall of Caius Marius* (1679).

Nonsuch. A country house near Mitcham in Surrey, begun by Henry VIII, granted to the Earl of Arundel in 1556, and finished by his son-in-law, Lord Lumley. Elizabeth bought it *c.* 1590, and used to like to go there in the autumn: 'Nonsuch ... of all other places she likes best.' It was demolished in the 1680s. (See J. Dent, *The Quest for Nonsuch*, 1962.)

Norden, John (1548–*c.* 1625), topographer, was appointed surveyor of the crown woods and forests, and in 1616 of the royal castles, in the southern counties. His *Speculum Britanniæ* was designed as a series of county guides, historical and descriptive, with maps. The first part, *Middlesex*, appeared in 1593, and contains his famous views of London and Westminster. He completed the survey, in manuscript, of five other counties, including the almost uncharted Cornwall, and designed maps for the 5th edition (1607) of *Camden's Britannia.* (See MAPS OF LONDON.)

Norfolk, Duke of. 1. In *3 Henry VI*, the 3rd Duke of the Mowbray creation appears in I, i and II, ii as a supporter of York. (John Mowbray, 1415–61.)

2. In *Richard III*, the 1st Duke of the Howard creation has 'the leading of the foot and horse' for Richard at Bosworth, where he is killed. (John Howard, *c.* 1430–85. See SURREY.)

3. In *Henry VIII*, Thomas Howard (1443–1524), the 2nd Duke, who first appears as Earl of Surrey in *Richard III*, is one of the bitterest opponents of Wolsey, against whom he warns Buckingham.

Norris's Men. 'Lord Norris players' are recorded as playing at Bath with the Admiral's sometime between the summer of 1593 and that of 1594. There is no other record of the company.

North, Sir Thomas (*c.* 1535–*c.* 1601), second son of the 1st Lord North. He probably went to Peterhouse, Cambridge, entered Lincoln's Inn 1557, was knighted 1591, and J.P. for Cambridge 1592 and 1597. He translated Guevara's *Reloj de Principes* as the *Diall of Princes* (1557), *The Morall Philosophie of Doni* (1570) from the Italian, and Plutarch's *Lives* from the French version of Jacques Amyot. This last was published in 1579 as *The Lives of the Noble Grecians and Romanes*, and was followed by editions with new *Lives* in 1595 and 1603. North's *Plutarch* was one of the most influential books of the age, both in subject and style, and furnished Shakespeare with material for *Julius Caesar*, *Timon of Athens*, *Coriolanus* and *Antony and Cleopatra*. Sometimes he takes long passages of North's prose and puts them into blank verse with little change, though he nearly always adds some touch that transfigures the whole. The most famous example is the description of Cleopatra on Cydnus (see PLUTARCH), with which should also be compared Dryden's version in *All for Love*. The death of Charmian is a good illustration of Shakespeare's close following of North, and of the addition of two words of Shakespearean magic:

> One of the soldiers, seeing her, angrily said unto her: 'Is that well done, Charmion?' 'Very well,' said she again, 'and meet for a princess descended from the race of so many noble kings.' She said no more, but fell down dead by the bed.

> GUARD. What work is here! Charmian, is this well done?
>
> CHAR. It is well done, and fitting for a princess
> Descended of so many royal kings.
> Ah, soldier! [*Dies.*

Northbrooke, John, a minister of Gloucester who wrote *A Treatise wherein Dicing, Dauncing, Vaine playes, or Enterluds, with other idle pastimes, &c., commonly used on the Sabbath day, are reproued by the Authoritie of the word of God and auntient writers* (1577). He mentions the Theatre and Curtain, which had just been built, as 'those places also, which are made vppe and builded for such playes and enterludes, as the Theatre and Curtaine is, and other such lyke places', and continues:

> Satan hath not a more speedie way, and fitter schoole to work and teach his desire, to bring men and women into his snare of concupiscence and filthie lustes of wicked whoredome, than those places, and playes, and theatres are; and therefore necessarie that those places, and players, shoulde be forbidden, and dissolued, and put downe by authoritie, as the brothell houses and stewes are ... They vse to set vp their billes vpon postes certain dayes before, to admonishe the people to make their resort vnto their theatres ...

However, he allows that it is occasionally 'lawefull for a schoolmaster to practise his schollers to playe comedies', provided that they are free from 'ribaudrie', 'wanton toyes of loue', and 'sumptious apparell', are generally in Latin, and not acted for profit but 'for learning and exercise sake'.

Northumberland, Earl of. 1. In *Richard II*, Henry Percy (1342–1408), 1st Earl, joins Bolingbroke when he returns to claim the estates of Lancaster and then the throne. He flatters Bolingbroke, bullies Richard in the deposition scene (IV, i), and orders him to Pomfret and his Queen to France.

In *1 Henry IV*, he promises to join his son, Hotspur, and his brother, Worcester, in their rebellion against Bolingbroke, now Henry IV, whom they consider ungrateful. However, he feigns sickness and is not present at the critical battle of Shrewsbury where Hotspur is killed and Worcester captured.

In *2 Henry IV*, after encouraging Archbishop Scrope in the belief that he will join his rebellion, he flies to Scotland for refuge. The news of his defeat 'with a great power of English and of Scots' is announced in IV, iv.

2. In *3 Henry VI*, Henry Percy (1421–61), 3rd Earl, and grandson of Hotspur, supports Henry and the Lancastrian cause. He pities the captured York at Wakefield, and is killed at Towton.

Northumberland, Lady. In *2 Henry IV*, she persuades her husband, the Earl, to fly to Scotland (II, iii).

Northumberland Manuscript. An Elizabethan MS. discovered at Alnwick Castle, the home of the Earls of Northumberland. It contains essays and speeches by Francis Bacon, a letter by Sidney, and a copy of *Leicester's Commonwealth*. On the first page is part of a table of contents, *Speaches for my Lord of Essex at the tylt*, etc.; the rest of the page is covered with scribbles in another hand, including *Mr ffrauncis Bacon, William Shakespeare, Rychard the second, Rychard the third, honorificabilitudine* misquoted from *Love's Labour's Lost*, v, i, a misquotation from *Lucrece* (1086), and *Ile of Dogs by Thomas Nashe*. The date seems to be 1597–1603; *The Isle of Dogs* affair was in 1597, and Bacon was knighted in 1603. The names *Dyrmonth* and *Adam* occur, and Chambers suggests that the scribbler may have been an Adam Dyrmonth.

Norton, Thomas (1532–84), dramatist, was born in London and educated at Cambridge; he became a secretary to the Protector Somerset, entered the Inner Temple in 1555, and Parliament a few years later. His first wife was the daughter, his second the niece, of Archbishop Cranmer. In 1571 he was appointed Remembrancer of London, and in an *Exhortation* of 1574 warned the Lord Mayor against 'unnecessarie and scarslie honeste resorts to plaies ... and especiallie the assemblies to the unchaste, shamelesse and unnaturall tomblinge of the Italion Woemen'. His fanatical puritanism got him into trouble in 1583, when he was thrown into the Tower, and he died soon after his release. Norton was a writer of verses, some of which were published in *Tottel's Miscellany*, but he is best known as the collaborator with Thomas Sackville in *The Tragedy of Gorboduc* (q.v.), acted in 1562.

'Notes and Queries.' A periodical founded by W. J. Thoms in 1849 as 'a Medium of Intercommunication for Literary Men and General Readers'. Many Shakespearean problems have first been raised in *Notes and Queries*: for example, Richard Simpson's query of 1 July 1871, 'Are there any extant MSS. in Shakespeare's handwriting?' which led to the serious study of the handwriting in *Sir Thomas More*.

Nottingham, 1st Earl of, and Nottingham's Men. See ADMIRAL'S MEN.

Novel, Italian. The modern European novel began in Italy with the composition, *c.* 1300, of the *Cento Novelle Antiche*, a collection of anonymous stories. These were followed in the 14th century by the *Documenti d'Amor* of Francesco da Barberino, the *Decameron* of Boccaccio written about 1350, and *Il Pecorone* of Giovanni Fiorentino, a collection of fifty tales written about 1378. The most important novels of the 15th century were those of the south Italian, Masuccio, whose *Novellino* were printed in 1476. The early Italian novel reached its climax in the 16th century with the *Novelle* (1554) of Matteo Bandello, the *Hecatommithi* (1565) of his contemporary, Cinthio, marking the beginning of the decline of this form of literature. Shakespeare owed something to Boccaccio for *All's Well* and *Cymbeline*, to Giovanni Fiorentino for *The Merchant of Venice*, to Masuccio for *Romeo and Juliet*, to Bandello for *Much Ado*, and to Cinthio for *Othello*. (See SOURCES.)

Nurse. 1. In *Romeo and Juliet*, perhaps the first great comic character of the plays, she acts as go-between for the lovers, but when Romeo is banished she advises Juliet to forget him and to marry Paris. She does not appear after her discovery of the apparently dead Juliet.

2. In *Titus Andronicus*, Aaron kills the nurse, one of the three witnesses of the birth of his bastard son (IV, ii).

Nym. In *The Merry Wives*, a man of hints whose favourite word is 'humour'. Falstaff economizes by dismissing him and Pistol from his service, and in revenge they tell Page and Ford of Falstaff's love-letters to their wives.

In *Henry V* he is a corporal. He was troth-plight to Mistress Quickly, who, however, marries Pistol, with whom he quarrels, but is reconciled. He goes on the French campaign, during which he and Bardolph are hanged for looting. ('Nym' was a cant term meaning 'to steal'. It is possible that Nym is a dig at Jonson with his comedies of humour.)

O

Oberon. In *A Midsummer Night's Dream*, King of the Fairies. He quarrels with Titania about the possession of a little changeling boy whom he obtains by anointing her eyes with a magic juice that makes her infatuated with Bottom. By the same magic he makes Demetrius fall in love with Helena. He leads the fairy masque in honour of the wedding of Theseus and Hippolyta. (See 'HUON DE BORDEAUX'.)

Octavia. In *Antony and Cleopatra*, sister of Octavius Caesar. She marries Antony in an attempt to heal the breach between him and Octavius, but his desertion of her for Cleopatra leads to war.

Octavius. See CAESAR.

Octavo, an abbreviation of *in octavo*, 'in an eighth'. A sheet of paper folded three times forms eight leaves, or sixteen pages, and is said to be in octavo. A book made up of pages folded three times is an octavo. Shakespeare's poems were generally published in octavo; after the initial Quartos, there were nine octavo editions of *Venus and Adonis*, 1595–1617, and five of *Lucrece*, 1598–1616. *The Passionate Pilgrim* was published in octavo, and the so-called Q1 of *The True Tragedy* (*3 Henry VI*) is really in octavo.

Office-book. Sir Henry Herbert's record of his tenure of the Revels Office, 1623–42. It has been lost, but extracts were made by Malone for his 1790 edition of *Shakespeare*, and repeated in the Third Variorum, vol. III, pp. 57–9, of which he writes:

> For the use of this very curious and valuable manuscript I am indebted to Francis Ingram, of Ribbisford near Bewdley in Worcestershire, Esq. Deputy Remembrancer in the Court of Exchequer. It has lately been found in the same old chest which contained the manuscript Memoirs of Lord Herbert of Cherbury ... who was elder brother to Sir Henry Herbert ...
>
> The office-book of Sir Henry Herbert contains an account of almost every piece exhibited at any of the theatres from August 1623 to the commencement of the rebellion in 1641, and many curious anecdotes relative to them ... This valuable manuscript, having lain for a considerable time in a damp place, is unfortunately damaged, and in a very mouldering condition: however, no material part of it appears to have perished.

Unfortunately the Variorum is unindexed, and the Office-book references are scattered throughout Malone's *Historical Account of the English Stage*, but they have been edited by J. Q. Adams as *The Dramatic Records of Sir Henry Herbert*, 1917. (See HERBERT, SIR HENRY; MASTER OF THE REVELS.)

Ogle. A maker of wigs and theatrical properties, mentioned in the *Revels Accounts* for 1572–3, and by Henslowe, 10 February 1600, as 'father ogell'. The allusions to him in *Sir Thomas More*, lines, 1,006 and 1,148, are not very helpful, therefore, in dating the play.

Okes, Nicholas (d. after 1636), printer of some of the work of Dekker and Heywood, and of George Wither's unlicensed satirical tract, *Wither's Motto* (1621), for which he was imprisoned. About 1608 he took over the business of George and Lionel Snowden, and he may therefore have been printer of the poor Q1 *King Lear* of that year, with the Snowden device on the title-page. He printed O4 *Lucrece* (1607) for John Harrison, and Q1 *Othello* (1622) for Thomas Walkley.

Oldcastle, Sir John (*c.* 1375–1417), the Lollard, was the son of Sir Richard Oldcastle of Almeley, Herefordshire, which county he represented in Parliament. He served in the Welsh campaigns of Henry IV, became a friend of Prince Henry, and in 1408 married Joan, heiress of Cobham, so acquiring the title of Lord Cobham. About this time he became converted to the doctrines of Wycliffe, and in 1413 was accused of heresy. The new king, Henry V, did his best to dissuade his old friend, but in vain, and he was convicted. He escaped from the Tower, led a Lollard conspiracy to seize the King, intrigued with the Scots, and was apparently concerned with the Cambridge-Scrope-Grey plot of 1415. In 1417 he was captured, and hanged and burned at St Giles's Fields. He is celebrated as a martyr in Foxe's *Book of Martyrs*.

Oldcastle is Prince Henry's boon companion in *The Famous Victories of Henry V*, the source-play of *Henry IV*, in the original version of which Shakespeare retained the name. It was probably owing to protests, either by William, 7th Lord Cobham (d. 1597), or Henry 8th Lord, that Shakespeare changed the name to Falstaff before the registration of Q1 *1 Henry IV* in February 1598. Traces of the original name are found in *1 Henry IV*, I, ii, 'my old lad of the castle'; in *2 Henry IV*, I, ii, where *Old.* appears as a speech-prefix in Q; in the Epilogue, 'for Oldcastle died a martyr', and in III, ii Falstaff is said to have been 'page to Thomas Mowbray', which was true of Oldcastle. The play *Sir John Oldcastle* (q.v.), 1599, was attributed to Shakespeare by William Jaggard in 1619. (See FULLER; COBHAM; PARSONS.)

'Oldcastle.' In a letter of 6 March 1600, Rowland Whyte says that 'Sir John Old Castell' was played by the Chamberlain's Men. This was presumably *Henry IV, 1* or *2*, as *Sir John Oldcastle* was an Admiral's play. On 29 May 1639 'ould Castel' was apparently acted at Court by the King's; presumably *Henry IV*.

Old Lady. In *Henry VIII*, the delightful minor character who talks Shakespearean bawdy to Anne Bullen in II, iii, and when in V, i the King asks her if Anne is delivered of a boy is so agitated that she replies:

> Ay, ay, my liege;
> And of a lovely boy: the God of heaven
> Both now and ever bless her! 't is a girl,
> Promises boys hereafter.

Old Stratford. An agricultural area to the north of the borough, and part of the original manor of Stratford, which was held, 1562–90, by Ambrose Dudley, Earl of Warwick, and *c.* 1591–1610 by the Grevilles of Milcote. The freehold estate bought by Shakespeare 1 May 1602 was in the open fields of Old Stratford:

> This Indenture made the firste daie of Maye ... Betweene William Combe of Warrwicke .... Esquier, and John Combe of Olde Stretford ... gentleman, on the one partie, And William Shakespere of Stretford vppon Avon ... gentleman, on thother partye, Witnesseth that the saide William Combe and John Combe, for and in consideracion of the somme of three hundred and twentie poundes ... have ... solde ... vnto the saide William Shakespere, All and singuler those errable landes, with thappertenaunces, conteyninge by estymacion fowre yarde lande of errable lande, scytuate ... within the parrishe, feildes or towne of Olde Stretford ... conteyninge by estimacion one hundred and seaven acres ... And also all the common of pasture for sheepe, horse, kyne or other cattle in the feildes of Olde Stretford ... And also all hades, leys, tyinges, proffittes, advantages and commodities whatsoeuer ... And the reuercion and reuercions of all and singuler the same bargayned premisses ... nowe or late in the seuerall tenures or occupacions of Thomas Hiccoxe and Lewes Hiccoxe ...
>
> Sealed and deliuered to Gilbert Shakespere, to the vse of the within named William

Shakespere, in the presence of Anthony Nasshe, William Sheldon, Humfrey Maynwaringe, Rychard Mason, Jhon Nashe.

The 'hades, leys, tyinges' may be the 'viginti acris pasture' mentioned with the 'centum et septum acris terre' in a fine of 1610, or the twenty acres of pasture may have been a new purchase.

In 1605 Shakespeare bought half a leasehold interest in a parcel of the corn and hay tithes (q.v.) in Old Stratford, Welcombe and Bishopton. That the proposed Welcombe enclosure (q.v.) of 1614 would not have affected his Old Stratford estate is clear from a survey of 5 September 1614 of the 'Auncient ffreeholders in the ffieldes of Oldstratford and Welcombe':

> Mr Shakspeare. 4, yard Land, noe common nor ground beyond gospell bushe, noe grownd in Sandfield, nor none in slowe hill field beyond Bishopton nor none in the enclosure beyond Bishopton.

However, Shakespeare secured himself against a fall in the value of his tithes by an agreement with William Replingham, one of the promoters of the scheme.

Old Vic. A theatre in the Waterloo Road, South London, opened in 1818 as the Royal Coburg, and renamed the Royal Victoria Hall in 1833. It was a low-class popular playhouse and music-hall until taken over in 1880 by the social worker Emma Cons, who converted it into a temperance hall, The Royal Victoria Coffee Music Hall, and provided lectures and concerts. In 1898 she was joined by her niece, Lilian Baylis (q.v.), who added concert performances of opera, and then opera in costume, until the Old Vic Opera Company was giving three performances a week.

At the beginning of the 1914–18 war, when Ben Greet joined her with his company, she 'turned in despair to Shakespeare' to fill the theatre. During the war, Sybil Thorndike played men's parts, in 1920 Robert Atkins became producer, and by 1923 every play of Shakespeare had been performed at the Old Vic, the first theatre to achieve this record. Then came the actors and actresses from the West End theatres to join the company for a season: Edith Evans, John Gielgud, Donald Wolfit, Ralph Richardson, Laurence Olivier, Peggy Ashcroft and others, to play in productions under the direction of Robert Atkins (1919–25), Harcourt Williams (1929–33), and Tyrone Guthrie (1933–4, 1936–45). In 1931 the Sadler's Wells theatre was reopened under the management of Lilian Baylis who, when she died in 1937, had made her two theatres into the National Homes of Shakespeare and Opera in English.

On her death, Tyrone Guthrie took over the direction, but in 1940 a bomb wrecked the Old Vic and for four years the Drama, Opera and Ballet companies were based at the Victoria Theatre, Burnley. In 1944 the Drama company returned to London, to the New Theatre, where, under the direction of Laurence Olivier, Ralph Richardson and John Burrell it went from triumph to triumph.

In 1950 the Old Vic was reopened with Hugh Hunt as Director. Michael Benthall succeeded him in 1953, and in the next five seasons the 36 plays of the Folio were produced, the last being *Henry VIII* with Edith Evans and John Gielgud as Katharine and Wolsey. In 1962 Michael Elliott was appointed Director, and the Government announced plans for a National Theatre, which would absorb, though not be formed from, the Old Vic organization. The last performance by the Old Vic Company was *Measure for Measure* on 15 June 1963. Until the National Theatre is built, the Old Vic will be the headquarters of the new company.

Old Vic companies have travelled all over the world, and the Old Vic is responsible for the Theatre Royal at Bristol, where the Bristol Old Vic Company presents seasons of plays, and a School of Acting is maintained. (See E. J. Dent, *A Theatre for Everybody*, 1945.)

Oldys, William (1696–1761), antiquary, was the illegitimate son of the Chancellor of Lincoln. He lost money in the South Sea Bubble, and 1724–30 lived mainly at Wentworth Woodhouse in Yorkshire with the Earl of Malton. On his return to London he sold his collection of books to Edward Harley, 2nd Earl of Oxford, who in 1738 appointed him his literary secretary. After Oxford's death in 1741 his library was sold to the bookseller Thomas Osborne, who employed Oldys and Dr Johnson in compiling the *Harleian Miscellany*. In 1751 Oldys was imprisoned for debt in the Fleet, whence he was rescued two years later by the Duke of Norfolk who, in 1755, appointed him Norroy King-at-Arms.

Oldys wrote a number of *Lives*, including those of Ralegh, Cotton, Edward Alleyn and Sir John Fastolf, and used to make notes for his biographies in the margins of books. According to him, before he left London in 1724 he had annotated a copy of Langbaine's *Dramatick Poets* (1691), which was sold during his absence to the bookseller, Thomas Coxeter, from whom it passed to Theophilus Cibber, who used it for his *Lives of the Poets*. Oldys annotated a second copy of *Langbaine*, now in the British Museum, and this contains a few notes on Shakespeare, though of no great value.

Oldys also professed to have written a *Life of Shakespeare*, now lost, but apparently used by Steevens in his edition of *Shakespeare*, 1778. In this, after the customary reproduction of Rowe's *Life*, Steevens prints *Additional Anecdotes* derived from Oldys, who 'had covered several quires of paper with laborious collections for a regular life of our author'. These few anecdotes include Pope's version of D'Avenant's being the natural son of Shakespeare; that of one of Shakespeare's younger brothers seeing him act, apparently the part of Adam in *As You Like It*; the first stanza of the 'bitter ballad' against Sir Thomas Lucy (q.v.); and a Jonson-Shakespeare story:

Verses by Ben Jonson and Shakespeare, occasioned by the motto to the Globe Theatre – *Totus mundus agit histrionem.*

Jonson.

If, but *stage actors*, all the world displays,
Where shall we find *spectators* of their plays?

Shakespeare.

Little, or much, of what we see, we do;
We are all both *actors* and *spectators* too.

Steevens introduces the *Additional Anecdotes* without much conviction: 'The following particulars, which I shall give in the words of Oldys, are, for aught we know to the contrary, as well authenticated as any of the anecdotes delivered down to us by Rowe.'

Oliver. In *As You Like It*, eldest son of the dead Sir Rowland de Boys. He ill-treats his brother Orlando, who hears that he is planning to kill him and runs away. Oliver follows him into the forest, where Orlando saves him from a snake and a lioness. He repents, promises his estate to Orlando, and marries Celia. (Called Saladyne in Lodge's *Rosalynde*.)

Olivia. In *Twelfth Night*, a young and wealthy Illyrian lady. Unable to return the Duke's love, she falls in love with Viola, who is disguised as the Duke's page. She mistakes Sebastian, Viola's twin brother, for Viola herself, and is betrothed to him. (Called Julina in Rich's *Apolonius and Silla*.)

Olivier, Laurence (b. 1907), made his first stage appearance in a boys' performance of *The Taming of the Shrew* at Stratford in 1922. He was with the Birmingham Repertory Company 1926–8, and in 1935 played both Romeo and Mercutio in John Gielgud's production. In 1937–8, at the Old Vic, he played Hamlet, Sir Toby Belch, Henry V, Macbeth, Iago and Coriolanus, in 1937 Hamlet at Elsinore, and in 1940 Romeo in New York. He was engaged with film work 1940–3, in 1944 became a co-director of the Old Vic Company, with whom he played Hotspur and Lear in 1945–6, and was knighted in 1947. At Stratford in 1955 he played Macbeth, Malvolio and Titus Andronicus, in 1959

Coriolanus. In 1962 appointed Director of the National Theatre. He has produced, directed and played the lead in the films of *Henry V*, *Hamlet* and *Richard III*.

O'Neill, Eliza (1791–1872), Irish actress, made her first stage appearance in 1811, and won fame as Juliet at Covent Garden in 1814. For the next five years she was talked of as the successor of Mrs Siddons, but in 1819 she married an Irish baronet and abandoned her career.

Onions, Charles Talbut (1873–1965), Fellow of Magdalen, Oxford, and Reader in English Philology 1927–49. He was joint editor of the *Oxford English Dictionary*, 1914–33, finished editing *Shakespeare's England*, 1916, in succession to Sir Sidney Lee, and in 1911 published *A Shakespeare Glossary*.

Onomatopoeia. The formation of a word in imitation of an action or sound, as *stumble*, *splash*. The device may be extended to the phrase:

The armourers, accomplishing the knights,
With busy hammers, closing rivets up.

And more subtly, word and phrase may suggest a mood or an emotion:

Even so my sun one early morn did shine
With all-triumphant splendour on my brow.

Nought's had, all's spent,
Where our desire is got without content.

It is probable that most of our words are onomatopoeic in origin, and certain words and combinations of words must have an elemental significance of which we are not consciously aware. Perhaps part of the secret of Shakespeare's poetry is the employment of this unconscious imagery.

Open Air Theatre, founded by Sydney Carroll in 1933; an enclosure in Regent's Park, London, for the summer production of plays by Shakespeare and others.

Opera. A drama in which all or most of the words are set to music, whereas in a play the music, if any, is incidental. The essential element in opera is recitative: narrative or dialogue sung to a musical accompaniment that approximates to the rhythms of speech; the aria is a more lyrical expression in song. The first regular operas are generally considered to be the lost *Daphne* (1597) and the *Eurydice* (1600) of the Italian Jacopo Peri, one of the earliest composers of recitative. In England the masque tended to develop into opera; Nicholas Lanier composed recitative for a masque as early as 1617, and Shirley's *Cupid and Death* (1653), with music by Matthew Locke and Christopher Gibbons, is on the border between the two forms. But the first real English opera was *The Siege of Rhodes* (1656) with libretto by D'Avenant, who had seen Italian opera in Paris, and music by M. Locke, H. Lawes, H. Cooke, C. Coleman and G. Hudson. This was produced during the interregnum while regular plays were forbidden. Purcell's 'grand opera' *Dido and Aeneas* was produced about 1689. With the arrival of Handel in England in 1711, the Italian form of opera was established as a fashionable form of entertainment. Shakespeare's use of music is dramatic, never operatic.

Among composers who have made operas of Shakespeare's plays are Nicolai, Gounod, Götz, Verdi, Saint-Saëns, Britten. (See REYNOLDS, FREDERIC.)

Ophelia. The heroine of *Hamlet*, and daughter of Polonius. She loves Hamlet, but at her father's order repulses his advances, and thinks her action is the cause of his apparent madness. When her lover kills her father, she goes mad and drowns herself.

Orchestra. From the Greek, 'to dance'. In the Greek theatre, the circular space in front of the stage; in the centre of the circle was an altar to Dionysus, about which the chorus danced. The orchestra of the Roman theatre no longer had any religious significance, and was a semicircle about which were ranged seats for the senators. In his drawing of the Elizabethan Swan theatre, De Witt labels the lowest gallery 'orchestra', probably because it suggested Roman seating arrangements: 'It appears to resemble a Roman building,' he wrote. The musicians took up their position in front of the stage, where the classical orchestra had been, about the end of the 17th century, when the apron stage had begun to retreat, though as early as 1667 there was an experiment at the Lincoln's Inn Fields theatre, where the D'Avenant-Dryden version of *The Tempest* was produced; cf. the first stage-direction:

> The front of the stage is opened, and the band of twenty-four violins with the harpsicals and theorbos, which accompany the voices, are placed between the pit and the stage.

Organ. Small portable organs were used in private houses, and sometimes in the theatre, at least in the Blackfriars. When the Duke of Stettin-Pomerania (q.v.) visited that theatre, in September 1602, he heard for a whole hour before the play 'eine köstliche musicam instrumentalem von Orgeln, Lauten, Pandoren, Mandoren, Geigen und Pfeiffen' as well as a boy singing. And an organ is mentioned with other instruments in Marston's *Sophonisba* (1606), a Blackfriars play.

'Original.' On the title-page of the Folio we are assured that Shakespeare's plays are 'Published according to the True Originall Copies', a claim that is repeated in the head-title above the list of actors, 'Truely set forth, according to their first Originall'. This has led to much misunderstanding. It does not mean that they were necessarily printed from Shakespeare's manuscripts (though many of them were) but from authoritative texts that represented the plays as acted in the theatre. In medieval times 'original' seems to have meant the authoritative copy of a play. When Humphrey Moseley published the Beaumont and Fletcher Folio of 1647 he made a similar claim to Jaggard's (or Heminge's and Condell's): 'now you have both All that was Acted, and all that was not; even the perfect full Originalls without the least mutilation'. But we know that the copy from which he printed had often undergone some stage adaptation. (See TRANSCRIPTS.)

Original Accounts. See CHAMBER ACCOUNTS.

Orlando. The hero of *As You Like It*, the Rosader of Lodge's *Rosalynde*.

'Orlando Furioso.' A play by Robert Greene, written about 1591, registered 7 December 1593 and printed by John Danter for Cuthbert Burby in 1594 as 'The Historie of Orlando Furioso One of the twelve Pieres of France. As it was plaid before the Queenes Maiestie'. *Orlando Furioso* is important as the only Elizabethan play for which an actor's part has survived, that of Orlando as played by Edward Alleyn. (See PARTS.)

Orleans, Bastard of. In *1 Henry VI*, John Dunois, illegitimate son of Louis, Duke of Orleans, introduces the Dauphin to Joan of Arc, in whose powers he believes.

Orleans, Charles, Duke of (1391–1465). In *Henry V*, friend and cousin of the Dauphin. Before Agincourt he boasts that a hundred Englishmen will soon be his prisoners, but he himself is captured in the battle.

Orrery, Roger Boyle, 1st Earl of (1621–79), the soldier and statesman who contrived to be in favour both with Cromwell and Charles II, was also a dramatist. His *Henry V* (1664), a 'noble play' seen by Pepys, is original and not based on Shakespeare. On 19 October 1667 Pepys saw the first performance of his *Black Prince*, the wit of which was similar to that of *Henry V* and *Mustapha*, but the play was spoiled by the reading of a long and unnecessary letter by the actor, Charles Hart (q.v.).

Orsino. In *Twelfth Night*, Duke of Illyria. (The Apolonius of Riche's *Apolonius and Silla*. See BRACCIANO.)

Osric. In *Hamlet*, an affected courtier, 'spacious in the possession of dirt', who tells Hamlet of the King's wager on the proposed fencing-match with Laertes. He presides at the match, and to him the dying Laertes confesses his treachery. (In the original story Osric is Amleth's foster-brother.)

Ostler, William (d. 1614). One of the 'Principall Actors' in Shakespeare's plays (see p. 90). With Field and Underwood he was a boy actor with the Children of the Chapel, and with them played in Jonson's *Poetaster* (1601). According to Cuthbert Burbage, 'in processe of time the boyes growing vp to bee men, which were Vnderwood, Field, Ostler', they 'were taken to strengthen the Kings service'. It was probably in 1608, after the deaths of Sly and Fletcher, that Ostler and Underwood joined the King's Men, for whom Ostler is first mentioned as playing in *The Alchemist* in 1610. He played Antonio in *The Duchess of Malfi*, and was in the casts of *The Captain*, *Valentinian* and *Bonduca*. John Davies had a high opinion of his acting, calling him 'the Roscius of these Times' in his *Scourge of Folly* (1611). In 1611 he married Thomasine, daughter of John Heminge, and in the following year his son Beaumont was born. At this time he became a housekeeper in the Blackfriars and Globe theatres, but died – a young man – intestate 16 December 1614. His theatre shares, which should have gone to Thomasine, were claimed by her father who, in spite of her suits brought against him, seems to have succeeded in keeping them. (See WALLACE.)

Oswald. In *King Lear*, Goneril's steward. For insulting Lear, Kent trips him up and then, when he finds him alone, beats him soundly. He is carrying a love-letter from Goneril to Edmund when he meets the blind Gloucester, whom he tries to kill, but is himself killed by the disguised Edgar.

'OTHELLO.'

WRITTEN: 1602–3. See 'HONEST WHORE'. There are borrowings from *Othello* in the 'bad' Q1 of *Hamlet*, 1603.

PERFORMED: 1604. 'By the Kings Maiesties plaiers. Hallamas Day being the first of Nouembar A Play in the Banketinge house att WhitHall Called The Moor of Venis.' (*Revels Account*.)

1610, April. 'Lundi, 30. S.E. [Prince Frederick of Württemberg, formerly Count of Mömpelgart] alla au Globe, lieu ordinaire ou l'on joue les Commedies, y fut representé l'histoire du More de Venise.'

1612–13. 'The Moore of Venice' was one of the twenty plays given by the King's Men at the Revels preceding the marriage of the Lady Elizabeth.

1629. 'The benefitt of the winters day from the kinges company being brought me [Sir Henry Herbert, Master of the Revels] ... upon the play of The Moor of Venise, comes, this 22 of Nov. 1629, unto 9^l. 16^s. 0^d.'

1635. 'Maij 6: not farre from home all day att ye bla: ffryers & a play y^{is} day called ye More of Venice.' (*Diary* of Sir Humphrey Mildmay.)

1636. 'The 8th of December at Hampton Court, the Moore of Venice.'

REGISTERED: '6° Octobris, 1621. Thomas Walkley. Entred for his copie vnder the handes of Sir George Buck, and Master Swinhoe warden. The Tragedie of Othello, the moore of Venice. vj^d.' Transferred 1628 to R. Hawkins, 1638 to Mead and Meredith, 1639 to W. Leake.

PUBLISHED: 1622, Q1. 'The Tragœdy of Othello, The Moore of Venice. As it hath beene diuerse times acted at the Globe, and at the Black-Friers, by his Maiesties Seruants. Written by William Shakespeare. London, Printed by N.O. for Thomas Walkley, and are to be sold at his shop, at the Eagle and Child, in Brittans Bursse. 1622.' The only Shakespeare Q divided into Acts. A good text, for Greg, set from a private transcript of foul papers; for Alice Walker, from a careless transcript of prompt-book. (See WALKLEY.)

1623, F1. 'The Tragedie of Othello, the Moore of Venice.' The tenth play in the

Tragedy section: pp. 310–39. Acts and scenes marked. 'The Names of the Actors' given at the end. A good text, set from Q collated with prompt-book, or (for A. Walker) with an authoritative MS.

1630, Q2. Set up from Q1, with reference to F.

1655, Q3. Later Qq in 1681, 1687, 1695, 1705.

SOURCE: A *novella* in Giraldi Cinthio's *Hecatommithi* (1565), though the story differs in detail from Shakespeare's. 'Disdemona' is the only character named; the Ensign loves her, and kills her, and the Moor is killed by her relations. Shakespeare seems to have read Cinthio's Italian, as no other contemporary version is known.

STAGE HISTORY: 1660. 'To the Cockpit to see "The Moor of Venice", which was well done. Burt acted the Moor: by the same token, a very pretty lady that sat by me called out, to see Desdemona smothered.' (Pepys 11 October.)

1660, 8 December. Killigrew's Vere Street production with Margaret Hughes as Desdemona: probably the first appearance of an actress on the public stage.

Othello was one of the few plays to escape 'improvement', and has always been steadily performed. It is very popular in the U.S.S.R.

Desdemona, daughter of Brabantio, a Venetian senator, falls in love with and secretly marries the Moor Othello, a general in the service of the Venetian republic. While he is explaining his conduct to the Duke and Senate, news arrives of a threatened Turkish attack on Cyprus, which Othello is sent to defend, Desdemona being allowed to follow him.

With Othello goes Iago, his ensign, who is jealous of Cassio because he has been promoted lieutenant. In revenge he makes Cassio drunk while he is on duty, and so secures his disgrace. He then persuades him to ask Desdemona to intercede for him with Othello, and at the same time warns Othello that he suspects Cassio of being Desdemona's lover, finally convincing him of her infidelity by contriving that Cassio shall find and display a handkerchief given to her by Othello.

Othello, now sure of Desdemona's guilt, smothers her in bed, while Iago persuades his dupe Roderigo to murder Cassio; but Roderigo fails and is himself killed by Iago lest he should betray him. Emilia, Iago's wife and Desdemona's gentlewoman, discovers the murdered Desdemona and proves her innocence to Othello before Iago silences her by stabbing her. Meanwhile incriminating letters have been found on Roderigo, and Iago is arrested. Othello is also arrested and disarmed, but he finds a sword, and after an attempt to kill Iago, stabs himself.

Ottewell, George. An actor with Strange's, 1590–91. The Chamber Accounts record payments for plays and 'for other feates of Activitye', performed 27 December 1590 and 16 February 1591, to 'George Ottewell and his company the Lorde Straunge his players'. But the Privy Council Register notes a warrant for plays and activities on these days by the Admiral's. It seems, therefore, that there was some sort of alliance between Strange's and the Admiral's as early as 1590. Little more is known of Ottewell, or Attewell, though he may have been with the Queen's in 1595.

Otway, Thomas (1652–85), dramatist, was born at Trotton in Sussex and educated at Westminster and Christ Church, Oxford. He made one attempt to be an actor, but had an attack of stage fright. Betterton produced his first play, *Alcibiades*, in 1675, the part of Draxilla being played by Mrs Barry with whom Otway became infatuated, and as she did not return his passion, he enlisted in the army in Holland, returning in rags the following year (1678–9). His three great tragedies are *Don Carlos* (1676), *The Orphan* (1680), and *Venice Preserved* (1682), the first in rhyme, the others in blank verse. His *History and Fall of Caius Marius* (1679) is a blend of Shakespeare's *Romeo and Juliet* and Plutarch's *Life of Marius*. The lovers are Young Marius and Lavinia, the latter part being played by Mrs Barry; Betterton was the elder Marius, and James Nokes the Nurse. The version was popular and lasted until Theophilus Cibber's adaptation of *Romeo and Juliet* in 1744. Otway died in great poverty when he was only 33.

Overdone, Mistress. In *Measure for Measure*, 'a bawd of eleven years continuance'. She deplores the ruin of her trade by the strict enforcement of the Viennese laws against immorality, and in III, ii is sent to prison.

Overy, Edward. One of the witnesses of Shakespeare's purchase and mortgage of the Blackfriars Gatehouse, 10–11 March 1613. He was the son of a tanner, was apprenticed to William Hickes, scrivener and merchant, and died a wealthy man in 1621, leaving his 'kind friend' John Jackson, Shakespeare's trustee, £5 and a ring for his wife.

Ovid (43 B.C.–A.D. 17). Publius Ovidius Naso was born at Sulmo and studied law at Rome and Athens, but his real love was poetry. He settled at Rome, where he lived fashionably, was honoured as a poet, married three times, and had one daughter. He was patronized by Augustus who, however, in A.D. 8, suddenly banished him to Tomi among the Goths (see *A.Y.L.I.*, III, iii) on the Black Sea, for being involved in a scandal affecting the imperial family. In spite of his appeal to and flattery of Augustus and his successor, Tiberius, Ovid lived the rest of his life at Tomi, where he was buried. His works include the *Amores*, *Ars Amatoria*, *Heroides*, *Fasti*, *Tristi* and the *Metamorphoses*, the last a narrative poem in fifteen books, written in hexameters, and describing the miraculous transformations of Greek and Roman mythology.

Shakespeare was well acquainted with Ovid, his favourite Latin poet, whom he must have read at school, particularly the *Metamorphoses*, which had been translated by Arthur Golding (q.v.) in 1567. The story of *Venus and Adonis* he took from the *Metamorphoses*, either Ovid's Latin or Golding's English, or probably both, and he quotes a couplet from the *Amores* on the title-page. *Lucrece* comes from the *Fasti*, of which there was no direct translation, though there were English and French versions of the story. There are numerous references to and quotations from Ovid in the plays, particularly in the early ones, and Meres compares the honey-tongued Shakespeare to the sweet and witty Ovid. A copy of the *Metamorphoses* in the Bodleian is signed 'W^m^ Sh^r^' on the title-page. (See HALL, W.)

Oxford, Earl of. In *3 Henry VI*, John de Vere, 13th Earl of Oxford (1443–1513), whose father and elder brother had been executed by Edward IV, supports Margaret and the Lancastrian cause. After Barnet he joins Margaret at Tewkesbury, where he is captured. In *Richard III* he joins Richmond and fights at Bosworth, but speaks only two lines (v, ii).

Oxford, Edward de Vere, 17th Earl of (1550–1604), succeeded to the title and the hereditary office of Lord Great Chamberlain on his father's death in 1562. He was educated at Cambridge, and brought up in the household of Lord Burghley, where Arthur Golding, translator of Ovid, was his tutor. In 1571 he married Anne, daughter of Lord Burghley, by whom he had three daughters. He became one of Elizabeth's favourite courtiers though he longed for a more active life, and incurred her displeasure by serving in Flanders without her consent, by fighting a duel with Thomas Knyvet, one of her gentlemen, and by quarrelling with Sir Philip Sidney, an episode that led to Sidney's disgrace. His first wife died in 1588, but he partly restored his dissipated fortunes by his marriage with Elizabeth Trentham, who bore him a son.

Oxford was a patron of poets, himself wrote verses, and was, according to Meres, one of 'the best for comedy amongst us', though none of his plays has survived. In 1920 J. T. Looney split yet again the anti-Stratfordian ranks by discovering in Oxford the real author of the poems and plays attributed to Shakespeare.

Oxford's Men. John de Vere, 16th Earl of Oxford, had a company of players traceable in the provinces from 1547 to his death in 1562. Until 1580 there are no further records, but in that year Warwick's Men forsook their old patron and became followers of Edward de Vere, 17th Earl. The company was weakened when two of its leading members, John and Laurence Dutton, joined the newly formed Queen's company. In 1584 'the Erle of Oxforde his servauntes' played for the first time at Court, their payee for performances on 1 January and 3 March being John Lyly, who was a follower of Oxford. These performances, however, may have been given by a boys' company in Oxford's service, for in the following December, Henry Evans, who was working with Lyly at the Blackfriars, where the Chapel and Paul's children performed, was payee for a Court performance of *Agamemnon and Ulysses* 'by the Earle of Oxenford his boyes'. A few days later, 1 January 1585, yet another company appears, when 'John Symons and other his fellowes Servantes to Therle of Oxforde' performed 'feates of actiuitye and vawtinge'. In January 1587 Oxford's were playing in London, and in 1602 were licensed to play with Worcester's 'togeather in one Companie' at the Boar's Head Inn. Oxford died in 1604, and his company was merged in Worcester's, after 1603 Queen Anne's Men.

Oxford New English Dictionary. A dictionary compiled 'on historical principles, founded mainly on materials collected by the Philological Society'. It includes all words that were current in 1150, and those that have since been added to the language, their forms and meanings being illustrated by quotation; in 1888, when the preface to the first volume was written, 1,300 readers had collected 3,500,000 quotations from 5,000 authors. The scheme originated in 1857 in a resolution passed by the Philological Society at the suggestion of R. C. Trench; the first editors were Herbert Coleridge (d. 1861) and F. J. Furnivall, then, from 1878 to his death in 1915, J. A. H. Murray was editor. It was planned to be completed in ten volumes, issued in parts, the first of which was issued in 1884; the first volume appeared in 1888, and the work was completed in 1928. It contains 414,825 words, the history of which is illustrated by 1,827,306 quotations. The completion of the dictionary has been a great aid to Shakespeare scholars.

Oxford University, like Cambridge, did not play directly a large part in the development of the popular Elizabethan drama, though the study and performance of classical and neo-classical plays in the earlier part of the 16th century gave form and structure to the native growth, and the universities produced many of the men who wrote the plays for the London theatres. The authors of the first regular English comedy and tragedy were university men: Nicholas Udall was at Oxford, Thomas Norton at Cambridge, and Thomas Sackville at both Oxford and Cambridge; of the University Wits who in the 1580s made such startling advances in the drama, Lyly, Peele, and Lodge were Oxford men, and Greene added an Oxford degree to his Cambridge M.A.; of Shakespeare's other contemporaries, Marston, Beaumont, and Massinger were at Oxford, and Chapman may have been at both universities. Shakespeare must have known Oxford well, as it lies half-way between Stratford and London.

The university plays were largely academic; some of them were seen by Elizabeth in Christ Church Hall on her visits in 1566 and 1592; there, too, three Latin plays and one English were performed when James I visited the town in 1605. The best-known Oxford author of academic plays is William Gager of Christ Church, who was bitterly attacked by the puritanical John Rainolds, Master of Corpus Christi. (See ACADEMIC DRAMA; D'AVENANT; BODLEIAN; WOOD, ANTHONY À; VOLPONE.)

P

Page. 1. Anne. In *The Merry Wives*, her father wants her to marry Slender, her mother Dr Caius, but she runs away with Fenton and is forgiven by her indulgent parents.

2. Master Page, father of Anne and William, called Thomas in I, i, but George in II, i and V, v. When Nym tells him that Falstaff is making love to his wife, he trusts her, and advises Ford to trust his wife.

3. Mistress Page, one of the merry wives, takes a prominent part in the fooling of Falstaff, and devises the plan of baiting him in Windsor Forest. Her husband calls her Meg (II, i).

4. William, the young brother of Anne. Parson Evans tests his Latin grammar in IV, i, a scene first printed in F.

Page to Falstaff. In *2 Henry IV*, a diminutive boy put into Falstaff's service by the Prince of Wales 'to set him off'. In *Henry V*, after the death of Falstaff, he serves as boy to the three 'swashers' and 'antics', Bardolph, Pistol and Nym, on the Agincourt campaign, in which he is killed by the French while helping to guard the 'luggage'. Presumably he is the Robin (q.v.) of *The Merry Wives*.

Pageants. In the Middle Ages the name given to the cars on which the Miracle plays were performed; in Tudor times applied to tableaux and entertainments of varying degrees of elaboration, generally given out of doors. They were inseparable from the royal progresses when the sovereign paid midsummer visits to the houses of the nobility, as when Elizabeth was entertained by Leicester at Kenilworth (q.v.) in 1575, and by the Earl of Hertford at Elvetham (q.v.) in 1591, where there were fireworks, fairies and water-pageants. Towns, too, greeted the sovereign on progress with a pageant, the gildsmen sometimes exhibiting scenes or tableaux from their traditional plays, as at Coventry in 1566 and at Wells in 1613. London had its own pageants, particularly those at the installation of the Lord Mayor on 29 October; and there were water-pageants on special occasions: for example, when Prince Henry was created Prince of Wales in 1610, 'London's Love' was demonstrated by 'meeting him on the River of Thames ... with a worthie fleete of her Cittizens'. In a device by Anthony Munday, Richard Burbage and John Rice of the King's Men, the one as Amphion representing Wales, the other as Corinea representing Cornwall, rode on the backs of fishes and delivered the speeches of welcome. Some of the ablest poets and dramatists were employed in devising these City pageants: Peele, Munday, Dekker, Jonson and Middleton.

Painter, William (*c.* 1540–94), was a Kentish man, educated at St John's, Cambridge. In 1561 he was appointed clerk of the ordnance in the Tower of London, a position that he held until his death, in spite of acknowledged charges of peculation. He is remembered as the compiler of *The Palace of Pleasure*, an anthology of 'pleasant histories and excellent novels', translations mostly from classical and Italian authors, including Plutarch, Livy, Boccaccio, Bandello and Cinthio. The first volume of 1566 contained sixty stories, that of 1567 added thirty-four more, and the second edition of 1575 another seven. The book was a storehouse for the Elizabethan dramatists, and partly accounts for the Italian themes of so many of their plays. Shakespeare took from it Boccaccio's story of *Giglietta di Nerbone* for his *All's Well*, and probably used it for *Romeo and Juliet* and *Timon of Athens*.

Paired Words. In his middle period Shakespeare's imagery often takes the form of two nouns qualified by an adjectival phrase, one of the nouns being typically Latin, abstract, polysyllabic and general, the other Saxon, concrete, monosyllabic and particular, as in *accident and flood of fortune*, *catastrophe and* *heel of pastime*. This device is extended to the more general pairing of words, until in *Hamlet* it becomes almost a mannerism:

The *expectancy and rose of the fair state*,
The *glass of fashion and the mould of form*,
The observ'd of all observers, quite, quite
  down!
And I, of ladies most *deject and wretched*,
That suck'd the honey of his music vows,
Now see that *noble and most sovereign reason*,
Like sweet bells jangled, *out of tune and
  harsh;*
That unmatch'd *form and feature of blown
  youth*
Blasted with ecstasy.

After *Hamlet* the device becomes less frequent, though there are many pairs in what may be the next play, *Troilus and Cressida*, and it gives to *Hamlet* a peculiar emphasis and distinction of style.

Palaces. The principal palaces of Elizabeth, where plays were performed, were Whitehall, Hampton Court, Greenwich, Richmond and Windsor. James I gave Richmond to Henry, Prince of Wales, and Greenwich to Queen Anne, so that the chief residences of James and the Court were Whitehall, Hampton Court and Windsor. (See I. Dunlop, *Palaces and Progresses of Queen Elizabeth*, 1962.)

Palamon. In *The Two Noble Kinsmen*, cousin, friend and rival of Arcite for the love of Emily, whom he eventually marries.

'Palamon and Arcite.' A lost academic play in two parts, performed before Elizabeth in Christ Church Hall on 2 and 4 September, when she visited Oxford in 1566. On the first night a wall near the entrance fell and killed three people, but the disaster did not interfere with the performance. The play is said to have been by Richard Edwardes (q.v.), who Englished it from a Latin version of Chaucer's *Knight's Tale*, and was congratulated by the Queen. It does not seem to have been a source of *The Two Noble Kinsmen*. (See QUEEN'S ARCADIA.)

Palladio, Andrea (1518–80), was born in Vicenza. He studied architecture in Rome, his text-books being the *De Architectura* of Vitruvius, the Roman architect of the 1st century B.C., and the *De Re Aedificatoria* of Alberti (1404–72). His own *I Quattro Libri dell'Architettura* (1570) greatly influenced European architects, in England particularly Inigo Jones, who published an edition with notes. Palladio designed many fine buildings in Rome and Venice and in his native Vicenza, where his last great work was the Teatro Olimpico, the erection of which was begun shortly before his death and completed in 1584 by his pupil Vincenzo Scamozzi.

The Teatro Olimpico is of the first importance, as it influenced theatrical design throughout Europe. It is based on the rules of Vitruvius for the construction of Roman theatres, similar to that at Orange; there is an orchestra, a long and narrow stage, and behind it the proscenium, a classical façade of three stories pierced in the centre by a large arch (the *porta regia* of Vitruvius), on either side of which are smaller doors. There is a door in the wall at each end of the stage, and above it two boxes, one above the other, which may have been used either by actors or spectators. Through the doors can be seen perspective streets of buildings which are supposed to converge on the court or square which is the stage. The theatre was designed, of course, for classical and neo-classical drama without change of scene – the first play to be acted there was the *Oedipus Tyrannus* of Sophocles in 1584 – and it seems improbable that it influenced the London theatres for which Shakespeare wrote.

'Palladis Tamia.' See MERES.

Pallant, Robert. An actor who played in *The Second Part of the Seven Deadly Sins*, performed probably by Strange's *c.* 1591. He was with Queen Anne's 1602–19. 'R. Pallant' played Cariola in the King's Men's revival of *The Duchess of Malfi* in 1619, but it is improbable that he is the actor in the *Deadly Sins* of thirty years before. Sons of Robert Pallant 'player' were baptized in 1611 and 1614, and Robert Pallant 'a man' was buried at St Saviour's on 4 September 1619.

Palmer, John (*c.* 1742–98), one of the best comedians of his age, and the original Joseph Surface in *The School for Scandal*. He excelled in secondary parts such as Mercutio, Jaques, Touchstone and Sir Toby Belch. He married the daughter of Hannah Pritchard.

Palsgrave. A Count Palatine; a title by which the Elector Palatine (q.v.) was sometimes known.

Pamphlets. Shakespeare lived in an age of popular pamphleteering. The pamphlet was a convenient vehicle of invective and unimportant enough to escape the licensing laws. The Jesuits and secular priests attacked each other in pamphlets. The puritans attacked the bishops, the bishops replied, and in the Martin Marprelate controversy (q.v.) called in the playwrights to their aid. Again, both playwrights and players were attacked by the puritans, and some of the playwrights attacked the players, Nashe for example, and Greene in his *Groatsworth of Wit*. Academic critics and popular writers carried on their literary squabbles in pamphlets, the Nashe-Harvey controversy covering the last decade of the 16th century. Towards the end of Elizabeth's reign, political pamphlets became more dangerous, and in 1599 the flood was checked by a tightening up of the licensing laws, but it continued to flow in the 17th century, the most notorious pamphlets being those of Prynne, who is credited with 160 of them.

Pandar. In *Pericles*, owner of the brothel in Mytilene to which Boult brings Marina, who almost ruins his trade by converting his clients.

Pandarus. In *Troilus and Cressida*, Cressida's uncle, who acts as go-between to the lovers. He brings Cressida the news that she is to be exchanged for Antenor. When Troilus discovers her infidelity, he turns on Pandarus with:

Hence, broker-lackey! ignomy and shame
Pursue thy life, and live aye with thy name!

(Chaucer first debased the Homeric hero to a 'pander'.)

'Pandosto.' A prose romance or novel by Robert Greene, published in 1588 as 'Pandosto, the Triumph of Time . . . Pleasant for age to avoyde drowsie thoughtes, profitable for youth to eschue other wanton pastimes'. In the edition of 1607 it is called *Dorastus and Fawnia*. The novel is the source of *The Winter's Tale*, though there are considerable differences. Pandosto (Leontes) falls in love with his daughter Fawnia (Perdita) and kills himself, and Bellaria (Hermione) really dies when she hears of her son's death. Shakespeare adds Paulina, Autolycus, Antigonus, and the Clown, reverses the kingdoms of Bohemia and Sicilia, and expands the sheep-shearing scene from a few lines by Greene. Alexander Hardy, the French playwright, dramatized the story, *c.* 1625, as *Pandoste*; the play is lost, but Laurent Mahelot's sketches for the settings survive, and are important examples of multiple setting (q.v.).

Pandulph. In *King John*, the papal legate who by excommunicating John forces the French King to break his newly-made alliance with England. After John's victory and capture of Arthur, Pandulph persuades the Dauphin to invade England, but when John acknowledges the supremacy of the Pope he vainly urges him to withdraw his forces. (In 1216 he became Bishop of Norwich, where he was buried in 1226.)

'Panecia.' A lost play. During the Court Revels of 1574–5, 'my Lord of Leicesters menne showed theier matter of Panecia'. It has been suggested that this entry in the Revels Accounts is an error for *Fenicia*. Fenicia is the heroine of the Bandello story that is the source of *Much Ado*, and corresponds to Shakespeare's Hero. It is just possible, therefore, that *Panecia* is an early dramatic form of the Hero-Claudio plot. (See ARIODANTE AND GENEVRA.)

Panthino. In *The Two Gentlemen of Verona*, servant of Antonio, to whom he suggests that Proteus, his son, should follow Valentine to the Emperor's court to be 'tutor'd in the world'.

'Papal Tyranny in the Reign of King John.' Colley Cibber's political adaptation of Shakespeare's *King John*, produced just before the 1745 Rebellion with Cibber himself as Pandulph, Quin as John, and Mrs Pritchard as Constance.

Parallel Texts. Of the 36 plays in the Folio, 18 have no Quarto. Of the other 18 there are 4 with 'bad' Quartos only. This leaves 14 good Quartos, and as they were used as copy for the Folio they have approximately parallel texts. They are:

Love's Labour's Lost
Romeo and Juliet
Much Ado
Midsummer Night's Dream
Merchant of Venice
1 Henry IV
2 Henry IV
Richard II
Hamlet
Othello
Troilus and Cressida
Richard III
King Lear
Titus Andronicus

The Q and F texts of the first two are almost identical; the others differ in varying degrees owing to reference to or collation with prompt-books or foul papers. (See Walker, *Textual Problems*.) The inexpert Compositor E of the Folio, incapable of dealing with MS copy, set *Titus*, *Romeo*, the beginning of *Troilus* and certain pages of *Hamlet*, *Lear*, and *Othello*. (See Hinman, *The Prentice Hand*.)

The *Bankside Shakespeare* (1886–1906) is a parallel text edition, giving Q and F texts. (See COPY.)

Paris Garden. The Liberty and Manor of Paris Garden formed the extreme western end of the Bankside; beyond it was Lambeth Marsh, and to the east the Liberty of the Clink. The Manor had been part of the dissolved monastery of Bermondsey, and in 1589 was bought from Thomas Cure by Francis Langley for £850. There Langley built his Swan Theatre about 1595, 150 yards due south of Paris Garden stairs. The origin of the name is obscure, but 'The Royal Game at Paris Garden' was the bear-baiting. This sport may have been held in Paris Garden until about 1540, but after that date shifted farther east, and in Norden's map of 1593 the Beare howse is shown near the Rose theatre in the Clink. It seems as though the name Paris Garden continued to be applied to the 'game' of bear-baiting, even after it had been transferred from its original site to that of Elizabeth's reign. In 1604 Henslowe and Alleyn became joint Masters of the Game at Paris Garden. (See BEAR GARDEN.)

'Parnassus.' A series of three plays: *The Pilgrimage to Parnassus*, *The Return from Parnassus*, Part 1, and *The Return from Parnassus*, Part 2, for convenience called *1, 2, 3 Parnassus*. The plays are in manuscript, but *3 Parnassus* was registered 16 October 1605, and published in 1606 as 'The Returne from Pernassus: Or The Scourge of Simony. Publiquely acted by the Students in Saint Iohns Colledge in Cambridge'. They are all Cambridge plays, and acted probably at the Christmases of 1598, 1599, 1601. The author is anonymous, but John Day has been suggested, and also William Dodd, a Fellow of John's from Cheshire, to which county there is a reference.

1 Parnassus describes allegorically the pilgrimage of the students Philomusus and Studioso to Parnassus, and their resistance of the temptations that beset them on their way.

In *2 Parnassus* the students return to London, picking up a living as best they can. In III, i the love-sick Gullio quotes the first two lines of *Venus and Adonis*, and, with slight variations, the whole of stanza two, then in IV, i exclaims:

> Let this duncified worlde esteeme of Spencer and Chaucer, I'le worshipp sweet Mr Shakspeare, and to honoure him will lay his Venus and Adonis under my pillowe.

3 Parnassus contains important references to Shakespeare, Jonson, and the Chamberlain's Men, Burbage and Kempe being introduced as characters. Iudicio asks in I, ii:

> Who loues not *Adons* loue, or *Lucrece* rape?
> His sweeter verse contaynes hart trobbing line,
> Could but a graver subiect him content,
> Without loues foolish lazy languishment.

In IV, iii Burbage gives Philomusus an audition:

> BUR. I like your face, and the proportion of your body for Richard the 3. I pray, M. *Phil*. let me see you act a little of it.
> PHIL. 'Now is the winter of our discontent, Made glorious summer by the sonne of York.'

And earlier in the scene Kempe observes:

> Few of the vniuersity men pen plaies well, they smell too much of that writer *Ouid*, and that writer *Metamorphosis*, and talke too much of *Proserpina & Iuppiter*. Why heres our fellow *Shakespeare* puts them all downe, I and *Ben Ionson* too. O that *Ben Ionson* is a pestilent fellow, he brought vp *Horace* giuing the Poets a pill, but our fellow *Shakespeare* hath giuen him a purge that made him beray his credit.

The reference is to 'the war of the theatres' or 'Poetomachia' (q.v.). In *The Poetaster* (1601), Horace (Jonson) gives Crispinus (Marston) pills to make him vomit his windy words. Dekker, also satirized in *The Poetaster*, replied in his *Satiromastix*, in which Jonson, as Horace, is untrussed. This is the obvious purge given to Jonson, but, though Marston probably had a hand in *Satiromastix*, it is improbable that Shakespeare had anything to do with it. It was acted by the Chamberlain's, and perhaps the author of *Parnassus* assumed that it was Shakespeare's, though it was published with Dekker's name in 1602, i.e. after the production of *3 Parnassus*, if Christmas 1601 is the right date. Jaques, Nym and Ajax have all been suggested as satirical portraits of Jonson, and the purge administered by Shakespeare.

The play ends with a curious echo of the attack on the players made a decade earlier by the University wits, Greene and Nashe, both of them John's men. The scholar poets refuse to work for the Chamberlain's:

> Better it is mongst fidlers to be chiefe,
> Then at a plaiers trencher beg reliefe.
> But ist not strange these mimick apes should prize
> Vnhappy schollers at a hireling rate.
> Vile world, that lifts them vp to hye degree,
> And treades vs downe in groueling misery.
> England affordes those glorious vagabonds,
> That carried earst their fardels on thier backes,
> Coursers to ride on through the gazing streetes,
> Sooping it in their glaring satten sutes,
> And pages to attend their maisterships:
> With mouthing words that better wits haue framed,
> They purchase lands, and now esquiers are namde.

The author must be thinking in particular of Alleyn or Shakespeare, or probably of both. (See *The Three Parnassus Plays*, ed. J. B. Leishman, 1949.)

Parolles. In *All's Well*, a follower of Bertram, whom he persuades to go to 'the Tuscan wars'. Everybody, except Bertram, knows him for a cowardly braggart, and even Bertram is convinced when Parolles is captured and blindfolded in a mock ambush, and eagerly gives his unseen companions information that would undo them.

Parsons, Robert (1546–1610), son of a blacksmith of Nether Stowey, the vicar of which secured his admission to Balliol College, where he became fellow and dean. In 1574 he resigned or was dismissed, and joined the Jesuit Society at Rome. In 1580 he and Campion were employed on a secret mission in England; Campion was captured, but Parsons escaped and became Rector of the English College at Rome. In his *Treatise of the Three Conversions of England: containing An Examen of the Calendar or Catalogue of Protestant Saints, by John Fox* (1603–4), he wrote:

> The second moneth of *February* is more fertile of rubricate Martyrs, than *Ianuary*, for that yt hath 8. in number, two Wickliffians, *Syr Iohn Oldcastle*, a Ruffian-knight as all England knoweth, & commonly brought in by comediants on their stages: he was put to death for robberyes and rebellion vnder the foresaid *K. Henry* the fifth.

This was answered in 1611 by the historian and cartographer John Speed, in his *History of Great Britain* (N.D., Nicholas Dolman, was a pseudonym of Parsons):

> That N.D. author of the three conuersions hath made *Ouldcastle* a Ruffian, a Robber, and a Rebell, and his authority taken from the *Stageplaiers*, is more befitting the pen of his slanderous report, then the Credit of the iudicious, being only grounded from this Papist and his Poet, of like conscience for lies, the one euer faining, and the other euer falsifying the truth, I am not ignorant.

'Parts' of Actors. When a play was first produced it would be in manuscript, i.e. 'the allowed book', the copy authorized by the Master of the Revels. It was necessary, therefore, to transcribe the individual parts of the actors. Only one of these parts is known, that of Orlando in Greene's *Orlando Furioso*, played by Alleyn probably in 1592. It was originally a roll some 17 feet long and 6 inches wide, made up of fourteen sheets of paper pasted together. The last word or words of the preceding speaker, the 'cue', is written before each of Orlando's speeches. His exits are indicated by ruled lines and generally by the word 'exit', and stage-directions are given in the left margin. The part is mainly in English script, with some mislineation of verse, the lines of which begin with small letters. Punctuation, which is slight, is by commas. (See PLOTS; Greg, *Dramatic Documents.*)

'Passionate Pilgrim.' A miscellany published in octavo by W. Jaggard in 1599, without registration and attributed to Shakespeare, presumably because his poems were selling so well (the 5th and 6th editions of *Venus and Adonis* appeared in 1599):

> The Passionate Pilgrime. By W. Shakespeare. At London. Printed for W. Iaggard, and are to be sold by W. Leake, at the Greyhound in Paules Churchyard. 1599.

This is the title-page of the 2nd edition. The 1st was probably published earlier in the same year. The unique copy (without title-page) in the Folger Library is made up of two quires of the 1st and two of the 2nd. (See the facsimile by J. Q. Adams, 1939.)

Of the twenty-one poems in *The Passionate Pilgrim*, only five are certainly by Shakespeare:

1. A version of Shakespeare's Sonnet 138.
2. A version of Shakespeare's Sonnet 144.
3. A version of Longaville's Sonnet to Maria in *L.L.L.* IV, iii.
4. The theme of this sonnet, like that of 6, 9, 11, is Venus and Adonis. Bartholomew Griffin wrote 11, so that he probably wrote 4, 6, 9, though they may be Shakespeare's.
5. A version of Biron's Sonnet to Rosaline in *L.L.L.* IV, ii.
6. See 4.
7. Author unknown. This, like 10, 13, 14, 15, 19, is in the six-line stanza of Shakespeare's *Venus and Adonis*.
8. From Richard Barnfield's *Poems in diuers humors*, 1598.
9. See 4.
10. See 7.
11. A version of Sonnet 3 in Bartholomew Griffin's sonnet-sequence, *Fidessa*, 1596.
12. Author unknown. 'Crabbed age and

youth' appeared in Thomas Deloney's *Garland of Goodwill* (1631) with some 90 lines of an inferior continuation. There may have been an earlier edition of Deloney's miscellany, but it is improbable that this poem is his.

13. See 7.
14.–15. See 7. These two form one poem, and are printed as such in the 1640 edition of Shakespeare's *Poems*.

(Here Jaggard printed a new title-page: *Sonnets To sundry Notes of Musicke*.)

16. Author unknown.
17. A version of Dumain's address to Kate in *L.L.L.* IV, iii.
18. In *England's Helicon* (1600), attributed to 'Ignoto', but so is 21, which is Barnfield's. Probably, therefore, 18 is also his. It was first printed, with music, in Thomas Weelkes's *Madrigals*, 1597.
19. See 7. This poem resembles *Willobie his Avisa*, canto xliv (1594), which is also in the six-line stanza.
20. Four verses of Marlowe's *Come live with me*, and one verse of Raleigh's *Reply*.
21. From Barnfield's *Poems in diuers humors*. See 8 and 18.

Jaggard issued O3 in 1612, with additional anonymous pieces taken from Heywood's *Troia Britannica* which he had himself printed in 1609:

> The Passionate Pilgrime Or Certaine Amorous Sonnets, betweene Venus and Adonis, newly corrected and augmented. By W. Shakespeare. The third Edition. Whereunto is newly added two Loue-Epistles, the first from Paris to Hellen, and Hellens answere backe againe to Paris. Printed by W. Iaggard, 1612.

In a note appended to his *Apology for Actors* (1612), Heywood protested against Jaggard's impertinent piracy and wrote, somewhat obscurely, that it looked as though he had stolen from Shakespeare, who had replied by publishing the poems in his own name:

> Here, likewise, I must necessarily insert a manifest injury done me in that worke, by taking the two Epistles of *Paris* to *Helen*, and *Helen* to *Paris*, and printing them in a lesse volume, vnder the name of another, which may put the world in opinion I might steale them from him; and hee to doe himselfe right, hath since published them in his owne name: but as I must acknowledge my lines not worthy his patronage, vnder whom he [Jaggard] hath publisht them, so the Author I know much offended with M. *Jaggard* that (altogether vnknowne to him) presumed to make so bold with his name.

As a result, Jaggard cancelled Shakespeare's name on his unsold copies. (See SQ, IX, 4.)

Patent. In Tudor and Stuart times letters patent were a common and increasingly unpopular way of exercising the royal prerogative. They are 'open letters' addressed by the sovereign to all who may be concerned, granting some office or privilege to the patentee. By the Act of 1572 companies of players were to be authorized by a baron of the realm or person of greater degree, and Elizabeth's patent of 1574, authorizing Leicester's Men to play anywhere in England, was exceptional. Under James I, companies obtained their authority from the Crown, and patents were issued to all the privileged London companies, now brought under royal patronage. Thus the patent for the King's Men of 19 May 1603 begins:

> Commissio specialis pro Laurencio Fletcher & Willelmo Shackespeare et aliis
>
> Iames by the grace of god &c. To all Iustices, Maiors, Sheriffes, Constables, hedborowes, and other our Officers and louinge Subiectes greetinge. Knowe yee that Wee of our speciall grace, certaine knowledge, & mere motion haue licenced and aucthorized and by theise presentes doe licence and aucthorize theiese our Servauntes Lawrence Fletcher, William Shakespeare, Richard Burbage, Augustyne Phillippes, Iohn Heninges, Henrie Condell, William Sly, Robert Armyn, Richard Cowly, and the rest of theire Associates freely to vse and exercise the Arte and faculty of playinge . . .

The Master of the Revels was appointed by patent, and in 1581 Edmund Tilney was granted, by patent, the important privilege of licensing plays for performance. The Porter's Hall theatre was licensed by a patent of 1615.

Pater, Walter (1839–94), was educated at King's School, Canterbury, and

Queen's, Oxford, becoming a fellow of Brasenose in 1864. Three essays on Shakespeare were published in *Appreciations* in 1889, though the first two were written much earlier: *Measure for Measure* (1874), *Love's Labour's Lost* (1878) and *Shakespeare's English Kings* (1889). They form a small, but valuable, contribution to Shakespeare criticism.

Pathetic Fallacy. The endowing of animals or inanimate objects with human qualities, a device characteristic of Richard II:

> Dear earth, I do salute thee with my hand,
> Though rebels wound thee with their horses' hoofs.

Patience. In *Henry VIII*, a gentlewoman to Queen Katharine. She is in attendance when the Queen is dying. (IV, ii.)

Patroclus. In *Troilus and Cressida*, a Grecian commander and friend of Achilles, whom he urges to take up arms again. His own death at the hands of the Trojans at length rouses Achilles (V, V).

Patrons. By the Act of 1572 actors had to secure the patronage of a baron of the realm or personage of greater degree. Thus the patrons of Shakespeare's company were the Lord Chamberlains, the 1st and 2nd Lords Hunsdon, and on James I's accession the King himself. The other authorized London companies were also brought under royal patronage by James, and licensed by patent.

If every actor had to find a patron, every poet tried to find one, the more exalted the better, to whom he might dedicate his work in the extravagant terms expected by that age of flattery. Shakespeare's own patron was the Earl of Southampton, to whom he dedicated *Venus and Adonis* and *Lucrece*. When Heminge and Condell, his fellow actors, collected his plays in the Folio of 1623, they dedicated the volume to the Earl of Pembroke, then Lord Chamberlain, and his brother the Earl of Montgomery.

Paulina. In *The Winter's Tale*, wife of Antigonus. She vehemently defends Hermione against Leontes's charge of unchastity, brings him the prison-born Perdita, and shortly afterwards announces Hermione's death. Sixteen years later she makes Leontes promise never to marry again without her consent and shows him Hermione's 'statue' which turns out to be Hermione herself. Leontes persuades Paulina to marry Camillo as her second husband.

Paul's Boys. See CHILDREN OF PAUL'S.

Pauses. The variation of the pause is the most important means of giving variety and vitality to blank verse. Early blank verse tended to be a succession of lines each grammatically complete in itself, a phrase, a clause or a sentence, with a well-defined pause at the end. Shakespeare varied this by increasingly running over the sense from the end of one line into the next (*enjambment*), by pausing in the middle of a line, and by varying the position of the pause within the line. (See RUN-ON LINES; MID-LINE PAUSES.)

Pavane. A slow and stately dance of the 16th and 17th centuries. It is sometimes called Padovana ('of Padua'), suggesting an Italian origin. Elizabethan composers began to write purely instrumental music to the measure of the pavane, and by following it with the lively galliard began the development of the suite. Cf. *Twelfth Night*, V, i: 'A rogue and a passy measures pavin'.

Pavier, Thomas (d. 1625). A publisher of dubious reputation.

1600, 11 August. He registered *1 Sir John Oldcastle* and published Q1, 1600.

1600, 14 August. Secured the copyright of the pirated *Henry V* by transfer, presumably from the publishers, Millington and Busby, and published Q2, 1602.

1602, 19 April. Secured the copyright in the pirated *2, 3 Henry VI* and in *Titus Andronicus* by transfer from Millington.

1608, 2 May. Registered *A Yorkshire Tragedy* and published Q1, 1608, as Shakespeare's.

1619. Was associated with the printer W. Jaggard in the publication of ten of 'Shakespeare's' plays, five of which were issued with false dates. Pavier's contribution was:

The Whole Contention (*2, 3 Henry VI*). 'Printed for T.P.'

Henry V. 'Printed for T.P. 1608.'

1 Sir John Oldcastle. 'Printed for T.P. 1600.'

A Yorkshire Tragedy. 'Printed for T.P. 1619.'

Pericles. 'Printed for T.P. 1619.'

Of these six plays, the first three were reprints of 'bad' Quartos; the next two were not Shakespeare's; and *Pericles*, perhaps only half Shakespeare's, had been registered by Blount in 1608, though it may have become derelict on his death. Pavier was in business 1600–25, and Junior Warden of the Stationers' Company in 1622.

Pavy, Solomon. In 1600, when he was a boy of ten and 'apprentice to one Peerce', he was pressed by Nathaniel Giles for service with the Chapel Children. At Blackfriars he acted in *Cynthia's Revels* and *The Poetaster*, and when he died in 1603 Jonson wrote his epitaph. (See BOY ACTORS.)

Pay of Actors. The actor-sharers *were* the company, and owners of its joint stock: costumes, plays, properties, etc. Their gross profit was the entrance money taken at their performances, but out of this they had to pay rent to the housekeepers or theatre owner, normally half the gallery takings; then they had to pay the hired actors, musicians, boys, gatherers, and all expenses incidental to their productions. In addition, new plays and stock were a constantly recurring charge. For a Court performance the company received £10, the King's averaging about twelve Court performances a year during 1603–16. Chambers estimates the net income of a sharer in the King's at about £90 for the year May 1634–May 1635.

Housekeepers were the theatre owners, and might themselves be actor-sharers like Shakespeare and Burbage, or like Henslowe, a business man. They received normally half the gallery takings as rent, but out of this had to pay ground-rent, licence-fee, to re-imburse themselves for the capital invested in the theatre, and to keep it in repair. The ground-rent of the Globe was £14 10s., the cost of the rebuilding of 1613 about £1,400, and the licence-fee paid to the Master of the Revels was by 1599 £3 a month. Chambers estimates that Henslowe received from the Rose an average gross rent of £360 a year for the period 1592–7, plus any profit made from letting the right of sale of refreshments. In 1615 the net rent of the Globe was about £280, and of the Blackfriars £140.

Twenty years later the figures were about £400 and £750 respectively. As there were then sixteen housekeeper's shares in the Globe and eight in the Blackfriars, this meant a profit of £25 and £90 on each share. (See INCOME OF SHAKESPEARE.)

Hired actors were employed and paid by the sharers. In 1579 Gosson gives their pay as 6s. a week; in 1597 Henslowe was paying 5s. to 8s.

Boys were apprenticed to individual actors, who trained them, and hired them to the company. Henslowe paid a premium of £8 for a boy, and in 1597 received 3s. a week for his services.

Payton, Mr. A Stratford alderman living at Shottery. Thomas Hart gave him the manuscript of John Shakespeare's 'spiritual will', which Payton sent to Malone *c.* 1789. John Jordan (q.v.) in his *Original Collections* (*c.* 1780), wrote:

> The large barns, built with bricks, still standing in the Gild-pits, by the side of the Birmingham road, and which are now possessed by Mr Peyton, have always been thought to have been built by [Shakespeare].

Peacham, Henry (*c.* 1576–*c.* 1643), son of the Rev. Henry Peacham, was educated at Trinity, Cambridge, became a schoolmaster, and then a private tutor.

He was in addition an artist, his first book *Graphice* (1606) being a treatise on drawing, and his famous *Compleat Gentleman* (1622) contains chapters on painters, painting and the 'art of limming'.

There exists a drawing which illustrates the first scene of *Titus Andronicus*: 'Tamora pleadinge for her sonnes going to execution'. Beneath it are written twenty lines adapted from Act I, and twenty from Act V, and in the left margin 'Henricus Peacham Anno m° q° g q^to', interpreted as 1595. If this is correct, it is, as Chambers calls it, 'the first illustration to Shakespeare', and shows that the Moor Aaron, and presumably therefore Othello, were conceived by the Elizabethans as negroes, and that there was some attempt at historical costume, at any rate for the chief characters. It is possible that the writing is later than the drawing and that the scribe attributed it to 'Henricus Peacham'. (See SS, I.)

Peaseblossom. In *A Midsummer Night's Dream*, one of Titania's fairies.

Peck, Francis (1692–1743), antiquary, was educated at Trinity, Cambridge, and became a clergyman and prebendary of Lincoln. In his *Notes on Shakespeare's Plays* (1740) he discovers a twin for the traditional 'Shakespearean' epitaph on John Combe (q.v.).

Pedant. In *The Taming of the Shrew*, Tranio, posing as Lucentio, frightens him into pretending to be Vincentio, father of the real Lucentio, and arranging his marriage to Bianca with her father. When the real Vincentio appears, he runs away, but is present at the feast in the last scene.

Pedro, Don. In *Much Ado*, Prince of Arragon. He arranges the betrothal of Claudio to Hero, but is later convinced of her infidelity and supports Claudio in exposing her. When he discovers his error, he does his best to make amends. He also arranges the plot whereby Benedick is persuaded that Beatrice loves him. (Called Piero d'Aragona by Bandello.)

Peele, George (*c.* 1557–96), one of the University Wits, was the son of a clerk of Christ's Hospital, at which school he was educated before going to Broadgates Hall (Pembroke), Oxford, in 1571, and Christ Church in 1574. In 1579, the year in which he took his M.A., the governors of Christ's Hospital, for reasons unknown, ordered his father 'to discharge his house of his son George Peele and all other his household which have been chargeable to him', and after staying in Oxford, Peele went to London about 1581 and married. He appears to have spent the rest of his life in London, though in 1583 he was in Oxford again, where he produced the *Rivales* and *Dido* of William Gager, who praised his lost play of *Iphigenia*, translated from Euripides. Most of the stories in *The Merry Conceited Jests of George Peele* (1607) are considerably older than Peele, but may contain some biographical matter, and suggest, but do not prove, that his life was a riotous one, and he died, according to Meres, 'by the pox'.

Peele's extant plays, in approximately chronological order, are *The Arraignment of Paris*, *The Battle of Alcazar* (?), *Edward I*, *David and Bethsabe* and *The Old Wives' Tale*. In addition he devised a number of Lord Mayors' Pageants. Meres accounted him one of the 'best for tragedy', and as early as 1589 the young Nashe wrote of him in his preface to Greene's *Menaphon*,

> For the last, though not the least of them all, I dare commend him to all that know him, as the chief supporter of pleasance now living, the Atlas of poetry, and *primus verborum artifex*; whose first increase, the Arraignment of Paris, might plead to your opinions his pregnant dexterity of wit and manifold variety of invention, wherein (*me iudice*) he goeth a step beyond all that write.

Peele is almost certainly one of 'those Gentlemen, his Quondam acquaintance' addressed by Greene in his *Groatsworth of Wit* (1592).

Like the other University Wits, Peele was a pioneer; his *Edward I* is a development of the old chronicle history in the direction of the historical *play*, but his greatest contribution to the drama was the vitality and new music that he gave to blank verse. (*The Life and Works of George Peele*, ed. C. T. Prouty.)

Peers, Edward. A Gentleman of the Chapel who, *c.* 1600, became Choir Master of the Children of Paul's (q.v.) when Richard Mulcaster (q.v.) was High Master of the school. He revived the Paul's plays which had been discontinued ten years earlier, and is named as payee for a Court performance of 1 January 1601: 'Edwarde Peers Mr of the children of Poules'. For similar performances on 1 January 1603 and 20 February 1604 his name is spelt Peirs and Pearce in the Chamber Accounts.

Pembroke, Earl of. 1. In *King John*, William Marshal, Earl of Pembroke (d. 1219), disapproves of John's submission to the Pope, accuses him of Arthur's murder, and with Salisbury and other lords joins the Dauphin's army of invasion. When they hear that the Dauphin plans their murder, they return to their allegiance. (Actually Pembroke remained loyal, though his son William joined the Dauphin.)

2. In *3 Henry VI*, a Yorkist whom Edward IV orders to levy men (IV, i). (William Herbert, beheaded 1469.)

Pembroke, Henry Herbert, 2nd Earl of (*c.* 1534–1601), succeeded to the title on his father's death in 1570, and in 1586 was appointed President of Wales. His third wife was the illustrious Mary Sidney (*c.* 1561–1621), sister of Sir Philip Sidney, and mother of William Herbert, 3rd Earl: 'Sidney's sister, Pembroke's mother' of William Browne's epitaph. For her Sidney wrote *The Countess of Pembroke's Arcadia*, and to her Spenser dedicated his *Ruines of Time*. In 1599 she entertained Elizabeth at Wilton House, and there the Court found refuge from the plague in 1603. Henry Herbert was the patron of Pembroke's Men (q.v.).

Pembroke, William Herbert, 3rd Earl of (1580–1630), son of Henry Herbert, 2nd Earl, and of Mary Sidney, succeeded to the Earldom on the death of his father in 1601, becoming Lord Chamberlain 1615–25 and Lord Steward 1626–30. In 1624 he was Chancellor of Oxford University when Broadgates Hall was refounded in his honour as Pembroke College.

James Boaden, in 1832, was the first to suggest that William Herbert was 'Mr W. H.', the 'lovely boy' of the *Sonnets* urged by Shakespeare to marry, and Chambers points out that there were in 1595 abortive negotiations for his marriage to Elizabeth Carey, granddaughter of Lord Chamberlain Hunsdon, patron of Shakespeare's company. It is just possible, also, that Shakespeare was one of Pembroke's Men before joining the Chamberlain's in 1594. It may therefore be significant that Heminge and Condell dedicated the Folio of 1623 to the 'brethren, William Earl of Pembroke ... and Philip, Earl of Montgomery', instead of to Southampton, Shakespeare's early patron, with perhaps the best claim to be Mr W. H. Pembroke, apparently a weak and dissolute man, was disgraced and imprisoned for a time in 1601, when his mistress, Mary Fitton (q.v.), a Court lady, bore him a child. In 1890 Thomas Tyler advanced the improbable hypothesis that she was the 'Dark Lady' of the *Sonnets*. (See G. B. Shaw, *The Dark Lady of the Sonnets*.)

Pembroke, Philip Herbert, 4th Earl of (1584–1650), younger brother of William Herbert, was a favourite of James I, who in 1605 created him Earl of Montgomery, so that when, in 1630, he succeeded to the Earldom of Pembroke he was styled Earl of Pembroke and Montgomery, a title borne by his successors. Charles I favoured him and created him Lord Chamberlain in 1626, but deprived him of his office when he sided with Parliament in 1640. He was Chancellor of Oxford University, 1641–3 and 1647–50. Heminge and Condell dedicated the First Folio of Shakespeare's plays to him and his elder brother in 1623, and in 1647, when the theatres were closed, the suppressed King's Men dedicated the Folio of Beaumont and Fletcher to him:

My Lord,

There is none among all the names of Honour, that hath more encouraged the legitimate Muses of this latter age, than that which is owing to your family; whose coronet shines bright with the native lustre of its own jewels, which, with the access of some beams of Sidney, twisted with their flame, presents a constellation, from whose influence all good may be still expected upon wit and learning...

But directed by the example of some, who once steered in our quality, and so fortunately aspired to choose your Honour, joined with your (now glorified) brother, patrons to the flowing compositions of the then expired sweet Swan of Avon Shakespeare; and since, more particularly bound to your Lordship's most constant and diffusive goodness, from which we did for many calm years derive a subsistence to ourselves, and protection to the scene (now withered, and condemn'd, as we fear, to a long winter and sterility) we have presumed to offer to yourself, what before was never printed of these Authors...

Your Honour's most bounden,

John Lowin,	Joseph Taylor,
Richard Robinson,	Robert Benfield,
Elyærd Swanston,	Thomas Pollard,
Hugh Clearke,	William Allen,
Stephen Hammerton,	Theophilus Byrd.

Pembroke's Men. These were the servants of Henry Herbert, 2nd Earl of Pembroke, and are first heard of in 1592, in the winter of which year they made their only appearance at Court, where they gave two performances. The plague year of 1593 hit them hard, for the London theatres were closed; like the other more firmly established companies they had to travel, and in September Henslowe wrote to Alleyn, who was leading the Strange-Admiral combination, 'As for my lord a Penbrockes which you desier to knowe wheare they be, they ar all at home and hausse ben this v or sixe weackes, for they cane not saue ther carges [charges: i.e. expenses] with trauell as I heare & were fayne to pane [pawn] ther parell for ther carge'.

They survived, however, and are traceable in the provinces 1595–6. In February 1597 they were joined by Richard Jones and Thomas Downton of the Admiral's, and the company contracted with Francis Langley to play for a year at his newly built Swan theatre. In July they performed Nashe's 'seditious and sclanderous' *Isle of Dogs* (q.v.) as a result of which three of the actors, Ben Jonson, Gabriel Spencer and Robert Shaw, were imprisoned and all the theatres closed. Before they were reopened, Jones and Downton returned to the Admiral's at Henslowe's Rose, an example followed by Spencer (killed by Ben Jonson a year later), Shaw and William Borne. Langley sued them for breach of contract, but they pleaded that when the theatres reopened Langley was unable to obtain a licence, and in October Henslowe noted in his *Diary*, 'The xj of October begane my lord Admerals and my lord of Penbrockes men to playe at my howsse 1597.' Perhaps the rump of Pembroke's never really recovered from the secession, for though they continued their provincial career, the last word of them is of being in the clutches of Henslowe for two unprofitable performances at the Rose in October 1600. Perhaps they joined Worcester's, formed at about this time.

It is just possible that Shakespeare was with Pembroke's before joining the Chamberlain's in 1594, for one of their plays was *The True Tragedy of Richard Duke of York* (Shakespeare's *3 Henry VI*), published – a 'bad' Quarto – in 1595 as 'sundrie times acted by the Right Honourable the Earle of Pembrooke his seruants', and when Q1 *Titus Andronicus* appeared in 1594 it had been 'plaide by the Right Honourable the Earle of Darbie, Earle of Pembroke, and Earle of

Sussex their Seruants'. The possibility that Pembroke's son, William Herbert, was the Mr W. H. of the *Sonnets* strengthens the hypothesis.

Penguin Shakespeare. See HARRISON, G. B. The New Penguin Shakespeare and the Penguin Shakespeare Library began publication in 1967.

Pepys, Samuel (1633–1703), son of a London tailor of good family. After going to St Paul's School and Magdalene, Cambridge, he married and entered the household of his cousin and patron, Sir Edward Montague, later Earl of Sandwich, who secured for him a clerkship in the Navy Office. In 1665 he became Surveyor-General of the Victualling Office, and in 1672 Secretary of the Admiralty, a post that he lost at the Revolution in 1689, after which he lived in retirement. He began his *Diary* 1 January 1660, and discontinued it 31 May 1669, owing to failing eyesight. It is written in cipher and shorthand, was translated by John Smith 1819–22, and first edited by Lord Braybrooke in 1825.

Pepys was an indefatigable play-goer, and his accounts of his visits to the theatres form an important part of the *Diary*. When they were reopened at the Restoration, there were two patent companies, the Duke's under D'Avenant at Lincoln's Inn Fields ('the Opera') and the King's under Killigrew at Drury Lane. Most of Shakespeare's plays that he saw were the 'improved' versions of the period; thus:

> I went to the Opera, and saw 'The Law against Lovers' [D'Avenant's version of *Measure for Measure*], a good play and well performed, especially the little girl's, whom I never saw act before, dancing and singing ... (18 *February* 1662).

> To the King's house, and there saw 'The Tameing of a Shrew' [John Lacy's version], which hath some very good pieces in it, but generally is but a mean play ... (9 *April* 1667).

Percy, Henry. See HOTSPUR.

Percy, Lady. Sister of Roger Mortimer, 4th Earl of March, and wife of Hotspur. In *1 Henry IV* she pleads with her husband to tell her what heavy business he has in hand, and follows him from Warkworth to Wales, where they join Mortimer and Glendower. In *2 Henry IV* she speaks proudly of her dead husband and urges her father-in-law, Northumberland, not to wrong his ghost by helping others in the rebellion in which he had failed to help his son.

Percy, Thomas (1729–1811), son of a grocer of Bridgnorth, he became Bishop of Dromore. His antiquarian research, particularly his essay on early blank verse, his reprint of *The Household Book of the Earl of Northumberland in 1512*, and his famous *Reliques of Ancient English Poetry* (1765), all helped in the reconstruction of the age of Shakespeare with which late 18th-century scholars were occupied.

Perdita. The heroine of *The Winter's Tale*, and daughter of King Leontes and Hermione. (In Greene's *Pandosto* she is Fawnia, daughter of Pandosto, King of Bohemia.)

Performances of plays in the public theatres began at two o'clock in the afternoon, and normally lasted some two or two and a half hours. In the private theatres, where in any event artificial light would be required, they may have begun later. Bills, or posters, advertised the play, the flag flew from the hut of the tiring-house to show that the theatre was open, and three trumpet soundings announced the beginning of the performance. If the play were a tragedy, the heavens were hung with black curtains. The gatherers collected the money at the entrance to the theatre, and extra payments at the gallery entrances. At the third sounding, the Prologue in traditional black cloak would appear, and the play would be acted, possibly without a break, though there were intervals for music at the private theatres, a practice probably adopted in a modified form by the public theatres at the beginning of the 17th century. After the play came the Epilogue, spoken by one of the actors, who begged the audience for a plaudite, and this was followed by a jig. When the audience had gone, the gatherers would produce their boxes, and the actor-sharers would hand over half the gallery takings as rent to the house-keepers (possibly themselves), pay the hired men their wages, and pocket the rest. (See COURT PERFORMANCES; INTERVALS.)

'PERICLES, PRINCE OF TYRE.'

WRITTEN: 1608–9.

PERFORMED: Sometime between 5 January 1606 and 23 November 1608, the Venetian Ambassador Zorzi Giustinian (q.v.) saw 'a play called *Pericles*'. About Christmas 1609 a Yorkshire company acted 'Perocles prince of Tire'.

1619. 'In the kinges greate Chamber they went to see the play of Pirrocles, Prince of Tyre, which lasted till 2 aclocke. After two actes, the players ceased till the French all refreshed them with sweetmeates brought on Chinay voiders, & wyne & ale in bottells, after the players begann anewe.' (*Letter of Sir Gerrard Herbert to Sir Dudley Carleton,* 20 May 1619.)

1631. 'Received of Mr Benfielde, in the name of the kings company, for a gratuity for the liberty gaind unto them of playinge, upon the cessation of the plague, this 10 of June, 1631, £3.10.0. This was taken upon Pericles at the Globe.' (*Office Book of Sir Henry Herbert.*)

REGISTERED: 1608, '20 Maij. Edward Blount. Entred for his copie vnder thandes of Sir George Buck knight and Master Warden Seton A booke called. the booke of Pericles prynce of Tyre.'

1626. Transferred by Pavier's widow to E. Brewster and R. Bird.

1630. Transferred by Bird to Richard Cotes.

PUBLISHED: 1609. Q1. 'The Late, And much admired Play, Called Pericles, Prince of Tyre. With the true Relation of the whole Historie, aduentures, and fortunes of the said Prince: As also, The no lesse strange, and worthy accidents, in the Birth and Life, of his Daughter Mariana. As it hath been diuers and sundry times acted by his Maiesties Seruants, at the Globe on the Banck-side. By William Shakespeare. Imprinted at London for Henry Gosson, and are to be sold at the signe of the Sunne in Pater-noster row, &c. 1609.' The text, the basis of later editions, is corrupt, and probably reported. (See TITLE-PAGES.)

1609, Q2; 1611, Q3; 1619, Q4 (see JAGGARD); 1630, Q5; 1635, Q6.

1664, F3, second issue. 'The much admired Play, called Pericles, Prince of Tyre. With the true Relation of the whole History, Adventures, and Fortunes of the said Prince. Written by W. Shakespeare, and published in his life time.' Acts marked and names of actors given. Set up from Q6.

It is not clear why Blount failed to publish a Quarto after his registration in 1608. The play was excluded from F1 (and F2), either because Heminge and Condell knew that it was not all Shakespeare's work, or because they could not find a good text to replace the bad one. Acts III–V are unmistakably his and contain some of his finest poetry. There is no reason to doubt the authenticity of the three brothel scenes in Act IV.

Apart from a few lines, Acts I and II are so inferior to the remainder that it has generally been held that they are not Shakespeare's. But Philip Edwards argues (SS, 5) that the whole play may be Shakespeare's, Q being a memorial reconstruction by two 'reporters', one responsible for the first two acts, the other for the last three.

The Painfull Aduentures of Pericles Prince of Tyre. Being the true History of the Play of Pericles, as it was lately presented by the worthy and ancient Poet Iohn Gower, a novel by George Wilkins (q.v.), was published in 1608. It seems to be a rendering of a performance of the play eked out with borrowings from Twine's story.

SOURCES: The old story of Apollonius of Tyre in Gower's *Confessio Amantis* (1393). Laurence Twine's *The Patterne of Painefull Aduentures*, a prose version of the story, registered 1576, published without date, and reprinted 1607. The name Pericles instead of Apollonius may come from Prince Pyrocles in Sidney's *Arcadia.*

STAGE HISTORY: 1660. At the Cockpit with Betterton as Pericles. Apparently the first production of a Shakespeare play after the Restoration.

1738. George Lillo's adaptation, *Marina*.

1854. Phelps staged a, for him, unusually elaborate production at Sadler's Wells.

1947. Nugent Monck's production at Stratford.

Prince Pericles, going to woo the daughter of King Antiochus, discovers their incestuous love, and to escape the father's threatened vengeance sets sail for Tarsus, leaving the government of Tyre in charge of his minister Helicanus. He is shipwrecked off Pentapolis, where in a tournament he wins Thaisa, daughter of King Simonides, and marries her. (Acts I and II.)

When Pericles hears that Antiochus is dead, and Helicanus advises him to return, he sails for Tyre, but in a storm Thaisa apparently dies in childbirth, and is buried at sea in a chest which is washed ashore at Ephesus. There she is restored to life by Cerimon, and thinking Pericles is drowned and uncertain whether she gave birth to a child, she enters the temple of Diana. Pericles returns to Tyre by way of Tarsus, where he leaves his baby daughter Marina to be brought up by the governor Cleon and his wife Dionyza. (Act III.)

Some sixteen years later, Dionyza, jealous because Marina surpasses her own daughter, plans her murder, but she is carried off by pirates and sold to a brothel-keeper in Mytilene. There she meets the governor Lysimachus, who gives her gold with which to buy her release. Meanwhile Pericles in a vision sees the tomb erected to Marina by Cleon and Dionyza, is stricken speechless with grief, and puts to sea. He arrives off Mytilene, where Lysimachus restores him with the aid of Marina, whom Pericles recognizes as his daughter. In another vision, Diana summons him to Ephesus, and there father and daughter are restored to Thaisa. Marina is betrothed to Lysimachus, and Gower as Chorus tells how Cleon and Dionyza have been burned by the infuriated citizens of Tarsus.

Perithous. In *The Two Noble Kinsmen*, an Athenian general who places the disguised Arcite in the service of Emilia. In the last scene he describes Arcite's fatal accident.

Perkins, Richard (b. 1579). An actor in the Worcester's-Queen Anne's company, 1602–19. In a note at the end of his *White Devil* (Q1 1612), produced at the Red Bull, Webster wrote, 'in particular I must remember the well-approved industry of my friend Master Perkins, and confess the worth of his action did crown both the beginning and the end'.

Perkins Folio. See COLLIER.

Personification. A figure of rhetoric whereby an abstraction or inanimate object is symbolized as a person, or given some quality of a person. The first form, which may be called 'simple personification', is the allegorical device of the 15th-century Morality plays, a little clumsy and wooden, not greatly affected by Shakespeare, and, as is to be expected, commonest in his earliest plays. It is, as Dr Spurgeon shows in her analysis, much the commonest in *King John*, which contains forty examples (Death, Grief, Commodity, etc.) to the twenty-one of its nearest rival, *Richard II*. In addition there are thirty-one images in which 'personification seems the most striking aspect', as in 'your city's eyes, your winking gates'. This abundant use of personification makes *King John* a play apart. (See PATHETIC FALLACY.)

Perspective. The discovery of the art, or science, of representing perspective by the Italian painters of the Renaissance was soon applied to the Italian stage. In 1508 Ariosto's *Cassaria* was produced at Ferrara against a painting of Mytilene, a 'perspective of a landscape with houses, churches, towers, and gardens'. In his *Architettura* (1551) Sebastiano Serlio (q.v.) illustrated standard designs for Tragedy, Comedy and Satyric plays, made up of a back-cloth painted in perspective, in front of which were lath and painted canvas buildings, also arranged in perspective. For his masques Inigo Jones improved on Serlio, changing his perspective scenes by a system of movable shutters and corresponding back-cloths. It is possible that perspective back-cloths were used for Court performances, perhaps also in the private, sometimes even in the public, theatres.

Peter. In *Romeo and Juliet*, the servant of Juliet's nurse. At the end of IV, V, he quotes Richard Edwardes's poem, 'When griping grief'.

Peter of Pomfret. In *King John*, he is imprisoned and hanged for prophesying that John shall deliver up his crown before the next Ascension-day.

Peter Thump. In *2 Henry VI*, he accuses his master, Horner, of saying that York is the rightful King, and in a trial by combat, fought with sand-bags, kills him (II, iii). (He was hanged for felony.)

Peto. In *1 Henry IV*, he helps Falstaff to rob the travellers, and later tells the Prince how he and his companions tried to disguise their cowardice. In IV, ii Falstaff calls him 'my lieutenant Peto'. In *2 Henry IV* he brings news of the rebellion to the Prince (II, iv). (See ROSSILL.)

Petrarch (1304–74). Francesco Petrarca spent his early childhood in a village on the Arno, then in 1313 his family moved to Avignon where, in 1327, he first saw Laura who, in life and death, inspired the odes and sonnets of his *Canzoniere*. In 1341 he was crowned Poet Laureate in Rome. For the next few years he was much engaged in politics, formed a friendship with Boccaccio, then in 1362 settled at Padua, and finally at Arqua, where he died.

Petrarch is most important as the founder of humanism, the rediscoverer of the pagan world, and the first man of the Italian Renaissance. As a poet he fixed the form of the sonnet, a verse-form much affected by Ronsard and other poets of the Pléiade in 16th-century France, and in England by Sidney, Spenser, Shakespeare and their contemporaries. Shakespeare's one reference to Petrarch is in *Romeo and Juliet* (II, iv), where Mercutio says of Romeo, 'Now is he for the numbers that Petrarch flowed in: Laura to his lady was but a kitchen-wench.' Drummond reports of Jonson (1619) that he 'cursed Petrarch for redacting verses to Sonnets; which he said were like that Tirrants bed, wher some who where too short were racked, others too long cut short'. At the same time, Donne, with his harshness and original imagery, checked the over-sweet and chilly mannerisms of the cult of Petrarchism.

Petruchio. In *The Taming of the Shrew*, the tamer of Katharina. Called Ferando in *A Shrew*.

Pettie, George (1548–89). Author of *A petite Pallace of Pettie his Pleasure* (1576), the earliest English book in the affected style imitated and popularized by Lyly in his *Euphues* (1579–80). Pettie was a Christ Church man, and friend of William Gager.

Phebe. In *As You Like It*, a shepherdess whom Silvius loves. She falls in love with the disguised Rosalind, who promises to marry her if ever she marries woman, provided that Phebe will marry Silvius if ever she refuses to marry her. (Also called Phebe in Lodge's *Rosalynde*.)

Phelps, Samuel (1804–78), was born at Devonport. After working in newspaper offices he made a name for himself as a tragic actor, but it was not until 1837 that the 'Provincial Celebrity' appeared in London – as Shylock at the Haymarket. After some years with Macready, he became theatrical manager of Sadler's Wells (q.v.), his period there (1844–62) being of the first importance. Not only did he produce all but seven of Shakespeare's plays (*1, 2, 3 Henry VI, Titus Andronicus, Richard II, Troilus and Cressida* and *Two Noble Kinsmen*), but in an age of lavish spectacle he reduced scenery and effects to reasonable proportions, and restored much of Shakespeare's text that had been cut or adapted by the 'improvers'. Phelps's example influenced William Poel, Granville-Barker, and other producers who have swept away the otiose spectacle and 'business' of the Kean-Irving-Tree tradition to make room for what Shakespeare really wrote. Phelps himself was a star actor and played many leading Shakespearean parts, mostly tragic, though he was at his best as Bottom. His last appearance was as Wolsey in *Henry VIII*, in 1878, the year of his death.

Philario. In *Cymbeline*, the friend of Posthumus's father. The banished Posthumus stays at his house in Rome where he meets Iachimo. Philario tries to prevent their wagering on Imogen's chastity.

'Philaster.' A tragi-comedy by Beaumont and Fletcher, registered and published in 1620 as 'Phylaster, Or Loue lyes a Bleeding. Acted at the Globe by his Maiesties Seruants. Written by Francis Baymont and Iohn Fletcher. Gent.' Q2 (1622) states that 'it hath beene diuerse times Acted, at the Globe, and Blacke-friers'. But the play was written by October 1610, when John Davies's *Scourge of Folly*, which contains a reference to '*Loue lies ableeding*', was registered. The King's Men gave two performances during the Revels of 1612–13. Critics find resemblances between *Philaster* and *Cymbeline*, and some try to prove that Shakespeare borrowed from Beaumont and Fletcher. It may be so, but the resemblances are not very remarkable, and *Cymbeline* may well have been written before *Philaster*.

Philemon. In *Pericles*, a servant of Cerimon (III, ii).

Philip II (1527–98), King of Spain, son of the Emperor Charles V, succeeded to the Spanish dominions on his father's abdication in 1556. Two years earlier he had married Queen Mary of England, but she died childless in 1558. For the remainder of his life Philip was the champion of the Roman Catholic church against the Protestant Dutch and English with whom he was involved in secret or open struggle. His attempt to invade England was defeated in 1588, when his Armada was destroyed, though for some years after that there remained the possibility of another attack. He was succeeded by the incompetent Philip III (1578–1621), his son by his fourth wife. Don Armado in *Love's Labour's Lost* has been thought to be a caricature of Philip II.

Philip II, King of France (1165–1223). In *King John*, he supports Arthur's claim to the English throne. (He was with Richard I on the 3rd Crusade.)

Philip the Bastard. In *King John*. See FAULCONBRIDGE.

Phillips, Augustine. One of the twenty-six 'Principall Actors' in Shakespeare's plays (see p. 90). He is mentioned as 'Mr Phillipps' in the cast of the *Seven Deadly Sins*, acted *c.* 1591, probably by Strange's, of which company he was a member when they travelled under Alleyn in 1593. He was probably an original member of the Chamberlain's, formed in 1594, and with them played in *Every Man in His Humour* (1598), *Every Man out of His Humour* (1599) and *Sejanus* (1603); he is in the King's Men's patent of 1603 and the Wardrobe account of 1604. In 1599 he became one of the original housekeepers of the Globe, and in 1601 made a deposition about the performance of *Richard II* by the Chamberlain's on the day before the Essex rising:

> The Examination of Augustyne Phillypps servant vnto the L. Chamberlyne and one of hys players taken the xviijth of Februarij 1600 vpon hys oth.
>
> He sayeth that on Fryday last was sennyght or Thursday Sr Charles Percy Sr Josclyne Percy and the L. Montegle with some thre more spak to some of the players in the presans of thys examinate to have the play of the deposyng and kyllyng of Kyng Rychard the second to be played the Saterday next

promysyng to gete them xls. more then their ordynary to play yt. Wher thys Examinate and hys fellowes were determyned to have played some other play, holdyng that play of Kyng Richard to be so old & so long out of vse as that they shold have small or no Company at yt. But at their request this Examinate and his fellowes were Content to play yt the Saterday and had their xls. more then their ordynary for yt and so played yt accordyngly.

Augustine Phillips.

Like Shakespeare, he moved to the Bankside *c.* 1596, but when he made his will shortly before his death in May 1605, he lived at Mortlake in Surrey, where he had bought a house. He appears to have been the most loyal of colleagues, and mentions most of his fellow King's Men (Heminge, Burbage and Sly were overseers):

Item I geve and bequeathe unto and amongste the hyred men of the Company which I am of, which shalbe at the tyme of my decease, the some of fyve pounds of lawfull money of England to be equally distributed amongeste them, Item I geve and bequeathe to my Fellowe William Shakespeare a thirty shillings peece in gould, To my Fellowe Henry Condell one other thirty shillinge peece in gould, To my Servaunte Christopher Beeston thirty shillings in gould, To my Fellowe Lawrence Fletcher twenty shillings in gould [and 'twenty shillings in gould' to his other fellows, Robert Armyne, Richard Coweley, Alexander Cook, Nicholas Tooley]. Item, I geve to Samuell Gilborne my late apprentice, the some of fortye shillings, and my mouse colloured velvit hose, and a white taffety dublet, a blacke taffety sute, my purple cloke, sword and dagger, and my base viall. Item I geve to James Sands my Apprentice the some of fortye shillings and a citterne a bandore and a lute, to be paid and delivered unto him at the expiracion of his terme of yeres in his indenture of apprenticehood. (See WITTER.)

The reference to his musical instruments suggests that he was primarily a musician. His sister Elizabeth had married Robert Gough of the King's, a witness of the will, and another sister, Margery Borne, may have been the wife of William Borne of Pembroke's (q.v.) and the Admiral's. Heywood pays a tribute to Phillips in his *Apology for Actors* (q.v.).

Phillips, Edward (1630–*c.* 1696), son of Edward Phillips and John Milton's sister, Anne, was educated by Milton, at Magdalen, Oxford, 1650–51, became a bookseller's clerk, and tutor to John Evelyn's son. His most important work is *Theatrum Poetarum* (1675), in which he writes,

Shakespear, in spight of all his unfiled expressions, his rambling and indigested Fancys, the laughter of the *Critical*, yet must be confess't a *Poet* above many that go beyond him in Literature some degrees....

William Shakespear, the Glory of the English Stage; whose nativity at *Stratford* upon *Avon*, is the highest honour that Town can boast of: from an Actor of Tragedies and Comedies, he became a *Maker*; and such a Maker, that though some others may perhaps pretend to a more exact *Decorum* and *œconomie*, especially in Tragedy, never any express't a more lofty and Tragic heighth; never any represented nature more purely to the life, and where the polishments of Art are most wanting, as probably his Learning was not extraordinary, he pleaseth with a certain wild and native Elegance; and in all his Writings hath an unvulgar style, as well in his *Venus and Adonis*, his *Rape of Lucrece* and other various Poems, as in his Dramatics.

Phillips, Sir Richard (1767–1840), a sheriff of London, publisher, and editor of *The Monthly Magazine*, in which in 1818 he wrote an account of his discovery of the Hart family at Tewkesbury and his subsequent investigations at Stratford. (Descendants of Shakespeare's sister, Joan Hart, lived as chair-makers at Tewkesbury *c.* 1780–1850. John Shakespeare Hart lived in Barton Street and was buried in the Abbey churchyard in 1800; he inherited the Swan and Maidenhead (the 'Woolshop', next door to Shakespeare's birthplace) in 1793, and leased the Birthplace to a cousin, Thomas Hornby. Mrs Mary Hornby (q.v.) lived there 1793–1820.)

The landlord of the Swan and Maidenhead ... assured the writer, that, when he re-laid the floors of the parlour, the remains of wool, and the refuse of wool-combing, were found under the old flooring, imbedded with the earth of the foundation ...

Mrs Hornby shows a very small deep cupboard, in a dark corner of the room in which Shakspeare was born; and relates that a letter was found in it some years since, which had been addressed by Shakspeare from the playhouse in London to his wife. She asserts that this letter was in her possession, and that she used to show it to visitors; that one morning, a few years since, she exhibited it to a company, who went from her house to the church; but presently sent a message to beg that she would send the letter for further inspection at the tomb, – a request with which she complied. She saw nothing further, however, of her letter.

Philo. In *Antony and Cleopatra*, a friend of Antony. He speaks the first fine opening speech of the play, but does not appear after I, i.

Philostrate. In *A Midsummer Night's Dream*, Master of the Revels, he arranges the entertainment for the wedding festivities of Theseus, warning him that the interlude of *Pyramus and Thisbe* is 'nothing in the world'. (In Chaucer's *Knight's Tale*, in which Theseus and Hippolyta appear, the disguised Arcite calls himself Philostrate.)

Philoten. In *Pericles*, daughter of Cleon and Dionyza. She is merely mentioned by Gower in the Chorus to Act IV, as so eclipsed by 'absolute Marina' that the jealous Dionyza plans Marina's murder. Lillo makes more of her in his adaptation, *Marina* (q.v.).

Philotus. In *Timon of Athens*, servant of one of Timon's creditors, who applies to Timon for payment of his master's debt (III, iv).

'Phoenix and Turtle.' In 1601 Richard Field printed for Edward Blount a poem by Robert Chester called 'Loves Martyr: Or, Rosalins Complaint. Allegorically shadowing the truth of Loue, in the constant Fate of the Phoenix and Turtle'. It celebrates the love of Chester's patron, Sir John Salisbury, and his wife Ursula, symbolized as the turtle-dove (Constancy) and the phoenix (Love), from whose union sprang their daughter Jane. To Chester's poem, the title-page continues, 'are added some new compositions of seuerall moderne Writers whose names are subscribed to their seuerall workes, vpon the first subiect: viz. the Phoenix and Turtle'. These 'new compositions' are introduced by a new title-page:

> Hereafter Follow Diuerse Poeticall Essaies on the former Subiect; viz: the Turtle and Phoenix. Done by the best and chiefest of our moderne writers, with their names subscribed to their particular workes: neuer before extant. And (now first) consecrated by them all generally, to the loue and merite of the true-noble Knight, Sir Iohn Salisburie.

There are fourteen of these 'Poeticall Essaies', two of which are attributed to Jonson, one each to Marston, Chapman and Shakespeare, the rest being anonymous or pseudonymous.

Shakespeare's poem (without a title), 'Let the bird of loudest lay', is the fifth in the series, and celebrates not a physical but a spiritual union 'leaving no posterity'. If the poem really is Shakespeare's, it was presumably commissioned for Chester's volume and written *c.* 1600. Critics differ as to its merits, and it is charged with obscurity. It is strange, but scarcely obscure; un-Shakespearean in form, but much of the phrasing has a Shakespearean ring, 'Augur of the fever's end', 'And thou treble-dated crow'. The volume was reissued in 1611 with a new title: 'The Anuals of great Brittaine'. (See ROYDON; SS, 15.)

Phoenix Theatre. This was the roofed Cockpit in Drury Lane, converted by Christopher Beeston, 1616–17, into a private theatre. It was damaged by the prentices in their Shrovetide riot of 4 March 1617, first occupied by Queen Anne's Men (1617–19), and became with the other private houses of Blackfriars (1608) and Salisbury Court (1629) one of the most important of the Caroline theatres. In 1639 Christopher's son, William, was 'governor of the kings and queenes young company of players ['Beeston's Boys'] at the Cockpit in Drury Lane.' According to a manuscript addition to Stow's *Annales*, 'The Phenix in Druery Lane, was pulled downe also this day, being Saterday the 24 day of March 1649, by the same souldiers ... set on by the sectuaries of these sad times'. But the fabric survived and was occupied by John Rhodes and his company of young players who produced *Pericles* there in 1660, the first of Shakespeare's plays to be revived after the reopening of the theatres. It was deserted after the building of the new Restoration houses in Vere Street (1660), Lincoln's Inn Fields (1661), and Drury Lane (1663). It is mentioned by Heminge and Condell in their epistle 'To the great Variety of Readers' in F1, 1623: 'And though you be a Magistrate of wit, and sit on the Stage at *Blacke-Friers*, or the *Cock-pit*, to arraigne Playes dailie, know, these Playes haue had their triall alreadie, and stood out all Appeales.'

Phrynia. In *Timon of Athens*, mistress to Alcibiades. Timon curses her and gives her gold (IV, iii).

'Pide Bull' Edition. This is Q1 *King Lear* (1608), which was to be sold by Nathaniel Butter 'at his shop ... at the signe of the Pide Bull'. It is called the Pide Bull to distinguish it from Jaggard's surreptitious reprint of 1619, falsely dated 1608, with which it used to be confused.

'Pierce Penilesse.' A satire by Thomas Nashe, registered 8 August 1592 and published in the same year, as 'Pierce Penilesse his Supplication to the Diuell'. It is in part an exposure of the vices of the age, in part a defence of poetry, 'the honey of all flowers, the quintessence of all sciences, the marrow of wit, and the very phrase of angels', of plays, and of players whom he had attacked three years earlier in his preface to Greene s *Menaphon*:

Our Players are not as the players beyond Sea, a sort of squirting baudie Comedians, that haue whores and common Curtizens to playe womens partes, and forbeare no immodest speech or vnchast action that may procure laughter; but our Sceane is more statelye furnisht than euer it was in the time of *Roscius*, our representations honourable, and full of gallant resolution, not consisting, like theirs, of a Pantaloun, a Whore, and a Zanie, but of Emperours, Kings, and Princes; whose true Tragedies (*Sophocleo cothurno*) they do vaunt. Not *Roscius* nor *Aesope*, those admyred tragedians that haue liued euer since before Christ was borne, could euer performe more in action than famous *Ned Allen*.

And it contains what is apparently the first certain reference to Shakespeare's work, to *1 Henry VI*, performed by Strange's 3 March 1592:

How would it haue ioyed braue Talbot (the terror of the French) to thinke that after he had lyne two hundred yeares in his Tombe, hee should triumphe againe on the Stage, and haue his bones newe embalmed with the teares of ten thousand spectators at least (at seuerall times) who, in the Tragedian that represents his person, imagine they behold him fresh bleeding?

'Pimlyco or Runne Red-Cappe.' A satirical and anonymous pamphlet registered 15 April 1609, and published in the same year. It celebrates the Pimlico ale of Hogsdon (Hoxton) which people of all classes swarm to taste, and contains a theatrical image that suggests that *Pericles* was equally popular:

Amazde I stood, to see a Crowd
Of *Ciuill Throats* stretched out so lowd;
(As at a *New-play*) all the Roomes
Did swarme with *Gentiles* mix'd with
  Groomes,
So that I truly thought all These
Came to see *Shore* or *Pericles*.

The word 'Pimlico' – apparently the native name of a West Indian wader – first occurs in *News from Hogsdon*, a tract of 1598, with a reference to 'Ben Pimlico's nut-browne'.

Pinch. In *The Comedy of Errors*, described in stage-direction of F as 'a schoole-master call'd Pinch', and by Antipholus of Ephesus as 'one Pinch, a hungry lean-faced villain, A mere anatomy, a mountebank'. He orders both Antipholus and Dromio of Ephesus to be 'bound and laid in some dark room' as men possessed (IV, iv). (Called Medicus in the *Menaechmi*.)

Pindarus. In *Julius Caesar*, a servant of Cassius who took him prisoner in Parthia. When Cassius thinks his friend Titinius captured and the battle of Philippi lost, he promises Pindarus his freedom if he will kill him with the sword that stabbed Caesar. Pindarus does so, and runs away (V, iii).

Pipe. A small flageolet with only three stops, which could be played with the left hand while the right played the tabor, or drum. There are well-known illustrations of Richard Tarlton playing the pipe and tabor, and of a man accompanying Kempe on the instruments as he danced to Norwich.

Piracy of Plays. The term applied to the publishing of plays (and other books) the 'copy' of which had been stolen, or the text of which had been surreptitiously acquired. Heminge and Condell, in their preface to F1, refer to earlier editions of *some* of Shakespeare's plays as 'diuerse stolne, and surreptitious copies, maimed, and deformed by the fraudes and stealthes of iniurious impostors, that expos'd them'. It does not follow that these pirated editions, now called 'bad' Quartos (q.v.), were unregistered. The Stationers' Company was concerned with preserving the copyright of the stationer who entered for his copy in the Register and paid his sixpence, and not with the means by which he had acquired his 'copy'. The players' companies, to whom the plays corporately belonged, could try to prevent piracy by getting a stationer to make a blocking entry (probably Roberts's registration of *Hamlet* was an unsuccessful attempt to do this), and by invoking the aid of their patron; for example, *The Merchant of Venice*, registered by Roberts, 22 July 1598, was not to be 'prynted by the said James Robertes or anye other whatsoeuer without lycence first had from the Right honorable the lord Chamberlen'.

There are six generally accepted 'bad' Quartos.

	Q1	*Registered*	*Publisher*
2 Henry VI	1594	1594, 12 Mar., Millington	Millington
3 Henry VI	1595	No original entry	Millington
Romeo & Juliet	1597	No original entry	Danter
Henry V	1600	1600, 4 Aug., 'to be staied' 1600, 14 Aug., Pavier	Millington & Busby
Merry Wives	1602	1602, 18 Jan., Busby 1602, 18 Jan., Busby to Johnson	Johnson
Hamlet	1603	1602, 26 July, Roberts	Ling & Trundell

Sometimes registration after publication of a 'bad' Quarto seems to have established copyright and even to have blocked the publication of a correct version (e.g. *The Spanish Tragedy*, 1592). Perhaps the registration of *2 Henry VI* implied that of *3 Henry VI* and blocked corrected Quartos, as also registration of *Henry V* and *The Merry Wives*. The unregistered *Romeo and Juliet* was followed by Busby's corrected Q of 1599, and Roberts's 1602 registration of *Hamlet* enabled him to print the 'good' Q of 1604. (See HEYWOOD, THOMAS; 'RAPE OF LUCRECE'.)

Pisanio. In *Cymbeline*, the servant of Posthumus who, when banished, leaves him in Imogen's service. In the last scene it is Pisanio who reveals that Lucius's page, Fidele, is really Imogen.

Pistol, an 'Irregular Humorist' (F) and ranting braggart who quotes scraps of bombast picked up at the theatres. He first appears in *2 Henry IV* as Falstaff's ancient, or ensign (II, iv). He brings Falstaff the joyful news that Henry IV is dead, but when Falstaff is disowned by Henry V he is carried off to prison with him.

In *The Merry Wives* Falstaff dismisses him when he refuses to take his love-letter to Mistress Ford, and in revenge he tells Ford of Falstaff's designs. He resolves to pursue and marry Mistress Quickly, with whom, as Hobgoblin to her Fairy Queen, he baits Falstaff in Windsor Forest.

In *Henry V* he is Mistress Quickly's husband and host of the Boar's Head. With Bardolph and Nym he goes on the Agincourt campaign, insults Fluellen, who cudgels him and forces him to eat a leek, and hearing that 'Doll' (Nell Quickly?) is dead, resolves to turn bawd and cutpurse.

Pit. In the private theatres, the area corresponding to the 'yard' for the groundlings of the public theatres. But the pit had seats, apparently expensive ones: cf. James Wright, *Historia Histrionica* (1699), 'Here they had "Pits" for the gentry, and acted by candlelight.' The word is derived from cockpit, probably from the Drury Lane Cockpit converted into a private theatre, the Phoenix, 1616–17; cf. Leonard Digges (1640):

> The cock-pit, galleries, boxes, are all full,
> To hear Malvolio, that cross-gartered gull.

(See ORCHESTRA.)

Plagiarism. In *The Poetaster* (1601), Jonson satirizes Crispinus (Marston) as 'poetaster and plagiary', and Demetrius (Dekker) as 'playdresser and plagiary'. He refers to the custom of employing hack-writers, as Henslowe employed the delightful and prolific Dekker, to revise and bring up to date other men's work. It is sometimes asserted that Shakespeare began his career as a dresser of old plays that came to be regarded as his. The Elizabethan dramatists had in Spenser a model for their poetry, and in the numerous collections of romantic stories a common store of plots, stock characters, and situations, so that a certain similarity in manner and matter is scarcely remarkable.

Plague. Plague and Puritans were the worst enemies of the players, for in time of plague the Privy Council had to agree with the City Corporation, who seized any opportunity to close the theatres, that plays must be prohibited to restrict infection. When the London theatres were closed, the companies had to resort to arduous and unprofitable competition with the established provincial companies. In 1584 the players themselves suggested that playing should be permitted as long as plague-deaths did not exceed fifty weekly, according to the plague-bill, an official weekly return from the City parishes and a few suburban ones. The Corporation replied that weekly deaths *from all causes* should be less than fifty for three consecutive weeks. Probably nothing came of this, but from 1604 to 1607 the theatres may have been closed automatically when weekly plague-deaths exceeded thirty, after 1607 when they exceeded forty. The *Office Book* of Sir Henry Herbert, Master of the Revels, illustrates the procedure in 1636:

> At the increase of the plague to 4 within the citty and 54 in all. – This day the 12 May, 1636, I received a warrant from my lord Chamberlin for the suppressing of playes and shews, and at the same time delivered my severall warrants to George Wilson for the four companys of players, to be served upon them.

A summary of the plague and its effect on playing in Shakespeare's lifetime is given below (see *Eliz. Stage*, IV, 345–51; SS, 15.)

1563 Severe plague. 20,000 deaths. Plays restrained from 30 Sept.

1564–87	Some plague in summer, and some short restraints.
1588–91	Little plague and no restraints.
1592–4	Severe plague. 11,000 deaths in 1593. Plays restrained most of the time between June 1592 and May 1594.
1595–1602	Little plague and no restraints.
1603	Severe plague. 30,000 deaths. Plays restrained March 1603, possibly to April 1604.
1604–8	Some plague and some restraints.
1609	Fairly severe plague. 4,000 deaths.
1610–16	Little plague and no restraints.

Planché, James Robinson (1796–1880), son of a London watchmaker of Huguenot descent, became a dramatist, his first piece being produced at Drury Lane in 1818. He wrote a number of burlesques for Mme Vestris when she became lessee of the Olympic theatre in 1831, and was engaged by her to write and design for the Lyceum, which she took over in 1847. Planché was also an antiquary, author of *The History of British Costumes*, one of the founders of the British Archaeological Association, and successively Rouge Croix Pursuivant and Somerset Herald.

His archaeological pursuits were dramatically important, for they led to the antiquarian Shakespearean productions of the 19th century. These were inaugurated in 1823 when he designed Charles Kemble's revival of *King John*, the first Shakespeare play to be produced with historically correct costumes, every character appearing 'in the precise Habit of the Period, the whole of the Dresses and Decorations being executed from indisputable Authorities such as Monumental Effigies, Seals, Illumined MSS. &c.' He also designed the spectacular, and therefore severely cut, production of *A Midsummer Night's Dream* staged by Charles Mathews and his wife Mme Vestris at Covent Garden in 1840. More important was the help he gave to a production of exactly the opposite kind, Benjamin Webster's Haymarket revival of *The Taming of the Shrew*, uncut and unadapted, the first of the honourable line of productions that sought to present what Shakespeare wrote in something the way in which he would have had it done. (See SS, 16.)

Plantagenet, Lady Margaret. In *Richard III*, a young daughter of Clarence, who, with her brother Edward, Earl of Warwick, mourns her father's death (II, ii). ('The last of the Plantagenets': b. 1473, cr. Countess of Salisbury 1513, beheaded 1541.)

Plantagenet, Richard. In *1, 2, 3 Henry VI*. See YORK, 3RD DUKE OF.

Platter, Thomas, a doctor of Basle, who was in England 18 September to 20 October 1599, and wrote in German (1604–5) an account of his travels of 1595–1600. The first reference in the following important extract is to a performance of a play of *Julius Caesar*, probably Shakespeare's, at the newly built Globe. The theatre in, or near, Bishopsgate must be the Curtain, the only theatre open on the north bank in the autumn of 1599.

> After dinner on the 21 September, at about 2 o'clock, I went over the river with my companions, and in the thatched-house' [streüwinen Dachhaus] saw the Tragedy of the first Emperor Julius Caesar, with at least 15 characters, acted very well. At the end of the play two of the actors in men's clothes and 2 in women's clothes performed a dance, as is their custom, wonderfully well together.
>
> On another occasion, also after dinner, I saw another play, not far from our lodging in the suburb, as far as I remember in Bishopsgate ... At the end they gave an admirable performance of both English and Irish dances. So, every day at 2 o'clock in the afternoon, two and sometimes three plays are acted at different places in the City of London, whereby the people are entertained, and those who do best have the biggest audience. The places are built so that they act on a raised platform, and everybody is able to see well. There are, however, separate galleries where one can stand more comfortably, and also sit, though it costs more. Thus, if you stand on the level you pay only

1 English penny, but if you wish to sit you are let in at another door where you pay another penny. If, however, you wish to sit on a cushion in the best place, where not only can you see well, but also be seen, you pay another penny at another door. When there is a pause in the play they carry round food and drink, so that you may buy refreshments.

The actors are very expensively and handsomely dressed, for it is an English custom that when distinguished gentlemen or knights die, almost their best clothes are given to their servants, but as it is not fitting that they should wear them they sell them cheaply to the actors.

Plaudite. It was customary, at the end of the performance of a play, for the Epilogue to ask for a plaudite, or applause, from the audience. Thus in *Every Man out of His Humour* the envious Macilente steps forward and says,

... marry, I will not do as Plautus in his *Amphytrio*, for all this, *summi Jovis causa, plaudite*; beg a plaudite for God's sake; but if you, out of the bounty of your good liking, will bestow it, why, you may in time make lean Macilente as fat as Sir John Falstaff. (See M., I.)

Plautus, Titus Maccius (*c.* 254–184 B.C.), dramatist, was born at Sarsina in Umbria, but went early to Rome, where he found some sort of employment in a theatre. He lost in a business venture what money he had managed to save, and was for a time reduced to grinding corn in a flour-mill, where he wrote three of his plays. Of these, twenty remain, all of them comedies taken from Greek originals, in particular from Menander, and most of them comedies of intrigue. Plautus was very popular in the days of the late Republic, considered a rough diamond in the polished Augustan Age, forgotten during the Middle Ages, but at the Renaissance rediscovered as one of the great dramatic poets of classical times, his plays, with those of Terence and Seneca, being acted in England at the schools and universities early in the 16th century, and the first English comedy, *Ralph Roister Doister* (*c.* 1550), is based on his *Miles Glorious.*

Shakespeare probably read some of his plays at school, and certainly knew the *Menaechmi* (q.v.) which is the main source of *The Comedy of Errors*, and probably the *Amphitruo* as well, in which a husband is locked out of his own house. William Warner registered his translation of the *Menaechmi* 10 June 1594; *The Comedy of Errors* was acted at Gray's Inn 28 December, but it had probably been written some time before then. *The Taming of the Shrew* owes something to the *Mostellaria*, including the names of Grumio and Tranio. (See also MANNINGHAM.) In *Hamlet* Polonius refers to the actors for whom 'Seneca cannot be too heavy, nor Plautus too light'.

Shakespeare's name is coupled with that of Plautus by three of his contemporaries; by Francis Meres (1598): 'As *Plautus* and *Seneca* are accounted the best for Comedy and Tragedy among the Latines: so *Shakespeare* among y[e] English is the most excellent in both kinds for the stage.' By Thomas Freeman (1614):

Besides in plaies thy wit windes like
Meander:
Whence needy new-composers borrow
more
Than *Terence* doth from *Plautus* or *Menander.*

And by Ben Jonson (1623):

The merry Greeke, *tart* Aristophanes,
Neat Terence, *witty* Plautus, *now not please*;
But antiquated and deserted lye
As they were not of Natures family.

Jonson himself combined the *Aulularia* and *Captivi* in his *Case is Altered*, and Heywood's *Silver Age*, *Captives* and *English Traveller* are adaptations of the *Amphitruo*, *Rudens* and *Mostellaria* respectively.

Play-bills. See 'BILLS'.

Play-dresser. See DEKKER; PLAGIARISM.

Players. 1. In the Induction to *The Taming of the Shrew* a company of players comes to entertain a Lord. He makes them perform the comedy of *The Taming of the Shrew* before the drunken Sly, to whom they are introduced as 'Your honour's players'.

2. In *Hamlet* a company of 'four or five players' comes to offer Hamlet service. He expects to find a King, Knight, Lover, 'Humorous' Man, Clown and Lady. They are forced to travel: 'their inhibition comes by the means of the late innovation', meaning either that their playing in the City has been prohibited because of the recent insurrection (Essex's Rebellion (?) February 1601), or that they have lost favour because of the popularity of the Chapel Children at the newly opened second Blackfriars theatre. In F, Rosencrantz refers to the Poetomachia (q.v.), or War of the Theatres, but in Q2 (1604) the passage is omitted, no doubt because Queen Anne had taken the Children under her patronage. Hamlet at once gets the first player to 'speak him a speech', and later to perform before the King *The Murder of Gonzago*, in which he inserts a speech of some dozen or sixteen lines, and tells the player how to speak it. Hamlet's advice to the players (III, ii) is of the greatest importance, as it illustrates the stylized convention of Elizabethan acting, each thought having a corresponding action of the body to make clear the meaning of the words to those who did not understand them.

Plays. The number of plays written in the twenty years during which Shakespeare was active, *c.* 1590–1610, must have been remarkable. Shakespeare himself wrote 39 if we include *Pericles*, *The Two Noble Kinsmen*, and *Cardenio*, an average of two a year; Jonson was twitted for writing only one a year (though he wrote *Volpone* in five weeks), but Heywood tells us in *The English Traveller* (1633) that he had 'an entire hand or at least a main finger' in 220 plays, an average of more than five in a writing career of about forty years. At the turn of the century there may have been some twenty full-time dramatists writing two to three plays a year, which with the occasional contributions of others would make 60 to 70 a year. This agrees well enough with Henslowe's 55 'ne' plays for the Admiral's in the three years June 1594–June 1597, an average of 18 a year, and the 12 for Worcester's in seven months of 1602–3. Thomas Platter wrote that in 1599 two, and sometimes three, plays were acted every afternoon in London; the demand would come mainly from the Chamberlain's, Admiral's, Worcester's (after 1600) and the Chapel Children. Plays were acted on the repertory system and never had a long run. Between 19 February and 23 June 1592 Strange's played for Henslowe at the Rose on every day except Sundays, Good Friday and two other days, 105 performances altogether. There were 23 plays, five of them 'ne', some of them played only once, *Jeronymo* 15 times, and rarely the same play twice in one week.

There was, therefore, a big demand for plays, and to satisfy it the astute Henslowe devised a system of mass production with division of labour whereby as many as five dramatists worked at one play, each concentrating on the part at which he excelled. In addition, there was voluntary collaboration, the classical example being that of Beaumont and Fletcher. Then old plays were revised, largely for Henslowe, by 'play-dressers' such as Dekker. But though there was much collaboration, many plays were one author's sole work: nearly all Shakespeare's and Jonson's for example.

A dramatist might, like Shakespeare, write always for one company in which he was an actor-sharer, or be under contract to Henslowe or Langley for a number of years, or he might be a free lance like Jonson. The author, or authors, sold the play to a company of actors whose joint property it became; Henslowe normally paid £6 for a play for Worcester's in 1602–3, though sometimes £7 or £8, but no doubt his prices were the lowest. Small wonder that plays were thought of as ephemeral affairs for the stage and not as literature for the study, and lightly treated by publishers and the Stationers' Company. Jonson, however, took the drama more seriously, and was taunted by Heywood for the careful publication of his plays as his 'Works' in the Folio of 1616. It should be remembered that though Shakespeare himself supervised the publication of *Venus and Adonis* and *Lucrece*, he took no part, as far as we know, in the publication of his plays.

When a play had been bought by a company it was trimmed to suit their resources and arranged for performance by the book-keeper under the direction of the sharers, transcribed, and sent to the Master of the Revels for his censorship and 'allowance' for performance, and after 1606 for printing as well.

Plays seem generally to have been kept unpublished by the company as a financial reserve, though there was always the risk that they would be pirated, as were six of Shakespeare's. The great majority, therefore, of Elizabethan-Jacobean plays have perished; of Heywood's 220 only about twenty remain and the names of about a dozen more, and without the Folio we should have only half of Shakespeare's plays and four of these in corrupt versions. When capital was required, however, the company might sell plays to a publisher; many were sold and published in the difficult plague year of 1593–4, and four of Shakespeare's unpirated Quartos were published in 1600, probably to help to pay for the building of the Globe. A play had to be licensed for printing, originally by the clerical deputies of the Archbishop of Canterbury, but after 1606 by the Master of the Revels, and entered in the Stationers' Register, which secured the publisher's copyright on his payment of the fee of 6d. (See PERFORMANCES; PROMPT-BOOK.)

Pléiade. The school of seven French poets of the mid 16th century: Ronsard, du Bellay, Tyard, Baïf, Belleau, Jodelle and Pelletier or Dorat. They freed French poetry from medieval conventions, turned to the classics, and established the alexandrine as the staple French line. Their sonnets, particularly those of Ronsard and du Bellay, inspired the Elizabethans: Spenser, Sidney and, directly or indirectly, Shakespeare. (The name 'Pleiad', derived from the seven stars of the constellation of the Pleiades, was first applied to seven Hellenist poets of the 3rd century B.C., of whom Theocritus was the chief.)

Pliny, The Elder (*c.* 23–79). Gaius Plinius Secundus is remembered as the author of the *Historia Naturalis*, a work 'as varied as nature herself'. He was a friend of the Emperor Vespasian, and a Stoic who thought all time wasted that was not given to study. His scientific desire to study the eruption of Vesuvius that overwhelmed Pompeii and Herculaneum led to his death. His *Natural History* was translated by Philemon Holland (q.v.) and published in 1601. There are references to it in *Othello*, and possibly in *Julius Caesar*.

'Plot'. An abstract, scene by scene, of the action of a play. This was probably made by the book-keeper (prompter) from a prompt-copy, and hung on a peg for his own use, or perhaps in the tiring-house for the benefit of the tire-man and actors. The abstract was written in a large hand in two columns, mounted on pasteboard, and pierced in the top centre by an oblong hole so that it could be hung on a wooden peg. Seven plots are known:

The Second Part of the Seven Deadly Sins. By R. Tarlton. Probably performed by Strange's, *c.* 1590.

The Dead Man's Fortune. An Admiral's or Strange's play, *c.* 1590.

Frederick and Basilea. An Admiral's play *c.* 3 June 1597.

The First Part of Tamar Cham. Now lost. Originally, probably a Strange's play, *c.* 1591. The actors named in the plot are the Admiral's, *c.* 1602.

The Second Part of Fortune's Tennis. Fragmentary. An Admiral's play: possibly Dekker's lost *Fortune's Tennis, c.* 1597–8.

Troilus and Cressida. Fragmentary, without title. Probably the *Troilus and Cressida* written for the Admiral's by Chettle and Dekker, 1599.

The Battle of Alcazar. Fragmentary. Originally, probably a Strange's play by Peele, *c.* 1589. The actors named in the plot are the Admiral's, *c.* 1600.

The first four of these were once in the possession of George Steevens, in whose *Variorum* (1803) the text is given, as also in Malone's *Variorum* (1821).

In the plots the names of the actors generally follow the characters they present. The scenes are carefully divided by rules, and in *Dead Man's Fortune* the end of the first four of the five acts is indicated by crosses, with directions for music in the margin, though these are later additions:

	Enter the prolouge
	Enter laertes Eschines and vrganda
	Enter pesscodde to him his father
	Enter *Tesephon* allgeryus laertes wth atendantes: Darlowe: lee: b samme: to them allcyane and statyra
	Enter validore and asspida at severall dores to them the panteloun
Musique	—×—×—×—×—×—×—×—×—×—×-

In *Tamar Cham* noises are indicated in the margin: *Sound Sennet, Alarum, Thunder, Wind horne*, etc.; and each act is introduced by a Chorus: *Enter Chorus Dick Jubie: Exit*. Properties for *Alcazar* include: *rawflesh, 3 violes of blood & a sheeps gather, Dead mens heads & bones.* The plot of the *Seven Deadly Sins* (q.v.) has the title, 'The Booke and Platt of the Second part of The 7 deadly Sinns', suggesting that the book (i.e. the theatre copy of the play) and the plot were kept together. (See Greg, *Dramatic Documents.*)

Plume, Thomas (1630–74), the Archdeacon of Rochester who founded the library at Maldon, in which are preserved his manuscript notes of *c.* 1657. Among them is a description of Shakespeare's father, John:

> He was a glovers son – Sir John Mennis saw once his old Father in his shop – a merry Cheekd old man – that said – Will was a good Honest Fellow, but he durst have crackt a jeast with him at any time. (See MENNIS.)

Plutarch (*c.* 50–130) was born at Chaeronea in Boeotia. After studying philosophy at Athens and visiting Egypt, he went to Rome where his teaching gained him the patronage of the Emperor Trajan, who appointed him consul, and governor of Illyricum. After Trajan's death he retired to Chaeronea, where he wrote his *Parallel Lives*, and died at an advanced age. This is his most celebrated work, forty-six scholarly biographies of famous Greeks and Romans, nearly all arranged in pairs; e.g. Theseus and Romulus, as founders of states. The book has had an immense influence both on writers and men of action; 'Plutarch is my man', said Montaigne, and both Napoleon and Wellington were his students. It was translated by Sir Thomas North (q.v.) from the French version of Jacques Amyot, and published in 1579 as *The Lives of the Noble Grecians and Romanes.* North's *Plutarch* was Shakespeare's source for his Greek and Roman tragedies, the most famous parallel passage being in *Antony and Cleopatra* (II, ii):

She disdained to set forward otherwise, but to take her barge in the river of Cydnus, the poope whereof was of gold, the sails of purple, and the owers of silver, which kept stroke in rowing after the sound of flutes, howboys, cythern, violls, and such other instruments as they played upon the barge....

The barge she sat in like a burnish'd throne,
Burn'd on the water: the poop was beaten
  gold;
Purple the sails, and so perfumed that
The winds were love-sick with them; the
  oars were silver,
Which to the tune of flutes kept stroke, and
  made
The water which they beat to follow faster,
As amorous of their strokes....

Poe, Edgar Allan (1809–49), was, at his best, a critic of real merit. His remark on Shakespeare and poetry is often misquoted. It occurs in the 'Letter to B—', printed in his preface to *Poems* (1831), and in the *Southern Literary Messenger* (1836), of which periodical he was for a time sub-editor:

What is Poetry? – Poetry! that Proteus-like idea, with as many appellations as the nine-titled Corcyra! 'Give me,' I demanded of a scholar some time ago, 'give me a definition of poetry.' 'Très volontiers'; and he proceeded to his library, brought me a Dr Johnson, and overwhelmed me with a definition. Shade of the immortal Shakespeare! I imagine to myself the scowl of your spiritual eye upon the profanity of that scurrilous Ursa Major. Think of poetry, dear B—, think of poetry, and then think of Dr. Samuel Johnson! Think of all that is airy and fairy-like, and then of all that is hideous and unwieldy; think of his huge bulk, the Elephant! and then – and then think of the Tempest – the Midsummer Night's Dream – Prospero – Oberon – and Titania! ...

Poel, William (1852–1934), son of William Pole, the engineer, adopted the name of Poel when he went on the stage in 1876. He continued the work of Benjamin Webster and Samuel Phelps in freeing the production of Shakespeare from the tyranny of spectacle, and restoring the original text to the theatre. In 1881 he produced the First Quarto version of *Hamlet* at St George's Hall under approximately Elizabethan conditions, was manager of the Royal Victoria Hall (the Old Vic) 1881–3, and stage-manager of F. R. Benson's company 1883–4. In 1895 he founded the Elizabethan Stage Society and then, over a period of twenty-five to thirty years, produced without scenery and without intervals a series of Shakespearean and other plays, including *Dr Faustus*, *The Duchess of Malfi*, *Edward III*, *The Alchemist* and *The Return from Parnassus.* Among his actors were Nugent Monck, who continued his work with the amateur Norwich Players, and Granville-Barker, who first applied his principles to the commercial theatre. Poel's writings include *Shakespeare in the Theatre* and *What is Wrong with the Stage?*

POEMS. The poems published as Shakespeare's are:

Venus and Adonis, 1593; *The Rape of Lucrece*' 1594. These were printed by Richard Field, a Stratford man, and probably a friend of Shakespeare. They are probably the only works the publication of which Shakespeare supervised, and are very carefully produced. Both are dedicated to the Earl of Southampton. They were very popular; *Venus and Adonis* went through sixteen editions before 1640, and *Lucrece* eight. After 1655, when *Lucrece* was published with John Quarles's *Banishment of Tarquin*, there were no more 17th-century editions. They were next printed with *The Passionate Pilgrim* in 1707.

The Passionate Pilgrim, 1599. W. Jaggard's pirated edition of two of Shakespeare's *Sonnets*, three of the lovers' poems from *Love's Labour's Lost*, and sixteen other poems, some anonymous, some by other authors, and all attributed to Shakespeare.

The Phoenix and Turtle, 1601. A short poem ascribed to Shakespeare, and one of the 'diverse poeticall essaies ... done by the best and chiefest of our moderne writers' appended to Robert Chester's *Love Martyr*.

Sonnets, 1609.

A Lover's Complaint, 1609. Appended to the *Sonnets* and ascribed to Shakespeare.

Poems, 1640. The first collected edition of some of Shakespeare's poems was registered in 1639:

4° Nouembris 1639 ... John Benson Entred for his Copie vnder the hands of doctor Wykes and Master Fetherston warden An Addicion of some excellent Poems to Shakespeares Poems by other gentlemen vizt. His mistris drawne, and her mind by Benjamin: Johnson. An Epistle to Beniamin Johnson by Francis Beaumont. His Mistris shade. by R. Herrick. &c. vj^{d}.

The volume was published in the following year as,

Poems: Written by Wil. Shake-speare. Gent. Printed at London by Tho. Cotes, and are to be sold by Iohn Benson, dwelling in St Dunstans Church-yard. 1640.

It contains,

(*a*) As frontispiece, Marshall's copy of the Droeshout engraving.

(*b*) An epistle by Benson 'to the Reader':

I Here presume (under favour) to present to your view, some excellent and sweetely composed Poems, of Master William Shakespeare, Which in themselves appeare of the same purity, the Author himselfe then living avouched; they had not the fortune by reason of their Infancie in his death, to have the due accomodation of proportionable glory, with the rest of his everliving Workes, yet the lines of themselves will afford you a more authentick approbation than my assurance any way can, to invite your allowance, in your perusall you shall finde them *Seren*, cleere and eligantly plaine, such gentle straines as shall recreate and not perplexe your braine, no intricate or cloudy stuffe to puzzell intellect, but perfect eloquence; such as will raise your admiration to his praise: this assurancc I know will not differ from your acknowledgement. And certaine I am, my opinion will be seconded by the sufficiency of these ensuing Lines; I have beene somewhat solicitus to bring this forth to the perfect view of all men; and in so doing, glad to be serviceable for the continuance of glory to the deserved Author in these his Poems. I.B.

(*c*) Commendatory verses on Shakespeare by Leonard Digges and John Warren.

(*d*) The Sonnets (omitting 18, 19, 43, 56, 75, 76), printed in a different order from that of 1609, and altered so that they appear to be addressed to a woman, each, or occasionally a group of two or three, being prefixed by a title.

(*e*) The poems of the 1612 edition of *The Passionate Pilgrim*, intermingled with the *Sonnets*.

(*f*) *A Lover's Complaint*.

(*g*) The *Replies* of Ralegh and Ignoto to Marlowe's 'Live with me, and be my love'.

(*h*) 'Take, O, take those lips away', from *Measure for Measure*, with the second verse from Beaumont and Fletcher's *Bloody Brother*, 1639.

(*i*) *The Phoenix and Turtle*.

(*j*) Orlando's verses from *As You Like It*, III, ii.

(*k*) Basse's Elegy on Shakespeare in F1, Milton's in F2, and an anonymous Elegy beginning.

I dare not do thy memory that wrong,
Unto our larger griefs to give a tongue.
I'll only sigh in earnest, and let fall
My solemn tears at thy great funeral.

(*l*) 'An addition of some Excellent Poems, to those precedent, of Renowned *Shakespeare*, By other Gentlemen', including Jonson, Beaumont, and Herrick.

In the 17th century a number of manuscript poems, were ascribed to Shakespeare (see JAMES, ELIAS), and Boswell (*Var.*, II, 481) quotes from 'a manuscript volume of poems ... written apparently about the time of the Restoration':

Shakespeare upon the King.

Crownes have their compasse, length of
dayes their date,
Triumphes their tombs, felicity her fate:
Of more than earth cann earth make none
partaker
But knowledge makes the king most like
his Maker.

Some anonymous poems have been, on internal evidence, attributed to Shakespeare (see FLORIO). (For further details see the titles of the various poems.)

'Poetaster, The.' A satirical comedy by Ben Jonson, registered 21 December 1601, published in Q 1602, and in F 1616:

Poëtaster, Or His Arraignment. A Comicall Satyre, Acted, in the yeere 1601. By the then Children of Queene Elizabeths Chappel. The Author B. I. ... The principall Comoedians were, Nat. Field, Ioh. Vnderwood, Sal. Pavy, Will. Ostler, Tho. Day, Tho. Marton. With the allowance of the Master of Revells.

Dekker is ridiculed as Demetrius, 'playdresser and plagiary', and Jonson himself appears as Horace and gives the poetaster Crispinus (Marston) a pill that makes him vomit his windy words. The play also satirizes actors, lawyers, and soldiers in the persons of Histrio, Lupus, and Tucca. Dekker and Marston replied in *Satiromastix*. (See POETOMACHIA.)

Poetomachia. The name given by Dekker to the 'war of the theatres' 1599–1602, when Marston was writing mainly for the Paul's Children, and Jonson for the Children of the Chapel at Blackfriars. In the Apologetical Dialogue appended to *The Poetaster*, and written probably in 1602, Jonson complains that 'Fellows of practised and laxative tongues ... three years They did provoke me with their petulant styles On every stage', and in 1619 he told Drummond that 'He had many quarrels with Marston, beat him, and took his pistol from him, wrote his Poetaster on him; the beginning of them were, that Marston represented him in the stage'.

1599. Marston introduced Jonson as the poet and philosopher Chrisoganus in his *Histrio-mastix*, and the portrait, though inoffensive, may have offended Jonson.

1599. Jonson apparently satirizes Marston's turgid style in *Every Man out of His Humour*, a Chamberlain's play, where Clove talks 'fustian a little ... as you may read in Plato's Histriomastix.' (III, i).

1600. Marston satirizes Jonson as Brabant Senior, the cuckold, in *Jack Drum's Entertainment*, a Paul's play.

1601. In *Cynthia's Revels*, a Chapel play, Jonson appears to satirize Marston as Hedon, 'a light voluptuous reveller', and Dekker as Anaides, 'a strange arrogating puff'.

1601. Marston satirizes Jonson as Lampatho Doria in his *What You Will*, probably a Paul's play.

1601. Jonson seems to have heard that Dekker was preparing an attack, and got in his blow first, with *The Poetaster*, a Chapel play, in which he attacks Dekker as Demetrius the 'playdresser and plagiary', and Marston as Crispinus the 'poetaster and plagiary'. Horace (Jonson) gives Crispinus a pill to purge him of his windy words.

1601. Dekker, probably aided by Marston, replied in *Satiromastix*, a Chamberlain's and Paul's play, in which Demetrius and Crispinus ridicule Horace, the laborious poet.

Shakespeare refers to the Poetomachia in *Hamlet*, II, ii (1601), where the adult actors are described as being forced to travel in the provinces owing to the popularity of the boys' companies, who presented most of the plays in the controversy. In *3 Parnassus* of the same year Will Kempe is made to refer to Shakespeare's having given the 'pestilent fellow' Jonson a 'purge' in return for his 'pill', but there is no other obvious indication of Shakespeare's being involved in the quarrel, which was made up by 1604, when Marston dedicated *The Malcontent* to Jonson. (See 'PARNASSUS'.)

Poetry. Shakespeare's poems were very popular in the first half of the 17th century; between 1593 and 1640 there were sixteen editions of *Venus and Adonis* and eight of *Lucrece*, and contemporary reference to these two poems is more frequent than to the plays. Most of Shakespeare's other poems were collected in Benson's edition of 1640, but after that they were all neglected, though occasionally published by 18th-century editors of Shakespeare's works as an afterthought or pious duty; Steevens, one of the most important, excluded the poems because 'the strongest Act of Parliament that could be passed would fail to compel readers into their service', and even Hazlitt's admiration of Shakespeare ceased with his plays.

After the Restoration, Shakespeare's plays were thought of as rough-hewn material to be shaped and polished by a more refined age (see ADAPTATION). As late as 1771, Garrick re-wrote the end of *Hamlet*, and it was not until about the middle of the 19th century that Shakespeare came to be preferred to his improvers, and it was later still before his full text was restored. At the same time,

Shakespeare was recognized as a supreme creator of character, and it was on this basis that his reputation was established. With a few exceptions, such as Gray and Morgann, the 18th-century critics seem to have been unaware that Shakespeare is primarily a poet, and it remained for the Romantic critics, particularly Coleridge and Hazlitt, to discover the poetry of Shakespeare's plays. Even then the 19th century continued to think of Shakespeare in terms of his characters and, with the entry of the German critics into the field, of his philosophy, and this remains today the popular conception of Shakespeare.

Shakespeare is profound, but it is as a poet and not as a thinker that he is profound; he *is* a supreme master of character, but he is so because he is a supreme poet. King John, Richard II, Hamlet, Macbeth, Othello, Lear, Antony and Cleopatra are so real and near to us, not because of what they do, not even because of what they say, but because of the way in which they say it: because, in short, of the poetry; because of the simple 'magic and evocatory phrase':

> Sound all the lofty instruments of war.
>
> Of moving accidents by flood and field.

and because of the powerful magic of metaphor:

> My way of life
> Is faln into the sear, the yellow leaf.
> And all our yesterdays have lighted fools
> The way to dusty death.

Twentieth-century scholars have been much occupied with Shakespeare's theatre and the transmission of his text; critics have been more concerned with his poetry, particularly with his imagery, than heretofore, but there is still no general recognition that Shakespeare is above all else a poet, and that it is his poetry that transfigures every other element in his plays.

Shakespeare was first a lyric poet, author of the *Sonnets* and two lyrical dramatic poems. In *Romeo and Juliet*, *Richard II*, *Love's Labour's Lost* and *A Midsummer Night's Dream*, he applied this poetry to tragedy, history and comedy, but it is often applied as decoration, and is by no means always the stuff of the play. From *Henry IV* to *Twelfth Night* (1597–1600) he subordinated verse to prose, and from this schooling learned to write the dramatic poetry of the great tragedies. In the romances he turned again to a more lyrical form, but the poetry never runs away with the dramatist as it did in the earliest plays. All through his career, Shakespeare continued to write pure lyric, from 'Who is Silvia?' in *The Two Gentlemen of Verona* to Ariel's songs in *The Tempest*.

Poins. A practical joker and friend of Prince Henry. In *1 Henry IV* he proposes the plan whereby they rob Falstaff and his gang of the booty filched from the travellers; and later he helps the Prince to make fun of Francis the drawer. In *2 Henry IV* he suggests the trick whereby he and the Prince observe Falstaff 'in his true colours', disguised as drawers.

Politics. In her Proclamation of 16 May 1559, Elizabeth ordered her licensing officers to forbid plays 'wherin either matters of religion or of the gouernaunce of the estate of the common weale shalbe handled or treated, beyng no meete matters to be wrytten or treated vpon, but by menne of aucthoritie, learning and wisedome, nor to be handled before any audience, but of graue and discreete persons'. This was strictly enforced; for example, in 1597 the theatres were closed because of the seditious *Isle of Dogs*, in 1605 Chapman was imprisoned for his part in the anti-Scot *Eastward Ho!*, and in 1601 the Chamberlain's got into trouble for their extraordinary performance of *Richard II* with the deposition scene. (See CENSORSHIP; LICENSING.)

Polixenes. In *The Winter's Tale* (q.v.), King of Bohemia. (In Greene's *Pandosto* the corresponding character is Egistus, King of Sicily.)

Pollard, Alfred William (1859–1944), bibliographer, was educated at King's College School, London, and St John's, Oxford. In 1883 he became Assistant in the Department of Printed Books in the British Museum, Assistant-Keeper in 1909, and Keeper in 1919, in which year he was appointed Professor of English Bibliography in the University of London. He was Hon. Sec. Bibliographical Society 1893–1934, and editor of *The Library* 1903–34. Among his publications are, *Shakespeare Folios and Quartos: A Study in the Bibliography of Shakespeare's Plays*, 1909; *A New Shakespeare Quarto: Richard II*, 1916; *Shakespeare's Fight with the Pirates, and the Problems of the Transmission of his Text*, 1917; *The Foundations of Shakespeare's Text*, 1923; *Shakespeare's Hand in Sir Thomas More* (with others), 1923. Pollard rendered invaluable service to Shakespeare scholarship by his bibliographical research, which completely changed ideas about the transmission of Shakespeare's text. (See TEXTUAL CRITICISM.)

Pollard, Thomas. A comedian with the King's Men after Shakespeare's death. In 1635 John Shank, who had joined the company about 1615, maintained that he had 'still of his owne purse supplyed the company for the service of his Majesty with boyes as Thomas Pollard ...' Pollard played Silvio in the revival of *The Duchess of Malfi*, *c.* 1620, and acted with Taylor in *Henry VIII*, possibly the Globe revival of 1628. (See WRIGHT, JAMES.)

Polonius. In *Hamlet*, Lord Chamberlain and father of Ophelia and Laertes. He sends his servant Reynaldo to spy on Laertes in France, orders Ophelia to reject Hamlet's advances and then spies on their meeting, which he arranges; finally, Hamlet kills him while he is spying behind the curtains when Hamlet is talking to his mother. (In Q1 Polonius is called Corambis. See 'BESTRAFTE BRUDERMORD'.)

Polydore. The name given to Guiderius in *Cymbeline*.

Pompey. In *Antony and Cleopatra*, Pompeius Sextus (75–35 B.C.), younger son of Pompey the Great, continues his father's struggle against the new rulers of Rome, but at Misenum concludes a treaty with the triumvirs whom he feasts in his galley. However, the struggle is renewed and his defeat by Octavius is announced III, v.

'Pompey.' A lost play performed at Court by the Children of Paul's under Sebastian Westcott on Twelfth Night 1581; one of the many plays on the Caesar theme, written before Shakespeare's *Julius Caesar*.

Pompey Bum. In *Measure for Measure*, 'a clowne', a bawd and servant to Mistress Overdone. He is sent to prison, where he becomes assistant to Abhorson the hangman.

Pope, Alexander (1688–1744), the second editor of Shakespeare, published his edition of the plays in six quarto volumes in 1725. A seventh volume, edited by Dr George Sewell, contained the *Poems*, and an essay on the history of the stage. In his *Preface* Pope exposed the inaccuracies of the First Folio, 'for in all respects else it is far worse than the quartos. ... These editions now hold the place of originals, and are the only materials left to repair the deficiencies or restore the corrupted sense of the author.' In his second edition of 1728 he printed a list of the twenty-nine Quartos which he knew, but he appears to have made little use of them, and his text is substantially that of Rowe, who used the Fourth Folio. His emendations were according to his personal taste, and what he did not like was 'degraded to the bottom of the page'. However, he marked the scenes 'so distinctly that every removal of place is specified', and he improved the punctuation and rhythm. The critical part of his *Preface* is uninspired and conventional. The short-comings of Pope's edition were revealed by Theobald in 1726, in his *Shakespeare Restored, or a Specimen of* *the many Errors as well Committed as Unamended by Mr Pope in his late edition of this Poet.* Pope retaliated by making Theobald the original hero of *The Dunciad* (1728). In his second edition of Shakespeare Pope wrote, 'Since the publication of *our* first edition, there having been some attempts upon Shakespear, published by Lewis Theobald ... *we* have inserted, in this impression, as many of 'em as are judg'd of any the least advantage to the poet; the whole amounting to about *twenty-five* words'. As a matter of fact, he incorporated many of Theobald's best emendations. In 1790 Malone wrote:

> In Mr Pope's edition our author was not less misrepresented [than by Rowe]; for though by examining the oldest copies he detected some errors, by his numerous fanciful alterations the poet was so completely modernized, that I am confident, had he 're-visited the glimpses of the moon,' he would not have understood his own works.

Pope, Thomas. A comedian and acrobat, and one of the twenty-six 'Principall Actors' in Shakespeare's plays (see p. 90). In 1586–7 he was one of the English players at the Courts of Denmark (q.v.) and Saxony, *c.* 1591 played in *The Seven Deadly Sins*, probably with Strange's, of which company he was a member when they toured the provinces under Alleyn in 1593. He was probably an original member of the Chamberlain's on their formation in 1594, was their joint payee 1597–9, and played in *Every Man in His Humour* and *Every Man out of His Humour* 1598–9. He was one of the original housekeepers of the Globe 1599, but as he is not mentioned in the lists of the King's Men he had probably retired by 1603, in which year he made his will and soon afterwards died. He lived in Southwark and does not appear to have been married. Samuel Rowlands, in his *Letting of Humour's Blood*, 1600, refers to Pope and to Singer, the comedian of the Admiral's,

> what meanes Singer then,
> And Pope, the clowne, to speak so borish, when
> They counterfaite the clownes upon the stage?

Heywood mentions him in his *Apology for Actors* (q.v.).

Porter. In *Macbeth*, II, iii, he admits Macduff and Lennox into Macbeth's castle, where they discover the murdered Duncan. (See GARNET. Coleridge thought 'the low soliloquy of the Porter' was written by some other hand; but see De Quincey's essay *On the Knocking at the Gate*.)

Porter, Endymion (1587–1649), of Aston-sub-Edge in Gloucestershire, courtier, agent, and friend of Charles I, in whose cause he impoverished himself. According to Anthony Wood, he was 'beloved by two kings: James I for his admirable wit, and Charles I for his general bearing, brave style, sweet temper, great experience, travels and modern languages'. He was a friend and patron of painters and poets, including D'Avenant and Dekker, and of Thomas Russell, overseer of Shakespeare's will. In 1626 he secured for the projectors Charles I's licence for the abortive scheme of building a great amphitheatre for plays and every kind of spectacle and entertainment. (See SS, 2.)

Porter, Henry (d. 1599), dramatist, was writing in 1589, and was by 1596 in the clutches of Henslowe, who paid him £5 in December, and lent him £4 in March 1597. In 1598–9 Henslowe bought five plays from him for the Admiral's, and in the latter year bound him to sell to him 'alle the bookes' in which he had a hand. The last references to him are in 1599, when, in return for Henslowe's loan of 1s., he bound himself in £10 for the repayment of a debt of 25s. His one extant play, published in 1599, is the rural comedy, *The Two Angry Women of Abingdon*, which has been compared to *The Merry Wives of Windsor*. In 1598 Meres mentioned him as one of 'the best for Comedy amongst us'. He collaborated with Chettle in the lost Admiral's play *The Spencers*, and with Chettle and Jonson in *Hot Anger Soon Cold*. He was stabbed and killed by John Day 6 June 1599.

Porter, Thomas, was in 1615 vicar of Hempnall, Norfolk, sometime before which date, when at Cambridge, he wrote a Latin epigram on Shakespeare:

> Gul: Shakespeare Poëtam lepidum.
> Quot lepŏres in Atho tot habet tua Musa lepôres
> Ingenii vena diuite metra tua.

Porter's Hall. When Philip Rosseter's lease of the Whitefriars theatre for the Chapel (Queen's Revels) Children expired, he and his partners, Philip Kingman, Robert Jones, and Ralph Reeve, secured a patent, dated 3 June 1615, to build on the premises

> scituate and being within the Precinct of the Blackeffryers neere Puddlewharfe in the Suburbs of London, called by the name of the lady Saunders house, or otherwise Porters hall, and now in the occupation of the said Robert Iones ... one convenient Playhouse for the said children of the Revelles, the same Playhouse to be vsed by the Children of the Revelles for the tyme being of the Queenes Maiestie, and for the Princes Players, and for the ladie Elizabeths Players ...

The exact position of the theatre is not clear, but it must have been a porter's lodge not far from the King's Men's Blackfriars theatre and Shakespeare's Gatehouse. The Corporation protested to the Privy Council who, after consulting Lord Chief Justice Coke, on 26 September 1615 ordered 'That there shalbe noe Play house erected in that place.' Apparently Rosseter and his friends had already 'pulled down a great Messuage in Puddle wharfe, which was sometimes the house of the Ladie Sanders within the Precinct of the Blackfryers' and were 'now erectinge a Newe Playhouse in that place'. And a Privy Council Minute of January 1617 states that 'there bee certaine persons that goe about to sett vp a Play howse in the Black ffryaers neere vnto his Maiesties Wardrobe, and for that purpose have lately erected and made fitt a Building, which is almost if not fully finished'. It seems that the venture was not stayed before the performance of some plays; Beaumont and Fletcher's *Scornful Lady*, registered and published in 1616, was acted 'by the Children of Her Maiesties Reuels in the Blacke Fryers', and Nathan Field's *Amends for Ladies*, published 1618, 'was acted at the Blacke-Fryers, both by the Princes Seruants, and the Lady Elizabeths'.

Portia. 1. The heroine of *The Merchant of Venice* (q.v.).

2. In *Julius Caesar*, Cato's daughter and wife of Brutus. Like Lady Percy, she pleads with her husband to tell her the cause of his strange behaviour, and Brutus promises to disclose his secret. Shortly before Philippi Brutus tells Cassius that anxiety for his safety has led to her suicide (IV, iii).

Portraits. We know that two representations of Shakespeare were made shortly after his death: the bust by Gheerart Janssen in Stratford Church, and the engraving by Martin Droeshout for the Folio of 1623. Presumably, Droeshout worked from an earlier portrait of Shakespeare as a comparatively young man, and a number of paintings have been claimed as the 'Droeshout original': the Flower portrait, for example. In the same way it has been maintained that the Hunt portrait is the original of the Janssen bust. In the last two hundred years many paintings have been put forward as authentic portraits of Shakespeare; some are genuine portraits of the period, but that they are of Shakespeare is another matter; others are old portraits that have been tampered with, and some are more recent forgeries. There is also the Kesselstadt Death Mask.

The most important of the paintings are the Ashbourne or Kingston, Chandos, Ely Palace, Felton, Flower, Hunt or Stratford, Janssen or Somerset, Lumley, Soest, and the three portraits attributed to

Zuccaro: the Bath, Boston and Cosway.

Of the miniatures, the Hilliard or Somerville, and the Auriol are the most important, and of later engravings those by W. Marshall and W. Faithorne.

After the Stratford bust there were no further sculptures of Shakespeare until the statue by Scheemakers was erected in Westminster Abbey in 1740. Of slightly later date are the Roubiliac statue and D'Avenant bust. (See under the various names, and SPIELMANN.)

Posthumus Leonatus. The hero of *Cymbeline* (q.v.).

Prefaces to Shakespeare. The prefaces of the 18th-century editors are conveniently printed in the Variorum editions. Thus, in the Third Variorum (1821), there is Rowe's *Life* the *Prefaces* of Pope, Theobald, Hanmer, Warburton, Johnson and Malone, the *Advertisements* of Steevens 1766, 1773, 1793, 1803, of Reed 1785, 1803, and the *Introduction* of Capell. Johnson's, a scrupulously fair but somewhat insensitive appreciation, is the best known; those of Theobald, Steevens, Capell and Malone are the work of serious scholars. Among later prefaces, Furnivall's Preface to the *Leopold Shakespeare*, 1877, Wilson's Textual Introduction to the *New Cambridge Shakespeare*, 1921, R. B. McKerrow's *Prolegomena for the Oxford Shakespeare*, and Granville-Barker's *Prefaces to Shakespeare* (1927–47) are important.

Priam. In *Troilus and Cressida*, King of Troy and father of Troilus. He asks his sons' advice about returning Helen to the Greeks (II, ii), and in V, iii pleads with Hector not to fight on that ominous day.

Prices. It is impossible accurately to compare the cost of living, that is the value of money, at the beginning of the 17th century with that of today, when we spend a large part of our income on commodities and services that were then unobtainable. Of things that can be compared, some manufactured goods were very expensive: for example, the actors' state or summer liveries of scarlet cost 26s. 8d. a yard, though their everyday 'watching' liveries were only 5s. a yard; on the other hand, many items of food and other essentials cost much less. Perhaps £1 in 1600 was roughly the equivalent of £20 today. This proportion would agree well enough with the £6 to £8 which a dramatist received for a play, and with the 1d. paid for standing room, and the 1s. for the best seats in the theatres.

Prince Henry's Men. See ADMIRAL'S MEN; HENRY FREDERICK, PRINCE OF WALES.

Princess's Theatre. The London theatre at which Charles Kean (q.v.) produced, 1850–9, a number of Shakespearean revivals remarkable for their extravagant spectacle, and scholarly, not to say pedantic, fidelity to detail. For example, in *Henry VIII* Buckingham was taken to the Tower in a barge, and the dresses for *The Merchant of Venice* were 'chiefly selected from a work by Cesare Vecellio', printed at Venice in 1590.

Printers and Printing. A list of the printers and publishers of Shakespeare's plays and of the entries in the Stationer's Register up to the publication of the First Folio in 1623, is given below. 'Bad' Quartos are marked with an asterisk.

Play	*Registered by*	*Printer*	*Publisher*
2 H. VI	1594 Millington	*Q1 1594 Creede	Millington
	1602 Millington to Pavier	*Q2 1600 Simmes	Millington
		*Q3 1619 Jaggard	Pavier
3 H. VI	No original entry	*Q1 1595 Short	Millington
	1602 Millington to Pavier	*Q2 1600 White	Millington
		*Q3 1619 Jaggard	Pavier

Play	*Registered by*	*Printer*	*Publisher*
T. And.	1594 Danter	Q1 1594 Danter	Danter
	1602 Millington to Pavier	Q2 1600 Roberts	White
		Q3 1611 Allde	White
R. III	1597 Wise	Q1 1597 Simmes	Wise
	1603 Wise to Law	Q2 1598 Creede	Wise
		Q3 1602 Creede	Wise
		Q4 1605 Creede	Law
		Q5 1612 Creede	Law
		Q6 1622 Purfoot	Law
L.L.L.	No original entry	Q1 1598 White	Burby
	1607 Burby to Ling		
	1607 Ling to Smethwick		
R. & J.	No original entry	*Q1 1597 Danter	Danter
	1607 Burby to Ling	Q2 1599 Creede	Burby
	1607 Ling to Smethwick	Q3 1609	Smethwick
		Q4 n.d.	Smethwick
R. II	1597 Wise	Q1 1597 Simmes	Wise
	1603 Wise to Law	Q2 1598 Simmes	Wise
		Q3 1598 Simmes	Wise
		Q4 1608 White	Law
		Q5 1615	Law
M.N.D.	1600 Fisher	Q1 1600 Allde or Bradock	Fisher
		Q2 1619 Jaggard	Jaggard
M. of V.	1598 Roberts	Q1 1600 Roberts	T. Heyes
	1600 Roberts to T. Heyes	Q2 1619 Jaggard	Jaggard
	1619 T. Heyes to L. Heyes		
1 H. IV	1598 Wise	Q1 1598 Short	Wise
	1603 Wise to Law	Q2 1599 Stafford	Wise
		Q3 1604 Simmes	Law
		Q4 1608	Law
		Q5 1613 White	Law
		Q6 1622 Purfoot	Law
2 H. IV	1600 Wise and Aspley	Q 1600 Simmes	Wise and Aspley
M.W.	{ 1602 Busby	*Q1 1602 Creede	Johnson
	{ 1602 Busby to Johnson	*Q2 1619 Jaggard	Johnson
Hen. V	1600 'to be staied'	*Q1 1600 Creede	Millington and Busby
	1600 Pavier	*Q2 1602 Creede	Pavier
		*Q3 1619 Jaggard	Pavier
M. Ado.	1600 'to be staied'	Q 1600 Simmes	Wise and Aspley
	1600 Wise and Aspley		
Ham.	1602 Roberts	*Q1 1603 Simmes	Ling and Trundell
	1607 Ling to Smethwick	Q2 1604 Roberts	Ling
		Q3 1611	Smethwick
T. & C.	1603 Roberts (provisional)	Q 1609 Eld	Bonian and Walley
	1609 Bonian and Walley		
Oth.	1621 Walkley	Q 1622 Okes	Walkley
Lear	1607 Butter and Busby	Q1 1608 Okes or Snowden	Butter
		Q2 1619 Jaggard	Butter
Per.	1608 Blount	Q1 1609 White	Goosson
		Q2 1609 White	Gosson
		Q3 1611 Stafford	
		Q4 1619 Jaggard	Pavier

Before issuing the First Folio in 1623, Blount and Isaac Jaggard registered sixteen of the eighteen unpublished plays. The title-page states that it was printed by 'Isaac Jaggard and Ed. Blount'; Isaac's father, William, had died shortly before publication, but Blount was a publisher, not a printer, his name appearing with those of the other three members of the publishing syndicate: W. Jaggard, Smethwick, and Aspley.

The Jaggards (whose 1619 reprints should be noted), Danter and Roberts were publishers as well as printers; the others acted merely as printers, and cannot, presumably, be held responsible for the issue of 'bad' Quartos. Their work varies in quality: Eld's *Troilus and Cressida* is so bad that Kirschbaum ranks it as a 'bad' Quarto; Valentine Simmes is the best, but even he made 69 errors in the good Q1 of *Richard II*, and when he printed Q2 from Q1, though he corrected 14, he added 123 new ones. Plays were not an important part of a printer's business, and probably no great care was taken with them. (See MOXON; FOLIOS; MISPRINTS; SPELLING; PUNCTUATION; PUBLISHERS.)

The printers and publishers of the Quartos of the plays added to F3 – *Locrine, Oldcastle, Cromwell, London Prodigal, Puritan, Yorkshire Tragedy* (*Pericles*, given in the previous table, first appeared in Folio in F3) – are:

Play	*Registered by*	*Printer*	*Publisher*
Loc.	1594 Creede	Q 1595 Creede	Creede
Old.	1600 Pavier	Q1 1600 Simmes	Pavier
		Q2 1619 Jaggard	Pavier
Crom.	1602 Cotton	Q1 1602 R. Read?	W. Jones
	1611 Jones to Browne	Q2 1613 Snodham	
L.P.	No entry	Q 1605 Creede	Butter
Pur.	1607 Eld	Q 1607 Eld	Eld
Y.T.	1608 Pavier	Q1 1608 Bradock	Pavier
		Q2 1619 Jaggard	Pavier

Of the poems, *Venus and Adonis* and *Lucrece* were beautifully printed by the Stratford man, Richard Field, in 1593 and 1594, and no doubt Shakespeare saw them through the press. It is improbable that he supervised the printing of any other poems; Jaggard pirated *The Passionate Pilgrim*; the *Sonnets* and *Lover's Complaint* were printed, not very well, by Eld for Thorpe, and *The Phoenix and Turtle* is merely one of many poems appended to Robert Chester's *Love's Martyr*, printed by Field for Blount. (See under the various names.)

Pritchard, Hannah (1711–68), actress, began her career as a singer in the booths of Bartholomew Fair, but made her name at the Haymarket where Theophilus Cibber engaged her. In 1747 she joined Garrick at Drury Lane and remained with him for the rest of her career, playing a great number of Shakespearean heroines, her last appearance being in 1768 as Lady Macbeth, her most famous part, though it is said that she had not read the rest of *Macbeth* when she first played it. According to J. P. Kemble, Johnson said of her: 'Pritchard, in common life, was a vulgar idiot; she would talk of her *gownd*; but, when she appeared upon the stage, seemed to be inspired by gentility and understanding.' Her daughter, also an actress, married the actor John Palmer, but left the stage on her mother's death.

Private Theatres. The name given to the roofed and enclosed theatres originally occupied by boy actors, to distinguish them from the open 'public' theatres of the men's companies. In Shakespeare's time the private theatres were: the first Blackfriars (1575–84); the second Blackfriars used by the Chapel Children, 1600–8, and after that by the King's; the Whitefriars, occupied by the King's Revels in 1608, by the Queen's Revels (Chapel Children) in 1609, and supplanted by the Salisbury Court theatre in 1629; the Paul's theatre; the Phoenix converted from the Drury Lane Cockpit in 1616; Porter's Hall, 1616–17.

The auditorium of the Paul's theatre was circular, as in the public theatres, but the Blackfriars and Whitefriars were rectangular like the halls of great houses, and the former had at least one gallery. Seats were provided in all parts of the house, and the prices of admission were higher than those of the public theatres: 6d. to 2s. 6d. as against 1d. to 1s. Plays were normally acted in the afternoon, but daylight was supplemented by candles and torches. Cf. James Wright's *Historia Histrionica*, 1699:

> The Blackfriars, Cockpit, and Salisbury Court were called Private Houses; and were very small to what we see now ... they were all three built almost exactly alike, for form and bigness. Here they had 'Pits' for the gentry, and acted by candlelight.

As the boys were all singers, music formed a more important part of the entertainment than in the public theatres; for example, the stage-directions of Beaumont's *Knight of the Burning Pestle*, a Blackfriars play, *c.* 1607, call for music between the acts. This musical tradition was continued by the King's Men when they occupied the theatre in 1608. (See STAGING.)

Privy Council. Originated in Norman times as the *curia regis*, a group of the most important officers of state and of the royal household within the *commune concilium*. The Tudors controlled it firmly and formed it into a body for the exercise of the royal prerogative. In 1553 there were forty members, at the beginning of Elizabeth's reign twenty-four, and by the end only thirteen. The most important officers of state were the Chancellor, Treasurer, Privy Seal and Admiral; of the royal household, the Steward, Chamberlain and Master of the Horse. As the Lord Chamberlain was ultimately responsible for the King's indoor entertainments (the Master of the Revels being directly responsible), the Privy Council exercised a control over the stage, defended it on behalf of the sovereign and the humanistic Court against the attacks of Puritans and the London Corporation, and even, until 1614, signed warrants for the payment by the Treasurer of the Chamber of actors for Court performances.

Procter, Bryan Waller (1787–1874), the poet, is better known by his pseudonym of Barry Cornwall. He published an edition of Shakespeare's works (1839–43) in 3 vols. with woodcuts by Kenny Meadows.

Proculeius. In *Antony and Cleopatra*, a friend of Ceasar who sends him to capture Cleopatra in the Monument in which she has taken refuge after Antony's death (v, i and ii).

Production of Shakespeare's Plays. (For Elizabethan and early 17th-century productions, see STAGING.) Production is determined largely by the size and construction of the theatre and stage. The Restoration theatres were 'private', roofed buildings with apron stages, proscenium doors, and a music room over the proscenium arch. By the beginning of the 18th century the orchestra had been brought to its present position in front of the stage, which was pushed farther and farther within the proscenium arch, until before the mid 19th century the apron, and with it the proscenium doors, had disappeared. The 19th-century stage, therefore, was bounded in front by the proscenium arch and a row of footlights, beyond which the actors had to do their best to make themselves heard. This was not easy in the gigantic new Covent Garden and Drury Lane which necessitated a more stylized form of acting, slower declamation, and more extravagant gestures. The size, greater possibilities of illusion, and improved lighting, all encouraged spectacular productions, though this meant the cutting and rearrangement of the text to find time for the long intervals devoted to scene-shifting, for stage 'business', and music. Benjamin Webster (*Taming of the Shrew*, 1844), and Samuel Phelps at Sadler's Wells (1844–62) were honourable exceptions. William Poel revolted and produced the full texts on a more or less bare stage; Nugent Monck built his Elizabethan stage at Norwich; and, inspired by Poel, Gordon Craig and the German theatre, Granville-Barker and Barry Jackson abolished the tyranny of footlights on the picture-frame stage, which they converted into something like the Elizabethan by building out an apron, erecting a false proscenium within the proscenium arch, and raising the back of the stage into a platform approached by two steps.

When the theatres were reopened in 1660, much of Shakespeare was produced in 'improved' versions, accompanied by song and dance, to please the French taste of the courtly and restricted audience. In the 18th century the theatre again became a more popular form of entertainment; for those who wanted them, pantomime and spectacle were separately purveyed at Lincoln's Inn Fields and the 'Opera', so that Shakespeare's plays were not so encumbered with these distractions, though they continued to be acted for the most part in the Restoration or later versions. Garrick, too, as manager of Drury Lane, 1747–76, was not above improving Shakespeare, but it was he who popularized his plays and firmly established his reputation; he introduced a greater realism by the natural style of his acting, and by employing De Loutherbourg and other artists as scenic designers, though there was still little attempt at historical costume. This movement towards a greater illusion of scene was carried further by J. P. Kemble at Drury Lane (1780–1802) and Covent Garden (1803–17), where also he began to dress his main characters in approximately historical costume, and still further by his brother Charles who, with the aid of J. R. Planché, at Covent Garden in 1823 began the vogue of antiquarian productions with his *King John* in which every character was dressed 'in the precise Habit of the Period'. The antiquarian-spectacular was elaborated by Charles Kean, son of Edmund Kean, first of the stars, who produced his famous series of Shakespearean spectacles at the Princess's theatre, 1850–9.

From this time Shakespearean productions split into two streams: the one, of star-actor-managers who appealed to the eyes of the audience – Charles Kean at the Princess's, Irving at the Lyceum, Tree at His Majesty's; the other of actor-managers and producers who appealed primarily to the ear – Benjamin Webster, Samuel Phelps at Sadler's Wells (1844–62), F. R. Benson, William Poel, Granville-Barker at the Savoy, Nugent Monck at the Maddermarket, Barry Jackson at Birmingham, Bridges Adams at Stratford and Robert Atkins, Harcourt Williams and Tyrone Guthrie at the Old Vic. Of the first group, Tree at least was prepared to sacrifice Shakespeare's text to the spectacle of live rabbits on the stage; those of the second did all they could to reduce spectacle, and therefore intervals, to a minimum, so that they could play the whole of the text.

By the middle of the 20th century, this last method has become the norm; a simple setting, a full text played with only one interval on a stage approximating to the Elizabethan, as at Stratford, and produced by a specialist who is responsible for sweeping all the elements into a harmonious whole. (See SS, 2.)

The specialist producer, or director, is a 20th-century phenomenon. Among the best-known modern producers of Shakespeare are: Michel Saint-Denis (b. 1897), who began his career with Jacques Copeau in Paris, and in 1962 became General Artistic Adviser at the Royal Shakespeare Theatre. Glen Byam Shaw

(b. 1904), Co-Director and Director of the Shakespeare Memorial Theatre 1952–9. John Burrell (b. 1910), produced for the Old Vic when at the New Theatre after the war. Since 1955 Director of the Training Academy of the American Shakespeare Theatre. George Devine (b. 1910). Director of the Old Vic 1946–51 and founder of the Young Vic. Hugh Hunt (b. 1911), Director of Old Vic Company 1949–53, since 1961 Professor of Drama at Manchester University. Michael Benthall (b. 1919), as Director of Old Vic 1953–8 produced all 36 plays of the Shakespeare Folio. Peter Brook (b. 1925), perhaps best known for his productions of *Titus Andronicus*, 1955, and *Lear*, 1962. Appointed Co-Director of the Royal Shakespeare Theatre 1962. Peter Hall (b. 1930), first produced at Stratford in 1956; Director of Royal Shakespeare Theatre and Aldwych Theatre 1962.

Prohibition of Plays. Plays were forbidden during Lent, on Thursdays, which were reserved for bear-baiting, in time of plague, after 1574 at the time of divine service on Sunday and on holidays, and after 1583 at any time on Sundays. The Council prohibited playing during the fatal illness of Elizabeth and on the death of Prince Henry in 1612, and occasionally closed the theatres when a play was considered seditious: cf. *The Isle of Dogs*, 1597. The theatres were closed by Act of Parliament during the Civil War and Interregnum, 1642–60, though there was some evasion of the law, drolls and opera contriving to escape the title of plays.

Prologue. The beginning of a play was announced by three soundings of a trumpet, after which the Prologue, traditionally dressed in a black velvet cloak, introduced the play; cf. *Hamlet* III, ii, and the Induction to *Cynthia's Revels*. In the 17th century the Prologue apparently became unfashionable; cf. Beaumont's *Woman Hater* (*c.* 1606): 'Gentlemen, Inductions are out of date, and a Prologue in Verse, is as stale as a black Velvet Cloak.' (See CHORUS; EPILOGUE; 'GULL'S HORNBOOK'.)

'Promos and Cassandra.' The only play written by George Whetstone, registered and published in 1578 as 'The Right Excellent and famous Historye, of Promos and Cassandra; Deuided into two Commicall Discourses ... The worke of George Whetstones Gent'. This was Shakespeare's main source for *Measure for Measure*. It is based on a story by Cinthio, which Whetstone translated again in his collection of prose tales, *An Heptameron of Civil Discourses* (1582), where he says that his play was 'yet never presented upon stage'. Both in Cinthio and Whetstone, the heroine sacrifices her virtue to save her brother from death.

Prompt-book. Sometimes called the 'stage-copy', and apparently kept by the prompter (book-keeper) with the 'plot' of the play. An author's original draft would be too confusing to serve as a prompt-book, and there is no surviving example of such an arrangement. Normally the prompt-book was a transcript prepared by the book-keeper, which, after submission to the Master of the Revels for licensing, became the 'allowed book'. A Quarto, if the play had been printed, would be less convenient, the pages so much smaller than the folio manuscript with 60 or 70 lines on a page, though if this were worn out or lost a printed Quarto might become the prompt-book. Philip Williams (SQ, iv) suggested that annotated Quartos served as prompt-books more often than is thought. When an actors' company sold a play, they would not send the prompt-book, the authorized copy, to the printer, but the author's original draft. Many of Shakespeare's plays, therefore, were set up from his foul papers. About a dozen prompt-books have survived. (See 'BELIEVE AS YOU LIST'; 'JOHN A KENT'; 'SECOND MAIDEN'S TRAGEDY'; MANUSCRIPT PLAYS; COPY; Greg, *Dramatic Documents*.)

Prompter. See BOOK-KEEPER.

Proof-reading. As proofs of a sheet of the Folio were read and corrected while printing was in progress, some copies have the corrected and others the uncorrected state. Moreover, corrected and uncorrected sheets were gathered at random to make up a copy of the book, so that few, if any, copies of F are exactly the same. In his *Printing of the First Folio of Shakespeare* (1932) E. E. Willoughby, generalizing from a page of *Antony and Cleopatra* in which some 20 errors were marked for correction, concluded that proof-reading of the Folio was reasonably careful. If, as he assumed, the page was representative of the other 900, there should be some 18,000 corrections in the Folio. But, with the aid of his collating machine, Charlton Hinman has recently shown that there are only about 500: about 70 in the Comedies, 70 in the Histories, and 370 in the Tragedies, nearly half of them in the 70 pages set into type by the apprentice compositor E. Only 134 of the 900 pages were proof-corrected. Moreover, most of the errors corrected are merely typographical, only a few dozen are attempts to correct a corruption of meaning, and many of these are wrongly altered, and for only two is it certain that the reader must have referred to copy.

In *The Shakespeare First Folio* (1955) Greg wrote: 'Of proof-reading in the early seventeenth century we know distressingly little.' We now know that proof-reading of the Folio was distressingly inadequate, and that there must be hundreds of corruptions in the text. (See C. K. Hinman, *The Printing and Proof-reading of the First Folio*.)

Properties. The joint stock of a company of players was composed mainly of plays, apparel and properties – probably in that order of value. Henslowe's inventories for the Admiral's stock in 1598 are concerned mostly with 'sewtes' and 'aparell', the properties including weapons, musical instruments, animal skins, a rock, a Hell mouth, 'the clothe of the Sone and Mone', a cauldron for the Jew, and so on. They do not appear to have been very extensive or elaborate. For Court performances the players were helped out by the Revels Office. The value of a share in the joint stock of a company in the early 17th century was £50 to £80, suggesting a total value of some £750. The plays of William Percy, written for the Paul's boys at their private theatre, 1600–6, are the only ones that give a list of the properties required. For the multiple setting of his *Faery Pastoral* he needed 'A kiln of Brick. A Fowen Cott. A Hollowe Oake with vice of wood to shutt to. A Lowe well with Roape and Pullye. A Fourme of Turves. A greene Bank being Pillowe to the Hed but. Lastly A Hole to creepe in and out.' He adds, however, the interesting note that if there are too many people on the stage the properties 'that be outward' may be replaced by their names in 'Text Letters'. (See THRONE.)

Proscenium. 'In front of the *skene*.' In the Greek theatre the *skene* was the dressing-room behind the stage. *Proskenion* was used to describe either the stage itself or the front wall of the *skene* that formed the architectural background to the stage. The latter is the more correct usage, though in de Witt's drawing of the Swan (*c.* 1596) the apron stage is labelled '*proscænium*', and in his *Dictionary* (1598) Florio defines *Scena* as 'a skaffold, a pavillion, or forepart of a theatre where players make them readie, being trimmed with hangings, out of which they enter upon the stage'. For the Elizabethans, then, *scene* might mean the tiring-house (*skene*), but primarily it meant its front wall (*proskenion*). The fully developed proscenium-arch first appears in the Teatro Farnese at Parma (1618–19), where it seems to have been the logical widening of the big central arch of the Teatro Olimpico to frame the open Serlian stage. At the beginning of the 17th century, Inigo Jones began to frame his masques within a proscenium arch made for the occasion, and later applied his method to the staging of Court plays. The stage of the Restoration theatres was framed by a proscenium arch, in front of which projected a correspondingly reduced apron.

Prose. Shakespeare's main use of prose is for comic scenes and interludes, particularly those of low life (Falstaff always speaks prose). In addition, he uses it for sub-plots (*Lear* and *Much Ado*); for contrast (the funeral orations of Brutus and Antony); to show highly wrought states of mind, and madness itself (Lady Macbeth and Lear); for letters, etc. This accounts for the fact that in the series of comedies and historical-comedies from *1 Henry IV* to *Twelfth Night*, 1597–1600, prose rivals or exceeds verse as a medium; in *Richard II* (1595), which has no comedy, there is no prose; in *Much Ado* there are some 2,000 lines of prose and only 700 of verse. This 'prose period' was salutary, for it taught Shakespeare to write functional dramatic verse instead of the lyrical poetry that had preceded it, and as a corollary to create out of verse tragic character as real as the comic characters created out of prose. But his prose, too, developed: from the brittle, artificial language of Lyly, as in *Love's Labour's Lost*, to the (apparently) simple naturalism of Lady Macbeth. (See VERSE-TESTS.)

Prospero. The chief character in *The Tempest* (q.v.), 'the right Duke of Millaine' (F). There was a 15th-century Prospero Adorno, Duke of Genoa, who was deposed. Some think that Shakespeare speaks in the person of Prospero when, in the last scene, he bids farewell to his art.

Protection of Players. The members of a company of actors, their hired men, musicians and 'other necessary attendants' were protected from arrest during the season of the Court revels, to prevent interference with the sovereign's entertainment. For example:

Theise are to Certifie you that Edward Knight, William Pattrick, William Chambers, Ambrose Byland, Henry Wilson, Jeffrey Collins, William Sanders, Nicholas Underhill, Henry Clay, George Vernon, Roberte Pallant, Thomas Tuckfeild, Roberte Clarke, John Rhodes, William Mago, Anthony Knight, and Edward Ashborne, William Carver, Allexander Buklank, William Toyer, William Gascoyne, are all imployed by the Kinges Maiesties servantes in theire quallity of Playinge as Musitions and other necessary attendants, And are at all tymes and howers to bee readie with their best endeavours to doe his Maiesties service (during the tyme of the Revells) In Which tyme they nor any of them are to be arested, or ... Press'd for Souldiers ... Without leaue firste had and obteyned of the Lord Chamberlyne ... or of the Maister of his Maiesties Revells ... Given att his Maiesties Office of the Revells Vnder my hand and Seale the xxviith day of December, 1624. H. Herbert.

Proteus. One of the Two Gentlemen of Verona (q.v.). He is the Felix of the *Diana* of Montemayor (q.v.).

Provincial Companies and Tours. In addition to the London companies of actors (after 1603 the royal patent companies) there were those who confined their activities to the provinces. They had no permanent theatres, but moved from town to town, some over the whole country, Stratford being a favourite centre, others within a more limited area. The most important of these were, after 1594, Queen Elizabeth's Men; some of the others were the servants of the Lords Stafford, Berkeley, Chandos, Morley and Dudley. It is probable that Shakespeare, before going to London, came across Berkeley's Men at Berkeley Castle in south Gloucestershire, and they were at Stratford in 1581 and 1583.

On arriving at a town the players would present their Lord's warrant to the Mayor, and if he granted them licence to play they would give their first performance in the Guildhall ('the Mayor's play'), to which the citizens or burgesses came free and for which the Mayor gave them a 'reward' of about

£1. After this they earned what they could by public performances in an inn yard, or any convenient place. The corporation limited their time of stay and frequency of visits, and prohibited playing on Sundays and in Lent. The players were generally welcomed, but occasionally they found a town, particularly after about 1615, where the Puritans were able to repulse them. Their repertories included mangled versions of London plays put together from memory and notes by hired actors who had played in them (see 'BAD' QUARTOS).

In time of plague and prohibition of playing in London for any other reason, the London companies had to take to the road and compete with these established provincial rivals. It was a hard life, the returns were meagre, and travelling was expensive, and if prolonged, as in the bad plague year of 1593–4, companies might be almost broken (see PEMBROKE'S). In that year Strange's, possibly Shakespeare with them, travelled under Alleyn of the Admiral's, visiting Maidstone, where the Mayor's play fetched 20s., Southampton, Bath (16s. 3d.), Bristol, Shrewsbury (40s.), Leicester (5s.) and Coventry (20s.). (See 'HISTRIO-MASTIX'; 'RATSEIS GHOST'; J. T. Murray, *English Dramatic Companies 1558–1642*, 1910.)

Provost. In *Measure for Measure*, the prison governor who is persuaded by the disguised Duke to execute Barnardine instead of Claudio, but when the pirate Ragozine dies in prison, the Duke agreeing, he sends his head to Angelo instead of Claudio's.

Prynne, William (1600–69), Puritan pamphleteer, was born at Swainswick near Bath, educated at Bath Grammar School and Oriel, Oxford, and entered Lincoln's Inn in 1621. In 1633 he published his *Histrio-mastix, The Players Scourge*, in which he maintained that

> popular Stage-playes (the very Pompes of the Divell which we renounce in Baptisme, if we beleeve the Fathers) are sinfull, heathenish, lewde, ungodly Spectacles, and most pernicious Corruptions; condemned in all ages, as intolerable Mischiefs to Churches, to Republickes, to the manners, mindes, and soules of men. And that the Profession of Play-poets, of Stage-players; together with the penning, acting and frequenting of Stage-playes, are unlawfull, infamous and misbeseeming Christians.

As the book contained references to the justly violent ends of Kings who favoured plays, and opprobriously attacked actresses at a time when Queen Henrietta Maria performed in masques, Prynne was sentenced to imprisonment for life, a fine of £5,000, and the loss of both ears. In 1637 the stumps of his ears were shaved off and his cheeks branded with S.L. (seditious libeller) for a pamphlet attacking the bishops. He was released in 1640 by the Long Parliament and attacked successively Laud, the Independents, the army, and the regicides; he was expelled from Parliament by Pride's Purge, and imprisoned 1650–3. He supported the Restoration of Charles II, was elected member for Bath, appointed Keeper of the Records in the Tower, and died the author of some two hundred books and pamphlets.

Psycho-analysis. Walter Whiter's *Specimen of a Commentary on Shakespeare* (1794) was a remarkable anticipation of the application of the modern knowledge of the unconscious mind to Shakespearean criticism. In 1910 came Ernest Jones's (q.v.) *Œdipus Complex as an Explanation of Hamlet's Mystery*, and in his *Introductory Lectures on Psycho-Analysis* (1915–17) Freud drew attention to the dramatic effectiveness of slips of the tongue in Schiller and Shakespeare (cf. Portia in *M.V.* III, ii; 'One half of me is yours, the other half yours, – Mine own, I would say.' *See also* Ella F. Sharpe, *A Psycho-Analytic View of Shakespeare*, 1950). J. L. Lowes's *Road to Xanadu*, written in 1919–20, is an exhaustive analysis of the working of Coleridge's unconscious mind as revealed in his imagery; and since then Shakespeare's imagery (q.v.) has been methodically examined, Jung as well as

Freud, mythology and anthropology, all being pressed into service.

Public Theatres. See THEATRES.

Publishers. Originally, the printer was also publisher and bookseller, but by Shakespeare's time there were specialist publishers who employed a printer to produce a book and sometimes a bookseller to retail it.

(For the publishers of Shakespeare's plays, see PRINTERS, and also under the various names.) The earliest publishers were men of dubious reputation. Thomas Millington published the 'bad' Quartos of *2 Henry VI*, *3 Henry VI*, and in spite of the blocking entry in the Stationers' Register, the 'bad' Quarto of *Henry V*. These he transferred to Thomas Pavier, who re-issued them, and in addition published *Oldcastle* and *The Yorkshire Tragedy*, the second of which he ascribed to Shakespeare. In 1619 he joined his friend Jaggard in the issue of the falsely dated reprints of ten of 'Shakespeare's' plays. John Danter published, without registration, the 'bad' Quarto of *Romeo and Juliet*, and John Busby, Millington's partner in *Henry V*, registered *The Merry Wives*, and at once transferred it to Arthur Johnson, who published the 'bad' Quarto.

Publishers of integrity were Andrew Wise, Matthew Law and Cuthbert Burby, the last of whom published the corrected *Romeo and Juliet*, and possibly his Quarto of *Love's Labour's Lost* was a corrected edition of a previously pirated Quarto.

The Jaggards, father and son, were partly responsible for the publishing of the ten 'Shakespearean' plays of 1619, and the First Folio of 1623, all of which they printed. (See STATIONERS' REGISTER.)

Publius. 1. In *Titus Andronicus*, son of Marcus Andronicus. He helps his uncle Titus in his revenge on Demetrius and Chiron (IV, iii; V, ii).

2. In *Julius Caesar*, a senator in II, ii and III, i, where he is 'quite confounded with this mutiny'.

Pucelle. See JOAN OF ARC.

Puck. In *A Midsummer Night's Dream* (q.v.). Originally a malicious spirit, but identified by Shakespeare with Hobgoblin, otherwise 'that shrewd and knavish sprite Call'd Robin Goodfellow', about whom Reginald Scot wrote in his *Discovery of Witchcraft* (1584). (See 'JOHN A KENT'.)

Punctuation. The main differences between Elizabethan and modern punctuation are: the colon was often used where we should use a comma, full-stop, or exclamation mark ('Angels and Ministers of Grace defend vs:'); the comma was used with less precision and sometimes served as a semi-colon, a stop rarely used, and with some uncertainty. Their punctuation was more natural and rhetorical than ours.

The punctuation of the Quartos, printed at different times and by different presses, naturally varies, some of it being very poor. When a Folio text was set up from a Quarto, the punctuation was often altered and a number of new stops inserted, particularly commas, and sometimes brackets (q.v.), which frequently serve as commas. In addition, the Folio capitalizes more nouns and adjectives. The following parallel passages (Horatio's speech in *Hamlet*, I, i) illustrate most of these points: (*a*) is the 'bad' Q1, 1603; (*b*) the corrected Q2, 1604; (*c*) F1, 1623.

(*a*) *Hor.* Mary that can I, at least the whisper goes so,
Our late King, who as you know was by Forten-
Brasse of *Norway*,
Thereto prickt on by a most emulous cause, dared to
The combate, in which our valiant *Hamlet*,
For so this side of our knowne world esteemed him,
Did slay this Fortenbrasse, ...

(*b*) *Hora*. That can I.
At least the whisper goes so; our last King,
Whose image euen but now appear'd to vs,
Was as you knowe by *Fortinbrasse* of *Norway*,
Thereto prickt on by a most emulate pride
Dar'd to the combat; in which our valiant *Hamlet*,
(For so this side of our knowne world esteemed him)
Did slay this *Fortinbrasse*, ...

(*c*) *Hor*. That can I,
At least the whisper goes so: Our last King,
Whose Image euen but now appear'd to vs,
Was (as you know) by *Fortinbras* of Norway,
(Thereto prick'd on by a most emulate Pride)
Dar'd to the Combate, In which, our Valiant *Hamlet*,
(For so this side of our knowne world esteem'd him)
Did slay this *Fortinbras*: ...

In 1911 Percy Simpson in his *Shakespearian Punctuation* showed how English punctuation had changed in the 19th century, and maintained that Elizabethan punctuation was rhythmical rather than logical. This theory, developed by Pollard, was accepted by Wilson: 'the stops in the Folio and Quartos ... are now seen to be not the haphazard peppering of ignorant compositors, as all previous editors have regarded them, but playhouse punctuation, directing the actors how to speak their lines.' The theory is no longer generally accepted. It now seems clear that the spelling, capitalization and punctuation of the Folio (and most of the Quartos) are the compositor's rather than Shakespeare's. Moreover a number of compositors set F, each tending to reproduce his own preferences. Passage *c* above was set by compositor B, who was less accurate and conservative than A, and added more parentheses, though A italicized more place-names. (See P. Alexander, *Shakespeare's Punctuation*, 1945.)

Puns. 'A quibble is to Shakespeare', Johnson wrote disapprovingly in a famous passage in his Preface, 'what luminous vapours are to the traveller ... A quibble was to him the fatal Cleopatra for which he lost the world, and was content to lose it.' All the Elizabethan dramatists tickled the ears of the groundlings with their quibbles, and there were certain words, 'angel' for example, on which it seems to have been almost a convention to pun, though some of them are much more subtle and must have been directed at the audience on the stage or in the more select parts of the galleries (cf. *Hamlet*, III, ii: 'The Mousetrap. Marry, how? Tropically'). Shakespeare, however, was fonder of puns than any of his contemporaries; they are indeed an important part of his imagery, but there is a world of difference between the frigid punning of the early plays, analogous to the conceit, of, for example, Juliet (*R. & J.* III, ii):

Say thou but 'I',
And that bare vowel 'I' shall poison more
Than the death-darting eye of cockatrice:
I am not I, if there be such an I,
Or those eyes shut, that make thee answer 'I'.
If he be slain, say 'I'; or if not, no:

and the concentrated pun, analogous to metaphor, in the later tragedies; of Hamlet's ferocious 'Is thy union here?'; of Lady Macbeth's,

I'll gild the faces of the grooms withal,
For it must seem their guilt.

And of Othello's lyrical development of,

Put out the light, and then put out the light.

Purcell, Henry (1658–95), was the son of a Gentleman of the Chapel Royal, to which he was himself admitted as a chorister. He was probably a pupil of John Blow, whom he succeeded as organist of Westminster Abbey in 1679, and three years later he was appointed in addition organist of the Chapel. He died at the age of 37, and was buried under the organ in Westminster Abbey.

Purcell is one of the greatest of English musicians; in addition to church music, instrumental music and opera (q.v.), he wrote much for the theatre, including an overture and masque for Shadwell's version of *Timon of Athens*, the music for Dryden's version of *The Tempest*, and for *The Fairy Queen*, Betterton's adaptation of *A Midsummer Night's Dream*. In 1699 his music was used for a masque of *Dido and Aeneas* introduced into Gildon's version of *Measure for Measure*.

Purchas, Samuel (*c.* 1575–1626), was born at Thaxted and educated at St John's, Cambridge, in 1604 becoming vicar of Eastwood, Essex, and in 1614 rector of St Martin's, Ludgate. In 1613 he published *Purchas, his Pilgrimage; or, Relations of the World and the Religions observed in all Ages*; in 1619 *Purchas, his Pilgrim. Microcosmus, or the Histories of Man*; and in 1625 *Hakluytus Posthumus or Purchas his Pilgrimes, contayning a History of the World in Sea Voyages and Lande Travells, by Englishmen and others* (4 vols.). This last is a continuation of Hakluyt's *Principall Navigations*, and contains (vol. iv) William Strachey's account of the wreck on the Bermudas, an event that partly inspired *The Tempest*. (Incidentally, *Purchas, his Pilgrimage* was the source of Coleridge's dream-poem, *Kubla Khan*.)

Purfoot, Thomas. The printer of Q6 *Richard III* and Q6 *1 Henry IV*, 'to be sold by Mathew Law', 1622. In 1629 he was Junior Warden, and in 1634 Senior Warden of the Stationers' Company.

'Puritan, The.' One of the seven plays attributed to Shakespeare and added to F3, 1664. It was registered and published in 1607:

> 6 Augusti. George Elde Entred for his copie vnder thandes of Sir George Bucke knight and the wardens a book called the comedie of the Puritan Widowe vj^{d}.

The Puritane Or The Widdow of Watling-streete. Acted by the Children of Paules. Written by W. S. Imprinted at London by G. Eld. 1607.

The play was first attributed to Shakespeare by the bookseller Edward Archer, in his play-list of 1656. Shakespeare is certainly not the author; the initials W. S. suggest Wentworth Smith, one of Henslowe's hacks, but Marston or Middleton is more likely. It is an anti-Puritan comedy of London life, mostly in prose, dealing with the tricks of George Pyeboard and Captain Idle to win the widow and her daughter. There are episodes from *The Merrie Conceited Jests of George Peele Gent*, Pyeboard being meant for Peele.

Puritans. The term 'Puritan' seems first to have been used in 1564, the year of Shakespeare's birth, to designate those who thought that the Reformation in England had not gone far enough. They were not originally dissenters – many of them were clergymen – but they attacked the established government of the Church, particularly the bishops, who savoured too much of the papal hierarchy. The movement received an impetus from the Marian persecution and the contact of Protestant exiles with Calvinism at Geneva, and by Shakespeare's time had developed a singularly austere and joyless creed with special emphasis on the observance of the Sabbath.

In the first half of the 16th century there had been an alliance between the Protestant church and the stage; the Catholic miracle plays had been discouraged, and anti-Catholic plays, such as Bale's *King John*, encouraged. The humanists, too, had encouraged classical and neo-classical plays that had an educational and ethical value, but by 1581 the Oxford Puritan, John Rainolds, was denouncing plays in the university, and during the nineties engaged in a controversy with the apologists, William Gager and Alberico Gentili.

The Puritan attack on plays in London came earlier, being occasioned by the opening of the first regular theatres in

1576, the Theatre, the Curtain, and the first Blackfriars. It was led by two clergymen, John Northbrooke's *Treatise wherein ... Vaine playes, or Enterluds ... are reproued* appearing in 1577, and Phillip Stubbes's *Anatomie of Abuses* in 1583, and seconded by two repentant playwrights, Stephen Gosson and Anthony Munday (whose conversion, however, was only temporary). The attack was not only on the immorality of the plays themselves, but also on the actors, the dressing up of boys as women, the occasion given to the practice of immorality at the theatres, and on the performance of plays on Sunday, the day when all London could attend. The Puritans were supported by the City Corporation, many of whom were of their persuasion, and also responsible for the health and good conduct of the citizens, and jealous of their privileges, threatened by the centralizing policy of the Privy Council, who were trying to secure control of plays and playing.

The theatres were defended by the humanists, the Queen, the Court, the Privy Council and the playwrights themselves, and the attack died down; but it flared up again in the 17th century, culminating in the denunciations of Prynne and the closing of the theatres in 1642. (See RAINOLDS; NORTHBROOKE; ACTORS.)

Pushkin, Alexander (1799–1837), Russian poet, was one of the leaders of the Romantic movement that swept Europe at the beginning of the 19th century. Like Goethe and Schiller in Germany, and Hugo in France, he was much influenced by Shakespeare; his *Boris Godunov* (1825) is a tragedy in the Shakespearean manner, and a revolt against the French classical drama. 'Read Shakespeare,' he wrote, 'that is my refrain.' (See SS, 5.)

Puttenham, George and Richard (*c.* 1530–1600). Their mother was the sister of Sir Thomas Elyot, who dedicated to her his *Education for the bringing up of Children*. One of them was the author of *The Arte of Poesie*, published anonymously by Richard Field in 1589, but mentioned by Camden in 1614 as 'Maister Puttenham'. Field was almost certainly a friend of Shakespeare, who would, no doubt, read the book. Its three parts treat of Poets and Poesie, of Proportion, and of Ornament, the last being much concerned with the rhetorical devices of balance and repetition. The author advises writers to avoid archaisms and to model their speech on the Court, London and the neighbouring shires.

Pyk, John. A boy actor who accompanied Alleyn on the provincial tour with Strange's in the plague year of 1593.

'Pyramus and Thisbe.' A play which, with a *Romeo and Juliet*, was acted at Nördlingen in Germany in 1604, probably by a company of English actors.

Pyrrhic Foot. A foot of two short, or unstressed, syllables. In his later plays Shakespeare frequently substitutes a pyrrhic for the normal iambic foot of blank verse, a spondee (two stressed syllables) often preceding or following it:

And 'twixt the green sea and the azured vault
Set roar | ing war: | tŏ thĕ | drēad rātt | ling thund | er ...

Q

Quarto. The size of a book, in which each sheet is folded twice to form four leaves, or eight pages.

Quartos. A company of players might buy a dramatist's play for £6 to £10, when it became their property. Comparatively few of these plays were printed (probably about 1 in 10), but sometimes the company sold them to a stationer who published them as Quartos. Between 1594, the date of Shakespeare's first printed plays, and 1616, the following first Quarto editions of plays were published in London (the third column shows which of these were Shakespeare's, an asterisk denoting a 'bad' Quarto):

1594	18	*2 Hen. VI; T.A.
1595	5	*3 Hen. VI (octavo)
1596	2	
1597	4	*R.J.; R. II; R. III
1598	7	L.L.L.; 1 Hen. IV
1599	7	(R.J. 'good' Q2)
1600	15	*Hen. V; 2 Hen. IV; M.V.; M.A.; M.N.D.
1601	6	
1602	10	*M.Wives
1603	3	*Hamlet
1604	5	(Hamlet 'good' Q2)
1605	13	
1606	10	
1607	24	
1608	11	Lear.
1609	6	T.C.; Per.
1610	2	
1611	6	
1612	7	
1613	7	
1614	2	
1615	8	

In addition there were seven Qq printed at Cambridge (six in 1598), three at Edinburgh, six were printed without dates, and eighteen were registered but apparently unpublished, including *As You Like It* and *Antony and Cleopatra*. There were also, of course, numerous reprints.

Of the 184 plays published in London, eighteen were Shakespeare's. *Othello* appeared in 1622, so that nineteen of his plays were issued as Quartos before the First Folio of 1623, in which all except *Pericles* were published. Of the thirty-six plays in F1:

Eighteen were previously unpublished.

Eighteen had at least one Quarto.

Two (*R.J.*; *Ham.*) had a 'bad' Q1, but a 'good' Q2.

Four (*2, 3 Hen. VI*; *Hen. V*; *M.W.*) had 'bad' Quartos only.

Fourteen have approximately parallel Q and F texts. (See PARALLEL TEXTS.)

The following editions of Shakespeare's Poems were published in Quarto:

Venus and Adonis: Q1 1593; Q2 1594; later reprints in octavo.

Lucrece: Q 1594; reprints in octavo.

Phoenix and Turtle: Q1 1601; Q2 1611.

Sonnets and *A Lover's Complaint*: Q 1609.

(See 'BAD' QUARTOS; PRINTERS; PUBLISHERS; PLAYS; FOLIOS; JAGGARD; 'REPORTED TEXTS'; TEXTUAL CRITICISM.)

Quayle, Anthony (b. 1913), actor and producer. His first stage appearance was in 1931. He has played both tragic and comic parts, from Othello to Falstaff. As Director of the Shakespeare Memorial Theatre, 1949–56, he produced *The Winter's Tale*, *Troilus and Cressida*, *Measure for Measure*, etc.

Queen. 1. In *Richard II*, she overhears a gardener talking of the deposition of Richard (III, iv), and in v, i bids him farewell as he goes to the Tower. (Richard's much-loved first wife, Anne of Bohemia, died in 1394. This Queen, therefore, is his child-wife, Isabel of France (*c.* 1383–1410).)

2. In *Cymbeline*, wife of Cymbeline and, by a former marriage, mother of Cloten, for whom she attempts to secure the throne by marrying him to Imogen. This failing, she seeks the same end by a plan to poison Imogen and Cymbeline himself. She also tries to poison Pisanio. She goes mad, and dies confessing her attempted crimes.

Queen Anne's Men. See WORCESTER'S MEN.

Queen Elizabeth's Men. The most important of the adult companies from 1583 to about 1590. On 10 March 1583 Edmund Tilney, Master of the Revels, was ordered 'to choose out a companie of players for her Maiestie'. Elizabeth had inherited her father's Interlude Players (q.v.), but neglected them for the Boys' companies who, in the first twenty years of her reign, played at Court more often than all the adult companies put together. But after the building of the Theatre and Curtain in 1576, and the appearance of the University Wits in the early eighties, Elizabeth turned more to the adult players for her entertainment. Stow's *Annales* (1615) relates how,

> Comedians and stage-players of former times were very poor and ignorant in respect of these of this time; but being now grown very skilful and exquisite actors for all matters, they were entertained into the service of divers great lords: out of which companies there were twelve of the best chosen, and, at the request of Sir Francis Walsingham, they were sworn the queens servants and were allowed wages and liveries as grooms of the chamber.

On 28 November 1583 the City Corporation licensed the new company, consisting of 'Robert Wilson, John Dutton, Rychard Tarleton, John Laneham, John Bentley, Thobye Mylles, John Towne, John Synger, Leonell Cooke, John Garland, John Adams, and Wyllyam Johnson' to play 'at the sygnes of the Bull in Bushoppesgate streete, and the sygne of the Bell in Gratioustreete and nowheare els within this Cyttye.' The selection of twelve of the best players was a crippling blow to the other companies; Wilson, Laneham and Johnson came from Leicester's; John Dutton, and his brother Laurence who joined later, were the two leading men of Oxford's; Tarlton and Singer were the two most popular clowns of the day. Small wonder that the leading company, Leicester's, and the rest were eclipsed by these men in the royal red liveries, who in the next seven years played twenty-one times at Court, first appearing there in the winter of 1583–4. Like the other London companies, they travelled fairly regularly in the summer months, being, for example, at Norwich in June 1583, where they killed a man, at Stratford in 1587, where Malone thinks Shakespeare may have joined them, and at Carlisle and perhaps even Scotland in 1589. When in London they performed for some time at the Theatre, retreating into the City inns for the winter months.

Tarlton died in September 1588, at a time when the competition from the Admiral's, for whom Alleyn was playing the tragic heroes of Marlowe, was growing more intense. At Christmas 1591, they appeared only once at Court, whereas the Strange-Admiral combination performed six times; in the following winter they did not appear at all, and in January 1594 they gave their last Court performance. It may be a sign of their weakness that, beginning 1 April, they combined with Sussex's under Philip Henslowe, who notes, 'beginninge at easter, the queenes men and my lord of Sussex together'. A month later Francis Henslowe borrowed £15 from his uncle Philip 'to lay downe for his share to the Queenes players when they broke & went into the contrey to playe'. 1594 is the year of the formation of the Chamberlain's company which included Shakespeare, Richard Burbage and Kempe, and against whom the Queen's, now denuded of much of its talent, were unable to compete. In that year they raised money by selling seven of their plays, and disappeared into the obscurity of the provinces, where, however, they are traceable up to the time of Elizabeth's death.

'Queen's Arcadia.' A play by Samuel Daniel, performed at Oxford, 30 August 1605, registered 26 November, and published in 1606 as 'The Queenes Arcadia. A Pastorall Trage-comedie presented to her Maiestie and her Ladies, by the Vniuersitie of Oxford in Christ's Church, In August last'. One of the shepherds is called Palamon. (See 'TWO NOBLE KINSMEN'; 'BARTHOLOMEW FAIR'; 'PALAMON AND ARCITE'.)

Queen's Revels. The name given to the Children of the Chapel (q.v.), 1603–5, and again after 1610.

Quickly, Mistress. Hostess of the tavern in Eastcheap (see BOAR'S HEAD).

In *1 Henry IV*: there are many references to her husband in III, iii, where Falstaff maintains that her 'house is turned bawdy-house; they pick pockets'.

In *2 Henry IV*, she says that she is 'a poor widow of Eastcheap' (II, i), and that Falstaff, whom she has known for twenty-nine years, has promised to marry her. She enters an action to arrest him for debt, but he persuades her to withdraw it, and she entertains him and Doll Tearsheet before he sets out for Gloucestershire. In v, iv she is carried off to prison with Doll, 'for the man is dead that you and Pistol beat amongst you'.

In *The Merry Wives*, she is the housekeeper of Dr Caius, or as Parson Evans has it, 'in the manner of his nurse, or his dry nurse, or his cook, or his laundry, his washer and his wringer'. She helps impartially all the suitors of Anne Page, and Falstaff in his pursuit of the merry wives. Pistol resolves to marry her. In the last scene she plays the part of the Fairy Queen (cf. s.d. of 'bad' Q1, obviously descriptive of a performance, 'Enter Sir Hugh like a Satyre, and boyes drest like Fayries, Mistresse Quickly, like the queene of Fayries').

In *Henry V*, 'Nell Quickly' has married Pistol, although Nym was 'troth-plight to her'. In lyrical prose she describes Falstaff's death, presumably at her inn, and bids farewell to Pistol as he sets out on the French campaign. In v, i Pistol says, 'News have I that my Doll is dead i' the spital Of malady of France.' This has generally been taken as a mistake for 'Nell'; but Wilson argues that Pistol's speech was originally intended for Falstaff, and that 'Doll' was the original and correct reading (see HENRY V).

Quiller-Couch, Sir Arthur (1863–1944). 'Q' was born in Cornwall and educated at Newton Abbot College, Clifton, and Trinity, Oxford. He was knighted in 1910, and appointed Professor of English Literature at Cambridge in 1912. He edited the *Oxford Books* of English Verse, of Ballads, of Victorian Verse and of English Prose. In addition to a number of novels, short stories and poems, he wrote *On the Art of Writing* and *On the Art of Reading*. His chief Shakespearean criticism, *Shakespeare's Workmanship*, which is an interpretation of some dozen of the plays, was delivered as a course of lectures at Cambridge and published in 1918. He was joint-editor with Dover Wilson of the *New Cambridge Shakespeare*, in the first volume of which, *The Tempest* (1921), he wrote the General Introduction.

Quin, James (1693–1766), was born in London and educated in Dublin, where he became an actor, but made his name at Drury Lane in 1715 as Bajazet in Rowe's *Tamerlane*. From 1716 to 1730 he was at the Lincoln's Inn Fields theatre, but after 1734 until his retirement in 1757 he was almost entirely at Covent Garden, where he rivalled Garrick at Drury Lane. Quin's acting, however, was very different from the new naturalism of Garrick, being the slow, formal, declamatory style of the old school. He played many Shakespearean parts, including Richard III, Henry VIII, Brutus, Coriolanus, Aaron, Othello, Lear and Macbeth, but his most famous impersonation was that of Falstaff. He retired to Bath, where he lived well, and was buried in the Abbey, the epitaph on his tomb being written by Garrick. He is described by Smollet in *Humphrey Clinker*; he was coarse and hot-tempered, and killed a fellow-actor in a duel, but he was generous, and once saved Rich's life from the assault of a drunken nobleman.

Quince, Peter. In *A Midsummer Night's Dream*, he produces the interlude of Pyramus and Thisbe, and himself speaks the Prologue. (The anonymous German farce, *Herr Peter Squentz* (1663), is derived from the clown element in *M.N.D.*)

Quiney, Adrian (d. 1607). A well-to-do mercer of Stratford, whose family bore arms and had long been settled in the town, where they were influential members of the Corporation. He was bailiff in 1559 and 1571, when with his Henley Street neighbour, 'Mr John Shakespere', the poet's father, he was appointed 'to deale in the affayres concerninge the commen wealthe of the borroughe'. His son and partner in his business was

Quiney, Richard (d. 1602), who, in 1580, married Elizabeth Phillips (d. 1632), and was bailiff in 1592–3 and 1601–2, dying after a short illness before his term of office had expired. His widow kept a tavern, and when in 1611 she sold a house, her future daughter-in-law, Judith Shakespeare, witnessed the conveyance with her mark.

The 'Quiney correspondence' contains the only letters in which Shakespeare is mentioned. In the winter of 1597–8, when Richard was in London negotiating with the Privy Council on behalf of the Stratford Corporation, he received a letter, dated 24 January, from Abraham Sturley, a brother member of the Corporation and possibly connected with the Quiney business, mentioning that as 'Mr Shaksper' was thinking of buying land near Shottery, he and Adrian thought it a good opportunity for Richard 'to move him to deale in the matter of our tithes'. These may have been the Old Stratford tithes bought by Shakespeare in 1605, and farmed by Richard in 1596, or perhaps the Clopton tithe-hay, farmed by Quiney and Sturley in 1590.

Richard went to London again in the autumn of 1598, and on 25 October wrote from the Bell in Carter Lane to his 'Loveinge good ffrend & contreyman Mr Wm. Shackespere' asking for a loan of £30 to help him out of his London debts. On the same day he wrote to Sturley, saying that Shakespeare promised them money, and Sturley replied, urging him to obtain £30 or £40 as quickly as possible if the terms were reasonable, while Adrian urged him to bring the money home with him if he could. The correspondence is tantalizingly brief, but it seems clear that Shakespeare had money to invest, that the Quineys and Sturley were in urgent need of money, and that Shakespeare was willing to oblige them. (See E. I. Fripp, *Master Richard Quyny*.)

Quiney, Thomas (1589–*c.* 1655), third son of Richard, was christened at Stratford, 26 February 1589. He appears to have been well educated, but nothing is known of his career before 1616, when he married Shakespeare's younger daughter, Judith, who was four years older than he (see p. 543). The date, 10 February, was within the prohibited period before Easter, and they were excommunicated by the Consistory Court at Worcester. This happened between Shakespeare's drafting his will in January and signing it with alterations in March, and it may be significant that most of these alterations concern Judith's portion, which is so carefully secured as to suggest that Shakespeare was uncertain of his new son-in-law. At the time of his marriage, Thomas was living at a small house on the west side of High Street, but shortly afterwards moved to the Cage, a bigger house on the other side, at the corner of High Street and Bridge Street, where he set up business as a vintner. He was Chamberlain to the Corporation, 1621–3, but retired from that body in 1630, in which year he was fined for swearing and encouraging tipplers in his shop. In 1633 he was in financial trouble, John Hall and Thomas Nash acting as trustees for his wife and children, Shakespeare (1616–17), Richard (1618–39) and Thomas (1620–39). About 1652 he is supposed to have gone to his elder brother Richard, a wealthy London grocer, and to have died there. Judith was buried at Stratford, 9 February 1662, the only direct descendant of Shakespeare then being her niece, the childless Lady Elizabeth Bernard. (See TLS, 1 May 1964.)

Quinton. A village five miles south of Stratford (see HACKET).

Quintus. In *Titus Andronicus*, one of the four sons of Titus (see MARTIUS).

R

Racine, Jean (1639–99), the French dramatic poet, is to the neoclassical drama what Shakespeare is to the romantic, so that much of the criticism of the 18th century was concerned with estimating the relative merits of the two. Racine chose to work within the conventions of the classical drama, excluding all irrelevancies, observing the unities, and reducing action on the stage to a minimum; Shakespeare, ignoring the rules, embraced comedy and anything that enriched, even if it confused, his material, and spread his action when he so wished over a period of a dozen years, and from Britain to Rome, or from Rome to Egypt. '"Comprehension",' wrote Lytton Strachey, 'might be taken as the watchword of the Elizabethans; Racine's was "concentration".' Racine's best plays are generally acknowledged to be *Andromaque* (1667), *Phèdre* (1677), *Athalie* (1690).

Rainolds (or Reynolds), **John** (1549–1607), was educated at Corpus Christi, Oxford, of which college he became a fellow in 1568 and President in 1598. In 1566 he played Hippolyta in Edwardes's *Palamon and Arcite*, but became a Puritan, and in the nineties engaged in controversy with Gager and Gentili as to the desirability of university plays, publishing *Th' Overthrow of Stage-Playes* in 1599. Elizabeth saw Gager's *Rivales* on her second visit to Oxford in 1592, when she 'schooled' Rainolds 'for his obstinate preciseness, willing him to follow her laws, and not run before them'. He was the most prominent of the Puritans at the Hampton Court Conference of 1604, and initiated the production of the Authorised Version, himself helping to translate the Prophets. (See ACADEMIC DRAMA; OXFORD UNIVERSITY.)

Rainsford, Sir Henry. Lord of the manor of Clifford Chambers (q.v.).

Ralegh, Sir Walter (*c.* 1552–1618), was born at Hayes in south Devon and educated at Oriel, Oxford. After serving in Ireland, he became a Court favourite of Elizabeth, who knighted him in 1584, but sent him to the Tower in 1592 for seducing one of her maids of honour, Elizabeth Throckmorton, to whom he was later happily married. After 1587, he was eclipsed by his rival Essex, and both at Court and in the country his greed, arrogance and suspected atheism made him unpopular. He was confined in the Tower by James, 1603–16, for his part in a conspiracy, released to go on an expedition to Guiana, but executed on his return for fighting against the Spaniards.

Don Armado, in *Love's Labour's Lost*, and Coriolanus have both been identified with Ralegh, and Sonnets 37 and 89, referring to the poet's 'lameness' (though presumably figurative), have been ascribed to the wounded Ralegh, and 25 may refer to his disgrace. *Love's Answer* (to Marlowe's 'Live with me'), one verse of which was published in *The Passionate Pilgrim*, and the complete poem in the 1640 edition of Shakespeare's *Poems*, is attributed to Ralegh, as in *England's Helicon*, 1600, it is signed S. W. R. (See A. L. Rowse, *Ralegh and the Throckmortons*, 1962.)

Raleigh, Sir Walter (1861–1922), was born in London and educated at University College, London, and King's, Cambridge. He was appointed Professor of English Literature at Liverpool, at Glasgow, and in 1904 at Oxford, and knighted in 1911. His *Shakespeare*, 1907, is one of the best short books on the subject, combining a romantic enthusiasm with a classical restraint.

'Ralph Roister Doister.' A comedy in rhyming doggerel, written *c.* 1553 by Nicholas Udall, registered 1566 and probably published in the same year, the only copy, without title-page, being preserved at Eton College. It is important as the first regular English comedy, applying classical construction to a native theme; though Ralph is the cowardly braggart of Plautus's *Miles Gloriosus*, the plot and dialogue are fresh and original. Ralph, incited by Mathew Merygreeke, makes love to Christian Custance, a widow betrothed to an absent sea-captain, who eventually drives him off with her maids armed with mops and pails.

Rambures, Lord. In *Henry V*, Master of the Cross-bows, and one of the French lords who jest and boast with the Dauphin before Agincourt, where he is killed.

'RAPE OF LUCRECE.'

WRITTEN: Presumably this is the 'graver labour' referred to in the *Dedication* to Southampton of *Venus and Adonis* (q.v.), registered 18 April 1593. *Lucrece*, therefore, was probably written between April 1593 and May 1594.

REGISTERED: 1594. '9 Maij Master Harrison Senior Entred for his copie vnder thand of Master Cawood Warden, a booke intituled the Ravyshement of Lucrece.'

PUBLISHED: 1594, Q. 'Lucrece. London. Printed by Richard Field, for Iohn Harrison, and are to be sold at the signe of the white Greyhound in Paules Church-yard. 1594.' It is dedicated

To the Right Honourable, Henry Wriothesley, Earle of Southampton, and Baron of Titchfield.

The loue I dedicate to your Lordship is without end: wherof this Pamphlet without beginning is but a superfluous Moity. The warrant I haue of your Honourable disposition, not the worth of my vntutored Lines makes it assured of acceptance. What I haue done is yours, what I haue to doe is yours, being part in all I haue, deuoted yours. Were my worth greater, my duety would shew greater, meane time, as it is, it is bound to your Lordship; To whom I wish long life still lengthened with all happinesse.

Your Lordships in all duety.
William Shakespeare.

Richard Field, Shakespeare's first publisher and printer, was a Stratford man, and no doubt this partly accounts for the excellence of the text. Harrison published O1, 1598; O2, 3, 1600; O4, 1607. In 1614 the copyright was transferred to Roger Jackson, who published O5 in 1616. There were other octavo editions in 1624, 1632, 1655.

SOURCES: The story is told by Ovid (*Fasti*, II, 711–852), and by Livy (I, 56–60), and it was from 'Ovyde and Titus Lyvius' that Chaucer took his version of 206 lines in *The Legend of Good Women*. It also occurs in Painter's *Palace of Pleasure* (1566–7), in a *novella* by Bandello, and in Belleforest's translation of Bandello in his *Histoires Tragiques*. Shakespeare probably knew all these versions of the story.

'Rape of Lucrece.' Thomas Heywood wrote, *c.* 1605, a play on the theme; it was registered 3 June 1608 and in the same year was published as 'The Rape of Lucrece. A True Roman Tragedie. With the seuerall Songes in their apt places, by Valerius, the merrie Lord amongst the Roman Peeres. Acted by her Maiesties Seruants at the Red Bull, neare Clarkenwell'. It was performed at Court (Greenwich) 13 January 1612 'by the Queens players and the Kings men'. In his Epistle, Heywood has the interesting note:

> Some of my Playes have (unknowne to me, and without any of my direction) accidentally come into the Printers hands (and therefore so corrupt and mangled, copied only by the eare) that I have beene as unable to know them, as ashamed to challenge them. (See PIRACY OF PLAYS.)

'Rare Triumphs of Love and Fortune.' An anonymous play published in 1589 as 'Plaide before the Queenes most excellent Maiestie'. This is probably the same as *A History of Love and Fortune*, for the Court performance of which by Derby's, in December 1582, the Revels Office supplied a canvas 'city' and 'battlement' (see COURT PERFORMANCES; STAGING). The play contains the name Fidelia, adopted by Imogen in *Cymbeline*, and that of Hermione (*Winter's Tale*).

Ratcliffe, Sir Richard. In *Richard III*, the willing instrument of Richard, he leads to execution Rivers, Grey, Vaughan and Hastings. He comes to arm Richard before Bosworth, where he is killed. (See CATESBY.)

Rathgeb, Jacob. The secretary of Frederick, Count of Mömpelgart, who wrote an account of his master's travels in his *Badenfahrt* (1602), partly translated by W. B. Rye in *England as seen by Foreigners in the Days of Elizabeth and James the First* (1865). (See BULL-BAITING.)

'Ratseis Ghost.' An anonymous quarto tract, registered 31 May 1605, and published in the same year, the unique copy being preserved in the library of Earl Spencer at Althorp, Northampton. Gamaliel Ratsey was a Northamptonshire highwayman hanged at Bedford 26 March 1605. One chapter describes 'A pretty Prancke passed by Ratsey upon certaine Players that he met by chance in an Inne', an important contemporary account of the life of travelling players. Ratsey calls one or two of them to his chamber:

I pray you, quoth Ratsey, let me heare your musicke, for I have often gone to plaies more for musicke than for action; for some of you not content to do well, but striving to overdoe and go beyond yourselves, oftentimes, by S. George, mar all; yet your poets take great paines to make your parts fit for your mouthes, though they gape never so wide. Other-some, I must needs confesse, are very wel deserving both for true action and faire deliverie of speech, and yet, I warrant you, the very best have sometimes beene content to goe home at night with fifteene pence share apeece. Others there are whom Fortune hath so wel favored that, what by penny-sparing and long practise of playing, are growne so wealthy that they have expected to be knighted.

A week later, when he is disguised, he meets them in another inn and asks them to give him a 'private play', which they do, but

not in the name of the former noblemans servants; for, like camelions, they had changed that colour; but in the name of another, whose indeede they were, although afterwardes, when he heard of their abuse, hee discharged them and tooke away his warrant. For being far off, for their more countenance they would pretend to be protected by such an honourable man, denying their lord and maister, and comming within twenty miles of him againe, they would shrowd themselves under their owne lords favour. Ratsey heard their play, and seemed to like that, though he disliked the rest, and verie liberally out with his purse and gave them fortie shillings, with which they held themselves very richly satisfied, for they scarce had twentie shillings audience at any time for a play in the countrey.

The next day Ratsey pursues them professionally, and forces them to hand back his forty shillings, with interest, then good-humouredly advises their leader to quit the provinces and make his fortune in London:

Get thee to London, for, if one man were dead, they will have much neede of such a one as thou art ... My conceipt is such of thee, that I durst venture all the mony in my purse on thy head to play Hamlet with him for a wager. There thou shalt learne to be frugall, – for players were never so thriftie as they are now about London – and to feed upon all men, to let none feede upon thee; to make thy hand a stranger to thy pocket, thy hart slow to performe thy tongues promise; and when thou feelest thy purse well lined, buy thee some place or lordship in the country, that, growing weary of playing, thy mony may there bring thee to dignitie and reputation; then thou needest care for no man, nor not for them that before made thee prowd with speaking their words upon the stage ... And in this presage and propheticall humor of mine, sayes Ratsey, kneele downe – Rise up, Sir Simon Two Shares and a Halfe; thou art now one of my knights, and the first knight that ever was player in England.

This reference to the successful London player may be to Shakespeare, though it would better fit Alleyn, who retired about this time and in 1605 bought the Manor of Dulwich. Burbage must be the 'one man' who played Hamlet.

Ravenscroft, Edward (*c.* 1640–97), an obscure Restoration dramatist, and author of twelve plays, mostly adaptations, one of which was *Titus Andronicus, or the Rape of Lavinia*, performed in 1678 and published in 1687. As an example of his art may be quoted the lines of the Moor when the Empress stabs their child:

She has outdone me, ev'n in mine own art,
Outdone me in murder, kill'd her own
child;
Give it me, I'll eat it.

After this he is racked and burned alive on the stage. Ravenscroft has certainly outdone Shakespeare. The *Address* to his play contains an important passage:

I think it a greater theft to Rob the dead of their Praise then the Living of their Money. That I may not appear Guilty of such a Crime, 'tis necessary I should acquaint you, that there is a Play in Mr *Shakespear's* Volume under the name of *Titus Andronicus*, from whence I drew part of this. I have been told by some anciently conversant with the Stage, that it was not Originally his, but brought by a private Author to be Acted, and he only gave some Master-touches to one or two of the Principal Parts or Characters; this I am apt to believe, because 'tis the most incorrect and indigested piece in all his Works; it seems rather a heap of Rubbish than a Structure.

This is the only piece of external evidence, if so it may be called, against the authenticity of any of the plays in the Folio. (See AUTHENTICITY.)

Rawlidge, Richard. Author of a puritanical pamphlet, *A Monster Lately Found out and Discovered, or the Scourging of Tipplers*, 1628. This seems to describe the pulling down of the inn-theatres some time after 1596 when, during the disastrous six months that Lord Cobham (q.v.) was Lord Chamberlain, the Privy Council agreed to the prohibition of public plays within the City. (This would add sauce to the mock play in the Boar's Head Tavern in *1 Henry IV*, written *c.* 1597: 'He does it as like one of these harlotry players as ever I see!' exclaims Mistress Quickly; and 'Play out the play' cries Falstaff before he is 'banished' (II, iv).)

London hath within the memory of man lost much of hir pristine lustre ... some of the pious magistrates made humble suit to the late Queene Elizabeth of ever-liuing memorie, and her priuy Counsaile, and obtained leaue from her Majesty to thrust those Players out of the Citty and to pull downe the Dicing houses: which accordingly was affected, and the Play-houses in *Gracious street*, *Bishops-gate-street*, nigh *Paules*, that on *Ludgate hill*, the *White-Friars* were put down, and other lewd houses quite supprest within the Liberties, by the care of those religious senators.

The Bell and Cross Keys were in Gracechurch Street, the Bull in Bishopsgate Street, and the Bel Savage in Ludgate Hill; the play-house 'nigh Paules' presumably means the private house of the Paul's boys; Whitefriars may be an error for the second Blackfriars theatre, which James Burbage was forbidden to open in 1596. (See INN-THEATRES.)

Raworth, Robert. The printer, for William Leake, of O6 *Venus and Adonis*, 1602.

Realism. Shakespeare made little attempt to be realistic in the sense of accurately representing the life of his own or any other time. Unlike Jonson, Marston, Middleton, Dekker and Heywood, he wrote no play of contemporary English life, though there is nothing but Falstaff to link *The Merry Wives* to the early 15th century, and the sub-plot in the Illyrian *Twelfth Night* is an accurate presentation of an Elizabethan household. Many of the plays take place in classical or Renaissance Italy, whence come so many of the romantic plots, and these plays abound in impossibilities, inaccuracies and anachronisms. Again, in real life people do not speak verse, still less do they speak poetry. Shakespeare's realism is of a different kind: that of the poet and dramatist who creates men and women, and by his art compels us to believe in the reality of what we see and hear.

Rebec. A medieval stringed instrument, something like a violin, played with a bow. It survived in popular use until the 18th century, but was scarcely treated as a serious instrument in Shakespeare's time, though Hugh Rebeck is one of the musicians in *Romeo and Juliet*, IV, v.

Recorder. A wooden, end-blown flute with whistle mouthpiece and eight holes. It was made in various sizes: sopranino, descant, treble, alto, tenor, and bass, music being composed for a consort of recorders. It was apparently of English origin, easy to play, and therefore very popular, the tin whistle being its descendant. The most famous literary reference to the recorder is in *Hamlet*, III, ii.

Recordings. All of Shakespeare's plays and poems have been recorded in the last few years by the Marlowe Dramatic Society of Cambridge, assisted by a few professional actors. The productions are sponsored by the British Council in association with the Cambridge University Press, and directed by George Rylands with Thurston Dart as musical director. The text is the uncut *New Cambridge* edition of Dover Wilson. The corresponding venture in America is that of the Shakespeare Recording Society, whose performances are essentially professional and directed by various producers. The German Gramophone Company has also brought out several records with scenes and passages from the plays spoken by well-known German actors and actresses.

Red Bull Theatre, was built in Clerkenwell, *c.* 1604, by Aaron Holland on a site that he rented from Anne Bedingfield, just north of Clerkenwell Green and west of St John Street. It was probably occupied by Queen Anne's (Worcester's) Men as soon as built; their patent of April 1609 authorized them to play 'at their usual houses of the Curtain and Red Bull', and they probably stayed there until 1617, when they moved to the new Phoenix (Cockpit) in Drury Lane. According to James Wright (*Historia Histrionica*, 1699), it was a public theatre like the Globe and Fortune, 'large houses, and lay partly open to the weather', and presumably resembled them in construction. (There is no authority for regarding the stage lit by footlights and candelabra in the frontispiece to Kirkman's *Wits*, 1672, as that of the Red Bull, as was once supposed.) Wright says that the King's company acted there in 1660, but according to D'Avenant, by 1663 it had 'no tenants but old spiders'. (See G. F. Reynolds, *The Staging of Elizabethan Plays at the Red Bull Theatre*, 1940; SS, 7.)

Red Lion Inn. The only record of this theatre is in a memorandum of the Carpenters' Company, dated 15 July 1567, when it was agreed that William Sylvester, carpenter, should repair for John Brayne 'suche defaultes ... aboute suche skaffoldes, as he the said Willyam hathe mad at the house called the Red Lion in the parishe of Stebinyhuthe [Stepney]'. Brayne was to pay him £8 10s., and 'after the playe, which is called the storye of Sampson, be once plaied at the place aforesaid', to deliver bonds to Sylvester for the performance of the bargain. Stepney was east of the City, and the Red Lion, therefore, was not one of the much frequented City inns. Nine years later Brayne (q.v.) helped James Burbage to build the Theatre.

Redgrave, Michael (b. 1908), actor and producer. With the Liverpool Rep. 1934–6 and Old Vic 1936–7. He has played numerous great Shakespearean parts both in England and abroad: Hamlet, Lear, Antony, Shylock, etc. Knighted 1959.

Reed, Isaac (1742–1807), was born in London, son of a baker. He became a solicitor at Staple Inn, but eventually confined himself to conveyancing and literature. In 1778 he edited Middleton's *Witch*, in 1780 a revised edition of Dodsley's *Old Plays*, and in 1782 published his valuable *Biographia Dramatica* (2 vols.), biographies of English dramatists and a critical account of their work. Reed was a great friend of the capricious Steevens whose 10-volume edition of Shakespeare he edited in 1785, and as his literary executor undertook the great 21-volume edition of 1803, the First Variorum, which was reprinted in 1813. This contains a short biography by his friend Nichols, who writes,

> With the late Dr. Farmer, the worthy master of Emanuel College, Cambridge, he was long and intimately acquainted, and regularly for many years spent an autumnal month with him at that pleasant seat of learning. At that period the theatricals of Stirbitch Fair had powerful patronage in the Combination-room of Emanuel, where the routine of performance was regularly settled, and where the charms of the bottle were early deserted for the pleasures of the sock and buskin.

And James Boswell, the elder, wrote of his 'steady friend Mr. Isaac Reed',

> whose extensive and accurate knowledge of English literary History I do not express with exaggeration when I say it is wonderful; indeed his labours have proved it to the world; and all who have the pleasure of his acquaintance can bear testimony to the frankness of his communications in private society.

Reformation. The reformers of the first half of the 16th century, inspired by the new humanism, were not opposed to plays, but they insisted that they should instruct as well as please, and they could hardly be expected to approve of those miracle plays which emphasised points of Roman Catholic doctrine. Less disinterested Protestants, such as Thomas Cromwell, actively encouraged playwrights like John Bale to attack the Catholic Church and to propagate the reformed religion. The hundred years 1550–1650 witnessed the attack of the extreme Protestants, the Puritans (q.v.), which the playwrights were called in by the bishops to repel during the Martin Marprelate controversy of the nineties. Fifty years later, however, the Puritans carried the day and succeeded in closing the theatres, 1642–60.

Regal. A musical instrument of the 15th–17th centuries; it was like a very small portable organ, but with reed instead of flue pipes, and a harsh tone. It may have been used in the theatres.

Regan. In *King Lear* (q.v.), the second daughter of Lear. When Cornwall has put out one of Gloucester's eyes she urges him to put out the other. 'She is the most hideous human being (if she is one) that Shakespeare ever drew' (A. C. Bradley).

Rehan, Ada (1860–1916), actress, was born in Limerick, but at the age of five was taken to the United States where she first appeared on the stage in 1874. In 1879 she joined Augustin Daly's company, and played the lead in all his adaptations from the German, and in most of Shakespeare's comedies, her best parts being, perhaps, Katharina the Shrew, Rosalind and Viola. She was well received in London on her tours with Daly. Her bust and her portrait as Katharina are at Stratford.

'Rehearsal, The.' A comedy (1671), attributed to the 2nd Duke of Buckingham, though probably largely the work of Samuel Butler and others. It satirizes the heroic tragedies of the Restoration, and in the person of the playwright Bayes, the laureates D'Avenant and Dryden, the principal authors of these plays. Bayes takes his friends to see a rehearsal of his heroic tragedy, a patchwork of parodies, and there is a hit at D'Avenant's Shakespearean productions when he says that the actors dance 'worse than the Angels in *Harry* the Eight, or the fat Spirits in *The Tempest*, I gad'. *The Rehearsal* was imitated by Fielding in *Tom Thumb* (1730), and by Sheridan in *The Critic* (1779).

Reignier (René), Duke of Anjou (1434–80). In *1 Henry VI*, titular King of Naples, Sicily, and Jerusalem, he loyally supports the Dauphin and Joan of Arc. However, when Suffolk captures his daughter, Margaret, he agrees to her betrothal to Henry VI, provided he may quietly enjoy Maine and Anjou (v, iii).

Reinhardt, Max (1873–1943), was born near Vienna and began his career in a Salzburg theatre, but moved to Berlin where, in 1903, he became manager of the Neues Theater, 1905–20, director of the Deutsches Theater, and, 1919–20, of the Grosses Schauspielhaus. In these theatres, with the aid of a revolving stage and symbolic lighting, he staged elaborate and spectacular productions of Shakespeare. Later, at the Redoutensaal in Vienna he turned to a simpler, formal method of production. In 1933 he went to America, where he died.

Religion in Plays. In her proclamation of 16 May 1559 Elizabeth ordered the licensers of plays to 'permyt none to be played wherin either matters of religion or of the gouernaunce of the estate of the common weale shalbe handled or treated'. Criticism of the established religion remained one of the forbidden subjects throughout Shakespeare's lifetime, and after the *Act to Restrain Abuses of Players*, 1606, the Master of the Revels, who had become licenser of plays, would be responsible for purging performances of profanity. Henry Herbert took this part of his duty very seriously. Criticism of Roman Catholicism, however, was allowed, at least after the disappearance of the Spanish menace (cf. *King John*), and the bishops themselves invoked the aid of playwrights against the Puritan Marprelate attack. In the early 17th century the playwrights took the offensive against the Puritans, as in *Bartholomew Fair*.

Religion of Shakespeare. It is possible that Shakespeare's father was a Roman Catholic (see JORDAN, JOHN), and Richard Davies, *c.* 1700, wrote that Shakespeare himself 'dyed a papist', a view supported by the Countess de Chambrun. The evidence of the plays is slight, though his allusions to the Prayer Book suggest his Protestantism. Certainly he does not seem to have had any sympathy with Puritanism (cf. *Twelfth Night*), and *King John* suggests that he sympathized with John's uncomplimentary remarks about the Pope. As his political philosophy was all on the side of the established order, and, in the absence of other evidence, it seems probable that he was a supporter of the established Protestant Church, though for political rather than religious reasons. With religious doctrine he does not seem to have been much occupied. (See BIBLE; H. S. Bowden, *The Religion of Shakespeare*.)

Renaissance. The rediscovery of Greek and Roman culture in England at the beginning of the 16th century led to the acting of classical and neo-classical plays by educated amateurs: schoolboys, undergraduates and Inns of Court men; the gildsmen still performing their medieval miracle plays, and the professional actors their native moralities, interludes and formless chronicle histories. The most influential classical plays were the comedies of Terence and Plautus, and the tragedies of Seneca, and it was these, or original plays based on their model, either in Latin or English, that came to be favoured by the cultured classes of Tudor England. This accounts for the overwhelming popularity of the boys of the Chapel Royal and of Paul's at Court until about 1580; Elizabeth allowed the old-fashioned, uncultured Court Interluders literally to die out, and turned to the boys for her entertainment. At the beginning of her reign, however, humanist playwrights applied classical manner to native matter: Udall in *Ralph Roister Doister*, and Sackville and Norton in *Gorboduc*; in 1576 the first permanent London theatres were built; and a few years later the University Wits began writing plays with a classical structure for the adult professional actors. Until about this date, therefore, the effect of the Renaissance on the English drama had, broadly speaking, been confined to a small educated class; when Shakespeare began to write, the University Wits had popularized their classical models by writing plays which combined a real plot and structure with a native vigour of action and excitement. Between 1576 and 1590 the adult companies performed at Court twice as often as the boys (69 times as against 32); in 1583 Elizabeth formed her own company of adult players; the boys disappeared altogether from Court 1590–1600, and only became dangerous rivals again for a short, but important, period at the beginning of the 17th century, when, however, they were rivals for popular favour, and not because they had better plays.

Renoldes, William. A crazy Elizabethan soldier who thought the Privy Council caused certain books to be published to persuade him that the Queen loved him. In a letter of 21 Sept. 1593 he wrote that *Venus and Adonis* had been published 'within these three days'. (See Hotson, *Shakespeare's Sonnets Dated*, p. 141.)

Repertory System. There was no such thing as a continuous run at the Elizabethan theatres. Plays were acted on the repertory system, and a play was rarely acted twice in the same week; thus, on the thirty days of playing for Henslowe, 26 December–6 February 1593–4, Sussex's performed thirteen plays, most of them twice, but some of them three or four times. The last twelve performances are given below; the third column indicates Henslowe's takings, the figures in brackets the number of the performance in that period:

Popular plays, such as those of Marlowe, were revived over a number of years, other old plays were refurbished, and new plays were continually being added; Henslowe bought some 55 for the Admiral's 1594–7, though it does not follow that all of them were acted.

Replingham, William, of Great Harborough, Warwickshire, married Alicia, cousin of Arthur Mainwaring (q.v.). (See WELCOMBE ENCLOSURE.)

'Reported Texts.' Texts of plays that are mutilated by paraphrase, omission, vulgarization, improvization, mislineation and so on. They are generally admitted to have been reconstructed from memory for provincial performance by actors who had taken part in the plays in London. The prompt-book thus put together was sometimes sold to a stationer for publication. This, briefly, is the probable history of the six 'bad' Quartos of Shakespeare's plays. *Richard III* and *Pericles* are rather different. Pollard's theory that some bad texts were shorthand reports taken in the theatre has been generally abandoned. (See SHORTHAND.)

Reprints. See QUARTOS; FOLIOS; EDITORS; FACSIMILES.

Restoration Productions of Shakespeare. See DUKE'S COMPANY; KING'S COMPANY; ADAPTATIONS; PRODUCTION.

Revels Accounts. 'Original Accounts', showing expenses incurred for the Court

Jan.	16	Richard the Confeser	xj^{s}	(2)
	17	Abram & Lotte	xxx^{s}	(2)
	18	Kinge Lude	xxij^{s}	(1)
	20	Frier Frances	xxx^{s}	(3)
	21	the Fayer Mayd of Ytaly	xxij^{s}	(2)
	22	Gorge a Grene	xxv^{s}	(4)
Jan.	23 ne	Titus & Ondronicous	iij^{li} viij^{s}	(1)
	27	Buckengam	xviij^{s}	(4)
	28	Titus & Ondronicous	xxxx^{s}	(2)
	31	Abrame & Lotte	xij^{s}	(3)
Feb.	4	the Jewe of Malta	l^{s}	(1)
	6	Tittus & Ondronicus	xxxx^{s}	(3)

performance of plays, were made out by the Revels Office and submitted to the Treasurer of the Chamber who paid upon warrant from the Privy Council. They give the names of the companies, and generally the titles of the plays. There are eleven extant audited accounts for Elizabeth's reign, covering the greater part of the years 1571–88, and two for that of James I (1604–5, 1611–12), the authenticity of which has been disputed, but they are now generally accepted as genuine (see CUNNINGHAM). Those for 1604–5 are unusually full, the first nine of the fourteen entries reading as follows:

The plaiers.		The poets wch mayd the plaies.
By the Kings ma^tis^ plaiers.	Hallamas Day being the first of Nouember A play in the Banketinge house att Whitehall called The Moor of Venis.	
By his Ma^tis^ plaiers.	The Sunday ffolowinge A Play of the Merry Wiues of Winsor.	
By his Ma^tis^ plaiers.	On St. Stiuens Night in the Hall A Play caled Mesur for Mesur.	Shaxberd.
By his Ma^tis^ plaiers.	On Inosents Night The Plaie of Errors.	Shaxberd.
By the Queens Ma^tis^ plaiers.	On Sunday ffolowinge A plaie cald How to Larne of a woman to wooe.	Hewood.
The Boyes of the Chapell.	On Newers Night A playe cauled: All Foulles.	By Georg Chapman.
By his Ma^tis^ plaiers.	Betwin Newers Day and Twelfe day A Play of Loues Labours Lost.	
By his Ma^tis^ plaiers.	On the 7 of January was played the play of Henry the fift.	
By his Ma^tis^ plaiers.	The 8 of January Aplay cauled Euery on out of his Umor.	

The Declared Accounts of the corresponding Chamber Accounts show that 'John Hemynges one of his Ma^tes^ players' was paid £60 for the six performances of 1, 4 November, 26, 28 December, 7, 8 January, the warrant being dated 21 January. John Duke was payee for Queen Anne's (Worcester's) Men, and Samuel Daniel and Henry Evans for the Chapel (Queen's Revels) Boys. Declared Accounts for the Revels, fairly complete, are preserved in the Audit Office and Pipe Office Accounts. They are very brief abstracts: e.g. 1583–4 'vj histories, one Comedie'. (See CHAMBER ACCOUNTS.)

Revels Children. See CHILDREN OF THE CHAPEL.

Revels Office. In 1547 Sir Thomas Cawarden, first permanent Master of the Revels (q.v.), found accommodation for himself and his officers, as well as workrooms and storerooms, in the buildings of the dissolved Blackfriars priory. After his death in 1560, their headquarters became the 'late Hospital of St. John of Jerusalem' in Clerkenwell. In 1608 they were moved to the Whitefriars, and the Master, Edmund Tilney, drew up a memorandum which gives a good idea of the work done by the Office in supplying and storing scenery, properties, and costumes for the Court performances of plays and other Revels:

> Which Office of the Revells Consistethe of a wardropp and other severall Roomes for Artifficers to worke in (viz. Taylors, Imbrotherers, Properti makers, Paynters, wyerdrawers and Carpenters), togeather with a Convenient place for the Rehearshalls and settinge forthe of Playes and other Shewes for those Services.
>
> In which Office the Master of the Office hath ever hadd a dwellinge Howsse for himself and his Famelie, and the other Officers ar to haue eyther dwellinge Howsses Assigned unto them by the Master (for so goeth the

wordes of ther Pattentes) or else a rente for the same as thei had before they Came unto St Johnes.

By 1612 the Office was 'upon St Peter's Hill', and later still in the parish of St Mary Bowe. (See 'APOLOGY FOR ACTORS'.)

Revenge Play. The type of Elizabethan tragedy popularized by Kyd in his *Spanish Tragedy*. It derives from Seneca (q.v.), in whose plays ghosts crying for revenge are a normal ingredient. The tragedy of revenge remained popular throughout Shakespeare's lifetime; *Titus Andronicus* and *Richard III* are examples of early Shakespearean revenge plays, as *Julius Caesar* and, above all, *Hamlet* of later. Other examples are Marston's *Antonio's Revenge*, Chapman's *Revenge of Bussy D'Ambois*, Webster's *Duchess of Malfi*, Tourneur's (or Webster's) *Revenger's Tragedy*, and Massinger's *Roman Actor*.

'Review of English Studies.' 'A Quarterly Journal of English Literature and the English Language', established in 1925.

Revision of Plays. Popular plays were often revived, and sometimes alterations were made; an old play might be given another name to pass it off as new, forgotten allusions might be cut and fresh ones added, and alterations made to fit it to another theatre and company. Dekker was a 'dresser of plays', and professional dressers must have made more extensive alterations: *Old Fortunatus* appears to have been reduced from two parts to one, low comedy has been added to *Dr Faustus*, and so on, but there is no evidence to show that substantial rewriting, either by the original author or a dresser, was a common practice, a practice that would have added to the difficulties of actors who had to memorize a dozen parts in their repertory at the same time. A 'newly corrected and augmented' Quarto, like Q1 *L.L.L.*, may merely be a good Q replacing a 'bad'.

Nor is there any external evidence save that of Ravenscroft (q.v.) to show that Shakespeare revised other men's work, though J. M. Robertson, on stylistic grounds, assigns inferior matter to the author of a play revised by him, and Dover Wilson, following bibliographical clues, finds evidence for the frequent revision by Shakespeare of his own work. (See AUTHENTICITY OF PLAYS; DISINTEGRATORS.)

Revivals. Before the closing of the theatres in 1642, mention of the performances of plays, apart from the early Henslowe's *Diary* (1592–1603), is confined mainly to those at Court as recorded in the Revels and Chamber Accounts and the *Office Book* of Sir Henry Herbert, so that revivals at the theatres generally pass unmentioned. After the reopening of the theatres in 1660, dramatic records are much more numerous in the form of stage histories, diaries, etc., and absence of mention is strong evidence against the revival of a play.

Reynaldo. In *Hamlet*, servant of Polonius, who sends him to spy on Laertes in Paris. (Called Montano in Q1.)

Reynolds, Frederic (1764–1841), between 1816 and 1828 produced operatic versions of a number of Shakespeare's comedies: 1816, *A Midsummer Night's Dream*; 1819, *The Comedy of Errors*; 1820, *Twelfth Night*; 1821, *The Two Gentlemen of Verona*; 1821, *The Tempest*; 1824, *The Merry Wives*; 1828, *The Taming of the Shrew*. Most of these had music by Henry Bishop, but *The Comedy of Errors* included music by Arne and Mozart, and incorporated 'When icicles hang by the wall' and the chorus from *Antony and Cleopatra*, 'Come thou monarch of the vine'. Reynolds was educated at Westminster School, entered the Middle Temple, but turned from law to the theatre, his first play being performed in 1785. He wrote nearly a hundred tragedies and comedies.

Reynolds, George Fullmer (1877–1963). American scholar, and Professor of

English Literature in the University of Colorado, 1919–45. He was one of the pioneers of the detailed study of Shakespeare's theatre. (See his *Some Principles of Elizabethan Staging* (1905), and *The Staging of Elizabethan Plays at the Red Bull.*)

Reynolds, William (1575–1633), the 'William Raynolds gent' to whom Shakespeare left 'xxvj^{s} viij^{d} to buy him A Ringe'. He was a Catholic, held land in Stratford, and was connected by marriage with the Combe family. In 1615 he married Frances de Bois, and had a daughter, Anne.

Rhodes, John. One of the 'necessary attendantes' of the King's Men in 1624. He may have been the John Rhodes who was 'wardrobe-keeper at the theatre in Blackfriars before the breaking out of the Civil Wars', later a bookseller, and at the Restoration lessee of the Cockpit, where Betterton first appeared. Baldwin thinks that he was book-keeper of the King's Men before Knight, and the scribe of *The Honest Man's Fortune* and *Bonduca*, and stage-reviser of *Believe as You List.* (See PROTECTION OF PLAYERS.)

Rhodes, R. Crompton. Author of *Shakespeare's First Folio* (1923), a tercentenary study in which he clearly stated the hypothesis that the first Quartos of *Romeo and Juliet, Henry V, The Merry Wives* and *Hamlet* were reported texts (q.v.). He also suggested that plays of which there was no Quarto or other 'copy' were set up for the Folio from the prompter's 'plot' and the actors' 'parts'. (See ASSEMBLED TEXTS.)

Rhyme. In his *Attempt to Ascertain the Order in which the Plays of Shakespeare were Written*, first published in 1778, Malone noted the frequency of rhyme in the early plays, and was 'disposed to believe (other proofs being wanting) that play in which the greater number of rhymes is found, to have been first composed'. Pentameter rhyme for dialogue, instead of blank verse, is commonest in the plays of the lyrical period: *L.L.L.* 62 per cent, *M.N.D.* 43 per cent, *Rich. II* 19 per cent, *R.J.* 17 per cent; but the proportion of rhyme to blank verse is no very accurate index to the chronology as a whole. Rhyming dialogue is not very common in Elizabethan drama, and Shakespeare seems to have experimented with it when he was writing *Venus and Adonis, Lucrece* and the *Sonnets*, and then to have discarded it as a staple medium, though he retained it for certain effects, to clinch an aphorism and to define a scene, and such minor uses of rhyme afford a limited index of chronology, for they gradually dwindle and ultimately disappear in the latest plays.

Rhyming lyrics and episodes are common to all the plays; e.g. the Mouse-trap scene in *Hamlet*, and the Masque in *The Tempest.* (See VERSE-TESTS.)

Rhyme Royal. A stanza of seven iambic pentameters, rhyming *ababbcc.* It may derive its name from its use in *The Kingis Quair* (book), attributed to James I of Scotland (1394–1437). It is the stanza of Chaucer's *Troilus and Cressid*, of Shakespeare's *Rape of Lucrece*, and of *A Lover's Complaint*:

From the besieged Ardea all in post,
Borne by the trustless wings of false desire,
Lust-breathed Tarquin leaves the Roman host,
And to Collatium bears the lightless fire,
Which, in pale embers hid, lurks to aspire,
And girdle with embracing flames the waist
Of Collatine's fair love, Lucrece the chaste.

Rice, John. One of the 'Principall Actors' in Shakespeare's plays and the last named in the Folio list (see p. 90). He was apprenticed to Heminge in 1607, and was still a boy with the King's Men when he took part with Burbage in the pageant (q.v.) of 1610. He joined the Lady Elizabeth's on their formation in 1611, and returned to the King's as a sharer, *c.* 1620, probably to replace Field who died 1619–20. He is mentioned in their Warrant for liveries, 7 April 1621, and played Pescara in their revival of *The Duchess of Malfi* of about the same date. He seems to have retired after 1625, when his name last occurs in their lists. In his will of 1630, Heminge left 20s. 'unto John Rice, Clerk, of St Saviour's in Southwark', and appointed his 'loving friends Mr. [Cuthbert] Burbage and Mr. Rice to be the overseers'.

Rich, Barnabe (*c.* 1540–1617), soldier and writer, served in the campaigns in France, the Low Countries and in Ireland, where he settled towards the end of his life. In 1616, when he was about seventy-six, he was rewarded with £100 as the oldest captain in the army. He wrote a number of tracts on Ireland, advocating a firm policy, and a number of romances, some of which were published in *Riche his Farewell to Militarie Profession conteining verie pleasaunt discourses fit for a peacable tyme*, 1581. Of the eight stories in this collection three are translations from the Italian, the other five Rich claims as his own, including *Apolonius and Silla*, though it really comes from a novel of Bandello. This story is important as the source of the main plot of *Twelfth Night*. Silla falls in love with Duke Apolonius, whom she follows from Cyprus to his court at Constantinople. She is shipwrecked, disguises herself as her brother Silvio, and becomes a page of Apolonius, who sends her to woo on his behalf the young widow Julina, who falls in love with her. Silvio arrives in Constantinople in search of his sister, meets Julina who mistakes him for Silla, and is betrothed to her. He continues his search, and Julina tells Apolonius that she is betrothed to his page, whom the Duke imprisons. Silla reveals her identity and her love, and Apolonius marries her, and Silvio returns to marry Julina.

The fifth story, about 'Two Bretheren and their Wives', may have been a source of *The Merry Wives*.

Rich may be the 'R. B. Gent', author of *Greene's Funeralls* (q.v.).

Rich, John (1692–1761), son of Christopher Rich, manager of Drury Lane. In 1714, the year of his father's death, he opened the New theatre in Lincoln's Inn Fields where, under the name of Lun in 1716, he appeared as Harlequin, so establishing the English pantomime with some of the characteristics of the *commedia dell'arte*. His production of *The Beggar's Opera* in 1728, was said to have 'made Rich gay and Gay rich'. In 1733 he opened the Covent Garden theatre, and in 1750 occurred the celebrated '*Romeo and Juliet* War', when Barry and Mrs Cibber played at Covent Garden against Garrick and Anne Bellamy at Drury Lane. Rich returned to something like Shakespeare's text, instead of D'Avenant's adaptations, in his productions of *Measure for Measure* (1720) and *Much Ado* (1721).

'RICHARD II.'

WRITTEN: 1595–6. Mentioned by Meres, 1598.

PERFORMED: 1595. Sir Edward Hoby invited Sir Robert Cecil to see a performance of 'K. Richard' at his house in Canon Row on 9 December.

1601. 7 February. At the Globe. (See ESSEX; PHILLIPS, AUGUSTINE.)

1607. 30 September. 'Captain Hawkins dined with me, wher my companions acted Kinge Richard the Second.' (*Journal* of Capt. W. Keeling when off Sierra Leone.)

(1611. The 'Richard the 2 At the Glob', seen by Simon Forman on 30 April, was not Shakespeare's.)

1631. 'Received of Mr. Shanke, in the name of the kings company, for the benefitt of their summer day, upon ye second daye of Richard ye Seconde, at the Globe, this 12 of June, 1631, – 5^l^. 6^s^. 6^d^.' (*Office Book* of Sir Henry Herbert.)

REGISTERED: 1597. '29° Augusti. Andrew Wise. Entred for his Copie by appoyntment from master Warden Man, The Tragedye of Richard the Second vj^d^.'

PUBLISHED: 1597, Q1. 'The Tragedie of King Richard the second. As it hath beene publikely acted by the right Honourable the Lorde Chamberlaine his Seruants. London Printed by Valentine Simmes for Andrew Wise, and are to be sold at his shop in Paules church yard at the signe of the Angel. 1597.' A good text, printed from foul papers.

1598, Q2. 'By William Shake-speare.' Set up from Q1, but adds 123 errors.

1598, Q3. Set up from Q2. (The only play of Shakespeare to have three editions in two years. See A. W. Pollard, *A New Shakespeare Quarto: Richard II*, 1916.)

1608, Q4. 'With new additions of the Parliament Sceane, and the deposing of King Richard, As it hath been lately acted by the Kinges Majesties seruantes, at the Globe.' The 'deposition scene' appears to have been part of the original play which was cut when Q1 was printed. The version in Q4 seems to be a report.

1615, Q5. Set up from Q4.

1623, F1. 'The life and death of King Richard the Second.' The second play in the History section: pp. 23–45. Acts and scenes marked. Set up from Q3 (and Q5) perhaps used as prompt-book.

1634, Q6.

The Elizabethans saw parallels between the reigns of Richard II and Elizabeth, and no doubt the deposition scene was censored, and only acted and printed when James I was safely on the throne. An extraordinary revival with the deposition scene was staged at the Globe at the request of Essex's supporters on 7 February 1601, the day before his rebellion.

SOURCES: Holinshed's *Chronicles*, the 2nd edition, 1587. The scene between the Queen and the gardener is Shakespeare's addition. (See FROISSART; 'THOMAS OF WOODSTOCK'; DANIEL.)

STAGE HISTORY: 1680. Nahum Tate's version at Drury Lane was suppressed for political reasons, and he failed to save it by changing the characters and the title to *The Sicilian Usurper*.

1719. Theobald's successful version at Lincoln's Inn Fields.

1738. Shakespeare's play revived at Covent Garden.

1815. Richard Wroughton's version with Edmund Kean as Richard.

Richard II was one of the few plays not produced by Phelps, but it was staged by Poel, with Granville-Barker as Richard, in 1899.

Henry Bolingbroke, son of John of Gaunt, Duke of Lancaster, and Richard's cousin, accuses Mowbray of the murder of Richard's uncle, the Duke of Gloucester, to which Mowbray retorts by calling Bolingbroke a 'most degenerate traitor'. Richard orders a trial by combat, but at the last moment exiles Mowbray for life and Bolingbroke for ten years.

John of Gaunt dies and Richard seizes his estates, which are now really the property of Bolingbroke, to pay for his Irish campaign, in spite of the protests of his uncle York, and of Northumberland, who hears that Bolingbroke is coming to claim his own, and goes to join him. Richard goes to Ireland, Bolingbroke lands in Yorkshire, and with Northumberland goes to Berkeley Castle where York, left as regent, is forced to receive them.

Richard lands in Wales and hears that his Welsh forces have dispersed or joined the popular Bolingbroke, who has executed two of his favourites, Bushy and Green. With York's son, Aumerle, he seeks refuge in Flint Castle, where he is taken prisoner by Bolingbroke, who protests that he has come only to recover his estates. III, iv is a lyrical interlude in which the Queen talks to a gardener of Richard's possible deposition.

Richard's favourite, Bagot, brought before Bolingbroke, accuses Aumerle of Gloucester's murder, and Bolingbroke orders the repeal of Mowbray to confront Aumerle, but the Bishop of Carlisle announces Mowbray's death at Venice. Richard is brought in, and surrenders his crown to Bolingbroke; Carlisle protests, and is arrested by Northumberland. Richard is sent to the Tower, and Carlisle and Aumerle 'plot to rid the realm of this pernicious blot', Bolingbroke.

Richard, on the way to Pomfret Castle instead of the Tower, parts from his Queen, who is sent to France. York discovers Aumerle's plot and rushes to tell Bolingbroke, now Henry IV, but Aumerle reaches him first and asks for pardon, which is granted at the request of the Duchess of York. At Bolingbroke's command Richard is murdered in Pomfret Castle by Sir Pierce of Exton.

Richard II (1367–1400), son of the Black Prince (d. 1376), succeeded to the throne on the death of his grandfather, Edward III, in 1377. After the death of his wife, Anne of Bohemia, in 1394, he asserted his authority, in 1397 secured the murder of his uncle Gloucester, Thomas of Woodstock, and banished his cousin Bolingbroke. *Richard II* deals with the years 1397–1400, from just after the murder of Gloucester to that of Richard himself.

'RICHARD III.'

WRITTEN: 1592–3. Mentioned by Meres, 1598.

PERFORMED: 1593, 30 December. The play of 'Buckingham' recorded by Henslowe in his *Diary*, as played by Sussex's may refer to *Richard III*. He did not mark it then as 'new'. It was popular and profitable, and repeated three times in the next month. (See REPERTORY.)

1633. 'On Saterday, the 17th of Novemb. being the Queens birthday, Richarde the Thirde was acted by the K. players at St James, wher the king and queene were present, it being the first play the queene sawe since her Maiestys delivery of the Duke of York.' (*Office Book* of Sir Henry Herbert.)

(See MANNINGHAM.)

REGISTERED: 1597. '20 Octobris. Andrewe Wise. Entred for his copie vnder thandes of master Barlowe, and master warden Man. The tragedie of kinge Richard the Third with the death of the Duke of Clarence vj^d.'

1603. 25 June. Transferred to Matthew Law.

PUBLISHED: 1597, Q1. 'The Tragedy Of King Richard the third. Containing, His treacherous Plots against his brother Clarence: the pittiefull murther of his iunocent nephewes: his tyrannicall vsurpation: with the whole course of his detested life, and most deserued death. As it hath beene lately Acted by the Right honourable the Lord Chamberlaine his seruants. At London. Printed by Valentine Sims, for Andrew Wise, dwelling in Paules Churchyard, at the Signe of the Angell. 1597.' Not a 'bad' Q, but perhaps an abridged memorial reconstruction by the company when on tour.

1598, Q2. 'By William Shake-speare.'

1602, Q3. 'Newly augmented'; but there are no additions.

1605, Q4.

1612, Q5. 'As it hath beene lately Acted by the Kings Maiesties seruants.'

1622, Q6.

1623, F1. 'The Tragedy of Richard the Third: with the Landing of Earle Richmond, and the Battell at Bosworth Field.' The ninth play in the History section: pp. 173–204. Acts and scenes marked. Omits about 40 lines in Q, but adds about 230 not in Q. Set up from Q6 corrected from foul papers that incorporated leaves from Q3?

SOURCES: The *Chronicles* of Holinshed (2nd edition, 1587) and Halle, both based on Polydore Vergil's *Anglicae Historiae*, and Sir Thomas More's *History of Richard III*. (See 'TRUE TRAGEDY OF RICHARD III'.)

STAGE HISTORY: 1700. Colley Cibber (q.v.) produced the most famous of all Shakespearean adaptations at Drury Lane, and himself played Richard until 1739. Cibber's version held the stage, both in England and America, for 150 years. Phelps gave the original Shakespeare at Sadler's Wells in 1845, but returned to Cibber in 1862. Irving finally succeeded in restoring Shakespeare, though severely cut, in 1877 at the Lyceum.

1953. Stratford (Ontario) Festival, with Alec Guinness.

Edward IV is dying, and six people stand between his brother Richard, Duke of Gloucester, and the throne: Edward's two boys, Edward Prince of Wales and the Duke of York, and his daughter Elizabeth; Richard's elder brother Clarence, and his young son and daughter. In the first act Richard succeeds in having Clarence murdered in the Tower, and woos and later marries the Lady Anne, who was betrothed to Henry VI's son, the Prince of Wales, stabbed by Richard himself at Tewkesbury. Margaret, Henry VI's widow, plays a choric part and warns the jangling Yorkists against Richard.

When Edward IV dies, Richard, backed by Buckingham, attacks the Queen's party, and executes her brother Lord Rivers, her son Lord Grey, and the loyal supporter of Edward's children, Lord Hastings. While the Prince of Wales and Duke of York are lodged in the Tower, Buckingham persuades the London citizens to proclaim Richard king.

As soon as Richard is crowned, he deals with his nephews and nieces; the Prince and his brother are murdered in the Tower, and he plans to marry Elizabeth on the death of his wife Anne, whose end he hastens. Clarence's daughter is to marry a 'mean-born gentleman', but as his son is 'foolish' he is not to be feared. Buckingham hesitates over the murder of the Princes, and when Richard discards him he goes to join Richmond, but is captured and executed.

Henry Tudor, Earl of Richmond, of the House of Lancaster, lands, and his army meets Richard's at Bosworth. On the night before the battle the ghosts of those whom Richard has killed appear to him and foretell his defeat. In the battle Richard is killed by Richmond, who is hailed as King Henry VII.

Richard III. See GLOUCESTER, RICHARD, DUKE OF.

'Richard, Duke of York.' An adaptation of *2 Henry VI*, probably by Edmund Kean, who produced it in 1817.

Richards, Nathaniel (fl. 1630–54), dramatist, son of the rector of Kentisbury, Devon, a position to which he himself apparently succeeded sometime after taking his degree from Caius, Cambridge, in 1634. His chief work was published in 1640:

The Tragedy of Messallina, the Roman Emperesse. As it hath been acted with generall applause divers times, by the company of his Maiesties Revells.

It is important for its title-page, which shows a stage similar to that in *Roxana* (q.v.), though with a curtained opening above. These two illustrations and that of De Witt (*c.* 1596) are the only extant ones of the interiors of theatres before they were closed in 1642.

Richardson, John. A farmer of Shottery. On 1 September 1581 he witnessed the will of Richard Hathaway, Anne's father. On 28 November 1582 he stood surety, with Fulk Sandells, for the legality of Shakespeare's marriage to Anne.

Richardson, Nicholas, elected a Fellow of Magdalen, Oxford, in 1614. A commonplace book, now in the Bodleian, formerly in the lodgings of the Principal of Brasenose, contains a number of Shakespearean quotations. Samuel Radcliffe was Principal 1614–48, and was probably the compiler. The passage quoted (*R.J.* II, ii) does not occur on p. 84 of any known Quarto.

Tis' almost morning I would haue thee gone
And yet no farther then a wantons bird,
That lets it hop a little from his hand,
Like a poore prisoner, in his twisted gyues,
Then with a silken thread plucks it back againe
So iealous louing of his liberty. Tragedy of Romeo and Juliet. 4°: pag. 84:
Said by Juliet: pro eadem.

This Mr Richardson Coll. Magd: inserted hence into his Sermon, preached it twice at St Maries 1620. 1621. applying it to gods loue to his Saints either hurt with sinne, or aduersity neuer forsaking thē.

Richardson, Sir Ralph, born at Cheltenham 1902, made his first stage appearance at Brighton in 1921 as Lorenzo in *The Merchant of Venice*, and toured the provinces in Shakespearean Repertory before joining the Birmingham Repertory in 1925. His first London appearance was at the Haymarket in 1926. At the Old Vic, 1930–2, he played Prince Henry, Caliban, Enobarbus, Henry V, Iago, etc., and Sir Toby Belch at the reopening of Sadler's Wells in January 1931. Since then he has had many seasons at the Old Vic, of which he became joint-director in 1944; he played Falstaff in 1945, and produced *Richard II* in 1947. His first New York appearance was in 1935 as Mercutio. Knighted in 1947.

Richardson, William (1743–1814), Professor of Humanity at Glasgow University, 1773–1814. He is one of the Shakespeare critics who wrote between the publication of Johnson's classical and balanced estimate of Shakespeare in his *Preface* of 1765, and the romantic criticism of the early 19th century. He is classical in his matter, in his insistence on Shakespeare's genius as a creator of character, romantic in his manner, in analysing the characters in greater detail. This he did, however, as 'an exercise no less adapted to improve the heart, than to inform the understanding . . . to make poetry subservient to philosophy'. In 1774 he published *A Philosophical Analysis and Illustration of some of Shakespeare's Remarkable Characters*, an analysis of Macbeth, Hamlet, Jaques and Imogen. This was followed in 1784 by an examination of Richard III, Lear and Timon, and in 1789 of Falstaff and the Female Characters.

'Richard Tertius.' See LEGGE.

Richmond, Henry Tudor, Earl of. First appears in *3 Henry VI* as a 'pretty lad' who Henry VI prophesies shall be King (IV, vi). In *Richard III* he lands with a Lancastrian army to contest the title with the Yorkist Richard, whom he defeats at Bosworth, and is hailed as Henry VII. (Henry VII (1457–1509) was the son of Margaret Beaufort, great-granddaughter of John of Gaunt, and of Edmund Tudor, Earl of Richmond.)

Richmond, Ludovick Stuart, Duke of (1574–1624), cousin of James I, Lord Steward 1615–24, and the most famous tilter of his day. (See LENNOX'S MEN.) Shortly before his death, his wife saw a Court performance of *The Winter's Tale*, recorded by Herbert in his *Office Book*.

> To the Duchess of Richmond, in the king's absence, was given The Winters Tale, by the K. company, the 18 Janu. 1623 [1624] – Att Whitehall.

In the preceding August, Herbert had authorized a new copy of the play, probably for the Court performance, as the old allowed copy was missing. (It may have been with the Jaggards, who were then printing the Folio):

> For the king's players. An olde playe called Winter's Tale, formerly allowed of by Sir George Bucke, and likewyse by mee on Mr Hemmings his worde that there was nothing profane added or reformed, thogh the allowed booke was missinge; and therefore I returned it without a fee, this 19 of August, 1623.

Richmond Palace. Richmond on Thames was originally called Sheen, but the name was changed by Henry VII, former Earl of Richmond in Yorkshire. The original palace of Sheen was 'thrown down and defaced' by Richard II when his wife, Anne of Bohemia, died there, restored by Henry V, burned down in 1498, and rebuilt by Henry VII. It was one of the five most important palaces frequented by Elizabeth, and plays were given in its great Hall (100 ft × 40 ft). James I gave it to Henry, Prince of Wales, after whose death in 1612 it was allowed to fall into decay.

Rinaldo. In *All's Well*, Steward of the Countess of Rousillon, whom he tells of Helena's love for her son Bertram (I, iii). He is called 'Steward' in the stage-directions, but the Countess calls him Rinaldo in III, iv, when he reads her Helena's letter of farewell.

Ristori, Adelaide (1822–1906), Italian tragic actress, was the daughter of strolling players. In 1855 she appeared in Paris, where playgoers literally fought over the rival merits of her and Rachel (1821–58). She also played in London and paid four visits to the United States. One of her most celebrated parts was Lady Macbeth.

'Rivals, The.' D'Avenant's adaptation of *The Two Noble Kinsmen*, produced in 1664 with Betterton as Philander (Palamon) and Henry Harris as Theocles (Arcite). Celania, daughter of the Jailer, now the prison Provost, marries Philander.

Rivers, Earl. Anthony Woodville (*c.* 1442–83), brother of Elizabeth, Queen of Edward IV, first appears in *3 Henry VI* (IV, iv), when Elizabeth tells him of Edward's capture by Warwick. In *Richard III* he is executed by order of Richard (III, iii). His father, Richard Woodville, Lord Rivers, appears in *1 Henry VI* as Lieutenant of the Tower (I, iii).

Roberts, James. A printer who in 1593 acquired from John Charlewood the monopoly of printing 'all manner of billes for players'.

1598, 22 July. He registered *The Merchant of Venice*, but the entry forbids its being printed by him or anyone else without licence first had from the Lord Chamberlain. On 28 October 1600 he transferred the play to Thomas Heyes for whom he printed a good text (Q1, 1600).

1600. He printed Q2 *Titus Andronicus* for Edward White.

1600. The following entry was made in the Stationers' Register:

My lord chamberlens mens plaies Entred
viz.

27 May 1600 To master Robertes	A moral of clothe breches and veluet hose
27 May To hym.	Allarum to London

4 Augusti

As you like yt, a booke
Henry the ffift, a booke
Every man in his humour, a booke
The Commedie of muche A doo about nothing a booke.
} to be staied.

Pollard suggests that Roberts acted as agent for the Chamberlain's, by his registration blocking piratical publication, though in fact *Henry V* was pirated in that year. Chambers thinks that he may have entered the plays to secure the printing rights when he transferred them to a publisher, though *Much Ado* was registered again by Wise and Aspley, 23 August 1600, and printed for them by Simmes.

1602, 26 July. He registered *Hamlet* and then, oddly enough, got the publisher of the 'bad' Q1 1603, Ling, to publish his own 'true and perfect' printing of Q2, 1604.

1603, 7 February. He registered *Troilus and Cressida* 'in full Court', an unusual procedure, with licence to print 'when he hath gotten sufficient aucthority for it'. However, he did not print, and Bonian and Walley registered it again in 1609. Possibly Roberts's copyright had lapsed.

About 1605, W. Jaggard (q.v.) bought Roberts's business, and in 1615 his monopoly of printing play-bills. In 1619 Jaggard printed ten of 'Shakespeare's' plays, including *The Merchant of Venice* and *A Midsummer Night's Dream*, both as 'Printed by J. Roberts 1600', though Roberts does not appear to have printed Q1 *M.N.D.* in 1600.

Roberts, John, reputed author of *An Answer to Mr. Pope's Preface to Shakespear . . . By a Strolling Player*, 1729. (See Bishop, Sir William.)

Robertson, John Mackinnon (1856–1933), began his career as a journalist. He was M.P. (1906–18), Parliamentary Secretary to the Board of Trade (1911–15), and P.C. (1915). His reverence for Shakespeare led him to pick out inferior passages in the plays and poems and to attribute them to other men, particularly Marlowe and Chapman, so that he became the most advanced of the 'stylistic disintegrators', finding in *A Midsummer Night's Dream* the only play completely by Shakespeare. In 1917 he published *Shakespeare and Chapman*, and 1922–32 the five volumes of *The Shakespeare Canon*, for the most part summarized in *The Genuine in Shakespeare*, 1930. His *Baconian Heresy. A Confutation* appeared in 1913. (See Disintegrators.)

Robin. In *The Merry Wives of Windsor*, Falstaff's page. Presumably he is the diminutive page (q.v.) of *2 Henry IV*, for he is described as 'little gallant', 'eyas-musket', and 'little Jack-a-Lent' (puppet). He carries Falstaff's love-letters to the merry wives, and takes part with them in the plot against his master.

Robin Goodfellow. See Puck.

'Robin Goodfellow.' On 15 January 1604 Dudley Carleton wrote to his friend, John Chamberlain that at Court 'On New yeares night we had a play of Robin goode-fellow'. This was probably *A Midsummer Night's Dream*, though

J. P. Collier forged an entry in Henslowe's *Diary*, giving to an unnamed play by Chettle, bought for Worcester's in 1602, the title of *Robin Goodfellow*. In the *Trevelyan Papers*, edited by Collier in 1863, occurs an entry in the accounts for 1595 of a servant of John Willoughby, 'Robin Goodfellow vj^{d}', which may be a forgery suggesting that there was an earlier edition of the pamphlet *Robin Goodfellow, his Mad Prankes and Merry Jests*, registered in 1627, or of the ballad, *The Mad Merry Prankes of Robin Goodfellow*, registered 1631.

Robinson, John. (1) One of the four witnesses of Shakespeare's will. A John Robinson was baptized at Stratford in 1589. He may have been (2) the tenant of the Blackfriars Gatehouse when Shakespeare made his will in 1616. The former tenant had been William Ireland, but his lease apparently expired in 1613, when Shakespeare bought the house. In 1639 a cordwainer called Dicks was living there. Shakespeare's tenant may have been the 'John Robbinson' who was one of the thirty-one inhabitants of Blackfriars who petitioned the Privy Council in November 1596 against the opening of Burbage's Blackfriars theatre.

Robinson, Mary ('Perdita') (1758–1800), actress, was born at Bristol. At sixteen, she married a London clerk, and shared his imprisonment for debt, during which time she completed two volumes of verse. Her great beauty led to her appearance with Garrick at Drury Lane as Juliet in 1776, and to the infatuation of the Prince of Wales (later George IV), when she played Perdita (whence her sobriquet) in Garrick's version of *The Winter's Tale* in December 1779. She became 'Prince Florizel's' mistress but, when he deserted her two years later, her fear of public opinion led to her retirement from the stage.

Robinson, Richard. One of the 'Principall Actors' in Shakespeare's plays (see p. 90). In 1611 he was a boy with the King's Men when, according to a s.d., he played the Lady in *The Second Maiden's Tragedy* (q.v.). In the same year he appeared with them in *Catiline*, and *Bonduca* in which he played was probably produced in 1611. He seems to have succeeded Richard Cowley as a sharer and comedian in 1619, in which year he appears in the Licence for the King's Men of 27 March. He may have married Richard Burbage's widow, for in 1635 she was Mrs Robinson. He was one of the King's Men who signed the dedication to the 4th Earl of Pembroke (q.v.) of the Beaumont and Fletcher Folio of 1647. 'Richard Robinson, a player' was buried at St Anne's, Blackfriars, 23 March 1648. (See WRIGHT, JAMES.)

Robinson, Richard (fl. 1576–1600), author, about whose life little is known, save that he was a freeman of the Leatherworkers' Company, and dedicated the third part of his *Harmony of King David's Harp* (1595) to Queen Elizabeth. In 1577 appeared his *A Record of Ancyent Historyes, entituled in Latin Gesta Romanorum* (q.v.) *Translated, Perused, Corrected, and Bettered.*

Roche, Walter, Master of Stratford Grammar School, 1569–71. He was a Lancashire man, entered Corpus Christi, Oxford, in 1555, took his B.A. in 1559, was elected a Fellow, and became rector of Droitwich in the year that he went to Stratford. In 1571 he resigned his mastership of the school, where he was succeeded by Simon Hunt, and became a lawyer in Stratford. He was also rector of Clifford Chambers, 1574–8, the lawyer of Shakespeare's cousin, Robert Webbe, in 1576, and in 1604 lived in Corn Street (No. 20), three doors from New Place.

Roderick, Richard (d. 1756), was of Queen's, Cambridge, became a Fellow of Magdalene, and in 1750 F.R.S. In the 6th edition of Edward's *Canons of Criticism*, 1758, was published an essay by Roderick *On the Metre of Henry VIII*, the first, and long neglected, application of verse-tests to Shakespeare's work.

Roderigo. In *Othello*, 'a gull'd Gentleman' (F) who is in love with Desdemona. Iago pretends to help him in his suit, but spends his money and uses him for his own ends. He persuades him that Cassio also loves Desdemona, to force a drunken quarrel that leads to Cassio's disgrace, and finally to murder him. In the attempt, however, Roderigo himself is wounded, and lest he should betray his plot, Iago kills him. Letters that incriminate Iago are found in his pocket. (There is no corresponding character in Cinthio.)

Rogero. In *The Winter's Tale*, the 'Second Gentleman' of Sicily, who reports that Perdita is found, and that Paulina has 'twice or thrice a day, ever since the death of Hermione, visited that removed house' where Hermione's 'statue' is kept (v, ii).

Rogers, Phillip. A Stratford (High Street) apothecary, who also sold tobacco, pipes, and ale. Between 27 March and 30 May 1604 Shakespeare sold him several bushels of malt for £1 19s. 10d. On 25 June Rogers borrowed 2s. from Shakespeare, and later paid back 6s. of his total debt of £2 1s. 10d. The date is uncertain, but it was probably late in 1604 that Shakespeare brought an action in the Stratford Court of Record for the recovery of the balance of £1 15s. 10d. His solicitor was William Tetherton.

'Roman Actor, The.' A play by Massinger, licensed by Herbert 11 October 1626, and published in 1629 as 'The Roman Actor. A Tragædie. As it hath diuers times beene, with good allowance Acted, at the private Playhouse in the Black-Friers, by the Kings Majesties Servants. Written by Phillip Massinger'. Massinger considered it 'the most perfect birth of my Minerva'. It deals with the love of the tyrant Domitianus Caesar for Domitia, and her love for the actor Paris, a part in which Betterton excelled. The play was ascribed to Shakespeare by the booksellers of the mid 17th century.

Romances. The name given to the plays of Shakespeare's final period, *c.* 1608–12: *Pericles*, *Cymbeline*, *The Winter's Tale*, *The Tempest*, and perhaps *The Two Noble Kinsmen*. They have certain common characteristics; they are wildly improbable; they are tragi-comedies in the manner popularized by Beaumont and Fletcher at the private Blackfriars theatre and the Jacobean Court; apart from Prospero, Ariel, Caliban and a few comic figures, the only memorable characters are the heroines, Marina, Imogen, Perdita and Miranda; and the poety is a return to the lyrical style of the early plays, though more mellow and profound. (See SS, 11.)

Romantic Movement. The revolt at the end of the 18th and beginning of the 19th century against the rules and cult of reason into which the classicism of the Renaissance had hardened: liberty, variety and emotion being set against restraint, unity and reason. The classical 18th century had admitted the genius of Shakespeare, but it was a wild, irregular genius; the Romantics seized on his wildness and irregularity, his comprehension and variety, as virtues: Herder, Goethe and Schlegel in Germany, Hugo in France, Pushkin in Russia, and classical drama with its unities, imposed by France on the continent of Europe, was overthrown under the banner of the liberating Shakespeare. In England, neoclassical doctrines had never been so firmly established, but Pope and Johnson had thought it necessary to apologize for Shakespeare's irregularity and lapses of judgement. Coleridge, however, proclaimed that Shakespeare's form was organic, not mechanical, and that his judgement was equal to his genius. And he and Hazlitt showed that Shakespeare was a poet as well as a dramatist. The Romantic Movement led to a more profound understanding of Shakespeare, but many of its followers accepted him uncritically as a symbol of liberty, and this led to the adulation and sentiment of the mid 19th century, against which the 'realists' in their turn revolted.

'ROMEO AND JULIET.'

WRITTEN: 1595–6. Mentioned by Meres, 1598.

PERFORMED: No record of an Elizabethan or Jacobean performance, but 'often plaid publiquely' before Q1 1597. Marston in his *Scourge of Villanie* (q.v.), 1598, says that '*Iuliat* and *Romio*' was played at the Curtain. (See DIGGES; RICHARDSON, NICHOLAS.)

PUBLISHED: 1597, Q1. 'An Excellent conceited Tragedie of Romeo and Iuliet. As it hath been often (with great applause) plaid publiquely, by the right Honourable the L. of Hunsdon his Seruants. London, Printed by Iohn Danter, 1597.' A 'bad' Quarto, degenerating as it proceeds. Perhaps reproduced from memory by actors who had played Romeo and Paris and tried to expand a shortened version into the full text. It is some 800 lines shorter than Q2. (See H. R. Hoppé, *The Bad Quarto of Romeo and Juliet*; SS, 8.)

1599, Q2. 'The Most Excellent and lamantable Tragedie, of Romeo and Iuliet. Newly corrected, augmented and amended: As it hath bene sundry times publiquely acted, by the right Honourable the Lord Chamberlaine his Seruants. London Printed by Thomas Creede, for Cuthbert Burby, and are to be sold at his shop neare the Exchange. 1599.' Q2 contains many errors, but may have been set up from foul papers with some use of Q1. Q2 has 'Enter Will Kemp' for the 'Enter Peter' of Q1 (IV, v, 102).

1609, Q3. 'As it hath beene sundrie times publiquely Acted, by the Kings Maiesties Seruants at the Globe.' Set up from Q2.

Q4. No date. 'Written by W. Shakespeare' in some copies.

1623, F1. 'The Tragedie of Romeo and Iuliet.' The fourth play in the Tragedy section: pp. 53–79. Set by compositor E. (Originally the play ended on p. 77, and *Troilus and Cressida* begun on 78, but then withdrawn; the leaf (pp. 77–8) was cancelled, *R.J.* finished on 79, and *Timon* begun on 80. *T.C.* was later inserted as the first of the tragedies, the Prologue on an unnumbered page, the text beginning on p. '78'.) *Actus Primus. Scœna Prima* alone marked. Set up from Q3, and therefore of no textual authority.

Pollard and Wilson argue in favour of Shakespeare's twofold revision of an old play, first of Acts I and II, and later of Acts III–V.

REGISTERED: 1607. '22 Januarij Master Linge Entred for his copies by direccon of A Court and with consent of Master Burby vnder his handwrytinge ... Romeo and Juliett ...'

1607. 19 November, transferred by Ling to Smethwick.

SOURCES: *The Tragicall Historye of Romeus and Iuliet* (1562), a poem by Arthur Brooke (q.v.). The story had previously been treated by Masuccio of Salerno (1476), Luigi da Porto (*c.* 1530), Bandello (1554) and Boaistuau (1559), from the last of whom Brooke made his version, as did Painter for his *Rhomeo and Iulietta* in his *Palace of Pleasure* (1565–7). Apparently it existed in dramatic form, for Brooke writes, 'Though I saw the same argument lately set foorth on stage with more commendation, then I can looke for: (being there much better set foorth then I haue or can dooe) yet the same matter penned as it is, may serue to lyke good effect.'

STAGE HISTORY: 1662. D'Avenant's revival, with Betterton as Mercutio, and his wife, Mary Saunderson, as Juliet; Harris played Romeo. *c.* 1670, the tragi-comedy version of James Howard.

1679. The *Caius Marius* adaptation by Otway which held the stage for seventy years.

1744. Theophilus Cibber's adaptation.

1748. Garrick's adaptation.

1750. 'The *Romeo and Juliet* War'; Garrick and Anne Bellamy of Drury Lane versus Barry and Mrs Theophilus Cibber of Covent Garden.

1845. Charlotte and Susan Cushman in America returned to Shakespeare's text.

1847. Phelps re-established the original play in England.

1960. Old Vic. Franco Zeffirelli's production.

The old feud between the rival families of Montague and Capulet in Verona breaks out in a street brawl, and Prince Escalus threatens with death anyone, who shall again disturb the peace. Romeo, a Montague, is in love with Rosaline, but when he makes one in a masque at the house of Capulet he falls in love with his daughter Juliet, hears her declare her love for him as he stands beneath her window in the garden, and secures her consent to marry him.

The next afternoon they are secretly married by Friar Laurence. Shortly afterwards Romeo meets the Capulet, Tybalt, who tries to pick a quarrel with him, and when Romeo, now Tybalt's cousin by marriage, refuses to fight, his friend Mercutio accepts the challenge and is killed. Romeo now draws on Tybalt and kills him, for which offence the Prince banishes him.

The distracted Romeo seeks the advice of Friar Laurence, who tells him to spend the night with Juliet as arranged, and then to go to Mantua until his friends have secured his recall. Meanwhile Capulet arranges Juliet's marriage to the County Paris, and when she makes excuses he insists. Her mother and nurse fail her in her need, and she goes to the Friar, who forms a desperate plan. He gives her a potion to drink the next night, that will make her appear dead for forty-two hours, and promises to send word to Romeo to come and fetch her at the hour of waking, from the Capulet vault where she will be laid.

Juliet drinks the potion and is placed in the vault, but the Friar's messenger fails to reach Romeo in Mantua, and he hears only that Juliet is dead. He goes by night to the tomb, where he meets the mourning Paris, who attacks him, but is killed. Romeo breaks into the tomb, drinks poison, and dies beside Juliet. The Friar, hearing that his plan has miscarried, hastens to rescue Juliet, who wakes as he enters, sees the dead Romeo, and stabs herself. The watch arrives, the Friar is caught and explains what has happened, and Montague and Capulet are reconciled over the bodies of their dead children.

Ronsard, Pierre de (1524–85), 'the prince of poets' and brightest star of the Pléiade (q.v.), was a page at the French Court, spent three years in Scotland and England (1537–40), and was later in the service of Charles IX of France. His sonnets influenced the Elizabethans, including Shakespeare; compare, for example, the conceit in *Amours pour Astrée*, vi,

Il ne falloit, maistresse, autres tablettes
Pour vous graver que celles de mon cœur
Où de sa main Amour, nostre vainqueur,
Vous a gravée et vos grâces parfaites.

with Shakespeare's Sonnets 24 and 122,

Mine eye hath play'd the painter and hath stell'd
Thy beauty's form in table of my heart ...

Thy gift, thy tables, are within my brain
Full character'd with lasting memory ...

Rosalind. The heroine of *As You Like It* (q.v.). She takes her name from Lodge's romance, and Shakespeare's source, *Rosalynde. Euphues golden legacie* (q.v.).

Rosaline. 1. In *Love's Labour's Lost*, one of the ladies attending on the Princess of France. Berowne falls in love with her,

A whitely wanton with a velvet brow,
With two pitch-balls stuck in her face for eyes,

and writes her the sonnet, 'If love make me forsworn'. She promises to marry him at the end of a year if he will spend the time visiting and cheering the sick.

2. In *Romeo and Juliet*, Romeo is to begin with, as in Brooke's poem, in love with Rosaline, Capulet's 'fair niece'. She is presumably one of the guests at Capulet's party, v, ii, but is not named. (It is worth noting that both Rosalines, like the lady of the *Sonnets*, are dark.)

'Rosalynde. Euphues Golden Legacie.' A romance written by Thomas Lodge on his voyage to the Azores and Canaries and published on his return, in 1590. It is taken from the pseudo-Chaucerian poem, *The Tale of Gamelyn*, and is itself the source of *As You Like It*.

Saladyne (Oliver) chains his brother Rosader (Orlando) to a post and gives it out that he is mad. Adam Spencer (the Steward) unfastens his fetters, and they attack Saladyne's friends when they come to mock the supposed madman, and then escape into the forest. Meanwhile, Rosalind and Alinda (Celia) are both banished by Duke Torismond; Rosalind disguises herself as a page, Ganymede, Alinda calls herself Aliena, and they too go to the Forest of Arden to find Rosalind's father. The rest of the story is similar to *As You Like It*, though Torismond is forced to restore the dukedom, and Shakespeare transmutes it by adding Touchstone, Jaques, William, Audrey and Sir Oliver Martext. Lodge writes in the balanced and alliterative style of Euphues:

Think that royalty is a fair mark, that crowns have crosses when mirth is in cottages; that the fairer the rose is, the sooner it is bitten with caterpillars; the more orient the pearl is, the more apt to take a blemish; and the greatest birth, as it hath most honour, so it hath much envy.

'Roscius Anglicanus.' See DOWNES.

Rose Theatre. On 24 March 1585 the lease of a property called 'the Little Rose with two gardens' was assigned to Philip Henslowe. It was on the Bankside in the Liberty of the Clink, between the river and Maid Lane; the lease had twenty years to run, and the rent was £7. On 10 January 1587 Henslowe formed a partnership with a John Cholmley to build a playhouse on a part of this ground, 94 feet square, Cholmley, a grocer, to have the right of supplying refreshments, but he seems to have died before 1592. It was built by April 1588, and is shown in Norden's map of 1593 as a round building, 'The play howse', just to the south-east of 'The Beare howse'. In his map of 1600, it is called 'The stare' (Star, a name otherwise unknown), and is in the same position, but now between the Bear Garden and the newly built Globe.

From Henslowe's account of repairs at the beginning of 1592, it appears that the theatre was built of timber and plaster on a brick foundation, with a thatched roof. He ceiled 'my lords room' and 'the room over the tirehouse', and made a 'penthouse shed at the tiring house door'. In 1595 he did it 'about with elm boards' and made a 'throne in the heavens'.

The first company recorded in Henslowe's *Diary* is Strange's, and on the assumption that all his entries refer to the Rose, the following companies played there:

1592	19 Feb.–June 22	Strange's
1592–3	29 Dec.–1 Feb.	Strange's
1593–4	26 Dec.–6 Feb.	Sussex's
1594	1–9 April	Queen's and Sussex's
1594–1600	The home of the Admiral's who, in the autumn of 1600, went to the newly built Fortune	
1600	28–9 Oct.	Pembroke's
1602–3	Aug.–May	Worcester's, who then went to the Boar's Head, and later to the Red Bull

Henslowe's *Diary* finishes in 1603, and there are no further records of companies at the Rose. His lease of the site expired in 1605, and in June 1603 he was unwilling to renew it at a rent of £20 a year. Malone says (*Var.*, III, 56) that the Swan and the Rose were shut up in 1613, but that 'after the year 1620, as appears from Sir Henry Herbert's office-book [now lost], they were used occasionally for the exhibition of prize-fighters'. Alleyn paid tithes 'due for the Rose' in 1622.

Rosencrantz. See GUILDENSTERN.

Ross, 7th Lord (d. 1414). In *Richard II*, with Northumberland he joins Bolingbroke after Richard's seizure of the Lancaster estates.

Ross, Thane of. In *Macbeth*, he visits Lady Macduff and defends the wisdom of her husband's action in going to England, but in the next scene (IV, iii) he has to tell Macduff that Macbeth has slaughtered his undefended 'wife and babes'. He joins the rebellion against Macbeth.

Rosseter, Philip (*c.* 1575–1623), lutenist in the royal household, composer of songs and chamber music, and friend of, and collaborator with, the poet Thomas Campion (d. 1619), who left Rosseter 'all that he had'. Rosseter joined Robert Keyser *c.* 1609 when the Children of the Chapel (Revels) moved to Whitefriars, and was mainly instrumental in buying off, with the King's Men at the other private theatre of Blackfriars, the threatened competition of the Paul's boys, for a dead rent of £20 a year. He was leader of the syndicate named in the new patent for the Queen's Revels of January 1610, and again of the new syndicate of October 1617. When the lease of the Whitefriars theatre expired in 1614, Rosseter received a patent, 3 June 1615, to build the Porter's Hall theatre (q.v.). (See DABORNE.)

Rossill. Qq and F, *1 Henry IV* (I, ii, 181), name 'Haruey, Rossill' as two of the thieves with Falstaff. In II, iv, 193–5–9 Qq assign speeches to *Ross.* which F redistributes. In Q *2 Henry IV* (II, ii) 'sir Iohn Russel' occurs in the stage-direction, but not in F. Apparently Shakespeare changed Rossill to Peto. (See HARVEY.)

Rotheram, Thomas (1423–1500). In *Richard III*, Archbishop of York. He resigns his seal to Elizabeth, widow of Edward IV, when he hears that Richard has imprisoned her brother Rivers and her son Grey (II, iv). (Rotheram was made Chancellor in 1475, and Ab. of York in 1480. He was imprisoned for supporting Elizabeth.)

Roubiliac, Louis François (1695–1762), French sculptor, was born at Lyons, but settled in London sometime after 1730, and became the most fashionable sculptor in England. A number of monuments in Westminster Abbey, including that of Handel, are by him, as is the statue of George II in Golden Square, and those of Newton and George II at Cambridge. The statue of Shakespeare, based on the Chandos portrait, was commissioned in 1758 by Garrick, who left it to the British Museum. The so-called D'Avenant bust of blackened terracotta, which was found in the old Lincoln's Inn Fields theatre, once the home of D'Avenant's Duke's company, is probably by Roubiliac. (See SCHEEMAKERS.)

Rounds. The medieval theatre was a 'round' in which religious, and no doubt secular, plays were still acted in some parts of the country in Shakespeare's day. These rounds were simply open arenas, fifty or sixty feet in diameter, encircled by wooden stands or earthen banks into which steps were cut to accommodate the audience. Two of these earthen rounds may still be seen in west Cornwall, and from the stage directions and plans in their manuscripts we can tell pretty well how the Cornish miracle plays were produced. Ranged round the arena or 'plain' (corresponding to the yard of the Elizabethan theatre) were small tents or 'houses', each representing a locality in the play, and here the characters remained when not performing. Good characters were at the south, worldly characters at the west, and evil ones at the north next to Hell's Mouth (the Admiral's had a 'Hell mought'). Heaven was a scaffold or stage at the east, with a throne for God and another tent beside it where angels played and sang. (Compare the throne and music room of the Elizabethan theatre.) Most of the action took place towards the middle of the plain, and here was the principal locality of the play, represented by some piece of scenery. A large open space was necessary for many of the more spectacular episodes, as when the Duke of Cornwall's host of twenty men defeats the heathen army of fifteen, whose leader escapes on horseback, as well as for the acrobatics of the stock comic characters. (See STAGE; YARD.)

Rousillon (Rossillion), Countess of. In *All's Well*, mother of Bertram and guardian of Helena. She approves of Helena's marriage to her son, and when he deserts her she does her best to bring them together. ('The most beautiful old woman's part ever written', wrote Bernard Shaw.)

Rowe, Nicholas (1674–1718), the first critical editor of Shakespeare, was born in Bedfordshire, educated at Westminster School, and in 1691 entered the Middle Temple, but after his father's death devoted himself to literature. His tragedies were well received, and Johnson pronounced *The Fair Penitent* one of the most pleasing tragedies in the language, though his comedy, *The Biter*, is said to have amused no one but himself. He had several minor political posts, and in 1715 succeeded Nahum Tate as Poet Laureate. He was buried in Westminster Abbey. His edition of Shakespeare's plays was published in six octavo volumes in 1709 (see GILDON), a second edition of nine volumes in 1714 included the *Poems*. Apart from the doubtful plays, which he relegated to the end, the order is that of the Folios, each play being preceded by an engraving. Unfortunately, he increased the difficulties of his task by using the debased text of the Fourth Folio, but made, nevertheless, many still accepted emendations, some of which are the correct readings of the First Folio and Quartos, which he did not consult. As a dramatist, he was able to complete the Folio division into acts and scenes, the location of which he sometimes indicated, to mark entrances and exits, and to prefix a list of *dramatis personae* to each play. In short, he made Shakespeare intelligible and accessible to 18th-century readers, and prepared the way for the great scholars of the second half of the century. He introduced the plays with the first formal life of Shakespeare, for most of the material of which he admitted that he was indebted to Betterton, both for the theatrical traditions passed on by D'Avenant, and for the information that Betterton collected at Stratford:

> I must own a particular obligation to him [Betterton], for the most considerable part of the passages relating to his Life, which I have here transmitted to the Publick; his Veneration for the Memory of *Shakespeare* having engaged him to make a Journey into *Warwickshire*, on purpose to gather up what Remains he could of a Name for which he had so great a value.

Rowe's short *Life* remained the standard biography until the appearance of Malone's *Life* at the end of the century, a shortened version being prefixed to editions of Shakespeare from that of Pope (1725) to the Third Variorum (1821). The following extracts show that he is not always accurate, and that much of his material is taken from Stratford tradition.

> His Family ... were of good Figure and Fashion there, and are mentioned as Gentlemen. His Father, who was a considerable Dealer in Wool, had so large a Family, ten Children in all, that tho' he was his eldest Son, he could give him no better Education than his own Employment. He had bred him, 'tis true, for some time at a Free-School. ... His wife was the Daughter of one *Hathaway*, said to have been a substantial Yeoman in the Neighbourhood of *Stratford* ... He ... engag'd ... more than once in robbing a Park that belong'd to Sir *Thomas Lucy* ... For this he was prosecuted by that Gentleman ... he was oblig'd to leave his Business and Family in *Warwickshire*, for some time, and shelter himself in *London*.
>
> It is at this Time, and upon this Accident, that he is said to have made his first Acquaintance in the Play-house. He was receiv'd into the Company then in being, at first in a very mean Rank ... I could never meet with any further Account of him this way, than that the top of his Performance was the Ghost in his own *Hamlet* ... Besides the advantages of his Wit, he was in himself a good-natur'd Man, of great sweetness in his Manners, and a most agreeable Companion ... If I had not been assur'd that the Story was handed down by Sir *William D'Avenant* ... I should not have ventur'd to have inserted, that my Lord *Southampton*, at one time, gave him a thousand Pounds, to enable him to go through with a Purchase which he heard he had a mind to ...
>
> The latter part of his Life was spent, as all Men of good Sense will wish theirs may be, in Ease, Retirement, and the Conversation of his friends ...
>
> He had three Daughters, of which two liv'd to be marry'd ...
>
> We are to consider him as a Man that liv'd in a State of almost universal License and Ignorance: There was no establish'd Judge, but every one took the liberty to Write according to the Dictates of his own Fancy.

Rowington. A village in the same Hundred as Stratford, but ten miles to the north. The manor had belonged to the Abbey of Reading, and was granted by Elizabeth to Ambrose, Earl of Warwick, on the death of whose widow in

1604 it reverted to the Crown. Two properties in Stratford belonged to the manor, one in Church Street, held by Henry and Hamnet Sadler, the other in Chapel Lane (q.v.), the copy-hold of which was transferred by Walter Getley to Shakespeare 28 September 1602. There were Shakespeares at Rowington, but as far as is known the Chapel Lane cottage is the poet's only connexion with the village.

Rowlands, Thomas (*c.* 1570–1630), a writer of tracts both in prose and verse, many of them satirizing middle-class life in London, and valuable as social documents. In his *Whole Crew of Kind Gossips* (1609), he writes,

The chiefest Art I have I will bestow
About a worke cald taming of the Shrow,

which suggests a Jacobean performance of Shakespeare's play. And, as late as 1620, in *The Night-Raven*, he refers to the original *Hamlet* play, 'I will not call, Hamlet Revenge my greeves'. One of his best known pamphlets is *The Letting of Humours Blood in the Head-vaine* (1600), a collection of epigrams and satires. (See POPE, THOMAS.)

Rowley, Samuel (d. *c.* 1630). An actor with the Admiral's-Prince's Men, for whom he wrote plays, the only extant one entirely by him being published in 1605, as,

When you see me, You know me. Or the famous Chronicle Historie of King Henry the eight, with the birth and vertuous life of Edward Prince of Wales. As it was playd by the high and mightie Prince of Wales his seruants. By Samuell Rowly, seruant to the Prince.

Shakespeare and his collaborator, probably Fletcher, may have consulted the play when they wrote *Henry VIII*. In November 1602, Henslowe paid Rowley and William Bird £4 for their additions to *Dr Faustus*, presumably the comic prose passages, and H. D. Sykes suggests Rowley's authorship of similar scenes in *The Taming of A Shrew*, and of *The Famous Victories of Henry V*.

Rowley, William. An actor and dramatist about whom little is known. He was writing for Queen Anne's in 1607, was with the Duke of York's-Prince Charles's 1610–19, and writing and acting for the King's 1623–5. In 1662 Francis Kirkman published *The Birth of Merlin* (q.v.) 'by William Shakespear and William Rowley'; Rowley may have been the author, but not Shakespeare. Pope suggested that *The Troublesome Reign of King John* was by Shakespeare and Rowley; the 1611 Quarto, published by John Helme, ascribed it to 'W. Sh.'. The non-Shakespearean parts of *Pericles* have also been claimed by some for Rowley. His extant plays are *A Shoemaker a Gentleman*; *A New Wonder*, *A Woman Never Vexed*; *A Match at Midnight*.

'Roxana.' William Alabaster's Latin version of *La Dalida* (1567) by Luigi Groto (q.v.), performed at Trinity, Cambridge, *c.* 1592, registered 1632 as 'A Tragedy in Latin called Roxana', and published in the same year, as,

Roxana Tragaedia olim Cantabrigiae, Acta in Col. Trin. Nunc primum in lucem edita, summaque cum diligentia ad castigatissimum exemplar comparata.

The volume is important, as the title-page has a picture of a stage, presumably that of a London theatre in Caroline times, and not Trinity, Cambridge, in 1592. The apron stage tapers towards the front and is enclosed by low rails; curtains hang in front of the tiring-house wall or 'scene'; and above are two boxes like the old 'lords room'. (See 'MESSALINA'.)

Alabaster (1567–1640) was Essex's chaplain on the Cadiz expedition, 1596, and died as vicar of Therfield, Herts.

Royal Shakespeare Theatre, originally the Shakespeare Memorial Theatre, was the offspring of the Shakespeare Tercentenary Festival (q.v.) of 1864.

Charles Flower of Stratford was mainly responsible for the first theatre, opened 23 April 1879 with performances by Barry Sullivan's company. From 1886 to 1919, with scarcely a break, Frank Benson and his company gave the festival performances. The theatre was incorporated under Royal Charter in 1925, but destroyed by fire in 1926, and the Festivals of 1926–31 were given in the local cinema. On 23 April 1932, thanks to the efforts of Archibald Flower, Charles's nephew, the new Memorial Theatre was opened, built with money raised by public subscription, half of it coming from America. The chief architect was Elisabeth Scott, the relief figures on the façade are by Eric Kennington, and it now seats an audience of 1,326. The annual Shakespeare season lasts from April to November, and between 1949 and 1960 the company played occasionally in London and visited 13 countries overseas.

After Benson the Directors have been: Bridges Adams 1919–34, Iden Payne 1935–42, Milton Rosmer 1943, Robert Atkins 1944–5, Barry Jackson 1946–8, Anthony Quayle 1949–52, Anthony Quayle and Glen Byam Shaw 1952–6, Glen Byam Shaw 1957–9; Peter Hall, appointed Director in 1960, acquired the Aldwych Theatre as a permanent London home for the company. In 1961 the theatre was renamed the Royal Shakespeare Theatre, and Michel Saint-Denis and Peter Brook were appointed to share with Peter Hall, as Managing Director, the direction of the Royal Shakespeare Company in Stratford and London. (See SS, 16.) In 1968 Trevor Nunn was appointed Artistic Director.

Roydon, Matthew (fl. 1580–1622), poet, friend of Chapman, and apparently a dramatist. He is mentioned by Nashe in his preface to Greene's *Menaphon* (1589), as one of the 'most able men to revive Poetry ... as he hath shewed himselfe singular in the immortall Epitaph of his beloved Astrophell, besides many other most absolute Comike inventions (made more publike by every mans praise, than they can be by my speech)'. His elegy on Sidney, appended to Spenser's *Astrophel*, 1586, resembles Shakespeare's *Phoenix and Turtle*, a phoenix, turtle-dove, eagle and swan taking part in the obsequies. G. B. Harrison attributes *Willobie his Avisa* to Roydon.

Rugby, John, in *The Merry Wives*, servant of Dr Caius, he speaks only in I, iv and II, iii. According to Mistress Quickly, he is 'an honest, willing, kind fellow ... no tell-tale nor no breed-bate ... his worst fault is, that he is given to prayer; he is something peevish that way'.

Rümelin, Gustav (1815–88), German statesman and sociologist, published his *Shakespeare Studies by a Realist* in 1864, the year of the tercentenary celebrations of Shakespeare's birth, as a counterblast to the exclamatory and adulatory criticism of the mid 19th century. He maintained that Shakespeare's plots are ill-constructed and unworthy of his poetry, and though his characters are superior to his action, there is little truth of dialogue because they all speak like Shakespeare. The book is important as the first publication of the new 'realist' criticism. Rümelin taught for a time at the University of Tübingen.

Rumour. In *2 Henry IV*, 'the Presentor' (F). In Q the s.d. reads '*Enter* Rumour *painted full of tongues*'. He brings the false news to Northumberland that his son Hotspur has won the battle of Shrewsbury. Rumour was a common figure in Jacobean masques; cf. Campion's *Masque of Squires*, 1613, with its Rumour 'in a skin coat full of winged tongues, and over it an antic robe; on his head a cap like a tongue, with a large pair of wings in it'. (See CHORUS.)

Rundall, Thomas, in 1849 published for the Hakluyt Society, *Narratives of Voyages towards the North-West*, which included the *Journal* of Capt. William Keeling (q.v.) with its notices of Shakespearean performances at sea. Lee considered it a forgery, but it is now generally accepted as genuine.

Run-on Lines. Verse in which the sense runs on, or flows over, from one line into the next (the French *enjambement*) as in the following passage from *Antony and Cleopatra*:

For his bounty
There was no winter in't; an autumn 't was
That grew the more by reaping: his delights
Were dolphin-like; they show'd his back above
The element they lived in: in his livery
Walk'd crowns and crownets; realms and islands were
As plates dropp'd from his pocket.

This should be compared with the passage quoted under 'End-stopped lines'. It is not always easy to decide which is a run-on line, for the end of the line usually coincides with some break in the grammar, however slight – such clear-cut examples as four of those above are exceptional – and the test is often a subjective one. Before Shakespeare's time most verse was end-stopped, as is his own early verse, but he added variety and fluidity by developing the run-on line, partly by shortening the clauses so that they did not coincide with the line, and there is a fairly steady increase in the proportion of run-on lines, from about 10 per cent in the early plays to 40 per cent in the later. This proportion is, therefore, helpful in determining the chronology of the plays. (See VERSE-TESTS; LIGHT ENDINGS; WEAK ENDINGS.)

Russell, Thomas (1570–1634). Shakespeare appointed 'Thomas Russell Esquier' one of the overseers of his will, and left him £5. He was the second son of Sir Thomas Russell of Strensham, on the Avon, five miles north of Tewkesbury. He went to Queen's, Oxford, and as his second wife married Anne, widow of Thomas Digges, and mother of Sir Dudley Digges of the Virginia Company and of Leonard Digges (q.v.), author of the verses in Shakespeare's Folio, and *Poems*, 1640. He lived at Alderminster, four miles south of Stratford. (See L. Hotson, *I, William Shakespeare*.)

Russia. Shakespeare became known in Russia in the 18th century in French and German translations, but towards the end of the century a beginning was made of translating some of the plays into Russian. A complete translation, made by eleven authors, was edited by Nekrasow and Gerbel in 1865, and another was made by P. A. Kanshin in 1893. Pushkin (1799–1837) and Lermontov (1814–41) were much influenced by Shakespeare and wrote poems inspired by his works, and the great 19th-century critic Belinsky, and the actor Mochalov did much to popularize the plays. On the other hand, Tolstoy (q.v.) had little use for Shakespeare.

Shakespeare has become very popular in the U.S.S.R. The Shakespeare Cabinet, a branch of the All-Russian Theatre Society, meets every two months for discussion and the reading of papers, and organizes an annual Shakespeare Conference where scholars meet actors and producers, scholarship and the theatre being intimately linked. The *Shekspirovski Sbornik* (*Shakespeare Miscellany*) is a valuable post-war periodical.

There have been many new translations, including those of Pasternak, Ostrovsky, Morozov, and Marshak, and an eight-volume *Complete Works*, edited by A. Smirnov and A. Anikst, was completed in 1950. The plays are widely performed in the various languages of the Union – Georgian, Mari, Uzbek, Azerbaijanian – the most popular being *Hamlet*, *Othello*, *Romeo and Juliet*, *Twelfth Night* and *Much Ado*. (See M. Morozov, *Shakespeare on the Soviet Stage*, 1947; A. Hirondelle, *Shakespeare en Russie*, 1912.)

Rutland, Edmund, Earl of (1443–60). In *3 Henry VI*, 3rd son of Richard Plantagenet, Duke of York, he is murdered by Clifford because 'Thy father slew my father' (I, iii).

Rutland, Francis Manners, 6th Earl of (1578–1632). The account of Thomas Screvin, Rutland's steward, has the entry,

> [1613] Item, 31 Martii, to Mr Shakspeare in gold about my Lordes impreso, xliiijs; to Richard Burbage for paynting and making yt, in gold xliiijs.

This was for the tilt of 24 March 1613, celebrating the anniversary of James I's accession, Shakespeare and Burbage apparently collaborating to make Rutland's *impresa.*

Imprese were paper or pasteboard shields bearing painted emblematic devices and mottoes, carried and interpreted by a knight's squire before a tilt. They were not used in the tournament. Compare the tilt in *Pericles* II, ii, where Thaisa describes the knights' *imprese*, that of Pericles being

> A wither'd branch that's only green at top;
> The motto, 'In hac spe vivo.'

Ryan, Lacy (*c.* 1694–1760), actor and friend of Quin, with whom he played at Lincoln's Inn Fields and after 1733, at Covent Garden. Some of his best parts were Cassius, Edgar, Iago, Posthumus and Macbeth.

Ryan, Richard (1796–1849), bookseller, and probable editor of *Dramatic Table Talk*, 1825, which contains an apocryphal story of Shakespeare and Queen Elizabeth (q.v.).

Rylands, George (b. 1902). Fellow of King's, Cambridge; Governor of the Old Vic; author of *Shakespeare's Poetic Energy* (BAL), *The Ages of Man*, etc. Producer of the British Council recordings of Shakespeare.

Rymer, Thomas (1641–1713), historiographer and critic, was educated at Sidney Sussex, Cambridge, and entered Gray's Inn in 1666. In 1674 appeared his translation of Rapin's *Reflections on Aristotle's Treatise of Poesie*, with a preface defending the classical rules, which he applied unsuccessfully in his own tragedy, *Edgar, or the English Monarch*, 1677. In 1678 came his *Tragedies of the Last Age Consider'd* and in 1693 his *Short View of Tragedy*. On the death of Shadwell in 1692, he was appointed Historiographer Royal and began his great work of collecting original historical documents, the first volume of which appeared in 1704.

Rymer was a fanatical believer in the rules of the Ancients, and according to Macaulay 'the worst critic who has ever lived'. He ridicules the way in which in Elizabethan drama, 'Fancy leaps and frisks, and away she's gone; while Reason rattles the chain, and follows after.' Shakespeare should have followed the model of *Gorboduc*; as it is, 'In Tragedy he appears quite out of his Element; his Brains are turn'd, he raves and rambles, without any coherence, any spark of reason, or any rule to controul him, or set bounds to his phrenzy.' And as for *Othello*, 'the tragical part is, plainly none other, than a Bloody Farce, without salt or savour.' (*Short View of Tragedy*.)

Ryther, Augustine (fl. 1576–1604), engraver, was born in Leeds. He engraved maps of a number of counties, one of England in 1579, and in 1590 published ten charts illustrating the defeat of the Armada. His Map of London, dated without evidence as *c.* 1604, is of little value for identifying the Bankside theatres, as it was published at Amsterdam by Cornelis Danckerts, 1635–45.

S

Sackbut. An early form of trombone; a trumpet with a slide to lengthen the tube and so deepen the pitch. In Shakespeare's day it was used in churches to support, or to replace, the organ, and in bands. Cf. *Coriolanus* V, iv:

> The trumpets, sackbuts, psalteries and fifes,
> Tabors and cymbals and the shouting Romans,
> Make the sun dance.

Sackville, Thomas. See DORSET, 1ST EARL OF.

Sadler, Hamlet (d. 1624). Shakespeare left 'Hamlett Sadler 26s. 8d. to buy him a Ringe'. He appears in Stratford records as Hamnet as well as Hamlet, and signed himself Hamnet as a witness to the poet's will. As his wife was Judith (Staunton of Longbridge), it is reasonable to suppose that Hamnet and Judith Sadler were the godparents of Shakespeare's twin children, Hamnet and Judith (b. 1585). Sadler was a baker in High Street, Stratford. (See ROWINGTON.)

Sadler's Wells. A theatre in Rosebery Avenue, north London. In 1683 a Mr Sadler discovered a medieval medicinal well, where he laid out a garden and built a 'Musick House' for the benefit of those taking the waters. A theatre was built in 1765, where Joseph Grimaldi, the clown, first appeared, and at the beginning of the 19th century Charles Dibdin produced his aquatic plays in a tank beneath the stage. Samuel Phelps (q.v.) was manager 1844–62, and there produced his historic series of Shakespeare's plays. By the beginning of the 20th century, the theatre was derelict, but thanks to the efforts of Lilian Baylis, and a grant from the Carnegie Trust, it was reopened in 1931 as a theatre similar to the Old Vic in south London, where seats for good plays were reasonably cheap. It has since become the home of opera and ballet.

St Mary Overy. See SOUTHWARK.

Sainte-Maure, Benoît de. A French trouvère of the 12th century, author of the *Roman de Troie*, *c.* 1160. This is a poem of 30,000 lines based, not on Homer, but on the Latin narratives of the 4th and 5th centuries A.D. The classical story, which covers the period from the Golden Fleece to the return of the Greeks after the fall of Troy, becomes a medieval romance, and contains the first version of the story of Troilus and Briseide (Cressida), one of the sources of Boccaccio's *Filostrato*, and through Chaucer, of Shakespeare's *Troilus and Cressida.* He makes the Homeric Calchas father of Cressida.

St Paul's. Little is known of the private theatre used by the Children of Paul's (q.v.). It was 'at Paules' or 'nigh Paules'; the auditorium was circular, and is suggestive, therefore, of the chapter-house. Apparently the musicians were aloft in a 'Music Tree'.

Saint-Saëns, Camille (1835–1921), French composer, studied under Gounod, and was organist at the Madeleine, 1861–77. His opera *Henry VIII* was produced in Paris in 1883, and at Covent Garden in 1898.

Saintsbury, George (1845–1933), was educated at King's College School, London, and Merton, Oxford. He was a schoolmaster, 1868–76, a journalist for ten years, and then Professor of Rhetoric and English Literature at Edinburgh University 1895–1915. He was one of the most authoritative critics of his time, and though he did not specialize in Shakespeare scholarship there is much important Shakespearean criticism in his voluminous writings, of which his *History of Elizabethan Literature* (1877), *A Short History of English Literature* (1898) and *A History of Criticism* (1900–4) are three of the best known.

Salanio, Salarino, Salerio. In *The Merchant of Venice*, friends of Antonio and Bassanio. The first two play unimportant parts, appearing together in I, i; II, iv and viii; III, i. In II, vi Salarino helps Lorenzo to carry off Jessica, and in III, iii meets Antonio under arrest. In III, ii, however, a new character, Salerio, a Venetian friend of Bassanio and Gratiano, arrives with Lorenzo in Belmont and reports Antonio's losses, and is present at the Court scene. It looks, therefore, as though Salerio is a mistake for Salarino, or possibly for Solanio. Q3, 1637, includes Salanio and Salarino in the 'Actors' names', but not Salerio. Wilson calls them 'The Three Sallies' and suggests that the original characters were Solanio and Salerio, and that Salarino is a confusion of the two.

Salisbury, Earl of. 1. In *King John*, William de Longspée (d. 1226), illegitimate son of Henry II. He disapproves of John's second coronation and, suspecting him of Arthur's death, joins the Dauphin. When, however, he hears of the Dauphin's intended treachery, he returns to his allegiance.

2. In *Richard II*, John de Montacute, 3rd Earl (d. 1400), is a loyal supporter of Richard, the dispersal of whose Welsh forces he tries to prevent (II, iv). He joins the rebellion against Henry IV, but is captured at Cirencester and beheaded.

3. In *Henry V*, Thomas de Montacute, 4th Earl (1388–1428), is present at Agincourt. In *1 Henry VI*, he is killed by a cannon-shot at the siege of Orleans (I, iv).

4. In *2 Henry VI*, Richard Neville, 1st Earl (1400–60), son of Ralph Neville, 1st Earl of Westmoreland (q.v.), married the daughter of Thomas de Montacute, their son being Warwick the Kingmaker (q.v.). He is the enemy of Suffolk, whose banishment he secures, and of Cardinal Beaufort, whose death he witnesses. In V, i he joins his brother-in-law, the Duke of York, and fights at St Albans. (He was captured at Wakefield, and beheaded by the victorious Lancastrians, so that Warwick's statement in *3 Henry VI* (III, iii) that 'by the house of York, my father came untimely to his death', is false.)

Salisbury, Robert Cecil, 1st Earl of. See CECIL, ROBERT.

Salisbury, Sir John (*c.* 1567–1613), of Llewenny, Denbighshire, became the heir of his brother Thomas, who was executed in 1586 for conspiring to liberate Mary Queen of Scots. His wife was Ursula, illegitimate daughter of Henry, 4th Earl of Derby. He had four sons and three daughters, Henry being the eldest and only surviving son. He was M.P. for Denbighshire in 1601, in which year Robert Chester 'consecrated' to him *Love's Martyr*, which contains *The Phoenix and Turtle* (q.v.).

Salisbury, Sir Henry. Eldest and only surviving son of Sir John of Llewenny, was made a baronet in 1619, and died 1632. It is probable that the following verses, *c.* 1623, from a MS. of the family, were written by him

To my good freandes m[r] John Hemings & Henry Condall.

To yowe that Joyntly with vndaunted paynes
vowtsafed to Chawnte to vs thease noble straynes,
how mutch yowe merrytt by it is not sedd,
butt yowe haue pleased the lyving, loved the deadd,
Raysede from the woambe of Earth a Ritcher myne
then Curteys Cowlde with all his Castelyne
Associattes, they dydd butt digg for Gowlde,
Butt yowe for Treasure mutch moare manifollde.

Salisbury Court Theatre. According to Edmund Howes (1631), in 1629 'there was builded a new faire Play-house, neere the white Fryers'. This was the private Salisbury Court theatre, which succeeded the old Whitefriars and Rosseter's short-lived Porter's Hall, and lay just to the west of the City walls, between Fleet Street and the river. It was occupied by Queen Henrietta's and by the Prince's Men, gutted by a company of soldiers 'set on by the sectuaries' in 1649, but used for a time at the Restoration, and replaced in 1671 by the Dorset Garden theatre near by.

Salvini, Tommaso (1829–1915), Italian tragic actor, joined Adelaide Ristori's company in 1847, and fought in the War of Italian Independence, 1849. He first played Othello in 1856, other famous Shakespearean parts being Hamlet, Macbeth, Coriolanus and Lear. He paid several visits to England and America, in 1886 playing Othello to the Iago of Edwin Booth.

Sampson. In *Romeo and Juliet.* See GREGORY.

Sandells, Fulk (1551–1624), yeoman of Shottery. In 1581 overseer of Richard Hathaway's will, and responsible for paying Anne £6 13s. 4d. 'at the day of her marriage'. In 1582 one of Shakespeare's sureties for his marriage-bond. (See SS, 12.)

Sands, James. A boy actor with the King's when, in 1605, Augustine Phillips left his apprentice, James Sands, 40s., 'a citterne, a bandore and a lute'. William Sly, too, left him a legacy in 1608. He was never a sharer with the King's, and about 1617 seems to have been with Queen Anne's.

Sands, Lord (d. 1540). In *Henry VIII*, he appears in I, iii, flirts with Anne Bullen in I, iv, and in II, i as Sir William Sands, accompanies Buckingham on his way to execution. (Sir William Sands was created Baron in 1523, and Lord Chamberlain in 1526.)

'Satiromastix.' A play registered 11 November 1601, 'Vppon condicon that yt be lycensed to be printed', and published in the same year:

> Satiro-mastix. Or The vntrussing of the Humorous Poet. As it hath bin presented publikely, by the Right Honorable, the Lord Chamberlaine his Seruants; and priuately, by the Children of Paules. By Thomas Dekker.

The play is the reply of Dekker, and probably Marston, to *The Poetaster* (q.v.). In that play Jonson had assumed the character of the virtuous Horace, and satirized Dekker and Marston as Demetrius and Crispinus, plagiary and poetaster. In *Satiromastix* Dekker and Marston appear again as Demetrius and Crispinus; they discover Horace (Jonson) ponderously composing a poem, are joined by Jonson's Captain Tucca from *The Poetaster*, and Horace is mercilessly baited, and finally crowned with nettles. The satire is slipped into a tragedy of William Rufus, Sir Walter Terill and his wife which bears no relation to the quarrel of the dramatists. (See POETOMACHIA.)

Saturninus. In *Titus Andronicus*, he is elected Emperor in place of his dead father, his rival Titus having withdrawn, and marries Tamora, the secret enemy of Titus. He orders the execution of two of Titus's sons on suspicion of having murdered his brother Bassianus. When Titus kills Tamora at the banquet, he kills Titus, and is himself immediately killed by Titus's remaining son, Lucius.

Saunder. A boy actor named in the 'plot' of *The Seven Deadly Sins* (q.v.). There is a Saunder in *The Taming of A Shrew*.

Saunderson, Mary (d. 1712), the actress who, in 1662, married Betterton, and with him played many of Shakespeare's tragic heroines, including Juliet, Ophelia, Lady Macbeth, Katharine in *Henry VIII*, Andromache, and Evandra, Timon's mistress, in Shadwell's version of *Timon of Athens*. Pepys calls her by her stage name, Ianthe, and on 30 September 1662 saw '*The Duchess of Malfi* well performed, but Betterton and Ianthe to admiration'.

'Sauny the Scot.' See LACY.

Savage, Richard. The first secretary and librarian of the Birthplace Trustees (1884–1910), and editor of *The Parish Registers of Stratford-on-Avon* (3 vols., 1897–1905).

Savage, Thomas (*c.* 1552–1611), with William Leveson (q.v.), one of the trustees appointed by Shakespeare and his fellows in 1599 to make the shares in the Globe tenancies held in common. He was born at Rufford in Lancashire, a member of the Goldsmith's Company, and one of the sea-coal measurers of London. He lived near Heminge, whose landlord he was, and was also the 'very loving friend' of John Jackson, Shakespeare's friend, whom he appointed overseer of his will.

Rufford was the home of Sir Thomas Hesketh, to whom in his will of August 1581 Alexander Houghton of Lea commended 'William Shakeshafte nowe dwellynge with me'. Hesketh had a company of players in 1587, and it is just possible that Shakespeare, using a variant of his grandfather's name was tutor and actor in these Lancashire families. (Cf. Aubrey, 1681: 'he had been in his younger yeares a Schoolmaster in the Countrey'.) At any rate, the connexion of William Shakeshafte and Thomas Savage with Rufford is interesting. (See E. K. Chambers, *Sources for a Biography of Shakespeare*; Hotson, *Shakespeare's Sonnets Dated*; Alan Keen, *The Annotator*.)

Saxo Grammaticus (*c.* 1150–*c.* 1206), Danish poet and historian. At the suggestion of Bishop Absalon, whose secretary he was, he wrote a Latin history of the Danish kings called *Historia Danica, or Gesta Danorum.* Books I–IX cover the legendary period of Danish history; X–XVI are more historical and bring the history to the reign of Valdemar I (d. 1182). The work was first published in 1514.

The Hamlet story occurs in Books III and IV, and tells how Horwendil kills the King of Norway and marries Gerutha, daughter of the King of Denmark, their son being Amleth. Horwendil is murdered by his brother Feng, who marries Gerutha, and Amleth feigns madness the better to carry out his revenge. The suspicious Feng sets a girl to trap him; Amleth kills an eavesdropper, wins his mother to his side, and is sent by Feng to England with two companions whose deaths he secures by altering their letter. After adventures in England he returns, and with his mother's assistance makes the courtiers drunk, sets fire to the palace, kills Feng with his sword and seizes his throne. Later, he is killed in battle.

Saxo's story appeared in French in Belleforest's *Histoires Tragiques* (1576), and in English in 1608 as *The Historie of Hamblet*, but this is later than Shakespeare's play, parts of which it incorporates, for example, Hamlet's 'A rat! a rat!'

Say, Lord (d. 1450). In *2 Henry VI*, Lord Treasurer. Cade captures him and accuses him of extortion, the surrender of Normandy, and the propagation of learning; he has his head struck off and fixed on a pole, as also that of Say's son-in-law, Sir James Cromer (IV, vii).

Scala, Bartolomeo Della (d. 1304), of the famous della Scala or Scaliger family that ruled Verona, 1260–1375. It was during the rule of Bartolomeo (1301–4) that the real Romeo and Juliet are said to have lived and died. 'Escalus' in *Romeo and Juliet* is a corruption of della Scala.

Scales, Lord (d. 1460). In *2 Henry VI*, is in command of the Tower during Cade's rebellion (IV, v). His capture at Patay is reported in *1 Henry VI* (I, i).

Scarlet, Elizabeth. An aunt of Shakespeare; a sister of Mary Arden, she married one Scarlet and lived at Newnham, a hamlet a mile to the east of Aston Cantlow, in which parish it lies.

Scarus. In *Antony and Cleopatra*, a friend of Antony. He describes the flight of Cleopatra's fleet at Actium (III, x); unlike Enobarbus, he remains loyal to Antony and fights 'As if a god in hate of mankind had Destroy'd in such a shape', so that Cleopatra promises him 'an armour all of gold' (IV, viii).

Scene Division. See ACT AND SCENE DIVISION.

Scenery. See STAGING; PERSPECTIVE.

Scheemakers, Peter (1691–1770), Flemish sculptor, was born in Antwerp, studied under Delvaux, and in Rome 1728–35. He lived in England 1735–70, returning to Antwerp shortly before his death. He was one of the most popular sculptors of his time, fifteen of his monuments being in Westminster Abbey. Of these the best known is the statue of Shakespeare, erected by public subscription in 1740. Though designed by William Kent, the work was carried out by Scheemakers, and is the first sculptured portrait to be based on the Chandos painting. (See ROUBILIAC.)

Schlegel, August Wilhelm von (1767–1845), was born at Hanover, educated at Göttingen, and in 1796 settling at Jena. Here he began his famous translation into German of Shakespeare's plays, sixteen of which were published 1797–1801, and *Richard III* in 1810. In this work he was helped by his wife Caroline, most brilliant of the Romantic women writers. In 1803 they were divorced; she married the philosopher F. W. Schelling, and the remainder of the plays were completed, under the direction of Ludwig Tieck, by Graf Wolf Baudissin and Tieck's daughter Dorothea. This translation was one of the most important achievements of the German Romantics, and established Shakespeare almost as a German national poet. In 1808 Schlegel delivered a course of lectures in Vienna *On Dramatic Art and Literature* (published 1809–11), in which he interpreted the genius of Shakespeare in much the same way as did Coleridge at about the same time, though in Schlegel there is more mysticism; for him Shakespeare is 'in strength a demi-god, in profundity of view a prophet, in all-seeing wisdom a protecting spirit of a higher order'. He supplied Madame de Staël with much of the material for her *De l'Allemagne* (1813), the book that revealed the importance of German literature. In 1818 he was appointed Professor of Literature at Bonn, where he died.

He and his brother, Friedrich (1772–1829), also poet, critic and scholar, were the real founders of German Romanticism and of the school of interpretative criticism, and by his work August Wilhelm made Shakespeare accessible to the German people, and prepared the way for the scholars and critics of the later 19th century.

Scholarship. The main branches of Shakespearean scholarship may be classed as dealing with: Biography; Background, personal, social, and literary; Theatre; Text, its establishment, annotation and transmission; Sources; Language; Verse; Chronology; Authenticity.

The 17th century added little to the knowledge of Shakespeare and his work. Fuller and Aubrey made a few notes about his life; Langbaine made some study of sources; Ravenscroft cast doubt on the authenticity of *Titus Andronicus*.

In the 18th century a succession of scholars attacked, though with little co-operation, most of the problems. In 1709 came Rowe's short *Life*; material was collected by Oldys, and at the end of the century Malone wrote his *Life*, incorporating a mass of fresh knowledge. The text was reduced to order and annotated principally by Rowe, Theobald, Capell, Steevens, and Malone, the last three of whom began the serious study of the Quartos, and they and Richard Farmer added immensely to the knowledge of Shakespeare's background. Sources were explored by Theobald and Charlotte Lennox. Malone wrote *An Historical Account of the English Stage* to which George Chalmers added *A Farther Account*. Theobald and Capell made studies of Shakespeare's verse, and in 1778 came Malone's *Attempt to Ascertain the Order in which the Plays were Written.* The prefatory matter to the Variorum editions of 1803, 1813, 1821, is an invaluable summary of the work of 18th-century scholarship.

The 19th century was a period of greater cooperation and organized progress. The first Shakespeare Society, 1840–53, was founded by J. P. Collier, and the New Shakspere Society, 1873–94, by F. J. Furnivall, and both societies published much valuable material. Halliwell-Phillipps and Furnivall were the dominating figures of the Victorian era, the former concentrating on biographical matter, the latter on an organized study of the development and 'oneness' of Shakespeare, largely by means of verse-tests. This was stimulated by the entry of German scholars into the field and the foundation of the Shakespeare-Gesellschaft with its *Jahrbuch* in 1865. In 1863–6 Clark, Glover, and Wright published the *Cambridge Shakespeare*, the text of which was long the standard one. A few years later came the first important contribution of American scholarship, the first volume of the *New Variorum*, 1871, edited by H. H. Furness, and in 1886 the New York Shakespeare Society began the publication of Appleton Morgan's *Bankside Shakespeare*. Later 19th-century scholars of importance were Dowden, Lee, Fleay, and Brandes the Dane.

The discovery of de Witt's drawing of the Swan theatre in 1888 stimulated interest in the Elizabethan playhouse, and early 20th-century scholarship was largely concerned with this theme: thus, from America came W. J. Lawrence's *Elizabethan Playhouse* (1912), A. H. Thorndike's *Shakespeare's Theater* (1916) and J. Q. Adams's *Shakespearean Playhouses* (1917), and in 1923 E. K. Chambers published the four volumes of his *Elizabethan Stage*. This in turn encouraged more specialized studies, such as L. B. Campbell's *Scenes and Machines* (1923), T. W. Baldwin's *Organization and Personnel of the Shakespearean Company* (1927), M. C. Bradbrook's *Elizabethan Stage Conditions* (1932), A. Harbage's *Shakespeare's Audience* (1941), and so on. This rediscovery of the Elizabethan theatre led to the reform of theatrical production by William Poel, Granville-Barker and, in France, Jacques Copeau, and to a 'realist' school of critics led by the Americans E. E. Stoll and Hardin Craig, and the German L. L. Schücking, who sought to place Shakespeare in his Elizabethan theatrical and, more broadly, social and literary environment.

Meanwhile the new 'Critical Bibliography' of Pollard, McKerrow and Greg was revolutionizing textual criticism (q.v.), the first phase of which may be said to have begun with Pollard's *Shakespeare Folios and Quartos* (1909); the second with Willoughby's *Printing of the First Folio* (1932) and the work of Charlton Hinman, Philip Williams, and Alice Walker after the war.

The study of imagery, which began in the 1930s, belongs more properly to criticism (q.v.), but mention should be made of the recent biographical discoveries of Leslie Hotson, and of his revolutionary reconstruction of the Elizabethan theatre in *Shakespeare's Wooden O*; of Baldwin's studies of the Elizabethan Grammar School, and of the work of K. Muir and G. Bullough on Shakespeare's sources.

Modern scholarship has been greatly aided in America by the concentration of so much material in the Folger and Huntington Libraries, and the foundation of the Shakespeare Association of America with its periodicals, the *Shakespeare Bulletin* and *Shakespeare Quarterly*; in England by the Shakespeare Institute at Stratford and *Shakespeare Survey*. (See EDITORS.)

'Schöne Sidea, Die.' A play by Jakob Ayrer (q.v.), with some of the elements of *The Tempest*, though otherwise unlike. There is no tempest and no magic island, but there is a prince who is a magician with a familiar spirit, and a daughter beloved of his enemy's son, who is made to carry logs, and whose sword he enchants. It seems clear that Shakespeare and Ayrer had a common, though unknown, source. English players in Germany performed *Celinde and Sedea* in 1604 and 1613, but nothing is known of 'Celinde'.

Schubert, Franz Peter (1797–1828), the German composer, set an enormous number of lyrics to music, mostly Goethe's and Schiller's, but also some of Shakespeare's. The two most famous, 'Hark, hark, the lark', and 'Who is Silvia?', were written on the same day, the former in a tavern where he rested on a walk in the afternoon, the latter on his return home in the evening.

Schücking, Levin Ludwig (1878–1964), German professor and literary historian, leader of the 'realist' school of criticism that sought to relate Shakespeare to his dramatic environment. Author of *Character Problems in Shakespeare's Plays*, 1922. (See SOLILOQUY.)

Scofield, Paul (b. 1922). In 1946 he and Peter Brook went with Barry Jackson to Stratford. In 1955 he played Hamlet at the Moscow Arts Theatre, and in 1962 Lear in Brook's Stratford-Aldwych production.

Scoloker, Anthony (fl. 1604), poet, was probably a relative of the printer and translator, Anthony Scoloker (fl. 1550). He was author of *Daiphantus, or the Passions of Loue* (1604), in the Epistle to which he writes of the popularity of *Hamlet*, and in the poem itself describes how Hamlet appeared in his shirt-sleeves:

> It should be like the *Neuer-too-well read Arcadia* ... or to come home to the vulgars *Element*, like *Friendly Shakespeare's Tragedies*, where the *Commedian* rides, when the *Tragedian* stands on Tip-toe: Faith it should please all, like Prince *Hamlet*.

> Puts off his cloathes; his shirt he onely weares,
> Much like mad-*Hamlet*; thus as Passion teares.

Scot, Reginald (1538?–1599), a Kentish man, educated at Hart Hall, Oxford, and M.P. for New Romney, 1588–9. He led the life of a country gentleman, and published the first English treatise on hop-culture, *The Perfect Platform of a Hop-garden*, 1574. Ten years later came his famous *The Discouerie of Witchcraft, wherein the Lewde dealing of Witches and Witchmongers is notablie detected, in sixteen books . . . whereunto is added a Treatise upon the Nature and Substance of Spirits and Devils*, 1584. It is in part an enlightened attack on superstition, and a defence of the wretches persecuted as witches. Scot was assailed, among others by James VI of Scotland, who published his *Daemonologie* in 1597, and on his accession to the English throne ordered Scot's *Discouerie* to be burned. The book furnished material for *Macbeth* and Middleton's *The Witch*. There also is Robin Goodfellow, and a story of transformation into an ass.

Scotland. In 1574 the General Assembly forbade the performance of plays 'maid of ye cannonicall Scriptures' and ordered that 'profaine playes' should be licensed by the local Kirk Session. In 1589 James VI asked if Queen Elizabeth's Men, then at Carlisle, might visit Scotland to play before his bride, Anne of Denmark; but, as her arrival was postponed, it is not certain that they went. English players, probably under Lawrence Fletcher, and to celebrate the baptism of Prince Henry, were at the Scottish Court in 1594. In October 1599 Fletcher and his company of English comedians arrived in Scotland and secured the King's warrant to play at 'an hous within the toun. Upon Moonday, the 12th of November, they gave warning by trumpets and drummes through the streets of Edinburgh, to all that pleased, to come to the Blacke Friers' Wynd to see the acting of their comedeis'. The Kirk Sessions tried to prevent the performances, but James bullied them into submission and proclaimed with sound of trumpet that the players were at liberty to perform. It appears that Fletcher and his company were taken into the King's service, for on 9 October 1601 they were at Aberdeen as 'his majesty's servants'. This must be the reason why Fletcher's name appears first in the patent of May 1603 to the King's (Chamberlain's) Men, with which company, however, he appears to have taken no active part. But because Fletcher apparently led Shakespeare's English King's company in 1603, and led 'his majesty's servants' in Scotland in 1601, Knight, Fleay and others have assumed that Shakespeare and his fellows visited Scotland in 1601, after the trouble caused by their performance of *Richard II* the day before Essex's rebellion, and that there Shakespeare gathered information for *Macbeth*. Wilson, too, thinks that Shakespeare fled to Scotland, where he wrote *Macbeth* (1601–2), which was performed at Edinburgh. But if they were at Aberdeen in the middle of October, they would have little time to get back to London and rehearse for the first of their four Court performances on 26 December. (See JAMES I; FLETCHER, LAWRENCE.)

Scott, Sir Walter (1771–1832). See FULBROOK.

'Scourge of Villanie.' A tract by John Marston, published 1598. In *Satyre 7* he parodies the famous line from *Richard III*: 'A man, a man, a kingdome for a man.' More important is his association in *Satyre 10* of *Romeo and Juliet* with the Curtain theatre, which suggests that the Chamberlain's played there after the reopening of the theatres in the autumn of 1597 to the autumn of 1599, when the Globe was ready for them:

Lucus, what's playd to day? faith now I know
I set thy lips abroach, from whence doth flow
Naught but pure *Iuliat* and *Romio*.
Say, who acts best? *Drusus* or *Roscio*?
Now I have him, that nere of ought did speake
But when of playes or Plaiers he did treate.
H'ath made a common-place booke out of plaies,
And speakes in print: at least what ere he sayes
Is warranted by Curtaine plaudeties.

Scroop (Scrope), Sir Stephen (d. 1408). In *Richard II*, he tells the King that Bushy and Green, and his own brother the Earl of Wiltshire, have been beheaded by Bolingbroke (III, ii). (Sir Stephen succeeded as 2nd Baron Scrope of Masham in 1391.)

Scrope, Lord (d. 1415). In *Henry V*, with Cambridge and Grey he plans to murder the King as he sets out on his French campaign, is discovered, and sent to execution. He was one of Henry's most trusted counsellors. (Henry le Scrope was 3rd Baron, and eldest son of Sir Stephen Scrope in *Richard II*.)

Scrope, Richard (d. 1405), Archbishop of York. In *1 Henry IV*, he joins Hotspur's rebellion, but is not present at Shrewsbury. In *2 Henry IV*, he is tricked by Prince John into dismissing his forces, and executed (IV, ii). (Richard le Scrope was 4th son of the 1st Baron.)

Sea-captain. 1. In *2 Henry VI*, he captures the Duke of Suffolk, whose head he has struck off 'on our long boat's side' (IV, i).

2. In *Twelfth Night*, the captain of the ship wrecked off the coast of Illyria. He promises to present Viola to Orsino, disguised as a page (I, ii). In V, i Viola tells Olivia that he is 'in durance, at Malvolio's suit'.

Seacole. In *Much Ado*, George Seacole is the Second Watchman, appointed constable, who arrests Borachio and Conrade (III, iii). Francis Seacole, mentioned by Dogberry as a scribe in III, v, is the sexton or clerk of IV, ii.

Sebastian. 1. In *Twelfth Night* (q.v.), twin brother of Viola. (In Riche's

Apolonius and Silla, he is called Silvio; in Bandello's *novella*, Paolo.)

2. In *The Tempest* (q.v.), brother of Alonso, King of Naples, whose murder he attempts.

'Second Maiden's Tragedy, The.' An anonymous manuscript prompt-book, once in the possession of John Warburton (d. 1759). It was allowed and endorsed by Buck 31 October 1611. Somebody has added 'By Thomas Goffe', which two later hands have altered, first to 'George Chapman', and then to 'Will Shakspear'. Warburton attributed the play to Chapman, so probably the Shakespeare attribution is later. It was evidently a King's play, for stage-directions note 'Mr Goughe' as Memphonius, and 'Rich Robinson' as the Lady. (See Greg, *Dramatic Documents*.)

Sedley, Sir Charles (*c.* 1639–1701), Restoration wit and dramatist, was educated at Wadham, Oxford. His most celebrated comedy is *Bellamira: or The Mistress* (1687). His *Antony and Cleopatra* (1667) is independent of Shakespeare, of whom, however, he was an ardent admirer, and wrote,

Shackspear whose fruitfull Genius, happy wit,
Was fram'd and finisht at a lucky hit,
The pride of Nature, and the shame of Schools,
Born to Create, and not to Learn from Rules.

Segar, Sir William (d. 1633), a scrivener who was preferred to the College of Arms, and succeeded Sir William Dethick as Garter King-of-Arms in 1603. His *Booke of Honor and Armes. Wherein is discoursed the causes of Quarrell and the nature of Iniuries, with their Repulses*, was published 1590. From it Shakespeare took the 'first and second cause' in duelling in *Love's Labour's Lost* and *Romeo and Juliet*.

'Sejanus.' A tragedy by Ben Jonson, registered 2 November 1604, and published in 1605 (Q1) as 'Seianus his fall'. A note at the end of the Folio text (1616) states that 'This Tragœdie was first acted, in the yeere 1603. By the Kings Maiesties Servants. The principall Tragœdians were, Ric. Burbadge, Will Shakespeare, Aug Philips, Ioh. Hemings, Will. Sly, Hen. Condel, Ioh. Lowin, Alex. Cooke.' This is the last recorded appearance of Shakespeare as an actor. In his *Epistle* to Q1 Jonson wrote,

I would informe you, that this Booke, in all numbers, is not the same with that which was acted on the publike Stage, wherein a second Pen had good share: in place of which I haue rather chosen, to put weaker (and no doubt lesse pleasing) of mine own, then to defraud so happy a *Genius* of his right, by my lothed vsurpation.

It has been suggested, on no other evidence than the word *Genius*, that Shakespeare was the collaborator in the original play, the text of which has perished.

Seleucus. In *Antony and Cleopatra*, Cleopatra's treasurer. When she gives Caesar an inventory of her possessions Seleucus warns him that only half are recorded (v, ii).

Sempronius. In *Timon of Athens*, 'another flattering Lord' (F) who, on the pretext of being the last to be asked refuses Timon a loan (III, iii).

Seneca, Lucius Annaeus (*c.* 4 B.C.–A.D. 65), son of Seneca the rhetorician, was born at Cordoba in Spain, but was taken to Rome as a child. His success as an orator excited the jealousy of Caligula, and on the accession of Claudius in 41 the Empress Messalina secured his exile to Corsica. However, when Agrippina married Claudius in 49, Seneca was recalled and made tutor to her son, who succeeded Claudius as the Emperor Nero in 54. For a time Seneca checked the excesses of the young Emperor, but Nero tired of his restraint and in 65 ordered him to commit suicide. Seneca opened the veins in his arms and legs, and his devoted wife died with him.

In his philosophical works, written in an artificial rhetorical style, Seneca preaches a stoicism that has something in common with Christian doctrine. His nine tragedies are written in an inflated verse form of his prose style, and were probably not meant to be acted. Their main characteristics are: division into five acts, observance of the unities, use of the chorus, stichomythia, revenge demanded by a ghost, a bloody theme, action divorced from the stage and replaced by long speeches of narrative and sententious rhetoric. Tragedy was to teach as well as please.

His tragedies had an immense influence on the drama of the Renaissance, the writers of which period had little first-hand knowledge of Greek tragedy, and modelled their plays on those of Seneca and the precepts of Aristotle as crystallized by the pedants. Jasper Heywood translated the *Troas*, *Thyestès* and *Hercules Furens c.* 1560. Early Senecan imitations were academic, written for a small educated audience, either in Latin or the vernacular, like those of Garnier in France, or Sackville and Norton's *Gorboduc*, performed by the Gentlemen of the Inner Temple. Kyd popularized Senecan tragedy in his *Spanish Tragedy* by discarding the duller elements, emphasizing the ghost-revenge-blood *motif*, and by bringing the action on to the stage. Other dramatists followed him, including Shakespeare, notably in *Titus Andronicus*, *Richard III*, *Julius Caesar* and *Hamlet* (see REVENGE PLAY). The defeat of the strict Senecan form was deplored by the scholars, even by Sidney (q.v.).

Sennet. Trumpet music of the fanfare type, but longer than the flourish, associated with the appearance of royalty; cf. *Macbeth* III, i; *Lear* I, i, etc.

'Sequel of Henry IV, The.' An adaptation of *2 Henry IV*, incorporating the first scene of *Henry V*, published *c.* 1720, as,

The Sequel of Henry IV with the Humours of Sir John Falstaff and Justice Shallow; as it is acted by his Majesty's Company of Comedians at the Theatre Royal in Drury Lane. Altered from Shakespeare by the late Mr. Betterton.

Serlio, Sebastiano (1473–1554), Italian architect, born at Bologna, was a pupil of Baldassare Peruzzi, whose influence he acknowledges in his *Architettura*, published in 1551 while he was working for Francis I of France at Fontainebleau, where he died. In this book, translated into English in 1611, Serlio describes and illustrates his idea of a theatre and its *mise-en-scène*, based on his knowledge of Roman theatres. It is rectangular in plan, with the seats built up Roman fashion in semi-circular tiers. There is a long shallow fore-stage on which most of the action takes place, and behind this is a raked stage, at the front and on either side of which are three-dimensional *case* or 'houses' of lath and canvas; behind these again are flat painted *case*, diminishing rapidly in perspective to a backcloth also painted in perspective. In the centre is an open space, and the effect is that of looking up a long street flanked by houses. For comedy the architecture is less formal than for tragedy; for pastoral plays a country road running through an avenue of trees flanked by cottages replaces the street. This is a classical and ordered form of the more haphazard medieval multiple setting (q.v.), and may have been practised in the Jacobean private theatres; it was certainly adopted by Inigo Jones.

Servilius. In *Timon of Athens*, one of the servants of Timon, for whom he tries to raise a loan from Lucius (III, ii).

'Seven Deadly Sins, The.' A play by Richard Tarlton (d. 1588), the famous comedian of the Queen's Men. It was in two parts, but all that remains is the 'plot' (q.v.) of Part 2, discovered by Steevens in the library of Dulwich College. He describes it:

The Platt (for so it is called) is fairly written out on pasteboard in a large hand, and undoubtedly contained directions appointed to be stuck up near the prompter's station. It has an oblong hole in its centre, sufficient to admit a wooden peg; and has been converted into a cover for an anonymous manuscript play entitled The Tell-tale.

The play was a kind of morality, the second part of which illustrates the disastrous consequences of Envy, Sloth and Lechery. (By inference, therefore, Part 1 dealt with Pride, Gluttony, Wrath and Covetousness.) There is an Induction in which the saintly Henry VI and Lydgate, the monk of Bury, appear, followed by three episodes; that of Porrex representing Envy, Sardanapalus Sloth and Tereus Lechery. The scenes are separated by rules, and after each episode Henry and Lydgate speak, and the Sin of the next episode passes over the stage. The actors named indicate a revival by Strange's, *c.* 1590, the company reorganized as the Chamberlain's and joined by Shakespeare in 1594. The text of the first episode is given below:

THE PLATT OF THE SECOUND PARTE OF THE SEUEN DEADLIE SINNS

A tent being plast one the stage for Henry the sixt · he in it A sleepe to him The Leutenãt A purceuaunt R Cowly Jo Duke and i wardere [J Holland] R Pallant: to them Pride · Gluttony Wrath and Couetousnes at one dore · at an other dore Enuie · Sloth and Lechery · The Three put back the foure · and so Exeunt

---

Henry Awaking Enter A Keeper J Sincler · to him a seruaunt T Belt · to him Lidgate and the Keeper · Exit then enter againe · Then Enuy passeth ouer the stag · Lidgate speakes

---

A sennit · Dumb show ·
Enter King Gorboduk wth 2 Counsailers · R Burbadg m^{r} Brian · Th Goodale · The Queene wth ferrex and Porrex and som attendaunts follow · saunder w sly Harry J Duke · Kitt · Ro Pallant · J Holland After Gordbeduk hath Consulted wth his Lords he brings his 2 sonns to to seuerall seates · They enuing on on other ferrex offers to take Porex his Corowne · he draws his weopon The King Queen and Lords step between them They Thrust Them away and menasing [ect] ech other exit · The Queene and Lords Depart Heuilie · Lidgate speaks

---

Enter ferrex Crownd wth Drum and Coulers and soldiers one way · Harry · Kitt · R Cowly John duke · to them At a nother dore · Porrex drum and Collors and soldie W sly · R Pallant · John Sincler · J Holland

---

Enter [Gorb] Queene · wth 2 Counsailors · m^{r} Brian Tho Goodale · to them ferrex and Porrex seuerall waies wth [his] Drums and Powers · Gorboduk entreing in The midst between · Henry speaks

---

A Larum wth Excurtions After Lidgate speakes

Enter ferrex and Porrex seuerally Gorboduke still following them · Lucius and Damasus m^{r} Bry T Good ·

Enter ferrex at one dore · Porrex at an other The fight ferrex is slayn: to them Videna The Queene to hir Damasus · to him Lucius ·

Enter Porrex sad wth Dordan his man · RP · w sly: to them the Queene and A Ladie Nick saunder and Lords R Cowly m^{r} Brian · to them Lucius Rūning

---

Henry and Lidgat speaks Sloth passeth ouer

Phillips and Pope appear in the second episode, like Bryan called 'Mr', presumably because they were sharers. Obviously this plot is of the first importance, as indicating the method of production at a public theatre, and the composition of Shakespeare's company at about the time he joined it. Greg suggests that he played Henry VI. (See Greg, *Dramatic Documents.*)

Seyton. In *Macbeth*, an officer attending on Macbeth. He speaks a few significant lines in v, iii and v:

All is confirm'd, my lord, which was
reported ...
It is the cry of women, my good lord ...
The queen, my lord, is dead.

Shadow. The roof that protected the apron stage in the open public theatres; cf. the contract for the building of the Fortune: 'with a shadowe or cover over the saide Stadge'. (See HEAVENS.)

Shadow, Simon. In *2 Henry IV*, one of the men pressed by Falstaff for the army, because 'he presents no mark to the enemy' (III, ii).

Shadwell, Thomas (1642–92), dramatist, was born in Norfolk, and educated at Bury St Edmund's, and Caius, Cambridge. His first play, *The Sullen Lovers*, was produced in 1668, and was followed by sixteen others, which are valuable mainly as pictures of contemporary England. When Dryden satirized Shaftesbury and the Whigs in *The Medal* (1682), Shadwell, a Whig, attacked him in *The Medal of John Bayes*, and Dryden retorted in his annihilating *MacFlecknoe*:

The rest to some faint meaning make pretence,
But Shadwell never deviates into sense ...
Heywood and Shirley were but types of thee,
Thou last great prophet of tautology.

Shadwell had his revenge when at the Revolution of 1688 he superseded Dryden as Poet Laureate and Historiographer Royal.

In 1674 Shadwell turned the D'Avenant-Dryden adaptation of *The Tempest* into an opera, *The Enchanted Island*, with music by Purcell. Five years later his very successful *History of Timon of Athens, the Man-Hater*, was produced at Dorset Garden theatre. When Timon is ruined, his fiancée, Melissa, returns to her former lover, Alcibiades, but his mistress, Evandra, shares his misfortunes and finally commits suicide over his body. Melissa attempts to regain Timon when he finds the gold, and so loses Alcibiades as well. Shadwell's version held the stage until the middle of the 18th century. (See DANCE, JAMES; SAUNDERSON, MARY.)

Shakeshafte. See SAVAGE, THOMAS.

Shakespeare. 'Whatever may have been the origin of the name, the family of Shakspeare is of great antiquity in the county of Warwick, and was established long before our poet's time, in the woodland part of it, principally at Rowington and Lapworth; from which places several of them branched out, and settled at Wroxall, Knowle, Claverdon, Warwick, Balsal, Stratford, Hampton, and Snitterfield' (Malone; *Var.* II, 15). Chambers (II, 354) lists records of Shakespeares before 1400 in Gloucestershire (the earliest: William Sakspere of Clopton, hanged for robbery in 1248), Essex, Surrey, Kent, Staffordshire, Cheshire, Cumberland, Nottingham, Warwickshire, Yorkshire and Ireland; after 1500 in Warwickshire, Cambridgeshire, Derbyshire, Gloucestershire, Leicestershire, Nottinghamshire, Yorkshire, London and Ireland. Biographically, the most important Warwickshire Shakespeares, besides those of Stratford itself, are those of Snitterfield, Budbrooke, Hampton Lucy, Clifford Chambers, Warwick, Wroxall and Rowington. Adam Shakespere of Baddesley Clinton held land by military service in 1389, and his is the only family known to have done so. The heroic derivation of the name by Camden (q.v.) and Richard Verstegan – 'Breakspear, Shakspear, and the lyke, have byn surnames imposed upon the first bearers of them, for valour and feates of armes' – is therefore open to doubt.

Chambers quotes eighty-three spellings of the name in these records, some of the most remote from the generally accepted 'Shakespeare' being Shakespert, Shaksbye, Schacosper, Shaxbee, Shexsper, Saxspere, Sashpierre, Sadspere, Sheftspere, Chacsper. The poet's grandfather, Richard, appears as Shakstaff (1533) and Shakeschafte (1541. See SAVAGE, THOMAS.). His father, John, is spelt in some twenty different ways, mostly beginning in Shaks, or Shax-, but we have no signature, as either he could not write or preferred to make his mark. The poet's name is generally printed Shakespeare in his published works and in contemporary literary references, but in written records at Stratford and on the monument the short *a* of Shaks- and Shax- is commoner. Of his six signatures, the three of his will are Shakspere, Shakspere, Shakspeare; the others Shaksp, Shakspẽ, Shakspẽ, so that it is almost certain that the Stratford and Shakespeare's own pronunciation of the name was with a short *a*.

Shakespeare, Richard (d. 1561), the poet's grandfather, is generally identified with the farmer who farmed land on the two manors of Snitterfield. On the one, held by the Hales family 1546–99, he is traceable, probably as a copyholder, from October 1535, when he was fined for keeping too many cattle on the common pasture, to October 1560, when every tenant was ordered to 'make his hedges and ditches betwixt the end of the lane of Richard Shakespere, and the hedge called Dawkins hedge'. This holding may have been to the north of the lane to Warwick, where there was a field called Dawkins Close.

On the other manor, held by Robert Arden, the poet's maternal grandfather, Richard is traceable as a tenant 1528–60. He died in the winter of 1560–2, for on 10 February 1561 'Johannes Shakespere de Snytterfyld agricola', son of 'Richard Shakespere deceased late while he lyved of the parishe of Snytterfyld', was granted the administration of his estate. (See BUDBROOKE.) Richard had another son, called Henry. (See pp. 542, 543.)

Shakespeare, Henry (d. 1596), son of Richard Shakespeare, and the poet's uncle, is traceable as a tenant on the Hales manor at Snitterfield 1574–96. He was fined several times, in October 1596 'for having a diche betweene Redd Hill and Burman in decaye for want of repayringe'. Halliwell-Phillipps notes that these extensive fields of Red Hill and Burman 'still known under those names, are at a short distance from the Church on the right-hand side of the highway proceeding towards Luscombe'. There were also several actions for debt, and in 1587 he is described as John's brother – 'Henricus Shakspere frater dicti Johannis' – when John was sued for £10 which he had guaranteed, being part of a total debt of £22 owed by Henry to Nicholas Lane. 'Henrey Sakspere was Bureyed' at Snitterfield 29 December 1596, and on 9 February 1597 'Margret Sakspere widow, being times the wyff of Henry Shakspere, was bured'. (See HAMPTON LUCY.)

Shakespeare, John (d. 1601), son of Richard Shakespeare, and the poet's father, must have left Snitterfield sometime before 1552, when he is first mentioned in the Stratford records, he, Humphrey Reynolds and Adrian Quiney each being fined 12d. for making a dunghill in Henley Street, where presumably he was living. In a suit of 1556 he is first called 'glover', a trade that he followed until at least 1586, when again he appears as glover; he did not sign his name, but made his mark, sometimes in the form of a pair of glover's dividers. He also traded in barley, timber and wool, and possibly in other commodities. In other documents he is styled yeoman, that is, a man of substance under the degree of gentleman. The twenty years 1556–76 are years of prosperity:

1556. Buys two houses; the 'Woolshop' in Henley Street and another in Greenhill Street.

1557. Marries Mary Arden (q.v.), daughter of his father's landlord at Snitterfield.

1558. Birth of his first child, Joan. (Six other children were born 1562–74, and Edmund in 1580.)

1557–62. Successively borough constable, affeeror (assessor of fines), and chamberlain.

1561. Administers his father's estate.

1564. Birth of William Shakespeare.

1565. Alderman; 1568 Bailiff (Mayor); 1571 Chief Alderman and J.P.

1575. Buys two more houses; sites unknown, but probably the Birthplace, and an adjoining house to the west, destroyed in the fire of 1594.

The twenty years 1576–96 appear to be years of adversity.

1577. He ceases to attend Council meetings.

1578–9. Mortgages his wife's Wilmcote property, lets Asbies, and sells her share in the Snitterfield estate.

1580. Fined £40 for failing to appear before the court of Queen's Bench to give security that he would keep the peace.

1586. Replaced by another alderman because 'Mr Shaxpere dothe not come to the halles when they be warned, nor hathe not done of longe tyme.'

1587. Sued for part of the debt of his brother Henry (q.v.).

1592. Included in a list of recusants 'for not comminge monethlie to the churche ... It is sayd ... for feare of process for debtte'.

His fortunes are restored 1596–1601, probably by the poet:

1596. The Grant of Arms (see ARMS).

1597. His son William buys New Place. Attempts to recover the mortgaged estate from John Lambert.

1599. Applies for leave to impale the arms of Arden.

1601. Again appears as a member of the borough council. On 8 September, 'Mr Johannes Shakspeare' was buried in Stratford churchyard.

(There was another John Shakespeare who lived in Stratford *c.* 1584–95. He was a shoemaker, probably from Warwick, who married Margery Roberts (d. 1587) and had three children, Ursula, Humphrey and Phillip, whose names occur in the Stratford parish register, and have sometimes been confused with the children of the alderman. The shoemaker seems to have returned to Warwick and died there in 1624. Hotson has discovered two others; a 'John Shakespeare of Stratford upon Avon, yeoman' in 1533; and 'John Shackspere of Stretford Apon Aven' in 1561. The latter was a son of Christopher Shakespeare of Packwood, a manor frequented by Holinshed (q.v.). (See CLIFFORD CHAMBERS; INGON; JORDAN, JOHN; PLUME.)

The children of John Shakespeare and Mary Arden, in order of birth, were (the records are taken from the Stratford Parish Register (q.v.).):

Joan i (b. 1558). 'Jone Shakspere daughter to John Shakspere' was christened 15 September 1558. Nothing more is known of her; presumably she died before the birth of the second Joan in 1569. She was probably named after her aunt, Joan Arden (Lambert).

Margaret (1562–3). 'Margareta filia Johannis Shakspere' was christened 2 December 1562 and buried 30 April 1563. Probably named after her aunt, Margaret, wife of Henry Shakespeare.

William (1564–1616). See below: SHAKESPEARE, WILLIAM.

Gilbert (1566–1612). 'Gilbertus filius Johannis Shakspere' was christened 13 October 1566. He is probably the haberdasher 'de parochia sancte Brigitte London' who in 1597 was one of the sureties for William Sampson, a cloakmaker of 'Stratford super Aven'. In 1602 the conveyance of the poet's purchase of 127 acres of land in Old Stratford was 'Sealed and deliuered to Gilbert Shakespere, to the vse of ... William Shakespere'. In 1610 he signed himself 'Gilbart Shakespere' as a witness to a Stratford lease. He seems to have been a bachelor, which probably accounts for the 'adolescens' in the entry of his burial, 3 February 1612: 'Gilbert Shakspere, adolescens'. Malone suggested that the adolescens was Gilbert's son; Lee that Gilbert was the 'younger brother' who, according to Oldys, 'lived after the Restoration' to tell how he saw William act the part of Adam in his own *As You Like It*. But Shakespeare mentions none of his brothers in his will. (See JONES, THOMAS.)

Joan ii (1569–1646). Married William Hart. (See HART, JOAN.)

Anne (1571–9). 'Anna filia magistri Shakspere' was christened 28 September 1571, and buried – 'Anne daughter to Mr John Shakspere' – 4 April 1579.

Richard (1574–1613). 'Richard sonne to Mr John Shakspeer' was christened 11 March 1574, and buried – 'Rich: Shakspeare' – 4 February 1613. This is all that is known of this younger brother who apparently lived all his life at

Stratford and died there unmarried at the age of thirty-nine.

Edmund (1580–1607). 'Edmund sonne to Mr John Shakspere' was christened 3 May 1580. He was much the youngest child, born when times were bad, and possibly unwanted. There were four surviving children: William, aged 16; Gilbert, 14; Joan, 11; and Richard, 6. He was probably named after his uncle, Edmund Lambert, to whom his mother's Wilmcote property had just been mortgaged. For 31 December 1607, the MS. note of the sexton of St Saviour's, Southwark, reads, 'Edmund Shakspeare, a player, buried in the Church with a forenoone knell of the great bell, xxs.'. The fee for burial in the churchyard was only 2s., and that for ringing the lesser bell only 1s., so that the funeral was an expensive one, probably paid for by his brother William.

Four months earlier, 12 August 1607, 'Edward sonne of Edward Shackspeere, Player: base-borne' was buried at St Giles's, Cripplegate.

Shakespeare, William (1564–1616). References to the extant official records relating to Shakespeare's life are given below. A few early literary references are included, as are the plays he may be assumed to have written each year, though the dates of these can be only approximate.

1564, 26 April. 'Gulielmus filius Johannes Shakspere' was christened at Stratford parish church. (See BRETCHGIRDLE; EDUCATION.)

1581. See SAVAGE, THOMAS; DURSLEY.

1582, 27 November. 'Item eodem die similis emanavit licencia inter Willelmum Shaxpere et Annam Whateley de Temple Grafton.' Entry in the Bishop of Worcester's Register, of the issue of a special licence for the marriage, with only once asking of the banns, of Shakespeare to Anne Whateley. (See TEMPLE GRAFTON.)

28 November. Fulk Sandells and John Richardson, farmers of Stratford, enter into a bond exempting the Bishop from all liability should the marriage of 'William Shagspere on thone partie, and Anne Hathwey of Stratford in the Dioces of Worcester maiden' prove unlawful. (This was the normal procedure when a marriage was to be expedited. Anne was pregnant. See HATHAWAY; LUDDINGTON.)

1583, 26 May. 'Susanna daughter to William Shakespeare' christened.

1585, 2 February. 'Hamnet & Judeth sonne and daughter to William Shakspere' christened.

1588. Mentioned in Bill of Complaint, *Shakespeare* v. *Lambert*. (See LAMBERT.)

1589–91. (*1, 2, 3 Henry VI.*)

1592, 3 March. Henslowe records performance of 'Harey the vj' by Strange's; almost certainly *1 Henry VI*.

September. Publication of Greene's *Groatsworth of Wit*, with its reference to 'the onely Shake-scene in a countrey', and the 'Tygers hart wrapt in a Players hyde', a parody of a line in *3 Henry VI*. This is almost certainly an attack on Shakespeare, then, apparently, a successful dramatist in London. (See CHETTLE.)

(*Richard III*; *Titus Andronicus*.)

1593. Publication of *Venus and Adonis*, dedicated to the Earl of Southampton by 'William Shakespeare'.

(*Comedy of Errors*; *Taming of the Shrew*.)

1594. Publication of *The Rape of Lucrece*, again dedicated to Southampton by 'William Shakespeare'.

The first literary mention of his name in the anonymous verses in *Willobie his Avisa* (Reg. 3 Sept.).

26, 27 December. 'Willm̃ Kempe, Willm̃ Shakespeare, & Richarde Burbage seruantes to the Lord Chamberleyne' were payees for Court performances on these dates. Presumably Shakespeare had joined the Chamberlain's company on its formation in the summer. (The Council Warrant for payment is dated 15 March 1594–5.)

28 December. Performance of *The Comedy of Errors*, presumably by the Chamberlain's, at Gray's Inn. (See 'GESTA GRAYORUM'.)

(*Two Gentlemen of Verona*; *Love's Labour's Lost*.)

1595. (*Romeo and Juliet*; *Richard II*; *Midsummer Night's Dream*.)

1596. 11 August. 'Hamnet filius William Shakspere' buried at Stratford.

Grant of Arms.

October. Living in parish of St Helen's, Bishopsgate, where assessed at 5s. on goods valued at £5.

November. 'Willelmus Wayte petit securitates pacis versus Willelmum Shakspere ...' (See WAYTE.) The writ of attachment, or order for the arrest of Shakespeare, was issued to the Sheriff of Surrey, so he must have moved to the south bank of the Thames, probably the Liberty of the Clink, Bankside (see 1600, below).

(*King John*; *Merchant of Venice*.)

1597, 4 May. 'Willielmus Shakespeare dedit predicto Willielmo Underhill sexaginta libras sterlingorum' as the price of New Place.

15 November. The petty collectors of 'St Ellen's parishe' report that 'William Shackspere', assessed at 5s. on goods valued at £5, is 'ether dead, departed, and gone out of the sayde warde'.

(*1, 2 Henry IV*.)

1598. Jan.–Nov. The Quiney Correspondence (q.v.).

4 February. 'Stratforde ... Chapple street warde ... Wm. Shackespere. x quarters.' (From the official return of those holding stocks of corn or malt contrary to the law in a time of dearth.)

September. Acted in *Every Man in His Humour*.

7 September. Registration of *Palladis Tamia* by Francis Meres (q.v.), with its important references to Shakespeare.

Publication of Q1 *Love's Labour's Lost*, 'By W. Shakespere'; the first play to be published with Shakespeare's name. It was unregistered.

1 October. 'William Shakespeare' assessed according to a new subsidy of 1597–8, for St Helen's parish, 13s. 4d. on goods valued at £5. 'pd to mr Shaxspere for on lod of ston xd.' (From Stratford Chamber Account (Xmas).)

(*Much Ado*; *Henry V*; *Merry Wives*.)

1599. 21 February. 'William Shakespeare' becomes one of the original housekeepers of the Globe, with a one-tenth share. (See 'SHARERS' PAPERS'.) 'Willelmus Shakespeare' returned as a defaulter on his debt of 13s. 4d. with no goods to distrain in St Helen's parish.

6 October. The debt of 'Willelmus Shakspeare' to the Exchequer entered on the Pipe Roll and referred for collection to the Sheriff of Surrey and Sussex.

(*Julius Caesar*; *As You Like It*.)

1600, 23 August. The first mention of Shakespeare's name in the Stationers' register: 'Muche a Doo about nothinge ... Wrytten by master Shakespere'.

6 October. The debt of 'Willelmus Shakspeare' to the Exchequer entered on the Sussex-Surrey Pipe Roll, and referred for collection to the Bishop of Winchester, within whose jurisdiction the Liberty of the Clink lay. A later marginal note "T[ot]' may indicate that the debt was paid.

1601, 7 February. Performance of *Richard II* at the Globe, followed by Essex's rebellion.

25 March. Will of Thomas Whittington (q.v.) of Shottery: 'I geve and bequeth unto the poore people of Stratford 40s. that is in the hand of Anne Shaxspere, wyf unto Mr Wyllyam Shaxspere.'

8 September. Burial of the poet's father, John.

(*Troilus and Cressida*.)

1602. 1 May. 'William Shakespere of Stretford vppon Avon ... gentleman' buys 127 acres of land in Old Stratford (q.v.) for £320 from William and John Combe.

28 September. Acquires copyhold from Walter Getley of a cottage in Chapel Lane, opposite New Place.

Michaelmas Term. 'Willielmus Shakespeare generosus' secures warranty for New Place by a new fine with Hercules Underhill.

(*All's Well*; *Othello*.)

1603. 19 May. 'We ... doe licence and aucthorize theise our Servauntes Lawrence Fletcher, William Shakespeare ...' (From Royal Licence for the King's Men.)

Winter. Acted in *Sejanus*; the last record of his acting. (See WILTON HOUSE.)

(*Measure for Measure*.)

1604, March. 'William Shakespeare' and the other sharers in the King's company each supplied with 4½ yards of red cloth for liveries for the coronation procession of James I. (See SOMERSET HOUSE.)

Lodging with Christopher Mountjoy (q.v.) in Silver Street, Cripplegate (see 1612).

'Willielmus Shexpere versus Phillipum Rogers' (q.v.) at Stratford.

24 October. Survey of Rowington Manor: 'William Shakespere lykewise holdeth there one cottage and one garden, by estimation a quarter of one acre, and payeth rent yeerlye iis. vjd.'

(*Timon*.)

1605, 4 May. Will of Augustine Phillips of the King's Men: 'I geve and bequeathe to my Fellowe William Shakespeare a thirty shillings peece in gould.'

24 July. 'William Shakespeare ... gent.' buys from Ralph Huband for £440 his interest in a lease of tithes in 'Stratforde, Olde Stratforde, Welcombe and Bushopton.'

(*Lear*; *Macbeth*.)

1606, 1 August. 'Willielmus Shakespere

tenet ... Domum mansionalem.' (From Survey of Rowington, showing Shakespear as a tenant of the Chapel Lane Cottage, though the rent is given as only 2s.)

(*Antony and Cleopatra.*)

1607. 5 June. Marriage of Shakespeare's daughter in Stratford: 'John Hall gentleman & Susanna Shaxspere.'

(*Coriolanus.*)

1608. 21 February. Shakespeare's granddaughter christened: 'Elizabeth dawghter to John Hall gentleman.' The only grandchild born in the poet's lifetime.

9 August. 'Willelmus Shakespeare' becomes one of the original housekeepers of the Blackfriars theatre, with a one-seventh share. (See 'SHARERS' PAPERS'.)

Dec.–June 1609. 'Willielmus Shackspeare' v. Johannes Addenbrooke (q.v.) at Stratford.

9 September. Burial of the poet's mother, 'Mayry Shaxspere wydowe'.

(*Pericles.*)

1609. (*Cymbeline.*) *Shake-speares Sonnets* published.

1610. 'Willielmus Shakespere generosus' assures the conveyance of the Old Stratford land brought in 1602 by means of a fine or *Finalis Concordia.*

It is generally assumed that Shakespeare settled at Stratford, in New Place, at about this time. (See KEYSAR.)

(*The Winter's Tale.*)

1611. Bill of Complaint brought by 'William Shackspeare, gentleman' and others against the Combes for not paying their share of the mean-rent due to J. Barker on the Stratford tithes (q.v.).

11 September. 'Mr William Shackspere' contributes 'towardes the charge of prosecutyng the Bill in parliament for the better Repayre of the highe waies.'

5 October. 'A lease of a barne that he holdeth of Mr Shaxper, xx^{li}.' (See JOHNSON, ROBERT.)

(*The Tempest.*)

1612, May–June. The Belott-Mountjoy Suit (q.v.). (1st signature of Shakespeare.)

(*Henry VIII.*)

1613, 28 January. Will of John Combe: 'I give to Mr William Shackspere five pounds.'

10 March. 'William Shakespeare of Stratford Vpon Avon ... gentleman' buys the Blackfriars Gatehouse from Henry Walker for £140. (2nd signature.)

11 March. 'William Shakespeare ... gentleman' mortgages the Gatehouse to Walker for £60. (3rd signature.)

31 March. 'Mr Shakspeare' is paid 44s. for his share in designing Lord Rutland's impresa.

29 June. The Globe burned down during a performance of *Henry VIII.*

(*The Two Noble Kinsmen.*)

1614. Sept.–Sept. 1615. The Welcombe Enclosure controversy (q.v.).

Christmas. 'One quart of sack and one quart of clarrett winne geuen to a precher at the newe place. xxd.' (From Stratford Corporation Accounts.)

1615, April–May. 'Willyam Shakespere, gent' one of the 'daylie oratoures' in a friendly Bill of Complaint with reference to the sale of Mathias Bacon's Blackfriars property.

Mentioned as a shareholder in the Globe in the suit of Ostler *v.* Heminge (q.v. See also WITTER; 'SHARERS' PAPERS'.)

1616, 10 February. Marriage of 'Tho Queeny tow Judith Shakspere', the poet's younger daughter.

25 March. Signs his Will (q.v.). (Three signatures.)

23 April. Death of Shakespeare.

25 April, Burial of 'Will. Shakspere, gent.' (See MONUMENT; DOWDALL.)

For Shakespeare's relations, see: Arden, Etkyns, Scarlet, Hewins, Stringer, Lambert, Webbe, Hart, Quiney, Nash, Bernard. (See also STRATFORD REGISTER.)

For Stratford friends: Combe, Lane, Nash, Quiney, Sturley, T. Greene, R. Field, Russell, Collins, Sadler, W. Reynolds, W. Walker, J. Shaw, J. Robinson, R. Whatcott. (See also STRATFORD, and p. 543)

For London friends: Burbage, Heminge, Condell, A. Phillips, and the other members of the Chamberlain's-King's company; Southampton, F. Greville, Jonson, Drayton, Daniel, J. Fletcher, R. Field, Florio, Mountjoy, W. Leveson, T. Savage, W. Johnson, J. Jackson, L. Digges.

For contemporary references see (the list is chronological):

E. Spenser; *Pierce Penilesse*; R. Greene; H. Chettle; R. Edwardes; B. Rich; W. Harvey; *Willobie his Avisa*; W. Covell; F. Meres; R. Barnfield; J. Marston; G. Harvey; J. Weever; *Parnassus*; B. Jonson; J. Manningham; R. Parsons; A. Scoloker; W. Camden; *Ratseis Ghost*; W. Barksted; J. Davies; J. Speed; J. Webster; T. Heywood; R. Carew; T. Freeman; W. Drummond; E. Howes; T. Porter; F. Beaumont; E. Bolton; W. Basse; J. Taylor; N. Richardson; *Folio*; H. Holland; L. Digges; 'M., I'; H. Salisbury; M. Drayton; J. Milton; J. Benson.

For later 17th- and 18th-century biographical material, largely traditional, see:

Hammond; N. L'Estrange; T. Fuller; T. Plume; A. Cokain; J. Ward; D. Lloyd; R. Dobyns; J. Aubrey; R. Davies; A. Wood; Dowdall; W. Hall; C. Gildon; J. Wright; J. Downes; N. Rowe; T. Hearne; J. Spence; J. Roberts; F. Peck; C. Macklin; W. Oldys; W. Chetwood; R. Shiels; *Bidford*; E. Capell; J. Jordan; E. Malone; J. Davenport; S. Ireland; W. H. Ireland; R. Phillips; W. Irving; *Hilliard miniature*; R. Ryan; *Fulbrook*.

(See also CRITICISM; EDITORS; PORTRAITS.)

William Shakespeare had three children:

Susanna (1583–1649), 'daughter to William Shakespeare', was christened 26 May 1583. On 5 June 1607, when she was 24, she married the Stratford physician John Hall (q.v.), her only child, Elizabeth, being christened 21 February of the following year. In 1613 she brought an action for slander against John Lane (q.v.). Her father left her his entailed estate: New Place, the Old Stratford acres, the Henley Street houses, Chapel Lane cottage and Blackfriars Gatehouse, and made her and Hall residuary legatees and executors of his will (q.v.). Elizabeth married in 1626 and Hall died in 1635. James Cooke (see p. 203), who translated Hall's case-book, tells how in 1642 he visited New Place, when Mrs Hall thought her husband's Latin manuscript was written by some other doctor, though her own ailments – she suffered from scurvy – and Hall's treatments are recorded. 'Mrs. Susanna Hall widow' was buried 16 July 1649, beside her husband in the chancel of Stratford church. On her stone is the inscription:

Heere lyeth ye body of Svsanna wife to Iohn Hall, gent: ye davghter of William Shakespeare, gent: shee deceased ye ij[th] of Iuly. A°. 1649, aged 66.

Witty above her sexe, but that's not all,
Wise to salvation was good Mistris Hall,
Something of Shakespeare was in that, but this
Wholy of him with whom she's now in blisse.
Then, Passenger, hast nere a teare,
To weepe with her that wept with all;
That wept, yet set her self to chere
Them up with comforts cordiall.
Her love shall live, her mercy spread,
When thou has't ner'e a teare to shed.

Hamnet (1585–96). 'Hamnet & Judeth sonne and daughter to William Shakspere' were christened 2 February 1585. Hamnet was 11½ when he was buried 11 August 1596: 'Hamnet filius William Shakspere'. (See SADLER.)

Judith (1585–1662), the twin sister of Hamnet. She was 31 when she married Thomas Quiney (q.v.) 10 February 1616 – 'Tho Queeny tow Judith Shakspere' – during the period in Lent when a special marriage licence was required, and their failure to obtain one led to their excommunication. Her father died a few weeks later, and it may be significant that he made many alterations in the first draft of his will, carefully securing her portion, before signing it on 25 March. He left her £300 and his 'broad silver gilt bole'. Judith's three children all died young: Shakespeare at 6 months, Richard at 11, and Thomas at 19. 'Judith vxor Thomas Quiney Gent.' was buried at Stratford 9 February 1662, but the site of her grave is unknown. John Ward, who was vicar of Stratford, 1662–81, has an entry in one of his note-books: 'A letter to my brother, to see Mrs Queeny, to send for Tom Smith for the acknowledgment'. (See also GREENE, THOMAS; CLIFFORD CHAMBERS; SNITTERFIELD; WROXALL.)

Shakespeare Allusion Book. See 'CENTURIE OF PRAYSE'.

Shakespeare Association. Was founded in 1916 by Sir Israel Gollancz, to promote the study, interpretation, and appreciation of Shakespeare. It arranged lectures and meetings for the promotion of Shakespeare studies, and published monographs, books, and facsimiles. Its series of Quarto facsimiles is in progress, now published by the Clarendon Press, Oxford.

Shakespeare Association of America. See UNITED STATES.

Shakespeare Birthplace Trust. Formed in 1847 with the purchase of the Birthplace (q.v.). The Chairman of the Governing Body is Denis Flower, and in addition to Life and Ex-Officio Trustees there are representatives from the Universities of Oxford, Cambridge, London, and Birmingham. The Director is Levi Fox. In 1961 they began the building of a new library (there are 20,000 volumes) and study centre flanking the west side of the Birthplace garden, to commemorate the 400th anniversary of Shakespeare's birth in 1964.

Shakespeare Festivals. What might have been the first Stratford Shakespeare Festival was thwarted by the puritanical corporation, who in 1622 paid the King's Men 6s. not to play in the town. The first Festival, therefore, was Garrick's Jubilee (q.v.) of 1769. Then in 1824 the Shakespeare Club was formed in Stratford to organize an annual celebration of the poet's birthday with a Jubilee every third year. A theatre was built in New Place garden and opened in 1827 with a performance of *As You Like It*, but the venture was unsuccessful. The last triennial Jubilee was in 1830, and in 1872 the theatre was demolished.

Meanwhile, the tercentenary of Shakespeare's birth had been celebrated in 1864. Financially the festival was a failure, yet it led to the building of the first Memorial Theatre and the annual Stratford Festivals that began in 1879. These lasted for only a few weeks, and it was not until 1933, after the building of the present theatre, that they were extended to six months.

The idea of the Festival has spread. The East African Shakespeare Festival was established before the last war; in 1947 Poland organized a great 'Konkurs Szekspirowski', and there is a Festival at Verona. In Canada the Earle Grey Players (SS, 10) ran a Festival at Toronto, 1949–58, and in 1953 the first Festival was celebrated at Stratford, Ontario. In the U.S.A. there are Festivals at Ashland (Oregon), San Diego, Antioch, Hofstra College (in J. C. Adams's replica of the Globe), Memphis, Philadelphia, Topeka. The New York Shakespeare Festival Company, established by Joseph Papp, performs in an open-air theatre in Central Park, with all seats free; and at Stratford, Conn., is the American Shakespeare Festival Theatre and Academy. (See SQ, I, VI, VII.)

Shakespeare Gallery. A picture gallery established by John Boydell in Pall Mall, London, in 1789. It contained paintings of scenes from Shakespeare by Reynolds, West, Smirke, Peters, Fuseli and many other well-known artists of the day. It failed in 1804, and the pictures were sold by auction. Engravings of many of them can be seen in Stratford; the allegorical group by Thomas Banks, which graced the pediment of the Gallery, is in New Place garden. (See John Boydell, *The Shakespeare Gallery*, 2 vols., 1803.)

Shakespeare-Gesellschaft. See DEUTSCHE; AUSTRIA.

Shakespeare Institute, Stratford-upon-Avon, was established in 1951 by Professor Allardyce Nicoll, who directed its work until his retirement in 1961. It is a centre for postgraduate study of 16th- and 17th-century life and literature, and it is part of Birmingham University. It is housed in Mason Croft, formerly the home of Marie Corelli, and also has a building on the University site at Edgbaston. The Institute has a large collection of microfilms and microprints, *Shakespeare Survey* was edited there (1951–61), and it is the scene of the biennial Shakespeare Conference.

Shakespeare Memorial Library. See BIRMINGHAM.

Shakespeare Memorial Theatre. See ROYAL SHAKESPEARE THEATRE.

'Shakespeare Miscellany' (*Shekspirovski Sbornik*), the organ of the Shakespeare Cabinet of the U.S.S.R., a branch of the All-Russian Theatre Society. Vol. 1 was published in 1948.

'Shakespeare Quarterly.' Since 1950, the organ of the Shakespeare Association of America, edited by J. G. McManaway and published in January, April, July, October. (See UNITED STATES.)

Shakespeare Society. The first Shakespeare Society was founded in 1840 by J. P. Collier, with a council that included the scholars G. L. Craik, A. Dyce, J. O. Halliwell (-Phillipps) and Charles Knight. In addition to their *Papers* (1844–5–7–9), the Society published a mass of original material: old plays and documents, some of the most important being Dyce's edition of *Sir Thomas More*, Peter Cunningham's *Accounts of the Revels*, and Collier's *Alleyn Papers, Henslowe's Diary*, and *Extracts from the Registers of the Stationers' Company*. Unfortunately, Collier inserted forged entries in his material, the Society was discredited, and came to an end in 1853. (See NEW SHAKSPERE SOCIETY.)

'Shakespeare Survey,' 'an Annual Survey of Shakespearian Study and Production', edited by Allardyce Nicoll, was first published in 1948. It is issued under the sponsorship of Birmingham University, Manchester University, the Shakespeare Memorial Theatre and the Shakespeare Birthplace Trust, and assisted by a grant from the Rockefeller Foundation. The core of each volume consists of a series of articles devoted to some particular aspect of Shakespearian study, introduced by a general survey designed to indicate what the past fifty years have contributed to this selected field of investigation. In 1966 (vol. 19) Kenneth Muir succeeded as editor.

Shakespeare Tercentenary Festival. This was celebrated at Stratford in 1864 in a Grand Duodecagonal Pavilion erected between New Place and the Church, where a circle of poplars now stands. Festivities began with a banquet on 23 April, and after performances of *Twelfth Night, Comedy of Errors, Romeo and Juliet* and *As You Like It*, concluded with a Fancy Dress Ball. This was followed by a 'People's Week', which included performances of *Othello* and *Much Ado*, a pageant and an abortive ascent of 'Coxwell's Monstre Balloon'. The Chairman of the Committee was the Mayor, E. F. Flower, whose exertions, and those of his son, C. E. Flower, led to the building of the first Shakespeare Memorial Theatre, opened in 1879. (See R. E. Hunter, *Shakespeare, Stratford, and the Tercentenary Festival*, 1864.)

Shallow, Robert, once of Clement's Inn, now a 'Country Iustice' (F) on the Cotswolds. In *2 Henry IV*, he supplies Falstaff, whom he claims as an old London acquaintance, with recruits (III, ii). On his return from his campaign, Falstaff stays with Shallow, and borrows from him £1,000 on the security of Henry V's accession (V, i, iii and v).

In *The Merry Wives*, Shallow, still Justice of the Peace in the county of Gloucester, with a 'dozen white luces' in his coat of arms, threatens to make a Star-chamber matter of Falstaff's beating his men, killing his deer, and breaking open his lodge (I, i). He tries to secure Anne Page for his cousin Slender (III, iv; V, ii).

(Richard Davies (q.v.), *c.* 1700, was the first to mention the episode of Shakespeare's 'stealing venison and Rabbits particularly from Sr Lucy', and to identify Lucy with 'his Justice Clodpate', or Shallow. Leslie Hotson, however, in his *Shakespeare versus Shallow*, 1931, identifies him with Justice William Gardiner (q.v.).)

Shank, John. One of the 'Principall Actors' in Shakespeare's plays (see p. 90). James Wright says he was a comedian. In 1635 he told Lord Chamberlain Pembroke that he was 'an old man in this quality, who in his youth first served your noble father, and after that the late Queene Elizabeth, then King James, and now his royall Majestye'. Before 1603, therefore, he had been a member of Pembroke's and of Queen Elizabeth's companies. He is listed with Prince Henry's-Elector Palatine's in 1610 and 1613, and may have joined the King's in 1615 to replace the comedian Robert Armin who died in that year. He is first mentioned in their patent of March 1619, and thereafter in official and actor lists until 1631. In 1605 he lived in Southwark, but afterwards in Golden Lane, and he died in January 1636. (See 'SHARERS' PAPERS'.)

Sharer. A full member of a company of actors, and a part owner of their joint stock. He received his share of the profits of the company, generally the theatre entrance money and half that of the galleries, from which had to be deducted their expenses, including the payment of hired actors. A sharer in a company must be distinguished from a sharer in a theatre, or housekeeper, though sharers were sometimes, like Shakespeare, housekeepers as well. (See ACTORS' COMPANIES.)

'Sharers' Papers.' When John Heminge died in 1630, his theatre shares passed to his son William, who sold, apparently secretly, three shares in the Globe and two in the Blackfriars to John Shank for £506. This sale led, in 1635, to the Petition to Lord Chamberlain Pembroke of the King's Men Benfield, Pollard, and Swanston for the right to buy shares, and Shank was ordered to sell them one share in each theatre. Cuthbert Burbage's *Answer* to the Lord Chamberlain tells us much about the theatres and Shakespeare's holdings in them:

The father of vs Cutbert and Richard Burbage was the first builder of Playhowses, and was himselfe in his younger yeeres a Player. The Theater hee built with many Hundred poundes taken vp at interest. The players that liued in those first times had onely the proffits arising from the dores, but now the players receaue all the commings in at the dores to themselues and halfe the Galleries from the Houskepers. Hee built this house vpon leased ground, by which meanes the landlord and Hee had a great suite in law, and by his death, the like troubles fell on vs, his sonnes; wee then bethought vs of altering from thence, and at like expence built the Globe with more summes of money taken vp at interest, which lay heauy on vs many yeeres, and to our selues wee ioyned those deserueing men, Shakspere, Hemings, Condall, Philips and others partners in the profittes of that they call the House, but makeing the leases for twenty-one yeeres hath beene the destruction of our selues and others, for they dyeing at the expiration of three or four yeeres of their lease, the subsequent yeeres became dissolued to strangers, as by marrying with their widdowes, and the like by their Children. Thus, Right Honorable, as concerning the Globe, where wee our selues are but lessees.

Now for the Blackfriers that is our inheritance, our father purchased it at extreme rates and made it into a playhouse with great charge and troble, which after was leased out to one Euans that first sett up the Boyes commonly called the Queenes Majesties Children of the Chappell. In processe of time the boyes growing vp to bee men, which were Vnderwood, Field, Ostler, and were taken to strengthen the Kings service, and the more to strengthen the service, the boyes dayly wearing out, it was considered that house would bee as fitt for our selues, and soe purchased the lease remaining from Evans with our money, and placed men Players, which were Hemings, Condall, Shakspeare, &c.

Sharpe, Richard. A boy actor with the King's Men. He played the Duchess in their revival of *The Duchess of Malfi*, *c.* 1620.

Sharpham, Edward (1576–1608), a Devonshire man of the Middle Temple, and author of two extant comedies, both written for the Revels Children: *The Fleir*, 1606; and *Cupid's Whirligig*, 1607. *The Fleir* (q.v.) helps to date *King Lear*.

Shaw, George Bernard (1856–1950), has some lively things to say about

Shakespeare, notably in his Prefaces to *The Dark Lady of the Sonnets*, *Caesar and Cleopatra* and *St Joan*, and he has rewritten the last act of *Cymbeline*. He had little respect for Shakespeare's intellect, but a great reverence for his poetry. 'Shakespeare's power lies in his enormous command of word-music, which gives fascination to his most blackguardly repartees, and sublimity to his hollowest platitudes.' (See Edwin Wilson, *Shaw on Shakespeare*.)

Shaw, Julius (1571–1629), one of the witnesses of Shakespeare's will, whose house was next to that later occupied by Thomas Nash, and therefore next but one to New Place. Shaw married Anne Boyes and in 1597 took a 21-year lease of the house. He was a wool merchant and also dealt in building materials, with which he supplied the Corporation, to which he was elected in 1603. In 1616, the year of his signing Shakespeare's will as witness, he was bailiff. His colleagues speak of his honesty and fidelity, and he was probably an intimate friend of Shakespeare.

'Sheep-shearing, The: or Florizel and Perdita.' An adaptation of part of *The Winter's Tale*, by McNamara Morgan (q.v.).

Sheldon Folio. A fine copy of the First Folio of Shakespeare, in the 17th century owned by the Sheldons of Long Compton, Warwickshire. It was apparently bought by William Sheldon in 1628 for £3 15s. 0d. It is important, as it shows that *Romeo and Juliet* was originally meant to be followed by *Troilus and Cressida*, whereas it is followed by *Timon*, *T.C.* being inserted at the last moment as the first of the Tragedies. This entailed cancelling the leaf (pp. 77–8) on the recto or front of which was printed the conclusion of *R.J.* and on the verso or back the beginning of *T.C.* In the Sheldon copy this cancelled leaf is bound in after the first leaf of *T.C.* (See BURDETT-COUTTS.)

Shelton, Thomas (fl. 1612–20), translator of *Don Quixote*, about whose life little is known, though he seems to have been related to his patron, the 2nd Earl of Suffolk, and engaged in Catholic intrigues with Spain. The first part of *The Delightful History of the Wittie Knight, Don Quishote* was registered in January 1611 and published in 1612, though Shelton claims to have translated it five or six years earlier. In 1620 he published the second part with a revised edition of the first. The lost play of *Cardenio*, registered in 1653 as by Fletcher and Shakespeare, was presumably taken from the story of Cardenio and Lucinda in Shelton's translation.

Shepherd. 1. In *1 Henry VI*, father of Joan of Arc. When Joan denies his parentage he tells her captors to burn her as 'hanging is too good'. (v, iv.) (In Holinshed he is called 'a sorie shepherd, James of Arc'.)

2. In *The Winter's Tale*, 'reputed Father of Perdita' (F). He discovers the baby Perdita by the seaside, and brings her up as his daughter. He is condemned to death by Polixenes for allowing her to meet Florizel, and flies with the lovers to Sicilia where he and his son are created 'gentlemen born'. (He is the Porrus of Greene's *Pandosto*.)

Sheridan, Richard Brinsley (1751–1816), dramatist, was the third son of Thomas and Frances Sheridan. In 1776–8, he and Thomas Linley and Dr Ford paid Garrick £70,000 for Drury Lane theatre. Twice during Sheridan's ownership it had to be rebuilt: in 1791–4 because it was unsafe, and again in 1809 after the Great Fire. J. P. Kemble was manager for Sheridan from 1788 to 1802. (See 'REHEARSAL, THE'.)

Sheridan, Thomas (1719–88), actor, was born in Dublin and educated at Westminster and Trinity College, Dublin. His first stage appearance in London was at Covent Garden in 1744, where he played Hamlet and other leading parts, and came to be considered, after Garrick, one of the best actors of his time. He wrote, and himself played the lead in *Coriolanus, or The Roman Matron*, adapted from Shakespeare and James Thomson's *Coriolanus*, and produced at Covent Garden in 1754. In later life he devoted himself to educational reform, though he found time to help his son in the management of Drury Lane. He married Frances Chamberlain, author of *The Discovery*, produced by Garrick at Drury Lane in 1763.

Shirley, Anthony (1565–*c.* 1635). An adventurer who fought in the Netherlands, raided Africa and Central America, served as a volunteer in Italy, was knighted by Henry of Navarre, created admiral of a fleet by the King of Spain, and a prince by the Shah of Persia. His younger brother, Robert, accompanied him to Persia and stayed there when Anthony returned to England in 1599 (he met Kempe in Rome in 1601). The fantastic adventures of the Shirley brothers may have inspired the Persian allusions in *Twelfth Night*. John Day wrote a play, registered June 1607, called 'The Travailes of the three English Brothers. Sir Thomas, Sir Anthony, Mr Robert Shirley. As it is now play'd by her Maiesties Seruants', 'at the Curten'.

Shirley, James (1596–1666). Last of the Elizabethan dramatists, in that he was the last to be born in Elizabeth's reign; in the words of Lamb, 'he was the last of a great race, all of whom spoke nearly the same language, and had a set of moral feelings and notions in common'. He was born in London, educated at Merchant Taylors', St John's, Oxford, and Catherine Hall, Cambridge, ordained, converted to Rome, and turned schoolmaster. Before the closing of the theatres in 1642 he had written more than thirty plays, and taken part in the attack on the Puritan Prynne. During the Civil War he served the King. According to Anthony Wood, he and his wife died of fright and exposure after the Great Fire of 1666.

Among his best works are the tragedies *The Traitor* (1631) and *The Cardinal* (1641), the last great play of the epoch that began with Marlowe and the University Wits, and the comedies *The Lady of Pleasure* (1635) and *The Royal Master* (1638). Though his flight is never very high, it is steady, and his comedies anticipate those of the Restoration. He wrote the fine masque, *The Triumph of Peace* (1633), produced by Inigo Jones with music by Lawes, but is best known by the lyric 'The glories of our blood and state' at the end of his *Contention of Ajax and Ulysses* (1659).

Shore. See EDWARD IV.

Shoreditch. The London district north of the City walls and east of Finsbury Fields. Shoreditch High Street runs north from Bishopsgate, and on its west side stood the Curtain and the Theatre.

Short Lines. Incomplete blank verse-lines, in which there are fewer than five feet. These are sometimes the result of cuts, or of errors in printing; Wilson stresses them as evidence of revision. But Shakespeare often used short lines for exclamations, greetings, farewells, and so on, and also for certain effects, as to indicate a pause; cf. *Richard III* (IV, iv):

Meantime, but think how I may do thee good,
And be inheritor of thy desire.
Farewell till soon. [*Exit Tyrrel.*
The son of Clarence have I pent up close ...

Short lines become commoner as Shakespeare's verse develops, when as often as not speeches end within a line, which is not always completed by the next speaker; cf. *Antony and Cleopatra* (II, ii):

ANT. I am not married, Caesar: let me hear Agrippa further speak.
AGR. To hold you in perpetual amity ...

Very roughly, the early plays average 1 short line in 40 of normal blank verse, the later tragedies 1 in 15, the romances 1 in 25. *A Midsummer Night's Dream* and *King John* are abnormal in having a proportion of only 1 in 150. (See MISLINEATION.)

Short, Peter (d. 1603). Printer at the Star, on Bread Street Hill, 1589–1603. He printed,

1595. Q1 *3 Henry VI* (*The True Tragedy*) for T. Millington. This is a 'bad' Quarto, but the piracy was Millington's, not Short's.

1598. Q1 *1 Henry IV* for Andrew Wise.

1599. O1 *Lucrece* for John Harrison.

1599. O3 *Venus and Adonis* for William Leake.

He also printed the *Palladis Tamia* of Meres (1598), and finished the printing of Foxe's *Acts and Monumentes* (1596–7). (See LOWNES.)

Shorthand. The art of shorthand was being developed in Shakespeare's lifetime. Timothy Bright's *Characterie* was published in 1588, Peter Bales's *Brachygraphie* in 1590 and John Willis's *Stenographie* in 1602. It used to be thought that some of the 'bad' and poor Quartos (e.g. *Lear*) were shorthand reports taken in the theatre, but G. I. Duthie's *Elizabethan Shorthand* (1949) seems to prove that there was no adequate way of reporting plays by shorthand in Shakespeare's time. (See REPORTED TEXTS; 'IF YOU KNOW NOT ME'.)

Shottery. A village one mile west of Stratford, where Anne Hathaway is supposed to have lived before she married Shakespeare (see HEWLAND). Fulk Sandells and John Richardson, sureties to Shakespeare's marriage bond, and overseer and witness respectively of Richard Hathaway's will, 1581, came from Shottery. At the beginning of 1598 Shakespeare seems to have contemplated buying some forty acres of land in Shottery, for on 24 January Abraham Sturley wrote to Richard Quiney: 'Mr Shaksper, is willinge to disburse some monei vpon some od yardeland or other att Shottri or neare about vs.'

Shutters. See FLATS.

Shylock. The chief character in *The Merchant of Venice* (q.v.). The name probably comes from the Hebrew *shalach*, the *cormorant* of Leviticus xi, 17, and Deuteronomy xiv, 17. (See LOPEZ; GRANVILLE; MACKLIN; HEINE.)

'Sicilian Usurper, The.' See TATE.

Sicinius Velutus. In *Coriolanus*, he and Junius Brutus (q.v.) are tribunes of the people.

Siddons, Sarah (1755–1831), the great tragic actress, was the first child of the strolling player Roger Kemble, and sister of John Philip and Charles Kemble. She was born in a public-house, The Shoulder of Mutton, in Brecon, began acting as a child, and in 1773 married the actor William Siddons. Her success in Cheltenham, where she appeared in 1774 as Belvidera in *Venice Preserved*, led to her being engaged by Garrick at Drury Lane, but she was not well received and spent the years 1778–82 at Bath. Her next appearance, at Drury Lane in October 1782, as Isabella in *The Fatal Marriage*, was a triumph and established her as the greatest tragic actress of her time. In 1785 she appeared for the first time in her most famous part, that of Lady Macbeth, and in 1788 in her favourite part of Queen Katharine in the production of *Henry VIII* by her brother John, the new manager of Drury Lane for Sheridan. Her other most famous Shakespearean parts were Desdemona, Ophelia, Volumnia, Constance in *King John* and Rosalind, though she did not excel in comedy. Dr Johnson promised to hobble to see her whenever she played Katharine, and wrote his name on the hem of her garment in Reynolds's painting of her as The Tragic Muse. She retired from the stage in 1819, and was buried in Paddington churchyard in 1831. (See MONUMENT.)

Sidney, Sir Philip (1554–86), son of Sir Henry Sidney and Lady Mary Dudley, the Protector Northumberland's daughter and Leicester's sister, was born at Penshurst and educated at Shrewsbury School and Christ Church, Oxford. He spent the greater part of the years 1572–7 in travel, after which he turned to literature, and became one of the Leicester House circle, known as the Areopagus, who advocated the introduction of classical metres into English. There he met Spenser, who dedicated his *Shepherd's Calendar* to him in 1579, and about this time he wrote his *Astrophel and Stella* sonnets (Sidney is Astrophel, and Stella is Penelope Devereux, daughter of the 1st Earl of Essex), the *Apology for Poetry*, and began the *Arcadia*, written 'only for and only to' his devoted sister Mary, now Countess of Pembroke, to whose home at Wilton he retired in 1580. In 1583 he was knighted and married Frances Walsingham; in the following year he was appointed Governor of Flushing, and served under his uncle Leicester in the campaign of 1586, in which he was mortally wounded at Zutphen. Spenser commemorated him in his pastoral elegy, *Astrophel*. (See GREVILLE, FULKE.)

On 24 March 1586 Sidney wrote to Walsingham from Utrecht,

> I wrote to yow a letter by Will, my lord of Lester's jesting plaier, enclosed in a letter to my wife, and I never had answer thereof ... I since find that the knave delivered the letters to my ladi of Lester.

This has been taken as a reference to Shakespeare, but as Will Kempe was in the Netherlands at this time it almost certainly refers to him. Sidney's *Stella* sonnets were published in 1591, and must have influenced Shakespeare in the writing of his sequence. From the *Arcadia* he may have taken some of the names for *Cymbeline*, *The Winter's Tale*, and that of Pyrocles for his *Pericles, Prince of Tyre*. More important, the sub-plot of *King Lear* comes from the story, in Book 2, of the King of Paphlagonia who was deprived of his kingdom and his sight by his unnatural son.

In the *Apology*, or *Defence* as it was called in the edition of 1598, Sidney maintains the classical position, insists on the necessity of the unities in drama, deplores tragi-comedy, and ridicules the abuse of 'place' and 'time':

> Our Tragedies, and Comedies (not without cause cried out against), observing rules neither of honest civility nor of skilful Poetry, excepting *Gorboduc* (again, I say, of those that I have seen), which notwithstanding, as it is full of stately speeches and well sounding Phrases, climbing to the height of *Seneca* his style, and as full of notable morality, which it doth most delightfully teach, and so obtain the very end of Poesy; yet in truth it is very defectious in the circumstances: which grieveth me, because it might not remain an exact model of all Tragedies. For it is faulty both in Place and Time, the two necessary companions of all corporal actions. For where the stage should always represent but one place, and the uttermost time presupposed in it should be, both by *Aristotle's* precept and common reason, but one day: there is both many days and many places, inartificially imagined. But if it be so in *Gorboduc*, how much more in all the rest? where you shall have *Asia* of the one side, and *Afric* of the other, and so many other under-kingdoms, that the Player, when he cometh in, must ever begin with telling where he is; or else the tale will not be conceived. Now ye shall have three Ladies walk to gather flowers, and then we must believe the stage to be a Garden. By and by, we hear news of shipwreck in the same place, and then we are to blame, if we accept it not for a Rock. Upon the back of that, comes out a hideous Monster, with fire and smoke, and then the miserable beholders are bound to take it for a Cave. While in the meantime, two Armies fly in, represented with four swords and bucklers, and then what hard heart will not receive it for a pitched field?
>
> Now, of time they are much more liberal. For ordinary it is that two young Princes fall in love: after many traverses, she is got with child, delivered of a fair boy; he is lost, groweth a man, falls in love, and is ready to get another child, and all this in two hours' space: which how absurd it is in sense, even sense may imagine, and Art hath taught, and all ancient examples justified: and at this day, the ordinary Players in Italy will not err in.

Signatures. There are six undisputed signatures of Shakespeare:

1612	May 11	Willm̃ Shaksp	Deposition in Belott-Mountjoy suit
1613	Mar. 10	William Shakspẽ	Conveyance of Blackfriars Gatehouse
1613	Mar. 11	Wm Shakspe	Mortgage of Blackfriars Gatehouse
1616	Mar. 25	William Shakspere	on the three sheets of his will
		Willm̃ Shakspere	
		By me William Shakspeare	

The 'By me' on the third sheet of the will is generally thought to be Shakespeare's. The writing is the awkward English script, akin to modern German script, though there is a trace of the flowing Italian hand that was beginning to replace it in the long s. From these signatures Sir E. Maunde Thompson concluded that part of the manuscript play of *Sir Thomas More* (q.v.) is in Shakespeare's hand. In his opinion the signatures on the will are clearly those of a sick man. More than one hundred so-called signatures of Shakespeare have been 'discovered', most of them forged by W. H. Ireland. See E. M. Thompson, *Shakespeare's Handwriting;* Tannenbaum, *Problems in Shakespeare's Penmanship.* (See also HALL, W.; MONTAIGNE; LAMBARDE.)

Silence. In *2 Henry IV*, a country justice and cousin of Shallow. He has a wife, a daughter Ellen and a son William at Oxford (III, ii). In v, iii he gets drunk, sings, and has to be carried to bed. Shakespeare seems to have spelt the word 'scilens'.

Silius. In *Antony and Cleopatra*, an officer in Ventidius's army. He appears only in III, i, when he urges Ventidius to pursue the defeated Parthians.

Silvia. In *The Two Gentlemen of Verona* (q.v.), 'beloued of Valentine' (F), and daughter of the Duke of Milan. (She is the Celia of the *Diana* of Montemayor (q.v.), and dies of love for the disguised Felismena (Julia).)

Silvius. In *As You Like It*, a shepherd whose love for Phebe is unrequited. However, she marries him when Rosalind reveals her sex. (The Montanus of Lodge's *Rosalynde.*)

Simmes, Valentine. Printer, in business 1585–1622. He printed:

1597	Q1	*Richard III*	for A. Wise.
1597	Q1	*Richard II*	for A. Wise.
1598	Q2	*Richard II*	for A. Wise.
1598	Q3	*Richard II*	for A. Wise.
1600	Q	*2 Henry IV*	for Wise and Aspley.
1600	Q	*Much Ado*	for Wise and Aspley.
1600	Q2	*2 Henry VI*	for T. Millington. A reprint of Millington's 'bad' Quarto of *The First Part of the Contention*, 1594.
1603	Q1	*Hamlet*	for Ling and Trundell. This is the 'bad' Quarto, for the piracy of which, however, Simmes would not be responsible.
1604	Q3	*1 Henry IV*	for M. Law.

Simmes was the best printer of Shakespeare's plays, *Much Ado* being 'one of the few Shakespeare play books that was decently printed' (McKerrow). Yet he was constantly in trouble for printing unauthorized books, and in 1622 was forbidden to work as a master printer.

Simonides. In *Pericles*, King of Pentapolis and father of Thaisa, in Act II. He crowns Pericles victor of the tournament, then, as Prospero calls Ferdinand traitor before giving him Miranda, so does Simonides call Pericles, to test him before giving him Thaisa.

Simpcox, Saunder. In *2 Henry VI*, an impostor who claims to have been cured of blindness at St Alban's shrine. Gloucester exposes his fraud, and 'cures' him of his pretended lameness as well, by having him whipped so that he runs away (II, i). (The story is in neither Holinshed nor Halle, but is first told by Sir T. More in his *Dialogue concerning Heresies.*)

Simple. In *The Merry Wives*, Slender's servant. Evans sends him with a letter asking Mistress Quickly to help Slender's wooing of Anne Page; Dr Caius discovers him and sends him back with a challenge to Evans. Falstaff makes fun of him in IV, v.

Simpson, Percy (1865–1962), educated at Selwyn, Cambridge, was a schoolmaster 1887–1913, becoming English Lecturer at Oxford in 1913, and Fellow of Oriel in 1921. Author of *Shakespearean Punctuation* and editor, with C. H. Herford, of the Works of Jonson. (See PUNCTUATION.)

Simpson, Richard (1820–76), Shakespeare scholar, was educated at Oriel, Oxford, and became vicar of Mitcham, Surrey, but resigned in 1845 on his conversion to Roman Catholicism. He was elected to the committee of the New Shakspere Society in 1874, when he had already published *An Introduction to the Philosophy of Shakespeare's Sonnets* (1868), and *The School of Shakespeare, No. 1* (1872). This was the first part of a reprint of Elizabethan plays in which it was thought that Shakespeare had some part. The complete work was issued in 2 vols. in 1878, with a preface by F. J. Furnivall, and included *Fair Em, Jack Drum's Entertainment, Histrio-mastix*, etc. In 1871 (*Notes and Queries*) Simpson claimed that part of *Sir Thomas More* (q.v.) was in Shakespeare's handwriting. He was one of the first to discuss *The Politics of Shakspere's Historical Plays* (*N.S.S. Trans.* 1874 p. 396):

> ... there was a political current in Shakspere's mind, which in the days of Elizabeth led him into opposition. If he welcomed the accession of James, he was soon undeceived, and when he set his hand to the history of Rome, the winter of his discontent had become gloomier than before. His tragedies point to the same conclusion, and show that the sentiments of the 66th Sonnet, and of Hamlet's 'To be or not to be,' were his real ones.

Simrock, Karl Joseph (1802–76), German poet and scholar, was born and educated at Bonn, where he became lecturer and professor, and where he died. In 1813 he published *Die Quellen des Shakespeare in Novellen, Märchen und Sagen*, the first collection of source material since Charlotte Lennox's *Shakespear Illustrated*, 1753–4. Simrock also translated Shakespeare's poems and many of the plays.

Sincler (Sinklo), John. An actor who first appears in small parts, e.g. Keeper, Soldier, Julio, in *The Seven Deadly Sins* (q.v.), probably a Strange's play, *c.* 1590. The F stage-directions of *3 Henry VI* show that 'Sinklo' played the First Keeper in III, i, possibly with Pembroke's, who acted it *c.* 1592. Similar directions (probably Shakespeare's) in F show that he was 'a Player' in the Induction to *T. of Shrew*, and in Q *2 Henry IV* that he was 'First Beadle' in IV, i. He is last noticed as playing in the King's Men's version of *The Malcontent*, 1604. Sincler was, therefore, with the Chamberlain's-King's, possibly from its formation in 1594 until sometime after 1604, though he was never a sharer. Apparently he was the company's stock thin man, for whom Shakespeare created minor parts: e.g., Pinch and Shadow. (See JEFFES.)

'Sir John Oldcastle.' A play, the two parts of which were registered 11 August 1600:

> The first parte of the history of the life of Sir John Oldcastell lord Cobham. Item the second and last parte of the history of Sir John Oldcastell lord Cobham with his martyrdom.

The first part was published in the same year:

> The first part Of the true and honorable historie of the life of Sir John Old-castle, the good Lord Cobham. As it hath been lately acted by the right honorable the Earle of Notingham Lord high Admirall of England his seruants.

This was reprinted in 1619 (dated 1600), by W. Jaggard in his 'False Folio' as 'by William Shakespeare', and included in the Third Folio of 1664. But on 16 October 1599 Downton of the Admiral's acknowledged:

> Received by me Thomas Downton of Philip Henslowe, to pay Mr Monday, Mr Drayton, Mr Wilson, and Hathway, for The first part of the Lyfe of Sir Jhon Ouldcastell, and in earnest of the Second Pte. for the use of the company, ten pound.

The play was deservedly a success, and in November and December 1599 the following entries occur in Henslowe's *Diary*:

> Received of Mr Hinchelo for Mr Munday and the reste of the poets, at the playinge of Sir Jhon Oldcastell, the firste tyme, xs. as a gifte.
>
> Received of Mr Henslowe, for the use of the company, to pay Mr Drayton for the second parte of Sir Jhon Ouldcasell, foure pound.

On 12 March 1600 Henslowe paid 'the litel taylor' 30s. 'to macke thinges for the 2 pte of owldcastell', and in August 1602, 40s. 'unto Thomas Deckers for his adicions in Owldcastell'.

The second part has been lost but the two plays were obviously the Admiral's reply to the Chamberlain's two parts of *Henry IV*, giving a 'true and honorable historie' of Oldcastle (q.v.), in place of Shakespeare's Oldcastle-Falstaff. The prologue to *Oldcastle* makes this clear:

> It is no pamperd glutton we present,
> Nor aged Councellor to youthfull sinne.
> ... Let fair Truth be grac'te,
> Since forg'de inuention former time defac'te.

'Sir Thomas More.' A manuscript play, edited by Dyce and printed for the Shakespeare Society in 1844, and by Greg for the Malone Society in 1911. The MS., now in a bad state, consisted originally of sixteen leaves, or thirty-two pages, the last of which is blank. It was censored by Edmund Tilney, Master of the Revels 1579–1610, and then revised: three leaves were torn out, and seven new leaves and two scraps inserted, containing additions by five different hands. Greg called the original scribe S, and the five revisers A–E. These have been identified as follows:

- S, Anthony Munday, the original scribe and part author.
- A, Henry Chettle, scribe and author of Addition I which he revised.
- B, Thomas Heywood? (identified by Tannenbaum).
- C, the professional scribe of the plot of *The Seven Deadly Sins*.
- D, Shakespeare? This addition is three pages, making 147 lines in which More pacifies the anti-alien riots of 1517.
- E, Thomas Dekker.

Probably Munday, Chettle, and B (Heywood?) were the original authors, and D (Shakespeare?) and Dekker revisers. If so, it looks like an Admiral's play, as Munday, Chettle and Dekker all worked for Henslowe, though it is not known that they did so before 1598. Greg suggests as date, *c.* 1593, when Shakespeare might have worked for the Strange-Admiral combination. But other evidence suggests a date, perhaps as late as 1600, when it is not easy to find a reason why Shakespeare should revise an Admiral's play.

As early as 1871–2, Richard Simpson and James Spedding, basing their conclusions partly on style, had claimed that part of the play was by Shakespeare, and in 1916 Sir E. Maunde Thompson, the palaeographer, after comparing the MS. with the six signatures of Shakespeare, pronounced that one of the Additions, that of D, was in Shakespeare's handwriting, but added that the case for Shakespeare's authorship must rest on 'the convergence of a number of independent lines of argument – palaeographic, orthographic, linguistic, stylistic, psychological – and not on any one alone'.

This evidence was forthcoming in *Shakespeare's Hand in the Play of Sir Thomas More* (by A. W. Pollard and others, 1923). Wilson claims that both D and Shakespeare were old-fashioned spellers, and that many misprints in the early texts were probably due to Shakespeare's forming certain letters in the same way as D; and R. W. Chambers shows that the political philosophy of Shakespeare and D was similar: a respect for order and rank, a sympathetic understanding of the mob, and a belief that it is susceptible to oratory. Then in 1935 Caroline Spurgeon in her *Shakespeare's Imagery* showed the resemblance between the imagery of Shakespeare and D; compare, for example, Sir Thomas More, Coriolanus and Ulysses:

For other ruffians, as their fancies wrought
With self same hand, self reasons, and self
  right,
Would shark on you, and men like
  ravenous fishes
Would feed on one another.

What's the matter,
That in these several places of the city
You cry against the noble senate, who,
Under the gods, keep you in awe, which
  else
Would feed on one another?

And appetite, an universal wolf,
So doubly seconded with will and power,
Must make perforce an universal prey,
And last eat up himself.

D is either Shakespeare or an author whose writing, spelling, psychology, verse and imagery closely resemble his; if he is not Shakespeare, it is difficult to say who he is. It is clear that three pages of writing in Shakespeare's hand, or in one very similar, are an invaluable aid to textual critics. (See SPELLING; SS, 2; SS, 8, 102; GOODALE.)

Sisson, Charles Jasper (1885–1966). Shakespeare scholar, editor of *The Modern Language Review* 1926-55, Professor of English Literature at London University 1928–51, and later Assistant Director and Senior Fellow of the Shakespeare Institute. An authority on Elizabethan life and thought, he was author of *Lost Plays of Shakespeare's Age*, *The Mythical Sorrows of Shakespeare* etc. and editor of a one-volume edition of the *Complete Works* (1954).

Siward. In *Macbeth*, Earl of Northumberland and uncle of Malcolm. In Act v he leads the force of ten thousand English sent by Edward the Confessor to help Malcolm against Macbeth. His son, young Siward, is killed in single combat with Macbeth.

Skeat, Walter William (1835–1912), philologist, became a Fellow of Christ's, Cambridge, and in 1878 Professor of Anglo-Saxon. He is best known for his Oxford edition of Chaucer and his *Etymological English Dictionary*. In 1875 he published *Shakespeare's Plutarch*, and in 1914, with A. L. Mayhew, a *Glossary of Tudor and Stuart Words*.

Slender. In *The Merry Wives*, a half-witted cousin of Shallow, who persuades him to pay court to Anne Page. He is incapable of speaking for himself, but his suit is favoured by Master Page, and it is arranged that he shall run away with Anne in the confusion of the baiting of Falstaff in Windsor Forest, and marry her. However, he runs off with 'a great lubberly boy'. (Hotson in his *Shakespeare versus Shallow* identifies Slender with William Wayte (q.v.).)

Sly, Christopher. The drunken tinker in the Induction to *The Taming of the Shrew* (q.v.), 'old Sly's son of Burton-heath, by birth a pedlar, by education a card-maker, by transmutation a bear-herd, and now by present profession a tinker'. In his drunken sleep he mentions

Stephen Sly and old John Naps of Greece
And Peter Turph and Henry Pimpernell.

There is a Christophero Sly in the source play, *A Shrew*, but there were also Slys in Stratford. Stephen Sly was one of the labourers set to dig a ditch by William Combe when he began the abortive Welcombe enclosure in 1615. (See BARTON-ON-THE-HEATH; HACKET; WINCOT.)

Sly, William (d. 1608). One of the 'Principall Actors' in Shakespeare's plays (see p. 90). He played Porrex in *The Seven Deadly Sins*, *c.* 1591, and may have joined the Chamberlain's on their formation in 1594, appearing in their first extant actor-list, 1598, and thereafter in all their lists until 1605. In that year he became a housekeeper of the Globe, and was appointed one of the executors and overseers of Augustine Phillips's will, in which he was left 'a boule of Silver' worth £5. In 1604 he appeared under his own name, with Burbage and others, in the Induction to the King's Men's version of *The Malcontent*, from an affected phrase in which Malone infers that he played Osric in *Hamlet*. He was one of the original housekeepers of the Blackfriars theatre in 1608, but died shortly afterwards, and was buried in St Leonard's, Shoreditch, from his house in Halliwell Street, on 16 August. By his nuncupative will of 4 August he left 'to Robert Brown his part of The Globe ... to James Saunder fortie pounds', and to Cuthbert Burbage his sword and hat. (See 'APOLOGY FOR ACTORS'.)

Smethwick, John (d. 1641). Bookseller. In 1607 Nicholas Ling transferred to him the copyright in *A Shrew*, *Love's Labour's Lost*, *Romeo and Juliet*, and *Hamlet*. He published,

1609 Q3 *Romeo and Juliet*.
1611 Q3 *Hamlet*. (Q4 without date; Q5 1637.)
1623 F1 'Printed at the Charges of W. Jaggard, Ed. Blount, I. Smith-weeke and W. Aspley.'
1632 F2 published by Allot, Smethwick, Aspley, Hawkins and Meighen.

Smethwick was in business 1596-1640. In his early days he was frequently fined for selling privileged books, but was Junior Warden of the Stationers' Company in 1631, Senior Warden 1635, and Master 1639. He was for a time a partner of William Jaggard's brother, John.

Smith, John Christopher (1712–95), musician, was the assistant and amanuensis of the blind Handel. He wrote the music for Garrick's operatic version of *The Tempest*, 1756.

Smith, Logan Pearsall (1865–1946), was born in U.S.A., educated at Harvard and Balliol, Oxford, and naturalized a British subject in 1913. At a time when scholars and critics were concerned mainly with Shakespeare as a man of the theatre, he preferred reading the plays to seeing them acted, and turned in his *On Reading Shakespeare* (1933) to the poetry. His anthology, *The Golden Shakespeare*, was published in 1949.

Smith, Ralph (b. 1578). A Stratford hatter, son of John Smith, alderman and vintner. (See LANE, JOHN.)

Smith, Wentworth. A dramatist about whom little is known, save that Henslowe records fifteen plays, now lost, in which he collaborated with Day, Chettle and others for the Admiral's and Worcester's, 1601–3. He may be the W. Smith, author of the extant *Hector of Germany* (published 1615). And he may be the author of *Locrine* (1595), *Thomas Lord Cromwell* (1602) and *The Puritan* (1607), three of the plays added to F3 and published originally as 'by W.S.', though it is improbable that one man wrote three such different plays. It is more probable that the initials were meant to suggest Shakespeare and attract buyers, at least of the last two.

Smith, William. A poet who published in 1596 a sequence of forty-eight sonnets, with three others addressed to Spencer, called *Chloris, or the Complaint of the passionate despised Shepheard*. In 1600 the Stationers' Register has the entry,

> 3 Januarij. Eleazar Edgar Entred for his copye vnder the handes of the Wardens. A booke called Amours by J D. with certen oy[r] sonnetes by W.S.

J. D. may be Sir John Davies, and W. S. may be William Smith, though William Shakespeare is also possible. The volume is unknown, and may not have been published.

Smith, the Weaver, in *2 Henry VI*, a follower of Cade, though with little faith in his claim to be a Mortimer (IV, ii and vii).

Smoking. See TOBACCO.

Snare. In *2 Henry IV*, one of the '2 Serieants' (F). See FANG.

Snitterfield. A village three miles north of Stratford, on one of the manors of which Robert Arden owned two farms, one of 100 acres with a house and cottage, the other of 60 acres with a house. Richard Shakespeare, the poet's grandfather, was the tenant of the second of these, 1528–60. He also farmed land on the other manor, belonging to Hales. John, the poet's father, was presumably born there (the Register begins only in 1561) and lived there until he moved to Stratford *c.* 1550. His brother Henry is traceable on the Hales manor, 1574–96.

There were other Shakespeares living in Snitterfield; on 10 March 1581 'Baptizatus fuet John filius Thome Shaxper'. Thomas is recorded as farming on the Hales estate, 1563–83, and there was an Anthony who may have been his brother, and the brother of John Shakespeare of Clifford Chambers, who died 1610 and left legacies to his brother Anthony, and to his nephew John, son of his brother Thomas.

Snodham, Thomas. Printer of Q2 (1613), *Thomas Lord Cromwell*, and O5 (1616), *Lucrece*. He was active 1603–25, married Elizabeth, sister of Cuthbert Burby, and died 1625.

Snout, Tom. In *A Midsummer Night's Dream*, an Athenian tinker, is cast as Pyramus' father (I, ii), though in fact he plays the part of Wall at the performance of the Interlude in V, i.

Snowden, George and Lionel. Printers, 1606–8, whose business was acquired by Nicholas Okes *c.* 1608. *King Lear* was registered by Butter and Busby 27 November 1607 and published in 1608, probably early in the year. The printer's name is not given on the title-page, only the Snowden-Okes device, so that either the Snowdens or Okes may have been responsible.

Snug. In *A Midsummer Night's Dream*, an Athenian joiner. As he is slow of study, he is given the part of Lion in the Interlude, as it is 'nothing but roaring'.

Soest Portrait. So called after the painter Gerard Soest or Zoust (b. 1637). In the 18th century it was 'in the collection of F. Wright, painter in Covent Garden', and made known to the world by J. Simon's engraving of it. James Granger (1723–76), the print-collector, says that Soest painted it in the reign of Charles II. It has recently been acquired by the Shakespeare Birthplace Trust. (See SS, 15.)

Soliloquy. An actor's address to the audience, a prolonged 'aside'; a convention accepted by Shakespeare, though used with greater skill and economy in the later plays. The effect may be comic, as in the soliloquies of Benedick and Malvolio. Sometimes the soliloquizer plays the part of narrator, as when Edgar (*Lear* II, iii) says that he is going to disguise himself, or of chorus commenting on the action, like Kent in the preceding scene. More often the soliloquy reveals character; in the early plays, quite simply, by a statement such as Richard III's 'I am determined to prove a villain'; in the later tragedies, much more subtly, by allowing the character to reveal himself by his thought, language, imagery, even by the rhythms of his speech. The tragic soliloquy is generally confined to the introspective characters: to Brutus, Hamlet, Macbeth; Antony and Coriolanus think outwards and do not confide in the audience.

According to Schücking, soliloquy is not always self-revelatory; for example, Prince Hal's explanation of his loose behaviour is only the old convention of assuring the audience that all will be well.

Solinus. In *The Comedy of Errors*, Duke of Ephesus. According to the law, he condemns to death Aegeon of Syracuse for landing in Ephesus, unless he can raise a ransom of 1,000 marks in the course of the day. In the last scene, when the errors are resolved, he pardons him.

Somers, Sir George (1554–1610), was born at Lyme Regis, saw much service at sea, was knighted 1603, and appointed admiral of the Virginia Company 1609. With Sir T. Gates (q.v.) he was wrecked on the Bermudas, to which he returned from Virginia in 1610, and died there from a 'surfeit of eating of a pig'. The Bermudas were also called the Somers or Summer Islands. (See JOURDAN; STRACHEY, WILLIAM.)

Somerset, Robert Carr, Earl of (*c.* 1590–1645). Scottish favourite of James I, who created him in rapid succession Viscount Rochester, Privy Councillor, Secretary, Earl of Somerset, and on 10 July 1614 Lord Chamberlain. He was deprived of this last office on 2 November 1615 for his part in the murder of Sir Thomas Overbury, and succeeded by the 3rd Earl of Pembroke on 23 December. Somerset was sent to the Tower, pardoned in 1624, but played no further part in history.

Somerset, Dukes of. In *Henry VI*. See BEAUFORT.

Somerset House. A palace built on the north bank of the Thames to the west of the City walls by the Protector Somerset, who was executed in 1552. It then reverted to the Crown, was altered by Inigo Jones, and pulled down at the end of the 18th century to be replaced by the present building, designed by Sir William Chambers (1726–96).

In 1604 the Spanish ambassador, the Constable of Castile, was lodged there during peace negotiations, and from 9 to 27 August, the King's Men, as Grooms of the Chamber, were in attendance. The Chamber Account reads:

> To Augustine Phillippes and John Hemynges for thallowaunce of themselves and tenne of theire ffellowes his ma^{tes} groomes of the chamber, and Players for waytinge and attendinge on his ma^{tes} service by comaundemente vppon the Spanishe Embassador at Som'sette howse the space of xviij dayes viz^{d} from the ixth day of Auguste 1604 vntill the xxvijth day of the same as appeareth by a bill thereof signed by the Lord Chamberlayne, xxj^{li}. xij^{s}.

No plays are recorded. Presumably Shakespeare was one of the Grooms on duty. Phillips and Heminge and ten of their fellows are noted, which seems to indicate that there were now twelve sharers in the company, which had therefore been increased from the nine in the Wardrobe Account of March 1604 for the supply of red cloth for the coronation procession. (See GROOMS OF THE CHAMBER.)

Somerville, Sir John. In *3 Henry VI*. He appears only in v, i, when he tells Warwick that Clarence and his forces are at hand.

Songs. Many of the songs introduced by Shakespeare into his plays are fragments of popular ballads, and it is not always possible to tell whether a song really is his or a later insertion. The following are almost certainly Shakespeare's (the date is approximately that of the play, though the songs may not be contemporary):

1594	*T.G.V.*	Who is Silvia? (IV, ii)
1594	*L.L.L.*	When daisies pied, (V, ii)
1595	*M.N.D.*	You spotted snakes, (II, ii)
1596	*M.V.*	Tell me, where is fancy bred? (III, ii)

1598	*M. Ado*	Sigh no more, ladies, (II, iii)
		Pardon, goddess of the night, (V, ii)
1599	*A.Y.L.I.*	Under the greenwood tree, (II, v)
		Blow, blow, thou winter wind, (II, vii)
		What shall he have that killed the deer? (IV, ii)
		It was a lover and his lass, (V, iii)
1600	*T.N.*	O mistress mine, (II, iii)
		Come away, come away, death, (II, iv)
		When that I was and a little tiny boy, (V, i)
1603	*M.M.*	Take, O take those lips away, (IV, i)
1609	*Cym.*	Hark, hark, the lark, (II, iii)
		Fear no more the heat o' the sun, (IV, ii)
1610	*W.T.*	When daffodils begin to peer, (IV, iii)
		Get you hence, for I must go. (IV, iv)
		Lawn as white as driven snow, (IV, iv)
1611	*Tempest*	Come unto these yellow sands (I, ii)
		Full fathom five thy father lies, (I, ii)
		Where the bee sucks, (V, i)
1612	*Hen. VIII*	Orpheus with his lute, (III, i)

It will be seen that the songs of 1594–1600 all come from comedies, and are rarely dramatically important. If there were no good singers in the company at the time, a man or a boy could be hired, and probably choir boys were brought in for *M.N.D.* and *The Merry Wives*, both written for special occasions. But there would tend to be more songs when there were good singers in the company; Robert Armin, for example, their new comedian, sang the songs in *Twelfth Night* (though 'Come away, death' seems originally to have been Viola's). The use made of song in 1600 suggests a reply to the renewed competition of the choir boys performing at the Blackfriars.

There are few songs in the Histories; *Henry VIII* is exceptional, but 'Orpheus with his lute' was written (possibly by Fletcher) when music, masque and spectacle were almost essential ingredients of a play.

The songs, so dramatically used, in the late tragedies (for example, those of the Fool (Armin) in *Lear*, the snatches of Ophelia, and the Willow Song of Desdemona) were for the most part popular songs of the day, and would be all the more effective for their familiarity.

In the romances Shakespeare turned again to the pure lyrics of his early comedies. (See MUSIC; JOHNSON, ROBERT; MORLEY; WILSON, JOHN; ARNE; SCHUBERT; SULLIVAN, ARTHUR SEYMOUR; C. Ing, *Elizabethan Lyrics*; SS, 15.)

SONNETS.

WRITTEN: The usually accepted date is 1592–8. The publication of Sidney's *Stella* sonnets in 1591 led to the Elizabethan vogue of sonneteering, which lasted 1592–8, during which period some twenty sonnet sequences were published. Some, probably most, possibly all, of Shakespeare's sonnets were written by 1598, when Meres refers to 'his sugred Sonnets among his priuate friends'. Versions of sonnets 138 and 144 were published in *The Passionate Pilgrim*, 1599. Parallels to the Sonnets are most frequent in *Venus and Adonis* and *Lucrece*, published 1593–4, and in the plays thought to have been written at this time: *Love's Labour's Lost, Romeo and Juliet, Richard II.*

On the other hand, Hotson, in *Shakespeare's Sonnets Dated*, argues ingeniously that Sonnets 107, 123, 124 were written by 1589, and on the assumption that the group 1–126 is chronological, that 'Shakespeare completed this main group of his sonnets by 1589.' If so, neither Southampton nor Pembroke, then aged 16 and 9, can well be Mr W. H., for if 104 is autobiographical, Shakespeare met his friend three years before writing that sonnet. (In 1899 Samuel Butler dated the series 1–126 between April 1585 and 1 December 1588.)

REGISTERED: (1600. '3 Januarij. Eleazar Edgar Entred for his copye vnder the handes of the Wardens. A booke called Amours by

J D. with certen sonnetes by W S.' The volume is unknown. J. D. may be Sir John Davies, and W. S. may be William Smith (q.v.) but possibly Shakespeare.)

1609. '20 Maij Thomas Thorpe Entred for his copie vnder thandes of master Wilson and master Lownes Warden a Booke called Shakespeares sonnettes.'

PUBLISHED: (1599. W. Jaggard's edition of *The Passionate Pilgrim* has versions of sonnets 138 and 144.)

1609. Q. 'Shake-speares Sonnets. Neuer before Imprinted. At London By G. Eld for T. T. and are to be solde by Iohn Wright, dwelling at Christ Church gate. [Some copies have 'by William Aspley'.] 1609.' The Sonnets are followed by *A Lover's Complaint*. Thorpe prefixed an enigmatic dedication:

TO . THE . ONLIE . BEGETTER . OF . THESE . INSVING . SONNETS . MR W.H. ALL . HAPPINESSE . AND . THAT . ETERNITIE . PROMISED . BY . OVR . EVER-LIVING . POET . WISHETH . THE . WELL-WISHING . ADVENTURER . IN . SETTING . FORTH. T.T.

The text is a fair one, but the errors suggest that Shakespeare did not see it through the press, though it is possible that he approved its publication, and that the volume was not pirated. (On 19 June 1609 Alleyn paid 5d. for a copy of 'Shakspers Sonnets'.)

1640. Benson's edition of 'Poems: Written by Wil. Shake-speare. Gent.' (See POEMS.)

1709. Added by Charles Gildon to Rowe's 1st octavo edition of Shakespeare's Works.

The 154 sonnets, as printed in Q 1609, fall into two main groups, the first of which may be subdivided:

1–126: addressed mainly to a young man, described as a 'sweet boy', 'my lovely boy', with a 'woman's face'.

> 1–17: an appeal to this friend to marry and reproduce his beauty in a child.
>
> 40–42: the friend steals the poet's mistress (see also 133, 134, 144).
>
> 78–86: a rival poet secures the favour of his friend, who also appears to be his patron.

127–52: addressed to his mistress, a dark, married woman. This series contains the so-called 'vituperative' sonnets.

153–4: two versions of a Greek epigram on Cupid. These may not be Shakespeare's.

Sonnets interesting for reasons additional to their poetry are:

13. The first use of the 2nd person plural instead of singular; 'you' instead of 'thou' is used in only thirty-four of the sonnets.

20. 'A man in hew all *Hews*, in his controwling' has been taken for a pun, and a clue to the identity of the 'lovely boy', a mythical William Hughes, and therefore the Mr W. H. of Thorpe's dedication.

26. Resembles the prose dedication of *Lucrece* to Southampton.

37. Shakespeare refers to himself as lame, figuratively of course, though it has been interpreted literally. (See also 89.)

99. Has fifteen lines.

104. States that the friendship has lasted three years.

107. Gives a clue to the date. 'The mortall Moone hath her eclipse indur'de' may mean that Elizabeth has survived her 'grand climacteric', her 63rd year, i.e. 1596; or, Elizabeth is dead, i.e. 1603. Hotson maintains that it means that the deadly, moon-shaped Armada has been defeated, i.e. 1588.

110–11. Seem to refer to Shakespeare's profession of actor.

123. Thy pyramyds buylt vp with newer might' may refer to the re-erection of four Egyptian obelisks by Pope Sixtus V 1586–9. (Hotson.)

124. Hotson thinks the reference is to the murder of Henri III in August 1589.

126. Only twelve lines and written in couplets, forming an envoy to the series addressed to 'my lovely boy'.

135–6. The 'Will' sonnets (q.v.). See also 143.

145. In octosyllabics.

Many interpretations have been put upon these *Sonnets*: among others, that they are allegorical; that they are dramatic and not personal; that Shakespeare wrote them merely as exercises in the fashionable sonnet-form. Some doubt the authenticity of the order of the *Sonnets*, others the authenticity of the *Sonnets* themselves. But assuming that Thorpe's order is approximately Shakespeare's and the poems to be a genuine autobiographical record, the main problems are:

THEIR DATE: discussed above.

MR W. H. One theory is that Thorpe's dedication is addressed to the procurer, 'the only begetter', of the *Sonnets* for him to print. (See HALL, WILLIAM; HARVEY, SIR WILLIAM.)

More probably, the 'begetter' of the *Sonnets* means the inspirer of them, Shakespeare's friend and patron, to whom they are mostly addressed. 135 suggests that his name was William. (See PEMBROKE, WILLIAM HERBERT; SOUTHAMPTON; WILLOBIE; HUGHES, WILLIAM.)

THE RIVAL POET. There are various candidates, George Chapman being the favourite, though as far as we know he dedicated nothing in Elizabeth's reign to Southampton or Herbert, or to any W. H. Other candidates are Daniel, Drayton, Barnes, Marlowe and Markham.

THE DARK LADY. There have been many guesses, but nobody really knows who she was. It seems reasonable to identify her with the mistress stolen from Shakespeare by his friend. Thomas Tyler first suggested Mary Fitton, Pembroke's mistress (see G. B. Shaw, *Dark Lady of the Sonnets*); perhaps Rosaline is a clue: the Rosalines of *Romeo and Juliet* and of *Love's Labour's Lost* are both black beauties. (See WILLOBIE.)

Soothsayer. 1. In *Julius Caesar*, he tells Caesar to 'beware the Ides of March' (I, ii), Portia that there is 'much that I fear may chance' (II, iv), and on the Ides of March warns Caesar that they are not gone (III, i).

2. In *Antony and Cleopatra*, tells Charmian and Iras that they will outlive Cleopatra (I, ii), and Antony that Caesar's fortune shall rise higher than his (II, iii).

3. In *Cymbeline*, foretells to Lucius 'success to the Roman host' (IV, ii), and interprets the 'label' of Posthumus's vision (V, v), where Lucius calls him Philharmonus.

'Sophonisba.' A tragedy by John Marston, registered 17 March 1606, and published in the same year, as 'The Wonder of Women Or the Tragedie of Sophonisba, as it hath beene sundry times acted at the Blacke Friers'. Marston often echoes Shakespeare, and A. C. Bradley (*Shakespearean Tragedy*, 471) detects several echoes of *Macbeth* in *Sophonisba*. This suggests a date for *Macbeth* not later than early 1606.

Sothern, Edward Hugh (1859–1933), actor, son of the actor Edward Askew Sothern, whom he joined in America in 1879. For a time he was with John McCullough. He first played Hamlet, in New York, in 1900, then 1904–16 he played largely in Shakespeare with Julia Marlowe, whom he married in 1911. Malvolio was his most famous part, though he sentimentalized it.

Soundings. Before the performance of a play at a public theatre there were three distinct trumpet calls, probably from the hut above the tiring-house and at intervals of a few minutes, warning people that the play was about to begin. After the third sounding, the Prologue entered (see 'GULL'S HORNBOOK'). Jonson often had an Induction between the second and third soundings (cf. *Every Man out of His Humour*). In the private theatres, the trumpet calls may have been replaced by the softer music of the cornet (Jonson mentions 'an unperfect Prologue, at third music' in *Cynthia's Revels*, a Blackfriars play), the first, second and third music of the Restoration and 18th century, reduced to the first and second music of 19th-century overtures.

Sources. Though Theobald drew attention to source-plays, the first serious attempt to trace the sources of Shakespeare's plays was made by Charlotte Lennox (q.v.) in 1753 (see also SIMROCK). They fall into four main groups, with a fifth more miscellaneous, but for the most part composed of romances similar to the Italian *novelle*:

Holinshed's *Chronicles*	for the English Histories, including *Macbeth* and part of *Cymbeline* but excluding *King John*. (For the early Histories, Halle was the main authority.)

Plutarch's *Lives*	for the Roman Histories: *Julius Caesar*; *Timon*; *Antony and Cleopatra*; *Coriolanus*.	
Old Plays	*Taming of A Shrew* for *The Shrew*.	
	The Troublesome Raigne for *King John*.	
	King Leir for *King Lear*; the sub-plot from Sidney's *Arcadia*.	
	The Famous Victories for parts of *Henry IV* and *V*.	
Italian Novels (mostly in translation)	Ser Giovanni for *Merchant of Venice*.	
	Bandello for *Much Ado* and *Twelfth Night*.	
	Cinthio for *Othello*, *Measure for Measure* and part of *Cymbeline*.	
	Boccaccio for *All's Well*.	
Miscellaneous	*Titus Andronicus*:	Seneca and Ovid.
	Comedy of Errors:	Plautus, *Menaechmi*.
	Hamlet:	Belleforest, *Histoires Tragiques*.
	Two Gentlemen:	Montemayor, *Diana Enamorada*.
	As You Like It:	Lodge, *Rosalynde*.
	Winter's Tale:	Greene, *Pandosto*.
	Romeo and Juliet:	Brooke, *Romeus and Juliet*.
	Tempest:	Jourdan, *Discovery of the Bermudas*.
	Pericles:	Gower, *Apollonius of Tyre*.
	Troilus and Cr.:	Chaucer, *Troilus and Criseyde*.
	Two N. Kinsmen:	Chaucer, *Knight's Tale*.
Shakespeare	*Love's Labour's Lost* *Midsummer Night's Dream* *Merry Wives of Windsor*	An interesting group, as all three plays were probably written for private performance on special occasions.

These are main sources only, and the plays incorporate a mass of minor borrowings, conscious or unconscious. But if Shakespeare rarely invented his plots, he transmuted them, rejecting, adding, expanding, contracting and above all infusing his material with his poetry. The old plays he completely rewrote, adding the parallel plot of Gloucester to the Lear story. Holinshed he used for his facts, rarely followed his language, and added Falstaff and a host of minor characters. The light and flimsy stories of the novels could be adapted and woven together at pleasure: Claudio and Hero taken from Bandello, hints for Benedick and Beatrice perhaps extracted from Castiglione, while the humour of Dogberry 'he happened to take at Grendon in Bucks'; or to a mixture of Secchi, Bandello and Cinthio, add Malvolio, Feste, Sir Toby, Sir Andrew and the piercing poetry of Viola, and call it what you will. The noble prose of North's translation of Plutarch (q.v.) Shakespeare often follows more closely, but even here he nearly always adds some touch that transfigures the whole. (For details see the plays; see also NOVEL; K. Muir, *Shakespeare's Sources*; G. Bullough, *Narrative and Dramatic Sources of Shakespeare*, 6 vols., 1957–.)

Southampton, Henry Wriothesley, 3rd Earl of (1573–1624), was the second son of Catholic parents, Henry Wriothesley, 2nd Earl, and Mary Browne, daughter of the 1st Viscount Montague. He was born at Cowdray House, near Midhurst, in October 1573, and was thus nine and a half years younger than Shakespeare. In 1581 his father died and he succeeded to the title, his elder brother being already dead. He entered St John's, Cambridge, in 1585, graduated in 1589, and then entered Gray's Inn. He became a patron of literature, employing John Florio as his tutor in Italian, and at Court he became a favourite of the Queen and a friend of Essex, whom he accompanied on his Cadiz and Azores expeditions in 1596–7. Meanwhile Essex's cousin, Elizabeth Vernon, had become his mistress, and as she was with child, he married her early in 1598, an action which incurred the wrath of the Queen, a short imprisonment and a long disgrace. In 1599 he went with Essex as his Master of Horse on the ill-fated Irish expedition, but was recalled by the Queen. When Essex was disgraced after his failure, Southampton joined his rebellion of February 1601, was captured and with Essex condemned to death, but Cecil secured the commutation of his sentence to life imprisonment.

On the accession of James I, Southampton was released and taken into favour. He played an active part in the affairs of the Virginia Company, then in 1624 led a body of English volunteers to help the Dutch against the Spaniards. With him went his elder son, but soon after landing they both contracted fever and died. They were buried in Titchfield church in December 1624.

The only certain connexion of Shakespeare with Southampton is his dedication to him of *Venus and Adonis* (q.v.) in 1593, and of *Lucrece* (q.v.) in 1594. In 1709 Rowe told the story 'handed down by Sir William D'Avenant ... that my Lord Southampton, at one time, gave him [Shakespeare] a thousand Pounds, to enable him to go through with a Purchase which he heard he had a mind to.' The sum is fantastically large, but it is possible that there is an element of truth in the story, and it has encouraged the belief that 'Mr W. H.' of the *Sonnets* (q.v.) was Henry Wriothesley, a theory first advanced by Nathan Drake in 1817. Wilson suggests that Shakespeare spent the plague year of 1593–4 at Titchfield, Southampton's Hampshire home, and there wrote a first version of *Love's Labour's Lost*, a play with which Southampton appears to have entertained Anne of Denmark at his London house in January 1605. (See COBHAM; C. C. Stopes, *The Life of Henry, Third Earl of Southampton*; A.L. Rowse, *William Shakespeare*, 1963.)

Southwark. A borough on the south bank of the Thames opposite the City of London, with which it was connected in Shakespeare's day only by London Bridge, though the watermen plied across the river, particularly between Blackfriars and Paris Garden. In the 14th century the City gained some control, and in 1550 it became the Bridge Ward Without, with an alderman elected by the other aldermen. The Tabard Inn of Chaucer's day was in Southwark. St Saviour's Church, now a cathedral, was, before the suppression of the monasteries, that of the Augustinian Priory of St Mary Overy ('over the river'), and here are buried Gower, Fletcher, Massinger and Edmund Shakespeare, the poet's brother. The Bankside (q.v.) is a district of Southwark.

Southwell, John. In *2 Henry VI*, a priest who helps to conjure up a spirit for the Duchess of Gloucester, is captured, and condemned to be 'strangled on the gallows' (I, iv; II, iii).

Southwell, Robert (*c.* 1561–95), poet, joined the Society of Jesus, and in 1586 accompanied Henry Garnet (q.v.), on his Jesuit mission to England. He visited Catholic houses, secretly administering the rites of his Church, was captured in 1592, imprisoned, and executed in 1595. Many of his poems, of which *The Burning Babe*, praised by Jonson, is the best known, were written in prison. *Saint Peter's Complaint* was published in 1595, and lines in the Epistle have been claimed as possible echoes of *Venus and Adonis* and *Love's Labour's Lost*:

Still finest wits are 'stilling Venus' rose ...
O sacred eyes! the springs of living light ...
Sweet volumes, stored with learning fit for saints.

Spain. During the first twenty years of Shakespeare's life a state of what we should now call 'cold war' existed between Catholic Spain and Protestant England. The Jesuit Order was founded in 1540, and from 1574 onwards Jesuit missionaries, such as Campion, Parsons, Southwell and Garnet worked secretly in England, to which the reply was the patriotic piracy of Drake and his followers. Open war began without a declaration in 1585; Leicester led a campaign in the Netherlands, 1585–7, whither Kempe and other English actors followed him and his nephew Sidney was killed. In 1588 came the Armada, the destruction of which reduced the danger of invasion, but the war drifted on with English help to the Dutch and Henry of Navarre. Peace was made in 1604, when the Spanish Ambassador came to England and stayed at Somerset House (q.v.), where the King's Men acted as Grooms of the Chamber.

Shakespeare used a Spanish source, the *Diana Enamorada* of Montemayor (though he was Portuguese) for *The Two Gentlemen of Verona*, and if he really wrote *Cardenio* with Fletcher he must have taken the story from the *Don Quixote* of his contemporary, Cervantes. Don Armado in *L.L.L.* is 'a fantastical Spaniard'; Queen Katharine in *Henry VIII* is a sympathetic portrait of a great Spanish lady.

Shakespeare was translated into Spanish by J. Clark (10 plays), 1870–4; by the Marques de Dos Hermanos, 1872–7; and by G. Macpherson, 1885. Today, Shakespeare is frequently acted, and the old, inadequate texts have been replaced since 1955 by L. A. Marin's translation of the *Obras Completas*. Salvador de Madariaga's book, *On 'Hamlet'*, appeared in 1948. (See PHILIP II.)

Spalding, William (1809–59), born at Aberdeen, called to the bar at Edinburgh, where he became Professor of Rhetoric, and from 1845 to his death Professor of Logic at St Andrews. In 1833, when he was only twenty-four, he published his *Letter on Shakespeare's Authorship of The Two Noble Kinsmen; and on the Characteristics of Shakespeare's Style*, an analysis that led to the methodical study of Shakespeare's verse, and ultimately to the verse-tests of Furnivall, who reprinted the *Letter* for the New Shakspere Society in 1876, as 'one of the ablest (if not the ablest) and most stimulating piece of Shakespeare criticism I ever read'.

'Spanish Tragedy, The.' A play registered by Abel Jeffes 6 October 1592, possibly after he had published a 'bad' Quarto. An undated Q appears to be the first extant edition:

> The Spanish Tragedie, Containing the lamentable end of Don Horatio, and Bel-Imperia: with the pittiful death of olde Hieronimo. Newly corrected, and amended of such grosse faults as passed in the first impression.

There were further Qq in 1594, 1599, and throughout the reign of James I; that of 1602 reads:

> Newly corrected, amended, and enlarged with new additions of the Painters part, and others, as it hath of late been diuers times acted.

The play deals with the revenge of Hieronimo, Marshal of Spain, for the murder of his son Horatio, in which he is helped by Bel-Imperia who loved Horatio. According to a reference by Heywood in his *Apology for Actors*, the author was Thomas Kyd. It was probably written *c.* 1589, but the original company to perform it is unknown. Strange's played '*Jeronymo*' sixteen times for Henslowe in 1592, the Admiral's in 1597, and in 1601–2 Henslowe paid Jonson for additions, though they read much more like Webster than Jonson. It was revived again by the Admiral's in 1602, and apparently played by the Chamberlain's at about the same time. (Henslowe's '*Jeronymo*' entries almost certainly refer to *The Spanish Tragedy*, which is to be distinguished from the lost, anonymous *Comedy of Jeronimo* (also called by Henslowe *The Spanish Comedy* and *Don Horatio*) played by Strange's in 1592, and from the later (*c.* 1604) extant *First Part of Jeronimo*.)

The play is important as the prototype of the Revenge Tragedy (q.v.), because of its popularity and influence on the succeeding drama, and because Kyd is thought to have written the original Hamlet play, or *Ur-Hamlet* (q.v.). Some of the mid 17th-century booksellers ascribed it to Shakespeare.

Spectacle. The love of spectacle at the Court of James I and Anne of Denmark, stimulated by the masque, led to more spectacular plays – Shakespeare's romances and *Henry VIII* have more to please the eye than the early comedies and histories – and often to the insertion of new spectacle in old plays; for example, the Hecate scenes in *Macbeth* must have been written in sometime between 1606 and 1623. They were elaborated at the Restoration into the famous scenes of the singing and flying witches, banished from the stage only in the 19th century.

Spedding, James (1808–81), born in Cumberland, educated at Trinity, Cambridge, and devoted the greater part of his life to the study and editing of Bacon, whose *Works, Life and Letters* he published 1857–74. In August 1850 he wrote an article in the *Gentleman's Magazine* called *Who wrote Henry VIII?*, in which, he maintained, basing his arguments on the different styles of the play, that the greater part was by Fletcher. In 1876 Furnivall reprinted his article and the *Letter* of Spalding for the New Shakspere Society, which was engaged in the scientific, quantitative study of Shakespeare's verse. In 1872, in *Notes and Queries*, Spedding followed up Richard Simpson's claim that part of the MS. of *Sir Thomas More* was in Shakespeare's handwriting.

Speech-prefixes. The names of characters printed before their speeches. In MS. plays these are normally written in Italian hand; in Qq and F they are printed, generally abbreviated, though not always consistently, in italics. Sometimes the book-keeper substituted the actor's name in the prompt-copy, and apparently Shakespeare sometimes wrote the name of the actor he had in mind for the part: e.g. Kempe for Dogberry. (See KEMPE; COWLEY; SINCLER.)

Speed. In *The Two Gentlemen of Verona*, 'a clownish seruant to Valentine' (F), whom he accompanies to Milan, and warns that Proteus is also in love with Silvia. He last appears in IV, i, when he and Valentine are captured by the outlaws.

Speed, John (1552–1629), historian and cartographer, was born in Cheshire, became a London tailor, but thanks to the patronage of Fulke Greville was enabled to turn antiquary. In 1611 appeared his *Theatre of the Empire of Great Britaine*, a series of maps, one of which is a View of London, engraved by J. Hondius in 1610, showing the Globe as round and the Bear Garden as polygonal. In the same year Speed published a *History of Great Britaine* in which he attacked the Jesuit Parsons (q.v.) and, indirectly, Shakespeare.

Spelling. If Shakespeare wrote with his own hand the three-page addition (II, *c*) in *Sir Thomas More*, he was an old-fashioned speller; thus lines 51–71 read,

moor	You[u] that haue voyce and Credyt w[t] the nvmber Comaund them to a stilnes
Lincolne	a plaigue on them they will not hold their peace the deule Cannot rule them
Moor	Then what a rough and ryotous charge haue yo[u] to Leade those that the deule Cannot rule good masters heare me speake
Doll	J byth mas will we moor thart a good howskeeper and I thanck thy good worship for my Brother Arthur watchins
all	peace peace
moor	look what yo[u] do offend yo[u] Cry vppō that is the peace, not on of yo[u] heare present had there such fellowes lyvd when yo[u] wer babes that coold haue topt the peace, as nowe yo[u] woold the peace wherin yo[u] haue till nowe growne vp

had bin tane from you[u], and the bloody tymes
coold not haue brought you[u] to the state of men
alas poor things what is yt you[u] haue gott
although we graunt you[u] geat the thing you[u] seeke

Bett marry the removing of the straingers w[ch] cannot choose but
much advauntage the poor handycraftes of the Cytty

(Note the speech-rules, lack of punctuation, verse-lines beginning with minuscules.) The compositors, accustomed to printing the work of scholars, appear to have modernized archaic spellings in the Quartos and Folio, though occasionally they slip through. Wilson strengthened the case for Shakespeare's hand in *Sir Thomas More* by showing that if Shakespeare spelt like the writer of Addition II, *c*, many of the misprints in the early texts of his plays could be explained. (See HARINGTON; PUNCTUATION; SS, 7.)

Spence, Joseph (1698–1768), was of New College, Oxford, Professor of Poetry, 1728–38, and a friend of Pope, whom he met about 1726. He left a number of notes which were published by S. W. Singer in 1820, as *Anecdotes ... Collected from the Conversations of Mr. Pope, and other eminent Persons of his Time.* He records Pope's story of D'Avenant's being the illegitimate son of Shakespeare, and a story of *c.* 1730:

It was a general opinion, that Ben Jonson and Shakspeare lived in enmity against one another. Betterton has assured me often, that there was nothing in it: and that such a supposition was founded only on the two parties, which in their lifetime listed under one, and endeavoured to lessen the character of the other mutually. Dryden used to think that the verses Jonson made on Shakspeare's death, had something of satire at the bottom; for my part, I can't discover any thing like it in them.

Spencer, Gabriel, actor, is probably the Gabriel of F stage-direction, *3 Henry VI* (I, ii, 48): 'Enter Gabriel' for the 'Enter Messenger' of Q. As the play was printed as Pembroke's in 1595, he may have been with them *c.* 1594, or he may have acted with the Chamberlain's as a hired man in a later revival. He deserted Pembroke's for the Admiral's in 1597, and was killed by Ben Jonson in a duel on 22 September 1598. Wilson suggests that the servant Gabriel in *The Shrew*, IV, i, is Spencer.

Spencer, Hazelton (1893–1944), American scholar, elected Professor of English at Johns Hopkins University in 1937; author of *Shakespeare Improved, The Art and Life of William Shakespeare*, etc.

Spenser, Edmund (*c.* 1552–99), was born in London, and educated at Merchant Taylors' School, and Pembroke, Cambridge, where he met Gabriel Harvey, a Fellow of the College, by whom he was introduced to Leicester and the literary circle known as the Areopagus. In 1579 he published *The Shepherd's Calendar* and began the *Faerie Queene*, and in the following year went to Ireland as secretary to the deputy, Lord Grey of Wilton. He bought Kilcolman Castle, County Cork, in 1588, spent part of 1589–91 in England, when he published the first three books of the *Faerie Queene*, returned to Ireland, and in 1594 married Elizabeth Boyle, celebrated in his *Amoretti* sonnets and *Epithalamium*. He was in England again 1595–7, and published Books IV–VI of the *Faerie Queene*. Shortly after his return to Ireland, Tyrone's rebellion broke out, his castle was burned, and he and his wife and four children fled to London, where he died in distress in January 1599.

The early poetry of Shakespeare was much influenced by the elaborate slow music and artificial imagery of Spenser, but *c.* 1597 the tempo quickens, his verse becomes more compressed and dramatic, and the imagery observed and original. Rowe, 1709, says that 'Men of the most delicate Knowledge and polite Learning' must have admired Shakespeare:

> Amongst these was the incomparable *Mr Edmond Spencer*, who speaks of him in his *Tears of the Muses*, not only with the Praises due to a good Poet, but even lamenting his absence with the tenderness of a Friend.

The Tears of the Muses was registered 29 December 1590 and published 1591. In it Spenser laments that 'Willy', the writer of comedies, is now silent. But this is scarcely true of Shakespeare who, in 1590, was just beginning to write, and Chambers ingeniously suggests Lyly, who stopped writing for the Paul's boys at about that date:

> And he the man, whom Nature selfe had made
> To mock her selfe, and Truth to imitate,
> With kindly counter under Mimick shade,
> Our pleasant *Willy*, ah is dead of late ...
>
> But that same gentle Spirit, from whose pen
> Large streames of honnie and sweet Nectar flowe ...
> Doth rather choose to sit in idle Cell,
> Than so himselfe to mockerie to sell.

Probably the reference in *A Midsummer Night's Dream*, v, i, to the 'satire, keen and critical' of

> The thrice three Muses mourning for the death
> Of Learning, late deceased in beggary.

is to *The Tears of the Muses.*

Of the catalogue of poets in Spenser's *Colin Clout's Come Home Again* (1591–5), Malone wrote (*Var.*, II, 273):

> But where, it may be asked, among all these distinguished votaries of the Muses, is Shakspeare found?,– He closes the poetical band, obscurely yet unquestionably shadowed in these lines:

> And then, though last, not least, is *Ætion*, –
> A gentler shepheard may no where be found;
> Whose Muse, full of high thoughts invention,
> Doth, like himself, heroically sound.

It may be so, yet O. Elton suggests that Drayton is more probably meant. (See W. B. C. Watkins, *Shakespeare and Spenser*, 1950.)

Spielmann, Marion Harry (1858–1949), writer on art and authority on the iconography of Shakespeare, was editor of the *Magazine of Art* and Lecturer at the Royal Institution, etc. His publications include *The Portraits of Shakespeare* (Stratford Town Edition, 1907), *The Title-Page of the First Folio*, and *Shakespeare's Portraiture.*

Split Line. A complete line of blank verse printed in two parts. This may be due to (*a*) a speech ending within a line which is completed by another speaker:

> Destroyed in such a shape.
> *Cleo.* Ile giue thee Friend ...

Such split lines become commoner with the increase in mid-line speech-endings (q.v.). (*b*) A pause for action, sometimes perhaps for emphasis:

> The Honour'd gashes whole.
> *Enter Cleopatra.*
> Giue me thy hand.

(*c*) The compositor's finding it difficult to print a speech-prefix and a complete verse in one line (see MISLINEATION):

> *King.* The Prince hath ta'ne it hence:
> Goe seeke him out.
> Is hee so hastie, that hee doth suppose ...

Split lines due to (*a*) and (*b*) become commoner in the later plays.

Spondee. A foot of two long or stressed syllables (– –):

> Blōw wīnds, | ănd crăck yŏur chēeks! | rāge! | blōw! |

('rage' and 'blow' must be scanned as heavily stressed monosyllabic feet.) Like other irregularities, spondees become more frequent as Shakespeare's verse develops.

Sport. There is plenty of evidence in the poems and plays, both in reference and imagery, of Shakespeare's interest in sport: in horses, hunting, coursing, hawking, swimming and fishing. See H. N. Ellacombe, *Shakespeare as an Angler*; D. H. Madden, *The Diary of Master*

William Silence; C. Spurgeon, *Shakespeare's Imagery*.

Spurgeon, Caroline (1869–1941), Professor of English in the University of London 1913–29. In 1928 she edited *Keats's Shakespeare*, the 7-vol. edition annotated by Keats. Her *Shakespeare's Imagery*, 1935, is the classical book on the subject, the study of which she reduced almost to a science.

Staël, Madame de (1766–1817), daughter of Jacques Necker, French finance minister, and of Suzanne Curchod, the early love of Gibbon, married Baron de Staël, the Swedish ambassador. Though her roots were in the 18th century, she recognized that the age of Voltaire was over, and in her *De la Littérature* (1800) admitted that England and Germany, Shakespeare and Schiller, were the models for France. Although she could not condone all the extravagances of Shakespeare, and incidentally ranked *Henry VI* with *King Lear*, her appreciation is far less qualified than Voltaire's; Shakespeare has his faults, but he is certainly not a buffoon. Her *De l'Allemagne* (1813), which revealed the importance of German literature (see SCHLEGEL), led to a conflict with Napoleon and her exile.

Stafford, Lord (of Southwick). In *3 Henry VI*, a Yorkist, is ordered by Edward IV to levy men. (The death of Lord Stafford, son of the 1st Duke of Buckingham (q.v.) is announced in I, i, 7.)

Stafford, Simon. The printer of Q2 (1599) *1 Henry IV* for Andrew Wise, and of Q3 (1611), *Pericles*. He also registered and printed *King Leir* (1605) for John Wright. He was in business 1596–1626.

Stafford, Sir Humphrey, and his brother William, in *2 Henry VI* attempt to stop Cade and his followers at Blackheath, but are killed (IV, ii and iii).

Stage. As the only description of an Elizabethan theatre is the building contract of the Fortune, and the only contemporary illustration of a playhouse interior a sketch of the Swan, any detailed reconstruction is largely a matter of inference and conjecture.

The Elizabethan public theatre appears to have incorporated elements from the medieval rounds and the old bull- and bear-baiting houses, but to have been built mainly on the model of the inns that were used as temporary, and sometimes as permanent, playhouses, the essential feature of which was a galleried yard into which projected a platform stage. Theatres varied in detail, and there must have been modifications in the fifty years between the building of Burbage's Theatre in 1576 and the rebuilding of the Fortune in 1623, but the main features were common and constant.

Probably most of the public theatres were round, though some may have been polygonal, and the first Fortune was square, 80 ft outside and 55 ft inside. The main structure was of wood, sometimes on brick foundations, with lath-and-plaster walls, though de Witt says the Swan walls were flint, and those of the second Fortune were brick. Galleries, usually three, surrounded the yard, and here spectators could sit on paying an extra 1d. or 2d., and have a seat in a 'private room' or box for 6d. or 12d. The gallery roof of the first Globe was thatched, of the second tiled.

Into the open yard, where the groundlings stood for 1d., projected the apron stage, raised about five feet from the ground with trap-doors for spectacular effects; the Fortune stage was 43 ft wide and 27½ ft deep. At the back was the tiring-house, or actors' quarters, from which two doors, one on either side, led on to the apron, and between them was a recess with another door, the inner stage, or 'study', across which curtains could be drawn. The middle gallery ran behind the stage and formed in the early theatres a box, the 'lords' room', used sometimes as a music-room, sometimes as an upper stage; in the later theatres, such as the Globe and Fortune, it was probably designed and always used as an upper stage. Above this, and a continuation of the upper gallery, was the music-room of the later theatres, and on a level with the top of it projected the roof or 'shadow' that covered the apron stage, at the front corners of which it was supported by pillars (the Hope had no pillars). At the top of the tiring-house, that is, above the music-room, and built partly over the shadow, was the hut with machinery and traps from which aerial ascents and descents could be made. The flag flew from the hut during a performance, and it was probably from there that the trumpet was blown to announce the beginning of the play. The Elizabethan public theatre, therefore, had three stages: an apron or outer stage where most of the action took place, an inner stage for smaller set scenes, and an upper stage to represent battlements, a balcony, a hill, etc., though action from the smaller stages might always be extended to the apron.

This is the orthodox view, though there is little definite evidence to support it. In the Swan sketch the lower gallery is divided into a number of boxes or 'rooms' apparently occupied by spectators (as in the *Roxana* and *Wits* illustrations), and there is no sign of an inner stage between the doors. Hotson, therefore, offers a revolutionary alternative. According to this, the Elizabethan production of plays, both in the public and private theatres, was, like the medieval, in the round, so that the galleries over the stage contained seats, the best seats, occupied by gallants and their ladies. The tiring-house was under the stage, on which the action was played transversely, that is from side to side, not from back to front. At each side of this stage was a row of two or three small 'houses', some with two stories, between the back wall and the columns supporting the canopy. Most entries were from traps within the 'houses', round which curtains could be drawn. These houses supplied any necessary 'within' and 'above' for a play's production.

The private theatres of Blackfriars and Whitefriars were roofed and rectangular (Paul's appears to have been round), with at least one gallery and seats for spectators in the 'pit'. It can be inferred from the plays that there were three stages as in the public theatres, though the shadow would be the ceiling of the hall, above which were machines and cannon balls for simulating thunder. (For the orthodox view see J. C. Adams, *The Globe Playhouse*, 1942, and SQ, Jan. 1951; for the unorthodox, L. Hotson, *Shakespeare's Wooden O*, 1959. See also G. Wickham, *Early English Stages*, and SS, 12.)

Stage-directions. It is now generally accepted that most of the directions in Elizabethan plays, even those in the imperative, are the author's rather than prompter's. They are to make the action clear, for a play had to be read by (or to) the company before acceptance to indicate the way in which the author wished it to be staged, and they sometimes describe an episode as he imagined it when writing:

'*Enter Volumnia and Virgilia, mother and wife to Martius.*' '*Enter the prince marching, and Falstaffe meetes him playing vpon his trunchion like a fife.*' '*A florish of trumpets and 2. peeces goes of.*' '*Bassanio comments on the caskets to himself.*'

The book-keeper added functional directions to the prompt-book. He was much concerned with entrances, often marking them a few lines earlier than required by the text, and sometimes adding preliminary warnings, as in *The Two Noble Kinsmen*: '*2. Hearses ready with Palamon: and Arcite: the 3. Queenes. Theseus: and his Lordes ready.*' (Compare the English directions in the late 15th-century Cornish miracle play *Meriasek*: '*her yerdis* [sticks] *aredy*', '*horse aredy*', '*her the dragon aredy in the place*'.) Such anticipatory directions in a printed text suggest that the copy from which it was set up was the prompt-book. But the substitution of actors' names for characters, as in Q *2 Henry IV*, '*Enter Sincklo*' instead of F '*Enter* ... *Beadles*', suggests foul papers as copy, for Shakespeare was thinking of this lean little actor when he wrote the part.

As we should expect, Shakespeare's early directions are full, but become slighter as he worked with the Chamberlain's. Towards the end, when he was probably writing in Stratford and no longer in daily contact with his company, they become more detailed and explanatory again.

Additional directions, particularly scene-localities, unmarked in Quartos and Folio, were added by Rowe and other 18th-century editors, who also completed division into acts and scenes, and added lists of Dramatis Personae. (See Greg, *First Folio*, Chap. 4.)

Staging. There are three kinds of performance to be considered: (*a*) Private performances, the most important of which were those given at night in the banqueting-hall at Court, similar to which were those of the Inns of Court, and the academic plays at the Universities. (*b*) Private theatre performances by artificial light, and, until 1608, by boys only. (*c*) Public theatre performances by daylight. Costumes and properties (q.v.) were probably similar at all three kinds of performance, but scenery is another matter.

In the early Elizabethan Court plays, where the action was generally in one locality, a Serlian method of staging, a concentrated multiple setting, with structural 'houses' and painted perspective, seems to have been adopted. As the drama became more romantic and the localities represented farther apart, the more diffuse kind of multiple setting, as practised at the Hôtel de Bourgogne, was adopted, whereby all the 'houses' were separate, and spaced about the stage. (See COURT PERFORMANCES.)

Both these Court forms of multiple setting appear to have been used by the boys at the first Blackfriars theatre for the staging of Lyly's plays. The same conventions were practised in the later private theatres, from 1600 onwards. Sometimes they may have used 'locality boards' to indicate the scene, and the ingenious staging of Court masques by Inigo Jones may have led to some attempts at scene changing.

A play can be staged in one of four ways: by having only one scene (the classical method); by changing the scene for every change of locality (the post-Restoration); by multiple setting, where all the scenes are on the stage at the same time (the medieval, Serlian and Hôtel de Bourgogne methods); by having no scenery at all. This last was the method of the early players, both of interludes in private houses and of plays in Public inns, and was continued in the public theatres. Some sort of set scene, it is true, could be arranged within a curtained inner stage (but this was a matter of properties rather than scenery) and lath and painted canvas 'houses' might be erected at the back of the apron stage. For the most part, however, plays in the public theatres were staged with little scenery (though not without properties), locality being indicated perhaps by locality boards, but mainly by dialogue, on which the attention of the audience was concentrated, though modern scholarship tends to favour a greater scenic realism than was once suspected. All this assumes that the stage was set against a back wall, as in the classical theatre. Hotson, however, argues that the stage was surrounded by the audience, both at Court (*First Night of 'Twelfth Night'*) and in the public theatres (*Shakespeare's Wooden O*), and that the method of staging was the medieval one with 'houses'.

In any event, the apron jutting into the yard without the division of a proscenium arch fused actors and audience together, while the subsidiary inner and upper stages and concentration on words and action instead of scenery made for great fluidity and speed of performance, something very different from the Kean-Irving-Tree tradition of the 19th century. (See ROUNDS; COURT PERFORMANCES; PRODUCTION; STAGE.)

Stage-keeper. One of the theatre attendants, part of his job being apparently to keep the theatre clean. An actor plays the part of Stage-keeper in the Introduction to *Bartholomew Fair* (q.v.), in which the Book-holder says to him, 'Your judgement, rascal! for what? sweeping the stage, or gathering up the broken apples for the bears within?' (The play was first acted at the Hope-Beargarden, 1614.) Stage-keepers sometimes appeared as supers.

Stanley, Ferdinando. See DERBY, EARLS OF.

Stanley, Sir John. In *2 Henry VI*, brother of Thomas, Lord Stanley; in *R. III*, he is given charge of the exiled Duchess of Gloucester, and takes her to the Isle of Man (II, iv).

Stanley, Sir Thomas (d. 1576), uncle of Ferdinando Stanley, Lord Strange, 5th Earl of Derby (patron of Strange's-Derby's company which Shakespeare joined in 1594, when it was reorganized as the Chamberlain's). Sir Thomas married Margaret Vernon (d. 1596), and both were buried in Tong church, Shropshire, where there is a monument bearing on the canopy a man in armour and a woman, and beneath the canopy another man in armour. Epitaphs were engraved at either end of the tomb, which Dugdale in his *Visitation of Shropshire*, 1664, says 'were made by William Shakespeare, the late famous tragedian'. There is a MS. of earlier date, *c.* 1630, which also ascribed them to Shakespeare:

Shakspeare
An Epitaph on Sr Edward Standly.
Ingraven on his Toombe in Tong Church.

Not monumentall stones preserves our Fame;
Nor sky-aspiring Piramides our name;
The memory of him for whom this standes
Shall out live marble and defacers hands
When all to times consumption shall bee given,
Standly for whom this stands shall stand in Heaven.

On Sr Thomas Standly
Idem, ibidem
Ask who lies heere but doe not wheepe;
Hee is not deade; Hee doth but sleepe;
This stony Register is for his bones,
His Fame is more perpetuall, then these stones,
And his owne goodnesse wth him selfe being gone,
Shall live when Earthly monument is nonne.

Sir Thomas's brother, Sir Edward, died 1609, his son Sir Edward in 1632. The monument is undated, and if the man and woman on the canopy are Sir Thomas and Lady Margaret, it is not clear which Sir Edward lies below. The first did not live at Tong; the second died sixteen years after Shakespeare. The first epitaph sounds as if it might be by Shakespeare, but certainly not the second. (See JAMES, ELIAS; MILTON.)

Stanley, Thomas, Lord (*c.* 1435–1504). In *Richard III*, he plays an ambiguous part, professing loyalty to Richard, who mistrusts him as his wife is Margaret Beaufort, Countess of Richmond, the mother by Henry Tudor of Henry Richmond (Henry VII). When Richmond lands, Richard keeps Stanley's son, George, as hostage; Stanley tells Richmond that he dares not help him openly at Bosworth, but at the last moment he refuses to help Richard. (Both in Qq and F Stanley is often wrongly called Derby. Henry VII created him 1st Earl of Derby shortly after Bosworth.)

Stanley, Sir William. In *3 Henry VI*, brother of Thomas Lord Stanley, he helps Edward IV to escape from Middleham Castle (IV, v). (It was he who turned the scales in Richmond's favour at Bosworth.)

Starveling, Robin. In *A Midsummer Night's Dream*, an Athenian tailor. In I, ii he is cast as Thisbe's mother, but apparently plays Moonshine at the performance of the Interlude.

Stationers' Company. In Shakespeare's time the London book trade was in the hands of the Stationers' Company of London, an organization that goes back to 1404. It was incorporated by royal charter in 1557, with an elected Master, two Wardens and a Court of Assistants, and save for books printed by the University presses had the monopoly of printing for the whole of England. All the London booksellers (publishers) and most of the printers (there were ninety-three enrolled in the Charter of 1557) were freemen of the Company, who by entering their 'copy' in the –

Stationers' Register, and by paying a fee of 4d., later 6d., secured the sole right of printing or selling a book. Books had to be licensed, and the normal procedure was for a member of the Company to secure licence to print, and then, shortly before publication, enter for his copy in the Register and pay his fee. (For examples see LICENSING OF PLAYS; FOLIOS.) The Company was not concerned with how its members obtained their copy. Many published plays were not registered, and therefore not copyright, though a transfer in the Register appears to have secured it: for example, *Romeo and Juliet*. It should be noted that non-entry does not account for 'bad' Quartos. Many bad texts were regularly entered. (See ARBER. For 'Staying Entries' see ROBERTS, JAMES.)

Staunton, Howard (1810–74), journalist and Shakespeare scholar. He published an edition of Shakespeare in three volumes, and a photolithographic facsimile of F1 (1866). Author of *Memorials of Shakespeare*, 1864.

'Staying Entries'. See ROBERTS, JAMES.

Steevens, George (1736–1800). The 8th editor of Shakespeare, was educated at Eton and King's, Cambridge. He settled at Hampstead, and in 1766 published *Twenty of the Plays of Shakespeare*, being reprints of Quarto editions. In 1773 he published, in ten volumes, his edition of Shakespeare, based on that of Johnson, but with the addition of his own Elizabethan scholarship. It was revised and reprinted in 1778 (10 vols.) and again revised by his friend Isaac Reed in 1785 (10 vols.). Malone's edition of 1790 excited his jealousy, and in 1793 he published his final edition in fifteen volumes, with somewhat reckless and perverse emendations and notes, but sauced with a malicious wit at the expense of two innocent clergymen, Richard Amner and John Collins, to whom he attributed various indecent interpretations, earning for himself the title of 'the Puck of Commentators'. Steevens is important because, like Capell and Malone, he began the serious study of the Shakespeare Quartos, instead of relying on the often less accurate text of the Folios, and because of his unrivalled knowledge of Elizabethan literature. 'Past editors,' he wrote, 'eminently qualified as they were by genius and learning for this undertaking, wanted industry.' The immense value of his work can best be appreciated, perhaps, from the Contents of the 346 pages of introductory matter to the 1778 edition, 'With the Corrections and Illustrations of Various Commentators; to which are added Notes by Samuel Johnson and George Steevens':

Head of Shakespeare, from an Engraving by Martin Droeshout, before the Folio 1623.

Preface by Johnson.

Advertisement by Steevens.

Extract from the Gull's Hornbook, by Dekker, concerning our ancient theatres, &c.

The Globe Theatre, from the Long Antwerp View of London in the Pepysian Library.

Catalogue of the earliest Translations from Greek and Roman Classicks.

Appendix to Colman's Terence, relative to the Learning of Shakespeare.

Dedication by Heminge and Condell to the Folio, 1623.

Preface by the same.

——— by Pope.

——— by Theobald.

——— by Hanmer.
——— by Warburton.
Advertisement prefix'd to Steevens's Twenty Plays, &c.
Rowe's Life of Shakespeare.
Ms. in the Herald's Office.
Licences to Shakespeare, &c. from Rymer's Fœdera, and his Mss.
Head of Shakespeare from that by Marshall, prefixed to the Poems 1640.
Fac-Simile of Shakespeare's Hand-writing.
Anecdotes of Shakespeare, from Oldys's Mss. &c.
Farmer's account of a Pamphlet imputed to Shakespeare; together with Remarks on a passage in Warton's Life of Dr. Bathurst.
Observations on Passages in the Preface to the French Translation of Shakespeare.
Registers of the Shakespeare Family.
Grainger's Catalogue of the Portraits of Shakespeare.
Ancient and Modern Commendatory Verses on Shakespeare, with Notes, &c.
List of Editions of Shakespeare's Plays, both ancient and modern; – of Plays alter'd from him; – of detach'd Pieces of Criticism, &c.
Entries of Shakespeare's Plays on the Books of the Stationers' Company.
An Attempt to ascertain the Order in which the Plays attributed to Shakespeare were written, by Edmond Malone, Esq.

Malone's *Attempt to ascertain the Order* was first published in this edition. The 1st and 2nd Variorum editions (q.v.) of 1803 and 1813 are based on Steevens's, which might itself be called a Variorum edition, and the 3rd Variorum, 'Boswell's Malone' of 1821, includes Steevens's notes. Steevens was scholar rather than critic, and excluded Shakespeare's poems because 'the strongest act of Parliament that could be framed would fail to compel readers into their service'.

Stephano. 1. In *The Tempest*, 'a drunken Butler' (F). He meets Caliban, who worships him for his wine and persuades him to murder Prospero and become king of the island. However, Prospero makes him forget his intention by hanging rich apparel in front of his cave, then drives him off, and Caliban and Trinculo, with 'spirits in shape of dogs'. 2. In *The Merchant of Venice*, a servant of Portia; he tells Lorenzo of her return to Belmont (v, i).

Stettin-Pomerania, Philip Julius, Duke of, was in England in 1602, and his secretary, Frederic Gerschow, kept a diary of his visit. On 13 September he saw an unidentified play, probably at the Globe, of the capture of Stuhl-Weissenburg by the Turks, on the 14th the Admiral's play of *Samson* at the Fortune, on the 16th more than two hundred dogs at the bear-baiting, and on the 18th the Chapel children at Blackfriars. He says that the boys acted a play each week, and describes the instrumental and vocal music for a whole hour before the performance. (See ORGAN.)

Stichomythia. Line-by-line dialogue typical of Seneca and the early Elizabethan drama. Shakespeare used it in his plays up to about the time of *King John*, *c.* 1597, from which the following passage comes (III, i):

PAND. I will denounce a curse upon his head.
PHIL. Thou shalt not need. England, I will fall from thee.
CON. O fair return of banish'd majesty.
ELIN. O foul revolt of French inconstancy.
JOHN. France, thou shalt rue this hour within this hour.

Stinkard. A term applied to the '*Groundling* and *Gallery Commoner*'; that is, to the playgoer who stood in the yard for 1d. or bought the cheapest gallery seat for another 1d.: 'stinkards sitting in the penny galleries of a theatre' (*Ant and Nightingale*, 1604).

Stoll, Elmer Edgar (1874–1959). American scholar, elected Professor of English at the University of Minnesota in 1915. He was one of the most trenchant of the realist school of critics whose aim was to reveal Shakespeare in relation to his contemporaries and his theatre. Author of *Art and Artifice in Shakespeare*, etc.

Stopes, Charlotte Carmichael, was born and educated in Edinburgh, married in 1879, settled in London, joined the New Shakspere Society, and devoted much of her time to research into the lives of Shakespeare's relations and contemporaries, from *Shakespeare's Family*, 1901, to *The Life of Henry, Third Earl of Southampton*, 1922. It was she who discovered the unexplained episode in the life of Shakespeare's father, when in 1580 he was fined £40 by the Court of Queen's Bench.

Stow, John (*c.* 1525–1605), born in London, brought up as a tailor by his father, but met William Camden and other antiquaries, and himself turned antiquary, in 1561 publishing *The Woorkes of Geffrey Chaucer*, and in 1565 a *Summarie of Englyshe Chronicles*. In 1580 came his *Annales, or a Generale Chronicle of England from Brute until the present yeare of Christ 1580*, reprinted 1592, 1601, 1605, and brought up to date by Edmund Howes in his editions of 1615 and 1631. Stow published his *Survey of London* in 1598, and issued a second edition in 1603, which was revised with additions by Anthony Munday in 1618 and 1633. He was buried in the church of St Andrew Undershaft, where there is a terra-cotta effigy erected by his widow. Stow's *Annales* and *Survey* give invaluable information about England and London in Shakespeare's time. (See HOWES.)

Strachey, Giles Lytton (1880–1932), educated at Trinity, Cambridge. His essay on *Shakespeare's Final Period*, 1906, is a 'realist' attack on the sentimental Victorian view, and his *Landmarks in French Literature*, 1912, contains one of the best short comparisons of the art of Racine ('concentration') with that of Shakespeare ('comprehension').

Strachey, William (fl. 1588–1620), may be the William Strachey of Saffron Walden who married in 1588, was alive in 1620, and whose grandson was living in Virginia in 1625. He prefixed an admirable commendatory sonnet to the 1605 Q of *Sejanus*. He was wrecked with Sir T. Gates (q.v.) on the Bermudas in 1609, and wrote an account, dated 15 July 1610, addressed to an unnamed Excellent Lady in England; the letter was circulated, but published only in 1625 in *Purchas his Pilgrimes*, as *A True Reportory of the wrack and redemption of Sir Thomas Gates, knight, upon and from the ilands of the Bermudas his coming to Virginia, and the estate of that colony*. Strachey describes the Bermudas, contradicting Jourdan's story that they were inhabited by 'divels', and adds an outspoken account of the deplorable condition of Virginia. The official report of 1610 was probably written mainly by Gates and Strachey, who had been appointed recorder of the colony. By 1612 he had written *The Historie of Travaile into Virginia Britannia expressing the Cosmographie and Commodities of the Country. Togither with the Manners and Customes of the People*, but the MS. was unpublished, as was a later one of 1618. Strachey was a friend of Sir Dudley Digges, member of the Council for the Virginia Company, and brother of Shakespeare's admirer, Leonard Digges.

Strange, Lord (Ferdinando Stanley). See DERBY, 5TH EARL OF.

Strange's Men. See DERBY'S MEN.

Stratford-upon-Avon. The manor of Stratford was granted by King Offa to the Bishopric of Worcester, and the borough came into existence *c.* 1195, when Bishop John de Coutances granted the inhabitants some self-government. The Gild of the Holy Cross, founded in the 13th century, became an additional organ of government, caring for its poor members, maintaining an almshouse and exercising control over the school which was attached to the Gild buildings in Church Street. These were rebuilt *c.* 1490 by Sir Hugh Clopton, who also built New Place opposite, and the bridge across the Avon. To the south of the town was the Church of the Holy Trinity (*c.* 1210); the aisles were added in 1330, and the chancel *c.* 1480. In 1332 a chantry for priests was founded, and in 1351 a 'college' was built to house them.

In 1547 Gild and College were dissolved, but the inhabitants were compensated by the grant of a charter of incorporation in 1553. There was to be a Bailiff and a Council of fourteen Aldermen and fourteen Capital Burgesses; the bailiff and one alderman were to act as justices of the peace, and the bailiff was to preside over the Court of Record with jurisdiction in civil cases up to £30. Part of the Gild property was transferred to the corporation, and out of it they had to maintain the almshouse and pay the schoolmaster and vicar, appointed by the lord of the manor, who also had the right of objecting to the bailiff elected by the Council, a right exercised by Edward Greville of Milcote when Richard Quiney was elected in 1592, though his cousin Sir Fulke Greville persuaded him to change his mind. In 1549 the Bishops of Worcester were deprived of the manor of Stratford; it remained with the Crown 1555–62, was granted to Ambrose Dudley, Earl of Warwick, 1562–90, was bought by Ludovic Greville of Milcote, and inherited by his son, Sir Edward. (A bailiff, unlike a mayor, was in theory the servant of the lord of the manor.) Some of the bailiffs of Shakespeare's time were:

1559–60 Adrian Quiney
1568–9 John Shakespeare
1592–3 Richard Quiney
1594–5 Thomas Rogers
1596–7 Abraham Sturley
1601–2 Richard Quiney
1615–16 Julius Shaw

The town formed a parallelogram bounded on the east by the Avon, on the north by the Gild Pits, on the west by Rother Market and Rother Street, and on the south by the church and College House. From Clopton Bridge the road ran west into Bridge Street, Middle Row, Wood Street, and so to Rother Market. Half-way along was the High Cross where Henley Street forked to the right, and on the left, intersecting the town from north to south, ran High Street, Chapel Street, Church Street.

Adrian Quiney, John and Mary Shakespeare, and the Harts lived in Henley Street; the poet bought New Place opposite the Gild Chapel in 1597; John Hall, his son-in-law, lived at Hall's Croft in the Old Town to the south, and his other son-in-law, Thomas Quiney, moved into The Cage (previously occupied by Quiney's brother-in-law William Chandler) at the corner of Bridge Street and High Street in 1616. When Thomas Greene left New Place he went to live in Church Way, near the Reynoldses, and Thomas Combe and his sons William and Thomas lived at College House. Abraham Sturley lived in Wood Street, Richard Quiney and Henry Walker in High Street, Hamlet Sadler at the corner of High Street and Sheep Street, and Julius Shaw moved from Henley Street to Corn Street near New Place.

There were serious fires in 1594 and 1595, when 120 houses and eighty other buildings were burned in the crowded north part of the town, including those of Adrian Quiney, Hamlet Sadler, and Thomas Rogers the bailiff. Much of Henley Street, Wood Street, Bridge Street, High Street and Sheep Street had to be rebuilt; the new house built in High Street by Rogers, grandfather of John Harvard, is now known as Harvard House.

Stratford was often visited by players on tour, when they would give an official performance in the Gild Hall (see PROVINCIAL COMPANIES), followed by performances in the inn-yards of Bridge Street. The visiting companies during Shakespeare's youth, the first when his father was bailiff, were:

1569 Queen's Interluders; Worcester's
1573 Leicester's
1575 Warwick's; Worcester's
1576 Leicester's; Worcester's
1579 Strange's; Countess of Essex's

1580 Derby's
1581 Worcester's; Berkeley's
1582 Worcester's; Berkeley's
1583 Berkeley's; Chandos's
1584 Oxford's; Worcester's; Essex's
1586 An unnamed company
1587 Queen's; Essex's; Leicester's; Stafford's; an unnamed company

Stratford Register. 'The earliest register preserved in the Church of the Holy Trinity, the only one in which there are entries respecting the great dramatist, is a narrow and thick folio consisting of leaves of vellum held in a substantial ancient binding, the latter being protected by metal at the outer corners. It bears on its original leather side the date of 1600, in which year all the entries from 1558 were transcribed into it from then existing records [probably by the vicar, Richard Byfield], the contents of each page being uniformly authenticated by the signatures of the vicar and the churchwardens. After this attested transcript had been made, the records of the later occurrences, taken probably from the sexton's notes, were entered into the book, and their accuracy officially therein certified, at frequent but unsettled intervals . . . so that there is not one amongst the following extracts which, in the manuscript, is more than a copy or an abridgment of a note made at the time of the ceremony.' (HALLIWELL-PHILLIPPS.)

The extracts referring to Shakespeare and his family are given below; C = Christening; M = Marriage; B = Burial; the three forming separate divisions in the register. [Pl. 1.]

1558	15 Sept.	C	Jone Shakspere daughter to John Shakspere
1562	2 Dec.	C	Margareta filia Johannis Shakspere
1563	30 Apr.	B	Margareta filia Johannis Shakspere
1564	26 Apr.	C	Gulielmus filius Johannes Shakspere
1566	13 Oct.	C	Gilbertus filius Johannis Shakspere
1569	15 Apr.	C	Jone the daughter of John Shakspere
1571	28 Sept.	C	Anna filia magistri Shakspere
1574	11 Mar.	C	Richard sonne to Mr John Shakspeer
1579	4 Apr.	B	Anne daughter to Mr John Shakspere
1580	3 May	C	Edmund sonne to Mr John Shakspere
1583	26 May	C	Susanna daughter to William Shakespeare
1585	2 Feb.	C	Hamnet & Judeth sonne and daughter to William Shakspere
1589	26 Feb.	C	Thomas sonne to Richard Queeny
1590	6 Mar.	B	Thomas Green alias Shakspere
1593	20 June	C	Thomas filius Anthonij Nash generosi
1596	11 Aug.	B	Hamnet filius William Shakspere
1600	28 Aug.	C	Wilhelmus filius Wilhelmi Hart
1601	8 Sept.	B	Mr Johannes Shakspeare
1603	5 June	C	Maria filia Wilhelmi Hart
1605	24 July	C	Thomas fil. Wilhelmus Hart Hatter
1607	5 June	M	John Hall gentleman & Susanna Shaxspere
1607	17 Dec.	B	Mary dawghter to Willyam Hart
1608	21 Feb.	C	Elizabeth dawghter to John Hall gentleman
1608	9 Sept.	B	Mayry Shaxspere, wydowe
1608	23 Sept.	C	Mychaell sonne to Willyam Hart
1612	3 Feb.	B	Gilbert Shakspere, adolescens
1613	4 Feb.	B	Rich: Shakspeare
1616	10 Feb.	M	Tho Queeny tow Judith Shakspere
1616	17 Apr.	B	Will. Hartt, hatter
1616	25 Apr.	B	Will. Shakspere, gent
1616	23 Nov.	C	Shaksper fillius Thomas Quyny gent
1617	8 May	B	Shakspere fillius Tho. Quyny, gent
1618	9 Feb.	C	Richard fillius Thomas Quinee
1618	1 Nov.	B	Micael filius to Jone Harte, widowe
1620	23 Jan.	C	Thomas filius to Thomas Queeney

1623	8 Aug.	B	Mrs Shakspeare [Anne Hathaway]
1626	22 Apr.	M	Mr Thomas Nash to Mrs Elizabeth Hall
1634	13 Apr.	C	Thomas filius Thomæ Hart
1635	26 Nov.	B	Johannes Hall, medicus peritissimus
1636	18 Sept.	C	Georgius filius Tho: Hart
1639	28 Jan.	B	Thomas filius Thomæ Quiney
1639	26 Feb.	B	Richardus filius Tho: Quiney
1639	29 Mar.	B	Willielmus Hart
1646	4 Nov.	B	Joan Hart, window
1647	5 Apr.	B	Thomas Nash, Gent
1649	16 July	B	Mrs Sussana Hall, widow
1662	9 Feb.	B	Judith, vxor Thomas Quiney Gent

Strato. In *Julius Caesar*, a servant of Brutus. After the defeat at Philippi he holds the sword on which Brutus kills himself. Octavius takes him into his service (v, v).

Stringer, Agnes. The poet's aunt, sister of Mary Arden. Her first husband was John Hewins, then in 1550 she married Thomas Stringer of Stockton, Shropshire, dying sometime before October 1576.

Stubbes, Philip (*c.* 1555–*c.* 1610), Puritan pamphleteer, was educated both at Cambridge and Oxford, but did not take a degree. His most popular work was *A Christal Glass for Christian Women*, 1591, but more important today is *The Anatomie of Abuses* (q.v.), with its attack on plays and players.

Sturley, Abraham (or Strelley), came from Worcester, entered Queens', Cambridge, in 1569, and was for a time employed by Sir Thomas Lucy of Charlecote. He settled at Stratford *c.* 1580, having married Anne, daughter of the bailiff Richard Hill, in 1575, became a member of the Corporation, and was himself bailiff in 1596. He calls his friend Richard Quiney his 'most lovinge Brother', possibly, Fripp suggests, because they were members of a religious brotherhood, or, as Chambers suggests, because they were both members of the Corporation. On 24 January 1598, when he was in difficulties after the Stratford fire of 1594, he wrote to Richard, who was then in London:

This is one speciall remembrance from v[r] fathers motion. It semeth bj him that our countriman, M[r] Shaksper, is willinge to disburse some monei vpon some od yardeland or other att Shottri or neare about vs; he thinketh it a verj fitt patterne to move him to deale in the matter of our tithes. Bj the instruccions v can geve him theareof, and bj the frendes he can make therefore, we thinke it a faire marke for him to shoote att, and not unpossible to hitt. It obtained would advance him in deede, and would do vs muche good. Hoc movere, et quantum in te est permouere, ne necligas, hoc enim et sibi et nobis maximi erit momenti.

Sturley often lapsed into Latin. The tithes referred to may have been the Clopton hay-tithes, farmed by Sturley and one of the Quineys in 1590. He died in 1614. (See QUINEY.)

Suffolk, Duke of (*c.* 1484–1545). In *Henry VIII*, he tells Wolsey of his disgrace, acts as High Steward at the coronation of Anne Boleyn, is one of the Councillors before whom Cranmer is arraigned, and is present at the christening of Princess Elizabeth. (Charles Brandon was a great favourite of Henry VIII, who created him Viscount Lisle in 1513, and Duke of Suffolk in 1514, before his marriage to Henry's sister, Mary Tudor.)

Suffolk, Earl of (1396–1450). In *1 Henry VI*, in the Temple Garden scene (II, iv) he shows himself a Lancastrian by plucking a red rose. At Angiers he captures Margaret, daughter of 'Reignier' Duke of Anjou, with whom he arranges her marriage to Henry VI, though he himself becomes her lover.

In *2 Henry VI*, he is created 1st Duke of Suffolk for arranging the marriage, and becomes very powerful, securing the disgrace of the Duchess of Gloucester and murder of the Duke, for which he is banished by the King. He is captured off the coast of Kent and beheaded by Walter Whitmore (IV, i). (William de la Pole succeeded his brother, killed at Agincourt (*H. V.*; IV, vi), as 4th Earl of Suffolk in 1415, and was created 1st Duke in 1448. His being the lover of Margaret is unhistorical.)

Sullivan, Arthur Seymour (1842–1900), collaborator with W. S. Gilbert in the D'Oyley Carte operas, made his name at the age of twenty when his incidental music for *The Tempest* was performed at the Crystal Palace in 1862. By 1864, the year of the tercentenary celebrations, he had written the *Kenilworth Cantata*, with the duet 'How sweet the moonlight', and five songs from Shakespeare, including 'O Mistress Mine', 'Orpheus with his Lute' and 'The Willow Song'. He also wrote incidental music for *Henry VIII* (1877), and for the flying witches in Irving's production of *Macbeth*.

Sullivan, Barry (1824–91), Irish actor, was born at Birmingham, made his first stage appearance at Cork, and his first appearance in London, as Hamlet, in 1852. One of his best parts was Richard III. When he was 55 he played Benedick to Helen Faucit's Beatrice in *Much Ado*, the play which opened the first Memorial Theatre at Stratford in 1879.

'Supposes.' See GASGOIGNE, GEORGE.

'Suppositi.' See ARIOSTO.

Surrey, Duke of. In *Richard II*, he defends Aumerle against Fitzwater's charge of treason (IV, i), joins the rebellion against Bolingbroke, but is captured and killed. (Thomas Holand, 3rd Earl of Kent (1374–1400), was created Duke of Surrey by Richard II in 1397, but deprived of his title by Bolingbroke in 1399. He is called Kent in V, vi.)

Surrey, Earl of. 1. In *2 Henry IV*, 'Of the Kings Partie' (F), he appears but does not speak in III, i. (Thomas Fitz-Alan, Earl of Arundel and Surrey (1381–1415).)

2. In *Richard III*, fights for Richard at Bosworth (V, iii). (Thomas Howard, Earl of Surrey (1443–1524), succeeded his father, killed at Bosworth, in 1485, as 2nd Duke of Norfolk, under which title he appears in *Henry VIII*.)

3. In *Henry VIII*, Thomas Howard (1473–1554) succeeded his father as 3rd Duke of Norfolk in 1524. He married Buckingham's daughter and was the father of the poet. Like his father, who was really dead by the time of the action of III, ii, he opposes Wolsey, and avenges Buckingham's death.

Surrey, Henry Howard, Earl of (*c.* 1517–47), succeeded to the courtesy title of Earl of Surrey when his father became 3rd Duke of Norfolk in 1524. He was executed on a fantastic charge of high treason in January 1547, a few days before the death of Henry VIII. Surrey was a friend of Sir Thomas Wyatt (q.v.). Both were poets; they brought the sonnet from Italy, and the earliest blank verse in English is Surrey's translation of books II and IV of the *Aeneid*.

Surveyor, to the Duke of Buckingham. In *Henry VIII* (I, ii), he falsely swears that Buckingham had threatened to kill the King. (Charles Knyvet, the surveyor, had been dismissed by Buckingham 'on the complaint o' the tenants'.)

Sussex's Men. Thomas Radcliffe, 3rd Earl of Sussex, became Lord Chamberlain in 1572, in which year his company first appeared at Court, and then fairly regularly until his death in 1583. They are sometimes called the Chamberlain's during this period. The year 1583 saw the formation of the favoured Queen's company, and under the patronage of

Henry, 4th Earl, they disappear from the Court records until January 1592. His son Robert became 5th Earl in December, 1593, during the plague year when all the companies had to travel. However, they played for Henslowe at the beginning of 1594, in a repertory of twelve plays, one of which was 'titus & ondronicous', Q1 of *Titus Andronicus* being published that year as having been 'Plaide by the Right Honourable the Earle of Darbie, Earle of Pembrooke, and Earle of Sussex their Seruants'. In April 'the queenes men and my lord of Sussex together' gave eight performances at Henslowe's theatre. Perhaps they joined the Queen's, for they are not heard of again as an independent company until 1602, after which they are traceable in the provinces for many years.

It is possible that the 4th Earl was the 'Lord' for whose company Kyd and Marlowe were writing in 1593, and also that Shakespeare wrote *Titus Andronicus* for them.

Swan Theatre, fourth of the London theatres, was built by Francis Langley (q.v.) in Paris Garden, at the western end of the Bankside and 150 yards south of Paris Garden stairs, probably in 1595, certainly by February 1597, when Pembroke's contracted with Langley to play there for a year, at which date it 'was then lately afore vsed to have playes in hit'. Hotson's discovery of Shakespeare's association with Langley (see WAYTE) suggests that the earlier company was the Chamberlain's who had migrated from the Theatre and gone to the new Swan in the autumn of 1596. De Witt's famous drawing of the interior of the Swan is also thought to date from 1596, so that the actors on the stage may be Shakespeare's company.

It depicts a circular building with three rows of seats in each of the three galleries, the bottom one of which is marked 'orchestra' (q.v.). The apron stage, which is not boarded in, projects into the 'arena' or yard, and half-way back supports the columns of the shadow. There is no central recess, or inner stage, only two doors in the wall of the 'mimorum aedes' or tiring-house. Above are six boxes, apparently occupied by spectators, and above the roof of the shadow is the hut from which a flag flies and a man seems to be sounding the trumpet, although the play has begun. There is no scenery, no curtains, and the only property is a bench. It is a fair drawing, though it looks like a rapid sketch from memory, and is puzzling: the unenclosed stage without traps for the effects that we know could be produced at the Swan; the slight projection of the shadow; the absence of an inner stage. A translation of de Witt's Latin description reads:

> Of all the theatres, however, the finest and the biggest is that whose sign is a swan (commonly called the Swan theatre), for it will seat 3,000 people, is built of a concrete of flints (which are very numerous in Britain), and is supported by wooden columns so painted that they would deceive the most acute observer into thinking that they were marble. As it appears to resemble a Roman building, I have drawn it above.

The Swan is clearly marked in Norden's map of 1600 as a round building, but so are the other theatres.

The disastrous *Isle of Dogs* episode occurred in July 1597, and there is no evidence of continuous occupation by a company. Langley died in 1601, and Paris Garden was bought by Hugh Browker. The Swan appears to have been used for various forms of spectacle until 1611, when Henslowe may have used it for the Lady Elizabeth's before building the Hope, which was modelled on it, in 1614. 'After the year 1620, as appears from Sir Henry Herbert's office-book, they [the Swan and the Rose] were used occasionally for the exhibition of prize-fighters.' (Malone, *Var.* III, 56.) In *Holland's Leaguer* (1632), it is described as 'now fallen to decay'.

Swanston, Eliard. An actor with the Lady Elizabeth's, he joined the King's company in 1624, stayed with them until the closing of the theatres in 1642, and signed the players' dedication to the 4th Earl of Pembroke (q.v.) of the Beaumont and Fletcher Folio of 1647. He was one of the three petitioners of the Sharers' Papers (q.v.). 'Swanston used to play Othello' (*Historia Histrionica*, 1699).

Sweden. English 'comoedianten und springer' were at Nyköping 28 August 1592 for the wedding of Duke Karl of Sweden and Princess Christina of Holstein. A Swedish translation of Shakespeare's plays was made by C. A Hagberg, 1847–51 (12 vols.). Thanks largely to the producer, Alf Sjöberg, Shakespeare is frequently performed, particularly *Hamlet* (recently translated by B. Collinder) and *The Taming of the Shrew*. Gustaf Freden's *William Shakespeare*, a critical study, appeared in 1958. (See Erik Wikland, *Elizabethan Players in Sweden, 1591–92*, 1962.)

Swinburne, Algernon Charles (1837–1909), an ardent admirer of all things Elizabethan, who did much, like Charles Lamb, to revive interest in the minor Elizabethan drama. An inspired interpreter, but an erratic critic who exhausts the superlatives of the language, he published in 1880 *A Study of Shakespeare* in which he maintained that 'rhyme was Shakespeare's evil angel', and Imogen 'the woman best beloved in all the world of song and all the tide of time'.

Syllabic Variation. The variation of the number of syllables in a line. A regular blank verse line has ten syllables (five iambic feet); the substitution of an anapaest or dactyl will give eleven, as will the redundant final syllable of a feminine ending. In a catalectic line there is a syllable missing, as in,

Hav | ing call'd | thee from | the deep! | O still

Like other irregularities, syllabic variation becomes more frequent in Shakespeare's later verse.

Symons, John. An acrobat with Strange's, first mentioned in the Chamber Accounts as payee for the company 'for showinge certen ffeates of actiuitye and Tomblinge' on 1 January 1583. Until 1587 he produced a fairly regular New Year turn at Court, in 1585 as servant to 'Therle of Oxforde'. In 1588 he joined the Queen's, possibly taking some of Strange's tumblers with him.

T

Tabor. A small drum, usually associated with the pipe (q.v.), the tabor being played with the right hand and the pipe with the left. Feste played the tabor (*Twelfth Night*, III, i).

Taine, Hippolyte (1828–93), French historian and critic in the Romantic tradition. The chapter on Shakespeare in his *Histoire de la Littérature Anglaise* (1865) is one of the most important 19th-century French contributions to the subject. He sees Shakespeare as the unrestrained and passionate genius of a passionate age: 'une nature d'esprit extraordinaire . . . toute puissante, excessive, également souveraine dans le sublime et dans l'ignoble . . .'

Talbot, Lord. In *1 Henry VI*, he is captured at Patay by Joan of Arc owing to the desertion of Sir John Fastolfe, whose cowardice he later exposes. He escapes from the Countess of Auvergne's trap, retakes Rouen, and is finally surrounded and killed with his son near Bordeaux (IV, vii). (John Talbot, 6th Baron, was created 1st Earl of Shrewsbury in 1442. He spent much of his life fighting against the Welsh, Irish and French, and was killed with his son, Lord Lisle, at Castillon in 1453. See 'PIERCE PENILESSE'.)

'Tamburlaine.' A tragedy in two parts, written *c.* 1587, registered 14 August 1590 as 'The twooe commicall discourses of Tomberlein the Cithian shepparde', and published in the same year, as,

Tamburlaine the Great. Who, from a Scythian Shephearde by his rare and wonderfull Conquests became a most puissant and mightye Monarque. And (for his tyranny, and terrour in Warre) was tearmed, The Scourge of God. Deuided into two Tragicall Discourses, as they were sundrie times shewed vpon Stages in the Citie of London, By the right honorable the Lord Admyrall, his seruantes.

The play could have been written by nobody but Marlowe, but there is little external evidence to show that it is his: mainly an allusion by Greene to 'that atheist Tamburlan'. The verse of *Tamburlaine* influenced Shakespeare, and Richard III probably owes something to the Scythian Shepherd. *The Taming of A Shrew* incorporates a number of lines from *Tamburlaine*.

'Tamer Tamed, The.' A comedy by John Fletcher, written *c.* 1605, and first published in the Beaumont and Fletcher Folio of 1647, as *The Woman's Prize, or The Tamer Tam'd*. It is a sequel to *The Taming of the Shrew*, in which Petruchio is tamed by his second wife, the chaste and witty Maria. (See KNIGHT, EDWARD.)

'Taming of a Shrew, The.' An anonymous play of *c.* 1589:

REGISTERED: 1594. 'Secundo die Maij. Peter Shorte, Entred vnto him for his copie vnder master warden Cawoodes hande, a booke intituled A plesant Conceyted historie called the Tayminge of a Shrowe.'

PUBLISHED: 1594, Q1. 'A Pleasant Conceited Historie, called The taming of a Shrew. As it was sundry times acted by the Right honorable the Earle of Pembroke his seruants. Printed at London by Peter Short and are to be sold by Cuthbert Burbie, at his shop at the Royall Exchange.'

1596, Q2. Printed by Short and sold by Burby.

1607. On 22 January Burby transferred the copyright to Nicholas Ling, who published Q3 (printed by Simmes) and then on 19 November transferred it to John Smethwick.

A Shrew and *The Shrew* were confused in the publishing trade; Blount and Jaggard did not register *The Shrew* in 1623 with the rest of the previously unpublished plays before publishing F, of which Smethwick was one of the publishing syndicate; he held the copyright of *A Shrew*, good enough for *The Shrew* of F, and for Q, which he published in 1631.

A Shrew is similar to *The Shrew*, though the sub-plot is less complicated. There are the three themes of Christopher Sly, the taming of Kate by Ferando (Petruchio) and the sub-plot, taken from Gascoigne's *Supposes*, of Philema-Aurelius (Bianca-Lucentio). Some of the verse reads like imitation Marlowe, and passages of *Tamburlaine* and *Faustus* are liberally pilfered. Chambers thinks *A Shrew* the source play of *The Shrew*; Alexander and Wilson that it is a 'bad' Quarto of *The Shrew*, put together by Pembroke's after selling *The Shrew* in 1593; Duthie that it is a 'bad' Quarto of an earlier *Shrew* play, from which *The Shrew* is also derived.

'TAMING OF THE SHREW, THE.'

WRITTEN: 1593-4. Not mentioned by Meres.

PERFORMED: 1594, 13 June: 'the Tamynge of A Shrowe'; Henslowe's entry when the Admiral's and Chamberlain's were playing at Newington. This may be either *A* or *The Shrew*, and was presumably a Chamberlain's play. (See ROWLANDS.)

1633. 'On Tusday night at Saint James, the 26 of Novemb. 1633, was acted before the Kinge and Queene, The Taminge of the Shrewe. Likt.' (*Office-book of Sir H. Herbert.*)

REGISTERED: See 'Taming of a Shrew'.

PUBLISHED: 1623, F1. 'The Taming of the Shrew.' The eleventh play in the Comedy section: pp. 208-29. Acts, except II, marked. A fair text, set up from foul papers (the name of the actor Sincklo occurs as a speech-prefix for *Player* in *Ind.* I, 88).

1631, Q. 'A Wittie and Pleasant Comedie Called The Taming of the Shrew. As it was acted by his Maiesties Seruants at the Blacke Friers and the Globe. Written by Will. Shakespeare. Printed by W. S. for Iohn Smethwicke, and are to be sold at his Shop in Saint Dunstones Churchyard vnder the Diall. 1631.'

SOURCES: See 'Taming of a Shrew'. The Bianca sub-plot, whether by Shakespeare or another, derives from the *Supposes* of Gascoigne (q.v.).

STAGE HISTORY: 1667, 9 April. John Lacy's prose adaptation, *Sauny the Scot*, was seen by Pepys.

1715. Christopher Bullock's *Cobler of Preston* at Lincoln's Inn Fields anticipated Charles Johnson's *Cobler of Preston* (1716) at Drury Lane, a mixture of Sly and the '15 rebellion.

1735. Drury Lane: 'A Cure for a Scold, a Ballad Opera, by James Worsdale. Taken from the Taming of the Shrew' – or rather from *Sauny the Scot*.

1754. *Katherine and Petruchio*, by Garrick at Drury Lane, a version that held the stage for 100 years. Tree produced it in 1897, the Lichfield Repertory Company in 1949.

1844. Benjamin Webster staged Shakespeare's play uncut, and without scenery.

1928. Barry Jackson's modern dress production at Birmingham.

Christopher Sly, a drunken tinker, is found asleep by a Lord and his huntsmen and taken to his house, where he is surrounded by every luxury and persuaded that he is the master, having been out of his mind for fifteen years. A page disguises himself as his wife, and a company of travelling players present The Taming of the Shrew before them.

The elder daughter of Baptista of Padua is Katharina, the shrew, who he insists shall be married before he consents to the marriage of her younger sister Bianca, who has many suitors. Petruchio, an adventurer from Verona, undertakes the wooing of Kate, partly to help his friend Hortensio to win Bianca, but mainly for the sake of her dowry. Once she is his property he carries her off to his country house and tames her by preventing her eating and sleeping, and then takes her back to Padua.

There, Lucentio has outwitted his rivals and won Bianca by pretending to be her schoolmaster, and the disgusted Hortensio consoles himself with a rich widow. At a feast in Lucentio's house, Lucentio, Petruchio, and Hortensio have a wager as to whose wife is the most submissive, and Petruchio wins easily. (See 'TAMER TAMED'.)

Tamora. In *Titus Andronicus* (q.v.), Queen of the Goths. (There was a Tamara, or Thamar, who was Queen of Georgia 1184–1212.)

Tannenbaum, Samuel Aaron 1874–1948, physician and writer, was born in Hungary and went to the U.S. in 1886. He was editor of the *Shakespeare Association Bulletin*, an authority on Elizabethan handwriting and forgeries, and an opponent of the theory that Shakespeare had a hand in *Sir Thomas More*. (See COLLIER.)

Tarlton, Richard, the most famous and popular comedian of the late 16th century, joined the Queen's Men on their formation in 1583, was one of the Queen's private jesters, an 'ordinary Groom of her Majesty's Chamber', and buried on 3 September 1588. Tarlton wrote *The Seven Deadly Sins*, originally a Queen's play, but revived by Strange's or the Admiral's *c.* 1590. Henry Chettle in his *Kind-Harts Dreame* describes his 'sute of russet, his buttoned cap, his taber, his standing on the toe, and other tricks', with which the wood-cut on the title-page of *Tarlton Jests* (*c.* 1599) agrees. This is a collection of old jests mixed with some biographical matter, telling how Tarlton played at the Curtain and the Bell Inn, and doubled the clown and judge in *The Famous Victories of Henry V* at the Bull in Bishopsgate. He has been claimed as the 'pleasant Willy' of *The Tears of the Muses* (see SPENSER), and as the original of Yorick in *Hamlet*. (See also Induction to BARTHOLOMEW FAIR.)

Tate, Nahum (1652–1715), was born in Dublin and educated at Trinity College, but settled in London, where he published his first volume of poems in 1677. He wrote the libretto for Purcell's *Dido and Aeneas*, collaborated with Nicholas Brady in the *New Version of the Psalms* (1696), and with Dryden in the second part of *Absalom and Achitophel*, succeeding Shadwell as Poet Laureate in 1692. His plays are mostly adaptations from the Elizabethans; for example, *The*

Cuckold's Haven from *Eastward Ho!*, and *Injured Love* from *The White Devil*; but he is best known for his adaptations of three of Shakespeare's plays. In 1680 his version of *Richard II* was produced at Drury Lane, but suppressed by the government, who disliked the deposition theme. Tate altered the scene and names of the characters, called it *The Sicilian Usurper*, and published a vindication in which he claimed that his play was 'full of respect to Majesty', but in vain. He was more successful with *Coriolanus*, produced at Drury Lane in 1681–2 as *The Ingratitude of a Common-Wealth*, a tragedy indeed: Aufidius is killed, young Martius is tortured to death, Volumnia goes mad, and Virgilia commits suicide. Meanwhile the most famous version, or perversion, of all had been produced at the Duke's theatre in 1681, *The History of King Lear*, in which the Fool is omitted, Edgar is made Cordelia's lover, and all ends happily with Lear restored and Cordelia married. Until 1823, when Kean restored the tragic ending, Tate's version held the stage – with the approval of Johnson – to the exclusion of Shakespeare's, which was only restored in full by Macready in 1838.

Taurus, Statilius. In *Antony and Cleopatra*, commander of Caesar's army at Actium. Caesar orders him, 'Strike not by land . . . till we have done at sea' (III, iii).

Tawyer, William. A hired actor with the King's in a revival, probably late, of *M.N.D.* In F, v, i, the interlude players are preceded by *Tawyer with a Trumpet before them*, a prompter's note. A 'William Tawier, Mr Heminges man' was buried at St Saviour's in June 1625.

Taylor, John (1580–1653), the 'Water-Poet', was born and educated at Gloucester, pressed for the navy, sailed with Essex on the Cadiz raid and Islands Voyage (1596–7), and then became a Thames waterman, styling himself 'the king's water-poet and the queen's water-man'. He celebrated his fantastic journeys, such as his attempted voyage to Queenborough in a paper boat, and accomplished visit to the Queen of Bohemia in Prague, in verse and prose pamphlets, sixty-three of which he published in his '*Works*' in 1630. At the beginning of the Civil War, he kept a public-house at Oxford, D'Avenant's native town; then, when the Royalists were expelled, he took The Crown in Long Acre, London. The jest reported by Thomas Hearne (q.v.) about Shakespeare's relationship to D'Avenant, without its later application, occurs in Taylor's *Wit and Mirth* (1629):

> A boy, whose mother was noted to be one not overloden with honesty, went to seeke his godfather, and enquiring for him, quoth one to him, Who is thy godfather? The boy repli'd, his name is goodman Digland the gardiner. Oh, said the man, if he be thy godfather, he is at the next alehouse, but I fear thou takest God's name in vain.

In *The Praise of Hemp-seed* Taylor sings,

> *Spencer*, and *Shakespeare* did in Art excell . . .
> Forgetfulnesse their workes would ouer run,
> But that in paper they immortally
> Doe liue in spight of death, and cannot die.

In 1614, when there were no theatres open on the Bankside, to the great loss of the watermen who were used to ferry spectators from the north bank to the Swan, Rose, Globe and Paris Garden, Taylor petitioned the King on their behalf to prohibit theatres within four miles of the City on the north bank. According to Taylor, it was seriously considered, and the King's Men, with their eyes on their Blackfriars theatre, prepared a counter-petition. However, the new Globe and the Hope were built in 1614, and Taylor was accused by his fellow watermen of treating secretly with the players, and nothing came of the petition. Taylor, however, wrote his defence in *The True Cause of the Watermen's Suit concerning Players.* (See JACKSON, JOHN; VINCENT.)

Taylor, Joseph. One of the 'Principall Actors' in Shakespeare's plays (see p. 90). He left the Prince's company for the King's in April 1619, presumably to replace Burbage who had died in March. Some of the parts he played were Truewit in *The Silent Woman*, Face in *The Alchemist*, Mosca in *Volpone*, Ferdinand in *The Duchess of Malfi*, Paris in *The Roman Actor*, Iago and Hamlet, in which part John Downes says he was trained by Shakespeare himself, but as Shakespeare died three years before Taylor joined the company, this seems improbable. After the deaths of Condell and Heminge, he and Lowin took over the management of the company, and in 1630 he acquired two shares in the Globe and one in the Blackfriars. In 1639 he was appointed Yeoman of the Revels under Sir Henry Herbert. Three years later the theatres were closed, and he was one of the players who signed the dedication to the 4th Earl of Pembroke (q.v.) of the Beaumont and Fletcher Folio of 1647. He died at Richmond, where he was buried 4 November 1652.

Tearsheet, Doll. In *2 Henry IV*, mistress of Falstaff with whom she sups at Mistress Quickly's Boar's Head Tavern, and quarrels with Pistol on his first appearance (II, iv). In V, iv she is dragged off to prison as a harlot about whom 'there hath been a man or two lately killed'. In *Henry V* (V, i), Pistol says 'my Doll is dead i' the spital'. (See QUICKLY.)

Teatro Olimpico. See PALLADIO.

'TEMPEST, THE.'

WRITTEN: 1611–12.

PERFORMED: 1611, 1 November. 'By the Kings players: Hallowmas nyght was presented att Whithall before ye kinges Maiestie a play Called the Tempest.' (*Revels Account.*)

1613. 'Item paid to John Heminges upon the Cowncells warrant dated att Whitehall xx^o die Maij 1613, for presentinge before the Princes Highnes the Lady Elizabeth and the Prince Pallatyne Elector fowerteene severall playes, viz: ... The Tempest, ... the some of iiij^xx xiij^li vj^s viij^d. (*Chamber Account.*)

REGISTERED: 1623, 8 November. One of the sixteen plays registered by Blount and Jaggard before publishing F1.

PUBLISHED: 1623, F1. 'The Tempest.' The first play in the Folio: pp. 1–19. Acts and scenes marked; 'Names of the Actors' given, and 'The Scene, an vn-inhabited Island'; the most detailed stage-directions in F. A good text. Set up from a transcript by Crane of foul papers prepared for production. It is possible that the masque was added for the wedding of the Lady Elizabeth in February 1613.

SOURCES: For the Island: Narratives of the wreck of Sir George Somers, Sir Thomas Gates, William Strachey, Sylvester Jourdan, Richard Rich and others on the Bermudas in July 1609:

Rich's ballad of *News from Virginia* (October 1610).

Jourdan's *A Discovery of the Barmudas* (October 1610).

A True Declaration of the Estate of the Colonie in Virginia (November 1610), an official report.

Strachey's *A True Reportory of the Wracke and Redemption of Sir Thomas Gates, Knight*, a MS report (1610) published 1625.

Shakespeare may have had the story from Sir Dudley Digges, who visited his step-father, Thomas Russell, at Alderminster, near Stratford, in September 1610.

For the plot: see AYRER, JACOB; 'SCHÖNE SIDEA'; 'LI TRE SATIRI'; PROSPERO. See also EDEN; MONTAIGNE.

STAGE HISTORY: There is no record of a public performance before the Restoration, though Dryden in the preface to his version says that it had been acted at Blackfriars.

1667. *The Tempest, or The Enchanted Island* at the Duke's theatre, where the first performance was seen by Pepys (7 November). This is the polished version by Dryden and D'Avenant; Miranda is balanced by a younger sister, Dorinda, Ferdinand by Hippolito who had never seen a woman, Caliban by his sister Sycorax, and Ariel by the female spirit Milcha. Purcell wrote the music.

1674. Shadwell turned the Dryden-D'Avenant version into an opera with music by Purcell.

1746. Shakespeare's *Tempest* at Drury Lane.

1756. Garrick's operatic version with music by J. C. Smith.

1838. Macready at Covent Garden returned to, and established, the original play, rarely performed before this date.

1857. Charles Kean's production 'requiring the aid of 140 operatives', to manage 'the scenic appliances'.

1959. D'Avenant-Dryden version at the Old Vic.

Prospero, Duke of Milan, more interested in his books and magic than in his dukedom, is expelled by his brother Antonio and put to sea in a rotten ship with his baby daughter Miranda. They reach an island inhabited by a half-human creature, Caliban, son of the witch Sycorax, who has imprisoned the spirit Ariel, and these two Prospero makes his servants.

Twelve years later, when the play begins, Prospero by his magic contrives the shipwreck of Alonso, King of Naples, and his followers, including his brother Sebastian, his son Ferdinand, the honest counsellor Gonzalo, and Prospero's own brother, Antonio. Ferdinand, who is separated from the others and thinks himself the only survivor, meets Miranda, and at once they fall in love, according to Prospero's design, though he pretends to think him a spy and by his magic forces him to do the work of a slave. Meanwhile, Sebastian and Antonio attempt to murder Alonso and Gonzalo, and Caliban, who has met Stephano and Trinculo, a drunken butler and a jester, persuades them to set out to murder Prospero. Prospero releases Ferdinand from his spell, gives Miranda to him, and makes Ariel present a masque before the lovers, but interrupts it to drive off Caliban, Stephano and Trinculo, and to bring the spellbound King and his courtiers to his cell. He forgives his brother Antonio, but makes him promise to restore his dukedom, and himself restores Ferdinand to Alonso. The ship and crew are found to be safe, Prospero renounces his magic, frees Ariel, and all prepare to set sail for Italy, leaving Caliban once more the sole occupant of the island. (Shakespeare here obeys the unities: the action takes place in one day and in the same place.)

Temple Grafton. A village five miles west of Stratford, where Shakespeare may have been married after obtaining a licence from the Bishop of Worcester to be married with only once asking of the banns. The sureties of Shakespeare (a minor) for the licence, Fulk Sandells and John Richardson, entered into a bond on 28 November 1582, which stated that 'William Shagspere' intended marrying 'Anne Hathewey of Stratford in the Dioces of Worcester maiden'. But the clerk's entry of the day before in the Bishop's *Register* states that a licence had been issued to 'Willelmum Shaxpere et Annam Whateley de Temple Grafton'. The bond can scarcely be incorrect, but the clerk may have muddled his entry in the Register, as a dispute involving William Whateley, though of Crowle, had been before the consistory court on the same day. Fripp suggests that Anne Hathaway lived with her mother at Temple Grafton after her father's death in 1581. The simplest explanation is that Temple Grafton was the church where the marriage was to be celebrated, though there is no register of the period. It should be remembered that the bond was discovered only in 1836, more than 100 years after Rowe had written that Shakespeare's 'Wife was the Daughter of one Hathaway . . . of Stratford'.

Nothing is known of Anne Whateley. There were Whateleys at Henley-in-Arden; George Whateley of Stratford presented John Whateley to the living of Crowle, the manor of the Combe family, and William Whateley was vicar in 1582. Ivor Brown suggests that she was a girl with whom Shakespeare ran away to be married, but was forced to marry the pregnant Anne Hathaway.

'Temple Shakespeare.' An edition of Shakespeare's Works in 40 vols. 8vo, edited by Israel Gollancz, 1894–6.

Ten Brink, Bernhard (1841–92), was of Dutch origin, but educated in Germany, in 1873 became Professor of English at Strassburg University. He was a great Chaucer scholar, and wrote an unfinished *History of English Literature*; his *Five Lectures on Shakespeare*, delivered at Frankfort, were published in 1893 (in English in 1895).

Terence (*c.* 185–159 B.C.). Publius Terentius Afer was born at Carthage and brought to Rome as a slave, where he was freed by his master, Terentius Lucanus, whose name he adopted. After writing six comedies he sailed for Greece, whence he never returned. His comedies are imitations of the New Comedy of Athens, particularly of Menander (342–291), but the purity of his style has always been admired, and he had a great influence on Latin literature and that of the Renaissance. The comedies of Terence and Plautus were much acted by the schools and universities in England, as well as at Court, in the first half of the 16th century, and served as models for the construction of native plays: for example, *Ralph Roister Doister*.

Terry, Ellen Alicia (1848–1928), was born at Coventry, and at the age of eight first appeared on the stage of the Princess's theatre as Mamillius in Charles Kean's antiquarian production of *The Winter's Tale*. In 1858 she played Arthur in *King John*, and in 1867, in Garrick's version of *The Taming of the Shrew*, Katharine to the Petruchio of Irving, who in 1878 engaged her as his leading lady when he began his management of the Lyceum. There, for the next twenty-five years, she acted in Irving's Shakespearean revivals: Ophelia, Portia (one of her greatest parts), Desdemona, Juliet, Beatrice, Viola, Lady Macbeth, Queen Katharine, Cordelia, Imogen and Volumnia. She paid several visits to the U.S.A. with the Lyceum company. In 1902 she played in Tree's production of *The Merry Wives* at His Majesty's, and again in 1911. Her stage-jubilee was celebrated in 1906, and her last regular performance was as the Nurse in *Romeo and Juliet* in 1919. She was created G.B.E. in 1925. She was married three times: to the painter G. F. Watts, to the actor E. A. Wardell, and in 1907 to the American actor James Carew. Her sisters Kate and Marion became well-known actresses, and her brother Fred a leading actor-manager in association with his wife Julia Neilson. Gordon Craig was her son.

Textual Criticism. In their address 'To the Great Variety of Readers' in the First Folio, Heminge and Condell wrote:

> As where (before) you were abus'd with diuerse stolne, and surreptitious copies, maimed, and deformed by the frauds and stealthes of iniurious impostors, that expos'd them: euen those, are now offer'd to your view cur'd, and perfect of their limbes, and all the rest, absolute in their numbers, as he conceiued them.

This was interpreted by most 18th- and 19th-century editors as meaning that *all* the Quartos were corrupt versions. Yet Heminge and Condell had reprinted them in the Folio. It followed that they were themselves injurious impostors, and their claim to have restored the text was false. New editors, therefore, despairing of ever recovering what Shakespeare really wrote, felt free to adapt the text to suit their tastes; Pope and Hanmer 'threw to the bottom of the page' any passage that displeased them, and amended by 'intuition', while Johnson wrote:

> They [the plays] were immediately copied for the actors, and multiplied by transcript after transcript, vitiated by the blunders of the penman, or changed by the affectation of the player; perhaps enlarged to introduce a jest, or mutilated to shorten the representation; and printed at last without the concurrence of the author, without the consent of the proprietor, from compilations made by chance or by stealth out of the separate parts written for the theatre: and thus thrust into the world surreptitiously and hastily, they suffered another depravation from the ignorance and negligence of the printers, as every man who knows the state of the press in that age will readily conceive ... no other editions were made from fragments so minutely broken, and so fortuitously reunited; and in no other age was the art of printing in such unskilful hands.

And no man, quite ignorant of his facts, ever spoke more confidently than Johnson. Yet even as late as 1902 Sidney Lee maintained:

> The greater number of the quarto editions of Shakespeare's plays which were published

in his lifetime seem to have been printed from more or less imperfect and unauthorized playhouse transcripts which were obtained by publishers more or less dishonestly.

Lee wrote when A. W. Pollard, helped by W. W. Greg, was studying the so-called 'False Folio', which he proved to have been printed by Jaggard (q.v.) in 1619. In 1909 he published his findings in his epoch-making *Shakespeare Folios and Quartos*. In this he showed that Heminge and Condell had been misunderstood and wrongly suspected of imposture. *Some* of the Quartos were corrupt, 'maimed and deformed', and these he labelled 'bad'; but the great majority were good. Some of them, he argued, were probably printed from prompt copies, and some of these prompt copies were probably in Shakespeare's handwriting. The Folio, therefore, had been set up from these good Quartos and, for those plays previously unpublished, from similar copy delivered to the printer by Heminge and Condell, whose claim to have restored the text to the best of their ability was true.

There is, however, no surviving example of a dramatist's original manuscript being used as prompt-book, and in *The Elizabethan Printer and Dramatic Manuscripts* (1931) R. B. McKerrow argued that the manuscript sent by a company of players to the printer was not the prompt-book, which they would want to keep as the licensed 'book', but the author's original manuscript, his 'foul papers'. It was even better than Pollard had dared to hope.

All this was revolutionary. Half of the plays had apparently been printed from foul papers, many of the remainder from transcripts of them, and very few at more than one remove from them. Emendation of the text, therefore, was no longer a matter of intuition but of 'critical bibliography': a knowledge of the copy and of Elizabethan printing. This was helped by the discovery that Shakespeare probably wrote three pages of the manuscript play *Sir Thomas More* (q.v.), for if we know the peculiarities of his handwriting, spelling and punctuation we know the kind of error that a compositior would be likely to make, and in 1921 Dover Wilson, applying this 'new scientific method' to the editing of Shakespeare, published the first play of the *New Cambridge* edition, *The Tempest*.

Since then, however, there have been doubts. In 1932 E. E. Willoughby's *Printing of the First Folio* broke new ground, and in recent years the Folio has been subjected to intensive bibliographical investigation, notably by two more Americans, Charlton Hinman and Philip Williams, some, though not all, of whose findings Greg was able to incorporate in his monumental *Shakespeare First Folio* (1955). In her *Textual Problems of the First Folio* (1953) Alice Walker argued that Jaggard (not unnaturally) preferred printed to written copy, and that several plays, including *Hamlet, Othello* and *2 Henry IV*, were printed from corrected 'good' Quartos. If so, the Folio is of less authority than Pollard and the older school of bibliographers supposed. Moreover, Miss Walker indicated the startling number of errors made in setting the text, and in his *Printing and Proof-Reading of the First Folio* (1963) Hinman has shown how incompetent was some of the typesetting and how inadequate the proof-reading, that there are hundreds of variant readings in the known copies of the Folio, that five compositors set it, and that their task was made more difficult by the setting of the text by formes and consequent casting-off of copy. In short, we are at the beginning of a new age of textual criticism involving the study of the characteristics of individual compositors (q.v.), and, aware of the number and kind of errors that they made, editors will have to be prepared to amend the text more boldly. (See Dover Wilson's *New Way with Shakespeare's Texts* in SS, 7, 8. 9, 11.)

Thaisa. In *Pericles* (q.v.), daughter of King Simonides of Pentapolis, wife of

Pericles and mother of Marina. (In Gower's *Confessio Amantis* Thaise is Pericles' daughter; in Twine's *Patterne of Paynfull Adventures* she is called Lucina.)

Thaliard. In *Pericles*, a lord of Antioch who appears only in Act I, where Antiochus orders him to kill Pericles whom he follows to Tyre, but finds that he has sailed to some place unknown. (The Thaliarchus of Twine's *Patterne of Paynfull Adventures.*)

Theatre, The. On 13 April 1576 Giles Allen leased to James Burbage a plot of land just to the north of Bishopsgate, in the parish of St Leonard's, Shoreditch. It was part of an estate, formerly a priory of Benedictine nuns with a Holy Well, whence its name and status, the Liberty of Holywell or Halliwell, outside the jurisdiction of the City. The lease was for twenty-one years at a rent of £14, renewable for a further twenty-one within the first ten years provided Burbage spent £200 on the buildings; the tenant was to be allowed to take away any theatrical buildings erected on the site, and Allen and his family were to have free seats 'in some one of the vpper romes' (Lords' room?). The theatre was built between Shoreditch High Street and the present Curtain Road; it cost about £650, most of which was contributed by Burbage's partner and brother-in-law, John Brayne (q.v.), and was open by August 1577 (see 'SHARERS' PAPERS'). Burbage was himself a joiner, and the Theatre, an amphitheatre according to De Witt, was built largely of timber, with three galleries and upper rooms, or boxes. The charge for admission was 1d., which went to the players, and another 1d. or 2d. for admission to the galleries, which went to the landlords as rent. The occupying companies appear to have been: Leicester's 1576–8, Warwick's-Oxford's 1579–82, Queen's on occasions between 1583 and 1589, Admiral's 1590–91, and Chamberlain's 1594–6. The Theatre was also used for activities other than plays: for fencing and other spectacles. In July 1597 all the theatres were closed for a time after the *Isle of Dogs* affair at the Swan, but the Theatre probably closed for good.

The quarrels of Burbage with Brayne (d. 1586), Brayne's widow (d. 1593) and her legatee Robert Miles over their share of the profits led to legal actions and blows. In 1596 he quarrelled with Allen over the renewal of the lease, due to expire in April 1597. Burbage himself died in February, and his son Cuthbert, to whom he had transferred the lease in 1589, began to pull down the Theatre on 28 December 1598, and on 20 January 1599 had the timber carried to the south bank where he began the building of the Globe. Allen brought an action in October 1600, but it was decided in favour of Burbage. (See CURTAIN THEATRE.)

Theatres. (For the structure of the theatres, see STAGE; for production of plays, see STAGING.)

The church hall of St Botolph without Aldersgate was let to players in 1557, and probably before, but the first public 'playing-places' in London were the Inns, the first recorded performances being in 1557 at the Boar's Head, Aldgate, and the Saracen's Head, Islington. The strict City regulations of 1574 led to the building of permanent theatres in areas outside the City jurisdiction, which was fortunate, for in 1596 the Corporation succeeded in prohibiting plays within the City. (See INN-THEATRES.)

The first two public theatres and the first private theatre were all built in Liberties on the north bank in 1576: James Burbage's Theatre and Henry Laneman's Curtain in the Liberty of Holywell, Shoreditch, and Richard Farrant's first Blackfriars theatre for the Chapel Children in the Liberty of Blackfriars. (Of the Bankside theatres, the Swan was in the Liberty of Paris Garden, the others in that of the Clink.) It should be remembered that until 1608 no adult company normally played in a private theatre, but the King's took over the Blackfriars in that year, and in the Caroline period (1625–42) private theatres superseded public ones in importance. The Paul's boys rehearsed plays for Court in their own private theatre 'nigh Paules' from 1559 onwards. In 1582–4 they appear to have joined the Chapel Children at Blackfriars. The following summary may be helpful:

North Bank

Theatre	1576–98	J. Burbage. Chamberlain's 1594–6?
Curtain	1576–1660?	Henry Laneman. Chamberlain's 1597–9? Queen Anne's
Blackfriars i	1576–84	Richard Farrant and Chapel Children
Blackfriars ii	1600–8	Henry Evans and Chapel Children
Fortune i	1600–21	Alleyn-Henslowe. Admiral's (Prince's)
Red Bull	1605–63?	Aaron Holland. Queen Anne's until 1617
Blackfriars ii	1608–55	King's
Whitefriars	1608–29	King's Revels, Queen's Revels
Porter's Hall	1616–17	Philip Rosseter. Queen's Revels; Prince's; Elizabeth's
Phoenix (Cockpit)	1617–61?	C. Beeston. Queen Anne's 1617–19
Fortune ii	1623–49	Alleyn. Palsgrave's
Salisbury Court	1629–70	Queen Henrietta's

South Bank

Newington Butts	*c.* 1580–95?	Henslowe? Chamberlain's, June 1594
Rose	1587–1622	Henslowe. Admiral's 1594–1600
Swan	1595–1640?	Langley. Chamberlain's 1596?
Globe i	1599–1613	C. and R. Burbage. Chamberlain's-King's
Globe ii	1614–44	
Hope (Beargarden)	1614–56	Henslowe. Lady Elizabeth's 1614

The theatres were closed 1642–60. After the Restoration there were two companies licensed by royal patent, each with the right to build a theatre, the King's (Killigrew's), and the Duke of York's (D'Avenant's). When Covent Garden was built in 1732, it and Drury Lane became the two patent theatres until 1843, though the Haymarket was granted a licence for summer performances in 1766 (see FOOTE). Restoration theatres were 'private' (i.e. roofed); in the 18th century they became bigger and the apron stage smaller, until in the 19th century the picture-frame stage with elaborate scenic effects was fully developed, a stage quite unsuited to the performance of Shakespeare's plays.

(The unauthorized Haymarket opened in 1720, and Goodman's Fields in 1729.) (For details see the theatres mentioned, and PRINCESS'S; LYCEUM; HIS MAJESTY'S; OLD VIC; SADLER'S WELLS; MADDERMARKET; ROYAL SHAKESPEARE THEATRE. See also MAPS OF LONDON; HOWES; RAWLIDGE; NEWCASTLE; WRIGHT, JAMES.)

Theobald, Lewis (1688–1744), the third editor of Shakespeare, was born in Kent, became a hack-writer, translator of the classics, dramatist, and assistant producer of pantomimes at Drury Lane. In 1726 he wrote, *Shakspeare Restored, or a Specimen of the many Errors as well Committed as Unamended by Mr Pope in his late edition of this Poet; designed not only to correct the said Edition, but to restore the true Reading of Shakspeare in all the Editions ever published.* Pope replied to this exposure of the deficiencies of his edition of 1725 by making Theobald the original hero of *The Dunciad* (1728):

In each she [Dulness] marks her image full
 express'd
But chief, in Tibbald's monster-breeding
 breast; . . .
Studious he sate, with all his books around,

	King's	Duke's
1660	Red Bull	Cockpit and Salisbury Court
1660	Tennis-court, Vere Street	
1661		Lincoln's Inn Fields i
1663	Drury Lane i	
1671		Dorset Garden, Salisbury Court
1672	Lincoln's Inn Fields i	
1674	Drury Lane ii	
1682		Drury Lane ii (amalgamation of companies)
1695		L.I.F. ii (Betterton's Company)
1705		The 'Opera', Haymarket
1708		Drury Lane ii (amalgamation of companies)
1714		L.I.F. iii
1732		Covent Garden

Sinking from thought to thought, a vast profound!
Plunged for his sense, but found no bottom there,
Yet wrote and floundered on, in mere despair . . .
There hapless Shakespear, yet of Tibbald sore,
Wish'd he had blotted for himself before.

It is in *Shakspeare Restored* that occurs the most famous of all emendations: *Henry V*, II, iii, for the old reading of Mistress Quickly's description of Falstaff's death, 'For his Nose was as sharp as a Pen, and a Table of greene fields', Theobald suggested, 'and a' babbled of green fields'. In 1733 he brought out his own seven-volume edition of Shakespeare, which proved him the first Shakespeare scholar. 'Nothing is altered', he wrote in his *Preface*, 'but what by the clearest reasoning can be proved a corruption of the true text; and the alteration, a real restoration of the genuine reading'; yet he made more than three hundred alterations that are still generally accepted. With a wide knowledge of Elizabethan literature he worked from the First Folio and a number of Quartos, and he was the first to draw attention to Shakespeare's sources: to the old plays of *King Leir* and *The Famous Victories of Henry V*, to Holinshed's *Chronicles* and North's *Plutarch*. For a century and a half Theobald's reputation was stunted by Pope's attack, and Malone was less than just to him: 'His knowledge of the contemporary authors was so scanty, that all the illustration of that kind dispersed throughout his volumes has been exceeded by the researches which have since been made for the purpose of elucidating a single play.' That may be true, but Theobald worked half a century before Capell and Steevens, Richard Farmer and George Chalmers: Malone was their contemporary. In 1895 Churton Collins acclaimed the despised and plundered Theobald as 'the Porson of Shakespearean critics'. (See 'CARDENIO'.)

Thersites. In *Troilus and Cressida*, a deformed and scurrilous Grecian. His bawdy cynicism is a foil to Troilus' romance, and his dramatic function is almost that of chorus. His particular butt is the slow-witted Ajax, and some critics think that he is meant to be Marston attacking Jonson in the Poetomachia. (Thersites does not occur in Shakespeare's medieval sources; he comes from Homer.)

Theseus. 1. In *A Midsummer Night's Dream*, 'Duke' of Athens. In four days' time he is to marry Hippolyta; meanwhile he counsels Hermia to obey her father and marry Demetrius, but when he finds that Demetrius loves Helena he sanctions her marriage to Lysander. The three pairs of lovers are married together, and witness the interlude of Pyramus and Thisbe.

2. In *The Two Noble Kinsmen*, now married to Hippolyta, he imprisons Palamon and Arcite, and then when they fall in love with Emilia orders them to

fight for her, eventually bestowing her on Palamon, the loser, but the survivor.

'Thomas Lord Cromwell.' An anonymous play registered and published 1602:

> 11° Augusti. William Cotton. Entred for his Copie vnder thandes of master Jackson and master Waterson warden A booke called the lyfe and Deathe of the Lord Cromwell, as yt was lately Acted by the Lord Chamberleyn his servantes.
>
> The True Chronicle Historie of the whole life and death of Thomas Lord Cromwell. As it hath beene sundrie times publikely Acted by the Right Honorable the Lord Chamberlaine his Seruants. Written by W. S. Imprinted at London for William Iones, and are to be solde at his house neere Holburne conduict, at the signe of the Gunne, 1602.

In 1611 Jones transferred his copyright in 'Lord Cromwell, by W: S.' to John Browne, and Q2 was published in 1613:

> The True Chronicle Historie of the whole life and death of Thomas Lord Cromwell. As it hath beene sundry times publikely Acted by the Kings Maiesties Seruants. Written by W. S. London: Printed by Thomas Snodham. 1613.

In his play-list of 1656 Edward Archer ascribed the play to Shakespeare, and it was published in F3, 1664. It is an interesting play – Schlegel thought it deserved 'to be classed among Shakespeare's best and maturest works', but few critics today would assign it to Shakespeare. (See SMITH, WENTWORTH.)

'Thomas of Woodstock.' An anonymous MS. play without title-page, but called for convenience either *Thomas of Woodstock* or *1 Richard II*. It seems to have been part of the collection of the bookseller William Cartwright, an actor with the King's Revels 1629–37, and was probably written 1592–5. Though it deals with an earlier part of the reign of Richard II than Shakespeare's play, there are some parallels which suggest that if Shakespeare worked from an older play this may be the first part. (See A. P. Rossiter, *Woodstock, A Moral History*.)

Thompson, Edward Maunde (1840–1929), palaeographer, educated at Rugby and University College, Oxford, was Director and Principal Librarian of the British Museum 1888–1909, knighted 1895. In 1916 he identified Shakespeare's handwriting in the MS. play of *Sir Thomas More* (q.v.).

Thompson, John. A boy actor with the King's Men. He played the Cardinal's mistress in their revival of *The Duchess of Malfi c.* 1621.

Thoms, William John (1803–85), antiquarian, founded *Notes and Queries* in 1849, was secretary to the Camden Society, and deputy librarian to the House of Lords. In 1865 he published *Three Notelets on Shakespeare*.

Thorndike, Ashley Horace (1871–1933), American scholar, succeeded Brander Matthews as Professor of English at Columbia University in 1900. With W. A. Neilson he edited the *Tudor Shakespeare* (1911–13), and in 1916 published *Shakespeare's Theater*.

Thorndike, Sybil (b. 1882), studied under Ben Greet, in 1904 made her first stage appearance with his players at Cambridge in *The Merry Wives*, for four years toured the U.S. with him playing in Shakespeare repertory, and with him joined Lilian Baylis at the Old Vic in 1914. There, during the war, she played not only women's parts but also Prince Henry, the Fool in *Lear*, Launcelot Gobbo and Ferdinand. She has several times returned to the Old Vic, in 1940–42 toured the mining villages with the company, and in 1945 France, Belgium, and Germany. She was created D.B.E. in 1931. With her brother, Russell Thorndike (producer at Old Vic, 1919), she wrote *Lilian Baylis* (1938).

Thorpe, Thomas, publisher, son of a Barnet innkeeper, was apprenticed to the stationer Richard Watkins in 1584 and became a freeman of the Stationers'

Company in 1594. His first registration was in 1604, of Marston's *Malcontent*, made jointly with William Aspley, his last in 1624, when he and Blount transferred Marlowe's *Hero and Leander* to Samuel Vicars. In 1609, he registered and published Shakespeare's *Sonnets* (q.v.) with an enigmatic dedication to 'Mr W. H.'.

Throne, or 'State'. Apparently a stock theatrical property used for Court scenes, probably a survival of the throne of God in the Miracle plays. It appears to have been a chair mounted on a dais, and let down from the 'Heavens' as required. On 4 June 1595 Henslowe paid £7 2s. 'for carpenters worke & mackinge the throne in the heuenes'. (See 'EVERY MAN IN HIS HUMOUR'.)

Thurio. In *The Two Gentlemen of Verona*, 'a foolish riuall to Valentine' (F), and the suitor favoured by the Duke for Silvia. When Valentine is banished, Proteus pretends to woo Silvia for Thurio, who follows her when she runs away, but renounces her when Valentine threatens him.

Thyreus. In *Antony and Cleopatra*; Caesar sends him to win Cleopatra from Antony by promising her anything she requires. Antony finds him kissing her hand and has him whipped (III, xii and xiii). (Called Thidias in F, and altered by Theobald to the Thyreus of Plutarch.)

Tieck, Johann Ludwig (1773–1853), German poet, novelist and critic, was born in Berlin, and became one of the leaders of the Romantic movement. His *Kaiser Oktavius* was inspired largely by Shakespeare. In 1811 he published *Altenglisches Theater*, two volumes of Elizabethan plays, and in 1817 came to England to gather material for a work on Shakespeare, which he did not finish. He edited the translation of Shakespeare by Schlegel, his own daughter Dorothea and Graf Wolf Baudissin. *Shakespeares Vorschule* appeared 1823–9. Supported by Karl Immermann, Tieck advocated a return to the apron stage for the production of Shakespeare. (See MENDELSSOHN.)

Tillyard, Eustace M. W. (1889–1962), Shakespeare scholar, Master of Jesus College, Cambridge, 1945–59. His publications include *The Elizabethan World Picture* and *Shakespeare's History Plays*, in which he argues that *Henry VI* to *Richard III* and *Richard II* to *Henry V* were conceived as tetralogies.

Tilney, Charles. See 'LOCRINE'.

Tilney, Edmund (d. 1610), Master of the Revels (q.v.), was the son of Thomas Tilney of Shelley, Suffolk, and a distant connexion by marriage of Lord Howard of Effingham. In 1568 he published a tract, *A Briefe and Pleasant Discourse of Duties in Mariage called the Flower of Friendshippe*, dedicated to Queen Elizabeth. He was appointed Master of the Revels in 1579, at a time when Court entertainments became more lavish, and his long period of office, 1579–1610, was one of great extension of the Master's authority. In 1603 his nephew, George Buck, received a grant by patent of the reversion to Tilney, much to the disappointment of Lyly, who had hoped for it, and Buck acted as his uncle's Deputy in most things until his death in 1610. (See 'LOCRINE'.)

Timandra. In *Timon of Athens*, a mistress of Alcibiades. Timon curses her and gives her gold (IV, iii).

Time. In *The Winter's Tale*, acts as Chorus to bridge the interval of sixteen years between Acts III and IV.

'Times Literary Supplement, The.' A weekly review of newly published books, issued by *The Times* newspaper, and an important organ for correspondence on bibliographical matters. It first appeared 7 January 1902, with Bruce Richmond as editor.

'TIMON OF ATHENS.'

WRITTEN: 1604–5. See 'HUMOUR OUT OF BREATH'.

PERFORMED: No record of any pre-Restoration performance.

REGISTERED: 1623, 8 November. One of the sixteen plays registered by Blount and Jaggard before publishing F1.

PUBLISHED: 1623, F1. 'The Life of Tymon of Athens': pp. (wrongly numbered) 80–2, 81–98. *Actus Primus. Scœna Prima.* Marked; 'The Actors Names' given. The play was inserted between *Romeo and Juliet* and *Julius Caesar* in the space, which it does not fill by nine pages, left by the withdrawal of *Troilus and Cressida.* It looks as though the original intention was not to publish it, perhaps because it was unfinished, but that it was then put in to fill the gap. Set up, apparently by compositor B, from unfinished foul papers which appear to have been confusing, for there is much mislineation, and printing of verse as prose and prose as verse.

SOURCES: Plutarch's *Lives of Antonius* and *Alcibiades*; Paynter's *Palace of Pleasure*; Lucian's dialogue, *Timon, or the Misanthrope*. *Timon*, a MS. academic play, *c.* 1585, has a faithful steward and a mock banquet not in the other sources.

STAGE HISTORY: 1678. At the Duke's theatre, Dorset Garden, *The History of Timon of Athens, the Man-hater:* the popular version by Shadwell (q.v.), later with music by Purcell.

1768. 'Timon of Athens. As it is acted at the Theatre Royal on Richmond Green. Altered from Shakespeare and Shadwell. By James Love' [James Dance].

1771. Drury Lane: Richard Cumberland's version, in which the dying Timon gives his daughter Evanthe to her lover Alcibiades.

1786. Covent Garden: Thomas Hull's version, 'altered from Shakespeare and Shadwell'.

1816. Drury Lane: George Lamb's adaptation.

1851. Sadler's Wells: the first recorded performance of Shakespeare's play, produced by Phelps.

1922. Old Vic production.

It has been suggested on the one hand that *Timon of Athens* is Shakespeare's revision of some other dramatist's work; on the other, that some other dramatist has revised the work of Shakespeare. George Wilkins is sometimes mentioned as 'the other dramatist'. But it may well be that the play is the unfinished work of Shakespeare: a series of uncoordinated scenes, some of them mere sketches. Possibly he abandoned *Timon* in favour of *Lear*, the theme of which – ingratitude – is the same. If so, it would justify Wilson's claim that *Timon* is the 'still-born twin' of *Lear*.

In spite of the warnings of his faithful steward Flavius, Timon, a noble and wealthy Athenian, ruins himself by his lavish entertainment of his friends. When he turns to them for help they all find excuses for refusing it. Timon, therefore, invites his ungrateful friends to a mock banquet, uncovers the steaming dishes which contain nothing but warm water, throws water and dishes at them, and drives them out.

Now a misanthrope, Timon retires to a cave near the seashore, where he finds gold while digging for roots, and this he cynically heaps on those who pass his way or seek him out: harlots, bandits, and flattering artists. He is discovered by Alcibiades, the Athenian general, who has been banished by the ungrateful Senate, and is on his way to attack Athens. Apemantus, the professional misanthrope, also visits him, but Timon outcurses him and drives him off, as he does the senators who offer him absolute power if he will help them to repel Alcibiades. He finds in Flavius the singly honest man, though he refuses to let him stay and comfort him. Alcibiades takes Athens, and hears that Timon is dead, 'Entomb'd upon the very hem o' the sea'.

Tireman. One of the hired men of a company, responsible for dressing and making up the actors, for moving properties, and, in the private theatres, for bringing in the lights.

Tiring-house. 'The attyring housse or place where the players make them readye' was behind the stage, the *mimorum aedes* of the Swan drawing. Hotson, however, argues that it was under the stage.

Titania. In *A Midsummer Night's Dream* (q.v.), Queen of the Fairies. Her quarrel with Oberon is about a 'little changeling boy' whom he wants for a henchman, but she refuses to surrender. (The name

Titania comes direct from Ovid, who applies it to Diana (*Met.* III, 173), but Golding translates as 'Titan's daughter'.)

Titchfield. Near Fareham; the Hampshire home of the Earls of Southampton. Elizabeth stayed there on her progresses of 1569 and 1591. Shakespeare's patron, Henry Wriothesley, was 3rd Earl of Southampton and Baron of Titchfield. (See 'LOVE'S LABOUR'S LOST'.)

Tithes. Stratford Corporation owned the corn and hay tithes in Old Stratford, Welcombe, and Bishopton, and 'other small and pryvie tythes' in the parish of Stratford. In 1544 William Barker had acquired a 91-years' lease of these tithes, which lease passed to John Barker; in 1580 he granted a sub-lease to Sir John Huband, who died in 1583 and left half his leasehold interest to his brother Ralph. It was this leasehold interest that Shakespeare bought from Ralph Huband for £440 on 24 July 1605. He had to pay the owners, the Corporation, a reserved rent of £17, and the owner of the original lease, John Barker, a mean rent of £5; but as the annual value of the tithes in 1611 was £60, he made a profit of £38 a year. The leasehold interest of the other half of this parcel of tithes was held by the Combes, and of another larger parcel by Richard Lane, the total mean rent due to Barker being £27 13s. 4d.

There were other tithe-holders as well, the sub-leases of whom derived from Barker, who had a right of re-entry in default of the payment of his mean rent 'in parte or in all', and as many of these leases were ill defined, they were not all paying their share. Lane and Shakespeare, therefore, drafted a Bill of Complaint, probably in 1611, urging that the Combes and others were not paying their share, so that they themselves were 'usually dryven to pay the same for preservacion of their estates'. William Combe replied that he did pay his £5, but was willing to pay another 6s. 8d. for other tithes, provided all the other parties paid their share.

Titinius. In *Julius Caesar*, a friend of Brutus and Cassius. At Philippi Cassius sends him to discover whether certain 'troops are friend or enemy'. They are Brutus's forces, but Cassius, thinking that they are the enemy who have taken Titinius prisoner, persuades Pindarus to kill him. When Titinius finds his body, he stabs himself with Cassius's sword (V, iii).

Title-pages. These served partly as the publisher's advertisement of the book, a more modest form of the 'blurb' on the jacket of a book today. They were generally composed by the publisher and printed separately so that extra copies could be distributed as leaflets. This accounts for the panegyrics and inaccuracies of many title-pages; e.g. Q1, *Pericles* ('Mariana' for 'Marina').

'Titus and Vespasian.' Henslowe's entry in his Diary for 11 April 1592, when Strange's (Derby's) were playing at the Rose, reads,

ne tittus & vespacia iij[ll] iiij[s].

It was a popular play, and six more performances were given during the season, which lasted until 23 June. Presumably 'ne' means 'new', but in exactly what sense is not always clear. On 14 January 1597 he marked *elexsander & lodwicke* as 'ne' and 'the fyrst tyme yt wasse playde', and generally it seems to mean this, the first performance of an absolutely new play. Sometimes, however, it may refer to a newly revised, corrected or augmented play, or to a play new to his theatre, or even to a certain company.

The title suggests a play about the destruction of Jerusalem by Vespasian and his son Titus, but Strange's had a play of *Jerusalem*, in their 1592 Rose repertoire; if it were about Titus and Vespasian, it is quite possible that Henslowe muddled his title, and by *Titus and Vespasian* meant *Titus Andronicus*. This is made more probable by the fact that Lucius, *Titus Andronicus's* eldest son who revenges his injuries, is called Vespasianus in a German version printed in 1620. There is a MS. note, probably of the Revels Office, *c.* 1619, which includes four of Shakespeare's plays and *Titus, and Vespatian.* On the whole it seems probable that by *tittus & vespacia* Henslowe meant *Titus Andronicus*, though it may not have been new in the strict sense, even in April 1592.

'TITUS ANDRONICUS.'

WRITTEN: 1592–3? See '*Knack to Know a Knave*'.

In *Bartholomew Fair* (1614) Jonson implies that '*Andronicus*' was twenty-five to thirty years old; i.e. 1584–9.

Titus and Vespasian (q.v.) was 'ne' in April 1592.

Mentioned by Meres in *Palladis Tamia*, 1598.

PERFORMED: 1592, 11 April. 'ne tittus & vespacia', by Strange's.

1593. January. 'titus' performed three times by Strange's.

1594. January–February. 'ne titus & ondronicus' performed three times by Sussex's.

1594, June. 'andronicous' performed twice by the Admiral's and/or Chamberlain's at Newington Butts.

1596, January. At Harington's house in Rutland, Burley-on-the-Hill, by 'Les commediens de Londres'. (SS, 14.)

(See PEACHAM.)

REGISTERED: 1594. 'vj^to^ die ffebruarii. John Danter. Entred for his Copye vnder thandes of bothe the wardens a booke intituled a Noble Roman Historye of Tytus Andronicus. vj^d^. John Danter. Entred also vnto him by warraunt from Master Woodcock the ballad thereof. vj^d^.' (See JOHNSON, RICHARD.)

1602, 19 April. Transferred by Millington to Pavier.

PUBLISHED: 1594, Q1. 'The Most Lamentable Romaine Tragedie of Titus Andronicus: As it was Plaide by the Right Honourable the Earle of Darbie, Earle of Pembrooke, and Earle of Sussex their Seruants. London, Printed by Iohn Danter, and are to be sold by Edward White & Thomas Millington, at the little North doore of Paules at the signe of the Gunne. 1594.' (Only one extant copy, discovered in Sweden 1904, and now in the Folger Library.) Set up from foul papers.

1600, Q2. 'As it hath sundry times beene playde by the Right Honourable the Earle of Pembrooke, the Earle of Darbie, the Earle of Sussex, and the Lorde Chamberlaine theyr Seruants.' Printed by James Roberts for Edward White. Set up from Q1.

1611. Q3. 'As it hath sundry times beene plaide by the Kings Maiesties Seruants.' Printed by Edward Allde for Edward White. Set up from Q2.

1623, F1. 'The Lamentable Tragedy of Titus Andronicus.' The third play in the Tragedy section: pp. 31–52. Acts marked. Set by compositor E from Q3 with the addition of III, ii.

SOURCES: Seneca: *Thyestes* for the cannibalism; *Troades* for the sacrifice in I, i. Ovid: *Metamorphoses* for the 'tragic tale of Philomel'. The themes of the murderous Moor and of the marriage of Moor and white woman were common (cf. *Othello*).

If the play were really new in 1594, it is crude work for Shakespeare at so late a date. If, however, the *Titus & Vespacia* of 1592 refers to *Titus Andronicus*, it is more reasonable to attribute it largely to Shakespeare, at least as reviser. Chambers suggests that Strange's transferred it to Pembroke's, and Pembroke's to Sussex's who had it revised to its present form. Some think it a revision of a play by Peele. (See RAVENSCROFT; SS, 10.)

STAGE HISTORY: 1678: Ravenscroft's (q.v.) version at Drury Lane. In the 18th century, Aaron was one of Quin's favourite parts; and I. F. Aldridge, 'the African Roscius', who also played Othello, took the part in a 19th-century revival. The Old Vic produced the play in 1923.

1955: Stratford. Peter Brook's production with Laurence Olivier as Titus and Anthony Quayle as Aaron.

Titus Andronicus, a Roman general, returns to Rome after a victorious campaign against the Goths, whose Queen, Tamora, and her three sons he brings home captives. The eldest of these is sacrificed by the four remaining sons of Titus to the spirit of their brother who has been killed in the wars. Titus is chosen Emperor by the people, but renounces his claim in favour of Saturninus, the late Emperor's eldest son, who promises to marry Titus's daughter Lavinia, to which proposal Titus readily agrees. However, Bassianus, Saturninus's brother, claims her as his betrothed; Titus's sons support him, and in the struggle Titus kills his youngest son, Mutius. Saturninus thereupon seizes the carrying off of Lavinia as an excuse for renouncing her, Titus and his family, and for marrying Tamora, who, however, persuades him to pretend reconciliation so that she can 'find a day to massacre them all.'

Tamora begins her revenge in conjunction with her lover Aaron, a Moor. She and her two remaining sons, Demetrius and Chiron, meet Bassianus and Lavinia; the sons kill Bassianus and throw him into a pit near which Aaron has hidden gold, ravish Lavinia, and cut off her hands and tongue. Aaron then contrives that Titus's sons, Quintus and Martius, shall fall into the pit, and be accused of murdering Bassianus for the gold. He then persuades Titus that they will be pardoned if he sends his hand in ransom; Titus chops off his hand, but receives it back together with the heads of his sons.

Titus, now crazed, discovers who has ravished Lavinia, and he, his brother Marcus and remaining son Lucius plot their revenge. Lucius goes to the Goths, enlists their aid against Rome and captures Aaron with his baby son by Tamora. Saturninus craves a parley, and they all meet in Titus's house. There Titus has prepared a banquet with a pie made of the flesh of Tamora's sons, whose throats he has cut. When Tamora has eaten, he first kills Lavinia, then Tamora. Saturninus kills Titus, and Lucius kills Saturninus. Lucius is chosen Emperor; he condemns Aaron to be set breast-deep in earth and famished and then turns to the not unurgent business of ordering well the state.

Titus Lartius. In *Coriolanus*, one of the Roman generals against the Volscians. In Act I he takes part in the capture of Corioli, of which city Cominius leaves him in command. In III, i he tells Coriolanus that Aufidius has 'made new head' and is retired to Antium.

Tobacco. Shakespeare makes no mention of tobacco in his works, but many of his contemporaries, particularly Jonson, have much to say about the new habit of 'drinking tobacco' in the theatre and on the stage; Shift, indeed, in *Every Man out of His Humour*, makes a profession of teaching the art: 'I will undertake in one fortnight to bring you, that you shall take it plausibly in any ordinary, theatre, or the Tiltyard.' *See also* Ind. to *Cynthia's Revels.*

Tolstoy, Count Leo (1828–1910). In 1906 he published *Shakespeare and the Drama*, a book in which he confesses his inability to appreciate the plays: the characters lack individuality, the situations lack naturalness, and all is lacking in sincerity. He is prejudiced against the 'insignificant and immoral works of Shakespeare' presumably because they do not square with his conception of art, which should transmit the highest religious feeling.

Tooley, Nicholas. One of the 'Principall Actors' in Shakespeare's plays (see p. 91). He was with the King's in May 1605, when Phillips in his will left him a legacy as his 'fellow'. He is not in the actor-list of *Volpone* (1605), but is in the next extant one, *The Alchemist* (1610), after which he appears fairly regularly. In 1619 he witnessed Richard Burbage's will, and made his own 3 June 1623:

> I Nicholas Tooley of London Gentleman being sicke in body ... doe give unto Mrs Burbadge the wife of my good friend Mr Cutbert Burbadge (in whose house I do now lodge) as a remembrance of my love in respect of her motherlie care over me the Some of tenn pounds ...

He also left £10 to her daughter, £10 to Alice Walker, sister of his 'late Master, Richard Burbadge', and £29 13s. to Burbage's daughter Sara, which sum was owed him by his fellow Richard Robinson. He forgave John Underwood and William Ecclestone their debts, left £5 to Mrs Condell, £10 to her daughter and £10 to Joseph Taylor. His 'loving friends Cuthbert Burbadge and Henry Condell' were his executors and residuary legatees. In a codicil he states that his former name was Wilkinson. From his will it appears that Tooley had been an apprentice of R. Burbage, and it is just possible that he was the 'Nick' in *The Seven Deadly Sins*. He was buried at St Giles's, Cripplegate, 5 June 1623, 'from the house of Cuthbert Burbidge, gentleman'. (See 'DUCHESS OF MALFI'.)

Tottell, Richard (d. 1593), was of Exeter, but was in London by 1552, when he received a patent for the printing of law books. In June 1557 he printed his famous 'Miscellany': *Songes and Sonnettes, written by the ... late Earl of Surrey and other* [Wyatt]. It was so popular that another edition was published in July, and six more before the end of the century. In *The Merry Wives*, Slender wishes for his 'Book of Songs and Sonnets', and the grave-digger in *Hamlet* quotes from it. Tottell's best work was as a law book printer, but he also printed Gerard Legh's (q.v.) *Accedens of Armorie* and Surrey's *Aeneid*. He tried to establish a paper mill in England, and was Master of the Stationers' Company in 1579 and 1584.

Touchstone. In *As You Like It*, the 'clownish fool' of Duke Frederick's court, who accompanies Celia and Rosalind to the forest of Arden, where he meets and marries Audrey. (There is no corresponding character in Lodge's *Rosalynde*; it is probably the first part that Shakespeare wrote for Robert Armin, who replaced Kempe in the Chamberlain's *c.* 1599.)

Tourneur, Cyril (d. 1626), dramatist, was a relation, perhaps the son, of Captain Richard Turnor who served in the Low Countries as water-bailiff and then Lieutenant-Governor of Brill 1585–96. In 1613 Cyril Tourneur was paid £10 for carrying 'letters for his Majesty's service' to Brussels. In 1625 he was appointed secretary to the council of war, and sailed with Sir Edward Cecil on the disastrous Cadiz expedition, on the return from which he was put ashore in Ireland, where he died in February 1626.

His first extant work is the satire, *The Transformed Metamorphosis*, 1600. *The Atheist's Tragedy*, 'written by Cyril Tourneur', was published in 1611. *The Nobleman*, a lost play, was registered 15 February 1612: 'A play booke beinge a Tragecomedye called, The Noble man written by Cyril Tourneur.' *The Revenger's Tragedy* was registered and published anonymously in 1607: 'The Revengers Tragœdie. As it hath been sundry times Acted, by the Kings Maiesties Seruants.' It was ascribed to Tourneur by Edward Archer and Francis Kirkman in their play-lists of 1656 and 1661.

The Atheist's Tragedy and *The Revenger's Tragedy* are both belated tragedies of revenge written mainly in blank verse, but here the resemblance ends. The first is crude and laughable melodrama, almost without poetry, the verse crumbling at its extremities into innumerable light and weak endings. The second is tragic and dramatic, the verse firm, and it contains some of the very finest poetry of the period. It is most improbable that Tourneur wrote both; Webster is almost certainly the author of *The Revenger's Tragedy*.

Tragedies. There are twelve plays in the Tragedy section of the Folio, including the Roman Histories. While printing, *Troilus and Cressida* was withdrawn, replaced by *Timon*, and then inserted in the unpaged limbo that lies between the last History, *Henry VIII*, and the first Tragedy of the Catalogue, *Coriolanus*, as *The Tragedie of Troylus and Cressida*. Neither *Troilus* nor *Cymbeline*, the first and last in the section, is a tragedy in the sense that it ends with the death of the tragic hero or heroine; *Cymbeline* is, in fact, a typical Jacobean tragi-comedy, and *Troilus* is called a comedy in its Epistle. The plays appear in the Catalogue of contents as follows (the dates prefixed are those, approximately, of their composition):

1607–8	The Tragedy of Coriolanus	*Fol.* 1
1592–3	Titus Andronicus	31
1595–6	Romeo and Juliet	53
1604–5	Timon of Athens	80
1599–1600	The Life and death of Julius Caesar	109
1605–6	The Tragedy of Macbeth	131
1600–1	The Tragedy of Hamlet	152
1605–6	King Lear	283
1602–3	Othello, the Moore of Venice	310
1606–7	Anthony and Cleopater	346
1609–10	Cymbeline King of Britaine	369

Tranio. In *The Taming of the Shrew*, a servant of Lucentio, whom he impersonates so that his master can woo Bianca in disguise. Tranio himself pretends to be a suitor for Bianca so that he can draw off Lucentio's rivals. He gains Baptista's consent to Bianca's hand, and finds a pedant who pretends to be Tranio-Lucentio's father and agrees to the match. Finally he is unmasked and runs away. (In *A Shrew* he is Valeria, in *I Suppositi* Dulippo.)

Transcripts. The prompt-book itself was probably a transcript of foul papers, written, annotated, and tidied up by the book-keeper. Some of Shakespeare's plays seem to have been printed from a transcript of foul papers or of the prompt-book made for the purpose. Corruptions in the text may be due to the scribe's writing what he remembered, or thought he remembered, of the play, instead of what he was supposed to be copying: e.g. Q *Lear*. Crane probably transcribed the first four plays and *Winter's Tale* for the Folio, and it looks as though transcription was the initial policy, the first play, *Tempest*, being a particularly well prepared text, perhaps meant to serve as model for the remainder. Professional scribes were sometimes commissioned to make calligraphic private transcripts. Crane transcribed *The Witch*, for example, and Humphrey Moseley wrote in 1647 of the Beaumont and Fletcher plays, that 'when private friends desir'd a Copy, they then (and justly too) transcribed what they Acted'. Q *Othello* may have been printed from a private transcript.

To account for certain peculiarities (e.g. Q *1 Henry IV* and F *2 Henry IV*) Alice Walker (*Textual Problems*) postulates another kind of transcript: one made from foul papers and used by the book-keeper when writing his prompt-book. A text printed from such an intermediate transcript would lack the characteristics of foul papers and prompt-book alike. (See COPY.)

Translations of Shakespeare. See FRANCE; GERMANY; ITALY; RUSSIA; SPAIN; SWEDEN, etc. For translations into other languages, see Ebisch and Schücking, *A Shakespeare Bibliography*, p. 158.

Trap-doors were set in the Elizabethan stage for sudden or mysterious appearances and disappearances; thus, in *The Tempest*, III, iii: *Thunder and Lightning. Enter Ariell (like a Harpey) claps his wings vpon the Table, and with a quient deuice the Banquet vanishes.* The region underneath the apron stage retained the medieval name of hell, as the 'shadow' retained that of the heavens. In Henslowe's 1598 'Enventary of all the properties for my Lord Admerelles men' occurs the item 'j Hell mought'. This would be the jaws of some monster that could be placed over the trap leading to 'hell'. Properties may sometimes have been moved on to the stage through traps, as the 'throne' was let down from the 'heavens'. (See 'JEW OF MALTA'.)

Travers. In *2 Henry IV*, a retainer who brings his master, Northumberland, news of Hotspur's defeat at Shrewsbury (I, i).

Traverse. A theatrical term first used in the interlude *Godly Queen Hester* (*c.* 1525) to indicate a curtain. It seems next to have been used in this sense by Jonson in *Volpone* (1606): 'Volpone peepes from behind a traverse', here, Chambers suggests, a movable screen. But Webster (*Duchess of Malfi*) uses it to indicate a curtain that can be drawn, presumably to discover an inner stage: 'Here is discovered, behind a travers, the artificial figures ...' In the Jacobean masque the painted proscenium curtain was sometimes called the traverse, and on the Restoration stage it came to mean the recess itself revealed by drawing the traverse; cf. *The Duke of Guise* (1683) by Dryden and Lee: 'The Traverse is drawn'; 'The scene draws, behind it a Traverse'. (See CURTAINS.)

Trebonius, Caius. In *Julius Caesar*, one of the conspirators. He agrees with Brutus that Antony should not be killed with Caesar; before the assassination 'he draws Mark Antony out of the way', and afterwards tells how he has 'fled to his house amazed' (III, i).

Tree, Beerbohm (1853–1917). Herbert Draper Beerbohm was the son of a London grain merchant of German parentage. In 1878 he became an actor, adopting the stage name of Beerbohm Tree, and was so successful that by 1887 he was lessee and manager of the Haymarket. There, in 1889, he staged *The Merry Wives* with himself as Falstaff and his wife (Maud Holt) as Anne Page, and followed this success in 1892 by playing Hamlet to Mrs Tree's Ophelia. In 1897 he moved to Her Majesty's (later His Majesty's), where he produced, in the tradition of Charles Kean and Irving, his famous series of lavishly spectacular Shakespearean revivals, from *Julius Caesar* in 1898 to *Henry VIII*, *Macbeth*, and *Othello* (1910–11–12). Such settings involved much cutting of the text and transposition of scenes, and it was against this un-Shakespearean elaboration that Poel and Granville-Barker revolted. In 1907 Tree took his company to Berlin; he was knighted in 1909. His daughter, Viola, acted with him, playing Beatrice to his Benedick, Ariel to his Prospero, and Viola to his Malvolio. Max Beerbohm (b. 1872) was Tree's half-brother.

'Trick to Catch the Old One.' A comedy by Thomas Middleton, and one of his best plays. Q1 was published anonymously in 1608, 'As it hath beene lately Acted, by the Children of Paules'; Q2 (1608), 'Composed by T. M.'; Q3 (1616), 'By T. Middleton'. It was ascribed to Shakespeare by the booksellers of the mid 17th century.

Trinculo. In *The Tempest*, 'a Jester' (F). In the storm he shelters under Caliban's cloak, where he is found by his friend Stephano. The three set out to kill Prospero, but are defeated by Ariel and his magic.

Trochee. A foot of two syllables: long-short, or stressed-unstressed (- ⏑). It is the inversion of the normal iambic foot of blank verse, a valuable variant, most natural after a pause, and commonest therefore at the beginning of a line, and after a mid-line pause:

He then unto the ladder turns his back,
Lŏoks ĭn | the clouds, | scorning | the base
  degrees ...

In *King Lear* (V, iii), at the climax of the tragedy, Shakespeare inverts all five feet:

Thou'lt come no more,
Never, never, never, never, never!

In his early verse Shakespeare often suggests a reversed rhythm by placing together in mid-line two important trochaic words and emphasizing them by assonance:

O, how shall *summer's honey* breath hold
  out.
And do a *wilful stillness* entertain.

This practice is extended by placing trochaic words at the end of a line, and before a mid-line pause, and linking them in assonantal sequences, so that a falling rhythm is imposed on the rising iambic one without a real substitution of feet. This counterpoint of sound and rhythm is one of the most important elements in the late poetry. Cf. *The Tempest*:

Therefore my son i' th' ooze is *bedded;* and
I'll seek him *deeper* than e'er *plummet
  sounded,*
And with him there lie *mudded.*

A similar effect is sometimes achieved by dactyllic words:

Goes to and back, *lackeying* the *varying* tide.

'TROILUS AND CRESSIDA.'

WRITTEN: 1601–2. (See 'HISTRIOMASTIX'; 'IRON AGE.')

PERFORMED: The first S.R. entry and the first state of Q both assert that the play had been acted, the latter 'at the Globe'. The second state of Q omits this record, and the Epistle expressly asserts that it is 'a new play, never stal'd with the Stage'. There is no record of a performance, though it may have been acted at Court or, as Alexander suggests, at an Inn of Court. Hotson goes further (*Shakespeare's Sonnets Dated*), and claims it as the *Loue labours wonne* mentioned by Meres: '*Love's Labour's Won* unquestionably means *Love's Sorrow is Gained*, and consequently it can be nothing else than the alternative title of *Troilus and Cressida*.' He thinks that it (and *Love's Labour's Lost*) was privately acted at the Middle Temple, one of whose members, probably Richard Martin, 'Prince d'Amour' on their 'grand nights', wrote the Epistle. This would mean that it was written, in some form, before the registration of *Palladis Tamia* in September 1598.

REGISTERED: 1603. '7 februarii. Master Robertes. Entred for his copie in full Court holden this day to print when he hath gotten sufficient aucthority for yt, The booke of Troilus and Cresseda as yt is acted by my lord Chamberlens Men vj^d^.'

1609. '28^uo^ Januarii. Richard Bonion Henry Walleys. Entred for their Copy vnder thandes of Master Segar deputy to Sir George Bucke and master warden Lownes a booke called the history of Troylus and Cressida vj^d^.'

PUBLISHED: 1609, Q (1st state). 'The Historie of Troylus and Cresseida. As it was acted by the Kings Maiesties seruants at the Globe. Written by William Shakespeare. London Imprinted by G. Eld for R. Bonian and H. Walley, and are to be sold at the spred Eagle in Paules Churchyeard, ouer against the great North doore. 1609.' Set up from the author's private transcript?

1609, Q (2nd state). 'The Famous Historie of Troylus and Cresseid. Excellently expressing the beginning of their loues, with the conceited wooing of Pandarus Prince of Licia. Written by William Shakespeare.'

To this issue was added an Epistle by 'A neuer writer, to an euer reader':

'Eternall reader, you haue heere a new play, neuer stal'd with the Stage, neuer clapper-clawd with the palmes of the vulger, and yet passing full of the palme comicall; for it is a birth of your braine, that neuer undertooke any thing commicall, vainely: And were but the vaine names of commedies changde for the titles of Commodities, or of Plays for Pleas; you should see all those grand censors, that now stile them such vanities, flock to them for the maine grace of their grauities: especially this authors Commedies, that are so fram'd to the life, that they serue for the most common Commentaries of all the actions of our liues shewing such a dexteritie, and power of witte, that the most displeased with Playes, are pleasd with his Commedies. And all such dull and heauy-witted worldlings, as were neuer capable of the witte of a Commedie, comming by report of them to his representations, haue found that witte there, that they neuer found in them selues, and have parted better wittied then they came: feeling an edge of witte set vpon them, more then euer they dreamd they had braine to grinde it on. So much and such sauored salt of witte is in his Commedies, that they seeme (for their height of pleasure) to be borne in that sea that brought forth *Venus*. Amongst all there is none more witty then this: and had I time I would comment upon it, though I know it needs not, (for so much as will make you thinke your testerne well bestowd) but for so much worth, as euen poore I know to be stuft in it. It deserues such a labour, as well as the best Commedy in *Terence* or *Plautus*. And beleeue this, that when hee is gone, and his Commedies out of sale, you will scramble for them, and set vp a new English Inquisition. Take this for a warning, and at the perrill of your pleasures losse, and Iudgements, refuse not, nor like this the lesse, for not being sullied, with the smoaky breath of the multitude; but thanke fortune for the scape it hath made amongst you. Since by the grand possessors wills I beleeue you should have prayd for them rather then beene prayd. And so I leaue all such to bee prayd for (for the states of their wits healths) that will not praise it. Vale.'

1623, F1. 'The Tragedie of Troylus and Cressida.' The printer began to set it up after *Romeo and Juliet*, but then it was withdrawn, probably owing to copyright difficulties, and later inserted as the first of the Tragedies: Prologue unpaged; 78–80; the rest unpaged. *Actus Primus. Scœna Prima*, marked only. Not included in the Catalogue. Set up from Q collated with prompt-book (Greg); from a corrected copy of Q (P. Williams and A. Walker).

SOURCES: For the medieval romantic version of Homer: Chaucer's *Troilus and Criseyde*, which is based on Boccaccio's *Filostrato;* Caxton's *The Recuyell of the Historyes of Troye*, and possibly Lydgate's *The Sege of Troye;* Henryson's *The Testament of Cresseid*.

For the Homeric story, including Thersites: Arthur Hall's *Ten Bookes of Homers Iliades* (i–x); Chapman's *Seaven Bookes of the Iliades* (i, ii, vii–xi), and *Achilles Shield* (xviii), published 1598.

STAGE HISTORY: The first performance on record is that of Dryden's elevated version at the Duke's theatre in 1679: *Troilus and Cressida, or Truth Found too Late*, with Betterton as Troilus and his wife as Andromache. Cressida flirts with Diomedes only to secure her father's return to Troy, and kills herself to prove her innocence to Troilus, who kills Diomedes. Achilles and the Greeks sack Troy, and 'all the Trojans dye upon the place. Troilus last.' There were some revivals of this version.

1907. Shakespeare's play produced in London. William Poel produced it, uncut, in London and Stratford, 1912–13, the Old Vic in 1923, Stratford in 1948. Tyrone Guthrie's Old Vic production 1956.

Parts of the play have been variously ascribed to other authors: to Dekker and Chettle who wrote a *Troilus and Cressida* (q.v.), to Chapman, and Marston. But there is no good reason to doubt Shakespeare's authorship of this fine play. Some think the uncomplimentary description of Ajax in I, i is aimed at Jonson, and is the 'purge' referred to in *Parnassus*.

Troilus, son of King Priam of Troy, loves Cressida, whose father, Calchas, has deserted the city for the Greek camp. She lives with her uncle Pandarus, who contrives to bring the lovers together, but Calchas persuades Agamemnon, the Greek commander, to exchange the Trojan prisoner Antenor for his daughter Cressida, and Diomedes is sent to bring her to the Greek camp.

Meanwhile, Priam and his sons debate whether to restore Helen, wife of the Greek Menelaus, carried off by Priam's son, Paris, and the cause of the Greek siege of Troy. They decide to keep her, and Hector, eldest son of Priam, sends a challenge of single combat to the Greeks. Their champion, Achilles, however, is sulking and will not fight, so Ulysses suggests, as a means of bringing him to his senses, offering the ponderous Ajax the honour of accepting the challenge. There is a general truce, Hector and Ajax fight but soon break off, and the Greeks feast the Trojans, though not before Achilles has insulted Hector and promised to meet him in battle the next day.

Troilus takes the opportunity of visiting Cressida, and is conducted by Ulysses who, however, warns him what to expect and, unseen, they find her embracing Diomedes, to whom she gives Troilus's token. 'O beauty! where is thy faith?' the heart-broken Troilus exclaims, and returns to Troy. The next day there is a great battle in which Achilles treacherously kills the unarmed Hector, but Diomedes escapes the vengeance of Troilus. The scurrilous Thersites comments cynically on the action throughout the play.

'Troilus and Cressida.' In April–May 1599 Henslowe advanced £5 in three instalments to Dekker and Chettle in earnest of their play 'Troylles and Creseda' for the Admiral's. It is lost, but there is a fragmentary 'plot' with the stage-direction 'Enter Cressida, wth Beggars', which may be that of their play. If so, it deals with the later history of Cressida, as told by Henryson (q.v.) in *The Testament of Cresseid*. (See Greg, *Dramatic Documents*.)

'Troublesome Reign of John.' The anonymous play used by Shakespeare as the source of his *King John*. Though it is only 300 lines longer than Shakespeare's, it was published in two parts in 1591:

> The Troublesome Raigne of Iohn King of England, with the discouerie of King Richard Cordelions Base sonne (vulgarly named, The Bastard Fawconbridge): also the death of King Iohn at Swinstead Abbey. As it was (sundry times) publikely acted by the Queenes Maiesties Players, in the honourable Citie of London. Imprinted at London for Sampson Clarke, and are to be solde at his shop, on the backeside of the Royall Exchange, 1591.
>
> The Second part of the troublesome Raigne of King Iohn, conteining the death of Arthur Plantaginet, the landing of Lewes, and the poysning of King Iohn at Swinstead Abbey. As it was ... 1591.

In 1611 the two parts were printed together by V. Simmes for John Helme as 'Written by W. Sh.'. Q3, 1622, was printed by Augustine Mathewes for Thomas Dewe as 'Written by W. Shakespeare'.

The Troublesome Reign was probably written about the time of the Armada,

1588, as John is made the patriotic champion against papal tyranny. The authorship has been assigned to Marlowe and others; Peele is perhaps the most likely. Shakespeare follows the action fairly faithfully and makes the same historical mistakes, confusing Austria and Limoges, for example, but he entirely rewrites it, condensing and omitting as he thinks fit, and expanding a hint into a speech, a speech into a scene. *T.R.* makes more of the poisoning of John; the monk is himself poisoned by drinking first of the cup, and the Bastard kills the Abbot who has absolved him. Pope and some later scholars think that Shakespeare himself wrote the play.

Truchman. See MASQUE.

'True Tragedy of Richard III.' An anonymous chronicle history play registered 19 June 1594 by Thomas Creede as 'an enterlude', and published by him in the same year:

> The True Tragedie of Richard the third: Wherein is showne the death of Edward the fourth, with the smothering of the two yoong Princes in the Tower: With a lamentable ende of Shore's wife, an example for all wicked women. And lastly the conjunction and ioyning of the two noble Houses, Lancaster and Yorke. As it was playd by the Queenes Maiesties Players.

It is a bad, and probably a reported text, and it is impossible to do more than guess at the author; Lodge or Peele, *c.* 1590, is possible. Shakespeare must have known the play, and a few slight resemblances to his *Richard III* have been detected, but they prove nothing, as a reported text often includes echoes from other plays. Hamlet's 'Come: the croaking raven doth bellow for revenge,' echoes the line in *The True Tragedy*: 'The screeking Raven sits croking for revenge.' (See SQ, III, 299–306.)

'True Tragedy of Richard Duke of York.' A play published in 1595, and once ascribed to Marlowe with Shakespeare as reviser, but now accepted as a 'bad' Quarto (Q1 is really in octavo) of *3 Henry VI* (q.v.). As early as 1864 Thomas Kenny in his *Life and Genius of Shakespeare* argued that *The First Part of the Contention and The True Tragedy* were corrupt versions of *2* and *3 Henry VI*. Peter Alexander came independently to the same conclusion in 1924 (*TLS*, 9 October, 13 November), and in 1929 published his *Shakespeare's Henry VI and Richard III*, the argument of which is generally accepted: that *The First Part* and *The True Tragedy* should go into Pollard's catalogue of 'bad' Quartos as reported versions of *2, 3 Henry VI* as printed in F. *The True Tragedy* is only about two-thirds the length of *3 Henry VI*, but though the text is garbled it is not as bad as that of *The First Part*. Alexander thinks that the reporter was an actor who had played Warwick and Clifford; Chambers that he was a prompter helped by a 'plot'.

Trumpet. The most important musical instrument in the theatre. The three 'soundings' to announce the beginning of a play were blown on the trumpet (see 'GULL'S HORNBOOK'), and the appearance of royalty on the stage was announced by a 'flourish' on the trumpet. It was usually associated with the drum (q.v.). The instrument was the natural trumpet, like that still used to proclaim the approach of a judge at an assize. (See TUCKET.)

Trundell, John. Bookseller, in business in Barbican at the sign of Nobody, 1603–26. He and Nicholas Ling published the 'bad' Q1 of *Hamlet* in 1603.

Tubal. In *The Merchant of Venice*, a Jew who brings Shylock the dismal news from Genoa that Jessica is squandering his ducats and his jewels, but comforts him with the report that Antonio has lost an argosy (III, i).

Tucket. A flourish on the trumpet, from Italian *toccata*. Cf. *M. of V.* (V, i) and *Henry V* (IV, ii):

[*A tucket sounds.*
LOR. Your husband is at hand; I hear his trumpet.

Then let the trumpets sound
The tucket sonance and the note to mount.

Tuckfield, Thomas. A hired actor with the King's Men in 1624. The book-keeper's (Edward Knight's) note has preserved his name in Q (1634) of *The Two Noble Kinsmen* (V, iii, 1): *Enter ... Attendants. T. Tucke: Curtis.* (See PROTECTION OF PLAYERS.)

'Tugend- und Liebesstreit.' A German play (1677) derived from the story of *Apolonius and Silla* in Barnabe Rich's *Farewell to Militarie Profession* (1581), which is also a source of *Twelfth Night. T- und L.* and *T.N.* have elements in common not found in Rich, and Creizenach (*Schauspiele der Englischen Komödianten*) thinks that a lost English play based on Rich may have been the source of both.

Tunstall, James. In 1583 an actor with Worcester's provincial company, and in the nineties with the Admiral's. He was a witness of James Burbage's dispute with the Admiral's, *c.* May 1591, which led to that company's leaving the Theatre for the Rose.

'TWELFTH NIGHT.'

WRITTEN: 1599–1600. (See BRACCIANO.)

PERFORMED: 1601, Twelfth Night, at Whitehall? (See Hotson, *The First Night of 'Twelfth Night'*.) 1602, 2 February. In the Middle Temple. (See J. MANNINGHAM.)

1618. 'To John Heminges . . . upon a warrant dated 20 April 1618 for presenting two severall Playes before his Maiesty, on Easter Monday Twelfte night the play soe called and on Easter Tuesday the Winters Tale xx[li].' (*Chamber Account.*)

1623. 'At Candlemas Malvolio was acted at court, by the kings servants.' (*Office Book of Henry Herbert.*)

1640. See DIGGES.

REGISTERED: 1623, 8 November. One of the sixteen plays registered by Blount and Jaggard before publishing F1.

PUBLISHED: 1623, F1. 'Twelfe Night, Or what you will.' The thirteenth play in the Comedy section: pp. 255–75. Acts and scenes marked. A good text, set up from the prompt-book.

SOURCES: The Olivia-Orsino, Viola-Sebastian plot from the story of *Apolonius and Silla* in Barnabe Riche's *Farewell to Militarie Profession* (1581). This is an adaptation of Belleforest's French version (1571) of a *novella* by Bandello (1554), based on the Sienese comedy of *Gl'Ingannati* ('*The Deceived*') 1531. The sub-plot and its characters are Shakespeare's creation. (See 'LAELIA'; TUGEND- UND LIEBESSTREIT; SHIRLEY, ANTHONY; MOLYNEUX.)

STAGE HISTORY: 1661. D'Avenant's version at the Duke's theatre, with Betterton as Sir Toby. Pepys saw it 11 September 1661, 6 January 1663, 20 January 1669, and thought it 'but a silly play'.

1703. William Burnaby's vulgar version, *Love Betray'd; or, The Agreeable Disappointment*, at Lincoln's Inn Fields.

1741. Shakespeare's play at Drury Lane, with Macklin as Malvolio, and Hannah Pritchard as Viola.

1820. Frederic Reynolds's operatic version, with music by Henry Bishop.

1912. Granville-Barker's production, with Henry Ainley as Malvolio, Leon Quartermaine as Sir Andrew, and Lillah McCarthy as Viola.

1916. Old Vic production, with Ben Greet as Malvolio.

1950. Hugh Hunt's production at re-opening of the Old Vic.

Viola, on a voyage from 'Messaline', is shipwrecked on the coast of Illyria and, thinking that her twin brother Sebastian has been lost in the storm, disguises herself as a page, Cesario, and takes service with the Illyrian Duke, Orsino. She falls in love with her master who, however, loves the rich young widow Olivia, and he employs her as a messenger to Olivia, who in turn falls in love with Viola-Cesario. When Sebastian appears, Olivia mistakes him for Cesario and easily persuades him to marry her. Orsino is furious at this apparent betrayal, but when Viola meets Sebastian and explains that she is his twin sister, the Duke discovers his love for her and marries her.

The sub-plot centres on Malvolio, Olivia's steward. By his humourless officiousness he has offended many of the members of the household: Olivia's drunken uncle Sir Toby Belch, her gentlewoman Maria, her jester Feste, and her foolish suitor Sir Andrew Aguecheek. Maria contrives a plot whereby Malvolio finds a letter, written by her but apparently from Olivia, bidding him take courage and make love to her. Malvolio behaves so strangely that he is imprisoned as a madman and only released at the end of the play when Olivia discovers the trick. Sir Toby is so enchanted by its success that he marries Maria.

Twine, Laurence (fl. 1564–76), son of John Twine, headmaster of Canterbury Grammar School, which he attended before going to All Souls, Oxford, of which he became a Fellow in 1564. In 1576 was registered,

The Patterne of Painefull Aduentures, containing the most excellent, pleasant and variable Historie of the Strange Accidents that befell vnto Prince Apollonius, the Lady Lucina his Wife, and Tharsia his Daughter. Wherein the Vncertaintie of this World and fickle state of man's life are liuely described. Gathered into English by Lavrence Twine, Gentleman.

There are two extant editions, one undated, but later than 1576, and another of 1607, a year before the registration of *Pericles* (q.v.).

'Twins, The: or, Which is Which?' A farcical adaptation of *The Comedy of Errors*, performed in Edinburgh, and published in 1780.

'TWO GENTLEMEN OF VERONA, THE.'

WRITTEN: 1594–5. Mentioned by Meres, 1598.

PERFORMED: No record of a pre-Restoration performance.

REGISTERED: 1623, 8 November. One of the sixteen plays registered by Blount and Jaggard before publishing F1.

PUBLISHED: 1623, F1. 'The Two Gentlemen of Verona.' The second play in the Comedy section: pp. 20–38. Acts and scenes marked. The names of all the Actors' given. A fair text. Wilson finds evidence of cutting and adaptation by another hand, and from the absence of stage-directions, save for exits and inclusive entries at the beginning of scenes, concludes that it is an 'assembled text' (q.v.). According to Greg, set up from Crane's transcript of the prompt-book.

SOURCE: *La Diana Enamorada:* a prose romance in Spanish by Jorge de Montemayor (q.v.), translated into French by N. Collin (1578), and into English by B. Yonge in 1582, though not published until 1598. (See 'FELIX AND PHILIOMENA'.)

STAGE HISTORY: 1762. The first recorded performance is that at Drury Lane 'with Alterations and Additions' (for Launce and his dog) by Benjamin Victor.

1784. Shakespeare's play at Covent Garden.

1821. F. Reynolds's operatic version at Covent Garden.

The original play has been revived from time to time in the last hundred years, but with little success, though it appears to be a favourite on the Continent.

The two gentlemen of Verona are the friends Valentine and Proteus, the former of whom goes to the court of the Duke of Milan to be 'tutor'd in the world'. There he falls in love with Silvia, daughter of the Duke, who, however, intends her to marry the foolish Thurio. Proteus stays in Verona to be near his love Julia, but his father insists on his joining Valentine at Milan. He too falls in love with Silvia, and secures the banishment of Valentine by telling the Duke that his former friend and present rival plans to run away with Silvia. Julia disguises herself as a page, Sebastian, and follows Proteus to Milan, where she finds him making love to Silvia, who rejects him with contempt and runs away to find Valentine.

Proteus, accompanied by 'Sebastian', follows her and rescues her from a band of outlaws who had previously captured Valentine and then made him their captain. He threatens to force Silvia, but Valentine comes to her aid, though he then offers to renounce her in favour of his friend. At this Julia swoons; on recovering consciousness she reveals her identity, and Proteus realises that he loves her better than Silvia. The Duke and Thurio find the lovers, but Thurio behaves in so cowardly a way that the Duke dismisses him and gives Valentine Silvia's hand in marriage. The outlaws, too, are pardoned. Low, but amusing comedy is supplied by Launce, Proteus's servant, and his dog.

'TWO NOBLE KINSMEN, THE.'

WRITTEN: 1613—14. (See BARTHOLOMEW FAIR'; MASQUE OF THE INNER TEMPLE.)

PERFORMED: 1619? A Revels Office note of 'The 2. Noble Kinesmen' may indicate a Court performance.

REGISTERED: 1634. '8° Aprilis Master John Waterson Entred for his Copy vnder the hands of Sir Henry Herbert and master Aspley warden a Tragi Comedy called the two noble kinsmen by John ffletcher and William Shakespeare. vj^{d}.'

1646. Waterson's copyright transferred to Humphrey Moseley, the entry in the Register describing 'The Noble kinsman' as 'by Mr Flesher'.

PUBLISHED: 1634. Q. 'The Two Noble Kinsmen: Presented at the Blackfriers by the Kings Maiesties servants, with great applause: Written by the memorable Worthies of their time; Mr John Fletcher, and Mr William Shakepeare. Gent. Printed at London by Tho. Cotes, for Iohn Waterson: and are to be sold at the signe of the Crowne in Pauls Churchyard. 1634.' A very good text, set up from the prompt-book (Greg) or foul papers (F. O. Waller) annotated by the book-keeper, probably Edward Knight. (See GREVILLE, CURTIS; TUCKFIELD.)

1679. Published in F2 of the plays of Beaumont and Fletcher: 'Fifty Comedies and Tragedies. Written by Francis Beaumont and John Fletcher, Gentlemen. All in one Volume. Published by the Authors Original Copies, the Songs to each Play being added.'

SOURCE: Chaucer: *The Knight's Tale*. (See 'PALAMON AND ARCITE'.)

STAGE HISTORY: 1664. D'Avenant's version, *The Rivals* (q.v.), with Betterton as Philander (Palamon) and Henry Harris as Theocles (Arcite). The play was seen by Pepys 10 September 1664: 'To the Duke's house, and there saw "The Rivalls" which is no excellent play, but good acting in it; especially Gosnell comes and sings and dances finely; but, for all that, fell out of the key, so that the musique could not play to her afterwards; and so did Harris also go out of the time to agree with her.'

The only external evidence that the play is partly by Shakespeare is that of the entry in the Register and the title-page of Q. Pope, 1725, ascribes it entirely to Shakespeare: '... The Two Noble Kinsmen, if that play be his, as there goes a tradition it was (and indeed it has little resemblance of Fletcher, and more of our author than some of those which have been received as genuine).' But there are clearly two authors; Fletcher must be accepted as one, and as Shakespeare was probably collaborating with him, *c.* 1613, in *Henry VIII* and *Cardenio*, and as parts of the play read like late Shakespeare, there is no good reason for doubting the authority of Q, though Beaumont, and Massinger the imitator of Shakespeare's style, have been suggested instead of him. There is fine, and occasionally great verse in Acts III and V, and Shakespeare must have been mainly responsible for I, i and ii; III, i; V, i and iii; especially for the invocations to Mars, Venus and Diana in V, i. The Tilburina-like sub-plot of the gaoler's daughter is at once laughable and revolting, and seems to be part of Fletcher's contribution; nothing could be more unlike Shakespeare. (See SS, 11.)

The two noble kinsmen, the cousins Palamon and Arcite, have decided to leave the court of their uncle Creon, the tyrannical and cruel King of Thebes, when they hear that Theseus, 'Duke' of Athens, is about to attack Creon at the request of three queens whose husbands he has killed. They fight for Thebes, but Theseus is victorious, captures them, and puts them in a prison from the window of which they see Emilia, sister of Theseus's queen, Hippolyta, and fall in love with her. Arcite is released though banished from Athens, but disguises himself and obtains service with Emilia. Palamon escapes from prison, meets his rival Arcite, and while fighting they are discovered by Theseus who orders their deaths, but at the intercession of Hippolyta and Emilia changes his doom and tells them to return in a month, each with three knights, when after a tournament the victor shall have Emilia and the other lose his head.

The cousins return with their knights; Arcite prays to Mars for victory, Palamon to Venus, and Emilia implores Diana to give the garland to the one who loves her best. Arcite is victorious, and Palamon is about to be beheaded when news comes that Arcite has been thrown from his horse and mortally injured. With his dying breath he gives Emilia to Palamon, and Theseus blesses the union.

This is substantially the Chaucer story, but the play is given a subplot. Palamon is loved by his gaoler's daughter, who releases him, and then goes mad for fear that he will be eaten by wolves, and that her father will be hanged. On the advice of a doctor, her wooer pretends to be Palamon and she is cured.

Tybalt. In *Romeo and Juliet*, nephew to Lady Capulet. He is angered by Romeo's attending the Capulet feast, and picks a quarrel with him. Romeo refuses to fight, but when Mercutio accepts the challenge and is mortally wounded, he attacks Tybalt and kills him (III, i).

Tyler, Thomas (1826–1902), biblical and Shakespeare scholar, was educated at London University. He was an original member of the New Shakspere Society, wrote *The Philosophy of Hamlet* (1874), and in his edition of Shakespeare's *Sonnets* (1890) first advanced the theory that the Dark Lady was Mary Fitton. (See G. B. SHAW, *Dark Lady of the Sonnets*.)

Tyrrel, Sir James. In *Richard III*, he undertakes the murder of the Princes in the Tower, suborns Dighton and Forrest to do the deed, and tells Richard that they are dead and buried (IV, ii and iii). (Tyrrel was a Yorkist, knighted 1471, appointed Master of the Horse by Richard III, and Governor of Guisnes by Henry VII who, however, had him executed in 1502.)

Tyrwhitt, Thomas (1730–86), scholar and critic, fellow of Merton, and a trustee of the British Museum. He devoted much of his life to classical scholarship, but in 1766 he published anonymously *Observations and Conjectures upon some passages of Shakespeare*, in which he suggested various emendations of the text: for example, of the famous crux in *J.C.* III, i, 'Know, Caesar doth not wrong, nor without cause Will he be satisfied'. He was the first critic to mention Meres's *Palladis Tamia*.

U

Udall, Nicholas (1504–56), was educated at Winchester and Corpus Christi, Oxford. In 1534 he became Headmaster of Eton, but in 1541 was brought before the Privy Council on charges of theft and immorality, and sent to the Marshalsea prison. He made a living by writing, and a warrant of December 1554 recites that he was diligent 'in sctting forth Dialogues and Enterludes' for Queen Mary. One of these was probably *Ralph Roister Doister* (q.v.), generally considered the earliest real comedy in English. He became Headmaster of Westminster in 1555 and died a year later.

Ulrici, Hermann (1806–84), in 1834 became a professor at Halle, where he remained until his death. He is best known as a philosopher, but in 1839 he produced his *Shakespeares dramatische Kunst*, one of the earliest attempts to trace the growth and development of Shakespeare's art. It was translated into English as *Shakespeare's Dramatic Art* in 1876, when it influenced Furnivall and the New Shakspere Society.

Ulysses. In *Troilus and Cressida*, one of the Grecian commanders. He restores some order to the confusion in the Grecian camp by making the famous speech on 'degree' and the importance of an ordered rule, and by suggesting the plan to make Achilles jealous of Ajax and so provoke him to fight again (I, iii). When Troilus goes to see Cressida, he accompanies him and tries to comfort him when he discovers her infidelity (V, ii).

Underhill, William (*c.* 1523–70), a lawyer of the Middle Temple, and a big owner of land in Warwickshire, including the manor of Barton-on-the-Heath, where Shakespeare's uncle, John Lambert, lived. In 1567 he bought New Place from William Bott for £40. It was from his son, William (*c.* 1554–97), that Shakespeare bought the house in 1597. Soon after this he was poisoned by his eldest son Fulke (b. 1579), and the Underhill estates passed to Fulke's brother Hercules when he came of age in 1602, which is the reason for the levying of a second fine on New Place in that year. Fulke was executed at Warwick in March 1599.

Underwood, John. One of the twenty-six 'Principall Actors' in Shakespeare's plays (see p. 91). With Field and Ostler he was with the Chapel Children at Blackfriars, where he played in *Cynthia's Revels* and *The Poetaster*, 1600–1. In 1608 Lawrence Fletcher and William Sly died, the King's Men moved into the Blackfriars theatre, and it was probably in this year that Underwood was 'taken to strengthen the Kings service' (see 'SHARERS' PAPERS'). He played with them in *The Alchemist*, 1610, and appears in most of the King's lists until his death in 1624. He was married and had five children to whom he left his shares in the Globe, Blackfriars and Curtain. He left his executors, of whom Condell was one, and his overseers, Heminge and Lowin, 11s. each to buy rings.

United States of America. The American contribution to the knowledge and appreciation of Shakespeare in the last hundred years has been a great one. The first Shakespeare play to be publicly performed in America seems to have been *Richard III*, in New York on 5 March 1750. The great American tragic actors of the 19th century were Edwin Forrest (1806–72), Edwin Booth (1833–93), one of the actor sons of J. B. Booth, John McCullough (1837–85), and Lawrence Barrett (1838–91). Charlotte Cushman was Forrest's contemporary, and was followed by Helena Modjeska and Mary Anderson. Fanny Davenport and Ada Rehan played largely in Shakespearean comedy in Augustin Daly's company, and Julia Marlowe with E. H. Sothern, who did much to popularize Shakespeare, as R. B. Mantell, Walter Hampden and Maurice Evans have done.

Despite the work of OrsonWelles and Katharine Cornell, the actress-manager, Shakespeare is not often produced on Broadway today, though there is vigorous activity elsewhere. Pioneering work was done by Margaret Webster who, after the failure of the short-lived American Repertory Theatre in 1947, organized a company that toured the states and Canadian provinces. Another touring group is the State Theatre of Virginia, the Barter Theatre, and it was with this company that Robert Breen produced and played *Hamlet* at Elsinore in 1949. Meanwhile the first American Shakespeare Festival had been established at Ashland, Oregon, and by 1960 there were at least ten Shakespeare Festivals (q.v.) throughout the country. In New York the City Shakespeare Festival is staged in Central Park, and eighty miles away is the American Shakespeare Festival at Stratford-on-the-Housatonic, Connecticut.

The first important American contribution to scholarship was the beginning by H. H. Furness of the great *New Variorum* edition in 1871. This was followed by J. A. Morgan's *Bankside* edition and, at the beginning of this century, the *Tudor* and *Yale*. At the same time American scholars were reconstructing Shakespeare's theatre and background, among others, A. H. Thorndike, J. Q. Adams, C. W. Wallace, W. J. Lawrence, Lily B. Campbell, T. W. Baldwin, H. Craig, G. F. Reynolds, A. Harbage, A. C. Sprague, J. C. Adams, G. E. Bentley and Madeleine Doran. The foundation of the Folger Shakespeare Library in 1932, with its concentration of early editions, encouraged the detailed study of the First Folio, and began a new phase in critical bibliography. E. E. Willoughby's *Printing of the First Folio* appeared in 1932, and among leading textual critics and editors today are C. K. Hinman, P. Williams, J. G. McManaway, F. Bowers, H. T. Price, M. A. Shaaber, H. E. Rollins, H.R. Hoppe and S. B. Hemingway.

American criticism has always been remarkable for its originality and refusal to be bound by accepted standards: that of Poe, Emerson, Lowell and Barrett Wendell in the 19th century, and of, for example, E. E. Stoll, W. W. Lawrence,

T. M. Parrott, O. J. Campbell, Mark van Doren and W. Farnham in the 20th. It should not be forgotten that L. P. Smith and T. S. Eliot were Americans by birth.

The Shakespeare Society of Philadelphia was founded in 1842 (SQ, III, 4), the Shakespeare Association of America (N.Y.) in 1925, and published 24 volumes of its *Bulletin* before being reorganized in 1949, when the *Bulletin* was changed to the *Shakespeare Quarterly*. The English *Shakespeare Survey* has been helped by a grant from the Rockefeller Foundation, and it was largely the generosity of John D. Rockefeller and other Americans that made possible the rebuilding of the Memorial Theatre at Stratford. (See E. C. Dunn, *Shakespeare in America*; CINEMA.)

Unities. See ARISTOTLE.

Universities. See ACADEMIC DRAMA; CAMBRIDGE; OXFORD; 'PARNASSUS'.

University Wits. The name given to the group of playwrights who, in the 1580s, transformed the native didactic interludes and shapeless chronicle histories into real plays by giving them dramatic form, and inspiring them with vigorous action and the energy of their poetry. Greene, Marlowe and Nashe were Cambridge men; Lyly, Peele and Lodge were Oxford. By 1594, when Shakespeare joined the Chamberlain's company, Greene and Marlowe were dead, and after 1590 the others wrote little, so that Shakespeare entered into their inheritance with no important rival in the field.

Upper Stage. It is possible that in the first public theatres the continuation of the gallery behind the apron was used as an upper room (see THEATRE, THE) or 'lords' room', and, as occasion demanded, as a music room and upper stage; and that in the later theatres, the Globe and Fortune, that part of the gallery was made into a permanent upper stage, consisting of a recess with a narrow balcony or 'tarras' in front of its curtains.

Yet there is little evidence for this: the illustrations of the Swan, *Roxana*, and *Wits* stages show spectators in the gallery, and Hotson argues that the upper stage was the upper storey of the 'houses' erected on the apron. (See STAGE; LORDS' ROOM; MUSIC ROOM; 'JEW OF MALTA'.)

'Ur-Hamlet.' The name given to the lost, pre-Shakespeare play of *Hamlet*, the proofs of the existence of which are as follows:

1. In his preface to Greene's *Menaphon* (1589) Nashe refers to 'whole *Hamlets*, I should say handfulls of tragical speaches', in a passage that apparently refers to Kyd (q.v.), author of the Senecan 'revenge' play of *The Spanish Tragedy*.

2. On 11 June 1594, Henslowe records a performance of *Hamlet*, not marked as new, by the Chamberlain's at Newington Butts.

3. In his *Wits Miserie* (1596), T. Lodge alludes to 'the Visard of y[e] ghost which cried so miserably at y[e] Theator like an oister wife, Hamlet, reuenge'. (The ghost in Shakespeare's play does not call 'Hamlet revenge'.)

4. In Dekker's *Satiromastix* (1601). Tucca says 'My name's Hamlet revenge: thou hast been at Paris Garden, hast not?', which suggests that the Chamberlain's took the play to the Swan theatre in Paris Garden, where Hotson has shown that they probably acted in the autumn of 1596.

It seems clear, then, that the Chamberlain's had an old 'revenge' play of *Hamlet*, probably by Kyd, and written as early as 1589; Malone first ascribed the play to Kyd, and it has since been named the *Ur-Hamlet*, or *Source-Hamlet*. But if Shakespeare used it as a source it probably bore no more resemblance to his play than *The Troublesome Reign* to *King John*. Some maintain that the 'bad' Q1 of Shakespeare's *Hamlet* is his revision of the *Ur-Hamlet*, and that even in Q2 fragments of the old play are incorporated and account for certain dramatic difficulties. (See 'BESTRAFTE BRUDERMORD'.)

Ursula. In *Much Ado*, one of Hero's gentlewomen. Aware that Beatrice is eavesdropping, she and Hero talk of Benedick and convince her that he loves her (III, i).

Urswick, Christopher. In *Richard III*, Derby (Stanley) sends him with a message to Richmond, later Henry VII. (Urswick was chaplain to Richmond's mother, Margaret Beaufort, Countess of Richmond.)

U.S.S.R. See RUSSIA.

V

Valentine. 1. Hero of *The Two Gentlemen of Verona* (q.v.). (There is no corresponding character in Montemayor's *Diana.*)

2. In *Twelfth Night*, one of Orsino's gentlemen; he appears only in I, i and iv.

'Valentinian.' A tragedy by John Fletcher, performed by the King's Men sometime between 1610 and 1614. It was published in F1 of the works of Beaumont and Fletcher (1647); F2 (1679) states that 'The principal Actors were, Richard Burbadge, Henry Condel, John Lowin, William Ostler, John Underwood'.

Valeria. In *Coriolanus*, a talkative friend of Virgilia, Coriolanus's wife (I, iii). She is with Volumnia and Virgilia when they persuade Coriolanus to spare Rome (V, iii).

Valerius. In *The Two Noble Kinsmen*, a Theban nobleman who tells Palamon and Arcite of Theseus's impending attack on Thebes, and of Creon's wrath (I, ii).

Vanbrugh, Violet (1867–1942), daughter of the Rev .R. N. Barnes of Exeter, where she was born. Her first London appearance as an actress was in 1886. In 1892 she played Anne Bullen in Irving's production of *Henry VIII*, and in 1910 Queen Katharine in Tree's equally lavish production. After her marriage to the actor-manager Arthur Bourchier in 1894 she played in many of his productions, notably as Portia to his Shylock, and as Lady Macbeth.

Her sister Irene (1872–1949) acted more in modern comedy, though she played Mistress Page to Violet's Mistress Ford in *The Merry Wives.*

Variorum Editions, are those 'with the notes of various people', *cum notis variorum.* Steevens's first four editions of Shakespeare's Plays (1773, 1778, 1785, 1793) almost merit the name, but it is the 5th and 6th, edited after his death by Isaac Reed, that go by the name of the First and Second Variorum editions.

FIRST VARIORUM, 1803, in twenty-one volumes. Steevens's editions of Shakespeare were based on that of Johnson, to which he added an immense amount of his own material. Steevens died in 1800, and his friend and literary executor, Isaac Reed, published 'The Plays of William Shakspeare. In Twenty-One Volumes. With the Corrections and Illustrations of Various Commentators. To which are added Notes, by Samuel Johnson and George Steevens. The Fifth Edition. Revised and Augmented by Isaac Reed, with a Glossarial Index.' The frontispiece is J. Neagle's engraving of the Felton portrait. It should be noted that the *Poems* are excluded.

Steevens's 2nd edition of 1778 contained 346 pages of introductory matter; this contains in the first three volumes 1,450 pages of prolegomena. The main additions to that of 1778 (see p. 474) are: reprints of the Prefaces of Capell and Malone to their editions of 1768 and 1790, Farmer's complete *Essay on the Learning of Shakspeare*, Malone's *Historical Account of the English Stage*, including extracts from the then recently discovered *Diary* of Henslowe, *Further*

Historical Account by G. Chalmers, with extracts from the Chamber Accounts, and a description by Steevens of four 'plots'. The whole represents the immense progress made in Shakespearean scholarship in the second half of the 18th century.

SECOND VARIORUM, 1813, in twenty-one volumes. Reed died in 1807, and this edition is a reprint of the First Variorum; that is, Johnson-Steevens-Reed. The frontispiece is William Holl's engraving of the Felton portrait.

THIRD VARIORUM, 1821, in twenty-one volumes. James Boswell the younger is to Malone what Isaac Reed is to Steevens. When Malone died in 1812, he left the material of his projected new edition of Shakespeare in the hands of the son of his old friend, James Boswell, Johnson's biographer, who published it in 1821 as 'The Plays and Poems of William Shakspeare, with the Corrections and Illustrations of Various Commentators: Comprehending a Life of the Poet, and an enlarged History of the Stage, by the late Edmond Malone. With a new Glossarial Index.' The frontispiece is Fry's engraving of the Chandos portrait. It is known as the Third Variorum, or 'Boswell's Malone'. The introductory matter in the first three volumes fills some 1,800 pages, most of it the same as that in the first two Variorum editions, but with the addition of Malone's *Life of Shakespeare*, incorporating the final form of his *Attempt to Ascertain the Order of Shakspeare's Plays*, and the *Essay on the Phraseology and Metre of Shakspeare*, which was finished by Boswell. Volume XX contains the *Poems*, with which Steevens would have nothing to do. It is, perhaps, the most important of all editions of Shakespeare, though infuriatingly unindexed.

NEW VARIORUM. An enormous and valuable work begun in 1871 by the American scholar, H. H. Furness (q.v.), who published eighteen volumes before his death in 1912. The work has been continued successively by H. H. Furness Jnr., J. Q. Adams and H. E. Rollins. Since 1936 it has been issued under the auspices of the Modern Language Association of America. It is the most comprehensive of all editions of Shakespeare, though much of the matter in the early volumes is out of date. For this reason the Shakespeare Association published a *Supplement* to *1 Henry IV* in 1956. (SQ, VII.)

Varrius. 1. In *Measure for Measure*, apparently a friend of the Duke, who speaks to him in IV, v. He is not mentioned in 'The names of all the Actors' in F, and his irrelevance suggests that the text as we have it is cut.

2. In *Antony and Cleopatra*, a friend of Pompey, whom he tells of Antony's expected arrival in Rome (II, i).

Varro. 1. In *Julius Caesar*, a servant of Brutus, in whose tent he sleeps before Philippi (IV, iii).

2. In *Timon*, two of 'Seuerall Seruants to Vsurers' (F). They take their name from their master, who does not appear, but sends them to press Timon to pay his debt (II, ii; III, iv).

Vaughan, Sir Thomas. In *Richard III*, he is executed with Rivers and Grey by order of Richard at Pomfret Castle (III, iii). (Vaughan was of Tretower Castle, Brecon, and an ancestor of Henry Vaughan, the 'Silurist', and his twin brother Thomas, the alchemist.)

Vaux. 1. Sir William, in *2 Henry VI*, tells the Queen that Cardinal Beaufort is dying (III, ii).

2. Sir Nicholas, in *Henry VIII*, is given charge of the condemned Buckingham (II, i). (Sir William was a Lancastrian, killed at Tewkesbury, 1471. His estates were forfeited but restored to his son, Sir Nicholas, by Henry VII.)

Venice, Duke (Doge) of. 1. In *The Merchant of Venice*, as judge in the Court of Justice he pardons Shylock his life provided that he becomes a Christian, surrenders half his estate to Antonio, and pays a fine to the state (IV, i).

2. In *Othello*, at the meeting of the Senate he appoints Othello to the command of Cyprus, and urges Brabantio to accept him as Desdemona's husband (I, iii).

Ventidius. 1. In *Timon*, 'one of Tymons false Friends' (F). Timon rescues him from a debtors' prison and refuses his offer of repayment, but when Timon is ruined Ventidius refuses to help him. (Called 'Ventigius' in 'The Actors Names'.)

2. In *Antony and Cleopatra*, one of Antony's generals. He routs the Parthians but refuses to pursue them lest over-success arouse Antony's jealousy (III, i).

'VENUS AND ADONIS.'

WRITTEN: 1592–3. Shakespeare calls it 'the first heire of my inuention', which may mean the first of his works to be written, or the first to be published.

REGISTERED: 1593. 'xviii° Aprillis. Richard Feild Assigned ouer to master Harrison senior 25 Junii 1594. Entred for his copie under thandes of the Archbisshop of Canterbury and master warden Stirrop, a booke intituled, Venus and Adonis, vj[d].'

Transferred to John Harrison in 1594, to William Leake in 1596, and to William Barrett in 1617.

PUBLISHED: 1593, Q1. 'Venvs and Adonis. *Vilia miretur vulgus: mihi flauus Apollo Pocula Castalia plena ministret aqua.* London. Imprinted by Richard Field, and are to be sold at the signe of the white Greyhound in Paules Church-yard. 1593.' The dedication reads,

'To the Right Honorable Henrie Wriothesley, Earle of Southampton, and Baron of Titchfield.

'Right Honourable, I know not how I shall offend in dedicating my vnpolisht lines to your Lordship, nor how the worlde will censure mee for choosing so strong a proppe to support so weake a burthen, onelye if your Honour seeme but pleased, I account my selfe highly praised, and vowe to take aduantage of all idle houres, till I haue honoured you with some grauer labour. But if the first heire of my inuention proue deformed, I shall be sorie it had so noble a god-father: and neuer after eare so barren a land, for feare it yeeld me still so bad a haruest, I leaue it to your Honourable suruey, and your Honor to your hearts content which I wish may alwaies answere your owne wish, and the world's hopefull expectation.

'Your Honors in all dutie,
'William Shakespeare.'

Richard Field, Shakespeare's first publisher and printer, was a Stratford man, probably a friend of Shakespeare, and the two produced an excellent text. Field published Q2 1594; Harrison, O1 1595?, O2 1596; Leake, O3 O4 1599, O5 1602?, O6 O7 O8 1602; Barrett, O9 1617. There were five more editions before 1640.

Meres testified to the poem's popularity in his *Palladis Tamia*, 1598: 'So the sweete wittie soule of *Ouid* lives in mellifluous & hony-tongued *Shakespeare*, witnes his *Venus* and *Adonis*, his *Lucrece*, his sugred Sonnets among his priuate friends, &c.'

SOURCES: *Venus and Adonis* is written in sesta rima, a quatrain followed by a couplet, used by Spenser in his *Astrophel*, and by Thomas Lodge in his *Scillaes Metamorphosis*. Lodge's poem and Ovid's *Metamorphoses* gave Shakespeare his theme and also suggestions for its treatment. He may have read Marlowe's *Hero and Leander* in manuscript.

(See RENOLDES.)

Verbruggen, Susanna (d. 1703), one of the leading actresses in Betterton's company. As her second husband she married John Verbruggen, who also acted with Betterton, playing Cassius to his Brutus in 1707.

Verdi, Giuseppe (1813–1901), produced his first Shakespearean opera, *Macbeth*, at Florence in 1847. Forty years later his *Otello* was produced at Milan, and was followed by *Falstaff* in 1893, when he was eighty. They are the most important of his operas and two of his greatest works. The libretti were written by Arrigo Boito, that of *Falstaff* being an adaptation of *The Merry Wives* with some additions from *Henry IV*. (See ITALY; SJ, XCII.)

Vere St Theatre, near Clare Market, was converted from Gibbons's indoor tennis-court and used by the King's Company (q.v.) of actors from 8

November 1660, when they left the Red Bull, to 7 May 1663, when the first Drury Lane theatre was ready for them.

Verges. In *Much Ado*, a headborough or petty constable. With Dogberry he instructs the watch, tells Leonato that they have arrested a couple of arrant knaves, and helps to examine Conrade and Borachio (IV, ii). (See COWLEY.)

Vergil, Polydore (*c.* 1470–1555), was born at Urbino and came to England in 1501 as collector of Peter's pence. He was appointed Archdeacon of Wells in 1508, naturalized an Englishman in 1510, but *c.* 1551 returned to Urbino where he died. He began his *Historia Anglica* in 1505, at the request of Henry VII, dedicated it to Henry VIII in 1533, and published it in 26 books in the following year. The 27th book, which covers the reign of Henry VIII to 1536, was added to the third edition of 1555. His history is particularly valuable for the Yorkist and early Tudor period, and was used by Halle and Holinshed, from whom Shakespeare took most of his material for *Richard III*.

Vernon, Elizabeth. Wife of Shakespeare's patron, Southampton (q.v.).

Vernon, George. A hired actor with the King's Men in 1624. Apparently he became a sharer. (See PROTECTION OF PLAYERS.)

Vernon, Sir Richard. In *1 Henry IV*, he joins the rebellion of his 'cousin' Hotspur, counsels caution at Shrewsbury, acquiesces in Worcester's decision not to tell Hotspur of the King's offer of peace, is captured, and led to execution. (Vernon came from Shipbrook, Cheshire.)

Vernon. In *1 Henry VI*, he plucks a white rose in the Temple-Garden scene (II, iv) and quarrels with the Lancastrian Basset. They ask permission to fight a single combat, but are refused (IV, i). (The incident is not in the chronicles. Vernon may be Sir Richard, Speaker of the House of Commons.)

Verreyken, Ludowic, Flemish ambassador in London. On 6 March 1600 Lord Chamberlain Hunsdon feasted him, probably at Hunsdon House, Blackfriars, and entertained him with a performance of *1 Henry IV* by Shakespeare and his fellows. On 8 March, Rowland Whyte wrote to Sir Robert Sidney,

> All this Weeke the Lords haue bene in London, and past away the Tyme in Feasting and Plaies; for Vereiken dined vpon Wednesday, with my Lord Treasurer, who made hym a Roiall Dinner; vpon Thursday my Lord Chamberlain feasted hym, and made him very great, and a delicate Dinner, and there in the After Noone his Plaiers acted, before Vereiken, Sir John Old Castell, to his great Contentment.

Verse. See BLANK VERSE; VERSE PARAGRAPH; RHYME; VERSE-TESTS.

'Verse Fossils'. Dover Wilson thinks that when Shakespeare revised a play he sometimes rewrote verse passages as prose (*Much Ado*, for example), and that fragments of the original verse remain embedded in the prose. These he calls 'verse fossils'.

Verse Paragraph. In Shakespeare's early blank verse (q.v.) most of the lines are end-stopped, so that the line itself is the normal unit. As the number of run-on lines increased and the position of the pause was varied along the line, the phrase of indefinite length or the 'paragraph' consisting of a number of lines beginning and ending anywhere within the line, became the unit. Compare the line as unit in *2 Henry VI* (II, iii) with the paragraph as unit in *The Winter's Tale* (IV, iv):

> Forbear to judge, for we are sinners all.
> Close up his eyes and draw the curtain close;
> And let us all to meditation.

It cannot fail but by
The violation of my faith; and then
Let nature crush the sides o' the earth
together
And mar the seeds within! Lift up thy
looks:
From thy succession wipe me, father, I
Am heir to my affection.

Verse-tests. These form a statistical analysis, as scientific and objective as possible, of the metre and construction of Shakespeare's verse, a knowledge of which is a valuable aid in determining the chronology and authenticity of the plays. As early as 1758, Richard Roderick noted abnormalities in *Henry VIII*, and wrote *On the Metre of Henry VIII*, published in the 6th edition of T. Edwards's *Canons of Criticism*. The first attempt to establish the chronology by means of verse-tests (the proportion of rhyme and of run-on-lines) was made by Malone, who published his *Attempt* in 1778. In 1833 William Spalding wrote on *Shakespeare's part in The Two Noble Kinsmen*, and in 1850 James Spedding returned to the question of *Henry VIII*. In 1857 came Charles Bathurst's *Remarks on the Differences* in Shakespeare's *Versification in Different Periods of his Life*, and verse-tests became one of the most important activities of Furnivall and the New Shakspere Society (1873–94). Furnivall himself wrote on *The 'Stopped Line' Test* (1873), and this was followed by the important, though not always accurate, metrical tables of Fleay, by Ingram *On the 'Weak Endings' of Shakespeare* (*N.S.S.* 1874), and by F. S. Pulling on *The 'Speech-Ending' Test* (*N.S.S.* 1879). Meanwhile in Germany, Hertzberg was working on similar lines (*Jahrbuch*, 1878); König's *Der Vers in Shakespeares Dramen* appeared in 1888, and Conrad published his findings, 1895–1909.

The following table is based on the researches of these 19th-century scholars. It illustrates the development of Shakespeare's verse from the comparative monotony and inflexibility of *Henry VI* to the variety and plasticity of *The Winter's Tale* and *The Tempest*, the high proportion of rhyme in the 'lyrical' period of *L.L.L.* to *M.N.D.*, and of prose in the histories and comedies from *Henry IV* to *Twelfth Night*. With a few interesting exceptions, the development is fairly steady; the most spectacular change is the sudden leap in the number of light and weak endings in *Antony and Cleopatra*.

The plays are printed in chronological order, or at least in an order that must approximate to that in which they were written. It should be added that the evidence of verse-tests is treated less seriously today. (See p. 516.)

Col. 1. Compiled by T. R. Smith and F. J. Furnivall from *Globe* edition (*N.S.S.* 1880–6).

Col. 2. The figures are mine, based on Fleay as corrected by Chambers. Fleay worked from the *Globe* edition. The proportion is that of lines of prose to the total number of lines in the play.

Col. 3. König's figure brought to the nearest whole number. It is important to note that the proportion is that of pentameter rhymes (couplets and alternate) to all pentameter lines (excluding prologues, epilogues, interludes, songs, etc.). It is *not* the proportion of rhyme to the total number of lines.

Cols. 4–6. König's figures brought to the nearest whole number.

Cols. 7, 8. Ingram's figures (*N.S.S.* 1874).

(The best and most detailed metrical tables are those of E. K. Chambers, *William Shakespeare*, II, 397–408).

Vestris, Elizabeth (1797–1856), born in London, granddaughter of Francesco Bartolozzi, the engraver. She married the ballet dancer Auguste Vestris in 1813, but he deserted her, and in 1838 she married the actor Charles James Mathews. She played mainly in light comedy and burlesque, though when she and her husband took over Covent Garden in 1839, she acted in Shakespearean comedy: Rosaline in *Love's Labour's Lost*, with which they opened their management, followed by *The Merry Wives* and *A Midsummer Night's Dream*.

	Proportion (%) of						Number of	
	1 Total Lines	2 Prose to Total	3 Rhyme to Verse	4 Feminine Endings	5 Run-on Lines	6 Mid-line Speech Endings	7 Light Endings	8 Weak Endings
1 H. VI	2677	0	10	8	10	1	3	1
2 H. VI	3162	18	3	14	11	1	2	1
3 H. VI	2904	0·1	3	14	10	1	3	0
R. III	3619	2	4	20	13	3	4	0
Tit. An.	2523	2	4	9	12	3	5	0
C.E.	1778	14	19	17	13	1	0	0
T. Sh.[1]	2649	23	4	18	8	4	1	1
T.G.V.	2294	29	7	18	12	6	0	0
L.L.L.	2789	39	62	8	18	10	3	0
R.J.	3052	15	17	8	14	15	6	1
R. II	2756	0	19	11	20	7	4	0
M.N.D.	2174	22	43	7	13	17	0	1
John	2570	0	5	6	18	13	7	0
M.V.	2660	24	5	18	22	22	6	1
1 H. IV	3176	47	3	5	23	14	5	2
2 H. IV	3446	53	3	16	21	17	1	0
M. Ado	2826	75	5	23	19	21	1	1
H. V	3380	42	3	21	22	18	2	0
M.W.W.	3018	88	6	27	20	21	1	0
J.C.	2478	7	1	20	19	20	10	0
A.Y.L.	2857	57	6	26	17	22	2	0
T.N.	2690	64	14	26	15	36	3	1
Ham.	3931	31	3	23	23	52	8	0
T.C.	3496	34	9	24	27	31	6	0
A.W.	2966	50	19	29	28	74	11	2
Oth.	3316	20	3	28	20	54[3]	2	0
M.M.	2821	41	4	26	23	51	7	0
Tim.	2373	29	9	22	33	63	16	5
Lear	3334	20	3	29	29	61	5	1
Mac.	2108	7	6	26	37	77	21	2
A.C.	3063	9	1	27	43	78	71	28
Cor.	3410	24	1	28	46	79	60	44
Per.[2]	(1140)	30	3	22	25	71[3]	15	5
Cym.	3339	16	3	31	46	85	78	52
W.T.	3075	28	0	33	38	88	57	43
Tem.	2064	22	0·1	35	42	85	42	25
H. VIII[2]	(1167)	0·6	0·5	32	39	72	45	37
T.N.K.[2]	(1131)	5	2	30	30	92[4]	50	34

[1] Whole play. [2] Shakespeare's part (Chambers's figures). [3] Bradley's figure. [4] My figure.

Victor, Benjamin (d. 1778), a London barber who became 'Poet Laureate' of Ireland in 1755, and treasurer of Drury Lane 1760–78. He published *Memoirs of Barton Booth*, and a *History of the Theatres of London and Dublin, 1710–71*. His adaptation of *The Two Gentlemen of Verona*, produced at Drury Lane by Garrick in 1762, when it ran for five nights, is the first recorded performance of any version of the play – this one with additions for Launce and his dog.

Viëtor, Wilhelm (1850–1918), German philologist and Professor at Marburg University. His *Shakespeare's Pronuncia-*

tion, 1906, is one of the standard works on the subject.

Vigny, Alfred de (1797–1863), French Romantic poet, lived in England for some time, and in 1828 married an Englishwoman. In 1835 he produced his successful play *Chatterton*, in 1829 his translation of *Othello*, and he also adapted *The Merchant of Venice* as *Shylock*.

Vincent, played as a boy in *The Seven Deadly Sins*, probably with Strange's, *c.* 1591. He may be the Thomas Vincent, 'prompter at the Globe playhouse', mentioned by John Taylor, the water poet, in *Taylor's Feast*, 1638.

Vincentio. 1. In *The Taming of the Shrew*, father of Lucentio. On his way from Pisa to Padua he meets Petruchio, who tells him that his son has married Bianca (IV, v). In Padua the Pedant who is impersonating him almost secures his imprisonment, but Lucentio confesses and Vincentio pardons him. (In *A Shrew* he is Jerobel, Duke of Cestus; in *I Suppositi* Filogono, a merchant of Catania.)

2. In *Measure for Measure* (q.v.) Duke of Vienna. (The only mention of his name in F is in 'The names of all the Actors': '*Vincentio: the Duke*'. In *Promos and Cassandra* he is the King of Hungary, in Cinthio the Emperor Maximilian.)

Viol. In Shakespeare's day, the most important of the stringed instruments. 'A chest of viols', so called because they were kept in a chest, was a set of instruments of various sizes, generally two trebles, two tenors, and two basses. They were played in consort, with the hand under the bow, and held downwards like a 'cello. The back of the viol is flat and generally has six strings. Cf. *Richard II*, I, iii:

And now my tongue's use is to me no
  more
Than an unstringed viol or a harp.

In *Pericles*, III, ii, viols help to restore Thaisa:

The rough and woful music that we have,
Cause it to sound, beseech you.
The viol once more: ...
The music there!

Viol da Gamba. The name given to the instruments of the viol family, 'leg viols', because they were held downwards between the knees or legs, to distinguish them from the violin and viola, *Viole da Braccio* or 'arm viols'. Viol da gamba, the viol-de-gamboys of Sir Toby Belch, came to be applied to the bass viol in particular.

Viola. The heroine of *Twelfth Night* (q.v.); daughter of 'Sebastian of Messaline' and twin sister of the young Sebastian, she assumes the name Cesario. (She is the Silla of Riche's *Apolonius and Silla*, who takes the name of Silvio. In Bandello she is Nicuolo–'Romolo', and in *Gl'Ingannati* Lelia–'Fabio'. In the *Inganni* of Curzio Gonzaga (1592) the heroine calls herself Cesare.)

Violenta. In *All's Well*, a friend of the widow of Florence. She appears only in III, v, but does not speak: an indication that the F text is incomplete.

Virgilia. In *Coriolanus*, the faithful and quiet wife of Coriolanus, who vows to keep her house till he returns from the wars. When he does, he fondly calls her 'My gracious silence'. She helps to persuade him to spare Rome (V, iii). (She is called Virgilia by Plutarch, but in the legends is Volumnia.)

Virginal. The earliest form of keyboard stringed instrument, which developed into the spinet and harpsichord. Their strings are plucked by plectra attached to wooden jacks, instead of being struck as in the clavichord and pianoforte. Cf. Sonnet 128:

How oft, when thou, my music, music
  play'st,
Upon that blessed wood whose motion
  sounds
With thy sweet fingers, when thou gently
  sway'st

The wiry concord that mine ear confounds,
Do I envy those jacks that nimble leap
To kiss the tender inward of thy hand ...

It was a domestic instrument, played mainly by ladies, and would not be powerful enough in tone for use in the theatre. (Cf. the image in *W.T.*, I, ii: 'Still virginalling upon his palm.')

'Virtuous Octavia.' A play by Samuel Brandon, about whom nothing else is known, registered 5 October 1598, and published in the same year, as 'The Tragicomœdi of the vertuous Octavia. Done by Samuel Brandon'. It may have given a hint to Shakespeare for *Antony and Cleopatra*, but like the *Cleopatra* of Daniel, it is classical in form and may not have been intended for the stage.

Visscher, J. C. 17th-century Dutch engraver of the famous *View of London*, '1616', though there is no proof that he was ever in England. (See MAPS OF LONDON; SS, I.)

Vocabulary of Shakespeare. See George Gordon, *Shakespeare's English*, 1928: the best short account (21 pages).

'Volpone.' A comedy by Ben Jonson, first published in Quarto in 1607 as 'Ben: Ionson his Volpone Or the Foxe', and dedicated 'To the Two Famous Universities, for the Love and Acceptance shown to his Poem in the Presentation'. In F (1616), Jonson adds,

This Comœdie was first acted, in the yeere 1605. By the K. Maiesties Servants. The principall Comœdians were, Ric. Burbadge, Ioh. Hemings, Hen. Condel, Ioh. Lowin, Will. Sly, Alex. Cooke.

The King's were in Oxford in October 1605, and must have played *Volpone* in Cambridge sometime between then and the publication of Q in 1607. As Shakespeare is not in the actor-list, it seems probable that he stopped acting between the production of *Sejanus*, in which he played in the winter of 1603, and that of *Volpone* in 1605.

Voltaire (1694–1778), whose real name was François Arouet, spent the years 1726–29 in exile in England, where he made friends with the Walpoles, Congreve, Pope and other men of letters, and was introduced to the works of Shakespeare. A firm believer in the classical rules, he published his views on Shakespeare in his *Lettres Philosophiques sur les Anglais* (1734): 'Il avait un génie plein de force et de fécondité, de naturel et de sublime, sans la moindre étincelle de bon goût et sans la moindre connaissance des règles.' When Letourneur (q.v.) began his prose translation of Shakespeare in 1776 and called him 'the God of the theatre', Voltaire abused him (Letourneur) as an 'impudent imbecile', and claimed that he had himself been the first to show the French the few pearls to be found in the enormous dung-hill of Shakespeare's works. His final verdict is summarized in a letter to Horace Walpole in 1768: 'C'est une belle nature, mais bien sauvage; nulle régularité, nulle bienséance, nul art, de la bassesse avec la grandeur, de la bouffonnerie avec du terrible; c'est le chaos de la tragédie, dans lequel il y a cent traits de lumière.'

Volumnia. In *Coriolanus*, mother of Coriolanus. She despises the plebeians as much as he, but advises him to conceal his contempt until he is consul (III, ii). It is she who persuades him to spare Rome when, to avenge his banishment, he is about to attack it with his Volscian allies (V, iii). (Plutarch calls her Volumnia, but in the legends she is Veturia, and Volumnia is Coriolanus's wife.)

Volumnius. In *Julius Caesar*, a schoolfellow of Brutus, whom he refuses to aid in his suicide (V, v). (Volumnius wrote an account of Brutus's death, which Plutarch made use of.)

Voragine, Jacobus de (*c.* 1230–98), a Dominican friar who became Archbishop of Genoa. His *Golden Legend*, or Lives of the Saints, was one of the most popular books of the Middle Ages, and was translated into English by Caxton in 1483. The legend of St Barlaam contains a moral story about four caskets, two covered with gold and two with pitch, the former containing bones, the latter diamonds and pearls. It is a possible source of the casket-choosing theme in *The Merchant of Venice*.

'Vortigern and Rowena.' A play: one of the Shakespearean forgeries of W. H. Ireland (q.v.). It reads rather like Savonarola Brown's tragedy, but is not bad for a boy of eighteen writing in 1795–6.

Voss, Johann Heinrich (1751–1826), German poet and professor at Heidelberg. His translation of Shakespeare's plays, completed with the help of his sons, was published 1818–29.

W

Walker, Sir Edward (1612–77). Through the patronage of the Earl of Arundel he entered the College of Arms, in the Civil War supported Charles I, who knighted him, and Charles II, who at the Restoration made him Garter King-of-Arms. He bought New Place in 1675, and by the marriage of his daughter Barbara to Sir John Clopton, the house returned to the family that built it. (See BAGLEY.)

Walker, Henry (d. 1616). In 1604 he bought the Blackfriars Gatehouse from Mathias Bacon for £100, and on 10 March 1610 sold it to Shakespeare for £140. In the conveyance he is called 'citizein and Minstrell of London'. He was born at Kington, Herefordshire, was a member of the Minstrel's Company of London, had a shop at his house in St Martin Ludgate, and left a considerable fortune.

Walker, William. Shakespeare's godson, to whom he left 'xx^{s}. in gold'. He was probably the son, baptized 16 October 1608, of Henry Walker, mercer, alderman and bailiff of Stratford. He died in March 1680.

Walkley, Thomas, bookseller. He registered *Othello* 6 October 1621. Q1 was well printed by Nicholas Okes 'for Thomas Walkley, and are to be sold at his shop, at the Eagle and Child, in Brittans Bursse, 1622.' To this he added an Epistle:

The Stationer to the Reader.

To set forth a booke without an Epistle, were like to the old English prouerbe, A blew coat without a badge, & the Author being dead, I thought good to take that piece of worke vpon mee: To commend it, I will not, for that which is good, I hope euery man will commend, without intreaty: and I am the bolder, because the Authors name is sufficient to vent his worke. Thus leauing euery one to the liberty of iudgement: I haue ventered to print this Play, and leaue it to the generall censure.

Yours,
Thomas Walkley.

Wallace, Charles William (1865–1932), American scholar, was educated at the University of Nebraska, where he was appointed Professor of English Dramatic Literature in 1910. Between 1907 and 1916 he and his wife examined more than five million original records in their Shakespearean and dramatic research, to finance which he entered the oil industry in 1918. He discovered the documents relating to the suits of *Ostler* v. *Heminge* (1615), *Witter* v. *Heminge and Condell* (1619), *Keysar* v. *Burbage* (1610), all of which yield invaluable information about the shares and Shakespeare's holdings in the Globe and Blackfriars. His finding of the suit of *Belott* v. *Mountjoy* is one of the most important of biographical discoveries.

Walley, Henry, publisher; with Richard Bonian he registered *Troilus and Cressida* 28 January 1609, although the play had been registered by James Roberts in 1603. Q was 'Imprinted by G. Eld for R. Bonian and H. Walley, and are to be sold at the spred Eagle in Paules Church-yeard, ouer against the great North doore. 1609.' An Epistle was added to a second issue of Q, though Hotson thinks that it was written not by the publishers, but by Richard Martin of the Middle Temple. (See 'TROILUS AND CRESSIDA'.)

War of the Theatres. See POETOMACHIA.

Warburton, William (1698–1779), the fifth editor of Shakespeare, was born at Newark, educated at Oakham and Newark grammar schools, intended becoming a solicitor, but in 1723 was ordained, and in 1729 received the living of Brant Broughton in Lincolnshire. His defence of the *Essay on Man* secured him the friendship of Pope, who introduced him to the wealthy Ralph Allen of Prior Park, Bath, who 'gave him his niece and his estate, and, by consequence, a bishopric'. The niece he acquired in 1745, the bishopric (of Gloucester) in 1759, and the estate (Prior Park), where he had lived for the most part since his marriage, in 1764. He died at Gloucester in 1779.

In 1747 Warburton published an edition of Shakespeare in eight volumes. In his Preface he claimed that he had 'communicated a great number of observations' to Theobald, 'a poor man', and to Hanmer, 'a poor critick', 'which they managed, as they saw fit, to the relief of their several distresses'. What Theobald 'read he could transcribe: but, as what he thought, if ever he did think, he could but ill express, so he read on: and by that means got a character of learning'. As for Hanmer, 'he was absolutely ignorant of the art of criticism, as well as of the poetry of that time, and the language of his author'. After this abuse, Warburton proceeded to incorporate the best things from Theobald, adding, in the words of Malone, 'his own chimerical conceits in the place of the author's genuine text'. The *Supplement to Warburton's Edition of Shakespeare* (1747), later known as *The Canons of Criticism*, by Thomas Edwards, is a satirical exposure of Warburton's incompetence. Warburton was a remarkable man, but not a remarkable editor of Shakespeare, and 'seems to have erected his throne on a heap of stones, that he might have them at hand to throw at the heads of all those who passed by'.

Ward, John (1629–81), Vicar of Stratford 1662–81. Shakespeare's daughter, Judith Quiney, was buried 9 February 1662, and in one of his note-books Ward wrote: 'A letter to my brother, to see Mrs. Queeny, to send for Tom Smith for the acknowledgement.' He cannot have had much time to gather information from Judith, but the Harts were living at the 'Birthplace', owned by Shakespeare's granddaughter Lady Bernard (Elizabeth Hall), who was still alive, though living at Abington, Northants. In his early days Ward had been a student of medicine, and in the late 18th century his note-books (now in the Folger Library) were acquired by the Medical Society of London and in 1839 edited by Dr C. Severn. One of these has the note, 'This booke was begunne Feb. 14, 1661 [1662], and finished April the 25 1663, att Mr. Brooks his house in Stratford-uppon-Avon', and contains the following entries:

> Shakespear had but 2 daughters, one whereof M. Hall, ye physitian, married, and by her had one daughter, to wit, ye Lady Bernard of Abbingdon.
>
> I have heard y^{t} M^{r}. Shakespeare was a natural wit, without any art at all; hee frequented ye plays all his younger time, but in his elder days lived at Stratford: and supplied ye stage with 2 plays every year, and for y^{t} had an allowance so large, y^{t} hee spent att ye Rate of a 1,000*l.* a year, as I have heard.
>
> Remember to peruse Shakespears plays, and bee versd in *them*, y^{t} I may not bee ignorant in y^{t} matter.
>
> Shakespear, Drayton, and Ben Jhonson, had a merry meeting, and itt seems drank too hard, for Shakespear died of a feavour there contracted. (See WINCOT.)

Ward, John, the actor. (See MONUMENT.)

Warner, Richard (*c.* 1713–75), botanist and Shakespeare scholar, was educated at Wadham, to which college he bequeathed his library. He thought of publishing an edition of Shakespeare, but when Steevens issued his advertisement in 1766, he changed his mind, and in 1768 wrote *A Letter to David Garrick Esq., concerning a Glossary to the Plays of Shakespeare*. At this glossary he worked until his death, leaving to Garrick the manuscripts now in the British Museum.

Warner, William (*c.* 1551–1609), poet, was educated at Magdalen Hall, Oxford. He is remembered for his long historical poem, *Albion's England* (1586), written in rhyming fourteeners and dedicated to Lord Chamberlain Hunsdon, afterwards patron of Shakespeare's company. In his *Continuance of Albion's England* (1606), he adds an account of Macbeth which, if inspired by Shakespeare's play, helps to date it. Warner also wrote a translation of the *Menaechmi* of Plautus, the main source of *The Comedy of Errors*. This was registered 10 June 1594, though apparently not published until 1595. *The Comedy of Errors* was produced at Gray's Inn at Christmas 1594, and it is possible that Shakespeare saw the manuscript 'Englished' by Warner 'for the use and delight of his private friends', though Shakespeare probably knew the original Latin. Some claim Warner as the 'Aetion' of *Colin Clout's Come Home Againe* (see SPENSER).

Warren, John, 17th-century minor poet, whose verses *Of Mr. William Shakespeare* were prefixed to Benson's edition of the *Poems*, 1640. They begin,

What, lofty *Shakespeare*, art againe reviv'd?
And *Virbius* like now show'st thy selfe twise liv'd,
Tis [Benson's] love that thus to thee is showne,
The labours his, the glory still thine owne.

Wart, Thomas. In *2 Henry IV*, Falstaff presses him for the army (III, ii).

Warton, Joseph (1722–1800), elder brother of Thomas Warton, was educated at Winchester and Oriel, Oxford. He became Headmaster of Winchester in 1766, resigning in 1793 when the boys rose against him for the third time. He was a romantic born in a classical age, wrote *The Enthusiast, or The Lover of Nature* (1744), and relegated Pope to the second rank of poets. In 1753–4 he contributed five articles on Shakespeare to *The Adventurer*, the first series to be written for a periodical, insisting that the 'finer features must be singly pointed out', and that general criticism is 'useless and unentertaining'.

Warton, Thomas (1728–90), one of the precursors of the romantic movement, was born at Basingstoke, educated at Trinity, Oxford, of which college he became a Fellow, appointed Professor of Poetry 1757, and Poet-Laureate 1785. The three volumes of his great work, *The History of English Poetry*, were published 1774–78–81. This reached only the close of the 16th century and his beloved Spenser, and did not, therefore, deal fully with Shakespeare, but it was an invaluable work for scholars like Capell, Steevens and Malone, who were trying to relate Shakespeare to his age. (See WISE, FRANCIS.)

Warwick, county town of Warwickshire, is on the Avon, nine miles north-east of Stratford. The castle of the Earls of Warwick stands above the river, and there Elizabeth was entertained by Ambrose Dudley, Earl of Warwick, on her progress of 1566, after a visit to his brother the Earl of Leicester at Kenilworth, and before a visit to Sir Thomas Lucy at Charlecote. She repeated her progress in 1572, when the entertainments at Kenilworth (q.v.) and Warwick Castle were on a princely scale. There were Shakespeares in Warwick; Thomas Shaxper, shoemaker, died in 1577 leaving three sons. William was drowned in the Avon in 1579. Thomas married the daughter of the mayor of Coventry, became bailiff of Warwick in 1612, and made his will in 1632. His son, John, was apprenticed to William Jaggard, printer of the Shakespeare Folio, from 1610 to 1617. Thomas's third son, John, is probably the shoemaker, or corvizer, who lived in Stratford *c.* 1584–95 and was buried at St Mary's, Warwick, in 1624. His children, Ursula, Humphrey and Phillip, baptized at Stratford, were apparently thought by Betterton and Rowe to be those of Shakespeare's father. Until the Dissolution one of the manors at Snitterfield, on which Shakespeare's grandfather Richard farmed, was held by the collegiate Church of St Mary, where Fulke Greville (q.v.) was buried in 1628.

Warwick, Ambrose Dudley, Earl of (*c.* 1528–90), third son of the Protector Northumberland. Like his younger brother, Robert, Earl of Leicester, he was a great favourite of Elizabeth, who created him Baron Lisle and Earl of Warwick in 1561, and in the following year granted him the manor of Stratford. Shakespeare's cottage in Chapel Lane was part of the manor of Rowington, also granted to Warwick. His third wife was Anne, daughter of the 2nd Earl of Bedford. Warwick was the patron of a company of players.

Warwick's Men. A company is traceable from 1559 to 1564–5, in the winter of which year they gave two plays at Court. In 1574–5 they appear again, at Stratford, and until 1580 they performed regularly at Court. John and Laurence Dutton were two of their leading actors, but in 1580 the whole company deserted Warwick for the Earl of Oxford, an action that occasioned some scurrilous verses, the introduction to which is informative:

> The Duttons and theyr fellow-players forsakying the Erle of Warwycke theyr mayster, became followers of the Erle of Oxford, and wrot themselves his *Comœdians*, which certayne Gentlemen altered and made *Camœlions*.

'Y[e] Erle of Warwiches' were at Ipswich in March 1592. The Earl had died without an heir in 1590, so perhaps the company was maintained by his widow, who died in 1604.

Warwick, Earl of. 1. In *2 Henry IV*, he comforts the King (III, i), and defends the character of the Prince of Wales (V, ii).

In *Henry V*, though present in IV, vii and V, ii, he speaks only one line, in IV, viii.

In *1 Henry VI*, he plucks a white rose (II, iv), and helps Plantagenet to recover his title of Duke of York (III, i). He is one of those who send Joan of Arc to the stake (V, iv).

(Richard Beauchamp, Earl of Warwick (1382–1439) fought against Glendower, and was Governor of Normandy, 1437–9, where he died. His tomb in St Mary's, Warwick, is one of the finest of its period. His daughter Anne married Richard Neville, 'the King-Maker', who succeeded to the Warwick earldom.)

2. In *2 Henry VI*, he accuses Suffolk of the murder of Gloucester, and quarrels with Somerset. With his father, Salisbury, he joins the Yorkists in the Wars of the Roses, and helps to win the first Battle of St Albans.

In *3 Henry VI*, he supports the claim to the throne of the Duke of York, after whose death he wins the Battle of Towton and has York's son crowned Edward IV. He goes to France to secure the Lady Bona as wife for Edward, but when he hears that he has married Lady Grey, he joins Queen Margaret and the Lancastrians. He captures Edward, takes off his crown and returns it to Henry VI, but is defeated and killed at Barnet. (Richard Neville, 'the King-Maker' (1428–71), was the son of the 1st Earl of Salisbury, and by marrying the daughter of Richard Beauchamp, Earl of Warwick, inherited the Warwick earldom. His daughter Isabel married the Duke of Clarence.)

3. In *Richard III*, the young son of Clarence appears with his sister Margaret (II, ii). He is imprisoned by Richard.

(Edward, Earl of Warwick (1475–99), was the son of Clarence and Isabel, daughter of the King-Maker. He was impersonated by Lambert Simnel and executed by Henry VII.)

Wayte, William (d. 1603). In 1930 Leslie Hotson discovered two writs of attachment issued to the sheriff of Surrey, *a.* returnable 3 November 1596, *b.* 29 November 1596. He translates the legal Latin:

a. Be it known that Francis Langley craves sureties of the peace against William Gardener and William Wayte for fear of death, and so forth.

b. Be it known that William Wayte craves sureties of the peace against William Shakspere, Francis Langley, Dorothy Soer wife of John Soer, and Anne Lee, for fear of death, and so forth.

Anyone craving sureties of the peace made oath before a justice that he stood in fear of his life or some bodily hurt, whereupon a judge would order the sheriff of the county concerned to attach the alleged threatener and make him enter a bond to keep the peace. Langley was owner of the newly built Swan theatre; Gardiner (q.v.), who died 26 November 1597, was a scoundrelly Surrey justice who defrauded his stepson, Wayte, described in a previous bill of complaint as 'a certain loose person of no reckoning or value, being wholly under the rule and commandment of the said Gardiner.' Of D. Soer, Anne Lee and of Shakespeare's part in the quarrel nothing is known.

From the fact that the writ to attach Shakespeare was issued to the sheriff of Surrey it seems clear that he had moved to the Bankside by November 1596, and from his association with Langley, Hotson concludes that the Chamberlain's was the company that acted at the Swan towards the end of 1596. From further evidence he concludes that Shallow and Slender are portraits of Gardiner and Wayte, that *The Merry Wives* was first produced at Westminster, 23 April 1597, and that the two parts of *Henry IV* were written 1596–7. (See Hotson, *Shakespeare versus Shallow*.)

Weak Endings. Monosyllabic prepositions and conjunctions at the end of a line, which 'are so essentially *proclitic* in their character that we are forced to run them, in pronunciation no less than in sense, into the closest connexion with the opening words of the succeeding line.' (Ingram: *N.S.S.* 1874.) They constitute, of course, an extreme form of run-on line:

These our actors,
As I foretold you, were all spirits, and
Are melted into air.

There are very few weak endings in Shakespeare's verse before *Antony and Cleopatra*, after which they increase from 1 to 3 per cent in his part of *Henry VIII*. (See LIGHT ENDINGS; VERSE-TESTS.)

Webbe, Alexander (d. 1573). The poet's uncle; first husband of Margaret, sister of Mary Arden. He was also brother of Agnes, widow of John Hill, Robert Arden's second wife. In Robert Arden's conveyance of two Snitterfield properties to his daughters in 1550, Webbe is described as of Bearley, a hamlet in the parish of Snitterfield. In 1560 Arden's widow, Agnes, leased the properties, in which she had a life interest, to Webbe for forty years at a rent of 40s. In his will, 15 April 1573, Webbe appointed 'John Shackespere of Stretford-upon-Aven' as one of his overseers, and 'Henry Shaxspere' was a witness.

His son was Robert Webbe. Agnes renewed the lease in his favour, and to him, 15 October 1579, 'John Shackspere and Marye his wyeffe' sold their share of the property for £4. By 1582 he had acquired all the reversionary interests in both the Arden estates in Snitterfield. In 1580 Thomas Mayowe, a descendant of the original owner, brought an action against Webbe for the recovery of the property which he claimed to have been entailed. John and Henry Shakespeare were called as witnesses, but the evidence and decision are unknown.

Webster, Benjamin (1797–1882), actor-manager and dramatist, was born in

Bath, son of a dancing master. From Drury Lane he went to the Haymarket, of which he became lessee 1837–53, then built the new Adelphi theatre, and was later manager of the Princess's and St James's. He was a prolific writer and adapter of plays and a great actor of character parts, retiring from the stage in 1874. His production of *The Taming of the Shrew* at the Haymarket in 1844 made history. Assisted by Planché, he staged the original play, not Garrick's version, without scenery, and with only curtains and locality boards. It lasted three and a half hours, but the experiment was well received by the audience.

Webster, John (fl. 1602–24). Little is known about his life. A John Webster was an actor with Robert Browne's company in Germany in 1596. As a playwright he first appears in Henslowe's *Diary* in 1602; and the City pageant, *Monuments of Honour* (1624), was published as 'invented and written by John Webster, Merchant-Taylor.' In 1602 he collaborated with Dekker and others in *Sir Thomas Wyatt*, in the lost *Caesar's Fall*, and in *Christmas Comes but Once a Year*. In 1604–5 he and Dekker wrote *Westward Ho!* and *Northward Ho!* for the Paul's boys, and in 1604 he adapted Marston's *Malcontent* for the King's. *Appius and Virginia* was registered and published as his in 1654, but some critics ascribe it mainly to Heywood. The additions to the 1602 Q of *The Spanish Tragedy* read like Webster, as does most of *The Revenger's Tragedy* (1607). His fame rests primarily on *The White Devil* (published 1612), a Queen's play, and *The Duchess of Malfi* (q.v.), acted by the King's 1613–14. After Shakespeare, Webster is perhaps our greatest dramatic poet, though he was almost forgotten until Charles Lamb rediscovered him. Of his contemporaries he wrote in his Epistle to *The White Devil*:

> Detraction is the sworne friend to ignorance: For mine owne part I haue euer truly cherisht my good opinion of other mens worthy Labours, especially of that full and haightned stile of Maister *Chapman*: the labor'd and vnderstanding workes of Maister *Johnson*; The no lesse worthy composures of the both worthily excellent Maister *Beaumont* & Maister *Fletcher*: And lastly (without wrong last to be named), the right happy and copious industry of M. *Shakespeare*, M. *Dekker*, & M. *Heywood*, wishing what I write may be read by their light: Protesting, that, in the strength of mine owne iudgement I know them so worthy, that though I rest silent in my owne worke yet to most of theirs I dare (without flattery) fix that of *Martiall*. – *non norunt Haec monumenta mori*.

(See TATE; *The Works of John Webster*, ed. F. L. Lucas.)

Weelkes, Thomas (*c.* 1575–1623), organist of Winchester College, and later of Chichester Cathedral. He wrote church music, and music for viols, but is best known for his madrigals. No. 18, 'My flocks feed not', in *The Passionate Pilgrim* was first printed with music by Weelkes in his *Madrigals*, 1597.

Weever, John (1576–1632), poet and antiquary, a native of Lancashire, educated at Queen's, Cambridge, and after travel in France and Italy settled in Clerkenwell, producing his well-known *Ancient Funerall Monuments* in 1631. His *Epigrammes in the oldest Cut, and newest Fashion* (1599) contains a sonnet to 'Honie-tong'd Shakespeare', which mentions Adonis, Venus, Lucretia, Tarquine and 'Romea Richard'. *The Mirror of Martyrs, or The Life and Death of Sir John Oldcastle* (published 1601, but 'some two years ago was made fit for the print.') refers to 'Brutus speach, that Caesar was ambitious', and to the reply of 'eloquent Mark Antonie'.

Welcombe Enclosure. Welcombe is a hamlet in Stratford parish about a mile north-east of the town. It gave its name to an open field, to the west of which were the hamlets and open fields of Old Stratford and Bishopton. In 1602 Shakespeare bought 127 acres of land in Old Stratford, then in 1605 the lease of part of the corn and hay tithes in the fields of all three hamlets. When, therefore, in the autumn of 1614, Arthur Mainwaring and William Replingham began proceedings for the enclosure of these fields, mainly Welcombe, Shakespeare was affected, though the scheme did not affect his estate in Old Stratford. As a tithe-holder he would stand to gain if enclosure led to better cultivation, though he would lose if arable land were converted to pasture; but on 28 October Replingham covenanted to compensate him and his 'cousin' Thomas Greene, another tithe-holder, for any loss. Greene was clerk to the Stratford Corporation, who strenuously opposed the enclosure and employed him to petition the Privy Council and to dissuade the promoters, who were joined by William Combe, a large landowner in Welcombe. Combe actually began the enclosure in January 1615 by digging a ditch, but was stopped by an order of the Warwick Assizes, and the enclosure was stayed. We cannot be certain what Shakespeare thought about the scheme, though it may be that he was not unfavourable, for on 23 December 1614 Greene made a note of letters from the Corporation and himself:

> Lettres wrytten one to Mr Manneryng another to Mr Shakspeare with almost al the copanyes hands to eyther: I alsoe wrytte of myself to my Cosen Shakespeare the Coppyes of all our oathes made then alsoe a not of the Inconvenyences wold grow by the Inclosure.

Unfortunately, Shakespeare's reply, if any, is lost.

Welles, Thomas. In her will, 29 January 1670, Shakespeare's granddaughter, Lady Bernard, left £50 to her 'cousin Thomas Welles of Carleton in the county of Bedford'. Welles was vicar of Carlton and Chellington, probably the son of Michael Welles, who married John Hall's sister.

Wendell, Barrett (1855–1919), American critic, was educated at Harvard, where he became Assistant Professor in 1888, and Professor in 1898. His *William Shakespere: a Study in Elizabethan Literature* is incisive and original criticism.

West, James (*c.* 1704–72), a native of Prior's Marston, Warwickshire, had a house at Alscot, three miles from Stratford. He was Secretary to the Treasury 1741–62, and President of the Royal Society, 1768–72. (See GREENE, JOSEPH; WINCOT.)

Westcott, Sebastian (d. 1582), Yeoman of the Chamber in 1545, and from *c.* 1557 to his death Master of the Choir School of St Paul's. During this period the Paul's boys gave twenty-seven performances at Court, considerably more than those given by any other company.

Westminster, Abbot of. In *Richard II*, is given charge of the arrested Bishop of Carlisle (IV, i), but with him and Aumerle he lays a plot against Bolingbroke. It is, however, discovered, and the death of 'the grand conspirator' is reported in the last scene. (The Abbot was either William de Colchester or Richard Harweden.)

Westminster School. The first record of a play by the boys is in 1521, the next in 1561, when they performed in the Lord Mayor's pageant. As at St Paul's, there was a choir-school attached to the grammar school, and between 1565 and 1574, one or the other, or perhaps both together, performed a number of Latin and English plays at Court.

Westmoreland, Earl of. 1. In *1 Henry IV*, a firm supporter of Henry, and an opponent of Worcester and the Percies. He is present at Shrewsbury.

In *2 Henry IV*, 'Of the Kings Partie' (F). He arranges the meeting between Prince John and the rebel leaders, and arrests them when they have dispersed their forces (IV, ii).

In *Henry V*, his wish for ten thousand more men at Agincourt occasions Henry's St Crispin speech. (Westmoreland was not present at Agincourt, nor was Warwick, to whom Q assigns the remark. Holinshed says 'one of the best' made it. Ralph Neville, 4th Baron (1365–1425), was created 1st Earl of Westmoreland by Richard II. He was a 'cousin' of Bolingbroke (Henry IV) by his marriage with Joan Beaufort, Bolingbroke's half-sister.)

2. In *3 Henry VI*, a Lancastrian, though he has no patience with Henry when he makes York his heir (I, i).

(Ralph, 2nd Earl (*c.* 1404–84), was grandson of the 1st Earl.)

'What You Will.' A comedy by Marston, registered and published in 1607, but probably written and acted by the Paul's boys in 1601 as a reply to Jonson's *Cynthia's Revels*. It is one of the plays in the War of the Theatres or Poetomachia (q.v.).

Whatcott, Robert. One of the witnesses of Shakespeare's will. He was principal witness for Susanna Hall at the Ecclesiastical Court of Worcester when she brought her action for slander against Ralph Lane in July 1613.

Whately, Anne. See TEMPLE GRAFTON.

Whately, Thomas (d. 1772), politician and critic, was M.P. 1761–72, and author of *Remarks on some of the Characters of Shakespeare*. Unfortunately he interrupted his work on this in order to finish his *Observations on Modern Gardening*, and died before he had written more than a comparison of Richard III and Macbeth, which was published by his brother, Dr Joseph Whately, in 1785. It is interesting as being a fragment from what would have been the first book to analyse Shakespeare's characters in detail.

'When You See Me, You Know Me.' A play by Samuel Rowley, which may have had some influence on *Henry VIII*. It was registered and published in 1605:

> When you see me, You know me. Or the famous Chronicle Historie of King Henry the eight, with the birth and vertuous life of Edward Prince of Wales. As it was playd by the high and mightie Prince of Wales his seruants. By Samuell Rowly, seruant to the Prince.

Whetstone, George (*c.* 1544–*c.* 1587), born in London, though connected with a wealthy family near Stamford. Having spent his small fortune, he enlisted in 1572 and served in the Low Countries, where he met George Gascoigne and Thomas Churchyard. His first book was the *Rocke of Regarde* (1576), prose and verse tales adapted from the Italian. In 1578 came his play *Promos and Cassandra* (q.v.), adapted from Cinthio, and the main source of *Measure for Measure*. There is a prose version in his collection of stories, *Heptameron of Civill Discourses* (1582). He sailed with Sir Humphrey Gilbert on the unsuccessful voyage of 1578–9, visited Italy in 1580, and fought at Zutphen, 1586. He was a friend of William Fleetwood, the puritanical Recorder of London, and like Gosson he turned Puritan and in 1584 attacked the abuse of the stage in his *Mirour for Magestrates of Cyties*, called in its second edition *A Touchstone for the Time*:

> Truly the use of them [Stage-plays] upon the Sabbath day, and the abuse of them at all times, with scurrility and unchaste conveyance, ministred matter sufficient for them [the godly Divines] to blame, and the Magistrate to reforme.

White, Edward, bookseller, whose shop was 'at the little north door of Paul's, at the sign of the Gun'. He and Millington were commissioned by Danter to sell Q1 *Titus Andronicus* (1594), and White himself published Q2 (1600) and Q3 (1611). He was active 1577–1612.

White, William, printer. Of Shakespeare's works he printed:

1598	Q1	*Love's Labour's Lost*	for C. Burby
1600	Q2	*3 Henry VI*	for T. Millington
1608	Q4	*Richard II*	for M. Law
1609	Q1	*Pericles*	for H. Gosson
1609	Q2	*Pericles*	for H. Gosson
1613	Q5	*1 Henry IV*	for M. Law

He was active 1588–1615; until 1596, at The White Horse in Fleet Lane, and then in Cow Lane. Like many other printers of plays, he dealt in ballads and other ephemeral literature.

Whitefriars Theatre. Whitefriars was a disreputable district to the west of the City walls, between Fleet Street and the river. It lay within the precinct of the dissolved priory of Carmelites or White Friars, and was a liberty until 1608, when it was brought within City control. Richard Rawlidge mentions a Whitefriars theatre, suppressed in Elizabeth's reign, but the first definite record of the private theatre is in the lease for nearly seven years from March 1608 of the 'mansion howse parcell of the late dissolved monastery', granted by Lord Buckhurst to Michael Drayton and Thomas Woodford. It was first occupied by the short-lived King's Revels company, then by the Queen's Revels, 1609–13, who were joined by the Lady Elizabeth's and Prince Charles's. The lease expired at the end of 1614, and Rosseter acquired Porter's Hall for the Revels, 1615–17. The Whitefriars lease was renewed, and the theatre seems to have been occupied by Prince Charles's. In 1629 it was replaced by the Salisbury Court theatre, which in turn was replaced by the Dorset Garden, *c.* 1670. (Salisbury Court was the house of the Bishops of Salisbury, later known as Dorset House, just to the east of the Whitefriars precinct.)

Whitehall Palace. The original building belonged to the Dominican monks of Holborn. In the 13th century they sold it to Walter de Grey, Archbishop of York, who left it to his successors as their London residence, so that it became known as York House or York Place. It was improved by Wolsey, who surrendered it to Henry VIII on his downfall, when it became known as White Hall from the name of one of the rooms in the old palace of Westminster; cf. *Henry VIII* (IV, i):

You must no more call it Yorke-place, that's past;
For since the Cardinall fell, that Titles lost,
'Tis now the Kings, and call'd White-Hall.

Henry VIII employed Holbein in its reconstruction, and made it his principal London residence. It lay between St James's Park and the river, on either side of the road from Westminster to the City. By the river were the main buildings and garden; the great hall where plays were performed was 100 ft by 45 ft and stretched across the present Horse Guards Avenue. The road was spanned by two gateways, the northern one by Holbein, over which galleries led to other lodgings, the cockpit, tennis-court and tilt-yard.

It became customary in the 16th century to build large temporary banqueting-houses for special entertainments. One was built at Whitehall in 1572, another made of wood in 1581 was replaced in 1606 by one of brick and stone, and this in turn was replaced in 1619 by the banqueting-house of Inigo Jones. Almost all the old palace was destroyed by fire in 1697.

Whiter, Walter. See IMAGERY; SQ, XIII, 2.

Whitgift, John (*c.* 1530–1604), born at Grimsby, educated at Queen's and Pembroke, Cambridge, became a Fellow of Peterhouse, and Professor of Divinity. He was Bishop of Worcester, March 1577–August 1583, so that it was from him that Shakespeare obtained the special licence for his marriage in 1582. From 1583 to his death, Whitgift was Archbishop of Canterbury, pursued an anti-Puritan policy, precipitated the Marprelate controversy, and in 1586 became responsible for the licensing for printing of all books, including plays. (See CANTERBURY, ARCHBISHOP OF.)

Whitmore, Walter. In *2 Henry VI*, in capturing Suffolk at sea he loses an eye, and in revenge strikes off his head (IV, i). (Halle mentions the incident, but not

Whitmore, who is unknown. He is 'Water Whickmore' in Q.)

Whittington, Thomas, husbandman of Shottery, is mentioned by Richard Hathaway as 'my sheepherd' in 1581. He died in April 1601, after making his will on 25 March. He was then living with 'John Pace, of Shottre, the elder'. Shakespeare's wife, Richard Hathaway's daughter, owed him 40s. which he left to the poor of Stratford, and her brothers John and William owed him almost £6, though he owed them 'for a quarter of an yeares bord'. It was customary for servants to bank with their masters.

'W. H., Mr.' See SONNETS.

Widow. 1. In *The Taming of the Shrew*, she is married by Hortensio when he despairs of winning Bianca. She is present in v, ii. (In *A Shrew* she is Emelia, a third daughter of Alfonso (Baptista).)

2. In *All's Well*, mother of Diana. She gives Helena lodging at Florence, and helps her in her plan to win back Bertram (III, vii).

Wieland, Christoph Martin (1733–1813), German poet, became acquainted with Shakespeare's works through the writings of Voltaire, and, fired with enthusiasm, between 1762 and 1766 published prose translations of twenty-two of his plays, so for the first time bringing Shakespeare to the German people. His translation was superseded by those of Eschenburg and Schlegel.

Wilkins, George (fl. 1603–8). Little is known about his life. In 1603 he wrote a pamphlet, *The Miseries of Barbary*, and in 1607, with Dekker, *Jests to Make You Merrie*. In the same year he collaborated with Day and Rowley in *The Travels of Three English Brothers* (see SHIRLEY, ANTHONY), and his own play, *The Miseries of Enforced Marriage*, was published. This deals with the murder, in 1605, by Walter Calverley (called Scarborow in the play) of his two children, and the attempted murder of his wife. It was registered as 'A tragedie', but the play ends in reconciliation. It is the theme of *A Yorkshire Tragedy* (*c.* 1606), published in 1608 as Shakespeare's.

In 1608 Wilkins published his novel, *The Painful Aduentures of Pericles Prince of Tyre. Being The true History of the Play of Pericles, as it was lately presented by the worthy and ancient Poet Iohn Gower*, and in his Argument refers to the play 'as it was ... by the Kings Maiesties Players excellently presented.' It is a prose version of *Pericles* (registered 20 May 1608), the last three acts of which are generally accepted as Shakespeare's, though it is less widely accepted that Wilkins was himself the author of the first two. The novel seems to have been taken from the play (and Twine's *Patterne of Painefull Aduentures*) and not the play from the novel.

Wilkinson, Tate (1739–1803), actor and manager, had a gift of mimicry that offended many of his acquaintances, including Garrick. He became manager of a number of Yorkshire theatres and spent most of his time in the provinces, where his Shakespearean interpretations were well received, though he made very free with the text.

Will. Shakespeare's will, preserved at Somerset House, is written in English hand on one side of each of three sheets, probably by a clerk of the Warwick solicitor, Francis Collins. It seems probable that Collins prepared a draft in January 1616, and that Shakespeare made alterations necessitating a new first sheet before signing on 25 March. The provisions are:

To Judith, his younger daughter, who had married Thomas Quiney on 10 February: £100 as marriage portion; £50 in consideration of her surrendering her rights in the Chapel Lane cottage to Susanna; the interest on a further £150; a broad silver-gilt bowl.

To his sister, Joan Hart: £20, all his 'wearing Apparell', and for life the Henley

Street house, where she was living, at a rent of 12d. To each of her three sons, £5. (Joan's husband, William Hart, died three weeks later.)

To his granddaughter, Elizabeth Hall: all his plate except Judith's bowl.

To the poor of Stratford, £10; Thomas Combe, his sword; Thomas Russell, £5; Francis Collins, £13 6s. 8d.; his godson William Walker, 20s.

To Hamlet Sadler, William Reynolds, Anthony Nash, John Nash and to his 'ffelowes John Hemynge Richard Burbage & Henry Cundell' 26s. 8d. each 'to buy them Ringes.'

To 'my wieff my second best bed with the furniture.' (Anne would have the widow's right to live at New Place, her dower of a third share for life in the real estate, except the Blackfriars house, and perhaps a similar share in the personal property.)

To his elder daughter Susanna (Hall): New Place, the old Stratford land, the two Henley Street houses, the Blackfriars Gatehouse, and any other real property 'with their Appurtennaunces' were entailed upon Susanna and her heirs male, Elizabeth and her heirs male, Judith and her heirs male, 'and for defalt of such issue to' his 'Right heires'. Susanna and her husband, John Hall, were residuary legatees.

The poet signed each sheet: 'William Shakspere'; 'Willm Shakspere'; 'By me William Shakspeare'. Collins also signed, as did the witnesses, 'Julyus Shawe John Robinson, Hamnet Sadler, Robert Whattcott'. The will was proved 22 June, but the inventory then exhibited has not been found. This may have included his library; presumably he had already disposed of his shares in the Globe and Blackfriars theatres; his leasehold interest in the Stratford tithes went with the residuary bequest to the Halls, who sold them in 1625 for £400.

After the death of the last of Judith Quiney's sons in 1639, the entail was barred and a series of settlements made, Elizabeth finally becoming free to dispose of the property as she wished. The Blackfriars house was sold *c.* 1647, probably to her 'kinsman' Edward Bagley, who by her will (1670) acquired New Place, which he sold to Sir Edward Walker in 1675, and the Old Stratford land. The Henley Street houses she left to the Harts. (See GREENE, JOSEPH.)

'Will Sonnets.' Sonnets 135 and 136, in which the word 'will' occurs eighteen times; in Q it is ten times printed *Will*, suggesting a pun on Shakespeare's Christian name, and perhaps that 'Mr W. H' was another William. The sonnets begin:

Whoever hath her wish, thou hast thy *Will*,
And *Will* to boot, and *Will* in over-plus ...

If thy soul check thee that I come so near,
Swear to thy blind soul that I was thy
Will ...

(See HUGHES, WILLIAM.)

William. In *As You Like It*, a simple peasant in love with Audrey from whom he is scared by Touchstone (v, i).

Williams, Harcourt (1880–1957). Began his stage career with Benson. A disciple of Granville-Barker, he produced at the Old Vic, 1929–34, a series of Shakespeare plays, speeding up the verse-speaking, shedding the traditional mannerisms, and earning the nickname of 'Harcourt Williams non-stop Shakespeare'. (See his *Four Years at the Old Vic.*)

Williams, John (1582–1650), Lord Keeper and Bishop of Lincoln in 1621, and Archbishop of York 1641. He got into trouble *c.* 1631 for having a private performance of a comedy at his house at Buckden, Hunts., on a Sunday night. The play was apparently *A Midsummer Night's Dream*, in which 'Mr Wilson' played Bottom. (See WILSON, HENRY.)

Williams, Michael. In *Henry V*, a soldier who quarrels with the disguised King on the night before Agincourt and, having exchanged pledges, promises to challenge him after the battle (IV, i). The King gives Fluellen Williams's pledge, and when they come to blows explains the joke and rewards Williams (IV, viii).

Willobie, Henry (b. *c.* 1575), son of a Wiltshire gentleman; he matriculated from St John's, Oxford, in 1591, but changed to Exeter College from which he took his degree in 1595. On 3 September 1594 was registered *Willobie his Avisa, or the true picture of a Modest Maid and of a chast and constant wife*. In an Epistle to the Reader, dated at Oxford 1 October, 'Hadrian Dorrell' (q.v.) says that he found the MS. among the papers of his 'chamber fellow', a promising scholar who had gone abroad on her Majesty's service. A Thomas Darell matriculated from Brasenose at the same time as Willobie, but 'Hadrian Dorrell' may be a pseudonym of Willobie himself.

The poem relates how Avisa, an innkeeper's wife, rejects the advances of numerous suitors, including Henrico Willobego, Italo-Hispalensis. In the Argument, H. W. tells how he confided his unrequited love to his 'familiar friend W. S.' who had just recovered from a like passion. W. S. 'determined to see whether it would sort to a happier end for this new actor, than it did for the old player. But at length this Comedy was like to have growen to a Tragedy ...' Then follows a long dialogue in verse between H. W. and W. S., in which W. S. says, echoing Sonnet 41,

Well, say no more: I know thy griefe,
And face from whence these flames aryse,
It is not hard to fynd reliefe,
If thou wilt follow good advyse:
  She is no Saynt, She is no Nonne,
  I thinke in tyme she may be wonne.

It is possible that Shakespeare is W. S. 'the old player', and that the reference is to his love affair, though probably not with Avisa, recorded in the *Sonnets*. Some see in H. Willobie the 'Mr W. H.' of the *Sonnets*. Commendatory verses prefixed to *Willobie his Avisa*, and signed 'Contraria Contrarijs: Vigilantius: Dormitanus', contain the first literary reference to Shakespeare by name:

Yet *Tarquyne* pluckt his glistering grape,
And *Shake-speare*, paints poore Lucrece rape.

Hotson identifies Vigilantius ('waker') and Dormitanus ('sleeper') with two boys who entered Balliol in 1590: Robert Wakeman and Edward Napper, and also strengthens the case for Shakespeare's being the W. S. of *Avisa*. When his friend Thomas Russell married his first wife, Katherine Bampfield, in 1590, Henry Willoughby's elder brother, William, married her sister. Russell, therefore, may have introduced Shakespeare to the Willoughbys, and Shakespeare may often have met Henry when he was an undergraduate at Oxford. A. Acheson (*Mistress Davenant*, 1913; *Shakespeare's Sonnet Story*, 1922) identifies Avisa with an Anne Bird (*avis*), whom he assumes to have been a first wife of John D'Avenant, the 'A. D.' mentioned by Dorrell in his preface, Shakespeare's mistress, the dark lady of the *Sonnets*, and the mother of William D'Avenant.

Willoughby, Lord. In *Richard II*, he deserts Richard, and with Ross joins Bolingbroke and Northumberland near Berkeley (II, i and ii). (William de Willoughby, 5th Baron, died 1409.)

Wilmcote. A hamlet three miles north-west of Stratford, in the parish of Aston Cantlow. Robert Arden, Shakespeare's maternal grandfather, lived there and farmed his freehold land called Asbies, and another copyhold estate. (See ARDEN; ASBIES; WINCOT.)

Wilson, Frank Percy (1889–1963), Professor of English Literature at Leeds 1929–36, London 1936–47, and Oxford 1947–57. His publications include *The Plague in Shakespeare's London*, *Shakespeare and the Diction of Common Life*, *Marlowe and the Early Shakespeare*.

Wilson, Henry. An actor; he played in Massinger's *Believe As You List* with the King's Men in 1631; cf. stage-direction: 'Harry: Willson: & Boy ready for the song at ye Arras.' He may be the 'Mr Wilson' of the play performed for John Williams (q.v.).

Wilson, John (1595–1674), singer and lutenist, Gentleman of the Chapel Royal, private musician to Charles I, and Professor of Music at Oxford (1656). His *Cheerful Ayres* (1660) contains his setting of Autolycus's song 'Lawn as white as driven snow'. He is probably the 'Iacke Wilson' who played Balthazar and sang 'Sigh no more, ladies', in *Much Ado* (q.v.), though there was another John Wilson (1585–*c.* 1641) who became a city wait. (See DONNE.)

Wilson, John Dover (1881–1969), educated at Lancing and Caius, Cambridge, Professor of Education at King's College, London, 1924–35, and Professor of English at Edinburgh University 1936–45. He was editor of the *New Cambridge Shakespeare* (q.v.) and author of *The Essential Shakespeare, The Fortunes of Falstaff, What Happens in Hamlet*, etc. (See RECORDINGS.)

Wilson, Robert (*c.* 1550–*c.* 1605), actor and dramatist, was with Leicester's in 1572, but joined the Queen's on their formation in 1583. Meres describes him (1598) as 'our wittie Wilson, who for learning and extemporall witte in this facultie [of 'extemporall verse'] is without compare.' He is probably the 'R. W.' who wrote the extant *Three Ladies of London*, published 1584, a play about a generous Jewish money-lender, perhaps a reply to *The Jew*, the lost play that may have been a source of *The Merchant of Venice*.

Wilton House, in Wiltshire, was built by William Herbert, 1st Earl of Pembroke, on the site of a dissolved convent. Sir Philip Sidney's sister, Mary, married the 2nd Earl in 1577, and the house is rich in associations with Sidney, Daniel, Jonson, Inigo Jones and others of the period. During the plague James I held his court at Wilton from October to December 1603, and on 3 December a warrant was issued from Wilton to pay the King's Men £30 for coming from Mortlake (London) to present a play before the King on 2 December. In 1865 Lady Herbert told William Cory that 'we have a letter, never printed, from Lady Pembroke to her son, telling him to bring James I from Salisbury to see *As You Like It*; "we have the man Shakespeare with us" ... he came.' The letter has not been found.

Winchester, Bishops of. See BEAUFORT, HENRY; GARDINER.

Winchester House, on Bankside, was from 1107 to the early 17th century the London residence of the Bishops of Winchester, who had jurisdiction over the liberty of the Clink where Shakespeare appears to have gone to live towards the end of 1596.

Wincot. The old provincial spelling or pronunciation of three Warwickshire villages; Wilmecote in Aston Cantlow, home of the Ardens, Little Wilmecote, with a water-mill, being a hamlet just to the south, within Stratford parish; Wilnecote, near Tamworth in north Warwickshire (see COKAIN); Wincot or Willicote four miles south of Stratford, between Clifford Chambers and Quinton. The last is probably the Wincot of *The Shrew*, Ind. ii (see HACKET).

Capell first published the anecdote in 1780:

> Wincot is in Stratford's vicinity, where the memory of the ale-house subsists still; and the tradition goes that 'twas resorted to by Shakespeare for the sake of diverting himself with a fool who belong'd to the neighbouring mill.

In 1770, Thomas Warton wrote in a note on *The Shrew*,

> *Wilnecote* is a village in *Warwickshire*, with which Shakespeare was well acquainted, near *Stratford*. The house kept by our genial hostess still remains, but is at present a mill.

In a letter of 1790 he explained that he had his information from 'Mr. Wise, Radclivian librarian' and that 'the place is Wylmecote, the mill, or Wilnicote, near Stratford, not Tamworth.'

The tradition of Shakespeare's drinking was well established. Steevens says that James West claimed to have the wooden bench on which Shakespeare sat, and 'an earthern half-pint mug out of which he was accustomed to take his draughts of ale at a certain publick house in the neighbourhood of Stratford every Saturday afternoon'. (See BIDFORD; WARD, JOHN (Vicar of Stratford).)

Windsor. The Chapel of St George in Windsor Castle is the scene of the installation of the Knights of the Garter, and the Garter and Mömpelgart references in *The Merry Wives* suggest that it was written for such an occasion. If the play were acted at Windsor, the Children of Windsor (q.v.) might have taken part in the last scene. Hotson thinks that it was first performed before the Queen at the feast at Westminster on St George's Day, 23 April 1597, when Frederick, Duke of Württemberg, formerly Count of Mömpelgart, and George Carey, Lord Hunsdon, patron of Shakespeare's company, were two of the new knights elected. The installation was at Windsor a month later, 24 May.

Winstanley, William (*c.* 1628–*c.* 1690), is of some importance as author of one of the first modern histories of English poetry. (Thomas Heywood's *Lives of All the Poets*, *c.* 1614, was the first to be projected; Edward Phillips's *Theatrum Poetarum*, 1675, was the first to be published.) But Winstanley's *Lives of the Most Famous English Poets*, 1687, adds nothing to our knowledge of Shakespeare, his account being taken from Fuller and Phillips.

'WINTER'S TALE, THE.'

WRITTEN: 1610–11. (See 'MASQUE OF OBERON.')

PERFORMED: 1611, 15 May, seen by Simon Forman at the Globe.

1611. 'The Kings players: The 5th of nouember A play Called ye winters nightes Tayle.' (*Revels Account.*)

1612–13. One of the seven plays of Shakespeare performed at Whitehall before the marriage of the Princess Elizabeth.

1618, 7 April: at Court.

1624. 'To the Duchess of Richmond, in the King's absence, was given The Winters Tale, by the K. company, the 18 Janu. 1623. Att Whitchall.' *Office Book.* (See RICHMOND, LUDOVICK.)

1634, 16 January. 'The Winters Tale was acted on Thursday night at Court, the 16 Janua. 1633, by the K. players, and likt.' (*Office Book.*)

REGISTERED: 1623, 8 November. One of the sixteen plays registered by Blount and Jaggard before publishing F1.

PUBLISHED: 1623, F1. 'The Winters Tale.' The last (14th) play in the Comedy section: pp. 277–303. Acts and scenes marked, and 'The Names of the Actors' given. Probably printed from Crane's transcript of foul papers, as the 'allowed book' (prompt-book) had been lost. (See HENRY HERBERT.)

SOURCE: Robert Greene's romance, *Pandosto or The Triumph of Time* (1588), reprinted as *Dorastus and Fawnia* (1607).

STAGE HISTORY: 1741, 1742. Revived at Goodman's Fields and Covent Garden.

1754. Covent Garden: *The Sheep-Shearing; or, Florizel and Perdita*, by McNamara Morgan.

1756. Drury Lane: Garrick's adaptation, mainly of Acts IV and V, *Florizel and Perdita*.

1802. Drury Lane: 'An Alteration' by J. P. Kemble, with himself as Leontes and Mrs Siddons as Hermione.

1847. Sadler's Wells: Phelps revives Shakespeare's play.

1856. Princess's Theatre: the antiquarian production of Charles Kean (q.v.).

1912. Savoy: Granville-Barker's production.

Leontes, King of Sicilia, persuades himself that his friend Polixenes, King of Bohemia, is the lover of his wife Hermione. He tries to poison Polixenes who, however, escapes. Hermione he puts in prison, where she gives birth to a daughter whom he calls 'a bastard by Polixenes', and orders the child to be exposed in some remote and desert place. During the trial news comes from the oracle at 'Delphos' that Hermione is chaste, and that 'the king shall live without an heir, if that which is lost be not found.' Leontes denies the truth of the oracle, but the terrible truth is confirmed when Paulina, the Queen's gentlewoman, announces that Hermione and his young son Mamillius are dead.

The baby girl is found on the coast of Bohemia by a shepherd, who brings her up as his own daughter, Perdita. When she is sixteen, Prince Florizel, son of Polixenes, falls in love with her, but his proposed marriage is discovered and prevented by his father. The lovers sail to Sicilia, where Leontes discovers that Perdita is his daughter, and Paulina restores to them Hermione, whose death was only apparent and who has been living in secret retirement. Polixenes and Leontes are reconciled and arrangements made for the marriage of their children, Florizel and Perdita.

Broad comedy is supplied by the rogue Autolycus, the shepherd, and his son.

'Wisdom of Doctor Dodipoll.' An anonymous play, acted by the Children of Paul's, registered 7 October 1600, and published in the same year. The remark, 'Then reason's fled to animals, I see', is almost the same as that in *Every Man out of His Humour* (1599), 'Reason long since is fled to animals, you know', and both seem to refer to *Julius Caesar* (III, ii):

O judgment! thou art fled to brutish beasts,
And men have lost their reason.

If so, *Julius Caesar* must have been written by 1599.

Wise, Andrew. Publisher of five of Shakespeare's plays:

Richard III: 1597, registered and published Q1, 1597 (printed by Simmes); Q2, 1598 (Creede); Q3, 1602 (Creede). Transferred to Law in 1603.

Richard II: 1597, registered and published Q1, 1597 (Simmes); Q2, 1598 (Simmes); Q3, 1598 (Simmes). Transferred to Law in 1603.

1 Henry IV: 1598, registered and published Q1, 1598 (Short); Q2, 1599 (Stafford). Transferred to Law in 1603.

2 Henry IV: 1600, with Aspley registered and published Q (Simmes).

Much Ado: 1600, with Aspley registered and published Q (Simmes).

Andrew Wise, or Wythes, was a bookseller at The Angel in St Paul's Churchyard, 1589–1603. He transferred his copyrights to Law in 1603, and is not heard of again.

Wise, Francis (1695–1767), Radcliffe librarian at Oxford in 1748. In 1790 Thomas Warton wrote:

My note about Wilnecote I had from Mr Wise, Radclivian librarian, a most accurate and inquisitive literary antiquary, who, about fifty years ago, made a journey to Stratford and its environs to pick up anecdotes about Shakespeare, many of which he told me; but which I, being then very young, perhaps heard very carelessly and have long forgot.

But some of the information that Wise gave Warton for his *Life of Sir Thomas Pope* was fabricated, though not necessarily by Wise. (See WINCOT.)

'Witch, The.' A tragi-comedy by Thomas Middleton, written probably 1609–11. It was not printed, but the MS. was found by Steevens and edited by Isaac Reed, 1778. The two songs referred to in the stage-directions of Macbeth, *Sing within. Come away, come away, &c.* (III, v), and *Musicke and a Song, Blacke Spirits, &c.* (IV, i), occur in full in *The Witch*, where they are sung by Hecate. This, and the fact that Middleton's witches echo Shakespeare's, make it almost certain that the tinkling iambics of Hecate and of the Witch at the end of IV, i in *Macbeth* are interpolations by, or based on Middleton. Cf. *The Witch*:

HECATE. Black spirits and white, red spirits and grey;
Mingle, mingle, mingle, you that mingle may.
Titty, Tiffin, keep in stiff in;
Fire-drake, Puckey, make it lucky;
Liard, Robin, you must bob in.
Round, around, around, about, about, about;
All Ill keep running in, all Good keep out.
WITCH 1. Here's the blood of a bat.
HECATE. Put in that, O, put in that.
WITCH 2. Here's libbard's bane.
HECATE. Put in again.
WITCH 1. The juice of toad; the oil of adder.
WITCH 2. Those will make the younker madder....

Witches. In *Macbeth*, they open the play, then in I, iii hail Macbeth as Thane of Cawdor, Thane of Glamis, and King hereafter; Banquo as one who shall beget kings. In IV, i they show him three Apparitions whose ambiguous messages suggest security. (Holinshed has, 'suddenlie in the middest of a laund, there met them three women in strange and wild apparell, resembling creatures of elder world'. But he only hints at IV, i: Macbeth 'had learned of certain wizzards in whose words he put great confidence (for that the prophesie had happened so right that the three fairies or weird sisters had declared unto him) how that he ought to take heede of Macduffe ...')

'Wits, The.' See KIRKMAN.

Witter, John. When the widow of Augustine Phillips (d. 1605) married John Witter in 1606, she forfeited her interest in her late husband's estate, but as executor of the will Heminge leased Phillips's share in the Globe to the Witters, but resumed possession when they were unable to meet their share of rebuilding the theatre after the fire of 1613. In 1619 Witter brought an unsuccessful action against Heminge and Condell for the recovery of interest. This is of importance because of the *Answer* of Heminge and Condell, in which they explain how the shares in the Globe were originally and subsequently divided: in 1599 Cuthbert and Richard Burbage kept half the total shares, and divided the other half among Shakespeare, Phillips, Pope, Heminge and Kempe. Difficulties and litigation arose when shares were alienated, as in the case of Witter. (See WALLACE.)

Woffington, Margaret (Peg) (1714–60), actress, was born in Dublin, and made her first London appearance in 1740. She played mainly in the fashionable comedy of the day, but also in Shakespearean comedy: Portia, Rosalind, Viola, Helena and also Constance in *King John*. She was Garrick's mistress, a generous benefactress, and retired from the stage in 1757.

Wolfit, Donald (1902–68), first appeared on the stage at York in 1920 as Biondello in *The Taming of the Shrew*. He joined the Old Vic for the 1929–30 seasons and played Cassius, Claudius, etc., played Hamlet in the production of the first Quarto *Hamlet* 1933, and Hamlet, Antony, etc., in the Stratford Festivals of 1936–7. In 1937 he formed his own Shakespeare company, toured the provinces and Canada, and opened his first London season of Shakespeare's plays during the Battle of Britain in 1940. He continued the work of Ben Greet in making Shakespeare known to as wide an audience as possible, and had seasons in Cairo, Paris and Brussels. In 1960 he made a world tour with Shakespeare recitals. Knighted 1957.

Wolsey, Cardinal. In *Henry VIII*, he helps to secure the execution of Buckingham and divorce of Queen Katharine, but opposes the King's marriage with Anne Boleyn. Papers showing his extorted wealth, and letters 'to the pope against the king' are intercepted, and bring about his downfall (III, ii). (Thomas Wolsey (*c*. 1475–1530) became Archbishop of York in 1514 and Cardinal in 1515. Griffith's defence of Wolsey after his death (IV, ii) is taken from Edmund Campion's *History of Ireland*, quoted by Holinshed.)

Wood, Anthony à (1632–95), born at Oxford where he spent all his life. He entered Merton College in 1647, took his M.A. in 1655, and dedicated himself to the study of antiquities. His *History and Antiquities of the University of Oxford* was published in 1674, followed in 1692 by *Athenae Oxonienses: an Exact History of all the Writers and Bishops who have had their Education in the University of Oxford from 1500 to 1690*.

Wood employed Aubrey (q.v.) to collect material for *Athenae Oxonienses*. Aubrey has a note in which he says that

Shakespeare used to visit Warwickshire once a year, and commonly stayed at the Crown Tavern at Oxford, kept by the 'grave and discreet' John D'Avenant, and that his son, Sir William D'Avenant, was 'contented enough' to be thought Shakespeare's son, 'in which way his mother had a very light report, whereby she was called a whore.' Wood refines the story and merely says that William was unlike his melancholy father, and was the only child that took after his witty and light-hearted mother. (See HEARNE.)

Woodville. In *1 Henry VI*, as 'Lieutenant of the Tower' he acts on the orders of Cardinal Beaufort and refuses to admit Gloucester and his men. (Richard Woodville (d. 1469) was created Baron Rivers in 1448. His eldest daughter, Elizabeth (q.v.), widow of Sir John Grey, married Edward IV in 1464.)

Woodward, Henry (1714–77), comic actor, was educated at Merchant Taylors' School, and in 1729 joined Rich at Lincoln's Inn Fields, where he played in *The Beggars' Opera.* He was at Goodman's Fields 1730–6, and then for most of the period 1737–58, at Drury Lane, where he played a great number of Shakespeare's comic parts, notably Mercutio. With Spranger Barry, he was joint-manager of the Crow Street Theatre, Dublin, 1758–62. His last appearance was as Stephano in 1777.

Wool-shop. So called by Halliwell-Phillipps: 'Upon the north side of Henley Street is a detached building, consisting of two houses annexed to each other, the one on the west having been known from time immemorial as Shakespeare's Birth-Place, and that on the east a somewhat larger one which was purchased by his father in the year 1556. It may fairly be assumed that in the latter the then "considerable dealer in wool" deposited not rifling portion of his stock.' (See MAIDENHEAD; PHILLIPS, RICHARD; *The Times*, 22 November 1930.)

Worcester. Stratford lies within the diocese of Worcester, the bishops of which, until 1549, held the principal manor and that of Bishop's Hampton. In the Register of the Consistory Court at Worcester are recorded: the bond of 'Johannes Shakespere de Snytterfyld agricola' for the proper administration of the estate of 'Richard Shakespere of Snytterfyld' (10 February 1561); the issue of a special licence for the marriage of 'Willelmum Shaxpere et Annam Whateley de Temple Grafton' (27 November 1582); the bond of Fulk Sandells and John Richardson as sureties for the marriage licence of 'William Shagspere ... and Anne Hathwey' (28 November 1582); the action for slander brought by Susanna Hall against John Lane (July 1613); the excommunication of Thomas Quiney and Judith Shakespeare (May 1616).

Worcester, Earl of. In *1 Henry IV*, he quarrels with the King and joins the rebellion of Northumberland and Hotspur. Before Shrewsbury the King offers to pardon him and the other rebels, but Worcester suspects that he will always live under suspicion and refuses to tell Hotspur of the offer. He is captured and sent to his death. (Thomas Percy (*c.* 1343–1403) was the younger brother of Northumberland and the uncle of Hotspur. He helped Bolingbroke to become Henry IV, but then rebelled against him.)

Worcester's (Queen Anne's) Men. A provincial company of William Somerset, 3rd Earl of Worcester, is traceable 1555–85, playing at Stratford in 1568–9 when Shakespeare's father was bailiff, and again in 1574–5, 1576–7, 1581–2. The names of the company are preserved in the records of the Corporation of Leicester, where in March 1584,

> Robert Browne, James Tunstall, Edward Allen, William Harryson, Thomas Cooke, Rychard Johnes, Edward Browne, Rychard Andrewes ... mett Mr Mayor in the strete ... who then craived lycense agayne to play

at there inn, & told them they shold not, then they went away & seyd they wold play, whether he wold or not, & in dispite of hym, with dyvers other evyll & contemptuous words.

This is the first mention of Edward Alleyn, then only sixteen, who soon afterwards joined the Admiral's.

In 1589 the 3rd Earl died, his son Edward, Lord Herbert, succeeding him, and after a break since 1585 the records begin again, either of this or of another company. On 3 January 1602 they gave a play at Court for which William Kempe and Thomas Heywood, the dramatist, were payees. In this year they absorbed Oxford's, and became one of the three privileged London companies, obtaining from the Privy Council a licence to play at 'the Bores head'. This was a modification of the Council's order of June 1600, 'that there shall bee about the Cittie two howses and noe more allowed to serue for the vse of the Common Stage plaies', the Globe for the Chamberlain's, and Alleyn's new Fortune for the Admiral's. Later in the same year, however, they were with Henslowe at the Rose, where in February 1603 they played Heywood's new *A Woman Killed with Kindness*.

In March 1603 Elizabeth died, and Worcester's came under the patronage of James I's consort, Anne of Denmark, henceforth being known as Queen Anne's Men. In April 1604 a Privy Council letter mentions the Curtain as their theatre, and a royal patent of about the same date calls their 'usual houses' the Curtain and Boar's Head, but that of April 1609 names 'theire nowe vsuall houses called the Redd Bull in Clarkenwell and the Curtayne in Hallowell'. The players are given as 'Thomas Greene, Christofer Beeston, Thomas Haywood, Richard Pirkyns, Richard Pallant, Thomas Swinnerton, Iohn Duke, Robert Lee, Iames Haulte, and Roberte Beeston'. They played at the new Cockpit theatre of Christopher Beeston 1617–19. As Queen Anne's Men they performed fairly regularly at Court, and there are records of extensive provincial tours, probably by more than one company. The company broke up soon after the Queen's death in 1619. (See RED BULL.)

Wordsworth, William (1770–1850). In his *Essay, Supplementary to the Preface to the Lyrical Ballads* (1815), Wordsworth summarizes contemporary opinion of Shakespeare; the French think him a buffoon; the Italians are unable to appreciate him; 'the Germans only, of foreign nations, are approaching towards a knowledge and feeling of what he is', and their appreciation is in some respects superior to that of the English, who still consider him 'a wild irregular genius, in whom great faults are compensated by great beauties'. How long will it be, he asks, before it is acknowledged that Shakespeare's judgement was equal to his genius? This was precisely the point that Coleridge set out to establish.

Worsdale, James (*c.* 1692–1767), a servant of Sir Godfrey Kneller, who by a pleasant manner and not over-scrupulous means became a fashionable though mediocre portrait painter. He was also an actor and author of a number of plays, one of which, *A Cure for a Scold*, was a ballad opera or farce based on *The Taming of the Shrew*, or rather on Lacy's *Sauny the Scot*, and acted at Drury Lane 1735 and Covent Garden 1750.

Wotton, Henry (1568–1639), was educated at Winchester and at New and Queen's Colleges, Oxford. For most of James's reign he was ambassador at Venice, and in 1624 was installed Provost of Eton, where he was buried. He was a friend of Izaak Walton, and a devoted admirer of Elizabeth of Bohemia, to whom he addressed his most famous lyric, 'You meaner beauties of the night'. In a letter to Sir Edmund Bacon he described the burning of the Globe theatre (q.v.).

Wright, James (1643–1713), antiquary and collector of plays, is generally thought to be the author of the anonymous tract, *Historia Histrionica: An Historical Account of the English Stage* (1699). It is written in dialogue form, and contains valuable information about early 17th-century actors and plays.

Lovewit. Pray, Sir, what master-parts can you remember the old 'Blackfriars' men to act, in Johnson's, Shakespeare's, and Fletcher's plays?

Truman. What I can at present recollect I'll tell you. Shakespeare (who, as I have heard, was a much better Poet than Player), Burbage, Hemmings, and others of the older sort, were dead before I knew the Town. But, in my time, before the Wars; Lowin used to act, with mighty applause, Falstaffe; Morose; Vulpone; and Mammon in the *Alchemist*; Melancius in the *Maid's Tragedy*. And at the same time, Amyntor was played by Stephen Hammerton: who was, at first, a most noted and beautiful Woman-Actor; but afterwards he acted, with equal grace and applause, a young lover's part.

Taylor acted Hamlet incomparably well; Jago; Truewit, in the *Silent Woman*; and Face, in the *Alchemist*.

Swanston used to play Othello.

Pollard and Robinson were Comedians. So was Shank ...

Before the Wars, there were in being, all these Play-Houses at the same time.

The 'Blackfriars' and 'Globe' on the Bankside. A winter, and summer house belonging to the same Company; called 'The King's Servants'.

The 'Cockpit' or 'Phoenix' in Drury Lane; called 'The Queen's Servants'.

The Private House in Salisbury Court; called 'The Prince's Servants'.

The 'Fortune' near White Cross Street: and the 'Red Bull' at the upper end of St. John's Street. The two last were most frequented by citizens, and the meaner sort of people.

All these companies got money, and lived in reputation: especially those of the 'Blackfriars', who were men of grave and sober behaviour ...

Lovewit. What kind of Playhouses had they before the Wars?

Truman. The 'Blackfriers', 'Cockpit', and 'Salisbury Court' were called Private Houses; and were very small to what we see now. The 'Cockpit' was standing since the Restoration; and Rhodes's company acted there for some time ... they were all three built almost exactly alike, for form and bigness. Here they had 'Pits' for the gentry, and acted by candlelight.

The 'Globe', 'Fortune', and 'Bull' were large houses, and lay partly open to the weather: and there they always acted by daylight ...

Plays were frequently acted by Choristers and Singing Boys ... Some of the Chapel Boys, when they grew men, became Actors at the 'Blackfriars'. Such were Nathan Field and John Underwood.

Wright, Thomas (1810–77), born near Ludlow, where he was educated, and at Trinity, Cambridge. He was one of the founders of the Shakespeare Society in 1840 and edited a number of valuable works, including *Queen Elizabeth and her Times, A Series of Original Letters* (1838), *The Chester Plays* (1843–7, for the *Shakespeare Society*), and with Halliwell-Phillipps a revised edition of Nare's *Glossary* of Shakespeare (1859).

Wright, William Aldis (1836–1914), educated at Trinity, Cambridge, of which college he was Vice-Provost, 1888–1912. With W. G. Clark he edited the 9-vol. *Cambridge* Shakespeare (1863–6), and the 1-vol. *Globe* (1864). He was an editor of the *Journal of Philology*, and literary executor of Edward FitzGerald, whose *Letters and Literary Remains* he published in 1889.

Wriothesley, Henry. See SOUTHAMPTON, 3RD EARL OF.

Wroxall. A village in Warwickshire about twelve miles north of Stratford. Shakespeares were on the manor from the early 15th century. There was a priory, and in the Register of the Guild of Knowle (q.v.) occurs the entry for 1503–4, 'Orate pro anima Isabella Shakspere quondam priorissa de Wraxale.' A Richard Shakespeare, bailiff of the manor, 1534–5, was identified by Yeatman with the poet's grandfather of Snitterfield, but Richard of Wroxall retired to a farm at Haseley, where he probably died *c.* 1559.

Württemberg, Frederick, Duke of. See MÖMPELGART.

Wyatt, Sir Thomas (1503–42), born at Allington Castle in Kent, educated at St John's, Cambridge, and died in 1542 while engaged on diplomatic service. He and Surrey brought the sonnet from Italy to England, and he experimented with various elaborate forms for his love poems, ninety-six of which were published in *Tottel's Miscellany*, 1557.

Wyndham, George (1863–1913). Educated at Eton; after serving in the army he entered Parliament and became Chief Secretary for Ireland (1900–5). He published an edition of Plutarch, and *The Poems of Shakespeare* (1898), both with introductory essays.

Wyntoun, Andrew of (*c.* 1350–*c.* 1420), a canon of St Andrews, and Prior of St Serf's in Lochleven. He wrote a verse history of Scotland, the *Orygynale Cronykil of Scotland*, from the earliest times to the accession of James I in 1406. This was used by Hector Boece for his *Scotorum Historiae* (1527), the main source for Holinshed's *Chronicle* of Scotland.

Y

'Yale' Shakespeare. Published 1917–27 in forty volumes, under the general editorship of W. L. Cross and Tucker Brooke.

Yard. In the public theatres this corresponded to the 'plain' of the medieval rounds (q.v.), in which most of the action took place. When Burbage built his Theatre in 1576 it seems likely that the actors, many of whom were comic tumblers and acrobats, would make use of the yard. By 1600 groundlings normally stood in the yard, but for certain plays it, or part of it, may have been kept free for the actors.

Yates, Mary Ann (1728–87), actress, daughter of William Graham, a ship's steward, married the comedian Richard Yates (*c.* 1706–96) with whom she often acted. She first appeared at Drury Lane with Garrick in 1753, and subsequently played many Shakespearean heroines: Portia, Rosalind, Viola, Imogen, Isabella, Hermione, Julia to her husband's Launce in Benjamin Victor's adaptation of *The Two Gentlemen of Verona* (1762) and Cleopatra to Garrick's Antony in the revival of the original play in 1759.

'Year's Work in English Studies.' Published since 1921 by the English Association, the original editor being Sir Sidney Lee. There is a section devoted to Shakespeare, in which new books are reviewed.

Yonge, Bartholomew (*c.* 1555–*c.* 1612), was of the Middle Temple, spent two years in Spain, *c.* 1577–8, and sometime after his return his friend Edward Banister of Idesworth gave him the *Diana Enamorada* of Montemayor to translate. His work was finished by 1582, but it was published only in 1598, with a dedication to Lady Rich (Essex's sister) 'from High Onger in Essex the 28 of Novemb. 1598'. Twenty-four of the lyrics in the book were published in *England's Helicon*, 1600. The story is the source of *The Two Gentlemen of Verona*.

York, Archbishop of. See SCROPE (*H. IV*); ROTHERAM (*R. III*).

York, Duchess of. 1. In *Richard II*, she persuades her 'son' Aumerle to confess his treason to Bolingbroke, and herself procures his pardon (V, ii and iii). (Aumerle's mother died in 1394, and this Duchess of York was his father's second wife, Joan Holland, a girl ten years younger than Aumerle.)

2. In *Richard III*, mother of Edward IV and Clarence, whose deaths she bewails (II, ii), and of Richard, whom she curses (IV, iv). (Cicely Neville, daughter of the 1st Earl of Westmoreland (q.v.), married Richard, 3rd Duke of York, in 1438.)

York, Duke of. 1. In *Richard II*, uncle of Richard and Bolingbroke between whom he tries ineffectively to keep the peace. He is left as Regent while Richard is in Ireland, but, after rebuking Bolingbroke for his rebellion, joins him and acknowledges him as Henry IV (IV, i). He reveals the plot of his son, Aumerle, to the new King (V, ii and iii). (Edmund of Langley (1341–1402), 5th son of Edward III, was created 1st Duke of York in 1385. His sons were Aumerle and Richard Earl of Cambridge (in *Hen. V*).)

2. In *Richard II*, Aumerle (afterwards 2nd Duke of York) is a cousin of Richard, whom he supports against his other cousin, Bolingbroke. He joins a conspiracy against the usurping Bolingbroke, but confesses and is pardoned (V, iii).

In *Henry V*, as Duke of York, he is given command of the vanguard at Agincourt where he is killed (IV, vi). (Edward (*c.* 1373–1415), elder son of Edmund of Langley, was created Earl of Rutland and Duke of Aumerle (Albemarle) by Richard II, and succeeded as 2nd Duke of York on the death of his father in 1402. He died childless, and the title passed to Richard, the son of his only brother, Cambridge, executed before Agincourt.)

3. In *1 Henry VI*, Richard 3rd Duke of York, an enemy of the Lancastrian Somerset, plucks a white rose in the Temple Garden scene (II, iv). He serves in France, fails to relieve Talbot, and condemns Joan of Arc.

In *2 Henry VI*, he objects to the marriage of Henry to Margaret of Anjou, and is sent to Ireland as Regent. On his return he finds Somerset still in favour and, supported by Salisbury and Warwick, claims the throne. He wins the Battle of St Albans, where he kills Clifford.

In *3 Henry VI*, he makes peace on the King's promising that he shall succeed to the throne, but breaks his oath and is captured and killed by Margaret and the Lancastrians at Wakefield. (Richard (1411–60), only son of Richard Earl of Cambridge, executed before Agincourt, was granted his uncle's title and became 3rd Duke of York. On the death of Edmund Mortimer in 1424 he became the representative of the elder branch of the royal family. His sons were Edward IV, George Duke of Clarence, and Richard III.)

4. In *Richard III*, the 5th Duke of York is murdered in the Tower with his brother Edward V, by order of his uncle Richard III. (Richard (1472–83) was the second son of Edward IV, who was himself 4th Duke of York, 1460–1.)

York, Mayor of. In *3 Henry VI*, with some reluctance he lets Edward IV into the town (IV, vii). (Edward's visit was in 1471 when Thomas Beverley was Lord Mayor.)

'Yorkshire Tragedy, A.'

WRITTEN: 1606–7.

REGISTERED: 1608. '2do die Maij. Master Pavyer Entered for his Copie vnder the handes of master Wilson and master Warden Seton A booke Called A Yorkshire Tragedy written by Wylliam Shakespere vjd.'

PUBLISHED: 1608, Q1. 'A Yorkshire Tragedy. Not so New as Lamentable and true. Acted by his Maiesties Players at the Globe. Written by W. Shakspeare. At London Printed by R. B[radock] for Thomas Pauier and are to bee sold at his shop on Cornhill, neere to the exchange. 1608.' (The Head-title reads, 'All's One, Or, One of The Four Plaies In One, Called A York-shire Tragedy As It Was Plaid by the Kings Maiesties Plaiers.')

1619, Q2. 'A Yorkshire Tragedie, Not so New, as Lamentable and True. Written by W. Shakespeare. Printed for T. P. 1619.' (This is one of Jaggard's reprints for the 'false Folio' of 1619.)

1664, F3 (2nd issue). One of the seven plays added to F3.

Though all the early evidence points to Shakespeare's authorship and it is a powerful though crude play, its exclusion from F1 and its un-Shakespearean theme and style lead most critics to reject it. It is the story of Walter Calverley, who murdered his children and was executed in August 1605.

Young, Charles Mayne (1777–1856), son of a surgeon. After acting in the provinces for some years, he appeared in London in 1807 as Hamlet. In 1812 he played Cassius to the Brutus of J. P. Kemble, whom he succeeded as the leading tragic actor of the day. He played the King in Charles Kemble's famous antiquarian revival of King John in 1823.

Z

Zuccaro, Federigo (1543–1609), one of the most successful portrait painters of his day. In 1574 he came to England, where he painted Queen Elizabeth and some of her courtiers. He did not stay long, however, returning to Rome to finish his painting of the vault of the Pauline chapel. He was decorating the Escorial for Philip II of Spain in the year of the Armada.

A number of so-called portraits of Shakespeare have been fathered upon Zuccaro, including the 'Boston Zuccaro', the 'Cosway Zuccaro', and the 'Bath' or 'Archer' portrait. According to M. H. Spielmann, the first is a good painting of the Flemish school, the second ill drawn and clearly not a portrait of Shakespeare, the third a good painting worthy of Zuccaro, but as he came to England when Shakespeare was only ten, and did not stay long, it is improbable that it is a portrait of Shakespeare.

APPENDIX I

THE COPY FOR THE PLAYS
(BASED ON GREG)

Folio Order	*Quarto*	*Folio*	*Act and Scene Division*
Tem.		Crane transcript of foul papers	A & S
T.G.V.		Crane transcript of prompt-book	A & S
M.W.W.	Report	Crane transcript of prompt-book	A & S
M.M.		Crane transcript of foul papers	A & S
C.E.		Foul papers	Acts
M.Ado	Foul papers	Q and prompt-book	Acts
L.L.L.	Foul papers	Q1	Acts
M.N.D.	Foul papers	Q2 and prompt-book	Acts
M.V.	Foul papers	Q1 and prompt-book	Acts
A.Y.L.I.		Prompt-book	A & S
Shrew		Foul papers	Acts*
A.W.W.		Foul papers	Acts
T.N.		Prompt-book	A & S
W.T.		Crane transcript of foul papers	A & S
John		Author's copy used as prompt-book?	A & S*
R. II	Foul papers	Q3 and Q5 used as prompt-book	A & S
1 H. IV	Foul papers	Q5 with some editing	A & S
2 H. IV	Foul papers	Q and prompt-book	A & S
H. V	Report	Foul papers	Acts*
1 H. VI		Author's copy used as prompt-book	A & S*
2 H. VI	Report	Author's copy used as prompt-book	None
3 H. VI	Report	Author's copy used as prompt-book	None
R. III	Memorial reconstruction	Q3, Q6 and foul papers	A & S
H. VIII		Foul papers	A & S
T. & C.	Author's transcript	Q and foul papers	None
Cor.		Foul papers	Acts
Titus	Foul papers	Q3 and prompt-book	Acts
R. & J.	1597 Report		
	1599 Foul papers and Q1	Q3	None
Timon		Unfinished foul papers	None
J.C.		Transcript of prompt-book	Acts
Mac.		Prompt-book	A & S
Hamlet	1603 Report		
	1604 Foul papers and Q1	Q2 and prompt-book	A & S*
Lear	Transcript of foul papers	Q1 and prompt-book	A & S
Oth.	Transcript of foul papers	Q and prompt-book	A & S
A. & C.		Foul papers	None
Cym.		Prompt-book	A & S
Per.	Report?	Q6	Acts

* Imperfectly divided. (All the Comedies, it will be noted, are divided into Acts.)

APPENDIX II

THE SHAKESPEARE FAMILY

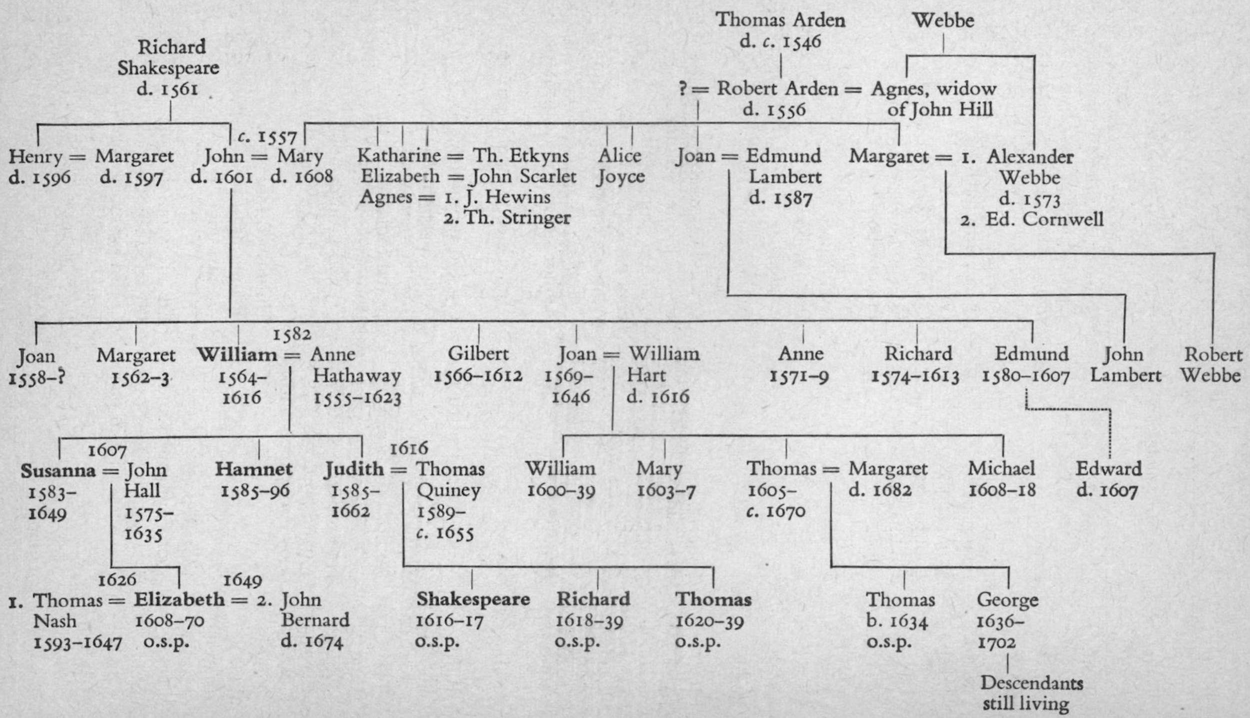

APPENDIX III

INTER-RELATIONSHIP OF THE FAMILIES OF

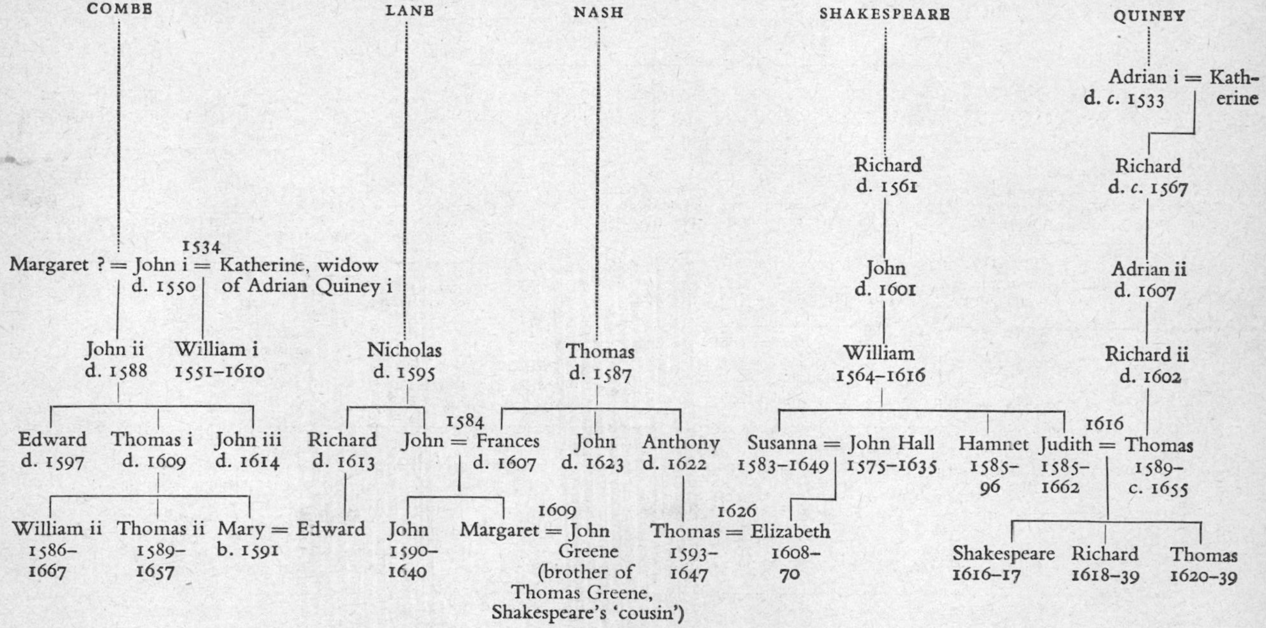

APPENDIX IV

GENEALOGICAL TABLE ILLUSTRATING SHAKESPEARE'S ENGLISH HISTORICAL PLAYS

EDWARD III
1312–77

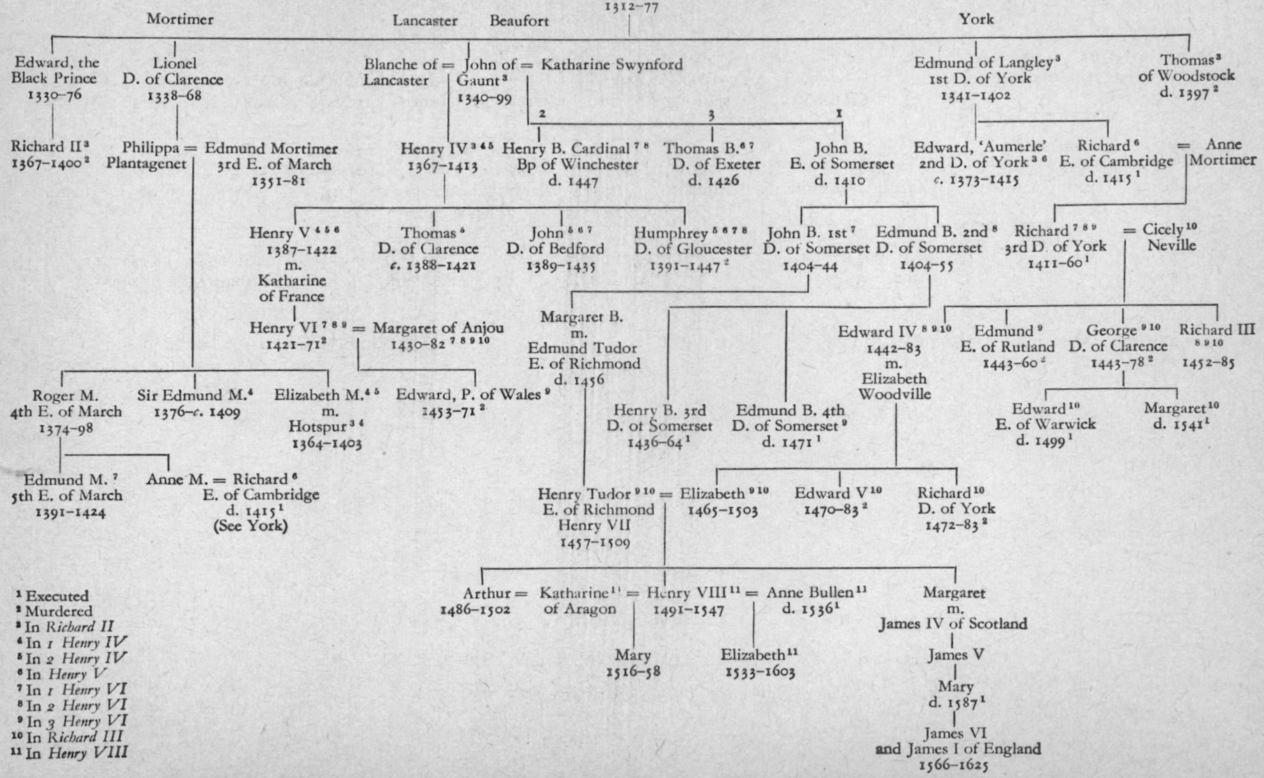

[1] Executed
[2] Murdered
[3] In *Richard II*
[4] In *1 Henry IV*
[5] In *2 Henry IV*
[6] In *Henry V*
[7] In *1 Henry VI*
[8] In *2 Henry VI*
[9] In *3 Henry VI*
[10] In *Richard III*
[11] In *Henry VIII*

Bibliography

The most complete bibliographies of Shakespeare are:

JAGGARD, W., *Shakespeare Bibliography: A Dictionary of every Known Issue of the Writings of our National Poet and of Recorded Opinion thereon in the English Language* (Stratford), 1911.

EBISCH, W., and SCHÜCKING, L. L., *A Shakespeare Bibliography* (Oxford), 1931. *Supplement for the Years 1930–35*, 1937.

The Cambridge Bibliography of English Literature, 1940. Vol. I, pp. 539–608. *Supplement*, 1957.

GORDON, R., *A Classified Shakespeare Bibliography* (4 vols.), Vol. I, 1963.

VELZ, JOHN W., *Shakespeare and the Classical Tradition, A Critical Guide to Commentary, 1660–1960* (Minneapolis), 1968.

Current publications are recorded in:

Annual Bibliography of English Language and Literature, 1920– . (Modern Humanities Research Association.)

Jahrbuch der Deutschen Shakespeare-Gesellschaft, 1865– .

Review of English Studies. A Quarterly Journal of English Literature and the English Language, 1925– .

Shakespeare Quarterly (N.Y.), 1950– .

Shakespeare Survey. An Annual Survey of Shakespearean Study and Production, 1948– .

The Year's Work in English Studies, 1920– . (There is a section for Shakespeare, giving short reviews of the most important publications.)

EDITIONS OF SHAKESPEARE

For collected editions 1623–1821, see EDITORS, p. 147. Apart from these, the most important 19th- and 20th-century editions in English are:

1795–6	S. Johnson (Philadelphia). 8 vols. (1st American ed.)
1805	A. Chalmers, 9 vols. (Fuseli's plates.)
1818	T. Bowdler. *Family Ed.* 10 vols.
1826	S. W. Singer, 10 vols.
1842–4	J. P. Collier, 8 vols.
1842–4	C. Knight. *Library Ed.* 12 vols.
1847	G. C. Verplanck (N.Y.). 3 vols.
1852–7	H. N. Hudson (Boston). 11 vols.
1853–65	J. O. Halliwell-Phillipps. 16 vols. Folio.
1854–65	N. Delius (Eberfeld). 8 vols. (Text used for *Leopold Sh.*)
1857	A. Dyce. 6 vols. 3rd ed. 10 vols. 1895–1901.

1857–66 R. G. White (Boston). 12 vols.
1858–60 H. Staunton, 3 vols.
1863–6 W. G. Clark, G. Glover, W. A. Wright. *Cambridge Ed.* 9 vols., much revised 1891–3. (The most important edition textually after the Third Variorum.)
1864 W. G. Clark, W. A. Wright. *Globe Ed.* 1 vol. (The standard edition for numbering lines.)
1871– H. H. Furness *et al. New Variorum Ed.* (Philadelphia). In progress.
1877 F. J. Furnivall. *Leopold Ed.* (Delius text), 1 vol.
1881 H. N. Hudson. *Harvard Ed.* (Boston). 20 vols.
1886–1906 J. A. Morgan. *Bankside Ed.* (N.Y.). 22 vols. (Parallel Text.)
1888–90 H. Irving, F. A. Marshall. *Henry Irving Ed.* 8 vols.
1892 W. J. Craig. *Oxford Ed.* 1 vol.
1894–6 I. Gollancz. *Temple Ed.* 40 vols.
1899–1903 C. H. Herford. *Eversley Ed.* 10 vols.
1899–1924 W. J. Craig, R. H. Case *et al. Arden Ed.* 37 vols.
1904–7 A. H. Bullen. *Stratford Town Ed.* 10 vols.
1906 W. A. Neilson (Boston). 1 vol.
1907–12 F. J. Furnivall, W. G. Boswell-Stone, F. W. Clarke. *Old Spelling Ed.* 17 vols., incomplete.
1911–13 W. A. Neilson, A. H. Thorndike *et al.* (N.Y.). *Tudor Ed.* 40 vols.
1917–27 W. L. Cross, C. F. T. Brooke *et al.* (New Haven). *Yale Ed.* 40 vols.
1921–63 A. T. Quiller-Couch, J. D. Wilson *et al. New Cambridge Ed.* One vol. for each play.
1929–34 H. Farjeon, *Nonesuch Press Ed.* 7 vols., reprinted 1953, 4 vols.
1936 G. L. Kittredge (Boston). 1 vol.
1938– R. E. C. Houghton *et al. New Clarendon Ed.* In progress. One vol. for each play.
1951 P. Alexander. 1 vol.
1951 H. Craig (Chicago). 1 vol.
1951– Una Ellis-Fermor (until 1958), H. F. Brooks, H. Jenkins *et al. New Arden Ed.* In progress. One vol. for each play.
1954 C. J. Sisson. 1 vol.
1954– H. Kökeritz, C. T. Prouty *et al.* Revised *Yale* edition. One vol. for each play.
1957 J. J. Munro. *London Shakespeare.* 6 vols.
1958 P. Alexander. *Heritage Shakespeare* (N.Y.). 3 vols.
1969 A. Harbage. *Complete Pelican Shakespeare*, 1 vol.

Recent paperback editions are the English *Penguin* (G. B. Harrison) and *New Penguin* (T. J. B. Spencer), and the American *Crofts* (R. C. Bald), *Pelican* (A. Harbage), *Folger Library* (L. B. Wright, V. A. LaMar), *Laurel* (F. Ferguson), *Yale*, *Signet* (S. Barnet).

Facsimile Editions. See p. 160.

Concordances, Glossaries, Indexes. See p. 113.

Translations. See BELGIUM, DENMARK, FRANCE, GERMANY, ITALY, NETHERLANDS, RUSSIA, SPAIN, SWEDEN. For translations into other languages, see Ebisch and Schücking: *A Sh. Bibliography*, p. 158. Current activities in other countries are reported in *Shakespeare Survey*.

Some of the most important books and essays on Shakespeare are listed below under the following headings, though many of them inevitably overlap:

Life

(*a*) General. (The standard, and fully documented work, is that of Chambers, though some material has been discovered since 1930. Most *Lives* contain critical matter as well.)

(*b*) Special Studies. (Shakespeare's friends and relations, his education, knowledge, etc.)

(*c*) Background. (Mainly political and social, but partly dramatic.)

Works

1. Scholarship
   (*a*) Text
   (*b*) Authenticity, Chronology, Language, Verse, etc.
   (*c*) Sources
2. Literary Criticism

Theatre

Shakespeare's theatre, contemporary drama, and histories of the drama, the stage, and Shakespearean productions to the present day. (The standard work on Shakespeare's theatre is E. K. Chambers, *The Elizabethan Stage*.)

(A valuable book with essays by eminent scholars, covering every aspect of Shakespeare, is *A Companion to Shakespeare Studies* (edited by H. Granville-Barker and G. B. Harrison), 1934.)

LIFE

The old conception of Shakespeare as a comparatively uneducated man has died hard; indeed, it is not yet dead. It began, perhaps, with Ben Jonson's 'small Latin and less Greek', was fostered by Voltaire, and accepted by 18th- and 19th-century scholars: Malone, R. Farmer, Carlyle, Halliwell-Phillipps and the rest. Today, however, scholars find in Shakespeare a well-educated man who moved easily in the most cultured society of his time. (See BIOGRAPHY, p. 63.)

(*a*) GENERAL

ADAMS, J. Q., *A Life of William Shakespeare*, 1923.

ALEXANDER, P., *Shakespeare's Life and Art*, 1938.

A Shakespeare Primer, 1951.

BAILEY, J., *Shakespeare*, 1929.

BEECHING, H. C., *William Shakespeare, Player, Playmaker, and Poet*, 1908.

BRANDES, G., *William Shakespeare*. Translated from the Danish by W. Archer. 2 vols., 1898. (An imaginative reconstruction.)

BROOKE, C. F. T., *Shakespeare of Stratford*, 1926.

BROWN, IVOR, *Shakespeare*, 1949.

CHAMBERS, E. K., *William Shakespeare. A Study of Facts and Problems*. 2 vols., 1930. (Chaps. i, iii. Appendices A, B, C, E.)

Sources for a Biography of Shakespeare, 1946.

CHAMBRUN, C. L. de, *Shakespeare: A Portrait Restored*, 1957.
CHUTE, M., *Shakespeare of London*, 1949.
ELZE, K., *William Shakespeare*, 1888.
FLEAY, F. G., *A Chronicle History of the Life and Work of William Shakespeare*, 1886.
FRIPP, E. I., *Shakespeare, Man and Artist*. 2 vols., 1938. (Authoritative on Stratford.)
FURNIVALL, F. J., and MUNRO, J., *Life and Work of Shakespeare*, 1908.
HALLIDAY, F. E., *The Life of Shakespeare*, 1961 (Penguin 1964).
HALLIWELL-PHILLIPPS, J. O., *Outlines of the Life of Shakespeare*. 7th ed., finally revised, 1887. (The basis of later *Lives*.)
HARRIS, F., *The Man Shakespeare and his Tragic Life Story*, 1909.
HARRISON, G. B., *Shakespeare at Work*, 1933.
KENNY, T., *The Life and Genius of Shakespeare*, 1864. (Suggests that *1 Contention* and *The True Tragedy* are 'bad' Quartos.)
LAMBERT, D. H., *Cartae Shakespeareanae*, 1904.
LAMBOURN, E. A. G., and HARRISON, G. B., *Shakespeare, the Man and his Stage*, 1923.
LEE, S., *A Life of William Shakespeare*, 1898. New ed. 1931. (The standard work until superseded by Chambers.)
LEFRANC, A., *À la Découverte de Shakespeare*, 1945. (Derbyite.)
MALONE, E., *The Life of William Shakspeare*. Third Variorum, 1821.
MASSON, D., *Shakespeare Personally*, 1914.
NEILSON, W. A., and THORNDIKE, A. H., *The Facts about Shakespeare*, 1913.
PARROTT, T. M., *William Shakespeare: a Handbook*, 1934.
PEARSON, H., *A Life of Shakespeare*, 1949.
QUENNELL, P., *Shakespeare*, 1963 (Penguin 1969).
RALEIGH, W., *Shakespeare*, 1907.
REESE, M. M., *Shakespeare: his World and his Work*, 1953.
ROWE, N., *Some Account of the Life of Mr William Shakespeare*, 1709. (The first formal *Life*.)
ROWSE, A. L., *William Shakespeare*, 1963.
WILSON, J. D., *The Essential Shakespeare: A Biographical Adventure*, 1932.

(*b*) SPECIAL STUDIES

ACHESON, A., *Shakespeare's Lost Years in London*, 1920.
BAKER, O. L., *In Shakespeare's Warwickshire, and the Unknown Years*, 1937.
BALDWIN, T. W., *William Shakspere's Petty School*, 1943.
William Shakspere's Small Latine & Lesse Greeke. 2 vols., 1944.
BARNARD, E. A. B., *New Links with Shakespeare*, 1930.
BOWDEN, H. S., *The Religion of Shakespeare*, 1899.
BRASSINGTON, W. S., *Shakespeare's Homeland*, 1903.
BROOKE, C. F. T. (Ed.) *Shakespeare's Sonnets*, 1936. (A biographical reconstruction.)
BROWN, IVOR, *How Shakespeare Spent His Day*, 1963.
CAMPBELL, J., *Shakespeare's Legal Acquirements*, 1859.
CHAMBERS, E. K., *Shakespearean Gleanings*, 1944.
CHAMBERS, R. W., *The Jacobean Shakespeare* (BAL), 1937.

COLLIER, J. P., *New Facts regarding the Life of Shakespeare*, 1835. (Contains a number of forgeries.)

COLLINS, J. C., *Studies in Shakespeare*, 1904.

COOPER, D., *Sergeant Shakespeare*, 1949. (That Shakespeare served with Leicester in the Netherlands.)

DE GROOT, J. H., *The Shakespeares and the Old Faith*, 1946.

ELLACOMBE, H. N., *Shakespeare as an Angler*, 1883.

The Plant-Lore and Garden-Craft of Shakespeare, 1896.

FARMER, R., *An Essay on the Learning of Shakespeare*, 1767. (3rd Var. I.)

FOX, L., *The Heritage of Shakespeare's Birthplace* (SS, 1), 1948.

FRENCH, G. R., *Shakespeareana Genealogica*, 1869.

FRIPP, E. I., *Master Richard Quyny*, 1924.

Shakespeare's Stratford, 1928.

Shakespeare's Haunts near Stratford, 1929.

Shakespeare Studies, Biographical and Literary, 1930.

GEIKIE, A., *The Birds of Shakespeare*, 1916.

GRAY, A., *A Chapter in the Early Life of Shakespeare*, 1926. (That Shakespeare was an usher in the family of Sir H. Goodere.)

GREEN, C. F., *The Legend of Shakespeare's Crab-Tree*, 1857.

GREENWOOD, G., *Shakespeare's Law and Latin*, 1916.

HARRISON, G. B. (Ed.), *Willobie his Avisa*, 1926.

HERFORD, C. H., *Shakespeare's Normality*, 1921.

HOTSON, J. L., *Shakespeare versus Shallow*, 1931. (Finds in Justice Gardiner the original of Shallow.)

I, William Shakespeare, 1937. (Mainly about Thomas Russell, Shakespeare's friend.)

Shakespeare's Sonnets Dated, 1949.

JORDAN, J., *Original Collections on Shakespeare and Stratford-on-Avon*, Ed. by J. O. Halliwell-Phillipps, 1864.

Original Memoirs and Accounts of the Families of Shakespeare and Hart. Ed. by J. O. H-P., 1865.

KNIGHTS, L. C., *Shakespeare's Politics* (BAL), 1957.

LAW, E. P. A., *Shakespeare as a Groom of the Chamber*, 1910.

LEE, S., *Stratford-on-Avon from the Earliest Times to the Death of Shakespeare*, 1885, 1907.

LEWIS, B. R., *The Shakespeare Documents*, 1941. (Facsimiles.)

LONG, J. H., *Shakespeare's Use of Music*, 1959.

LOOTEN, C., *Shakespeare et la Religion*, 1924.

MADDEN, D. H., *The Diary of Master Silence*, 1897, 1907. (Shakespeare's knowledge of sport.)

Shakespeare and his Fellows, 1916.

MARCHAM, F., *William Shakespeare and his daughter Susannah*, 1931.

MITCHELL, C. M., *The Shakespeare Circle. A Life of Dr John Hall*, 1947.

MUIR, K., and O'LOUGHLIN, S., *The Voyage to Illyria*, 1937. (Biography based on Shakespeare's imagery and sources.)

NAYLOR, E. W., *Shakespeare and Music*, 1928.

NOBLE, R., *Shakespeare's Biblical Knowledge*, 1935.

PLIMPTON, E. A., *The Education of Shakespeare*, 1933.
SANDYS, J. E., 'Education' in *Shakespeare's England*, 1916.
SAVAGE, F. G., *The Flora and Folk-lore of Shakespeare*, 1923.
SCOTT-GILES, C. W., *Shakespeare's Heraldry*, 1950.
SIMPSON, R. R., *Shakespeare and Medicine*, 1959.
SISSON, C. J., *The Mythical Sorrows of Shakespeare* (BAL), 1934.
SMART, J. S., *Shakespeare: Truth and Tradition*, 1934.
SPIELMANN, M. H., *The Title-page of the First Folio* (Shakespeare's Portraiture), 1924.
STAUNTON, H., *Memorials of Shakespeare*, 1864.
STOPES, C. C., *Shakespeare's Family ... with some Account of the Ardens*, 1901.
Shakespeare's Warwickshire Contemporaries, 1907.
The Life of Henry, Third Earl of Southampton, 1922.
SYKES, H. D., *Sidelights on Shakespeare*, 1919.
TANNENBAUM, S. A., *A New Study of Shakespeare's Will*, 1926.
THOMSON, J. A. K., *Shakespeare and the Classics*, 1952.
WALLACE, C. W., *The Newly Discovered Shakespeare Documents* (University Studies of the University of Nebraska, v), 1905.
Shakespeare and his London Associates as Revealed in Recently Discovered Documents (University Studies of the University of Nebraska, x), 1910. (The Belott-Mountjoy papers.)
WILSON, F. P., *Shakespeare's Reading* (SS, 3), 1950.

(*c*) BACKGROUND (see also THEATRE)

AKRIGG, G. P. V., *Jacobean Pageant, or, The Court of King James I*, 1962.
ALLEN, J. W., *A History of Political Thought in the 16th Century*, 1928. *English Political Thought, 1603–60*, 1938.
ANDERSON, R. L., *Elizabethan Psychology and Shakespeare's Plays*, 1927.
BABB, L., *The Elizabethan Malady: A Study of Melancholia in English Literature from 1580 to 1642*, 1951.
BIRCH, T., *Memoirs of the Reign of Queen Elizabeth, 1581–1603*, 2 vols., 1754.
The Court and Times of James I, 2 vols., ed. 1848.
BYRNE, M. St C., *The Elizabethan Home*, 1930.
Elizabethan Life in Town and Country, 1933.
The Social Background (*Companion to Shakespeare Studies*), 1934.
CAMDEN, WILLIAM, *The History of Elizabeth*, 1631.
CHAMBERLAIN, J., *Letters during the Reign of Queen Elizabeth*, ed. 1861.
CHAMBERS, E. K., *The Elizabethan Stage*, 1923. Book I: 'The Court.'
COLLINS, A. (Ed.) *Letters and Memorials of State, in the Reigns of Queen Mary, Queen Elizabeth, King James*. 2 vols., 1746. (Known as *The Sidney Papers*.)
CRAIG, H., *The Enchanted Glass: the Elizabethan Mind in Literature*, 1936, 1950.
DORAN, M., *Endeavors of Art: A Study of Form in Elizabethan Drama*, 1954.
DRIVER, T. F., *The Sense of History in Greek and Shakespearean Drama*, 1960.
FARNHAM, W., *The Medieval Heritage of Elizabethan Tragedy*, 1936, 1956.
FORD, B. (Ed.), *The Age of Shakespeare* (Penguin Books), 1955.
GREEN, A. W., *The Inns of Court and Early English Drama*, 1931.
HALLIDAY, F. E., *Shakespeare in his Age*, 1956.

HARINGTON, J., *Nugae Antiquae*. Ed. T. Park. 2 vols., 1804. (Original papers, including many of Harington's letters.)

HARRISON, G. B., *England in Shakespeare's Day*, 1928.

An Elizabethan Journal, 1591–94, 1928.

A Second Elizabethan Journal, 1595–98, 1931.

A Last Elizabethan Journal, 1599–1603, 1933.

A Jacobean Journal, 1603–1606, 1941.

HARRISON, W., *Description of England*, 1587. (Ed. for NSS.)

ING, C., *Elizabeth Lyrics*, 1951.

INNES, A. D., *England Under the Tudors*, 1905.

JOSEPH, M., *Shakespeare's Use of the Arts of Language*, 1947.

JUDGES, A. V., *The Elizabethan Underworld*, 1930. (A collection of Tudor and early Stuart tracts and ballads.)

MADARIAGA, S. de, *Don Juan as a European Figure*, 1946.

NEALE, J. E., *Queen Elizabeth*, 1934.

NICOLL, A., *The Elizabethans* (extracts from Elizabethan writers), 1957.

NICHOLS, J., *The Progresses and Public Processions of Queen Elizabeth*. 3 vols. 1788–1807. 2nd ed. 1823.

The Progresses, Processions and Magnificent Festivities of King James the First. 4 vols. 1828.

PUTTENHAM, G., *The Art of English Poesie*. Ed. Willcock, G. D., and Walker, A., 1936.

RALEIGH, W. (Ed.) *Shakespeare's England. An Account of the Life and Manners of his Age*. 2 vols., 1916, 1926.

ROWSE, A. L., *The England of Elizabeth*, 1950.

RYE, W. B., *England as seen by Foreigners in the Days of Elizabeth and James the First*, 1865.

SCOT, REGINALD, *The Discouerie of Witchcraft*, 1584. Ed. by M. Summers, 1930.

SISSON, C. J., *Lost Plays of Shakespeare's Age*, 1936. (Relates the drama to contemporary life.)

Studies in the Life and Environment of Shakespeare since 1900. (SS, 3), 1950.

STOLL, E. E., *Shakespeare Studies: Historical and Comparative in Method*, 1927.

STOPES, C. C., *Shakespeare's Environment*, 1914, 1918.

STOW, J., *Annales, or, a General Chronicle of England, Begun by J. Stow. Continued and Augmented unto 1631 by E. Howes*, 1580–1631.

A Survey of London, 1598. Ed. C. L. Kingsford. 2 vols., 1908.

TILLYARD, E. M. W., *The Elizabethan World Picture*, 1943.

TREVELYAN, G. M., *England Under the Stuarts*, 1904.

English Social History, 1942. Chaps. vi, vii: 'Shakespeare's England'.

SPENCER, T., *Death and Elizabethan Tragedy: A Study of Convention and Opinion in the Elizabethan Drama*, 1936.

WATSON, C. B., *Shakespeare and the Renaissance Concept of Honor*, 1960.

WILLEY, B., *The Seventeenth-Century Background: Studies in the Thought of the Age in Relation to Poetry and Religion*, 1934.

WILSON, F. P., *The Plague in Shakespeare's London*, 1927.

Elizabethan and Jacobean, 1945.

WILSON, J. D., *Life in Shakespeare's England*, 1911. New ed. 1949. (Contemporary accounts.)

WILSON, T., *Wilson's Arte of Rhetorique*, 1560. Ed. G. H. Mair, 1909.

WINWOOD, R., *Memorials of Affairs of State in the Reigns of Elizabeth and James I.* Original Papers of Sir Ralph Winwood. 3 vols., 1725.

WRIGHT, L. B., *Middle Class Culture in Elizabethan England*, 1935.

YOUNG, G. M., *Shakespeare and the Termers* (BAL), 1947. (The possible influence of the Inns of Court on Shakespeare.)

WORKS

I. SCHOLARSHIP. (*a*) TEXT

It should be emphasized that textual criticism (q.v.) was revolutionized in the first half of the 20th century by the bibliographers A. W. Pollard, W. W. Greg and R. B. McKerrow. The annual reviews of Textual Studies by J. G. McManaway in *Shakespeare Survey* provide a valuable summary of contemporary work. *Shakespeare Quarterly* also has an annual review.

BLACK, M. W., and SHAABER, M. A., *Shakespeare's Seventeenth Century Editors, 1632–85*, 1937.

BOWERS, F., *On Editing Shakespeare*, 1955.

Textual and Literary Criticism, 1959.

CHAMBERS, E. K., *William Shakespeare*. 2 vols., 1930. (Chaps. iv, v, vi: 'The Book of the Play'; 'The Quartos and the First Folio'; 'Plays in the Printing-House'.)

DUTHIE, G. I., *Elizabethan Shorthand and the First Quarto of King Lear*, 1949.

The Bad Quarto of Hamlet, 1941.

FLATTER, R., *Shakespeare's Producing Hand*, 1948.

GOLLANCZ, I. (Ed.) *Studies in the First Folio*, 1924. (Shakespeare Association, to celebrate the tercentenary of F1. J. D. Wilson: *The Task of Heminge and Condell.* R. C. Rhodes: *The First Folio and the Elizabethan Stage.* W. W. Greg: *The First Folio and its Publishers.* A. Nicoll: *The Editors of Shakespeare from First Folio to Malone.*)

GREG, W. W., *Two Elizabethan Stage Abridgements: 'The Battle of Alcazar' & 'Orlando Furioso': an Essay in Critical Bibliography*, 1923. (Argues that bad texts were reproduced from memory rather than shorthand.)

Principles of Emendation in Shakespeare, 1928. Reprinted in *Aspects of Shakespeare*, 1933.

The Editorial Problem in Shakespeare, 1942. 2nd ed. 1951.

The Shakespeare First Folio, 1955. (A summary of this century's scholarship and of the problems yet to be solved.)

Some Aspects and Problems of London Publishing between 1550 and 1650, 1956.

HART, A., *Stolen and Surreptitious Copies*, 1942.

HINMAN, C. K., *Six Variant Readings in the First Folio of Shakespeare*, 1961.

The Printing and Proof-Reading of the First Folio, 1963.

HOPPÉ, R., *The Bad Quarto of Romeo and Juliet*, 1948.

JACKSON, A., *Rowe's Edition of Shakespeare* (*The Library*), 1930.

KIRSCHBAUM, L., *Shakespeare and the Stationers*, 1955.

LOUNSBURY, T., *The Text of Shakespeare*, 1906. (A history of the text from the Quartos to Theobald.)

MCKERROW, R. B., *A Dictionary of Printers and Booksellers, 1557–1640*, 1910.

Printers' and Publishers' Devices, 1455–1640, 1913.

An Introduction to Bibliography for Literary Students, 1927.

The Elizabethan Printer and Dramatic Manuscripts, 1931.

The Treatment of Shakespeare's Text by his Earlier Editors, 1709–68, 1933.

Prolegomena for the Oxford Shakespeare: a Study in Editorial Method, 1939.

POLLARD, A. W., *Shakespeare Folios and Quartos: A Study in the Bibliography of Shakespeare's Plays, 1594–1685*, 1909. (Showed that most of the Quartos used as copy for F1 were 'good', and established the first Quartos of *R.J.*, *Hen. V*, *M.W.W.*, and *Hamlet* as 'bad'. A revolutionary book.)

'King Richard II.' A New Quarto, 1916.

Shakespeare's Fight with the Pirates and the Problems of the Transmission of his Text. (Sandars Lectures, 1915. Published 1917.) (Maintains that some of the First Quarto editions were printed from Shakespeare's own autograph MS.)

The Foundations of Shakespeare's Text (BAL), 1923.

'Shakespeare's Text' in *Companion to Shakespeare Studies*, 1934.

POLLARD, A. W., GREG, W. W., THOMPSON, E. M., WILSON, J. D., CHAMBERS, R. W., *Shakespeare's Hand in the Play of 'Sir Thomas More'*, 1923. (Maintains that 147 lines are in Shakespeare's handwriting.)

RHODES, R. C., *Shakespeare's First Folio: a Study*, 1923.

SCHROEDER, J., *The Great Folio of 1623: Shakespeare's Plays in the Printing House*, 1956.

SIMPSON, P., *The Bibliographical Study of Shakespeare* (Oxford Bibliographical Society), 1923.

Proof-reading in the 16th, 17th, and 18th Centuries, 1935.

SISSON, C. J., *New Readings in Shakespeare*, 1956.

THOMPSON, E. M., *Shakespeare's Handwriting*, 1916.

WALKER, A., *Textual Problems of the First Folio*, 1953. (The editorial implications of the use of corrected quartos as Folio copy.)

WILLIAMS, P., *New Approaches to Textual Problems in Shakespeare* (*Studies in Bibliography* VIII), 1955.

WILLOUGHBY, E. E., *The Printing of the First Folio of Shakespeare*, 1932.

WILSON, F. P., 'The New Bibliography', pp. 76–135 of *Studies in Retrospect* (Bibliographical Society), 1945.

WILSON, J. D., *Textual Introduction* to *The Tempest* (*New Cambridge Shakespeare*), 1921. Also 'The Copy for the Text' in subsequent volumes. (The application of Pollard's 'critical bibliography' to the editing of Shakespeare.)

The New Way with Shakespeare's Texts: An Introduction for Lay Readers, SS, 7, 8, 9, 11. 1954–5–6–8.

(*b*) AUTHENTICITY, CHRONOLOGY, LANGUAGE, VERSE, ETC.

ABBOTT, E. A., *A Shakespearian Grammar*, 1872.

ALEXANDER, P., *Shakespeare's Punctuation*, 1945.

Shakespeare's Henry VI and Richard III, 1929.

BALD, R. C., '*Macbeth*' *and the* '*Short*' *Plays* (RES), 1928.
The Booke of '*Sir Thomas More*' *and its Problems* (SS. 2), 1949.
BALDWIN, T. W., *William Shakspere's Five-Act Structure. Shakspere's Early Plays on the Background of Renaissance Theories of Five-Act Structure from 1470*, 1947.
BARTLETT, J., *A New and Complete Concordance or Verbal Index or Words, Phrases, & Passages in the Dramatic Works of Shakespeare, with a Supplementary Concordance to the Poems*, 1894.
BRADLEY, H., 'Shakespeare's English' in *Shakespeare's England*, 1916.
BROOKE, C. F. T. (Ed.) *The Shakespeare Apocrypha: being a Collection of fourteen Plays which have been ascribed to Shakespeare*, 1918.
BYRNE, M. ST C., *Elizabethan Handwriting for Beginners* (RES), 1927.
CHAMBERS, E. K., *The Disintegration of Shakespeare* (BAL), 1924. (Refutes the disintegrators.)
William Shakespeare, 1930. Chaps. vii, viii deal with Authenticity and Chronology. Metrical Tables: Appendix H, Vol. II, pp. 397–408.
CRANE, M., *Shakespeare's Prose*, 1951.
DORAN, M., *Henry VI Parts II and III: their Relation to the* '*Contention*' *and the* '*True Tragedy*', 1928.
DOUCE, F., *Illustrations of Shakespeare*, 1807.
DOWDEN, E., *Shakspere Primer*, 1877. (Gives his chronology.)
DUTHIE, G. I., *Elizabethan Shorthand, and the first Quarto of King Lear*, 1949.
EVANS, B. I., *The Language of Shakespeare's Plays*, 1952.
FLEAY, F. G., *Shakespeare Manual*, 1876, 1878. (Gives his chronology.)
FRANZ, W., *Shakespeare-Grammatik*, 1900, 1939.
FURNIVALL, F. J., *Preface* to the *Leopold Shakespeare*, 1877. (A summary of mid-Victorian scholarship, giving his chronology.)
Preface to the *Shakespeare Commentaries* of Gervinus, 1883.
GIBSON, H. N., *The Shakespeare Claimants*, 1962.
GORDON, G. S., *Shakespeare's English*, 1928.
HOTSON, J. L., *Shakespeare's Sonnets Dated, and other Essays*, 1949. (Includes an essay on *Love's Labour's Won*, which he identifies with *Troilus and Cressida*.)
HULME, H. M., *Explorations in Shakespeare's Language*, 1962.
HUNTER, J., *New Illustrations of Shakespeare*. 2 vols., 1845.
INGLEBY, C. M., *A Complete View of the Shakspere Controversy, concerning the authenticity and genuineness of manuscript matter affecting the works and biography of Shakspere, published by J. P. Collier*, 1861.
Shakespeare, the Man and the Book. 2 vols., 1877, 1881. (Includes a paper on metrical tests by F. G. Fleay.)
ISAACS, J., 'Shakespearian Scholarship' in *Companion to Shakespeare Studies*, 1934.
JESPERSON, O., *The Growth and Structure of the English Language* ('Shakespeare and the Language of Poetry'), 1926, 1943.
JOSEPH, SISTER M., *Shakespeare's Use of the Arts of Language*, 1947.
KÖKERITZ, H., *Shakespeare's Pronunciation*, 1953.
KÖNIG, G., *Der Vers in Shakespeares Dramen*, 1888.
MAHOOD, M. M., *Shakespeare's Word-Play*, 1957.
MCKNIGHT, G. H., *Modern English in the Making*, 1928. (Chaps. v–xi.)

McMANAWAY, J. G., *Recent Studies in Shakespeare's Chronology* (SS, 3), 1950.
MAIR, J., *William Ireland and the Shakespeare Papers*, 1938.
MALONE, E., *An Attempt to Ascertain the Order in which the Plays of Shakspeare were Written*, 1778. Final form in *Variorum*, 1821. (The first serious attempt to establish the chronology.)
An Inquiry into the Authenticity of Certain Miscellaneous Papers and Legal Instruments, 1796. (The Ireland Forgeries.)
MUIR, K., *Shakespeare as Collaborator*, 1960.
NARES, R., *A Glossary; or, Collection of Words, Phrases, Names, and Allusions to Customs, Proverbs, etc.*, 1822. Revised and expanded by J. O. Halliwell and T. Wright. 2 vols., 1872.
NESS, F. W., *Use of Rhyme in Shakespeare's Plays*, 1941.
NEW ENGLISH DICTIONARY, 1888–1933.
ONIONS, C. T., *A Shakespeare Glossary*, 1911, 1953.
PARTRIDGE, A. C., *The Problem of Henry VIII Reopened*, 1949. (Supports the Spedding-Hickson division of the play between Shakespeare and Fletcher.)
PARTRIDGE, E., *Shakespeare's Bawdy: A Literary and Psychological Essay and a Comprehensive Glossary*, 1947.
POLLARD, A. W. (Ed.), *Shakespeare's Hand in the Play of Sir Thomas More*, 1923.
PROUTY, C. T., *'The Contention' and Shakespeare's 2 Henry VI*, 1954.
ROBERTSON, J. M., *The Shakespeare Canon*, 1922–30. (By the chief of the stylistic disintegrators.)
SCHMIDT, A., *Shakespeare-Lexicon*. 2 vols., 1874–5. 3rd. ed. by G. Sarrazin, 1902.
Shakespeare Survey 7. The central theme is Shakespeare's style, 1954.
SIMPSON, P., *Shakespearian Punctuation*, 1911. (Considers punctuation dramatic and independent of syntax, a theory not generally accepted.)
SIMPSON, R., *The School of Shakespeare*. 2 vols., 1878.
SPURGEON, C., *Shakespeare's Imagery*, 1935.
STOKES, F. G., *A Dictionary of the Characters and Proper Names in the Works of Shakespeare*, 1924.
SUGDEN, E. H., *A Topographical Dictionary to the Works of Shakespeare and his Fellow Dramatists*, 1925.
TILLEY, M. P., *A Dictionary of the Proverbs in England in the Sixteenth and Seventeenth Centuries*, 1950.
TUVE, R., *Elizabethan and Metaphysical Imagery: Renaissance Poetic and Twentieth-Century Critics*, 1947.
WENTERSDORF, K., *Shakespearean Chronology and the Metrical Tests* (Shakespeare-Studien), 1952.
WILLCOCK, G. D., 'Shakespeare and Elizabethan English' in *Companion to Shakespeare Studies*, 1934.
WILSON, F. P., *Shakespeare and the Diction of Common Life*, 1941.
Marlowe and the Early Shakespeare, 1953.
WILSON, J. D., 'Act- and Scene-Division in the Plays of Shakespeare' RES iii, 1927. (Favours the 'seamless' structure.)
'They Sleepe all the Act' RES iv, 1928.
WYLD, H. C., *A History of Modern Colloquial English*, 1920, 1925.

(e) SOURCES

ANDERS, H. R. D., *Shakespeare's Books: A Dissertation on Shakespeare's Reading and the Immediate Sources of his Works*, 1904.

ATTWATER, A. L., 'Shakespeare's Sources' in *Companion to Shakespeare Studies*, 1934.

BROOKE, T., *Shakespeare's Plutarch*, 1909.

BULLOUGH, G., *Narrative and Dramatic Sources of Shakespeare*, 6 vols., 1957–.

CHAMBRUN, C. L. DE, *Shakespeare, Actor-Poet*, 1927. (The influence of Montaigne.)

CLEMEN, W., *Die Tragödie vor Shakespeare*, 1955. Trans. as *English Tragedy before Shakespeare*, 1961.

GOLLANCZ, I. (Ed.), The Shakespeare Classics (1907–13). A series of reprints, including *Menaechmi, Apollonius and Sylla, Pandosto, Romeus and Juliet, Rosalynde, King Leir, Taming of A Shrew, Troublesome Raigne*, Holinshed, Plutarch.

GREEN, H., *Shakespeare and the Emblem-Writers*, 1870.

GUTTMAN, S., *The Foreign Sources of Shakespeare's Works*, 1947.

HALLE, E., *The Union of the Two Noble and Illustre Families of Lancastre and Yorke*, 1548. Reprinted 1809.

HART, A., *A New Shakespearean Source-Book*, 1934.

HAZLITT, W. C., *Shakespeare's Library. A Collection of the Plays, Romances, Novels, Poems, and Histories employed by Shakespeare*. 6 vols., 2nd ed., 1875.

HOLINSHED, R., *Chronicles of England, Scotland, and Ireland*, 1577, 1587. Reprinted 6 vols. 1807–8.

LENNOX, C., *Shakespeare Illustrated*, 1753. (The first study of sources.)

LUCAS, F. L., *Seneca and Elizabethan Tragedy*, 1922.

MACCALLUM, A. W., *Shakespeare's Roman Plays and their Background*, 1910, 1925.

MUIR, K. (Ed.), *The Painfull Adventures of Pericles Prince of Tyre, by G. Wilkins*, 1953. *Shakespeare's Sources*, 2 vols., 1957–.

NICOLL, A. AND J. (Eds.), *Holinshed's Chronicle as Used in Shakespeare's Plays*, 1927.

NOBLE, R. S. H., *Shakespeare's Biblical Knowledge, and Use of the Book of Common Prayer*, 1935.

PAINTER, WILLIAM, *The Palace of Pleasure*. 3 vols., ed. by J. Jacobs, 1890.

PROUTY, C. T., *The Sources of Much Ado about Nothing*, 1950.

ROUSE, W. H. D. (Ed.), *Shakespeare's Ovid, Golding's Translation of the Metamorphoses*, 1961.

SCHANZER, E., *Shakespeare's Appian*, 1956.

SIMROCK, K., *Die Quellen des Shakespeare in Novellen, Märchen und Sagen*, 1831, 1870. (The first collection of sources after that of Charlotte Lennox.)

SKEAT, W. W., *Shakespeare's Plutarch*, 1892.

SPENCER, T. J. B. (Ed.), *Shakespeare's Plutarch*, 1964, 1968. *Elizabethan Love Stories*, 1968.

TAYLOR, G. C., *Shakespeare's Debt to Montaigne*, 1925.

THALER, A., *Shakespeare and Sir Philip Sidney*, 1947.

WHITAKER, V. K., *Shakespeare's Use of Learning: An Inquiry into the Growth of his Mind and Art*, 1953.

2. LITERARY CRITICISM

For a brief account of Shakespeare criticism, see p. 120. A short history is given in *A*

Companion to Shakespeare Studies, 1934, and for the years 1900–1950 in *Shakespeare Survey* 4.

Summaries, though not a history, in spite of its title, of the chief critical works and essays in English, German, and French are given in:

RALLI, A., *A History of Shakespeare Criticism*. 2 vols., 1932.

Anthologies of English criticism are:

Variorum Editions, 1803, 1813, 1821: contain a number of 18th-century critical essays.

DRAKE, N., *Memorials of Shakespeare; or, sketches of his character and genius, by various writers*, 1828.

INGLEBY, C. M., *Shakespeare's Centurie of Prayse*, 1875. (The *Shakespeare Allusion Book*, 1909; see p. 88.) Contains most of the 17th-century allusions and criticisms, including Dryden's.

WARNER, B., *Famous Introductions to Shakespeare's Plays by the notable Editors of the 18th century*, 1906.

SMITH, D. N., *Eighteenth Century Essays on Shakespeare*, 1903, 1963.

Shakespeare Criticism: A Selection (World's Classics), 1916. (English criticism 1623–1840, Jonson to Carlyle, with a valuable Introduction.) There are two companion volumes: 1919–35 (ed. A. Bradby), 1935–60 (ed. A. Ridler).

HALLIDAY, F. E., *Shakespeare and his Critics*, revised ed. 1958.

ABERCROMBIE, L., *A Plea for the Liberty of Interpreting Shakespeare* (BAL), 1930.

ALEXANDER, P., *Hamlet Father and Son*, 1955.

Shakespeare's Life and Art, 1939.

ARMSTRONG, E. A., *Shakespeare's Imagination. A Study of the Psychology of Association and Inspiration*, 1946.

BAGEHOT, W., *Shakespeare – the Man*, 1853.

BAKER, G. P., *The Development of Shakespeare as a Dramatist*, 1907.

BARBER, C. L., *Shakespeare's Festive Comedy*, 1959.

BAYLEY, J., *The Characters of Love*, 1960.

BENTLEY, G. E., *Shakespeare and Jonson*, 2 vols., 1945.

BICKERSTEITH, G. L., *The Golden World of 'King Lear'*, 1947.

BLUNDEN, E., *Shakespeare's Significances*, 1929. (On *King Lear*.)

BOAS, F. S., *Shakspere and his Predecessors*, 1896.

BRADBROOK, M. C., *Shakespeare and Elizabethan Poetry*, 1951.

BRADLEY, A. C., *Shakespearean Tragedy:* Lectures on *Hamlet, Othello, King Lear, Macbeth*, 1904. (A classic. See L. B. Campbell: *Bradley Revisited* (Studies in Philology), 1947.)

Oxford Lectures on Poetry, 1909 (pp. 245–393).

BRANDES, G., *William Shakespeare*, 1898.

BROOKE, C. F. T., *Essays on Shakespeare*, 1948.

BROWN, J. R., *Shakespeare and his Comedies*, 1957.

CAMPBELL, L. B., *Shakespeare's Histories; Mirrors of Elizabethan Policy*, 1947.

Shakespeare's Tragic Heroes: Slaves of Passion, 1930.

CAMPBELL, O. J., *Shakespeare's Satire*, 1943.

Shakespeare and the 'New' Critics (*J. Q. Adams: Memorial Studies*), 1948.

CHAMBERS, E. K., *Shakespeare: A Survey*, 1925. (Essays on all the plays.)

CHARLTON, H. B., *Shakespearian Comedy*, 1938.
Shakespearian Tragedy, 1948.

CLEMEN, W., *The Development of Shakespeare's Imagery*, 1936, 1951.

COLERIDGE, S. T. See *Coleridge's Shakespeare Criticism*. Ed. by T. M. Raysor, 2 vols., 1930. Or, *Coleridge's Essays and Lectures on Shakespeare* (Everyman edition). *Coleridge on Shakespeare*, ed. T. Hawkes, 1969.

CONKLIN, P. S., *A History of 'Hamlet' Criticism, 1601–1821*, 1947.

CRAIG, H., *In Interpretation of Shakespeare*, 1948. (The historical approach: 'Shakespeare as an Elizabethan'.)

CROCE, B., *Ariosto, Shakespeare, and Corneille*, 1920. New Italian ed. of *Shakespeare* section, 1948, with Introduction and Notes by N. Orsini.

DANBY, J. F., *Shakespeare's Doctrine of Nature. A Study of 'King Lear'*; 1949.

DE QUINCEY, T. See p. 132.

DOREN, M. van, *Shakespeare*, 1939, 1941.

DOWDEN, E., *Shakspere: A Critical Study of his Mind and Art*, 1875. (The first book in English on 'Shakespeare as a whole', but somewhat sentimental.)

DRYDEN, J., *Critical Essays*, ed. W. P. Ker, 2 vols. 1900.

DUTHIE, G. I., *Shakespeare*, 1951.

ECKHOFF, L., *William Shakespeare*, 1948. (A Norwegian appraisal.)

ELIOT, T. S., *Selected Essays*, 1932.
Essays on Elizabethan Drama, 1957.

ELLIS-FERMOR, UNA, *Some Recent Research in Shakespeare's Imagery*, 1937.
Shakespeare the Dramatist, ed. K. Muir, 1961.

EMERSON, R. W., *Shakspeare: or, the Poet*. (Vol. IV, Works, 1903–4.)

EMPSON, W., *Seven Types of Ambiguity*, 1930, 1961.

FARNHAM, W., *The Medieval Heritage of Elizabethan Tragedy*, 1936.
Shakespeare's Tragic Frontier, 1950.

FLATTER, R., *Hamlet's Father*, 1949.

FLUCHÈRE, H., *Shakespeare, Dramaturge élisabéthain*, 1948. Tr. 1953.

GERVINUS, G. G., *Shakespeare*. 4 vols., 1849–50. Trans. by F. E. Bunnett as *Shakespeare Commentaries*, 1863. Ed. 1883 with introduction by F. J. Furnivall. (The first book to trace Shakespeare's development.)

GOETHE, J. W. His famous estimate of Hamlet's character is in *Wilhelm Meister*, 1795.

GOLLANCZ, I. (Ed.), *A Book of Homage to Shakespeare*, 1916.

GORDON, G. S., *Shakespearian Comedy and Other Studies*, 1944.

GRANVILLE-BARKER, H., *Prefaces to Shakespeare*. 5 vols. I: *Love's Labour's Lost, Julius Caesar, King Lear*, 1927. II: *Romeo and Juliet, Merchant of Venice, Antony and Cleopatra, Cymbeline*, 1930. III: *Hamlet*, 1937. IV: *Othello*, 1946. V: *Coriolanus*, 1947. 4 vols. 1964. (Studies by a scholar, dramatist, actor and producer.)

GUNDOLF, F., *Shakespeare und der deutsche Geist*, 1911.

HALLIDAY, F. E., *The Poetry of Shakespeare's Plays*, 1954.

HARBAGE, A., *As They Liked It. An Essay on Shakespeare and Morality*, 1947. (Though primarily engaged with ethics, admits the greater importance of the poetry.)

HARRISON, G. B., *Shakespeare's Tragedies*, 1951.

HAZLITT, W., *Characters of Shakspear's Plays*, 1817. (The first book to consider the characters and poetry of each play in detail.)

On Shakespeare and Milton (*Lectures on the English Poets*), 1818.

HEILMAN, R. B., *This Great Stage: Image and Structure in King Lear*, 1948.

Magic in the Web: Action and Language in Othello, 1956.

HEINE, H., *Shakespeares Mädchen und Frauen*, 1839.

HERFORD, C. H., *A Sketch of Recent Shakespearean Investigation*, 1923. (A survey of Shakespearean criticism 1893–1923.)

HOLLOWAY, J., *The Story of the Night: Studies in Shakespeare's Major Tragedies*, 1961.

HUGO, V., *Préface de Cromwell*, 1827. (The proclamation of the Romantic faith in France.)

JOHNSON, S., *Preface* to his Edition of Shakespeare, 1765. (A judicial balancing of Shakespeare's genius against his want of taste.)

Observations on the Plays. Short critical notes on each play, reprinted in the *Variorum* editions. See *Dr Johnson on Shakespeare*, ed. W. K. Wimsatt, 1969.

JONES, E., *Hamlet and Oedipus*, 1949.

JONSON, B. See *Conversations with William Drummond*, 1618–19; *Elegy*, in F1. 1623; *Timber: or Discoveries*, 1641; *De Shakespeare nostrati*.

KEATS, J., *The Letters* ed. M. B. Forman, 2 vols., 1931.

KENNEDY, M. B., *Oration in Shakespeare*, 1942.

KITTREDGE, G. L., *Shakspere: an Address*, 1916. (A short introduction to the historical approach.)

KNIGHT, G. W., *The Wheel of Fire*, *The Imperial Theme*, *The Shakespearian Tempest*, *The Olive and the Sword*, *The Crown of Life*, *The Mutual Flame*, *The Sovereign Flower*, 1930–58. (Interpretation based upon poetic symbolism.)

KNIGHTS, L. C., *Explorations*, 1946.

Some Shakespearean Themes, 1959.

An Approach to Hamlet, 1961.

LAMB, C., 'On the Tragedies of Shakespeare, considered with reference to their fitness for Stage Representation', 1811. ('The plays of Shakespeare are less calculated for performance on a stage than those of almost any other dramatist whatever.')

LASCELLES, M., *Shakespeare's Measure for Measure*, 1953.

LAWLOR, J., *The Tragic Sense in Shakespeare*, 1960.

LAWRENCE, W. W., *Shakespeare's Problem Comedies*, 1931 (Penguin 1969).

LEAVIS, F. R., *The Common Pursuit*, 1952.

LEECH, C., *Shakespeare's Tragedies and Other Studies in Seventeenth Century Drama*, 1950.

LEISHMAN, J. B., *Themes and Variations in Shakespeare's Sonnets*, 1961.

LESSING, G. E., *Hamburgische Dramaturgie*, 1767. ('The man who first valued Shakespeare according to his full desert was indisputably Lessing' – *Gervinus*.)

LOUNSBURY, T. R., *Shakespeare as a Dramatic Artist*, 1901.

Shakespeare and Voltaire, 1902.

MACKAIL, J. W., *The Approach to Shakespeare*, 1930.

MADARIAGA, S. DE, *On Hamlet*, 1948.

MARRIOTT, J. A. R., *English History in Shakespeare*, 1918.

MASEFIELD, J., *William Shakespeare*, 1911, 1954. (An essay on each play.)

MENON, C. N., *Shakespeare Criticism*, 1938.

MONTAGU, E., *Essay on the Genius and Writings of Shakespear*, 1769.

MORGANN, M., *On the Dramatic Character of Sir John Falstaff*, 1777. (A remarkable anticipation of romantic criticism.)

MOULTON, R. G., *Shakespeare as a Dramatic Artist*, 1885. 3rd ed., 1906, enlarged.

MUIR, K., *Shakespeare and the Tragic Pattern*, 1959.

MUNRO, J., *The Shakespeare Allusion Book, 1591–1700*. (See INGLEBY: *Shakespeare's Centurie of Prayse*.)

MURRY, J. M., *Shakespeare*, 1936.

Countries of the Mind, 1922, 1931.

NICOLL, A., *Studies in Shakespeare*, 1928. (On the four great tragedies.)

NOBLE, R. S. H., *Shakespeare's Use of Song*, 1923.

O'CONNOR, F., *The Road to Stratford*, 1948.

PALMER, J. L., *Political Characters of Shakespeare*, 1945.

Comic Characters of Shakespeare, 1946.

PARROTT, T. M., *Shakespearean Comedy*, 1949.

PATER, W. See p. 356.

PETTET, E. C., *Shakespeare and the Romance Tradition*, 1949.

POPE, A., *Preface* to his edition of Shakespeare, 1725. (The Augustan view; conventional and general criticism.)

QUILLER-COUCH, A., *Shakespeare's Workmanship*, 1918. (Lectures delivered at Cambridge on about twelve of the plays.)

RALEIGH, W., *Shakespeare*, 1907.

REESE, M. M., *The Cease of Majesty. A Study of Shakespeare's History Plays*, 1961.

REYTHER, P., *Essai sur les idées dans l'œuvre de Shakespeare*, 1947.

RICHARDSON, W., *A Philosophical Analysis and Illustration of Some of Shakespeare's Remarkable Characters*, 1774.

RIGHTER, ANNE, *Shakespeare and the Idea of the Play*, 1962 (Penguin 1967).

ROSEN W., *Shakespeare and the Craft of Tragedy*, 1960.

RYLANDS, G. W. H., *Words and Poetry*, 1928.

'Shakespeare the Poet' in *Companion to Shakespeare Studies*, 1934.

RYMER, T., *The Tragedies of the Last Age Consider'd and Examin'd by the Practice of the Ancients, and by the Common Sense of all Ages*, 1678. (*The Critical Works*, ed. C. A. Zimansky, 1956.)

A Short View of Tragedy, 1693. (The most extreme of the English Neo-Classic school; 'In tragedy Shakespeare raves and rambles.')

SCHLEGEL, A. W., *A Course of Lectures on Dramatic Art and Literature*, pub. 1809–11, tr. 1846.

SEN GUPTA, S. C., *Shakespearian Comedy*, 1950.

SCHÜCKING, L. L., *Die Characterprobleme bei Shakespeare*, 1919. Trans. as *Character Problems in Shakespeare's Plays*, 1922.

Baroque Character of the Elizabethan Tragic Hero, 1939.

Shakespeare und der Tragödienstil seiner Zeit, 1947. (The 'realist' and historical approach.)

SEWELL, A., *Character and Society in Shakespeare*, 1951.

SHAW, G. B. See p. 449.

SISSON, C. J., *Shakespeare's Tragic Justice*, 1962.

SITWELL, E., *A Notebook on William Shakespeare*, 1948. (Notes on most of the plays.)

SMITH, L. P., *On Reading Shakespeare*, 1930.

SPENCER, H., *The Art and Life of William Shakespeare*, 1939. New ed. 1948. (Vigorous and original criticism of each play, with sources and stage-history.)

SPENCER, T., *Shakespeare and the Nature of Man*, 1943.

SPIVACK, B., *Shakespeare and the Allegory of Evil*, 1959.

STAUFFER, D., *Shakespeare's World of Images: The Development of his Moral Ideas*, 1949.

STEWART, J. I. M., *Character and Motive in Shakespeare. Some Recent Appraisals Examined*, 1949. (In part an attack on the 'realist' and historical school of Stoll and Schücking.)

STIRLING, B., *Unity in Shakespearian Tragedy*, 1956.

STOLL, E. E., *Shakespeare Studies: Historical and Comparative in Method*, 1927.
Art and Artifice in Shakespeare, 1933.
Shakespeare and other Masters, 1940. (Stoll was a leader of the 'realist' and historical school: that the full appreciation of Shakespeare depends on a knowledge of his theatre and times.)

STRACHEY, L., *Shakespeare's Final Period*, 1906. (*Books and Characters*, 1922.) (Suggests a Shakespeare 'bored with everything except poetry'.)

SUARÈS, A., *Shakespeare, poète tragique*, 1921.

SWINBURNE, A. C., *A Study of Shakespeare*, 1880. (Important, though rhapsodic.)

TEN BRINK, *Five Lectures on Shakespeare*. Trans. J. Franklin, 1895.

TILLYARD, E. M. W., *Shakespeare's Last Plays*, 1938.
Shakespeare's History Plays, 1946.
Shakespeare's Problem Plays, 1949.

TOLSTOY, L., *Shakespeare and the Drama*. Trans. A. Maude, 1906. (Finds Shakespeare's view of life immoral, and his works detestable.)

TRAVERSI, D. A., *Shakespeare, the Last Phase*, 1954.

ULRICI, H., *Shakespeares dramatische Kunst*, 1839. Trans. L. D. Schmitz as *Shakespeare's Dramatic Art*, 2 vols., 1876.

VOLTAIRE. See p. 518.

VYVYAN, J., *The Shakespearean Ethic*, 1959.

WALKER, R., *The Time is out of Joint: A Study of Hamlet*, 1948. *The Time is Free: A Study of Macbeth*, 1949.

WENDELL, B., *William Shakspere: a Study in Elizabethan Literature*, 1894.

WHATELY, T. See p. 526.

WHITER, W., *A Specimen of a Commentary on Shakspeare*, 1794.

WILSON, H. S., *On the Design of Shakespearian Tragedy*, 1957.

WILSON, J. D., *The Fortunes of Falstaff*, 1943.
What Happens in Hamlet, 1935, 1959.
Shakespeare's Happy Comedies, 1962.

YODER, E. A., *Animal Analogy in Shakespeare's Character Portrayal*, 1947.

YOUNG, K., *Samuel Johnson on Shakespeare*, 1923.

THE THEATRE

Dekker's *Gull's Hornbook*, 1609, gives a little information about Shakespeare's theatre. The first real accounts, very sketchy, are Flecknoe's, 1664; Wright's (?),

1699; and Downe's, 1708. The first formal history is that of Malone, 1790, enlarged in the 1821 Variorum, to which Chalmers contributed *A Farther Account.*

In the 19th century came Collier's *History*, 1831; Jusserand's *Théâtre en Angleterre*, 1878; and Fleay's *Chronicle History*, 1890.

Interest in the structure and conduct of the theatres, and in the original staging of Shakespeare's plays was stimulated by Gaedertz's publication in 1888 of the De Witt sketch of the Swan, and the first half of the 20th century has been a time of immense advance by English, American and Continental scholars. The way was cleared by the work of W. W. Greg, and by the researches of C. W. Wallace, J. T. Murray and others. Between 1912 and 1917 came W. J. Lawrence's *Elizabethan Playhouse*, A. H. Thorndike's *Shakespeare's Theater*, and J. Q. Adams's *Shakespearean Playhouses.*

All this preliminary work was brought together in the four great volumes of E. K. Chambers's *Elizabethan Stage*, 1923, a work continued by G. E. Bentley in the *Jacobean and Caroline Stage*, 7 vols. 1941–68, and by J. L. Hotson in the *Commonwealth and Restoration Stage*, 1928. Studies have become more detailed: Baldwin on Shakespeare's company, Bradbrook on stage conditions, Reynolds on the Red Bull, J. C. Adams on the Globe, Sprague, Bennett and Harbage on Shakespeare's audience, Baskerville on the jig, Linthicum on costume, Naylor on music, L. B. Campbell on machines, and so on.

Wider surveys of the theatre have been made by Creizenach, *Geschichte des neueren Dramas*, 1893–1916, of Vol. V of which *The English Drama in the Age of Shakespeare* is a translation, by Mantzius, and by Allardyce Nicoll in his series of histories of the theatre.

Current productions of Shakespeare's plays are recorded in *Shakespeare Survey* and *Shakespeare Quarterly*.

ADAMS, J. C., *The Globe Playhouse*, 1942.
The Original Staging of King Lear (*J. Q. Adams: Memorial Studies*), 1948.

ADAMS, J. Q., *Shakespearean Playhouses: a History of English Theatres from the Beginnings to the Restoration*, 1917.
Ed. *The Dramatic Records of Sir Henry Herbert, Master of the Revels, 1623–73*, 1917.

ALBRECHT, A., *Das englische Kindertheater*, 1883.

ALBRIGHT, V. E., *The Shakespearian Stage*, 1909.

ARBER, E., *A Transcript of the Registers of the Company of Stationers of London, 1554–1640.* 5 vols., 1894.

ARTS COUNCIL. *History of Shakespearian Production*, 1948.

BABCOCK, R. W., *The Genesis of Shakespeare Idolatry, 1776–99*, 1931.

BALDWIN, T. W., *The Organization and Personnel of the Shakespearean Company*, 1927.

BASKERVILLE, C. R., *The Elizabethan Jig and Related Song Drama*, 1929.

BENNETT, H. S., *Shakespeare's Audience* (BAL), 1944.

BENTLEY, G. E., *The Jacobean and Caroline Stage*, 1941.
Shakespeare and the Blackfriars Theatre (SS, 1), 1948.

BOAS, F. S., *University Drama in the Tudor Age*, 1914.

BRADBROOK, M. C., *Elizabethan Stage Conditions*, 1932.
The Rise of the Common Player, 1962.

BRAINES, W. W., *Holywell Priory and the Site of the Theatre, Shoreditch*, 1915.
The Site of the Globe Playhouse in Southwark, 1921.

BROADMEIER, C., *Die Shakespeare-Bühne nach den alten Bühnen-Anweisungen*, 1904. (The 'alternation' theory, now rejected, that Shakespeare so constructed his plays that scenes were alternately performed on the apron and inner stages. See REYNOLDS, G. F.)

BYRNE, M. ST C., *Fifty Years of Shakesperian Production: 1898–1948* (SS, 2), 1949.

CAMPBELL, L. B., *Scenes and Machines on the English Stage during the Renaissance*, 1923.

CHALMERS, G., *The Rise and Progress of the English Stage* (*Third Variorum*), 1821.

CHAMBERS, E. K., *The Mediaeval Stage*. 2 vols., 1903.
The Elizabethan Stage. 4 vols., 1923. (The standard work.)

CHILD, H., Stage Histories of the Plays in the *New Cambridge Shakespeare*, 1921–44.
Shakespeare in the Theatre (*Companion to Shakespeare Studies*), 1934.
The Shakespearian Productions of John Philip Kemble, 1935.

CIBBER, C., *An Apology for the Life of Colley Cibber*. Ed. R. W. Lowe, 1888.

COHN, A., *Shakespeare in Germany in the 16th and 17th Centuries: An Account of English Actors in Germany and the Netherlands, and of the Plays Performed by Them*, 1865.

COLLIER, J. P., *The History of English Dramatic Poetry to the Time of Shakespeare: and Annals of the Stage to the Restoration*. 3 vols., 1831.

COWLING, G. H., *Music on the Shakespearian Stage*, 1913.

CREIZENACH, W., *Schauspiele der englischen Komödianten*, 1889.
The English Drama in the Age of Shakespeare, 1916.

CUNNINGHAM, P., *Extracts from the Accounts of the Revels at Court, in the Reigns of Queen Elizabeth and King James* (Shakespeare Society), 1842.

DAVIES, W. R., *Shakespeare's Boy Actors*, 1939.

DEKKER, T., *The Gull's Hornbook*, 1609. Ed. R. B. McKerrow, 1904.

DENT, E. J., *Shakespeare and Music* (*Companion to Shakespeare Studies*), 1934.
A Theatre for Everybody. The Story of the Old Vic and Sadler's Wells, 1945.

DOBRÉE, B., *Shakespeare and the Drama of his Time* (*Companion to Shakespeare Studies*), 1934.

DODSLEY, R., *A Select Collection of Old Plays*. 12 vols., 1744. 4th ed. by W. C. Hazlitt, 15 vols., 1874.

DOWNES, J., *Roscius Anglicanus, or an Historical Review of the Stage from 1600 to 1706*, 1708. Ed. J. Knight (facsimile reprint), 1886. Ed. M. Summers, 1927.

FARJEON, H., *The Shakespearean Scene*, 1949. (Productions of the last 20–30 years.)

FARMER, J. S. (Editor), *Tudor Facsimile Texts*, 1907–13. (Reproductions of printed and MS. plays.)

FEUILLERAT, A. (Editor), *Documents relating to the Office of the Revels in the Time of Queen Elizabeth*, 1908.

FLEAY, F. G., *A Chronicle History of the London Stage, 1559–1642*, 1890.
A Biographical Chronicle of the English Drama, 1559–1642. 2 vols., 1891.

FLECKNOE, R., *A Short Discourse of the English Stage*, 1664 (Reprinted in Hazlitt, *The English Drama and Stage*.)

FOAKES, R. A., and RICKERT, R. T. (Eds.), *Henslowe's Diary*, 1961. (The editors question Greg's opinion of Henslowe as an illiterate philistine.)

GAEDERTZ, K. T., *Zur Kenntnis der altenglischen Bühne*, 1888. (Contains the first reproduction of De Witt's sketch of the Swan theatre.)

GENEST, J., *Some Account of the English Stage, 1660–1830*. 10 vols., 1832. (The basis of all later histories of the stage.)
GILDERSLEEVE, V. C., *Government Regulation of the Elizabethan Drama*, 1908.
GILDON, C., *The Lives and Characters of the English Dramatic Poets*, 1699.
GRAVES, T. S., *The Court and the London Theatres during the Reign of Elizabeth*, 1913.
GREG, W. W., *A Bibliography of the English Printed Drama to the Restoration*. 4 vols. 1939–59. (A monumental work.)
Henslowe's Diary. 2 vols., 1904–8.
Henslowe Papers, 1907.
Ed. *Malone Society Reprints* (include type-facsimiles of plays), 1907–
Dramatic Documents from the Elizabethan Playhouses. 2 vols., 1931. (Invaluable reproductions, with commentary, of 'plots', actors' parts, MS. plays, etc.)
HALLIDAY, F. E., *The Cult of Shakespeare*, 1957.
HARBAGE, A., *Shakespeare's Audience*, 1941.
Shakespeare and the Rival Traditions, 1952.
HARTNOLL, P. (Ed.), *The Oxford Companion to the Theatre*, 1951.
HAZLITT, W. C., *The English Drama and Stage under the Tudor and Stuart Princes, 1543–1664, illustrated by a series of Documents, Treatises, and Poems*, 1869.
HERFORD, C. H., *A Sketch of the History of the English Drama in its Social Aspects*, 1881.
HERZ, E., *Englische Schauspieler und englisches Schauspiel zur Zeit Shakespeares in Deutschland*, 1903.
HEYWOOD, T., *An Apology for Actors*, 1612. (Shakespeare Society Reprint, 1841.)
HILLEBRAND, H. N., *The Child Actors. A Chapter in Elizabethan Stage History*, 1926.
HODGES, C. W., *Shakespeare and the Players*, 1948.
The Globe Restored, 1953.
HOGAN, C. B., *Shakespeare in the Theatre, 1701–1800*. 2 vols., 1952, 1957.
HOLMES, M., *Shakespeare's Public*, 1960.
HOTSON, L., *The Commonwealth and Restoration Stage*, 1928.
Shakespeare's Motley, 1952. (A study of the Elizabethan 'fool'.)
The First Night of Twelfth Night, 1954.
Shakespeare's Wooden O, 1959.
ISAACS, J., *Production and Stage-Management at the Blackfriars Theatre*, 1933.
JOSEPH, B., *The Tragic Actor*, 1959.
Acting Shakespeare, 1962.
JUSSERAND, J. J., *Le Théâtre en Angleterre depuis la Conquête jusqu'aux prédécesseurs immédiats de Shakespeare*, 1878.
KNIGHT, G. W., *Principles of Shakespearian Production*, 1936. New ed. 1949.
LAMB, C., *Specimen of English Dramatic Poets who lived about the time of Shakespeare*, 1808.
LANGBAINE, G., *Momus Triumphans: or, the Plagiaries of the English Stage*, 1688.
An Account of the English Dramatick Poets, 1691.
LAWRENCE, W. J., *The Physical Conditions of the Elizabethan Public Playhouse*, 1927.
Speeding up Shakespeare: Studies in the Bygone Theatre and Drama, 1937.
LEA, K. M., *Italian Popular Comedy: a Study in the Commedia dell'Arte, 1590–1620, with special reference to the English Stage*. 2 vols., 1934.

LEE, S., *Shakespeare and the Modern Stage: with other Essays*, 1906.

LINTHICUM, M. C., *Costume in the Drama of Shakespeare and his Contemporaries*, 1936.

LONDON COUNTY COUNCIL, *Bankside* (Vol. XXII of the *Survey of London* Series), 1950.

LOWE, R. W., *Thomas Betterton*, 1891.

MALONE, E., *Historical Account of the English Stage*, 1790. Enlarged in Third Variorum, 1821.

MALONE SOCIETY REPRINTS, 1927– . Suspended during the war, they were resumed in 1948 with the reprint of the 1594 Q of Lyly's *Mother Bombie*. See GREG, W. W.

MANTZIUS, K., *A History of Theatrical Art in Ancient and Modern Times*. 6 vols., 1897–1907. English trans. 1903–21.

MERCHANT, W. M., *Shakespeare and the Artist*, 1959. (A visual history of the production of the plays.)

MERMAID SERIES. *The Best Plays of the Old Dramatists*. 22 vols., 1887–95. Later reprints.

MOROZOV, M. M., *Shakespeare on the Soviet Stage*, trans. by D. Magarshak, with an introduction by J. D. Wilson, 1947.

MURRAY, J. T., *English Dramatic Companies, 1558–1642*. 2 vols., 1910.

NAGLER, A. M., *Shakespeare's Stage*, 1958.

NICOLL, A., *Dryden as an Adapter of Shakespeare* (Shakespeare Association), 1922.

Stuart Masques and the Renaissance Stage, 1937.

Studies in the Elizabethan Stage since 1900 (SS, 1), 1948.

The Development of the Theatre: A Study of Theatrical Art from the Beginnings to the Present Day, 1927, rev. 1948.

NUNZEGER, E., *A Dictionary of Actors and of other persons associated with the public representation of plays in England before 1642*, 1929.

ODELL, G. C. D., *Shakespeare from Betterton to Irving*. 2 vols., 1920.

POEL, W., *Shakespeare in the Theatre*, 1915.

PURDOM, C. B., *Producing Shakespeare*, 1950.

REYHER, P., *Les masques anglais*, 1909.

REYNOLDS, G. F., *Some Principles of Elizabethan Staging*, 1905. (Refutes the alternation theory of Brodmeier (q.v.).)

What we know of the Elizabethan Stage (Modern Philology), 1911.

'*Troilus and Cressida*' *on the Elizabethan Stage* (J. Q. ADAMS: *Memorial Studies*), 1948.

The Staging of Elizabethan Plays at the Red Bull Theater, 1940.

RHODES, R. C., *The Stagery of Shakespeare*, 1922. (Based on the stage-directions of the Quartos.)

RIBNER, I., *The English History Play in the Age of Shakespeare*, 1957. New ed. 1965.

SCHELLING, F. E., *The English Chronicle Play: a Study in the Popular Historical Literature Environing Shakespeare*, 1902.

Elizabethan Drama, 1558–1642, 2 vols., 1908.

SHAKESPEARE ASSOCIATION, *Shakespeare and the Theatre*, 1927.

SHAKESPEARE SURVEY 1 and 12 (devoted largely to the Elizabethan theatre), 1948, 1959.

SHAPIRO, I. A., 'The Bankside Theatres: Early Engravings', SS, 1, 1948.
SIMPSON, P., and BELL, C. F., *Designs by Inigo Jones for Masques and Plays at Court*, 1924.
SISSON, C. J., *The Elizabethan Dramatists, except Shakespeare*, 1928.
Le Goût Public et le Théâtre Élisabéthain jusqu'à la Mort de Shakespeare, 1921.
'The Theatres and Companies' in *Companion to Shakespeare Studies*, 1934.
Lost Plays of Shakespeare's Age, 1936.
SMITH, I., *Shakespeare's Globe Playhouse; A Modern Reconstruction*, 1956.
SOUTHERN, R., *The Medieval Theatre in the Round*, 1957.
SPENCER, H., *Shakespeare Improved: the Restoration Versions in Quarto and on the Stage*, 1927. (Includes a history of the Restoration stage.)
SPENS, J., *Elizabethan Drama*, 1922.
SPRAGUE, A. C., *Shakespeare and the Audience*, 1935.
Shakespeare and the Actors, 1944.
Shakespearian Players and Performances, 1953.
STAHL, E. L., *Shakespeare und das deutsche Theater*, 1947.
STOPES, C. C., *Burbage and Shakespeare's Stage*, 1913.
William Hunnis and the Revels of the Chapel Royal, 1910.
SUMMERS, M., *Shakespeare Adaptations*, 1922. (Reprints the Dryden-D'Avenant *Tempest*, *The Mock Tempest* of T. Duffet, and Tates's *King Lear*; with introduction and notes.)
SWINBURNE, A. C., *Contemporaries of Shakespeare*, 1919.
SYMONS, A., *Studies in the Elizabethan Drama*, 1920.
THALER, A., *Shakspere to Sheridan*, 1922.
THORNDIKE, A. H., *Shakespeare's Theater*, 1916.
TIEGHEM, P. VAN, *Le préromantisme. La découverte de Shakespeare sur le continent*, 1947.
WALLACE, C. W., *The Children of the Chapel at Blackfriars, 1597–1603*, 1908.
The Evolution of the English Drama up to Shakespeare, with a History of the First Blackfriars Theatre, 1912.
WARD, A. W., *History of English Dramatic Literature to the Death of Queen Anne*. 2 vols., 1875; 3 vols., 1899.
WATKINS, R., *Moonlight at The Globe*, 1946.
On Producing Shakespeare, 1950.
WATSON, E. B., *Sheridan to Robertson: A Study of the Nineteenth-Century London Stage*, 1926.
WELLS, H. W., *Elizabethan and Jacobean Playwrights*, 1939.
WELSFORD, E., *The Court Masque; a Study in the Relationship between Poetry and the Revels*, 1927.
WICKHAM, G., *Early English Stages 1300–1660*, 2 vols. 1959, 1963.
WICKLAND, E., *Elizabethan Players in Sweden, 1591–92*, 1962.
WRIGHT, J. (?), *Historia Histrionica. An Historical Account of the English Stage ... In a Dialogue of Plays and Players*, 1699. Facsimile Reprint, 1872.

SHAKESPEARE'S COMEDIES

LAURENCE LERNER

Laurence Lerner's new anthology of criticism on Shakespeare's comedies follows the pattern of his successful volume, *Shakespeare's Tragedies*. Once again he has collected together some of the best modern Shakespearean criticism, mostly written in this century, and arranged it to throw light on nine of the comedies. (He excludes the last plays and the so-called problem plays.) A general section on comedy includes passages from Ben Jonson and Meredith.

Excellence, not inaccessibility, has been the criterion for a book which is designed to interest the general reader of Shakespeare as much as the student of literature. The contributors, therefore, run from Shaw, Freud and Quiller-Couch to Granville-Barker, Middleton Murry, Auden, and Empson, and on to more recent critics such as C. L. Barber, Anne Righter, and Cyrus Hoy.

SHAKESPEARE'S TRAGEDIES

LAURENCE LERNER

Shakespeare's tragedies have always been fertile acres for comment and criticism. The same dramas which inspired a Keats to write poetry appealed to A. C. Bradley – or to Ernest Jones, the psycho-analyst – as studies of character; and where the New Criticism has been principally interested in language and imagery, other critics in America have seen the plays as superb examples of plot and structure. Most of Aristotle's elements of tragedy have found their backers, and – as the editor points out in his introduction – these varying approaches to Shakespeare are by no means incompatible.

In what *The Times Literary Supplement* described as an 'excellent collection' Laurence Lerner has assembled the best examples of the modern schools of criticism and arranged them according to the plays they deal with. With its 'Suggestions for Further Reading' and the general sections on tragedy, this is a book which will stimulate the serious reader and do much to illuminate Shakespearian drama.

LIFE IN SHAKESPEARE'S ENGLAND

JOHN DOVER WILSON

Many people who have learned to enjoy Shakespeare feel they would like to know more about his life and times, and this authoritative book is the answer. It is not a biographical study, but an anthology collected from many contemporary sources so as to illuminate the conditions, the appearance, the habits, pastimes, and beliefs of Shakespeare's time. Professor Dover Wilson's methods of assembling this panorama of the period is to pin-point the clues provided by scores of passages in the plays and follow them up by relevant supporting evidence from what we nowadays call the 'documentary' writers of the time. Thus we are able to see city and countryside, school and university, court and theatre, as the man of Shakespeare's day saw them with his own eyes. We observe at close quarters his sports, his superstitions, his daily life at home or abroad, his experiences in childhood and age. Actor, sailor, courtier, traveller, and beggar relate, in their own words, what living was like in the great days of sixteenth-century England.

A Peregrine Book

THE GROWTH AND STRUCTURE OF ELIZABETHAN COMEDY

M. C. BRADBROOK

Her published works on Elizabethan drama are evidence that Miss Bradbrook is uniquely qualified to carry out a full-scale survey of the comedy of the period, to which so little attention has been given. As she states in her introduction to this book: 'Comedies outnumber tragedies on the Elizabethan stage by nearly three to one. Sweet and bitter comedy, romantic and satiric comedy, or Shakespearian and Jonsonian comedy have all been used as terms of description for the two main divisions, of which the first may be said to be characteristically Elizabethan, and the second Jacobean. In the following chapters I have tried to trace the evolution and the interaction of these two comic forms.'

In this scholarly study she follows the course of English comedy from its beginnings, commenting on the plays of Shakespeare, Jonson, Lyly, Peele, Greene, Nashe, Dekker, Marston, Middleton, Day, Chapman, and Fletcher. In addition she discusses the significant period of the War of the Theatres (1599–1602).

'The criticism of individual playwrights is fresh and penetrating, and at times Miss Bradbrook's writing has the compression and force of epigram' – *Listener*

'An invaluable guide to the whole corpus of "sweet and bitter comedy" from Lyly to Fletcher' – J. I. M. Stewart in the *New Statesman*

SHAKESPEARE'S PLUTARCH

EDITED BY T. J. B. SPENCER

'Worthy to stand with Malory's *Morte d'Arthur* on either side the English Bible' – George Wyndham on North's Plutarch (1895)

Shakespeare's use of his sources has always been of absorbing interest, and North's translation of Plutarch's *Parallel Lives* of Greek and Roman heroes is among the most important of these. In this volume an important editorial task has been undertaken by Professor T. J. B. Spencer, Director of the Shakespeare Institute and Professor of English at Birmingham University. Four lives from North's Plutarch – those of Julius Caesar, Brutus, Marcus Antonius, and Coriolanus – have been collated with extracts from the plays for which they were the main sources. In this way the reader can see, almost at a glance, how and why Shakespeare adapted his source.

These colourful biographies must have been a rich reading experience in an age when books were scarce. Plutarch's understanding of character and North's refreshingly vigorous use of the young English language ensure that they are still a joy to read in themselves. And for anyone who has sensed the creative vitality of the great plays, this volume offers a new and exciting opportunity to explore their workmanship.

Also by F. E. Halliday

THE LIFE OF SHAKESPEARE

On 26 April 1564 'Gulielmus filius Johannes Shakspere' was christened at Holy Trinity Church at Stratford-upon-Avon, and on 25 April 1616 'Will Shakspere, gent' was buried at the same church. In between lived the man we know as William Shakespeare.

Modern scholarship has enormously enriched our understanding of Shakespeare's plays and of the world in which he moved and wrote, yet it is now over ten years since the last full-scale biography of Shakespeare was written. Mr Halliday, using recent research – in particular the work of Leslie Hotson and T. W. Baldwin – steers a lively course between the meagre dust of contemporary records and the higher fancies of Shakespeare's 'lost years'.

'A quick-moving and workmanlike biography ... admirably compact and comprehensive . . . we are given as much information as others have provided in twice the length' – Ivor Brown in the *Observer*